Company Law

Farrar's

Company Law

Third edition

John H Farrar   LLM, PhD
Barrister of the High Courts of New Zealand and Australia
Professor of Law at Victoria University of Wellington

Nigel E Furey   LLM
Solicitor of the Supreme Court
Senior Lecturer in Law, University of Bristol

Brenda M Hannigan   MA, LLM
Solicitor, Ireland
Senior Lecturer in Law, University of Southampton

With a chapter on taxation by

Philip Wylie   LLB, FCA
Senior Lecturer in Law, Cardiff Law School

Butterworths
London, Dublin, Edinburgh
1991

United Kingdom	Butterworth & Co (Publishers) Ltd, 88 Kingsway, LONDON WC2B 6AB and 4 Hill Street, EDINBURGH EH2 3JZ
Australia	Butterworths Pty Ltd, SYDNEY, MELBOURNE, BRISBANE, ADELAIDE, PERTH, CANBERRA and HOBART
Canada	Butterworths Canada Ltd, TORONTO and VANCOUVER
Ireland	Butterworth (Ireland) Ltd, DUBLIN
Malaysia	Malayan Law Journal Sdn Bhd, KUALA LUMPUR
New Zealand	Butterworths of New Zealand Ltd, WELLINGTON and AUCKLAND
Puerto Rico	Equity de Puerto Rico, Inc, HATO REY
Singapore	Malayan Law Journal Pte Ltd, SINGAPORE
USA	Butterworth Legal Publishers, AUSTIN, Texas; BOSTON, Massachusetts; CLEARWATER, Florida (D & S Publishers); ORFORD, New Hampshire (Equity Publishing); ST PAUL, Minnesota; and SEATTLE, Washington

A CIP Catalogue record for this book is available from the British Library.

First edition 1985
Second edition 1988

ISBN 0 406 50930 1

Typeset by Phoenix Photosetting, Chatham, Kent
Printed and bound in Great Britain by
Mackays of Chatham PLC, Chatham, Kent

Preface

Company law does not stand still. Since the second edition of this book there has been the Companies Act 1989 and much activity in the EC in the lead-up to 1992. These changes have necessitated considerable revision of the book.

The chapter on Harmonisation of Company Law in the EC has been enlarged and moved up into Part I of the book to mark the increasing importance of the topic to English company law.

Chapter 7 on Corporate Personality and Limited Liability has been considerably revised in the light of recent cases, literature and some observations arising from the second edition.

Chapter 8 takes account of the conversion of Companies House into an Executive Agency.

Chapter 9 on Constitutional Issues takes account of developments in the US literature about whether the company constitutes a contract and the extent to which company law regimes should be mandatory.

Chapter 10 on Memorandum of Association and Corporate Capacity takes account of the Companies Act 1989 reforms to ultra vires. In this edition we have treated these reforms within a discussion of the evolution of the ultra vires doctrine. This is because the new edition comes at a time of transition and to understand the new reforms one needs to review the earlier law.

Chapters 14, 15, 16 and 18 have been rewritten by Brenda Hannigan and Chapter 19 has been revised by John Farrar to take account of the Companies Act 1989. The chapter on Ownership and Control of the Listed Public Company has been moved into Part V of the book as it seems to fit more logically under Structural Problems and Change.

Chapter 29 on Investigation and Inspection has been revised in the light of the Companies Act 1989.

Chapter 32 on Groups has been revised in the light of the Companies Act 1989 and Chapter 37 on Receiverships has been rewritten by Nigel Furey. John Farrar has added a new chapter in Part VII on Cross Frontier Mergers in the light of its increasing importance in the lead-up to 1992. This chapter contains a detailed discussion of the relevant developments in the EC.

We are glad that this book, whatever its defects, has stimulated an interesting debate in recent law reviews. We have learnt some things from our critics although we do not necessarily agree with them on everything.

The responsibility for the chapters in this edition is as follows:

John Farrar—Chapters 1–13, 17, 19, 21, 29–32, 34, 36 and 40–42.
Nigel Furey—Chapter 22, 28, 33, 35 and 37–39.
Brenda Hannigan—Chapters 14–16, 18 and 23–27.
Philip Wylie—Chapter 20.

The law is stated as at 1 January 1991.

John Farrar
Nigel Furey
Brenda Hannigan
Philip Wylie

Contents

x *Contents*

Glossary of terms

Administration Administration is a procedure introduced by the Insolvency Act 1985 to provide an alternative to receivership and winding up in the case of a company experiencing financial problems. The aim of the procedure is the rehabilitation of the company or its business. The present provisions are contained in Pt II of the Insolvency Act 1986.

Agency theories of the firm The theory of the firm is that part of economics which seeks to explain the theory of production. Firms are not real firms but theoretical constructs. The agency theories of the firm explain the firm by reference to a nexus of agency contracts.

Allotment In relation to shares the process by which a person acquires the unconditional right to be included in the company's register of members in respect of those shares: s 738, Companies Act 1985.

Amalgamation A merger of at least two companies usually characterised by the formation of a third company to act as holding company.

Annual general meeting A meeting of members of the company held once a year in pursuance of the statutory obligation under s 366(1), Companies Act 1985.

Annual return A return to be made by a company to the Registrar of Companies every year giving prescribed details: Companies Act 1985, s 363(1).

Arbitrage To take advantage of differences in price or rate between one market and another. This concept was developed in respect of foreign exchange but is also used in the futures and stock markets.

Articles of Association The internal regulations of the company.

Audit committee A committee usually of three members of the Board of Directors, two of whom are non-executive directors. The functions of the committee are to review with the external auditors and company financiers the accounting policies of the group and external control of the group's assets.

Auditor A person who audits the accounts of a company.

Bear A bear is an investor who sells a security short in the belief that the market will fall. See *Short selling*.

Bearer bond A bond transferable by delivery.

Big Bang The term refers to the day when minimum commissions on The London Stock Exchange were abolished. However, it has eventually become a shorthand expression for a whole range of developments on world financial markets and in the City of London in particular. These include the increased use of technology and the development of global trading in securities.

Board of Directors   The directors of a company as a collective body.

Bona vacantia   Property belonging to no one. On the dissolution of a company all property vested in it is deemed to be *bona vacantia* and belongs to the Crown, the Duchy of Lancaster or the Duke of Cornwall: Companies Act 1985, s 658(1).

Bond   A type of debenture usually characterised by a certificate giving a right to receive a specified sum on maturity and interest in the meantime. In the USA debentures are usually called bonds.

Bonus share   A share given by the company to a member usually proportionate to his existing holding and requiring no fresh consideration to be provided by him. Such shares usually result from a capitalisation of net profits.

Bull   A bull is someone who trades on the expectation of a price rise.

Call   A demand made on a member by the company to pay up the amount remaining or part of the amount remaining unpaid on his or her shares.

Capital redemption reserve   A reserve constituted by a transfer of a notional amount on the redemption or purchase by a company of its own shares: Companies Act 1985, s 170.

Certificate of incorporation   A document issued by the Registrar of Companies evidencing the formation of the company.

Charge   An encumbrance on property which is either fixed or floating. A fixed legal charge is a statutory creation, a fixed equitable charge a creation of equity. A floating charge is a species of equitable charge which does not attach to specified assets until crystallisation. See *Floating charge*.

Class   In company law usually a reference to an issue of company shares characterised by certain class rights.

Class rights   Rights expressly described in the memorandum, articles or terms of issue as rights attaching to a class of shares or rights which relate to dividends, return of capital or voting. To this concept has been added rights which although not attached to any particular shares are conferred on the beneficiary in the capacity of member or shareholder of the company: *Cumbrian Newspapers Group Ltd v Cumberland & Westmorland Herald Newspaper & Printing Co Ltd* [1987] Ch 1.

Commencement of winding up   The date when a winding up is deemed to have started.

Commercial paper   A US term which is catching on in the UK referring to short term unsecured debt or loan capital.

Committee of inspection   A committee consisting of creditors and members appointed to assist a liquidator in winding up.

Company limited by guarantee   A company, the liability of whose members is limited by guarantee.

Company limited by shares A company, the liability of whose members is limited by shares.

Compulsory winding up A winding up by the court.

Contributory A person liable to contribute to the assets of a company in the event of its being wound up. It usually refers to a shareholder.

Control contract means a contract in writing conferring such a right of control authorised by the memorandum or articles of the undertaking in question and permitted by the law under which that undertaking is established (CA 1985, Sch 10A para 4(2)). Such contracts are common in relation to groups in Germany and although mentioned in the Seventh EEC Directive and CA 1989 are rare in the United Kingdom.

Convertible Usually a debenture or debenture stock which can be converted at a later date into shares in an issuing company. The actual mechanics of this involve using the money to subscribe for shares at an agreed price.

Debenture A written acknowledgement of indebtedness by a company.

Debenture stock That part of the debt or loan capital of a company consolidated into stock and constituted by a debenture stock trust deed.

Directive An EC source of law directed to the government of a member state to implement.

Director A person who is a member of the Board of Directors having in that capacity overall direction of the company's business or affairs. See also *Executive* and *Non-executive director*.

Dissolution of company The corporate equivalent of death. It usually follows winding up.

Dividend A distribution out of the profits of a company to a shareholder in proportion to his/her shares and in accordance with his or her rights. Once declared a dividend constitutes a debt.

Dominant influence means a right to give directions with respect to the operating and financial policies of another undertaking which the directors of that undertaking are obliged to comply with whether or not they are for the benefit of that undertaking (CA 1985, Sch 10A para 4(1)). This is to establish whether there is a group relationship for the purpose of consolidated accounts.

Equity In investment language it usually refers to ordinary shares of a company which are the residual claimants to the profits of the company. Hence an analogy with equity of redemption.

Eurodollar A US dollar held by a non-resident of the US outside the US. These have become a type of international currency and the dealings in them have contributed to the international financial revolution.

Executive director A director who is full-time or under an obligation to devote a substantial amount of his time to the management of his or her company. Not all executives are directors and not all directors are executive directors. Some directors are non-executive directors. See *Non-executive director*.

Extraordinary general meeting   A general meeting other than an annual general meeting.

Extraordinary resolution   A resolution passed by a majority of not less than three-fourths of the members voting in person or by proxy at a general meeting of which adequate notice has been given: Companies Act 1985, s 378(1).

Firm   In ordinary language a business organisation. In economic theory something more abstract and in its true nature only capable of comprehension by a few economists.

Flotation   The process by which the shares or debentures of a company are offered to the public for subscription or purchase. The term refers to new issues not to the secondary market in those shares or debentures. The secondary market is a market by individual shareholders or debenture holders rather than the company itself or an issuing house.

Floating charge   A species of equitable charge created by a company (or in England by farmers) which only becomes a fixed equitable charge on crystallisation.

Futures contract   A contract to buy or sell at a future date.

Gearing   The relationship of debt to equity in a company's capital structure. The more long term debt there is the higher the gearing. Shareholders benefit to the extent that the return on the borrowed money exceeds the interest costs. Also known as leverage in the USA.

General meeting   A meeting of the members of the company entitled to attend and vote thereat. The articles may permit proxies to attend and vote in their stead. The general meeting and Board of Directors are the two principal decision making organs of the company.

Holding company   A company which controls a subsidiary company. A parent company of a group of companies.

Insider dealing or trading   Improper use of price sensitive information in respect of listed securities by a person for private gain.

Issue at a discount   An issue of shares or debentures at an amount less than their par value.

Issue at a premium   An issue of shares or debentures at a price above their par value.

Issued share capital   That part of a company's share capital which has been issued.

Leverage   See *Gearing.*

Liquidation   See *Winding up.*

Loan capital   The debt capital of a company as opposed to its share capital. Whereas share capital is normally permanent capital loan capital is usually not permanent capital although it is technically possible to have irredeemable debentures.

Liquidator   A statutory officer charged with the responsibility of winding up the company.

Listed securities Securities which are listed on a recognised stock exchange.

Market charge means a charge granted in respect of obligations on a recognised investment exchange, clearing house or transfer system in respect of market contracts. See CA 1989, sub-s 173(1). See also the concept of market property defined in s 177.

Managing Director A director of the company appointed to deal with the day to day management of the company.

Member Usually another name for a registered shareholder or stockholder.

Memorandum of association One of the two constitutional documents of a company, the other being the articles of association. A memorandum states the first name of the company, the country in which its registered office is situated, its objects, the basis of limitation of liability of members and its initial share capital.

Merger An ambiguous term which refers in English law to a reconstruction, amalgamation or takeover.

Minority shareholders Shareholders who are not in the majority. The meaning of minority is determined by what constitutes the majority for the matter in hand. The Companies Act requires different majorities for different purposes.

Negative pledge An undertaking given by a company to a creditor that it will not create any security. This is often accompanied by a provision for equal participation if any security is to be created. The term is sometimes used to describe a restrictive clause in a floating charge to similar effect.

Nominal capital The legal measure of the share capital with which the company is initially formed or as subsequently increased and up to which the company can issue shares.

Nominee shareholder A shareholder who holds his or her shares as nominee for another person.

Non-executive director A term of variable meaning which usually refers to a director who is not under an obligation to devote the whole or substantially the whole of his or her time to the affairs of the company. The two main roles of non-executive directors are to act as a check on management and to give an external perspective. Non-executive directors are often directors of a number of companies. Some of them are put on boards because of a connection with a financial institution.

Officer A broad generic term which includes a director, manager or secretary: Companies Act 1985, s 744.

Official notification A formal procedure involving proof by the Registrar of Companies of receipt of certain documents.

Official receiver A civil servant attached to the court for bankruptcy purposes. He or she also deals with winding up of companies.

Options A contract giving the purchaser the right to buy (a call option) or sell (a put option) a given security within or at a specified time.

Ordinary resolution   A resolution passed by a simple majority of members present at a general members.

Ordinary share   A share entitling its holder to any dividend which is declared after dividends have been paid on preference shares. Sometimes called an equity share.

Par value   The authorised or nominal value of a share.

Parent company   See *Holding company*.

Poll   A method of voting whereby each member can vote for or against a resolution according to the number of shares which he or she holds.

Pre-emption   A right given to shareholders to purchase the shares of any member wishing to sell his or her shares. The term is also used to refer to the right of certain shareholders to subscribe for further shares on a new issue.

Preference shares   A share giving its holder preferential rights in respect of dividends, and/or return of capital on a solvent winding up. Such shares usually have limited voting rights.

Preferential debts   Certain unsecured debts which on the grounds of public policy are given preferential status on the insolvent winding up of a company.

Pre-incorporation contract   A contract entered into before a company has been incorporated.

Private company   A company which is not a public company.

Privatisation   A loose term used to refer to the process by which a nationalised industry is sold off to the public through the medium of shares. It is to be contrasted with corporatisation whereby the particular enterprise continues under public ownership but is run on corporate lines.

Promoter   A person who takes steps to form a company or set it in motion. The term can also extend to someone involved in its subsequent flotation.

Prospectus   An invitation to the public to subscribe for shares or debentures of the company.

Proxy   A person appointed by a shareholder to vote for him or her at a meeting.

Public company   A company limited by shares or limited by guarantee and having a share capital which states in its memorandum that it is to be a public company and in respect of which the formalities laid down by the Companies Act for public companies have been complied with.

Quorum   The minimum number of persons necessary to constitute a valid meeting.

Receiver   A person appointed by a debenture holder or debenture stock trustee to take over the whole or part of the property of a company on default by the company. In the former case the receiver will be an administrative receiver.

Reconstruction   Where one company transfers the whole of its undertaking and property to a new company in consideration of the issue of shares by the new company to the shareholders in the old company.

Redeemable shares Shares of a company which can be redeemed by the company.

Reduction of capital The diminution or extinguishment of the share capital of a company. Normally this requires the consent of the court.

Register of charges This refers to either a register of charges created by the company kept by the company itself or the register kept by the Registrar of Companies.

Register of members A register kept by the company of membership of the company.

Registrar of companies A public official recognised by the Companies Act whose responsibility is primarily to register certain documents under the Companies Act 1985. He or she also is the person responsible for official notification under s 711 of the Companies Act 1985. This is the public notice by him or her in the Gazette of receipt and issue of a sub-class of registrable documents.

Regulation An EC source of law which is immediately binding in member states.

Regulations A term sometimes used to describe the articles.

Resolution A formal decision by a majority of the members of the company or the Board of Directors.

Rights issue A right given to a shareholder to subscribe for further shares usually at an advantageous price.

Scheme of arrangement A compromise or arrangement between the company and its creditors or between the company and its members.

Share A unit in the share capital of a company.

Share capital That part of the permanent part of the capital of a company which is constituted into shares. It is usual to think of the share capital as a fund.

Share premium account A notional account to which is credited in the books of the company a sum equal to the amount of any premiums on the issue of shares.

Short selling Sale of a security not actually held without the cover of an actual purchase in the hope of a decline in price.

Special resolution A resolution passed by a majority of not less than three-fourths of members voting at a general meeting of the company of which not less than 21 days' notice has been given: Companies Act 1985, s 378(2).

Stag Someone who buys on a new issue with the intention of selling immediately at a profit.

Stock In the strict sense the aggregate of fully paid shares which have been consolidated. In practice such consolidation is rare. In the USA stock is the usual term used for a share. Stock can also refer to debenture stock.

Stock exchange An exchange which provides a primary and secondary market for securities.

Subscriber of memorandum   A person who signs the memorandum of association. As such this person is one of the original members of the company.

Subsidiary company   A company controlled by another company. For the definition of control see s 736(1), Companies Act 1985.

Table A   A model set of articles of association originally contained in the Companies Act but now contained in a statutory instrument.

Takeover   A loose term used to describe the situation whereby one company ('the bidder') makes an offer to the shareholders of another company ('the target'). A takeover bid can be made over the heads of existing management. In the USA this is described as a tender offer.

Transfer   This normally refers to a form of transfer of shares or debentures or debenture stock. For listed securities a simple form is prescribed.

Transmission   The vesting of a member's shares in another person by operation of law.

Ultra vires   An act in excess of powers. Normally it refers to something not authorised expressly or impliedly by the objects clause of a company. Sometimes the phrase is used to describe an act by directors which is in excess of authority. Since the CA 1989 reforms its significance is largely in respect of the latter.

Undertaking   means a body corporate or partnership, or an unincorporated association carrying on a trade or business with or without a view to profit (s 259(1) CA 1985). Undertakings may be members of a group in which case they are either a parent undertaking or a subsidiary undertaking for the purpose of group accounts.

Underwriting   An arrangement under which a person promises to take up shares on a public issue which are not taken up by the public.

Unlisted Securities Market (USM)   A misnomer which refers to a list of companies which are not on the Official List of The London Stock Exchange. It was set up in 1980 to help small companies to raise capital. The criteria are less rigorous than for a listing on the main exchange. The intention is that such companies will eventually progress to a full listing.

Voluntary arrangement   An arrangement with creditors which does not take the form of a scheme of arrangement sanctioned by the court: see Pt I of the Insolvency Act 1986.

Winding up   The process of liquidation of a company. This can either be compulsory, ie winding up by the court or voluntary. Voluntary winding up can either be a members' voluntary winding up in case of solvency, or a creditors' winding up in case of insolvency.

Table of statutes

References in this Table to *Statutes* are to Halsbury's Statutes of England (Fourth Edition) showing the volume and page at which the annotated text of the Act will be found. Page references printed in **bold** type in this Table indicate where the section of the Act is set out in part or in full.

Table of cases

H

PART I

Incorporation and its consequences

CHAPTER 1

The company as a business medium

THE NATURE AND PURPOSE OF BUSINESS ENTERPRISE

This book is about the law relating to companies and unless otherwise stated, references are to the Companies Act 1985 (abbreviated as CA 1985). 'Company' is an ambiguous term with no strictly technical meaning[1]. It can refer loosely to a group of persons associated together for a common purpose such as a partnership of businessmen or it can refer to a species of business corporation. We are concerned here with the latter but it will be useful at the outset to discuss the nature and history of business enterprise in general and the place of the business corporation within it. Business enterprise is a wide term which connotes a unit of ownership in pursuit of profits[2]. Economists usually prefer to use the term 'firm' while lawyers refer to the exact species.

Firms in Western societies are creatures of a market economy. In such an economy, the price system is the final arbiter of production and consumption[3]. Instead of central planning by the state as in the USSR[4], the vital questions of who produces what goods in which quantities and in which places are answered by countless decisions by numerous people acting without knowledge or with limited knowledge of the others. The co-ordinating mechanism is the 'invisible hand'[5] of the price system of the market. This is the theory at any rate. It is a characteristic of the modern economy that production is typically carried out by firms, not by individuals. This is not a logically necessary consequence of the price system[6]. It is theoretically possible that all production could be carried out by individuals who specialised in producing particular goods or services. This is true of simple societies, but as society and technology grow more complex, the problems of co-ordination by the price system become increasingly difficult and costly. The firm represents to some extent an alternative to the price

---

1 *Re Stanley* [1906] 1 Ch 131 at 134.
2 See N S Buchanan *The Economics of Corporate Enterprise* (1940) p 15.
3 *Buchanan*, ibid, pp 10–15.
4 Today the Russian system is in a state of flux which has been termed 'Perestroika'. Central planning and inefficient management have resulted in increasing difficulties. There are experiments with democratisation and increasing recognition of private property but the USSR lags behind Hungary and Poland in its concept of business enterprise and its development of efficient markets. There is a risk that if the reforms fail or do not conspicuously succeed that reactionary or neo-Stalinist methods will be resorted to with more repression and greater centralisation. See Anders Aslund *Gorbachev's Struggle for Economic Reform* (1989 Cornell University Press) pp 194–195.
5 Adam Smith *An Inquiry into the Nature and Causes of the Wealth of Nations* (New York: Modern Library, 1937) p 423.
6 *Buchanan*, op cit, p 13.

system for the various factors involved in production[7]. One eminent writer, Professor Alfred Chandler Jr of Harvard Business School, has defined the modern industrial firm as 'a collection of operating units, each with its own specific facilities and personnel, whose combined resources and activities are co-ordinated, monitored and allocated by a hierarchy of middle and top managers'[8]. Instead of a host of market transactions and the time and cost involved in negotiating them, the firm purchases some agents of production and hires others. The defining characteristic of the firm is in 'a *team* use of inputs and a centralised position of some party in the contractual arrangements of *all* other inputs'[9]. In a sense it is a specialised surrogate market[10]. As Ronald Coase, an economist at Chicago Law School, once wrote: 'Within the firm, these market transactions are eliminated and in place of the complicated market structure with exchange transactions is substituted the entrepreneur-coordinator who directs production'[11]. This produces economies in transaction costs.

Business decisions are frequently taken in conditions of uncertainty and risk. Risk averseness[12] as well as lack of capital probably accounts for particular people becoming employees rather than individual owners and, as we shall see, it enters into the decision to spread one's investment over a number of firms. It does not, however, necessarily account for the existence and organisation of the classical firm which is more due to economies in transaction costs although it helps to explain the evolution of the form of the modern limited liability company which restricts the liability of investors.

A basic issue in the theory of the firm is the nature of profit and its allocation. Profit is another ambiguous term. In economics it usually refers to the excess of total revenue over total cost including what are called the opportunity costs of equity or risk capital[13]. Opportunity costs mean the return necessary to attract that kind of capital from alternative uses. Accountants and lawyers treat the opportunity costs as part of profit. Profit in economics serves to attract and allocate additional investment, entre-preneurial skills and other scarce resources[14].

The next question is who shares in the profit and in what proportions? Is it to go to management as quasi-entrepreneurs, to shareholders, or to other constituents of the firm, and on what basis? This requires decision-making hierarchies and monitoring procedures.

THE TAXONOMY OF FIRMS

The sole trader

The simplest economic and legal unit is the sole trader—that is, an individual carrying on business either entirely alone or employing others. As an

---

7 Ronald H Coase (1937) 4 Economica (NS) 386, *The Firm, the Market and the Law* (1988); A A Alchian and H Demsetz (1972) 62 Am Econ Rev 777.
8 *Scale and Scope: The Dynamics of Industrial Capitalism* (1990), p 13.
9 Alchian and Demsetz, op cit.
10 See note 7.
11 Coase, op cit. For a discussion of this and neoclassical and managerialist theories of the firm see John Coffee Jr (1987) 85 Mich L Rev 1.
12 For a useful recent discussion of risk see Coffee, op cit, pp 16–24.
13 R A Posner and K E Scott *Economics of Corporation Law and Securities Regulation* (1980) p 2.
14 Ibid.

economic unit, he is very vulnerable since he can be made personally bankrupt for his business debts. Until 1861[15], this was an advantage in the sense that only traders could be made bankrupt and escape perpetual harassment from their creditors and the risk of the Debtors' Prison. Since 1861, bankruptcy applies to non-traders as well. Today, English law does not distinguish between traders and non-traders except in some areas of consumer protection. Most civilian systems perpetuate the basic distinction.

Partnership

Partnership is a relationship of two or more persons carrying on a business in common with a view to profit. Partnership is a species of contract involving principles of commercial agency. The utilitarian reform philosophy of the nineteenth century combining with commercial self-interest culminated in the codification of the law in the Partnership Act 1890. This Act, while comprehensive, is not a complete code, since the administration of partnership assets on death or bankruptcy and the question of goodwill are not dealt with[16], and the existing rules of common law and equity prevail unless they are inconsistent with the Act. The Act, unlike Scots and European systems, does not confer legal personality on the partnership. Partners are collectively called a 'firm' in s 4 of the Act but the firm is not a body corporate. The firm is the aggregate of partners who share profits, have individual authority to bind the firm for transactions in the course of business and are ultimately liable to the extent of their personal fortunes for the debts of the partnership. To overcome the risks and administrative disadvantages, partners often incorporate their business and in the case of partnerships of more than 20, incorporation is mandatory. Section 716(1) of CA 1985 provides inter alia:

No company, association or partnership consisting of more than 20 persons shall be formed for the purpose of carrying on any business that has for its object the acquisition of gain by the company, association, or partnership or by its individual members, unless it is registered as a company under this Act or is formed in pursuance of some other Act of Parliament, or of letters patent.

However, certain professions are prevented by the rules of their professional bodies from incorporating and statutory recognition of this is given by s 716(2) and (3) which relax the rule of a maximum of 20 partners in the case of solicitors, accountants, stockbrokers and other partnerships exempted by the Secretary of State by regulations made under the latter subsection. Architects, chartered engineers, estate agents and surveyors inter alia have been exempted.

Unincorporated associations

Section 716(1) refers not only to 'company' and 'partnership' but also to 'association'. This is a reference to unincorporated associations. Most of these do not in fact have as their object the acquisition of profit but exist for the mutual benefit and often the recreation of their members and thus escape the compulsion to incorporate in s 716(1). Unlike some other systems, English law does not recognise that association predicates corpo-

---

15 Until 1861, bankruptcy in England and Wales only applied to traders. Non-traders could not be made, nor could they make themselves, bankrupt.
16 See *Lindley on the Law of Partnership* (15th edn, 1984) p 4.

rateness[17] and treats such bodies in a rather complicated way. The mechanism of the trust has proved useful for the holding of property by such associations but difficult questions have arisen over the extent of personal liability of the executive and members[18]. For these reasons some of these associations voluntarily incorporate as companies.

Corporations

Sir Edward Coke in *The Case of Sutton's Hospital* in 1612[19] described a corporation as 'invisible, immortal', and existing 'only in intendment and consideration of the Law'. *Kyd on Corporations*[20] defined a corporation as 'a collection of many individuals, united into one body, under a special denomination, having perpetual succession under an artificial form, and vested, by the policy of the law, with the capacity of acting, in several respects, as an individual . . .'. Some jurists have seized upon such statements as support for the proposition that a corporation is essentially a legal fiction[21]. However, all that Coke and Kyd were putting forward was a theory of law, a statement of how a corporation is to be treated legally. In law all persons recognised by law are legal persons and hence, in a sense, legal fictions. The theory thus rests on a tautology[22]. The most rational approach to the concept of legal corporateness lies in a concentration on the ways in which the legal requirements for corporations have been worked out by analogy with the legal relations between individuals and the reasons why this has taken place[1]. Perhaps too much emphasis in the past has been put on the separate legal personality of corporations. This has created metaphysical problems which have had to be solved before the courts could get down to the practical issues, and has obscured the fact that corporations are distinct and developing methods of owning and holding property and organising production by individuals or groups which in their turn determine certain relationships of control, agency and monitoring of agency performance.

Corporation is a genus with two traditional species—sole and aggregate. Corporations sole confer corporate status on the single holder of an office, e g the Archbishop of Canterbury. Corporations aggregate confer corporate status on a group of persons. There is a criss-crossing classification into charitable and civil corporations. The type of company with which we are principally concerned— the company limited by shares—is a sub-species of civil corporation.

Economists look upon the company as a way of organising capital by a firm which has acquired distinctive legal attributes. We have seen how the firm represents an alternative arrangement to the market by the various factors in production represented by the company. This tells us why much economic activity takes place in firms but not why many of those firms are companies. The answer is, as Richard Posner[2] has pointed out, that the

---

17 See F W Maitland *Selected Essays* (1936) ed H D Hazeltine et al, p 209.
18 See Harold A J Ford *Unincorporated Non-Profit Associations* (1959) and S Stoljar *Group and Entities* (1973) passim.
19 (1612) 10 Co Rep 1a at 32b.
20 Vol 1, p 13.
21 Pope Innocent IV, Savigny and Salmond. For a discussion of the other theories such as the 'purpose', 'enterprise', 'bracket' and 'concession' theories, see R W M Dias *Jurisprudence* (5th edn, 1985) chapter 12.
22 See *Max Weber on Law in Economy and Society* (1954) ed Max Rheinstein, p 156.
 1 See H L A Hart (1954) 70 LQR 37.
 2 R Posner *Economic Analysis of Law* (3rd edn, 1986) p 368; see also P Halpern, M Trebilcock and S Turnbull (1980) 30 U of TLJ 959. Cf Coffee, op cit, p 16 et seq.

company is primarily a method of solving problems encountered in raising substantial amounts of capital. As such it is a kind of standard form contract. Capital is raised by many risk-averse investors contributing to a common fund. The capital raised enables a potentially elaborate organisation to be set up with professional management. Instead of a series of separate investment contracts and contracts with the various factors in production, there is substituted the master contract constituted by the company. This produces economies in transaction costs on both fronts. Most companies have limited liability for their members but not of course themselves. This transfers the ultimate risks of business failure to their creditors but in practice this only means trade and involuntary creditors since financial creditors take guarantees from the principal shareholders and directors in private companies[3]. On the other hand the use of the corporate form involves the cost of monitoring the performance of management and employees to prevent shirking and manipulation of corporate assets for personal advantage. Here one has to balance these agency costs against the benefits derived[4]. The shareholders retain the authority to change the membership of the management and over major decisions affecting the structure of the company. Economic theories of transaction costs, information and monitoring provide insights not only into incorporation but also the financing, management and growth of companies. They also help to explain why some companies merge and why some companies fail. We shall consequently refer to them from time to time where this is helpful.

The concept of the enterprise and undertaking

German law recognises the concept of the enterprise as such but has problems in giving a clear definition to the concept and marking the relationship with firm. It seems to be a broader concept than firm taking into account sociological as well as legal and economic phenomena[5]. The concept is occasionally used in English company law as a basis for piercing the corporate veil in the case of related companies. The reality of the economic enterprise is then looked at. Recently, the Companies Act 1989, implementing the Seventh EC Directive on Harmonisation of Company Laws, has used the term 'undertaking' which conveys some of the same looseness as 'enterprise'. It is broader than company and corporate group. There it is used in a modest sense in connection with accounts of associated business entities.

MAJOR ECONOMIC THEMES IN THE DEVELOPMENT OF MODERN COMPANY LAW

There are seven major economic themes which characterise the development of modern company law. The first is a growth of larger business units. The history of limited liability companies is one of increasing concentration. This

---

3 *Posner*, op cit, p 370; Coffee, op cit, p 67 et seq.
4 See N Wolfson (1980) 34 Miami LR 959; M Jensen and W Meckling (1976) 3 J Financial Econ 305; Coffee, op cit, p 31 et seq.
5 See G Teubner 'Enterprise Corporatism: New Industrial Policy and the Essence of the Legal Person' 36 Am J of Comp L 130 (1988). See also T Reiser. 'The Theory of Enterprise Law in the FDR' ibid 111.

is the logic of the system. The mechanism of this species of corporation enabled capital to be accumulated from a number of small investors and the natural tendency is towards monopoly. As Berle and Means stated in their classic study, *The Modern Corporation and Private Property*[6]: 'The corporate system has done more than evolve a norm by which business is carried on. Within it exists a centripetal attraction which draws wealth together into aggregations of constantly increasing size, at the same time throwing control into the hands of fewer and fewer men.' This was one of the central theses of their book and one of their conclusions was that such organisations had passed beyond the realm of private enterprise and had become 'nearly social institutions'. Later, they wrote: 'The law of corporations . . . might well be considered as a potential law for the new economic state, while business prestige is increasingly assuming the aspect of economic statesmanship.' This undoubtedly overstated the case. The relationship of such companies to the market is one of the more controversial areas of economics. Are they the creature or the controller of the particular market? In the UK there has been an increasing degree of concentration, especially in the last 30 years. Like West Germany and France, it has experienced a substantial upward trend in average manufacturing industry concentration levels. A survey by Professor K George of 157 product lines in the UK revealed a 10% point average increase in five firms' sales concentrating ratios between 1958 and 1968[7]. The weight of evidence from a number of surveys indicates that UK industries are on average more concentrated than US industries[8]. Government policy has at times been somewhat mixed in its attitudes. Sometimes it has favoured concentration and has actively fostered it, as in the setting up of the Industrial Reorganisation Corporation by the first Wilson government. Sometimes it has sought to curb restrictive trade practices and monopolies. The principal instrument for the latter has been not company law but separate legislation originating with the Monopolies and Restrictive Practices (Inquiry and Control) Act 1948 and now contained in the Fair Trading Act 1973 and the Competition Act 1980. A similar attitude characterises the EC's attitude to concentration. Company law measures, such as the draft convention on transnational mergers and the European company project favour concentration, but there are strong provisions in the Treaty of Rome on concentration and the abuse of a dominant position[9].

A second theme is the development of increasingly elaborate structures. The simplest corporate structure is a single company whose constitutional organs are the board of directors and general meeting of shareholders. Their precise relationship to each other is partly a matter of law, partly a matter of contract constituted by the memorandum and articles of association[10]. Sometimes this is supplemented by an extrinsic agreement and some managerial systems are sometimes superimposed on the legal framework. In a large company there will often be an elaborate vertical chain of command extending from the Board through middle management to the workforce. In this century, the group of companies developed as an extension of the

6 Revised edition, 1968, p 18.
7 K D George (1975) 85 Economic Journal 124; S Prais *The Evolution of Giant Firms in Britain* (1976) p 16.
8 F M Scherer *Industrial Market Structure and Economic Performance* (2nd edn, 1980) p 72.
9 See arts 85 and 86.
10 See Chapters 10 and 11, post.

corporate concept[11]. This originally arose as a method of expansion and pooling of resources which extended the surrogate market. When the private company was introduced, the use of subsidiary private companies enabled a public company to devolve parts of its business to subsidiaries and escape the disclosure requirements imposed on public companies. Later, this was curtailed by changes in the disclosure requirements. The group enterprise has created problems for the law which have not yet been solved. The group enabled not only vertical integration but also horizontal integration. As a result of the latter, there have developed large groups known as conglomerates with subsidiaries in a number of different industries. The American Federal Trade Commission in its statistical analyses in fact breaks these down into five separate categories: horizontal extension, where the firms are actual competitors in some relevant market; vertical extension, where the firms occupy adjacent stages in some vertical chain of production and distribution; product extension, where the firms, although not in actual competition, sell products functionally related in terms of manufacture or distribution; market extension, where the firms sell in geographically distinct markets; and pure conglomerates, where the firms are in essentially unrelated fields[12].

The third theme is a shift from ownership to control of the firm[13]. The early entrepreneurs both owned and managed their businesses. With the growth of the modern company as a mode of diversified ownership there has been a gradual shift of power from those who own to those who control or manage such companies. In many large public companies the top management have relatively small personal shareholdings. On the other hand, they have functional control of the enterprise. This again is a central thesis of Berle and Means' analysis of US companies in 1930. Although as a theory it had been anticipated by Marx and others, Berle and Means were the first to give it empirical content. Berle and Means traced the development of the concept of *control* which they recognised to be somewhat amorphous. They identified five different types of control in the modern company:

(1)   control through almost complete ownership;
(2)   majority control;
(3)   control through legal devices without majority ownership e g pyramiding, the use of non-voting shares, voting trusts;
(4)   minority control; and
(5)   management control.

The first three rest on a legal base. The last two are extra-legal. The trend is to the last two because of the dispersion of share ownership in the larger public companies. With this divergence of ownership and control comes a divergence of interest. The shareholder is interested more in income and capital appreciation of his investment rather than the company as an enterprise. Management is interested in the enterprise for a diversity of motives ranging from professional pride to the most naked self-interest in the pursuit of power.

---

11 See Chapter 32, post.
12 *Scherer*, op cit, p 558.
13 See *Berle and Means*, op cit; C S Beed (1966) 1 Journal of Economic Studies 29; J H Farrar, 'Ownership and Control of Listed Public Companies: Revising or Rejecting the Concept of Control' in *Company Law in Change* (1987) (ed B Pettet) p 39 et seq.

While some economists challenge the divergence of interest argument, most subsequent research has tended to confirm Berle and Means' major findings in substance. Those who subscribe to their separation theory are known as the school of Managerialists. This is a broad heading and there is considerable diversity within it. While Marxists agree on separation of ownership and control, they use the theory as part of a larger enquiry. As Michel de Vroey has written[14]: 'While Managerialists just ask the question "who . . . rules the corporation?", Marxists' main question is: "For which class interests are the corporations ruled?"'. Thus to Marxists there is a dispersion of *legal* ownership but not economic ownership in the sense that the latter remains in the hands of the dominant class.

While much of the discussion has taken place at the level of theory, Berle and Means did test their theory against the evidence. In the UK, an empirical study by Sargent Florence in 1961 adopting several alternative criteria concluded that two-thirds of the large companies in 1951 were not owner-controlled[15]. A recent study by S Nyman and A Silberston of Nuffield College, Oxford[16] is critical of these findings. They argue that the extent of managerial control is more limited than has been thought and there may not be an inexorable tendency to increase. However, the situation differs from industry to industry and this probably affects earlier empirical findings. They favour a flexible, more realistic approach to the concept of control, arguing that firms controlled by families, professional managers, other firms or by financial institutions may display different behavioural characteristics. In particular, they stress the need to accommodate potential control and what we call our fourth theme.

The fourth theme is the ever increasing ownership of ordinary shares in UK companies by institutional investors ie pension funds, insurance companies, unit trusts and investment trusts who manage other people's savings[17]. The combined holdings of such bodies amounted to 54.1% of the market value of listed UK equities and 63.8% of listed UK company bonds in 1981[18]. In the past institutional investors have been reluctant to use their voting strength and be active at general meetings. This contrasts very sharply with the role of financial institutions in France and Germany where they play a more positive part in corporate governance. In the UK, such institutions came under some criticism by the Committee on the Functioning of Financial Institutions[19]. Recently there have been signs of a more active role by institutional investors as minority shareholders[20]. The full implications of this trend have not been worked out[1]. Obviously it represents a change in

---

14 (1975) 7 Review of Radical Political Economy 2.

15 Florence *Ownership, Control and Success of Large Companies* (1961).

16 (1978) 30 Oxford Economic Papers 74.

17 See eg R Dobbins and T W McRae *Institutional Shareholders and Corporate Management* (1975) but see also R C Clark 94 Harv L Rev 561 where he argues that there is a further stage beyond this—the age of the group savings planner through pension schemes. We subsume this under institutional investment.

18 *The Stock Exchange Fact Book*, cited by J Oakley and L Harris *The City of Capital* (1983) pp 106–7.

19 Cmnd 7937 (1980).

20 See *Prudential Assurance Co Ltd v Newman Industries Ltd (No 2)* [1981] Ch 257, where the Prudential took action as a minority shareholder against a fraudulent management. However, the result was expensive and rather unsatisfactory.

1 See J H Farrar and M Russell (1984) 5 Co Law 107.

one's model of the typical shareholder. For management, it represents a possible institutional check on their abuses. On the other hand, it may represent a source of useful support in a takeover, in corporate planning and as a source of further funds for expansion. We deal with this question in detail in Chapter 34.

A fifth theme is the ever increasing amount of government intervention in corporate affairs. The early Companies Acts were a blend of intervention and laissez-faire. By providing for incorporation on registration they encouraged the growth of this form of business medium. On the other hand, they required disclosure of an increasing amount of information regarding the company. Disclosure[2] has long been recognised as the dominant philosophy of most modern systems. It is a sine qua non of corporate accountability. It can be justified on the following main policy grounds:

(1)   it leads to a better informed and consequently more efficient stock market;
(2)   it minimises the risk of fraud;
(3)   it prevents excessive secrecy and the distrust which this engenders; and
(4)   it facilitates equality of opportunity.

Counter arguments can be put forward in terms of confidentiality, lack of utility and excessive cost.

The UK corporate system is distinctive in that until recently the law and the government have been less involved in the regulation of public companies than in most other larger economies. This has been because of the strong tradition of self-regulation of the City of London financial institutions. The Stock Exchange, the Takeover Panel and the Council for the Securities Industry have supplemented Parliament and the courts. Some argue that the system is in need of root and branch reform and generally favour the creation by legislation of a Securities Commission which would have public participation in its membership, rule formulation and procedures. The latest thinking under the Financial Services Act 1986 is, however, to develop the present system of self regulation within a statutory framework[3]. The new system is a pyramid of power, descending from the Secretary of State for Trade and Industry through the Securities and Investments Board (SIB) to a number of self-regulatory agencies. The Director General of Fair Trading has a watching brief to report on restrictive trade practices.

Another area of government intervention, as we have seen, has been the regulation of concentration. Nationalisation has also taken place in various sectors of the economy and from time to time, government has invested public money in companies in key sectors. However, the recent trend has been in the opposite direction. Since 1973 the United Kingdom's membership of the EC has meant that its laws are increasingly influenced by the EC institutions.

Sixth, a point related to increasing government intervention, is the increasing legal impact of economic integration through membership of the European Community (EC). Since 1973 the United Kingdom has been a

---

2 For a valuable discussion of the concept of disclosure, see W Grover and J C Baillie in *Proposals for a Securities Market Law for Canada*, vol 3, p 350 ff.
3 See the Gower Report on Investor Protection (Cmnd 9125) 1984; The Times, 18 October 1984; the White Paper, *Financial Services in the United Kingdom* (Cmnd 9432) 1985.

member state of the EC which has adopted an elaborate programme for harmonisation of company law and securities regulation. Since 1972 this had had an important influence on domestic law reform. As the EC moves towards the Single Market in 1992 the momentum increases, as we shall see in later chapters.

Seventh, there has been the growth of multinational enterprises which in capital and power have begun to rival the nation state[4]. There is an increasing call in the OECD, United Nations and EC to lay down guidelines to regulate the activities of multinationals[5].

Historically the UK has been the headquarters of some of the early multinationals such as Imperial Chemical Industries plc, formed in 1926, which was designed from its incorporation to be multinational in its interests. Its objects were inter alia to 'extend the operations of the company to any foreign country, colony or state, by establishing and carrying on there all or any' of the businesses mentioned in its Memorandum. ICI now has manufacturing companies in more than 40 countries and selling companies in more than 60. Since the end of the First World War we have seen the phenomenal growth and spread of American multinationals. The growth of multinational companies has had an impact on the corporate form, labour practices, the transfer of technology and on tax in the host countries. In macro-economic terms they have sometimes caused balance of payments problems for smaller countries and threatened the very sovereignty of those countries. A small country like New Zealand, for example, with a population of less than the size of London or Sydney is often not in a very strong position to regulate a multinational oil or aluminium corporation. This particular trend in company law, therefore, necessarily raises problems of international law.

Lastly, there have been the changes in the world economy from being international to transnational. The transnational economy is shaped by money flows as much as trade in goods and services[6]. Part of this transition has been the so-called international financial revolution[7]. The causes are many and complex (indeed some may be effects)—the growth of the Euro-dollar market and its consequences—the reduction of money to a commodity in its own right and the move towards deregulation of capital markets; the massive developments in technology which provide ever more efficient information and communication systems; increasing competition in banking, brokerage and insurance—the whole marketing of financial services; and the breakdown of barriers between different financial markets. Today the monetary and tax policies of nation states increasingly react to movements in the transnational money and capital markets rather than try to shape them[8].

The principal beneficiaries of this revolution have been the larger listed companies, especially the multinational ones. Taking advantage of their status in the market place they are now able to achieve great flexibility

---

4 There is a plethora of literature on this subject. See e g R Vernon *Sovereignty at Bay* (1971), N Fatemi et al *Multinational Corporations* (2nd edn revised, 1976) and R Eels *Global Corporations* (1972).
5 See *International Investment Guidelines for Multinational Enterprises* (Cmnd 6525).
6 See Peter Drucker *The New Realities* (1989) pp 115–116.
7 See A Hamilton, *The Financial Revolution* (1986); J L Jones (1986) 7 Co Law 99.
8 Drucker, op cit, p 115.

through individual contracting in their financial affairs. It is a world of syndicated loans; futures, options; convertibles and swaps characterised by flexibility, diffusion of risk and the rapid trading of commercial paper. Some aspects of these developments are tax driven to take advantage of loopholes in national tax regimes and tax havens. Now, more than at any other time in the past, the financial world in which companies operate is fluid and the changes fast moving. The effects of this on conventional concepts of company law are yet to be assessed.

THE UNDERLYING INTERESTS

Underlying any discussion of company law and any rational debate about reform is the question of interests. The limited liability company does not simply represent one interest. It represents an arena in which there is a potential clash of many interests. We may identify the interests underlying it as:

(1) investors—share capital
              —loan capital
(2) outside creditors—commercial finance
                    —trade creditors
(3) employees
(4) consumers
(5) the public.

Investors either provide share or loan capital to the company. Generally the former have a permanent stake in the profits of the business which they can nevertheless realise. The latter usually have a fixed income and are investors for a limited time. Their interest is often secured.

Outside creditors are principally trade creditors who are usually unsecured and concerned with the company as a credit risk. Commercial finance creditors are institutions such as banks who are invariably secured creditors but do not regard themselves as investors.

The employees are a species of creditor but with an interest in the company as a source of job security.

Consumers are members of the general public who are interested in the company as a source of products and service.

The public interest can embrace investor and consumer protection but also covers residual matters such as regional development, resource management and the national interest. Under the law as it stands, the directors of a company primarily owe their duties to the company as an abstract entity. Since this abstract entity potentially covers all the interests mentioned above, directors have to weigh them up in practice and resolve the conflict between them. The law is unsatisfactory in that if the directors consider consumers and the public interest at the expense of investors and employees they may be held to have committed a breach of duty and yet pressure might have been put on them by the government to do this. Until the Companies Act 1980[9] they would have been in breach of duty by considering employees. The formulation of the duties of management of the modern company needs

_____
9 Sections 46 and 74.

more thorough and realistic appraisal[10]. Modern business enterprise is often very large and complex. This size and complexity gives it considerable resources of power which can be used to control and influence others. The regulation of companies and management is a vital matter of social control calling for a sensitive balancing of efficiency and fairness. It cannot be solved by any simple formula, economic or otherwise.

10 See Philip A Joseph (1980) 14 UBCLR 75 for a valuable discussion of the relationship of corporate management to labour.

CHAPTER 2

A brief general history of English company law

To understand modern company law, one needs to know something of the economic, social and legal history of business enterprise. In some of the chapters which follow we will give more detailed discussion of the history of particular branches of company law where this is helpful to an understanding of the modern law, but we will start by giving a brief general survey[1]. The history can be divided into four main periods:

(1) from earliest times until the South Sea Bubble;
(2) from the Bubble Act until the first Companies Act 1844;
(3) from 1844 until the United Kingdom's accession to the Common Market; and
(4) from 1972 until the present day.

1 THE EARLY PERIOD UP TO THE SOUTH SEA BUBBLE

The simplest and earliest form of business organisation is the sole trader. In the Middle Ages the principal trades were regulated by the guilds of merchants which roughly resembled modern trade protection associations with the ceremonial and social activities of organisations such as City Livery Companies and the Free Masons[2]. The guilds regulated a broad branch of trade or conferred on their members a monopoly of dealing in a particular kind of commodity. Their regulations also covered apprenticeships and the employment of journeymen, i e qualified employees. The medieval guild was part of the structure of municipal organisation in England, closely linked with the borough[3], and thus existed as much for social as economic purposes. There was a fellowship between the members and a concern for welfare as well as business standards. It represented a closed economic group of sole traders characterised by corporate monopoly and privilege, albeit usually of a local extent[4]. As with a modern cartel the standard of regulation was set by the least efficient economic unit[5]. The purpose of the guild was to ensure an adequate level of profit to the poorest business. The effect of this was

---

1 See Sir William Holdsworth *A History of English Law* (1932) vol VIII, chapter IV, para 4; R R Formoy *The Historical Foundations of Modern Company Law* (1923); C A Cooke *Corporation Trust and Company* (1950); W R Scott *Joint Stock Companies to 1720* (1912); A B DuBois *The English Business Company after the Bubble Act 1720–1800* (1938), H R Hahlo [1982] JR 139; Bishop Hunt *The Development of the Business Corporation in England 1800–1867* (1936); and L C B Gower *Principles of Modern Company Law* (4th edn, 1979) chapters 2 and 3.
2 *Gower*, op cit, p 23.
3 *Cooke*, op cit, chapter 11.
4 See Julien Freund *The Sociology of Max Weber* (1968) p 154 ff.
5 *Cooke*, op cit, p 22.

necessarily to increase the wealth and power of the most efficient members. Through the guild and the borough merchants were able to throw off the feudal yoke. Through the craft guild and the trading company, associations of merchants were able to throw off local public control. The result of this was eventually to make the whole country the economic unit and to lead to national economic policies[6].

The two earliest business organisations which bear some resemblance to the modern partnership are the *Commenda* and the *Societas*[7]. The *Commenda*, which was found in Babylonian and Arabic as well as Western law[8], was a cross between a modern partnership and a loan and involved one person advancing money to a trader on terms that he should have a return which varied with the profits. Originally this was a temporary association for a particular transaction. The *Commenda* has largely disappeared from the English scene but still exists in the other Continental European members of the EC. The *Societas* was a more permanent association which was the forerunner of the modern partnership. As such it developed as a form of commercial agency and gradually the common law and equitable rules coalesced into specialised partnership principles. The reason given for the relative unimportance of *Commenda* and the development of *Societas* in England is that English business practice lagged behind that of Continental countries in book-keeping. 'If a limit to individual liability is to be operated it requires a separation of the accounts of the firm from the capital accounts of the capitalist partners'[9], *Commenda* is the earliest transaction in which we see a method of capitalistic accounting[10]. This type of accounting did not generally develop in England until much later. The normal convention was a simple division of profits and simple participation in the business with no capital account.

At common law, the only means of incorporation were by Royal Charter or statute although there is some suggestion that before the Reformation Papal Charters were recognised[11]. Incorporation by Royal Charter was relatively rarely given to traders. The original purpose of incorporation by Royal Charter seems to have been to confer protection and status[12]. The grant was often for charitable purposes such as the founding of a new college or incorporation of an existing college at Oxford or Cambridge. Later, in the Elizabethan period, the dominant purpose was to regulate a particular trade[13]. This became necessary when the guild system had declined and become the subject of abuse. Some of these grants amounted to monopolies. Underlying the grant, however, was the idea of public purpose. The concept of public purpose and benefit in incorporation declined due to a number of factors—the Stuart abuse of the Royal prerogative, the increase of trade and manufacture and the growth of overseas trade, originally as privateering expeditions. This is the beginning of the rise of capitalistic enterprise whose dominant characteristic is to produce a more open economic group[14], but this is to anticipate later events.

6 *Cooke*, op cit, p 34.
7 See *Holdsworth*, op cit, p 195 ff.
8 See *Max Weber on Law in Economy and Society* (1954) ed Max Rheinstein, p 148.
9 *Cooke*, op cit, p 46.
10 *Weber*, op cit.
11 For religious and educational bodies.
12 *Cooke*, op cit, p 52.
13 Ibid, p 53.
14 *Freund*, op cit.

With the development of overseas and especially colonial trade we see the rise of 'merchant ventures'. The merchant venturers gave rise to 'regulated companies' which extended the guild system into overseas trade. The pattern was for each member to trade on his own stock but as a member of the 'company'. From the beginning of the fifteenth century the Crown made extensive grants of privileges to companies of merchants trading overseas. Later these were Royal Charters providing for incorporation and a monopoly of trade in a particular region. The objects of such grants are to provide for proper organisation of the trade, to develop a new trade or colonisation. The interest of merchants was not in separate legal personality as such so much as the exercise of governmental power and trading privilege.

The next development is the concept of joint stock[15]. Historically this seems to have been linked with the grant of a monopoly. The grant is made to a 'company' of individuals who raise stock for the exploitation of the monopoly. Joint stock represents a combination of association and exploitation of a privilege. This concept was particularly useful with overseas trading ventures. At first each voyage was a separate venture but later more permanent accounting took place. The East India Company was the first to combine incorporation, overseas trade and joint stock raised from the general public. This development was summed up well by a Committee of the House of Commons in 1604. 'A whole Company', it said, 'by this means, is become as one man'[16]. Although some joint stock ventures obtained incorporation, many did not and were in essence partnerships describing themselves loosely as 'companies'. Stocks and shares in both incorporated and unincorporated ventures began to be dealt in on the developing stock market which Parliament found it necessary to regulate in 1696. By the beginning of the eighteenth century, therefore, there was considerable diversity in the forms of business organisation and added to this there was some trade in the charters of defunct chartered corporations. Further, in 1694 in return for money lent to the government by a group of individuals, a Royal Charter incorporated the group as a joint stock company. This was the Governor and Company of the Bank of England[17]. Underlying this was the idea that the money lent to the state constituted a fund of credit on which loans could be made by the bank. It did not take long for the next stage to be reached whereby a company might venture to take over the whole national debt. Such a company would be granted trading privileges and exchange its shares for existing holdings of government stock. It is against this background that one must now consider the South Sea Bubble[18]. This had its origin in 1711 when a lawyer and financier, John Blunt, formed a company styled 'The Company of Merchants of Great Britain Trading to the South Seas'. The main object of the company was to secure the trade in the South Seas. The company prospered so much that in 1719 it offered to take over the National Debt, buying out either for cash or for shares all other creditors. The company proposed to pay £7.5 m for this privilege and to reduce the interest

15 *Cooke*, op cit, chapter IV.
16 Report of Committee on the Bill for Free Trade: Journals of the House of Commons I, p 218 in respect of the Muscovy Company.
17 For the background, see *Scott*, op cit, vol 1 and J Carswell *The South Sea Bubble* (1960) chapters 1 and 2.
18 See *Scott*, op cit; L Melville, pseud (LS Benjamin) *The South Sea Bubble* (1921); *Carswell*, op cit, on which what follows is based.

which the country was paying. At this time the National Debt stood at £31 m and rumours were circulating that the country was facing bankruptcy. The government of the day regarded the scheme as the answer to its problems. It did so all the more willingly as Blunt had bribed some of the Ministers. The company persuaded Parliament to pass the South Sea Act which empowered the company to pay anyone who had a government annuity the amount which was due to him. Payment was not, however, to be in cash, but in shares in the company. It was anticipated that the close connection with the government would act as great publicity for the company and inspire confidence in its business. For a time this was indeed the case. People were remarkably ignorant about trading in the South Seas but they were tremendously impressed by the size of the enterprise and its close connection with the government. Everyone, merchants, professors, doctors, clergymen and even the Canton of Berne invested in the company. Within a few days the £100 shares went up to £1,000. Blunt and his colleagues made huge fortunes. The success of the South Sea Co led to numerous similar schemes with a rich variety of objects. These companies were floated to fatten elephants, fix quicksilver and even for 'a certain design which will hereafter be promulgated'. People's credulity knew no bounds and there was such an urge to invest in anything that resembled a share that stalls were set up in the streets. The size of this investment reached incredible proportions. At one time the amounts invested in such companies amounted to £500 m, twice the then value of all the land in England.

However, in 1720 the bubble inevitably burst. The immediate cause seems to have been proceedings against other joint stock companies. Whether these were instigated by or at the behest of the directors of the South Sea Co is a matter of controversy[19]. People began to realise that the shares could not possibly be worth the amount they had paid for them and they tried to get rid of them. The South Sea Co itself was unable to meet its liabilities and the whole tower came tumbling down. In the resulting confusion there was great fury and cries for vengeance. It was suggested that the directors of the South Seas Co should be given a Roman execution. A government enquiry was set up. A Bill was passed for the confiscation of the property of those guilty of fraud. A sum of £2 m was provided for compensation. A number of Ministers were disgraced. The South Sea Bubble and the resulting Bubble Act set back the development of joint stock companies for some time.

2 THE PERIOD FROM 1720–1844

The Bubble Act (6 Geo 1, c 18) prohibited a company from acting as a body corporate and from raising transferable stocks and shares without the legal authority of a Royal Charter or Act of Parliament. Any scheme contravening the Act was illegal and void. On the other hand it exempted a number of undertakings *including the South Sea Co itself* and contained a proviso that nothing in the Act prohibited the carrying on of business in partnership. The Act is a poor commencement of English company legislation which Maitland said 'seems to scream at us from the Statute Book'[20].

---

19 See L C B Gower (1952) 68 LQR 214.
20 F W Maitland *Collected Papers* vol 3, 'Trust and Corporation' p 390.

However, only one prosecution under the Act is reported until the beginning
of the nineteenth century[1]. Whether this was due to the prolixity of the Act
or the popular distrust of the joint stock concept as a medium of investment
is not clear. Maitland explained the matter thus: 'In its panic, Parliament
had spoken much of mischief to the public, and judges, whose conception of
the mischievous was liable to change, were able to declare that where there
was no mischievous tendency there was no offence'[2]. In the resulting hiatus,
given that Royal Charters and Acts of Parliament were difficult to obtain,
much was left to the ingenuity of legal draftsmanship. The principal development was the 'deed of settlement company' drafted so as to comply with
the Act[3]. This was a combination of trust and association. Its assets were
held on trust by trustees but its business was managed by managers or
directors. What the investor obtained was an interest in the trust fund.
Attempts were made from time to time to make such interests transferable
and the resultant provisions often attained through complexity the practical
effect, if not the letter, of limited liability. However, deed of settlement
companies were vulnerable to prosecution under the Bubble Act, despite
the fact that they were becoming increasingly common in business. In the
early nineteenth century, after a crop of cases on the Act, an enquiry was
carried out into the working of the Act and it was eventually repealed in 1825
at the behest of the Board of Trade. There was nevertheless doubt as to the
legality of deed of settlement companies at common law until 1843[4].

It is with the growth of the railway companies that we see a considerable
impetus for legislative reform. Railways needed to raise capital from the
public. It was cumbrous and expensive for such enterprises to obtain incorporation by Act of Parliament and they were not likely to obtain the grant of
a Royal Charter. There were gradual and piecemeal reforms. An attempt to
pass a general Companies Act in 1838 was defeated in the House of Lords by
opposition led by Lord Brougham[5]. It is odd that in this respect Brougham
should find himself at odds with John Austin[6] and John Stuart Mill[7]. The
latter was to compare the English position very unfavourably with that of
America in the 1840s. However, the immediate cause of the first Companies
Act was business fraud. A Select Committee was set up in 1841 'to inquire
into the State of the Laws respecting Joint Stock Companies (except for
Banking), with a view to the greater Security of the Public'. This came under
the chairmanship of William Gladstone in 1843 and reported in 1844 that
there was a need for legislation providing for registration of deed of
settlement documents with a public official. This was enacted as 7 & 8 Vict,
c 110 and is the first modern Companies Act. The deed of settlement
company, when registered, was invested with the qualities and incidents of
corporations, although the full effect of this was not recognised until later in
the nineteenth century. The effect of this legislation was to shift from the
privilege of incorporation to the right of incorporation provided the

---

1 *R v Cawood* (1724) 2 Ld Raym 1361.
2 *Maitland*, op cit, p 391.
3 See *Gower*, op cit, p 32 ff, for a useful discussion of such 'companies'.
4 See *Gower* op cit, p 39.
5 See P L Cottrell *Industrial Finance 1830–1914* (1980) p 44.
6 See (1825) Parliamentary History and Review 711.
7 See J S Mill *Principles of Political Economy* (1909) Book V, chapter IX.

statutory conditions were fulfilled[8]. Nevertheless, traces of the old privilege idea lingered on in the case law.

3 THE PERIOD FROM 1844–1972

In 1844, there were about 970 deed of settlement companies of which 170 were in insurance[9]. The 1844 Act provided for incorporation on registration. It did so by a system of provisional registration which was later made complete. Until then the company was not fully incorporated. It did not provide for limited liability nor for a separate regime for the winding up of companies. Between 1844 and 1856, 910 companies were registered under the Act of which 219 were in insurance, 211 in gas and water, 85 in markets and public halls, 46 in shipping and 41 in lending. The Act thus seems to have had relatively little effect on the organisation and financing of manufacturing industry. Only 106 such companies were registered, of which the largest group was 13 cotton companies.

The introduction of limited liability

The companies formed under the 1844 legislation were unlimited companies in the sense that their shareholders still had unlimited liability for the debts of the company[10]. Limited liability could be the subject of individual contracting between the shareholders and the creditors. Indeed, complex drafting of deeds of settlement and cumbrous legal procedures produced the effect, if not the letter, of limited liability, since creditors had to sue each shareholder in a separate action and, in practice, sued the richest. There was a question about the validity of clauses purporting to create limited liability but such a clause was upheld in 1852 in *Hallett v Dowdall*[11]. The Court of Exchequer Chamber held that it was valid and could bind third parties with express notice.

After some debate, limited liability was introduced in the Limited Liability Act 1855. It was introduced by Bouverie, the Vice President of the Board of Trade, as a progressive reform measure which would help to vitalise British business. He argued that increasing numbers of companies were seeking incorporation under French and American laws to achieve limited liability. Twenty 'English' companies had been formed in France from 1853 to 1854[12].

Other arguments in favour were:

(1)   it enabled small capital to be turned to profitable employment;
(2)   it was a question of free trade against monopoly;
(3)   unlimited liability was impracticable and impeded work such as railways, canals and docks;
(4)   it prevented prudent men from becoming members of companies which were consequently being formed by the rash and reckless.

---

8 See J W Hurst *The Legitimacy of the Business Corporation in the US 1780–1970* (1970) p 58.
9 *Cottrell*, op cit, pp 44–45.
10 See H N Butler (1986) 6 International Review of Law and Economics 169.
11 (1852) 21 LJQB 98.
12 139 Official Report (3rd series) (1855) p 321.

The main arguments against it were that:

(1) it was not a privilege to be given to partners but a right to be taken from creditors;
(2) it encouraged people to trade beyond their means;
(3) it led to speculation and fraud;
(4) there was adequate capital available without it[13].

Liability was limited to the amount unpaid on the shares in the case of members of companies which had:

(1) at least 25 members holding £10 shares, of which 20% had been paid up;
(2) three-quarters of their capital subscribed; and
(3) the word 'limited' after the company's name[14].

The first requirement was introduced in the House of Lords because of a reluctance to extend the principle of limited liability to small trading companies. The Act was rapidly replaced by the Joint Stock Companies Act 1856, a comprehensive measure which abolished the old system of provisional registration and introduced the modern form of constitution consisting of memorandum and articles of association and separate winding-up procedures. Incorporation and limited liability could be had by any company mustering seven subscribers. The safeguards of 1855 were brushed aside in the name of laissez-faire. Only the label 'Limited' and the facility of searching the public register protected the public. From then on we see the growth of the modern companies legislation. The first modern Companies Act is said to be the Act of 1862 which was a more comprehensive measure than the earlier legislation and was described by Sir Francis Palmer, the Victorian company law expert, as the 'Magna Carta of co-operative enterprise'. It was a major act of consolidation and also introduced companies limited by guarantee and unlimited companies, as well as more detailed provisions on winding up. It is after this Act that we see the incorporation for the first time of many industrial enterprises.

It is possible as Maitland[15] argued that if limited liability had not been introduced as a matter of law, it would have developed as a matter of contract. Its importance from an economic point of view[16] was that it eliminated the need for a number of separate contracts and substituted the separate capital of the company for the private property of the individual shareholders who might constantly change. In doing so it cheapened transaction costs, reduced risk for investors by transferring it to trade creditors and thereby also cheapened the cost of credit. It thus facilitated the raising of large masses of capital and the development of new industries at home and abroad. The number of incorporations rose dramatically in the period after 1856.

13 See B C Hunt *The Development of the Business Corporation in England 1800–1867* (1936) chapter VI; R R Formoy *The Historical Foundations of Modern Company Law* (1923) section V and (1855) XXIV Law Times 142.
14 18 & 19 Vict c 133.
15 *Maitland*, op cit, p 392.
16 See R Posner *Economic Analysis of Law* (3rd edn, 1986) chapter 14; P Halpern, M Trebilcock and S Turnbull (1980) 30 U of TLJ 117; O E Williamson (1981) 19 J Econ Lit 1537.

Major trends in the law between 1862 and 1972

Since much of what followed will be dealt with in detail later, we shall concentrate on the major trends in the legislation and case law between 1862 and the present day. The practice developed of having major reviews and consolidation statutes approximately every 20 years. Thus there was major legislation in 1908, 1929 and 1948. This was broken in the period after 1948 when successive governments failed to implement the totality of the Jenkins Report. There was piecemeal reform but no major consolidation until 1985.

In this period there are two rival approaches to companies—what we might call the *utility* approach and the *responsibility* approach[17]. The 1844 and 1855 Acts were largely based on the utility approach—the recognition that the company performed rational economic and social ends and was to be encouraged. Consistent with this approach was the permission given to companies to reduce their capital, to alter their objects clauses, the recognition and privileges given to the private company and the gradual recognition of management autonomy and the parent and subsidiary relationship. In the case law the same trend is marked by the recognition of the floating charge as a flexible species of security over the undertaking of companies and the reluctance of the courts to overrule business judgments.

However, it is arguable that the trend towards responsibility has been even stronger. From the beginning there has been a policy of requiring disclosure by companies of basic data by registration with the Registrar of Companies. Today the disclosure obligations extend to a wide range of information. This is mainly statute law. In the case law, the trend towards responsibility is manifest in the ultra vires doctrine which restricted corporate activity to the objects in the objects clause and matters incidental thereto. In fact the justification of the doctrine contained some recognition of the privilege approach to incorporation. The trend towards responsibility can also be seen in the development as a protection for creditors of the capital maintenance doctrine which prohibited the watering down of share capital by transactions at patent undervalue, the trafficking by a company in its own shares and the distribution of improper dividends. Gradually the courts realised that minority shareholders in a small incorporated firm could be locked in and unable to curb the power of the majority within the orthodox decision-making framework. A balance was struck between the business judgment rule and the need for intervention to prevent manifest wrongdoing or an interference with private rights. The case law, however, did not provide a particularly satisfactory system of minority shareholder remedies and this was eventually supplemented by statute. Whereas shareholders generally have some part in the constitutional structure of the company, creditors do not. Their remedies are essentially contractual and centre around the presence or absence of security and the type of security which they hold. Creditors' remedies were improved by the modern system of winding up—a form of corporate bankruptcy—which started in 1856 and assumed its modern form ultimately in 1929.

Much modern reform legislation has been aimed at safeguarding the market for investment capital and more recently the market for control. The first is concerned with disclosure on public issues of securities, continuing disclosure and the prevention of fraudulent market practices. The second is

17 *Hurst*, op cit, passim.

concerned with the regulation of mergers and takeovers of companies. In both these areas the public interest is involved.

An important development in the post-war period was the growth of a sophisticated system of self-regulation which supplemented the legislation and case law[18]. Historically the burden of supervision has rested with The Stock Exchange which from its earliest period has evolved rules to deal with membership of the Exchange and market practice[19]. It has more recently formulated detailed regulations with which companies whose shares are listed or dealt in on The Stock Exchange must comply. These have been the subject of EC directives and the present law is set out in the Financial Services Act 1986. Also the Bank of England as the centre of the City of London's financial activities maintains a general oversight of the financial system, and in particular the financial securities markets. The Bank of England has taken a leading role in the development of self-regulation of the securities market. It was on the instigation of the Governor of the Bank of England that the City Working Party was set up in 1959 which led to the formulation of a City Code on Takeovers and Mergers and the establishment of a Panel on Takeovers and Mergers, the latter with an appellate structure. There are a number of other city institutions which represent various sectors of the securities industry and all of these were represented on the Council for the Securities Industry (CSI) which was set up in 1978 to exercise general supervision of the industry. There has since been a trend towards increased legal regulation[20].

4 1972 UNTIL THE PRESENT DAY

On 1 January 1973, the UK joined the European Economic Community. This meant that it became subject to the provisions of the Treaty of Rome which dealt with the harmonisation and unification of company laws. We will discuss the relevant provisions of the Treaty and the various measures in Chapter 3 so here we shall be brief[1]. In s 9 of the European Communities Act 1972, the UK implemented the First Directive of the EEC on company law harmonisation. The major effect of this was to add a complicated gloss to the ultra vires doctrine and directors' authority[2]. The Companies Act 1980 implemented the Second Directive of the EEC which deals with share capital and classification of companies[3] and the Companies Act 1981 implemented the Fourth Directive on company accounts. The Stock Exchange (Listing) Regulations 1984[4] issued under the 1972 Act gave effect to three directives of the EC[5] to harmonise the law and practice of the grant and maintenance of listings on stock exchanges of member states. These are now consolidated in the Financial Services Act 1986. There are a number of

---

18 See B Rider and E Hew (1977) 19 Mal L Rev 144.
19 See its evidence to the Committee to Review the Functioning of Financial Institutions.
20 The Gower Report on Investor Protection (Cmnd 9125) 1984; The Times, 18 October 1984; the White Paper, *Financial Services in the United Kingdom* (Cmnd 9432) 1985.
 1 See Chapter 3, post.
 2 See Chapter 10, post.
 3 See Chapter 4, post.
 4 SI 1984/716.
 5 See Sch 1 to SI 1984/716.

further measures in the pipeline, prominent amongst which are worker participation in corporate decision making and the project for a European Company, which would be a genuine transnational company.

In 1985–86, the companies legislation was the subject of a major consolidation with an attempt to restate the law in a more rational shape and to modernise the language. The principal act is now the Companies Act 1985. There are separate acts dealing with business names and insider trading. An Insolvency Act was passed in 1985 which was consolidated in the Insolvency Act 1986. This legislation attempts to co-ordinate personal and corporate insolvency into the same statute. It does this by a mixture of consolidation and reform. In the Financial Services Act 1986 a new regime was set up to replace the CSI. This introduced a system of self-regulation within an over-arching legal framework. The new system is a pyramid of power descending from the Secretary of State for Trade and Industry through the Securities and Investments Board (SIB) to a cluster of self-regulatory agencies. The Financial Services Act requirements replace the earlier law contained in the Prevention of Fraud (Investment) Act 1958 and the Stock Exchange (Listing) Regulations 1984. It is hoped that the new system will enable the United Kingdom to cope with the international financial revolution. Whether this will be so remains to be seen. It may be that domestic regimes are incapable of controlling the financial forces which have been unleashed by the new developments.

As if to demonstrate the innate capacity of UK corporate laws to resist rational and systematic structure Parliament enacted the Companies Act 1989[6]. This implements the Seventh EC Directive on Consolidated Accounts[7] and the Eighth Directive on Regulation of Auditors[8]. The remainder of the act attempts to complete the reform of ultra vires and constructive notice, makes interim reforms to company charges, strengthens the range of investigatory powers of the DTI, reforms the competition rules governing mergers, deregulates private companies, modifies the insolvency rules applicable to settlement and clearing systems on financial markets as well as making further amendments to the companies and financial services legislation. Apart from deregulation of private companies relatively little attention seems to have been paid to the transaction costs of compliance with UK corporate laws, as opposed to the achievement of small economies in the Civil Service.

If there is one characteristic which distinguishes UK and EC corporate laws from the USA it is the level of sophistication of the discussion of policy issues. With rare exceptions[9] there is little sophistication in the law reform debate. The rules often seem to have a mind and will of their own, which, coupled with the increasing bureaucratisation of the reform process, makes formal and substantive rationalisation a difficult goal.

6 See C Swinson *A Guide to the Companies Act 1989* (1990).
7 26 OJL 193, 18 July 1983.
8 27 OJL 126, 12 May 1984.
9 Notably the work of Gower, Diamond, Prentice and Sealy on financial services, company charges, ultra vires and private companies respectively.

CHAPTER 3

Harmonisation of company law in the EC

There have been European influences on the development of English company law from an early date. The first concepts of corporateness and partnership, as well as the system of double entry bookkeeping, were derived from European ideas[1]. In the nineteenth century the adoption of the modern form of constitution was partly influenced by French ideas, and later the German reforms, which gave legal recognition to private companies, indirectly influenced the adoption of the private/public dichotomy in the UK[2]. Alarm at the rapid technological and scientific advances of Germany at the end of the century was the cause of the adoption of what is now s 4 of CA 1985, which enables a company to alter its objects clause[3]. Connected with these legal influences is the close geographic proximity of England to Europe and the inevitability of trade with Europe. Thus, before 1973 a UK company such as ICI Ltd could find itself brought before the European Court for violation of the anti-trust laws of the EC[4].

ECONOMIC INTEGRATION UNDER THE TREATY OF ROME

On 1 January 1973, the UK became a member state of the European Communities. The Communities are the European Economic Community, the European Coal and Steel Community and the European Atomic Energy Community. It is with the EC that we are presently concerned. The EC, as Dr Walter Hallstein, the first President of the EEC Commission, wrote 'is a remarkable legal phenomenon. It is a creation of the law; it is a source of law; and it is a legal system . . . The basic law of the European Economic Community, its whole philosophy, is liberal. Its guiding principle is to establish undistorted competition in an undivided market.'[5] In other words, it is equality of treatment between nationals of member states. This philosophy seems based on Adam Smith and Ricardo. The essential doctrine is that there is a general presumption in favour of customs unions and other forms of economic integration. Added to this is the more modern argument of increasing returns from economies of scale. However, the market economy is tempered by social welfare considerations, strong public control of agriculture and transport and a measure of public control over the economy[6]. The EC marks a number of steps on the road from a loose co-operation of nation states towards a federation. At the moment the EC

---

1 See Cooke *Corporation, Trust and Company* (1950).
2 See Chapter 2, ante.
3 See *Re Jewish Colonial Trust (Jeudische Colonial Bank) Ltd* [1908] 2 Ch 287.
4 *Case 48/69 ICI Ltd v EC Commission* [1972] ECR 619.
5 *Europe in the Making* (1973) p 30.
6 See E Stein *Harmonization of European Company Laws* (1971) p 6. See too *Programme of the Commission for 1989* EEC Bull Supp 2/89, pp 7–8.

remains far from being a single integrated unit and at the same time is faced with increasing international competition which is beginning to erode living standards. In 1985 the Commission published proposals to create a Single European Market. This called for 300 regulatory changes leading to a complete elimination of trade barriers and to the free movement of goods, services, capital and people. This was reviewed by the governments of the member states who committed themselves to it through the package of reforms which were known as the Single European Act with 1992 as the target date. Advocates of the Single Market wish to see an unobstructed market of great size governed by market forces, not politics or geography[7].

The UK's membership of the Communities resulted from Treaties of Accession which were given internal effect by the European Communities Act 1972. The 1972 Act provided for the recognition and enforcement of enforceable community rights created or arising by or under the treaties. Thus, we are concerned with the provisions of the Treaty of Rome, further treaties made thereunder or by way of amendment, and secondary legislation adopted by the appropriate institutions under the treaties[8]. Article 189 of the Treaty of Rome defines the principal secondary legislation. A *regulation* has general application. It is binding in its entirety and directly applicable in all member states. A *directive* is binding, as to the result to be achieved, upon each member state to which it is addressed, but leaves to the national authorities the choice of form and methods. A *decision* is binding in its entirety upon those to whom it is addressed, and *recommendations* and *opinions* have no binding force. It is further provided under art 190 that regulations, directives and decisions shall state the reasons on which they are based and shall refer to any proposals or opinions which are required to be obtained pursuant to the treaty. Under s 3(1) of the European Communities Act 1972, any question as to the meaning or effect of any of the treaties, or as to the validity, meaning or effect of any community legislation, is to be treated as a question of law and, if not referred to the European Court, be for determination in accordance with the principles laid down by and any relevant decision of the European Court. Section 3(2) provides that judicial notice shall be taken of the treaties, the Official Journal of the Communities and of any decision or expression of opinion by the European Court. If a member state fails to comply with its obligations under the treaties, it can be brought before the European Court under arts 169 and 170. These articles provide for the action to be brought by the Commission or by another member state. A complicated jurisprudence has developed over the meaning of direct applicability and direct effect. If a provision of the treaty or secondary legislation has direct effect, then an individual or a company may have locus standi. This is a developing, complicated area of law with which it is not possible to deal in detail here[9].

Relevant provisions of the Treaty of Rome

Article 2 of the Treaty sets out the goals of the EC. These are, by establishing a common market and progressively approximating the economic policies of

---

7 See generally Ernst and Whinney *Europe 1992: The Single Market* (1988); N Colchester and D Buchan *Europe Relaunched* (1990); M Silva and B. Sjögren *Europe 1992 and the New World Power Game* (1990).

8 For a useful discussion see T C Hartley *The Foundations of European Community Law* (2nd edn, 1988).

9 Ibid, chapter 7.

member states, to promote throughout the community a harmonious development of economic activities, a continuous and balanced expansion, an increase in stability, an accelerated raising of the standard of living and closer relations between the states belonging to it. Article 3 provides that for the purposes set out in art 2, the activities of the Community shall include, inter alia, (c) the abolition, as between member states of obstacles to freedom of movement for persons, services and capital, and (h) the approximation of the laws of member states to the extent required for the proper functioning of the common market.

The Treaty recognises certain basic freedoms. These include the right of establishment. Article 52 provides for the abolition of restrictions on the freedom of establishment of nationals of a member state in the territory of another. This includes freedom to set up and manage undertakings, in particular companies or firms within the meaning of art 58. Article 58 gives a broad definition of companies or firms. It means companies or firms constituted under civil or commercial law, including co-operative societies, and other legal persons governed by public or private law, save for those which are non-profitmaking. Article 54 provides for the drawing up of a general programme for the abolition of existing restrictions on freedom of establishment within the Community. Under art 54(3)(g) the Council and the Commission are instructed to carry out their duties 'by co-ordinating to the necessary extent the safeguards which, for the protection of the interests of members and others, are required by member states of companies or firms within the meaning of the second paragraph of art 58 with a view to making such safeguards equivalent throughout the Community'.

Article 100 is a general provision on approximation of laws. It provides that the Council shall, acting unanimously on a proposal from the Commission, issue directives for the approximation of such provisions laid down by law, regulation or administrative action in member states and directly affect the establishment or functioning of the common market. The Parliament and the Economic and Social Committee shall be consulted in the case of directives whose implementation would, in one or more member states, involve the amendment of legislation. Articles 100A and 100B which were added later provide for qualified majorities in certain cases.

Article 220 provides that member states shall, so far as is necessary, enter into negotiations with a view to securing inter alia the mutual recognition of companies or firms within the meaning of the second paragraph of art 58, the retention of legal personality in the event of transfer of their seat from one country to another, and the possibility of mergers between companies or firms governed by the laws of different countries; the simplification of formalities governing the reciprocal recognition and enforcement of judgments of courts or tribunals and of arbitration awards. These negotiations will lead to international treaties which will supplement the existing treaties.

Lastly, art 235 contains sweeping-up provisions. If action by the Community proves necessary to attain one of the objectives of the Community and the Treaty of Rome has not provided the necessary powers, the Council shall, acting unanimously on a proposal from the Commission and after consulting the Parliament, take the appropriate measures.

Patterns of legal integration

The three basic legal techniques of integration used are, therefore:

(1)   the removal of all restrictions which discriminate on the basis of nationality;
(2)   the putting into effect of common rules and common policies;
(3)   the approximation of national laws under art 3(h)[10].

The Treaty also uses the terms 'harmonisation', which English lawyers tend to prefer, and 'co-ordination', but there seems to be little consistency in the way in which they are used and there seems to be no meaningful difference between them[11]. All three terms fall short of unification.

The usual pattern is for drafts of proposals to be prepared by the Commission. They may then be discussed in a group convened by the Commission and consisting of 'experts' (ie officials) from member states and may be circulated by the Commission to interested outside bodies. After adoption by the Commission as formal proposals, they are sent to the European Parliament and the Economic and Social Committee for their opinions. In the light of these opinions the Commission may amend their proposals, before presenting them to the Council of Ministers for discussion in a working group of officials from the various member states. Such discussions are normally chaired by officials from the Member State holding the Presidency of the Council of Ministers. They are subsequently referred to the Committee of Permanent Representatives (COREPER) which in turn refers them to the Council of Ministers itself for final decision[12].

Under the European Communities (Amendment) Act 1986, which implements the Single European Act signed at Luxembourg and The Hague on 17 and 28 February 1986, proposals based on arts 7, 49, 54(2), 56(2) (second sentence), 57 (excluding the second sentence of para 2), 100A, 100B, 118A, 130E and 130Q(2) of the Treaty are now subject to qualified majority voting and to a new 'cooperation procedure' with the European Parliament. The latter gives the Parliament the opportunity to express a second opinion but leaves the last word with the Council.

PROGRESS TO DATE

Within the EC, some progress has been made on three broad fronts. First, there are the directives prepared under the provisions of art 54(3)(g); secondly, there are treaties drawn up under art 220, and thirdly, there is a draft regulation providing a statute for a European company drawn up under art 235. Let us look at each of these in turn.

The First Directive (68/151/EEC)[13]   This was adopted on 9 March 1968 and mainly provided for relief against the doctrine of ultra vires and limits on directors' authority as well as providing for some basic publicity. The

---

10   *Stein*, op cit, pp 6–9. See also R M Buxbaum and Klaus J Hopt *Legal Harmonisation and the Business Enterprise* (1988), Chapters 3 and 4.
11   Ibid, p 9. On Community policy with regard to approximation of laws, see the lecture given by Dr C D Ehlermann, Director General of the Legal Service of the Commission published in App 3(b) of 'Approximation of Laws under Article 100 of the EEC Treaty' 22nd Report (1977–78) of the House of Lords Select Committee on the European Communities ('HLSC') (HL 131) (1977–78).
12   This summary of procedure is taken more or less verbatim from *The Single Market— Company Law Harmonisation* published by the Department of Trade and Industry.
13   OJ Special edition 1968(1), pp 41–45.

Directive was implemented by the U K in s 9 of the European Communities Act 1972[14].

The Second Directive (77/91/EEC)[15]   This Directive provides for minimum requirements regarding the formation of companies and the maintenance, increase and reduction of capital. It provides amongst other things for a new classification of private and public companies and introduces compulsory valuation for non-cash consideration provided to a public company in consideration of its allotment of its shares. This Directive was implemented by the Companies Act 1980 in the U K[16]. Some of the other member states have failed to implement this Directive and the Commission has commenced infringement proceedings against them.

The Third Directive (78/855/EEC)[17]   This provides for co-ordination of procedures applying to internal mergers within a member state. It only applies to public companies and to what in English company law are known as reconstructions. It will be applicable mainly where by means of a scheme of arrangement under s 425 of CA 1985 the assets and liabilities of company A are transferred to another, B, in consideration of the issue of shares in B issued to the shareholders of A. A is then dissolved. This procedure is rarely used and is mainly used on a merger of investment trusts. In some minor respects, it is stricter than English law and required changes in ss 425–430. The Directive[18] does not apply to a takeover by acquisition of shares. The Companies (Mergers and Divisions) Regulations 1987, SI 1987/1991 implement it by inserting s 427A and Sch 15A in the CA 1985.

The Fourth Directive (78/660/EEC)[19]   This deals with disclosure of financial information and the contents of a company's annual accounts. This Directive was revised in the light of the U K's membership and now contains a basic requirement that the accounts give 'a true and fair view'. The Directive was implemented in the U K by the Companies Act 1981[20].

Draft Fifth Directive[1]   This deals with the important topics of company structure and worker participation and has been the subject of much controversy[2]. The present position is that the Commission's amended proposals

14 See D D Prentice (1973) 89 LQR 518; J H Farrar and D G Powles (1973) 36 MLR 270; J G Collier and L S Sealy (1973) CLJ 1. See now CA 1985, ss 35 and 35A.
15 20 OJ, L 26, 31 January 1977, pp 1–13.
16 See D D Prentice *The Companies Act 1980* (1980); J Tinnion *The Companies Act 1980* (1980).
17 21 OJ, L 295, 20 October 1978, pp 36–43.
18 See 'Implementation of the Third EC Directive on Company Law', and explanatory and commentative note by the Department of Trade, London 1982.
19 21 OJ, L 222, 14 August 1978, pp 11–31.
20 See G W Eccles and J Cox *Companies Act 1981* (1982).
 1 This Directive was first proposed in 1972; see Official Journal of the European Communities 1972 No C 131/49. The current version is that put forward in 1983 as amended in 1989. 26 OJ, C 240, 9 September 1983, pp 2–38. See the Green Paper on Employee Participation and Company Structure in the European Communities, EEC Bull Supp 8/75. See C M Schmitthoff [1983] JBL 456 and the memoranda of the Law Society's Company Law Committee of March 1984 and April 1990.
 2 See J Welch (1983) 8 ELR 83. See also W Kolvenbach (1990) 11 University of Pennsylvania J of International Business Law 709 at 720–733.

were issued in July 1983 and are under consideration by a Council Working Group of officials from member states and the Commission. It is anticipated that discussion of the draft will take several years. The new draft provides for a distinction between directors of a public limited company who will be responsible for management and those responsible for their supervision. At the end of 1983, the Commission announced an alteration so that this distinction could be achieved either through a two-tier board or a conventional one-tier board as in the UK. On the one-tier board, there would be a division between executive directors who would manage, and non-executive directors who would supervise. The implementation of this distinction as a matter of law would require changes to English law.

Employee participation in corporate decision-making would be required to take one of the following forms.

(1)   through board representation at the supervisory level;
(2)   by means of a works council; or
(3)   through collective agreements giving the same rights as (1) or (2).

Further options are included in respect of employee participation in groups of companies.

In addition to these major provisions, the latest draft also includes provision in respect of (a) the duties and liability of directors; (b) the powers of the general meeting; (c) the rights of shareholders and in particular minority shareholders; (d) approval of annual accounts; and (e) the functions and liability of auditors. With regard to (a) there is a general provision for personal liability for loss suffered by the company as a result of breaches of law, the corporate constitution or other wrongful acts. Liability is to be joint and several which would involve a change in English law and arguably lead to more effective monitoring of management by management. An individual director may be exonerated if he can prove that no fault is attributable to him personally. The draft does not define the standard of care required of directors although the Commission's Explanatory Memorandum to the original proposal in 1972 suggested that 'other wrongful acts' might include negligence and would arguably go further than the current law. With regard to (b), shareholders are given slightly more rights in respect of the convening of meetings. As regards (c), arts 16–18 allow a minority shareholder to bring a derivative action on behalf of the company, even where the general meeting has expressly renounced its right to bring proceedings provided that the plaintiff shareholder voted against the resolution or made objection which was recorded in the minutes. Proceedings can be instituted by a simple majority of the shareholders or in the case of a derivative action by shareholders holding 5% of the issued capital or shares to the value of 100,000 ECUs. An unsuccessful shareholder who fails to establish reasonable grounds for commencing the proceedings may be ordered to pay costs. Presumably in English law, the new interlocutory procedures would protect him against this risk. Under the original art 19, a derivative action could also be brought by a creditor who was unable to obtain payment and such an action would not be affected by any waiver by the company of a breach of duty. This has been deleted and replaced by a vague provision which leaves the matter to be determined by the laws of the member state.

Other important provisions prevent a shareholder from voting on an issue where there is a conflict of interest between the company and him personally.

This would go further than the existing English law. Another provision renders void shareholder agreements whereby a shareholder undertakes always to vote in a certain way. This would involve an alteration of the English law. There are provisions for compulsory reserves and appropriation of profits. The latter would have the effect of shifting the power to determine dividends to the general meeting. Both of these would involve a change in English law.

We will not comment on the detailed provisions in respect of auditors and accounts.

In addition there is also a draft Directive on procedures for informing and consulting employees which overlaps with the Fifth Directive[3]. This is sometimes known as the Vredeling Directive. It does not form part of the company law harmonisation programme as it applies to other employers as well as companies. It would require head offices of large companies to inform and consult employees of subsidiaries or separate establishments through local management. The Department of Employment and the Department of Trade and Industry issued a consultative document in November 1983 on both draft directives. The basic attitude of the government was in favour of voluntary rather than compulsory adoption. It took the view that the introduction of community-wide legislation in this area would contribute nothing to the establishment of a common market in goods and services but would increase employers' costs and damage the competitive position of industry in the community. Legislation of this kind would do nothing to cope with rising unemployment but at the same time be likely to disrupt existing industrial relations practices. This undoubtedly overstates the case. Many of the proposals are attractive and would involve considerable improvement to English law. On the other hand, the cost factor must be weighed up and reforms should not be introduced if the costs are prohibitive.

The Sixth Directive (82/891/EEC)[4]   This was adopted on 17 December 1982 and deals with scissions or divisions. 'Scission' means the transaction whereby a public company ('plc') transfers to a number of public companies ('plcs') within the same member state which are already incorporated or yet to be formed, all its assets and liabilities in exchange for the issue of shares to the shareholders of the original company. It is the logical opposite of merger and might be termed demerger. The Directive should have been implemented by 1 February 1986 but this was delayed. It is now implemented by the Companies (Mergers and Divisions) Regulations 1987, SI 1987/1991.

The Seventh Directive (83/349/EEC)[5]   This deals with group accounts and supplements the Fourth Directive. It was adopted on 13 June 1983 and was implemented by CA 1989.

---

3 26 OJ, C 217, 12 August 1983, pp 3–16.
4 25 OJ, L 378, 31 December 1982, pp 47–54. See 'Company Law: Scissions' 43rd Report (1979–80) of the HLSC (HL 206) (1979–80).
5 26 OJ, L 193, 18 July 1983, pp 1–17. See 'Group Accounts' 18th Report (1981–82) of the HLSC (HL 214) (1981–82). See (1984) 9 ELR 143; S Turley (1986) 7 Co Law 10.

The Eighth Directive (84/253/EEC)[6]   This deals with the qualifications and independence of auditors of both public and private companies[7] and was adopted on 10 April 1984. This was implemented by CA 1989.

Draft Ninth Directive   This deals with certain aspects of the group relationship[8] and is in the course of preparation. The preliminary draft had been greatly influenced by the German law relating to groups. A revised text was circulated informally to member states in December 1984. The revised text seeks to provide an organised legal structure for the 'unified management' of a plc which is controlled by any other undertaking (whether a company or not) and of that other undertaking. The Directive will also set out rules for the conduct of groups which are not subject to 'unified management' although in this case the rules would apply to the relations between the parent or dominant undertaking and those members of the group which are plcs. Unless the dominant undertaking formalises its relationship by one of the methods specified by the Directive it will be liable for any losses sustained by the dependent company resulting from that influence and attributable to a fault in management or to action which was not in its interests. There are to be two methods for constituting a group – the control contract or a unilateral declaration of control. In addition, the Directive would leave member states free to introduce other methods of achieving the same result. The revised text was the subject of a consultative document published in 1985.

Proposal for a Tenth Directive[9]   This proposal is designed to facilitate on a Community-wide basis the type of merger between plcs dealt with in the Third Directive. Work on a draft convention on this subject started before the enlargement of the EC but was then suspended. Meetings were resumed in 1984 at which it was decided that the draft convention should be converted into a proposal for a Directive which was adopted by the Commission on 4 January 1985. The proposal is currently under consideration.

The Eleventh Directive[10]   The Commission has adopted a proposal for a directive dealing with disclosure requirements in respect of branches opened in a member state by certain types of companies governed by the law of another state. The Department of Trade and Industry issued a consultative memorandum on this on 19 August 1987.

The Twelfth Directive[11]   This allows private companies with only one member. This is permitted already in a number of jurisdictions.

Proposal for a Thirteenth Directive[12]   This deals with takeovers and is influenced by the City of London Takeover Code. It is dealt with in detail in Chapters 35 and 41. The UK government is concerned that it is too inflexible and may inhibit takeovers.

---

6 27 OJ, L 126, 12 May 1984, pp 20–26.
7 See 'Qualifications of Company Auditors', 12th Report (1979–80) of the HLSC (HL 60) (1979–80).
8 See F Woolridge *Groups of Companies* (1981); T Hadden *The Control of Corporate Groups* (1983) p 42; J Welch (1986) 7 Co Law 112.
9 Bull Supp 1985/3; 28 OJ, C 23, 25 January 1985, pp 11–15. See J Welch (1986) 7 Co Law 69.
10 32 OJ 1989, L 395, 30 December 1989.
11 32 OJ 1989, L 395/40, 30 December 1989.
12 32 OJ, C 64, 14 March 1989, pp 8–14.

Directive on prospectuses[13]   This relates to the issue and contents of prospectuses and the object is to co-ordinate national requirements for the admission of securities to listing. This was implemented in the UK by The Stock Exchange (Listing) Regulations 1984[14] made under the European Communities Act 1972, together with further directives (79/279/EEC) and (82/121/EEC) which relate to admission to listing on a stock exchange and continuing disclosure. These are now consolidated in the Financial Services Act 1986. There is a further Directive adopted on 22 June 1987 providing for mutual recognition of listing particulars. This requires a prospectus and vetting by the competent authority[15] which in the UK is the Council of the Stock Exchange.

Amongst other matters that have been or are currently under consideration are European economic interest groupings[16], takeover formalities and defences in different member states[17], liquidations, reservations of property clauses, insider trading and disclosure of substantial shareholdings. A European Economic Interest Grouping means a new legal form enabling undertakings in different member states to establish common, non-profit support activities with unlimited liability. The regulation came before the House of Lords Select Committee on the European Communities in 1984 and was adopted by the Council of Ministers on 25 July 1985[18]. This was supplemented by the European Economic Interest Grouping Regulations 1989 (SI 1989 No 638).

There is a report by Professor Scholten on what amounts to a members' voluntary winding up. A revised draft is being prepared. Work on reservation of property clauses is now closely tied in with the Council of Europe's draft convention on the topic.

On 29 February 1968, the original member states of the EC other than the Netherlands signed the convention on the mutual recognition of companies and legal persons[19]. The convention was to apply to all companies incorporated in any member state and would include an English partnership. Recognition was to be accorded when the company has its statutory registered office in one of the member states. This would be subject to certain exceptions based on the principle of the real seat. After much discussion, the member states have now decided to abandon the project. Mutual recognition occurs in practice anyway, without the necessity of a Convention.

A draft convention has been prepared dealing with bankruptcy, winding-

---

13 See 22 OJ, L 66, 16 March 1979, pp 21–32; 23 OJ, L 100, 17 April 1980, pp 1–26; 25 OJ, L 48, 20 February 1982, pp 26–29; 30 OJ, L 185, 4 July 1987, pp 81–83. See too 32 OJ, C 101, 22 April 1989, p 13; 32 OJ, L 124, 5 May 1989, pp 8–15.
14 SI 1984/716.
15 See also EEC Draft Directive for Prospectuses for Unlisted Securities (80/893) which is the subject of the 43rd Report (1980–81) of the HLSC (HL 271) (1980–81).
16 See 31 OJ, C 153, 11 June 1987, pp 8–10; S Israel (1988) 9 Co Law 14; 25th Report of the HLSC 1984.
17 See C Bradley (1986) 7 Co Law 131; J Dine (1988) 9 Co Law 56.
18 28 OJ, L 199, 31 July 1985, pp 1–9.
19 EEC Bull Supp 2/69; B Goldman *European Commercial Law* (1973) p 389; G K Morse [1972] JBL 195.

up, arrangements, compositions and similar proceedings[20]. This supplements the convention on mutual recognition of judgments which has now been given internal effect by legislation[1]. It has undergone a great deal of revision, particularly as a result of U K membership and the latest draft convention and report is contained in Bulletin Supplement 2/82. This in essence provides for the rationalisation of bankruptcy, winding up and analogous proceedings in the EC. First, it sets out detailed rules to enable bankruptcy jurisdiction to be vested in a single and appropriate national court. Secondly, it seeks to secure that the liquidator appointed by the court has extensive authority to administer the insolvent estate, wherever situated in the EC. Thirdly, it aims at simplification of the liquidator's duties in collecting assets and determining claims by a limited meaure of harmonisation and identification of applicable law. Fourthly, it aims at simplification of the rules and reduction of the cost for a foreign creditor making a claim. The draft convention was debated in the House of Lords Select Committee on the EC in 1981 and a Council Working Group carried out a second reading of the text in 1984. There are still a number of points upon which agreement has not been reached. The Council for Legal Services was asked to advise on the implications of a convention which is not necessarily applied to all member states. The matter was then considered by the Working Party and a further report was submitted to COREPER.

A further draft convention dealing with international mergers of companies[2] has been superseded by the proposal for the Tenth Directive and considerable work has been done on harmonisation of the law relating to disclosure of information to employees on a merger[3]. An EC Mergers Regulation was adopted in 1990 to implement a new regime of competition law within the Community. This is dealt with in Chapter 41[4].

The last measure to be discussed is the most ambitious. This is the *draft regulation for a European company*[5]. The proposal goes beyond harmonisation and provides for an additional form of incorporation which will have registration with the Community. It will be available when two or more limited companies merge or form a joint holding or subsidiary company.

Much work on this project was done by Professor Pieter Sanders of the Netherlands, although the French claim some responsibility for the paternity of

20 See Report of the Advisory Committee on the Draft Convention (Cmnd 6602). See also 'Bankruptcy Convention' 26th Report (1980–81) of the HLSC (HL 175) (1980–81). See M Hunter QC (1972) 21 ICLQ 682, (1976) 25 ICLQ 310; I Fletcher (1977) 2 ELR 15; J H Farrar [1977] JBL 320.
1 The Convention on Jurisdiction and the Enforcement of Judgements in Civil and Commercial Matters, dated 27 September 1968 and amended on 9 October 1978. (1978) OJC 304, 30 October; (1979) OJC 59, 5 March.
2 See 'International Mergers' 28th Report (1977–78) of the HLSC (HL 159) (1977–78).
3 See 'Employee Consultation' 37th Report (1980–81) of the HLSC (HL 250) (1980–81). See also 'Comparative survey of the protection of employees in the event of the insolvency of their employer in the Member States of the European Communities' Doc V/305/1/76 final (Professor G Schnorr).
4 (1990) OJ, L 257/13 in force 21 September 1990.
5 See Bull Supp 4/75; Proposal for a European Company Statute—A Consultative Document (DTI) December 1989. See Report of the Select Committee on the EEC, HL. Session 1989–90, 19th Report (HL Paper 71-I); J Dine (1990); 11 Co Law 208. For some earlier discussion see 'Memorandum de la Commission de la CEE sur la création d'une société commerciale européenne' SEC (66) 1250 22 April 1966; 'Projet d'un statut des sociétés anonymes européennes' Doc 16.205/IV/66, December 1966; See generally *Quo vadis, Jus Societatum?*, ed P Zonderland (1972) and Chapter 42, post.

the project. The project has been under debate for twenty-five years but has now acquired a momentum as part of the proposals for 1992. The Commission adopted a new draft on 12 July 1989 and this is the subject of a Consultative Document by the Department of Trade and Industry. The draft is discussed in Chapter 41, post, when we consider cross frontier mergers.

The European company may be compared with the proposal for a European Economic Interest Grouping. The latter is intended to facilitate joint ventures and hence is very flexible. The European Company Proposal, after lying somewhat dormant, has been adopted as part of the programme for 1992. It is seen as a vehicle for cross frontier mergers.

THE FUTURE

The tactics employed by the Commission have in the past been described as 'salami tactics'. In other words, they approached the matter slice by slice. This approach was criticised on the basis that it was difficult to agree upon any particular directive without knowing, at least in broad terms, what else was to be done. The counter-argument was that elaboration of a complete uniform Companies Act would take a lot of time and bog down reform within the Community for a long time. In any event, it has been said that the statute for the European company would provide some sort of blueprint. Be that as it may, certain changes took place under the Jenkins presidency.

There was a suspension of work on certain projects and a determination to concentrate on certain key areas. Some real progress was made with company accounts and listing requirements. Work on the draft Fifth Directive has continued, although in its nature it is controversial. The key areas on which the Commission is currently engaged are disclosure, the group relationship and cross frontier mergers. With regard to disclosure, the Commission has participated in the negotiations in the ad hoc expert group on accounting of the United Nations Centre on Multinationals. On groups the original draft, based heavily on German law, has been the subject of controversy in other member states. This and codetermination have presented obstacles to the implementation of a number of other proposals, including the European Company Proposal. All of these, however, have been caught up in the momentum to 1992.

In considering harmonisation as a whole, remarkably little attention seems to have been paid to the US experience, where at first sight an effective market system seems to work without harmonisation of corporate laws. Indeed, there is said to be a market for corporation statutes. Certainly, there is diversity, but the extent of its importance can be exaggerated. Most of the major corporations are registered in Delaware and many others are incorporated in states which are based on the Model Business Corporation Act. Also, securities regulation is largely federal law. Conversely, US corporate lawyers are beginning to look at the EC laws carefully in the build-up to 1992.

Although from time to time, strong criticisms are made of the effect of membership of the EC on reform of English company law, it is interesting to note that the U K is one of the member states that has been most effective in translating the directives into national law. In doing so, however, it is severing many of the traditional links with the U S and the Commonwealth and losing many of the benefits of developments in those countries. As Dr Hans Claudius Ficker, a member of the Commission staff, argued expressing his personal view: 'the future development of the harmonised national law must be carried out in common, so that the member states lose their right to independent law reforms. Otherwise new disparities will arise obstructing all common efforts'. The year of 1973 marked a change of direction in English company law reform, the full implications of which are only just beginning to be appreciated.

CHAPTER 4

Classification of firms and companies

We saw in Chapter 1 how economists concentrate on the firm as a unit of
ownership and production which comprehends sole traders, partnerships
and companies and regard the company as a method of capital raising
whereas lawyers put the emphasis on the particular legal forms. The lawyers'
attempt to equate firm and company through the conferment of abstract
legal personality on the latter leads to strains and tensions in legal decision
making. The logic of the former sometimes conflicts with the practicality and
justice of the factual situation. It is useful at this stage to compare the
economists' and lawyers' alternative systems of classification, since it would
be puzzling if there was too wide a divergence between them and the
difference would need to be explained. Indeed economic reasoning may
sometimes afford a corrective to the abuses of legal logic. One must recognise that the *purposes* of classification may differ. Economics is concerned
with a variety of purposes—analysis, explanation, prediction and
evaluation—but mainly in the context of rational choice and allocation of
scarce resources. Law is principally concerned with social control and regulation. A regulatory scheme should, however, proceed on a rational basis
and economics in its new and broadest sense provides an instrumental
approach which is compatible with the law pursuing non-economic
objectives[1].

CLASSIFICATION OF FIRMS BY SIZE

Business firms are classified by economists in many ways. One obvious way
is to attempt some kind of factual classification based on size, but this begs
many questions relating to the criteria to be used to measure size. The
amount of assets, the aggregate market value of shares, turnover or net
income after tax, the return on capital, the number of employees and the
number of shareholders[2] can be used but they are all problematic. The use of
assets for instance gives a disproportionate prominence to capital intensive
industries and consequently sales are often taken as an index for some
companies. Businesses are roughly classified into small, medium or large,
whatever criteria are used. Indeed some are so large that they transcend the
corporate form and the nation state as we shall see in Chapter 42. These are
called multinationals. Thus there is considerable diversity in size. Coupled
with this is diversity of production and organisational structure.

Most firms start as small firms and grow until they reach minimum efficient

---

1 See Cento Veljanovski 'Legal Theory, Economic Analysis and the Law of Torts' in W
Twining, *Common Law and Legal Theory* (1986) pp 215, 216.
2 See P I Blumberg *The Megacorporation in American Society* (1975) p 21.

size. Some firms operate beyond minimum efficient size incurring diseconomies of scale. Some go through the progression to medium and then to large size but the particular events which lead to this and the speed of transition often differ greatly. Much depends on the capacity of the market to absorb new firms.

Small firms

Small firms are either run as sole traders, partnerships or companies. What is a small firm differs according to the type of industry concerned and this also seems to influence the use of the corporate form. The Bolton Committee in 1972[3] adopting this relativist approach, defined small firms as follows:

Industry	Small firms			
	Definition: maximum of	*As % of all firms*	*Employment as % of all firms*	*Average numbers employed per small firm*
Manufacturing	200*	94	20	25
Retailing	£50,000+	96	49	3
Wholesaling	£200,000+	77	25	7
Construction	25*	89	33	6
Mining & quarrying	25*	77	20	11
Motor trades	£50,000+	90	32	3
Miscellaneous services	£50,000+	90	82	4
Road transport	5"	85	36	4
Catering	All'	96	75	3

* employees
+ turnover
" vehicles
' excluding multiple chains

Particularly interesting is the differing extent of the use of the corporate form amongst small firms in different sectors. Thus in manufacturing the position was as follows[4]:

Legal status of small firms—manufacturing

Size of firm (no of employees)	*Quoted cos %*	*Non-quoted cos %*	*Unlimited cos %*	*Partnerships %*	*Sole proprietors %*	*Total*
1– 24	0.0	77.2	2.6	7.4	12.6	100
25– 99	1.0	94.6	1.1	2.3	1.0	100
100–199	5.4	91.7	1.6	0.7	0.7	100
1–199	0.4	81.0	2.3	6.2	10.0	100

Bolton Committee: *Research Report No 17*

3 Cmnd 4811 (1971). See further R E Thomas *The Government of Business* (2nd edn, 1983) chapter 3.
4 Bolton Committee: Research Report No 17.

In other words there was widespread use of the corporate form in manufacturing industry which increased with the number of employees. In non-manufacturing the position was as follows[5]:

Legal status of small firms—non-manufacturing

Industry	Quoted cos %	Non-quoted cos %	Unlimited cos %	Partnerships %	Sole proprietors %	Total
Catering	0.0	6.5	0.0	24.7	68.8	100
Construction	0.0	72.4	0.2	9.1	18.3	100
Motor trades	0.0	46.7	0.3	21.4	31.5	100
Retail distribution	0.4	34.5	0.6	22.6	41.8	100
Road transport	0.8	35.2	0.0	19.5	44.5	100
Wholesale distribution	0.7	82.7	1.8	4.6	10.2	100
Total	0.3	33.3	0.4	20.3	45.8	100

Bolton Committee: *Research Report No 17*

Here it is particularly noticeable that small catering firms tended not to use the corporate form and the substantial majority of firms were sole traders. The incidence of sole traders overall was quite high except in construction and wholesale as opposed to retail distribution. This reflects the risks involved in the latter. Construction is cyclical and tends to operate with higher costs and a longer time lag between commencement and end of production. Wholesale distribution is subject to high financial risk since goods are usually supplied on credit.

The latest definition of smallness is in relation to accounting exemptions for small companies in CA 1985. Such a company must satisfy at least one of the following three criteria set out in s 248(1):

(1) its turnover must not exceed £2 m;
(2) its balance sheet total must not exceed £975,000; and
(3) its average number of employees on a weekly basis must not exceed 50.

As can be seen these figures are much higher than the criteria used by the Bolton Committee even allowing for inflation. Where the corporate form is adopted, it will usually be the private company limited by shares, and will be used not to amass capital so much as to limit the liability of its members. We examine the problems of small incorporated firms in Chapter 31 but in essence they involve the absence of a secondary market for the shares making valuation of the shares difficult; possible conflicts over dividend policies; inability to rely on the stock market as a monitoring device for management performance; and above all a general fusion of ownership and control of the company, which is a mixed blessing[6].

---

5 Bolton Committee: Research Report No 17.
6 Frank Easterbrook and Daniel Fischel (1986) 38 Stanford L Rev 271.

Medium sized firms

The only definition of medium size we have is given in s 248(2) of CA 1985. A medium sized company must satisfy two out of the following three criteria:

(1)   its turnover must not exceed £8 m;
(2)   its balance sheet total must not exceed £3.9 m; and
(3)   its average number of employees on a weekly basis must not exceed 250.

A medium sized firm is likely to be a private company or private group of companies. The 1985 Act allows such companies to file modified accounts with the Registrar. Some medium sized companies may have shares dealt in on the USM (the unlisted securities market).

Large firms

One could pursue the implicit logic of the 1985 Act and say that a large firm is one which satisfies two out of three of the following criteria:

(1)   its turnover exceeds £8 m;
(2)   its balance sheet total exceeds £3.9 m; and
(3)   its average number of employees exceeds 250.

A large firm will almost certainly be incorporated as a limited liability company and is likely to be a public company. Indeed it will usually be a public company whose shares are listed on The Stock Exchange. If so, it will be subject to the rules of The Stock Exchange contained in the Admission of Securities to Listing (popularly known as the Yellow Book) and provisions of the Financial Services Act 1986 insofar as the latter are not contained in the former. The Stock Exchange generally does not favour applications for listing from companies whose expected total capitalisation is less than £700,000 in the case of shares. On the other hand, there is no minimum figure for the Unlisted Securities Market although capitalisation in the region of £2 m has been the normal level. In January 1983, of 5,335 public companies on the register, only 2,279 had securities listed on The London Stock Exchange. The total population of companies in 1983 was 855,700[7]. Thus the listed companies represented 0.266% of all domestic registered companies. Nevertheless the market value of their securities on 30 June 1983 was £603,935.7 m and they dominated most aspects of production and marketing. The Times' top 1,000 companies for 1983–84 had sales of £372,419,866,000 from a total capital employed of £175,410,442,000[8]. Thus one could say, at the risk of sounding banal, that the largest of the large are very large by all the principal criteria with the possible exception of return on capital (since some companies may be too large, operating beyond minimum efficient scale). Let us give a few examples. The largest company in the UK by market capitalisation at July 1986 was British Telecom with a market

7 *The Stock Exchange Official Year Book 1983–84* p 923. Cf T Hadden *Company Law and Capitalism* (2nd edn, 1977) p 39.
8 *The Times 1000 1983–1984,* p 8. See also D A Hay and D J Morris *Industrial Economics* (1979) pp 240–241. For an earlier detailed survey see P Sargeant Florence *Ownership, Control and Success of Large Companies* (1961).

capitalisation of £1,200.2 m. Particulars of its shareholdings are shown on the page opposite. Its pre-tax profit for the year ended 31 March 1986 was £1,828 m on a turnover of £8,387 m[9]. The eighth largest company in the UK by market capitalisation was Marks & Spencer plc, a household name, which in 1986 had group net assets of £1,462.9 m, turnover of £3,734.8 m and net profit of £222.4 m. It employed an average of 56,500 staff in 1986[10]. Where the company operates in more than one country it may be regarded as a multinational. We consider multinational operations in Chapter 42. Thus British Petroleum Company plc, the second largest British company by capitalisation and parent company of a worldwide group of more than 1,900 subsidiaries and related companies, had total group net assets of £13,428 m, turnover of £27,171 m and net profit of £916 m in 1986. It employed 28,700 UK employees and 98,000 non-UK employees in 1986[11].

Such firms came into existence because entrepreneurs needed to raise capital from a relatively large number of investors. They are characterised by specialised management which tends to be separate from the capital investors and indeed performs a discrete economic function. It has also been argued[12] that limited liability flows logically from the concept of the company as a capital raising mechanism. It should, however, be noted that the argument is not that corporate personality per se entails limited liability but that the capital raising characteristic of public companies does so. It allows individuals to invest a small part of their savings without risking ruin if the company becomes insolvent. Such companies provide a market for investment capital and liquidity for investment through the buying and selling of their securities on the Stock Market. They are also active in the market for corporate control as the bidder or target for a takeover bid. The market for investment capital and the market for corporate control provide ways of monitoring performance of the management of such companies. The price of the company's securities reflects many factors, but prominent amongst these is the market's appraisal of the efficiency of management. If the price declines, particularly if it falls below asset valuation, it will attract the attention of a bidder who will feel that he can make more efficient use of the assets. These market forces all affect the relevant legal norms[13]. Large firms are thus essentially different from small firms in matters other than size.

It seems pretty obvious, therefore, that the size and capital raising characteristics of a firm are useful starting points for legal classification since larger companies usually:

(1)   have specialised management;
(2)   have separation of ownership and control;
(3)   provide a market for investment capital;
(4)   participate in the market for corporate control more regularly.

It is patently unjust to subject a small firm to a disclosure regime appropriate to a large company or multinational[14]. Also the structural problems of such companies are vastly different as we shall see in later chapters.

---

9 Report and Accounts 1986.
10 Annual Report and Accounts, 31 March 1986.
11 Annual Report and Accounts, 1986.
12 See H G Manne (1967) 53 Virginia Law Review 259.
13 See *Hadden*, op cit, passim.
14 See Buchanan *The Economics of Corporate Enterprise* (1937) p 23.

Analysis of shareholders of British Telecom

Classification of ordinary shareholders at 31 May 1986

	Shareholders	Ordinary shares of 25p each	
	Number of holdings	Number of shares held (millions)	Percentage of total
HM Government (a)	1	2,988	49.8
Trustees of the Employee Share Ownership Scheme (b)	1	53	0.9
Pension funds	504	200	3.3
Insurance companies	374	264	4.4
Banks	1,915	5	0.1
Other corporate bodies (c)	10,320	1,731	28.9
Individuals	1,566,790	758	12.6
Held by Lloyds Bank Plc on behalf of others (d)	1,936	1	
	1,581,841	6,000	100.0

Size of shareholding at 31 May 1986

	Shareholders		Interest in ordinary shares of 25p each	
	Number of holdings	Percentage of total	Number of shares held (millions)	Percentage of total
1–399	457,144	28.9	90	1.5
400–799	760,582	48.1	347	5.8
800–1,599	337,773	21.3	274	4.6
1,600–9,999	23,173	1.5	55	0.9
10,000–99,999	1,855	0.1	59	1.0
100,000–999,999	957	0.1	302	5.0
1,000,000–999,999,999 (c)	356		1,885	31.4
1,000,000,000 and above	1		2,988	49.8
	1,581,841	100.0	6,000	100.0

(a)   It is likely that HM Government will sell its 49.8% holding in due course as part of its privatisation policy.

(b)   Under the Employee Share Ownership Scheme, 53 million ordinary shares of the company were held in trust on 31 May 1986 by British Telecom Employee Shares Trustees Limited on behalf of 221,906 participants who were beneficially entitled to the shares under special arrangements made at the time of the Offer for Sale.

(c)   Approximately 17 million shares were represented by American Depositary Receipts, which are listed on the New York and Toronto Stock Exchanges. A further 43 million shares, held by Japanese investors, are traded on the Tokyo Stock Exchange. Analyses by classification and size were not available for these holdings.

(d)   849,540 shares on which the final instalment of 40p per ordinary share, due to be paid to HM Government on 9 April 1986, remained outstanding at 31 May 1986.

CLASSIFICATION OF FIRMS BY REFERENCE TO BASIS OF COMPETITION IN WHICH THEY OPERATE

For the purpose of economic analysis it is also useful to distinguish firms on the basis of the competitive situation in which they operate. Bigness in the economy is not necessarily synonymous with market concentration. There are in theory four basic types of situation: perfect competition, monopolistic competition, monopoly and oligopoly.

A firm operates in perfect competition when the price at which it can profitably sell its product is determined by market forces outside its control.

Each business is so small in relation to the total sources of supply that its influence on the price is infinitesimal. Monopoly is the other side of the coin. Here a single seller occupies the whole market, and the product it sells cannot be replaced by close substitutes. Monopolistic competition puts the emphasis on each seller selling a differentiated but substitutable product. Oligopoly is where there are a few sellers in the market and these regard themselves as interdependent.

The common law dealt with competition by the doctrine of restraint of trade. This favours competition and prohibits unreasonable restraints of trade. Popular hostility to abuse of monopolies has been the case throughout much of English history. It is reflected in the classical economic writings of Adam Smith who thought that the principle underlying the successful functioning of a market economy was a pursuit of individual self-interest, controlled through competition. This was his famous 'invisible hand' which led individual self-interest to the common good[15]. We have seen in the previous chapter that early corporateness was associated with monopoly. It should be noted, however, that this was usually in relation to foreign trade and was an early means of social control. Smith was hostile to monopoly and suspicious of the joint stock company. His theory and indeed the common law have been affected by subsequent more complex economic conditions. This has led to monopolies and restrictive practice legislation in the post-war period. Added to this is EC law under arts 85 and 86 of the Treaty of Rome which regulate competition and prohibit abuse of a dominant position. We touch on these in a later chapter.

Although some small firms are able to exploit a monopoly or oligopolistic position for a short time, high profits will attract new entrants, who will compete, given the absence of substantial barriers to entry. Since perfect competition does not exist, most small firms operate in an environment of effective competition in the real world. Indeed, the same is true of most medium sized and large firms. Some large companies and multinationals are, however, able to exploit an oligopolistic position. Competition affects the growth of the firm and the elimination of competition, economies of scale and access to capital are all motives in takeovers and mergers. Competition is also a factor in business failure.

LEGAL CLASSIFICATION OF COMPANIES UNDER THE COMPANIES ACTS

There are two basic systems of legal classification of companies under the Companies Acts, neither of which is now directly concerned with size, but both of which have some bearing on the raising of capital. These are (1) by reference to the liability of members and (2) the public/private dichotomy.

Dealing with (1), registered companies may be:

(a)   Companies limited by shares. (This was introduced in 1855.)
(b)   Companies limited by guarantee. (This was introduced in 1862.)
(c)   Unlimited companies. (This is the oldest type of company and ultimately dates back to 1844.)

---

15 *An Inquiry into the Nature and Causes of the Wealth of Nations* (1937).

In the case of (a), which is the most common type in practice, each member must contribute to the company's assets the amount unpaid on his shares. Under s 74(1) of the Insolvency Act 1986, past members are also liable if they were members within one year before the commencement of the winding up and it appears to the court that the existing members are unable to satisfy the contributions required of them but past members are only liable to the extent unpaid on their former shares before they ceased to be members and for debts contracted before they ceased to be members. The limited liability of members effectively transfers the risk of business failure from them to the creditors. In practice this means trade creditors and involuntary creditors, since finance creditors usually take security and personal guarantees in the case of small firms. In the case of larger firms the limited liability greatly facilitates capital raising from the public.

In the case of (b), the member is contingently liable for the amount which he has undertaken to contribute in the event of insolvent winding up. In the case of (c) the member's liability is unlimited if the company is insolvent, although the company has legal personality.

In practice, (b) and (c) are rare. (b) is mainly used for educational or other charitable bodies as an alternative to the trust mechanism.

Until 1907, there was just one basic type of company under the Companies Acts. In that year the public/private dichotomy was introduced. The introduction of the private company was almost by accident. Originally the Loreburn Committee had simply intended it as the basis of exemption from the statement in lieu of prospectus but in the House of Lords it was successfully proposed that it should be exempt from filing a balance sheet. English law did not, like German law, recognise the private company as an institution, sui generis but simply as as a species of the genus, limited company[16].

The basis of the dichotomy was restrictions on offers to the public of its shares, share transfers and the number of shareholders. Thus to some extent size entered into the classification. The private company was intended for small businesses, the public company for large businesses. However, the method of capital raising was fundamental to the classification.

Because public companies are able to incorporate private companies as subsidiaries, the 1948 Act limited the privilege of not filing accounts to the exempt private company, which corresponded roughly to the small incorporated firm. This continued until the Companies Act 1967 abolished the concept. Apart from the accounting advantages conferred on small and medium sized companies by CA 1985, private companies have had basically the same disclosure obligations as a public company. However, the Companies Act 1989 has relaxed a number of the legal requirements as part of a policy of 'de-regulation'. We shall deal with the matter in more detail later.

The rational basis of classification of the 1900s was abandoned in 1980 in order to implement the Second Directive of the EC. Now CA 1985 defines a public company explicitly and a private company by exclusion. A public company is defined in s 1(3) as a company limited by shares or limited by guarantee and having a share capital (a) whose memorandum states that it is to be a public company and (b) which has complied with the provisions for registration of such a company. This means that its memorandum must be in

---

16 See C M Schmitthoff 'How the English Discovered the Private Company' in *Quo Vadis, Jus Societatum?* ed P Zonderland (1972) p 183.

the form specified by regulations under the Act by virtue of s 3 and it must have a minimum capital of at least £50,000. With effect from 22 December 1980, a company cannot be formed as or become a company limited by guarantee with a share capital. A private company is a company which is not a public company. The only provision still expressly concerned with size and capital raising is s 81 which makes it a criminal offence for a private company (other than a company limited by guarantee and not having a share capital) to offer its securities to the public directly or indirectly. This is now the only real disadvantage of incorporation as a private company which otherwise has substantial advantages over public companies.

The following is a list of the other legal differences between public and private companies:

(i)   public companies must have at least two directors whereas private companies need only have one (CA 1985, s 282(1));

(ii)   in the case of public companies, two or more directors cannot be appointed by a single resolution unless a resolution that it shall be so has first been agreed to without any vote being given against it (s 292);

(iii)   proxies appointed to attend and vote instead of a member of a private company have the same right to speak as the member;

(iv)   accounting records need only be kept for three years in the case of a private company whereas they must be kept for six years in the case of a public company (s 222(4));

(v)   the period for laying and delivering accounts by a private company is ten months after the end of the account period whereas it is seven months for public companies (s 244(1));

(vi)   the company secretary of a public company must be suitably qualified (s 286);

(vii)   certain pre-emptive rights conferred by ss 89 and 90 may be excluded by a provision in the memorandum or articles of a private company (s 91);

(viii)   the stringent rules for payment for shares which regulate non-cash consideration only apply to public companies (s 99 et seq);

(ix)   the obligation to convene an extraordinary general meeting in the event of a serious loss of capital only applies to a public company (s 142);

(x)   the rules relating to treatment of shares held by or on behalf of a company in itself only apply to public companies (s 146);

(xi)   the rules restricting liens and charges by a company on its shares only apply to public companies (s 150);

(xii)   the rules restricting payment of dividends to an amount which does not diminish a company's net assets below its called up share capital and undistributable reserves only apply to public companies (s 264);

(xiii)   the directors of a private company are under fewer restrictions in their financial relationship to their company and need make less disclosure in the accounts (s 330 et seq);

(xiv)   the public company registered as such on its original incorporation must obtain a certificate before it carries on business or borrows.

The principal significance of this is that the private company does not have to have a minimum capital;

(xv)   a private company may purchase or redeem its own shares out of capital (s 171 et seq);

(xvi)   a private company may provide financial assistance for the purchase of its own shares (s 155 et seq);

(xvii)   private companies are not subject to the disclosure of interests in shares provisions of Pt VI of the Act.

(xviii)   private companies have been 'deregulated' by CA 1989, ss 113, 116 by allowing written resolutions and elective resolutions to relax formalities in respect of authority to allot shares, laying accounts before general meetings, holding annual general meetings, short notice of meetings and dispensing with the annual appointment of auditors.

Patterns of registration

Table A shows the numbers of private and public companies on the register in Great Britain between 1983–86 and 1988–89[17]. From this it can be seen that public companies are a small percentage which has more than doubled in this period. This has reversed the downward trend from 2.97% in 1970. No doubt the tightening of requirements on public companies in the 1980–81 legislation had some bearing on the sharp decline.

Table B shows an analysis on the basis of amount of nominal capital which is a crude index of size and capitalisation[18]. The old pattern was for most companies to be formed with a share capital of £100. Now since 1987–88 the majority have been formed with a share capital of £1,000–£4,999 in England and Wales although not in Scotland.

Groups

Many companies and undertakings belong to a group. This introduces the further classification of companies and undertakings into parent or holding companies or undertakings and subsidiaries. The simplest group relationship is:

P controls S.

However, there can in practice be sub-holding companies and subsidiaries. Thus:

SS   SS

---

17   *Companies in 1988/89.*
18   Nominal capital is simply the legal measure of the capital fund. It does not necessarily reflect the value of the fund.

Table A
Public and private companies incorporated and on the register, 1983 to 1986 and 1986–87 to 1989–90

Thousands of companies

	1983	1984	1985	1986	1986–87	1987–88	1988–89	1989–90
Public Companies								
New registrations	0.1	0.2	0.5	0.7	0.6	0.8	3.2	1.2
Conversions from private	0.1	0.2	0.2	0.3	0.4	0.6	0.8	1.1
Dissolved	—	—	—	—	—	0.1	0.2	0.3
In liquidation/course of removal	0.1	0.1	0.1	0.3	0.3	0.2	0.6	0.7
Effective number on registers at end of period	3.4	3.7	4.3	5.1	5.2	6.6	9.8	11.1
Public companies as percentage of effective register	0.4%	0.4%	0.5%	0.6%	0.6%	0.7%	1.0%	1.1%
Private Companies								
New registrations	96.1	97.7	104.1	116.6	117.2	125.4	131.9	125.1
Conversions from public	0.1	0.1	0.2	0.1	0.1	0.1	0.1	0.3
Dissolved	44.9	53.9	61.6	104.7	84.2	78.3	118.1	85.33
In liquidation/course of removal	100.6	109.8	181.1	209.9	198.7	203.8	159.7	165.0
Effective number on registers at end of period	852.4r	887.3	858.7	842.3	862.1	904.7	963.1	998.7
of which: Unlimited	''	''	''	''	''	4.8	4.6	4.5

Table B

Number of new registrations of companies having a share capital: analysed by amount of nominal capital, 1983 to 1986 and 1986–87 to 1988–89

Nominal share capital	1983	1984	1985	1986	1986–87	1987–88	1988–89	*Thousands of companies* 1989–90
England and Wales								
Up to £100	56.2	53.0	56.4	62.5	59.5	45.3	45.6	41.9
Over £100 & under £1,000	0.6	0.9	0.6	0.6	0.5	0.6	0.5	0.5
£1,000 & under £5,000	21.0	24.4	28.1	32.2	35.9	57.0	63.1	59.6
£5,000 & under £10,000	1.6	1.4	1.3	1.2	1.2	1.3	0.8	0.7
£10,000 & under £20,000	5.7	6.1	5.5	6.2	6.4	6.2	5.4	5.6
£20,000 & under £50,000	1.2	1.1	1.0	0.9	0.9	0.9	0.8	0.8
£50,000 & under £100,000	1.2	1.4	1.4	1.5	1.5	1.8	2.4	2.0
£100,000 & under £200,000	1.8	2.1	2.3	2.8	2.9	3.3	5.5	3.8
£200,000 & under £500,000	0.3	0.3	0.3	0.4	0.4	0.4	0.4	0.5
£500,000 & under £1m	0.2	0.2	0.2	0.3	0.3	0.4	0.4	0.4
£1m & over	0.3	0.4	0.5	0.7	0.6	0.8	0.9	1.1
All companies	90.0	91.3	97.5	109.3	110.1	117.7	125.7	116.9
Total nominal share capital (£m)	2,299	2,672	7,015	3,129	5,285	4,752	4,687	9,140
Scotland								
Up to £100	3.2	3.5	3.8	4.1	3.9	3.0	2.7	2.8
Over £100 & under £1,000	—	—	—	—	—	—	—	—
£1,000 & under £5,000	0.3	0.3	0.4	0.5	0.5	1.8	2.6	2.3
£5,000 & under £10,000	0.1	0.1	0.1	0.1	0.1	0.1	0.1	—
£10,000 & under £20,000	0.3	0.4	0.4	0.4	0.4	0.4	0.4	0.4
£20,000 & under £50,000	0.1	0.1	0.1	0.1	0.1	0.1	0.1	0.1
£50,000 & under £100,000	0.2	0.2	0.2	0.2	0.2	0.2	0.2	0.2
£100,000 & under £200,000	0.2	0.2	0.2	0.2	0.2	0.3	0.3	0.4
£200,000 & under £500,000	—	—	—	—	—	0.1	—	0.1
£500,000 & over	—	—	0.1	0.1	0.1	0.1	0.2	0.3
All companies	4.6	4.9	5.3	5.8	5.6	6.1	6.7	6.7
Total nominal share capital (£m)	93	126	154	154	173	160	410	650

With the larger firms, group structures become increasingly complex and sometimes the legal picture is not an accurate reflection of the actual organisational structure. Some subsidiaries may be little more than shells or may be run as agents for other companies in the group. Some groups such as ICI operate a division structure which is superimposed on the legal group structure. Management may be organised on a divisional basis rather than a company basis. This may make the monitoring of management performance by external agencies more difficult. Both the group structure and the other more elaborate operational structures pose difficulties for outside creditors. Normally these only surface when the difficulties give rise to insolvency. Here the de jure separation of entities may be contradicted de facto both by business operations and the practice of finance creditors of taking group guarantees and security.

We examine the question of groups in Chapter 32.

Legislative reform

The reforms introduced by the Companies Act 1981 allowed modified accounts by small and medium sized companies. These were consolidated in Part VII of the CA 1985. Recently the CA 1989 allowed a measure of 'deregulation' in respect of private companies. Written resolutions are allowed as are elective resolutions to relax a number of Company Law formalities. Other reform proposals have been for a new simpler form of incorporation for small businesses[19]. Such reforms have taken place in South Africa and Australia. We discuss this in Chapter 31. A further reform which has been contemplated is a greater recognition of the single economic enterprise of a group of companies when a member of a group becomes insolvent. Such reforms have been introduced in New Zealand but the Cork Committee on Insolvency Law and Practice[20] made no recommendation of this kind, preferring to leave it to a general review of company law.

THE EMERGENCE OF A FACT-BASED JURISPRUDENCE

English law has traditionally been unconcerned with whether the private company was a *kapitalgesellschaft* or *personalgesellschaft*[1]. It was simply regarded as a species of limited liability company. The public/private dichotomy was almost exclusively regarded as the basis of statutory disclosure requirements and nothing else. However in the last 50 years there have been signs of the development of a more fact based jurisprudence in the cases. The various trends can be summarised as follows:

(1)   There has been a tendency to disregard the corporate form where the interests of justice require it. These cases are usually referred to as piercing the corporate veil[2].

(2)   There is a trend towards recognition of something like a *personalgesellschaft*—a relationship of personal confidence with a network of

---

19 A New Form of Incorporation for Small Firms—A Consultative Document 1981.
20 Cmnd 8558 (1882).
  1 Literally, capital company and personal company. See Schmitthoff, op cit.
  2 See Chapter 7, infra.

equitable obligations—behind the corporate form in the case of small incorporated firms[3]. This development started under the just and equitable ground for winding up but has been used as the basis of control over a majority shareholder in two English and one Canadian case[4]. The *locus classicus* is a speech of Lord Wilberforce in *Ebrahimi v Westbourne Galleries Ltd*[5] in 1972 where he said[6]:

> . . . a limited company is more than a mere judicial entity, with a personality in law of its own: . . . there is room in company law for recognition of the fact that behind it, or amongst it, there are individuals, with rights, expectations and obligations inter se which are not necessarily submerged in the company structure. That structure is defined by the Companies Act and by the articles of association by which the shareholders agree to be bound. In most companies and in most contexts, this definition is sufficient and exhaustive, equally so whether the company is large or small. The 'just and equitable' provision does not, as the respondents suggest, entitle one party to disregard the obligation he assumes by entering a company, nor the court to dispense him from it. It does, as equity always does, enable the court to subject the exercise of legal rights to equitable considerations; considerations, that is, of a personal character arising between on individual and another, which may make it unjust, or inequitable, to insist on legal rights, or to exercise them in a particular way.

At the present time it is difficult to see how far this development will go. In a way it is a potentially wide doctrine which could change much of established company law as it relates to small and medium sized firms.

(3)   In a number of cases starting with *Baroness Wenlock v River Dee Co*[7] in 1883 the courts have shown a willingness to bypass the strict legal formalities prescribed by the Companies Acts in the case of small incorporated firms. However, this is usually on the basis of unanimity or estoppel or waiver, which are established legal doctrines.

Thus in *Re Duomatic Ltd*[8] Buckley J said:

> I proceed on the basis that where it can be shown that all shareholders who had a right to attend and vote at a general meeting of the company assent to some matter which a general meeting of the company could carry into effect, that assent is as binding as a resolution in general meeting would be.

As we have seen this has now been allowed by the CA 1989 for all unanimous written resolutions of private companies as part of a scheme for 'deregulation'.

(4)   In some, but not all, cases of groups of companies the courts have shown a willingness to look to the group enterprise as a whole in spite

---

3 See Chapters 31 and 27, infra.
4 *Clemens v Clemens Bros Ltd* [1976] 2 All ER 268; *Pennell v Venida Investments Ltd* (25 July 1974, unreported) discussed in (1981) 44 MLR 41; *Diligenti v RWMD Operations Kelowna Ltd* [1976] 1 BCLR 36.
5 [1973] AC 360, HL.
6 Ibid, at 379b-d.
7 (1883) 36 Ch D 675n. See also *Re George Newman & Co* [1895] 1 Ch 674, CA; *Re Express Engineering Works Ltd* [1920] 1 Ch 466, CA; *Re Oxted Motor Co Ltd* [1921] 3 KB 32; *Parker & Cooper Ltd v Reading* [1926] Ch 975; *Re Pearce Duff & Co Ltd* [1960] 3 All ER 222; *Re Duomatic Ltd* [1969] 2 Ch 365; *Re Moorgate Mercantile Holdings Ltd* [1980] 1 All ER 40; *Cane v Jones* [1981] 1 All ER 533. See J Birds (1981) 2 Co Law 68; C Baxter [1983] CLJ 96.
8 [1969] 2 Ch 365 at 373.

of conventional legal principles which emphasise the separate interests of individual companies.

In *DHN Food Distributors v London Borough of Tower Hamlets*[9] Lord Denning MR said:

We all know that in many respects a group of companies are treated together for the purpose of general accounts, balance sheet and profit and loss account. They are treated as one concern. Professor Gower in his book on company law says: 'there is evidence of a general tendency to ignore the separate legal entities of various companies within a group, and to look instead at the economic entity of the whole group'. This is especially the case when a parent company owns all the shares of the subsidiaries, so much so that it can control every movement of the subsidiaries. These subsidiaries are bound hand and foot to the parent company and must do just what the parent company says.

It must be conceded, however, that there have been signs recently of a return to legal orthodoxy in the cases[10]. It is difficult to provide any general theoretical framework for these trends. Perhaps they represent no more than a reluctance by the judiciary to make a fetish of legal classification where this is too much at odds with economic theory and common sense. We shall return to this question in Chapter 31 when we look at small incorporated firms in more detail.

9 [1976] 3 All ER 462 at 467, CA.
10 See Chapter 7, infra.

CHAPTER 5

Promotion and pre-incorporation contracts

PROMOTERS

Promoter, like company, is a word with a variety of meanings. It was the old name for a common informer and the technical term for the prosecutor of a suit in the ecclesiastical courts. We are, however, not concerned with those meanings nor with promotion at large, but simply with the promotion of a company. Speaking in general terms, the promoters of a company are those who are the leading lights in its formation or flotation or, to adopt the metaphor of an American writer, who are 'the midwife of the business'[1]. Before incorporation a company does not exist. Someone must act on it's behalf. Formalities need to be attended to. Professionals need to be instructed and paid. The business proposition may need to be appraised. Initial finance may need to be arranged. The legal approach to these commercial facts has never fully crystallised. Promotion was not a legal term of art at common law and is not given an exhaustive statutory definition. Consequently the courts have been reluctant to pin themselves down to any precise definition, at the same time imposing strict obligations on those who fall within the category. The obligations have been built up by the courts relying on agency and trust principles supplemented from time to time by statute. On the whole, however, the legislative reforms have been piecemeal.

The small trader who takes steps to incorporate his business is engaged in promotion. From the seventeenth century onwards there have been people who have specialised in the promotion of public companies although in the early period they usually had a number of other interests as well. Thus Nicholas Barbone[2], son of Cromwell's General Praise-God Barbone, was a physician, Member of Parliament and property developer as well as promoter of a fire insurance company and bank. Most professional promoters of public companies have been connected with the City of London and have been men of repute, but in the period 1860–1920 there were a number of company promoters who perpetrated frauds which the courts sought to combat by means of the development of specific fiduciary duties. In recent years, most leading companies have started off life as private companies or unlisted public companies and then 'gone public' later after establishing a sound profit record. In this process they have been assisted by stockbrokers or specialist financial institutions known as issuing houses. An issuing house, which will usually be a merchant bank, organises the raising of capital by

---

1 H G Henn and J A Alexander *Laws of Corporations* (3rd edn, 1983) p 237. Midwife of the birth of the company is perhaps more apt.
2 See E V Morgan and W A Thomas *The Stock Exchange: its History and Functions* (2nd edn, 1969) p 25. For a description of some of the professional promoters see ibid pp 136–139, 206 ff.

new issues of securities. The stockbrokers and issuing houses are promoters
if they perform more than mere ministerial acts. In the nineteenth century,
promoters were sometimes classified into three types—professional, occasional and ad hoc[3]. The issuing houses are professionals. The individual
professional promoter of public companies has disappeared because he
often considered the question whether the company would float rather than
whether it would succeed as the question of greatest importance. Occasional
promoters were persons of greater status who never took part in a scheme
unless its bona fides and prospects were beyond question. They too are rare
today as are ad hoc promoters. Issuing houses have taken over much of the
new issue business and have improved standards. The Radcliffe Report said
that some 60% of new issues were sponsored by issuing houses. Today the
figure would be higher. 'In sponsoring an issue [an issuing house] accepts the
responsibility for the bona fides of the company seeking listing. The public of
course get to know those houses on whose reputation they can rely in their
reputation for bringing sound companies to the market . . . in a way a good
issuing house provides its own guarantee of success in much the same way as
the Good Housekeeping Seal of Approval does[4].' Thus changes in commercial practice have now rendered the case law on promoters largely of
historical interest in the case of public companies but the principles are still
relevant to private companies.

The concept of promotion

The concept has been judicially described but not exhaustively defined. The
policy reasons for the lack of a definition are said to be four[5]:

(1)   The cases coming before the courts involve misfortune or fraud which
       has brought the company into difficulties. In these circumstances the
       judges have been satisfied that the retention of secret profits would be
       inequitable and, therefore, by a process of ex post facto rationalisation
       they call the person who made them a promoter.
(2)   It is thought that the term is best left as a business term.
(3)   The lack of a precise definition makes evasion and avoidance of the
       legal rules difficult.
(4)   The wide variety of companies promoted makes a unifying definition
       impossible.

Let us now examine the judicial descriptions.

In *Erlanger v New Sombrero Phosphate Co*[6] in 1878, Lord Blackburn said
that the term was 'a short and convenient way of designating those who set in
motion the machinery by which the Act . . . enables them to create an
incorporated company'. This is not enough. In *Whaley Bridge Calico Printing Co v Green*[7] in 1879, Bowen J was a little more explicit. He said: 'The
term promoter is a term not of law, but of business, usefully summing up in a

---

3 This was the classification adopted by Sir Francis Palmer in his *Company Precedents*
   (1956–60).
4 Michael Richardson *Going Public* (1976) p 16.
5 See Joseph H Gross *Company Promoters* (1972) pp 19–20. This chapter was also published
   in (1970) 86 LQR 493 at 498.
6 (1878) 3 App Cas 1218, HL.
7 (1879) 5 QBD 109.

single word a number of business operations familiar to the commercial world by which a company is generally brought into existence'[8]. The trouble with this is that it begs the question of what those business operations are. In *Twycross v Grant*[9] the Court of Appeal in fact found that the defendants who had planned the formation of the company, found directors, paid the preliminary expenses, arranged contracts, and were to receive substantial remuneration from the vendors were undoubtedly promoters. Cockburn CJ said that the term meant 'one who undertakes to form a company with reference to a given project and to set it going, and who takes the necessary steps to accomplish the purpose'. The most comprehensive description was given by Lindley J in *Emma Silver Mining Co v Lewis & Son* where he said[10]:

It is now clearly settled that persons who get up and form a company have duties towards it before it comes into existence: see *Bagnall v Carlton* (1877) 6 Ch D 371 and per Lord Cairns LC in *Erlanger v New Sombrero Phosphate Co* (1878) 3 App Cas 1218 at 1236. Moreover, it is in our opinion an entire mistake to suppose that after a company is registered its directors are the only persons who are in such a position towards it as to be under fiduciary relations to it. A person not a director may be a promoter of a company which is already incorporated, but the capital of which has not been taken up, and which is not yet in a position to perform the obligations imposed upon it by its creators.

This shows that promotion can in certain circumstances extend to subsequent flotation. In *Tracey v Mandalay Pty Ltd*[11] in 1953 the majority of the High Court of Australia (Dixon CJ, Williams and Taylor JJ) held that it was not only the persons who take an active part in the formation of a company and the raising of capital who were promoters. Persons who leave it to others to get up the company upon the understanding that they also will profit from the operation may become promoters.

Ultimately, however, the question is one of fact to be determined in the light of all the circumstances.

Examples of promotion

CLEAR CASES OF PROMOTION

The clearest case is the person who plans the scheme for the formation of a company, has the documents prepared and registered, finds the directors, negotiates the preliminary contracts and deals with the drafting, printing, registration and circulation of any prospectus[12]. He has done all the things one associates with promotion. It will, however, be sufficient to do some of these things in co-operation with others[13].

LESS CLEAR CASES

A vendor of property may be and often is a promoter but he is not a

---

8 (1880) 5 QBD 109 at 111.
9 (1877) 2 CPD 469 at 541, CA.
10 (1879) 4 CPD 396 at 407. Followed in *Tracy v Mandalay Pty Ltd* (1952) 88 CLR 215.
11 (1952) 88 CLR 215.
12 *Emma Silver Mining Co v Grant* (1879) 11 Ch D 918; *Re Olympia Ltd* [1898] 2 Ch 153, CA; *Re Leeds & Hanley Theatres of Varieties Ltd* [1902] 2 Ch 809.
13 *Emma Silver Mining Co v Grant* (1879) 11 Ch D 918.

promoter when he merely acts as vendor[14]. A person who assists in the flotation but took no part in the formation of a company may be a promoter[15]. People who appear at first sight to be acting as agents or employees of another may sometimes be held to be promoters if they share in the remuneration or have some say in the promotion[16]. Thus the director of a promoting company may be held to be a promoter if he acts otherwise than as a director of that company[17].

CASES OF NON-PROMOTERS

A person who acts as agent or servant of a promoter is not per se a promoter[18]. Thus the solicitor, accountant, printer, stockbroker and bank are not promoters provided they merely act in a ministerial way.

The fiduciary duties of promoters

A promoter is not an agent of the company which he is forming for the simple reason that it does not then exist[19]. Neither is he treated as a trustee in normal circumstances, despite the doctrinal possibility[20]. Upon incorporation he does, however, stand in a fiduciary position towards the company which begins when the promotion itself began and ends after the company is formed or the promotional plan is completed. It is often superseded by new fiduciary duties where the promoter becomes a director of the company. The essence of the promoter's fiduciary duties are good faith, fair dealing and full disclosure[1]. Lord Blackburn said in *Erlanger v New Sombrero Phosphate Co*[2] that the Companies Act gave to promoters 'an almost unlimited power to make the corporation subject to such regulations as they please, and for such purposes as they please, and to create it with a managing body whom they select, having such powers as they choose to give to those managers'. He continued: 'I think those who accept and use such extensive powers are not entitled to disregard the interests of that corporation altogether. They must make a reasonable use of the powers which they accept from the legislature . . . and consequently they do stand, with regard to that corporation, when formed, in what is commonly called a fiduciary relation to some extent'. *Erlanger*'s case was the first case to recognise the existence of a fiduciary relationship.

THE DUTIES

There are three basic fiduciary duties. These are owed to the company and are:

(1)   A duty not to make a secret profit at the expense of the company. A

---

14 *Erlanger v New Sombrero Phosphate Co* (1878) 3 App Cas 1218.
15 *Emma Silver Mining Co v Lewis* (1879) 4 CPD 396.
16 See Pearson J in *Lydney and Wigpool Iron Ore Co v Bird* (1885) 31 Ch D 328 at 339.
17 *Re Darby, ex p Brougham* [1911] 1 KB 95.
18 *Re Great Wheal Polgooth Co Ltd* (1883) 53 LJ Ch 42.
19 *Kelner v Baxter* (1866) LR 2 CP 174.
20 See *Re Leeds & Hanley Theatres of Varieties Ltd* [1902] 2 Ch 809 at 819; *Rita Joan Dairies Ltd v Thomson* [1974] 1 NZLR 285 at 293; P D McKenzie (1973) 5 NZULR 117.
 1 Cf H A Henn and J A Alexander *Corporations* (3rd edn, 1983) p 239.
 2 (1878) 3 App Cas 1218 at 1236, 1268.

profit is not secret if it is disclosed but the disclosure must be full and frank. It must be made to either:

(a)   an independent board of directors[3] *or*

(b)   the existing and intended shareholders[4].

Independence in (a) is a question of fact; (b) is satisfied where all the members of a private company are aware of the facts and there is no intention to 'go public'. It is satisfied in the case of a public company by full disclosure of the facts in the articles or a prospectus. It will also be satisfied where the company in a general meeting, at which neither the promoter nor the holders of any shares in which he is beneficially interested vote in favour of the transaction, elect not to rescind it[5]. Even if they do vote in favour of it this will probably be valid.

In *Erlanger's* case[6] a syndicate headed by Erlanger acquired a lease of an island in the West Indies said to contain valuable phosphates for £55,000 and then formed a company to acquire the lease and to work the mines. The lease was sold to the company through a bare nominee for the syndicate for £100,000 without the circumstances of the sale being disclosed. The facts were found out later when the first phosphate shipments had been a failure. The shareholders removed the old board and sought rescission. It was held that the syndicate were promoters and that since they had failed to disclose their secret profit the contract could be rescinded.

In *Salomon v A Salomon & Co Ltd*[7] the House of Lords recognised that where there was not an independent board there may be sufficient disclosure if all the original shareholders are told of the material facts. In *Gluckstein v Barnes*[8], however, it was held that the promoter will not be exonerated in these circumstances if the original shareholders are not independent and the scheme is designed as a fraud on the public. An eloquent moral indignation characterises the speech of Lord Macnaghten in that case. He said that where 'gentlemen set about forming a company to pay them a handsome sum for taking off their hands a property which they contracted to buy with that end in view . . . appoint themselves sole guardians and protectors of this creature of theirs, half-fledged and just struggling into life, bound hand and foot while yet unborn by contracts tending to their private advantage, and so fashioned by its makers that it could only act by their hands and only see through their eyes', and the company goes to the public for share subscriptions '"Disclosure" is not the most appropriate word to use when a person who plays many parts announces to himself in one character what he has done and is doing in another. To talk of disclosure to the thing called the company, when as yet there were no

3 *Erlanger*, supra; *Gluckstein v Barnes* [1900] AC 240.
4 *Salomon v A Salomon & Co Ltd* [1897] AC 22; *Larocque v Beauchemin* [1897] AC 358 at 364, PC.
5 *Lagunas Nitrate Co v Lagunas Syndicate* [1899] 2 Ch 392, CA. As to whether the promoter and his nominess should abstain, cf Ghana Companies Code, s 12(4)(c) and L C B Gower's discussion in his Report thereto.
6 (1878) 3 App Cas 1218, HL.
7 [1897] AC 22.
8 [1900] AC 240.

shareholders, is a mere farce. To the intended shareholders there was no disclosure at all"[9].

(2)   When the promotion has started the promoter must account to the company for the benefit of any subsequent contract for the acquisition of property which he intends to sell to the company, since this belongs in equity to the company which can insist on taking it at cost[10]. Where the promoter acquired the property on his own account before the commencement of the promotion it belongs to him in law and equity and he can sell at a profit provided he discloses the facts[11]. If he does not make disclosure the contract is liable to be rescinded[12].

(3)   A promoter must not exercise undue influence or fraud[13] and in particular must not hide his interest through a nominee[14].

REMEDIES OF THE COMPANY

The company's remedies are rescission, recovery of the secret profit and damages for breach of fiduciary duty or deceit.

Rescission   We have seen that in *Erlanger*'s case the company was entitled to rescind the contract for the purchase of the lease of the island. Rescission is an equitable remedy which involves unscrambling the contract and return of the consideration and will be lost:

(a)   if the parties cannot be substantially restored to their original position[15] unless this is due to the fault of the promoter;
(b)   if third parties have acquired rights for value[16].

   In *Re Leeds & Hanley Theatres of Varieties Ltd*[16] promoters made a profit by selling through a nominee and failed to disclose the facts. Meanwhile a mortgagee sold the property. It was held that rescission was no longer possible but damages could be recovered.

Recovery of the secret profit   Where the company has affirmed the contract it can still sue the promoter to account for the secret profit. The action for recovery of the secret profit is either in equity on the basis of a constructive trust or at law as a claim for money had and received[17]. It can also be the subject of a misfeasance summons in the winding up of the company[18] and is provable in the bankruptcy of the promoter[19].

   In *Gluckstein v Barnes*[20] Gluckstein and others, intending to buy the Olympia exhibition hall and promote a company, first bought up charges on

9 Ibid, at 248–249.
10 *Hichens v Congreve* (1829) 1 Russ & M 150n; *Re Leeds & Hanley Theatres of Varieties Ltd* [1902] 2 Ch 809; *Re Cape Breton Co* (1885) 29 Ch D 795, CA; *Jacobus Marler Estates Ltd v Marler* (1913) 85 LJPC 167n; *Tracy v Mandalay Pty Ltd* (1952) 88 CLR 215 at 239.
11 *Erlanger*'s case, supra.
12 *Ladywell Mining Co v Brookes* (1887) 35 Ch D 400, CA.
13 *Erlanger*'s case, supra; *Gluckstein v Barnes*, supra.
14 *Erlanger*'s case, supra; *Cavendish-Bentinck v Fenn* (1887) 12 App Cas 652 at 671, HL.
15 *Lagunas Nitrate Co v Lagunas Syndicate* [1899] 2 Ch 392.
16 *Re Leeds & Hanley Theatres of Varieties Ltd* [1902] 2 Ch 809.
17 L S Sealy *Cases and Materials in Company Law* (4th edn, 1989) p 25.
18 *Re Caerphilly Colliery Co, Pearson*'s case (1877) 5 Ch D 336, CA.
19 *Re Darby, ex p Brougham* [1911] 1 KB 95.
20 [1900] AC 240, HL.

the property at below par. They later bought the property and sold it to their new company at a profit. They also procured repayment of the charges at par. They then disclosed the profit on the sale but not on the charges. The House of Lords held that the company could recover the secret profit from the promoters who were jointly and severally liable. In computing the secret profit all bona fide expenses of the promotion can be deducted. Thus in *Emma Silver Mining Co v Grant*[1] a defendant was allowed sums expended in securing the services of directors and in payments to brokers and the press.

Damages for breach of fiduciary duty   We have seen in *Re Leeds & Hanley Theatres of Varieties* (supra) that damages for breach of fiduciary duty may be awarded in lieu of rescission. Where property is acquired before the promotion commenced by the promoter in his own right but which he failed to disclose, the company cannot affirm the contract and claim damages or recover the secret profit[2]. The reason is that in this case the property does not belong in equity to the company and for the court to order damages or recovery of the secret profit would amount to variation of the contract. The law is that the promoter must not make a *secret* profit in respect of the sale of his own property, not that he should sell at a lower price.

Damages for deceit   The facts will usually warrant an action in deceit against the promoter for a misrepresentation inducing the company to enter into the contract.

LIABILITY TO AND REMEDIES OF SHAREHOLDERS AND CREDITORS

In English law promoters do not owe fiduciary duties to shareholders and creditors[3] in the absence of special facts giving rise to such a relationship which go beyond the ordinary aspects of promotion[4]. The shareholders and creditors may, however, have actions at common law for deceit, misrepresentation or negligence. In addition there may be actions for compensation under ss 150–152 of the Financial Services Act 1986 in the case of listed securities and ss 166–168 in the case of unlisted securities against the persons responsible for the issue of the listing particulars or prospectus. We shall examine these remedies in more detail when we discuss raising capital, in Chapter 33.

THE IMPACT OF S 103

Section 103 provides that a public company must not allot shares as fully or partly paid for a consideration other than cash unless there has been a valuer's report by an independent person. The necessity for such a report will cut down the possibility of fraud by promoters but as we have seen the possibility for this in the case of promoters of companies whose shares are publicly quoted in practice is negligible anyway.

If the promoter is a subscriber to the memorandum and the transaction takes place within two years of receipt of the certificate to commence

---

1 (1879) 11 Ch D 918.
2 *Re Cape Breton Co* (1885) 29 Ch D 795, CA; *Jacobus Marler Estates Ltd v Marler* (1913) 85 LJPC 167n; *Tracy v Mandalay Pty Ltd* (1952) 88 CLR 215 at 239.
3 Cf American law. See *Henn and Alexander*, op cit, p 244.
4 Cf *Coleman v Myers* [1977] 2 NZLR 225 (NZCA).

business under s 117, the further requirements of s 104 apply. These require approval by an ordinary resolution of the company as well as valuation.

Remuneration of promoters

To claim remuneration the promoter must establish a contract under seal at least in respect of formation, since the consideration will be past consideration. The promoter cannot rely for this purpose on a provision in the articles[5] except perhaps if he is a member and claims the general right to have the company's business conducted in accordance with the articles[6].

Disclosure of the remuneration paid in the two preceding years must be made in any prospectus[7].

PRE-INCORPORATION CONTRACTS

Before the company is incorporated it is often necessary for the promoters to enter into negotiations with third parties on its behalf. If these proceed to the contract stage, the question arises, who is to be liable on the contract and in particular is the promoter personally liable? The position at common law is quite complicated but to some extent this has been superseded by s 9(2) of the European Communities Act 1972, now re-enacted with minor amendments in s 36C of CA 1985. The problems usually arise in connection with small private companies.

Let us first briefly consider the position at common law. This can be summed up in the following principles:

(1) Since the company was a non-existent principal at the time of the contract, it cannot be bound nor take any benefit under it[8].

(2) For the same reason ratification is impossible[8].

(3) There may be evidence of the substitution of a new contract by novation but merely accepting the old contract and carrying it into effect after incorporation does not give rise to novation[9]. On the other hand a variation of one of the terms may be sufficient[10].

(4) There will normally be a presumption of personal liability on the part of the agent although the matter is ultimately one of construction and personal liability may be rebutted[11].

(5) Even if the agent is not liable on the contract he may possibly be liable for breach of warranty of authority[12].

(6) The use of the trust device appears to be ineffective to bind the unborn company and to exonerate the agent from personal liability[13].

5 *Melhado v Porto Alegre Rly Co* (1874) LR 9 CP 503.
6 See p 125 post.
7 Section 57.
8 *Kelner v Baxter* (1866) LR 2 CP 174; *Newborne v Sensolid (GB) Ltd* [1954] 1 QB 45, CA.
9 *Re Northumberland Avenue Hotel Co Ltd* (1886) 33 Ch D 16, CA.
10 *Howard v Patent Ivory Manufacturing Co* (1888) 38 Ch D 156.
11 *Black v Smallwood* (1965) 117 CLR 52 (Aust HC); *Marblestone Industries Ltd v Fairchild* [1975] 1 NZLR 529.
12 *Black v Smallwood,* supra and *Lomax v Dankel* [1981] 29 SASR 68 but cf *Newborne v Sensolid* supra and *Hawke's Bay Milk Corpn Ltd v Watson* [1974] 1 NZLR 236 at 239.
13 *Rita Joan Dairies Ltd v Thomson* [1974] 1 NZLR 285.

Article 7 of the First Directive of the EC provides that any person who enters into a transaction on behalf of a company 'which is in the process of formation', shall be personally liable on the transaction unless the company, on formation, assumes the obligation, or there is an agreement negating such liability. Section 36C of the CA 1985 (which replaces the old s 36(4) of that Act which in its turn replaced s 9(2) of the European Communities Act) provides:

36C. Pre-incorporation contracts, deeds and obligations
(1) A contract which purports to be made by or on behalf of a company at a time when the company has not been formed has effect, subject to any agreement to the contrary, as one made with the person purporting to act for the company or as agent for it, and he is personally liable on the contract accordingly.

It can be seen that s 36C does not deal with case law rules (1), (2), (3), (5) and (6). It simply clarifies (4) in a very marginal way[14]. The scope of the subsection was explored by the Court of Appeal in *Phonogram Ltd v Lane*[15]. The material facts were that prior to the incorporation of a company called Fragile Management Ltd the defendant contracted with the plaintiff for a loan of £12,000 to finance a pop group, Cheap Mean and Nasty. The plaintiff wrote a letter to the defendant in which it referred to him undertaking to repay. He nevertheless was required to sign and return a copy 'for and on behalf of Fragile Management Ltd'. The company was, however, never formed. The group never performed under the contract and the defendant was held personally liable under s 9(2) to repay the amount advanced.

Ingenuous arguments based on the wording of art 7 of the Directive 'in the course of formation' and 'purport' were rejected. Lord Denning MR said that s 9(2) obliterated the old subtleties which turned on the wording adopted. It applied whatever formula was adopted. The reference to 'subject to any agreement to the contrary' means 'unless otherwise agreed'. Unless there is a clear exclusion of personal liability the subsection applies. Shaw LJ agreed. Oliver LJ did not think that the pre-1973 position depended on subtle verbal distinctions but on what was the real intent revealed by the contract. However, he agreed that the subsection had made the old cases irrelevant. As regards contracting out his Lordship did not think that an agreement to the contrary could be inferred by the fact that a contract was signed by a person acting as agent.

How marginal is the effect of s 36C as so construed on the case law? It is submitted that what was formerly a rebuttable presumption of construction is now a rule of law but one which can be excluded by a clear agreement to the contrary. Anything short of an express exclusion of liability will be insufficient in practice if not in theory.

The Jenkins Report[16] favoured a reform which not only dealt with the position of the agent but also enabled a company unilaterally to adopt

---

14 See D D Prentice (1973) 89 LQR 518 at 530–533 for a useful discussion of s 9(2) which predates *Phonogram Ltd v Lane* [1982] QB 938, CA.
15 [1982] QB 938, CA. See also *Rover International Ltd v Cannon Films Sales Ltd (No 2)* (1987) 3 BCC 369 and the unreported cases of *Bitar v Al Sanea* (27 April 1983, unreported) and *Janfred Properties Ltd v Ente Nationale Haliane etc* (14 July 1983, unreported) discussed by N N Green (1984) 47 MLR 671. See also *Cotronic (UK) Ltd v Wendaland Builders Ltd* (25 February 1991 unreported) (dissolved company not within section but quantum meruit claim possible).
16 Cmnd 1749 (1962) para 54(b).

contracts which purported to be made on its behalf or in its name prior to incorporation. Such a reform has now been adopted in Ghana, Ireland, Canada, Australia and New Zealand[17] and should be introduced in the UK to complete reform of this topic.

17 See a useful summary of the various reforms in *Pre-incorporation Contracts*, Report No 8 of the Law Reform Commissioner of Victoria, p 9 ff.

CHAPTER 6

The mechanics of company formation

The Companies Act 1844 provided for incorporation by registration of deeds of settlement. The modern company is no longer formed in this way although vestiges of those days still survive in the form of subscription of the memorandum of association by the initial subscribers and the wording of s 14 of CA 1985 which refers to the corporate constitutional documents when registered as binding the company and its members to the same extent as if they respectively had been signed and sealed by each member. We shall examine this wording in detail in Chapter 11. Every company must have at least two members[1]. Originally this was seven[2] but when the public/private dichotomy was introduced in 1907, private companies were allowed a statutory minimum of two[3]. The number was reduced to two in the case of public companies by the Companies Act 1980[4]. If a company falls below the statutory minimum and carries on business for more than six months, those members who know are personally liable for its debts[5]. This is an exception to the separate legal personality of the company and the limited liability of members of a company limited by shares.

CHOOSING THE APPROPRIATE FORM

Once the decision has been reached in principle to incorporate, the question arises what particular form of company to adopt.

The parties today will rarely seek incorporation by Royal Charter unless they are concerned with education or some other charitable or public purpose. This form is mainly used for new universities set up by the state and the recognition of the governing bodies of certain key professions. It requires a petition addressed to the Crown accompanied by a draft charter[6] and is dealt with by the Privy Council.

It will also be rare today that the parties will choose to promote a statutory company which requires the passing of a specific public Act of Parliament[7]. This form is only used today for public corporations such as the nationalised industries and is usually conventionally regarded as constitutional rather than company law.

The most common form is to incorporate as a species of registered company under the Companies Acts. The basic choices here are (1) between

---

1 Section 1(1) of CA 1985.
2 Joint Stock Companies Act 1856, s 3.
3 Companies Act 1907.
4 Section 2(1) of the Companies Act 1980.
5 Section 24.
6 For the procedure, see Gower *Modern Company Law* (4th edn, 1979) p 297.
7 See *Gower*, op cit, p 297.

an unlimited or a limited company, and (2) between a public and a private company. The unlimited company confers separate legal personality, but the members remain personally liable for its debts in full. This form in practice is usually only adopted by such professions as stockbrokers who seek the administrative convenience of incorporation but who are subject to professional rules which do not allow them to limit their liability. A company can be limited by shares or by guarantee. A company limited by shares is one whose members are liable to pay up the full amount of the nominal value of their shares in the event of its winding up but no more[8]. These are by far the most common species of company. A company limited by guarantee is one whose members are liable to pay up the amount specified in their guarantee in the memorandum and no more. This form in practice is often used by educational bodies. Examples are the London School of Economics, the College of Law and modern polytechnics. Prior to the Companies Act 1980, companies limited by guarantee could also have a share capital for other purposes such as attributing votes to members. Since 22 December 1980, a company limited by guarantee may not be formed with a share capital but this does not affect existing companies which have such capital[9].

A further choice as far as limited companies are concerned is between public and private status. Under the law in force before 1980, the public/private dichotomy was worked out by reference to the definition of a private company in s 28 of the Companies Act 1948. A public company was one which was not a private company. A private company was characterised by three attributes:

(a)   a restriction on the right to transfer its shares;
(b)   a limit on its membership to 50, excluding employees and ex-employees;
(c)   a prohibition on making an invitation to the public to subscribe for its shares or debentures.

This has now been repealed and s 1(3) of CA 1985 defines a public company as:

a company limited by shares or limited by guarantee and having a share capital, being a company—
(a)   the memorandum of which states that it is to be a public company, and
(b)   in relation to which the provisions of the Act or the former Companies Acts as to the registration or re-registration of a company as a public company have been complied with on or after 22 December 1980.

A public company must now have a minimum share capital of £50,000. The requirement of limited liability rules out unlimited companies and the requirement of a share capital excludes companies limited by guarantee formed on or after 22 December 1980.

A private company is a company which is not a public company.

In practice most companies will probably continue to be formed as private companies and will be converted into public companies only when they want to 'go public' ie to invite public investment in their shares or debentures.

---

8   This does not include any premium since this technically does not form part of the share capital: *Neimann v Smedley* [1973] VR 769.
9   Companies Act 1980, s 1(2) which came into force on 22 December 1980. See now s 1(4) of CA 1985.

This will often precede a flotation of their shares or debentures on a Stock Exchange when the company's business has been built up to the requisite size.

THE FORMATION FORMALITIES

The modern company is formed by the registration of certain documents with the Registrar of Companies. There are separate registers for England and Wales, Scotland and Northern Ireland.

Name

STATUTORY RULES

Before this is done, prior to 1981, it was usual to apply for consent to the incorporation of the company with a particular name. The reason was that the Registrar had a discretion under s 17 of the Companies Act 1948 which stated quite simply that no company should be registered by a name which in the opinion of the Department of Trade was undesirable. Although the Act conferred a broad discretion the Registrar issued a practice direction describing the way in which he exercised his discretion. The main points were that the name must not be misleading or suggest a connection with the Crown, government departments, local authorities, statutory undertakings or foreign governments. In addition the use of certain words such as 'Bank', 'Insurance' and so on had to be justified as appropriate[10]. The Registrar normally made a search in the Register and in the Trade Marks Register and refused to consent if there was likely to be confusion.

Because of the element of uncertainty, incorporators usually proffered a number of alternative names. The rate of incorporations has increased considerably in recent years. The result of all this was a considerable volume of work for the Registrar's staff both prior to and on incorporation which resulted in delays.

Sections 17 and 18 of the Companies Act 1948 were repealed by s 119(5) of, and Sch 4 to, the Companies Act 1981. The new system, now set out in Pt I, Ch II of CA 1985, provides, first, that no name will be permitted if it is the same as a name on an index of names maintained by the Registrar or if the Secretary of State in certain circumstances objects, secondly, that certain specified words are unacceptable and, thirdly, circumstances in which the Secretary of State may request a company to change its name.

The index referred to in s 26(1)(c) must include the names inter alia of:

(a)   companies within the meaning of the Act;
(b)   overseas companies (i e companies incorporated abroad who have filed documents with the Registrar under s 691 and which 'do not appear to the registrar of companies not to have a place of business in Great Britain). The reason for the ugly double negative is to safeguard the Registrar from fly by night foreign companies which he may as a result keep on the Register (s 714(1)).

The purpose of the index is to enable the company itself to check whether its proposed name is the same as one already on the Register.

---

10 For a fuller discussion see *Gower*, op cit, p 302 ff.

Unacceptable names are those:

(1)   the use of which in the opinion of the Secretary of State constitutes a criminal offence (s 26(1)(d));
(2)   which in his opinion are offensive (s 26(1)(e));
(3)   which in his opinion are likely to give the impression that the company is connected with either government or a local authority (s 26(2)(a));
(4)   which include a word or expression specified in regulations made under s 29 which necessitates prior approval of the Secretary of State or relevant body[11] (s 26(2)(b)).

The Secretary of State has power to exempt a company from (3) and (4).

Section 28 sets out three circumstances in which the Secretary of State may direct a company to change its name. These are:

(1)   where it is the same as a name that appears or should have appeared at the time of registration in the index;
(2)   where it is in the opinion of the Secretary of State 'too like' a name which is on, or should have appeared in, the index (s 28(2)(a) and (b));
(3)   where the company provided misleading information in order to be registered with the name or gave undertakings which it has not fulfilled (s 28(3)).

Obviously (2) is a broad category.

Under s 18 of the Companies Act 1948, it was formerly necessary for a company to obtain consent for a change of name. This has now been abolished. All that the company need do is pass a special resolution, but of course if the name falls within the sections discussed above, the company may be required to effect a further change.

The result of these elaborate reforms, accompanied as they are by the abolition of the Business Names Registry, which kept a record of other business names, is to reduce staff and to 'privatise' this area. More obligations are cast upon companies, which ignore them at their peril. The law as opposed to the administrative practice of company names has increased in importance.

One organisation which has stepped in to fill the gap is sponsored by the principal Chambers of Commerce and provides a name check service which is based on the information on the public records which have been computerised.

THE TORT OF PASSING OFF

Any person who is aggrieved by the incorporation of a company with a name which is likely to cause confusion in relation to his goods may be able to bring proceedings for an injunction to prevent the tort of passing off[12]. The basis of the action is a right not so much in the name itself but in the goodwill engendered by the use of the name in connection with the plaintiff's business[13]. The existence of the goodwill is a question of fact. However, a person

---

11   A regulation has been made entitled The Company and Business Names Regulations 1981, SI 1981/1685.
12   See J D Heydon *Economic Torts* (2nd edn, 1978) for a discussion of this tort.
13   *Spalding & Bros v A W Gamage Ltd* (1915) 113 LT 198, HL; *Ad-Lib Club Ltd v Granville* [1971] 2 All ER 300. See also *Star Industrial Co Ltd v Yap Kwee Kor* [1976] FSR 256, PC.

may carry on business under his own name even if it does cause confusion with competitors provided he does not intend to deceive the public in relation to the goods[14]. The courts may infer such an intent. Thus in *Ewing v Buttercup Margarine Co Ltd*[15] the plaintiff carried on an unincorporated business under the trade name Buttercup Dairy Co. The defendant company was incorporated to trade in similar products and had adopted the name innocently. The Court of Appeal held that nevertheless the plaintiff was entitled to an injunction since confusion must result. Where the name of a new company may lead to the suggestion that it has taken over an existing business, this may be the ground for an injunction. Thus the Manchester Brewery Co was granted an injunction against the North Cheshire and Manchester Brewery Co[16] on the basis that it was calculated to deceive. Where there is similarity as to name, there may be no risk of confusion because of different geographical areas in which the parties operate[17] or different areas of business. Where one company carried on specialised insurance business and the other general insurance business it was held in a Scottish case that no confusion was likely to result[18].

A company cannot claim a monopoly in a descriptive word even where it was the first to use it. Thus the British Vacuum Cleaner Co could not prevent a company called New Vacuum Cleaner Co from using the words 'vacuum cleaner'[19]. It is interesting to note that Parker J also held that the plaintiff company, by allowing subsidiary companies to be formed to work particular areas under names using the words 'vacuum cleaner', had admitted that another company with a name containing those words would not necessarily be confused with the plaintiff company. This seems very questionable.

It is not necessary to prove an intention to deceive, at least to obtain an injunction. The fact of passing off per se gives rise to a right to nominal damages if damage is probable but actual damage can be pleaded and recovered. In equity, relief could be obtained where the passing off was innocent whereas at common law it was necessary to prove fraud. The position since the Judicature Acts is not clear[20]. There are strong policy grounds for holding that fault should be necessary before the company is held liable in damages. On the other hand absence of fault need not bar the grant of an injunction.

LIMITED AND PUBLIC LIMITED COMPANY

The word 'limited' must appear at the end of the name of a private company and the words 'public limited company' at the end of the name of a public company. Section 19 of the Companies Act 1948 enabled a company to apply for dispensation from the obligation to put the word limited at the end of its name. Most companies which successfully applied were companies limited by guarantee. The dispensation was negated to some extent by s 9 of

14 *Hall-Gibbs Mercantile Agency Ltd v Dun* (1910) 12 CLR 84.
15 [1917] 2 Ch 1, CA.
16 *North Cheshire and Manchester Brewery Co v Manchester Brewery Co* [1899] AC 83, HL.
17 *Empire Typesetting Machine Co of New York v Linotype Co Ltd* (1898) 79 LT 8, CA. Cf, however, *Maxim's Ltd v Dye* [1978] 2 All ER 55.
18 *Scottish Union and National Insurance Co v Scottish National Insurance Co* 1909 SC 318.
19 *British Vacuum Cleaner Co Ltd v New Vacuum Cleaner Co Ltd* [1907] 2 Ch 312. See also *Aerators Ltd v Tollitt* [1902] 2 Ch 319 ('Aerators').
20 See *Heydon*, op cit.

the European Communities Act 1972 which required disclosure of the company's limited liability on its letter headings. Section 19 was repealed by the Companies Act 1981 and replaced by s 15 of that Act. Section 15 of the 1981 Act has now been re-enacted in s 30 of CA 1985, and s 9(3) of the European Communities Act 1972 in s 35(1) of the 1985 Act. In future private companies limited by guarantee and those companies limited by shares which had dispensation under s 19 on 25 February 1982 are exempt provided they satisfy the criteria set out in s 30(3)(a) and (b). These provide respectively:

(a)   'that the objects of the company are (or, in the case of a company about to be registered, are to be) the promotion of commerce, art, science, education, religion, charity or any profession, and anything incidental or conducive to any of those objects; and
(b)   that the company's memorandum or articles of association
    (i)   require its profits (if any) or other income to be applied in promoting its objects,
    (ii)   prohibit the payment of dividends to its members, and
    (iii)   require all the assets which would otherwise be available to its members generally to be transferred on its winding up either to another body with objects similar to its own or to another body the objects of which are the promotion of charity and anything incidental or conducive thereto (whether or not the body is a member of the company)'.

The effect of these changes is to reduce the class of companies having dispensation.

The documents to be filed

The principal documents which are registered are the memorandum and articles of association which have superseded the deeds of settlement. The basic form of these dates back to the Joint Stock Companies Act 1856 and was influenced by the New York Business Corporations Act. The current forms are set out in regulations made by the Secretary of State under ss 3 and 8 of CA 1985[21]. The memorandum of association of a company limited by shares states the name and country in which the company's registered office is situated, its objects and powers, the basis of liability, the initial share capital and the number of shares into which it is divided. If the company is a public company, this too must be stated in the memorandum. It is subscribed by the original members of the company and states their name, address and the number of shares they subscribe. The main function of the memorandum of association is to describe the essential attributes of the particular company and its relationship with the outside world. Section 3 provides for the form to be set out in regulations made by the Secretary of State.

The articles of association deal with such matters as classes of shares, class rights, transfer and transmission of shares, procedures at general meetings and meetings of directors, and dividends—in other words, the internal organisation of the company. Most companies adopt a modified version of the model set out in Table A, formerly set out in Sch 1 to the Companies Act

21 The Companies (Table A–F) Regulations 1985, SI 1985/805.

1948 and now set out in regulations made under s 8[20]. Section 7 provides that there may in the case of a company limited by shares and there shall in the case of a company limited by guarantee or unlimited, be registered with the memorandum, articles of association signed by the subscribers and prescribing regulations for the company. Section 8(1) provides that the articles may adopt the whole or any part of Table A and s 8(2) provides that in the case of a company limited by shares:

if articles are not registered or if articles are registered but do not exclude or modify Table A, Table A applies as in force at the date of the company's registration.

However, the statutory precedents are a guide, not a straitjacket. They indicate form or arrangement, not substance. They do not have to be followed literally. They are directory, not mandatory, forms[1]. Thus provisions which differ from them, or conflict with them, may still be valid.

Accompanying the memorandum and articles there must be a Statement on Formation of a Limited Company[2] and a Declaration of Compliance[3] which is a statutory declaration made by the solicitor engaged in the formation or by a person named as the first director or secretary in the articles. Capital duty[4] and the registration fee[5] must be paid and it is now obligatory to file the Particulars of Registered Office[6] and Particulars of Directors and Secretary[7] at this stage.

THE ROLE OF THE REGISTRAR

The role of the Registrar in respect of incorporation is administrative. He has to be satisfied that the documents are in order and that the formalities prescribed by the Companies Acts have been complied with. He has no power to conduct a judicial enquiry. Section 1(1) of CA 1985 requires the members to be associated 'for a lawful purpose'. In *R v Registrar of Joint Stock Companies, ex p More*[8] some Irishmen wanted to incorporate an English company to market Irish Sweepstake tickets. It was lawful to do this in Eire but not in the UK. The Registrar consequently refused registration and the Irishmen sought mandamus. The court refused to upset the Registrar's decision. On the other hand if the purpose is lawful and all the statutory conditions have been complied with, the Registrar must issue the certificate of incorporation and if he refuses to issue it, an order of mandamus will be made against him[9].

The certificate of incorporation

On the registration of the company the Registrar gives a certificate that the company is incorporated and, in the case of a limited liability company, that its liability is limited (s 13(1)). Under s 711(1)(a), the Registrar must advertise

1 Per Megarry J in *Gaiman v National Association for Mental Health* [1971] Ch 317 at 328.
2 Form PUC 1.
3 Section 12(2). Form 41a.
4 Finance Act 1973, s 47.
5 Now a fixed flat rate fee of £50; see Companies (Fees) Regulations 1988, SI 1988/887.
6 Section 10(6).
7 Section 10(2).
8 [1931] 2 KB 197, CA.
9 *R v Registrar of Companies, ex p Bowen* [1914] 3 KB 1161.

the issue of the certificate in the Gazette, the official newspaper. The effect of the certificate is specified in s 13(3) and (4).

From the date of incorporation the subscribers of the memorandum, together with people who subsequently become members, constitute a body corporate capable forthwith of exercising all the functions of an incorporated company but with such liability on the part of the members to contribute to its assets in the event of winding up as is provided by the Act. In the case of a public company an additional certificate under s 117 as to the amount of the allotted share capital must be obtained before it can commence business or borrow.

Section 13(7) provides that the certificate of incorporation is conclusive evidence (a) that the requirements of the Act in respect of registration and of matters precedent and incidental thereto have been complied with and that the association is a company authorised to be registered, and is duly registered under the Act; and (b) if the certificate contains a statement that the company is a public company, that the company is such a company. The ample scope of this provision is illustrated by *Jubilee Cotton Mills Ltd v Lewis*[10] where it was held that the certificate was conclusive as to the date of incorporation even though it was wrong. Also, in *Cotman v Brougham*[11], the House of Lords felt that an earlier provision to similar effect prevented them from vetoing a clause in a memorandum which they did not like. The clause in question treated every paragraph in the objects clause as a separate object and became known as a *Cotman v Brougham* clause which appears in most objects clauses today. We examine this question in detail in a later chapter. On the other hand the certificate is only conclusive that the formalities have been complied with and is not conclusive of the legality of the company's objects. In *Bowman v Secular Society*[12], it was held that the Attorney General could apply for certiorari to have the registration cancelled in the event of its object being unlawful[13].

The effect of the section is to exclude from English company law the doctrine of nullity of incorporation which exists in continental systems. This allows judicial annulment for irregularities in formation and was the subject of Section III of the First EC Directive[14].

One last matter to which we shall briefly refer is that it is possible to convert a company incorporated as a private company into a public company, and vice versa, provided the formalities set out in ss 43 and 53 respectively are complied with. In practice most public companies are incorporated as private companies. Under s 43, this means that a special resolution must be passed, an application made in the prescribed form accompanied by certain documents and the requirements of s 43(2) and (3) and ss 44 and 45 must be complied with.

There are also procedures laid down for converting from limited to unlimited form and vice versa but s 49(3) provides that no *public* company or a company previously registered as unlimited may apply to be re-registered as an unlimited company[15].

10 [1924] AC 958, HL.
11 [1918] AC 514, HL.
12 [1917] AC 406, HL.
13 See too the unreported case of the incorporated prostitute *R v Registrar of Companies, ex p A–G* (17 December 1980, unreported) set out in *Hahlo's Cases and Materials on Company Law* (3rd edn, 1987) H R Hahlo and J H Farrar, p 176. Cf *Princess of Reuss v Bos* (1871) LR 5 HL 176.
14 On nullity see R R Drury (1985) 48 MLR 644.
15 For a detailed discussion of these specialised topics, see *Palmer's Company Law* (24th edn, 1987) vol 1, para 5–05 ff.

CHAPTER 7

Corporate personality and limited liability

THE CONCEPT OF CORPORATE PERSONALITY

A company is a species of corporation. This means that it is 'a body of bodies; technically, an artificial person composed of natural persons'[1]. For the purposes of much legislation it ranks as a person along with natural persons unless the context otherwise requires[2].

The early companies legislation merely referred to the subscribers forming themselves into an incorporated company and did not spell out the consequences in any detail[3]. As a learned commentator in the Law Quarterly Review of 1897 stated: 'Our Legislature . . . delivered itself on the Companies Acts in its usual oracular style, leaving to the Courts the interpretation of its mystical utterances'[4]. The separate legal personality of a limited liability company was firmly established by the House of Lords in the leading case of *Salomon v A Salomon & Co Ltd*[5], although the courts have subsequently, for reasons of policy, disregarded this personality in a minority of cases.

The facts of *Salomon v A Salomon & Co Ltd* were as follows: Aron Salomon was a boot and shoe manufacturer trading as a successful sole trader in the East End of London for over 30 years. There was family pressure to give them a share in the business and he wished to extend the business. He, therefore, formed a company and sold his business to the company. At the time the legislation required a company to have a minimum of seven members. A Salomon and Co Ltd had Salomon himself and six members of his family who held one share each as nominees. Thus the company was in reality a 'one-man company'. The price paid by the company for the transfer of the business was on paper over £39,000, 'a sum which', Lord Macnaghten said, 'represented the sanguine expectations of a fond owner rather than anything that can be called a businesslike or reasonable estimate of value'[6]. Although worthy of comment, this fact ultimately had no bearing on the case in the House of Lords. The purchase price was to be paid as to £30,000[7] out of money as it came in, which Salomon immediately returned to the company in exchange for fully paid shares, £10,000 in debentures and the balance (except for £1,000) to be used to pay

1 Harry G Henn and J A Alexander *Corporations* (3rd edn, 1983) p 145.
2 Interpretation Act 1978, s 5 and Sch 1.
3 Joint Stock Companies Act 1856, s 3.
4 (1897) 13 LQR 6. For useful recent discussions of the economic and legal background to the case, see P Ireland 'Triumph of the Company Legal Form 1856–1914' and G R Rubin 'Aron Salomon and his Circle' in *Essays for Clive Schmitthoff* ed J Adams (1983) pp 29 ff and 99 ff respectively.
5 [1897] AC 22, HL.
6 [1897] AC 22 at 49, HL.
7 Lord Macnaghten's speech (ibid) seems wrong on this point.

the debts. The debentures were an acknowledgement of indebtedness by the company secured on its property and effects. At the end of the day Salomon received about £1,000 in cash, £10,000 in debentures and half the nominal capital of the company in issued shares. The company fell upon hard times. There was a great depression in the trade and strikes of workmen. In view of the latter, contracts with public bodies on which the company relied were farmed out amongst a number of different firms. Salomon attempted various strategies to get the company back on its feet. He and his wife lent it money. He mortgaged his debentures to obtain the necessary funds which he loaned to the company. The mortgagee was registered as the holder of the debentures. Still the company did not prosper and it went into receivership and then liquidation. There was a forced sale of its assets. There was enough to enable the liquidator, if he wished, to pay the mortgagee but not enough to repay the debentures in full or the unsecured creditors. In the course of the liquidation the mortgagee of the debentures brought a claim under the debentures against the company. The liquidator attempted to resist the claim by arguing that the debentures were invalid on the ground of fraud. At first instance[8] Vaughan Williams J, a bankruptcy expert[9], looked upon the case with a jaundiced eye. He disapproved of the one-man company which was then a new practice[10] and thought he detected fraud. He held that the company was merely acting as Salomon's nominee and agent and therefore Salomon as principal had to indemnify the company's creditors himself. Salomon appealed to the Court of Appeal which turned down his appeal, but largely on the different ground that Salomon was a trustee for the company which was his mere shadow[11]. Both the first instance judge and the Court of Appeal thought that a one-man company was an abuse of the Companies Act. Salomon appealed to the House of Lords which totally rejected the rulings below. A one-man company was not an abuse of the Companies Act, all the relevant formalities had been complied with and the Act was silent on the question of beneficial interests and control. A Salomon and Co Ltd was different from Salomon as an individual. Lord Halsbury LC[12] saw the view of the Court of Appeal as involving a logical contradiction. Sometimes it regarded A Salomon and Co Ltd as a company and sometimes it did not. Lord Watson[13] mentioned a new point, namely that the creditors of the company could have searched the Companies Register to find out the name of the shareholders and their failure to do so should not impute a charge of fraud against Salomon. Lord Herschell[14] largely based his speech on the intention of the statute to protect shareholders by limiting their liability. The speech of Lord Macnaghten, which is more comprehensive, is a legal classic. He states at p 51 quite firmly that:

The company is at law a different person altogether from the subscribers to the Memorandum and, although it may be that after incorporation the business is precisely the same as it was before, and the same persons are managers, and the same hands receive the profits, the company is not in law the agent of the subscribers or

8 [1895] 2 Ch 323.
9 He was author of *Williams on Bankruptcy*.
10 See Lindley LJ at [1895] 2 Ch 323 at 336.
11 [1895] 2 Ch 323 at 336.
12 [1897] AC 22 at 31.
13 Ibid, at 40.
14 Ibid, at 45.

trustee for them. Nor are subscribers as members liable, in any shape or form, except to the extent and in the manner provided by the Act. That is, I think, the declared intention of the enactment.

The House of Lords' decision in *Salomon* has been criticised as going too far. The contemporary comment of the Law Quarterly Review[15] was that the House of Lords had recognised that one trader and six dummies would suffice and that the statutory conditions were mere machinery. 'You touch the requisite button and the company starts into existence, a legal entity, an independent *persona*.' The decision recognised that the one-man company fell within the policy of the Act. There was nothing startling in that. Once limited liability was recognised the creditors must look at the capital—the limited fund—and that only. Nevertheless, from the point of view of statutory construction it was thought that such a decision would have been impossible twenty or thirty years earlier. The reference in the Act to the persons being 'associated' would then have predicated a partnership. A more drastic modern criticism was that of the late Professor Otto Kahn-Freund[16] who thought that the decision was 'calamitous'. The courts, while developing fiduciary principles to protect shareholders, had failed to mitigate 'the rigidities of the "folklore" of corporate entity in favour of the legitimate interests of the company's creditors'. Not only this but the incongruity permeated the whole of legal business life. He thought that the answer lay in:

(a)   raising the cost of incorporation;
(b)   the introduction of minimum capital for all companies not exempted by the Department of Trade and a minimum subscription on incorporation;
(c)   the abolition of private companies;
(d)   a general clause deeming those companies under the control of ten persons to be the agents of those persons.

As we have seen, a minimum capital has now been introduced for public companies. Most of Professor Kahn-Freund's other suggestions are probably too draconian but variations on the theme of (d) received some consideration by the Insolvency Law Review Committee of the Department of Trade which preferred not to express a final view on the matter.

We saw in the first chapter how all legal personality is in a sense fiction—the creation of legal artifice. *Corporate* personality is essentially a metaphorical use of language clothing the formal group with a single separate legal identity by analogy with a natural person. Metaphors in fact abound in this area of law, both to support and to reject the separate legal personality of the company. As Cardozo J said in the American case of *Berkey v Third Avenue Rly*[17]: 'Metaphors in law are to be narrowly watched, for starting as devices to liberate thought, they often end by enslaving it'. It is certainly the case that the application of the *Salomon* principle has on occasions led to some extreme results. Thus in the Northern Irish case of *Macaura v*

15 (1897) 13 LQR 6.
16 (1944) 7 MLR 54.
17 244 NY 84 at 94–5 (1926).

Northern Assurance Co[18] Macaura was the controlling shareholder of a company and effected fire insurance in his own name in respect of the property of the company. The question in issue was whether he had an insurable interest in the property of the company. The House of Lords held that only the company had an insurable interest in its property. Macaura had no insurable interest and, therefore, could not claim on the policies. This seems a rather harsh application of the principle although it may be that the House was influenced by the charges of fraud which had been unsuccessful in the earlier arbitration. Certainly there seems to have been less than a month between the taking out of one of the policies and the fire. The converse also applies. In the Canadian Supreme Court case of *Wandlyn Motels Ltd v Commerce General Insurance Co*[19] it was held that a company has no insurable interest in the assets of the principal shareholder.

A more humane application of the principle which really pushes it to its logical extreme is *Lee v Lee's Air Farming Ltd*[20]. This was a New Zealand appeal to the Privy Council. Lee was the controlling shareholder, sole governing director and chief pilot of the company. A governing director has all the powers of management vested in him. Lee died as a result of an air crash while top-dressing. The question was whether he was an employee of the company for the purpose of the workmen's compensation legislation. The New Zealand Court of Appeal had held that he was not, as he was not sufficiently separate from the company. The Privy Council overruled this, applying a strict application of the *Salomon* principle. The company and Lee were separate legal persons and it was possible for a controlling shareholder and governing director to have a contract with his company which could be the basis of a claim.

LEGITIMATE USE OF THE CORPORATE FORM AND PIERCING THE VEIL

The courts have on occasion not applied the *Salomon* principle. However, they have not done this in a systematic way by defining the proper ends of incorporation. Instead they have moved from case to case.

As Rogers AJA said in the New South Wales Court of Appeal in *Briggs v James Hardie & Co Pty Ltd*[1]:

The threshold problem arises from the fact that there is no common, unifying principle, which underlies the occasional decision of courts to pierce the corporate veil. Although an ad hoc explanation may be offered by a court which so decides, there is no principled approach to be derived from the authorities . . .

---

18 [1925] AC 619, HL. Cf however *Constitution Insurance Co of Canada v Kosmopoulos* (1987) 34 DLR (4th) 208 (Supreme Court of Canada) and *American Indemnity Co v Southern Missionary College* 260 SW 2d 269 (1953) which allowed claims in the case of a sole shareholder. In the *Kosmopoulos* case the court concentrated on the concept of insurable interest and did not regard itself as piercing the corporate veil. For earlier comment on the case see Jacob Ziegel (1984) 62 Can Bar Rev 95. It is always possible to insure the shares themselves. See *Paterson v Harris* (1861) 1 B & S 336; *Wilson v Jones* (1867) LR 2 Exch 139.
19 (1970) 12 DLR (3d) 605.
20 [1961] AC 12, PC.
 1 [1989] 16 NSWLR 549 at 567.

It is difficult to start to rationalise the cases except under the broad, rather question-begging heading of policy and by describing the main legal categories under which they fall[2]. These are:

(1)   agency;
(2)   fraud;
(3)   group enterprises;
(4)   trusts;
(5)   tort;
(6)   enemy;
(7)   tax;
(8)   the companies legislation;
(9)   other legislation.

We will deal with each of these in turn and then attempt a summing up.

1 Agency

The *Salomon* case held that a company was not automatically the agent of its shareholders. It did not exclude the possibility of there being an agent relationship in fact. Occasionally the courts have seemed willing to construe an express or implied agency of the company for its members[3]. It has, however, been held that a 98% controlling interest in a company by itself does not create or manifest an agency relationship[4]. The authorities were reviewed by Atkinson J in *Smith, Stone & Knight Ltd v Birmingham Corpn*[5] where he attempted, not particularly successfully, to identify the underlying principles. The facts of the case were that a company took over a business and continued it through a subsidiary company which was treated as a department. The parent company claimed compensation on the basis of injury by the corporation's use of its powers of compulsory acquisition over the subsidiary's land. Piercing the corporate veil was essential to the plaintiff's claim since the corporation would otherwise escape paying compensation altogether by virtue of s 121 of the Lands Clauses Consolidation Act 1845 which enabled purchasers to get rid of occupiers with short tenancies by giving them notice. Counsel for the parent company used agency and group arguments and Atkinson J accepted at the end of the day that the parent company could recover. He said that the overall question of whether the subsidiary was carrying on the business as the parent's business or its own was a question of fact. In answering it, six factors were to be weighed:

2 See Murray Pickering (1968) 31 MLR 481; M Whincup (1981) 2 Co Law 158; Gower *Principles of Modern Company Law* (4th edn, 1979) p 123; *Henn and Alexander*, op cit, p 344 and the bibliography cited by the latter at pp 345–346. However, for attempts to break away from this unsatisfactory approach see P Carteaux (1984) 58 Tulane L Rev 1089; A Domanski (1986) 103 SALJ 224; A Beck 'The Two Sides of the Corporate Veil' in *Contemporary Issues in Company Law* (1987) (ed J H Farrar), 69; S. Ottolenghi (1990) 53 MLR 338. Dr Ottolenghi distinguishes between peeping behind, penetrating, extending and ignoring the corporate veil. See too JS Ziegel (1990) 31 Les Cahiers de Droit 1075.
3 See *Rainham Chemical Works Ltd v Belvedere Fish Guano Co* [1921] 2 AC 465, HL; *Southern v Watson* [1940] 3 All ER 439, CA; *Clarkson Co Ltd v Zhelke* (1967) 64 DLR (2d) 457. For a detailed survey see R Flannigan (1986–7) 51 Sask Law Rev 23.
4 *Kodak Ltd v Clark* [1903] 1 KB 505, CA.
5 [1939] 4 All ER 116.

(a)   were the profits of the subsidiary those of the parent company?
(b)   were the persons conducting the business of the subsidiary appointed by the parent company?
(c)   was the parent company the 'head and brains' of the trading venture?
(d)   did the parent company govern the adventure?
(e)   were the profits made by the subsidiary company made by the skill and direction of the parent company?
(f)   was the parent company in effective and constant control of the subsidiary?

As can be seen, (d), (e) and (f) cover very much the same ground. At the end of the day Atkinson J held that the subsidiary was the 'agent or employee; or tool or simulacrum of the parent'. For all its faults *Smith, Stone & Knight* was followed by Else-Mitchell J in the New South Wales Supreme Court case of *Hotel Terrigal Pty Ltd v Latec Investments Ltd (No 2)*[6] where His Honour disregarded a purported sale by a mortgagee company of the mortgaged property to its wholly owned subsidiary for an improper purpose. The emphasis in compulsory acquisition cases has shifted more recently to the group enterprise argument. This has proved successful in the English Court of Appeal but not elsewhere as we shall see.

Professor Otto Kahn-Freund in a note in [1940] 3 MLR 226 distinguished between two kinds of control, 'capitalist control' and 'functional control' and argued that the *Salomon* case was about capitalist control. 'Capitalist control', which means control by ownership of a company's share capital, does not necessarily mean there is an agency. Functional control is concerned with who is actually running the company and, therefore, is relevant to the determination of an agency. As can be seen most of the factors mentioned by Atkinson J are concerned with 'functional control'.

US corporation laws recognise functional control under the instrumentality doctrine which is sometimes linked with unity of interest. A clear statement of principle appears in the judgment of Alcorn J in *Zaist v Olson* 227 A 2d 552 (1967) at p 558 where he said:

The instrumentality rule requires, in any case but an express agency, proof of three elements: (1) control, not mere majority or complete stock control, but complete domination, not only of finances but of policy and business practice in respect to the transaction attacked so that the corporate entity as to this transaction had at the time no separate mind, will or existence of its own; and (2) such control must have been used by the defendant to commit fraud or wrong, to perpetuate the violation of a statutory or other positive legal duty, or a dishonest or unjust act in contravention of plaintiff's legal rights; and (3) the aforesaid control and breach of duty must proximately cause the injury or unjust loss complained of . . .

As we will see in a moment there is a link between agency in fact, instrumentality and the concept of the group enterprise.

2 Fraud

The courts are prepared to pierce the corporate veil to combat fraud. They will not allow the *Salomon* principle to be used as an engine of fraud. Fraud

6 [1969] 1 NSWLR 676.

here includes equitable fraud. In *Gilford Motor Co Ltd v Horne*[7], a managing director of a company entered into a covenant in a service agreement not to solicit customers from his employers. Upon leaving the company's employment he formed a company to solicit customers. It was held by the Court of Appeal that his company was a mere sham to cloak his wrongdoings and, therefore, he could be restrained from committing a breach. Similarly, in *Jones v Lipman*[8] a man contracted to sell property but then changed his mind. In order to avoid an order for specific performance he transferred the property to a company. Russell J held that specific performance could be ordered against the company. It was 'the creature of the first defendant, a device and a sham, a mask which [he] held before his face to avoid recognition by the eye of equity'[9].

Again, in *Re Bugle Press Ltd*[10] the use of a company as a device to fall within the provisions of s 209 of the Companies Act 1948 was disallowed. Section 209 which is re-enacted in s 428 of CA 1985 enables a takeover bidder who falls within the section and has acquired the requisite proportion of shares to acquire the minority compulsorily. Here there were three shareholders, and two wanted to buy out the third, who refused. As things stood the facts did not fall within the section so the majority formed a company to make an offer for all the shares in order to bring the matter within the section. The Court of Appeal, looking to substance rather than form, disregarded the company as a mere sham or simulacrum. The minority shareholder, said Harman LJ, had only to shout and the walls of Jericho fell flat.

It should, however, be noted that the courts have not shown any great willingness to step in to protect creditors from abuse of the corporate form due to reckless as opposed to fraudulent trading. Where fraudulent trading has taken place, s 630 enables the court to pierce the corporate veil. The Cork Report favoured an extension of this to wrongful trading, and this concept was introduced by the Insolvency Act 1985, the relevant provision now being consolidated in s 214 of the Insolvency Act 1986.

3 Group enterprises

The courts have sometimes shown a willingness to look upon a group of companies as one economic unit[11]. This is done by the accounting and disclosure provisions of the companies legislation to some extent and is now carried on by the courts on occasion. Indeed the legislation has been used as a justification for the case law even though not strictly relevant. In *Littlewoods Mail Order Stores v McGregor*[12] Lord Denning stated that the

---

7 [1933] Ch 935, CA.
8 [1962] 1 All ER 442.
9 Ibid, at 445 c–d.
10 [1961] Ch 270, CA.
11 See *Gower*, op cit, p 128 ff. For an interesting recent analysis see H Collins (1990) 53 MLR 731. For recent case law discussion see *Adams v Cape Industries plc* [1990] BCC 786, CA. See too the discussion of Salomon, groups and undertakings in *Istituto Chemioterapico Italiano SpA and Commercial Solvents Corpn v EC Commission* Case 6, 7/73 [1974] ECR 223, ECJ, Advocate General Warner at p 263. For the relationship with factual control and agency see above and *Adams v Cape Industries plc* (supra) and *Revlon Inc v Cripps and Lee Ltd* [1980] FSR 85, CA.
12 [1969] 3 All ER 855 at 860, CA.

doctrine laid down in *Salomon* had to be carefully watched. It has often been supposed to cast a veil over a limited liability company through which the courts could not see. This was not true. The courts can and often do draw aside the veil and look at what really lies behind. Parliament had shown the way: the courts should follow suit. A similar line was taken in the recent case of *DHN Food Distributors Ltd v London Borough of Tower Hamlets*[13]. This was a case of compulsory acquisition. The facts were that one company in the group owned the freehold and another company which carried on the business on the premises was a bare licensee. The Court of Appeal was prepared to recognise the economic unit of the group as a single entity to enable them to recover their compensation. The different members of the Court of Appeal seem to have been influenced by different factors. Lord Denning MR referred to the fact that the subsidiaries were wholly owned, but thereafter lapsed into metaphor. Goff LJ made it clear that not every group would be treated in this way but pointed to ownership, no separate business operations and the nature of the question to be answered. Shaw LJ pointed to common directors, shareholdings and common interest.

This approach seems to go too far and is inconsistent with the view of the High Court of Australia in *Industrial Equity Ltd v Blackburn*[14] where it was said that the group account provisions did not operate to deny the separate legal personality of the company. The *DHN* case was not followed by the House of Lords in the Scottish appeal of *Woolfson v Strathclyde Regional Council*[15]. A similar approach again more consistent with *Salomon*'s case was taken by the New Zealand Court of Appeal in the case of *Re Securitibank Ltd (No 2)*[16]. This involved an in-house bill where the client drew a bill of exchange on Merbank which was then discounted by another member of the group, Commercial Bills. Counsel sought to argue that this involved an infringement of the money lending legislation because the essence of the transaction was a loan if one pierced the corporate veil. The Court of Appeal referred to the *Littlewoods* case and thought that it was putting the matter the wrong way round. The starting point should be the application of the *Salomon* principle and any departure from it must be looked at very carefully. *Woolfson v Strathclyde RC* and *Re Securitibank Ltd* were considered by Young J in the New South Wales case of *Pioneer Concrete Services Ltd v Yelnah Pty Ltd*[17]. This was a case of a complicated commercial agreement involving a group of companies which had been entered into with full legal advice. His Honour held that the court would only pierce the corporate veil where it could see that there was in law or in fact a partnership between the companies or where there was a mere sham or facade. Here there was a good commercial reason for having separate companies perform different functions and the veil should not be pierced.

The *Pioneer* decision was referred to by Rogers AJA in the recent New South Wales Court of Appeal decision of *Briggs v James Hardie & Co Pty*

---

13 [1976] 3 All ER 462, CA.
14 (1977) 137 CLR 567 at 577.
15 (1978) 38 P & CR 521, HL. See F Rixon (1986) 102 LQR 415. For discussion of recent Northern Irish cases see G Dee (1986) 7 Co Law 248.
16 [1978] 2 NZLR 136.
17 [1986] 5 NSWLR 254. See also *National Dock Labour Board v Pinn and Wheeler Ltd* [1989] BCLC 647.

Ltd[18] where His Honour made an interesting analysis of what he called 'the unity of enterprise theory' relying on Commonwealth and US authorities. The majority gave a liberal interpretation to section 58 of the Limitation Act NSW 1969 to allow an extension of the limitation period in a case of multiple defendants and Rogers AJA said that the mere potential to exercise control over a subsidiary was not enough to justify piercing the corporate veil. The exercise of some control in fact was also insufficient. Dominance may be part of the test but Commonwealth company law was not settled on this or on the degree of control or the extent of reliance or under capitalisation. The Salomon principle had survived the growth of corporate groups, and domination and control were not per se sufficient to pierce the corporate veil. It is unfortunate that His Honour does not appear to have been referred to the US instrumentality doctrine which, when read in the context of the US approach overall, completes the picture. In *Re a Company*[19] in 1985 the Court of Appeal was prepared to pierce the corporate veil by granting an injunction restricted to companies controlled by the defendant where the evidence showed that the defendant had created a corporate network to dispose of his assets and there was an allegation of fraud.

One area where the courts have been particularly reluctant to recognise the concept of group entity is in relation to corporate debts. It is not possible in the absence of an agency or trust relationship or wrongful trading[20] to hold one group company liable for the debts of another. In the USA equitable doctrines are sometimes applied in this context and in New Zealand and the Irish Republic there is legislation giving the court power to order a pooling of assets.

4 Trust

Occasionally, the courts may pierce the corporate veil to look at the characteristics of the shareholders. In *Abbey Malvern Wells Ltd v Ministry of Local Government and Planning*[1] a school was carried on in the form of a company, but the shares were held by trustees on educational charitable trusts. The court was prepared to pierce the corporate veil and look at the terms on which the trustees held the shares.

5 Tort

Although there are isolated cases where English courts have used tort remedies to pierce the corporate veil, it is not common in Commonwealth jurisdictions outside Canada. In Canada, however, there is an increasing use of tort to bypass *Salomon*'s case. Inducing a breach of contract[2], deceit[3] and

18 [1989] 16 NSWLR 549.
19 [1985] BCLC 333, CA.
20 For a case where a claim under s 332 of the 1948 Act failed see *Re Augustus Barnett & Son Ltd* (1986) 2 BCC 98, 904. Noted by D D Prentice (1987) 103 LQR 11. For a recent case where the House of Lords seemed willing to pierce the corporate veil or use the alter ego approach in equity, see *Winkworth v Edward Baron Development Co Ltd* [1987] 1 All ER 114, HL.
1 [1951] Ch 728.
2 *McFadden v 481782 Ontario Ltd* (1984) 47 OR (2d) 134; *BG Preeco I (Pacific Coast) Ltd v Bon Street Holdings Ltd* (1989) 60 DLR (4th) 30.
3 *BG Preeco* (supra).

conspiracy[4] have all been used in recent cases. Thus in the British Columbia Court of Appeal case of *BG Preeco I (Pacific Coast) Ltd v Bon Street Holdings Ltd*[5] the Court held that *Salomon*'s case was to be adhered to but that there was a direct remedy in deceit against the principal directors and shareholders where they had misled the plaintiff by switching the name of a company with assets to a shell company. The end result turned out to be the same. There would appear to be great potential here for undermining the rigour of the *Salomon*[6] principle and this perhaps reflects the fact that its application in the tort area has always been less justifiable than in contract. Many tort victims have no choice in the selection of tort feasor. Here domination and under-capitalisation seem particularly relevant to piercing the veil.

6 Enemy

In times of war the court is prepared to pierce the corporate veil to see who are the controlling shareholders of companies. This was done in *Daimler Co Ltd v Continental Tyre and Rubber Co (GB) Ltd*[7] where shares in an English company were held by Germans in the First World War.

7 Tax

From time to time for reasons of fiscal policy tax legislation disregards the separate legal personality of companies. Also the courts are prepared to disregard the separate legal personality of companies in the case of tax evasion or over-liberal schemes of tax avoidance without any necessary legislative authority. In such cases the courts frequently dismiss the company as a mere sham[8]. The question of form and substance in tax law is quite complex and this is merely part of it.

8 Companies legislation

The companies legislation contains a number of provisions disregarding the separate corporate entity. Thus s 24 of CA 1985 provides that in the case of the reduction of the membership of a company below the statutory minimum, the continuing members who are cognisant of the fact shall be personally responsible for the company's debts without limitation of liability. Section 213 of the Insolvency Act 1986 provides that where in the winding up of a company it appears that the company's business has been carried on with the intent to defraud the creditors or for any fraudulent purpose, the court may declare persons who were knowingly parties to the carrying on of the business personally liable without limitation of liability[9]. As we have seen this has been extended to wrongful trading by what is now s 214 of the Insolvency Act 1986.

4 *Lehndorff Canadian Properties Ltd v Davis & Co* (1987) 10 BCLR (2d) 342.
5 Ibid.
6 See Rogers AJA in *Briggs v James Hardie & Co Pty Ltd* [1989] 16 NSWLR 549 at 578, 580.
7 [1916] 2 AC 307.
8 See *Gower*, op cit, pp 120–1, chapter 11.
9 See too ss 238(3), (4), (5) and 240. See A Wilkinson (1987) 8 Co Law 124. See also s 349(4) (misdescription of the company); and the group provisions of the Companies Acts.

9 Other legislation

The locus classicus for legislation in general is perhaps the speech of Lord Diplock in *Dimbleby & Sons Ltd v National Union of Journalists*[10] where he said:

My Lords, the reason why English statutory law, and that of all other trading countries, has long permitted the creation of corporations as artificial persons distinct from their individual shareholders and from that of any other corporation even though the shareholders of both corporations are identical, is to enable business to be undertaken with limited financial liability in the event of the business proving to be a failure. The 'corporate veil' in the case of companies incorporated under the Companies Acts is drawn by statute and it can be pierced by some other statute if such other statute so provides: but in view of its raison d'être and its consistent recognition by the courts since *Salomon v Salomon & Co Ltd* [1897] AC 22, one would expect that any parliamentary intention to pierce the corporate veil would be expressed in clear and unequivocal language. I do not wholly exclude the possibility that even in the absence of express words stating that in specified circumstances one company, although separately incorporated, is to be treated as sharing the same legal personality of another, a purposive construction of the statute may nevertheless lead inexorably to the conclusion that such must have been the intention of Parliament.

In that case the House of Lords held that the phrase 'an employer who is a party to the dispute' did not extend to another company which had identical shareholdings and the same parent company as the actual employer.

Conclusion

It is difficult to sum up these exceptions except to say that the departures from the *Salomon* principle seem to be based on policy decisions. The general principle seems to be that *Salomon* will be applied until some reason to the contrary appears. There is a range from legitimate purposes where it will be applied to dishonest purposes where it will not be applied. Where there is unity of interest and ownership and the concept of separate legal personality is being used to defeat public convenience, justify wrong, protect fraud, or defend crime, the law will tend to regard the company as an association of the natural persons comprising it[11]. Reduction of potential tort liability (short of fraud) will not suffice[12]. In between are cases where the court might disregard it to achieve a just result. There seems to be a general reluctance to apply the principle in a pedantic way where the result will cause injustice. It should, however, be noted that the argument for piercing the corporate veil will not usually be the sole argument in the case. It will usually be incidental to some other argument of substance. A similar but not identical point was made by Stone J in the American case of *Re Clark's Will*[13], when he said:

Many cases present avowed disregard of corporate entity . . . But they all come to just this—courts simply will not let interposition of corporate entity or action prevent a judgment otherwise required. Corporate presence and action no more than those of an

10 [1984] 1 WLR 427 at 435 B-G.
11 *Henn and Alexander*, op cit, p 344.
12 See *Adams v Cape Industries plc* [1990] BBC 786, CA; *Walkovszky v Carlton* (1966) 18 NY 2d 414. For interesting law and economics analysis of *Walkovszky* see Halpern, Trebilcock and Turnbull (1980) 30 U Toronto LJ 117, 145–146.
13 204 Minn 574 at 578 (1939). See also Wilson J in *Constitution Insurance Co of Canada v Kosmopoulos* (1987) 34 DLR (4th) 208 at 213-14 and a note in (1982) 95 Harv L Rev 853.

individual will bar a remedy demanded by law in application to facts. Hence the process is not accurately termed one of disregarding corporate entity. It is rather and only a refusal to permit its presence and action to divert the judicial course of applying law to ascertained facts. The method neither pierces any veil nor goes behind any obstruction, save for its refusal to let one fact bar the judgment which the whole sum of facts requires. For such reasons, we feel that the method of decision known as 'piercing the corporate veil' or 'disregarding the corporate entity' unnecessarily complicates decision. It is dialectically ornate and correctly guides understanding, but over a circuitous and unrealistic trail. The objective is more easily attainable over the direct and unencumbered route followed herein.

It is submitted, however, that this describes judicial policies rather than legal principle. To state a policy is not to provide a substitute for legal principle. However, as a frank avowal of judicial policy it is welcome.

CONSEQUENCES OF SEPARATE CORPORATE PERSONALITY

As a species of corporation the company has the following traditional and modern corporate attributes[14].

(1)   It has perpetual succession. Until dissolved a company continues to exist and survives the death of its directors and shareholders. As Grant wrote in 1850 'This unbroken personality, this beautiful combination of the legal characters of the finite with essentials of infinity appears to have been the primary object of the invention of incorporations'[15].

(2)   It owns its own property. The assets of a company do not belong to the shareholders. The only interest which they have in the assets of the company is indirectly through the medium of their shares. They have no proprietary rights to the underlying assets. Similarly creditors of the company are not creditors of the shareholders. The creditors must go against the company and it is only if the company is being wound up and there is some evidence of fraud that they may possibly have recourse against the shareholders.

(3)   As a separate legal person the company can sue or be sued in its own name.

(4)   A company can create a floating charge. This is a type of equitable security which can only be granted by companies and others who are empowered under specific legislation. The essence of a floating charge is that it floats over the undertaking or class of assets until an event occurs which causes it to crystallise, whereupon it becomes a fixed equitable charge. Until then the company can dispose of its assets in the ordinary course of business.

(5)   Although it is not perhaps a logically necessary attribute of separate legal personality in modern law, the liability of the members of a limited company is limited and the two concepts are closely linked in practice[16]. Members are only liable for the amount unpaid on nominal

---

14 See *The Case of Sutton's Hospital* (1612) 10 Co Rep 1a at 23a and 30b and 1 Bl Comm 456 at 463–6; CA 1985, s 13(3), (4).
15 *Grant on Corporations* (1850) Butterworths, p 4.
16 Chartered corporations usually involved this. The first companies under the general Companies Acts did not. This status became possible in 1855.

value of their shares. In the case of a company limited by guarantee they are only liable for the amount of their guarantee.

(6)   As the price of separate legal personality, the company must comply with the formalities of the Companies Acts. This requires payment of the registration fee, capital duty and the regular filing of documents and accounts with the Registrar of Companies. These are the costs of transacting business in this particular way.

THE RELATIONSHIP OF LEGAL PERSONALITY TO LIMITED LIABILITY

Although there is a tendency to equate the two, legal personality and limited liability are two separate concepts. A company can be a separate legal person but its shareholders may still have unlimited liability for its debts. Unlimited companies which existed in England between 1844–1855 as the norm, still continue as the exception. Limited liability can be the subject of individual contracting between a company's shareholders and its creditors. Complex drafting of deeds of settlement and cumbrous legal procedures produced the effect if not the letter of limited liability before the 1855 Act. Creditors had to sue each shareholder in a separate action and in practice sued the richest. The latter had no recourse. The reforms in the Joint Stock Companies Winding Up Act 1848 put an end to this de facto limited liability and reduced the attractiveness of shares to smaller investors. However, in 1852 in *Hallett v Dowdall*[17] the validity of a limited liability clause was upheld by the Court of Exchequer Chamber and it was held to bind third parties with express notice. The result was widespread use of such clauses which may have accounted for the change in public opinion in favour of limited liability[18].

Alternatively the company might take out insurance to cover its liabilities, thereby adding to its costs which it will pass on to its consumers. The third possibility is that adopted from 1855 onwards of institutionalised limited liability under the Companies Acts.

Limited liability under the Companies Acts means that shareholders are under no obligation to the company or its creditors beyond their obligations on the par value of their shares or under their guarantee in the case of a company limited by guarantee. Limited liability arguably reduces the costs involved in the separation of ownership and control. Generally this will only be relevant in the case of public companies. First, limited liability reduces the need to monitor management and other shareholders. Secondly, limited liability and free transfer of shares with which it is arguably linked facilitate the market for control. This acts as an incentive to management to perform efficiently. Thirdly, limited liability, in adding to the marketability of shares, improves the information fed to the market place by the increased volume of transactions. Fourthly, limited liability allows shareholders to diversify their holdings. Fifthly, it facilitates optimal investment decisions since a positive attitude to risk taking will ensue[19].

English company law, unlike US corporation laws, does not link limited

17   (1852) 21 LJQB 98.
18   H N Butler (1986) 6 International Review of Law and Economics 169.
19   See F Easterbrook and D Fischel (1985) 52 U Chi L Rev 89, 94 et seq.

liability with adequate capitalisation of the company. In some cases in the US jurisdictions it has been suggested that inadequate capitalisation is in itself a sufficient basis for piercing the corporate veil[20]. However, the orthodox view is that it is only one factor[1]. US courts have been more willing than English courts to pierce the corporate veil in cases of insolvent one-man companies and groups prior to winding up. Underlying this is perhaps some idea that the corporate privilege must be used for legitimate business purposes. The problem with this is to define what such purposes are.

It has been argued by Meiners, Mofsky and Tollinson[2] that the primary reasons for the corporate form of business are not in fact related to the principle of limited liability. These reasons are said to be:

(1)   The marketability of shares (although this is only the case in public listed companies)
(2)   perpetual existence
(3)   flexible financing methods
(4)   specialisation of management
(5)   majority rule.

These could exist without limitation of liability. The argument is a variation on the theme of Coase's theorem that if transaction costs are zero the ultimate use of the property will not depend on the initial assignment of property rights. Here the argument is that free contracting will vitiate the impact of the rule of liability on credit terms. Such contract based arguments do not, however, deal with the immunity of shareholders from liability to *involuntary* creditors. This is seen as a question of allocation of risk. Limited liability for tort transfers the obligation to insure on to the consumer who arguably pays lower prices in consequence.

In recent years there has been an increased call for abolition or at least restriction of limited liability and inroads have been made into the concept by s 214 of the Insolvency Act 1986 which deals with wrongful trading and supplements the law on fraudulent trading. Other alternatives are to introduce effective minimum capital requirements or compulsory insurance for certain involuntary creditors[3].

MOTIVES FOR AND AGAINST INCORPORATION

In practice, the privilege of limited liability is whittled away to some extent by the requirement of banks that the controllers of small incorporated firms give a guarantee in respect of the company's indebtedness. The result of this is that commercially the corporate veil is pierced for financial creditors. The limitation of liability is, however, still very relevant as regards trade creditors and involuntary creditors such as claimants in tort. A second motive for incorporation is taxation although at the end of the day there are taxation arguments either for or against incorporation. The use of the corporate form is a useful means of spreading income amongst members of a family. It is also

20 *Minton v Cavaney* 364 P (2d) 473 (1961).
1 *Pearl v Shore* 17 Cal App (3d) 608 (1971).
2 (1979) 4 Delaware Journal of Corporate Law 351.
3 F Easterbrook and D Fischel (1985) 52 U Chi L Rev 89, 101 et seq.

useful for spreading ownership of wealth. Shares in a company are convenient subjects for gifts by wealthy relatives to the junior members of their family. A third motive for incorporation is organisation. A business often outgrows a sole trader or partnership and there is a need for a more sophisticated administrative structure. However, it must be admitted that the legal structure envisaged by company law is rather simplistic and outdated in practice. Modern companies have developed a managerial structure and chain of command which give recognition to middle management and the work force in addition to the basic company law requirements. A fourth motive for incorporation is to take advantage of the floating charge. We have briefly discussed the nature of the floating charge above. It is understood that banks and other financial institutions put pressure on businesses to incorporate so that they can be granted a floating charge as security over stock in trade and book debts.

Incorporation is not without its price. First there is the cost of incorporation and of maintaining proper secretarial and accounting systems. Trading as an incorporated company involves a lot of paperwork and constant disclosure. As far as a proprietor of a solvent business is concerned, as a sole trader he owes no duties to anyone in respect of his control of his business except that he must pay his taxes and comply with other general legislation applicable to him. Once the business is incorporated and he becomes a director, he is a fiduciary, and owes duties not to make secret profits and not to use his powers for an improper purpose[4]. These duties can be enforced by the company in general meetings[5] by exercising its powers of removal and can be the subject matter of an investigation by the Department of Trade and Industry[6]. In practice, shareholders in public companies are not active in monitoring management and prefer to vote with their feet by selling their shares rather than get involved in a corporate row. Also, the track record of the Department of Trade and Industry for investigating corporate fraud and mismanagement is not particularly impressive, as we shall see in a later chapter. Nevertheless, the market for control and the market for management provide some control over management behaviour. A mismanaged company may be taken over and management prefer to be associated with a winner rather than a loser. To that extent they may be self-policing. If the company goes into liquidation, a person who is party to carrying on the business with intent to defraud creditors will be liable for fraudulent trading[7]. Indeed, he can be liable for fraudulent or wrongful trading before the company goes into winding up. These are some of the costs which a person must pay if the corporate form is adopted.

4 See Chapter 25, post.
5 See Chapter 27, post.
6 See Chapter 29, post.
7 See Chapter 39, post.

CHAPTER 8

The companies registration system and the concepts of constructive notice and official notification

THE COMPANIES REGISTRATION SYSTEM

Part of the price which the incorporators of a company pay for incorporation is a continuing obligation to file certain documents with the Registrar of Companies. This obligation is in addition to the obligation to keep proper books and records at the company's registered office. When the Registrar grants a certificate of incorporation he opens a file for the new company and allots it a number. (The name and number so allotted have to be disclosed on the company's letter headings[1].) The documents lodged on registration are placed in the file together with a copy of the certificate of incorporation. If the company has been incorporated as a public company the declaration made for the purposes of obtaining a certificate to carry on business under s 117 will also appear on the file.

An annual return has to be filed[2] which gives up-to-date particulars about the company and, unless the company is an exempted unlimited company, it must file its accounts.

Other important documents which must be filed include the following:

(1) notice of the situation of the registered office or any change[3];
(2) particulars of directors or secretary or any change[4];
(3) copies of all special and extraordinary resolutions and an ordinary resolution increasing the capital of the company[5];
(4) copies of the memorandum or articles as altered by any statutory provision other than a special resolution under s 4[6];
(5) copies of any prospectus[7];
(6) the valuation of a non-cash consideration provided for the shares in a public company[8];
(7) particulars of registrable charges[9];
(8) resignation of auditors[10];
(9) appointment of a receiver[11] or liquidator[12];
(10) office copy of an administration order[13].

---

1 Section 351(1).
2 Section 363.
3 Section 10(6).
4 Section 10(2).
5 Sections 123 and 380 (4)(a) and (b).
6 Section 18.
7 Section 64(1).
8 Section 111.
9 Section 395.
10 Section 390(3).
11 Sections 53 and 54 of the Insolvency Act 1986.
12 Section 109(1) of the Insolvency Act 1986.
13 Section 21(2) of the Insolvency Act 1986.

This is not an exhaustive list but gives an idea of the range of information contained on the company's file.

The main office of the Registrar of Companies for England and Wales was formerly in City Road, Islington in London. Now the main office is in Maindy Way, Cardiff, but a smaller office is still kept in London[14]. There are separate registries for companies incorporated in Scotland and Northern Ireland.

When a member of the public makes a search he obtains a microfiche copy of the company's file.

THE PURPOSES OF THE SYSTEM

The companies registration system has grown up in a piecemeal way but the original purpose in 1844 was that it was part of a constitutive act whereby a deed of settlement company was transformed into a body corporate[15]. It was a state formality which involved a degree of publicity. The Registrar's file was open to the public and thus provided a source of information about the company. The main worry that people had at that time was to ascertain the authority of people to bind such companies. Registration on a public file of the constitutional documents afforded the public the means of checking the authority of persons purporting to bind the company. On the other hand there was no express provision such as is found in the Law of Property Act 1925 providing that registration should amount to notice. However, Lord Wensleydale said in *Ernest v Nicholls*[16] in 1857:

The Legislature then devised the plan of incorporating these companies in a manner unknown to the common law, with special powers of management and liabilities, providing at the same time that all the world should have notice who were the persons authorised to bind all the shareholders, by requiring the co-partnership deed to be registered, certified by the directors, and made accessible to all; and, besides, including some clauses as to the management, as in the Act 7 and 8 Vict c 110, s 7, etc. All persons, therefore, must take notice of the deed and the provisions of the Act. If they do not choose to acquaint themselves with the powers of the directors, it is their own fault, and if they give credit to any unauthorised persons they must be contented to look to them only, and not to the company at large. The stipulations of the deed, which restrict and regulate their authority, are obligatory on those who deal with the company; and the directors can make no contract so as to bind the whole body of shareholders, for whose protection the rules are made, unless they are strictly complied with.

The company's file which started off life as part of a constitutive act became a definitive source of information about the company's powers and directors' authority. Persons who dealt with companies were affected with notice of all that was contained in the registered constitution and, not only that, they were taken to understand the documents according to their proper meaning. The latter point was no doubt due to the principle 'ignorance of the law is no excuse'. Most of the cases involve shareholders and in *Oakbank Oil*

14　There was much criticism of this move. See e g L S Sealy (1981) 2 Co Law 51 at 52.
15　For a discussion of the distinction between constitutive and declaratory effect, see E Stein *Harmonisation of European Company Laws* (1971) p 277.
16　(1857) 6 HL Cas 401 at 418–419. See also *Mahony v East Holyford Mining Co* (1875) LR 7 HL 869 at 893 per Lord Hatherley. See J Montrose (1934) 50 LQR 224 at 236 ff.

Co v Crum (1882) 8 App Cas 65 at 71 Lord Selborne LC described their position in this way:

Each party must be taken to have made himself acquainted with the terms of the written contract contained in the articles . . . and the Acts of Parliament, so far as they are important. He must also in law be taken (though that is sometimes different from what the fact may be) to have understood the terms of the contract according to their proper meaning; and that being so he must take the consequences, whatever they may be . . .

Although the authorities are less clear it appears that a similar principle was applied to outsiders. Eventually, however, this was reduced to a form of estoppel and to a negative doctrine. It cut down the scope of apparent authority but could not be relied on by one who did not know of the terms of a particular article. This doctrine became known as the doctrine of constructive notice. Starting off life as a doctrine about the constitution, it was later extended to non-constitutional matters when registration of charges with the Registrar was introduced. Again there was no express provision for constructive notice and it had been held that registration under the Bills of Sale legislation did not give rise to it. When it came it was again as a result of judicial lawmaking[17]. Notice was, however, confined to the existence of a charge as disclosed in the registered particulars and not its contents. Copies of the charge do not appear on the Register; furthermore, although non-registration of a charge will invalidate it as against the liquidators and creditors, registration does not amount to a conclusive priority point for the charge. This is usually the date of creation. The system of registration of charges is thus an incomplete registration system. A complete registration system would conclusively determine all these questions.

We can sum up the purposes of the company registration system, therefore, as threefold:

(1)   constitutional
(2)   informational
(3)   validatory.

It is possible to identify further purposes of the system of disclosure at large, such as monitoring corporate management but we shall discuss these in later chapters under those headings[18].

THE DOCTRINE OF CONSTRUCTIVE NOTICE

The doctrine of constructive notice was originally developed in equity in property cases. An intending purchaser or mortgagee had a duty to investigate deeds the existence of which was disclosed or which he discovered where such deeds could affect the title[19]. Historically it was different from the common law concept of actual knowledge which would be inferred where a person had been wilfully blind, although in practice the same facts could

---

17 See W J Gough *Company Charges* (1978) p 359.
18 See generally Sealy, op cit and *Hahlo's Cases and Materials on Company Law* (3rd edn, 1987) by H R Hahlo and J H Farrar, chapter 8 and materials cited.
19 See *English and Scottish Mercantile Investment Co Ltd v Brunton* [1892] 2 QB 700, CA and J H Farrar (1974) 38 Conv (NS) 315.

fall under both concepts. Constructive notice as applied to companies developed originally as a constitutional doctrine. Here one was not concerned with title but with capacity and authority. Constructive notice in this sense was originally an evidential rule concerning public documents. It was a necessary corollary of this that matters which could not be verified by a search could not bind a member of the public.

The doctrine was extended beyond the memorandum and articles and particulars of directors to special resolutions[20]. When registration of charges was introduced, the judges extended the doctrine of constructive notice to them, although here as we have seen the purpose of registration was different[1]. Non-registration operated to invalidate charges. The doctrine of constructive notice of registered particulars of charges, however, operated (albeit inconclusively) to postpone subsequent charges and was thus similar to the original equitable doctrine.

Dr W J Gough in his book *Company Charges*[1] argues that the extension of the doctrine to registered charges was bogus since the original company law doctrine was a constitutional doctrine. This seems to take too rigid a view of company registration. The purposes of registration evolved as we have seen, and as they developed the doctrine of constructive notice changed. As it related to company charges, it assumed a character closer to the original equitable doctrine.

A further question remains. How far does the company doctrine extend? It is clear law that before 1973 it extended to the memorandum and articles and special resolutions[2]. It is also clear that it continues to apply to company charges[3]. It is submitted that for documents other than charges distinctions can be drawn between those documents which are constitutional and those non-constitutional documents whose validity nevertheless depends on registration on the one hand, and those documents which fall outside these categories and whose function is merely to supply information on the other hand[4]. In the latter category would fall accounts and annual returns.

Even before 1973 the rigours of constructive notice were mitigated by the rule in *Royal British Bank v Turquand*[5] whereby outsiders were not to be concerned with internal irregularities and could rely on the evidential maxim *omnia praesumuntur rite et solemniter esse acta*—everything is presumed to have been done properly and solemnly which ought to have been done so[6]. The doctrine was substantially abolished as far as constitutional matters were concerned by the European Communities Act 1972, s 9(1) which was consolidated in CA 1985, s 35. The reforms were completed by the CA 1989 which make further amendments to the ultra vires doctrine and then purport to abolish what the act calls 'deemed notice' by the insertion of a new s 711A in the CA 1985. This reads as follows:

20 *Re London and New York Investment Corpn* [1895] 2 Ch 860.
1 Page 361.
2 *Irvine v Union Bank of Australia* (1877) 2 App Cas 366, PC; *Re London and New York Investment Corpn* [1895] 2 Ch 860.
3 *Re Standard Rotary Machine Co Ltd* (1906) 95 LT 829; *Wilson v Kelland* [1910] 2 Ch 306.
4 Cf *Palmer's Company Law* (24th edn, 1987) vol 1, para 21–02 and W J Gough *Company Charges* (1978) p 359 which adopts a distinction between public documents and non-public (sic) documents.
5 (1856) 6 E & B 327.
6 Discussed in detail in Chapter 22, post.

711A Exclusion of deemed notice (1) A person shall not be taken to have notice of any matter merely because of its being disclosed in any document kept by the registrar of companies (and thus available for inspection) or made available by the company for inspection.

(2) This does not affect the question whether a person is affected by notice of any matter by reason of a failure to make such inquiries as ought reasonably to be made.

(3) In this section 'document' includes any material which contains information.

(4) Nothing in this section affects the operation of—

(a)   section 416 of this Act (under which a person taking a charge over a company's property is deemed to have notice of matters disclosed on the companies charges register), or

(b)   section 198 of the Law of Property Act 1925 as it applies by virtue of section 3(7) of the Land Charges Act 1972 (under which the registration of certain land charges under Part XII, of Chapter III of Part XXIII, of this Act is deemed to constitute actual notice for all purposes connected with the land affected).

Section 711A(2) retains the doctrine of inferred actual knowledge on the basis of wilful blindness and section 711A(4) retains constructive or deemed notice for charges registered under CA 1985 or the property legislation.

We discuss these reforms in Chapters 10, 19 and 22, post.

OFFICIAL NOTIFICATION[7]

The 1972 Act, while partially abolishing constructive notice, introduced the additional formality of official notification for a subclass of registrable documents. The formalities are that *the Registrar* must give notice in the Gazette of the *issue* or *receipt* of the following documents specified in s 711(1) of CA 1985. These are:

(a)   any certificate of incorporation of a company;

(b)   any document making or evidencing an alteration in a company's memorandum or articles;

(c)   any notification of a change among the directors of a company;

(d)   any copy of a resolution of a public company which gives, varies, revokes or renews an authority for the purposes of s 80 (allotment or relevant securities);

(e)   any copy of a special resolution of a public company passed under s 95(1), (2) or (3) (disapplication of pre-emption rights);

(f)   any report under ss 103 or 104 as to the value of a non-cash asset;

(g)   any statutory declaration delivered under s 117 (public company share capital requirements);

(h)   any notification (given under s 122) of the redemption of shares;

(j)   any statement or notice delivered by a public company under s 128 (registration of particulars of special rights);

(k)   any documents delivered by a company under s 241 (annual accounts);

(l)   a copy of any resolution or agreement to which s 380 applies and which—

    (i)   states the rights attached to any shares in a public company, other than shares which are in all respects uniform (for purposes of s 128) with shares previously allotted; or

    (ii)   varies rights attached to any shares in a public company; or

---

7   For a discussion of the evolution of this doctrine and the influence of the German Commercial Code and case law see *Stein*, op cit, pp 278–279 and the German materials there cited. The provisions represent a series of political compromises and remind one of the definition of a camel as a horse designed by a committee.

(iii)   assigns a name or other designation, or a new name or designation, to any class of shares in a public company;

(m)   any return of allotments of a public company;

(n)   any notice of a change in the situation of a company's registered office;

(p)   any copy of a winding-up order in respect of a company;

(q)   any order for the dissolution of a company on a winding up;

(r)   any return by a liquidator of the final meeting of a company on a winding up.

[Provisions (i) and (o) are omitted from the statutory list.]

Official notification is not a constitutive act and does not give rise to constructive notice[8]; it is a source of information and failure to deliver such documents gives rise in some cases to a form of statutory estoppel under s 42(1) which prevents the company from relying on the relevant event against a third party who was unaware of it. This statutory estoppel is not quite the same as invalidity. The act in question is valid but the company cannot rely on it as against a person who could not have been aware of it. What we have in effect is a subclass of the subclass specified in s 711(1). Section 42(1) refers to:

(a)   the making of a winding-up order in respect of the company, or the appointment of a liquidator in a voluntary winding up of the company; or

(b)   any alteration of the company's memorandum or articles; or

(c)   any change among the company's directors; or

(d)   (as regards service of any document on the company) any change in the situation of the company's registered office.

Section 42(1) also provides that in any event there is a 15-day leeway period after gazetting during which the company cannot rely on the relevant event against a person who was unavoidably prevented from knowing of it during that period. It is not clear what 'unavoidably prevented' means here. Presumably it does not obligate a person to make a search.

In *Re Peek Winch & Tod Ltd*[9] it was held that a company and its receiver could not rely on the making of a winding-up order until it was gazetted and the statutory period had expired, as against a party who had no actual notice of it.

COMPANIES HOUSE, AN EXECUTIVE AGENCY

The Registry of Business Names was abolished and effectively superseded by a private system operating under the aegis of the principal Chambers of Commerce. There was an announcement on 24 November 1982 by the Minister of Consumer Affairs that he was considering 'privatising' the whole or part of the companies registration system[10]. The aim of this was to reduce government spending. It was later dropped in the absence of commercial interest. The main arguments for retention of the present system were:

(1)   Company registration is treated as a public matter in all common law countries.

---

8 See *Official Custodian for Charities v Parway Estates Developments Ltd* [1984] 3 All ER 679, CA—official notification by gazetting of a winding-up order held not to give rise to notice or knowledge of the winding up.

9 (1980) 130 NLJ 116, CA.

10 For an attack on this see (1983) 4 Co Law 2.

(2)   It is basic to effective disclosure which runs throughout our company law.
(3)   There needs to be public control over the creation of companies and access to information.
(4)   Enforcement of the statutory disclosure requirements needs to be handled by a public official.
(5)   The systems of constructive notice and official notification could not operate as part of a private system.

The main arguments in favour of 'privatisation' were:

(1)   Many EEC member states use chambers of commerce for a number of these purposes. We could do the same.
(2)   The role of the Registrar need not be totally abolished but could be cut down to a formal receipt and policing function.
(3)   The information carried by the companies registration systems needs to be computerised and the government is currently unwilling to invest this money whereas private enterprise might be. Computers can store the information more efficiently and cut down costs in the long run.
(4)   If a system is centred on regional Chambers of Commerce as part of a computer link up, then searching can be decentralised to the advantage of consumers.
(5)   Constructive notice has been abolished for constitutional matters. For charges what is needed is a complete registration system integrated with the land registration system. Official notification could continue as part of a more limited role for the Registrar of Companies.

On 3 October 1988 a compromise was reached. Companies House became an Executive Agency within the Department of Trade and Industry and the occasion was suitably marked by the unveiling of a commemorative slate plaque. The aim of the Agency is 'to operate with a greater degree of autonomy, leading to the prospect of increased efficiency and the delivery of an improved service to the customer'[11].

In conclusion one can say that traditional assumptions of company law are being challenged. Economic recession, like the prospect of being hanged, concentrates the mind. Increasingly our system of companies registration has seemed a costly and inefficient storage house of information whose practical relevance has often seemed small[12]. If the primary objective of the system is now seen as the provision of up-to-date and accurate information then the increased use of computers and the new developments in optical disc and imaging technology are an obvious prerequisite. It will be interesting to see whether the new Agency can achieve a marked improvement in the system.

11   *Companies in 1988–89*, p 13.
12   See Sealy, op cit and *Company Law and Commercial Reality* (1986).

PART II

The corporate constitution

CHAPTER 9

Constitutional issues

The constitution of a modern company consists of two documents usually bound up as one—the memorandum and articles of association. These are all that is prescribed by law. Sometimes, however, they are supplemented by shareholders' agreements, and other similar arrangements. Overall there is considerable freedom of choice in the drafting of the original documents but this freedom is more restricted when it comes to constitutional change. In the case of the memorandum, there are considerable restrictions on change, but even in the case of the articles freedom is curtailed to protect minorities from oppression. Thus provisions which would be valid if in the original constitution, such as an exclusion of the rules of natural justice may not subsequently be adopted or there will at least be a heavy onus on those seeking the change.

The purpose of the constitution is to provide for the distribution of *profit*, *risk* and *control* within the company. Profits will be distributed in accordance with shareholders' rights which may be specified in the memorandum but nowadays are more usually set out in the articles. The memorandum sets out the basis of liability of members—limited or unlimited and limited by shares or guarantee. Allocation of control between the company in general meeting and the board of directors is dealt with in the articles. However, profit and control and allocation of risk amongst the proprietors per se are often the subject matter of shareholders' agreements where these are used. Shareholders' agreements are mainly used in the case of private companies and joint ventures between larger companies.

In broad terms, the memorandum governs the relationship between the company and the outside world. The company identifies the name by which it is first incorporated and the purposes and objects for which it is formed. Originally incorporation was regarded as a privilege and there was a natural tendency on the part of the courts to restrict it. This led to the development of the ultra vires doctrine which protected some creditors at the expense of others. Shareholders and intra vires creditors were protected from unauthorised depletion of the capital fund. The history of the ultra vires doctrine is a history of a struggle between two competing models of incorporation—the *legal privilege model* and the *freedom of contract model*. Whereas the legal privilege model emphasised responsibility through restriction and the fulfilment of conditions, the contract model emphasises the utility of the right to incorporate and the freedom of choice of incorporators under a liberal economy state concerned with facilitating rather than restricting business. The legal privilege model is the oldest model of incorporation and dates back to the Middle Ages. Indeed, early business corporations were often regarded as arms of the state or means of extending state control. This model continued as the dominant model even after the liberal reforms of 1844–1856. The origins of the freedom of contract model perhaps lie in the 1844 Act, although some commentators stress that this represented state intervention as well. It grew in strength as a result of the Limited Liability Act 1855 and the adoption of the modern form of constitution in 1856. The reform of the 1890s which provided for alteration of objects and the growing liberalism of judicial decisions on ultra vires from the turn of the century added to this trend. It perhaps reached its logical extreme in 1972 when in *Ebrahimi v Westbourne Galleries Ltd* [1973] AC 360, the House of Lords allowed the contract greater significance than the legal constitution, an equitable doctrine which had some of its roots in the earlier jurisprudence of the substratum cases. This supremacy of the contract/equitable model, however, is at the moment limited to winding up on the just and equitable ground and the statutory minority shareholder's remedy and is of uncertain scope and significance elsewhere. It is a potentially wide doctrine which may need to be kept in check.

Recently the debate about the two models has taken a distinctly economic perspective in the USA as the result of an important symposium sponsored by the Columbia Law School Center for Law and Economic Studies, entitled 'Contractual Freedom in Corporate Law'[1]. It is impossible to do justice here to the sophistication of this debate and to understand it one must see it in its US context. There is no such thing as US company law. Each state has its own corporation law statute. In a sense there is a market for corporation law statutes. Business people are free to choose their state of incorporation. Some state statutes are more lax than others. There is diversity although many of the major corporations incorporate in Delaware, a small state which has a tradition of permissiveness and a pro-management attitude. People of the Chicago School argue the freedom of contract principle, relying on the law and economics analysis of the company as a nexus of contracts[2]. The primary function of corporate law should be to facilitate the private contracting process by providing a set of non-mandatory 'standard-form' provisions, leaving it to the parties to opt out. They argue that there is little convincing justification for many mandatory rules. This argument, which is simply made, has put more traditionally minded commentators on the defensive. To deal with the argument they maintain that to treat the company as a nexus of contracts is reductionist. The most effective spokesman is Professor Melvin Eisenberg[3] who argues that contract here does not mean contract but a modified and specialist conception of implicit contract taken from labour economics where it means neither contract nor even bargain. They are forms of private ordering but not contracts. Professor Eisenberg sees many of the rules of company law being determined by the unilateral action of corporate organs or officials, some by contract or other forms of agreement and others determined by law. He classifies the rules into *enabling rules, suppletory or default rules* and *mandatory rules*. The first

---

1 See the November 1989 issue of the Columbia Law Review, especially the Foreword by Lucian Bebchuk 'The Debate on Contractual Freedom in Corporate Law' 89 Col LR 1395 (1989).
2 Frank Easterbrook and Daniel Fischel 'The Corporate Contract' ibid 1416.
3 Melvin Eisenberg 'The Structure of Corporation Law' ibid 1461, for other useful analysis see John C Coffee Jr 'The Mandatory/Enabling Balance in Corporate Law: An Essay on the Judicial Role' Ibid 1618; Jeffrey Gordon 'The Mandatory Structure of Corporate Law' ibid 1529; see too Roberta Romano 'Answering the Wrong Question; the Tenuous Case for Mandatory Corporate Laws' ibid 1599; and for an over aggressive polemic which at times hides some sound criticisms see Fred McChesney 'Economics, Law and Science in Corporate Field: A Critique of Eisenberg' ibid 1530.

gives legal effect to rules that corporate actors adopt. The second apply
unless the corporate actors adopt other rules. The third cannot be varied.
Mandatory rules are only part of this complex picture. Examples of enabling
rules are the provisions for the conferral of authority and the rules for
increase or reduction of capital although all of these have mandatory
aspects. Examples of suppletory rules are the regulations of Table A.
Examples of mandatory rules are the rule against insider trading, the disclosure rules, the provisions for alteration of articles and the principal fiduciary
duties. There is a justification for many mandatory provisions. Some are not
totally mandatory in any event. They can be avoided by a restructuring of
the transaction. It is, therefore, necessary to make a close study of each rule.
Further, the libertarian argument conspicuously falls down in respect of
constitutional change as opposed to the original adoption of the corporate
constitution[4]. Freedom of contract here would lead to the tyranny of the
majority.

The EC harmonisation programme relies heavily on mandatory rules
and rejects the idea of a market for company law statutes. English and EC
discussions of principle and policy pay too much attention to existing legal
rules and often fail to take in the broader perspective. The policy issues
raised by the US debate suggest that greater sophistication is needed in
London and Brussels. The issues are not clear cut and the problems are not
necessarily solved by more intervention. Professor Eisenberg's analysis is
helpful in coming to terms with the innate complexity of corporate law.

Reverting to domestic company law, not only is the memorandum a source
of definition of the purpose and capacity of the company, it is sometimes
used as a place in which to entrench class rights of shares. Before 1980, to
insert such rights in the memorandum without a variation of rights clause
rendered them immutable save by a scheme of arrangement under what is
now s 425 of CA 1985. This was modified slightly by the Companies Act 1980.

Whereas the memorandum deals with the company's relationship with the
outside world, the articles regulate the internal affairs of the company. The
statutory regulation is permissive to a greater extent than in the case of the
memorandum. This is particularly so in the case of constitutional change.
The model articles in Table A are merely a guide and it is possible to contract
out. The statutory model envisages a democratic board of directors and
general meeting operating by majority rule. It does not mandate compliance
with natural justice although occasionally the courts will imply it. It envisages the company's dirty linen being laundered within the company but on
the whole is pretty silent on the matter of resolving disputes. Its approach to
the board of directors is collegiate and egalitarian with the exception of the
managing director's authority and the chairman's casting vote. The working
democracy so constituted, however, grants no franchise to employees or
creditors. The equitable concept of the good of the company which company
law inherited from partnership as the yardstick at general meetings, has
traditionally meant in practice the good of the shareholders, although the law
is currently undergoing change. At the moment, however, English law has
not developed a concept of fiduciary obligation on majority shareholders
such as exists in the USA.

---

4 Bebchuk, op cit, and his 'Limiting Contractual Freedom in Corporate Law: the Desirable
Constraints on Charter Amendments' 102 Harv LR 1820 (1989).

The articles are a source of rights, but only for members, and there is some complicated jurisprudence about their enforcement. Outsider rights in articles are difficult to enforce in the absence of an extrinsic contract which incorporates them. Where the rights constitute class rights and they are varied there is also a further degree of procedural complication involved.

From the point of view of legal theory, the corporate constitution represents a complicated area where public law joins agency, contract and equity. In the development of company law, ideas have been borrowed from each of these branches of law. However at the end of the day it must be recognised that the corporate constitution is sui generis. Mistakes can arise if any analogy is pushed to extremes. The corporate constitution serves a multiplicity of business organisations of differing size and with differing pressures. The statutory model although regarded by some economists as a standard form contract which rational contractors would independently adopt has proved rather limited in practice and has been supplemented by both judicial equity and self-help by incorporators and their legal advisers. Within the bounds set by illegality and public policy, the latter have been allowed considerable freedom. The greatest restriction on freedom of contract is the inability of a director as fiduciary to abuse his position. The fiduciary concept is perhaps the most potent modern weapon in the judicial armoury in spite of its intellectual limitations. Laskin J in the Canadian Supreme Court case of *Canadian Aero Service Ltd v O'Malley*[5] described this as:

an updating of the equitable principle whose roots lie in the general standards that I have already mentioned, namely, loyalty, good faith and avoidance of a conflict of duty and self-interest. Strict application against directors and senior management officials is simply recognition of the degree of control which their positions give them in corporate operations, a control which rises above day [sic] accountability to owning shareholders and which comes under some scrutiny only at annual general or at special meetings. It is a necessary supplement, in the public interest, of statutory regulation and accountability which themselves are, at one and the same time, an acknowledgement of the importance of the corporation in the life of the community and of the need to compel obedience by it and by its promoters, directors and managers to norms of exemplary behaviour . . .

This emphasises the public interest in the corporate constitution and the regulation of corporate and corporate executive conduct.

Even here certain aspects of the strict fiduciary principles have been relaxed in relation to directors contracting with their companies. The law is dealt with in Chapter 25 and to understand it fully one needs to know the tortuous path which has led the law from a strict trust rule to relaxation and then to restrictions on contracting out.

To sum up, law and economics writers, echoing the earlier debate on freedom of contract, argue that the fiduciary rules and principles are an elaborate standard form which obviates the need for individual contracting with its resulting transaction costs. A number of traditional scholars are prepared to accept this as a useful insight but are not prepared to countenance free contracting out of these particular rules and principles. These rules and principles are mandatory on the grounds of public policy. In the case of

5 (1974) 40 DLR (3d) 371, 384.

public listed companies shareholders would generally not be in a position to exercise informed choice and are subject to a contract of adhesion[6].

6 V Brudney 'Corporate Governance, Agency Costs and the Rhetoric of Contract' 85 Col LR 1403 (1985); Melvin Eisenberg 'The Structure of Corporation Law' 89 Col LR 1461 at 1474 et seq (1989), but cf Henry Butler and Larry Ribstein 'Opting out of Fiduciary Duties: A Response to the Anti-Contractarians' 65 Wash LR 1 (1990).

CHAPTER 10

The memorandum of association and the question of corporate capacity

THE EVOLUTION OF THE MODERN FORM OF MEMORANDUM

The first Companies Act of 1844 provided for incorporation by registration of deeds of settlement[1]. The modern form of memorandum of association, however, dates from the Joint Stock Companies Act 1856[2]. This legislation was introduced by Robert Lowe MP, then President of the Board of Trade, based on the model of the New York Business Corporation Act[3]. This modern form is different from a deed although, as we have seen, it still retains the old characteristic of subscription and s 14(1) of CA 1985 gives the memorandum effect as if it had been signed and sealed by each member and contained covenants on the part of each member to observe all its provisions. The basic legal requirements are set out in s 2 and Tables D and F[4]. These require the memorandum to state:

(1) the name of the company, which in the case of a private limited company must end with the word 'limited' and in the case of a public company the words 'public limited company';
(2) in the case of a public company, the fact that it is such a company;
(3) whether the registered office is to be situated in England and Wales or Scotland;
(4) the objects of the company;
(5) in the case of a company limited by shares or guarantee that the liability of its members is limited;
(6) in the case of a company limited by guarantee the amount of the guarantee;
(7) in the case of a company with a share capital the amount of the share capital with which the company proposes to be registered and its division (except in the case of an unlimited company).

Section 3A provides that where the memorandum states that the object of the company is to carry on business as a general commercial company—

(a) the object of the company is to carry on any trade or business whatsoever, and
(b) the company has power to do all such things as are incidental or conducive to the carrying on of any trade or business by it.

The procedural requirements are:

(a) in the case of a company with a share capital, no subscriber of the

1 See Chapter 2, ante.
2 Ibid, s 5 and Schedule Form A.
3 Hansard, vol CXL (1856), col 133.
4 The Companies (Tables A to F) Regulations 1985 (SI 1985/805) Schedule.

memorandum may take less than one share and against his name must be shown the number of the shares he takes;

(b)   the memorandum and articles must be signed by each subscriber in the presence of at least one witness who must attest the signature. The original is dated and filed with the Registrar of Companies.

CORPORATE CAPACITY AND THE RISE AND FALL OF THE ULTRA VIRES DOCTRINE

Conceptual questions

The memorandum of association governs the relationship between the company and the outside world. In particular it defines the capacity of the company. The Act of 1844 required a statement of the business or purpose of the company in the deed of settlement but this could be altered by the members. Section 25, however, defined its main powers and privileges which included power 'to perform all other Acts necessary for carrying into effect the Purposes of such Company, and in all respects as other Partnerships are entitled to do'. The latter words are important. The 'company' under the 1844 Act was still a partnership on which certain corporate attributes had been conferred. It was not subject to the ultra vires doctrine. However, the intention of the legislature from 1856 onwards was for capacity to be defined by the simple specification of an object which could not be changed. Object has never been defined in the legislation but the precedents set out in the Companies Acts seem to imply some notion of purpose[5] or the description of the nature of the company's trade or business in a broad generic way[6]. A distinction is drawn in the cases between objects and powers. Power has been defined as 'a legal ability by which a person may create, change or extinguish legal relations'[7]. Power is thus an aspect of capacity. It seems to be generally accepted that a power is something less than an object in the sense that it is a means, while the object is the end. Anything outside the objects and powers of a company is ultra vires. Sometimes it is also said to be illegal but this is a misuse of terms. This point was made clear by Lord Cairns LC in the leading case of *Ashbury Railway Carriage and Iron Co Ltd v Riche*[8] in 1875 where he said:

I have used the expressions extra vires and ultra vires. I prefer either expression very much to one which occasionally has been used in the judgments in the present case, and has also been used in other cases, the expression 'illegality'.

In a case such as that which your Lordships have now to deal with, it is not a question whether the contract sued upon involves that which is *malum prohibitum* or

---

5   See *Re Governments Stock Investment Co* [1891] 1 Ch 649, a case on alteration of objects. Chitty J discusses both terms at 655.

6   Section 7 of the 1844 Act referred to 'business or purpose'. Section 5 of the Joint Stock Companies Act 1856 used the term 'objects' and the form set out in the Schedule for the Eastern Steam Packet Company Ltd provided:
The objects for which the company is established are, 'the Conveyance of Passengers and Goods in Ships or Boats between such Places as the Company may from Time to Time determine, and the doing of all such other Things as are incidental or conducive to the Attainment of the above Object'.

7   Seavey (1920) 29 Yale LJ 859 at 861.

8   (1875) LR 7 HL 653 at 672.

malum in se, or is a contract contrary to public policy, and illegal in itself. I assume the contract in itself to be perfectly legal, to have nothing in it obnoxious to the doctrine involved in the expressions which I have used. The question is not as to the legality of the contract; the question is as to the competency and power of the company to make the contract.

A second sense in which the phrase ultra vires can be used was mentioned by Vinelott J in *Rolled Steel Products (Holdings) Ltd v British Steel Corpn*[9] when he referred to a wider sense where a transaction ostensibly within the scope of the powers of the company express or implied is entered into in furtherance of a purpose which is not authorised. Although this was perhaps a useful way of explaining earlier authority involving loans to companies it was potentially a dangerous doctrine capable of producing uncertainty in commercial transactions and the Court of Appeal did not accept it[10]. Sometimes the phrase 'ultra vires' is used in a third sense to refer to the acts of directors outside their authority. This usage is not improper, but undesirable. It is better to limit the phrase 'ultra vires' to the capacity of the company and use the term 'lack of authority' to refer to the directors to avoid equivocation.

The doctrine of ultra vires does not apply to chartered corporations. At common law chartered corporations seem to have been regarded as having all the powers of a natural person in spite of the practice of specifying express objects in the charter. From Coke onwards this seems to have been regarded as the law[11]. This does not mean, however, that a chartered corporation can never be stopped from acting outside its charter. In *Institution of Mechanical Engineers v Cane*[12], Lord Denning in the House of Lords thought that anyone injured thereby could apply for an injunction to prevent a chartered corporation acting outside its objects. The more orthodox view, however, is that only a member has locus standi[13]. In addition, the Attorney General can apply for revocation of the charter if the corporation persistently acts outside its objects[14].

The development of the doctrine of ultra vires in relation to registered companies[15]

THE BASIC RULE

Although the doctrine of ultra vires was modified by s 9(1) of the European Communities Act 1972 (now s 35 of CA 1985) it is still necessary to trace the development of the doctrine in order to understand the full implications of the reforms. In the eighteenth century there were occasional references to corporate assets being held on trust. There seems to have been an equation of corporate bodies with a trust[16]. However, this reflected the loose usage of

---

 9 [1982] 3 All ER 1057 at 1076 and 1077.
10 [1984] BCLC 466.
11 See the case of *Sutton Hospital* (1612) 10 Co Rep 1a 23a.
12 [1961] AC 696 at 724.
13 See *Jenkin v Pharmaceutical Society of Great Britain* [1921] 1 Ch 392; *Pharmaceutical Society of Great Britain v Dickson* [1970] AC 403, HL.
14 See *Jenkin v Pharmaceutical Society of Great Britain*, supra, at 398.
15 See *Brice on Ultra Vires* (3rd edn, 1893); *Street on Ultra Vires* (1930); Horrwitz (1946) 62 LQR 66; Hornsey (1949) 61 Jur Rev 263; Holt (1950) 66 LQR 493.
16 See CA Cooke *Corporation, Trust and Company* (1950) p 69 ff.

that time and although it may have been strictly accurate in relation to deed of settlement companies it ceased to have any relevance after 1856. In the early nineteenth century with the growth of statutory companies, the question arose as to whether they were to be treated in the same position as chartered corporations. After some fluctuation of opinion a view came to be accepted that they had the powers of a natural person except in so far as these were cut down by the legislation or their objects clause[17]. This view, however, was decisively rejected by the House of Lords in *Ashbury Railway Carriage and Iron Co Ltd v Riche*[18]. The facts of the case were that the company was incorporated under the Companies Act 1862 and had as its objects the following:

The objects for which the company is established are to make and sell, or lend on hire, railway-carriages and wagons, and all kinds of railway plant, fittings, machinery, and rolling-stock; to carry on the business of mechanical engineers and general contractors; to purchase and sell, as merchants, timber, coal, metals, or other materials; and to buy and sell any such materials on commission, or as agents.

It entered into a contract to finance the building of a railway in Belgium by Riche but later wanted to get out of the contract. It consequently argued that it was ultra vires. In the courts below, much had turned on whether or not the transaction had been ratified because the company had an old deed of settlement clause in its articles which provided for extension of the objects by special resolution. The House of Lords held that the transaction was ultra vires. The company had only such objects as were specified in its objects clause. Benjamin QC had argued the ratification point but the House of Lords rejected this argument on the basis that the act was void and it was not possible to ratify a void act. This point was of considerable significance at the time as there was no possibility of altering an objects clause from 1856 until 1890. The immediate policy behind the decision seems to be that incorporation is a privilege only to be granted in respect of the objects specified. In other words, the court adopted the legal privilege model of incorporation. This is extremely unrealistic, as the company can choose its own objects. The underlying policy is far from clear-cut. There seem to be elements of investor protection, creditor protection and public interest. These interests are not necessarily reconcilable and have motivated the courts to different decisions at different times, as we shall see[19].

IMPLIED POWERS

Shortly after the *Ashbury* case, the House of Lords realised that its ruling had been somewhat draconian, and in the case of *A-G v Great Eastern Rly Co*[20], it relaxed the rule by recognising implied powers which were reasonably incidental to the carrying out of the express objects.

---

17 See *Taylor v Chichester & Midhurst Rly* (1867) LR 2 Exch 356, and *Riche v Ashbury Railway Carriage and Iron Co Ltd* (1874) LR 9 Exch 224.
18 (1875) LR 7 HL 653.
19 For a full discussion, see L Getz (1963) 3 UBCLR 30, and the Consultative Document of the Department of Trade and Industry, *Reform of the Ultra Vires Rule*, Pt II, Report by Dr D D Prentice, Chapter III.
20 (1880) 5 App Cas 473, HL.

THE MAIN OBJECTS RULE OF CONSTRUCTION AND *COTMAN V BROUGHAM*
CLAUSES

Businessmen, however, were not satisfied with the *Ashbury* case, even as relaxed in *A-G v Great Eastern Rly Co*. They required further protection. The practice grew up of extending the objects clause by a proliferation of objects and powers. The patronising and moralising attitude of some of the Chancery judiciary of the time to such practices can be seen from the speech of Lord Wrenbury in *Cotman v Brougham*[1] where he said:

There has grown up a pernicious practice of registering memoranda of association which under the clause relating to objects contain paragraph after paragraph not specifying or delimiting the proposed trade or purpose, but confusing power with purpose and indicating every class of act which the corporation is to have power to do. The practice is not one of recent growth. It was in active operation when I was a junior at the Bar. After a vain struggle I had to yield to it, contrary to my own convictions. It has arrived now at a point at which the fact is that the function of the memorandum is taken to be, not to specify, not to disclose, but to bury beneath a mass of words the real object or objects of the company, with the intent that every conceivable form of activity shall be found included somewhere within its terms.

That these views were not universally held is made clear by Sir Francis Palmer in his *Company Precedents* where he wrote[2]:

No doubt some persons have argued that what the Legislature really intended was that the principal objects should be specified—not the powers by which those objects are proposed to be attained—and proceeding from this premise maintain that once a main or primary 'object' is specified it is improper to set out in the memorandum further objects which merely confer 'powers'. But there is nothing in the Act to give colour to this contention, or to show an intention to discriminate between main objects and objects merely conferring powers. Every object stated, whether main or auxiliary, in effect endows the company with a power or powers. To exclude objects conferring powers is to nullify the Act.

Beside these critics there is another class who complain of what may be called the multifariousness of the contents of a memorandum of association. The objects clause, according to their view, ought to specify the leading objects, be they one or many; and that is enough! To go on and specify as an object anything which is implied or may possibly be implied as incidental, on a reasonable construction of the leading object or objects, is irregular and improper. There ought to be no overloading, overlapping, repetition or surplusage. But here again the answer is that it is a matter for the subscribers' discretion.

The courts reacted to this development by adopting the main objects rule of construction in *Re Haven Gold Mining Co*[3]. Under this rule, where the objects are expressed in a series of paragraphs, the courts seek for the paragraph which appears to contain the main or dominant object and treat all the other paragraphs, however generally expressed, as ancillary to this main object and limited thereby[4]. Businessmen were not happy with this at all and the practice grew up of including a clause at the end of the objects clause providing that the objects set out should not be restrictively construed and that each of the paragraphs should be regarded as conferring a separate

1 [1918] AC 514 at 523, HL.
2 *Palmer's Company Precedents* (11th edn, 1912) vol 1, pp 458–9.
3 (1882) 20 Ch D 151, CA. See also *Re German Date Coffee Co* (1882) 20 Ch D 169, CA.
4 See *Palmer*, op cit, p 470.

and independent object[5]. Such a clause was ignored in *Stephens v Mysore Reefs (Kangundy) Mining Co Ltd*[6] in 1902 by Swinfen Eady J who disapproved of the stringing together of wide powers. The validity of such a clause was raised in the leading case of *Cotman v Brougham*[7]. The facts of the case were that the company was a rubber company with a long objects clause ending with this clause. It underwrote an issue of shares by an asphalt company. The validity of the underwriting could be upheld by accepting that underwriting was a separate object. The House of Lords considered that it could not decide the issue of validity of the clause because the Act said that the Registrar's certificate was conclusive that the formalities had been complied with. This took the matter out of their hands. Numerous members of the House, in particular Lord Wrenbury, expressed strong disapproval of such clauses. Nevertheless, now known as *Cotman v Brougham* clauses, they have become standard form, and it is very unusual not to find one at the end of an objects clause of a modern company. In *Re Introductions Ltd*[8], however, we see perhaps a last ditch stand by the courts when a restrictive view was taken of the effect of a *Cotman v Brougham* clause. The company was incorporated to promote exhibitions at the time of the Festival of Britain. It later went into pig breeding and was unsuccessful. A bank had lent them money for the pigbreeding business and in the insolvency of the company the efficacy of the bank's security was raised. There was no reference to pig breeding in the objects clause and to validate the security it was necessary to argue that the borrowing clause existed as an independent object by virtue of the *Cotman v Brougham* clause. The Court of Appeal held that it did not. A *Cotman v Brougham* clause could not convert something which was intrinsically a power into an object, and borrowing was intrinsically a power.

SUBJECTIVE OBJECTS CLAUSES

In addition to *Cotman v Brougham* clauses, draftsmen sometimes preceded the leading objects with the words 'as an independent object' or drafted the leading objects very widely. A further development which has taken place is the appearance of so-called subjective objects clauses. These provide for the carrying on of any business which the company or the directors think fit. The clause in the *Stephenson* case was an example. A common clause is 'To do all such other things as the company may think conducive to the attainment of the above objects or any of them'. Such a clause was accepted in *Peruvian Railways Co v Thames and Mersey Marine Insurance, Re Peruvian Railways Co*[9] where Cairns LJ said:

Anything, therefore, which, in the opinion of the company (how to be expressed we shall see afterwards) is incidental or conducive to the main object of the company—which was the acquisition of concessions for railways—they may do. If, therefore, there comes to be a concession for a railway which is to be paid for by instalments, it is, I think, beyond all possibility of dispute, that if they think it incidental or conducive to the attainment of the concession, when the instalments become or are

5 The practice was probably started by Sir Francis Palmer in 1891. See op cit (5th edn, 1905) p 207.
6 [1902] 1 Ch 745.
7 [1918] AC 514, HL.
8 [1970] Ch 199, CA. Noted by Leigh (1970) 33 MLR 81.
9 (1867) 2 Ch App 617 at 624.

about to fall due, in place of making calls on their shareholders, they should give a bill of exchange, payable at a future day, for the amount of the instalments, they may do so. The words seem to me so wide that they necessarily include a power of that kind. This is a power which, of course, may require to be exercised by a general meeting of the shareholders, or it may be capable of being exercised by the directors.

There is some suggestion in the cases that such clauses may not have been adequate compliance with the Companies Acts[10]. However, the practice of the Registrar was to accept such clauses and in a number of modern cases they have been accepted as valid.

In *Bell Houses Ltd v City Wall Properties Ltd*[11] the validity of such a clause was upheld by the Court of Appeal. The facts were that a property development company had know-how and contacts in the financial world, and had agreed to introduce another company to financiers to enable it to obtain development finance. It charged a commission for the introduction which the other company having first accepted then refused to pay. The question of ultra vires was raised. The Court of Appeal, faced with this defence, recognised that the commission was valid on the basis of the subjective objects clause which read 'To carry on any other trade or business whatsoever which can, in the opinion of the board of directors, be advantageously carried on by the company in connection with or as ancillary to . . . the general business of the company'. The court emphasised, however, that the transaction was ancillary to the existing business.

THE CORPORATE GIFTS AND GRATUITOUS TRANSACTIONS CASES

In practice, companies make gratuitous payments to charities, hospitals, and even to the Conservative Party[12]. These are regarded as being justified on the basis of social responsibility. In America, the validity of charitable payments is clearly recognised[13]. This is not necessarily the case in the UK, although their validity is assumed perhaps in s 235(3) of CA 1985, which requires disclosure in the directors' report. Indeed the case law on this topic has grown progressively more complex and has raised fundamental questions about the relationship of the ultra vires doctrine to directors' authority and duties and minority shareholders' remedies.

In *Hutton v West Cork Rly Co*[14] Bowen LJ said that there should be 'no cakes and ale except such as are required for the benefit of the company' and that 'charity has no business to sit at boards of directors qua charity'. In *Re Lee, Behrens & Co Ltd*[15] Eve J laid down three tests for the validity of corporate gifts. He said: 'Whether they be made under an express or implied power, . . . the validity of such grants is to be tested . . . by the answers to

10 See *Re Crown Bank* (1890) 44 Ch D 634.
11 [1966] 1 QB 207. Noted by Wedderburn (1966) 29 MLR 673; Polack [1966] CLJ 174; Baker (1966) 82 LQR 463. The case went back to Mocatta J to be tried on the facts and he decided in favour of City Wall because Bell Houses had never earned their commission. Bell Houses again appealed, this time unsuccessfully. The second hearing and appeal were never reported. We are grateful to Prof J Milnes Holden for this information. Prof Milnes Holden was junior counsel for City Wall.
12 Gifts by the League Against Cruel Sports, a company limited by guarantee, to the Labour Party were ruled ultra vires in *Simmonds v Heffer* [1983] BCLC 298. The matter was treated as one of construction. See P Davies [1983] JBL 485.
13 See H G Henn and J Alexander *Corporations* (3rd edn, 1983) p 350.
14 (1883) 23 Ch D 654, CA.
15 [1932] 2 Ch 46.

three pertinent questions: (1) Is the transaction reasonably incidental to the carrying on of the company's business? (2) Is it a bona fide transaction? and (3) Is it done for the benefit of and to promote the prosperity of the company?'.

As can be seen (1) is the test of an implied power and it seems to be inappropriate to an express power (2) seems to be an ingredient in directors' duties, not corporate capacity and (3) seems to add nothing to (1) and (2). Nevertheless, these tests were applied in later cases which have only recently been considered at appellate level. In *Parke v Daily News*[16] the defendant company was proposing to close down its operation. The Cadbury family which held the majority of shares wished to make gratuitous payments to redundant employees. This was before the Redundancy Payments Act 1965 which made it compulsory to make such payments. The proposed payments were challenged by Parke who was a minority shareholder. Plowman J applied the *Lee Behrens* tests and held that the proposed redundancy payments were ultra vires. The immediate effect of *Parke v Daily News* has now been negated by ss 309 and 719 of CA 1985. Section 309 enables the directors of a company to have regard to the interests of employees as well as shareholders and s 719 gives power to the company to provide for employees on the cessation or transfer of a business. The tests were also applied in the case of *Re W & M Roith Ltd*[17]. In that case a director had no pension arrangements with the company. He fell ill and the company entered into a service agreement with him, making provision for his wife after his death. It was held, applying the *Lee Behrens* tests, that the agreement was ultra vires. This case has been criticised on the grounds that it was not really a case of ultra vires, but one of directors' breach of duty. The *Lee Behrens* tests were, however, rejected by Pennycuick J in the case of *Charterbridge Corpn Ltd v Lloyds Bank Ltd*[18]. This was a case involving a group guarantee. The bank had advanced money to the property development subsidiary in the group on condition that each other company in the group gave a guarantee of the indebtedness secured by a debenture on its assets. The question arose as to whether the guarantees and debentures given by the other companies were ultra vires. There was an express provision in their objects clauses providing for the giving of guarantees and securities. Pennycuick J rejected the *Lee Behrens* tests on the above grounds and said that where the transaction was expressly authorised, that was the end of the matter. He also expressed the basis of an alternative ratio by saying that if the motivation of the directors was relevant one need not see whether they had actually considered the transaction to be for the good of the company if an honest and reasonable director, standing in their shoes, would have believed that it was for the good of the company. There is much to commend in both the *Charterbridge* approaches. Two matters, however, arguably weaken the decision. *Parke* and *Roith* were not cited and, also, the judge did not consider the object/power distinction. Such transactions may be rejected on the basis that the power to give a guarantee or security cannot be an independent object. *Charterbridge* was followed in Scotland in *Thompson v J Barke & Co (Caterers) Ltd*[19] and a similar approach was taken

16 [1962] Ch 927.
17 [1967] 1 All ER 427.
18 [1970] Ch 62.
19 1975 SLT 67.

by Oliver J in *Re Halt Garage (1964) Ltd*[20] when he held that once a transaction was intra vires the proper test lay in the genuineness and honesty of the transaction—was it a genuine exercise of the power—not on some abstract test of the benefit of the company. If claims are made for remuneration the real question is—are the payments in question genuine remuneration? He said:

I cannot help thinking, if I may respectfully say so, that there has been a certain confusion between the requirements for a valid exercise of the fiduciary powers of directors (which have nothing to do with the capacity of the company but everything to do with the propriety of acts done within that capacity), the extent to which powers can be implied or limits be placed, as a matter of construction, on express powers, and the matters which the court will take into consideration at the suit of a minority shareholder in determining the extent to which his interests can be overridden by a majority vote. These three matters, as it seems to me, raise questions which are logically quite distinct but which have sometimes been treated as if they demand a single, universal answer leading to the conclusion that, because a power must not be abused, therefore, beyond the limit of propriety it does not exist.

The matter was further reviewed this time by the Court of Appeal in *Re Horsley & Weight Ltd*[1]. This case is particularly interesting because the court included Buckley LJ who had also sat in *Re Introductions Ltd*. The issue was whether a pension policy for a director and employee was ultra vires and amounted to misfeasance by the director in question in the liquidation of the company. The court held that there was an express provision to grant pensions which constituted a *substantive object* and not merely an ancillary power. That being the case, the benefit and prosperity of the company were immaterial. The *Lee Behrens* tests and *Re W & M Roith Ltd* were doubted and *Charterbridge* approved. The policy was intra vires and there was no misfeasance.

Buckley LJ[2] said that the objects of a company need not be commercial; they could be charitable or philanthropic or whatever the original incorporators wished, provided they were legal. There was no reason why a company should not part with its funds gratuitously or for non-commercial reasons if this was within its declared objects.

All three judges were of the opinion that the scope of a paragraph in an objects clause was a matter of construction. The significance of this is highlighted by the later case of *Rolled Steel Products (Holdings) Ltd v British Steel Corpn*[3]. Here the facts were considerably more complicated but the essential issue was the validity of a guarantee and debenture given by a company which was in excess of the company's own indebtedness and stood to benefit others. There was a power to lend and advance money in the objects clause but Vinelott J held that as a matter of construction this was not a substantive object but an ancillary power. Not only that but he distinguished between powers conferred for the furtherance of commercial purposes and those which were not. Powers in the first category must be exercised for commercial purposes which overlapped if they did not in fact coincide with the *Lee Behrens* requirement of benefit and prosperity of the

20 [1982] 3 All ER 1016. Noted (1980) 2 Co Law 141 and (1983) 46 MLR 204.
 1 [1982] Ch 442, [1982] 3 All ER 1045, noted (1981) 2 Co Law 70. See also Wedderburn (1983) 46 MLR 204; McMullen [1983] CLJ 58.
 2 [1982] Ch 442 at 450, [1982] 3 All ER 1045 at 1052.
 3 [1982] Ch 478, [1982] 3 All ER 1057, noted by Birds (1982) 3 Co Law 123.

company. Vinelott J regarded the pension power in *Re Horsley & Weight Ltd* as an example of the first category although this seems at odds with what Buckley LJ had said.

The Court of Appeal[4] did not accept Vinelott J's classification but restated the law in the following principles. A clear distinction should be drawn between transactions which are beyond the capacity of the company and those which are in excess or an abuse of power of directors. The term ultra vires should be used for the former. The question of capacity of the company must depend on a true construction of the memorandum. Although each provision of the memorandum is to be given its full effect, a particular provision might by its very nature be incapable of constituting a substantive object or its wording might indicate that it was only intended to constitute a power ancillary to the other objects. However, even where a particular transaction was capable of being performed as something reasonably incidental to the attainment or pursuit of the company's objects, it will not be rendered ultra vires merely because the directors entered into it for purposes other than those set out in the memorandum. The transaction would be binding on the company on the basis of the apparent authority of the directors to bind the company unless the other party had notice or knowledge of the directors exceeding their authority. Such a person could be liable as constructive trustee of the company's property which came into his hands. Where a power is limited to be only exercisable for the purpose of the company or the company's business this does not put a third party on inquiry as to whether it has been so exercised.

Re Lee Behrens & Co Ltd (supra) was disapproved of and rejected. The tests laid down in that case have now been laid to rest as far as ultra vires is concerned. These principles are consistent with *Re Horsley & Weight Ltd* and add to the clarification of the law attempted in that case. Vinelott J's analysis had muddied waters which were beginning to clear.

In *Brady v Brady*[5] the Court of Appeal held that in the broadest terms a company could not give all its assets away. Theoretically it could reserve to itself such a power but in the real world of trading companies would not be likely to do so. The majority of the court put emphasis on the need to safeguard assets for the protection of the creditors and rejected an argument that it might be in the interests of the company to survive at any cost, including giving half its assets away. Such a transaction could not be justified on the basis of an express power which was not explicit nor as an implied power. The House of Lords, however, allowed an appeal holding that the transactions were expressly authorised by the objects clauses and did not involve misfeasance by the directors. There was no suggestion of fraud or bad faith. The case also involved the question of companies financing the purchase of their own shares and is considered later.

CONSEQUENCES OF ULTRA VIRES PRIOR TO 1973

In *Ashbury Railway Carriage and Iron Co Ltd v Riche*[6], it was held that an ultra vires act was void. This did not mean, however, that there was no possibility of relief. There could be the following relief:

4 [1984] BCLC 466, CA. Noted (1986) 102 LQR 169.
5 [1989] AC 755, [1988] 2 All ER 617, HL. See also *Aveling Barford Ltd v Perion Ltd* [1989] BCLC 626.
6 (1875) LR 7 HL 653.

(1)   The person dealing with the company could enforce the transaction if he or she did not know of its ultra vires character[7]. This seems odd and it may be that the authorities which suggest this were not cases of ultra vires but cases of intra vires powers being used for an improper purpose by the directors[8] or alternatively ultra vires in the sense used by Vinelott J in the *Rolled Steel* case. In any event the scope of this was severely curtailed by the doctrine of constructive notice.

(2)   A guarantor of the company's obligation might be liable depending on the wording of his or her guarantee[9].

(3)   Directors who negotiated the transaction might be liable to the third party for breach of warranty of their authority[10], deceit[11] or negligent misstatement[12] provided the representation was in respect of fact, not law.

(4)   Any payment could be recovered if it was possible to trace it in equity[13].

(5)   By an equitable right akin to subrogation, any ultra vires loan which was applied to pay intra vires creditors conferred on the ultra vires lender a right to stand in the shoes of the intra vires creditors who had been paid except that he was not entitled to any securities which they had held[14].

It appears that the following could plead ultra vires[15]:

(a)   the company[16];

(b)   the other party to the transaction. There was some confusion in the cases but the better view seems to be that the other party could plead ultra vires except possibly where the contract had been performed by the company[17];

(c)   a shareholder[18];

(d)   a creditor generally could not unless he or she was a debenture holder whose security was threatened by the proposed payment[19];

(e)   normally a stranger could not but in *Charterbridge Corpn Ltd v Lloyds Bank Ltd*[20] a purchaser of leasehold property, who was concerned to get a good title, was allowed to seek a declaration that the bank's mortgage was ultra vires the vendor company. The company was not even joined as a party to the action.

7   *Re David Payne & Co Ltd, Young v David Payne & Co Ltd* [1904] 2 Ch 608, CA.
8   See Baxter [1970] CLJ 280.
9   *Garrard v James* [1925] Ch 616.
10   *Chapleo v Brunswick Permanent Building Society* (1881) 6 QBD 696, CA.
11   *Derry v Peek* (1889) 14 App Cas 337, HL.
12   *Hedley Byrne & Co Ltd v Heller & Partners Ltd* [1964] AC 465, HL.
13   *Sinclair v Brougham* [1914] AC 398, HL.
14   *Re Wrexham, Mold and Connah's Quay Rly Co* [1899] 1 Ch 440, CA; *Blackburn Building Society v Cunliffe Brooks & Co* (1882) 22 Ch D 61, CA; affd sub nom *Cunliffe Brooks & Co v Blackburn and District Benefit Building Society* (1884) 9 App Cas 857, HL.
15   See *Street on Ultra Vires*, p 30; Furmston (1961) 24 MLR 717; *Gore-Brown on Companies* (44th edn, 1985) by Boyle and Sykes, paras 3–18.
16   See Collier and Sealy [1973] CLJ 1, pp 2–3; Farrar and Powles (1973) 36 MLR 270, p 273 ff; Prentice (1973) 89 LQR 518, p 524 ff.
17   *Anglo-Overseas Agencies Ltd v Green* [1961] 1 QB 1; *Re KL Tractors Ltd (in liquidation)* (1960) 106 CLR 318 and *Bell Houses Ltd v City Wall Properties Ltd* [1966] 2 QB 656 at 694.
18   *Parke v Daily News Ltd* [1962] Ch 927.
19   *Cross v Imperial Continental Gas Association* [1923] 2 Ch 553.
20   [1970] Ch 62.

Approaches to the reform of ultra vires

It is generally accepted by law reform bodies that the doctrine of ultra vires is unsatisfactory[1]. It represents a pluralism of policies which are not easy to reconcile—investor protection, creditor protection and the public interest[2]. There are four basic approaches to the reform of the doctrine:

(1)   Total abolition. This means that a company is given all the powers of a natural person either expressly or impliedly. As we have seen this is the position of chartered corporations at common law. This approach has been adopted in a number of overseas jurisdictions, notably Canada, New Zealand and Australia where it has been combined with (2).

(2)   Abolition as regards third parties but retention as an internal doctrine. This means that third parties are protected but that an ultra vires act can be the subject of internal redress against the directors. This is the approach which was recommended by the Cohen Committee in 1945.

(3)   Partial abolition as regards third parties, but retention as an internal doctrine. This involves the protection of a limited class of persons. Thus s 34(2) of the New Zealand Companies Act 1955 protects a lender or other person dealing with the company from the company exceeding a borrowing limit provided that he or she does not have express notice. The Jenkins Committee in 1962 recommended the protection of persons contracting with the company in good faith[3]. As we shall see, s 9 of the European Communities Act 1972 (now s 35 of CA 1985) adopted a solution on these lines.

(4)   The specification of a list of ancillary objects and powers which are implied unless excluded. This was adopted in New Zealand[4], Australia[5] and Canada[6] and was also recommended by the Jenkins Committee[7]. It is only a partial solution to the problems created by the doctrine since the objects and powers are ancillary to the express objects and may not cover a particular transaction in any case.

There is much to be said for the first and second approaches which logically require the abolition or modification of the doctrine of public notice whereby everyone has constructive notice of documents in the public file. They guarantee the security of commercial transactions and leave no doubt about their operation. However, as we have seen, the UK, by becoming a member of the EC, was obliged to adopt the third approach which is in line with the recommendations of the Jenkins Report.

The effect of CA 1985, s 35

Section 9(1) of the European Communities Act 1972 was passed to implement art 9 of the First Directive of the Council of the EC, 9 March 1968.

---

1   See Cohen Report (Cmd 6659) 1945, para 12; Jenkins Report (Cmnd 1749) 1962, para 35 ff.
2   See Farrar [1978] 8 NZULR 164.
3   Paragraph 42.
4   Companies Act 1955, Sch 2. However this now only applies to companies registered before 1 January 1984 which have not assumed the powers of a natural person—Companies Amendment (No 2) Act 1983, s 6.
5   UCA 1961, Sch 3, Powers, Companies Code 1981, Sch 2. Since repealed in 1983.
6   Iacobucci, op cit.
7   Paragraph 43.

This directive was made under art 54(3)(a) of the Treaty of Rome to harmonise the protections afforded to members and others. Article 9 provides as follows:

(1) Acts done by the organs of the company shall be binding upon it even if those acts are not within the objects of the company, unless such acts exceed the powers that the law confers or allows to be conferred on those organs.

However, Member States may provide that the company shall not be bound where such acts are outside the objects of the company, if it proves that the third party knew that the act was outside those objects or could not in view of the circumstances have been unaware of it; disclosure of the statutes shall not of itself be sufficient proof thereof.

(2) The limits on the powers of the organs of the company, arising under the statutes or from a decision of the competent organs, may never be relied on as against third parties, even if they have been disclosed.

(3) If the national law provides that authority to represent a company may, in derogation from the legal rules governing the subject, be conferred by the statutes on a single person or on several persons acting jointly, that law may provide that such a provision in the statutes may be relied on as against third parties on condition that it relates to the general power of representation; the question whether such a provision in the statutes can be relied on as against third parties shall be governed by Article 3.

The text is set out in full so that comparisons may be made with CA 1985, s 35 which replaced s 9 of the 1972 Act.

The original section 35 provided:

(1) In favour of a person dealing with a company in good faith, any transaction decided on by the directors is deemed to be one which it is within the capacity of the company to enter into, and the power of the directors to bind the company is deemed to be free of any limitation under the memorandum or articles.

(2) A party to a transaction so decided on is not bound to enquire as to the capacity of the company to enter into it or as to any such limitation on the powers of the directors, and is presumed to have acted in good faith unless the contrary is proved.

The effect of s 35 which was later reformed in the CA 1989 was to add a complicated gloss to the ultra vires doctrine[8]. It did not abolish the doctrine but simply protected a limited class of person dealing with the company. The company itself could not rely on it. In order to be protected the person had to (1) be dealing with the company, (2) be in good faith and (3) the transaction must be decided on by the directors. These three requirements gave rise to a number of problems of interpretation. It was not clear whether a broad or a narrow meaning was to be given to the word 'dealing'. Dealing normally predicates reciprocity and is capable of limitation to commercial transactions[9]. It can also be used in an extended sense. The Jenkins Report limited the protection to persons contracting with the company but as can be seen above, art 9 simply talks about third parties in general. There is no reference to dealing. Probably the better view is that 'dealing' was used in an extended sense[10]. Whether it is wide enough to cover a corporate gift or other gratuitous transaction was not clear. It was arguable that it should not.

---

8 See Collier and Sealy, op cit; Farrar and Powles, op cit; Prentice, op cit; Wyatt (1978) 94 LQR 182; LCB Gower *Modern Company Law* (4th edn, 1979) p 184 ff.
9 See Farrar and Powles, op cit, pp 272–3; Prentice, op cit, p 525.
10 See *Gower*, op cit, p 185; Prentice, op cit, p 525; see too *Re Halt Garage (1964) Ltd* [1982] 3 All ER 1016. Cf *International Sales and Agencies Ltd v Marcus* [1982] 3 All ER 551.

The whole purpose of the Directive, indeed the EC itself, is economic. The use of the word 'transaction' seems to presuppose reciprocity[11]. A pension such as in *Re Horsley & Weight Ltd* may be covered where there is a long-standing relationship, whereas a one-off gift may not be protected, certainly where the company is improperly used as the vehicle for another's generosity. The concept of good faith was not defined[12]. Unlike some other systems such as the German, good faith is not a general requirement of English commercial and company law. It occurs in different areas of law with differing meanings. Thus it is a requirement of English law that an insured must show uberrima fides. This means that he must make full disclosure. In equity, equitable interests are enforceable against all except a bona fide purchaser for value without notice. In the Bills of Exchange Act 1882[13], the Sale of Goods Act 1979[14], and the Law of Property Act 1925, good faith is used and defined. The term 'good faith' was not used in the final version of the Directive because its usage differed between member states[15]. Instead, art 9 talks about knowledge and what amounts to wilful blindness. In the context of s 35 it was not clear whether good faith simply meant without notice or imported some further requirement of fairness. Clearly, if a person had actual knowledge or notice of the lack of corporate capacity he would not be protected. It was arguable in the light of art 9(1) that he would also not be protected if he had been wilfully blind, i e shut his eyes to the need to make further inquiry. Constructive notice of the objects clause, however, no longer applied[16].

The requirement that the transaction had to be decided on by the directors gave rise to further difficulties[17]. It seemed to predicate the necessity for a board decision and it was arguable that the act of a single director, even one who is a managing director, did not confer the protection of the section unless he had been given a general authority by the board as a whole. Even in the latter case it was necessary to adopt a liberal construction of the wording. Here, art 9 does not really help. It refers to 'organs', which is an ambiguous term in English company law. English law has never fully received the organ theory of German law. It applies in the area of tort and crime, where, arguably, different policies apply. The phrase in s 35 seemed to cover (1) a decision of the majority of a duly constituted board meeting; (2) a transaction entered into by a duly authorised director; (3) a transaction entered into by a managing director[18]. In *International Sales and Agencies Ltd v Marcus*[19] Lawson J resolved some but not all of the above problems.

---

11 Farrar and Powles, *Gower* and Prentice, op cit.
12 See Collier and Sealy, pp 2–3; Farrar and Powles, p 273 ff; Prentice, p 524 ff.
13 Section 90.
14 Section 62.
15 See W Fikentschen and B Grosfield (1964–5) CML Rev 259.
16 Collier and Sealy, op cit, p 2; Farrar and Powles, op cit, p 272.
17 Collier and Sealy, op cit, pp 3–4; Farrar and Powles, p 273 ff; Prentice, op cit, p 526; *Gower*, op cit, p 187; S N Frommel (1987) 8 Co Law 11. See too *Friedrich Haaga GmbH*: Case 32/74 [1974] ECR 1201, [1975] 1 CMLR 32, ECJ. It has been argued by the Commission that the UK government has failed to implement fully the First Directive in not specifying which persons represent the company (OJ 1977, C289/1).
18 This would be consistent with art 9(3). See now *International Sales and Agencies Ltd v Marcus* [1982] 3 All ER 551; and *TCB Ltd v Gray* [1986] Ch 621 (agreement of all directors individually). Noted by J Birds (1986) 7 Co Law 104; J Collier [1986] CLJ 207. Upheld on appeal on other points (1987) 3BCC 503.
19 [1982] 3 All ER 551, [1982] 2 CMLR 46. The former contains an error at p 559 ff.

The material facts of the case were that loans were made to a major shareholder in two companies. He became ill, and said his friend M would see the lender was repaid if he died. The shareholder died and M, who was a director and effectively controlled the two companies, repaid the lender with cheques drawn on the companies. The companies reclaimed the moneys. The lender claimed the protection of s 9(1), now s 35 of CA 1985. Lawson J held that (1) M was in breach of his fiduciary duty and was a constructive trustee of the moneys; (2) the payments were ultra vires; (3) the lender was liable as a constructive trustee of the moneys since he had actual notice that the moneys belonged to the companies and the payment was in breach of trust; and (4) the lender was not protected by s 9(1), now s 35, CA 1985, which did not affect the operation of a constructive trust. Lawson J[20] said:

Whilst s 9(1) [now s 35, CA 1985] reflects 'if it proves that the third party knew the act was outside those objects', it does not directly reflect in so many words, the alternative 'or could not in view of the circumstances have been unaware of it'. Which seems to me very close to turning a blind eye. In my judgment I am entitled to look at the Council's Directive as an aid to the interpretation of s 9(1) of the Act. I conclude, firstly, that s 9(1) relates only to legal obligations of the company under transactions with third parties, whether or not they be within or without its powers; secondly, that s 9(1) is designed to give relief to innocent third parties entering into transactions with companies against the operation in England of the old ultra vires doctrine; thirdly, that the test of lack of good faith in somebody entering into obligations with a company will be found either in proof of his actual knowledge that the transaction was ultra vires the company or where it can be shown that such a person could not in view of all the circumstances, have been unaware that he was a party to a transaction ultra vires.

His Lordship said that the onus of proof was on the lender to establish a 'dealing' but on the companies to establish lack of good faith. There was no dealing with the company since M simply used the company as the vehicle of his generosity. Since M was sole effective director to whom all actual authority to act for the companies had been effectively delegated the transactions were decided on by the directors. The results of the *Marcus* case were thus:

(1)   The onus of proving 'dealing' was on the third party and there was no dealing where the companies' funds were wrongly used to the third party's knowledge.
(2)   A single effective director could constitute 'directors'.
(3)   Good faith was to be interpreted in the light of art 9 of the Directive.
(4)   The section did not protect a constructive trustee.

In *Barclays Bank Ltd v TOSG Trust Fund Ltd* in 1984 Nourse J considered the matter at first instance[1]. The case which went on appeal on other points involved complicated facts surrounding the collapse of holiday tour operators and an argument about double proof of debts in a winding up. Nourse J considered s 9(1) of the European Communities Act 1972 and found that the

---

20 [1982] 3 All ER 551 at 559. Noted (1983) 46 MLR 204, [1982] CLJ 244. See too *Rolled Steel Products (Holdings) Ltd v British Steel Corpn* [1986] Ch 246, CA; *Barclays Bank Ltd v TOSG Trust Fund Ltd* [1984] BCLC 1; *International Factors (NI) Ltd v Streeve Construction Ltd* [1984] NIJB.
1 [1984] BCLC 1 at 17-18.

transactions in question were intra vires. In approaching the section he thought that he would only have recourse to the First Directive if the language of the Act was either ambiguous or doubtful in some other respect. With respect to his Lordship this is not strictly correct. The courts are on judicial notice of the contents of the Official Journal and this includes the text of the Directive. His Lordship then went on to say that the expression 'in good faith' was one whose meaning was well established and understood in the law and that it did not admit to any ambiguity or doubt. This statement is remarkable and it is difficult to see any rational basis for it. However, taking that view, his Lordship did not think it necessary to rely on the Directive and preferred to follow his own chauvinistic line. His general view of the section was that it had abolished the rule that a person who deals with a company is automatically affected with constructive notice and its objects clause but by retaining the requirement of good faith it ensured that a defence based on absence of notice should not be available to anyone who had not acted genuinely and honestly in his dealings with the company. Notice and good faith, although two separate concepts, were often inseparable. His Lordship went on to say that a person who deals with a company in circumstances where he ought to know that the company has no power to enter into the transaction will not necessarily act in good faith. A fortiori where he actually knew. His Lordship emphatically refuted the suggestion that reasonableness was a necessary ingredient of good faith. In his Lordship's view a person acted in good faith if he acted genuinely and honestly in the circumstances of the case. Reading his Lordship's judgment highlights the folly of the British government in seeking to implement this directive by the use of some part of the draft prepared by the Jenkins Committee. This leads the court into more subjective dimensions than were intended by the First Directive. It is submitted that the approach of Lawson J is preferable both as to resort to the Directive and also in the interpretation of the section. It is interesting to note that the Irish Republic has the same problems resulting from the earlier enactment of a reform influenced by the Jenkins Report[2].

Section 35 thus led to a most unsatisfactory reform of ultra vires.

The CA 1989 reforms

The topic of ultra vires and the related topic of directors' authority were the subject of a consultative document issued by the Department of Trade and Industry entitled 'Reform of the Ultra Vires Rule'[3]. This was prepared by Dr D D Prentice of Pembroke College, Oxford. The document itself reflected earlier consultation which Dr Prentice had with the public. Part V of the CA 1989 largely gives effect to the Prentice proposals. Section 108 of the Act enacts a new s 35 of the Companies Act 1985. Section 35(1)–(4) now reads as follows;

(1) The validity of an act done by a company shall not be called into question on the ground of lack of capacity by reason of anything in the company's memorandum.

(2) A member of a company may bring proceedings to restrain the doing of an act which but for subsection (1) would be beyond the company's capacity; but no such

2 See P Ussher *Company Law in Ireland* (1985) pp 123 et seq.
3 See R R Pennington (1987) 8 Co Law 103; S N Frommel (1987) 8 Co Law; B Hannigan [1987] JBL 173.

proceedings shall lie in respect of an act to be done in fulfilment of a legal obligation arising from a previous act of the company.

(3) It remains the duty of the directors to observe any limitations on their powers flowing from the company's memorandum; and action by the directors which but for subsection (1) would be beyond the company's capacity may only be ratified by the company by special resolution.

A resolution ratifying such action shall not affect any liability incurred by the directors or any other person; relief from any such liability must be agreed to separately by special resolution.

(4) The operation of this section is restricted by section 30B(1) of the Charities Act 1960 and section 112(3) of the Companies Act 1989 in relation to companies which are charities; and section 322A below (invalidity of certain transactions to which directors or their associates are parties) has effect notwithstanding this section.

This achieves most of the major reforms effected by the Canadian federal reforms of 1975, which have influenced reforms in Australia and New Zealand as well as in other Canadian jurisdictions[4].

The new English section, like the original Ontario reform of 1970[5], still does not expressly confer on companies all the powers of a natural person, but it removes the effects of lack of capacity. It will no longer be necessary to resort to verbose drafting and in effect ultra vires now becomes more clearly a question of directors' authority. As in the Canadian reforms, it remains open to a member of the company to bring proceedings under s 35(2) to restrain a threatened ultra vires transaction as well as seek internal redress against the directors for exceeding their authority under s 35A(4) and (5) which distinguish between executory and executed contracts. However, the wording of the new s 35(2) is rather obscure. It provides inter alia that 'no such proceedings shall lie in respect of an act to be done in fulfilment of a legal obligation arising from a previous act of the company'. This seems to distinguish between contract and conveyance, a distinction not adopted in other systems but one which arguably has roots in the case law of ultra vires. If this is so then the use of the words 'to be done' instead of 'done' is unfortunate. An act by directors outside the capacity of the company can be ratified by *special* resolution and such resolution does not affect any underlying liability of the directors.

A new s 35A deals with the lack of authority by directors and unfortunately reproduces some of the unsatisfactory wording of s 9(1) of the European Communities Act 1972 and the old section. The new section is dealt with in Chapter 23, post, but a few remarks will be made here. The section still only operates 'in favour of a person dealing with a company in good faith'. Thus, the unsatisfactory concept of good faith which was removed from the final wording of the first directive[6] is retained although there is now a provision in s 35(A)(2)(b) whereby a person is not to be regarded as acting in bad faith by reason of his knowing that an act is beyond the powers of the directors under the company's constitution. A new s 35(B) provides that a party to a transaction is not bound to inquire as to whether it is permitted by the company's memorandum or as to any limitation on the

---

4 Canada Business Corporations Act, s 15. See Ziegel, Daniels, Johnston & MacIntosh, op cit, pp 293 et seq.
5 Business Corporations Act 1970, s 16.
6 Vide supra; see too F Wooldridge (1989) 133 Sol J 714. Dr Wooldridge's article contains a useful critique of the legislation at bill stage in the House of Lords.

powers of the board of directors to bind the company or authorise others to do so.

However, the clarity of these reforms is obscured by a further provision in CA 1989, s 142, which deals with the abolition of the doctrine of what it calls 'deemed notice'. Section 142(1) purports to abolish the doctrine of 'deemed notice', by the insertion of a new s 711A in the CA 1985. Unfortunately, a further subsection provides that this does not affect the question whether a person is affected by notice of any matter by reason of a failure to make such inquiries as are reasonably to be made. In other words, there is still the possibility of actual knowledge and actual notice and this may in certain circumstances include inferred actual knowledge or notice at common law. The retention of this in the wording of the section is likely to strengthen the hand of a conservative judge who is unsympathetic to the reform. This is unfortunate and differs from the approach adopted in respect of company charges. Another distinctive characteristic of the new reforms is an express provision that a transaction in excess of authority entered into with parties which include directors of the company or its holding company, or any person connected with such a director or a company with whom such a director is associated, is voidable at the instance of the company. It is assumed that such persons should know of limitations and ensure compliance. This reform is provided for in a new s 322A of the CA 1985. There are exceptions in s 322A(5), which include the intervention of third party rights and ratification by *ordinary* resolution.

ALTERATION OF THE MEMORANDUM OF ASSOCIATION

Section 2(7) of CA 1985 expressly forbids the alteration of the conditions contained in the memorandum 'except in the cases, in the mode and to the extent for which express provision is made by this Act'.

Firstly, under s 28(1) of CA 1985, a company may by special resolution change its name.

Secondly, a company may only with considerable difficulty alter the country in which its registered office is situated. Usually this involves formation of a new company in the other jurisdiction[7].

Thirdly, it is possible under s 4 to alter the objects clause by special resolution.

As we have seen, between 1856 and 1890 a company could not alter its objects clause. The only solution was to form another company which was not as burdensome as it sounds since this could usually be a subsidiary. The policy behind the Companies (Memorandum of Association) Act 1890 was not so much reform of ultra vires as to assist companies to develop their business along more efficient and technological lines[8]. Initially, the change which was effected by special resolution was limited to seven specified purposes and needed confirmation by the court. This was changed in 1948 to dispense with confirmation by the court unless the holders of not less than 15% of the nominal capital of the company or any class thereof or not less

7 See further *Palmer's Company Law* (24th edn, 1987) vol 1, paras 8–10–11.
8 Per Eve J in *Re Jewish Colonial Trust (Juedische Colonial Bank) Ltd* [1908] 2 Ch 287 at 295.

than 15% of the company's pre-1947 debenture holders[9] object. This is now contained in CA 1985, s 5, although CA 1989 removed the old limitation in s 4 that the alteration of objects had to be for one of the seven specified purposes[10]. In practice, few cases now go to court and there is little check on the company's power to alter its objects.

Fourthly, it is possible to alter the clause dealing with limitation of liability. Under the Act as we have seen in Chapter 6, it is possible for a limited liability company to become unlimited and vice versa[11].

Fifthly, it is possible to alter the company's share capital. Section 121(2)(a) of CA 1985 gives a general power to increase the capital[12]. On the other hand, generally speaking, a reduction of capital (other than by redemption or purchase under Pt V, Ch VII) can only take place with the consent of the court[13]. This is necessary to protect creditors and to achieve fairness between the different classes of shareholders.

Lastly, s 17 contains a rather odd provision which is not found in most other systems. This provides that any condition which could lawfully have been contained in the articles instead of the memorandum may be altered by special resolution. This is subject, however, to the following restrictions:

(1)   It does not apply where the memorandum provides for or prohibits alteration of such conditions (s 17(1)(b)).
(2)   It does not authorise the variation or abrogation of class rights (s 17(2)(b)).
(3)   An application can be made to the court to cancel the alteration (s 17(1)).
(4)   Nothing can be done to increase the liability of any member to contribute or subscribe without his consent (s 16).
(5)   The power is subject to any restriction imposed by the court under s 459. Section 459 is the statutory remedy for minority shareholders and gives the court wide powers.

It should be noted that s 17 does not apply if the relevant provision has been inserted in the objects clause[14].

Since the only matter of this kind likely to be inserted is a class rights provision, s 17 is not very useful. As we shall see later, if class rights are set out in the memorandum it is difficult to alter them. Whether this is a good thing or not depends on the circumstances.

---

9 The debentures must have been issued before 1 December 1947 (s 5(8)).
10 CA 1989, s 110(2).
11 Sections 49–52.
12 See e g Table A, reg 32(a).
13 Section 136.
14 *Re Hampstead Garden Suburb Trust Ltd* [1962] Ch 806.

CHAPTER 11

Articles of association

THE SCOPE AND CONSTRUCTION OF THE ARTICLES

The articles of association are the domestic regulations of the company and govern its internal administration. They determine how the powers conferred on the company by the memorandum of association shall be exercised. The matter was put succinctly by Lord Cairns LC in *Ashbury Railway Carriage and Iron Co Ltd v Riche*[1] in 1875 when he said: 'The memorandum is, as it were, the area beyond which the actions of the company cannot go; inside that area the shareholders may make such regulations for their own government as they think fit.'

The articles are subordinate to the memorandum in the sense that they cannot confer wider powers than the memorandum. If there is any inconsistency between them the memorandum prevails and any alteration to the articles which conflicts with the memorandum is void to the extent of the conflict[2]. The articles cannot be resorted to to fill in any gap in the memorandum in respect of any matter which by law is required to be in the memorandum[3]. The reason is that such conditions are introduced for the benefit of creditors and the outside public as well as the shareholders[4]. In this respect at least, the memorandum is dominant. This, for instance, covers objects but not powers since the former but not the latter are required to be specified in the memorandum[5]. On the other hand in other cases the articles must be read together with the memorandum so far as may be necessary to explain any ambiguity in the memorandum or to supplement it upon any matter as to which it is silent[6]. In Scotland[7] it was held prior to 1980 that it is permissible to refer to a variation of rights clause in the articles which were filed contemporaneously with the memorandum although this was not referred to in the memorandum itself. Both cases involved applications to the court to confirm reduction of capital which had been approved by the shareholders so arguably they do not establish a general principle and in any event the English courts did not go so far[8]. However, s 125(4)(a) of CA 1985 adopts the Scots solution. If the class rights are set out exhaustively in the memorandum and this contains no variation of rights clause, such rights are

---

1 (1875) LR 7 HL 653 at 671. See also Bowen LJ in *Guinness v Land Corpn of Ireland* (1882) 22 Ch D 349 at 379, CA.
2 *Ashbury v Watson* (1885) 30 Ch D 376, CA.
3 *Guinness v Land Corpn of Ireland* (1882) 22 Ch D 349, CA.
4 Per Bowen LJ at 381.
5 Ibid at 383–4.
6 *Angostura Bitters (Dr JGB Siegert & Sons) Ltd v Kerr* [1933] AC 550 at 554, PC.
7 *Re Oban and Aultmore-Glenlivet Distillers Ltd* (1903) 5 F 1140; *Marshall, Fleming & Co Ltd* 1938 SC 873. See also *Harrison v Mexican Rly Co* (1875) LR 19 Eq 358 at 365, but cf *Guinness v Land Corpn of Ireland,* supra, at 377, 381.
8 See eg *Duncan Gilmour & Co Ltd v Inman* [1952] 2 All ER 871.

unalterable except by unanimous consent of all the members of the company under s 125(5) or by a scheme of arrangement under s 425 which requires application to the court[9]. In practice it is rare to insert class rights in the memorandum today. The subject of class rights is dealt with in detail in Chapter 17.

The first set of articles in the modern form were set out in Table B of the Schedule to the Joint Stock Companies Act 1856 and most modern companies now have articles which are based to some extent on the form set out in Table A. There are express provisions in the Act dealing with articles. Section 7 provides that there may, in the case of a company limited by shares, and there shall, in the case of a company limited by guarantee or unlimited, be articles registered with the memorandum. Section 8(1) provides that the articles of association may adopt all or any of the regulations contained in Table A and s 8(2) provides that in the case of the company limited by shares, if articles are not registered or if articles are registered, in so far as the articles do not exclude or modify Table A, the regulations of Table A as in force at the date of the company's registration shall constitute the company's articles. Section 8(4) provides that the articles of companies limited by guarantee with and without share capital, and an unlimited company having a share capital, shall be respectively in the forms set out in Tables D, C and E as prescribed in regulations made by the Secretary of State or as near that form as circumstances admit. The statutory forms are directory, not mandatory. They are intended as guides, not strait-jackets[10] and there is a greater measure of choice in the content of the articles than in the memorandum.

The courts regard articles as commercial documents and apply a liberal construction to them. Jenkins LJ in *Holmes v Keyes*[11] described their approach as follows:

I think that the articles of association of a company should be regarded as a business document and should be construed so as to give them reasonable business efficacy, where a construction tending to that result is admissible in the language of the articles, in preference to a result which would or might prove unworkable.

This is important because the articles cannot be rectified by the courts[12]. The power to alter is purely statutory. Any alteration must be effected by special resolution of the company under s 9. If there is any inconsistency between different parts of the articles, the courts will follow the ordinary canons of construction and look to the whole, seeking to achieve harmony between the different provisions and compliance with the law[13]. The relationship of express articles to the statutory model in Table A can give rise to problems of construction if the articles are not well drafted. Thus, in the New Zealand

---

9 The Jenkins Report 1962 (Cmnd 1749) para 190 recommended the adoption of the Scots rules.
10 *Gaiman v National Association for Mental Health* [1971] Ch 317.
11 [1959] Ch 199 at 215, CA. Such construction may lead the court to imply terms—see *Mutual Life Insurance Co of New York v Rank Organisation Ltd* [1985] BCLC 11, at 21. However, the particular terms were arguably simply a paraphrase of the existing law. See also *Re Hartley Baird Ltd* [1955] Ch 143 at 146.
12 *Scott v Frank F Scott (London) Ltd* [1940] Ch 794 at 801–3, CA.
13 *Oakbank Oil Co v Crum* (1882) 8 App Cas 65, HL. Cf *Elderslie SS Co v Borthwick* [1905] AC 93 at 96, HL, a case on bills of lading where the ordinary canons of construction are discussed by Lord Halsbury LC at 96.

case of *McNeil v McNeil's Sheepfarming Co Ltd*[14] the company's own articles provided for one man, one vote, but the Table A provision of one vote per share also applied. The court held that the express article took precedence. On the other hand, the mere fact that the articles deal with the matter in question does not necessarily exclude Table A. In *Fischer v Black & White Publishing Co*[15] the articles provided that the company's profits available for dividend should be applied in a certain order between different classes of shareholders. Some regulations of Table A were excluded, but the Court of Appeal held that the regulations of Table A which allowed directors to set aside reserves out of profits before paying any dividend at all, applied. Sometimes the commercial construction adopted by the court is so liberal that it almost amounts to rectification. Thus in *Rayfield v Hands*[16] the judge interpreted an article referring to directors as if it referred to members to enable a provision requiring them to buy the plaintiff's shares at fair value to take effect. The court may resort to the memorandum to resolve ambiguities in the articles but if there is a conflict between the two the memorandum prevails[17].

The articles must not contain anything which is illegal or contrary to public policy. Thus in the Australian case of *Re Victoria Onion and Potato Growers' Association Ltd v Finnigan, Ryan and Farrell*[18] an article was held void as being in unreasonable restraint of trade[19]. In theory this should be rejected by the Registrar, but in practice this seldom happens in relation to articles as opposed to objects clauses.

THE LEGAL EFFECT OF THE ARTICLES

Section 7 of the 1844 Act required a deed in the form specified in the section and Sch A under the hand and seals of the members. This had to contain 'a Covenant on the Part of every Shareholder, with a Trustee on the Part of the Company to pay up the Amount of the Instalments on the share taken by such Shareholder and to perform the several Engagements in the Deed contained on the Part of the Shareholders'. This meant there was an actual contract. Section 26 required any new shareholder to execute the deed or a deed referring thereto. This constituted novation. As we have seen in Chapters 2 and 6, the modern form of memorandum and articles was adopted by the Joint Stock Companies Act 1856. Sections 7 and 10 of that Act catered for the transition from registered deed of settlement to the modern form, by providing that the memorandum and articles, when registered, bound the company and the shareholders 'to the same Extent as if

14 [1955] NZLR 15.
15 [1901] 1 Ch 174, CA.
16 [1960] Ch 1. See the comments of L C B Gower (1958) 21 MLR 401 at 657 and K W Wedderburn [1958] CLJ 148. See also *Re Caratti Holding Co Pty Ltd* (1975) 1 ACLR 87 but cf *Cohen & Sons Pty Ltd v Brown* [1969] 2 NSWR 593.
17 *Duncan Gilmour & Co Ltd v Inman* [1952] 2 All ER 871.
18 [1922] VLR 384.
19 See also *Otaraia Cooperative Co v Flynn* [1930] GLR 74; *Heron v Port Huon Fruitgrowers Co-operative Association Ltd* (1922) 30 CLR 315; *Parker & Co Ltd v Woollands* (1924) 26 WALR 172; *Tasmanian Hopgrowers Pool Ltd v Wilton* (1926) 22 Tas LR 16; *St Johnstone Football Club Ltd v Scottish Football Association Ltd* 1965 SLT 171. See also *Invercargill Sports Depot Ltd v Patrick* [1939] NZLR 161 which dealt with alteration of articles.

each Shareholder had subscribed his Name and affixed his Seal thereto or otherwise executed the same, and there were in such Articles contained, on the Part of himself, his Heirs, Executors and Administrators, a Covenant to conform to all the Regulations of such Articles, subject to the Provisions of this Act'. This obviated the need for every incoming member to execute the memorandum and articles. Although the 1856 Act provided for incorporation, the consequences of the separate legal personality of the company were not fully appreciated at the time and this is probably the reason for the wording[20]. The modern wording is contained in s 14(1) of CA 1985, which provides that, subject to the provisions of the Act, the memorandum and articles, when registered, bind the company and its members to the same extent as if they respectively had been signed and sealed by each member, and contained convenants on the part of each member to observe all the provisions of the memorandum and of the articles. Section 14(2) provides that all money payable by any member to the company under the memorandum or articles shall be a debt due from him to the company, and in England and Wales, of the nature of a specialty debt. The reason for s 14(2) is most likely to have been to resolve any doubt as to whether money payable by a *subsequent* member was a debt at all[1]. The wording of s 14 sometimes produces some strange results. In *Re Compania de Electricidad de la Provincia de Buenos Aires Ltd*[2] Slade J drew attention to the fact that the section did not say that the articles took effect as if they had been sealed by the company. There was deemed to be a contract and the company was bound but the contract was only under seal as far as members were concerned. This had the effect that money owed by members to the company was a specialty debt as s 14(2) in fact states but money owed by the company was a simple contract debt. The period of limitation is consequently different— twelve years in the first case, six years in the second. The position of the company has been explained by Jordan CJ in *Australian Coal and Shale Employers' Federation v Smith*[3]. He said that it can be regarded as an application of the equitable principle that a party who takes the benefit of a deed is bound by it although he does not execute it.

The nature of the statutory contract created by s 14(1) has been much discussed by the courts and legal commentators. The following principles and contradictions arise from the cases.

(1)   It has been held that the articles constitute a 'social contract[4]' but this is just a sophisticated way of saying that they constitute the constitution of an association[5]. The deemed contract has some rather odd characteristics. First, the section says that it is subject to the provisions of the Act. These provisions include s 9 which gives the company unilateral power to alter the contract by special resolution. Secondly, the

---

20 See Gower *Modern Company Law* (4th edn, 1979) p 315; Pennington *Company Law* (6th edn, 1990) chapter 2.
1 3 Bl Com 153 states that a debt is a sum due by certain and express agreement.
2 [1978] 3 All ER 668 at 697g–698a.
3 (1937) 38 SRNSW 48 at 55.
4 See the Australian cases of *Dutton v Gorton* (1917) 23 CLR 362 at 395; *Wood v W and G Dean Pty Ltd* (1929) 43 CLR 77.
5 Cf *Re Chas Jeffries & Sons Pty Ltd* [1949] VLR 190 at 194 where it was described by Fullagar J as 'A Rousseau-esque synonym for the articles of association'. Indeed the phrase is perhaps as meaningless here as it is in the context of society as a whole.

normal remedies for breach of contract do not necessarily apply[6]. It is generally accepted that the remedies of a member for external redress are limited to an injunction or a declaration although in the case of *Moffatt v Farquhar*[7], Mallins VC directed an inquiry as to damages where directors acting in excess of their powers refused to register share transfers. It has been held that rectification is not available although as we have seen the commercial construction adopted by the courts sometimes comes close to rectification.

(2) The articles bind members qua members only. It has been held that the articles create a contract binding each member of the company but that the member is only bound qua member. In the leading case of *Hickman v Kent or Romney Marsh Sheep-Breeders' Association*[8], the articles provided for reference of disputes between members and the company to arbitration. The plaintiff brought an action against the company in connection with his expulsion from the company. Astbury J held that the company was entitled to have the action stayed because the articles amounted to a contract between the company and the member and referred such matters to arbitration[9]. In *Beattie v E and F Beattie Ltd*[10] there was a dispute between a director and his company. The director sought to have the dispute referred to arbitration under one of the articles. The Court of Appeal, following *Hickman* regarded this as a dispute qua director not member, and refused although it has been suggested that since the director was also a member it fell within the articles and his right as a member to have the company's business conducted in accordance with the articles[11].

(3) Although the section does not provide that the articles bind the company and the members as if they had been sealed by the company, it has been held in numerous cases that the section gives rise to a contract binding the company to the members on which it can sue and be sued. In *Pender v Lushington*[12] the articles limited a shareholder's vote at a general meeting to 100 in all. Certain shareholders before a meeting transferred shares to nominees to increase their voting power. The chairman ruled the latter out of order and the plaintiff's votes were rejected on this ground. The court held that he was entitled to an injunction against the directors because he had a right to have his vote recorded. In substance, his claim appears to have been against the company although he technically joined the company as a co-plaintiff.

(4) The articles constitute a contract between individual members. Normally this will be enforceable through the company but it may be possible in certain circumstances to have direct redress. *Hickman's* case left open the question as to whether the articles constitute a

6 See *Gower*, op cit, p 316.
7 (1878) 7 Ch D 591.
8 [1915] 1 Ch 881. See also *Gore Bros v Newbury Dairy Co Ltd* [1919] NZLR 205; Chantler (1976) 12 UWAL Rev 333; Bastin [1977] JBL 17.
9 Cf *St Johnstone Football Club Ltd v Scottish Football Association Ltd* 1965 SLT 171 where it was held that an article prohibiting a member from taking legal proceedings against the company was contrary to public policy and void.
10 [1938] Ch 708, CA.
11 Wedderburn [1957] CLJ 193.
12 (1877) 6 Ch D 70.

contract between the members inter se. In *Welton v Saffery*[13], Lord Herschell dissenting said: 'It is quite true that the articles constitute a contract between each member and the company, and that there is no contract in terms whatever between the individual members of the company; but the articles do not any the less, in my opinion, regulate their rights inter se. Such rights can only be enforced by or against a member through the company . . .'. The same view was expressed by Scott LJ in *London Sack and Bag Co v Dixon and Lugton*[14] and by Harman J in *Re Greene, Greene v Greene*[15]. On the other hand in *Wood v Odessa Waterworks Co*[16] Stirling J said that the articles took effect between each individual shareholder and every other, although the issue before him was an application by shareholders for an injunction against the company and its directors. In *Rayfield v Hands*[17], Vaisey J adopted the latter view and allowed direct enforcement without joinder of the company. There, the articles of a private company provided that any member intending to transfer his shares should inform the directors who should take the shares equally between them at fair value. Vaisey J adopting a commercial construction regarded the reference to directors as a reference to members and held that the article was directly enforceable. The cases cited above which appear to require enforcement through the company were cited but his Lordship gave them short shrift. The decision has been criticised as going too far[18] but can perhaps be justified on the basis that (1) it appears to have been an innocent drafting error of a mechanical kind and the intention was clear; (2) the company in question was analogous to a partnership; and (3) (more convincingly) the action is explicable as being an example of a personal right being infringed which is one of the recognised exceptions to the rule in *Foss v Harbottle* which requires an action to be brought through the company[19].

(5)   The articles do not per se constitute an enforceable contract between a company and an outsider[20]. This is no doubt due to privity of contract and lack of mutuality. Outsider means a person who is not a member or a member acting in a capacity other than that of a member. Even a director is normally treated as an outsider for this purpose[1]. Any right claimed by an outsider must be conferred by a separate contract or relationship outside the articles. In *Eley v The Positive Government*

---

13 [1897] AC 299 at 315, HL.
14 [1943] 2 All ER 763 at 765, CA.
15 [1949] Ch 333 at 340.
16 (1889) 42 Ch D 636 at 642.
17 [1960] Ch 1.
18 See Gower (1958) 21 MLR 401, 657; Wedderburn [1958] CLJ 148.
19 See Chapter 27.
20 *Hickman v Kent or Romney Marsh Sheep-Breeders' Association* [1915] 1 Ch 881 at 897, 903. This may not apply in Scots law which recognises a jus quaesitum tertii. See also *Woodlands Ltd v Logan* [1948] NZLR 230 for a case where enforcement by legal proceedings was unnecessary. It is arguable that this rule does not apply to New Zealand law in any event because of s 4 of the Contracts (Privity) Act 1982 which abolishes the doctrine of privity of contract subject to certain exceptions.
 1 See *Beattie v E and F Beattie Ltd*, supra.

Security Life Assurance Co Ltd[2] an agreement was made between a promoter and the plaintiff that the latter should advance the costs of formation and in return be appointed permanent solicitor. The plaintiff advanced £200 and prepared the articles. The articles provided that the plaintiff should be the solicitor of the company and should not be removed except for misconduct. He was allotted 200 shares in satisfaction of the advance made by him. His employment as solicitor was terminated and he sued for damages for breach of contract. It was held he could not claim as a solicitor relying on the articles. There are two important points about this case. First, the court did not like the original arrangements and second, there had been insufficient disclosure of it to shareholders. An extrinsic contract may be made by the company with an outsider on the basis of the articles and such a contract may even be inferred from the conduct of the parties. In *Eley's* case the court said that there was nothing but the fact of employment in favour of such a view and this was insufficient. However, in *Swabey v Port Darwin Gold Mining Co*[3], *Re International Cable Co*[4], and *Re New British Iron Co, ex p Beckwith*[5], the courts were prepared to imply an extrinsic contract from service upon the terms of the article. *Swabey* was a Court of Appeal decision. There the directors had served the company without any express service contract. An article provided for remuneration at a fixed rate per annum. The company purported to reduce this by a retrospective special resolution. A director sued. The Court of Appeal held that although the articles did not themselves form a contract one could nevertheless get from them the terms upon which the director was serving. This was followed by Stirling J in *Re International Cable Co*[4] and a similar approach was adopted by Wright J in *Re New British Iron Co*[5] where the two earlier cases were not cited. Such a contract will be on the basis that the article as a term can be unilaterally changed by the company by special resolution under s 9 but such alteration must not be retrospective[6].

(6) It is sometimes maintained that in any event there is a roundabout way of enforcing outsider rights on the basis of every member of a company having a right to have the company's business conducted in accordance with the articles[7]. However, clear authority for this proposition is somewhat limited[8]. In *Richmond Gate Property Co Ltd*[9] the argument was used to defeat a director's claim. This was a case of a claim in contract or quasi contract for remuneration as a director[10]. There was no express service agreement. There was a provision in the articles that

2 (1876) 1 Ex D 88, CA. This was followed in *Browne v La Trinidad* (1887) 37 Ch D 1, CA. See the analysis of *Eley* in *Cumbrian Newspapers Group Ltd v Cumberland and Westmorland Herald Newspaper and Printing Co Ltd* [1986] 3 WLR 26 at 36–7.
3 (1889) 1 Meg 385, CA.
4 (1892) 66 LT 253.
5 [1898] 1 Ch 324.
6 *Swabey v Port Darwin Gold Mining Co* (1889) 1 Meg 385, CA.
7 See Wedderburn [1957] CLJ 193.
8 See *Quin and Axtens v Salmon* [1909] AC 442, HL and *Re H R Harmer Ltd* [1958] 3 All ER 689, CA. See also *Kraus v J G Lloyd Pty Ltd* [1965] VR 232 at 235–6; *Hogg v Cramphorn Ltd* [1967] Ch 254 and *Bamford v Bamford* [1970] Ch 212, CA.
9 [1964] 3 All ER 936.
10 See Wedderburn (1965) 28 MLR 347 and Evans (1966) 29 MLR 608.

directors' remuneration was to be fixed by the Board. None had been fixed. Indeed there had been an understanding that none would be paid to the managing director until the company got on its feet. Plowman J held that there was no claim in quantum meruit. For quantum meruit there must be no contract. Here there was a contract —the contract constituted by the articles. Under the terms of that contract, the remuneration was to be fixed by the directors. It had not been fixed. Therefore, there was no claim to remuneration. This decision can be criticised on two grounds. First, it seems to ignore the fact that this was using the contract argument in an outsider right situation and second, it is then using the argument to defeat the outsider's claim. This seems to be wrong in principle and unjust in effect although the decision can be justified on its facts.

It is arguable that this roundabout way of enforcement rests on the questionable proposition that all outsider rights conferring articles are true articles. Although Table A is directory, not mandatory, the further one gets from it the harder it is to justify the provision as an article. There is some authority to the effect that provisions in articles conferring commercial rights in a capacity other than that of a member derive no binding force from s 14(1). Any binding force which they have must be derived from a separate contract outside the articles[11]. This view is consistent with what Astbury J said in *Hickman*'s case. The matter has been the subject of an interesting but inconclusive academic debate. The argument that since every member has a right to have the company's business conducted in accordance with the articles a member can indirectly enforce outsider rights qua member was first developed by Lord Wedderburn in 1957[12]. Professor Gower put forward the more orthodox view that s 14 gives the articles contractual effect only in so far as they confer rights or obligations on the member in his or her capacity as member but acknowledged the force of Wedderburn's argument[13]. Mr Goldberg tacked a middle course[14]. An outsider right can only be enforced if this is incidental to the enforcement of the member's contractual right under s 14(1) to have the company's affairs conducted by the particular organ of the company specified in the Act or the memorandum or articles. A refinement of this was put forward by Mr G N Prentice[15]. He argues that:

(1) it is misleading solely to ask whether a member sues qua member or qua outsider;

(2) it is not enough to shift the emphasis on to the organ of the company concerned;

(3) it is necessary to go one stage further and ask whether the provision in question affects the power of the company to function in the circumstances in question and it is only where there is some

11 See *London Sack and Bag Co Ltd v Dixon and Lugton Ltd* [1943] 2 All ER 763, CA; *Eltham Co-operative Dairy Factory Co Ltd v Johnson* [1931] NZLR 216; *Black, White and Grey Cabs Ltd v Gaskin* [1971] NZLR 552 and *Ryans Cartage Services Ltd v Connor* (1981–3) 1 NZCLC 95–071.
12 [1957] CLJ 193.
13 Gower *Modern Company Law* (4th edn, 1979) p 317.
14 (1972) 35 MLR 362. See too (1985) 48 MLR 158.
15 (1980) 1 Co Law 179.

interference with the power of the company to function that a member will have a remedy.

Robust support for Wedderburn is provided by R Gregory who argues that there is more basis in the authorities for the thesis than had been thought. The cases on which he relies mainly involve directors[16] and it must be admitted that it seems rather absurd to regard directors as outsiders since they stand in a fiduciary relationship to the company which in part is defined by the articles. To sum up, a member qua member has rights which are either (1) personal rights covering the incidents of his shares or (2) constitutional rights to have the company function properly in accordance with the basic statutory scheme. Any other rights are not within s 14(1) and must be the subject of an extrinsic contract. The position of directors is, however, somewhat problematic. In some cases they have been allowed to sue on the articles[16]. In other cases such as *Swabey v Port Darwin Gold Mining Co* the courts have readily implied an extrinsic contract. In other cases they have been denied redress[17]. The position is most unsatisfactory particularly since directors are clearly bound by the articles qua directors and it seems odd to say that they have obligations but not rights under the articles[18].

(7) A clause providing for exclusion, if in the original articles, will be regarded as falling within the contract and the rules of natural justice will not necessarily be implied. In *Gaiman v National Association for Mental Health*[19] Megarry J recognised that there can be such a power which need not conform with the principles of natural justice. It is also possible to provide in the articles expressly that the rules of natural justice shall not apply[20]. However, it is one thing to adopt such a provision on incorporation and another to attempt to alter the articles to adopt such a provision. In the latter case it may be rejected by the courts as not being for the good of the company[1]. Also it may be that where the company is an entity such as a football club or association and seeks to operate the provision to deprive a person of his livelihood, the courts will import a requirement of natural justice[2].

ALTERATION OF ARTICLES

Under s 9, subject to the provisions of the Act and to the conditions contained in its articles, a company may by special resolution alter its

---

16 (1982) 44 MLR 526 citing *Orton v Cleveland Fire Brick and Pottery Co* (1865) 3 H & C 868; *Pulbrook v Richmond Consolidated Mining Co* (1878) 9 Ch D 610; *Imperial Hydropathic Hotel Co, Blackpool v Hampson* (1882) 23 Ch D 1, CA; *Hayes v Bristol Plant Hire Ltd* [1957] 1 All ER 685.

17 *Browne v La Trinidad* (1887) 37 Ch D 1 at 14–15, CA.

18 For yet another view—this time using relational contract analysis—see R R Drury [1986] CLJ 219.

19 [1971] Ch 317. Noted by Prentice (1970) 33 MLR 700. See also H H Mason (1975–6) 1 ABLR 226.

20 *Thorborn v All Nations Club* (1975) 1 ACLR 127. Cf *McNab v Auburn Soccer Sports Club Ltd* [1975] 1 NSWLR 54 at 59.

1 See p 128.

2 See *Enderby Town Football Club Ltd v Football Association Ltd* [1971] 1 All ER 215 at 219, CA.

articles. There are a number of rules and principles which have been introduced either by the Companies Acts or by the cases which regulate the exercise of this power. These were conveniently summarised in the judgment of Latham CJ in the Australian case of *Peter's American Delicacy Co Ltd v Heath* (1938–9) 61 CLR 457. We shall follow His Honour's basic analysis. The rules and principles are as follows:

(1)   A company cannot deprive itself of its statutory power to alter its articles either by agreement or by provision in its articles. Any provision to that effect is void[3]. It is, however, possible to put an entrenched provision in the memorandum of association and if this provides for class rights which are not to be alterable then the provision is immutable except by unanimous consent of all the members or a scheme of arrangement under s 425.
(2)   The contract constituted by the articles must be regarded as containing a provision that the articles may be altered by special resolution under s 9. Such an alteration may amount to a breach of an extrinsic contract but this does not invalidate the resolution[4].
(3)   Subject to compliance with class rights procedures and s 127, it is possible to alter members' rights in this way[5] and the fact that the alteration prejudices or diminishes the rights of some members is not per se a ground for attacking the validity of the alteration[6].
(4)   The power to alter must, however, be exercised bona fide for the benefit of the company as a whole[7]. This is a concept inherited by company law from partnership law where it is used as a curb on a majority exercising a power of expulsion[8]. Its nature was described but its scope not defined by Lindley MR in *Allen v Gold Reefs of West Africa Ltd*[9] where he said:

> Wide, however, as the language of Section 10 is, the power conferred by it must, like all other powers, be exercised subject to those general principles of law and equity which are applicable to all powers conferred on majorities and enabling them to bind minorities. It must be exercised, not only in the manner required by law, but also bona fide for the benefit of the company as a whole, and it must not be exceeded. These conditions are always implied, but are seldom, if ever, expressed.

Thus in *Allen's* case an article was altered in such a way as to prejudice one shareholder. The articles gave a lien on partly-paid shares for debts of members. Zuccani owed money in respect of unpaid calls on partly-paid shares but was the only holder of fully-paid shares. After his death insolvent, an alteration was made to give the company a lien on fully-paid shares as well. The court held that it was for the benefit of the company to recover moneys due to it and the alteration in its terms

---

3   *Malleson v National Insurance and Guarantee Corpn* [1894] 1 Ch 200; *Allen v Gold Reefs of West Africa Ltd* [1900] 1 Ch 656, CA.
4   *Allen's* case, supra, at 672.
5   *Allen's* case, supra; *Sidebottom v Kershaw, Leese & Co Ltd* [1920] 1 Ch 154, CA; *Shuttleworth v Cox Bros & Co (Maidenhead) Ltd* [1927] 2 KB 9, CA.
6   *Sidebottom's* case, supra; *Shuttleworth's* case, supra.
7   *Allen's* case, supra. See F Rixon (1986) 49 MLR 446 for a lucid analysis of the concept.
8   *Blisset v Daniel* (1853) 10 Hare 493.
9   Discussed in *Shuttleworth v Cox Bros & Co (Maidenhead) Ltd* [1927] 2 KB 9.

related to all holders of fully-paid shares. The fact that Zuccani was the only member of that class at that moment did not invalidate it.

In *Greenhalgh v Arderne Cinemas Ltd*[10] Evershed MR explained the test in the following way:

> I think it is now plain that 'bona fide for the benefit of the company as a whole' means not two things but one thing. It means that the shareholder must proceed upon what, in his honest opinion, is for the benefit of the company as a whole . . . the phrase, 'the company as a whole', does not (at any rate in such a case as the present) mean the company as a commercial entity, distinct from the corporators: it means the corporators as a general body. That is to say, the case may be taken of an individual hypothetical member and it may be asked whether what is proposed is, in the honest opinion of those who voted in its favour, for that person's benefit.

(5) It is not for the court to impose on a company its ideas as to what is for the benefit of the company. It is for the shareholders to determine whether the alteration is or is not for the benefit of the company subject to the proviso that the court will step in if the decision is such as no reasonable man could have reached. In other words, this is a prima facie general rule, not an absolute rule[11]. The courts will interfere if the alteration is 'so oppressive as to cast suspicion on the honesty of the persons responsible for it, or so extravagant that no reasonable man could really consider it for the benefit of the company'. The test is thus analogous to that which a court of appeal applies in quashing the verdict of a jury[12]. It is probably easier to approach it by phrasing it in the negative—the majority must not exercise their powers so that the result will not be for the good of the company, and to instance cases of the latter[13]. Evershed MR in *Greenhalgh v Arderne Cinemas Ltd* put the matter thus:

> I think that the matter can, in practice, be more accurately and precisely stated by looking at the converse and by saying that a special resolution of this kind would be liable to be impeached if the effect of it were to discriminate between majority shareholders and the minority shareholders, so as to give to the former an advantage of which the latter were deprived. When the cases are examined in which the resolution has been successfully attacked, it is on that ground.

On the other hand the court in that case took a narrow view of discrimination. The letter of the rights remained the same and the court did not consider the question of the enjoyment of the rights.

(6) The benefit of the company cannot be regarded as a criterion which is capable of solving all the problems in this branch of law. An alteration which is made bona fide and for the benefit of the company, if otherwise within the power, will be good. But it is not the case that it is necessary that the shareholders should always have the benefit of the company in view. In cases where the question which arises is simply a

---

10 [1951] Ch 286 at 291, CA.
11 *Carruth v ICI Ltd* [1937] AC 707, HL.
12 Per Bankes LJ in *Shuttleworth*'s case, supra, at 18.
13 Cf JL Austin *Sense and Sensibilia*. The concept of the benefit of the company as a whole is probably a 'trouser word' in that the negation of the concept 'wears the trousers' ie controls the definition.

question as to the relevant rights of different classes of shares, the problem cannot be solved in any event by regarding merely the benefit of the company[14]. The shareholders are not trustees for the company or for one another, nor are they to be regarded as partners[15]. A shareholder can vote in his own interests but the power to alter articles must not be exercised fraudulently or for the purpose of oppressing a minority[16].

(7) When the validity of a resolution altering the articles is challenged the onus of showing that the power has not been properly exercised is on the person complaining. The courts will not presume fraud or oppression or other abuse of power[17].

Let us now consider some of the cases in which these principles have been applied. In *Brown v British Abrasive Wheel Co*[18] the company had two distinct groups of shareholders. One group had a large majority and was prepared to inject more money into the company on condition that the articles were changed to get rid of the recalcitrant minority. The alteration was challenged by the minority and the court held that it was not for the good of the company. Similarly in *Dafen Tin Plate Co Ltd v Llanelly Steel Co (1907) Ltd*[19] a power to buy out a minority at fair value was held to be not for the good of the company. On the other hand in *Sidebottom v Kershaw, Leese & Co Ltd*[20] one of the shareholders was a competitor of the company and the others wanted to get rid of him. They consequently proposed an alteration of the articles providing for the compulsory purchase at a fair price of the shares of any members who competed with the business of the company. The Court of Appeal held that this was for the good of the company. Lord Sterndale MR held that the question whether the directors introduced the alteration for the benefit of the company was ultimately one of fact. Evidence of malicious motive and discrimination would negate the bona fides. Similarly, in *Shuttleworth v Cox Bros & Co (Maidenhead) Ltd*[1] the articles contained a provision for one person to be a permanent director of the company. He failed to account to the company for moneys belonging to the company and failed to resign when called upon to do so. The company passed a special resolution altering the articles providing for terminating of office by the permanent directors on a request in writing by all the other directors. The Court of Appeal held that this was for the good of the company.

It seems from these cases that an alteration of the articles which provides for expropriation will not generally be regarded as for the good of the company. However, the courts will be prepared to regard it as for the good of the company if there are some valid commercial reasons for the provision and the alteration provides for fair compensation.

14 *Pender v Lushington* (1877) 6 Ch D 70 at 75, 76; *Mills v Mills* (1938) 60 CLR 150. For a lucid analysis of the concept of the good of the company see F Rixon (1986) 49 MLR 446.
15 *Phillips v Manufacturers' Securities Ltd* (1917) 116 LT 290, CA.
16 *Cook v Deeks* [1916] 1 AC 554 at 564, PC; *Menier v Hooper's Telegraph Works* (1874) 9 Ch App 350; *Shuttleworth*'s case, supra, at 27; *Carruth v ICI Ltd* [1937] AC 707, HL.
17 *Peter's American Delicacy Co Ltd v Heath* (1938–9) 61 CLR 457 at 482. See P Xuereb (1985) 6 Co Law 199, 206 et seq; Rixon, op cit.
18 [1919] 1 Ch 290.
19 [1920] 2 Ch 124.
20 [1920] 1 Ch 154, CA.
 1 [1927] 2 KB 9, CA.

In *Greenhalgh v Arderne Cinemas Ltd*[2] the Court of Appeal upheld an alteration as being for the good of the company which discriminated in fact if not in law. The company had a nominal capital of £31,000 divided into 21,000 10 shilling preference shares and 205,000 2 shilling ordinary shares. The plaintiff held 4,213 ordinary shares. The articles contained a pre-emption clause. The majority shareholder agreed to sell ordinary shares to an outsider and a notice of meeting was sent out proposing the alteration of the articles by the addition of a clause authorising a sale to a transferee if sanctioned by an ordinary resolution. The court rejected the plaintiff's claim that it was not for the good of the company since it negated his enjoyment of his rights. *Greenhalgh* represents a harsh decision but one which nevertheless is consistent with the cases on variation of class rights as we shall see in Chapter 17. The court seems to concentrate on form and ignore substance.

Occasionally the courts have had resort to mainstream principles of the law of contract. Thus in the New Zealand case of *Invercargill Sports Depot Ltd v Patrick*[3] the adoption of a proposed article restricting competition was held to be invalid for reasons of restraint of trade. This seems to go beyond the concept of the good of the company and in some ways to be inconsistent with it. The company exists for an economic rationale which may be served by restrictions on trade. Activities which are in restraint of trade may be for the good of the company in an economic sense. On the other hand there is no reason why parties should be in any preferential position under the general law of contract merely because they have assumed the corporate form for their particular arrangements.

The sixth principle laid down by Latham CJ in the *Peters Delicacy* case must now be regarded as subject to a possible qualification. His Honour said that shareholders are not trustees for the company or one another. In New Zealand it was held as long ago as 1879 in *Stanford v Gillies*[4] that where a shareholder entered into a secret agreement with an intending purchaser of the company's property to be paid a sum of money to use his influence with the other shareholders to promote the sale at a certain price, the agreement was founded on an illegal consideration, and fraudulent, and the shareholder was a trustee for the company in respect of the money received. In this case the shareholder was active in getting shareholder approval in general meeting and was in league with another shareholder who was also a director. Although they were two of the largest shareholders they only held 91 out of a total of 300 shares. The court largely based its decision on cases involving co-owners and *Menier v Hooper's Telegraph Works*[5] but it can also perhaps be explained in terms of constructive trust. The shareholder was knowingly a party to the director's breach of duty. In the U S A, the courts have developed a doctrine of fiduciary obligations on controlling shareholders to the other shareholders[6] in certain circumstances and in the recent cases of *Clemens v Clemens Bros Ltd*[7]

2 [1951] Ch 286, CA.
3 [1939] NZLR 161.
4 (1880) OB & F (SC) 91.
5 (1874) 9 Ch App 350.
6 See eg *Jones v Ahmanson* 81 Cal Rptr 592 (1970).
7 [1976] 2 All ER 268. Noted by D Prentice (1976) 92 LQR 502; and see G R Sullivan (1978) 41 MLR 169. See also L S Sealy 'Equitable and Other Fetters on the Shareholder's Freedom to Vote', *The Cambridge Lectures 1981* (1981) ed Eastham & Krivy, p 80 ff, especially pp 84–85. See also the unreported case of *Pennell v Venida Investments Ltd* in 1974 discussed by S Burridge (1981) 44 MLR 40.

and *Estmanco* (*Kilner House*) *Ltd v Greater London Council*[8] there is perhaps some limited support for that doctrine. The facts of *Clemens* were that the plaintiff held 45% and her aunt 55% of the shares in the defendant company. Thus she had negative control in the sense that she could block a special resolution which required a three-quarters majority. There was a pre-emption provision in the articles under which the plaintiff would in the normal course get complete control of the company on her aunt's death. The aunt and four non-shareholders were the directors. The directors proposed a capital increase which would result in the non-shareholder directors getting shares and the balance going to a trust for employees. The requisite ordinary resolutions were duly passed. The effect of this was to dilute the plaintiff's holdings and to remove her present negative and future actual control. The plaintiff challenged the resolutions on the ground of oppression. The case did not involve an actual alteration of the articles but an effective de facto negation of the plaintiff's rights. It raised the question of the aunt's duties as director and majority shareholder. At the end of the day, Foster J thought it unwise to try to formulate a principle 'since the circumstances of each case are infinitely varied'. He was prepared to say, however, that the aunt was not 'entitled as of right to exercise her votes as an ordinary shareholder in any way she pleases'. The right was subject to equitable considerations which might make it unjust to exercise it in a particular way. He cited Evershed MR in *Greenhalgh v Arderne Cinemas Ltd* and equated the niece with the hypothetical shareholder for whose benefit the power must be exercised. This seems an improper use of Evershed MR's rather impractical test. In the *Estmanco* case the GLC owned a block of flats which it decided to sell on long leases. A management company was formed and one share was to be allocated to each flat. The shares were to have voting rights when all the flats had been sold but until then all voting rights vested in the GLC. After 12 flats had been sold, the GLC decided to let the remainder to council tenants. The company issued a writ to prevent this. The GLC in an extraordinary general meeting used its votes to obtain a resolution instructing the directors to withdraw the action. A minority shareholder brought an action and Megarry VC allowed the action to proceed. The case, like *Stanford v Gillies* and *Clemens*, is not an alteration of articles case but Megarry VC said some interesting things about the alteration of articles cases and their relevance to a minority shareholder's action. He held that:

Although a majority shareholder, unlike a director, owed no fiduciary duty to the company and was entitled to vote in his own interest, that did not give him an unrestricted right to pass a resolution depriving a minority shareholder of its rights or property merely because the majority shareholder reasonably believed that his actions were in the best interests of the company.

He drew attention to the difficulty of wedding the alteration of articles cases to the fraud on the minority exceptions to the rule in *Foss v Harbottle*. The cases indeed are more consistent with the rule which equates the company with the majority than with the exceptions. He said at p 444 g–j:

Now the question is how far authorities such as these on the validity of making alterations in the articles fit in with the rule in *Foss v Harbottle* (1843) 2 Hare 461, 67 ER 189, and its exceptions; for counsel for the council accepted, as he had to, that

---

8 [1982] 1 All ER 437. See R Gregory (1982) 45 MLR 584.

the line of authority on altering the articles has not yet been applied to the rule in *Foss v Harbottle* and its exceptions. I do not think that counsel ever succeeded in answering that question satisfactorily. Plainly there must be some limit to the power of the majority to pass resolutions which they believe to be in the best interests of the company and yet remain immune from interference by the courts. It may be in the best interests of the company to deprive the minority of some of their rights or some of their property, yet I do not think that this gives the majority an unrestricted right to do this, however unjust it may be, and however much it may harm shareholders whose rights as a class differ from those of the majority. If a case falls within one of the exceptions from *Foss v Harbottle*, I cannot see why the right of the minority to sue under that exception should be taken away from them merely because the majority of the company reasonably believe it to be in the best interest of the company that this should be done. This is particularly so if the exception from the rule falls under the rubric of 'fraud on a minority'.

Clemens shows the difficulty of applying the good of the company test to a private company and the need to resort to some broader conception of fairness between shareholders. In the past this has generally been limited to classes of shares but in a two shareholder company it seems appropriate since the fact that there are two shareholders with different holdings give them a de facto position analogous to different classes. This was the approach adopted in *Re Hellenic and General Trust Ltd*[9] in relation to the concept of class for the purposes of the scheme of arrangement procedures in s 425. Equitable considerations enable one to transcend the legal form of the company on such occasions. As we shall see such considerations arise on a petition to wind up the company on the just and equitable ground under s 122(1)(g) of the Insolvency Act 1986. Indeed Foster J in the *Clemens* case relied on the leading case in that area, *Ebrahimi v Westbourne Galleries Ltd*[10]. *Ebrahimi* was not cited in *Estmanco* but the decision is consistent with it. What *Estmanco* reveals is the difficulty of fitting together the alteration of articles cases with the fraud on the minority exception to the rule in *Foss v Harbottle*. It seems to follow from this that an alteration may be validly effected but still capable of being regarded as fraud on the minority and the subject of a minority shareholder's action. *Stanford v Gillies, Clemens* and *Estmanco* do not, however, go as far as the American cases. There is not yet full recognition of fiduciary duties on controlling shareholders as such. Nevertheless the jurisprudence of fairness which is emerging from equitable principles of restraints on powers and the statutory remedies under s 459, CA 1985 and s 122(1)(g) of the Insolvency Act 1986 are leading courts in that direction. It will be easier for the courts to think in fiduciary terms in the case of a quasi partnership company than in the case of a listed public company. We look in more depth at the special problems of the latter in Chapter 34[11].

It is interesting to see that the latest draft of the Fifth EC Directive contains articles which prevent a shareholder from voting on an issue where there is a conflict of interest between the company and him personally (art 34) and for avoiding shareholder agreements which fetter a shareholder's vote (art 35). While these fall short of general fiduciary obligations on controlling share-holders, they will prevent many of the abuses in practice.

---

9 [1975] 3 All ER 382.
10 [1973] AC 360, HL.
11 See further J H Farrar, 'Duties of Controlling Shareholders' in *Contemporary Issues in Company Law* (1987) ed J H Farrar, pp 185–202.

Sometimes a proposed alteration of the articles involves class rights. Professor Gower has described class rights as rights relating to dividends, voting and surplus assets on a winding up[12]. In *Cumbrian Newspapers Group Ltd v Cumberland and Westmorland Herald Newspaper and Printing Co Ltd*[13] in 1986 Scott J defined rights or benefits contained in articles into three different categories. First, there are rights or benefits which are annexed to particular shares. He regarded as classic examples of these, dividend rights and rights to participate in surplus assets on a winding up. Secondly, there are rights or benefits conferred on individuals, not in the capacity of members or shareholders of the company, but for ulterior reasons, connected with the administration of the company's affairs or the conduct of its business. These are the outsider rights discussed above. Thirdly, there was an intermediate category of rights or benefits which, although not attached to any particular shares, are nevertheless conferred on the beneficiary in the capacity of member or shareholder of the company. His Lordship thought that the first and third categories were 'rights attached to a class of shares' for the purposes of s 125, CA 1985. It is usual for a company to have an express variation of rights clause. Where there is no such clause s 125 now sets out procedures to be complied with. The procedures must be followed by members of the class prior to the general meeting at which the special resolution is proposed. The question arises, must the variation of rights procedure be complied with before there can be a valid alteration of articles? On this, prior to the statutory reforms of 1980 now contained in s 125, there were two conflicting Australian decisions. In *Fischer v Easthaven Ltd*[14] the judge held that articles can be freely altered by special resolution in spite of a variation of rights clause. On the other hand in *Crumpton v Morrine Hall Pty Ltd*[15] the judge came to the opposite conclusion and was prepared to restrain the company from acting on an alteration which did not comply with the variation of rights clause. In an earlier English decision in *Lord St Davids v Union Castle Mail SS Co*[16] in 1934 which was never fully reported, Clauson J appears to have thought that the variation of rights clause must be complied with and in *Rights and Issues Investment Trust Ltd v Stylo Shoes Ltd*[17], Pennycuick J appeared to take the same view. Section 125 now seems to make that view the law in all cases in future. We shall examine this question in more detail in Chapter 17.

The effect of articles and alterations to articles on contracts[18]

There are three main possibilities. First, the articles may be the only form of legal relationship between a company and a member. Second, there may be an extrinsic contract between the company and a member which refers to the articles. Third, there may be an extrinsic contract between the company and an outsider which refers to the articles.

---

12 Op cit, pp 562–3.
13 [1986] 3 WLR 26 at 36–7. Noted by J Birds (1986) 7 Co Law 202; K Polack [1986] CLJ 399.
14 [1964] NSWR 261.
15 [1965] NSWR 240.
16 (1934) 78 Sol Jo 877; see also *Australian Fixed Trusts Pty v Clyde Industries Ltd* (1959) SR NSW 33.
17 [1965] Ch 250.
18 See generally M J Trebilcock [1967] 31 Conv (NS) 95 and L G S Trotman, 'Articles of Association and Contracts' in *Contemporary Issues in Company Law* (1987) ed J H Farrar.

WHERE THE ARTICLES ARE THE ONLY LEGAL RELATIONSHIP WITH A MEMBER

In this first case the articles are freely alterable under s 9, subject to the alteration being for the good of the company and complying with class rights procedures.

WHERE THE MEMBER HAS AN EXTRINSIC CONTRACT WITH THE COMPANY WHICH REFERS TO THE ARTICLES

In this case the case law is rather complex. In *Punt v Symons & Co Ltd*[19] Byrne J held that a company cannot by contract—even an extrinsic contract—exclude the power to alter its articles and no injunction would be granted to restrain it from effecting the alteration. In the House of Lords case of *Southern Foundries (1926) Ltd v Shirlaw*[20], which technically involved an outsider, there is some limited support for this proposition. The facts of the case were that a man was appointed managing director of the company under an express service agreement for ten years. There was a provision that he would cease to be managing director if he ceased to be a director. The company altered the articles to allow a principal shareholder to remove directors. The House of Lords held by a majority of three to two that the managing director was entitled to damages for wrongful dismissal. The House of Lords recognised that a company could always alter its articles and could not contract out of that power but it also recognised that to do so may make it liable to a claim for damages if the terms of the contract are such that the alteration amounts to a breach. Lord Porter said obiter that the courts will not grant an injunction to prevent the adoption of new articles. On the other hand there is earlier authority which is inconsistent with this. In *Baily v British Equitable Assurance Co*[1] the Court of Appeal held that a company cannot by altering its articles alter an extrinsic contract and could be restrained by declaration from adopting articles which infringed the profit-sharing rights of its policy holders. That decision was reversed by the House of Lords on a point of construction on the basis that the terms of the articles were incorporated into the contract in question and consequently the statutory power to alter them. The Court of Appeal's decision was, however, followed in *British Murac Syndicate Ltd v Alperton Rubber Co Ltd*[2] by Sargeant J, who mistakenly thought that *Punt v Symons* had been over-ruled by *Baily's* case. He therefore granted an injunction. In the recent case of *Cumbrian Newspapers Group Ltd v Cumberland & Westmorland Herald Newspaper & Printing Co Ltd* Scott J said obiter that if a company had agreed that its articles would not be altered he could see no reason why it should not 'in a suitable case' be injuncted from initiating the calling of a general meeting with a view to the alteration of the articles. However, he thought that this should not be granted to prevent a company from discharging its statutory obligations to call a general meeting on a members' requisition, for example under s 368, CA 1985. As His Lordship's reasoning is

19 [1903] 2 Ch 506.
20 [1940] AC 701, HL. See too *Cumbrian Newspapers Group Ltd v Cumberland and Westmorland Herald Newspaper and Printing Co Ltd* [1986] 3 WLR 26 at 43–44 where Scott J obiter agreed with Lord Porter's obiter dicta. Cf *Carrier Australasia Ltd v Hunt* (1939) 61 CLR 534 (High Court of Australia).
 1 [1904] 1 Ch 374, CA.
 2 [1915] 2 Ch 186.

premised on the right to alter being a right of the members, not the company, this seems logical. However, his initial premise seems questionable. It is not a right of the members. It is a corporate power exercisable by the appropriate majority of the members.

A distinction can perhaps be drawn between granting an injunction to stop a company from altering its articles and granting an injunction to stop a company from acting in breach of contract under an altered article[3]. Whereas it is possible to argue that no injunction will be granted to stop a company from altering its articles, an injunction may possibly still lie to prevent a company acting in breach of contract. However, against this can be argued that to grant an injunction to stop a company from acting in accordance with the altered article so far negates the exercise of the power to alter the articles that it almost negates the power itself. To this argument perhaps there is a rejoinder to the effect that this does not stop the company acting on the article in respect of persons other than the other party to this particular contract.

A residual question is whether the shareholders inter se can contract against the alteration of the company's articles, e g unless there is unanimous consent. There is no authority directly in point but the courts have allowed weighted voting rights and it has been argued[4] that such an agreement is analogous to a weighted voting provision on the basis that it does not purport to deprive a company of its statutory power. Rather it purports to contrive majorities for or against a resolution when the statutory power is being exercised.

WHERE THE COMPANY HAS AN EXTRINSIC CONTRACT WITH AN OUTSIDER WHICH REFERS TO THE ARTICLES

An extrinsic contract between the company and an outsider is governed by normal contract principles. Complications arise when the contract in some way is affected by the articles or incorporates them.

We have seen that the articles per se cannot give rise to a contract with an outsider[5] but may be evidence of an implied contract[6]. If the articles are a term of the contract the matter is largely one of construction. If the article was incorporated qua article the court may say that the original contract has impliedly incorporated the statutory power to alter it[7] but an alteration cannot be made retrospectively. The effect of this is that the company has a unilateral power of variation of the contract or at least that term of the contract[8]. The position is rather analogous to members of a club. One joins the club subject to the rules for the time being.

In *Read v Astoria Garage (Streatham) Ltd*[9] a managing director was appointed under the articles but without any extrinsic service agreement. Article 68 of Table A, which applied, enabled the company to dismiss him without notice by resolution in general meeting. It was held by the Court of Appeal that a term as to reasonable notice was not to be implied. A different

3 Cf M J Trebilcock [1967] 31 Conv (NS) 95 at 114.
4 P Finn [1978] ABLR 97 at 102.
5 *Hickman v Kent or Romney Marsh Sheep-Breeders' Association* [1915] 1 Ch 881.
6 *Re New British Iron Co, ex p Beckwith* [1898] 1 Ch 324.
7 See *Swabey v Port Darwin Gold Mining Co* (1889) 1 Meg 385, CA.
8 See *Malleson v National Insurance and Guarantee Corpn* [1894] 1 Ch 200.
9 [1952] Ch 637, CA. Noted by L C B Gower (1953) 16 MLR 82.

construction, however, was reached in *Shindler v Northern Raincoat Co Ltd*[10] where there was an extrinsic service agreement which expressly provided for a term of ten years. Diplock J held that there was an implied term that the company would not do anything of its own motion to put an end to that state of affairs. This latter view is consistent with *Nelson v James Nelson & Sons Ltd*[11] and reconcilable with *Southern Foundries (1926) Ltd v Shirlaw* (supra). It was held by the Court of Appeal in *Nelson v James Nelson & Sons Ltd* that where the company had entered into a service agreement with a managing director for a fixed term the company could not rely on an article which enabled them to revoke such appointment at will or otherwise than in accordance with the agreement. It is to be noted that here the article in question was already there. There was no question of alteration. What the court was holding was that the company relying on one provision in the articles to enter into a commitment could not later renege relying on another provision. Nevertheless, neither *Shindler* nor *Nelson* were cases of alteration of articles and the company cannot exclude its statutory power to alter its articles by special resolution although as we have seen a particular alteration may give rise to an action for damages for breach of contract by the outsider. The principles are the same as those we have discussed above in relation to an extrinsic contract with a member.

CONCLUSION

This rather summary discussion of the cases indicates that it is important to distinguish between the statutory 'contract' on the one hand and all other contracts on the other. The statutory contract is a special contract governed by the principles of company law. Other contracts are ordinary contracts governed by the law of contract. One should not perhaps let the fact that some of the terms of an ordinary contract are found in the articles confuse the issue. As far as possible the latter should be governed by the ordinary principles of the law of contract[12].

---

10 [1960] 2 All ER 239.
11 [1914] 2 KB 770, CA.
12 See Trotman, op cit, for a more detailed and convincing argument along these lines.

CHAPTER 12

Supplementing the statutory constitution

Since 1856, the Companies Acts have provided for a constitution in the form of memorandum and articles of association. The proprietors of a company sometimes wish to supplement these for a variety of reasons. Although they value the limitation of personal liability as regards the outside world they wish to agree among themselves how risk, profit and control shall ultimately be distributed. Let us first examine some of their reasons and then some of the methods of supplementation.

REASONS FOR SUPPLEMENTATION[1]

First, it may be felt in the case of an incorporated partnership or joint venture company that the statutory form provides an inadequate record of their understanding. Some additional agreement is necessary to deal with the composition of the board, removal of directors, the entitlement of members to office, the exercise of corporate powers to borrow, pay dividends or wind up and the right of a shareholder to be bought out given the absence of a ready market for shares in such companies.

Secondly, it may be necessary to supplement the statutory methods of resolution of disputes. The statutory model provides a simple model. Disputes are resolved by majority decision in general meetings, although certain matters require a three-quarters majority, such as a change of the constitution. A supplementary arrangement may provide for arbitration, rights of pre-emption or voluntary winding up in such circumstances.

Thirdly, in the past the rights of minority shareholders to bring an action for oppression have been severely curtailed by the rule in *Foss v Harbottle* and the limitations of the statutory remedy under s 459 of CA 1985. A supplementary agreement can expressly provide against oppression and breach of the agreement will carry all the normal contractual remedies, unlike the statutory deemed contract under s 14.

Fourthly, since the House of Lords decision in *Ebrahimi v Westbourne Galleries Ltd*[2] the courts are prepared to consider such arrangements in order to assess whether one or more of the proprietors are reneging on their equitable obligations. One written agreement may save hours of oral testimony and cross examination if litigation results.

One Swedish jurist attempted to categorise the basic types of supplementary arrangement as (1) those which concentrate control (2) those which

---

1 See P Finn [1978] ABLR 97, 102–4; B N Apple QC *Special Lectures on Law Society of Upper Canada 1968* (1968) pp 41–64. See also F Hodge O'Neal *Close Corporations* (3rd edn, 1988) vol 1, chapter 5; and C M Roose (1971) 15 Scandinavian Studies in Law 163 and B Gomard (1972) 16 Scandinavian Studies in Law 97.
2 [1973] AC 360, HL.

distribute control and (3) those which transfer control. However, not all such arrangements are necessarily concerned with control unless the term is used in the broadest possible sense. Dispute resolution, for instance, is not a matter of control except in the sense of social control[3].

METHODS OF SUPPLEMENTATION

There are four methods of supplementation which have found favour[4]— shareholders' agreements, voting trusts, irrevocable proxies and management agreements. We deal with each of these in turn although only shareholders' agreements are common in the United Kingdom.

1 Shareholders' agreements

Shareholders' agreements are usually one of three kinds:

(a)   an agreement between the company and the members collateral and supplementary to the articles;
(b)   an agreement between all the shareholders inter se;
(c)   an agreement between some of the shareholders.

(A) AGREEMENT BETWEEN THE COMPANY AND THE MEMBERS

Here the position was described with characteristic lucidity by Salmond J in the New Zealand case of *Shalfoon v Cheddar Valley Co-operative Dairy Co Ltd*[5] in 1924 where he said:

There are two distinct ways in which an obligation may come into existence as between a company and one of its shareholders. In the first place, it may have its source in a regulation validly made by the company and inserted in the articles of association . . . In the second place, it may have its source in a contract made between the company and the individual shareholder. This distinction is of practical importance for several reasons. In the first place, an obligation imposed by a regulation is not merely personal, but is appurtenant to the shares of the company so as to run with those shares in the hands of successive owners and to bind all shareholders for the time being; but a contractual obligation is purely personal and binds only the individual shareholder who has become a party to the contract, and cannot be made to run with the shares as appurtenant thereto in the hands of successive owners. In the second place, a regulation can always be altered or repealed by the company, and the rights and obligations created thereby may be thus modified or destroyed; whereas a contract between the company and a shareholder can only be altered or cancelled by the mutual consent of both parties. In the third place, a regulation to be valid must be within the scope of the legislative authority given by the Companies Act to a company over its shareholders; whereas a contract made between a company and a shareholder is subject merely to the general provisions of the law of contract, a company being entitled to make any contract with a shareholder which it might lawfully make with an outsider. A shareholder may therefore take upon himself by contract with the company many obligations which

---

3 Roose, op cit, p 166.
4 *O'Neal*, op cit; M Pickering (1965) 81 LQR 248; NCSC Commentary, 'Regulation on the Use of Proxies, Voting Trusts and Arrangements' in the *NCSC* (Australia) *Manual:* Release 404; P Xuereb (1987) 8 Co Law 16.
5 [1924] NZLR 561.

could not be imposed upon him by the company by the making of regulations.

The existence and importance of this distinction between a contract and a regula-tion are not affected by the circumstances that the regulations of a company have themselves the effect of a contract between the company and the shareholders by virtue of section [14].

Thus an agreement between the company and its member can range wider than the articles and cover outsider rights but this remains personal to the particular members and only binds their transferees if there is a novation. A collateral agreement between the company and *all* its members is perfectly legitimate. However, in the USA recently some large companies are enter-ing into what are called 'standstill agreements' with major shareholders. Such agreements are long-term contracts in which the contracting sharehol-der generally agrees that it will not buy or sell any of the company's stock without management's written approval and will vote as they direct on certain issues. In exchange the contracting shareholder gets its nominee on the board of directors and may be given other rights. Insofar as standstill agreements involve a sale of the contracting shareholder's votes they are illegal and void under US laws as contrary to public policy. We examine the latter question in (b) below. The risk of such agreements—even informal agreements—is that they may effectively disenfranchise other shareholders.

(B) AGREEMENT BETWEEN ALL THE SHAREHOLDERS INTER SE[6]

Such agreements are often used to supplement the articles and usually relate to participation in management, the right to be bought out and the circum-stances in which the company will be put into voluntary liquidation.

While there is nothing improper in all the shareholders agreeing to vote in a particular way at general meeting such agreements are of doubtful efficacy if they:

  (i)   provide for a pecuniary benefit to a particular shareholder for voting in a particular way;
 (ii)   purport to bind members qua directors as to how they should vote as directors;
(iii)   purport to fetter the company's power to alter its articles.

In addition they may be held to be limited in terms of time to a reasonable time or the length of time the shares are held[7]. In the USA, in certain states, a maximum period has been stipulated[8]. Professor Finn has argued that type (i) is illegal either on the basis that they constitute a bribe or that they amount to a fraud on other shareholders[9] but that these bases do not seem to be rele-vant if the shareholders' agreement is an open one supported primarily or solely by mutual promises. The case he cites is *Elliott v Richardson*[10] in 1870 which was an agreement between two shareholders A and B in a company which was being wound up compulsorily that in consideration of A agreeing to use his influence to postpone a call about to be made and to support B's

---

6 P Finn [1978] ABLR 97; G Hornstein (1950) 59 Yale LJ 1040. However, see now the latest provisions of the Fifth Directive of the EC discussed in Chapter 3. These would avoid many such agreements.
7 *Greenhalgh v Mallard* [1943] 2 All ER 234, CA.
8 See O'Neal *Close Corporations* (3rd edn, 1988) vol 1, para 5–09.
9 Op cit, p 99.
10 (1870) LR 5 CP 744.

claim as a creditor of the company B would pay all calls on A's shares. It was held that the agreement was contrary to the policy of the winding-up provisions of the Companies Acts and void. Willes J also expressed the opinion that the agreement to support B's claim was void as being against the spirit of the law against maintenance. It is submitted, however, that while there is a well-established body of law against contracting out of the winding-up scheme and against fraud on creditors, the mere passing of a money consideration should not invalidate such an agreement in a situation where there is no winding up. It is established that a member's vote is an item of personal property and he is entitled to consider his own interests without regard to the interests of other shareholders[11] subject to a duty on the majority voting in a general meeting to consider the interests of the company as a whole. Where the consideration is part of a sale of the shares[12] or a mortgage advance on the security of the shares[13] the member has been obliged to honour his agreement. Also where instead of providing for a consideration for voting in a particular way the agreement provides a penalty for not voting in a particular way, it has been upheld[14].

On the other hand it has been held in New Zealand in *Stanford v Gillies*[15] that a shareholder who enters into a secret agreement with a purchaser of the company's assets to receive a bribe to promote the sale with the other shareholders is liable as a trustee for the company. In the particular case the shareholder was in league with another shareholder who was also a director. Together they were two of the largest shareholders holding 91 out of 300 shares. The four significant features of this case were the secrecy, the bribe, the active promotion of the sale in general meeting and the complicity in a breach of duty by the director. The shareholder was in effect a constructive trustee.

Article 35 of the latest draft of the Fifth Directive of the EEC avoids agreements whereby a shareholder undertakes to vote in one of the following ways:

(a)   always to follow the instructions of the company or one of its organs;
(b)   always to approve the proposals of the company or one of its organs;
(c)   to vote in a specified manner or abstain in consideration of special advantages.

Except in the case of puppet shareholders, (a) and (b) will be rare in practice. (c) is the most far reaching and covers the situation which we have discussed above. It arguably goes further than *Elliott v Richardson* in making such agreements void. It is questionable whether such a provision ought to apply where a voting arrangement is part of an agreement for sale of shares or a mortgage advance.

Type (ii) agreements (above) are proscribed on the basis of the fiduciary duties of a director[16]. Where a shareholders' agreement binds them in their

---

11 *Coronation Syndicate Ltd v Lilienfeld and New Fortuna Co Ltd* 1903 TS 489 at 497.
12 *Greenwell v Porter* [1902] 1 Ch 530; *Thorby v Goldberg* (1964) 112 CLR 597.
13 *Puddephatt v Leith* [1916] 1 Ch 200. See S Krüger (1978) 94 LQR 557, (1981) 10 Anglo American LR 73 for a comparison with US law.
14 *Ringuet v Bergeron* (1960) 24 DLR (2d) 449 (Supreme Court of Canada). The penalty here was a transfer of the shares of the defaulting shareholder.
15 (1880) OB & F (SC) 91.
16 Finn, op cit, p 100; Delaney (1950) 50 Col LR 52.

capacity as a director, it is invalid as constituting a fettering of their discretion although valid portions of the agreement may be severed and remain in force[17]. For this reason an agreement requiring unanimity by the directors in every decision is void[18]. On the other hand, if, when a contract is negotiated on behalf of a company the directors bona fide think it in the interests of the company as a whole that the transaction should be entered into, they may bind themselves by the contract to do whatever is necessary to effectuate it[19]. The limits of this latter doctrine are hard to define although it appears to have been adopted in Australia[19] and England. In the unreported English case of *Pennell v Venida Investments Ltd*[20] in 1974, Templeman J appears to have accepted that an oral shareholders' agreement existed to perpetuate an existing status quo with regard to the ratio of shareholdings within a 'quasi-partnership' company and this could not be unilaterally altered by the majority shareholder and its nominee directors. This goes further than the Australian authority.

Type (iii) has given rise to more case law which we have already considered in the previous chapter. Basically, a company cannot contract out of its power to alter its articles although to act on the alteration may amount to a breach of contract.

A residual question is whether the shareholders inter se can contract against the alteration of the company's articles e g unless there is unanimous consent. There is no authority directly in point but the courts have allowed weighted voting rights and it has been argued[1] that such an agreement is analogous to a weighted voting provision on the basis that it does not purport to deprive a company of its statutory power. Rather it purports to contrive majorities for or against a resolution when the statutory power is being exercised.

(c) AGREEMENT BETWEEN SOME OF THE SHAREHOLDERS[2]

The principles are the same as in (b) above but the exercise of the contractual provisions can work oppressively on members who are not parties to the contract and may for that reason give rise to minority shareholder remedies[3] although the wronged shareholder will face problems of proof.

2 Voting trusts

A voting trust involves the voting rights of all or some of the shares in a company being settled upon trust[4]. The shares are usually transferred as there is doubt as to whether votes can be separated from ownership of the shares. Such a trust can be a very flexible instrument of control. The trustees may be given a free hand or a very limited discretion. 'In effect a voting trust confers a joint irrevocable proxy with general or restricted powers[5]'. It is,

---

17 *Motherwell v Schoof* [1949] 4 DLR 812.
18 *Atlas Development Co Ltd v Calof and Gold* (1963) 41 WWR 575.
19 *Thorby v Goldberg* (1964) 112 CLR 597.
20 (25 July 1974, unreported). See the valuable article by Susan Burridge (1981) 44 MLR 40.
 1 Finn, op cit, p 102.
 2 Finn, op cit.
 3 See Chapter 27, infra.
 4 M Pickering (1965) 81 LQR 248 at 257; *O'Neal*, op cit, para 5.31.
 5 Pickering, ibid.

however, a more formal device than a shareholders' agreement since the trustees get title to the shares. This can sometimes have disadvantages for the original shareholder who may lose his membership rights and not be able to control the trustees.

Voting trusts are much more common in the USA than in the UK although it was formerly common here to settle shares on trustees as part of a settlement. Voting trusts are still used where there is need to maintain a particular tradition or viewpoint e g in a newspaper. The use of voting trusts has been restricted by specific state legislation in the USA where trust has an 'antitrust' connotation in the sense that they were used to further monopolies and restrictive trade practices.

3 Irrevocable proxies

A proxy is an authority to exercise voting rights given by a member to another person to act on his behalf. Unlike the voting trust a proxy does not have the title to the shares vested in him.

In order to be irrevocable the grant of the proxy must be coupled with an interest and to secure the interest. 'Interest' is a rather vague concept which Bentham said was a primitive term with no known genus and it may be sufficient if the proxy is given for valuable consideration[6]. If the latter is the case then it can be regarded as a species of voting agreement.

It is uncertain whether a proxy can be compelled to attend company meetings and vote as directed[7]. In *Second Consolidated Trust Ltd v Ceylon Amalgamated Tea and Rubber Estates Ltd*[8] it was held by Uthwatt J that a chairman at a meeting holding proxies was under an obligation to use them to demand a poll to ensure that the real sense of a meeting was given effect. In *Oliver v Dalgleish*[9] Buckley J said obiter that the principal might be in a position to complain if the proxy did not perform the duty.

It is common for companies to send out proxy forms in favour of the board but the Admission of Securities for Listing of The Stock Exchange direct the despatch of two-way proxy forms for companies whose shares are listed on a Stock Exchange. These enable the shareholder to mandate the proxy to vote for or against a resolution.

4 Management agreements[10]

It is possible for a company itself to delegate the whole or part of its management to a member or an outsider under an express agreement. This is common in relation to investment trusts and companies carrying on business abroad[11]. Another similar mechanism is the appointment of a governing director where the general authority to manage the company's

---

6 See Pickering, op cit, p 262; *O'Neal* op cit, para 5.36. See also R Powell *The Law of Agency* (2nd edn, 1961) p 392 but cf *Bowstead on Agency* (15th edn, 1985) art 135.
7 Pickering, op cit, p 263.
8 [1943] 2 All ER 567.
9 [1963] 3 All ER 330.
10 Pickering, op cit, pp 267–268; *O'Neal*, op cit, para 5.39.
11 Such an agreement was regarded as valid in *Investment Trust Corpn Ltd v Singapore Traction Co Ltd* [1935] Ch 615 at 626 where the Court of Appeal held that it was not ultra vires the company to enter into a proposed agreement to terminate the management contract.

affairs is vested in one man. This gives rise to problems of definition of the responsibilities of the other members of the board. Both mechanisms are to be distinguished from a delegation of *part* of their functions by the board of directors to a committee or individual where final power is left with the board.

In the USA management contracts have sometimes been impugned on the basis of violation of a statutory provision whereby management is vested in the board of directors or the board not having authority to bind the corporation to a long-term contract on such matters. The validity of a management contract seems to depend to a large extent on the number and importance of the powers delegated and the length of time involved[12]. In the only English authority where such a contract was considered, *Investment Trust Corpn Ltd v Singapore Traction Co Ltd*[13], it was for so long as the company was entitled under a local law to operate the undertaking and was assumed by the Court of Appeal to be valid. The case, however, was concerned with whether a subtantial payment for termination was intra vires.

Other non-constitutional methods of control

In addition to these quasi-constitutional arrangements, it is possible for control to be exercised by:

(1)   a group structure
(2)   crossholding of shares[14]
(3)   circular holdings of shares.

We shall discuss the group relationship in Chapter 32. It exists where one company called the parent company is a member of and controls other companies which are called subsidiaries. Crossholdings normally involve two or more companies which hold a majority of each other's shares. If the directors are common to all the companies or have some agreement to act together their position is impregnable. This can be represented thus:

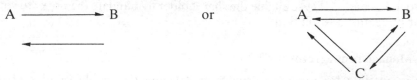

Circular holdings differ from crossholdings of the second type in that shares in one company are normally only held by one other company. This can be represented thus:

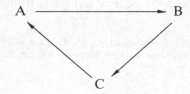

---

12 *O'Neal*, op cit, para 5.39.
13 [1935] Ch 615, CA.
14 See Pickering, op cit, pp 265–6 on which this is based.

THE LEGITIMACY OF SUPPLEMENTARY DEVICES

We have considered the question of the legal validity of particular methods. The ultimate policy question remains—should such variation of the statutory constitution be allowed?[15]

The main reasons why people attempt to do this are either that they are individual shareholders in a private company and desire to be shareholders to the outside world but partners among themselves[16] or that they are companies in a joint venture enterprise who wish to keep their arrangements secret. The first highlights a defect in the present law in the way it fails to cater for such businesses, a matter to which we shall return in Chapter 31. In the absence of such a provision, it is arguably justifiable to supplement the present statutory scheme in this way, provided outsiders do not suffer. The latter represents a legitimate business goal which the law should protect.

A final question remains: granted the legitimacy of the reasons for such supplementation, should the proprietors be allowed to use illegitimate devices to achieve their ends? The answer to this is clearly No. Bribery, fraud, distortion of the facts and evasion of statutory obligations to outsiders should not be countenanced. The ends do not justify the means.

---

15 Pickering, op cit, p 272 ff.
16 See Bradley 'Toward a More Perfect Close Corporation—Need for More and Improved Legislation' (1966) 54 Geo LJ 1145 at 1148.

PART III

Financial structure and membership

CHAPTER 13

The concept of capital and the financing of companies

THE ECONOMIC CONCEPT OF CAPITAL

There is probably no concept in economics which is quite so ambiguous and confusing as capital. According to the context the word may mean wealth, a factor or means of production, the value of those means of production, the net worth of a business enterprise, the present value of a future sequence of receipts, money, the money value of assets and possibly other things as well. Capital is thus thought of in physical terms, in value terms and in money terms[1], an ambiguity which has sometimes been carried over into law as we shall see in a later chapter.

The etymology of the word seems to be the Latin 'caput' meaning head or principal. In medieval Latin, there are constant references to *capitalis pars debiti*, that is, the principal sum as distinct from interest. Originally the term seems to be confined to loans of money. Later it took in other assets and acquired a wider meaning than loan. The word is then said by some to be an adjective used elliptically as a substantive[2]. The full phrase is said to be capital stock. Capital was used for capital stock at least as early as 1635[3]. Dyche and Pardon's *English Dictionary* in 1735 had an entry on Capital— 'Chief, head, or principal; it relates to several things, as the capital stock in trading companies it is the fund or quantity of money they are by their charter allowed to employ in trade'[4]. To understand this transition in usage one needs to examine the history. In the Guild system there was little need for capital stock[5]. The principal asset of the business was the skill and connection of the tradesman. The only capital he needed was to build or rent a house, purchase tools or stock and set himself up. These funds could usually be acquired by savings as a journeyman working for another established trader. By the sixteenth century, however, with the expansion of the money supply there is a growth of a distinctly capitalist class and with them the concept of capital as a fund of money. The removal of the prohibitions on usury facilitated this development. For a time such capitalists ran the risk of being held to be partners. The *commenda* never gained a strong foothold in English law because of the backwardness of English accounting methods. Nevertheless certain accounting developments took place. First, there was the idea of the value of a business as a going concern and not just as a chain of

---

1 See N S Buchanan *The Economics of Corporate Enterprise* (1940); A A Alchian and W R Allen *University Economics* (3rd edn, 1974) p 387.
2 Murray's *New English Dictionary* (1888–1928).
3 See Dafforne *Merchant's Mirrour* Ex No 96.
4 For a dated but nevertheless interesting discussion of the history of the concept of capital see R H I Palgrave *Dictionary of Political Economy* (1901–06) vol 1—Capital.
5 See C A Cooke *Corporation, Trust and Company* (1950) p 39 ff, on which this paragraph is based.

single instances. Secondly, there was the growth of double entry book-keeping which enabled a separation of the accounts of the business from those of the capitalists. The concept of the business as a separate accounting unit reached a more sophisticated stage of development in the joint stock company. The penultimate stage of the development was when the company was regarded as a separate legal person and the ultimate stage was when the liability of the members was limited and the fund of share capital was regarded at the end of the day as the company as far as creditors were concerned.

THE MODERN LEGAL CONCEPT OF CAPITAL

As Latham CJ said in the Australian case of *Incorporated Interest Pty Ltd v Federal Commission of Taxation* (1943) 67 CLR 508 at 515: 'It is impossible to say that "capital" has a single technical meaning which prima facie should be attributed to the word in any statutory provision'.

The legal concept of capital crops up in the law of trusts and revenue law as well as company law. In trust law it describes the original trust fund and any assets which replace the items in the original fund. A distinction is drawn between capital and income and problems arise with some borderline cases. On the whole the trust law concept of capital is a relatively simple one since the legal title to the fund vests in the trustees and the beneficiaries have reasonably well defined interests in the equitable ownership of the fund[6]. In revenue law, there is the same capital/income distinction. Here the distinction is resolved by reference to accounting principles and the authorities. The distinction was formerly crucial as most capital gains were not taxable at all. That is no longer the case but the distinction is still of some consequence as the taxation of the two is different.

Capital is used in modern company law to cover:

(1)   *share* capital—the funds subscribed by members;
(2)   *loan* capital—the fund provided by commercial finance providers and investors holding debentures or debenture stock;
(3)   all funds whether provided by members, creditors or by retention of profits; and
(4)   the assets in which all the funds have been invested.

The memorandum specifies the initial *authorised* share capital of the company. This is sometimes known as the *nominal* capital. The whole or part of this may be *paid-up*. Hence the terms fully-paid and partly-paid share capital. Thus we have the legal measure of the fund and the amount actually subscribed by investors. This money or other value transferred does not usually lie idle. It is invested in assets for the purposes of the company's business. This is sometimes called *real* capital from the Latin 'res' meaning 'a thing'.

In the Canadian case of *St Michael Uranium Mines Ltd v Rayrock Mines Ltd*[7] Le Bel, JA distinguished between the various meanings of capital in the following dictum:

---

6 R R Pennington *Company Law* (6th edn, 1990) chapter 6.
7 (1958) 15 DLR (2d) 609 (Ont CA).

I think . . . . it is right to say that there is confusion commonly existing regarding the meaning of the term capital in corporation financing. To the economist it usually signifies tangible instruments of production, that is, physical assets used in the creation of other goods or of services. The average man frequently thinks of 'money' as 'capital' and uses the terms synonymously, and bankers often use the word capital, in the sense of net worth. However, in business parlance the term ordinarily means the investment in an enterprise, which from the legal point of view, may be thought of as being represented by money or by money's worth consisting of property and valuable tangible assets the corpus of the corporate business. . . . And capital and share capital are not the same: *Re Ontario Express and Transportation Co* (1894) 21 OAR 646, CA.

Although share capital is represented by real capital the value of shares does not always correspond to that of the underlying net assets. The value of shares depends on the number of shares offered by sellers and sought by buyers at any particular time[8]. Where the shares represent control of a company which is a small incorporated firm, the shares will tend to reflect the net asset value of the business. A minority holding in such a company will not generally have as high a value[9]. For most articles of such companies, there will be a pre-emption clause enabling the other shareholders to buy at fair value to be certified by the auditor. In the case of companies whose shares are listed in a recognised stock exchange the value will be at or around the current list price although such quotations are sometimes unreliable[10]. There are a number of criteria used by investment analysts and accountants in valuing shares. These include capital cover, dividend yields and the price:earnings ratio. Capital cover is not the same as an assets valuation. It is a calculation based on the extent to which net assets are sufficient to repay share capital. It is merely a factor, not a conclusive factor, since the other criteria might compensate for inadequate capital cover. Dividend yield is calculated by reference to the price and is affected by government restraints on dividends. The price:earnings ratio puts the emphasis on profitability not dividend yield. The question of the value of the share capital is thus potentially a more complicated question than the question of the value of the underlying real capital used in the business.

We saw above that the original usage of the word 'capital' referred to a loan. Capital in modern company law is used to cover not only share capital provided by the proprietors but also the loan capital provided by creditors. Whereas the former represents a right in the company the latter represents a right *against* the company[11]. The debt may be unsecured or secured. If there is at least a written acknowledgement of the debt it is usually called a debenture[12]. The value of debentures will depend on a number of factors— security, the position of the company, the interest rate and the date of repayment. Debentures listed in the Stock Exchange stand at a figure below par. This represents the discount which the loan creditor takes for the company's use of his money. Thus the company pays or suffers the discount and has to pay interest on the par value of the loan capital.

The real capital into which both share and loan capital is invested is

---

8 *R R Pennington*, op cit, chapter 6. This contains a useful analysis of the fundamentals of valuation of shares. See too V Krishna (1987) 8 Co Law 66; (1987) 13 Can Bus LJ 132.
9 See, however, *Re Bird Precision Bellows Ltd* [1984] Ch 419; normally there is no such discount in valuation for purposes of s 459. See Chapter 27, post.
10 A V Adamson *The Valuation of Company Shares and Businesses* (5th edn, 1975) Law Book Co, Sydney, pp 138–140.
11 See L C B Gower *Modern Company Law* (4th edn, 1979) at p 399.
12 See Chapter 19, post.

divided by economists into *fixed* and *circulating* capital. The distinction which has been traced back as far as the Physiocrats[13] and was adopted by Smith, Mill and Marx, was said by Ricardo to be not 'essential', and one in which the line of demarcation cannot be accurately drawn[14]. In other words they are relative terms. Hayek in *The Pure Theory of Capital*[15] thought that such a simple dichotomy probably does more harm than good. Nevertheless the courts have adopted the distinction which seems to have passed into law as a result of Sir Horace Davey's argument in a leading case[16]. In *Ammonia Soda Co v Chamberlain*[17] in 1918, Swinfen Eady LJ said fixed capital was:

That which a company retains, in the shape of assets upon which the subscribed capital has been expended, and which assets either themselves produce income, independent of any further action by the company, or being retained by the company are made use of to produce income or gain profits.

Circulating capital was:

A portion of the subscribed capital of the company intended to be used by being temporarily parted with and circulated in business, in the form of money, goods or other assets, and which, or the proceeds of which, are intended to return to the company with an increment, and are intended to be used again and again, and to always return with some accretion. Thus the capital with which a trader buys goods circulates; he parts with it, and with the goods bought by it, intending to receive it back again with profit arising from the resale of the goods . . . It must not, however, be assumed that the division into which capital thus falls is permanent . . . The terms 'fixed' and 'circulating' are merely terms convenient for describing the purpose to which the capital is for the time being devoted when considering its position in respect to the profits available for dividend.

As we shall see in the next chapters, the usage in the Companies Acts and the cases is loose and it is often difficult to say in which sense the word capital is being used. This has led to confusion in the past although the reforms in the Companies Act 1980 (now contained in Pt VIII of the CA 1985) settle much of the earlier confusion in the law of company dividends.

SOURCES OF CAPITAL[18]

Share capital and loan capital such as debentures are usually sources of long-term capital for the company. Once started it will hopefully generate profits and these can be used in whole or in part as a source of internal finance.

For the smaller company[19] bank borrowing on a short- to medium-term

---

13 See J Gold (1945) 6 UTLJ 14 at 26.
14 D Ricardo *The Principles of Political Economy and Taxation* (1926) (Everyman edn) p 19n.
15 (1941) p 323.
16 See *Lee v Neuchatel Asphalte Co* (1889) 41 Ch D 1, 7, 13, CA.
17 [1918] 1 Ch 266, CA.
18 See generally J M Samuels and F M Wilkes *Management of Company Finance* (3rd edn, 1980) chapters 3, 4 and 11.
19 See J Bates *The Financing of Small Business* (2nd edn, 1971) chapters 7 and 8 and M Chesterman *Small Businesses* (2nd edn, 1982) chapter 4.

basis and trade credit are common methods of financing. The problems about bank borrowing are that banks generally require a fixed and floating charge and personal guarantees by directors, and the company to some extent can be subject to the vagaries of bank policy. Trade credit can also be an unreliable source since it can be affected by the pressures on suppliers from their creditors in turn.

To improve their cash flow position, an increasing number of companies factor their trade debts, which means that they receive payment in advance but at a discount from a credit factor who then collects the debts.

Hire purchase is a common method of buying goods on credit but the cost is expensive. An increasingly common method of obtaining the use of plant and machinery without the capital outlay is plant hire. The assets are simply hired rather than purchased and the cost of hire is a trading expense for tax purposes.

Financial prudence

In this book we shall concentrate on share and loan capital and look at each in turn in the following chapters, but first let us examine elementary canons of financial prudence. A high risk firm will have to pay a higher return on loan capital than a lower risk firm. This is usually called a risk premium and varies according to the lender's perception of the risk. Obviously payment of the premium does not eliminate the risk but on average the losses from default should be offset against the gains from the receipt of risk premiums. Loan capital servicing is a first charge on profits. Share capital represents a residual return although the entitlement to the residue will differ where there are different classes of shares. The interest of the shareholder is to receive an income return, capital appreciation and a surplus on a solvent winding up. Internal financing by retention of profits which is sometimes together with share capital referred to as equity finance is not free of cost. There is opportunity cost to the shareholders which may be reflected ultimately in a lower market price of the shares because shareholders have decided to liquidate their investment in the company[20].

Mainly for taxation reasons, loan capital tends to be a cheaper source of finance for a company than share capital. Also in the long term, equity shareholders will require a higher return than creditors since they are always at risk in the event of a decline in profits or insolvency[1]. Nevertheless according to traditional thinking the advantages of loan capital can only be carried up to a point. This is because of the concept of gearing. Gearing[2] (called leverage in the USA) means the relationship between fixed interest capital and capital with variable remuneration. The greater the proportion of the former, the higher the gearing. If gearing becomes too high, both types of investor will demand a higher return to compensate for the risk of insolvency. The levels of gearing beyond which it is imprudent to go differ according to time and the particular sector.

---

20 See J Freear *The Management of Business Finance* (1980) chapter 6.

1 Royal Commission on the Distribution of Income and Wealth Report No 2, *Income from Companies and its Distribution* (Cmnd 6172) p 73.

2 Royal Commission on the Distribution of Income and Wealth, Background paper No 1, *The Financing of Quoted Companies in the United Kingdom* p 13.

Another view is that put forward by Modigliani and Miller[3] in 1958, where they argued that what counts is the future earnings stream of the company, not how it is financed. The total market value of a company is independent of its capital structure since investors can through market operations eliminate differences in value. However their theory is predicated on certain assumptions such as there being no corporation taxes and perfect capital markets. When the institutional facts to the contrary are taken into account and allowance is made for transaction costs in arbitrage, we seem to be back to the traditional approach[4].

Apart from the question of gearing there is the additional point that for smaller businesses, long-term debt is unpopular because of the fear of loss of independence. Directors of unlisted companies generally prefer to finance their activities where possible out of retained earnings.

Sources and uses of funds 1986/7–1988/9

We set out an Income and Appropriation Account and Sources and Uses of Funds 1986–87 to 1988–89 which give details of the financing of (i) the top 2,000 companies, (ii) smaller companies, and (iii) all companies. From this it can be seen that the top 2,000 raised a larger proportion of finance from new issues compared with smaller companies but both relied on retained income and increased bank and short-term loans and creditors. Both increased their expenditure on fixed assets in this period.

The special problems of financing small firms

In recent years, five possible gaps in the financing of small firms have been identified—the equity gap, the loan gap, the short- to medium-term finance gap, the venture capital gap and the technological gap[5]. Both main political parties have accepted that there is a congeries of problems facing such firms. The Wilson Committee to Review the Functioning of Financial Institutions[6] in 1980 made a number of recommendations. In particular they favoured the establishment of a loan guarantee scheme on an experimental basis, the creation of an English Development Agency to parallel the existing Welsh and Scottish Agencies, and the encouragement of a new form of investment trust—small firm investment companies, the purchase of whose shares by individuals would attract tax relief. They also favoured the development of the Unlisted Securities Market. We discuss the small incorporated firm and the USM in Chapters 31 and 33. The tax position of close companies and tax relief for investment in small firms is discussed in Chapter 20. Useful details about sources of finance are set out in the Bank of England and City Communication booklet, *Money for Business*.

3 F Modigliani and M Miller (1958) 48 Am Econ Rev 261.
4 See R Posner and K Scott *Economics of Corporation Law and Securities Regulation* (1980) p 235 and the materials there cited.
5 *Freear*, op cit, p 371 ff.
6 Cmnd 7937, para 1408.

Accounts of industrial and commercial companies: Income and Appropriation Account, and Sources and Uses of Funds, 1986–87 to 1988–89

(i) Top 2,000 companies

£billion

	1986–87	Accounting year ending during: 1987–88	1988–89
Income and Appropriation Account			
Gross trading profit	47.1	58.8	71.3
Other revenue income	6.4	6.9	7.8
Less:			
Interest on bank and short-term loans	5.4	6.1	8.6
Gross income	48.1	59.6	70.5
Less:			
Depreciation and amounts written off	15.7	15.3	17.3
Interest on long-term loans	2.3	2.0	3.5
Profit before tax	30.1	42.3	51.5
Less:			
Taxation due	10.3	13.4	15.7
Dividends	9.6	11.4	14.4
Minority shareholders' interest	0.8	1.1	1.2
Retained income	9.4	16.4	20.3
Sources and Uses of Funds			
Gross income	48.1	59.6	70.5
Net receipts from issues	11.8	18.0	17.8
Increase in bank and short-term loans	1.8	0.5	8.7
Increase in creditors	7.0	14.0	16.0
Exchange differences and other capital receipts	0.6	–3.6	0.4
Total sources of funds	69.3	88.4	113.5
Payments out of income	20.8	24.9	28.3
Expenditure on fixed assets etc	33.9	50.8	59.3
Increase in current assets and investments	14.6	12.7	25.8
Total uses of funds	69.3	88.4	113.5

Table (continued)

Accounts of industrial and commercial companies; Income and Appropriation Account, and Sources and Uses of Funds

(ii) Smaller companies	Accounting year ending during:		£billion
	1986–87	1987–88	
Income and Appropriation Account			
Gross trading profit	11.4	14.2	
Other revenue income	1.2	1.0	
Less:			
Interest on bank and short-term loans	3.2	2.9	
Gross income	9.3	12.3	
Less:			
Depreciation and amounts written off	3.9	4.3	
Interest on long-term loans	0.2	0.2	
Profit before tax	5.2	7.9	
Less:			
Taxation due	2.2	3.0	
Dividends	0.8	1.1	
Minority shareholders' interest	—	—	
Retained income	2.2	3.7	
Sources and Uses of Funds			
Gross income	9.3	12.3	
Net receipts from issues	0.5	0.9	
Increase in bank and short-term loans	–0.3	2.0	
Increase in creditors	1.8	5.6	
Exchange differences and other capital receipts	0.5	0.5	
Total sources of funds	11.7	21.3	
Payments out of income	1.7	2.9	
Expenditure on fixed assets etc	5.1	8.1	
Increase in current assets and investments	5.0	10.2	
Total uses of funds	11.7	21.3	
Number of companies (000s)	329	336	

and Sources and Uses of Funds

(iii) *All companies*

£billion

	Accounting year ending during:	
	1986–87	*1987–88*
Income and Appropriation Account		
Gross trading profit	58.5	73.0
Other revenue income	7.6	7.9
Less:		
Interest on bank and short-term loans	8.6	9.0
Gross income	57.4	72.0
Less:		
Depreciation and amounts written off	19.6	19.6
Interest on long-term loans	2.5	2.2
Profit before tax	35.4	50.2
Less:		
Taxation due	12.4	16.4
Dividends	10.5	12.5
Minority shareholders' interest	0.9	1.1
Retained income	11.6	20.1
Sources and Uses of Funds		
Gross income	57.4	72.0
Net receipts from issues	12.3	18.9
Increase in bank and short-term loans	1.5	2.4
Increase in creditors	8.8	19.6
Exchange differences and other capital receipts	1.1	–3.1
Total sources of funds	81.0	109.7
Payments out of income	22.5	27.8
Expenditure on fixed assets etc	38.9	59.0
Increase in current assets and investments	19.6	22.9
Total uses of funds	81.0	109.7
Number of companies (000s)	331	338

Note: As the figures for smaller companies were not available the figures for all companies were not able to be compiled.
Source: *Companies in 1988–89.* Table E2.

CHAPTER 14

Raising share capital

Our concern in this Chapter is to consider the rules surrounding the raising of share capital by companies, in particular those regarding payment for shares, something which concerns shareholders and creditors alike. Here the rules are predominantly statutory, mainly as a result of the Companies Act 1980 which implemented the requirements of the Second EC Directive in this regard. We start, however, with some of the central concepts of share capital which need first to be understood before proceeding to look in detail at the rules governing payment for share capital and the doctrine of capital maintenance.

Nominal capital

Section 2(5)(a) requires that a company's memorandum of association state the amount of the share capital with which the company proposes to be registered and the division of the share capital into shares of a fixed amount. This is known as the nominal or authorised capital. A company may decide, for example, to have a share capital of £100 divided into 100 £1 shares, so the nominal or authorised share capital is £100 and each share has the nominal or par value of £1. The company may issue shares up to that amount, ie it may issue 100 shares, and if it wishes to go beyond that figure it may alter the limit set in the memorandum by an ordinary resolution under s 121, discussed in Chapter 16.

Minimum authorised capital of public companies

Private companies in the UK do not have to have a minimum capital although this is common in continental systems. We saw in Chapter 4, however, that public companies do have to have a minimum capital. Indeed it is a feature of many of the capital rules, as we shall see, that stricter requirements have been imposed on public companies.

The reason for the imposition of a minimum authorised capital was to implement art 6 of the Second Directive. It was felt that discrepancies between the various member states on this question would affect freedom of establishment and attract capital to countries with the most liberal regimes. It is arguable that underlying this idea of a minimum authorised share capital is the naive economic assumption that the capital in the sense of real capital will remain intact. This may well prove not to be the case since capital may be lost[1] through trading although the capital maintenance rules, which we

---

1 Note that where a public company has suffered a serious loss of capital, where its net assets are half or less of its called up share capital, then the directors have to call an extraordinary general meeting to consider what steps to take about the situation, CA 1985, s 142.

shall consider in this and the following Chapter, at least reduce the risk of real capital being depleted by, for example, improvident dividends or other methods of returning capital to shareholders.

Section 118(1) defines 'the authorised minimum' as £50,000 or such other sum as the Secretary of State may by order made by statutory instrument specify[2]. The figure chosen was stricter than the EC requirement of 25,000 European Units of Account (roughly £16,000). This was with a view to ensuring some greater measure of substance in public companies.

Under s 117(1), a company registered as a public company on its original incorporation cannot do business or exercise any of its borrowing powers unless the registrar of companies has certified that the minimum capital requirements have been complied with, or the company is re-registered as a private company. The registrar will only issue a certificate if he is satisfied that the nominal value of the company's allotted share capital is not less than the authorised minimum[3]. A statutory declaration in the prescribed form confirming this must be filed with the registrar.

If the company does commence trading without this certificate, then the company and any officer in default is liable to a fine[4] but the validity of any transaction entered into by the company is not affected[5]. If, however, a company enters into a transaction in contravention of this section (ie when it is without a certificate), and fails to comply with its obligations in that connection within 21 days of being called upon to do so, then the directors are jointly and severally liable to indemnify the other party in respect of any loss or damage suffered by him by reason of the company's failure to comply with these obligations[6]. It is unlikely that much use will be made of this provision, first, for few public companies are likely to attempt to trade without this certificate and, secondly, it would be difficult to establish that the loss or damage suffered was by reason of the company's failure to comply with these obligations.

Nominal or par value

As noted above, the amount of the nominal share capital will be divided into shares of fixed nominal or par value, a figure which will usually be set quite low, for example, £1, 50p or 25p. If the company's nominal share capital is £100 divided into 100 shares of £1 each, £1 is the nominal or par value of each share and each shareholder must pay £1 (at least) for each share allotted to him by the company. £1 at least, because the market value of that share may be £1.10 or £1.50 or any other price and the shareholder will have to pay whatever amount is the market price for the share. The only relevance of par value to the shareholder is that the company may not issue its shares for less than the par value, something which is discussed in greater detail below, hence the need to pay at least £1.

---

2 Despite the power to alter (meaning, for all practical purposes, to increase) the minimum figure, the DTI has not taken the opportunity to do so, and it remains as set in 1980.
3 CA 1985, s 117(2).
4 CA 1985, s 117(7). Note also that a public company which has not obtained a s 117 certificate and more than a year has expired since it was registered as a public company may be wound up by the court, Insolvency Act 1986, s 122(1)(b).
5 CA 1985, s 117(8).
6 Ibid.

The upper limit of the shareholder's liability to contribute to the company will be the price at which he has agreed to take the shares, so if the company issues £1 shares at £1.50 and the shareholder has agreed to purchase 10 shares, then he is liable to pay £15 to the company. The minimum he could have been required to pay is £10 and in fact the company is able to sell the shares at £15.

Companies used to have shares of a high par value but today lower par values are preferred as they are seen to increase the marketability of the shares and are preferred by investors. Many other jurisdictions have dispensed with the idea of par value and shares of no par value have long been allowed in the USA. The Gedge Committee in 1954 and the Jenkins Committee in 1962 recommended that no par value shares be permitted in the UK but no action was taken[7]. The objection to par value is that it is misleading to unsophisticated investors for it quickly ceases to have any relevance to the market value of the shares[8]. If a shareholder buys shares at £1.50 (nominal value £1) and subsequently sells for £1.90 or £1.30 then he has either made a profit or a loss, but in neither case is the par value of £1 relevant. No par value shares, on the other hand, can be issued for such consideration as the directors decide is in the best interests of the company. Shareholders would simply hold a number of shares, whose value would depend, as now, on the value of the company and the market's perception of that value, but without being confused by the historical figure of nominal value.

Issue at a premium

It is quite common for companies to issue shares at a premium, ie at more than par value, especially when capital is raised at a later stage after incorporation, although the initial subscribers may take at the nominal or par value. So a £1 share may subsequently be issued for £1.30, £1.50 or even £2. A premium can equally arise if the shares are issued for a non-cash consideration, ie for an asset worth £2. The point arose in *Henry Head & Co Ltd v Ropner Holdings Ltd*[9] where there was an amalgamation of two shipping companies through the formation of a new holding company. There was a one-for-one exchange of shares by the shareholders of the two companies for shares in the holding company. The assets of the companies were under-valued and were worth £5m more than the nominal value of the shares in the new holding company. The question was whether it was correct for the holding company to transfer £5m to a share premium account. The court found that it was, and this decision was followed by Walton J in *Shearer (Inspector of Taxes) v Bercain Ltd*[10], although its effects have been mitigated by ss 131–134, noted below.

There is no requirement for companies to issue shares at a premium[11]. It depends on the circumstances of each case whether it will be prudent or even

---

7 Cmnd 9112 and Cmnd 1749, respectively. An attempt to introduce such reforms in the Companies Act 1967 failed but no par shares have been legalised in a number of Canadian jurisdictions, see Welling *Corporate Law in Canada* (1984) pp 577–580.
8 Sealy *Cases and Materials in Company Law* (4th edn, 1989), p 334 makes the point that if shares were originally issued at a premium or in exchange for non-cash consideration, the shares may never have been worth their face value and after issue their market value will never again bear any resemblance to the historic figure once ascribed to it.
9 [1952] Ch 124, [1951] 2 All ER 994.
10 [1980] 3 All ER 295.
11 *Hilder v Dexter* [1902] AC 474, HL; *Lowry (Inspector of Taxes) v Consolidated African Selection Trust Ltd* [1940] AC 648, [1940] 2 All ER 545, HL.

possible to do so, and it is a question for the directors to decide[12]. A good example of forgoing some of the available premium is where the company makes a rights issue, discussed in detail below, to raise further capital from its shareholders and does so, as is normally the practice, at a price which is at a discount to the market price. It is in the interests of the company to make the price attractive to encourage people to buy further shares in the company. In some circumstances, however, directors may be in breach of their duties to the company in not obtaining the greatest financial return from the shares[13].

As regards what use may be made of the share premium, the old rule was that the company could distribute the premium as a dividend since it was not share capital. That rule was changed by statute, and CA 1985, s 130 now requires that share premium be treated in most respects as share capital. It is therefore subject to many of the constraints laid down on the use of such funds by the company.

Section 130(1) provides that when the company issues shares at a premium, whether for cash or otherwise, a sum equal to the aggregate amount or value of the premiums on those shares has to be transferred to an account called 'the share premium account' which can only be resorted to for limited purposes and is subject to the provisions on reduction of capital[14]. The limited purposes for which it can be used are:

(a)　paying up unissued shares to be allotted as fully paid bonus shares (discussed below);
(b)　writing off:
　　(i)　preliminary expenses;
　　(ii)　expenses or commission or discount in connection with an issue of shares or debentures of the company;
　　(iii)　providing for any premium payable by the company on the redemption of any debentures.

Exceptions to this requirement to transfer any premium to a share premium account are provided by ss 131–134 which set out certain circumstances in which either a share premium account is not required or only a limited amount need be transferred to such an account. This is in response to the decisions in *Henry Head & Co Ltd v Ropner Holdings Ltd*[15] and *Shearer (Inspector of Taxes) v Bercain Ltd*[16], noted above, and the net effect is to allow certain reconstructions and mergers to take place without a transfer to a share premium account so releasing certain assets which may be distributed as a dividend.

Prohibition on issue at discount

While a company can issue shares for a premium, it cannot issue shares at a discount, ie for less than the nominal value, a point established in the last

12 *Hilder v Dexter* [1902] AC 474 at 480, per Lord Davey.
13 Ibid, at 481, per Lord Davey, where the arrangement is improvident or an abuse or in excess of the powers of management committed to the directors.
14 CA 1985, s 130(2) and (3).
15 [1952] Ch 124, [1951] 2 All ER 994.
16 [1980] 3 All ER 295.

century[17]. In the leading case of *Oregum Gold Mining Co of India v Roper*[18] in 1892, a company purported to issue £1 preference shares credited with 15 shillings paid up, leaving only five shillings to be paid on allotment. The House of Lords held that there was no power under the Companies Acts to do this, that it was therefore ultra vires and the allottees were liable to pay the full amount on their shares. Lord Macnaghten made the point that in a limited liability company shareholders purchase immunity from liability beyond the amount due on their shares on the basis that they remain liable up to that limit. 'Nothing but payment and payment in full, can put an end to that liability'[19].

The basic rule is now contained in s 100 which prohibits the issue of shares at a discount by any company[20]. If shares are allotted in contravention of the provision, the allottee is liable to pay the company an amount equal to the amount of the discount, with interest at the appropriate rate[1].

A limited exception to the no discount rule is found in s 97 which permits companies to pay underwriting commissions, provided such payments are authorised by their articles and the amount involved does not exceed specified limits[2]. Underwriting involves the use of professional intermediaries by companies seeking to raise funds from the public by the issue of shares. These intermediaries, for example, merchant banks and institutional investors, undertake to subscribe or procure subscriptions for those shares in return for a fee. This fee could be prohibited as a discount on the shares if it were not for this explicit provision permitting such payments.

There is, however, one major loophole in the no discount rule, namely that while a company may not issue shares at less than the nominal value, it may accept as payment for those shares money or money's worth and where money's worth is received, the courts will not inquire into the adequacy of the consideration unless it is illusory or manifestly inadequate. In such circumstances, it is possible that the shares are issued at a discount. This is a topic to which we return below.

Issued, allotted and paid-up share capital

'Issued' and 'allotted' are often used interchangeably although the main provisions dealing with share capital, ss 99–116 of the 1985 Act, refer to allotment which is arguably more appropriate to a public offer or offer for sale where shares are allotted on letters of allotment than to private companies. Allotment for the purposes of the Act is defined by s 738 as meaning when a

17 *Ooregum Gold Mining Co of India v Roper* [1892] AC 125, HL; *Re Eddystone Marine Insurance Co* [1893] 3 Ch 9, CA; *Welton v Saffery* [1897] AC 299, HL. A rights issue is not at a discount for these purposes because it is at a discount to the market price, not the nominal value.
18 [1892] AC 125, HL.
19 [1892] AC 125 at 145. Equally, the company cannot thereafter increase the member's liability to contribute to the company's share capital, CA 1985, s 16.
20 The rule cannot be evaded by issuing convertible debentures at a discount which are capable of being immediately converted to ordinary shares, *Mosely v Koffyfontein Mines Ltd* [1904] 2 Ch 108, CA. See also *Re Eddystone Marine Insurance Co* [1893] 3 Ch 9, CA.
 1 CA 1985, s 100(1). Directors who allot shares at a discount are guilty of a breach of duty to the company and are liable to pay the amount of the discount and interest to the company if that amount cannot be recovered from the allottee or holder of the shares, as where the shares have passed into the hands of a bona fide purchaser for value from the original allottee, *Hirsche v Sims* [1894] AC 654, PC.
 2 See CA 1985, s 97 as amended by the Financial Services Act 1986, s 212(2), Sch 16, para 16.

person acquires the unconditional right to be included in the company's register of members in respect of the shares. Allotted or issued capital, as opposed to nominal, is the amount actually issued. So if a company has a nominal share capital of £100 divided into 100 £1 shares and 10 shares have been issued, the company has a nominal capital of £100, an issued capital of £10 and an unissued capital of £90.

Issued shares may be fully or partly paid-up. In the latter case the company can make calls on the shareholder up to the amount of the share price which has not been paid[3]. So if a share is a £1 share of which 50p is paid up, the company can later call up the balance of 50p. The practice used to be that only part of the price was paid on allotment, the remainder being paid later when called. This is less common today as most shares are issued fully paid. Public companies, in any event, must not allot a share except as paid up at least as to one quarter of its nominal value and the whole of any premium[4]. If this rule is contravened the allotment is still valid but the share allotted in contravention is to be treated as if one quarter of its nominal value together with any premium has been paid and the allottee must pay that amount less any consideration actually applied in payment[5].

The one notable recent exception, as far as the issue of fully paid up shares is concerned, has been the privatisation issues where, with a view to encouraging the greatest number of small shareholders, the shares were usually issued partly paid to enable individuals to spread their payments for the shares over a period of time. In all other cases, companies prefer to issue shares as fully paid which means that they obtain the capital which they wanted to raise and can avoid the administrative difficulties of making calls. For shareholders, the advantage is that they are not subject to any further liability to the company.

Bonus issue

A bonus issue[6] of shares occurs where the company capitalises profits or revenue reserves or some other permissible fund[7] and applies the proceeds in paying up bonus shares which normally go to existing members in proportion to their entitlement to dividend[8]. The process involves the use of the funds mentioned above to provide the shareholders with additional, fully paid (usually), shares in the company[9]. It is essentially an accounting exercise as the company's reserves are reduced but its share capital fund is increased. From the point of view of the shareholders, calling the issue a bonus is somewhat misleading because the company, and therefore their

---

3 A company may by special resolution resolve that it will not call up any uncalled capital except in the event of winding up, CA 1985, s 120. The creation of such reserve capital is most unusual now.
4 CA 1985, s 101(1).
5 Ibid, s 101(3) and (4).
6 Also known as capitalisation issues, or script issues.
7 The company may also use its share premium account or capital redemption reserve to finance a bonus issue. Note *Re Cleveland Trust plc* [1991] BCC 33 where a bonus issue was declared void on the ground of common mistake when the directors and shareholders were mistaken as to the availability of profits which could be capitalised.
8 See Table A, art 110.
9 As this appears to be a case of the company allotting shares without receiving money or money's worth, it would seem to fall foul of s 99(1) but, as we saw above, s 99(4) specifically provides that s 99(1) does not prevent the company from making a bonus issue.

shares in the company, is still worth the same as before the issue, so the total value of their shareholding has not altered[10]. All that has happened is that they hold more shares, but each is worth less than before. One advantage as far as the company and shareholders are concerned is that a bonus issue is not a distribution for the purposes of the rules[11] in Part VIII of the 1985 Act (which are discussed in Chapter 15), so funds which would not be available for distribution as dividends may be used for this purpose.

Rights issue

A rights issue, not to be confused with a bonus issue, occurs where the company offers a new issue of shares to its existing shareholders in proportion to their existing shareholdings. Such pre-emption rights, if taken up, enable the existing shareholders to retain their proportionate shareholdings in the company and prevents the dilution of their holdings which would occur if the company could by-pass its existing shareholders and offer shares directly to the public or other selected groups of investors. As such issues are usually offered at a discount to the market price[12], requiring the company to offer the shares to the existing shareholders also means that they get the benefit of that discount rather than outsiders.

In the continental European member states of the EC, companies are generally obliged to offer their shares to their existing shareholders before going outside. In the case of UK listed companies there was such a requirement under the Stock Exchange regulations in the case of equity capital, but it became a statutory requirement for all companies only in the Companies Act 1980, implementing art 29 of the Second EC Directive. The present provisions are now contained in ss 89–96 of CA 1985 which are considered below. The present Stock Exchange position has also altered somewhat and it too is outlined below.

THE GENERAL RULE

The general rule set out in s 89(1) is that a company proposing to allot equity securities[13] must not allot them to any person unless it has first made an offer to each person holding relevant shares[14] to allot to him[15], on the same or more favourable terms, a proportion of those securities which is as nearly as practicable equal to the proportion in nominal value of the shares held by him.

---

10 Of course, it is not strictly accurate to say that there is no difference in value before and after a bonus issue, for the market may respond favourably to a bonus issue so the shares may gain a little in value, but essentially the shareholder's position does not alter.
11 CA 1985, s 263(2)(a).
12 A rights issue, although at a discount to the market, does not infringe the no discount rule because it is not a discount on the nominal value.
13 Equity security is defined in s 94(2) as meaning a relevant share other than a subscriber share or bonus share and includes options and convertible securities.
14 Relevant shares is defined in s 94(5) as meaning any shares other than:
　(a)　shares which as respects dividend and capital carry a right to participate only up to a specified amount in a distribution, and
　(b)　shares held or to be held under an employees' share scheme.
15 If the shares are allotted by means of renounceable letters of allotment, a person in whose favour they are renounced may be allotted shares without any breach of s 89(1), s 89(4).

The effect of the definitions of equity and relevant shares in s 94 is that s 89(1) applies to any allotment by a company of shares which are not subscriber shares, bonus shares, shares which as respects dividends and capital carry a right to participate only up to a specified amount in a distribution, or employee shares. Any allotment outside of those categories must therefore be done on a pro rata basis in accordance with the statute.

This pro rata offer must be made to any existing shareholder holding relevant shares, ie shares other than those with a limited right to capital and dividend on a distribution and employee shares. It must be in writing[16] and must state a period of not less than 21 days during which it may be accepted, and the offer shall not be withdrawn before the end of that period.

EXCEPTIONS

It would seem therefore that practically all allotments must be on this pro rata basis. However, there are a large number of instances when s 89(1) does not apply.

It does not apply to:

(1)   an allotment of securities when they are allotted on a pre-emptive basis to a class of shares in pursuance of a class right to that effect[17]. In this instance s 89(1) imposing statutory pre-emption rights does not apply because there is an internal provision applying a pre-emptive right in any case. If the holder of those shares or anyone in whose favour he has renounced his right to their allotment accepts the shares, then s 89(1) has no application. If they are not so accepted then any subsequent offer of those shares has to be in accordance with s 89(1), ie on a pre-emptive basis to the rest of the shareholders rather than to the general public. So in these cases, the order of allotment is to the holder of the class of shares, then to the existing shareholders generally, and only then to the general public.

(2)   an allotment of equity securities if these are, or are to be, wholly or partly paid up otherwise than in cash[18], s 89(4). This obviously offers an easy method of avoiding pre-emption rights, since so long as any part of the consideration is paid otherwise than in case then s 89(1) does not apply.

(3)   an allotment of securities which would, apart from a renunciation or assignment of the right to their allotment, be held under an employees share scheme, s 89(5).

(4)   an allotment of securities by a *private* company if the company has expressly excluded it (s 91):

    (a)   by an express provision contained in the memorandum or articles; or

    (b)   by an inconsistent provision in the memorandum or articles which

---

16 CA 1985, s 90(2), unless the holder cannot be contacted when a notice in the Gazette will suffice, s 90(5).

17 CA 1985, ss 89(2) and (3). A class of shares is defined for these purposes in s 94(6) as shares to which the same rights are attached as to voting and as to participation, both as respects dividends and as respects capital, in a distribution.

18 See CA 1985, s 738.

is treated as excluding s 89(1). However, a class right of pre-emption is not to be regarded as an inconsistent provision excluding the general right, for as we have seen under 1 above, a class right does not exclude the general right when the holders of the class do not accept the shares offered to them.

(5)   an allotment of securities by *any* company, if it has been disapplied in accordance with s 95 which links the issue to the authority given to directors to allot shares under s 80 et seq. The section offers two permutations.

First, there is the situation where the directors have been given a general authority to allot under s 80: then s 95(1) provides that the company may by its articles or a special resolution provide that s 89(1) shall not apply or that it shall apply but with such modifications as the directors may determine.

So a general authority to allot (which may be granted for up to five years[19]) may be accompanied, whether by a provision in the articles or a special resolution, by a general disapplication of the pre-emption rights or their application as modified to the directors' wishes[20]. It is very common for this method of opting out of the statutory provisions to be adopted.

Secondly, there is the situation where the directors have either a general or specific authority to allot, and the company does not wish to opt for the general disapplication of s 89(1) as above: then s 95(2) provides that the company may by special resolution resolve that the pre-emption provisions shall not apply to a specified allotment of equity securities or that it should only apply in a modified form. So this is a more limited disapplication done on an individual basis with regard to a specified allotment.

A special resolution to this effect under s 95(2) must be recommended by the directors and they must circulate to the shareholders, with the notice of the meeting at which the resolution is proposed, a written statement setting out their reasons for making the recommendation, the amount to be paid to the company in respect of the equity shares to be allotted and the directors' justification of that amount[1].

As noted before, CA 1989, s 113 now permits private companies to do by written resolution anything which may be done by resolution in general or class meetings. As far as s 95(2) is concerned, any private company wishing to proceed by written resolution obviously is not in a position to circulate a statement of directors before a meeting and instead is required to supply

---

19 CA 1985, s 80(4). Since the CA 1989 a private company by an elective resolution may grant authority for an indefinite period, see s 80A, inserted by CA 1989, s 115.

20 Note that because of the link to the authority to allot granted under s 80, the power to disapply s 89(1) given under s 95(1) ceases to have effect when the authority to which it relates is revoked or would (if not renewed) expire; but if the authority is renewed, the power to disapply may also be renewed, for a period no longer than that for which the authority is renewed, by a special resolution of the company, s 95(3).

 1 CA 1985, s 95(5). Section 95(6) provides that a person who knowingly or recklessly authorises or permits the inclusion in a statement so circulated of any matter which is misleading, false or deceptive in a material particular is liable to imprisonment or a fine, or both.

such a statement to each member at or before the time at which the written resolution is supplied to him for signature[2].

CONSEQUENCES OF BREACH

Section 92 confers a civil remedy for compensation for breach of the pre-emption rights[3] against the company and every officer who knowingly authorised or permitted the contravention. The company and the officers are jointly and severally liable to compensate any person to whom an offer should have been made under the subsection or provision contravened for any loss, damage, costs or expenses which the person has sustained by reason of the contravention. Any claim for compensation must be brought within two years of the delivery of the return of allotment in question. A failure to comply may also be grounds for a petition alleging unfairly prejudicial conduct under s 459[4] which is considered in detail in Chapter 27.

LISTED COMPANIES AND PRE-EMPTION RIGHTS

As mentioned previously the Stock Exchange did insist, as a requirement of listing, that a company offer its shares on a pre-emptive basis unless the shareholders in general meeting otherwise permitted. In other words, each specific allotment had to be put to the shareholders for their approval if it was going to be allotted other than on a pro rata basis.

Following Big Bang in 1986, it was felt that this was too restrictive and hindered companies' freedom to raise capital as quickly and as cheaply as possible. The Stock Exchange therefore decided in October 1986 that companies should be entitled, with shareholder approval, to use the procedure available under s 95(1) to exclude the statutory rights conferred by s 89, subject to certain constraints[5].

The main concern was the period during which directors might be able to make issues other than on a pre-emptive basis. As we saw above, it is possible under s 95(1) to grant the directors authority to allot without regard to pre-emption rights for a period of five years, which the Stock Exchange thought granted too much freedom of manoeuvre to directors. Instead the Stock Exchange decided that shareholder approval might take the form of either general disapplication of the statutory pre-emption requirements not more than 15 months prior to the issue, or prior approval of a specific issue. The Stock Exchange will not therefore accept a s 95 disapplication which is intended to run for a longer period. This ensures that each year the shareholders have an opportunity to scrutinise how the directors have exercised their powers to allot, free of any pre-emptive constraints, in the previous

---

2 CA 1985, Sch 15A, para 3, as inserted by CA 1989, s 114.
3 This applies to a breach of the rights conferred by s 89(1) but also to a breach of any class pre-emption right under s 89(3) which had the effect of precluding the application of s 89(1), s 92(1).
4 See *Re a Company (No 005134 of 1986), ex p Harries* [1989] BCLC 383 at 396. Indeed even an issue made in accordance with the statutory provisions may be the subject of a s 459 petition, see *Re a Company* [1985] BCLC 80.
5 Admission of Securities to Listing, Section 1, Ch 2, para 18. See also Section 5, Ch 2, para 37; Section 6, Ch 2, para 7.

year. If they feel that their position has been jeopardised by the directors' actions then they can refuse to renew the powers under s 95 for the following year. Details of issues other than on a pre-emptive basis must also be included in the annual report and accounts[6].

However, a major group of investors, namely the institutional investors[7], opposed this dilution of their statutory rights and their opposition was sufficiently effective to result in additional guidelines being drawn up in 1987 after discussion between the institutional investors, corporate treasurers and the Stock Exchange. The guidelines set out that the Stock Exchange will continue to require companies to seek shareholders' approval annually for a special resolution to disapply pre-emption rights. For their part, the institutions will not oppose resolutions which seek to disapply pre-emption rights in respect of ordinary share capital up to an amount equal to 5% of the issued ordinary share capital at the relevant time. This is subject to a rolling limit of 7.5% in any three-year period. The discount available when shares are offered on a non pre-emptive basis is also limited[8].

Quite apart from the legal position then, as dictated by the Companies Acts or by the regulatory bodies such as the Stock Exchange, these further constraints have to be taken into account. The hope is that this compromise will facilitate flexible fund raising by companies without risking serious dilution of the interests of major shareholders and indeed it seems that there is now a degree of harmony concerning these matters. Recently, however, there have been suggestions that the Government may be considering abolishing altogether the statutory right of pre-emption in the interests of wider share ownership[9]. The argument is that with the institutions owning somewhere in the region of 70% of listed UK equities, true wider share ownership cannot be achieved so long as they have first claim on any fresh issues of shares under the statutory provisions. However, no such reform featured in the Companies Act 1989, so for the moment at least the position remains as stated above but clearly this is an area which will continue to concern shareholders, companies and the regulatory bodies.

Quasi-capital

In addition to share capital properly so-called there are two notional funds which are by law required to be created, and which appear in the balance sheet of a company as a kind of quasi-capital. Subject to certain exceptions, they can only be distributed or returned to shareholders in the same restricted way as share capital. The two notional funds are share premium account and capital redemption reserve. The former is required by s 130 when shares are issued at a higher price than their par value and was discussed above: the latter is required by s 170 where shares are redeemed or purchased by a company in certain circumstances and is discussed in Chapter 15.

6 Ibid, Section 5, Ch 2, para 21(q).
7 In particular, those institutions represented by the Association of British Insurers and the National Association of Pension Funds.
8 The guidelines have been further relaxed recently where the company wishes to issue new shares to overseas investors, July 1990.
9 See 'Pre-emption Rights Still on Agenda', *Financial Times* 4 May 1989; 'Study on Share Privileges Set Up', *Financial Times* 5 May 1989.

RAISING OF CAPITAL AND CAPITAL MAINTENANCE

Having considered the basic concepts, we now turn to the more detailed rules concerning payment for share capital. To understand those rules, they have to be placed against the background of the capital maintenance doctrine.

The doctrine of capital maintenance

With the advent of limited liability, the courts' concern at the end of the last century turned to the protection of creditors and they developed the doctrine of capital maintenance with a view to providing that protection. This doctrine regards the company's share capital as a fund which is a safeguard for creditors. As Jessel MR explained in *Re Exchange Banking Co, Flitcroft's Case*[10]:

The creditor has no debtor but that impalpable thing the corporation, which has no property except the assets of the business. The creditor, therefore, I may say, gives credit to that capital, gives credit to the company on the faith of the representation that the capital shall be applied only for the purposes of the business, and he has therefore a right to say that the corporation shall keep its capital and not return it to the shareholders, though it may be a right which he cannot enforce otherwise than on a winding up.

Of course, the courts cannot guarantee that this fund will be intact when the creditors need to resort to it and this is recognised in those early decisions. Lord Watson in *Trevor v Whitworth*[11] noted:

Paid-up capital may be diminished or lost in the course of the company's trading; that is a result which no legislation can prevent; but persons who deal with, and give credit to a limited company, naturally rely upon the fact that the company is trading with a certain amount of capital already paid . . . and they are entitled to assume that no part of the capital which has been paid into the coffers of the company has been subsequently paid out, except in the legitimate course of business.

Nevertheless, within the limits of what the law can achieve, the courts set about developing a set of rules concerning the establishment and maintenance of share capital which have since been modified by the Companies Acts. Whether the protection afforded by these rules is now real or illusory we shall endeavour to assess, as we examine each of them in this and subsequent chapters.

There are essentially two aspects to the doctrine, one concerned with raising share capital in the first place and the other with ensuring that it is not then returned to the shareholders ahead of a winding up. Obviously, if share capital is to be a creditors' fund then every care must be taken to ensure appropriate payment is received by the company for the shares, so we start in this Chapter by considering the various rules governing payment. Having raised the capital, it is then essential that the company does not return that capital to the shareholders, as where the company purchases back the

---

10 (1882) 21 Ch D 519 at 533, CA. See also *Ooregum Gold Mining Co of India v Roper* [1892] AC 125 at 133, per Lord Halsbury LC, HL.
11 (1877) 12 App Cas 409 at 423, HL.

shares, or funds the original purchase by providing financial assistance to the purchaser, or simply depletes the company's assets through improper dividends, funded not out of profits but out of capital. All of these aspects are discussed in Chapter 15. Finally, in Chapter 16, we consider the stringent procedure which must be followed if a company wishes formally to reduce its capital fund.

Payment for shares—the basic rules

Our starting point, as we saw above, is that a company cannot make a gratuitous allotment of its shares[12]. The allottee must pay, in full, at least the nominal value of the shares and will probably pay a premium as well.

Money or money's worth

Having established that the company must receive at least the nominal value of the shares, s 99(1) provides that shares allotted by a company, and any premium on them, may be paid up in money or money's worth (including goodwill and know-how), although s 99(4) provides that this does not preclude the company allotting bonus shares.

The one, not very significant, exception to the rule that money or money's worth will suffice is that shares taken by a subscriber to the memorandum of a public company in pursuance of an undertaking of his in the memorandum, and any premium on the shares, must be paid up in cash[13].

Obviously, where cash[14] is obtained for the shares, as where a company allots 100,000 shares for £100,000 and receives £100,000, then no problem arises. What is the position, however, if, instead of receiving £100,000, the company receives a plot of land in return for the shares? How can the company, or more particularly the other shareholders, be certain that the plot of land is in fact worth £100,000 or more? If it is worth less, then the company will have effectively issued its shares at a discount which is prohibited by s 100. This practice of transferring shares for an undervalue by accepting non-cash assets is known in America as stock watering. It is damaging to the creditors and to the other shareholders as it dilutes the value of the capital fund and their shares. Here the rules distinguish between public and private companies.

---

12 *Re Wragg Ltd* [1897] 1 Ch 796, CA; *Ooregum Gold Mining Co of India v Roper* [1892] AC 125, HL; *Re Eddystone Marine Insurance Co* [1893] 3 Ch 9, CA.

13 CA 1985, s 106. No attention has been paid to the plea of Vaughan Williams LJ in *Mosely v Koffyfontein Mines Ltd* [1904] 2 Ch 108 at 117, CA, that in all cases the nominal value of shares should be paid in cash, in order to end the abuses arising from acceptance of money or money's worth.

14 A share in a company is deemed paid up in cash or allotted for cash if the consideration for the allotment or payment up is cash received by the company, or is a cheque received in good faith which the directors have no reason for suspecting will not be paid, or is a release of a liability of the company for a liquidated sum, or is an undertaking to pay cash to the company at a future date, CA 1985, s 738(2). An assignment of a debt is not an undertaking to pay cash at a future date for these purposes, see *System Control plc v Munro Corporate plc* [1990] BCLC 659.

Private companies

The position as far as a private company is concerned is that such a company is entitled to issue fully paid up shares in return for property or services provided, as Lindley LJ noted in *Re Wragg Ltd*[15], it acts honestly and not colourably, and provided it has not been so imposed upon as to be entitled to be relieved from its bargain. There is a danger that the company may over-value the consideration so that the transaction is essentially the issue of shares at a discount but 'so long as the company honestly regards the consideration given as fairly representing the nominal value of the shares in cash, its estimate ought not to be critically examined'[16]. It is only where the consideration is illusory or it is manifest on the face of the instrument that the shares are issued at a discount that the court will be prepared to consider the adequacy of the consideration. This judicial attitude is in keeping with the courts' traditional reluctance to interfere in business matters. The result, given that the vast majority of companies are private, is that there are no real constraints on issuing shares at a discount provided the consideration is money's worth rather than cash[17].

Public companies

Many continental jurisdictions countered such abuses by requiring expert valuation reports[18] and this was adopted in art 10 of the Second EC Directive. The Companies Act 1985 reflects those requirements and imposes more stringent requirements on public companies in a number of respects.

(A)   ALLOTMENTS FOR CONSIDERATION OTHER THAN CASH

Section 103(1) sets out the basic position as follows:

A public company shall not allot shares as fully or partly paid up (as to their nominal value or any premium on them) otherwise than in cash unless—
(a)   the consideration for the allotment has been independently valued under s 108; and
(b)   a report with respect to its value has been made to the company by a person appointed by the company (in accordance with that section) during the six months immediately preceding the allotment of the shares; and
(c)   a copy of the report has been sent to the proposed allottee.

These requirements do not apply to an allotment of shares in connection with:

---

15   [1897] 1 Ch 796 at 830, CA. See also *Mosely v Koffyfontein Mines Ltd* [1904] 2 Ch 108, CA; *Re White Star Line Ltd* [1938] Ch 458, [1938] 1 All ER 607, CA.
16   *Ooregum Gold Mining Co of India v Roper* [1892] AC 125 at 137, HL, per Lord Watson.
17   The inconsistency between prohibiting a discount but allowing payment in money's worth was noted by Lindley LJ in *Re Wragg Ltd* [1897] 1 AC 796 at 831, CA who accepted that the difference between issuing shares at a discount and issuing them at a price put upon property or services by the vendor and agreed to by the company may not always be very apparent in practice. In his opinion, however, the two transactions were essentially different, and whilst the one is ultra vires the other is intra vires.
18   France, Belgium, Germany and Italy. See further E Stein *Harmonisation of European Company Laws* (1971) p 321.

(a)   a share exchange for the shares of all the holders of shares in another
       company or of a particular class of shares; or
(b)   a proposed merger of the company with another[19].

The section also makes clear that bonus issues are not caught by these
provisions[20]. Note that the consideration need not be wholly in non-cash
assets but may be part cash and part non-cash.

Independent valuation and report

Section 108 governs the independent valuation and report. Its provisions
have been described by Harman J in *Re Ossory Estates plc*[1] as curious and
arcane.

Under s 108 the valuation and report must be made by an independent
person ('the valuer'), that is to say a person qualified at the time of the report
to be appointed, or continue to be, an auditor of the company. So the
existing auditor may be appointed as the valuer for these purposes.

However, s 108(2) provides that where it appears to the valuer to be
reasonable for the valuation of the consideration to be made (or for him to
accept a valuation made) by another person who appears to him to have the
requisite knowledge and experience to value the consideration, and who is
not a connected person of the company in any of the ways specified in
s 108(2)(b)[2], he may arrange for or accept the other person's valuation. The
company's existing auditor is excluded from the categories of persons
specified in s 108(2)(b) and so may act as the valuer for these purposes also,
ie as someone brought in by the valuer.

The report must be in the following form:

(1)   It must state[3]:
       (a)   the nominal value of the shares in question;
       (b)   the amount of any premium payable on the shares;
       (c)   the description of the consideration, the method of valuation
              (where he himself has valued it) and the date of valuation;
       (d)   the extent to which the nominal value of the shares and any
              premium are to be treated as paid up (i) by the consideration and
              (ii) in cash.
(2)   Where the valuation is by a person other than the valuer, the latter's
       report must state that fact and also state[4]:
       (a)   the former's name, knowledge and experience;
       (b)   the description of the consideration, the method of valuation and
              the date of the valuation.
(3)   In all cases the valuer's report must state[5]:

19 See s 103(5) which defines 'merger' for these purposes.
20 Section 103(2).
 1 [1988] BCLC 213 at 215.
 2 To be independent the person must not be an officer or servant of the company, or any other
      body corporate which is that company's subsidiary or holding company or a subsidiary of
      that company's holding company, or a partner or employee of such an officer or servant,
      s 108(2)(b).
 3 CA 1985, s 108(4).
 4 Ibid, s 108(5).
 5 Ibid, s 108(6).

(a)   that the method of valuation (and any delegation of responsibility) was reasonable in all the circumstances;

(b)   that it appears to the valuer that there has been no material
change in the value of the asset since the valuation; and

(c)   that the value of the consideration together with any cash by
which the nominal value of the shares or any premium payable on
them is to be paid up, is not less than so much of the aggregate of
the nominal value and the whole of any such premium as is
treated as paid up by the consideration and any such cash.

Under s 110(2), it is an offence for any person knowingly or recklessly to
make a statement which is misleading, false or deceptive in a material
particular in connection with the preparation of such report. A valuer who
makes an erroneous report so causing loss to the company could be liable in
negligence to the company[6].

If the proposed allottee has not received a report under this section or he
knows or ought to have known of any other contravention of these requirements for valuation and report he is liable to pay an amount equal to the
aggregate of the nominal value of the shares plus any premium, with interest
at the appropriate rate[7].

Section 111 requires a copy of the report to be filed with the registrar of
companies together with the return of allotments which is required by
s 88(2) to be filed within one month of an allotment.

(B)   NON-CASH ASSETS ACQUIRED FROM SUBSCRIBERS

Section 104 sets out special rules which apply to a transfer of non-cash assets[8]
by subscribers to the memorandum of public companies[9]. We briefly
referred to these in Chapter 5 in relation to promoters. It should be noted
that by s 106, the original subscription must be paid up in cash so the concern
here is with other allotments of shares to subscribers.

For a period of two years from the date of the s 117 certificate (discussed
above) of entitlement to do business, any transfer[10] of non-cash assets from a
subscriber to the company for a consideration equal in value to 10% or more
of the nominal value of its issued capital at that time will be void unless the
following conditions are complied with:

---

6 But not apparently to the shareholders individually in this instance, *Caparo Industries plc v
Dickman* [1990] 1 All ER 568, [1990] BCLC 273, HL.

7 CA 1985, s 103(6). The effect is to create an immediate liability, as if the allottee had agreed
to take up the shares for cash, *Re Bradford Instruments plc* [1990] BCC 740. See also *Re
Ossory Estates plc* [1988] BCLC 213, which is discussed further below, and *System Control
plc v Munro Corporate plc* [1990] BCLC 659.

8 Defined in s 739(1) as meaning any property or interest in property other than cash.

9 The section also applies to companies which are re-registered as a public company, in which
case it applies to persons who were members of the company on the date of re-registration
and any transfer of non-cash assets between them and the company within two years
beginning with that date, s 104(3).

10 Defined s 739(2). A reference to the transfer or acquisition of a non-cash asset includes the
creation or extinction of an estate or interest in, or a right over, any property and also the
discharge of any person's liability, other than a liability for a liquidated sum.

(a)   the consideration to be received by the company, and any considera-
      tion other than cash to be given by the company, must have been
      independently valued by a valuer in the same way as outlined above
      and a report[11] on the consideration must have been made to the
      company during the six months immediately preceding the date of the
      agreement;
(b)   the terms of the agreement must have been approved by an ordinary
      resolution of the company. Copies of the resolution and report must
      have been available before the meeting to members and to the other
      party to the agreement if not then a member of the company[12].

Under s 104(6), the rules do not apply to (i) acquisitions in the ordinary
course of business, a potentially wide category, or (ii) acquisitions as a result
of a court order or under court control.

There is clearly a degree of overlap between ss 103 and 104 and it is
important to appreciate the differing scope of each provision. Section 103
applies whenever a public company accepts a non-cash consideration from
anyone as consideration for an allotment of shares. Section 104 applies to
any transfer of a non-cash asset from a subscriber to a public company within
the first two years, whether the consideration for the transfer is an allotment
of shares or something else. There are different exceptions to each.

It is possible for both sections to be applicable in the same instance, since
the provisions are not mutually exclusive. Thus any allotment of shares for
a non-cash consideration to a subscriber within the two-year period is
potentially within both provisions which is not unduly burdensome for the
company as both sections require essentially similar independent valuations
and reports. However, in addition, s 104 requires transactions within its
ambit to be approved by the company in general meeting by an ordinary
resolution. In other words, the informed consent of the shareholders will
have to be sought. As we will see later, the general meeting has lost much of
its authority as an effective monitor of this type of transaction as a result of
directors' control of proxy votes and the indifference of the average
shareholder. Nevertheless, many provisions in the Companies Acts still
require matters such as this to be presented for their approval. There is
another loophole, however, namely that s 104 does not apply where it is part
of the company's ordinary business to acquire such assets as have been
transferred. This may exclude the vast majority of suspect transactions from
s 104 and leaves them subject solely to s 103.

The type of transaction which is within s 104 but not within s 103 is where
the transaction does not involve an allotment of shares but is simply a
transfer of non-cash assets by a subscriber to the company within the two-
year period. That is subject to independent valuation and requires the
consent of the company in general meeting unless it can be shown, as will
frequently be the case, that it is part of the company's business to acquire
assets of that description. So even in this instance, s 104 can be sidestepped,
all of which suggests it is of little more than nuisance value.

---

11 The contents of the report are set out in s 109 and are essentially the same as those required
    under s 108 outlined above.
12 Copies of the report and the resolution must also be filed with the registrar of companies
    within 15 days of passing the resolution, s 111(2).

(C) UNDERTAKINGS TO DO WORK OR PERFORM SERVICES

Section 99(2) provides that a public company shall not accept at any time, in payment up of its shares or any premium on them, an undertaking by a person that he or another should do work or perform services for the company or for any other person. If a public company accepts such an undertaking in payment up of its shares, the holder of the shares shall be liable to pay the company an amount equal to their nominal value together with any premium[13]. The rule does not prevent a bonus issue of shares to its members[14]. Given the difficulty in valuing services, it is not surprising that this loophole is shut.

(D) RESTRICTION ON LONG-TERM UNDERTAKING

Section 102 prohibits the allotment of shares by a public company as fully or partly-paid as to their nominal value or any premium in consideration (in whole or in part) for an undertaking which is to be or may be performed more than five years after the date of the allotment[15]. In the event of breach the allottee is liable to pay to the company an amount equal to the aggregate of the nominal value and the whole of any premium due.

Consequences of breach

The consequences of breach of any of the above rules concerning inadequate consideration is relatively uniform. As a general rule, the allottee remains liable to pay an amount equal to the nominal amount and any premium due together with interest[16]. Subsequent holders are jointly and severally liable unless they are purchasers for value and did not have actual notice of the contravention or they took from a holder who was not himself liable under these provisions[17].

These penalties can be quite onerous, as Harman J noted in *Re Ossory Estates plc*[18], where property and £1.495m in cash had been transferred to the company in return for 8m shares (cost £1.76m). As this was the allotment of shares for a non-cash consideration, an independent valuation and report was required. No such report was ever made, so, applying the statutory provisions, the vendor, having transferred the property to the company, was liable to pay the company a further £1.76m as the price of the shares. This outcome was described by Harman J as a somewhat startling conclusion.

13 CA 1985, s 99(3).
14 Ibid, s 99(4).
15 The provision equally applies to a contract which did not originally contravene this provision but is subsequently varied and results in a contravention. In such cases the variation is void; equally caught is the situation where an undertaking was to have been performed within five years but was not, ss 102(3) and (5).
16 The effect is to create an immediate liability, as if the allottee had agreed to take up the shares for cash, *Re Bradford Instruments plc* [1990] BCC 740.
17 CA 1985, s 112(3). Prentice *The Companies Act 1980* (1980) p 50 commends the compromise effected by these provisions between protecting corporate creditors and enhancing the transferability of shares.
18 [1988] BCLC 213, noted Birds (1989) 10 Co Law 67. See also *System Control plc v Munro Corporate plc* [1990] BCLC 659.

However, these penalties are subject to the court's powers under s 113 to give relief where it is just and equitable to do so, having regard to the matters mentioned in s 113(3), which essentially involves having regard to amounts already paid or services performed by the allottee or any other person in respect of the amounts due. Section 113(5) provides that in determining whether to exempt an applicant from the whole or part of any liability, the court shall have regard to the principle that a company which has allotted shares should receive money or money's worth at least equal in value to the aggregate of the nominal value of those shares and the whole of any premium. On the facts in *Re Ossory Estates plc*, Harman J found that the company had since sold on some of the property transferred at a substantial profit and had undoubtedly received at least money or money's worth equal in value, and probably exceeding in value, the aggregate of the nominal value of the shares and any premium[19]. It was indeed just and equitable that the vendor should be relieved from any further liability.

Where there is a breach of the provisions the company and officers in default are also guilty of an offence and liable to a fine[20]. This incrimination of the company is unnecessary and by requiring the company to pay a fine can obviously work to the detriment of the creditors, the protection of whom is the major policy behind the legislation. Directors may also be in breach of duty and liable to make good any damage suffered by the company as a result of these contraventions[1]. Despite breaches of these provisions, any undertaking given by any person to do work or perform services or to do any other thing remains enforceable by the company[2].

Conclusion

Having considered the rules, it will be apparent that the statutory provisions are of a type which has become quite prevalent in English company law, ie they seek to cover every conceivable eventuality and in the process submerge the basic principles beneath a welter of detail. As Sealy noted, this is a pretty large sledgehammer to crack a fairly small nut[3].

In any event, as *Re Harmony and Montague Tin and Copper Mining Co, Spargo's Case*[4] made clear many years ago, rules about allotting shares for non-cash assets are easily evaded by the simple process of dividing the transaction into two stages. First, the individual sells assets to the company and the company becomes indebted to him for a stated amount. Secondly, the company allots fully-paid shares to him and in return the company is released from the liability to pay the stated sum. The transaction is no longer the allotment of shares for a non-cash consideration but an allotment of shares for cash. In that case, Sir W M James LJ explained that it is not necessary that the formality of the money being handed over and taken back again should be gone through. If the two demands are set off against each

---

19 [1988] BCLC 213 at 215. Contrast the position in *System Control plc v Munro Corporate plc* [1990] BCLC 659 where there was absolutely no evidence that the company had received full value for the shares.
20 CA 1985, s 114.
 1 *Hirsche v Sims* [1894] AC 654, PC.
 2 CA 1985, s 115 subject to s 113.
 3 Sealy *Cases and Materials in Company Law*, (4th edn, 1989) p 338.
 4 (1873) 8 Ch App 407.

other, the shares have been paid in cash[5]. The point is confirmed by CA 1985, s 738(2) which provides that a share is allotted for cash if the consideration for the allotment is, inter alia, the release of a liability of the company for a liquidated sum.

5 (1873) 8 Ch App 407 at 412.

CHAPTER 15

Corporate self-dealings, distributions and the capital maintenance doctrine

Having considered the rules relating to the receipt of share capital in the first instance, we turn now to consider provisions which attempt to prevent the return of that capital in various ways to the shareholders ahead of a winding up. The share capital maintenance rules which were developed by the courts but are now in statutory form prohibit companies from acquiring their own shares, or giving financial assistance to a purchaser of their shares or paying dividends out of capital. The basic rules remain but, as we shall see, they have been modified by statute, in some case strengthening, in others diminishing, the doctrine of capital maintenance.

PURCHASE AND REDEMPTION BY COMPANIES OF THEIR OWN SHARES

Background

It was laid down in 1887 by the House of Lords in *Trevor v Whitworth*[1] that it was unlawful for a company to purchase its own shares, even though this was authorised by its constitution. In the words of Sealy:

'This case settled a controversy which had existed, at least potentially, ever since the passing of the 1856 Act. It was only slowly recognised that the issue was not a domestic matter concerned with compliance with the articles, or even a question of vires dependent upon the powers set forth in the memorandum, but a matter of legality under the Companies Act itself'[2].

The very idea of a company purchasing its own shares was thought by Lord Macnaghten in *Trevor v Whitworth* to be

'contrary to the plain intention of the Act of 1862 and inconsistent with the conditions upon which, and upon which alone, Parliament has granted the privilege of limiting their liability to individuals'[3].

The basis for the objections was a need to protect creditors against a reduction of capital in this way without the company adhering to the statutory provisions on reduction (now CA 1985, s 135) which require the reduction to be confirmed by the court. Opposition to companies purchasing their own shares remained an element of English law thereafter and was ultimately included in statutory form in the Companies Act 1980, in what is now s 143 of the CA 1985.

Section 143(1) provides that a company limited by shares may not acquire

---

1 (1887) 12 App Cas 409.
2 Sealy *Cases and Materials in Company Law* (4th edn, 1989) p 330.
3 (1887) 12 App Cas 409 at 433.

its own shares, whether by purchase, subscription or otherwise[4]. However, s 143(3) goes on to provide that the prohibition in ss (1) does not apply in relation to—

(a)   the redemption or purchase of shares in accordance with Chapter VII of this Part,
(b)   the acquisition of shares in a reduction of capital duly made,
(c)   the purchase of shares in pursuance of an order of the court under s 5 (alteration of objects), s 54 (litigated objection to resolution for company to be re-registered as private) or Part XVII (relief to members unfairly prejudiced), or
(d)   the forfeiture of shares, or the acceptance of shares surrendered in lieu, in pursuance of the articles, for failure to pay any sum payable in respect of the shares.

(a) is the subject of much of this Chapter. (b) and (d) are discussed in Chapter 16 and (c) is discussed as and when the statutory provisions mentioned are considered.

This dramatic shift from the rule in *Trevor v Whitworth*[5], reflected in s 143(3), was brought about by the Companies Act 1981 which permitted companies to issue redeemable shares, purchase back their own shares and, in the case of private companies, to purchase back out of capital. The power to issue redeemable shares was not new, for companies had been able since 1929 to issue redeemable preference shares. The purchase powers, however, were entirely novel. Before considering the statutory requirements in detail, it is worth considering why, after almost a century, the rule in *Trevor v Whitworth*[6] was relaxed in this way.

Reasons for the change of approach

These statutory provisions allowing companies to issue redeemable shares and to purchase back their own shares were just one of a series of measures introduced by the Government in the early 1980s which were designed to attract equity investment in small businesses[7]. The difficulties which smaller companies face in trying to raise equity investment have been well documented[8]. Many small businesses are family concerns where the individuals concerned, much as they might welcome an injection of capital, are reluctant to raise it through an issue of shares for fear of losing control of the business to an outsider. Outsiders, for their part, are reluctant to contribute their capital to an enterprise whose shares are not easily marketable and where they risk being locked-in.

Any scheme to assist such companies would have to be flexible enough to increase the marketability of the shares without necessarily depriving the

---

4 See CA 1985, s 23, as inserted by CA 1989, s 129, which also prohibits a company from being a member of its holding company. Section 23 is discussed in greater detail in Ch 18.
5 (1887) 12 App Cas 409.
6 Ibid.
7 Another example would be the various tax incentives offered under schemes such as the Business Expansion Scheme to make equity investment more attractive for individuals.
8 See the Interim Report of the Committee to Review the Functioning of Financial Institutions, Cmnd 7503 (1979); Bolton Committee Report of Inquiry into Small Firms, Cmnd 4811 (1971); Chesterman *Small Businesses* (2nd edn, 1982), Ch 4.

existing owners of control and without further jeopardising the position of the company's creditors[9].

These are just the advantages which are seen to come from having the power to issue redeemable shares and the power to purchase back its own shares, as Professor Gower outlined in Part II of the consultative document, 'The Purchase by a Company of its Own Shares', which preceded the legislative changes[10]. The provisions complement one another and provide together a flexible equity capital structure for such companies. The company may issue redeemable shares, envisaging that the commitment will be a short-term one, or at least for a definable period. So the company has the use of the capital for this period while the investor knows that he will not be locked-in. The purchase back powers, on the other hand, enable the company at some point in the future to buy back shares without having to anticipate that eventuality at the time of issue. As far as investors are concerned, there always is the possibility that the company itself will be in the market, or will create a market for the shares, so increasing the possibility of realising their investment and reducing the chances of being locked-in.

It was also thought that these new powers might accommodate family re-arrangements, for example, by enabling founding shareholders to resign and realise their investment without the remaining family members being required personally to fund the purchase back of their shares. They might also offer a means of buying out discontented shareholders or providing employee shareholdings which the company might purchase back when the employment was terminated.

All of these factors pointed towards these powers being of greatest use in the private company. Indeed in the Green Paper on 'The Purchase by a Company of its Own Shares'[11], Professor Gower found it difficult to identify reasons as to why public companies needed these powers, questions of marketability and equity finance gaps being irrelevant there. The reasons suggested were that these powers would enable such companies to use up surplus funds, eliminate fractional shareholdings and generally give them a more flexible capital structure also.

After a slow start, an increasing number of public companies have sought authority from their shareholders to purchase back. Many of these companies have openly conceded that one of the purposes behind their purchases is to enhance the earning value of the remaining shares, a purpose not necessarily envisaged when the legislation was enacted. There is also the possibility that public companies will use these powers to buy up shares in the market which might otherwise be available to a would-be bidder, so providing existing boards with a further defensive mechanism against takeover bids. Whether such behaviour is in the best interests of the company and the shareholders are questions which have yet to be addressed.

Whatever the justification for giving these powers to public companies, the fact remains that the power is available and it has become a standard

---

9 For an excellent discussion of the difficulty in reconciling all the interested parties in purchase back schemes, see Dugan Repurchase of own shares for New Zealand in *Contemporary Issues in Company Law* (1987) ed Farrar.
10 Cmnd 7944 (1980).
11 Ibid, para 16.

feature of annual general meetings to see public companies asking their shareholders for authority to buy back their own shares.

Already then we have a hint of the sorts of conflicts which can arise from stepping away from the rule in *Trevor v Whitworth*[12] in this fashion. These potential problems were recognised by Parliament, as we shall see, and dealt with by the imposition of very stringent procedural requirements which are set out in the statutory provisions. These are designed to ensure that the powers can only be exercised in certain circumstances, using certain funds and in the full glare of publicity.

Strict adherence to the procedures is required, for it is only purchases or redemption in accordance with the statutory provisions which are permissible. Any other scheme will fall foul of the prohibition on purchase in s 143(1): the company will be liable to a fine, every officer of the company who is in default will be liable to imprisonment or a fine, and the purported acquisition will be void, s 143(2).

The statutory requirements

The statutory provisions are rather complex[13], so it may be useful to start with a very brief summary of the position. Basically, redemption or purchase back needs to be authorised by the articles and must be carried out by way of special or ordinary resolution (although private companies will in future be able to avail themselves of the written resolution procedure provided by the Companies Act 1989). Only certain specified funds may be used to finance the scheme and there are onerous disclosure requirements to ensure that the transaction is done openly. On purchase or redemption, the shares are cancelled so reducing the company's issued capital. However, because of the requirement to establish a capital redemption reserve, discussed below, a reduction of capital does not occur, save in the exceptional case where a private company actually purchases back or redeems out of capital.

Authorised by the articles

Looking at the procedural requirements in more detail. In order for a company to purchase or redeem its own shares, it must be authorised to do so in the articles[14]. Given that prior to 1980, companies could not have had a provision for purchase back in their articles, this requirement means that all of the companies which have taken this power on board have had to ask their shareholders for authority to do so. This is not a power which can be automatically assumed by the board. To that extent, therefore, and allowing for the natural apathy of shareholders, the question of purchase back has been specifically brought to the attention of the shareholders.

While the purchase back power may be given quite generally in the articles, s 159A, inserted by CA 1989, s 133(4), has laid down more specific requirements regarding the issue of redeemable shares[15]. In particular, the

---

12 (1887) 12 App Cas 409.
13 See the trenchant criticisms of the legislation by Sealy *Company Law and Commercial Reality* (1984) pp 8–14.
14 CA 1985, ss 159(1) and 162(1). Articles 3 and 35 of Table A are typical provisions.
15 The DTI has issued a Consultative Document, 'The Redemption of Redeemable Shares', November 1990, explaining the background to this provision.

date on or by which, or dates between which, the shares are to be or may be redeemed must be specified in the articles or, if the articles so provide, fixed by the directors, and in the latter case, the date or dates must be fixed before the shares are issued. Any other circumstances in which the shares are to be or may be redeemed must also be specified. The amount payable on redemption must also be specified in, or determined in accordance with, the company's articles, and in the latter case the articles must not provide for the amount to be determined by reference to any person's discretion or opinion. Any other terms and conditions of redemption shall also be specified in the company's articles.

General requirements

Redeemable shares cannot be issued unless the company has other shares in issue which are not redeemable[16] and equally, the company must after purchase back have other shares in issue, at least some of which are not redeemable[17], and the company must be left with at least two members[18]. The shares to be redeemed or purchased must be fully paid up[19] (otherwise the creditors would lose a valuable asset on liquidation, namely uncalled capital) and payment must be made at the time when the shares are purchased or redeemed[20] (to prevent companies from oppressing shareholders by redeeming or purchasing their shares so depriving them of their status as members but without actually paying over the proceeds). This requirement also resolves difficulties of timing and valuation.

More specific requirements then apply depending on whether the purchases are off-market or market purchases.

Off-market and market purchases

A purchase by a company of its own shares is off-market if the shares either—

(a)   are purchased other than on a recognised investment exchange, or
(b)   are purchased on a recognised investment exchange but are not subject to a marketing arrangement on that investment exchange[1].

A market purchase is any purchase which is not an off-market purchase[2]. The purpose behind the distinction is to impose a lower level of regulation on market purchases in recognition of the fact that the market authorities impose their own regulatory requirements[3] which, coupled with the higher degree of publicity attaching to such purchases, should be sufficient to deter the more blatant abuses of the procedure.

---

16 CA 1985, s 159(2).
17 Ibid, s 162(3).
18 Ibid, s 24.
19 Ibid, ss 159(3), 162(2) as inserted by CA 1989, s 133(4).
20 Ibid.
 1 Ibid, s 163, as amended by the Financial Services Act 1986.
 2 Ibid, s 163(3).
 3 See Admission of Securities to Listing, Section 5, Ch 2, paras 17, 21(p), 30.4 and Section 9, Ch 1, para 13.

Thus, in relation to an off-market purchase, a specific contract of purchase[4] (a copy of which or a written memorandum of whose terms must have been available to the members at the company's registered office for 15 days prior to the meeting and at the meeting itself) must be approved by the company in general meeting by a special resolution[5]. The authority conferred by the company in general meeting may be varied, revoked or from time to time renewed by a further special resolution[6]. In the case of a public company, the authority must specify a date on which it is to expire[7].

It should be noted, with respect to off-market purchases, that the special resolution is not effective if any member of the company holding shares to which the resolution relates exercises the voting rights carried by any of those shares in voting on the resolution and the resolution would not have been passed if he had not done so[8].

Following the CA 1989, it will be possible for private companies to deal with these matters by way of a unanimous written resolution instead of by resolution in general meeting[9]. One or two consequential changes have to be made in that case[10]. First, the disenfranchisement referred to above does not arise because it would mean that unanimity could not be achieved. Instead the member holding shares to which the resolution relates is not for these purposes regarded as a member whose consent to the resolution is required. He simply does not participate in the written process. Secondly, instead of details of the contract being available before the meeting, details must have been supplied to each member at or before the time when the resolution was supplied to him for signature.

As for market purchases, the company may be given a general authority to purchase by an ordinary resolution in general meeting[11]. The authority may be general or limited to the purchase of shares of any particular class or description, and may be conditional or unconditional[12] but it must specify the maximum number of shares which may be acquired, determine both the maximum and minimum price which may be paid for the shares[13] and specify a date on which the authority is to expire[14], which must in any event be not later than 18 months from the date of the resolution[15].

---

4 CA 1985, s 165 allows a company to enter into a contingent contract for an off-market purchase, on the same terms as outlined in the text in respect of specific contracts, if authorised by special resolution. Section 165 defines what is a contingent contract for these purposes.

5 CA 1985, s 164(1), (2) and (6).

6 Ibid, s 164(3).

7 Ibid, s 164(4), and in a resolution conferring or renewing authority that date must not be later than 18 months after that on which the resolution is passed.

8 Ibid, s 164(5).

9 CA 1985, s 381A, inserted by CA 1989, s 113(2). This is subject to the ability of the auditors to require the company to call a meeting, s 381B.

10 Provided for by CA 1985, Sch 15A, para 5, inserted by CA 1989, s 114.

11 CA 1985, s 166(1) and (2). The written resolution procedure, being limited to private companies, is not relevant to market purchases.

12 Ibid, s 166(2).

13 Ibid, s 166(3). The price may be determined either by specifying a particular sum or providing a basis or formula for calculating the price in question without reference to any person's discretion or opinion, CA 1985, s 166(6). This is obviously to ensure that the directors are not in a position to enter into transactions at varying prices, depending on their relationship with the vendors.

14 CA 1985, s 166(3).

15 Ibid, s 166(4).

No question of disenfranchising any shares arises in this context since the authority is not specifically aimed at any particular shares but is a general authority.

Disclosure requirements

As always, disclosure requirements play an important role in the regulatory requirements. It has already been mentioned that the specific contract in an off-market purchase has to be available for inspection both for 15 days prior to the meeting at which it is approved and at the meeting itself[16]. There are other disclosure requirements to note.

Any resolution, whether ordinary or special, conferring, varying, revoking or renewing an authority to purchase has to be sent to the registrar of companies within 15 days[17]. Within 28 days of any shares purchased being delivered to the company, a return must be delivered to the registrar of companies stating the number and nominal value of the shares and the date on which they were delivered to the company[18]. In the case of a public company further details, relating to the aggregate amount paid by the company for the shares, and the maximum and minimum paid by the company for shares of each class, have to be included[19]. A copy of any contract of purchase, whether on or off-market or contingent, or a written memorandum of its terms must be kept at the company's registered office for 10 years[20] and shall be available for inspection by the members, or if it is a public company, by any person. Details of any purchases must also be given in the directors' report[1].

Financing redemption and purchase back

A crucial element in any redemption or purchase back scheme, obviously, is the source of the funding which will pay for it. Here the danger to creditors is that the company will be effectively stripped of assets which are returned to the shareholders leaving a shell with inadequate assets to pay off the company's creditors in full. The legislation attempts to prevent that happening by providing, subject to one major exception, that companies must fund redemption or purchase back out of:

(i)   distributable profits[2], or
(ii)   the proceeds of a fresh issue of shares made for the purpose[3].

---

16 Ibid, s 164(6).
17 Ibid, s 166(7) and s 380. This is an exception to the general rule that ordinary resolutions do not have to be filed.
18 CA 1985, s 169(1).
19 Ibid, s 169(2).
20 Ibid, s 169(4).
 1 Ibid, Sch 7, Part II.
 2 Defined in accordance with the statutory provisions on distribution in CA 1985, s 263(2), s 181.
 3 CA 1985, s 160, and s 162(2) as inserted by CA 1989, s 133(4). As a general rule, any premium on redemption or purchase must be paid out of distributable profits, s 160(1), subject to certain exceptions where the shares redeemed or purchased back were originally issued at a premium in which case the proceeds of a fresh issue made for the purposes of the redemption may be used to a limited extent, see s 160(2).

In other words, the company must use funds (distributable profits) which could have gone to the shareholders anyway in the form of dividend, or must substitute for the capital which they are repaying new capital brought in by a fresh issue. Neither, it will be appreciated, has any impact on the company's creditors, so there is not in fact any erosion of the capital maintenance doctrine. To ensure that this is in fact the case, the company must set up a capital redemption reserve fund.

Capital redemption reserve

The position regarding the creation of a capital redemption reserve is governed by s 170. It provides that when shares are redeemed or purchased wholly or partly out of profits then a transfer must be made to the capital redemption reserve of an amount equal to the nominal value of the shares purchased or redeemed. Where shares are redeemed or purchased wholly or partly out of the proceeds of a fresh issue, then the difference between the nominal value of the shares redeemed or purchased, less the proceeds of the fresh issue, must be transferred to the capital redemption reserve[4]. Section 170(4) provides that the reserve must be treated as if it were share capital although it may be used for the allotment of fully-paid bonus shares.

Private companies—redemption or purchase out of capital

A provision which potentially has a significant impact on creditors is that in s 171 which allows private companies in certain circumstances to redeem or purchase back out of capital. Given the potential danger to creditors, it is not surprising that the statutory provisions surround such purchases with even more stringent requirements than those already noted.

As before, the starting point is that the company must be specifically authorised by its articles to redeem or purchase back out of capital[5]. The payment out of capital must be approved by a special resolution[6] and the resolution is ineffective if any member of the company holding shares to which the resolution relates exercises the voting rights carried by any of those shares in voting on the resolution and the resolution would not have been passed if he had not done so[7].

As noted above, following the CA 1989, it will be possible for private companies to deal with these matters by way of a unanimous written resolution instead of by resolution in general meeting[8], with one or two consequential changes to the procedure[9]. First, the disenfranchisement referred to above does not arise because it would mean that unanimity could not be achieved. Instead the member holding shares to which the resolution relates is not, for these purposes, regarded as a member whose consent to the resolution is required. He simply does not participate in the written process.

4 CA 1985, s 170(2).
5 CA 1985, s 171(1). An authority to purchase is insufficient, it must specifically make provision for purchase out of capital. Article 35 of Table A is an example.
6 CA 1985, s 173(2).
7 Ibid, s 174(2).
8 CA 1985, s 381A, inserted by CA 1989, s 113(2). This is subject to the ability of the auditors to require the company to call a meeting, s 381B.
9 Provided for by CA 1985, Sch 15A, para 6, inserted by CA 1989, s 114.

Secondly, instead of the statutory declaration and auditors report, discussed below, being available before the meeting, details must have been supplied to each member at or before the time when the resolution was supplied to him for signature.

Statutory declaration and auditors' report

The directors must make a statutory declaration as required by s 173(3) stating, in particular, that having made full inquiry into the affairs and prospects of the company, they have formed the opinion[10]—

(a) as regards its initial situation immediately following the date on which the payment out of capital is proposed to be made, that there will be no grounds on which the company could then be found unable to pay its debts; and

(b) as regards its prospects for the year immediately following that date that, having regard to their intentions with respect to the management of the company's business during that year and to the amount and character of the financial resources which will in their view be available to the company during that year, the company will be able to continue to carry on business as a going concern (and will accordingly be able to pay its debts as they fall due) throughout that year.

Annexed to this declaration must be a report by the company's auditors stating that they have inquired into the company's state of affairs and that they are not aware of anything to indicate that the opinion expressed by the directors in their declaration is unreasonable in all the circumstances[11].

This declaration and the auditors' report must be available to any member or creditor for inspection in the five weeks after the passing of the resolution[12]. Any director who makes this statutory declaration without having reasonable grounds for the opinion expressed in the declaration is liable to imprisonment or a fine or both[13].

Much more significant, however, is s 76 of the Insolvency Act 1986 which applies where a company is being wound up and it has made a payment out of capital in respect of purchase or redemption and the aggregate of its assets and the amounts paid by way of contribution is not sufficient for the payment of its debts and liabilities and the expenses of winding up. In those circumstances, if the winding up commenced within one year of the date on which the relevant payment out of capital was made, then the person from whom the shares were redeemed or purchased, and the directors who signed the statutory declaration are, so as to enable the insufficiency to be met, liable to contribute to the company's assets. A person from whom any of the shares were redeemed or purchased is liable to contribute an amount not exceeding so much of the relevant payment as was made by the company in respect of his shares and the directors are jointly and severally liable with that person to contribute that amount. A director will be excused liability if he shows

---

10 In forming this opinion, the directors shall take into account the same liabilities (including contingent and prospective liabilities) as would be relevant under s 122 of the Insolvency Act 1986 to the question whether a company is unable to pay its debts, CA 1985, s 173(4).
11 CA 1985, s 173(5).
12 Ibid, s 175(6).
13 Ibid, s 173(6).

that he had reasonable grounds for forming the opinion set out in the declaration. Presumably he will claim that he was justified in relying on the auditors who, after all, agreed with his opinion.

Permissible capital payment

As for the amount which may be paid out of capital, the company must first use any available distributable profits[14] and the proceeds of any fresh issue made for the purpose of purchase or redemption, before resorting to capital, with the amount then needed being described as the permissible capital payment[15]. The amount of the permissible capital payment must be stated by the directors in their statutory declaration and the auditors' report must confirm that it has been correctly determined[16].

The payment out of capital must be approved by a special resolution passed on or within the week immediately following the date on which the directors make their statutory declaration[17]. The actual payment out of capital must be made no more than 5 and not later than 7 weeks after the date of the resolution[18].

Disclosure requirements

Various disclosure requirements also apply here which are aimed at bringing the proposed payment to the attention of creditors, who may wish to apply to the court for an order prohibiting payment.

Section 175 provides that, within the week immediately following the date of the resolution for payment out of capital, the company must cause to be published in the Gazette a notice—

(a)   stating that the company has approved a payment out of capital for the purpose of acquiring its own shares by purchase or redemption (as the case may be);

(b)   specifying the amount of the permissible capital payment and the date of the special resolution;

(c)   stating that the directors' statutory declaration and the auditors' report are available for inspection at the company's registered office; and

(d)   stating that any creditor of the company may at any time within the 5 weeks immediately following the date of the resolution apply to the court under s 176 for an order prohibiting payment.

A similar notice must be published in a national newspaper or a notice in writing must be given to each creditor[19]. A copy of the directors' statutory declaration and the auditors' report must also be sent to the registrar of companies at the same time[20].

---

14 Defined in this instance in accordance with s 172 rather than ss 270–275 which apply generally.
15 CA 1985, s 171(3).
16 Ibid, ss 173(3) and (5).
17 Ibid, s 174(1).
18 Ibid.
19 Ibid, s 175(1) and (2).
20 Ibid, s 175(5).

Objections by creditors or members

In recognition of the potential for abuse when companies are permitted to redeem or purchase back out of capital and the fact that this essentially allows companies to reduce capital without the sanction of the court as required by CA 1985, s 135, provision is made for an application by an objecting creditor or member to the court to have the resolution authorising the payment cancelled[1]. It should be noted that no such procedure is available in respect of purchase or redemption in any other instance.

Those entitled to apply to the court are any member of the company other than one who consented to or voted in favour of the resolution; and any creditor of the company[2]. The application must be within 5 weeks of the date on which the resolution was passed[3].

No minimum shareholding or debt is required but obviously the more insignificant the amounts, the less weight is likely to be attached to the objections. In any event, the difficulty for those objecting, particularly if they are members, is to persuade the court to set aside something which in the case of an off-market purchase, has been approved by a special resolution, ie by 75% of those voting, which did not include the interested shareholders. The court in such circumstances tends to refuse redress, stating that the members know best and that it is not for the court to interfere in what is essentially a difference as to business policy[4].

The jurisdiction of the court on an application under s 176 is quite open-ended. The only specific guidance provided is that, under s 177(1), the court may adjourn the proceedings in order that an arrangement can be made for the purchase of the interests of dissentient members or for the protection of dissentient creditors (as the case may be). Without prejudice to that power, the court shall make an order[5] on such terms and conditions as it thinks fit either confirming or cancelling the resolution. The court's order may, in particular, provide for the purchase by the company of any shares of any members and for the reduction of the company's capital accordingly.

Cancellation

It should finally be noted that regardless of the type of company or source of funding, once the company has purchased or redeemed any shares then it must cancel those shares, thus reducing the company's issued (but not authorised) capital[6]. This is designed to prevent companies trafficking in their shares and to reduce the impact which purchase back can have within the company. For example, the directors are not able to retain the shares and vote them as they see fit. They are able to re-issue shares, of course, up to the authorised limit. Cancellation should increase the earnings of the

---

1 Ibid, s 176.
2 Ibid.
3 Ibid.
4 We have already seen the difficulties which minority shareholders face when trying to challenge alterations to the articles, also approved by a special resolution. See the discussion above, Ch 11.
5 Within fifteen days of any order being made, or such longer period as the court may direct, the company must deliver an office copy of the order to the registrar of companies, CA 1985, s 176(3)(b).
6 CA 1985, ss 160(4) and 162(2) as inserted by CA 1989, s 133(4).

remaining shares, although this depends on factors such as the market's perception of the wisdom of redemption or purchase, the price paid and whether there has been a fresh issue of shares.

Effect of a company's failure to redeem or purchase its own shares

Section 178 governs the position when the company fails to purchase or redeem shares and provides that the company is not to be liable in damages in respect of any such failure. Specific performance may still be available, but not if the company shows that it is unable to meet the costs of redeeming or purchasing the shares in question out of distributable profits[7].

Tax aspects of redemption and purchase by a company of its shares

Under tax law, before the Finance Act 1982 a redemption or purchase by a company of its own shares was normally treated as a distribution giving rise to advance corporation tax. The Finance Act 1982, the provisions of which have now been consolidated in the Income and Corporation Taxes Act 1988, changed the position, enabling an unlisted company to purchase or redeem without suffering this tax consequence provided certain conditions are fulfilled. If they are fulfilled the transaction will be treated as a capital gains transaction by the member which may mean that less tax is payable. The qualifying conditions are as follows. First, the company that is buying its own shares must be an unquoted trading company or the holding company of a trading group. Secondly, the purpose behind the purchase of shares must be to benefit its trade. Thirdly, the vendor must be resident or ordinarily resident within the UK for tax purposes. Fourthly, he must have owned the shares for at least five years. Fifthly, the company need not purchase all the vendor's shares provided that his shareholding is substantially reduced. The detailed tax rules are contained in the Income and Corporation Taxes Act 1988, ss 219–229.

As can be seen, these conditions are restrictive. Only private companies and unlisted public companies are eligible. Although the category of trade is wide, it excludes investment companies other than the holding company of a trading group. The benefit of a trade and the non-tax avoidance requirements are particularly restrictive although tax relief can be obtained if the former is the main purpose. The new tax rules confer much discretion on the Revenue and as the matter seems to be handled at local level, it is possible that the exercise of the discretion may vary from area to area.

FINANCIAL ASSISTANCE BY A COMPANY FOR THE ACQUISITION OF ITS OWN SHARES

Background

Having originally prohibited companies from purchasing their own shares, it soon became apparent that an equally unacceptable practice was that of companies giving financial assistance to enable persons to buy their own

---

7 Ibid, s 178(3). Section 178(4)–(6) deals with the position where the company goes into winding up.

shares. The classic abuse was for a bidder to borrow money from a bank and then to repay the bank out of the company's funds after the takeover. The Jenkins Committee in 1962 explained the concerns about this sort of practice as follows:

If people who cannot provide the funds necessary to acquire control of a company from their own resources, or by borrowing on their own credit, gain control of a company with large assets on the understanding that they will use funds of the company to pay for their shares, it seems to us all too likely that in many cases the company will be made to part with its funds either on inadequate security or for an illusory consideration[8].

It then noted that when the facts are ultimately discovered, the company's remedies against the bidder will be worthless, either because he has disappeared, has disposed of his assets, or is insolvent, and minority shareholders and creditors suffer accordingly[9]. This is the classic asset-stripping abuse of financial assistance.

Another type of abuse arising from financial assistance which has been much to the fore in recent years is the use of company funds to fund share support schemes as an element of a takeover strategy. In the 1980s many takeovers were carried out on a share-for-share basis, so shareholders in the target company were offered, not cash for their shares, but shares in the bidder. For the scheme to work, the value of the shares in the bidder had to be maintained at a level which made them attractive to the shareholders in the target. This might be done by giving financial assistance to persons to buy shares in the bidder, for example, by indemnifying them against any loss incurred on their purchases. The effect, of course, was to manipulate the company's share price and to deceive the market as to the true nature of the purchases. So the practice can have an adverse impact on an individual company but in the wider context it can also distort the equity markets.

The Greene Committee reporting in 1927[10] recommended a statutory extension to the prohibition on companies purchasing their own shares which was introduced in the Companies Act 1929 to curb this additional abuse and the Jenkins Committee in 1962 in turn recommended that the provisions should be retained and strengthened[11]. The original section was s 45 of the Companies Act 1929 which became s 54 of the Companies Act 1948 which gave rise to a number of interesting cases. However, s 54 presented various problems of interpretation[12] and it was repealed and replaced by the Companies Act 1981. The current statutory prohibition is to be found in CA 1985, ss 151 to 158.

It should be noted, however, that private companies may now give financial assistance provided they are solvent and adhere to the statutory procedure provided.

---

8 Report of the Company Law Committee, Cmnd 1749, para 173.
9 Ibid, para 176.
10 Company Law Amendment Committee Report, Cmnd 2657.
11 Cmnd 1749, para 173.
12 Section 54 made it an offence for a company to give financial assistance for the purpose of or in connection with the acquisition, by purchase or subscription, of its own shares. The concerns as to the width of this prohibition heightened following *Belmont Finance Corp Ltd v Williams Furniture Ltd (No 2)* [1980] 1 All ER 393, CA which queried whether a transaction entered into in the ordinary course of business, even if for fair value, might be caught if any part of the purpose for the transaction was to provide financial assistance.

Basic position

Section 151(1) provides that where a person is acquiring or proposing to acquire[13] any shares in a company, it is not lawful for the company or any of its subsidiaries to give financial assistance, directly or indirectly, for the purpose of that acquisition before or at the same time as the acquisition takes place. Equally, a company or any of its subsidiaries is prohibited by s 151(2) from giving financial assistance, directly or indirectly, after the acquisition of shares in the company for the purpose of reducing or discharging any liability incurred in so doing[14].

Financial assistance is widely defined in s 152 to include, inter alia, financial assistance given by way of gift, guarantee, security or indemnity, or a loan or any other agreement under which any of the obligations of the person giving the assistance are to be fulfilled at a time when, in accordance with the agreement, any obligation of another party to the agreement remains unfulfilled, or any other financial assistance given by a company the net assets[15] of which are thereby reduced to a material extent or which has no net assets[16]. In *Charterhouse Investment Trust Ltd v Tempest Diesels Ltd*[17] Hoffmann J considered the meaning of financial assistance under s 54 but his comments are still of use in considering financial assistance under the new provision. In his opinion, the commercial realities of the transaction as a whole must be considered in deciding whether it can properly be described as the giving of financial assistance by the company, bearing in mind that the section is a penal provision and should not be strained to cover transactions which are not fairly within it[18].

The key elements[19] then are the acquisition of shares in the company and the giving of financial assistance, directly or indirectly, to the person who acquired the shares, by the company or a subsidiary, before or after the acquisition occurred, for the purpose of the acquisition or to reduce any liability incurred in the acquisition.

If a company acts in contravention of this section, it is liable to a fine[20] and

13 Note that acquisition is wider than s 54 which covered acquisition by purchase or subscription only.
14 See CA 1985, s 152(3) which further defines incurring a liability and giving financial assistance for the purpose of reducing or discharging a liability.
15 Net assets is defined as the aggregate of the company's assets less the aggregate of its liabilities, CA 1985, s 152(2).
16 Pennington *Company Law* (6th edn, 1990) p 382 makes the point that this final provision raises problems of interpretation and if, as is probable, it means any transaction where the financial assistance is not balanced by the company acquiring assets of equivalent value, then it adds nothing to the specific items in the definition which precede it.
17 [1986] BCLC 1.
18 Ibid, at 10.
19 As the facts in many financial assistance schemes can be extremely complex, it may be useful to keep in mind Lord Denning's basic approach, set out in *Wallersteiner v Moir* [1974] 3 All ER 217 at 238, [1974] 1 WLR 991 at 1014, CA where he said: 'You look at the company's money and see what has become of it. You look at the company's shares and see into whose hands they have gone. You will then soon see if the company's money has been used to finance the purchase.' In the more serious cases, the use of nominee shareholders may cloud the picture, but nevertheless this is a good starting point.
20 CA 1985, s 151(3). Sealy *Cases and Materials in Company Law* (4th edn, 1989) p 342, makes the point that the draftsman has thoughtlessly made liable the very company whose protection it is his concern to promote.

every officer in default is liable to imprisonment or a fine or both. There are also civil consequences, discussed below.

The basic scheme of the provisions then is tolerably clear, even if, as we shall see, the detail gives rise to many difficulties of interpretation. Moreover, s 153 goes on to set out a large number of circumstances when the prohibition does not apply.

Exceptions

The exceptions fall into three distinct categories:

(i)   the purpose exceptions in s 153(1) and (2) which are designed to ensure that the width of the prohibition does not inadvertently catch genuine commercial transactions which are in the interests of the company;

(ii)   transactions specified as not being within the prohibition, really for the avoidance of doubt: most are subject to alternative statutory regimes. For example, a dividend payment lawfully made may be used to purchase shares in the company without infringing the prohibition;

(iii)   exemptions for those companies whose business it is to give financial assistance in the ordinary course of business and various exemptions designed to facilitate employee share schemes.

(i) is the category which causes most difficulty.

(i)   THE PURPOSE EXCEPTIONS

Section 153(1) provides that s 151(1) does not prohibit a company from giving financial assistance for the purpose of the acquisition of shares in it or its holding company if:

(a)   the company's principal purpose in giving it is not to give it for the purpose of any such acquisition, or the giving of the assistance for that purpose is but an incidental part of some larger purpose of the company; and

(b)   the assistance is given in good faith in the interests of the company.

An identical exception is s 153(2) applies to the prohibition on giving financial assistance after the shares have been acquired to relieve or discharge a liability incurred in so doing. This purpose exception has attracted most comment, as its scope is rather uncertain, but it has now been considered in detail by the House of Lords in *Brady v Brady*[1].

The facts of this case were extremely complicated but essentially revolved around a scheme of reorganisation of a group of companies which was designed to enable two brothers to split a family business after disagreements between them meant it was impossible to continue as a joint venture[2]. Without going into the labyrinthine complexities of the scheme it suffices for our purposes to say that M purchased all of the shares in B from

---

1   [1989] AC 755, [1988] 2 All ER 617, HL; revsd [1988] BCLC 20, CA. See Greaves and Hannigan (1989) 10 Co Law 135, also noted (1988) CLJ 24, 359; [1988] JBL 65, 412.

2   For a subsequent case on very similar facts, see *Plaut v Steiner* (1988) 5 BCC 352 where *Brady* was applied.

O and therefore incurred a liability in so doing, namely the purchase price. That liability was then partly reduced by the transfer of half of B's assets to O who passed the assets on to A. So a liability incurred on the acquisition of B's shares is partly reduced or discharged by B's assets. This question was whether this prima facie case of financial assistance was saved by being within the purpose exception in s 153(2), outlined above.

What was the principal purpose for the transfer of the assets? Was it incidental to a larger purpose? In either case, was it in the best interests of B? The Court of Appeal, for varying reasons, thought that the purpose element was satisfied in one way or another but did not accept that the assistance was given in good faith in the interests of the company[3]. The House of Lords, for its part, would have accepted that the assistance was given in good faith in the interests of the company but would not accept that the purpose element had been satisfied.

The starting point was the wording of s 153(2). In the words of Lord Oliver, it was clear that sub-paragraph (a), set out above, contemplated two alternative solutions[4]. The first envisaged a principal and a subsidiary purpose. In Lord Oliver's view, the principal purpose of the financial assistance was simply and solely to reduce the indebtedness incurred by M in acquiring B and therefore the transaction was not saved under the first part of the subsection. As for the second part of the subsection, here it was not suggested that the financial assistance was intended to achieve any object other than the reduction or discharge of the indebtedness but that result, it was said, was merely incidental to some larger purpose. The key to being within that element, in Lord Oliver's opinion, was finding some larger overall corporate purpose in which the resultant reduction or discharge of liability was merely incidental. In construing purpose in the context of this provision, he noted[5]:

. . . there has always to be borne in mind the mischief against which s 151 is aimed. In particular, if the section is not, effectively, to be deprived of any useful application, it is important to distinguish between a purpose and the reason why a purpose is formed. The ultimate reason for forming the purpose of financing the acquisition may, and in most cases probably will, be more important to those making the decision than the immediate transaction itself. But 'larger' is not the same thing as 'more important' nor is 'reason' the same as 'purpose'.

The House of Lords thus concluded that the purpose of the transaction was to assist in the financing of the acquisition of the shares, although the reason was to facilitate a break up of the business which would divide it equally between the two brothers and leave each with a viable business. Both the principal purpose and the larger purpose of the transaction therefore was to give financial assistance and so the requirements of s 153(2)(a) were not satisfied. In approaching the transaction in this manner the House of Lords focused narrowly on the immediate transaction itself without regard to the financial and commercial advantages in the wider context which were considered by their Lordships to be mere by-products[6]. The transaction did therefore amount to the giving of financial assistance contrary to s 151 which

3 See Greaves and Hannigan (1989) 10 Co Law 135 at 137 on the Court of Appeal position.
4 [1989] AC 755 at 778, [1988] 2 All ER 617 at 632.
5 [1989] AC 755 at 779, [1988] 2 All ER 617 at 633.
6 [1989] AC 755 at 780, [1988] 2 All ER 617 at 633.

was not saved by s 153(2). However, as the company was a private company, the parties could have used the provisions of s 155 which permits private companies to give financial assistance in certain circumstances. This is discussed further below.

Finally, it must be remembered that there is a further limb to the purpose exceptions, namely that the assistance is given in good faith in the interests of the company. On this aspect, Lord Oliver stated that the words 'in good faith in the interests of the company' form a single composite expression and require that those responsible for procuring the company to provide the assistance act in the genuine belief that it is being done in the company's interests[7]. This was undoubtedly the case in *Brady* where the scheme was necessary to save the company from probable liquidation and so was properly perceived as calculated to advance Brady's corporate and commercial interests and the interests of its employees. It was in the company's interest that it should continue in being under proper management unhampered by insoluble differences between the directors. As the company was solvent, there was no risk to the interests of present creditors and their position in the long term would be further improved by the restructuring[8]. However, this was not sufficient to save the scheme.

(ii)   TRANSACTIONS SPECIFIED AS PERMISSIBLE

These transactions are listed in s 153(3) which provides that s 151 does not prohibit—

(a)   a distribution of a company's assets by way of dividend lawfully made or a distribution made in the course of a company's winding up,
(b)   the allotment of bonus shares,
(c)   a reduction of capital confirmed by order of the court under s 135,
(d)   a redemption or purchase of shares under the statutory provisions outlined above,
(e)   anything done in pursuance of an order of the court under s 425 (compromises and arrangements with creditors and members),
(f)   anything done under an arrangement made in pursuance of s 110 of the Insolvency Act 1986 (acceptance of shares by liquidator in winding up as consideration for sale of property), or
(g)   anything done under an arrangement made between a company and its creditors which is binding on the creditors by virtue of Part 1 of the Insolvency Act 1986.

The reason why these exceptions are listed is readily understood once it is remembered that the prohibition of the giving of financial assistance is essentially based on the need to protect creditors against a return of capital to shareholders ahead of a winding up and to prevent the company from having its assets misused[9]. All of the schemes mentioned in categories (c) to (g) are subject to elaborate statutory requirements designed to ensure the protection of creditors and prevent the misuse of assets, and in a number of cases the schemes require the confirmation of the court. There is no need

7 [1989] AC 755 at 777, [1988] 2 All ER 617 at 632.
8 [1989] AC 755 at 778, [1988] 2 All ER 617 at 632.
9 *Wallersteiner v Moir* [1974] 3 All ER 217 at 239, [1974] 1 WLR 991 at 1014, CA, per Denning LJ.

therefore to subject such transactions to the requirements of s 151. As for (a), this simply removes any doubt about the validity of using a dividend payment to fund a purchase of shares or reduce a liability already incurred in the acquisition of shares. The risk of improvident dividend payments being made simply to provide financial assistance is eliminated by the stringent distribution rules, discussed below, which now govern the area. The allotment of bonus shares which might otherwise infringe the section as it is worded, is also specifically exempted, but as we saw above in Chapter 14, a bonus issue is in any event more in the nature of a book-keeping exercise than an attempt to return capital to shareholders, so there is no risk to creditors there either.

(iii)   TRANSACTIONS IN THE ORDINARY COURSE OF BUSINESS AND EMPLOYEE SHARE SCHEMES

This third category provides exemptions for those companies whose business it is to give financial assistance in the ordinary course of business and various exemptions designed to facilitate employee share schemes.

Section 153(4) allows financial assistance in the ordinary course of business where the lending of money is part of the ordinary business of the company. The financial assistance must take place in the ordinary course of business and must not be a loan given specifically to enable shares in the company to be purchased[10].

Secondly, the company is not prohibited by s 151 from providing, in good faith in the interests of the company, financial assistance for the purposes of an employees' share scheme[11]. In addition, quite apart from any employees' scheme, a company can give financial assistance for the purpose of enabling or facilitating transactions in shares in the company between, and involving the acquisition of beneficial ownership of those shares by, employees, former employees and various relatives[12]. Finally, s 153(4)(c) enables a company to make loans to employees (other than directors) with a view to enabling those persons to acquire full-paid shares in the company or its holding company to be held by them by way of beneficial ownership.

It should be noted that these exemptions in category (iii) may only be relied on by a public company if the company has net assets which are not thereby reduced, or to the extent that those assets are thereby reduced, the financial assistance is provided out of distributable profits[13].

Financial assistance by private companies

As we have already seen, the statutory provisions on redemption and purchase are relaxed for private companies[14], and this is also the position regarding financial assistance. This relaxation of the prohibition has proved

---

10 *Steen v Law* [1964] AC 287, [1963] 3 All ER 770.
11 CA 1985, s 153(4)(b) as substituted by CA 1989, s 132. The wording is slightly changed from the previous provisions with a view to widening this category in keeping with current Government policy in favour of employees' share schemes. Employee share scheme is defined in CA 1985, s 743.
12 CA 1985, s 153(4)(bb) as amended by CA 1989, Sch 18, para 33.
13 Ibid, s 154(1). Sub-s (2) defines net assets for these purposes.
14 As we saw above, they alone are entitled to fund redemption or purchase back out of capital, s 171.

of great importance in practice, particularly in terms of facilitating management buy-outs which have become quite common in recent years[15].

Section 155 provides that a private company may give financial assistance for the acquisition of its own shares[16] if the company has net assets[17] which are not thereby reduced or, to the extent that they are reduced, the assistance is provided out of distributable profits[18]. In other words, either the company receives a quid pro quo for its assistance, for example, where it provides a loan which is to be repaid with interest, in which case the net assets are not reduced, or if they are to be reduced then it must come out of the fund which would otherwise be available to the shareholders for dividends, namely the distributable profits. Creditors therefore are not disadvantaged in such circumstances.

The procedural requirements are extensive, and in many respects identical to those already considered in relation to redemption or purchase out of capital[19]. The giving of assistance must be approved by special resolution of the company in general meeting[20] or the company may opt to use the written resolution procedure provided by the CA 1989[1]. A statutory declaration from the directors and an auditor's statement in support is also required.

Statutory declaration and auditors' report

The directors must make a statutory declaration as required by s 156 one week before the special resolution is passed by the company[2]. The declaration must state, in particular, that they have formed the opinion[3], as regards the company's initial situation immediately following the date on which the assistance is proposed to be given, that there will be no ground on which the company could then be found unable to pay its debts, and either—

(a)   if it is intended to commence the winding up of the company within 12 months of that date, that the company will be able to pay its debts in full within 12 months of the commencement of the winding up, or

---

15 See Lumsden [1987] JBL 111.
16 Or the acquisition of shares in its holding company, if it is a private company, s 155(1); but a subsidiary may not give financial assistance for the acquisition of shares in the holding company if the subsidiary is also a subsidiary of a public company which is itself a subsidiary of the holding company, s 155(3).
17 Defined CA 1985, s 154(2), s 155(2).
18 Ibid, s 155(2).
19 Interestingly, the Jenkins Committee Report, Cmnd 1749, paras 178–187, would have applied these requirements to all companies. This would have avoided many of the complex questions of interpretation which arise under ss 151–153 but is not possible now with regard to public companies in the light of the requirements of the Second EC Directive, art 23. However, the Law Society's Standing Committee on Company Law is urging the Department of Trade and Industry to review the scope of s 151 arguing that the provisions are much stricter than the Second Directive requires. See discussion below of their proposals.
20 Except where the company proposing to give the financial assistance is a wholly-owned subsidiary when no resolution is required, s 155(4). Where the financial assistance is given by a subsidiary for the acquisition of shares in the holding company, then the approval of the holding company's general meeting by special resolution is also required, see s 155(5).
1 CA 1985, s 381A, as inserted by CA 1989, s 113(2).
2 Ibid, s 157(1).
3 In forming their opinion for these purposes, the directors shall take into account the same liabilities, (including contingent and prospective liabilities) as would be relevant under s 122 of the Insolvency Act 1986 to the question whether the company is unable to pay its debts, CA 1985, s 156(3).

(b)   in any other case, that the company will be able to pay its debts as they fall due during the year immediately following that date.

Annexed to this declaration must be a report by the company's auditors stating that they have inquired into the company's state of affairs and that they are not aware of anything to indicate that the opinion expressed by the directors in their declaration as to any of the matters specified is unreasonable in all the circumstances[4].

The special resolution is not effective unless this declaration and the auditors' report is available for inspection by members of the company at the meeting at which the resolution is passed[5]. Where a private company opts to use the unanimous written resolution procedure provided by the CA 1989, then these documents must be made available to the member at or before the time at which the resolution is supplied to him for signature[6]. Any director who makes this statutory declaration without having reasonable grounds for the opinion expressed in the declaration is liable to imprisonment or a fine or both[7], but unlike in the case of redemption or purchase out of capital, no civil liability attaches under the Insolvency Act in the event of insolvency within 12 months of the payment of the financial assistance.

Strict time limits must be complied with and the financial assistance must not be given before the end of a period of four weeks after the resolution is passed[8]. This is because, as we shall see, objecting shareholders have 28 days in which to apply to the court. However, the financial assistance must be given not more than eight weeks after the statutory declaration is made[9]. This is to prevent the assistance being given a long time after the statutory declaration has been made and which is then out of date.

Objecting members may apply to the court

Under s 157(2), where a special resolution has been passed authorising the giving of financial assistance by a private company, an application for its cancellation may be made to the court within 28 days by the holders of not less than 10% in nominal value of the company's issued share capital or any class thereof[10]. Such an application cannot be made by any person who consented to or voted in favour of the resolution[11]. It will be noted that this procedure is not available to creditors who are already adequately protected by the restrictions on the funds which may be used and the need for a statutory declaration by the directors supported by the auditors.

At the hearing the court has wide powers. It shall make an order either cancelling or confirming the resolution and may, if it thinks fit, adjourn the proceedings in order that an arrangement may be made for the purchase of the interests of dissentient members and may give such directions and make

---

4 CA 1985, s 156(4).
5 Ibid, s 157(4). The declaration and auditors' report must also be delivered to the registrar of companies together with any special resolution required to be passed by s 155, s 156(5).
6 CA 1985, s 381A(7), as inserted by CA 1989, s 113; Sch 15A, para 4, as inserted by CA 1989, s 114.
7 CA 1985, s 156(7).
8 Ibid, s 158(2), unless all members entitled to vote at general meetings voted in favour of the resolution.
9 Ibid, s 158(4).
10 Such applications are governed by the procedure laid down in s 54, s 157(3).
11 CA 1985, s 157(2).

such orders as it thinks expedient for facilitating such arrangements[12]. Where the court's order provides for the purchase by the company of any member's shares it may provide accordingly for the reduction of the company's capital. Notice of any application to the court must be given forthwith to the registrar of companies and notice of any court order within 15 days of the making of it. No financial assistance can be given where an application has been made by a member until the final determination of the application unless the court orders otherwise[13]. For the reasons noted above in relation to members objecting to private companies redeeming or purchasing shares out of capital, it is difficult to see shareholders enjoying much success under this provision. They may have a greater chance of success simply in alleging unfairly prejudicial conduct under CA 1985, s 459, discussed in detail in Chapter 27.

It must not be forgotten that the other exemptions already outlined above apply equally to private companies so it is not necessary to follow this s 155 route. However, the great advantage in using s 155 is that companies do not face the uncertainties as to the scope of the purpose exceptions. Despite the procedural requirements, therefore, it is much the preferred method of proceeding.

Consequences of breach

As already noted, s 151(3) provides that if a company acts in contravention of this section, it is liable to a fine and every officer in default is liable to imprisonment or a fine or both. The statutory provisions do not, however, deal with the civil consequences of a company entering into a transaction in breach of the provisions[14].

Clearly, a director who authorises the giving of financial assistance in breach of the statutory provisions will be in breach of his duties to the company and liable to make good any losses suffered by it as a consequence[15].

A shareholder may seek an injunction to restrain the giving of financial assistance in breach of the statutory provisions but once the transaction is completed then he can only bring a derivative action[16] on behalf of the company to recover the sums expended[17]. That derivative action may be blocked, according to *Smith v Croft (No 2)*[18], despite the wrongdoers being in control of the company, if a majority of the independent shareholders believe that such an action is not in the best interests of the company[19].

Third parties who receive funds or who knowingly participate in the directors' breach of duty may be liable to the company as constructive

---

12 CA 1985, s 54(5), (6).
13 Ibid, s 158(3).
14 See generally, *Palmer's Company Law* (24th edn, 1987), paras 39–12 to 39–14.
15 *Belmont Finance Corpn Ltd v Williams Furniture Ltd (No 2)* [1980] 1 All ER 393, CA; *Wallersteiner v Moir* [1974] 3 All ER 217, [1974] 1 WLR 991, CA; *Selangor United Rubber Estates Ltd v Cradock (No 3)* [1968] 2 All ER 1073, [1968] 1 WLR 1555; *Steen v Law* [1964] AC 287, [1963] 3 All ER 770.
16 Discussed in detail in Ch 27.
17 *Smith v Croft (No 2)* [1988] Ch 114, [1987] 3 All ER 909.
18 Ibid.
19 The decision in this case is not without its difficulties, see Prentice [1988] 104 LQR 341, and is discussed in greater detail in Ch 27.

trustees. This is so if they received the funds with actual knowledge of the directors' breach of duty or in circumstances where they ought to have known of the breach[20]. Those who dishonestly participate in the scheme without actual receipt of the funds are liable to account if they knew of the breach of duty or wilfully shut their eyes to it[1]. Imposing liability on third parties is important as their participation, for example, as bankers, is often crucial to the success of the scheme.

Another issue which arose under s 54 was whether a transaction entered into in pursuance of the illegal financial assistance was itself invalid. For example, if a debenture or guarantee is the method of providing the financial assistance, is it enforceable? The question was considered in *Victor Battery Co Ltd v Curry's Ltd*[2], the facts of which were typical of many financial assistance schemes. J bought the whole of the share capital of VB, using a bank loan to finance the transaction. Once in control, he had the company, VB, take over the loan and give a debenture in respect of it to the bank. The question was whether that debenture was enforceable by the bank. Roxburgh J held that it was. The case was much criticised[3] and in *Heald v O'Connor*[4] the court refused to follow the earlier decision holding a debenture in similar circumstances to be void and unenforceable. Fisher J noting that such a result best furthered the policy of the Act in that it was likely to deter potential lenders from lending money on security which might be held to contravene the statute.

A related issue was whether an agreement to acquire shares which had yet to be performed but which had envisaged the use of financial assistance could be severed so as to cast aside the illegal element but enable the basic agreement to purchase shares to be enforced. The balance of authorities seems to support the view that such severance should take place if possible[5]. In *Carney v Herbert*[6], the Privy Council decided that severance could take place provided that the financial assistance is ancillary to the overall trans-

---

20 *Belmont Finance Corpn Ltd v Williams Furniture Ltd (No 2)* [1980] 1 All ER 393, CA; *Karak Rubber Co Ltd v Burden (No 2)* [1972] 1 All ER 1210, [1972] 1 WLR 602; *Selangor United Rubber Estates Ltd v Cradock (No 3)* [1968] 2 All ER 1073, [1968] 1 WLR 1555.

1 *Belmont Finance Corpn Ltd v Williams Furniture Ltd (No 2)* [1980] 1 All ER 393, CA; *Re Montagu's Settlement Trusts* [1987] Ch 264, [1987] 2 WLR 1192; *Lipkin Gorman v Karpnale Ltd* [1987] 1 WLR 987; on appeal [1989] 1 WLR 1340, [1989] BCLC 756n, CA, noted [1989] JBL 255; *Agip (Africa) Ltd v Jackson* [1990] Ch 265; affd (1991) Times, 9 January, Financial Times, 18 January, CA; *Eagle Trust plc v SBC Securities Ltd* (1991) Times, 14 February, Financial Times, 5 February. *Selangor United Rubber Estates Ltd v Cradock (No 3)* [1968] 2 All ER 1073, [1968] 1 WLR 1555 suggests that it is sufficient if the third party ought to have known of the breach of duty but this has not been generally accepted although *Baden, Delvaux and Lecuit v Société Général* [1983] BCLC 325 might be thought to support it. This confusion as to the degree of knowledge required under this heading has been the subject of much academic comment, see Millett (1991) 107 LQR 71; Harpum [1987] 50 MLR 217; Vroegop [1988] JBL 437; Arora [1990] JBL 217.

2 [1946] Ch 242, [1946] 1 All ER 519.

3 While it was followed in *Curtis's Furnishing Stores Ltd v Freedman* [1966] 2 All ER 955, it was doubted in *Selangor United Rubber Estates Ltd v Cradock (No 3)* [1968] 2 All ER 1073, [1968] 1 WLR 1555 and in many overseas jurisdictions, see *Heald v O'Connor* [1971] 2 All ER 1105, [1971] 1 WLR 497, where Fisher J outlines the history of the *Victor Battery* decision.

4 [1971] 2 All ER 1105, [1971] 1 WLR 497.

5 *South Western Mineral Water Co Ltd v Ashmore* [1967] 2 All ER 953, [1967] 1 WLR 1110 which was endorsed by the Privy Council in *Carney v Herbert* [1985] AC 301, [1985] 1 All ER 438. See also *Lawlor v Gray* (1980) 130 NLJ 317.

6 [1985] AC 301, [1985] 1 All ER 438, PC.

action and its elimination would leave unchanged the subject matter of the transaction, ie the sale of the shares, the nature of the illegality not being such as to preclude severance[7].

Reform

The difficulties in applying these provisions are evident from *Brady v Brady*[8] and the Guinness trial where the s 151 charge was withdrawn from the jury by the judge. Practitioners are frequently concerned, particularly when dealing with the acquisition of other companies, with the application of the financial assistance provision and are unhappy with the lack of certainty surrounding its possible application. These concerns have prompted the Law Society's Standing Committee on Company Law to make submissions to the Department of Trade and Industry urging the DTI to make changes to the provisions to resolve some of the present uncertainties[9]. The Committee has urged the Department to decriminalise the section and to allow companies to give financial assistance in the circumstances currently applicable to private companies under s 155, namely where the financial assistance does not reduce net assets or, to the extent that they are reduced, the assistance is provided out of distributable profits. The only limit on the application of that provision should be the requirements of the Second EC Directive on Company Law which requires that public companies be prohibited from giving financial assistance. However, as the wording of the Directive is narrower than that in s 151, the Committee feels there is scope for relaxing the provisions in the CA 1985 while still complying with the EC requirements.

The DTI's only response to date has been to indicate that it will issue guidelines to companies regarding the circumstances under which they can spend money to promote their own shares. This is a more limited issue which has been raised by those anxious to promote wider share owneship who feel that s 151 impedes a company's promotional activities. It does not address the more fundamental issues raised by the Law Society's paper which would require amendments to the legislation as it now stands.

DIVIDENDS

Background

The particular problem which the rules attempt to address in this area is the risk that directors and shareholders will attempt to swell the dividend fund, creating fictitious profits and otherwise distributing the company's assets during its lifetime, thus depleting the capital assets of the company to the ultimate detriment of the company's creditors who, on liquidation, will find the company stripped of its assets. Its significance in the context of capital maintenance is obvious.

Before 1980 the position was governed entirely by case law rules which,

7 [1985] AC 301 at 314, [1985] 1 All ER 438 at 446, PC.
8 [1989] AC 755, [1988] 2 All ER 617, HL.
9 See The Law Society's Standing Committee on Company Law, Companies Act 1985, s 151, Memorandum No 233, September 1990.

while prohibiting the payment of a dividend out of capital[10], were in other respects rather lax and out of step with modern accounting practice. For example, they permitted dividends to be paid out of current trading profits, without making good losses in fixed capital[11] or trading losses in previous years[12]; they allowed dividends to be paid out of an unrealised capital gain resulting from a bona fide revaluation of fixed assets[13] and did not require companies to provide for depreciation[14]. Many of these legal rules were commercially unwise and contrary to good accounting practice but the courts were reluctant to interfere with the directors' discretion as men of business[15].

The position altered, however, with the Companies Act 1980, and statutory provisions, found in CA 1985, ss 263–281, now govern the area, displacing in most instances the old common law rules. To a very considerable step, Parliament has intervened where the courts felt they could not. The result is a series of statutory requirements which curb the more dubious dividend payments for the protection of the creditors generally[16]. If a company does not have distributable profits as defined by these provisions, then it cannot declare a dividend. Even if it has distributable profits, it must be remembered that the rules lay down the minimum requirements which must be met before a company may declare a dividend and there may be further restrictions on the directors' freedom of action in the memorandum and articles of association[17].

The rules cannot provide complete protection, of course, and it has to be borne in mind that many private companies have been accustomed to not declaring dividends and so have not been constrained by these rules but have instead distributed profits by way of directors' remuneration over which there are few controls, as we shall see. In the past, this practice was dictated by taxation requirements but the position has now altered and there is no longer the tax disincentive against distributions which previously existed. Indeed there may now be tax savings to be made by paying dividends, thus avoiding, for example, paying national insurance contributions on salary. The question of dividends or salary is therefore a matter to be determined now in the light of the individual's position rather than by any general taxation requirements. A further complication in private companies is that a persistent failure to pay dividends when distributable profits are available may justify a petition under CA 1985, s 459, alleging unfairly prejudicial conduct, discussed in detail in Chapter 27.

---

10 *Re Exchange Banking Co, Flitcroft's Case* (1882) 21 Ch D 591, CA; *Verner v General and Commercial Investment Trust* [1894] 2 Ch 239, CA.
11 *Verner v General and Commercial Investment Trust* [1894] 2 Ch 239, CA; *Lee v Neuchatel Asphalte Co* (1889) 41 Ch D 1, CA.
12 *Ammonia Soda Co v Chamberlain* [1918] 1 Ch 266, CA; *Re National Bank of Wales* [1899] 2 Ch 629, CA.
13 *Dimbula Valley (Ceylon) Tea Co Ltd v Laurie* [1961] Ch 353, [1961] 1 All ER 769.
14 *Lee v Neuchatel Asphalte Co* (1889) 41 Ch D 1, CA; *Bolton v Natal Land and Colonization Co* [1892] 2 Ch 124.
15 *Lee v Neuchatel Asphalte Co* (1889) 41 Ch D 1 at 18, CA, per Cotton LJ, at 21 per Lindley LJ; *Re National Bank of Wales* [1899] 2 Ch 629, CA.
16 See *Precision Dippings Ltd v Precision Dippings Marketing Ltd* [1986] Ch 447 at 455, [1985] BCLC 385 at 388, CA, per Dillon LJ. However, a creditor does not have locus standi to seek an injunction to prevent an unlawful dividend, only a shareholder can do that.
17 CA 1985, s 281.

The statutory position

The basic rule, set out in s 263, is that a company shall not make a distribution except out of profits available for the purpose.

By distribution we usually mean the payment of a dividend but the term is defined in s 263(2) to apply to every description of distribution of a company's assets to its members, whether in cash or otherwise, with certain exceptions. The excepted categories are distributions by way of—

(a)   an issue of shares as fully or partly-paid bonus shares, discussed in Chapter 14,

(b)   the redemption or purchase of any of the company's own shares out of capital (including the proceeds of any fresh issue of shares) or out of unrealised profits in accordance with Chapter VII of Part V, discussed above,

(c)   the reduction of share capital by extinguishing or reducing the liability of any of the members on any of the company's shares in respect of share capital not paid up, or by paying off paid up share capital, discussed in Chapter 16, and

(d)   a distribution of assets to members of the company on its winding up, discussed in Chapter 39.

The profits available for distribution are defined by s 263(3) as the company's accumulated, realised profits, so far as not previously utilised by distribution or capitalisation, less its accumulated realised losses, so far as not previously written off in a reduction or reorganisation of capital duly made. The requisite elements of the definition are then in turn further defined.

Realised profits and losses[18]   The key point is that it is only realised profits or losses which enter the equation. 'Realised profits' was defined in *Re Oxford Benefit Building and Investment Society*[19] as meaning reduced to actual cash in hand or at least rendered tangible for the purpose of division. The reason for this requirement is to prevent companies from relying on estimated or expected profits which might never actually materialise. In deciding whether something is realised or not, it is a question of considering standard accounting practice in these matters. This statutory requirement that the profit be realised reverses the much criticised common law rule laid down in *Dimbula Valley (Ceylon) Tea Co Ltd v Laurie*[20] which enabled a company to declare a dividend on an unrealised profit occurring on a revaluation of assets. Equally, depreciation which formerly was not provided for[1], now must be treated as a realised loss[2]. On the other hand, unrealised losses are not take into account unless the company is a public company, discussed below.

---

18   Profits and losses covers revenue and capital profits and losses, CA 1985, s 280(3).
19   (1886) 35 Ch D 502. For criticism of the usefulness of this approach, see Noke [1989] JBL 37 at 42.
20   [1961] Ch 353, [1961] 1 All ER 769.
 1   *Lee v Neuchatel Asphalte Co* (1889) 41 Ch D 1, CA; *Bolton v Natal Land and Colonization Co* [1892] 2 Ch 124.
 2   CA 1985, s 275(1). An exception arises where the value of a fixed asset is diminished in a revaluation of all fixed assets or all fixed assets other than goodwill.

Accumulated losses   Equally crucial is the requirement that the amount of accumulated realised losses must be deducted before any distribution can be made. This abrogates the old common law rule, noted above, that losses made in previous accounting periods did not have to be made good. Now accounting periods can no longer be regarded in isolation from one another. Hence the need in many cases to write off losses in a reduction of capital duly made before resuming the payment of dividends[3].

Public companies

There are further requirements, set out in s 264, as far as public companies are concerned. This is in keeping with the capital provisions generally in the Companies Act 1985 which, as we have seen, commonly impose more stringent requirements on public companies.

In addition to having profits available for distribution as outlined above, a public company must satisfy two further conditions before it makes a distribution.

Section 264 provides that a public company may only make a distribution at any time

(a)   if at that time, the amount of its net assets is not less than the aggregate of its called-up share capital and undistributable reserves, and

(b)   if, and to the extent that, the distribution does not reduce the amount of those assets to less than that aggregate.

Net assets for these purposes is defined by s 264(2) as meaning the aggregate of the company's assets less the aggregate of its liabilities.

Called up share capital is widely defined in s 737 to include capital to which a company will become entitled but which it has not received and situations where a call has been made but not paid.

A company's undistributable reserves are[4]:

(a)   the share premium account;

(b)   the capital redemption reserve;

(c)   the amount by which the company's accumulated unrealised profits (not previously utilised by any capitalisation) exceeds its accumulated unrealised losses (not previously written off in a reduction or reorganisation of capital duly made); and

(d)   any other reserve which the company is prohibited from distributing by any enactment or by its memorandum or articles.

The net effect of these additional requirements for public companies means that a public company must allow for any unrealised loss (in excess of an unrealised profit) which may exist. That unrealised loss must be covered before the company can declare a dividend.

---

3   We shall see in Ch 16 that there has been an increased use of the capital reduction provisions because of these dividend rules which require a reduction to be made if the company is to resume payment of dividends after a period of losses.

4   CA 1985, s 264(3).

Accounts

All of these matters must be determined in accordance with the company's accounts, ie the company's last annual accounts prepared in accordance with the requirements of the Act[5], which accounts must have been duly laid before the general meeting[6]. If the auditors have qualified the accounts, then they must state in writing whether, in their opinion, the substance of the qualification is material for determining the legality of the proposed dividend and a copy of that statement must also have been laid before the company in general meeting[7].

The significance of this statement by the auditor was considered by the Court of Appeal in *Precision Dippings Ltd v Precision Dippings Marketing Ltd*[8]. In this case, no auditor's statement had been made, let alone laid before the company in general meeting. A dividend was paid and the company later went into liquidation. The liquidator claimed to recover the amount of the dividend from the recipient (Marketing). The defence to the claim was that this requirement of an auditor's statement was a mere procedural requirement and so the failure to comply with it did not invalidate the payment. Dillon LJ rejected this argument, stating that it was not a mere procedural requirement but an important part of the scheme provided by the statutory provisions as a major protection for creditors. The wording of the provision showed that the auditor's statement had to be available to the shareholders before the distribution was made. As it had not been available then the statutory provisions had been contravened.

Liability

Where a distribution is made which is in contravention of the requirements of the Act on distributions, then s 277(1) provides that any member who, at the time of the distribution, knew or had reasonable grounds for believing that it was so made, is liable to repay the distribution to the company. This statutory liability is, by s 277(2), without prejudice to any other obligation imposed on a member to repay a distribution unlawfully made to him.

Following on from the finding noted above, that the failure to comply with the requirements concerning the auditor's statement meant that the dividend payment was in breach of the statutory requirements, the court in *Precision Dippings Ltd v Precision Dippings Marketing Ltd*[9] then turned to the issue of liability. Marketing, as the recipient of the dividend, claimed that while it knew all the facts concerning the payment of the dividend, it did not in fact know the terms of the statutory provisions and therefore was not within s 277(1). The Court of Appeal decided that it was unnecessary to examine the wording of s 277(1) since s 277(2) covered the position. The payment of the dividend was an ultra vires act of the company. Marketing,

---

5 Ibid, s 271(2) and (3).
6 Ibid, s 270(3). If the company is a private company which has elected to dispense with the laying of accounts and reports before the company in general meeting, then the accounts must have been sent to the members instead, CA 1985, s 252 as inserted by CA 1989, s 16.
7 Ibid, s 271(4). If the company is a private company which has elected to dispense with the laying of accounts and reports before the company in general meeting, then the statement must have been sent to the members instead, CA 1985, s 252 as inserted by CA 1989, s 16.
8 [1986] Ch 447, [1985] BCLC 385, noted Parkinson, (1986) 7 Co Law 26.
9 [1986] Ch 447, [1985] BCLC 385, CA.

when it received the money, had notice of the facts and would be liable as a constructive trustee for the company[10]. Marketing was accordingly liable to account to the company. Directors who recommend dividends in breach of the rules are also liable to account to the company for the sums paid out[11].

Declaration of dividends

Assuming at this stage that a company does have distributable profits as determined in accordance with the rules set out above, the next question is whether this automatically entitles the shareholders to a dividend. It will do so where the articles provide for the payment of a fixed dividend where the company has distributable profits[12], but in other cases the articles will commonly require a declaration of the company in general meeting by ordinary resolution following a recommendation by the directors[13]. In the exercise of this as of any other power, the directors are obliged to act bona fide in the interests of the company as a whole[14] and prudent financial management may require putting a certain percentage of the funds to reserves rather than distributing the entire amount[15]. A persistent failure to pay dividends when funds are available may be unfairly prejudicial conduct under s 459[16] or warrant a winding up on the just and equitable ground[17].

Only when a dividend has actually been declared does it become payable and due to the members[18]. It need not be paid in cash, but if a non-cash consideration is to be provided, eg in the form of additional shares[19], then specific authorisation to that effect must be included in the articles[20].

10 [1986] Ch 447 at 458, [1985] BCLC 385 at 390, per Dillon LJ, applying *Rolled Steel Products (Holdings) Ltd v British Steel Corpn* [1986] Ch 246, [1985] 3 All ER 52, CA. See also *Re Cleveland Trust plc* [1991] BCC 33.
11 *Re Exchange Banking Co, Flitcroft's Case* (1882) 21 Ch D 519, CA; *Re Oxford Benefit Building and Investment Society* (1886) 35 Ch D 502.
12 *Evling v Israel and Oppenheimer* [1918] 1 Ch 101.
13 See Table A, art 102. The general meeting may decrease but not increase the amount to be distributed. The directors have power to declare an interim dividend, art 103.
14 This will include an obligation in some circumstances to have regard to the interests of creditors, see discussion in Chapter 25, which may preclude the payment of a dividend, see *Hilton International Ltd v Hilton* (1988) 4 NZ CLC 64 at 721.
15 The Draft Fifth EC Directive on Company Law, art 49, would require the compulsory transfer of at least 5% of the profits in each financial year to a statutory reserve until that reserve amounts to not less than 10% of the subscribed capital. It further provides for limitations on the way in which the statutory reserve may be used. The UK is opposed to this proposal, see Amended Proposal for a Fifth Directive on the Harmonisation of Company Law, Consultative Document, January 1990.
16 *Re Sam Weller & Sons Ltd* [1990] Ch 682, [1990] BCLC 80. *Re a Company (No 00370 of 1987), ex p Glossop* [1988] 1 WLR 1068, [1988] BCLC 570 had suggested that s 459 was not available because the conduct complained of, the failure to pay adequate dividends, affected all of the members and therefore could not be unfairly prejudicial to some of the members. Peter Gibson J did not agree with that approach in *Re Sam Weller* and the position has now been clarified by CA 1989, Sch 19, para 11 which has altered the wording of s 459 to cover conduct unfairly prejudicial to the interests of the members generally or of some part of the members.
17 *Re a Company (No 00370 of 1987), ex p Glossop* [1988] 1 WLR 1068, [1988] BCLC 570.
18 *Bond v Barrow Haematite Steel Co* [1902] 1 Ch 353.
19 See Table A, art 110.
20 *Wood v Odessa Waterworks Co* (1889) 42 Ch D 636.

CHAPTER 16

Share capital alteration

As has already been explained, the amount of a company's share capital and the division thereof is set out on incorporation in the company's memorandum of association, as required by CA 1985, s 2(5). Section 2(7) further provides that a company may not alter the conditions contained in the memorandum except in the cases, in the mode and to the extent, for which express provision is made by the Act. Our concern in this Chapter is to consider the two statutory provisions which do permit the alteration of the share capital provision in the memorandum, namely s 121 dealing with alterations which do not involve a reduction of capital and s 135 which provides for reduction. We shall deal with each in turn.

ALTERATIONS OTHER THAN REDUCTION

Section 121 enables a company limited by shares or limited by guarantee with a share capital, if so authorised by its articles, to alter its memorandum provisions relating to share capital in the following ways.

The company may—

(a) increase its share capital by new shares of such amount as it thinks expedient;
(b) consolidate and divide all or any of its share capital into shares of larger amount than its exisiting shares;
(c) convert all or any of its paid-up shares into stock, and re-convert that stock into paid-up shares of any denomination;
(d) sub-divide its shares, or any of them, into shares of smaller amount than is fixed by the memorandum;
(e) cancel shares, which at the date of the passing of the resolution to cancel them, have not been taken or agreed to be taken by any person, and diminish the amount of the company's share capital by the amount of the shares so cancelled.

Various procedural points common to all these categories should be noted before considering each in turn. First, the company's articles must authorise the alteration in question. Article 32 of Table A is commonly adopted for this purpose and it provides that these alterations may be effected by an ordinary resolution. The one omission from art 32 is any provision in respect of (c) above which reflects the fact that it is rare now for companies to convert their shares into stock.

Secondly, s 121(4) provides that the power conferred by the section must be executed by the company in general meeting which prior to the Companies Act 1989 ruled out the use of written procedures. However, as far as private companies are concerned, this is now subject to the written resolution procedure provided by the CA 1989. Section 381A of the 1985 Act, as inserted by CA 1989, s 113(2), provides that anything which in the case of a private company may be done by a resolution in general meeting (or in a class meeting) may be done, without a meeting, by a resolution in writing signed by or on behalf of all the members of the company. The procedure is subject to the right of the company's auditors to require that a meeting be held, in the circumstances set out in s 381B. The written resolution procedure is explained in detail in Chapter 22.

Thirdly, there are the standard disclosure requirements which are common where there is a change to the constitutional documents. Notice of any alteration authorised by s 121 and provided for by the company's articles must be given within one month of alteration[1] (within 15 days if the alteration relates to an increase in share capital)[2] to the registrar of companies. In all cases, the company must also send to the registrar a copy of the memorandum as altered[3]. Default in respect of any of these obligations leaves the company and any officer in default liable to a fine[4].

Increasing share capital

This is the most common alteration. Its purpose is to lift the ceiling on the company's share capital imposed by the terms of the memorandum. A company incorporated in 1980 may find that the limit originally set, for example, £500,000 divided into 500,000 £1 shares, is inadequate for the expansion of the business in 1991. It may wish to increase that figure to £1m divided into 1m £1 shares, so as to enable it to raise further equity capital by issuing another 500,000 shares.

It should be noted that the passing of a resolution to increase the authorised share capital under s 121(2)(a) does not operate as a grant of authority to the directors to proceed to allot those shares. Authority to allot is a separate matter governed by CA 1985, s 80 and discussed in detail in Chapter 25.

Consolidation

Consolidation means combining a number of shares into a new share of commensurate nominal value. Thus ten £1 shares may be consolidated into one £10 share. This process is less common now as the preference is for shares of lower rather than higher nominal value but it is sometimes used as an element of a capital rearrangement scheme which has left the company with unwieldy nominal value shares. Thus 12.5p shares may be consolidated into 50p or £1 shares. This exercise has no financial impact on the shareholders who now hold fewer shares but of greater nominal value.

Conversion of shares into stock and vice versa

Section 121(2)(c) provides for easy conversion from shares to stock and vice versa although it is of limited significance now, as it is rare for UK companies to make use of these powers. The starting point in the UK is that stock

---

1 CA 1985, s 122.
2 Ibid, s 123.
3 Ibid, s 18(2).
4 Ibid, ss 122(2), 123(4), 18(3).

cannot be issued directly by the company[5] but arises from a conversion of fully-paid shares into stock. There were two reasons, in particular, for converting shares in this way. First, shares could not (and cannot) be dealt with in fractions, whereas stock may be. Secondly, shares have to be numbered but stock does not. However, these supposed advantages are less significant now. While, strictly speaking, stock may be dealt with in fractions, in practice a company's articles will prescribe the minimum dealing unit which is usually the same as one share, so stock is not necessarily any more flexible than shares. Equally, the administrative advantages of unnumbered stock are available in respect of shares, as s 182(2) permits numbers to be dispensed with where all the issued shares in a company, or of a particular class, are fully paid up and rank pari passu for all purposes.

The limited significance[6] of conversion explains why it alone, of the categories of alteration specified is s 121, is omitted from art 32 of Table A which, as we saw, is the model authorisation provision for companies wishing to use s 121. Any company wishing to convert will have to ensure that it does have authority in its articles to do so. Article 32 of itself is insufficient.

Sub-division

This is quite a common process and is simply the opposite process to consolidation which was described above. Sub-division involves dividing a share into a number of new shares and is usually done to increase the marketability of shares where companies feel their nominal value is too high. Thus £1 shares can be sub-divided in four 25p shares or ten 10p shares.

Cancellation

Section 122(2)(e) deals with the cancellation of nominal capital which at the date of the relevant resolution has not been taken or agreed to be taken by any person[7]. For example, a company may have been incorporated with a share capital of £200,000 divided into 200,000 £1 shares. The company's plans prove over-optimistic and it is only trading in a limited way for which share capital of £50,000 is adequate. The company might wish to cancel £100,000 of that outstanding capital since it cannot envisage ever raising that amount of share capital. The only effect of this is to reduce the scope for issuing further shares but power to do so can be restored at any time by simply increasing the share capital back to £200,000 if circumstances so warrant.

This alteration results in the reduction of the company's authorised capital, not its issued capital[8], and is therefore to be distinguished from such a reduction which is discussed below. A reduction of issued capital may have

---

5 *Re Home and Foreign Investment and Agency Co Ltd* [1912] 1 Ch 72.
6 The Jenkins Committee on Company Law reporting in 1962, Cmnd 1749, para 472, noted that the advantages of conversion seemed to be negligible and recommended that steps be taken to phase out the use of stock but this was never acted upon.
7 It is not sufficient to rule out s 122(2)(e) that someone has offered to take the shares proposed to be cancelled; there must be a contract to take the shares, *Re Swindon Town Football Co Ltd* [1990] BCLC 467.
8 A point explicitly made in s 121(5).

implications for a company's creditors as they look to the share capital as a creditors' fund whereas a cancellation of capital not yet taken up or agreed to be taken up has no effect on creditors. Given its limited significance, this power is rarely used other than again as part of an overall scheme of reconstruction.

REDUCTION OF CAPITAL

Here we are concerned not with cancelling unissued shares, as above, but with reducing the share capital previously raised by the company. Given our overriding concern with share capital as a creditors' fund, it is not surprising that it is a basic principle of English company law that capital cannot generally be reduced without the consent of the court. The position was explained by Lord Watson in *Trevor v Whitworth*[9] as follows:

Paid up share capital may be diminished or lost in the course of the company's trading; that is a result which no legislation can prevent; but persons who deal with, and give credit to a limited company, naturally rely upon the fact that the company is trading with a certain amount of capital already paid, as well as upon the responsibility of its members for the capital remaining at call; and they are entitled to assume that no part of the capital which has been paid into the coffers of the company has been subsequently paid out, except in the legitimate course of its business[10].

Having said that, business realities require that there should be provision for a number of exceptional circumstances when capital may be reduced. These must be considered against the background of the general prohibition, however, so we shall see that reduction is permitted only in limited instances and surrounded by measures designed to ensure that creditors, in particular, are not jeopardised.

Briefly, reduction may occur in the following ways:

(a)   reduction by special resolution in accordance with the requirements of CA 1985, s 135. This procedure is discussed in detail below;

(b)   reduction as a consequence of a redemption of shares or a purchase back of shares by a *private* company *out of capital*[11] (discussed in Chapter 15) which has the effect of a reduction of capital for such companies without requiring the confirmation of the court as required by s 135. Creditors and members are protected in such circumstances, however, by the elaborate procedural requirements imposed by the statutory provisions which authorise such schemes and by the ability to object to the court under CA 1985, s 176;

(c)   reduction as a consequence of a court order for the purchase of shares of an objecting member by a company under a variety of provisions, such as s 54 (objection to public company going private), s 157

---

9 (1887) 12 App Cas 409, HL. For a recent example of a breach of the basic principle that capital may not be returned, see *Aveling Barford Ltd v Perion Ltd* [1989] BCLC 626. Disguising the transaction as a sale (at a gross undervalue) will not hide the true nature of the transaction.

10 Ibid, at p 423.

11 Reduction does not occur in the case of redemptions or purchases otherwise than out of capital since, in those instances, an amount equivalent to the amount redeemed or purchased must be transferred to the capital redemption reserve which, as we saw in Ch 15, is treated as if it were share capital, CA 1985, s 170(4).

(objection to private company giving financial assistance for the purchase of its own shares), s 177 (objection to purchase or redemption of shares by private company out of capital) and s 459 (relief for unfairly prejudicial conduct);

(d)   reduction as a result of forfeiture or surrender by members, discussed below.

Having outlined the possible methods of effecting a reduction, we will concentrate in this Chapter on (a) the statutory mechanism for reduction provided by CA 1985, s 135. (b) has been discussed in Chapter 15; (c) is discussed where the relevant provisions are considered; and (d) is considered briefly at the end of this Chapter.

CA 1985, s 135

Section 135(1) allows a company, if so authorised by its articles, and subject to confirmation by the court, by special resolution to reduce its capital in any way and sub-s (2) goes on to specify three methods of reduction, in particular, which companies may wish to use[12]. They are:

(a)   the extinction or reduction of any liability on shares not fully paid up;

(b)   the cancellation of paid-up share capital which is lost or unrepresented by available assets;

(c)   the payment off of any paid-up share capital in excess of the company's wants.

(a)   THE EXTINCTION OR REDUCTION OF LIABILITY ON SHARES NOT FULLY PAID UP

Reduction in this instance appears to endanger creditors as it extinguishes a liability, namely the obligation on the part of the holders of partly-paid shares to pay the amount due on those shares, which would be a valuable asset to the creditors in the event of a winding up[13]. In practice, however, this category is rarely used, as it is unusual now for shares to be issued as partly-paid. It is seldom therefore that there is any question of there being any unpaid share capital outstanding.

(b)   THE CANCELLATION OF PAID-UP SHARE CAPITAL WHICH IS LOST OR UNREPRESENTED BY AVAILABLE ASSETS

The cancellation of paid-up share capital which is lost or unrepresented by available assets appears to have an impact on creditors, as it reduces the minimum level of assets which must be maintained by the company. However, if a company had at one time a paid-up share capital of £200,000, but following trading losses, its net assets now amount only to £50,000, little is achieved by maintaining the figure of £200,000 as the capital yardstick. Reduction in that instance is an exercise to restore reality to the company's

---

12 The courts have emphasised on many occasions that there is no question of sub-s (2) limiting or controlling the power available to the company to reduce its capital *in any way* as provided by s 135(1): *British and American Trustee Corpn v Couper* [1894] AC 399, HL; *Poole v National Bank of China* [1907] AC 229, HL; *Re Thomas de la Rue & Co Ltd* [1911] 2 Ch 361; *Ex p Westburn Sugar Refineries Ltd* [1951] AC 625, [1951] 1 All ER 881, HL.

13 Assuming that those shareholders were in a position to meet their liability on those shares.

accounts. Reduction will also be crucial to the company's ability to make or resume dividend payments to its shareholders and it is important to appreciate the impact of the dividend rules, discussed in detail in Chapter 15, in this context.

Under these rules, a company may only distribute profits as defined by CA 1985, s 263, namely the amount by which its accumulated realised profits, so far as not previously utilised by distribution or capitalisation, exceed its accumulated realised losses, so far as not previously written off in a reduction or reorganisation of capital duly made. A public company, moreover, may only declare a dividend if the amount of its net assets is not less than the aggregate of its called-up share capital and undistributable reserves which include the capital redemption reserve and share premium account[14].

The net effect of the need to have regard to accumulated profits and losses means that accrued losses have either to be made good, a process which could take an inordinate amount of time, or more likely it will be necessary to reduce capital to take account of the loss. Equally, public companies with a significant share capital account and undistributable reserves may find that the effect of these rules is to preclude them from declaring dividends out of current profits. The share capital and share premium accounts need to be reduced in such cases, so lowering the threshold which must be crossed before the company can declare dividends.

A failure to maintain or resume the payment of dividends will result in a depressed share price which may make the company vulnerable to takeover. It also makes it more difficult for the company to raise additional equity capital as shares with no dividend return would be unattractive to investors.

In so far as the capital must be lost, the court will want to be satisfied that it is indeed lost, for if it is not permanently lost then a cancellation of paid-up share capital will prejudice the interests of the creditors[15]. In *Re Jupiter House Investments (Cambridge) Ltd*[16] Harman J held that where loss of capital was sought to be proved, loss meant permanent loss, as far as was presently foreseeable, and not a temporary fall in the value of some capital asset. However, where the loss could not be proved to be permanent[17] but the company had given an undertaking which ensured that if the loss of capital was in fact recovered, it would not be distributed as dividends, the court could, in the exceptional circumstances, confirm the proposed reduction. The effect of the undertaking was to ensure that there was no risk of moneys which in truth represented capital of the company being used to pay dividends[18]. On the other hand, in *Re Grosvenor Press plc*[19], Nourse J was loath to require such undertakings, noting that there were already statutory safeguards to protect the interests of future creditors and shareholders in that the publicity requirements surrounding the reduction and the need for the company's accounts to give a true and fair view of the state of its affairs meant that they would be fully informed of the position. There was no need,

---

14 CA 1985, ss 264(1), (3).
15 *Re Grosvenor Press plc* [1985] 1 WLR 980 at 982, [1985] BCLC 286 at 288, per Nourse J.
16 [1985] 1 WLR 975, [1985] BCLC 222. See Milman (1986) 7 Co Law 68.
17 In this instance, the loss arose from defects in a substantial building which the company owned. The company had been advised that it had more than an even chance of recovering the loss by an action for damages against a third party.
18 [1985] 1 WLR 975 at 979, [1985] BCLC 222 at 225, per Harman J.
19 [1985] 1 WLR 980, [1985] BCLC 286. Noted Milman (1986) 7 Co Law 68.

except in special circumstances, for the court to require a reserve to be set aside indefinitely.

It might finally be noted at this point that CA 1985, s 142 requires directors of a public company to call an extraordinary general meeting promptly upon discovering that the net assets are half or less of its called-up share capital for the purpose of considering whether any steps should be taken to deal with the situation. One possibility clearly is to seek a reduction of capital.

(c)   THE PAYMENT OFF OF ANY PAID-UP SHARE CAPITAL IN EXCESS OF THE COMPANY'S WANTS

As for (c), the payment off of paid-up share capital in excess of the company's needs, this clearly poses no risk to creditors and may simply reflect a shrinking of the company's activities[20]. It might be noted that it is only in this instance that capital is actually returned to the shareholders. In (a) the capital has never been received and in (b) the capital is lost.

It is not necessary that the shareholders should actually receive cash; non-cash assets may be used instead[1] and in that case there need not be an exact correlation between the capital reduced and the value of the assets transferred[2]. This may appear to offer some opportunity for abuse but the courts have indicated that the important matter is not how much is returned to the shareholders but how much is retained for the protection of creditors[3]. However, the disparity in value may well adversely influence the court in the exercise of its discretion to confirm the reduction.

Having identified the reasons for and the circumstances in which a reduction might be used, we turn now to consider the manner in which a reduction is effected.

Procedure for reduction

First, the company must be authorised by its articles to reduce capital and art 34 of Table A is typical of the provisions which are adopted. It provides that, subject to the provisions of the Act, the company may by special resolution reduce its share capital, any capital redemption reserve and any share premium account[4] in any way. This is frequently qualified in public companies

---

20 Many of the earlier cases of reductions under (c) related to companies whose business had been nationalised and which were reducing their activities to some limited venture of their own or in some cases heading for liquidation.

1 *Ex p Westburn Sugar Refineries Ltd* [1951] AC 625, [1951] 1 All ER 881, HL; *Re Thomas de la Rue & Co Ltd* [1911] 2 Ch 361. It might also be noted that a distribution whether of cash or assets in a reduction is not a distribution for the purposes of CA 1985, Part VIII, s 263(2), hence there is no need to have distributable profits as therein defined.

2 In *Ex p Westburn Sugar Refineries Ltd* [1951] AC 625 at 631, [1951] 1 All ER 881 at 885, Lord Reid made the point that this must be the position because in many cases it is impossible to make any exact valuation of the non-cash assets. It is therefore possible that the shareholder may receive more or less than the value of his capital but if what is offered to the shareholder is illusory then the court will refuse to confirm the reduction: *Re Thomas de la Rue & Co Ltd* [1911] 2 Ch 361.

3 See, for example, Lord Normand in *Ex p Westburn Sugar Refineries Ltd* [1951] AC 625 at 630, [1951] 1 All ER 881 at 884.

4 The share premium account and capital redemption reserve are treated as share capital and so are subject to the same constraints on reduction, see CA 1985, ss 130(3) and 170(4) respectively.

by providing that the reduction shall not have the effect of reducing the share capital below the authorised minimum for a public company[5].

A special resolution in general meeting is therefore required, subject to the availability now of a written resolution in the case of private companies[6].

When the company has passed the special resolution then it may apply to the court for an order confirming the reduction, which the court may make on such terms and conditions as it thinks fit[7], subject to the position of the company's creditors having been safeguarded, as discussed below.

In practice, the position of two groups, the creditors and the shareholders, will be relevant to the court's decision, although it must be appreciated that in many instances the reduction will have no effect on the creditors whose co-operation and agreement the company will have ensured and is not opposed by the shareholders. In such cases the court's role is little more than to endorse the company's plans.

CREDITORS

Creditors are not left, as shareholders are, to rely on the court in the exercise of its discretion to protect them. Instead, in recognition of the potential risk to creditors when companies exercise a power to reduce capital, specific statutory provision is made for their protection.

Section 137(1) provides that the court is required to be satisfied with respect to every creditor of the company who under s 136 (discussed below) is entitled to object to the reduction of capital that either (a) his consent to the reduction has been obtained; or (b) his debt or claim has been discharged or has been determined, or has been secured, before it makes an order confirming the reduction on such terms and conditions as it thinks fit.

Section 136(2) provides that where the proposed reduction involves either a diminution of liability in respect of unpaid share capital or the payment to a shareholder of any paid-up share capital, and in any other case if the court so directs, then the procedure specified in s 136(3)–(5) must be adhered to unless the court exercises its discretion under s 136(6), having regard to the special circumstances of the case, to disapply sub-ss (3)–(5).

The procedure under s 136(3)–(5) is that a list of creditors entitled to object is settled and the court has to be satisfied that any such creditor has either (a) consented to the reduction, or (b) his debt or claim has been discharged or has been determined, or has been secured, before it makes an order confirming the reduction on such terms and conditions as it thinks fit. In practice, because reduction is frequently part of an overall reconstruction, the company will

---

5 CA 1985, s 117(2) requires that the nominal value of a public company's allotted share capital must not be less than the authorised minimum, which by CA 1985, s 118(1) is £50,000. This provision does not rule out a reduction by a company which momentarily reduces the company's capital to nil before following it with an increase in capital to above that minimum, *Re M B Group Ltd* [1989] BCLC 672.

6 See CA 1985, s 381A, as inserted by CA 1989, s 113. This removes the doubts expressed in *Re Barry Artists Ltd* [1985] 1 WLR 1305, [1985] BCLC 283 as to whether written resolutions are acceptable for s 135 purposes.

7 The court can confirm a resolution even if there is a factual error in it, provided that it is so insignificant that no one could be thought to be prejudiced by its correction: *Re Willaire Systems plc* (1987) BCLC 67, CA. See also *Re European Home Products plc* [1988] BCLC 690 where a more significant error occurred but the court reluctantly confirmed the reduction as creditors were not affected and no shareholder regarded the mistake as being of such importance as to seek the court's refusal.

usually have reached an agreement with its creditors who have either consented to the scheme subject to bank guarantees being forthcoming covering amounts due to them or who have been paid off. Applications under sub-s (6) to dispense with the settling of the list are therefore very common and frequently granted[8].

It is clear from the above that it is rare for the position of creditors to be at risk as a result of a reduction of capital. Instead it is frequently the shareholders, or more specifically particular classes of shareholders, who are aggrieved when a company decides to exercise this power to reduce capital.

SHAREHOLDERS

There are no specific statutory provisions dealing with shareholders and so objecting shareholders must persuade the court not to exercise its discretion in favour of the reduction. The general approach of the courts and the nature of the jurisdiction to confirm a reduction is set out most clearly in Lord Cooper's (dissenting) judgment in *Scottish Insurance Corp Ltd v Wilsons and Clyde Co Ltd*[9]:

In the early days, the courts took this jurisdiction very seriously and refused to confirm many reductions, often on the dubious ground that they were ultra vires. This tendency was corrected in *British and American Trustee Corpn*[10]; *Balmenach-Glenlivet Distillery*[11]; *Poole v National Bank of China*[12], and *Caldwell & Co*[13], which progressively narrowed the court's powers and inaugurated in company practice what might be called an era of self determination and laissez-faire. Nevertheless, emphasis was again and again laid by the House of Lords upon the proposition that the courts had a 'discretion' to confirm or not to confirm, which it was their duty to apply in 'every proper case', and that this discretion fell to be exercised by reference to the test of whether the scheme would be 'fair and equitable', 'just and equitable', 'fair and reasonable', or 'not unjust or inequitable', expressions sometimes qualified and explained by the addition of the words 'in the ordinary sense of the term' or 'as a matter of business'. . . . it is abundantly plain from those decisions that the court's jurisdiction is a discretionary one, not confined to verifying the technical correctness of the formal procedure, nor even to determining according to strict law the precise rights of the contending parties, but involving an application of broad standards of fairness, reasonableness and equity . . .

Having established the discretionary nature of the jurisdiction involving the application of broad standards of fairness and equity, and so presumably raising the possibility of dissenting shareholders succeeding in getting reductions set aside on these grounds, he continued:

---

8 In considering whether to dispense with the list of creditors, the court will consider whether a company holds sufficient cash and gilt-edged securities to cover all provable liabilities with a reasonable margin of safety as well as the amount which it is proposed to be returned to the shareholders, although its consideration is not limited to cash and gilt-edged and it may also take into account sums due to a company by its sundry debtors provided that the said sums have been written down so as to exclude bad debts, *Re House of Fraser plc* [1987] BCLC 293; *Anderson Brown & Co Ltd* 1965 SC 81; *Re Lucania Temperance Billard Halls (London) Ltd* [1966] Ch 98, [1965] 3 All ER 879.
9 1948 SC 360, CS; affd [1949] AC 462, [1949] 1 All ER 1068, HL.
10 [1894] AC 399, HL.
11 (1906) 8 F 1135.
12 [1907] AC 229, HL.
13 1916 SC (HL), 120.

Nothing could be clearer and more reassuring than these formulations of the duties of the court. Nothing could be more disappointing than the reported instances of their subsequent exercise. Examples abound of the refusal of the courts to entertain the plea that a scheme was not fair or equitable, but it is very hard to find in recent times any clear and instructive instance of the acceptance of such an objection. The explanations may be that the modern company meeting never deviates by a hair's breadth from fairness and equity, and that the 'proper case' for the exercise of the court's discretionary control never nowadays occurs; but I find it difficult to regard this explanation as convincing.

So despite the existence of this clear discretionary equitable jurisdiction vested in the courts, it is rare for the courts to refuse to confirm a reduction. Lord Cooper went on to indicate why he thought this was the case:

It is important to observe that nearly all the cases in which the court has refused to listen to the complaint of a minority has been marked by one or both of two significant features: (a) that the dissentient minority was very small and usually merely obstructive, and (b) that the company was a going concern, recasting its capital structure in the general interests of the company as a trading entity, or staving off the threat of ruin in the interests of all concerned. When such features are present it is easy to understand the hint dropped by Eve J *(Thomas de la Rue & Co)*[14] that in ninety-nine cases out of a hundred the court should not interfere, and to appreciate the importance rightly attached by Stirling LJ *(Welsbach Incandescent Gas Light Co)*[15] to the bona fide judgment of businessmen on a matter of business in which they themselves are largely interested.

These factors are familiar to all dissentient shareholders and we have encountered similar arguments in other areas, for example, in seeking to challenge an alteration to the articles of association. The scheme is always supported by a large majority of the shareholders (necessarily so, for many matters require special resolutions) and, equally necessarily, presents issues of internal management and business judgment which are for the company to decide upon and not the courts[16].

Little has changed in the more recent cases with Harman J in *Re Ratners Group plc*[17] noting:

The court has over the years established . . . three principles on which the court will require to be satisfied. Those principles are, first, that all shareholders are treated equitably in any reduction. That usually means that they are treated equally, but may mean that they are treated equally save as to some who have consented to their being treated unequally, so that counsel's word 'equitably' is the correct word which I adopt and accept. The second principle to be applied is that the shareholders at the general meeting had the proposals properly explained to them so that they could exercise an informed judgment on them. And the third principle is that creditors of the company are safeguarded so that money cannot be applied in any way which would be detrimental to creditors.

---

14 [1911] 2 Ch 361.
15 [1904] 1 Ch 87, CA.
16 See *Poole v National Bank of China Ltd* [1907] AC 229 at 236, per Lord Loreburn '. . . it is no part of the business of a court of justice to determine the wisdom of a course adopted by a company in the management of its own affairs.'
17 [1988] BCLC 685. See also *Re Thorn EMI plc* [1989] BCLC 612. The other qualification on the court's discretion noted by Harman J in both of these cases was that the court must not be asked to confirm a reduction which was for no discernible purpose but was a hollow and pointless act. It seems unlikely that companies or their professional advisers would make a practice of such pointless applications.

It was noted above that in many instances the creditors, shareholders and company are in complete agreement about the proposal and the court's role is limited to endorsing their plans. It will equally be appreciated, in the light of the judicial attitude outlined above, that even the presence of dissentient shareholders is unlikely to alter the courts' general tendency to approve such schemes. This is so even if the proposed scheme does not affect all shareholders of the same class in the same fashion, although the courts will scrutinise such schemes very closely to ensure that they do not work unfairly or inequitably[18]. However, more recently the court did indicate that if the scheme is to treat one part of a class differently from another part of the same class, the court would prefer to see it carried out through a scheme of reconstruction under CA 1985, s 425[19].

What has troubled the courts to a slightly greater degree in some of the cases has been the claim by preference shareholders that the effect of a reduction is to vary or abrogate their class rights and so requires their consent before it can be confirmed by the courts[20].

Reduction of capital and class rights

The main focus of shareholder discontent is, in practice, on whether the reduction is fair and equitable as between the different class of shareholders.[1] The approach of the courts on this issue has been that in determining fairness and equity between shareholders the court looks at what the class rights would have been in a winding up and compares that with the position which would arise under the proposed reduction.

Thus, if capital has been lost and the classes rank pari passu for these purposes, then prima facie the loss should be borne equally[2] but where there are class rights, then these should be complied with.

If therefore there are preference shares which have preference as to a return of capital, and the company is reducing capital because it is lost or unrepresented by available assets, then the ordinary shares must bear the loss first[3], as they would do if the company were being wound up. Equally, if surplus capital is being returned, it will normally be returned to the preference shareholders who will usually have priority as to repayment of capital in a winding up[4]. It is in this context of being paid off first that many disputes have arisen as preference shareholders have been reluctant to be

18 *British and American Trustee Corpn v Couper* [1894] AC 399, HL.
19 *Re Robert Stephen Holdings Ltd* [1968] 1 All ER 195n, [1968] 1 WLR 522. In this case the court did confirm the reduction despite it affecting shareholders of the same class in different ways but no shareholder appeared to oppose the confirmation.
20 Class rights and the variation thereof are discussed in detail in Ch 17.
1 *British and American Trustee Corpn v Couper* [1894] AC 399, HL; *Poole v National Bank of China Ltd* [1907] AC 229, HL; *Scottish Insurance Corpn Ltd v Wilsons and Clyde Co Ltd* 1948 SC 360; affd [1949] AC 462, HL; *Ex p Westburn Sugar Refineries Ltd* [1951] AC 625, [1951] 1 All ER 881, HL.
2 *Bannatyne v Direct Spanish Telegraph Co* (1886) 34 Ch D 287, CA, where the preference shareholders had no preference as to capital, only as to dividend.
3 *Re Floating Dock Co of St Thomas Ltd* [1895] 1 Ch 691.
4 *Re Chatterley-Whitfield Colleries Co Ltd* [1948] 2 All ER 593, CA; affd sub nom *Prudential Assurance Co Ltd v Chatterley-Whitfield Colleries Ltd* [1949] AC 512, [1949] 1 All ER 1094, HL; *Scottish Insurance Corpn Ltd v Wilsons and Clyde Co Ltd* 1948 SC 360; affd [1949] AC 462, HL; *Re Fowlers Vacola Manufacturing Co Ltd* [1916] VR 97; *Re Saltdean Estate Co Ltd* [1968] 3 All ER 829, [1968] 1 WLR 1844.

'expelled' from the company in this way, particularly when it means an end to high dividend returns and a share in the company's continued prosperity. Here too the judicial attitude has generally been unsympathetic, with the courts on many occasions rejecting any claim by such shareholders to be entitled to continued participation[5].

The problem surfaced most recently in *House of Fraser v ACGE Investments Ltd*[6] where the ordinary shareholders in general meeting passed a special resolution approving the paying off of the whole of the preference share capital of the company as being in excess of the wants of the company. No class meetings of the preference shareholders were held to approve or disapprove the reduction. The company's articles provided that the special rights attached to any class of shares could only be modified, commuted, affected or dealt with, with the consent of the holders of the class of shares. The preference shareholders argued that the failure to obtain their consent meant that the court could not confirm the reduction.

In the House of Lords, Lord Keith[7] found that the position had been definitively stated by Buckley J in an earlier case on almost identical facts, *Re Saltdean Estate Co Ltd*[8]:

It has long been recognised that at least in normal circumstances where a company's capital is to be reduced by repaying paid-up share capital, in the absence of agreement or the sanction of a class meeting to the contrary, that class of capital should first be repaid which would be returned first in a winding up of the company (see *Re Chatterley-Whitfield Collieries Ltd*[9], per Lord Greene) . . . In the present case the preference shareholders are entitled to prior repayment of capital in a winding up and, consequently, if the company has more paid up capital than it needs and wishes to repay some part of it, the first class of capital to be repaid should prima facie be the preferred shares.

. . . it is said that the proposed cancellation of the preferred shares will constitute an abrogation of all the rights attached to those shares which cannot validly be effected without an extraordinary resolution of a class meeting of preferred shareholders under art 8 of the company's articles. In my judgment, that article has no application to a cancellation of shares on a reduction of capital which is in accord with the rights attached to the shares of the company. Unless this reduction can be shown to be unfair to the preferred shareholders on other grounds, it is in accordance with the right and liability to prior repayment of capital attached to their shares. The liability to prior repayment on a reduction of capital, corresponding to their right to prior return of capital in a winding up, is a liability of the kind to which Lord Greene in the passage I have referred to, said that anyone has only himself to blame if he does not know it. It is part of the bargain between the shareholders and forms an integral part of the definition or delimitation of the bundle of rights which make up the preferred share. Giving effect to it does not involve the variation or abrogation of any rights attached to such shares.

Buckley J concluded as far as preference shareholders were concerned:

The fact is that every holder of preferred shares of the company has always been at risk that his hope of participating in undrawn or future profits of the company might

---

5 Ibid.
6 [1987] AC 387, [1987] BCLC 478, HL; affg [1987] BCLC 293, CS. There may, in the appropriate case, be some scope here for petitions under CA 1985, s 459, alleging unfairly prejudicial conduct, see [1987] JBL 165.
7 [1987] AC 387 at 393, [1987] BCLC 478 at 483, with whom the rest of their Lordships agreed.
8 [1968] 3 All ER 829 at 831, [1968] 1 WLR 1844 at 1849.
9 [1948] 2 All ER 593 at 596, CA.

be frustrated at any time by a liquidation of the company or a reduction of capital properly resolved upon by a majority of his fellow members. This vulnerability is, and has always been, a characteristic of the preferred shares. Now that the event has occurred, none of the preferred shareholders can, in my judgment, assert that the resulting state of affairs is unfair to him[10].

Lord Keith in the *House of Fraser* case was in complete agreement with this approach, finding that the proposed reduction of capital involved an extinction of preferred shares in strict accordance with the contract embodied in the articles of association, to which the holders of the preferred shares were party. The preferred shareholders had a right to a return of capital in priority to other shareholders and that right was not affected, modified, dealt with or abrogated but was given effect to[11].

This is so in any instance where the preference shareholders have priority as to a return of capital, even if they also have further rights of participation as regards dividend[12]. It is not clear whether preference shares which are participating as to surplus on a winding up could be dealt with in this way although *Re William Jones & Sons Ltd*[13] suggests that they can. In that instance, however, the preference shareholders raised no objection to being paid off, probably because they were to be paid off in full although the shares stood at less than par. Moreover, there was no present prospect of the company being wound up, so any enjoyment of surplus on a winding off would not occur for many years.

Preference shareholders must then appreciate the impact which the company's ability to reduce capital may have on their position. The difficulties of preference shareholders in these situations is recognised to some extent in listed companies, which often protect such shareholders by means of what is called the *Spens* formula which entitles the shareholders to at least the quoted market value of their shares on a reduction, and gives them voting rights in the general meeting on the special resolution required by s 135.

As for any scheme of reduction which does vary or abrogate class rights[14] as opposed to fulfil them, despite suggestions to the contrary in the older cases[15], it is hard to envisage that the courts would confirm such reductions without the consent of the class, in the light of the requirements of s 125 which are discussed in detail in Chapter 17.

Public interest

One final point to note is that many of the earlier cases refer to the need to have regard to the interests of creditors, shareholders *and* to the interests of those members of the public who may be induced to take shares in the company[16]. The interests of future shareholders or creditors are unlikely to

---

10 See also *Bannatyne v Direct Spanish Telegraph Co* (1886) 34 Ch D 287, CA; *Scottish Insurance Corpn Ltd v Wilsons and Clyde Coal Co Ltd* 1948 SC 360; affd [1949] AC 462 at 487, per Lord Normand, HL.
11 [1987] AC 387 at 393, [1987] BCLC 478 at 484.
12 *Re Saltdean Estate Co Ltd* [1968] 3 All ER 829, [1968] 1 WLR 1844.
13 [1969] 1 All ER 913, [1969] 1 WLR 146.
14 Of course, on the court's interpretation of variation or abrogation, very few schemes will have such an effect.
15 For example, *Re William Jones & Sons Ltd* [1969] 1 All ER 913, [1969] 1 WLR 146.
16 *Poole v National Bank of China Ltd* [1907] AC 229 at 239, HL, per Lord Macnaghten, see also *British and American Trustee Corpn v Couper* [1894] AC 399 at 411, HL.

have much impact on the courts today, for as Nourse J noted in *Re Grosvenor Press plc*[17], they are already adequately protected in that the publicity requirements surrounding the reduction and the need for the company's accounts to give a true and fair view of the state of its affairs means that they would be fully informed of the position. So long as creditors and shareholders are not prejudiced, wider public concerns do not influence the court and it is not concerned with any ulterior purpose for the reduction provided it is lawful. Thus reduction schemes for reasons of tax avoidance (as opposed to evasion) or to avoid some of the consequences of nationalisation have in the past been approved[18].

After confirmation

Once the court confirms the reduction, a copy of the court order and of a minute approved by the court setting out the alteration to the company's capital must be filed for registration with the registrar of companies and the reduction is not effective until this has been done[19]. The registrar then certifies the registration and this certificate of registration is conclusive evidence that all the requirements with respect to the reduction of share capital have been complied with and the court minute sent to the registrar is deemed to be substituted for the corresponding part of the memorandum[20].

Where the court makes an order confirming a reduction of a public company's capital which brings its nominal value below the authorised minimum, the registrar of companies must not register the order unless the court otherwise directs or the company is first re-registered as a private company[1].

FORFEITURE AND SURRENDER

The articles of association of a company may provide that shares may be forfeited for non-payment of calls in respect of sums remaining unpaid on the shares. This does not fall foul of CA 1985, s 143(1), prohibiting a company from acquiring its own shares, for s 143(3)(d) specifically excepts shares acquired by forfeiture or surrender in lieu of forfeiture. Such provisions are regarded as penal provisions and must be construed strictly[2]. Forfeiture occurs under Table A, art 19, on a resolution of the directors and, like all powers conferred on directors by the articles, this power must be exercised by them for a proper purpose. They equally have a power under art 20 to cancel the forfeiture on such terms as they think fit.

Article 20 goes on to provide that subject to the provisions of the Act a forfeited share may be sold, re-allotted or otherwise disposed of in such terms and in such manner as the directors determine.

---

17 [1985] 1 WLR 980 at 985, [1985] BCLC 286 at 291.
18 *Ex p Westburn Sugar Refineries Ltd* [1951] AC 625, [1951] 1 All ER 881, HL.
19 CA 1985, s 138(1) and (2). The court may also order further publication of the reduction, s 138(3).
20 Ibid, s 138(4) and (5).
 1 Ibid, s 139. The nominal value of the company's allotted share capital must be not less than the authorised minimum which by CA 1985, s 118(1) is set at £50,000.
 2 *Johnson v Lyttle's Iron Agency* (1877) 5 Ch D 687, CA.

A person whose shares have been forfeited shall cease to be a member and must surrender the share certificate in respect of those shares but remains liable to the company for all moneys which at the date of forfeiture were payable by him to the company in respect of those shares. A statutory declaration by a director that a share has been forfeited shall be conclusive evidence of the facts stated in it as against all persons claiming to be entitled to the share and the declaration shall constitute a good title to the share and any person to whom the share is disposed of is not affected by any irregularity in or invalidity in the forfeiture proceedings.

The position regarding forfeiture in public companies is further governed by s 146(2) which provides that, unless the shares are previously disposed of, a company must not later than the end of three years from the date of their forfeiture, cancel them and diminish the amount of share capital by the nominal value of the shares. A failure to do so is an offence under s 149(2). Where the effect of this cancellation will be to bring the company's allotted share capital below the authorised minimum, it may apply for re-registration as a private company, stating the effect of the cancellation. The company or its nominee must not exercise any voting rights in respect of the shares and any purported exercise of those rights will be void by virtue of s 146(4).

A company's articles may also provide for the surrender of shares and it is common to find such a provision to be exercised in lieu of a power of forfeiture. A surrender of shares in a public company is subject to the provisions of s 146 and governed by the same rules as those applying to forfeiture.

CHAPTER 17

Classes of shares and class rights

HISTORICAL BACKGROUND

The division of share capital into different classes first arose in England. There are cases of preference shares even as early as the seventeenth century[1]. Nevertheless, in the early period of modern company law, it was common to have shares of only one class[2]. These were of high nominal value but were usually only partly paid. This was in a period when partnership ideas were predominant and the nature of the shares arguably presupposed active participation by the investor in the company. From as early as 1830, a number of companies incorporated under special acts had been given power to issue preference as well as ordinary shares but it was not until the 1860s that the power was conferred generally.

From about 1880, the fashions changed. It was the rise of the small shareholder who invested in the company but did not participate in management. We see in this period the issue of shares of smaller nominal value on which a higher proportion of the price was paid up on issue. However, this aspect of the second phase may have begun as early as the period 1830 to 1844. One leading writer in the Edinburgh Review in 1836 wrote that any person with 'ten or twenty shillings to spare' might become a shareholder[3]. It should be noted nevertheless that the Limited Liability Act 1855 required the shares of limited liability companies to be of not less than £10 *nominal* value. This was repealed in 1856. In this second period we also see the rise of the preference share as a fashionable hybrid between ordinary shares and debentures. It suited the needs of those who were more interested in a fixed yield. It also proved useful to those companies who wished to raise further capital without risking a loss of control by the existing equity shareholders. In times of economic recession preference shares were sometimes issued in satisfaction of a trade debt. In the USA, preference shares were favoured as a means of financing holding companies commonly known as 'trusts' and were also used in many railway and public utility reorganisations to repay debentures on which there had been default. In this second period also there was a growth in deferred or founders' shares taken by promoters partly for financial reasons and partly for publicity, since it indicated their faith in the enterprise being promoted. It was then the age of sophistication and indeed complexity in share capital structures.

Since the 1920s there has been an increasing counter-trend towards

---

1 See W R Scott *Joint Stock Companies to 1720* (1912) vol 1, chapter VII. For a study of preference shares in the period 1775–1850, see G H Evans *British Corporation Finance 1775–1850* (1936).
2 See L C B Gower *Principles of Modern Company Law* (4th edn, 1979) pp 405–6.
3 J R McCulloch (1836) LXIII Edinburgh Review 419 at 428. See Bishop Hunt *The Development of the Business Corporation in England 1800–1867* (1936).

greater simplicity. Founders' shares and an excessive variety of preference shares have gradually disappeared and shares have tended to be issued fully paid. Indeed the latter is now normally required by The Stock Exchange for the listed shares of a public company. Smaller nominal values are more common today. The Labour Government's fiscal legislation of the mid-1960s led to a decline in the popularity of preference shares since the dividends were to be paid out of taxed income whereas interest on debentures is a charge on income for corporation tax purposes.

THE CONCEPT OF A CLASS AND CLASS RIGHTS

To a logician, a class is the number of individual objects or cases marked by the possession by each of a certain set of characteristics[4]. Where the general idea of a class can be thus defined it is a class concept, or more briefly, a concept. Used as a legal term in this context, class is somewhat vague but can probably be defined as 'those persons whose rights are not so dissimilar as to make it impossible for them to consult together with a view to their common interest'[5]. Common character and common interest seem primary requirements as with class gifts in the law of trusts and succession[6]. Dissimilar interests alone, not arising from legal rights under the corporate constitution, cannot generally be regarded as sufficient ground for the separation of classes[7].

In company law, however, it has been stated by Professor Gower[8] that there cannot be class rights until the shares of the members are somehow divided into separate classes in the sense that some have rights different from those of the others[9]. These apparently paradoxical views are strictly correct[10]. There is classification but it has no significance. If there is only one possible class, then all shares fall within it. There is only one set of rights—shareholder rights. Class *rights* presupposes separate classes. Once there are separate classes then the following are regarded as class rights whether they be in the memorandum, articles, resolution or terms of issue:

(1)　class rights expressly stated in the memorandum, articles or relevant resolution;

(2)　rights to dividends, voting or return of capital or a winding up;

4　S H Mellone *An Introductory Textbook of Logic* (19th edn, 1950) p 23.
5　Per Bowen LJ in *Sovereign Life Assurance Co v Dodd* [1892] 2 QB 573 at 583, CA: see also *Re Jax Marine Pty Ltd* [1967] 1 NSWR 145 at 149 where Street J puts it in the positive; but cf *Re Hellenic and General Trust Ltd* [1975] 3 All ER 382 noted by J A Hornby (1975) 39 MLR 208 and D D Prentice (1976) 92 LQR 13. See also *Borgelt v Millman NO* 1983 (1) SA 757 at 769 A–B and *New Zealand Forest Products Ltd v NZ Stock Exchange* (1984) 2 NZCLC 99–051, 2 NZCLC 99–159, CA. Some of these were cases of classes of creditors but similar principles apply.
6　In the class gift cases in the law of succession, class is characterised by persons bearing a common character of coming within a certain category or description defined by a general or collective formula (*Re Chaplin's Trusts* (1863) 12 WR 147 at 148).
7　*Borgelt v Millman NO*, supra, and *New Zealand Forest Products Ltd v NZ Stock Exchange*, supra. Cf *Re Hellenic and General Trust Ltd*, supra.
8　*Gower*, op cit, p 562.
9　Cf *Re John Smith's Tadcaster Brewery Co Ltd* [1953] Ch 308 at 319, 320, CA per Jenkins LJ. *Palmer's Company Law*, op cit, states that a separate class is constituted when the principal rights carried by the shares differ from those carried by other shares.
10　Cf *Hodge v James Howell & Co* [1958] CLY 446, discussed below.

(3)   the right to have a variation of rights clause complied with[11].

Where there are different classes, even a right which is identical to those of another class but which is appurtenant to each class would appear to be capable of being a class right, although it may not necessarily constitute a 'preference or special privilege'[12].

It has been held that where there are preference and ordinary shares the rights of ordinary shares are not class rights[13]. This seems wrong in principle and the case is inadequately reported.

In *Cumbrian Newspapers Group Ltd v Cumberland and Westmorland Herald Newspaper and Printing Co Ltd*[14] in 1986 Scott J defined rights or benefits contained in articles into three different categories. First, there are rights or benefits which are annexed to particular shares. He regarded as classic examples of these dividend rights and rights to participate in surplus assets on a winding up. Secondly, there are rights or benefits conferred on individuals not in the capacity of members or shareholders of the company, but for ulterior reasons, connected with the administration of the company's affairs or the conduct of its business. These are the outsider rights discussed in Chapter 11. Thirdly, there is an intermediate category of rights or benefits which, although not attached to any particular shares, are nevertheless conferred on the beneficiary in the capacity of member or shareholder of the company. His Lordship thought that the first and third categories were 'rights attached to a class of shares' for the purposes of s 125 of the CA 1985.

An interesting further question is whether one can have sub-classes of shares. In *Re Powell-Cotton's Re-Settlement, Henniker-Major v Powell-Cotton*[15] Roxburgh J held that there could be. Thus there could be a division of ordinary shares into preferred and deferred ordinary shares. However, this was not a company law case, but involved construction of the wording of the particular settlement. It seems likely that each sub-class would be regarded as a separate class for the purposes of variation of rights in company law[16].

CLASSES OF SHARES

The power to create different classes of shares may be set out in the objects clause of the memorandum. This is now unusual. It is usually dealt with in the articles. Thus Table A, reg 2 expressly provides for this, requiring the approval of the company by ordinary resolution in general meeting. Formerly, it was thought that this power should be reserved from the

---

11 *Gower*, op cit, p 563; cf the Jenkins Report (Cmnd 1749) para 198(b) which thought that the position regarding (3) should be clarified. This was dealt with by s 32(7) of the Companies Act 1980, now s 125(7) of CA 1985. See later.
12 *Re Stewart Precision Carburettor Co* (1912) 28 TLR 335.
13 *Hodge v James Howell & Co Ltd* [1958] CLY 446, CA.
14 [1986] 3 WLR 26 at 36–7. Noted by J Birds (1986) 7 Co Law 202; K Polack [1986] CLT 399.
15 [1957] Ch 159.
16 See *Palmer*, op cit, para 34–07 and cf *Re Hellenic and General Trust Ltd* [1975] 3 All ER 382, [1976] 1 WLR 123 (different shares in same class in one company held by subsidiary of company which was being taken over by that company held to be separate classes for purpose of a scheme of arrangement). See notes by J A Hornby (1976) 39 MLR 207 and D D Prentice (1976) 92 LQR 13.

incorporation[17] but now it is clear that this can be adopted at any time provided that there is no conflict with the memorandum[18].

In order to give shares special rights, it is not enough to use some broad generic label like 'preference share' since the rights must be set out and will not be implied[19]. It is interesting to note that the Canadian Business Corporations Act has abolished the formal distinction between ordinary or common shares as they call them and preference shares. It was thought that such descriptions assumed that each type of share had a precise meaning—an assumption which the draftsmen rejected[20]. Section 24(3) now simply provides that the articles may provide for more than one class of share having the rights, privileges, restrictions and conditions set out therein. At least one class must have voting rights. While a description such as 'preferred' has no precise meaning, the term 'ordinary' is reasonably precise and it could be argued that the new Canadian federal solution will confuse investors more than the present English practice.

In any case of conflict between rights in the memorandum and those in the articles or the resolution authorising the issue, the memorandum prevails[1]. Resort can be made to the articles to resolve an ambiguity in the memorandum[2]. Resort cannot be made to any prospectus for this purpose[3].

The most usual classes of shares in practice are ordinary shares and preference shares. Both of these can be redeemable.

In addition there are non-voting ordinary shares[4], and in some jurisdictions outside the UK, labour shares and no par value shares. This does not exhaust the gamut of variety but other shares are usually variations on the themes of the above.

Ordinary shares

Ordinary shares are often called 'equities' in financial circles which probably comes from equity of redemption which connotes the residual rights after discharge of prior commitments.

Ordinary shares normally carry the residual rights of participation in the income and capital of the company which have not been granted to other classes. They carry the risk but stand to gain the most in a prosperous company. They have no right to a fixed dividend. Indeed they have no right to a dividend at all, until it is declared. However, directors of public companies will not hold office for long if they decline to propose dividends. After the fixed dividends to preference shareholders, the ordinary shareholder enjoys the remainder of the distributable surplus actually distributed as

---

17 *Hutton v Scarborough Cliff Hotel Co Ltd B* (1865) 2 Drew & Sm 521.
18 *Andrews v Gas Meter Co* [1897] 1 Ch 361, CA.
19 See *Gore-Browne on Companies* (44th edn, 1985) by Boyle and Sykes, para 14–2.
20 See F Jacobucci et al *Canadian Business Corporations* (1977) p 110.
1 *Guinness v Land Corpn of Ireland* (1882) 22 Ch D 349, CA.
2 *Angostura Bitters (Dr JGB Siegert & Sons) Ltd v Kerr* [1933] AC 550, PC.
3 *Re Chicago and North West Granaries Co Ltd* [1898] 1 Ch 263 (an issue of debentures).
4 See the Jenkins Report (Cmnd 1749), paras 123–140; White Paper on Company Law Reform (Cmnd 5391), para 48.

dividend by the directors unless the company has issued participating preference shares.

Ordinary shares usually carry one vote per share. Preference shares on the other hand only usually have restricted voting rights: these are limited to meetings which in some way affect their rights. Ordinary shares therefore normally carry voting control in general meetings. Non-voting ordinary shares can be issued but they are not common and are disapproved of by The Stock Exchange, although capable of being listed. The words 'non-voting' must appear in their description[5].

Ordinary shares usually scoop the pool of surplus assets in a solvent winding up after the return of capital to all other shareholders. Sometimes, however, preference shares have a right to participate in surplus assets.

Deferred shares

These are also sometimes called founders' shares. As we have seen they used to be common but are now quite rare although they are referred to in the Act[6]. They were taken up by the promoters of the company to indicate faith in their enterprise. The rights are sometimes specified in the memorandum but vary considerably. Usually they provide for a right to a dividend after a dividend of a particular percentage has been paid on other shares. They often had disproportionally high voting rights and were used by promoters as a method of fraud. Other investors generally disliked them and the increasing strictness of Stock Exchange regulations regarding prospectuses has cut them down. Many public companies which had issued them have now converted them into ordinary shares[7].

Labour shares

Employee share schemes are common, especially in the larger companies. They usually provide for the acquisition by employees directly or through trustees of shares in the company. Such shares are usually ordinary or preference shares. In New Zealand, there is power under s 67 of the Companies Act 1955 to issue labour shares which have no nominal value and have restrictions on transfer. There is provision for surrender on leaving the company's employment. Insofar as they do not form part of the nominal capital, it is arguable they are not truly shares. They are anomalous and rare and the Macarthur Report[8] recommended their abolition.

No par value shares

No par value shares are allowed in the U S A and Canada but not in the U K. No par value means that the undertaking is divided into fractions, the value

---

5 Admission of Securities to Listing, 9.04.
6 Schedule 3, para 1.
7 See R R Pennington *Company Law* (6th edn, 1990) chapter 7.
8 See Final Report of the Special Committee to Review the New Zealand Companies Act (1973), paras 151–152. See also H S Hancock 'Profit Sharing Reform with particular reference to the French Law of 1967' (1937) 7 VUWLR 36 at p 39 ff.

of which fluctuates without the misleading additional factor of a nominal value attributed to the shares. The Gedge Committee[9] in 1954 favoured the legislation of such shares but no action was taken. The Jenkins Committee[10] also favoured their introduction. Professor Gower[11] has argued for the total abolition of nominal value with the result that there would merely be a stated capital, covering paid-up capital and share premium account, and all shares would be no par value shares. He introduced this into his draft Companies Code for Ghana[12]. An attempt to introduce them in the UK in 1967 failed and the White Paper of the Heath government[13] published in 1973 was against their introduction. Although it recognised there was logic in the argument, it did not feel there was a practical need. The introduction of no par value shares is currently being considered in New Zealand.

Preference shares

Preference shares have preferential rights as to (a) dividend or (b) return of capital in a solvent winding up or (c) both as to dividend and capital. The right to dividend, which is usually expressed as a percentage of the nominal value of the share may be cumulative or non-cumulative. The latter means that the dividend is only payable out of the available profits of the particular year. Preference shares are sometimes given a further right to participate in profits or assets. Usually the voting rights of preference shares are restricted to meetings considering a variation of their rights.

In some ways, preference shares are more like debentures than ordinary shares[14]. They normally carry dividends at a fixed rate which thus resembles the fixed interest payable on a debenture. They normally have a measure of priority over ordinary shareholders in a winding up although unlike a debenture this is limited to a solvent winding up. Like debenture stockholders, their voting rights are usually limited to meetings where their rights are affected but unlike debenture stockholders, they have votes at general meetings in such circumstances.

In times of inflation, there are disadvantages in a fixed income security since they do not appreciate in value as much as ordinary shares and the fixed income is worth less. Also, they may not keep pace with high interest rates. Lastly, they have certain fiscal disadvantages, as we have seen, in that the dividend is not deductible from gross income. Compared with ordinary shares, they are a marginally safer investment from a shareholder's point of view in troubled times but if times are really bad and the company goes into liquidation, they rank after secured and unsecured creditors. An American writer has consequently described their existence as 'a monument to the perennial irrationality of the securities markets'[15].

Preference share rights have given rise to a number of cases on construction which have not always shown the courts at their best. Such cases always

9 Cmnd 9112.
10 Cmnd 1749, paras 32–34.
11 Op cit, p 238.
12 Ghana Companies Code 1963, s 66.
13 Cmnd 5391, para 49.
14 See Charlesworth and Cain *Charlesworth's Company Law* (13th edn, 1987) p 270.
15 Alfred F Conard *Corporations in Perspective* (1976) p 265.

turn on the meaning of the particular words used but we will endeavour to extract some general canons[16] or presumptions.

CANONS OF CONSTRUCTION

There are two basic axioms:

(1)   A presumption of equality between shares. This is easily rebutted by contrary wording. This was expressed by Lord Macnaghten in *Birch v Cropper, Re Bridgewater Navigation Co Ltd* in 1889[17] when he said:

> Every person who becomes a member of a company limited by shares of equal amount becomes entitled to a proportionate part in the capital of the company, and, unless it be otherwise provided by the regulations of the company, entitled as a necessary consequence, to the same proportionate part in all the property of the company . . . When the company is wound up, new rights and liabilities arise.

(2)   Where rights are stated over any matter the statement of rights is presumed exhaustive in that particular respect. This is less easily rebutted. This canon was clearly expressed by Sargant J in *Re National Telephone Co* in 1914[18] where he said:

> . . . the weight of authority is in favour of the view that, either with regard to dividend or with regard to the rights in a winding up, the express gift or attachment of preferential rights to preference shares, on their creation, is, prima facie, a definition of the whole of their rights in that respect, and negatives any future or other right to which, but for the specified rights, they would have been entitled.

In addition to these basic axioms there are a number of particular canons which are almost exclusively deductions therefrom and which can be conveniently divided into two groups: (a) where the company is a going concern and (b) where the company is being wound up[19].

A WHERE THE COMPANY IS A GOING CONCERN

(1)   A preferential right to a dividend is presumed to be a right to a cumulative dividend[20]. The right to a cumulative dividend means that if there is a shortfall of profits in any particular year, the arrears of preferential dividend must be carried forward and paid in a following year before the dividend on ordinary shares. This can be rebutted by wording which indicates that the dividend is non-cumulative or is payable out of yearly profits[1]. This is perhaps an example of equality.
(2)   Preference shares are presumed not to participate in surplus profits[2].

---

16 Canon meaning rule. The canons here, like the canons of construction of deeds and statutes, are not rules but presumptions of or pointers to intention. See *Gower*, op cit, generally for the historical development of the present canons.
17 (1889) 14 App Cas 525 at 543, HL.
18 [1914] 1 Ch 755 at 774.
19 This classification is based on Charlesworth and Cain *Charlesworth's Company Law* (13th edn, 1987) p 266 ff.
20 *Webb v Earle* (1875) LR 20 Eq 556.
 1 *Adair v Old Bushmills Distillery* [1908] WN 24.
 2 *Will v United Lankat Plantations Co Ltd* [1914] AC 11, HL; *Re National Telephone Co* [1914] 1 Ch 755.

This is clearly rebutted where shares are expressly declared to be participating preference shares with a right of participation after a certain percentage dividend has been paid on the ordinary shares.

(3)   There is a presumption of equality of voting rights with other shares[3]. This is frequently rebutted by limiting the voting rights to situations such as where preferential dividends are in arrears or their rights are being varied.

B WHERE THE COMPANY IS BEING WOUND UP

(1)   Arrears of preferential dividend are presumed not to be payable on a winding up unless the dividend has been declared[4]. This is frequently rebutted in practice.

(2)   Preferential shares are presumed to have no priority as to repayment of capital in a winding up. This too can be rebutted[5].

(3)   Surplus assets after repayment of capital on a winding up are presumed to be divisible pro rata amongst all classes of shares[6]. This is frequently rebutted.

Since there is an insufficiency of assets to pay creditors on an insolvent winding up, shareholders get nothing and the above questions do not arise.

Although these canons are inherently fair and rational their application has given rise to difficulties in the cases. Each case ultimately turns on the particular wording used. There is much to be said for providing in a schedule to the Companies Act a list of particular rights which would attach to preference shares in the absence of a contrary provision. Such a suggestion was, however, rejected by the Jenkins Committee in 1962 on the ground that they questioned the wisdom of attempting to define by statute the basic rights of preference shares of which there are so many varieties[7].

Privatisation and the 'golden share'

Under the Thatcher Government a number of firms were 'privatised' in the sense that the business was placed in the private sector or, if already in the private sector, the public were invited to invest in the business through private ownership. In most sales the Government sold all its holding in the firm, but important ownership restrictions were put in the articles. In a number of cases the maximum individual shareholding could not exceed 15% and foreign ownership was not permitted. To back up these restrictions the Government retained what has become known as a 'golden share'[8]. This is held by the relevant minister and permits him or her to prevent a takeover or the amendment of the articles without the Government's prior consent.

---

3 See s 370(6).
4 *Re Crichton's Oil Co* [1902] 2 Ch 86, CA.
5 *Birch v Cropper, Re Bridgewater Navigation Co Ltd* (1889) 14 App Cas 525, HL.
6 *Williamson-Buchanan Steamers Ltd Liquidators* 1936 SLT 106; *Scottish Insurance Corpn Ltd v Wilsons and Clyde Coal Co* [1949] AC 462, HL.
7 Cf Ghana Companies Code, s 51.
8 See Cento Veljanovski *Selling the State* (1987); pp 127–128. This gives a excellent treatment of the subject from a law and economics perspective. See Chapter 6 on 'Selling the Assets' and the interesting subsequent chapters on the regulatory changes needed to balance privatisation with the public interest. See, too, C Graham and T Prosser 'Privatising Nationalised Industries' (1987) 50 MLR 16, 33–34.

VARIATION OF CLASS RIGHTS[9]

Companies having issued shares of different classes sometimes wish to vary the rights attaching to them. Much depends on (a) where the class rights are set out and (b) the procedure laid down in the relevant variation of rights clause. Then the question is whether the proposed alteration falls within the relevant provisions. Next there is a statutory power under s 127 to disallow variations in certain circumstances even where the variation of rights formalities have been complied with. Finally, where the company is unable to vary the rights under these procedures it may still be possible to make use of the scheme of arrangement provisions of s 425.

At one time it was thought that whatever appeared in the memorandum was immutable. Thus in *Hutton v Scarborough Cliff Hotel Co Ltd A*[10] *in 1865, it was held that where the memorandum divided the capital into so many shares of a certain value the company could not alter its articles to issue preference shares. In other words the cases decided that the capital was all of one class. It was probably because of this case that the practice developed of inserting a division into separate classes in the memorandum. In Ashbury v Watson* in 1885[11] it was held that where this was done the rights could not be altered by altering the articles. In *Andrews v Gas Meter Co*[12] in 1897, on the other hand, it was held that where the memorandum did not specify different classes, preference shares could be created by the articles. The *Hutton* case was overruled.

The *Hutton* case had also made a distinction between two types of articles—managerial articles which could be altered by special resolution and fundamental constitutional articles which could not. This distinction was also rejected in *Andrews v Gas Meter Co*. However, the fallacious distinction probably accounted for the view that unless there was a variation of class rights clause in the memorandum or articles, class rights could not be altered.

Class rights in the memorandum

Here there are three possibilities. First, the memorandum may prohibit a variation in which case there is no joy except by a scheme of arrangement under s 425. The memorandum cannot be altered by the company in this respect. Secondly, the memorandum may provide a variation of rights procedure. Here the clause must be complied with and s 127 may be applicable. Thirdly, the memorandum may not provide for a variation of rights.

It was held in two Scots cases, *Oban and Aultmore, Glenlivet Distilleries Ltd*[13] and *Marshall, Fleming & Co Ltd*[14] that where the memorandum and articles were issued contemporaneously and the articles contained a variation of rights clause this was effective. Section 17(2)(b) which gives power to alter conditions in the memorandum which could have been contained in the articles, does not authorise any variation or abrogation of the special rights of any class of members.

---

9 See D G Rice [1958] JBL 29 for a discussion of the old law.
10 (1865) 2 Drew & Sm 514.
11 (1885) 30 Ch D 376, CA.
12 [1897] 1 Ch 361, CA.
13 (1903) 5 F 1140.
14 1938 SC 873.

The matter now seems to be resolved by s 125(4) and (5). Section 125(4) seems to adopt the Scots approach. In s 125, variation includes abrogation (s 125(8)). In any case, where the class rights are set out in the memorandum and the memorandum and articles do not contain a variation of rights clause, those rights may only be varied if *all* the members of the company agree to the variation (s 125(5)). Note the requirement is all the members of the company, not all the members of the class.

Class rights in the articles

Here there are two possibilities. First, the articles may provide a variation of rights procedure. Secondly, the articles may not provide a variation of rights procedure. Formerly it was thought that variations could only be effective if the power was in the articles when the shares were issued[15]. This is a view which has long been discredited[16]. Articles in practice usually provide something to the effect that class rights can be altered by the consent in writing of the holders of a specified proportion or by an extraordinary resolution in a class meeting[17]. The question then is, must this be complied with before a special resolution is passed altering the class rights? As we have seen, s 9 provides that 'subject to the provisions' of the Act, and to the conditions contained in its memorandum, a company may alter its articles. Is there, then, anything in the Act enforcing compliance with the procedure laid down in the articles? Section 127, which we shall look at in more detail later, refers to such a clause and presupposes that it will be complied with. Before 1897, as we have seen, it was thought that constitutional articles could not be altered at all. The decision in *Andrews v Gas Meter Co* seems to have put an end to that doctrine. A trace of it remained in that it was thought that class rights could not be altered unless there was a variation of rights clause and it was complied with[18]. That view, which may have influenced the drafting of what is now s 127, seems to be unsound. In *Palmer's Company Law* (12th edn, 1924) which was the current edition at the time of the Greene Committee's deliberations[19], it was stated that: 'probably such interference with the rights of a class by a majority proposing to benefit themselves at the expense of the class so dealt with would be restrained as unfair and oppressive, and an abuse of the power to alter articles'. Palmer thought that the insertion of a clause 'does not necessarily prevent the rights of classes of shares so far as they depend on the articles from being altered by special resolution, but might make it more difficult to justify such a course if the alteration was attacked as unfair[20]'. Section 127 was passed to provide a

15 See Jessel MR in *Griffith v Paget* (1877) 5 Ch D 894 at 899.
16 See *Andrews v Gas Meter Co* [1897] 1 Ch 361, CA.
17 See the Companies Act 1948, Sch 1, Pt 1, Table A, reg 4. The new Table A does not contain such a provision.
18 See Gower *Modern Company Law* (4th edn, 1979) p 564 and Ford *Principles of Company Law* (5th edn, 1990) para 1703–5. Cf the Australian cases cited at 7 and 8 below.
19 Cmnd 2657, paras 22–23.
20 Ibid, pp 92–3 citing *Menier v Hooper's Telegraph Works* (1874) 9 Ch App 350 and Romer LJ in *Allen v Gold Reefs of West Africa* [1900] 1 Ch 656, CA. See too *Carruth v ICI Ltd* [1937] AC 707 at 765, HL; *Re Suburban and Provincial Stores Ltd* [1943] 1 All ER 342 at 344, CA. For a recent discussion see Scott J in *Cumbrian Newspapers Group Ltd v Cumberland and Westmorland Herald Newspaper and Printing Co Ltd* [1986] 3 WLR 26 at 40–1 where His Lordship seems to agree with this view of the old law.

summary remedy for abuse of such clauses[1]. Failure to comply raised a very strong presumption that the alteration was not for the good of the company.

Now s 125(4) makes compliance with a variation clause mandatory in any event and s 125(2) provides for a statutory variation of rights procedure where the articles do not contain one. This is similar to reg 4 of the former Table A in the First Schedule to the Companies Act 1948. It requires either (i) the holders of three-quarters of the issued shares of the class in question to consent in writing to the variation, or (ii) an extraordinary resolution passed at a separate class meeting sanctioning the variation. This implements the Jenkins Committee's recommendations[2]. Any contravention of s 125 renders the purported alteration ineffective[3].

Class rights outside the memorandum or articles

The rights may be set out in a shareholders' agreement. The company may alter its articles in breach of such an agreement but might be liable for damages. It is clear that an injunction will not be granted to restrain the alteration of articles but it may be granted to restrain the company acting in breach of the contract[4].

In practice class rights are not often created in this way. Such agreements are only really found amongst private companies. We have discussed the nature and effect of such agreements in Chapter 12. In such a case, s 128 now requires registration of particulars of the rights and variations thereof with the Registrar of Companies. Section 128(1) provides that where a company allots shares with rights which are not stated in its memorandum or articles or in any resolution or written agreement equivalent to a resolution which has to be filed with the Registrar under s 380, the company shall file a statement in the prescribed form containing particulars of those rights unless the shares are in all respects uniform with shares previously allotted. Shares allotted with such rights are not to be treated as different from shares previously allotted by reason only of the fact that the former do not carry the same rights to dividends as the latter in the 12 months immediately following the former's allotment. Where rights are varied in this manner, a statement giving particulars of the variation must be filed (s 128(3)). This extends to a change of names (s 128(4)). There are criminal penalties for default on the company and every officer (s 128(5)).

Construction of variation of rights clauses

The courts generally adopt a restrictive construction of such clauses. The policy seems to be a reluctance to bog down the affairs of companies with unnecessary impediments. It is an oversimple policy which has led to a distinction which lends no credit to the sagacity of the courts. The distinction

1 See Lord Maugham in *Carruth v ICI Ltd* [1937] AC 707 at 765, HL. Cf the Australian cases cited at 7 and 8 below.
2 Cmnd 1749, para 198(a). Cf the Australian reforms discussed by J Cotton (1986) 4C & SLJ 227.
3 See *Cumbrian Newspapers Group Ltd v Cumberland and Westmorland Herald Newspapers and Printing Co Ltd*, supra. For the interpretation of 'rights attached to a class of shares' in s 125 by Scott J, see above.
4 *Allen v Gold Reefs of West Africa* [1900] 1 Ch 656, CA.

is drawn between the rights and the value or enjoyment of those rights. This was strikingly illustrated in the House of Lords case of *Adelaide Electric Supply Co Ltd v Prudential Assurance Co Ltd*[5] in 1934 where it was held that the alteration of the place of payment of a preference share dividend from England to Australia did not vary the right of the preference shareholder, notwithstanding that the Australian pound was worth less than the English pound. Lord Tomlin said that notwithstanding this potential loss, the change of place of payment was not a reduction in dividends within the meaning of the articles.

Similarly in *Greenhalgh v Arderne Cinemas Ltd*[6] a subdivision of a class of ten shilling ordinary shares into two shilling shares was held not to *vary* the rights of a holder of existing two shilling ordinary shares although this altered control of the company.

A similar restrictive approach has been adopted to the word 'abrogated' and even 'affected'. In *White v Bristol Aeroplane Co Ltd*[7], the defendant company proposed to increase its capital by a bonus issue of 660,000 £1 preference stock, ranking pari passu with the existing 600,000 £1 preference stock and 2,640,000 ordinary shares of ten shillings each. All the new shares were to be issued to the existing ordinary shareholders and paid for out of the reserves of the company. Article 68 of the company's articles provided:

All or any of the rights or privileges attached to any class of shares forming part of the capital for the time being of the company may be *affected, modified, varied, dealt with or abrogated* in any manner with the sanction of an extraordinary resolution passed at a separate meeting of the members of that class . . . [The emphasis has been added.]

The plaintiff was a preference stockholder who brought proceedings on behalf of himself and all other preference stockholders. He sought an injunction to restrain the company from convening a general meeting without the sanction of an extraordinary resolution passed at a separate meeting of the holders of the preference stock in accordance with art 68. Article 62 of the company's articles conferred on the company in general meeting power to issue the proposed new shares while art 83 stipulated that the holders of preference stock were not to receive notice of a general meeting or to attend and vote there unless the meeting was convened, inter alia, 'to consider a resolution directly affecting their rights or privileges' as a separate class. It was argued by the plaintiff that the word 'affect' was wide and must be taken to cover a transaction which though not necessarily modifying or varying rights would in some way otherwise affect them. This argument was accepted by Danckwerts J, but was rejected by a strong Court of Appeal consisting of Sir Raymond Evershed MR, Denning and Romer LJJ ie two Chancery lawyers and one common lawyer. Sir Raymond Evershed MR[8] stated:

there is to my mind a distinction, and a sensible distinction between an affecting of the rights and an affecting of the enjoyment of the rights, or of the stockholder's capacity to turn them to account . . .

5 [1934] AC 122. As to the meaning of a reference to particular currency see *Re Scandinavian Bank Group plc* (1987) 3 BCC 93 where Harman J disagreed with a dictum of Lord Wright in the *Adelaide* case.
6 [1946] 1 All ER 512, CA.
7 [1953] Ch 65, [1953] 1 All ER 40, CA.
8 Ibid, at 74.

The Court of Appeal, therefore, held that the proposed issue of new capital did not affect the rights or privileges of the existing preference stockholders. They might be affected as a matter of business by the new preference stock which would be in the possession of ordinary shareholders and have a majority over the existing preference stock, but this would affect only the enjoyment of the rights and not the rights themselves. The original class rights had not been varied or abrogated as a matter of law[9].

The court's powers under s 127

This section originally only applied where there was a variation of rights clause under the memorandum or articles and it was complied with. Variation includes abrogation but not affect. Prior to 1980 it was unclear what happened if the variation of rights clause was not complied with. Strictly speaking it fell outside the section which seems absurd. The protection of the section would thus be denied in the very circumstances where it was needed although this would not prevent a challenge to the alteration of the articles as not being for the good of the company. In Australia[10] it has been held that a variation of rights clause procedure must be followed before the variation is effective. On the other hand in another earlier case[11] the opposite was held. The prevailing English view seems to support the former[12] although as we have seen this is not necessarily a true reflection of the history. The matter was resolved in any event by s 32(8) of the Companies Act 1980 which made compliance with the clause or the procedures set out in s 32(2) mandatory if there was no clause[13]. These are now re-enacted in ss 125 and 127(1) and (1)(b). The only gap now left is where the class rights are set out in the memorandum and the memorandum and articles do not contain a variation of rights clause. Section 127(1)(b) only refers to s 125(2) and not to s 125(5). However it is submitted that if s 125(5) is not complied with there can be no variation of rights at all.

Section 127 enables a dissentient 15% of the issued shares of the class to apply to the court within 21 days to have the variation cancelled. If application is made the variation is not effective unless sanctioned by the court.

The sole ground for intervention by the court is that the court is 'satisfied, having regard to all the circumstances of the case, that the variation would unfairly prejudice' the shareholders in question. This seems to be a more precise criterion than the concept of the good of the company. A variation may be for the good of the company but may still unfairly prejudice a class of

---

9 See Evershed MR at 80. See also *Re Saltdean Estate Co Ltd* [1968] 3 All ER 829, where Buckley J held that the class rights attached to shares were not 'varied' or 'affected' if the shares were cancelled. This seems to carry the rule to its logical conclusion. See too *House of Fraser plc v ACGE Investments Ltd* (1987) 3 BCC 201, HL.

10 *Crumpton v Morrine Hall Pty Ltd* [1965] NSWR 240.

11 *Fischer v Easthaven Ltd* [1964] NSWR 261. See also *Lord St Davids v Union Castle Mail SS Co* (1934) Times, 24 November; *Greenhalgh v Arderne Cinemas Ltd* [1946] 1 All ER 512, CA; *White v Bristol Aeroplane Co Ltd* [1953] Ch 65, CA; *Re John Smith's Tadcaster Brewery Ltd* [1953] Ch 308, CA.

12 *Rights and Issues Investment Trust Ltd v Stylo Shoes Ltd* [1965] Ch 250. See further *Cumbrian Newspapers Group Ltd v Cumberland and Westmorland Herald Newspaper and Printing Co Ltd,* supra.

13 *Cumbrian Newspapers Group Ltd v Cumberland and Westermorland Herald Newspapers and Printing Co Ltd,* supra.

shareholders. It also seems to involve proof of something less than oppression. It is interesting that the same concept is now used by the statutory minority shareholder remedy in s 459 of the Companies Act 1985.

OTHER REMEDIES

Other remedies which are potentially available to minority shareholders in the case of a variation of class rights are:

(1)   actions under the exceptions to the rule in *Foss v Harbottle*;
(2)   a statutory action under s 459; and
(3)   a winding-up petition on the just and equitable ground.

   Each of these remedies is dealt with in detail in Chapter 27.

CHAPTER 18

Legal incidents of membership and share ownership

INTRODUCTION

In the previous chapters we have considered issues relating to the raising of share capital, its maintenance and the nature of the rights attached to a share and different classes of shares. Now we turn to consider membership of a company, how it is attained, what restrictions may be imposed, the signifi-cance of entry on the company's register of members, and the role of the share certificate. Mortgages and liens on shares are also discussed.

In this section, we shall use the terms 'member' and 'shareholder' inter-changeably, and indeed in most cases a member is a shareholder. There are, however, two circumstances where this is not the case. In the case of a company limited by guarantee without a share capital, an individual is clearly a member but not a shareholder, while equally the holder of a bearer share warrant is a shareholder but not a member because his name has not been entered on the register of members which, as we shall see, is decisive in determining who is a member.

DEFINITION OF MEMBER

CA 1985, s 22, provides the starting point in identifying who is a member. It states:

(1) The subscribers of a company's memorandum are deemed to have agreed to become members of the company, and on its registration shall be entered as such in its register of members.
(2) Every other person who agrees[1] to become a member of a company, and whose name is entered in its register of members, is a member of the company.

It should be noted that entry on the register of members is not essential to membership in the case of the subscribers but is in all other cases[2], as where members obtain their shares as a result of allotment by the company itself, or transfers from existing members (whether as a gift or for valuable considera-tion) or on transmission, that is, a transfer by operation of law on the death or bankruptcy of an existing member.

A person can thus become a member of a company in one of four ways:

(i) by subscribing to the memorandum upon the incorporation of the company;

---

1 This requirement is satisfied when a person assents to become a member and it does not require that there should be a binding contract between the person and the company: *Re Nuneaton Borough Association Football Club Ltd* [1989] BCLC 454, CA.
2 See *Re Florence Land and Public Works Co, Nicol's Case, Tufnell and Ponsonby's Case* (1885) 29 Ch D 421, CA.

(ii)   by application and allotment followed by entry on the register of members;
(iii)   by transfer from another member followed by registration;
(iv)   by transmission on death or bankruptcy followed by registration.

We will deal with each of these in turn. Categories (i) and (iv) are of limited significance whilst (ii) and (iii) are the most common methods by which persons become members. (ii) has already been discussed in Chapter 14 and is further considered as far as public companies are concerned in Chapter 33, so only (iii) needs to be considered here in detail.

First, it is important to note certain restrictions on membership which will prevent (a) minors and (b) companies from being members under any of these methods in certain instances.

RESTRICTIONS ON MEMBERSHIP

Minors

The general position is that there is no prohibition on minors[3] being members, although the company may refuse to accept a minor as a shareholder[4]. However, applying ordinary contract law rules, the contract is voidable by the minor before or within a reasonable time of attaining his majority. If the minor repudiates the contract, he will not be liable for future calls but cannot recover the purchase price unless there has been a total failure of consideration[5], which is unlikely to be the case. Given that shares are normally issued fully paid now, there is little reason for repudiation and it is rare for problems with minors to arise, unlike in the late nineteenth century when there were many cases of heirs and heiresses seeking to repudiate contracts for shares. Until the minor repudiates, the minor has full rights of membership.

Companies

A company cannot be a member of itself, a point originally established in *Trevor v Whitworth*[6] and now stated in s 143 which provides that any purported acquisition of its own shares is void and an offence by the company and any officer in default. However, the prohibition does not apply, as we saw in Chapters 15 and 16, where a company acquires any of its own fully-paid shares otherwise than for valuable consideration; or on a redemption or purchase or reduction of capital properly authorised; or as a result of forfeiture or surrender in lieu; or pursuant to a court order[7].

Section 23, as inserted by s 129 of the CA 1989, further provides that, subject to certain exceptions, a company cannot be a member of its holding

---

3 That is anyone under 18 years of age in England and Wales, Family Law Reform Act 1969, s 1.
4 *Re Asiatic Banking Corpn, Symons' Case* (1870) 5 Ch App 298.
5 *Steinberg v Scala (Leeds) Ltd* [1923] 2 Ch 452, CA.
6 (1887) 12 App Cas 409, HL.
7 CA 1985, s 143(3). See also ss 144 and 145. Section 146 applies to a public company acquiring its own shares in certain circumstances (particularly applicable to forfeiture and surrender) and requires it to disenfranchise such shares and to cancel them within a certain period (generally three years) if it has not previously disposed of the shares.

company and any allotment or transfer of shares in a company to its subsidiary is void. The policy behind s 23 too was to reinforce the rule in *Trevor v Whitworth*[8] and prevent any reduction of capital. The prohibition cannot be avoided by using a nominee, as s 23(7) provides that this section applies to a nominee acting on behalf of a subsidiary as to the subsidiary itself. 'Holding company' and 'subsidiary' are defined by s 736, as substituted by CA 1989, s 144 and are discussed in Chapter 32.

The exceptional circumstances when a subsidiary may hold shares in its holding company are:

(a) where the subsidiary is concerned only as personal representative or trustee unless, in the latter case, the holding company or a subsidiary of it is beneficially interested under the trust[9];

(b) where the subsidiary is a market maker under the Financial Services Act 1986 and holds the shares in the holding company as a market maker;

(c) where the subsidiary held the shares before 1 July 1948; or held the shares between 1 July 1948 and 1 November 1990 (the commencement date for s 129) in circumstances in which it was not caught by the provisions of the old s 23, but now falls within the prohibition (because of the changed definitions of holding and subsidiary companies). In these circumstances it may continue to be a member of the holding company (and to receive bonus issues in respect of its holding) but it has no right to vote those shares in general or class meetings;

(d) where a company becomes a holder of shares in another company and subsequently becomes a subsidiary of that other company, it may continue to hold those shares (and receive bonus issues in respect of them) but may not vote those shares at general or class meetings.

Subject to these cases, a company can be a member of another company and may appoint a corporate representative under s 375 of the CA 1985 to attend meetings.

BECOMING A MEMBER

(I) Subscribers of the memorandum

Section 22(1) provides, as we saw, that the subscribers of the memorandum are deemed to have agreed to become members and on its registration shall be entered as such in the register of members[10]. The memorandum will indicate the number of shares which the subscribers have undertaken to purchase and every subscriber in the case of a company having a share capital must take at least one share[11]. As noted previously, shares taken by a subscriber to the memorandum of a public company in pursuance of an under-

---

8 (1887) 12 App Cas 409, HL.
9 Section 23(2)(a) and (b) proceeds to define when the holding company or a subsidiary is so interested. (a) in particular excludes any interest held only by way of security for the purposes of a transaction entered into by the holding company or subsidiary in the ordinary course of a business which includes the lending of money.
10 See generally Smith (1982) 3 Co Law 99.
11 CA 1985, s 2(5).

taking of his in the memorandum, and any premium on the shares, must be paid up in cash as required by s 106.

The subscriber is obliged to take up from the company the number of shares specified in the memorandum and it is not sufficient for a subscriber to acquire the requisite number of shares by transfer from other members[12]. The subscriber will be released from this obligation to subscribe if the company has allotted all of its capital to other persons[13], in which case there are no shares available for the subscribers[14], but this is rare in practice, particularly when so many companies are set up as shelf companies with the two subscribers each subscribing for one £1 share.

(II)   By application, allotment and registration

Allotment of shares by the company to existing or new investors is a matter for the directors, subject to certain statutory constraints. The powers of directors in this regard are discussed in Chapter 25, while the statutory constraints have already been discussed in Chapter 14. In Chapter 33 we shall examine in more detail the mechanics of allotment by public companies. Suffice it to say that the final requirement here too must be entry on the register of members as required by s 22.

(III)   Transfer followed by registration

A person may acquire shares from an existing member by purchase or gift, but in either case the transferee does not become a member until he is entered on the register as required by s 22.

BASIC POSITION

The basic position on share transfer[15], set out in *Re Smith, Knight & Co, Weston's Case*[16], is that a shareholder has a prima facie right to transfer his shares and directors have no discretionary powers, independent of the powers given them by the articles, to refuse to register a transfer[17]. That the question of share transfer is essentially a contractual matter is confirmed by s 182(1) of the Companies Act 1985 which provides that the shares of any member in a company are personal estate and are transferable in the manner provided by the company's articles[18].

---

12 *Re South Blackpool Hotel Co, Migotti's Case* (1867) LR 4 Eq 238; *Re London, Hamburgh and Continental Exchange Bank, Evans's Case* (1867) 2 Ch App 427.
13 *Re Tal y Drws Slate Co, Mackley's Case* (1875) 1 Ch D 247.
14 If, however, some of the allottees do not take up their shares or the company increases its share capital thereafter, the subscriber's obligation to take the agreed number of shares revives, see *Re London, Hamburgh and Continental Exchange Bank, Evans's Case* (1867) 2 Ch App 427.
15 For a more detailed discussion of share transfer, see Hannigan (1990) 11 Co Law 170.
16 (1868) 4 Ch App 20.
17 Ibid. See also *Re Copal Varnish Co Ltd* [1917] 2 Ch 349; *Re Bede Steam Shipping Co Ltd* [1917] 1 Ch 123, CA.
18 Subject to the Stock Transfer Act 1963 as amended which enables securities of certain descriptions to be transferred by a simplified process.

The articles need not impose any restrictions on transfer[19], although restrictions are usually justified in a private company[20] on the basis that they ensure that the existing members have control over who is admitted to the company, something which is regarded as essential, given that many private companies are analogous to partnerships[1].

TYPICAL RESTRICTIONS

The current Table A contains restrictions which enable directors to refuse to register (a) a transfer of a share which is not fully paid to a person of whom they do not approve and (b) a transfer of a share on which the company has a lien (art 24). They may also refuse to register a transfer unless (a) it is lodged at the office or at such other place as the directors may appoint and is accompanied by the certificate for the shares to which it relates and such other evidence as the directors may reasonably require to show the right of the transferor to make the transfer; (b) it is in respect of only one class of shares; and (c) it is in favour of not more than four transferees (art 24).

These are very limited provisions and it is customary for private companies to adopt, in addition, art 3 of Part II of the old Table A, previously contained in Sch 1 to the Companies Act 1948, which provides that the directors may, in their absolute discretion and without assigning any reason therefor, decline to register any transfer of any share, whether or not it is a fully-paid share.

In addition to these provisions giving the directors a discretion to refuse to register transfers, some type of pre-emption provision is commonly included which ensures that existing members have the first opportunity to buy any shares which may be for disposal.

The net effect of these provisions usually is that a member wishing to sell will be permitted to transfer his shares to an existing member without restriction but where he seeks to transfer to an outsider then a pre-emption provision will come into effect. This will normally require notice to the company secretary who must notify the other members that there are shares available for purchase. If the shares are not taken up by those entitled to do so under the pre-emption provision, then the transferor is usually entitled at that stage to offer his shares to an outside purchaser, subject to the proviso that the directors may refuse to register a transfer in such circumstances.

Any scheme of transfer laid down by the articles must be adhered to and the directors have no power to authorise registration in circumstances where there would be a breach of the articles[2].

---

19 This will be the position in relation to the transfer of fully-paid quoted shares which the Stock Exchange requires should not be restricted by the articles in any way, see the Admission of Securities to Listing (the Yellow Book), Section 9, Ch 1, para 1.
20 Until 1980 it was mandatory for private companies to include a restriction on the transfer of their shares in the articles, see Companies Act 1948, s 28, repealed by the Companies Act 1980, Sch 4.
 1 *Re Smith & Fawcett Ltd* [1942] Ch 304, [1942] 1 All ER 542, CA. See generally Andre (1979) 53 Tulane L Rev 776.
 2 *Tett v Phoenix Property and Investment Co Ltd* [1986] BCLC 149, CA, see in particular Goff LJ at pp 167–168. See also *Curtis v J J Curtis & Co* [1986] BCLC 86 where the New Zealand Court of Appeal came to a similar conclusion.

A DESIRE TO TRANSFER

The first step in the transfer process normally involves establishing that a shareholder wishes/desires/intends to transfer his shares. Recent controversy has centred on whether this covers an attempt to transfer the legal title to the shares or whether it is sufficiently all-encompassing to include dealing with the beneficial interests attached to those shares so that such dealing triggers the mechanism provided by the articles. The point was considered in *Safeguard Industrial Investments Ltd v National Westminster Bank Ltd*[3], where the bank, as the executor of a deceased shareholder, had been registered in respect of the deceased's holding. The bank held the shares as trustees for two beneficiaries to whom (for the moment at least) it did not propose to transfer the shares. One of the existing members argued that the bank's position (it could at any moment be required to transfer the shares to the beneficiaries) was such that it should be regarded as proposing to transfer for these purposes and should be required to serve a transfer notice.

The Court of Appeal, affirming the decision of Vinelott J at first instance, did not agree. 'Transfer' in the articles only embraced the transfer of the legal title and was inapt to apply to the transfer of beneficial interests. The mere fact that there is someone who can make an immediate demand for the transfer of a share does not make the existing member a proposing transferor for these purposes.

The court distinguished the position in *Safeguard* from that which had arisen in an earlier case, *Lyle and Scott Ltd v Scott's Trustees*[4].

In that case, a number of shareholders entered into an agreement with a third party under which they received £3 per share and bound themselves, inter alia, to vote as he desired, so putting him as fully in control of the company as they could without actually presenting transfers for registration. It was alleged that they were desirous of transferring and so the pre-emption provision in the articles came into effect.

In this instance the House of Lords agreed. Having agreed to sell and having received the purchase price, the vendors held the shares as trustees for the purchasers. They were bound to do everything to perfect the title of the purchaser. It was impossible that they could have done as they did unless they desired to transfer.

Oliver LJ in *Safeguard* thought the two cases were clearly distinguishable. In *Lyle*, the parties had entered into an unconditional agreement to sell, which obliged the shareholders to transfer when requested on payment of the price, which price had been paid and which agreement remained uncancelled and unrepudiated at the time of the hearing. This, in his opinion, was a thousand miles away from the position in *Safeguard*[5]. The fact that the bank in *Safeguard* was under a duty to transfer the shares on request did not mean that it had the necessary desire to transfer for the purpose of the articles. Duty does not equal desire.

---

3 [1980] 3 All ER 849; affd [1982] 1 All ER 449, CA. The first instance decision is noted by Birds (1981) 2 Co Law 69.
4 [1959] AC 763, [1959] 2 All ER 661, HL, noted Sealy (1960) CLJ 38. *Hunter v Hunter* [1936] AC 222, HL which might also initially appear to support the view that dealing in beneficial interests is caught, instead turns on its particular facts, namely that the mortgagee purported to exercise a power of sale which had not in fact arisen, see Pettet (1985) 48 MLR 220.
5 [1982] 1 All ER 449 at 454, CA. See also Vinelott J at first instance who was equally unconvinced that the two cases were similar, [1980] 3 All ER 849 at 859.

Another example of dealing with beneficial interests in a way which does not trigger the pre-emption mechanism is to be found in *Theakston v London Trust plc*[6].

In theory the transfer under scrutiny was from one member of the company (London Trust) to another (Paul) so avoiding the pre-emption provision. However, the transfer was being financed by an outsider, Matthew Brown (MB). MB also paid the stamp duty due and gave Paul certain tax indemnities. The agreement also provided that P would:

(i)   endeavour to have the shares registered in MB's name;
(ii)   charge the shares in favour of MB;
(iii) vote the shares as directed by MB;
(iv)   account to MB with respect to any distributions received in connection with the shares;
(v)   accept any offer for the shares as and when made by MB and endeavour to have MB registered as the owner of the shares; and
(vi)   not accept any other offer for any shares in the company.

The question was whether the effect of this agreement was such that the transfer from London Trust to Paul was really a transfer to MB (an outsider), so triggering the pre-emption provisions.

Harman J, looking at what had occurred, accepted as a fact that London Trust had sold its block of shares to Paul. He in turn had charged the shares to MB. In other words, in keeping with the *Safeguard* position, the court looked to see what had happened to the legal title to the shares. Moving on from that conclusion, the next suggestion was that, given the relationship between Paul and MB, Paul should be regarded as proposing to transfer his shares to MB, so triggering the mechanism at this second stage.

Having reviewed *Lyle* and *Safeguard*, Harman J thought the mere presence of an option in the agreement did not mean of itself that Paul should be regarded at that time as proposing to transfer. Some further steps would need to be taken under the agreement before the question of triggering the mechanism could arise and any steps taken would have to be examined to see whether they were sufficiently unequivocal to indicate that he was then proposing to transfer[7].

The effect of these decisions, as Lord Sorn anticipated in *Lyle*[8], is to leave open the obvious manoeuvre of dealing in the beneficial interest, thus defeating the draftsman's attempt to retain control within the company through the use of a pre-emption provision[9].

Assuming that the shareholder has triggered the mechanism, the next requirement is to notify the company, probably through the company

---

6 [1984] BCLC 390.
7 See also *Re a company (No 005685 of 1988), ex p Schwarcz* (No 2) [1989] BCLC 427, also reported as *Re Ringtower Holdings plc* (1988) 5 BCC 82, where Peter Gibson J, applying *Theakston*, found that a conditional agreement to sell subject to several events occurring (which were not within the control of either party to the agreement) did not constitute a present and unequivocal desire to transfer or dispose of shares.
8 1958 SC 230 at 250.
9 As Vinelott J stressed at first instance in the *Safeguard* case, [1980] 3 All ER 849 at 860, this gap in the articles cannot be filled by construction and if the parties wish to preclude dealing in the beneficial interest in this way then they must do so expressly.

secretary, indicating the number of shares which the member wishes to transfer[10]. The company secretary, in turn, will inform those members who are entitled under the pre-emption provision to make an offer to purchase the shares in question. The articles may also provide a means of determining the price to be paid, often simply that the price is to be the fair value[11] as certified by the company's auditors whose opinion is binding and conclusive. This sometimes creates problems as the transferor finds himself dissatisfied with the figure determined under this method but the courts are reluctant to permit challenges to such valuations save in exceptional circumstances, as where the valuers have departed from their instructions in a material respect[12].

REFUSAL TO REGISTER

One of the greatest difficulties arises when, having gone through the various stages outlined above, the transfer is blocked by a refusal by the directors to register the transfer. The significance of entry on the share register has already been explained.

As far as the directors' power to refuse is concerned, there are two possibilities: either the directors have an absolute discretion to refuse to register or the power is much more circumscribed.

With regard to an absolute discretion, here the typical provision will state that the directors may, in their absolute discretion, decline to register any transfer of any share. The leading authority on this provision is *Re Smith & Fawcett Ltd*[13] where the Court of Appeal accepted that where the articles contain a provision such as this, drafted in the widest possible terms, there is no limitation on the exercise by directors of that power other than the standard requirement that, as a fiduciary power, it must be exercised bona fide in what they consider—and not what a court may consider—to be in the interests of the company, and not for any collateral purpose[14]. Subject to that qualification, an article in this form gives the directors what it says, an absolute and uncontrolled discretion. It enables them to take into account any matter which they consider to be in the interests of the company. Obviously in such instances, it is very difficult to challenge a refusal to register, particularly as the directors cannot be required to give reasons to justify their decision[15].

10 Notification operates as an invitation to treat, subject to any provision in the articles, and it is for would-be purchasers to make an offer to purchase, leaving the transferor to decide whether to accept or not: *Tett v Phoenix Property and Investment Co Ltd* [1986] BCLC 149, CA.
11 See *Re Howie and Crawford's arbitration* [1990] BCLC 686 on the meaning of fair market value.
12 *Jones v Sherwood Computer Services plc* [1989] EGCS 172, CA; *Burgess v Purchase & Sons (Farms) Ltd* [1983] Ch 216, [1983] 2 All ER 4, noted Birds (1983) 4 Co Law 215; *Dean v Prince* [1954] Ch 409, [1954] 1 All ER 749, CA. It may not be possible to use CA 1985, s 459 (the unfairly prejudicial remedy) to challenge these procedures, although that issue has not yet been definitively resolved, see the discussion on s 459 in Ch 27.
13 [1942] Ch 304, [1942] 1 All ER 542.
14 [1942] Ch 304 at 306, [1942] 1 All ER 542 at 543. See also *Re Bell Bros, ex p Hodgson* (1891) 7 TLR 689; *Re Coalport China Co* [1895] 2 Ch 404, CA.
15 *Re Gresham Life Assurance Society, ex p Penney* (1872) 8 Ch App 446; *Berry and Stewart v Tottenham Hotspur Football and Athletic Co* [1935] Ch 718; *Duke of Sutherland v British Dominions Land Settlement Corpn Ltd* [1926] Ch 746.

With regard to a more limited power, the provisions vary greatly from company to company. For example, the articles might provide that the directors may refuse to register any transfer:

(a)   where the company has a lien on the shares;
(b)   where it is not proved to their satisfaction that the proposed transferee is a responsible person;
(c)   where the directors are of opinion that the proposed transferee is not a desirable person to admit to membership[16].

Here too the basic obligation is that the directors must act bona fide in what they consider to be in the interests of the company and not for any collateral purpose. More specifically, they must act within the limits laid down by the provisions in the articles which will be strictly construed[17].

The possibilities of challenging a refusal are greatest, obviously, where the power is a limited power. *Re Bede Steam Shipping Co*[18] illustrates the point. The articles there provided that the directors might decline to register a transfer if, in their opinion, it was contrary to the interests of the company that the proposed transferee should be a member thereof. The directors admitted that no inquiry had been made as to the fitness of the transferees. Instead the transfers in question had been rejected because a majority of the board objected to the transferor disposing of single shares or small lots of shares to individuals with a view to increasing the number of shareholders who would support him. The Court of Appeal found that the articles required the directors to focus on the qualities of the transferee and identify reasons why he was unsuitable. The particular objections which the directors had focused on were more concerned with the motives and attitudes of the transferor. These were not grounds provided for by the articles and so the transferee should be registered.

DECISION WITHIN TWO MONTHS

Registration may be secured, however, despite opposition, as a result of the failure of the directors to exercise their discretion within the requisite time period. There are two requirements in this context. The first is that the directors must actively exercise their discretion. They must take a decision to refuse to register a transfer, pass a board resolution to that effect and notify the transferee of it, otherwise the prima facie right to transfer will prevail[19]. Secondly, the decision by the directors must be taken within a reasonable time and a reasonable time for these purposes is within two months of the transfer being lodged with the company[20]. If that period has elapsed then the directors will no longer be able to exercise their discretion and an application can be made under s 359 of the Companies Act 1985 to

16 *Re Coalport China Co* [1895] 2 Ch 404, CA. Other examples can be found in *Re Gresham Life Assurance Society, ex p Penney* (1872) 8 Ch App 446; *Berry and Stewart v Tottenham Hotspur Football and Athletic Co* [1935] Ch 718.
17 *Re Smith & Fawcett Ltd* [1942] Ch 304, [1942] 1 All ER 542, CA.
18 [1917] 1 Ch 123. See also *Re Bell Bros, ex p Hodgson* (1891) 7 TLR 689; *Re Ceylon Land and Produce Co, ex p Anderson* (1891) 7 TLR 692.
19 *Re Hackney Pavilion Ltd* [1924] 1 Ch 276; *Moodie v W and J Shepherd (Bookbinders) Ltd* [1949] 2 All ER 1044, HL; *Re Swaledale Cleaners Ltd* [1968] 3 All ER 619, [1968] 1 WLR 1710, CA; CA 1985, s 183(5).
20 *Re Swaledale Cleaners Ltd* [1968] 3 All ER 619, [1968] 1 WLR 1710, CA; CA 1985, s 183(5).

have the register rectified by the inclusion of the name of the transferee.

Where the directors have correctly exercised their discretion so making the decision to refuse unimpeachable, there remains the question as to the position between the vendor and the purchaser of the shares who cannot now complete the transaction by having the purchaser registered. The position on a contract for the sale of shares is that the equitable title to the shares passes to the purchaser once the contract is made and payment received and the legal title passes on completion and registration by the company[1]. Unless the contract so provides, the vendor does not promise to secure registration and if the directors do refuse to register the transfer he is not liable in damages for breach although he will hold the shares as bare trustee for the purchaser. Where the parties are agreeable to such an outcome, then they can negate the effect of the directors' refusal to register.

(IV)   Transmission

Transmission arises by operation of law on the death, or bankruptcy of a member. On the death of a shareholder, the shares are transmitted to his personal representative and s 187 provides that the production of the grant of probate of the will, or letters of administration of the estate, shall be accepted by the company as sufficient evidence of the grant notwithstanding anything in the articles to the contrary. Whether the personal representative can actually be registered as a member depends on the provisions of the articles, but in any event under s 183(3), a personal representative may transfer the shares even though he is not registered[2]. In the case of bankruptcy, the beneficial interest in the shares vests in the trustee in bankruptcy whose position is similar to that of the personal representative.

The position is generally governed by articles similar to those in Table A, art 30 of which provides that a person becoming entitled to a share in consequence of death or bankruptcy may elect either to become a holder of the share or to have someone else registered as the transferee. In either case, the decision takes effect as a decision to transfer by the member, as if death or bankruptcy had not occurred. In other words, the election by the personal representative or trustee in bankruptcy has the effect of triggering any pre-emption provisions which may exist[3].

On being registered, the personal representative or trustee in bankruptcy enjoys the same rights as any other holder. Before that occurs, by virtue of art 31, they enjoy the same rights as any other holder except the right to attend and vote at general or class meetings.

1 *Hawks v McArthur* [1951] 1 All ER 22.
2 Further, CA 1985, s 459(2) now enables a person to whom shares have been transmitted to apply to the court to grant relief where the affairs of the company are being carried on in a manner which is unfairly prejudicial. This would cover the case where the directors unfairly refuse registration.
3 Oliver LJ in *Safeguard Industrial Investments Ltd v National Westminster Bank Ltd* [1982] 1 All ER 449 at 451, CA, discussed in detail above, made the point that had the company's articles in that case contained this Table A provision on transmission on death which treats an election by a personal representative to be registered as an event triggering any provisions applicable on transfer, the bank would have been required to serve a transfer notice. As it was, the company had excluded such a provision from its articles and so the bank was entitled as personal representative to be registered without any restriction coming into play; see also *Scott v Frank F Scott (London) Ltd* [1940] Ch 794, [1940] 3 All ER 508, CA.

THE REGISTER OF MEMBERS

Section 352 provides that every company shall keep a register of its members giving details of the names, addresses and holdings of its shareholders[4]. The register must disclose the date of entry on the register as a member and the date of ceasing to be a member, dates which may be of considerable significance with regard to voting and dividend rights.

The register provides creditors and investors with information as to the identity of those behind the corporate form which may affect any decision to invest or provide credit. It is also constantly monitored by public companies in order to detect bidders for the company building up a stake with which to launch a takeover bid. The usefulness of the register in such companies is reduced, however, by the widespread use of nominee shareholdings, discussed below.

The register must be kept at the registered office except that:

(a)   if the work of making it up is done at another office of the company, it may be kept there; and

(b)   if the company arranges with another person to make it up on behalf of the company, it may be kept at the office of that person provided in both cases the latter office is not outside the country of registration[5].

The registrar of companies must be notified of the place where it is kept.

Section 356 currently provides that the register may be inspected during business hours by members without charge and by any other person on payment of a fee[6]. Copies of the register or part of it may also be obtained. The position on these matters will in future be governed by regulations to be made under CA 1985, s 723A, as inserted by CA 1989, s 143, which will make provision for the hours of access, the provision of copies and the relevant fee. The decision to provide for such matters by regulation is in part a response to representations by the largest companies which have had to incur significant costs in providing access to, and copies of, their registers to commercial users who have used the information for their own purposes, for example, as mailing lists. It is hoped to curb some of these abuses by allowing companies to charge more realistic fee levels although this must be balanced with the need not to unreasonably deter private individuals from exercising their right of access to this information[7].

By s 361, the register is prima facie but not conclusive[8] evidence of any matters directed or authorised by the Act to be inserted in it. The details in the register can be challenged, for instance, on the grounds of mistake, but any shareholder wishing to challenge an entry must act promptly[9]. If there is

---

4 Where the shares are numbered, the numbers must be given. Where there are separate classes, the class must be specified. The amount paid up or agreed to be considered as paid up must also be disclosed, CA 1985, s 352.

5 CA 1985, s 353.

6 The register may be closed for not more than 30 days in each year after notice has been published in a newspaper, CA 1985, s 358.

7 See 'Proposals for Introducing Regulations on Inspection and Copying of Company Records, A Consultative Document', DTI, 1990.

8 See *Reese River Silver Mining Co v Smith* (1869) LR 4 HL 64 at 80.

9 *Re Scottish Petroleum Co* (1883) 23 Ch D 413 at 434, CA.

an error in the register, it can be corrected by the court[10] under s 359 which provides a summary procedure for rectification of the register where:

(a)   the name of any person is, without sufficient cause, entered in or omitted from the register; or

(b)   default is made or unnecessary delay takes place in recording the fact that a person has ceased to be a member.

The person aggrieved, or any member of the company, or the company may apply for rectification and the court has a discretion to refuse the application or order rectification and payment of damages[11]. The court will only act under s 359, however, if the matter is relatively straightforward. If the court cannot decide the case on affidavit evidence it will decline to deal with the case under the section and it will be necessary to bring normal rectification proceedings by action[12].

The limits to this jurisidiction under s 359 were explored recently in *Re Piccadilly Radio plc*[13]. In this instance, shares in a radio company were transferred without obtaining the consent of the IBA as required by the articles of association. Other shareholders in the company, with a view to preventing certain proposals being agreed to at a general meeting, sought rectification of the share register under s 359 by deleting the names of the transferees and restoring the name of the original transferor. Millett J, despite finding that there had been a breach of the articles, refused rectification. Section 359, he noted, provided a discretionary remedy. It was not automatic. The court must consider the circumstances in which and the purpose for which the relief was sought. The circumstances here did not warrant rectification for a number of reasons. The applicants had no interest in the shares and were not seeking to have their own names restored to the register. Instead they were searching for a means to disenfranchise opposition to the proposals to be put to the general meeting. They had seized on a breach of an article of which the IBA itself did not complain. The transferor did not seek rectification and the company itself did not support the application. A less meritorious claim was difficult to imagine. Their purpose in making it was foreign to the statutory remedy which they invoked.

Notice of trusts

A company registered in England and Wales is not concerned with trusts over its shares[14]. Section 360 provides that no notice of any trust, express, implied or constructive, shall be entered on the register, or be receivable by the registrar, in the case of companies registered in England and Wales.

---

10   Whether the company can correct the register without going to the court under s 359 is uncertain, see *Re Derham and Allen Ltd* [1946] Ch 31 which says that it cannot, cf *Reese River Silver Mining Co v Smith* (1869) LR 4 HL 64.

11   CA 1985, s 359(2). Gower *Principles of Modern Company Law* (4th edn, 1979) p 432 makes the point that the reference to damages in the Act is a misnomer and that any payment would be by way of compensation rather than damages.

12   *Re London, Hamburgh and Continental Exchange Bank, Re, Ward and Henry's Case* (1867) 2 Ch App 431; *Re Diamond Rock Boring Co Ltd, ex p Shaw* (1877) 2 QBD 463, CA.

13   [1989] BCLC 683.

14   *Société Générale de Paris v Walker* (1885) 11 App Cas 20, HL.

Article 5 of Table A provides that, except as required by law, no person shall be recognised by the company as holding any share upon any trust and (except as otherwise provided by the articles or by law) the company shall not be bound by or recognise any interest in any share except an absolute right to the entirety thereof in the holder. The company is consequently not liable to beneficiaries in the case of breach of trust.

The only way a beneficiary can protect his position is by means of a stop notice[15]. A stop notice is effected by filing an affidavit of the facts and a notice in the right form with the court and serving office copies of the affidavit and notice on the company[16]. The effect of a stop notice is that the company may not register a transfer of the shares affected or take any other steps restrained by the stop notice until fourteen days after sending notice thereof to the person on whose behalf the stop notice was filed. Where a stop notice has been filed then the company must act as stated but in all other respects the company treats the trustee as if he were the outright owner of the shares and in the same position as any other member.

Nominee holdings

Nominee shareholdings, by which are meant holdings registered in the name of someone holding the shares directly or indirectly on behalf of the true owner, are valid and common. They are particularly common in public companies where nominees are used to mask the identity of those holding shares in the company. This may be for reasons of privacy and commercial convenience but is too often a means of disguising insider dealing, accommodating share support schemes contrary to the statutory provisions (ss 151–153) and camouflaging would-be bidders for the company who may be trying to evade the requirements of the City Code on Takeovers and Mergers.

The Companies Act contains a number of provisions aimed at curbing such abuses. These are to be found in Pt VI of CA 1985, as amended by CA 1989, s 134, and include an obligation under s 198 to notify any known interests in voting shares in a *public* company within two days (reduced from five days by the 1989 Act) of the obligation arising. An interest for this purpose means a 3% interest (reduced from 5% by the 1989 Act) in the shares of the company but the Secretary of State is given extensive power by s 210A to vary these thresholds and time limits by regulations. There is also a requirement to notify particulars of certain family and corporate interests under s 203; and notification of group interests of persons acting together under s 204. Section 211 requires a register of interests in shares to be kept by every public company and s 212 gives the company power to require information with respect to interests in its voting shares. These provisions are supplemented by the powers of investigation conferred on the Department of Trade and Industry by Pt XIV which we deal with in Chapter 29.

---

15 Governed by the Charging Orders Act 1979 and RSC Ord 50, rr 11–14.
16 RSC Ord 50, rr 11–15.

SHARE CERTIFICATES

Under s 185, every company must issue a share certificate within two months of allotment or the lodging of a transfer, unless the conditions of issue otherwise provide. For the moment, this certificate is the proper and indeed only documentary evidence of title in the possession of the shareholder[17], although there are radical plans to change this, as discussed below, in relation to the securities of listed companies.

Section 186 provides that the certificate is prima facie (but not conclusive) evidence of title. The presumption arising from it can be rebutted. However, there are a number of authorities establishing estoppel in this context. For example, if the company issues certificates which describe shares as fully paid up when they are not and a third party relies on the certificate, then the company is estopped from denying that they are fully paid[18]. In *Bloomenthal v Ford*[19] in 1897, a lender to the company took shares in the company as collateral security. The certificate said he was the holder of 10,000 fully-paid ordinary shares when the shares were not in fact fully-paid. It was held by the House of Lords that the company was estopped from denying the certificate. The lender could have found out the true position by enquiry, but there was no actual notice and he was in good faith. The reason seems to be, in the words of Lord Halsbury, that the company is not allowed to say 'I told you so-and-so but you ought not to have believed me'[20]. The onus will be on the company to prove actual notice[1]. Where there is a subsequent transfer and the transferor has acquired a good title by estoppel, the transferee acquires a good title even if he had actual notice that the shares were only partly-paid[2].

However, if a certificate was issued following the presentation of a forged transfer then the company is not estopped from denying its validity. This is because the person presenting the transfer impliedly warrants the authenticity of the transfer[3]. A purchaser from such a person is in a better position. He can claim compensation from the company if he is displaced by the true owner since he relied not on a forged transfer but on the certificate issued by the company[4].

Electronic recording and transfer of shares

Major changes in the way in which shares are transferred and certificates issued are currently under development as the London Stock Exchange's

---

17 Per Lord Selborne in *Société Générale de Paris v Walker* (1885) 11 App Cas 20 at 29, HL. See also Lord Fitzgerald at 44.
18 See *Burkinshaw v Nicolls* (1878) 3 App Cas 1004, HL; *Re A W Hall & Co* (1887) 37 Ch D 712.
19 [1897] AC 156, HL.
20 Ibid, at 162.
 1 *Burkinshaw v Nicolls* (1878) 3 App Cas 1004, HL; *Re A W Hall & Co* (1887) 37 Ch D 712.
 2 *Re Stapleford Colliery Co, Barrow's Case* (1880) 14 Ch D 432, CA. Cf *Re London Celluloid Co* (1888) 39 Ch D 190 at 197, CA. Gower *Principles of Modern Company Law* (4th edn, 1979) p 439 justifies this outcome on the ground that otherwise the shares might become unmarketable and the estoppel of little value.
 3 *Re Vulcan Ironworks Co* [1885] WN 120; *Sheffield Corpn v Barclay* [1905] AC 392, HL; *Yeung Kai Yung v Hong Kong and Shanghai Banking* [1981] AC 787, [1980] 2 All ER 599, PC.
 4 *Re Bahia and San Francisco Rly Co* (1868) LR 3 QB 584; *Balkis Consolidated Co v Tomkinson* [1893] AC 396, HL; *Dixon v Kennaway & Co* [1900] 1 Ch 833.

TAURUS (Transfer and Automated Registration of Uncertificated Stock) programme[5]. This programme, which has been under discussion for most of the last decade, aims to abolish share certificates and replace them with electronic records. On the current schedule, the Stock Exchange hopes to see the system go 'live' by May 1992 with significant progress towards the elimination of share certificates for the securities of listed companies by 1993.

The reason for wishing to change from paper records to an electronic method of recording transfers is to ensure that London has a fast, efficient and economic method of recording transactions which will enable it to remain as the leading equity market within the European time zone. Problems with paper settlement were evident in the bull markets in 1986 and 1987 when the volume of trades threatened to swamp the paper system.

The proposal is that share certificates and stock transfer forms will no longer be used in every purchase and sale of shares in any listed company which has joined TAURUS. Instead transfers will be recorded on computer by controllers and transmitted by them to the TAURUS Operator—the central computer system—which in turn will transmit the information to the company registrars who will use the information, as now, to maintain the company's own register of members.

The Government has indicated that as far as practicable it intends to recreate the effect of existing law in the new environment of electronic recording and transfer of shares. Membership will require entry on the company's register of members as now and this will not happen until notification by the Operator and entry by the company registrar. An investor will not therefore automatically become a member of a company on being entered in the controller's records but must wait for the company's decision, as is the position at the moment. Moreover, the register would not be updated continuously as at present but only at specified dates known to the investor. However, the register must be updated once a month. In the intervening period between entry on the controller's records and entry in the company's register, the investor will be given a precisely defined package of procedural rights, called entitlement, which will include the right to sell the shares.

With the abolition of share certificates, it is not proposed that investors should be issued with any piece of paper which is prima facie evidence of title, instead they will simply obtain from the controller a statement like a bank statement showing details of their holdings and containing an authorisation code which must be used in any transfer. If an investor suffers from a failure of the controller, as where the controller sells shares belonging to an investor without his consent, then his remedy initially will be a civil remedy against the controller but provision is also made for a compensation scheme.

Of course, in view of s 185 which requires share certificates, any change to

---

5 See A Borrowdale 'Settlement of Stock Exchange Bargains' in *Contemporary Issues in Company Law* (1987) ed J H Farrar, p 227 which considers TAURUS and other similar schemes in the US, Australia and New Zealand.

electronic registration needs to be specifically authorised and provision is made for this by s 207 of the CA 1989, which provides that the Secretary of State may make provision by regulations for enabling title to securities to be evidenced and transferred without a written instrument. The DTI has consulted interested parties as to the content of these regulations and the scheme outlined above is as it appeared in the draft regulations issued in May 1991[6]. It is hoped that the final version will be laid before Parliament in November 1991.

Not everyone is happy with the prospect of electronic recording, however, because individual shareholders are uneasy about giving up the certificate as evidence of their holding, while the larger companies are concerned that the new system will make it more difficult and costly for them to identify who owns their shares and to serve s 212 notices requiring disclosure of ownership which help warn them of any impending takeover bid.

MORTGAGES OF SHARES

There are two species of share mortgage: legal and equitable. A legal mortgage, which affords the greatest security, is effected by a transfer of the shares followed by registration of the mortgagee as the holder of the shares. The mortgagor's equity of redemption cannot be noted by the company and the only protection which the mortgagor can obtain is by use of a stop notice, a process outlined above. Otherwise the mortgagee is treated by the company as the absolute owner of the shares. When the mortgage is repaid, the shares are retransferred. Despite the security offered by a legal mortgage there are drawbacks involved. If the company's articles contain restrictions on transfer then that mechanism will be triggered by the attempt to have the mortgagee registered. Equally, if the mortgagee is registered in respect of partly-paid shares, then the mortgagee as holder of the shares is liable to pay any calls which the company may make in respect of those shares.

An equitable mortgage, which is much more common, is effected by delivery of the share certificate and a blank transfer executed by the mortgagor. Once the mortgagee is in possession of these documents, he may exercise a power of sale in the event of default without having to apply to the court for an order for sale[7]. It is common for the parties also to draw up a memorandum setting out the basis on which the shares have been charged and dealing with such matters as dividend and voting rights. The memorandum will frequently contain an irrevocable power of attorney authorising the mortgagee to complete the share transfer form in the event of foreclosure or to exercise a power of sale on default.

---

6 The Uncertificated Securities Regulations, A Consultative Document, May 1991; 'Electronic Recording and Transfer of Shares, A Consultative Paper', July 1990.
7 *Stubbs v Slater* [1910] 1 Ch 632, CA.

LIENS ON SHARES

At common law a company has no lien on the shares of its members but the articles may provide that the company shall have a lien for unpaid calls and other debts. Under English law, such a lien takes effect as an equitable charge[8].

The position regarding liens varies depending on whether the company is public or private. If it is a private company, then its articles may provide that the company shall have a first and paramount lien over the member's shares in respect of amounts due in respect of the shares[9]. Alternatively, provision may be made for the company to have a lien in respect of any indebtedness of the shareholder to the company. As regards enforcement, the articles normally grant the directors an express power of sale. Complicated questions often arise with regard to priorities as between a lien and other charges. Article 8 of Table A provides that the company shall have a first and paramount lien. Where a third party gives notice of his interest before the company's lien arises he will have priority. Thus, in *Bradford Banking Co v Briggs, Son & Co*[10] the articles gave the company a first and paramount lien for debts due from the shareholder. The shareholder created an equitable mortgage by depositing all his share certificates with a bank and the bank gave notice of the equitable mortgage to the company. The shareholder then became indebted to the company and the company's lien thereby came into operation. It was held by the House of Lords that the bank had priority because the notice was served on the company before the company's lien came into operation.

The position as far as public companies are concerned is governed by s 150, which provides that a lien or other charge of a public company on its own shares is void unless it falls within the following categories:

(1)   liens on partly-paid shares for any sums payable in respect of those shares;
(2)   liens which are in the ordinary course of business of a lending or credit company;
(3)   liens created by private companies which were in existence prior to re-registration as public companies.

Categories (2) and (3) are obviously very restricted in their application, leaving (1) as the most common kind of lien, but even that is of limited value in this context since public companies usually issue their shares as fully-paid.

---

8 *Everitt v Automatic Weighing Machine Co* [1892] 3 Ch 506.
9 See arts 8–11 of Table A. Art 8 provides that the company shall have a first and paramount lien on every share, not being a fully-paid share, for all moneys (whether presently payable or not) payable at a fixed time or called in respect of that share.
10 (1886) 12 App Cas 29.

CHAPTER 19

Loan capital

In this chapter we are concerned with medium and long term loan capital, not short term debt such as trade credit and hire purchase. However, within the concept of loan capital, we include bank overdrafts which in practice if not in theory often represent medium term financing for healthy companies in normal credit conditions in addition to term loans. There are three important characteristics which have traditionally distinguished loan from share capital. First, loan capital represents a set of rights against the company, not rights in the company. Secondly, the rights arise out of a relationship of debtor and creditor, and thirdly, although debt is common enough with natural persons there are certain legal forms which are only employed by companies. Let us examine each of these characteristics in a little more detail.

Since the loan creditor's rights are against the company, he has only limited control over the company's affairs. He is not a member of the company. Such controls as he can exercise arise contractually from the loan agreement until default. After default, these are augmented by the normal creditors' remedies which are often extended by contract. The most common remedy is the appointment of a receiver and manager. Sometimes loan capital is 'convertible' into share capital, that is, the investor can require his loan to be applied in the purchase of shares. Thereafter he has such rights of participation as the shares themselves confer.

The essence of the legal relationship is debt, although loan creditors fall into two main categories, commercial finance providers and investors. The first covers financial institutions who are conventionally not regarded as investors. Investment creditors cover a wide range of people and institutions whose common link is that in fact they invest for a safe fixed return since loan capital does not produce capital appreciation for the loan creditor. Their investment is usually remunerated at a fixed rate of interest. There is often flexibility as to when the debt must be repaid. The debt constitutes a prior charge on the profits of the company and on its assets in a liquidation in the sense that the claims of the loan creditor must be met before shareholders are paid. Since loan capital is debt, not share, capital, it is not subject to the share capital maintenance rules. It can be issued at a discount and be repurchased by the company and reissued. Interest on it may be paid out of capital.

Loan capital is a common method of financing business enterprise and for successful companies, particularly listed companies, there is an increasing variety of debt capital available. Much of this is handled privately by financial institutions and does not involve public listing on stock exchanges. Listed debt capital is thus becoming less common.

What is distinctive about corporate debt is the frequent use of the debenture stock trust deed and floating charge. By the former, we mean that instead of having a large number of individual loan creditors with their separate rights and remedies, larger companies often enter into a trust deed with a financial institution as trustee, creating debenture stock. The investor takes up the stock and his rights are enforced through the trustee. This form has been common since the end of the nineteenth century and avoids the difficulties which would arise from having thousands of individual debenture holders. By a floating charge, we refer to a species of equitable charge which relates but does not specifically affix to a class of assets. The company can dispose of particular assets in the ordinary course of business until crystallisation when the floating charge attaches as a fixed equitable charge. We shall consider the floating charge in more detail later. For top listed companies there has been an increasing use of the negative pledge in lieu of security. A negative pledge which we consider later involves a contractual obligation by the debtor company *not* to create security in favour of other lenders. Some argue that even the negative pledge will become obsolete for such companies.

THE HISTORICAL DEVELOPMENT OF LOAN CAPITAL

In the seventeenth century the share capital of the leading companies was oversubscribed, and the number of shareholders relatively small and mainly concentrated in the merchant classes. Such companies made increasing use of loan capital. The advantages of this were:

(1) the loan capital could be issued at an interest rate below the expected yield on the shares; and
(2) this concentrated the profits in the hands of a small number of investors.

The nature of the loan capital at this time was bonds and annuities. Scott[1] described bonds, which were an acknowledgement of debts under seal, as 'a striving towards the modern debenture'. Originally bonds were short term loans repayable at three or six months or at call. Later, although they retained this nominal character in practice, they were rolled over and became longer term capital. There was an advantage from the company's point of view in that it could renegotiate the interest rate from time to time. Terms were often extended or the bonds replaced by a new issue. Annuities which gave the investor a right to a fixed annual payment were popular with the government and the main companies at this time. Consols—the Consolidated Annuity of the Bank of England—date from the eighteenth century. The East India Company, for example, traded heavily in such loan capital[2].

Bonds were popular with 'persons not familiar with the wayward habits of the embryo stock market', especially women[3]. Women held only about 2–4% of India stock but about 20% of India bonds in 1685. The figures for the African Company were 10% and 20% respectively. Trustees and even a

---

1 *Constitution and Finance of English, Scottish & Irish Joint Stock Companies to 1720* (1910–1912) vol 1, p 304.
2 'Britannia Languens' in *A Select Collection of Early English Tracts on Commerce* (1953) ed J R McCulloch, p 341.
3 K G Davies 'Joint Stock Investment in the Later Seventeenth Century' in *Essays in Economic History* (1954) ed E M Carus-Wilson, vol II, p 289.

few institutions such as the Drapers Company, a City livery company, held bonds. This is a pattern which continues to the present day.

Turning next to the eighteenth century, there is difficulty in distinguishing between investment and trade creditors since the ordinary trade creditor often received a sealed obligation. The methods of raising loan capital varied. An issue could be made by a direct public offer or an offer for sale to one person who then sold to the public. The African Company left a broad discretion to the directors as to choice of method. Sometimes it was provided that the interest on particular bonds would be paid in preference to all other debts of the company.

Mr DuBois in *The English Business Company After the Bubble Act 1720–1800* states: 'In general during the eighteenth century, the differentiation between the creditors' and the proprietors' position was not always clearly defined'[4]. He cites[5] a proprietor at a general court of the East India Company on 9 August 1732 which was considering a reduction of the dividend on the stock arguing for a reduction of the interest on bonds on the basis: 'This Company consists of two sorts of proprietors, to wit, Stock Proprietors and Bond Proprietors; but why should the Burden be all laid on the stock?'. It was thought necessary in 32 Geo 3 c 101 (1792) which incorporated the Company of Proprietors of the Lancaster Canal Navigation to provide expressly: 'that no Person to whom any such Mortgage or Assignment shall be made or transferred as aforesaid shall be deemed a Proprietor . . . or capable of acting or voting for or on Account of . . . such Mortgage or Assignment'. Sometimes there was an option given to bondholders to become stockholders and sometimes bonds were repaid in stock.

As regards investor protection, the loan creditor could sue for default in payment of interest or principal. In addition, he could petition one of the Houses of Parliament for the appointment of a committee of investigation. Petitions were made in respect of the York Buildings Company, the Charitable Corporation in 1733 and the Royal African Company in the 1740s. Such petitions maintained that this was their only remedy in the absence of bankruptcy provisions for chartered corporations[6]. It is clear, however, that loan creditors were in a weaker position than stockholders in not having a representative in the active management of the company. From time to time committees of loan creditors grew up on an ad hoc basis[7]. Loan creditors of deed of settlement companies were generally in a better position in that they could in theory sue the stockholders but in practice this was curtailed by complex drafting. They also lacked participation in management and adequate representation.

On the whole, bondholders seem to have recovered their loans if the company foundered, but with the industrial revolution came a vast expansion of credit for current transactions. When companies failed, bondholders often found they were one of a number of competing unsecured creditors. Investment creditors then began to insist on security and this raised the question of what security the company could give[8]. Loan capital was still

---

4 *DuBois* (1938, reprinted 1971) p 372.
5 Ibid, p 429.
6 Ibid, p 431.
7 Ibid.
8 See R R Pennington (1960) 23 MLR 630.

usually issued for relatively short terms, no more than five years. It was not until the 1880s that long term loan capital became common.

Let us look first of all at the rights of a bondholder, prior to 1862. The bond was a chose in action which could not be assigned at law. In equity it could be assigned, but only subject to equities. This made the title to the debentures vulnerable and restricted their marketability.

From the 1860s onwards, steps were taken to achieve negotiability in the case of bearer debentures and freedom from equities in the case of other debentures. The Judicature Act reforms improved the position by allowing legal assignment of choses in action.

From the point of view of security at common law, the company could only give a legal mortgage of land and a pledge of chattels. Equity was more flexible and the floating charge was developed in the 1870s as an equitable security over an undertaking or class of assets whose members changed in the course of business. Professor Pennington[9] has argued that there were three influences at work—equity, railway undertaking mortgages and insurance policy clauses, although the influence of the latter was problematic. Dr W J Gough[10] argues that the only influence was the equitable assignment of future property cases which allowed transfer of future assets by a present act which was later completed by identification or appropriation. The floating charge was conceptualised in the period 1870 to 1910 but unfortunately largely in the language of metaphor. To say that a floating charge 'floats' and does not attach to any specific assets until crystallisation and yet is a present charge and present security over shifting assets, is potentially contradictory. This use of metaphorical language, rather than sharp analytical terms, has led to conceptual confusion which we shall explore later in this chapter. By the end of the nineteenth century, companies found it useful to adopt a debenture stock trust deed for large scale issues. The advantages of the deed were that it enabled the company to create one security and it provided clear procedures during the subsistence of the security and on default.

There have been further developments in this century. Debt capital has become popular due to tax advantages—the interest being deductible against gross profits and only taxable in the hands of the recipients. Added to this is the substantial increase in the number of flexible types of debt financing offered by international financial institutions, particularly for the larger companies. Nevertheless the risks attaching to high gearing are driving some companies back to equity financing or to greater use of convertibles.

FORMS OF LOAN CAPITAL

Debentures

Nearly every document evidencing indebtedness by a company is commercially called a debenture, although it would be a mistake to equate the two completely. The term is not usually applied to routine correspondence. Also, loan capital can be raised by means of bills of exchange and other negotiable instruments which evidence debt but these are not usually called

---

9 (1960) 23 MLR 630.
10 Gough *Company Charges*, p 80 ff.

debentures. This is a matter of convention. We shall not deal with such instruments here. Generally, if not always, there will also be a covenant or agreement to repay[11].

Although it is an ancient term[12], there is no precise legal form of a debenture. Various forms of instruments are usually called debentures. There are mortgage debentures which create a charge on some kind of property. There are bonds which are under seal. There are others which are nothing more than a formal acknowledgement of indebtedness. They all seem to have the common characteristic that they are documents which either create or acknowledge a debt[13]. The use of the term is not necessarily conclusive as to the nature of the instrument. A debenture can be issued singly or in a series. The statutory definition contained in s 744 of CA 1985 provides that the term 'debenture' *includes* debenture stock, bonds and any other securities of a company, whether constituting a charge on the assets of the company or not. The word security is used here in a narrow sense. Debenture covers a mortgage issued to a single mortgagee[14].

Debenture stock

A debenture is an instrument evidencing a debt with or without security. There are two parties—the company and the loan creditor. Debenture stock is not an instrument but an equitable interest under an instrument (generally a debenture stock trust deed) which evidences a collective debt divided into units. Debenture stock is 'borrowed capital consolidated into one mass for the sake of convenience'[15]. Whereas a single debenture is only usually transferable in its entirety, a holding of debenture stock may be disposed of in whole or in part like a holding of shares. Sometimes the debenture stock trust deed or terms of issue restrict transfers to particular multiples of stock. The trust deed contains covenants by the company with the trustee to repay the capital sum and interest, and to observe and perform other covenants relating to the conduct of its business. It also usually contains security in the sense of a fixed or floating charge or both and the normal mortgage provisions. It invariably contains administrative provisions dealing with such matters as transfer of stock and meetings of stockholders.

The early forms of debenture trust deed supplemented individual debentures but usually contained the security offered by the company. The modern form replaces individual debentures and the holder of loan stock is now not usually a direct creditor of the company[16]. He is a beneficiary under the trust by which the trustee holds the debt. Most trust deeds provide for action to be taken by the trustee and pre-empt individual action by a

---

11 *Topham v Greenside Glazed Fire-Brick Co* (1887) 37 Ch D 281 at 292 per North J.
12 See the historical usage discussed in *Palmer's Company Precedents*, Pt III (Debentures) (16th edn, 1956–1960) p 1.
13 *British India Steam Navigation Co v IRC* (1881) 7 QBD 165 at 172–173; *Edmonds v Blaina Furnaces Co* (1887) 36 Ch D 215 at 219–221; *Levy v Abercorris Slate and Slab Co* (1887) 37 Ch D 260 at 263–264; *Union Bank of Australia Ltd v South Canterbury Building and Investment Co Ltd* (1894) 13 NZLR 489 at 512; *Lemon v Austin Friars Investment Trust Ltd* [1926] Ch 1, CA; *R v Findlater* [1939] 1 KB 594 at 599, CA.
14 *Knightsbridge Estates Trust Ltd v Byrne* [1940] AC 613, HL.
15 *Palmer's Company Law* (24th edn, 1987) vol 1, para 44–04.
16 R R Pennington *Company Law* (6th edn, 1990) chapter 12.

stockholder whose main remedy is against the trustee, to compel it to exercise its powers under the trust deed.

Redeemable and irredeemable debentures

Debentures may be redeemable at the option of the company or irredeemable. At common law, when a debenture was redeemed or transferred to the company, the debt was discharged and the debenture ceased to exist. Now where debentures have been redeemed, s 194 enables the company to reissue them or issue other debentures in their place:

(a)   unless any express or implied provision to the contrary is contained in the articles or in any contract entered into by the company; or
(b)   unless the company has, by passing a resolution to that effect or by some other act, manifested its intention that the debentures should be cancelled.

On a reissue of redeemed debentures, s 194(2) provides that a person entitled to the debentures has the same priorities as if the debentures had never been redeemed.

Formerly, there was some doubt about whether a company could issue irredeemable debentures or debentures payable at a long time in the future. It was thought that this might involve a clog on the equity of redemption. To remove doubts, s 193 contains a provision which was first introduced in 1907. This provides that, notwithstanding any rule of equity to the contrary, a condition in a debenture should not be invalid by reason only that the debentures are thereby made (a) irredeemable or (b) redeemable on a contingency or (c) on the expiration of a period (however long)[17].

It has been held by the House of Lords in *Knightsbridge Estates Trust Ltd v Byrne*[18] that a mortgage of land to a single mortgagee by a company is within the section. In practical terms, it is unlikely that a lender will wish to have his or her money out on mortgage for so long at least if the interest rate is fixed. Even where it is variable by reference to some index, like the minimum lending rate of a particular bank, a lender will lose the benefit of capital appreciation of his or her investment in this kind of long term loan.

Issue of debentures and debenture stock

We saw in Chapter 13 that a company cannot issue shares at a discount. Debentures may be issued at a discount unless the memorandum or articles forbid it. Indeed, they usually are issued at a discount in the case of large scale issues by public companies. However, it is not possible to use convertible debentures to avoid the rule applicable to shares. Thus in *Mosely v Koffyfontein Mines Ltd*[19] in 1904 a debenture issued at a discount provided for immediate conversion into fully paid shares equal to par. It was held to be objectionable.

Debentures may be issued payable to registered holder or to bearer. The latter have been rare in the last thirty years because of exchange control

---

17 Note the limits of the section. Other provisions may in fact and in equity constitute a clog.
18 *Knightsbridge Estates Trust Ltd v Byrne* [1940] AC 613, HL.
19 [1904] 2 Ch 108, CA.

restrictions, but since these have recently been lifted, we may see a return to this type of security.

Issues of debentures are subject to the provisions of the Financial Services Act 1986 which we will deal with later in Chapter 33. They are also subject to The Stock Exchange regulations where a listing is sought.

There is now no loan capital duty on the issue of debentures. This was abolished by the Finance Act 1973, s 49(2).

In equity, an agreement to issue a debenture by way of charge gives rise to a charge[20] since equity looks on that as done which ought to be done. The agreement must, however, be registered under s 395 as we shall see. Specific performance of a contract to make a loan will not normally be granted. The policy is that the borrower can borrow elsewhere. While this will generally be so, it may not be so in the case of an agreement to make a substantial advance or to enter into an offer for sale of debenture stock when the market subsequently declines. For these reasons s 195 makes specific performance available to a company. It will be lost, however, where the company has forfeited the debentures.

ISSUES IN A SERIES AND PARI PASSU CLAUSES

Debentures are sometimes issued in a series. When this is done and the debentures do not contain a pari passu (ie equality) clause they rank according to the date of issue or if all issued on the same day, by their numbering. This negatives their marketability. It is usual, therefore, to set out a pari passu clause on the following lines[1]: 'The debentures of this series are all to rank pari passu in point of charge without any preference or priority one over another.'

The effect of this is to place all the debentures on the same level as to security so that if it is enforced, the proceeds are divided pro rata amongst the debentureholders according to the amount paid up, and if more interest is due on some of the debentures, in proportion to the total amount due in respect of principal and interest. When debenture stock is issued, such a clause is not strictly necessary in view of the nature of the stockholder's interest but in practice it is usual to include such a clause in the trust deed.

Although the precedents usually mention a maximum fixed sum for the series it is more common today in the case of public issues of debenture stock to have a formula in the debenture stock trust deed rather than a fixed amount[2].

SUBORDINATION OF DEBENTURES

Sometimes debentures contain express provision for subordination of debts. Obviously there are problems of privity of contract as far as the benefiting creditors are concerned. These can probably be overcome either by a separate deed to which they are parties or by an express covenant in the debenture in favour of the company and the creditors intended to benefit or by arguing a trust or agency by the company in their favour. A further argument might be possible on the ground of waiver and estoppel if it can be

---

20 *Levy v Abercorris Slate and Slab Co* (1887) 37 Ch D 260.
1 Taken from *Palmer's Company Law* (24th edn, 1987) vol 1, para 44–16.
2 See *Pennington*, op cit, chapter 12.

proved that the new creditors suffered a detriment by relying on the pur-ported subordination[3]. We look at subordinated debt later in this chapter as a new form of loan capital.

Transfer of debentures and debenture stock

A debenture is a species of chose in action. Section 183 requires a proper instrument of transfer to be delivered to the company except in cases of transmission by operation of law.

Debentures which are fully paid registered debentures are usually trans-ferred by means of a form under the Stock Transfer Act 1963, or if they are dealt in on the Stock Exchange, by the new Talisman system which we have discussed in relation to shares. Bearer debentures are transferable by delivery. Otherwise the form of transfer will often be specified in the terms of issue.

A transfer of a debenture which is not a bearer debenture takes place subject to equities unless the terms of issue provide that transfers shall be free of equities. Thus in *Re Rhodesia Goldfields Ltd*[4], A, a debenture stockholder transferred stock to B who was registered. A was also a director and the company had a claim against him for money had and received. It was held that B had to suffer a deduction of the company's claim against A before he could be paid. It is usual, however, to provide for payment of principal and interest to the registered holder free of equities. This amounts to a contract by the company that it will not rely on such equities. In a case somewhat similar to *Re Rhodesia Goldfields Ltd*, but where the debentures contained such a clause, a transferee from a delinquent director was held entitled to payment in full[5]. On the usual wording, it will be necessary for the transferee to be registered to obtain the benefit of the clause[6].

It has been held[7] that bearer debentures are negotiable instruments. Although bearer debenture stock has not been the subject of a court decision it is treated by commercial custom as negotiable[8].

Redemption

The terms of the particular debenture stock trust deed usually specify a procedure for redemption. The three most common methods are (i) out of a sinking fund set aside for the purpose, (ii) by annual drawings normally done by lot, and (iii) by purchase in the market or by tender[9]. In addition, the debentures can be redeemed out of the proceeds of a fresh issue of shares or debentures although there are certain problems in this method due to the difficulty of getting the timing and pricing right.

---

3 See *Pennington*, op cit, chapter 12. Cf *Gough*, op cit, p 415 and R M Goode *Legal Problems of Credit and Security* (2nd edn, 1988) pp 95 et seq.
4 [1910] 1 Ch 239.
5 *Re Goy & Co Ltd* [1900] 2 Ch 149.
6 *Re Palmer's Decoration and Furnishing Co* [1904] 2 Ch 743.
7 *Bechuanaland Exploration Co v London Trading Bank* [1898] 2 QB 658.
8 See *Pennington*, op cit, p 483.
9 See further *Palmer's Company Law*, vol 1, para 44–43.

COMPANY CHARGES

Fixed charges[10]

The basic rules here are the normal mortgage rules applicable to an individual. The most common asset charged is land and the most common mortgage is a charge by way of a legal mortgage. The charge specifically attaches and the company cannot dispose of the land without the debenture holder's consent. An equitable mortgage can be given over a legal or an equitable interest in land. An equitable charge is created where land is made liable to the discharge of a debt.

A fixed charge on chattels in the case of an individual must be effected under the Bills of Sale legislation which requires registration of a schedule of all assets secured. The legislation is cumbrous and outdated and in practice has been superseded by hire purchase and credit sales. Such a charge in the case of a company need only be registered at the Companies Registry. Equitable mortgages and charges can also be created on chattels. Intangible property such as shares in another company can be the subject of a fixed legal or equitable charge. The former requires transfer into the name of the chargee, whereas the latter does not.

The most common securities created by a company are a fixed charge over land and sometimes intangibles such as book debts, and a floating charge over the undertaking and current assets of the company.

Floating charges

Floating charges were first recognised by the Court of Appeal in Chancery in *Re Panama, New Zealand and Australian Royal Mail Co*[11] in 1870. Their juridical nature, however, was not finally worked out until the 1900s[12], and even today there are some crucial ambiguities. There was at first some doubt as to whether they were securities in the stricter sense before they crystallised, but it is now settled that a floating charge is a present equitable charge which is not specific but shifting until crystallisation, when it settles and becomes a fixed equitable charge[13].

In *Governments Stock and Other Securities Investment Co v Manila Rly Co Ltd*[14], Lord Macnaghten described a floating charge as follows:

A floating security is an equitable charge on the assets for the time being of a going concern. It attaches to the subject charged in the varying condition in which it happens to be from time to time. It is of the essence of such a charge that it remains

---

10 See *Fisher & Lightwood's Law of Mortgage* (10th edn, 1988). For an interesting economic analysis, see T H Jackson and A T Kronman 'Secured Financing and Priorities Among Creditors' (1979) 88 Yale LJ 1106. See also A Schwartz 'Security Interest and Bankruptcy Priorities: A Review of Current Theories' (1981) 10 J Legal Stud 1.
11 (1870) 5 Ch App 318. See W J Gough *Company Charges*; J H Farrar (1974) 38 Conv (NS) 3, 5; (1976) 40 Conv (NS) 397.
12 See *Re Yorkshire Woolcombers Association Ltd* [1903] 2 Ch 284, CA; on appeal sub nom *Illingworth v Houldsworth* [1904] AC 355, HL; *Evans v Rival Granite Quarries Ltd* [1910] 2 KB 979, CA.
13 See e g Lord Macnaghten in *Illingworth v Houldsworth*, supra, at 358; Buckley LJ in *Evans v Rival Granite Quarries Ltd*, supra, at 999.
14 [1897] AC 81 at 86, HL.

dormant until the undertaking charged ceases to be a going concern, or until the person in whose favour the charge is created intervenes.

Seven years later he said in *Illingworth v Houldsworth*[15]:

I should have thought there was not much difficulty in defining what a floating charge is in contrast to what is called a specific charge. A specific charge I think, is one that without more fastens on ascertained and definite property or property capable of being ascertained and defined; a floating charge, on the other hand, is ambulatory and shifting in its nature, hovering over and so to speak floating with the property which it is intended to affect until some event occurs or some act is done which causes it to settle and fasten on the subject of the charge within its reach and grasp . . .

The three common characteristics of a floating charge are now recognised to be that (1) it is a charge on a class of assets of a company present and future, (2) that class is one which in the ordinary course of business changes from time to time, (3) by the charge it is contemplated that until some future step is taken by or on behalf of the chargee the company may carry on its business in the ordinary way[16].

A FLOATING EQUITABLE INTEREST

Dr Gough in his *Company Charges*[17] argues that a floating charge, though a present charge and present security, does not create any proprietary or equitable interest until crystallisation. At most it amounts to a mere equity or bundle of equities which arise out of the security contract. It is submitted that this view, which is based on the idea of appropriation, is not an adequate explanation of the floating charge[18]. It has been held that a floating charge which extends to land creates an interest in the land before crystallisation for the purposes of the Statute of Frauds[19]. It has also been held in Western Australia in *Landall Holdings Ltd v Caratti*[20] that a floating charge creates a floating equitable interest before crystallisation but a contrary view has recently been taken in Queensland in *Tricontinental Corpn Ltd v FCT*[1] where it was held that there was no proprietary interest in the property which would defeat a notice under s 218 of the Income Tax Assessment Act 1936. The reasoning in both recent cases repays close study. Williams J in the *Tricontinental* case recognised that the holder of a floating charge has the right before crystallisation to intervene and to obtain an injunction to prevent the company dealing with its assets otherwise than in the ordinary course of business. However, His Honour and his brethren were impressed by the fact that the reasoning in the early English cases to the effect that the floating charge is not a specific security until crystallisation had been cited

---

15 [1904] AC 355 at 358, HL.
16 See Romer LJ in *Re Yorkshire Woolcombers Association Ltd* [1903] 2 Ch 284 at 295, CA. In fact the members of the class change rather than the class itself. See also *Re Croftbell Ltd* [1990] BCC 781.
17 Op cit.
18 See J H Farrar (1980) 1 Co Law 83.
19 *Driver v Broad* [1893] 1 QB 744, CA; *Wallace v Evershed* [1899] 1 Ch 891. Cf also *Re Dawson* [1915] 1 Ch 626, CA; *Dempsey and the National Bank of New Zealand v Traders Finance Corpn Ltd* [1933] NZLR 1258; *Re Manurewa Transport Ltd* [1971] NZLR 909.
20 [1979] WAR 97.
1 (1987) 5 ACLC 555.

with approval in a number of High Court cases[2]. If there is such an interest it is only defeasible by a transaction in the ordinary course of business. A transaction not in the ordinary course of business takes subject to the equitable interest created by the charge, even though crystallisation may not have taken place[3]. If the transaction is substantial, it may occasion crystallisation on the basis that the company has ceased to be a going concern[3].

THE POWER OF THE COMPANY TO CARRY ON BUSINESS

What is the precise legal basis of the company's power to dispose of the assets in the ordinary course of business, notwithstanding the charge? Professor Pennington in an article in the Modern Law Review in 1960[4] and also in his book on company law[5] argues that there are two theories adopted by the judges. The older theory which he calls the 'licence' theory explains the matter by implying a licence from the lender. The newer theory which he calls 'the mortgage of future assets' theory explains the matter by reference to the fact that the charge does not attach specifically to any of the assets until crystallisation.

There is in fact little clear-cut authority for the 'licence' theory[6]. It is suggested that the basis of the company's power is not actual authorisation[7] by the lender but its capacity under its memorandum and articles of association and the general law. In fact one could say without begging the question that this power is now part of the law relating to floating charges[8]. The lender is under a disability, to use Hohfeld's[9] language, and his floating equitable interest is defeasible pro tanto. The matter can be modified by the terms of the particular debenture but if this power is excluded the document ceases to be a floating charge. This has now passed from being a matter of wording of a particular charge to a general requirement of law[10]. This view of the company's power is consistent with the 'mortgage of future assets' theory but not dependent on it.

What is the scope of the power? First, it has been suggested that there is a general requirement of good faith on the part of the company[11]. Although this is clearly relevant as regards the person dealing with the company it seems to have the same dubious relevance as regards the company here as it had as one of the three tests of gratuitous payment laid down in *Re Lee*,

---

2 See, e g, *Barcelo v Electrolytic Zinc Co of Australasia Ltd* (1932) 48 CLR 391 at 420; *Luckins v Highway Motel Pty Ltd* (1975) 133 CLR 164 at 173–4; and *United Builders Pty Ltd v Mutual Acceptance Ltd* (1980) 144 CLR 673 at 686. See too *Clyne v Federal Comr of Taxation* (1981) 150 CLR 1. The point is not purely academic as it affects priorities.

3 *Hamilton v Hunter* (1983) 7 ACLR 295; *Torzillu Pty Ltd v Brynac Pty Ltd* (1983) 8 ACLR 52. As to ordinary course of business see too *Reynolds Bros (Motors) Pty Ltd v Esanda Ltd* (1984) 8 ACLR 422; *Julius Harper Ltd v F W Hagedorn & Sons Ltd* [1989] 2 NZLR 471.

4 (1960) 23 MLR 630.

5 Pennington *Company Law* (6th edn, 1990), chapter 12.

6 See Farrar (1974) 38 Conv (NS) 3. See, however, *Reynolds Bros (Motors) Pty Ltd v Esanda Ltd* (1984) 8 ACLR 422.

7 Cf R M Goode *Legal Problems of Credit and Security* (2nd edn, 1988) Chapter III where it is said to be based on apparent 'authority'. Usually the 'authority' will be actual.

8 See Romer LJ in *Re Yorkshire Woolcombers Association*, supra, see also *National Provincial Bank of England Ltd v United Electric Theatres* [1916] 1 Ch 132.

9 See Hohfeld *Fundamental Legal Conceptions* (reprinted edn, 1966) p 36.

10 See Fletcher Moulton LJ in *Evans v Rival Granite Quarries Ltd* [1910] 2 KB 979 at 993, CA.

11 See *Hamer v London City and Midland Bank Ltd* (1918) 87 LJKB 973.

Behrens & Co Ltd[12]. The courts have recognised the following transactions as dealings in the ordinary course of business—sales, leases, mortgages, charges, liens, payment of debts and other transactions effected with a view to carrying on the concern[13]. Ultimately, however, it depends on the nature of the particular company's business[14] and in determining the matter the courts will consult the memorandum and articles of association. Matters which are exceptional may nevertheless be regarded as being in the ordinary course of business if they are intra vires[15]. This seems a little paradoxical if the test is, as it appears to be, the *ordinary* course of business[16].

The nature of crystallisation

CRYSTALLISATION—CLEAR CASES

What then is crystallisation and when does it occur? It was referred to in *Re Victoria Steamboats Ltd*[17] in 1897 by Kekewich J as a 'newly-adopted term'. It is the process whereby the equitable charge attaches specifically and finally to all the items of the class of mortgaged assets which the company owns at that date or subsequently acquires if future assets are within the scope of the particular charge. The latter assets become subject to the fixed charge as they come into existence. In relation to debts, the fixed charge operates as a completed equitable assignment[18].

It is settled law that crystallisation occurs on the winding up of the company—even, it seems, where the winding up is a members' voluntary winding up[19]. It is settled law that it occurs where a receiver is appointed[20] but it is insufficient that steps are merely being taken to appoint a receiver[1].

12 [1932] 2 Ch 46 which was followed in *Parke v Daily News Ltd* [1962] Ch 927 and *Re W & M Roith Ltd* [1967] 1 All ER 427. See however, *Rolled Steel Products (Holdings) Ltd v British Steel Corpn* [1986] Ch 246, CA.
13 See *Gore-Browne on Companies* (44th edn, 1985) p 422. A fraudulent transaction is not to be treated as in the ordinary course of business. See *Williams v Quebrada Railway, Land and Copper Co* [1895] 2 Ch 751.
14 *Re Old Bushmills Distillery Co, ex p Brett* [1897] 1 IR 488, CA. This seems to be close to the 'reasonably incidental' test of an implied power. See *A-G v Great Eastern Rly Co* (1880) 5 App Cas 473, HL.
15 See *Re Borax Co* [1901] 1 Ch 326, CA. Cf *Hubbuck v Helms* (1887) 56 LJ Ch 536 and *Re H H Vivian & Co Ltd* [1900] 2 Ch 654.
16 Although the word 'ordinary' constantly appears in the cases, Lord Ashbourne C in *Re Old Bushmills*, supra, at 495 thought it had 'no place properly at all in the phrase'. It is submitted that he was wrong. On the meaning of the phrase, see now *Reynolds Bros (Motors) Pty Ltd v Esanda Ltd* (1984) 8 ACLR 422; *Julius Harper Ltd v F W Hagedorn & Sons Ltd* [1989] 2 NZLR 471.
17 [1897] 1 Ch 158 at 161. The concept of crystallisation as such has no place in Scots law (see now Pt XVII, Ch 1), although it appeared in the original Bill which led to the Companies (Floating Charges) (Scotland) Act 1961.
18 *NW Robbie & Co Ltd v Witney Warehouse Co Ltd* [1963] 3 All ER 613, CA.
19 *Re Colonial Trusts Corpn, ex p Bradshaw* (1879) 15 Ch D 465 at 472 per Jessel MR. This is so even if the voluntary winding up is for the purposes of reconstruction, see *Re Crompton & Co Ltd* [1914] 1 Ch 954.
20 *Re Panama, New Zealand and Australian Royal Mail Co* (1870) 5 Ch App 318; *Re Florence Land and Public Works Co, ex p Moor* (1878) 10 Ch D 530, CA; *George Barker (Transport) Ltd v Eynon* [1973] 3 All ER 374.
1 *Re Colonial Trusts Corpn, ex p Bradshaw* (1879) 15 Ch D 465 at 472; *Government Stock Investment and Other Securities Co v Manila Rly Co* [1895] 2 Ch 551, CA; *Re Roundwood Colliery Co* [1897] 1 Ch 373, CA; *Re Hubbard & Co Ltd* (1898) 68 LJ Ch 54.

It has recently been held in *Re Brightlife Ltd*[2] that the service of notice pursuant to a clause in a debenture may constitute intervention, giving rise to crystallisation.

CRYSTALLISATION—UNCLEAR CASES

Ceasing to be a going concern or to carry on business   There are some passages in the authorities which suggest that a floating charge crystallises on the company ceasing to be a going concern, although they were ignored by practically all the leading English company law textbooks[3]. Until recently there was no express decision on the point[4] although it is clear that ceasing to be a going concern is one of the grounds for the appointment of a receiver by the court[5]. It was first treated as constituting crystallisation in the fifth edition of *Palmer's Company Precedents* in 1891[6] and there were subsequent dicta to this effect[7]. Occasionally, the crystallisation event has been put in terms of ceasing to carry on business[8]. Of the two phrases, 'ceasing to be a going concern' provides a rather imprecise and subjective test. It is a phrase taken from the context of valuation for accounting purposes where valuation as a going concern takes into account continuity and is contrasted with valuation on a break-up basis[9]. It has the advantages in that context that people are using it conveniently to describe what they know anyway, not to prescribe a particular future event. 'Ceasing to carry on business' on the other hand allows the possibility of more objective assessment although it is arguably wider in scope. Anyone is capable of discerning the presence or absence of business activity. Such activities are, however, capable of being conducted *after* the company has ceased to be a going concern, e g a closing-down sale. The main drawback with both tests is that they do not involve any intervention by the lender and might possibly be unknown to him or third parties. This is quite likely with ceasing to be a going concern and quite

---

2 [1986] 3 All ER 673.
3 In *Hubbuck v Helms* (1887) 56 LJ Ch 536 at 538, Stirling J refers to this as a ground for appointing a receiver. In *Robson v Smith* [1895] 2 Ch 118, the matter is fully argued before Romer J who accepts stoppage of business as a ground for crystallisation but finds on the facts that there had been no stoppage of business (ibid, at 124–125). In his famous dicta in *Governments Stock and Other Securities Investment Co Ltd v Manila Rly Co Ltd* [1897] AC 81 at 86, HL, Lord Macnaghten refers to ceasing to be a going concern as constituting crystallisation. His dicta are adopted in obiter dicta by Vaughan Williams and Fletcher Moulton LJJ in *Evans v Rival Granite Quarries Ltd*, supra, at 990 and 993. In *Edward Nelson & Co v Faber & Co* [1903] 2 KB 367 at 367–377, Joyce J refers to ceasing to carry on business, and Fletcher Moulton LJ uses the same phrase in the *Evans* case, supra, at 997. The English authorities do not apply to Scots law which is governed by Pt XVII, Ch 1.
4 See now *Re Woodroffes (Musical Instruments) Ltd* [1986] Ch 366 and *Hamilton v Hunter* (1983) 7 ACLR 295.
5 *Hubbuck v Helms* (1887) 56 LJ Ch 536; *Re Borax Co* [1901] 1 Ch 326, CA.
6 Op cit, by F B Palmer assisted by C Macnaghten (son of Lord Macnaghten), p 476.
7 See the cases cited in footnote 3 supra.
8 See the cases cited in footnote 3 supra.
9 Statement of Standard Accounting Practice, No 2 issued by the Institute of Chartered Accountants in England and Wales defines the 'going concern' concept as follows: 'the enterprise will continue in operational existence for the foreseeable future. This means in particular that the profit and loss account and balance sheet assume no intention or necessity to liquidate or curtail significantly the scale of operation'.

possible with ceasing to carry on business. The latter has now been accepted as a ground for crystallisation in *Re Woodroffes (Musical Instruments) Ltd*[10].

Automatic crystallisation clauses A more important and troublesome question is whether crystallisation occurs when an event happens which is expressly mentioned in the floating charge as a crystallisation event. Originally such clauses, which refer to varieties of default and breach of covenant, were not common but they seem to be used more frequently today.

There is some English and Commonwealth authority on the point. The English authority[11] which appears to support it, is all obiter dicta and is arguably equivocal[12]. The Commonwealth cases represent conflicting views. In the New Zealand case of *Re Manurewa Transport Ltd*[13] the matter was expressly considered at first instance. Here, the facts were that the company operated a carrying business and had created a floating charge which contained the usual form of restrictive clause forbidding the creation of further mortgages without consent. There was also an express automatic crystallisation clause which provided that the charge should 'attach and become affixed' on the happening of a number of events, one of which was breach of the restrictive clause.

After delay by the company in the payment of its garage bills, a garage firm seized a truck and refused to release it until they were given security for their account. A chattel security was created over the truck and registered. The consent of the debenture holder was never obtained and the matter fell for decision on the company's insolvency. Speight J decided in favour of the debenture holder. He held that under the New Zealand legislation there was constructive notice not only of the existence of a floating charge but also of its contents including a restrictive clause, as far as it related to chattels. The floating charge, therefore, had priority. Secondly, he expressly upheld Professor Pennington's view of the law that crystallisation can take place without intervention on the happening of an automatic crystallisation event. He relied on some of the English dicta and a New Zealand case of *Paintin & Nottingham Ltd v Miller Gale and Winter* [1971] NZLR 164, where North P had paraphrased Lord Macnaghten's dictum in the *Illingworth* case[14]. Speight J continued:

After all, a floating charge is not a term of art, it is a description for a type of security contained in a document which may provide a variety of circumstances whereupon crystallisation takes place[15].

---

10 [1986] Ch 366. Noted by L Sealy [1986] CLJ 25. See too *Hamilton v Hunter* (1983) 7 ACLR 295. Cf *Halpin v Cremin* [1954] IR 19.
11 See *Re Horne and Hellard* (1885) 29 Ch D 736; *Davey & Co v Williamson & Sons* [1898] 2 QB 194 at 209; *Illingworth v Houldsworth* [1904] AC 355 at 358, HL and *Evans v Rival Granite Quarries Ltd* [1910] 2 KB 979 at 1000, CA. Cf, however, 986, 993.
12 See Farrar (1976) 40 Conv (NS) 397. Cf A J Boyle [1979] JBL 231.
13 [1971] NZLR 909. See D W McLauchlan 'Automatic Crystallisation of a Floating Charge' (1972) NZLJ 300 and cf Farrar, *Gough* and Boyle, op cit; R Dean (1982) 1 C & SLJ 185.
14 Speight J's decision can also be supported by the New Zealand Court of Appeal's decision in *Geoghegan v Greymouth-Point Elizabeth Rly and Coal Co Ltd* (1898) 16 NZLR 749 at 768, 771, which was not cited and is not referred to in the New Zealand textbooks.
15 [1971] NZLR 909 at 917.

Re Manurewa Transport Ltd has been followed in the Australian case of *Deputy Commissioner of Taxation v Horsburgh*[16] and a similar view was taken in *Re Obie Pty Ltd (No 2)*[17]. A different view, however, was taken by Berger J in the Canadian case of *R v Consolidated Churchill Copper Corpn Ltd*[18]. This involved a claim by the Province of British Columbia that its statutory lien had priority over a floating charge. This depended on the charge not having crystallised. Berger J held that the charge had not crystallised inter alia because the relevant clause only provided for enforceability not crystallisation, and in any event the English authorities did not afford clear support. There were strong policy reasons against adopting the *Manurewa* view. It would render the filing obligation in respect of the appointment of a receiver redundant and would enable the company's assets to be immune from execution since another creditor would not know from the public file whether the floating charge had crystallised or not and the wording of a particular clause might make the levying of execution a ground for automatic crystallisation. In the recent case of *Re Brightlife Ltd*[19] Hoffmann J said obiter that he preferred *Re Manurewa* to the *Churchill Copper* case.

Thus the position is still not completely clear. An express automatic crystallisation may be regarded as effective, but where the particular floating charge merely provides that the company shall be at liberty to deal with the property charged until the happening of a specific event (ie it does not *expressly* make the event terminate the power to carry on business), the charge continues to float after the happening of the event until a receiver is appointed or the company goes into liquidation[20]. The receiver must actually be appointed. It is not enough merely to issue a writ[1]. It is crucial, therefore, to look at the precise wording of the particular charge. In the light of the cases the true view seems to be that if the clause does not clearly purport (a) to make such an event cause the charge to cease to float or (b) to terminate the company's power to carry on business or (c) otherwise to constitute automatic crystallisation[2] then it appears to be overridden by the company's power *under the law* to carry on business in the ordinary course until intervention or winding up.

Floating charges which are caught by Part VI of the Insolvency Act 1986 (transactions at undervalue etc) will be caught notwithstanding the presence of an automatic crystallisation charge in view of the definition of floating

---

16 [1983] 2 VR 591.
17 (1984) 2 ACLC 69.
18 [1978] 5 WWR 652.
19 [1986] 3 All ER 673. Noted by A Wilkinson (1987) 8 Co Law 75; A H Silvertown (1986) 83 L S Gaz 2895. See too *Re Permanent Houses (Holdings) Ltd* [1988] BCLC 563.
20 *Governments Stock and Other Securities Investment Co v Manila Rly Co Ltd* [1897] AC 81, HL; *Edward Nelson & Co v Faber & Co* [1903] 2 KB 367; *Evans v Rival Granite Quarries Ltd* [1910] 2 KB 979, CA, quaere if the company in the meantime ceases to be a going concern. *Biggerstaff v Rowatt's Wharf Ltd* [1896] 2 Ch 93, CA is also cited by 7 Halsbury's Laws (4th edn), for this proposition but this case in fact was concerned with an automatic crystallisation clause taking effect on default. There had been no default at the relevant time.
 1 *Re Hubbard & Co Ltd* (1898) 68 LJ Ch 54.
 2 The courts may equate *enforceability* and crystallisation but a mere reference to the amount secured or the stock becoming repayable is probably insufficient in the light of the *Government Stock* case, supra. Cf, generally, A J Boyle [1979] JBL 231.

charge in s 251. This covers a charge 'which, as created, was a floating charge'. There is provision in CA 1989 for the introduction of registration of notices of crystallisation by regulations made by the Secretary of State.

RESTRICTIVE CLAUSES

As we have seen, as part of its general power to carry on business in the ordinary course, the company implicitly retains the particular power to mortgage and charge its property. This was not at first recognised[3] but it is now accepted that the company is at liberty to create specific mortgages ranking in priority to the floating charge or after it[4]. The rationale of this apparently is that to hold otherwise would destroy the very object for which the money was borrowed—the carrying on of the company's business. This is not an argument that bears close scrutiny since such drastic consequences will not always necessarily ensue. In a later case it was argued that where the subsequent charge is only an equitable security it ought not to have priority over the floating charge. This was the view rejected in *Wheatley v Silkstone and Haigh Moor Coal Co*[5] even though the floating charge purported to confer a first charge. It was sufficient, North J said, that this should be so on crystallisation.

On the other hand in *Re Benjamin Cope & Sons Ltd*[6] in 1914 it was held that a company could not create a floating charge ranking prior to or pari passu with an existing floating charge. Sargant J appeared to view the above cases rather critically and thought that to extend them to the situation before him would be 'acting contrary to all professional and commercial views on the subject'. In the later case of *Re Automatic Bottle Makers Ltd*[7] in 1926 the Court of Appeal held that notwithstanding *Re Benjamin Cope*, a later floating charge over *part* of the assets could rank in priority to or pari passu with the earlier floating charge where power to create such a charge had been reserved in the first charge. Although there are suggestions that this might apply without such a power, it is submitted that this would be to confuse the specificity of the subject matter of a charge with the specificity of its legal character. After all a floating charge on part is still a floating charge, not a specific charge.

Because of the latitude shown by the courts to companies who have created floating charges, it has become the general practice to insert a clause forbidding the creation of any mortgage or charge ranking in priority to or pari passu with the floating charge. The clause (which, when it appears in a floating charge will be referred to hereafter as a 'restrictive clause' and, when it appears alone, as a 'negative pledge') appears to have been originally introduced as a suggestion in the first edition of *Palmer's Company Precedents*

3 *Re Panama etc Mail Co* (1870) 5 Ch App 318 at 322.
4 *Re Florence Land and Public Works Co, ex p Moor* (1878) 10 Ch D 530, CA.
5 (1885) 29 Ch D 715. Cf *Re Robert Stephenson & Co Ltd* [1913] 2 Ch 201, CA and *Re Camden Brewery Ltd* (1911) 106 LT 598n, CA—expressly 'subject to'.
6 [1914] 1 Ch 800 at 806. See also the briefly reported earlier case of *Smith v English and Scottish Mercantile Investment Trust* [1896] WN 86, 40 Sol Jo 717 to the same effect. This does not appear to have been cited.
7 [1926] Ch 412.

in 1877[8]. Such a clause 'is on its face a restriction on dealing in the course of business'[9]. The courts nevertheless proceed on the assumption that it is valid although they recognise that it must be strictly construed[10]. In no case does the validity of such a clause appear to have been challenged. It might have been argued that since this fettered the power of the company to carry on business, it was inconsistent with the nature of a floating charge, but it would now seem too late for this point to be raised.

Conversely, a point which would still seem tenable is that the subsequent mortgage must be granted by the company in good faith and in the ordinary course of business[11]. It is strongly arguable that the subsequent mortgage, being granted in breach of the restrictive clause, can be neither. In other words, it is arguable that it is evidence of equitable fraud by the company[12]. Where a restrictive clause is used outside a debenture and as a substitute for secured indebtedness it is commonly called a negative pledge. Such usage is increasingly common with larger companies, particularly those with international operations. We discuss this later in this chapter.

It is now clearly established that knowledge of the existence of such a clause operates in equity to prevent a subsequent mortgagee obtaining priority. This seems to be consistent with the equitable fraud argument. The onus appears to be on the subsequent chargee to prove that he is a bona fide chargee for value without notice, not on the first chargee to prove that he has knowledge or notice. A difficult question is what exactly knowledge and notice mean in this context. It is firmly established that although there is deemed notice of the existence of the floating charge (s 416(1)) there is no constructive notice of a restrictive clause[13] since there is no place for it in the registered particulars in England and Wales. The position is different in Scotland[14]. Such clauses are now very common and banks frequently endorse particulars on the form registered at the Companies Registry. There is no deemed notice achieved thereby (s 416(2)) but the possibility of actual knowledge[15]. Indeed, even where a subsequent purchaser or chargee does not search, the fact that such clauses are very common and the possibility for an existing creditor to inspect the copy of the charge in the company's own register of charges or for a prospective lender to request a copy, might give rise to an inference of such knowledge, particularly in a conveyancing transaction. Inferred knowledge is different from constructive notice. It is a

---

8 See *Palmer's Company Precedents* (16th edn, 1956–1960) p 55. *Buckley on the Companies Acts* (13th edn, 1981) p 265, on the other hand, maintains that the clause was introduced into debentures as a result of *Wheatley v Silkstone and Haigh Moor Coal Co*, supra. Charles J in *English and Scottish Mercantile Investment Co Ltd v Brunton* [1892] 2 QB 1 at 9 shares the same view. See also Edward Manson 'The Growth of the Debenture' (1897) 13 LQR 418 at 422 where he states that such a clause is of 'doubtful expediency'.

9 Per Walker C in *Cox v Dublin City Distillery Co* [1906] 1 IR 446 at 456.

10 *Brunton v Electrical Engineering Corpn* [1892] 1 Ch 434 and *Robson v Smith* [1895] 2 Ch 118.

11 See Sankey J in *Hamer v London City and Midland Bank Ltd* (1918) 87 LJKB 973 at 976.

12 See Kekewich J in *Williams v Quebrada Railway, Land and Copper Co* [1895] 2 Ch 751 at 755; see also *Cox v Dublin City Distillery* [1906] 1 IR 446.

13 *Re Valletort Sanitary Steam Laundry Co Ltd* [1903] 2 Ch 654; *Re Standard Rotary Machine Co* (1906) 95 LT 829; *Wilson v Kelland* [1910] 2 Ch 306; *G & T Earle Ltd v Hemsworth RDC* (1928) 140 LT 69, CA; *Welch v Bowater (Ireland) Ltd* [1980] IR 251.

14 See *Gore-Browne on Companies*, op cit, para 18–40.

15 See further Farrar (1976) 40 Conv (NS) 397; Cf *Gough*, op cit, *Goode*, op cit, for contrary views.

rebuttable rather than an irrebuttable presumption. Under the CA 1989 amendments to Part XII of the CA 1985, however, there is now provision for the introduction of new prescribed particulars which are certain to include requirements in line with Scots law. We shall attempt a summary of the priority rules when we have considered the provisions for registration.

THE EFFECT OF A FLOATING CHARGE ON JUDGMENT CREDITORS

In *Davey & Co v Williamson & Sons Ltd*[16] the Divisional Court held that seizure under execution is not in the ordinary course of business. It is generally thought that this goes too far[17] and that the crucial question is whether the floating charge has crystallised before execution is completed[18]. When execution is regarded as completed differs according to the method adopted[19]. The execution creditor is also entitled to retain moneys paid by the company before crystallisation to avoid sale of goods taken in execution even though the execution is uncompleted at the date of crystallisation[20]. Having said this, it is arguable that where execution is levied on the chattels of the company in such a way as to frustrate its business then this may give rise to crystallisation on the ground of cesser of business or ceasing to be a going concern. Such an event may also be an express crystallisation event.

REGISTRATION

The terms of a debenture stock trust deed usually require the company to keep a register of debenture holders. Section 190(3) provides that if one *is* kept, it should be kept at one of the places where the register of members is kept. If this is elsewhere than the registered office the company must notify the Registrar of Companies. There are two systems of registration of charges under CA 1985—the first is in a register kept by the company itself, the second in the register kept by the Registrar of Companies. The first was first introduced in s 43 of the Companies Act 1862, the second in s 14 of the Companies Act 1900. The present law is contained in Part XII of the CA 1985 which was substantially revised by the CA 1989.

Due to historical reasons there is overlap but not identity in the charges covered by the two sets of provisions. Every charge falling within ss 395–396 is registrable under s 411 but in addition, there are certain charges which fall outside s 395 but which fall within s 411. *Palmer's Company Law*[21] mentions as examples of the latter mortgages by deposit of certain commercial documents and charges on a concession. There is sense, therefore, in searching the company's own register for the sake of completeness, but in practice this is rarely done and persons dealing with the company tend to content themselves with a search of the company's file at the Companies Registry coupled with express inquiry of the company. Let us now examine each system.

Registration in the company's own register

Section 411 provides that every company shall keep at its registered office a register of charges containing entries for each charge, giving a short

16 [1898] 2 QB 194.
17 See *Pennington*, op cit, chapter 12; R J Calnan (1982) 10 NZULR 111.
18 *Robson v Smith* [1895] 2 Ch 118; *Taunton v Sheriff of Warwickshire* [1895] 2 Ch 319, CA.
19 *Pennington*, op cit, chapter 12.
20 *Robinson v Burnell's Vienna Bakery Co* [1904] 2 KB 624.
21 Ibid, para 46–01.

description of the property charged, the amount of the charge and (except in relation to bearer securities) the names of the persons entitled thereto. Under s 411(1), copies of the instruments of charge must be kept with the register. Failure to enter a charge in the register does not invalidate the charge but the company and any officer of the company in default is liable to a fine under s 411(4). Under s 412, the register and the copies of the instruments of charge may be inspected by a member or existing creditor without fee. A member of the public may inspect the register on payment of such fee as may be prescribed.

Registration at the Companies Registry

Section 396 provides for registration of particulars of certain categories of charge. Section 396(1) lists the following categories of charge:

(a)   a charge on land or any interest in land, other than—
   (i)   in England and Wales, a charge for rent or any other periodical sum issuing out of the land,
   (ii)   in Scotland, a charge for any rent, ground annual or other periodical sum payable in respect of the land;
(b)   a charge on goods or any interest in goods, other than a charge under which the chargee is entitled to possession either of the goods or of a document of title to them;
(c)   a charge on intangible movable property (in Scotland, incorporeal moveable property) of any of the following descriptions—
   (i)   goodwill,
   (ii)   intellectual property,
   (iii)   book debts (whether book debts of the company or assigned to the company),
   (iv)   uncalled share capital of the company or calls made but not paid;
(d)   a charge for securing an issue of debentures; or
(e)   a floating charge on the whole or part of the company's property.

We shall examine first what constitutes a charge in general within s 395 and then, secondly, some of the more complex particular categories.

The concept of a registrable charge

Under s 395(2), 'charge' means any form of security interest (fixed or floating) over property, other than an interest arising by operation of law, and 'property' includes future property. The key concept of 'security interest' is not defined but arguably expands the concept of charge and may be wide enough to cover a reservation of property clause or hire purchase or conditional sale agreement if the substance rather than the form is looked at[1]. The charge must be created by the company. A charge is created when the instrument is executed, even though the advance is made later[2]. Where there is a series of debentures, the charge is created when the first of the series is issued[3].

---

1 See, however, E Feiran and C Mayo [1991] JBL 152. The authors adopt a definition of security interest by Professor R Goode as a right in the asset of another to secure payment or performance. This seems unduly restrictive. Cf UCC article 1–201(37) which covers even 'simple' reservation of property or title. See further 'A Review of Security Interests in Property (1989) (The Diamond Report)' 3.14–3.10 discussed on p 281. See also G McCormack [1990] Lloyd's Maritime and Commercial Law Quarterly 520.
2 See further *Gough*, op cit, chapter 15.
3 *Re Spiral Globe Ltd (No 2), Watson v Spiral Globe Ltd* [1902] 2 Ch 209.

Where a charge arises by operation of law, it is not created by the company and is not registrable under the section[4]. Thus an unpaid vendor's lien is not within the section. An express contractual lien in a lien by operation of law situation is created by the company but is not within the section because it does not create a charge[5]. In any event s 396(1)(b) expressly excludes charges with a right to possession of goods or documents of title to goods. Since 'charge' now means any form of security interest this seems to exclude all possessory securities.

An agreement to create a security at some future date is not within the section until the security is actually given[6].

A charging order over shares or land is not within the section[7].

Let us now look at some of the more important categories.

CHARGES ON LAND

This covers legal and equitable mortgages or charges of land, even where the land is situated abroad. A charge on the land for rent or other periodic payment is excluded from the category. So if the company has entered into a lease or agreed to pay a rent charge payable out of its land, these are not registrable, but a mortgage over the company's own leasehold interests or rent charges would be.

Specific charges on unregistered land after 1 January 1970 must be registered under the Land Charges Act 1972 as well as at the Companies Registry[8]. All specific charges on registered land must be registered at the Land Registry and the Companies Registry. A floating charge over unregistered land need only be registered at the Companies Registry. A floating charge over registered land can only be protected by a notice if the land certificate can be produced and by a caution against dealings if it cannot[9]. Generally, unless this is done, a purchaser under a registered disposition is not concerned, whether or not he has notice 'express, implied or constructive'[10]. If the company is registered as the proprietor of land, or of a charge, the company's registered number will also be entered on the land register if it is provided or stated on any document lodged for registration[11].

When an instrument creates both a fixed and floating charge, it will normally be registered as a charge under ss 25 and 26 of the Land Registration Act 1925 as to the fixed provisions so that a copy of the deed would

---

4 Section 395(2); *London and Cheshire Insurance Co Ltd v Laplagrene Property Co Ltd* [1971] Ch 499, [1971] 1 All ER 766.
5 See *George Barker (Transport) Ltd v Eynon* [1974] 1 All ER 900, CA; *Waitomo Wools (NZ) Ltd v Nelsons (NZ) Ltd* [1974] 1 NZLR 484 (NZ CA).
6 *Re Gregory Love & Co* [1916] 1 Ch 203.
7 *Re Overseas Aviation Engineering (GB) Ltd* [1963] Ch 24, CA.
8 What follows is based on the author's revisions to *Palmer's Company Law* (24th edn, 1987) vol 1, para 46–06.
9 Section 3(7) and (8), Land Charges Act 1972. See *Property Discount Corpn Ltd v Lyon Group Ltd* [1980] 1 All ER 334, (registration of a charge on an equitable interest under s 395 effective for the purpose of s 3(7) of the 1972 Act, even though it was registered against the company which created the charge and not against the estate owner). See the useful note by D J Hayton (1980) 1 Co Law 144.
10 Land Registration Act 1925, ss 49(1)(f), 54, 60 and 64; Administration of Justice Act 1977, s 26 (abolition of mortgage caution). See Ruoff, Roper and Prentice *Law and Practice of Registered Conveyancing* (5th edn) pp 573–4; J H Farrar (1974) 38 Conv (NS) 315 at 324–5. See also Practice Direction dated 17 January 1977, noted (1977) 121 Sol Jo 72.
11 Land Registration Act 1925, ss 59(6) and 110(7).

either be bound up in the charge certificate or be issued as part of it. So far as registered land is affected by the floating provisions, it can be protected by notice under s 40 of the Act.

When debentures or trust deeds which create floating charges are noted on the register under s 49 and they contain a restrictive clause, the entry on the register will refer to the clause and be to the following effect: 'By a Trust Deed dated . . . of . . . Limited, the land is charged as security for the moneys therein mentioned. The charge is expressed to be by way of floating security but not so as to permit the creation of charges in priority thereto or pari passu therewith.'

If the floating charge is protected by a caution under s 54 of the Act the Registry will neither see nor possess a copy and anyone interested in the land learning of the caution will need to go to the deed itself for full information about it.

An agreement to create a mortgage or charge over land amounts to an equitable mortgage[12] and is registrable. Any mortgage or charge subsequently created is also registrable, and its validity is unaffected by non-registration of the agreement[13].

An equitable charge arising by presumption of law by deposit of title deeds is nevertheless contractual and does not arise by operation of law[14]. The presumption reads into the contract the charge which is implied. The charge is, therefore, registrable. This applies even where the debt secured is owed by a third party. If the charge is avoided, everything ancillary to it is also void. Accordingly, no separate lien on the deeds and documents will be recognised[15].

A lien arising by operation of law such as a solicitor's lien is not registrable[16]. An unpaid vendor's lien is thus not registrable[17]. Neither is a right of subrogation to an unpaid vendor's lien[18]. However, it is not normally possible to allege an unpaid vendor's lien if a valid but unenforceable charge is obtained as security[19]. It is otherwise if the latter charge is void from inception; in this case one can rely on the unpaid vendor's lien[20]. The unpaid vendor's lien will be excluded if the intention was simply the creation of an unsecured loan[1]. Where an equitable charge is duly registered and under a

---

12 *Eyre v McDowell and Wheatley* (1861) 9 HL Cas 619, but cf *Williams v Burlington Investments Ltd* (1977) 121 Sol Jo 424, HL where a contract to create a legal charge on a particular event was held not to be registrable as it did not create a present equitable right to a security but was merely an agreement that in some future circumstances a security would be created.
13 *Re Columbian Fireproofing Co Ltd* [1910] 2 Ch 120, CA.
14 *Re Wallis & Simmonds (Builders) Ltd* [1974] 1 All ER 561.
15 *Re Molton Finance Ltd* [1968] Ch 325, CA.
16 *Brunton v Electrical Engineering Corpn* [1892] 1 Ch 434.
17 *London and Cheshire Insurance Co Ltd v Laplagrene Property Co Ltd* [1971] Ch 499.
18 *Burston Finance Ltd v Speirway Ltd* [1974] 3 All ER 735. Cf *Coptic Ltd v Bailey* [1972] Ch 446, which was not followed.
19 *Re Beirnstein* [1925] Ch 12; *Capital Finance Co Ltd v Stokes* [1969] 1 Ch 261, CA; *London and Cheshire Insurance Co Ltd v Laplagrene Property Co Ltd* [1971] Ch 499. Cf Sunnucks (1970) 33 MLR 131.
20 *Thurstan v Nottingham Permanent Benefit Building Society* [1902] 1 Ch 1, CA; on appeal sub nom *Nottingham Permanent Benefit Building Society v Thurston* [1903] AC 6, HL; *Ghana Commercial Bank v Chandiram* [1960] AC 732, PC; *Congresbury Motors Ltd v Anglo-Belge Finance Co Ltd* [1971] Ch 81, CA; *Greendon Investments Ltd v Mills* (1973) 226 Estates Gazette 1957; *Burston Finance Ltd v Speirway Ltd* [1974] 3 All ER 735.
 1 *Paul v Speirway Ltd (in liquidation)* [1976] Ch 220.

term thereof a legal mortgage is later executed, the latter need not be registered[2].

Under s 396(3), the holding of debentures entitling the holder to a charge on land shall not be deemed to be an interest in land for the purposes of the section. A charging order over land by way of execution is not registrable under the section, but must be registered under the Land Registration Act 1925[3].

CHARGES ON GOODS OR ANY INTEREST IN GOODS

Formerly there was awkward cross-referencing to the Bills of Sale Acts but this has now been replaced by the more straightforward language of s 395(1)(b) which defines goods as any tangible movable property. However, given differing definitions of goods in other contexts there may still be problems of interpretation. The category now covers a wider range of goods and extends to charges whether or not they are created or evidenced by an instrument in writing. Charges arising by operation of law or which are purely possessory such as common law liens or pledges are excluded. There is some uncertainty as to whether reservation of property clauses, hire purchase, conditional sale agreements and finance leases are covered. If the court adopts a substance rather than form approach and a liberal interpretation of the term 'security interest' in s 395(2) then they will be covered even though not expressly mentioned. Complex reservation of property clauses have been regarded as registrable charges in any event[4].

CHARGES ON BOOK DEBTS

Formerly this was a separate category of charge. Section 396(1)(c)(iii) now subsumes book debts under the general category of a charge on intangible movable property (in Scotland, incorporeal movable property). Book debts are covered whether book debts of the company or assigned to the company. There is no definition of book debt although it is intended to deal with this under regulations made under s 396(4). Until then one has to rely on the case law.

Book debts are debts connected with and arising in the course of trade of any business, due or growing due to the proprietor of that business and entered or commonly entered in books[4a]. They are a species of chose in action and are assets of the company.

Assignments of book debts by way of security for a debt owing by the company are within s 396(1)(e)[5]. This is so whether or not the debt is entered in the books. A charge on *future* book debts is registrable[6] and it is

---

2 *Cunard SS Co Ltd v Hopwood* [1908] 2 Ch 564; *Re William Hall (Contractors) Ltd* [1967] 2 All ER 1150.
3 *Re Overseas Aviation Engineering (GB) Ltd* [1963] Ch 24, CA.
4 See eg *Clough Mill Ltd v Martin* [1984] 3 All ER 982; *Feiran and Mayo* op cit, 153–4.
4a *Shipley v Marshall* (1863) 14 CBNS 566.
5 *Saunderson & Co v Clark* (1913) 29 TLR 579; *Re Welsh Irish Ferries Ltd* [1986] Ch 47.
6 *Independent Automatic Sales Ltd v Knowles and Foster* [1962] 3 All ER 27.

possible in equity to have a fixed charge over future book debts[7]. A letter authorising moneys to be paid to the company's bank where the company was in debt, which was expressed to be irrevocable, has been held to be within the section[8]. Section 396(2)(e) excludes a debenture which is part of an issue or series and s 396(2)(d) excludes a deposit by way of security of a negotiable instrument given to secure the payment of book debts. The first are separately covered and the second is excluded on grounds of expediency. In New Zealand, it has been held rather illogically that cash at the bank is not a book debt although the relationship of banker and customer is that of debtor and creditor[9]. This view was also taken by Hoffmann J in *Re Brightlife Ltd*[10] notwithstanding the Registrar's practice of accepting registration of particulars in respect of them. Moneys in a trust account held by the company in order to pay its liabilities to third parties incurred in the interest of the settlor are not book debts registrable under s 396 and even if the right of the third parties in the moneys in the special account were charges and void for non-registration, the settlor's equitable right would not be avoided under s 396[11]. A shipowner's contractual lien on subfreight is not a charge on book debts and registrable[12]. A right of retention giving rise to set-off is not a charge on book debts[13].

CHARGES ON UNCALLED SHARE CAPITAL OR CALLS MADE BUT NOT PAID

This is subsumed under s 396(1)(c)(iv) as a species of intangible movable property.

CHARGE FOR THE PURPOSE OF SECURING ANY ISSUE OF DEBENTURES

This particular category could be used as a catch-all category for all other types of charge not specifically listed. Until the CA 1989, there was no English authority on the matter but it seems probable that the legislature intended the issue of a series of debentures. Indeed Professor Pennington argues that it refers to a 'large scale issue' of a series[14]. In the New Zealand Court of Appeal decision in *Automobile Association (Canterbury) Inc v Australasian Secured Deposits Ltd*[15], Richmond J assumed that this was what the legislature had primarily in mind and for this reason considered that a charge supporting such an issue was sufficiently significant to require registration. This was a case of deposits on 24 hours' call for which the

---

7 *Siebe Gorman & Co Ltd v Barclays Bank Ltd* [1979] 2 Lloyd's Rep 142. *Re Keenan Bros Ltd* [1986] BCLC 242. *Re Permanent Houses (Holdings) Ltd* [1988] BCLC 563. Cf *Re Lakeglen Construction Ltd (in liquidation)* [1980] IR 347; the Northern Irish case of *Re Armagh Shoes Ltd* [1982] NI 59; and *Re Brightlife Ltd* [1986] 3 All ER 673. See further R R Pennington (1985) 6 Co Law 9; G McCormack (1987) 8 Co Law 3; R A Pearce [1987] JBL 18. See also Byrne and Tomkin (1985) 135 NLJ 443.
8 *Re Kent and Sussex Sawmills Ltd* [1947] Ch 177.
9 *Watson v Parapara Coal Co* [1915] 17 GLR 791. See Goode, op cit, pp 124–5.
10 [1986] 3 All ER 673. See too *Re Permanent Houses (Holdings) Ltd* [1988] BCLC 563.
11 *Carreras Rothmans Ltd v Freeman Matthews Treasure Ltd* [1985] Ch 207.
12 Section 396(2)(g) reversing *Re Welsh Irish Ferries Ltd* [1986] Ch 47.
13 *Re Charge Card Services Ltd* [1987] Ch 150; on appeal [1989] Ch 497; [1988] BCLC 711, CA.
14 Pennington's *Company Law* (5th edn, 1990) p 503.
15 [1973] 1 NZLR 417. See the discussion in *Gough*, op cit, p 277.

appellant received as security local authority stock with unregistered executed transfers. The Court of Appeal held that issue must be construed as referring in a collective sense to the aggregate of a number of individual debentures issued by the company and that as the three charges in question were distinct, they were not registrable. Separate charges on such stock were not a registrable category. Now s 396(2)(a) seems to adopt the New Zealand interpretation.

CHARGES ON SHIPS

These are no longer expressly referred to but are technically goods. Legal mortgages are effected in accordance with the form laid down in the Merchant Shipping Act 1894 and registered at the ship's port of registry. Equitable mortgages need not comply with these formalities.

CHARGES ON AIRCRAFT

These were not originally covered by s 95(2) of the Companies Act 1948 and are not covered by s 396. However, under the Civil Aviation Act 1982[16] there is provision for a Register of Aircraft Mortgages to be kept by the Civil Aviation Authority and for registration at the Companies Registry[17].

CHARGES ON GOODWILL AND INTELLECTUAL PROPERTY

Section 396(2)(d) defines intellectual property as:

(i)   any patent, trade mark, service mark, registered design, copyright or design right, or
(ii) any licence under or in respect of any such right.

Mortgages and charges of patents[18], registered trademarks[19] and registered designs[20] must be notified to the Patents Office.

Procedure for registration

Under s 398(1) it is the responsibility of the company to deliver the prescribed particulars in the prescribed form to the Registrar for registration within 21 days after the date of the charge's creation or acquisition. However, it is possible for any person interested to deliver the particulars to the Registrar and it will usually be safest for a chargee or his or her solicitors to do so. The fees can be recovered from the company (s 398(2)). It is no longer necessary to produce the charge itself.

Effect of registration

Under s 416(1) 'A person taking a charge over a company's property shall be taken to have notice of any matter requiring registration and disclosed on

---

16 See also the Mortgaging of Aircraft Order 1972, SI 1972/1268, operative since 1 October 1972.
17 Ibid, art 16(2).
18 Patents Act 1977, s 32(2).
19 Trade Marks Act 1938, s 25(1).
20 Registered Designs Act 1949, s 19(1).

the register at the time the charge is created.' In other words, there is constructive or deemed notice. Apart from this, there is no inferred knowledge, or notice of additional matters actually put on the register. This is made clear by s 416(2). Insofar as notice of restrictive clauses is likely to be a required particular the question of the scope of s 416(2) is largely academic.

Effect of non-registration

If the charge is not registered within 21 days after the date of creation or, as the case may be, after the date of acquisition, the company and every officer in default is liable to a fine (s 398(3)).

A charge which is not registered by the company[1] within 21 days of its creation is not totally void. Under s 399(1), it is void against:

(a)   an administrator or liquidator of the company, and
(b)   any person who for value acquires an interest in or right over property subject to the charge, where the relevant event occurs after the creation of the charge, whether before or after the end of the 21 day period, but subject to late delivery of particulars under s 400.

The relevant event is defined in relation to (a) as the beginning of insolvency proceedings and in relation to (b) as the acquisition of the interest or right (s 399(2)).

A purchaser is now potentially protected by s 399(1)(b) unless he or she purchased expressly subject to the charge.

A charge is not void for non-registration as against a person acquiring an interest in a right over property where the acquisition is expressly subject to the charge (s 405(1)).

In *Mercantile Bank of India Ltd v Central Bank of India*[2] in 1937, letters of hypothecation over goods in India were held by Porter J to constitute floating charges and should have been registered. However, since the charges remained valid against the company the chargee was able to convert the charges into fixed charges and perfect them by seizure before liquidation and this was good against the liquidator. Until seizure, the security in the charges was void against other creditors[3].

It is the security not the contract to repay which is void. The latter continues and ranks in a liquidation as an unsecured debt. Section 407(1) makes the whole of the sum secured payable forthwith on demand when the security becomes void. Until a relevant event, the chargee has all the remedies of a mortgagee but cannot claim priority over a subsequent creditor whose charge is registered before his[4] or hers.

---

1   I e, if presented particulars are not filed in time. See *Sun Tai Cheung Credits Ltd v AG of Hong Kong* (1987) 3 BCC 357 (PC appeal from Hong Kong).
2   [1938] AC 287, PC.
3   Ibid.
4   *Re Monolithic Building Co* [1915] 1 Ch 643, CA.

Registration and priorities[5]

Under the case law rules, a subsequent legal charge ranks before an earlier equitable charge provided the holder of the legal charge is bona fide and without notice. Amongst equitable charges where the equities are otherwise equal, the rule in *Dearle v Hall* applies and the first in time prevails. Registration has the following effects on those priorities. First, an unregistered charge which is void under s 399 loses its priority. Secondly, registration under s 398 gives rise to deemed notice of the charge but priority is otherwise determined by the date of creation of the respective charges. Deemed notice is of the charge but not its contents unless these are required particulars.

The following table attempts to apply the basic rules. LC = legal charge, FC = floating charge, FEC = fixed equitable charge, RC = restrictive clause, K = knowledge or notice, UR = unregistered. The order of creation is indicated by the sequence; the order of priority by the numbers. 1–8 assume both charges are duly registered. 9–11 illustrate the effect of non-registration where a relevant event has occurred. The position in 7 is arguably based on the presence in the relevant case of a clause enabling a subsequent floating charge over part to be created ranking in priority (*Re Automatic Bottlemakers Ltd* [1926] Ch 412) since otherwise it is logically inconsistent with 6. It is the specificity of the charge not the specificity of its subject matter which influences priorities.

1	LC	FC
	1	2

2	FC	LC
	2	1

3	FC		LC
		RC	(K)
	1		2

4	FC	FEC
	2	1

5	FC		FEC
		RC	(K)
	1		2

6	FC	FC
	1	2

7	FC whole	FC part
	2	1

8	FC whole + RC	FC part (K)
	1	2

---

5 Cf the Diamond Report, 21.2.8, which recommended a scheme based on date of registration which unfortunately was not accepted by the Government.

9	LC	FC	
	(UR)	1	
	void		
10	FC	LC	
	RC (UR)	(K)	
	void	1	
11	FC	FC	
	(UR)		
	void	1	

As can be seen the rules are still complex and it is a great pity that the Government failed to implement a simplified statutory set of rules.

Late delivery of particulars

The old law required an application to the High Court if particulars were not delivered by the due date. This is now replaced by s 400 which allows the prescribed particulars to be delivered for registration more than 21 days after creation. This will not affect the rights of creditors which have been acquired by the happening of a relevant event even if this took place in the 21 day period.

Suppose charge A is created on 1 July but particulars are not registered in the 21 day period. Charge B is created on 15 July and duly registered on 23 July. Late delivery of particulars in respect of A is made on 30 July. Charge B will have priority because of s 399(1)(b) if value has been received by the company.

Further, s 400(2) provides that late delivery is of no effect where the company is then or, as a consequence of the transaction in respect of which the charge was granted, will be unable to pay its debts and insolvency proceedings begin before the end of the relevant period beginning with the date of delivery of particulars. The relevant period is two years in the case of a floating charge in favour of connected persons, one year in respect of other floating charges and six months in any other case (s 400(3)(b)).

Supplementing or varying registered particulars

It is no longer necessary to apply to the High Court to rectify the registered particulars. Now it is enough to deliver further particulars signed by or on behalf of both the company and chargee under s 401 at any time. If there is an extension of the charge it may be necessary to deliver fresh particulars.

Effect of errors and omissions in registered particulars

Under the old law the certificate of registration was conclusive. Hence the need to present the original charge with the particulars. Now the certificate (if issued) merely gives rise to an irrebuttable presumption that the particulars were delivered not later than the date shown and a rebuttable presumption that they were delivered not earlier than the date shown (s 397(5)). A certificate will now only be issued on request (s 397(3)).

The consequences of inaccurate particulars in future will be that pro tanto the charge will be void if a relevant event occurs unless the court orders otherwise (s 402(1) and (2)). The court's discretion is governed by s 402(4).

It may order the charge effective as against an administrator or liquidator if the error was not likely to have misled materially any unsecured creditor to his or her prejudice or no person became an unsecured creditor while the registered particulars were incomplete. Also under s 402(5) the court may make such an order if it is satisfied that a person acquiring an interest or right over property subject to the charge did not rely on the registered particulars.

Registration of discharge

This is still optional although the Diamond Report recommended that it be compulsory. Section 403 provides that a memorandum may be delivered to the Registrar for registration provided it is in the prescribed form signed by or on behalf of both the company and the chargee (s 403(1) and (2)). If such a memorandum is delivered in a case where the charge in fact continues to affect the company's property it is void against the administrator or liquidator and any person who for value acquires an interest in or right over property subject to the charge where the relevant event occurs after the delivery of the memorandum (s 403(5)).

NEW DEVELOPMENTS IN CORPORATE DEBT FINANCING

Reference has been made in earlier chapters and at the beginning of this chapter to developments in international finance. In the context of corporate debt financing there is a decreasing separation of long term and short term lending and between debt and equity. The emphasis is on flexibility through individual contracting. Short term debt can be rolled over into medium term finance, bonds can be converted into equity and interest separated from principal. It is a world of syndicated loans, convertibles and swaps characterised by flexibility, diffusion of risk and rapid trading of commercial paper. Some of these developments are tax driven to take advantage of loopholes in national tax regimes and tax havens. Three common forms taken by the new corporate debt financing are negative pledges, debt defeasance and subordinated debt.

As we saw earlier in this chapter a *negative pledge* is a restrictive clause which does not appear in a debenture or floating charge. Indeed its logical character is the opposite of security. It is an agreement not to give security to anyone, or at least anyone other than certain specified lenders. In the US there have been arguments that certain forms of negative pledge can give rise to an equitable lien. Thus in *Connecticut Co v New York, NH and HR Co*[6] bonds issued by a railway company contained a covenant whereby if the company should subsequently mortgage any of its present property the bonds would participate in such security. The court held that the bonds created an equitable lien or charge which would attach on the making of a new mortgage. Indeed in a Californian case in 1964[7] it was held that an equitable lien might arise if a negative pledge was broken even if it did not provide for the creation of equal security. However, this seems to go too far. In English law the most that one can say is that it may be possible in certain

---

6 107 A 646 (1919).
7 *Coast Bank v Minterhout* 392 P (2d) 265 (1964).

circumstances to establish either an equitable charge or an equitable mortgage[8]. Normally the agreement will do no more than give a future and contingent charge and until this contingency occurs there is no charge and no need for registration. It might also be possible to argue that the torts of inducing a breach of contract or conspiracy and even equitable fraud apply in appropriate circumstances[9].

Debt defeasance is a concept sometimes linked with the negative pledge[10]. The lender under a negative pledge will usually be unhappy to see an earlier debenture or debenture stock trust deed continue to exist. Debt defeasance provides one possible solution. It involves the borrower company not necessarily discharging the prior debenture but setting aside securities to provide cash flow to service the debt and adequate cover for satisfaction of the debt. As well as providing a solution in the case of a negative pledge the company may wish to engage in debt defeasance (a) to improve reported profits, (b) to provide greater freedom to deal with its assets, (c) to use up cash so that a 'crown jewel' is removed to thwart a hostile takeover bid. There are two main types of debt defeasance—legal defeasance and 'in substance' defeasance. Legal defeasance is where the original debt is released. 'In substance' defeasance is where there is no formal release but satisfactory arrangements are made using the mechanism of a trust or some contractual undertaking by third parties to be responsible for the debt. The latter is sometimes known as the 'assumption' method. There is no legal or accounting regulation of debt defeasance at the moment in the UK. In the US the Financial Accounting Standards Board in consultation with the SEC issued a practice statement outlawing some of the more extreme forms of 'in substance' defeasance. Now in the US there needs to be a release or the use of a trust over cash or other essentially risk free monetary assets.

Brief reference was made earlier in this chapter to subordination of debt. *Subordinated debt* is increasingly popular as an alternative to equity capital. English law is less tolerant of subordination than US laws. There seems to be no great problem while the debtor company is solvent but on insolvency subordinated debt runs foul of the pari passu principle. It is arguable that subordination arrangements purport to contract out of the statutory scheme applicable in winding up and for that reason are contrary to public policy. However, much depends on how the documents are drawn up. It may be possible to provide for subordination after winding up to take the form of arrangements which only take effect after the statutory procedures have been completed. Also it may be possible to use the mechanism of a trust to operate outside the winding-up scheme in any event. While a trust over book debts may possibly require registration as a covert charge on book debts, a trust over dividends accruing on winding up is not a charge on book debts and there is no need for registration[11].

On the whole the new forms of corporate debt financing operate outside the scheme of the CA 1985. It can be argued that there is a need for registration of details to complete the picture of a company's finances. It would, however, be difficult to introduce such legislation while the practice is in a state of flux.

8 *Re Gregory Love and Co* [1916] 1 Ch 203.
9 See J H Farrar 'Negative Pledges, Debt Defeasance and Subordination of Debts' in *Contemporary Issues in Company Law* (1987) ed J H Farrar, pp 35 et seq.
10 For further detailed discussion see Farrar, op cit, p 142.
11 For further detailed discussion see Farrar, op cit, pp 155–6.

REMEDIES OF LOAN CREDITORS

If a company defaults, it is often indicative of business failure. We shall consider this concept and the main legal procedures in Chapters 36–38. Here we shall simply summarise the loan creditor's remedies:

(1)   He or she can sue for principal and interest.
(2)   He or she can present a winding-up petition.
(3)   He or she can apply to the court to appoint a receiver or a receiver and manager.
(4)   He or she can apply to the court for orders of foreclosure or sale of any secured property.

Usually the debenture contains provisions enabling the loan creditor or trustee to appoint an administrative receiver without resort to the court and in practice this is the most common remedy.

Debenture stock trust deeds usually provide for action to be taken by the trustee and restrict the rights of an individual stockholder to take action. It is rare to have an individual or class action by a debenture stockholder today.

FURTHER REFORM

The general question of loan creditors' rights was considered as part of the review of insolvency law and practice by the Cork Committee and a subsequent White Paper. Some but not all of the reforms recommended by the Cork Report were introduced in the Insolvency Act 1985. This act was then consolidated in the Insolvency Act 1986. We consider the relevant reforms in Chapters 37–39 in relation to receivership, administration and winding up.

In 1986 the Department of Trade and Industry commissioned Professor A L Diamond to produce a report on security interests in property other than land. As part of that exercise Professor Diamond addressed the question of registration of company charges as an interim measure and many of his recommendations were enacted in the CA 1989 revisions to Part XII. His final report[12] favoured a comprehensive reform on the lines of article 9 of the US Uniform Commercial Code as it has been adapted in Canada. This involves an integrated system of registration of all consensual security interests created by individuals as well as companies and adopts a functional approach, based on substance, rather than form. This is currently under consideration[13].

---

12 *A Review of Security Interests in Property* by Prof A L Diamond (1989) HMSO.
13 See E Feiran and C Mayo [1991] JBL 152; G McCormack [1990] Lloyd's Maritime and Commercial Law Quarterly 520. For a complacent and somewhat incoherent response from the profession see the Law Society's Company Law Committee's Report referred to in that article. In New Zealand, professional response to a similar proposal has been much more positive.

CHAPTER 20

The taxation of companies

CONCEPTS

It is a fundamental concept of company law that a company is a legal entity distinct from its shareholders, and company law textbooks concentrate on the rights and obligations of a company as an independent legal person. However, the starting point to an understanding of company taxation is economics, not law. Although taxes may be imposed on, and paid by, legal entities such as trusts or companies, tax is ultimately borne by individuals. Concentration on corporation tax as solely a tax on companies without considering its implications for shareholders and others will result in a misleading overall picture. For example, assume a tax system which has no corporation tax and a company which makes profits of £100,000. Subsequently tax is introduced at 50%. One of the effects of the new tax is to reduce from £100,000 to £50,000 the funds available for distribution to shareholders or, if the company retains rather than distributes its profits, to reduce the increase in the market value of the shares which would otherwise have occurred. Corporation tax has therefore had a direct effect on individuals, the shareholders. It is an oversimplification to assume that only shareholders are affected by the imposition of, or alteration to the rates of, corporation tax, as a company may seek to pass on the burden of corporation tax in a number of ways. It may increase its prices to customers in an attempt to maintain its post-tax profits at pre-tax levels; it may reduce, or restrain an increase in, the prices it is prepared to pay its suppliers for goods or services, and it may reduce or restrain the wages it is prepared to pay its employees. The exact interaction of these different methods of shifting the burden of corporation tax is a matter for argument among economists[1], but it is at least clear that corporation tax is ultimately borne by individuals and that one of the groups of individuals affected is the company's shareholders. Any consideration of corporation tax would therefore be incomplete without a discussion of the related tax implications for individual shareholders.

In the UK the principal direct taxes paid by individuals are income tax, capital gains tax, and inheritance tax. Income tax is imposed on the worldwide income of a UK resident and domiciled individual, after deduction of authorised expenditure such as mortgage interest, and after deduction of personal allowances. For 1991/92, the first £23,700 of taxable income

---

1 See e g Kay and King *The British Tax System* (4th edn, 1986) pp 154–159; *First Report of the Irish Commission on Taxation* July 1982, paras 24.2–24.9; *Report of the Canadian Royal Commission on Taxation* (the Carter Commission) 1966, vol 4, pp 19–27; *1955 British Royal Commission on the Taxation of Profits and Income* (Cmnd 9474) paras 44–57; A R Prest 'The Select Committee on Corporation Tax' [1972] BTR 15; S Cnossen 'Corporation Taxes in OECD Member Countries' [1984] Bulletin International Bureau of Fiscal Documentation 483.

is taxed at 25%[2] (the basic rate) with any excess being taxed at a single higher rate of 40%[3]. Capital gains tax on chargeable gains, computed after deducting an annual exemption, used to be imposed at a flat rate of 30%, so that a higher rate income tax payer saved tax if he could realise profits as capital gain rather than as income. However, in the March 1988 Budget the Chancellor Nigel Lawson announced two major changes of policy which were implemented by the 1988 Finance Act. First, after deducting an annual exemption, which is currently the first £5,500 of chargeable gains[4], the excess gains are added to the taxpayer's income and taxed as if they were the top slice of his income[5]. Thus a higher rate income tax payer now pays CGT at 40%, and the tax advantage in receiving a profit as capital gain rather than as income has largely been removed. Second, to prevent capital gains tax being a tax on gains due solely to the effects of inflation, the tax was rebased to 31 March 1982, so that only gains accruing since that date are now taxed[6]. Additionally the taxpayer can claim an inflation indexation allowance the effect of which is that the 31 March 1982 market value of the asset, or its cost if it was acquired after that date, is increased by the percentage increase in the retail prices index from 31 March 1982, or the date of acquisition if later, to the date the asset is disposed of[7]. Thus only real, as opposed to inflationary, gains are now taxed. No capital gains tax is payable on assets transferred on a death, but the donee acquires the assets at their market value on the date of death[8], thus effectively exempting any gain accruing to the deceased from CGT.

Transfers of capital may also be subject to inheritance tax. Apart from a number of exempt transfers, such as the transfer of assets between husband and wife[9], the first £140,000 of a deceased's chargeable estate is taxed at a nil rate, and any excess value is taxed at 40%[10]. Inter vivos gifts are now generally exempt from inheritance tax provided the gift is an outright gift with no reservation of benefit to the donor[11]. However, gifts made within the seven years preceding the taxpayer's death remain taxable as part of his estate[12]. They are taxed in the order in which they were made, and are entitled to tapering relief varying with the length of time the donor has survived the transfer[13]. Certain inter vivos gifts, such as transfers into discretionary trusts[14] and the alteration of share capital in a close company[15], remain taxable when made, but with the benefit of the £140,000 nil rate band, and the

---

2 Finance Bill 1991, CL 20(1).
3 FB 1991, CL 20(1).
4 CGTA 1979, s 5(1A). References to current tax legislation are to the original legislation as amended and in force for 1991/92. The amended legislation is contained in *Butterworths Yellow and Orange Tax Handbooks* for 1991/92.
5 FA 1988, s 98.
6 FA 1988, s 96.
7 FA 1982, ss 86 and 87.
8 CGTA 1979, s 49(1).
9 ITA 1984, s 18(1).
10 ITA 1984, s 7(1) and Sch 1.
11 ITA 1984, s 3A(4).
12 ITA 1984, s 3A(4).
13 Eg, if the donor survives four years only 60% of the inheritance tax otherwise due will be levied, ITA 1984, s 7(4).
14 ITA 1984, ss 3, 3A.
15 ITA 1984, s 98. Gifts by close companies also remain chargeable, ibid, s 94 with s 3A(6).

rate of tax chargeable is 20% (half the death rate)[16]. If such transfers are made within seven years prior to the donor's death they are cumulated with his estate, and are charged to the higher of the inter vivos rate or the death rate, with credit being given for any inter vivos tax paid[17]. All inter vivos gifts, whether initially chargeable, or chargeable only because the donor dies within seven years, are entitled to an annual exemption of £3,000 in computing the value transferred[18].

When considering corporation tax, it is therefore necessary to keep in mind:

(1)   tax paid by a company on corporate profits;
(2)   tax paid by a company on corporate capital gains;
(3)   income tax paid by an individual shareholder on distributions from a company;
(4)   capital gains tax paid by individual shareholders on the disposal of shares;
(5)   to a lesser extent, inheritance tax payable by individual shareholders on the transfer of shares.

HISTORICAL BACKGROUND TO CORPORATION TAX

Until as recently as 1965, the UK had no separate corporation tax. Originally, companies were taxed like trusts and paid standard rate income tax on their profits. When these profits were distributed as dividend, a shareholder was taxed on a gross dividend of the cash amount he received grossed up by the standard rate of tax[19], but was credited with having paid this standard rate tax. Thus, at least to the extent that profits were distributed, the tax rate on companies was effectively a payment in advance of the shareholders' income tax liability. As there was no capital gains tax, retained profits suffered only standard rate income tax[20]. To fund an armaments build up before the Second World War, a National Defence contribution of 5% of company profits was imposed in 1937. In 1939, this was supplemented by an excess profits tax. Neither of these taxes was credited to shareholders if profits were distributed. After the war these taxes were replaced by a profits tax designed to encourage the retention of profits to finance the post-war regeneration of British industry[1]. Thus, under the system which existed in 1955 when the Royal Commission on the Taxation of Profits and Income[2] reported, companies paid standard rate income tax on their profits, plus an additional 22½% profits tax on profits in excess of £2,000. If profits were retained, profits tax at the rate of 20% was refunded. If profits were distributed, there was no refund of profits tax but the shareholder, while

16 ITA 1984, s 7(2).
17 ITA 1984, s 7(5).
18 ITA 1984, s 19.
19 Which tax had already been paid by the company as income tax on its profit.
20 For historical background to corporation tax, see eg Boydon's *Modern Income Tax and Surtax Practice* (1933); *1955 Royal Commission Report* (Cmnd 9474) paras 49 and 50; R White 'The Changing Face of Taxation—Corporation Tax' [1981] BTR 349; 1982 Green Paper on the Reform of Corporation Tax, App 1 (Cmnd 8456).
1 See *1955 Royal Commission Report*, paras 518–540.
2 Cmnd 9474.

taxed on the dividend grossed up at the standard rate, was credited with having paid standard rate tax, thus leaving the profits tax as an unrecoverable tax on distributed profits[3]. This tax system encouraged the retention, rather than the distribution, of profits, with a further incentive being the absence of a capital gains tax on the disposal of shares. The 1955 Royal Commission recommended no change in the basic system of company taxation[4], although they did recommend the abolition of non-distribution relief for profits tax[5], a recommendation implemented in the 1958 Finance Act[6]. However, the Royal Commission Report contained a minority report by G Woodcock, H L Bullock and N Kaldor which recommended the introduction of a capital gains tax[7] and a separate tax on company profits, distributed or retained, with shareholders paying income tax on dividends but receiving no credit for the underlying comporation tax paid by the company[8]. The minority recommendations became Labour Party policy and were implemented in the 1965 Finance Act.

Corporation tax was imposed at a flat rate of 40% on company profits, whether retained or distributed. If a dividend was paid the company deducted, *and paid over to the Revenue*, standard rate tax at 41.25% from the gross dividend. The shareholder was then subject to income tax on the gross dividend, but was credited with having paid the 41.25% tax withheld[9]. This system of company taxation, which is known as the Classical system, had the advantage of maintaining the company law demarcation between the company and the shareholder, but also had the economic disadvantage of discriminating in favour of retained profits and against distributed profits. £100 profits were subject to £40 tax if retained in the company but to £64.75 tax if distributed to a standard rate taxpayer, the whole of this tax being paid by the company. Although retention of profits did not normally confer significant tax advantages on shareholders other than high rate taxpayers, as capital gains tax at 30% was now imposed on any gain on the disposal of shares, it was thought to distort the capital market by encouraging inefficient as well as efficient companies to retain profits, rather than distribute them and enable shareholders to reinvest in more productive companies[10].

In 1971, the Conservative government issued a Green Paper, 'The Reform of Corporation Tax[11]' which discussed three alternative systems of corporation tax all of which were designed to preserve neutrality between tax on retained and distributed profits. The first alternative was a return to the pre-1965 system, which the government rejected (because, without

---

3 *1955 Royal Commission Report*, paras 47 and 48. The profits tax was not levied on non-corporate businesses, and thus some differentiation in the taxation of companies existed prior to 1965.
4 Ibid, para 553.
5 Ibid, para 540.
6 FA 1958, s 25(1).
7 Ibid, p 365 ff.
8 Ibid, p 382 ff.
9 The rates quoted are those effective for 1965/66. A detailed outline of the 1965 corporation tax provisions is contained in an Inland Revenue booklet on corporation tax issued in February 1966 under reference no 570 (1966).
10 Chancellor of the Exchequer Mr Barber's Budget Statement for 1971, 814 HC Official Report (5th series) (1970–71). See also evidence of Alan Lord to the House of Commons Select Committee established to review the 1971 Green Paper on Corporations Tax, HC 622, HMSO.
11 Cmnd 4630, March 1971.

complex provisions, it could result in the crediting of shareholders with payments of tax which had never been received from the company). The remaining two were the two rate system of corporation tax, then operated by West Germany, and the partial imputation system, then operated by France[12]. Under a two rate system[13] a company pays corporation tax at, say, 50% on its profits. If it distributes profits it withholds and pays over to the Revenue tax at the basic rate of income tax on the gross dividend, but pays a reduced rate of corporation tax (37.5% if the basic rate is 25%) on the profits it has distributed. The shareholder pays income tax on the gross dividend, but is credited with having paid the income tax withheld by the company. The net effect is that the company pays 50% tax to the Revenue whether its profits are retained or distributed, with no additional tax charge to a basic rate shareholder if profits were distributed. Under a partial imputation[14] system, a company pays tax at a flat rate of, say, 50% on its profits, whether distributed or retained, but is not required to withhold income tax on payment of a dividend. A shareholder in receipt of a dividend is taxed on the cash dividend received grossed up by a portion of the underlying corporation tax, but is credited with having paid this tax. In practice, grossing up is normally at the basic rate of income tax, which is traditionally lower than the corporation tax rate, and hence the title 'partial imputation' rather than 'full imputation' as a shareholder is only being credited with part, and not the whole, of the underlying corporation tax paid by the company. Again the net effect is that a company pays 50% tax on its profits, whether retained or distributed, and there is no additional tax charge to a basic rate taxpayer if profits are distributed.

As one of the effects of changes in the Finance Act 1984, discussed later, is that the UK is now moving from a partial towards a full imputation system, and in the case of small companies has already implemented a full imputation system, it is important that the differences between the two should be understood. The distinction may best be illustrated by an example. Assume that, for a particular year, a company has pre-tax profits of £1,000. The rate of corporation tax is 50%, the company distributes the whole of its after tax profits, and on distribution shareholders are entitled to a tax credit of $^{25}/_{75}$ of the cash dividend. This fraction is arbitrary, but is equivalent to basic rate tax of 25% on the dividend plus the credit, which has been the method used in the UK since 1973 to determine the fraction. The company therefore pays corporation tax of £500, leaving £500 available for distribution. The shareholders receive £500 dividend plus a tax credit of $^{25}/_{75} \times$ £500, or £167. The shareholders are then taxed on income of £667, but are credited with having already paid £167 income tax. It will readily be seen that part, but not the whole, of the £500 corporation tax paid has been transferred as a credit to the shareholders, and the system is a 'partial imputation' system. Now, assume the rate of corporation tax is reduced to 25%, but all other facts

---

12 For a summary of corporation tax systems operated by a number of other countries, including Germany and France, see App 7 of the 1982 Green Paper on the Reform of Corporation Tax (Cmnd 8456) and see also Thomas Knatz 'Corporation Tax Systems' [1972] BTR 33; S N Frommel 'The New German Imputation System and Foreign Investors' [1976] BTR 269; S Cnossen 'Corporation Taxes in OECD Member Countries' [1984] Bulletin International Bureau of Fiscal Documentation 483.
13 See 1971 Green Paper (Cmnd 4630) paras 15–38.
14 See ibid, paras 39–42.

remain the same. The company pays £250 corporation tax leaving £750 available for distribution. The shareholders received £750 cash plus a tax credit of $^{25}/_{75}$ × £750, or £250. The shareholders are then taxed on income of £1,000 but are credited with having paid £250 income tax. Effectively, the whole of the company's profits and tax payments have been flowed through to the shareholders, and the system is a 'full imputation' system.

If international considerations could be ignored, the two rate and partial imputation systems are identical in their practical effect. Under both the company has the same total burden whether it retains or distributes profits, and under both there is no additional tax charge to a basic rate shareholder on distributed profits. In 1971 the government initially favoured the two rate system[15] but a House of Commons Select Committee established to consider the Green Paper, recommended firmly in favour of the partial imputation system[16]. The recommendation was accepted by the government and legislation implementing a partial imputation system was contained in the Finance Act 1972 and took effect on 1 April 1973. A major reason for the change of mind was the international implications of the two systems[17]. Business is increasingly conducted by multinational groups of companies, and foreign countries also impose corporation tax. To ensure that there is no unnecessary net loss to the UK of tax, or of national income, when foreign companies repatriate the profits of a UK subsidiary in comparison with the repatriation by UK parent companies of the profits of foreign subsidiaries, there must be no significant difference between the total tax imposed by a foreign country on a UK-owned foreign subsidiary as compared with the UK tax imposed on the profits of a foreign-owned UK subsidiary. In practice it was thought easier to achieve this balance with an imputation system, which retains the same (high) rate of corporation tax whether profits are retained or distributed, than with the two rate system which charges a lower rate of corporation tax if profits are distributed, thus potentially benefiting foreign parent companies.

In 1973, the UK joined the European Economic Community. One of the objectives of the European Commission is to harmonise the corporation tax systems of member countries as an aid towards the free flow of profits and capital within the Community. To this end, the Commission submitted to the Council of Ministers on 1 August 1975[18] a draft directive recommending that all member states should adopt a partial imputation system of corporation tax similar to that then operated by France and the UK. However, the directive made no subsequent progress, so that the Irish Commission on Direct Taxation, which reported in July 1982 and recommended a full imputation tax system for Ireland[19], said that they did not consider the EEC draft directive to be a significant constraint on their recommendation[20]. In January 1982, the

---

15 See 1971 Green Paper (Cmnd 4630) para 10.
16 Report of the Select Committee on Corporation Tax, Session 1970/71, HC 622, HMSO, November 1981. See also A R Prest 'The Select Committee on Corporation Tax' [1972] BTR 15; R White 'The Changing Face of Taxation—Corporation Tax' [1981] BTR 349.
17 Report of the Select Committee on Corporation Tax, supra.
18 Official Journal of the European Communities 5/11/1975 No C 253/2, and see J Chown 'The Harmonisation of Corporation Tax in the EEC: The Commission's Programme' [1981] BTR 329 at 337.
19 First Report of the Commission on Taxation, July 1982, para 27.35. In so recommending they agreed with a similar recommendation of the Canadian Royal Commission on Taxation, 1966, vol 4, p 83.
20 First Report of the Commission on Taxation, supra, para 29.22.

UK Conservative government issued a further Green Paper[1] on the reform of corporation tax which made virtually no mention of the need to harmonise corporation tax within the EEC. In the light of these and other developments the European Commission have therefore recently recommended to the Council and the European Parliament that it is not now appropriate to proceed with proposals for major reforms of company taxation within member states to bring the systems more closely in line with one another.[2]

Sir Geoffrey Howe, then Chancellor of the Exchequer, announced in his March 1983 budget[3] that, in the light of representations received on the Green Paper, no major change in the structure of the tax was now envisaged. However, after the June 1983 General Election, Nigel Lawson was appointed Chancellor of the Exchequer and in his March 1984 Budget, while retaining the imputation system, he announced a number of important changes[4]. First, he considered the then current 52% rate of corporation tax to be much too high, penalising profits and discouraging commercial risk-taking. The rate was therefore progressively reduced to 35% with the reduction fully implemented from 1 April 1986. The rate for small companies was reduced to 30% immediately and thereafter in practice further reduced in line with reductions in the basic rate of income tax. Secondly, two significant corporation tax reliefs, stock relief and first year capital allowances (or accelerated depreciation), were withdrawn, either immediately or progressively. In 1984 the Chancellor expected the effect of these changes to be that companies' taxable profits would be increased but the tax payable on those profits would be reduced with, on balance, a net gain to the corporate sector[5]. In practice there appears to have been a significant increase in the corporation tax yield during the transitional period between 1984 and 1986 attributable to the change in tax structure. Thereafter, if there are no major changes in the economy, the yield under the new structure is likely to be less than if the pre 1984 structure had been retained[6]. For 1990/91 the forecast corporation tax receipts are £20.7 billion, or 13.02% of total tax receipts, which compares with £8.2 billion, or 9.22% of tax receipts, in 1984/85 and £13.4 billion, or 13.66% of tax receipts, in 1986/87[7]. The detailed implications of the changes are discussed later in the chapter, but their overall effect is to convert the UK corporation tax structure to a full imputation system for small companies and virtually a full imputation system for large companies, thus implementing the recommendations of the Irish Commission on Direct Taxation. It is clear that these changes were made for domestic reasons with little regard to the international considerations which

1 Corporation Tax 1982 (Cmnd 8456). The Green Paper provides an excellent analysis of the current corporation tax system and its effect.
2 'Guidelines on Company Taxation' (SEC (90) 601 final).
3 39 HC Official Report (6th series) col 149 (1982–83).
4 [1984] Simon's Tax Intelligence (STI) 196; 56 HC Official Report (6th series) col 295 (1983–84).
5 But see Institute for Fiscal Studies Report Series No 1, on corporation tax, which predicted that the tax burden for large companies in manufacturing and distribution would increase when the 1984 Budget changes were fully implemented.
6 M Devereaux 'On the Growth of Corporation Tax Revenues' (1987) vol 8 no 2 Fiscal Studies 77.
7 Figures taken from the Financial Statement and Budget reports for 1985/86, 1987/88, and 1990/91.

played such an important part in the original debate over the adoption of an imputation or two rate system of corporation tax.

UK IMPUTATION CORPORATION TAX[8]

Legislation on income tax and corporation tax is contained in a succession of annual Finance Acts. Periodically these Acts are consolidated. The most recent consolidation is the Income and Corporation Taxes Act 1988, which took effect on 6 April 1988 for individuals, and for accounting periods ended after 5 April 1988 for companies[9]. Corporation tax is imposed annually in a Finance Act for a financial year. A financial year runs from 1 April–31 March[10], and should be contrasted with the tax year for individuals, the fiscal year, which runs from 6 April to 5 April[11]. Thus the 1991 financial year, runs from 1 April 1991 to 31 March 1992. From the inception of the imputation system of corporation tax in 1973, until the financial year 1982, the rate of corporation tax was 52%, but this rate has now been progressively reduced to 33%. To enable companies to plan ahead, the Finance Act 1984 prescribed the rate both for the financial year 1983 and the next three financial years. In his March 1987 Budget the Chancellor announced that he proposed to continue this practice, and that the rate for the financial year 1987 would remain at 35%[12]. This remained the rate until the financial year 1990, but it was announced in the 1991 Budget that the rate for 1990 would be retrospectively reduced to 34%, and that the rate for 1991 would be 33%. For ease of exposition, the remainder of this chapter will assume a rate of corporation tax of 33%, the rate in force for the financial year ended 31 March 1992.

Traditionally, the corporation tax rate has been higher than the basic rate of income tax, currently 25%[13], and this might be considered to discriminate against the conducting of a small business through a company rather than as a sole trader or in partnership. Small companies therefore pay corporation tax at a reduced rate, known as the small companies rate. This rate remained at 42% from 1973 to 1978, reduced to 40% for 1979–1981, and to 38% for the financial year 1982. As part of the general reduction of corporation tax rates, it was reduced to 30%, the same as the basic rate of income tax, for the financial year 1983[14], and has since been further reduced in line with the fall in the basic rate of income tax, so that it is 25% for the financial year 1991[15]. However, to call it a rate for small companies is something of a misnomer, as the criterion is the amount of a company's profits, not the value of its assets or the number of its shareholders or employees. For the financial year 1991, if a company's profits, which have an extended definition for this purpose, do not exceed £250,000[16] the whole of its taxable profits are taxed at 25%. If

---

8 A clear exposition of the basic principles of corporation tax is provided in the Inland Revenue booklet, Corporation Tax, IR 18, obtainable free of charge from any Inspector of Taxes' office. See also *Simon's Taxes*, vol D, Butterworths, and Bramwell *The Taxation of Companies and Company Reconstructions* (4th edn, 1988) both of which provide a more detailed exposition of the tax.
9 ICTA 1988, s 843(1).
10 ICTA 1988, s 834(1).
11 Ibid, s 2(2).
12 FA 1987, s 21.
13 FB 1991, CL 20(1).
14 FA 1984, s 20.
15 FB 1991, CL 24(1).
16 ICTA 1988, s 13(3).

its profits exceed £1,250,000[17] the whole of its taxable profits are taxed at 33% with no relief for the first £250,000 profits. The income of a company with profits between £250,000 and £1,250,000 is taxed under a formula[18] the approximate effect of which is to tax the first £250,000 at 25% with the excess over £250,000 being taxed at 35%[19]. If a company has associated companies the limits are divided by one plus the number of associated companies[20]. If a company has an accounting period of less than 12 months, the limits are proportionately reduced[1]. The practical significance of the small companies rate has been considerable. The 1982 Green Paper estimated that about 95% of companies either take advantage of the small companies rate provisions or pay no tax at all, all but 3% or 4% of them having profits below £80,000, the then lower limit for the small companies rate[2]. Conversely the top 5% of all active companies contribute over 85% of the total corporation tax yield[3]. For the financial year ended 31 March 1991, the total yield from corporation tax is estimated at £20,700 m which represents 13.02% of total UK tax receipts and compares with a yield from income tax of £55,000 m (34.56%) and from value added tax of £32,100 m (20.19%)[4].

Computation of taxable profits

Corporation tax is imposed by reference to accounting periods[5]. A company's first accounting period begins when a company first comes into charge to corporation tax and ends with the earliest of the following events[6]:

(a)   12 months after its commencement;
(b)   the company's own termination date for its accounting period;
(c)   the company ceasing to trade, to be resident in the UK, or to be liable to corporation tax;
(d)   the commencement of the winding up of the company, when a new accounting period starts[7].

If a company's own accounts are prepared for a period exceeding 12 months, the first 12 months constitute one accounting period, with the balance of the period being a separate accounting period for tax purposes[8]. For companies who regularly prepare accounts to the same financial year end, the accounting period for corporation tax will coincide with the period covered by their own accounts. Where an accounting period straddles two financial years, the profits are apportioned on a time basis and taxed at the appropriate rate for each financial year[9]. Thus a company preparing annual financial accounts to 31 December 1991 will have one-quarter of the taxable

17 Ibid.
18 ICTA 1988, s 13(2).
19 The greater the gap between the main CT rate and the small companies rate, the greater is the tax on profits in excess of £250,000.
20 Ibid, s 13(3)(b).
1 Ibid, s 13(6).
2 Cmnd 8456, para 16(6).
3 1982 Green Paper on Corporation Tax (Cmnd 8456) App 4, para 10.
4 HM Treasury Financial Statement & Budget Report 1990–91 (the Red Book), p 6.
5 ICTA 1988, ss 8(3) and 12(1).
6 Ibid, s 12(3).
7 Ibid, s 12(7).
8 Ibid, s 12(2) and (3).
9 ICTA 1988, s 8(3).

profits of that account taxed at the corporation tax rate for the financial year ended 31 March 1990 and three-quarters taxed at the rate for the financial year 1991.

Companies resident in the UK are liable to corporation tax on their worldwide profits[10], although credit may be given against their UK tax liability for foreign tax paid on foreign income[11]. Non-resident companies are only liable to UK corporation tax on their profits from a branch or agency in the UK[12]. Prior to 15 March 1988 the test for company residence was based solely on case law and depended on where the company was centrally managed and controlled. A company was only resident in the UK for tax purposes if it was centrally managed and controlled here irrespective of its country of incorporation[13]. However, under ICTA 1988, s 765(1)(a) it was a criminal offence for a company which was resident in the UK to become non-resident without the consent of the Treasury, which would almost certainly have been refused if the purpose of the change of residence was tax avoidance. In *R v HM Treasury, ex p Daily Mail and General Trust plc*[14] the validity of this offence was challenged before the European Court with respect to a transfer of a company's residence to another EC country. The European Court held that the Treaty of Rome gave no right to a company incorporated in one state to transfer its central management and control to another member state in contravention of national legislation.

Perhaps because the Government anticipated losing the *Daily Mail* case, statutory changes to the law on company residence were made in FA 1988. As from 15 March 1988 the central management and control test remains the test for residence of companies which are not incorporated in the UK. The criminal sanction against such companies becoming non-resident has been repealed[15], but they must first notify the Revenue and make arrangements to pay any outstanding tax liabilities[16]. Additionally the company will be deemed to have disposed of all its assets with a consequent possible tax charge on its capital gains[17]. Companies which are incorporated in the UK are deemed to be resident in the UK for tax purposes irrespective of where they are centrally managed and controlled[18], but there is transitional relief for UK incorporated companies centrally managed and controlled abroad before, or shortly after, 15 March 1988. A company which, prior to 15 March 1988, was carrying on a business and had ceased to be resident in the UK in pursuance of a Treasury consent, will remain non-resident until the later of 15 March 1993 or the date it ceases to carry on business or, if the consent was a general consent, it ceases to be taxable in a foreign country[19]. If a UK

10 Ibid, s 8(1).
11 Ibid, ss 788–816. The credit is limited to the UK corporation tax which would otherwise have been payable on the income.
12 Ibid, s 11(1), (2), (3).
13 Bramwell *Taxation of Companies and Company Reconstructions* (4th edn, 1988) paras 12.02–12.05; *De Beers Consolidated Mines Ltd v Howe* [1906] AC 455, HL; *Unit Construction Co Ltd v Bullock* [1960] AC 351, HL; and see Inland Revenue Statement of Practice SP 1/90, and Sheridan 'The Residence of Companies for Taxation Purposes' [1990] BTR 78.
14 [1988] STC 787.
15 FA 1988, s 105(b), 148 and Sch 14, Pt IV.
16 FA 1988, ss 130 and 131, and see SP 2/90 which provides guidance on the arrangements for emigrating companies.
17 FA 1988, s 105.
18 FA 1988, s 66(1).
19 FA 1988, Sch 7, para 1.

incorporated company ceases to be resident after 15 March 1988 in pursuance of a Treasury consent[20] and is carrying on business immediately after 15 March 1988, it retains non-resident status until the later of 15 March 1993 or the date it ceases to carry on business[1]. Any other UK incorporated company which was non-resident under the central management and control test on 15 March 1988 will become resident in the UK from 15 March 1993[2]. A company within any of the categories which resumes actual residence in the UK becomes subject to the new rules from that date[3].

A UK-resident company computes its profits for corporation tax in the same way as an individual computes his income for income tax[4], except that the preceding year basis, which applies for some income tax purposes, does not apply for corporation tax[5]. The assessable profits of a company are those actually earned in an accounting period[6]. Apart from trading profits, assessable profits include income from land, interest received, and dividends from foreign companies. They do not include dividends from other UK-resident companies, technically known as franked investment income, which have already borne corporation tax and are not charged to this tax again if received by a resident company[7]. Additionally, a company is charged to corporation tax on its post 31 March 1982 capital gains less any allowable capital losses[8]. Companies are entitled to the indexation allowance in computing their chargeable gains[9], but do not receive the £5,500 annual exemption[10]. Capital gains made by companies, and retained in the company rather than distributed, will increase the value of a company's shares, but, unless the company is a unit or investment trust[11], a shareholder is given no relief for the potential double taxation of the same capital gain initially to the company and subsequently to the shareholder on disposal of his shares. It may therefore be sensible tax planning for small family companies to keep appreciating assets, such as land, outside the company to avoid this double taxation[12]. Alternatively the company should consider distributing its realised capital gains as dividend, rather than retain them. The gains will effectively remain liable to corporation tax, but double taxation will be avoided unless the shareholder is liable to higher rate income tax.

From its gross profits a company may deduct charges[13], which include interest paid on loans, including debentures, which have been used for

---

20 As the need to obtain such a consent has been abolished, this should only cover transitional applications.
1 FA 1988, Sch 7, para 2.
2 FA 1988, Sch 7, paras 3 and 4.
3 FA 1988, Sch 7, paras 1(3), 2(3), 3(2) and 4(2).
4 ICTA 1988, s 9(1).
5 Ibid, s 9(6).
6 Ibid, ss 8(3), 70(1).
7 Ibid, s 208.
8 Ibid, s 345.
9 FA 1982, s 86(1)(a).
10 The section conferring the exemption, CGTA 1979, s 5(1), refers only to individuals.
11 Investment and unit trusts are exempt from tax on capital gains which they make on the disposal of investments (FA 1980, s 81(1)), but a share or unit holder is chargeable to CGT on any gains he makes on the disposal of his shares or units.
12 Although other tax considerations may militate against this e g the inability to obtain roll-over relief if an unincorporated business is being transferred to a company, see p 308.
13 ICTA 1988, s 338(1).

business purposes[14]. A deduction as a charge on income can be claimed for gifts to charity under a deed of covenant which is capable of lasting for more than three years[15]. Provided certain formalities are complied with, a deduction is also available for single donations to charity[16]. For accounting periods beginning on or after 19 March 1991 there is no maximum deduction[17]. Prior to that there was a maximum deduction of £5,000,000 or 3% of the dividends for the period on the company's ordinary share capital, whichever was the greater[18]. If the company is a close company the minimum net of tax payment is £600[19], there is now no maximum amount[20], and there must be no collateral conditions or right to repayment attached to the gift[1].

The balance of gross profits less charges is then subject to corporation tax. Corporation tax is payable nine months after the accounting year end, or 30 days after assessment if later[2]. The longer delay which used to exist if the trade originally commenced before 6 April 1965 has been abolished[3]. From a date to be announced, but which will not be before 1993[4], under proposals known as Pay and File[5], a company will be required to estimate and pay its corporation tax liability not more than nine months after the end of an accounting period, whether or not an assessment has been received. It must then file its corporation tax return not more than twelve months after the relevant accounting period. Unless it has a reasonable excuse, a company will incur automatic penalties for the late filing of a return, and will have to pay interest calculated from the original due date for payment if it has underestimated its corporation tax liability. Conversely, the Revenue will repay tax with interest if the estimated payment turns out to have been excessive.

For most companies, the most significant item in their corporation tax computation is trading profit. A company's taxable trading profit is initially computed applying normal commercial accounting principles, but is then subject to adjustment[6]. Only the historical cost method of preparing accounts is currently recognised for tax purposes[7]. This system gives little or no recognition to the proportion of a company's profits attributable solely to inflation, and therefore tends to result in an overstatement of real profit and an increased tax burden on companies. This failure to permit a system of inflation accounting for tax purposes has had a significant impact on the real

14 Ibid, s 338(3) and (6).
15 Ibid, s 338(2), (3) and (5).
16 Ibid, ss 338(2)(b) and 339.
17 FB 1991, CL 63(1).
18 ICTA 1988, s 339A(1) and (3).
19 Ibid, s 339(3A).
20 FB 1991, CL 63(1).
 1 ICTA 1988, s 339(3B)–(3E).
 2 Ibid, s 10(1)(b).
 3 ICTA 1988, Sch 30, para 1. The reduction was phased in three annual steps, so that all companies are on the same basis as from 1990.
 4 See IR press release 13 April 1989 [1989] STI 327.
 5 Contained in F(No 2)A 1987, ss 82–88.
 6 See, e g, *Odeon Associated Theatres Ltd v Jones* [1973] Ch 288, CA; *Heather (Inspector of Taxes) v P-E Consulting Group Ltd* [1973] Ch 189; *BSC Footwear Ltd v Ridgway (Inspector of Taxes)* [1972] AC 544, HL.
 7 *Lowe v IRC* [1983] STC 816, PC, a New Zealand case, but the same decision would almost certainly be reached in the UK.

tax burden borne by companies. The 1982 Green Paper on corporation tax estimated that the effective rate of U K tax on company income of U K-based industrial and commercial companies, excluding those engaged on North Sea oil and gas production, earned over the period of 1976 to 1980 averaged roughly 25%[8] on the basis of historical cost profits but roughly 65% on the basis of inflation adjusted profits[9]. For financial companies, the figures were 30% and 40% respectively[10]. As yet the accountancy bodies have made only limited progress in agreeing on an acceptable system of inflation accounting[11], and the Revenue have been unwilling to accept any system other than historical cost accounting without it first being agreed and generally implemented as standard accounting practice[12].

The principal adjustments made to historical cost accounting profits for tax purposes involve the disallowance of some expenditure items properly deducted in computing accounting profit, such as the entertainment of customers[13], donations to political parties[14] and, most significantly, depreciation[15]. Depreciation is disallowed because technically it is the write-off of capital expenditure, which is itself disallowable for tax purposes. The total disallowable expenditure increases the taxable profit. From this increased profit, a number of deductions are authorised. Until the changes announced in the March 1984 Budget, the most significant of these were stock relief and capital allowances. Stock relief represented one of the few specific concessions by government for the effects of inflation on profit[16], and was designed to eliminate from profit the appreciation in value attributable to inflation of trading stock and work in progress still retained by a company at the end of its accounting period[17]. However, with greatly reduced inflation

---

8 This apparently low rate is explained largely by the effect of tax reliefs attributable to capital allowances and stock relief.
9 1982 Green Paper on Corporation Tax (Cmnd 8456) App 6, para 6.
10 Ibid, App 6, para 7.
11 A Statement of Standard Accountancy Practice (SSAP 16) required, for an experimental period, that large companies should include a statement showing the effect of inflation on profit for accounting periods beginning on or after 1 January 1980 applying a method known as current cost accounting. The standard has been the subject of considerable criticism and a revised proposed standard 'Accounting for the effects of changing prices' (ED 35) was issued by the Accounting Standards Committee of the Joint Accounting Bodies in July 1984. The revised proposals were themselves the subject of controversy and have now been abandoned. SSAP 16 was made voluntary in June 1985 by all CCAB bodies. They have since proposed that the standard be withdrawn, but support further work towards a new standard (*Accountancy*, November 1986, p 153).
12 The Irish Commission recommended against the use of inflation accounting for tax purpose until appropriate principles have been recommended for universal application by the accountancy bodies; Irish Commission on Direct Taxation, para 26.37, July 1982. The British government seems to be adopting the same approach: see the Chancellor of the Exchequer's Budget statement 1983, 39 HC Official Report (6th series) col 151 (1982–83).
13 ICTA 1988, s 577.
14 See the Chancellor of the Exchequer's statement, 460 HC Official Report (5th series) col 25 (18 January 1949).
15 *Forder v Handyside* (1876) 45 LJQB 809, and see J R Edwards 'Tax Treatment of Capital Expenditure and the Measurement of Accounting Profit' [1976] BTR 300.
16 Another is the indexation of the cost base of assets for CGT purposes for inflation occurring after acquisition or after March 1982 if later (FA 1982, s 86).
17 Stock relief was the invention of N Kaldor and was described by D Healey as his most valuable contribution to his work at the Treasury, see *The Time of My Life* p 393 (paperback).

and increased company liquidity, stock relief was abolished in respect of any period of account beginning after 12 March 1984[18].

Capital allowances are, in effect, statutory depreciation. Not all capital expenditure qualifies for capital allowances[19], but the rate of allowance for expenditure which does qualify has traditionally been substantially greater than the depreciation charged in a company's commercial accounts, because successive governments used capital allowances to encourage industry to increase its capital investment by permitting a rapid write-off of the expenditure for tax purposes. This was achieved by a combination of generous initial or first year allowances with an annual writing down allowance for any expenditure remaining unrelieved. Thus, until the 1984 Budget, a company which erected or acquired a new industrial building was permitted to claim an initial allowance of 75% of the expenditure[20], with the balance being written off annually at the rate of 4% of the total cost of the building[1]. Similarly, a company which purchased plant or machinery was entitled to a first year allowance of 100%[2] of the cost. The company was free to disclaim this allowance[3], in which case it received a writing down allowance of 25% per year of the declining balance of expenditure not yet written off[4]. In his 1984 Budget, the Chancellor of the Exchequer stated that he considered this policy of high initial write-off of capital expenditure for tax purposes to have been misguided because it encouraged the purchase of assets which tax allowances made appear profitable, but which did not generate a good commercial return[5]. In a major change of policy, initial and first year allowances for industrial buildings and plant machinery have therefore been progressively withdrawn so that, for expenditure after 1 April 1986[6], only an annual writing down allowance is given[7].

The significance of the pre-1984 stock relief and capital allowances can be seen by noting that in 1980/81 total corporation tax receipts were £4.65 billion[8] whereas the tax relief attributable to capital allowances was £6.7 billion and to stock relief £2.05 billion[9]. The anomaly of a tax system under which the value of tax reliefs are almost twice the tax yield was one of the reasons leading to demands for reform of the corporation tax structure and the 1984 Budget changes, now that they are fully effective, should rectify the anomaly. A further effect of stock relief and high capital allowances was that a company's profit for tax purposes was normally significantly lower than its accounting profit which, after deduction of corporation tax payable, becomes its distributable profit. The 1984 Budget changes have reduced this difference but they have not eliminated it, as, in many cases, annual capital

18 FA 1984, s 8.
19 For example, no relief is given for the construction of buildings which are not industrial buildings.
20 Capital Allowances Act 1968, s 1(2), as in effect for 1983/84.
 1 Ibid, s 2(2).
 2 FA 1971, ss 41 and 42 as in effect for 1983/84.
 3 Ibid, s 41(3).
 4 Ibid, s 44.
 5 56 HC Official Report (6th series) cols 295, 6 (1983/84).
 6 FA 1984, s 8 and Sch 12. The capital allowances legislation has now been consolidated in the Capital Allowances Act 1990 with effect for chargeable periods ended after 5 April 1990.
 7 In a limited number of cases, such as qualifying buildings in enterprise zones, generous initial allowances are still available.
 8 1982 Green Paper on Corporation Tax (Cmnd 8456) App 4, Table 7.
 9 Ibid, App 5, Table 2.

allowances still exceed the depreciation a company has charged in its commercial accounts. This difference between profit for tax purposes and distributable profit has important implications for the tax treatment of company distributions.

Distributions

It will be recalled that under the U K imputation system of corporation tax, company profits are taxed at 33%, or at 25% if the small companies rate applies. If profits are subsequently distributed to a shareholder a portion of the corporation tax paid is attributed to the shareholder who is subject to income tax on the actual dividend received plus the tax attributed, but is credited with having already paid the tax attributed. In effect the corporation tax has become an advance payment of income tax. If a company's pre-tax accounting profit and its profit for tax purposes were always identical, distributions would pose no problems. The company would pay corporation tax and be left with a net of tax profit which could then be distributed to shareholders to the extent desired with no further tax implications for the company. But we have seen that, in practice, profits for tax purposes may be materially lower than its distributable profits for company law purposes. The consequent reduction of the corporation tax bill may be further increased if a company has foreign income, as foreign tax paid on the foreign income will generally be creditable against any U K tax liability on the same income. The Revenue consider it to be a fundamental principle that they should not be required to credit a shareholder in receipt of a dividend with having paid tax unless they have actually received that tax from the distributing company. In the absence of further provisions, this could not be guaranteed as a company may well have distributable profits for company law purposes but have little or no corporation tax liability.

To deal with the problem, a system of advance corporation tax has been added to the basic imputation corporation tax structure. Advance corporation tax is payable where a company makes a distribution which is also a 'qualifying distribution'[10]. Distributions are widely defined to include not only dividends but distribution of capital profits and the transfer of assets other than as a return of capital on liquidation[11]. The capitalisation of profit followed by the issue of bonus shares does not constitute a distribution, although a shareholder may be liable to income tax if he is given the option to receive either a dividend or bonus shares[12]. With very limited exceptions, such as a bonus issue of redeemable share capital, all distributions are also qualifying distributions[13]. On, or within a short time after making a qualifying distribution, a company is required to pay over to the Revenue advance corporation tax (ACT) at a rate related to the basic rate of income tax[14] and which is currently $^{25}/_{75}$ of the amount distributed[15]. The rate has

10 ICTA, 1988, s 14(1).
11 Ibid, s 209.
12 Ibid, s 249.
13 Ibid, s 14(2).
14 Ibid, s 14(3). Distributions between 1 and 5 April, the overlap between the corporation tax and income tax year, continue to attract the previous year's rate of ACT (ICTA 1988, s 246(6)).
15 Ibid, s 14(3).

traditionally been fixed at a rate equivalent to the basic rate of income tax on an amount equal to the actual distribution plus the ACT and, since 1986, a change in the basic rate of income tax automatically triggers a change in the ACT rate[16]. However, it needs to be emphasised that there is no necessary connection between the rate of ACT and the basic rate of income tax[17]. ACT is not withholding of income tax, it is an advance payment of the company's liability for corporation tax for the year in which the qualifying distribution is made. Accordingly, a company may deduct any ACT actually paid from its corporation tax liability for the year, but this right to deduct is subject to important limitations[18]. The deduction may not exceed the amount of ACT which would have been payable by a company, had it distributed an amount which, together with the ACT on it, equals the company's profits, including capital gains, for the period[19].

EXAMPLE

For an accounting period a company has taxable profits of £900,000. During the period it paid cash dividends of £700,000. Its tax liability for the year is as follows, assuming a corporation tax rate of 33% and an ACT rate of $^{27}/_{75}$:

(a)	Payment of ACT on payment of dividends	
	£700,000 × $^{25}/_{75}$	£233,333
(b)	Corporation tax liability	
	Taxable profits	£900,000
	Corporation tax @ 33%	£297,000
	Less ACT, restricted to	
	£675,000 × $^{25}/_{75}$	(225,000)
	(£675,000 + £225,000	
	= £900,000, the company's profits	
	for the period)[20]	
	Mainstream corporation tax	£72,000

The company has therefore paid £305,333 (£233,333 + £72,000) tax to the Revenue of which £297,000 is its corporation tax liability for the year, and £8,333 is unrelieved ACT.

The system ensures that the Revenue is always paid tax which it has to credit to shareholders. Unrelieved ACT may be carried back for six years and set against mainstream corporation tax of prior accounting periods, taking later periods before earlier periods[1], and carried forward indefinitely

---

16 Ibid, s 14(3) consolidating FA 1986, s 17.
17 Indeed one of the concerns of the Revenue at the introduction of an imputation, rather than a two rate, system of corporation tax was that the rate of ACT would be subject to erosion under political pressure (evidence of the Revenue to the 1971 House of Commons Select Committee on the Corporation Tax Green Paper, HC 622, HMSO). In practice no erosion occurred, and the automatic relationship with the basic rate of income tax was made statutory in 1986.
18 ICTA 1988, s 239(1).
19 Ibid, s 239(2).
20 Put another way, £675,000 is the amount which, with ACT on it of £225,000, equals the company's profits of £900,000. The maximum ACT credit against the company's mainstream CT liability is therefore £225,000.
 1 Ibid, s 239(3).

against corporation tax due on profits of future accounting periods[2]. However, carry forward of unutilised ACT will be denied if within any period of three years there is both a major change of ownership of the company and a major change in the company's trade[3]. This is to prevent the purchase of companies with unutilised ACT solely for the purpose of utilising the ACT against the future profits of a quite different trade, and follows rules which disallow the carry forward of trading losses where there is a change of ownership of a company and a change of trade[4].

The tax treatment of qualifying distributions in the hands of UK-resident[5] shareholders depends on whether the recipient is an individual (or other person liable to income tax such as a trustee) or a company. An individual is treated as having received income taxable under ICTA 1988, Sch F of the actual distribution plus the tax credit attached to it[6] but is credited with having paid as income tax the amount of the tax credit[7]. Thus an individual in receipt of a dividend of £75 will also have a tax credit of £25 ($^{25}/_{75}$ × £75) and will be taxed on £100 gross income on which he is treated as having already paid £25 tax. The basic rate taxpayer therefore has no additional tax to pay, a higher rate taxpayer will have to pay more, and an individual not liable to tax will receive a £25 tax repayment on making a claim to the Revenue. Qualifying distributions received by companies are not liable to corporation tax in the hands of the recipient company[8]. The qualifying distributions plus the tax credit are together known as franked investment income[9]. The tax credit is only rarely repayable to the recipient company[10]. Franked investment income is primarily used to cover qualifying distributions made by the recipient company, so that when a recipient company makes a qualifying distribution of its own it is only required to pay ACT to the extent that its franked payments (qualifying distributions plus related ACT) exceed its franked investment income[11]. The practical effect is to flow through the distribution from the first company to the shareholders of the recipient company in priority to the distribution of other profits of the recipient company.

Groups of companies

It is common for an organisation with a number of different businesses to use separate companies for each business. For company law purposes, each company is a legal entity distinct from other companies in the group, but this legal demarcation could have considerable disadvantages from a tax viewpoint with, for example, losses in one company not being available for

---

2 Ibid, s 239(4).
3 Ibid, s 245. A similar rule applies if a trade becomes negligible and there is a change of ownership before it revives.
4 Ibid, s 768.
5 Special rules may apply if the recipient shareholder is not resident in the UK.
6 ICTA 1988, s 20(1).
7 Ibid, s 231(1).
8 Ibid, s 208.
9 Ibid, s 238(1).
10 Where the company is resident in the UK and exempt from corporation tax, or only not exempt in respect of trading profits, or the distribution is specifically exempted (ICTA 1988, s 231(2)).
11 Ibid, s 241.

deduction from profits of another company in the group. The corporation tax legislation therefore contains provisions which enable a group of companies to be taxed as if they were one entity, but care must be taken in applying the provisions as not all inter-group transactions are covered, and the definition of a group may vary from one provision to another. It is a basic principle of all the reliefs that they only apply to a group of UK-resident companies, so that they will not apply, for example, to a wholly owned UK subsidiary of a foreign parent company. The principal reliefs are outlined in the following paragraphs.

Under the ICTA 1988, s 240 a UK-resident parent company may surrender to UK-resident subsidiaries in which it has more than 50% of the share capital[12] all or any part of ACT which it has paid on dividends, but not on other qualifying distributions[13]. ACT may be surrendered even if the parent company has a corporation tax liability and, where there are a number of subsidiaries, in such proportions as may be desired[14]. Surrendered ACT may be used to reduce the subsidiary's mainstream corporation tax liability[15]. It may not be carried back, although it is relieved in priority to any ACT actually paid by the subsidiary[16]. It may be carried forward indefinitely against the subsidiary company's future mainstream corporation tax liability provided that, throughout the relevant accounting period, it remained a subsidiary of the surrendering parent company[17], but if it ceases to be a subsidiary, the benefit of any surrendered but unutilised ACT is lost unless both surrendering and receiving companies remain subsidiaries of a third company[18]. As from 13 March 1989 the ability of the subsidiary company to carry forward surrendered ACT will be lost if there is both a change of ownership of the subsidiary company and a major change in the business of the surrendering company within three years before, or three years after, the change of ownership[19]. A recipient company may make a payment to the surrendering company up to the value of the ACT surrendered without the payment being taken into account for corporation tax purposes[20]. Apart from ensuring relief for ACT, the surrender rules may provide a useful mechanism for the transfer of funds within the group.

In the absence of special provisions, whenever a subsidiary company paid a dividend, or made an annual payment, to a parent company it would have to account for ACT or withhold income tax[1], leaving the parent to utilise the ACT or recover the income tax from the Inland Revenue. Relieving provisions are therefore contained in ICTA 1988, s 247 to deal with the transfer of 'group income'. These provisions apply to transfers between 51%

---

12 ICTA 1988, s 240(10)—indirect shareholdings through non-resident companies are excluded, as are shareholdings which are trading stock of any company. Anti-avoidance provisions exist to prevent the relief from being abused (Ibid, s 240(11)).
13 Ibid, s 240(1).
14 Ibid, s 240(1)(b).
15 Ibid, s 240(2).
16 Ibid, s 240(4).
17 Ibid, s 240(5).
18 Ibid, s 240(5).
19 Ibid, s 245A.
20 Ibid, s 240(8).
 1 Although annual payments are normally tax deductible to a company, it must usually withhold and pay over to the Revenue under ICTA 1988, s 349 basic rate income tax on the gross payment, which is then treated as having been paid by the recipient.

subsidiaries and a parent company[2], but ownership of more than 50% of the share capital is only sufficient if the parent is also beneficially entitled to more than 50% of the profits available for distribution and more than 50% of the assets of the subsidiary were it to be wound up[3]. The provisions also apply to consortia[4]. A consortium exists for the purposes of s 247 if 75% or more of the ordinary share capital of a trading or holding company is owned by UK-resident companies with no company needed to make up the 75% owning less than 5% of the shares or entitled to less than 5% of the distributable profits or the assets available for distribution on a winding up[5]. A trading or holding company does not qualify for consortium relief if it is a 75% subsidiary of another company, or arrangements exist under which it could become one[6]. A holding company is a trading company, or a company the business of which consists wholly or mainly in the holding of shares or securities of trading companies which are its 90% subsidiaries[7]. If s 247 applies, payer and recipient may jointly elect that dividends, but not other qualifying distributions, should be paid without accounting for ACT but, even if an election for group income is in force, the payer company remains entitled to give notice that it will account for ACT on all or part of the dividend[8]. Similar provisions apply to authorise the payment gross of annual payments, such as interest, by a subsidiary[9] but these provisions are extended to include annual payments from a parent company to its 51% subsidiary[10], although not from a member of a consortium to a consortium subsidiary in which it has less than a 51% interest. If the payer company wishes to revert to accounting for income tax the election for group annual payments must be revoked.[11]

Perhaps the most economically significant group relief provisions are those in ss 402 and 403 of the ICTA 1988, which enable losses of one member of a group or consortium to be set against the profits of another, and allow loss relief for consortia, but the definition of a group or consortium is more restricted than under the ACT surrender or group income provisions. A group comprises a UK-resident parent company plus UK-resident[12] subsidiaries in which it has 75% interest[13]. 'Interest' for this purpose means ownership of 75% of the ordinary share capital plus entitlement to 75% of the profits available for distribution to equity holders plus entitlement to 75% of the assets of the subsidiary on its winding up[14]. A consortium exists if 75% of the share capital of a relevant company is owned by UK-resident companies, with none of the members of the consortium owning less than 5%[15]. A relevant company is a trading company which is owned by the consortium but is not a 75% subsidiary of any single company[16], or a holding company which is

2 ICTA 1988, s 247(1)(a).
3 ICTA 1988, s 247(8A) and Sch 18.
4 Ibid, s 247(1)(b).
5 Ibid, s 247(1)(b), s 247(9)(c) and Sch 18.
6 ICTA 1988, s 247(1A).
7 Ibid, s 247(9)(a).
8 Ibid, s 247(1), (2), (3).
9 Ibid, s 247(4)(a).
10 Ibid, s 247(4)(b).
11 There is no equivalent of ICTA 1988, s 247(3), which applies only to dividends.
12 Ibid, s 413(5).
13 Ibid, s 413(3)(a).
14 Ibid, s 413(7).
15 Ibid, s 413(6)(a).
16 Ibid, s 402(3)(a).

owned by the consortium and which has a trading company as a 90%
subsidiary which is not a 75% subsidiary of any other company[17], or is a
holding company owned by the consortium and not a 75% subsidiary of
another company[18]. Relief is only given if companies are members of a
qualifying group or consortium throughout the whole of the relevant
accounting periods of both surrendering and claimant companies[19]. If the
conditions are satisfied, trading losses[20], unutilised capital allowances[1], and
unrelieved charges on income[2] may be transferred up or down, and set
against the profits of the claiming member of the group or consortium for its
corresponding accounting period[3]. The claimant company is required to
utilise other available relief before group relief[4] and, in the case of a
consortium claim, only a fraction of losses appropriate to the consortium
member's interest in the subsidiary may be transferred up or down[5]. Where
a loss making company is both a member of a consortium and a member of a
group it may surrender any loss for which group relief is unavailable to
members of the consortium[6]. Further, if a consortium member is in receipt
of a loss under consortium relief which it cannot use, and is itself the member
of a group, it may surrender the loss to other members of its group[7]. A
consortium company's interest in a subsidiary is the lower of its percentage
entitlement to share capital, or profits, or assets on a winding up[8]. Anti-
avoidance provisions exist to prevent the group relief provisions being
abused[9]. A payment may be made by the claimant company and, to the same
extent that it does not exceed the loss surrendered, it may be ignored for
corporation tax purposes[10].

Relief from tax on capital gains exists where assets are transferred
between companies which are members of a 75% group[11]. A 75% group
exists if a parent company, the principal company, owns more than 75% of
the ordinary share capital of a subsidiary[12]. If the subsidiary in turn has a
75% subsidiary all the companies are members of a group[13], with the top
company as the principal company[14]. Additionally, each subsidiary must be
a 51% effective subsidiary[15]. By this is meant that the parent must be
beneficially entitled to more than 50% of the distributable profits of the
subsidiary and more than 50% of its assets on a winding up[16]. A company can
only be a member of one group, and ICTA 1970, s 272(1D) provides tests to

17 Ibid, s 402(3)(b).
18 Ibid, s 402(3)(c).
19 Ibid, s 409(1).
20 Ibid, s 403(1), (2).
 1 Ibid, s 403(3).
 2 Ibid, s 403(7).
 3 Ibid, s 403(1). 'Corresponding accounting period' is defined in s 408.
 4 Ibid, s 407(1)(b).
 5 Ibid, s 403(9).
 6 Ibid, s 405(1)–(3).
 7 Ibid, s 406.
 8 Ibid, s 413(8).
 9 Ibid, s 410.
10 Ibid, s 402(6).
11 ICTA 1970, ss 272–279. These provisions, which relate to capital gains tax, have not been
consolidated.
12 ICTA 1970, s 272(1A)(a) with ICTA 1970, s 272.
13 ICTA 1970, s 272(1A)(a).
14 ICTA 1970, s 272(1B).
15 ICTA 1970, s 272(1A)(b).
16 ICTA 1970, s 272(1E) with ICTA 1988, Sch 18.

determine to which group a company should be allocated if it would other-wise be a member of more than one group.

Assets transferred within the group are deemed to be transferred on a basis which ensures no gain or loss to the transferor company[17], but the transferee company takes over the asset at the transferor's cost base and date of acquisition[18]. If the recipient company leaves the group within six years, otherwise than on a liquidation, still retaining the asset, or a replacement asset into which the gain has been rolled over, there is a notional disposal of the asset for the purposes of the tax on capital gains[19]. Under the capital gains tax code, where business assets are replaced, any gain on the asset disposed of can generally be 'rolled over' into the new asset, so that a chargeable gain is deferred until the new asset is ultimately disposed[20]. For this purpose all the trades carried on by members of a 75% group of companies are treated as if they were carried on by one company[1].

Anti-avoidance provisions exist to prevent a company milking its subsidiaries of assets, disposing of the shares in the subsidiary and claiming a capital loss on the disposal[2], and these anti-avoidance provisions apply even if one of the relevant companies is non-resident[3]. Anti-avoidance provisions also exist in ICTA 1988, s 770 to prevent artificial prices being placed on transfers of trading stock between associated companies (roughly members of a 51% group but including foreign companies) unless both are resident in the UK[4]. Such a provision against artificial inter-company pricing is needed to ensure that profits earned in the UK are not transferred to a foreign country by the simple expedient of placing artificially low or high prices on goods transferred to or from foreign companies in the group.

Close companies and close investment-holding companies

Since 1922 there have been special rules to ensure that conducting business through, or holding investments in, a small family company (called a close company in the tax legislation) does not confer significant tax advantages in comparison with the conduct of the same activities without incorporation[5]. Historically the reason for such rules has mainly been the difference between income tax rates and corporation tax rates. For example, in 1976/77 the top marginal rate of income tax on unearned income was 98% and on earned income 83% whereas the main rate of corporation tax was 52% and the small companies rate was 42%. Prior to 1989/90 if a company was a close company and did not distribute a required proportion of its profits to shareholders the Revenue were entitled to apportion the undistributed profits among shareholders and tax them as if the company had distributed a dividend of the amount apportioned. With the reduction in income tax rates

17 Ibid, s 273(1). Where the asset is not trading stock of one company but was or becomes trading stock of the other, the transfer will give rise to a notional disposal and reacquisition for the purposes of CGT and the computation of trading profit (s 274).
18 Ibid, s 273(1); s 275(2).
19 Ibid, s 278(1) and (3).
20 CGTA 1979, ss 115–121.
 1 ICTA 1970, s 276(1).
 2 Ibid, ss 280 and 281.
 3 Ibid, ss 280(7) and 281(3).
 4 ICTA 1988, s 770.
 5 FA 1922, s 21.

from 1979 the apportionment provisions were repealed for trading companies by FA 1980 but remained for non-trading companies, with different distribution requirements for income from trading and land and for other income. With the subsequent reduction in income tax rates to almost the same level as corporation tax rates, and the taxation of capital gains realised by an individual at his marginal rate of income tax, in his March 1989 Budget the Chancellor announced the apportionment provisions had outlived their usefulness and would be repealed. However, special provisions would still be needed for the small minority of close companies, estimated at less than 5% of the total[6], which were largely concerned with passive investments. This type of company is termed a close investment-holding company. The repeal of the apportionment provisions did not affect other anti-avoidance legislation which applies to close companies, so that now there are provisions which apply to all close companies and provisions which only apply to close companies which are also investment-holding companies.

Under the current law a company is a close company if it satisfies one of the following conditions and is not otherwise exempt:

(a)   It is controlled by five or fewer participators[7]. Control is widely defined in ICTA 1988, s 416 as general control over the company's affairs, including entitlement to a majority of the share capital, or share capital which confers entitlement to a majority of the distributable income of the company, or of its assets on a winding up. 'Participator' is defined in ICTA 1988, s 417(1) to include a shareholder and a loan creditor[8] and, in counting the shares or interests of a participator, there has to be included any shares or interests in the company owned by the participator's 'associates'. A participator's associates include his spouse, parents, grandparents, children, brothers and sisters, partners, and trustees of related trusts[9]. No double counting is permitted, so that a wife's shares must either be counted as her own or her husband's, but if any combination results in five or fewer people having control, the company is close.

(b)   It is controlled by its directors[10], however many[11].

(c)   Five or fewer participators, or the directors, have rights, whether or not arising through their ownership of share capital which would entitle them on a winding up of the company the majority of its assets[12].

Even if any of these tests is satisfied, a company is not a close company in any of the following circumstances[13]:

(a)   it is controlled by an 'open' company[14];

(b)   it is non-resident[15];

---

6 See IR press release [1990] STI 202.
7 ICTA 1988, s 414(1).
8 Which is itself defined in s 417(7).
9 Ibid, s 417(3) and (4).
10 Defined in s 417(5).
11 Ibid, s 414(1).
12 Ibid, s 414(2).
13 This list of circumstances is not exhaustive, but includes the principal exemptions.
14 Ibid, s 414(5).
15 Ibid, s 414(1)(a).

(c)   it is a quoted company which satisfies the conditions that[16]:
  (i)   its shares have been quoted on a UK stock exchange in the past 12 months[17]; and
  (ii)   the shares quoted have been dealt with in the last 12 months[18]; and
  (iii)   35% of the voting stock excluding preference shares are held by the public[19], and have been quoted and dealt with as in (i) and (ii)[20]; and
  (iv)   85% of the stock is not held by five or fewer principal members[1].

A close company is also a close investment-holding company unless throughout the whole of the relevant accounting period it exists wholly or mainly for one or more of the following purposes[2]:

(a)   the carrying on of a trade on a commercial basis[3];
(b)   making investments in land which is not let to anyone connected with the company or a relative[4];
(c)   as a holding company for one or more companies which satisfy either of the first two conditions, or to co-ordinate the administration of two or more such companies[5];
(d)   to facilitate a trade carried on on a commercial basis by a company which is not a close investment-holding company, or is its parent company[6];
(e)   to facilitate the investment in land within (b) by a company which is not a close investment-holding company, or is its parent company[7].

If a company is a close company, whether or not it is also a close investment-holding company, the following special rules apply. First, if it provides for a participator or his associate[8] any living accommodation, entertainment, domestic or other services, or any other benefits of whatever nature, the expense incurred by the company, less any amount reimbursed, is treated as a distribution[9]. The expense is therefore not tax deductible to the company, ACT has to be paid on it[10], and the value of the benefit plus the tax credit[11] is taxed as income of the participator. The rules do not apply if the participator is also a director or higher paid employee of the company[12] as the payment will then be treated as additional pay taxable under Sch E[13].

16 Ibid, s 415.
17 Ibid, s 415(1)(b).
18 Ibid, s 415(1)(b).
19 Ibid, s 415(1)(a).
20 Ibid, s 415(1)(b).
 1 Ibid, s 415(2) and (6).
 2 Ibid, s 13A.
 3 Ibid, s 13A(2)(a).
 4 Ibid, s 13A(2)(b).
 5 Ibid, s 13A(2)(c) and (d).
 6 Ibid, s 13A(2)(e).
 7 Ibid, s 13A(2)(f).
 8 Ibid, s 418(8).
 9 Ibid, s 418(2).
10 Because the distribution is not excluded from being a qualifying distribution (ICTA 1988, s 14(2)).
11 Ibid, ss 20(1) and 231(1).
12 Ibid, s 418(3)(a).
13 Ibid, s 153 or s 154.

For living accommodation the exemption extends to all employees[14], as the benefit will be taxed under ICTA 1988, s 145. Secondly, if a close company makes a loan to a participator, otherwise in the course of a normal lending business, it must pay to the Revenue an amount equivalent to ACT on the loan[15]. At this stage there are no tax consequences for the participator and, if the loan is repaid, the ACT will be refunded[16]. To prevent avoidance, ACT is payable, subject to the right to claim a refund, even if the loan has been repaid before the company has been assessed to ACT[17]. However, if the loan is written off, the participator is treated as having received unearned income of the amount written off plus the related ACT, but on which non-refundable basic rate income tax has been paid[18]. He may therefore become liable to higher rate tax. The notional ACT paid by the company is never credited against its mainstream corporation tax liability. The loan provision does not normally apply to loans to participators who are also directors or employees of the company unless the loan exceeds £15,000[19]. Thirdly, if a close company transfers assets to any person for less than their market value under a bargain which is not at arm's length the difference between the market value and the actual transfer value is apportioned among the share-holders and reduces the cost of their shares for CGT purposes[20]. Finally, companies are not normally liable to inheritance tax, but if a close company makes a gift of assets inheritance tax may be charged on the company or, if it fails to pay, on the participators or recipients proportionate to their respective interests in the company, although there is no tax charge on anyone with less than a 5% interest[1]. An inheritance tax charge may also arise if there is an alteration to a close company's share capital resulting in a transfer of value from some shareholders to others[2].

If a close company is also a close investment-holding company it is not entitled to claim the small companies rate of corporation tax[3], and will consequently be taxed at 33% on its taxable profits, including chargeable gains. In the proposals in the 1989 Finance Bill it was envisaged that a company would have to satisfy an acceptable distribution test and, to the extent that it failed to do so, its profits would be taxed at 40%, equivalent to the top rate of income tax. However, during the progress of the Finance Bill through Parliament these proposals were withdrawn by the Government and replaced by a 35% tax on all the company's profits, since reduced to 33%. It was recognised that this gives a small incentive to a higher rate taxpayer to shelter income in a company, but it was considered that the small difference, coupled with a capital gains tax charge on the disposal of shares in the company, was sufficient to deter widespread abuse. Provisions also counteract the effect of a close investment-holding company paying dividends to particular shareholders primarily to enable them to reclaim from the

---

14 Ibid, s 418(3)(b).
15 Ibid, s 419(1).
16 Ibid, s 419(4).
17 Ibid, s 419(3).
18 Ibid, s 421(1).
19 Ibid, s 420(2).
20 CGTA 1979, s 75.
 1 ITA 1984, s 94.
 2 Ibid, s 98.
 3 ICTA 1988, s 13(1)(b).

Revenue the tax credit attaching to the dividends[4]. For example, in the absence of anti-avoidance provisions, child shareholders could be allocated shares with limited voting rights but high entitlement to dividend, so that company profits distributed to them which did not exceed their personal allowance would be free of income tax. If it appears to an inspector that arrangements exist to achieve this objective he may restrict any repayment of the tax credit to a shareholder to the extent that it appears to him to be just and reasonable[5]. The anti-avoidance provisions do not apply if, throughout the relevant accounting period, the company had only one class of shares and no shareholder waived his entitlement to dividends[6].

Business reorganisations

One of the objectives discernible in tax legislation is that some attempt should be made to ensure that a business reorganisation which is merely a change of form without a significant change of substance should not attract adverse tax consequences. The achievement of this objective is inevitably patchy, and in practice it is important that, once a business decision of substance has been reached, a tax specialist should be consulted to ensure that the implementation of that decision attracts the most favourable tax treatment. The following paragraphs give some indication of the reliefs which may be available, but each relief contains qualifying conditions and it is vital to study the actual legislation before reliance can be placed on its availability in a given situation.

Under ICTA 1988, s 343 where one company ceases to carry on a trade or part of a trade which is then taken over by another company, the trade may be treated as a continuous trade for corporation tax purposes, if, at the time of the transfer or within two years thereafter, at least three-quarters of both the old and new trades are in common ownership. For this purpose, shareholders in a company are treated as owners of a trade carried on by the company in proportion to their shareholdings[7]. No relief is available under this section for the transfer of a trade by an individual to a company, and relief may be restricted if the transferor company is insolvent at the time of the transfer[8].

If as part of a company reorganisation or amalgamation the business of a UK-resident company is transferred to another UK-resident company[9], any chargeable gain on the assets transferred may be deferred until the assets are disposed of by the acquiring company, providing the transferring company receives no consideration for the transfer other than the assumption of its liabilities by the acquiring company[10]. This relief is available where a company is put into liquidation and the liquidator agrees to transfer the old business or part of it to a new company and issues shares in the new company directly to the shareholders of the old company.

---

4   Ibid, s 231(3)–(3D).
5   Ibid, s 231(3A).
6   Ibid, s 231(3B).
7   ICTA 1988, s 344(2).
8   Ibid, s 343(4).
9   A company which is non-resident by virtue of a tax treaty and exempt from CGT does not qualify, ICTA 1970, s 267(2A).
10   ICTA 1970, s 267.

If a company disposes of a chargeable capital asset used in its trade and, within one year before or three years after the disposal, acquires another chargeable asset for use in its trade, it will often be able to defer any CGT liability arising on the disposal of the original asset[11]. For the purposes of this relief, all trades carried on by a company and its 75% UK-resident subsidiaries are treated as a single trade[12]. Both the disposed and acquired assets must be within a list of 'approved' assets[13] which comprises land and buildings, fixed plant and machinery, ships, aircraft and hovercraft, satellites, space stations and spacecraft, and milk and potato quotas[14].

Relief for demergers is available under ICTA 1988, ss 213–218. If a UK-resident trading company or member of a trading group[15] distributes to its shareholders the shares in one or more of its 75% subsidiaries[16], which must also be a trading company or holding company of a trading company[17], the distribution is not treated as a distribution of profit for corporation tax purposes[18], nor is it treated as a disposal for CGT[19]. Instead it is treated as a reorganisation of share capital[20] so that the cost of a shareholder's shares in the distributing company is apportioned between those shares and the shares received on the demerger, and a CGT charge will only arise on the subsequent disposal of any of the shares[1]. Similar relief may be available where a distributing company transfers a trade or trades, or shares in a 75% trading subsidiary company, to another company, and shares in that other company are in return issued to the members of the distributing company[2].

The reorganisation of a company's share capital, such as the creation of separate classes of ordinary shares, the issue of bonus shares, or the issue of shares under a rights issue, has few if any CGT consequences[3]. The cost of the original holding is merely apportioned to the revised holdings[4], although money paid by a shareholder to acquire shares under a rights issue will increase the cost base of his total shareholding[5]. If bonus shares are offered as an alternative to a dividend, both company and shareholder are taxed as if there had been a distribution of revenue profits equivalent to the amount of the cash dividend which could have been claimed, or the market value of the bonus shares issued if significantly different[6]. Apart from this, reorganisations of share capital normally have no income tax consequences, but any attempt to use a reorganisation to distribute income to shareholders disguised as capital is liable to be caught by anti-avoidance provisions in

11 CGTA 1979, s 115.
12 ICTA 1970, s 276(1).
13 CGTA 1979, s 115(1).
14 Ibid, s 118.
15 ICTA 1988, s 213(4) and (5).
16 Ibid, s 213(3)(a).
17 Ibid, s 213(5).
18 Ibid, s 213(2).
19 FA 1980, Sch 18, para 9(a).
20 Ibid, Sch 18, para 9(b).
 1 CGTA 1979, ss 77–81.
 2 ICTA 1988, s 213(3)(b) with CGT relief being provided by FA 1980, Sch 18, para 10, although on an apparently more limited basis than for demergers within s 213(3)(a).
 3 CGTA 1979, ss 77–82.
 4 Ibid, s 78.
 5 Ibid, s 79(1).
 6 ICTA 1988, s 249.

ICTA 1988, s 703, a section which is designed to counteract artificial devices used to turn revenue profit into capital distributions. It is important to check this section if any capital reorganisation is contemplated. It is a defence to an assessment under ICTA 1988, s 703, that a transaction was carried out for bona fide commercial reasons which did not have as their main object, or one of their main objects, the avoidance of tax[7], and it is possible to obtain advance clearance from the Revenue that they will not seek to charge a particular transaction under s 703[8].

Tax relief exists to assist an individual currently carrying on business as a sole trader or in partnership who wishes to transfer the trade to a company. Provided all the assets of the business, or all the assets other than cash, are transferred to the company, any gain on the assets transferred may be deducted from the value of the shares received in exchange[9], thus deferring a CGT charge until the shares are disposed of. If the transferor receives consideration additional to shares in the new company, the chargeable gain is apportioned between the shares and the other consideration, and only the CGT on the portion attributed to the shares may be deferred[10]. A drawback of this relief is that it requires all the assets except cash to be transferred[11], thus precluding, if the relief is to be claimed, the retention of land outside the company which might be desirable for other tax reasons. There is no equivalent relief for income tax purposes, so that the transfer of a trade to a company will be taxed as the termination of one trade and the commencement of a new one[12]. However, if the old trade has unrelieved losses these losses may, subject to certain conditions, be carried forward and deducted from future income that the proprietor of the business takes from the company[13]. Although some reliefs exist to assist the incorporation of a business there are no equivalent reliefs to assist disincorporation. The demerger provisions only give tax reliefs where groups of companies are broken down into smaller units. They do not give relief where a company disincorporates with its business thereafter being carried on by the shareholders either as sole traders or in partnership. With the increased volume of companies legislation, and the resulting increased administrative and compliance burdens imposed on companies, the proprietors of many small companies may wish now to disincorporate their business to avoid the company law obligations of incorporation. Currently tax considerations militate against this, and the government has come under pressure to enact legislation which removes the tax disadvantages of disincorporation[14]. However, no proposals for legislation have yet emerged[15].

7   ICTA 1988, s 703(1).
8   Ibid, s 707.
9   CGTA 1979, s 123.
10   Ibid, s 123(2), (3) and (4).
11   Ibid, s 123(1).
12   ICTA 1988, s 113(1). Any trading stock will be treated as transferred at sale price or market value (ICTA 1988, s 100(1)), with a resultant taxable profit to the transferor trade.
13   ICTA 1988, s 386.
14   See, e g [1987] STI 456 where it is reported that the IR and the DTI have published a joint consultative document on disincorporation. This seeks views on possible changes in tax and company law to facilitate a move from running a business as a company to running it as a sole trader or in partnership.
15   In practice no progress has been made since 1983, when the government first acknowledged that there might be a need for legislation, see the August 1983 edition of *Accountancy*, p 13.

Business incentives

It is government policy to encourage new businesses and the expansion of small businesses, and a number of tax incentives exist to promote this which are relevant to company taxation. Under the ICTA 1988, ss 289–312, if an individual unconnected with a company subscribes for shares in an unquoted trading company he may, subject to a number of restrictions, claim a deduction for income tax purposes of the amount invested subject to a minimum investment of £500[16] and a maximum relief of £40,000[17]. With the introduction of independent taxation from 5 April 1990 a husband and wife now each have separate limits[18]. The amount invested is tax deductible for all income tax purposes[19], so that the net cash cost of a £40,000 investment to a taxpayer paying income tax at the top rate of 40% is £24,000. To avoid withdrawal of relief, the shares must be retained for five years[20], but thereafter the first sale of the shares is exempt from CGT[1]. Any gain over the net of tax amount invested becomes, in effect, completely tax free, and the investor incurs a loss only if the sales proceeds ultimately received are lower than his net of tax investment. This scheme, known as the Business Expansion Scheme, has attracted considerable investment[2]. It was due to expire in April 1987, but has been extended indefinitely[3]. However, companies principally involved in land dealing, property development, or whose principal purpose is to invest in appreciating assets such as paintings or fine wines, are now excluded from the scheme[4]. The maximum amount which a BES company can raise in any six month period, or from 6 April to the date of issue if longer, is £750,000[5], but the limit is £5,000,000 if the company's trade is the operation or leasing of ships, or the building of residential accommodation for letting[6]. To prevent the bunching of investments towards the end of the tax year up to half an investment made in the first half of the following year may be carried back for deduction from income of the previous year, subject to a maximum total carry back of £5,000[7].

Further protection against loss for an investor in an unquoted company is provided by ICTA 1988, s 574. This section enacts that if an individual subscribes for shares in a qualifying company, basically an unquoted trading company, and subsequently disposes of those shares at loss, he may claim to deduct the loss for income tax purposes[8]. To avoid double relief under the business expansion scheme provisions and this section, any capital loss must be reduced by any relief claimed for a business expansion investment[9].

One disadvantage of investing in shares of an unquoted company is that

---

16 ICTA 1988, s 290(1).
17 Ibid, s 290(2).
18 FA 1988, Sch 3, para 12(1).
19 Ibid, s 289(5).
20 ICTA 1988, s 289(10) and (12).
1 CGTA 1979, s 149(C).
2 See March 1986 Budget Statement, 94 HC Official Report (6th series) cols 174, 175 (1985–96).
3 FA 1986, s 40(2).
4 ICTA 1988, ss 294 and 297.
5 Ibid, s 290A with SI 1990 No 862.
6 Ibid, s 290A(6) and (7), and FA 1988, Sch 4, para 3.
7 Ibid, s 289(6) and (7).
8 ICTA 1988, s 574(1).
9 CGTA 1979, s 149(C)(2) and (3), inserted by ICTA 1988, Sch 29, para 29.

the shares may prove difficult to resell. The Companies Act 1981 therefore contained provisions (now ss 162 ff of CA 1985) authorising companies to repurchase their own shares in specified circumstances. In the absence of special provisions, such a repurchase might have tax disadvantages as the purchase price would be treated as a distribution by the company and would be liable to income tax in the hands of the shareholder[10]. Relieving provisions are therefore contained in the ICTA 1988, ss 219–229. Provided a number of conditions are satisfied, the purchase price will be treated as a capital receipt, with any profit liable to CGT rather than income tax[11]. The most important conditions are that the acquiring company must be an unquoted trading company[12], it must make the purchase to benefit its trade[13] or to enable the vendor to pay inheritance tax[14], and it must acquire substantially the whole of the investor's shareholding[15]. The investor must be resident and ordinarily resident in the U K[16], and must have owned the shares for at least five years[17].

TAX ADVANTAGES AND DISADVANTAGES OF INCORPORATION

Prior to the changes made in the 1980s to the structure of both income tax and corporation tax there were significant tax advantages to be gained by conducting business through a company. The top rates of corporation tax were much lower than the top rates of income tax, thus enabling more profits to be retained for reinvestment in the business if it was incorporated. However, the tax system is now much more neutral, and considerations other than tax are more likely to determine whether the incorporation of a business is desirable. The following tax considerations remain relevant to any decision on incorporation versus non-incorporation.

If a business is conducted outside a company the proprietor is liable to higher rate income tax of 40% to the extent that his taxable income, including business profits, exceeds £23,700[18]. He is liable to Class II National Insurance contributions of £5.15 a week plus Class IV contributions of 6.3% on profits between £5,900 and £20,280[19]. The maximum tax deductible amount he can contribute to a pension scheme is 17½% of his earnings until he attains the age of 36, when the percentage gradually increases to 40% from the age of 61[20]. The profits of a business which is not incorporated are assessable on a preceding year basis[1], whereas company profits are assessable on an actual year basis, thus allowing the self-employed at least a 12 month delay[2] in paying tax, which results in real tax savings in times of high inflation. The proprietor

10 The possible tax disadvantages have been considerably reduced now that capital gains are taxed at income tax rates.
11 ICTA 1988, s 219(1).
12 Ibid, s 219(1), or an unquoted holding company of a trading group.
13 Ibid, s 219(1)(a).
14 Ibid, s 219(1)(b).
15 Ibid, s 221.
16 Ibid, s 220(1).
17 Ibid, s 220(5).
18 ICTA 1988, s 1(2)(b).
19 [1990] STI 960.
20 ICTA 1988, s 640.
 1 ICTA 1988, s 60(1).
 2 If the business's accounting year ends early in the tax year the delay will be much longer.

of a business is liable to capital gains tax at his top rate of income tax on capital gains from the disposal of business assets, subject to an annual exemption of £5,500[3], generous retirement relief if he is over 55[4], and the right to defer a charge if the disposal proceeds are reinvested in new qualifying business assets[5].

If a business is incorporated and its profits do not exceed £250,000 they are taxed at the small companies rate of 25%[6], thus apparently conferring a tax advantage over non-incorporation for profits in excess of £23,700. However, if profits are distributed they will be taxed at the proprietor's appropriate rate of income tax. If they are retained the proprietor will eventually be taxed at income tax rates on the capital gain accruing to his shares. The difference in tax rates is thus not as great as might at first sight appear. If a proprietor takes money out of a company as salary the amount paid will be taxed as his income rather than as the company's[7], but Class I National Insurance contributions will be payable both by the proprietor and by the company. If the proprietor is in a contracted out pension scheme his contributions average 7% on earnings between £52–£390 a week, and the company must pay an average of 6.65% on earnings up to £350 per week and 10.4% on any excess with no upper limit[8]. Total national insurance contributions are therefore likely to be higher than if the business was unincorporated. If profit is taken out of the company as dividend rather than as salary it is effectively only taxed as the income of the proprietor provided the company's profits remain below £250,000 and so taxable at the small companies rate, and no national insurance contributions are payable. However, this method of withdrawing profits from the company may restrict the pension which the proprietor can receive on retirement. Pension scheme arrangements for company employees are, in general, more generous than for the self-employed because payments by a company to an employee pension scheme are tax deductible to the company, but not taxable income of the employee, to the extent that they are designed to produce a retirement pension not exceeding two-thirds of the employee's final salary[9]. If an employee is elderly this can result in tax relief being available for much larger payments than if he had remained self-employed. Capital gains realised by a company which are retained in the company are subject to a double tax charge, first to the company when the gains are realised and later to the proprietor when he disposes of his shares in the company, which will have increased in value to reflect the gain. However this double charge can be eliminated if the company is liable to tax at the small companies rate and the capital gain is distributed as dividend, although the proprietor will not then have the benefit of the exemption of the first £5,500 chargeable gains. Retirement relief is available against capital gains arising on the disposal of shares in a family company if the proprietor is over 55 on terms equivalent to those available to the self-employed[10].

---

3 CGTA 1979, s 5(1A).
4 FA 1985, s 69 and Sch 20. FB 1991, CL 87 reduced the age from 60 to 55 from 19 March 1991.
5 CGTA 1979, s 115.
6 ICTA 1988, s 39.
7 Because it will be deductible in computing the company's taxable profit.
8 [1990] STI 960.
9 ICTA 1988, s 590(3)(a).
10 FA 1985, s 69 and Sch 20.

PART IV

Corporate power and its regulation

CHAPTER 21

The distribution and regulation of power in a company

We saw in Chapter 1 how some economists look at a company as legal recognition of a nexus of contracts by a group of persons pooling their capital and delegating management to specialist managers who agree to work for a given salary[1]. This represents a particular sophisticated network of property holdings. The members of this group possess an underlying investment interest and a vote which bear a complex relationship to each other as we saw in Part III. They are not only individual owners of rights but they also share in the less tangible legal personality of the company, a metaphysical relationship which plagues the law and generates many contradictions. Another simpler way of looking at a company is in relation to the accumulation and distribution of power and control both de jure and de facto. In the classic small private company, ownership and control are often vested in the same people subject to financial control sometimes resting with an outside institution. In such companies there is a natural tendency to informality, with a blurring of managerial and shareholder functions. This raises few problems unless there is conflict within the company or pressure from a loan creditor. In the larger company there is frequently a separation of ownership and control and a wide dispersal of share ownership. This gives management considerable scope for the exercise of power by virtue of their strategic position and control over the proxy machinery for general meetings. On the other hand, the ever increasing extent of institutional investment means that there is a potentially countervailing power. The emphasis to date is on the potential since institutions have generally been passive shareholders.

A CLOSED SYSTEM?

The received legal model of the company is a closed system of power and control. The two organs of the company recognised by company law are the general meeting of shareholders (which may not necessarily include all the shareholders, since some shares may not carry votes and preference shareholders may have limited voting rights) and the board of directors. The board of directors manages the company and makes business policy decisions and the general meeting of the shareholders as a body elects the board and decides on organic change. Company officers are answerable to the board but the board is only answerable to the company as a whole not the shareholders as such. This is at any rate the received general legal theory[2]

---

1 It should be noted, however, that directors have no right to be paid for their services in the absence of authority under the articles—*Re George Newman & Co* [1895] 1 Ch 674 at 686, CA.
2 M A Eisenberg *The Structure of the Corporation; a Legal Analysis* (1976).

although it is belied to some extent by the market for control. Dissatisfied shareholders may sell and this may depress the share price in the case of a listed company. They will also be inclined to accept a takeover offer.

In the case of the larger companies with debenture stock, there will usually be debenture stockholders' meetings and class meetings of the various classes of shares but the status of both of these is largely contractual and ad hoc. There is no recognition of the work force in the organic structure of the company although the board may now legitimately consider their interests in making decisions. This latter reform perhaps marks a closer equation by the law of the company with the economic concept of the firm. Collective bargaining nevertheless operates outside the company structure. Government and community pressures are also outside the corporate system. However, the reality of corporate decision making is that it must be open to outside influences in order to survive particularly in a time of recession. Trade union negotiations, the activities of competitors, the constraints of government and local authorities, the pressures of international trade are all influences on corporate decision making in the real world. In the U K some commentators detected in the period prior to 1979 a move towards 'corporatism' or the 'corporate state'[3]. This was seen in the active role of government in the promotion of mergers, in direct shareholding in certain key sectors and in a willingness to intervene in industrial disputes. Things have changed somewhat since then. There has been a retreat from intervention and a return to a more laissez-faire approach. Meanwhile in the EEC, plans have long been in gestation to give greater recognition to the employee and consumer interests in the structure of the company. This is more a reflection of welfare and political considerations than a positive economic reflex.

Active and latent control[4]

When companies are controlled by owner managers, active power and control are merged. For instance, the early coal and steel companies in the later part of the nineteenth century were run like this. The general tendency in the larger companies is for ownership and control to separate. The separation of ownership and control, instead of producing pure management control because of the dispersal of shareholding, has often resulted in the continuation of significant non-managerial ownership, which frequently is in the hands of financial institutions. Where this is the case the extent of control is often hard to assess and has been labelled by one American writer as latent power[5]. Such power is usually negative in nature. It rests on powers of veto in loan agreements or the power of constraint by influence on the board. The concept of control is considered further in Chapter 34. Although the general body of shareholders may be said to have latent power in the sense of certain residual rights of intervention and control, differences between shareholders in wealth, tax position, and investment objectives as well as the lack of a countervailing institutional framework parallel to that of management all tend to weaken this power in practice[6].

3 See J Winkler (1975) 2 BJLS 103.
4 Edward Herman *Corporate Control, Corporate Power* (1981) chapter 4.
5 Ibid.
6 Ibid, p 23.

THE STRATEGIC POSITION OF THE BOARD

Although in the nineteenth century management was frequently thought of as the agent of the company in general meeting which could be controlled by the general meeting, the change of wording in the standard form of article by the early twentieth century vested wider powers in the board of directors and curtailed the rights of the general meeting to interfere[7]. In a word it legitimated centralised management[8].

As Henry Manne has put it:

Management is a discrete economic service or function and the selection of individuals to perform that function, whether undertaken at the outset or during the later life of a company, is a part of the entrepreneurial job. Centralising management serves simply to specialise these various economic functions, and to allow the system to operate more efficiently[9].

Day to day control then rests with the board of directors which in theory must act as a collegiate body. In practice much authority is delegated to a managing director and other executives. The law has not fully come to terms with the variety of management structures and practices in modern companies. Although there is evolving a sensible law based on a modern view of agency principles this sometimes seems a little over-simplified and remote from reality. The law relating to the authority of an individual director and a manager to bind the company is not very satisfactory. Another conceptual approach which is mainly adopted in tort and criminal law is the attribution to the company of the acts of certain officers as its alter ego. This approach known also as the organic theory has been developed more fully in German law.

The practice of appointing outside directors particularly in larger companies is increasing but it is questionable whether this is more than window dressing in many companies. Such directors are often passive and do what management wants of them.

Control by the board of the proxy machinery has important strategic consequences, since few shareholders turn up at general meetings. However, the Stock Exchange requirements of two-way proxies which enable the shareholder to mandate the directors to give effect to his wishes curtail this somewhat.

Given that management usually has strategic control, in whose interests is it exercised? Obviously where there is ownership and control vested in the same hands there is no great problem unless the proprietors sacrifice the interests of creditors by fraudulent or reckless trading. It is thought that in publicly-held companies, management generally runs company affairs without regard to its own self interest as far as business decisions are concerned. On the other hand when it comes to structural decisions such as a merger or takeover, conflicts of interest arise[10]. Management and shareholders do not then necessarily have the same interest[11]. Management reward is frequently

---

7 See L C B Gower *Modern Company Law* (4th edn, 1979) p 143.
8 See H G Manne (1967) 53 Virginia LR 259.
9 Ibid.
10 *Eisenberg*, op cit, chapter 4.
11 Cf however, George J Benston (1973) 63 Am Econ Rev 132, who argues that the evidence does not support this conclusion.

unconnected with share ownership and in any event is only one of the operative motives of managerial conduct. These motives include the urge to power and prestige and the desire for security.

THE ECONOMICS OF THE RIGHT TO VOTE[12]

Voting rights exist because someone must have residual power to act where the contracts are incomplete[13]. The contractual nexus cannot cover every future contingency expressly. Decisions may have to be made which are felt by the law or the founders to need the backing of investors. The rights, however, usually attach to the ordinary shares as the residual claimants to the company's income. They receive most of the marginal gains and suffer most of the marginal costs. Hence it is felt that they are the appropriate group to exercise voting rights.

Ordinary shareholders normally have one vote per share at general meetings. Preference shareholders usually have only limited voting rights. Debenture holders have no right to vote at general meetings. Voting in any case is not compulsory and for many shareholders there is a strong disincentive to vote. To attend a meeting in person may be expensive. The exercise of one's votes does not give one any privileges unless one has control or one's votes can be decisive. Given the cost, the difficulty and the uncertainty of outcome many investors rely on the market and tend to spread their risks by investing in a number of companies. On the other hand, the right to vote is not without value. The value is at a minimum when the need to exercise it is remote and rises to a maximum when the exercise of voting rights assumes significance. Also the market recognises that shares can have a nuisance value. Thus, even in the case of winding up or a major reconstruction, shares carrying votes will have some value depending on what the support or opposition of the holders is thought to be worth.

THE LEGAL REGULATION OF MANAGEMENT

The legal regulation of management can be broadly divided into a free enterprise approach and a public interventionist approach. The first, which is the product of case law augmented by statute, is represented by two tiers of protection. The director owes a mixture of case law and statutory duties to the company. Some of these are characterised as fiduciary obligations and are owed to the company, not the individual shareholders or creditors of the company. For wrongs done to the company, the company is the proper plaintiff. The majority generally represents the company. The purpose of this latter doctrine was to curb the number of suits, and it is perhaps implicit in the economics of public companies. As Henry Manne has argued, the function of the shareholder is to put money at risk for use by entrepreneurs

---

12 See M S Rix *Stock Exchange Economics* (1954) p 53; F H Easterbrook and D R Fischel (1983) 26 J of Law & Econ 395; R Hessen *Defence of the Corporation* (1979) chapter 5, cf R Nader *Taming the Giant Corporation* (1976). For a discussion of share voting in mergers see H Manne 'Some Theoretical Aspects of Share Voting' in *The Economics of Legal Relationships* (1975) ed H Manne, p 534.
13 Easterbrook and Fischel, op cit, p 403.

and managers: 'Apart then from having the shareholders' funds used in the corporation's interest and his contracted-for return paid . . . economics suggests no other relationship between investors and managers.' Manne later equates the concept of centralised management with majority rule. It is not that management necessarily owns a majority of shares but that it has the means of control of them. There are, however, exceptions to the proper plaintiff rule when a minority shareholder is allowed to sue and to these can be added the statutory remedy under s 459 and winding up on the just and equitable ground. These remedies are somewhat draconian and arguably less important in the policing of management behaviour than market forces, particularly in the market for securities and the market for corporate control. Unless a public company whose shares are listed is efficiently managed, the price of its shares will decline and this will lower the price at which an outsider can take over the company[14]. Small firms, however, are not subject to the same market forces since the market for a minority interest will usually only be the majority. In the case of both types of company the rights of loan creditors to intervene depend on their contract with the company, their security and the general law.

The public interventionist approach is largely concerned with policing disclosure and commercial fraud. The Department of Trade and Industry has a number of statutory powers of investigation and inspection. Added to these are the specialist powers of the Director General of Fair Trading and the EEC Commission in respect of monopolies and restrictive practices which we shall consider in the next part of the book. The legal regulation of management has recently come under attack by some economists. It is said to be based on the largely unproven empirical assumptions that the separation of ownership and control is not economically optimal and that the legal treatment of the problem reduces or eliminates the inefficiencies at a cost less than the benefits obtained. The whole elaborate structure is thought to be built up on guesswork. Another unproven hypothesis is that market controls are not sufficient to police management shirking and abuse of discretion. Such critics argue[15]:

(1)   Separation of ownership and control is simply another example of joint effort and the inevitability of 'agency costs'. These costs include the cost of monitoring to deter shirking and abuse by management.
(2)   Monitoring is worthwhile only when the costs of monitoring management behaviour are less than the benefits derived.
(3)   Government intervention might force the incurring of monitoring costs which exceed the benefits derived.
(4)   Market forces will cause managements to seek to prove that they are honest and efficient. This will encourage investment in the company, ward off a takeover and improve their own marketability.
(5)   It is better to think of shareholders not as owners but as risk takers, since this more accurately analyses their position.

These arguments provide a valuable perspective and powerful critique of the

---

14 Manne, op cit.
15 See e g N Wolfson (1980) 34 Univ of Miami LR 959; E Fama 'Agency Problems and the Theory of the Firm' (1980) 88 Journal of Political Economy 288; M C Jensen and W H Meckling 'Theory of the Firm; Managerial Behaviour, Agency Costs and Ownership Structure' (1976) 3 Journal of Financial Economics 305.

law. They suffer, however, from one signal weakness. The law is not exclusively concerned with economic factors. Certain goals are thought worthy of public pursuit which are not necessarily cost effective. This is because of the close interface of law and social morality. Even if the benefits of policing management fraud were outweighed by the costs we should still feel obliged to incur them. Whether this applies to lack of care and inefficiency in management is more problematic. Although to some limited extent it affects the public interest, it is probably better left to private law enforcement by the shareholders through the company.

CHAPTER 22

Company general meetings

The law relating to company meetings is not the most exciting or interesting topic in company law. It is important to students of company law, however, in three ways. First, the relatively mundane one of understanding and being able to use correctly the terminology of meetings and resolutions which inevitably reappears throughout every other branch of company law. This chapter will therefore try to concentrate on the more important aspects, but attempts to simplify statutory language often lead to inaccuracy and some detail is thus unavoidable. Secondly, meetings and resolutions are important in that they represent the way in which shareholders can make their voices heard to the management of the company. Certainly if small shareholders in companies with a large number of shareholders wish their views to be known, the way they can do this is via resolutions passed at general meetings[1]. Although larger or institutional shareholders may give their views to the management in private they too may find that the expression of them or the threat to express them in general meetings is the more effective method[2]. Thirdly, the law relating to meetings and resolutions forms an important aspect of the deregulation of private companies which is one of the topical issues in company law reform[3]. Following suggestions made in a report published by the Institute of Directors[4] two procedures were introduced in the Companies Act 1989 designed to ease the burden of running a small private company. One allows shareholders by unanimous 'elective resolution'[5] to disapply certain Companies Act formalities. The other introduces a statutory procedure for passing resolutions by written agreement[6]. One final word of introduction. The conduct of company meetings, although affected by statutory provisions is very much a matter of the company's own regulations. Frequent reference will therefore be made in this chapter to the provisions of Table A as illustrating the most common practice in this area. In addition The Stock Exchange Rules contain some provisions affecting

---

1 From time to time shareholders may form action groups to co-ordinate pressure on the board of directors. A well known one during the 1970s was the Burmah Oil Shareholders Action Group formed as a result of that company's sale of its shares in British Petroleum to the Bank of England. See (1981) 2 Co Law 220. On more recent examples see the article by Charles Batchelor in the *Financial Times*, 14 November 1985. A Private Member's Bill proposed the establishment of a shareholders' committee for all public companies: see *The Times*, 21 February 1987.
2 The attempts by Lonrho plc to influence the management of House of Fraser plc provided valuable illustrations of the law and practice of meetings, circulars and resolutions.
3 Once a more coherent classification of public and private companies was introduced by the Companies Act 1980 it was to be expected that there would be an increasing divergence in the legislation relating to each type of company. Deregulation should be seen as a part of this process.
4 'Deregulation for Small Private Companies' (1986).
5 See pp 333–334, below.
6 See pp 338–340, below.

meetings of listed companies and these too will be referred to when appropriate.

Annual general meeting

Every company must hold at least one general meeting each calendar year[7] which it must designate in notices calling the meeting its annual general meeting[8]. There is no limit to the number of general meetings a company may hold each year but it must hold at least one, called the annual general meeting. The articles will usually provide for the meeting to be called by the directors[9] but if they fail to do so then any member of the company can ask the Department of Trade and Industry to call, or direct the calling, of a meeting[10].

The minimum period of notice that must be given of an annual general meeting is 21 days and the company's articles cannot provide for any shorter period[11]. However, if all the members entitled to attend and vote at an annual general meeting agree, the period of notice laid down in the Act or, if longer, in the company's articles can be waived[12]. Although there are no items of business which the Companies Act requires to take place at the annual general meeting, certain items are by convention usually dealt with, such as declaring a dividend, consideration of the accounts, balance sheets and the reports of the directors and auditors, the election of directors in place of those retiring and the appointment and remuneration of the auditors[13].

Members have a common law right to propose resolutions at an annual general meeting but notice must have been given to every member and in a large public company with a widely dispersed shareholding, this is likely to prove extremely expensive. The company may, of course, be willing to circulate members' resolutions with the notice calling the meeting but the company can now be compelled to do so[14] by members holding not less than 5% of the voting rights or 100 members holding an average paid up capital of

---

7   *Gibson v Barton* (1875) LR 10 QB 329.
8   Section 366(1). This is one of the provisions the members of a private company may elect to disapply. Under s 366A a private company may, by elective resolution, dispense with holding an annual general meeting unless required to do so by a member.
9   See Table A, art 37. If the articles make no provision for the calling of meetings then a minimum number of members may do so: s 370(3).
10   Section 367(1).
11   Section 369(1), (2). See also Table A, art 38. Reference to a number of days' notice means clear days ie excluding the day notice is given and the day the meeting is held: *Re Railway Sleepers Supply Co* (1885) 29 Ch D 204; *Re Hector Whaling Ltd* [1936] Ch 208 (cf the Scottish case of *Re Neil M'Leod & Sons Ltd, Petitioners* 1967 SC 16 which allowed the day of the meeting to be counted). Table A expressly refers to 'clear' days and defines this as excluding both the day notice is given or deemed to be given and the day the meeting is held: art 1. In calculating the precise period of notice, therefore, it is also necessary to take account of any provision as to when notice is deemed to be given. Under Table A notices are deemed to be given 48 hours after posting: art 115. For the problems raised by a postal strike see *Bradman v Trinity Estates plc* [1989] BCLC 757.
12   Section 369(3)(a). The attention of members must be drawn to the fact that the required notice has not been given for their consent to be valid: *Re Pearce, Duff & Co Ltd* [1960] 3 All ER 222, [1960] 1 WLR 1014.
13   It used to be the case that under Table A articles, such items were designated 'ordinary' business of an annual general meeting. All other business at the annual general meeting was, under the former Table A articles, deemed 'special' business, the consequence being that the general nature of such business had to be specified in the notice calling the meeting.
14   Section 376(1)(a).

£100 per member[15]. The members requisitioning the resolution must give notice to the company at least six weeks before the annual general meeting is due to take place[16]. They must also pay the company's expenses unless the company resolves otherwise, and may be required to deposit a sum to cover these expenses in advance[17].

The annual general meeting is the best opportunity shareholders have of questioning the management of the company. Nevertheless, it appears that many annual general meetings are routine affairs in which little information is either asked for or supplied. A survey[18] of attendance of annual general meetings in 1969 found that the average (mean) attendance was 80 and the median attendance was 47, ie half the companies surveyed had attendances of less than and half of more than 47. The survey also found that it was unusual for the shareholders present to represent more than 1% of the total voting capital and the average length of annual general meetings was 23 minutes.

Extraordinary general meetings

The articles of association of a company will usually provide for the directors to convene meetings apart from the annual general meeting[19]. These additional meetings are commonly referred to as extraordinary general meetings[20]. Of course, if the members' views are to be heard, a meeting will be necessary for the views to be formulated and resolutions passed and if the directors suspect those views will be critical they may be unwilling to call a meeting. It is important, therefore, that since 1900, provided they have sufficient support, shareholders have been able to requisition the directors to convene an extraordinary general meeting[1]. The requisition must state the objects of the meeting[2] and must be supported by holders of not less than 10% of the voting paid up capital or, in the case of a company with no share capital, by members representing not less than 10% of the voting rights in the company[3]. If there is a valid requisition, the directors must convene a meeting within 21 days, otherwise the requisitionists may themselves convene one[4]. Formerly the section did not specify a time within which the meeting convened by the directors had to take place and, provided a meeting was convened within 21 days, the requisitionists were prevented from calling one themselves[5]. It is now provided[6] that the meeting convened

---

15 Section 376(2).
16 Section 377(1)(a)(i).
17 Section 377(1)(b).
18 Midgley (1974) 114 Lloyds Bank Review 24. There is also an entertaining account of the effect that offering free refreshment at the meeting can have on attendance in Alex Rubner *The Ensnared Shareholder* (1965) pp 112–116.
19 See Table A, art 37. If the articles make no provision for the calling of meetings then a minimum number of members may do so: s 370(3).
20 Ibid, art 36.
 1 Section 368.
 2 Section 368(3).
 3 Section 368(2).
 4 Section 368(4).
 5 *Re Windward Islands Enterprises (UK) Ltd* [1983] BCLC 293.
 6 Section 368(8), inserted by the Companies Act 1989, Sch 19, para 9.

by the directors must take place not more than 28 days[7] after the notice convening it.

The minimum period of notice for extraordinary general meetings laid down by the Act is 14 days[8] unless the meeting is one at which a special resolution is to be proposed in which case at least 21 days' notice must be given[9]. The company's articles cannot provide for any shorter period but the minimum periods, whether those laid down by the Act or longer periods specified in the company's articles, can be waived if sufficient of the members entitled to attend and vote at the meeting agree[10]. There must be a majority in number of such members who must together hold at least 95% in nominal value of the shares giving a right to attend and vote at the meeting[11].

Power of the court to call meetings

Despite the number of provisions relating to the calling of meetings, it may still happen that it is impracticable to call a meeting or to conduct one in the manner prescribed by the articles or the Act. In these circumstances, the court may order a meeting to be held and conducted in such manner as the court thinks fit[12]. In particular, the court is authorised to direct that one member of the company present in person or by proxy shall constitute a meeting[13]. The court may exercise this power either of its own motion or on the application of any director of the company or of any member of the company who would be entitled to vote at the meeting[14].

Notices relating to meetings

TO WHOM MUST NOTICE BE GIVEN

Unless the articles otherwise provide, notice of general meetings must be given to every member of the company[15]. Thus, although members without

---

7 The maximum permissible time between receipt of the requisition and the holding of the meeting is thus seven weeks. Table A, art 37 allows a maximum of eight weeks and will therefore need amending.
8 Section 369(1), (2). This will normally mean clear days: see note 11 above.
9 Section 378(2). Likewise as to clear days, see note 11 above (p 322). Under Table A, if a resolution appointing a director is to be proposed then 21 clear days' notice is required: art 38.
10 Sections 369(3)(b) and (4) and 378(3). As to drawing the members' attention to such consent, see note 12 above (p 322). A private company may by elective resolution reduce the 95% majority needed for consent to short notice under these provisions, but to not less than 90%.
11 Ibid.
12 Section 371(1).
13 Section 371(2). See *Re El Sombrero Ltd* [1958] Ch 900, [1958] 3 All ER 1; *Re HR Paul & Son Ltd* (1973) 118 Sol Jo 166; *Re Opera Photographic Ltd* [1989] 1 WLR 634.
14 See note 12.
15 Section 370(2). Notice must also be given to the auditors who are entitled to attend general meetings of the company and to be heard at general meetings on matters concerning them as auditors: s 390(1). Table A also requires notice to be given to all persons entitled to a share in consequence of the death or bankruptcy of a member and to the directors: art 38. Note that under Table A a director is entitled to attend and speak at meetings, even if he is not a member: art 44. It is not entirely clear what happens if notice is not given to a director or if a director is prevented from attending and speaking in breach of the relevant Table A articles. If the director is not also a member of the company he will not be a party to the contract in

votes at general meetings normally have no right to attend[16], they will normally have the right to receive notice of any meetings. Again, except in so far as the articles otherwise provide, the manner in which notice of meetings must be served is that laid down by Table A as for the time being in force[17]. At common law, a meeting cannot be held unless every member entitled to receive notice has done so[18]. It is usual therefore for articles to provide that accidental omission to give notice or the non-receipt of notice shall not invalidate proceedings at the meeting[19].

CONTENTS OF NOTICES

Apart from indicating the time and place at which a meeting is to be held, the notice of a meeting[20] must also give members a sufficient indication of the business to be transacted at the meeting as will enable them to decide whether they need to attend or not. The notice will therefore also set limits on what may be decided at a meeting and if a resolution is passed of which proper notice was not given a member will be entitled to a declaration that it was invalid[1]. It is normally sufficient for the notice to indicate the general nature of the business to be transacted at the meeting[2] but certain resolutions may need to be set out in full. Thus a notice of a meeting called to pass an extraordinary, special or elective resolution must specify that the resolution is to be proposed as such[3] and must set out either the text or the entire substance of the resolution[4]. Similarly, the notice of an annual general meeting must set out the exact text of any resolution to be proposed as a result of a requisition by shareholders[5]. Finally, as part of the directors' duty to ensure that the members are fully aware of what is to be discussed at the meeting, the notice must disclose any benefit the directors will obtain as a

the articles and so will not be able to raise the breach of the articles as a breach of contract. Although another member might be entitled to challenge the meeting on the grounds of breach of the articles, none might be bothered to do so. And yet failure to give notice of meeting to all those entitled to it can have serious consequences for the validity of the meeting and what takes place there: see notes 18 and 19 below.

16 *Re Mackenzie & Co Ltd* [1916] 2 Ch 450.
17 Section 370(2). The relevant provisions of Table A are arts 111–116.
18 *Smyth v Darley* (1849) 2 HL Cas 789.
19 See Table A, art 39. This provision was going to be made statutory in the Companies Bill 1973, cl 73(4). It covers inadvertently not sending a notice to a member (*Re West Canadian Collieries Ltd* [1962] Ch 370, [1962] 1 All ER 26) but not deliberately not giving someone notice because of a mistaken view that they were not entitled to it (*Musselwhite v CH Musselwhite & Son Ltd* [1962] Ch 964, [1962] 1 All ER 201).
20 This section deals with notices of meetings but note that under Table A where, at a general meeting, a person is to be appointed director or re-appointed (unless retiring by rotation) a notice including the person's name, address, nationality and other directorships must be given to all those entitled to notice of the meeting between 7 and 28 days before the meeting: art 77.
1 *MacConnell v E Prill & Co Ltd* [1916] 2 Ch 57.
2 See Table A, art 38. Where the articles of a company distinguish between ordinary and special business, the effect is usually to enable a company to transact the ordinary business of that meeting without any notice of the items of business at all. Thus a company could, simply by giving notice of its annual general meeting, transact any items designated as ordinary business of the annual general meeting.
3 Sections 378(1), (2) and 379A(2).
4 *MacConnell v E Prill & Co Ltd* [1916] 2 Ch 57; *Re Moorgate Mercantile Holdings Ltd* [1980] 1 All ER 40, [1980] 1 WLR 227; *Re Willaire Systems plc* [1987] BCLC 67, CA.
5 Section 376(3).

result of the passing of any resolution[6]. This rule has been made statutory for meetings of members and creditors considering a scheme of arrangement[7] and the obligation in such cases extended to require the disclosure of any interests held by trustees for debenture holders[8]. The Jenkins Committee thought that the whole topic of the contents of notices of meetings should be the subject of a general provision declaratory of the existing law to 'serve as a reminder to directors and other officers of duties of which they may not be fully aware', but no such provision has been enacted[9].

SPECIAL NOTICE

Three types of resolution referred to in the Companies Act require what is called special notice. This means that the persons intending to move such a resolution must give *to the company* at least 28 days' notice before the meeting at which the resolution is to be moved[10]. The company must then give notice of the resolution to the members at the same time, and in the same manner, as the notice of the meeting. If that is not practicable, for example because notices of the meeting have already been sent out, the company must give notice either by advertisement or in any other mode allowed by the articles in which case the notice must be given at least 21 days before the meeting[11]. The three types of resolution for which special notice are needed are:

(1)   to remove a director by ordinary resolution[12];
(2)   to appoint an auditor in certain circumstances or to remove an auditor from office[13]; and
(3)   to allow a director to serve beyond retiring age[14].

Circulars

Besides sending a notice of meeting to the members, the directors have a common law duty to give members such explanations and additional information as may be necessary to understand the implications of any proposed transactions[15]. Provided the directors honestly believe that the policy they are promoting is in the best interests of the company, they will be

6 *Kaye v Croydon Tramways Co* [1898] 1 Ch 358, CA; *Tiessen v Henderson* [1899] 1 Ch 861; *Baillie v Oriental Telephone and Electric Co Ltd* [1915] 1 Ch 503, CA.
7 Section 426(2).
8 Section 426(4).
9 Report of the Company Law Committee (Cmnd 1749) paras 465–467. The proposal was included in the Companies Bill 1973, cl 74.
10 Section 379(1). The company might try and invalidate the notice by convening a meeting to take place in less than 28 days so it is provided that if this is done, notice shall be deemed to have been properly given: s 379(3).
11 Section 379(2). *Fenning v Fenning Environmental Products Ltd* [1982] LS Gaz R 803. But notice that the section cannot be used as a way of enabling a member to have a resolution he wishes to propose notified to all members: *Pedley v Inland Waterways Association Ltd* [1977] 1 All ER 209.
12 Section 303(2).
13 Sections 388(3) and 391A(1).
14 Section 293(5).
15 The Stock Exchange requires listed companies to send an explanatory circular with any notice of meeting which includes business other than routine business at an annual general meeting: Admission of Securities to Listing, s 5, ch 2, para 31.

entitled to exhort members to vote in support of the board and to pay for any circulars or advertisements involved out of company funds[16].

The ability to use the machinery and money of the company to make their views known to the members places the directors in a strong position compared to that of members who are critical of the board's policy. In order to help critics get their views across, there is a provision whereby a certain proportion of members can require the company to circulate a statement not exceeding 1,000 words relating to the business of a meeting[17]. The proportion of members supporting the requisition must either represent not less than 5% of the total voting rights or be not less than 100 members holding shares in the company on which an average of at least £100 per member is paid up[18]. The requisition must reach the company at least one week before the meeting and the company may require the requisitionists to deposit a sum reasonably sufficient to meet the company's expenses[19]. The company will then be obliged to circulate the statement to all members entitled to notice of meetings in the same manner and at the same time as the notice of meeting (a crucial provision if the members are to hear the critics' views before they send in their proxies) or as soon as practicable thereafter[20]. The word limit and the fact that the critics can be required to pay the company's expenses mean that they are still at a considerable disadvantage compared to the board of directors. Whether, if the critics are ultimately successful and their policy is accepted as being in the best interests of the company, they are entitled to be reimbursed by the company is as yet undecided but there are at least two US decisions supporting the view that they are[1]. It may sometimes happen that an argument as to the policy to be adopted by a company results from a split in the boardroom itself. Although in such a case boards of directors normally act by majority decision, it is arguable that both sets of directors have a duty to advise shareholders on what they honestly believe to be the best interests of the company and are therefore entitled to spend the company's money in doing so.

Proxies

One reason why the circulars sent to members are so important is that if members vote at all, they are far more likely to do so via the proxy voting machinery than to attend in person at the meeting and vote there. The information members receive before the meeting will be crucial therefore in persuading them to vote in a particular way. In fact, as we shall see, the proxy voting machinery may further reinforce the advantage held by the board in seeking support for their policy.

The term 'proxy' refers both to the instrument of appointment and to the person so appointed. Any member of a company with a share capital may

---

16 *Peel v London and North Western Rly Co* [1907] 1 Ch 5, CA; *Campbell v Australian Mutual Provident Society* (1908) 77 LJPC 117. As with notices of meetings The Stock Exchange requires proofs of circulars to be submitted for approval and final copies forwarded when circulars are issued: Admission of Securities to Listing, s 5, ch 2, paras 31 and 35.
17 Section 376(1)(b).
18 Section 376(2).
19 Section 377(1).
20 Section 377(3), (4) and (5).
 1 *Steinberg v Adams* 90 F Supp 604 (1950); *Rosenfield v Fairchild Engine and Airplane Corpn* 309 NY 168 (1955).

appoint a proxy who need not be a member of the company[2] and any notice calling a meeting of such a company must include a statement of this right.[3] The board of directors could try and prevent the opposition case being heard if it could require proxies to be returned to the company before the opposition have had a chance to mobilise. To prevent this, it is provided that any provision requiring proxies to be returned to the company more than 48 hours before the meeting is void[4]. Nevertheless, the board have considerable advantages in regard to the proxy voting machinery. They may send proxy forms out with the notice of meeting which may invite members to appoint a named member of the board to vote on their behalf in favour of board resolutions. Only in the case of companies listed on The Stock Exchange is there a requirement for companies to send out two-way proxies giving shareholders the equal opportunity to vote for or against resolutions[5]. Furthermore, it is perfectly permissible, provided directors honestly believe this is in the best interests of the company, to use the company's money to pay for the cost of sending out and returning proxy forms, even if they only invite members to appoint one of the directors to vote in favour of the board's policy[6]. The only control over this is that if invitations to appoint proxies are issued at the company's expense, they must be sent to every member entitled to notice of and to vote by proxy at the meeting[7]. The directors cannot just send invitations to those people they think will support them.

A proxy has the right to attend all meetings[8] but he may vote on a show of hands only if the articles permit[9]. He may, however, always vote on a poll and may be counted towards any minimum demand necessary for a poll[10]. In a private company, a proxy has the same right to speak as the member appointing him but in a public company the right to speak will depend on the articles[11]. If the appointment of the proxy is an entirely gratuitous transaction, the proxy will not, however, be under any duty to the member appointing him actually to cast his vote. The authority to vote in a particular way by implication excludes any authority to vote in a different way but does

2 Section 372(1). The Jenkins Committee recommended extending the right to appoint proxies to companies without a share capital: Report of the Company Law Committee (Cmnd 1749) para 462. Despite being included in the Companies Bill 1973, cl 75(1) this has not been enacted.
3 Section 372(3).
4 Section 372(5).
5 Admission of Securities to Listing, s 5, ch 2, para 36.
6 *Peel v London and North Western Rly Co* [1907] 1 Ch 5, CA. The importance of whether the company supplies proxy voting cards and whether they are pre-paid is illustrated by Midgley (1974) 114 Lloyds Bank Review 24. He found one company where reply-paid proxies had produced an average of 1,700 returns each year; when no cards were supplied only one proxy was submitted and when proxy cards were supplied but not pre-paid, 300 were returned. The resistance of shareholders to paying to return proxies is illustrated by another company where proxies were not pre-paid and although 820 were returned, 343 shareholders had failed to put a stamp on! It is not obvious that companies should supply pre-paid proxy cards. As Midgley points out, most business is routine and non-contentious and is decided by a show of hands without the proxy votes ever even being looked at.
7 Section 372(6).
8 Section 372(1).
9 Section 372(2). Table A does not permit proxies to vote on a show of hands: see art 59.
10 Section 372(2). Where a poll is taken on a procedural motion, a proxy will be entitled to vote: *Re Waxed Papers Ltd* [1937] 2 All ER 481, CA.
11 Section 372(1).

not impart an obligation actually to attend and vote. It will be different if the proxy is under a contractual obligation or an equitable obligation arising from a fiduciary duty, and it may be that where proxies are given to the chairman of a meeting, part of his duty of ensuring that the will of the meeting is heard entails his exercising proxies vested in him[12].

The form of the instrument appointing a proxy will usually be set out in the articles[13] but minor discrepancies or variations will not invalidate the proxy as long as they could not mislead members invited to make use of them[14]. It is usual for articles to provide that the qualification of any voter can only be challenged at the meeting or any adjournment thereof, and that the chairman's decision thereon is final, and this will apply to challenging the validity of any proxy form as well[15].

A proxy appointment is conditional on the member himself not attending the meeting and if he does so the proxy is ineffective[16]. A proxy may also be determined at any time[17], and will be determined automatically in certain circumstances[18]. Since this may happen without the company or other shareholders being aware of it, it is common for the articles to provide that despite any determination of authority, a vote cast by a proxy shall be valid unless the company has been notified in writing before the meeting, adjourned meeting or time appointed for taking a poll[19]. Such provision will not affect the position as between the member and the proxy, but it will protect the company if it treats as valid a vote cast by a proxy whose authority, unknown to the company, had ended. Such a clause does not, however, prevent a member from attending and voting in person, in which case the company must count the member's votes and not the proxy's[20].

CORPORATE REPRESENTATIVES

A corporation as an artificial legal person obviously cannot attend meetings in person. It could appoint a proxy but as we have seen proxies are subject to various disabilities compared to members attending in person[1]. So the Companies Act provides for the directors or other governing body of corporate members to appoint representatives who can exercise all the

12 *Second Consolidated Trust Ltd v Ceylon Amalgamated Tea and Rubber Estates Ltd* [1943] 2 All ER 567 at 570.
13 See Table A, arts 60 and 61. Companies listed on The Stock Exchange must send members two-way proxy forms which must state that if they are returned without an indication as to how the proxy shall vote on any particular matter the proxy will exercise his discretion. The form of proxy must also remind shareholders of their right to appoint a proxy of their own choice and provide a space for such nomination: Admission of Securities to Listing, s 5, ch 2, para 36.2.
14 *Isaacs v Chapman* (1915) 32 TLR 183; affd (1916) 32 TLR 237, CA; *Oliver v Dalgleish* [1963] 3 All ER 330, [1963] 1 WLR 1274.
15 See Table A, art 58.
16 *Cousins v International Brick Co Ltd* [1931] 2 Ch 90, CA.
17 Unless the proxy has been given to protect some interest of the appointee, for example, where share certificates are deposited as security for a loan.
18 For example, by the death of the member.
19 See Table A, art 63.
20 *Cousins v International Brick Co Ltd* [1931] 2 Ch 90, CA.
 1 For example, they cannot normally vote on a show of hands or speak at meetings of public companies.

powers of individual members[2]. Appointments may be made in respect of meetings of members, classes of members or creditors (including debenture holders) and unlike the appointment of a proxy, at least under Table A articles, they do not need to be notified to the company holding the meeting.

Quorum

For business to be validly transacted at a meeting the meeting must be quorate. Unless the articles provide otherwise, the quorum for a company is two members[3] personally present[4] but it is common to provide that two members present in person or by proxy will suffice[5]. The question has arisen whether the latter formulation allows one member holding a proxy from another member or one person holding proxies from two different members, to constitute a quorate meeting. The answer has always been No, because of the common law rule that there must be at least two people present for a meeting to take place at all[6] and that one person's presence on behalf of two people does not suffice[7]. It ought to be possible for a company's articles to exclude the common law rule and to provide instead that one person can constitute a meeting and to provide for a quorum of one[8]. This would not only avoid problems of dual capacity but also remove one of the devices whereby the minority can thwart the wishes of the majority[9]. If, on the other hand, the articles provide for a quorum of *more* than two members present in person or by proxy, it is thought that, provided there were at least two people present to constitute a meeting at common law, any person present could be counted for the purposes of the quorum as representing the number of members for whom he held proxies[10].

At common law, if a meeting becomes inquorate, it is dissolved but Table A provides[11] that in such circumstances, or, if the quorum has not been

---

2 Section 375. Representatives can, for example, be counted towards a quorum: *Re Kelantan Coconut Estates Ltd and Reduced* [1920] WN 274; see also Table A, art 40.

3 At present the minimum number of members for any company is two: s 1(1). Under the Twelfth Directive 89/667/EEC OJ 1989 L 395/40 (which member states should implement by 1 January 1992) member states must permit private companies at least to be formed with just one member who it is provided shall exercise all the powers of the general meeting: art 4.

4 Section 370(4). Although there is no specific provision that only members with votes at the meeting may be counted towards the quorum, it has been described as 'a practical absurdity' if members without votes could be counted, per Kekewich J in *Young v South African and Australian Exploration and Development Syndicate* [1896] 2 Ch 268 at 277. Under Table A, only members entitled to vote can be counted towards the quorum: art 40.

5 See Table A, art 40.

6 There seems to be no reason why the two people present need to be in each other's presence physically. It has been recognised that for a meeting everyone does not need to be face to face; it suffices if electronically they can hear and be heard and see and be seen by the others attending: *Byng v London Life Association Ltd* [1990] Ch 170 at 183, [1989] 1 All ER 560 at 565, CA. In that case there was more than one person in each room but the principle should enable a meeting to take place between persons none of whom is in the same room.

7 *Sharp v Dawes* (1876) 2 QBD 26, CA where the only member to turn up took the chair and having conducted the meeting resolved 'that a vote of thanks be given to the chairman'! *Re Sanitary Carbon Co* [1877] WN 223; *Re Prain & Sons Ltd* 1947 SC 325; *Re M J Shanley Contracting Ltd* (*in voluntary liquidation*) (1979) 124 Sol Jo 239.

8 But in *Re Prain & Sons Ltd* 1947 SC 325 it was stated obiter that this would not be possible.

9 See *Re El Sombrero Ltd* [1958] Ch 900, [1958] 3 All ER 1; *Re H R Paul & Son Ltd* (1973) 118 Sol Jo 166; *Re Opera Photographic Ltd* [1989] 1 WLR 634.

10 See *Re Neil M'Leod & Sons Ltd, Petitioners* 1967 SC 16.

11 Table A, art 41.

reached within 30 minutes of the time when the meeting should have started, it stands adjourned to the same day of the following week at the same time and place or to such time and place as the directors decide[12]. Finally, it should be noted that at a class meeting in connection with the variation of class rights, the quorum at such a meeting, other than an adjourned meeting, is two persons holding or representing by proxy one-third in nominal value of the issued shares of the class[13]. At an adjourned meeting, the quorum is one person holding shares of the class in question or his proxy[14]. Since it is perfectly possible for one member to hold the whole of one class of shares, references to class meetings must be construed accordingly and it has been held that a member holding all the shares in one class may validly meet by himself[15].

Chairman

Unless the articles make provision for the appointment of a chairman of the meeting the members may elect one of their number to be chairman[16]. Table A provides for the chairman of the board of directors or, in his absence, some other director nominated by the directors to be chairman at general meetings[17]. If the chairman or any such nominee is more than 15 minutes late, or unwilling to act, then the directors present may elect one of their number to be chairman[18]. If no director is willing or they are all more than 15 minutes late then the members present and entitled to vote may appoint one of themselves chairman[19].

Adjournments

One of the questions most likely to land the chairman in controversy is that of adjourning the meeting. At common law, the power to dissolve or adjourn meetings rests with the members[20]. However, the chairman has power to do so where it is impracticable for the members to pass a resolution. This has been held to apply where unruly conduct prevented the continuation of business[1]. It has also been applied where a meeting was unable to proceed to business at all because the venue was not large enough for all those entitled to attend to take part in the debate and to vote[2]. More mundanely, it also allows the chairman to suspend a meeting where a poll has been demanded on a motion to adjourn and the poll cannot be taken

---

12 As to the exercise of the directors' discretion, see p 332, below.
13 Section 125(6)(a).
14 Ibid.
15 *East v Bennett Bros Ltd* [1911] 1 Ch 163.
16 Section 370(5).
17 Table A, art 42.
18 Ibid.
19 Table A, art 43.
20 *National Dwellings Society v Sykes* [1894] 3 Ch 159.
 1 *John v Rees* [1970] Ch 345, [1969] 2 All ER 274. Megarry J's decision was that the disorder was not sufficient to warrant an adjournment. 'Certainly there was noise, disorder, and, in a few cases, bodily contact; but whatever affronts to dignity there may have been, there was nothing that could really be called violence:' at 383, 294.
 2 *Byng v London Life Association Ltd* [1990] Ch 170, [1989] 1 All ER 560, CA. The cinema at which the meeting was to take place could accommodate 300. Over 800 turned up and when one of the doors of the cinema was forced open it let in a 'muted roar' from the foyer!

forthwith[3]. The chairman is not prevented from exercising this common law power by a provision in the articles authorising the chairman to adjourn 'with the consent of the meeting'. Such a power can only apply where it is practicable to obtain the consent of the meeting and therefore does not exclude the chairman's common law power where it is impracticable to obtain such consent[4]. Even where the articles empower the chairman to dissolve or adjourn meetings with the consent of the meeting, it has been held that the chairman may refuse to do so even against the wishes of the meeting[5]. Hence it is common to provide that the chairman is not only empowered to adjourn the meeting with its consent, but is also obliged to do so if the meeting directs[6].

In exercising the common law power a chairman must not only act in good faith but must act reasonably in the light of the purposes for which the power exists[7]. At a company meeting a member is entitled not only to vote but also to hear and be heard in the debate. Accordingly, the impact of the proposed adjournment on those seeking to attend the original meeting and the other members must be a central factor in considering the validity of the chairman's decision to adjourn[8].

Minutes

Minutes of all proceedings at general meetings must be entered in books kept for the purpose[9] and members have statutory rights to inspect and to request copies of them[10]. If the minutes are signed by the chairman of that meeting or of the next succeeding meeting they constitute evidence of the proceedings[11] and where minutes have been duly made, it raises a rebuttable presumption that the meeting was properly convened, that all proceedings were properly conducted and all appointments of directors, managers or liquidators valid[12].

Resolutions

There are four types of resolution referred to in the Act: ordinary, extraordinary, special and elective.

3 *Jackson v Hamlyn* [1953] Ch 577, [1953] 1 All ER 887.
4 *Byng v London Life Association Ltd*, note 2 above.
5 *Salisbury Gold Mining Co Ltd v Hathorn* [1987] AC 268, PC.
6 See Table A, art 45, which also provides that if a meeting is adjourned for 14 days or more, fresh notices must be served, whereas at common law no notice of an adjourned meeting is necessary: *Wills v Murray* (1850) 4 Exch 843.
7 *Byng v London Life Association Ltd*, note 2 above, at 188–191, 569–571. *Quaere* whether any such requirement of reasonableness applies to adjournment decisions taken by the meeting itself.
8 In *Byng v London Life Association Ltd*, note 2 above, it was held not reasonable to adjourn to a larger venue two hours later when the chairman knew that several members would be unable to attend, despite the fact that had the meeting begun on time and merely carried on into the afternoon the same members would presumably have been unable to stay. This decision is probably, therefore, restricted to cases where the meeting as originally convened was unable to proceed to business. In such a case a member is effectively denied any opportunity to attend any part of the meeting.
9 Section 382(1).
10 Section 383. Under s 273A, inserted by the Companies Act 1989, s 143, new regulations are likely to be made governing the inspection and copying of records held by the company.
11 Section 382(2).
12 Section 382(4).

ORDINARY RESOLUTIONS

An ordinary resolution, apart from being specified on certain occasions, will also suffice whenever the Act does not specify any other type of resolution or require any particular majority. It is passed by a simple majority of votes cast in person or by proxy. There are no particular requirements as to notice of an ordinary resolution. Amendments at the meeting are therefore permissible provided they fall within the scope of the notice of the original resolution and are not such as would have caused any member to decide differently about attending the meeting[13].

EXTRAORDINARY AND SPECIAL RESOLUTIONS

An extraordinary or a special resolution is passed by a majority of not less than 75% of the votes cast in person or by proxy at a general meeting of which notice specifying the intention to propose the resolution as an extraordinary or special resolution was given[14]. The difference between them is that in the case of a special resolution at least 21 days' notice of the meeting must have been given[15]; for an extraordinary resolution no special period of notice is required so it will be 21 days or 14 days according to whether the meeting is an annual or an extraordinary general meeting. Since in the case of an extraordinary general meeting, the requirement for 14 days' notice can be waived by a sufficient majority of members and the same majority can waive the 21-day period required for a meeting at which a special resolution is to be passed[16], it will be apparent there is today very little difference between extraordinary and special resolutions. There used to be considerable difference because a special resolution had to be confirmed by a separate meeting but since that was repealed there is now no justification for keeping extraordinary resolutions and the Jenkins Committee recommended their replacement by special resolutions[17]. Because notice must be given of the resolution where it is to be proposed as an extraordinary or special resolution, it has been held that no amendment which will alter the substance of the resolution can be allowed at the meeting[18]. What will be permitted are corrections to grammatical or clerical errors, reducing the words of the notice into formal language or reducing it into the form of a new text but provided in each case that the substance remains identical[19].

ELECTIVE RESOLUTIONS

An elective resolution is a procedure by which a private company can disapply certain Companies Act requirements. The idea originated in a report from the Institute of Directors[20] suggesting that shareholders could be

---

13 *Choppington Collieries Ltd v Johnson* [1944] 1 All ER 762, CA.
14 Section 378(1) and (2). These sub-sections refer to a three-quarters majority of members who vote but this has been drafted on the basis of a show of hands. On a poll, the appropriate majority is three-quarters of the votes cast: s 378(5).
15 Section 378(2).
16 Section 369(3) and (4) and s 378(3).
17 Report of the Company Law Committee (Cmnd 1749) para 461. The nearest this came to implementation was inclusion in the Companies Bill 1973, cl 77(4).
18 *Re Moorgate Mercantile Holdings Ltd* [1980] 1 All ER 40, [1980] 1 WLR 227.
19 Ibid at 54 and 242; *Re Willaire Systems plc* [1987] BCLC 67, CA.
20 'Deregulation for Small Private Companies' (1986).

permitted to dispense with certain formalities and requirements where this would not affect creditors or other outside parties. At present there are five provisions which companies can elect to disapply[1], although the Secretary of State has power to extend elective resolutions to cover other areas of internal administration or procedure[2]. Eventually it may be possible to pass a single resolution adopting the entire deregulation package or 'elective regime'[3] but for the time being separate elective resolutions are needed to disapply each provision.

The key principle governing shareholders' decisions to opt for a more deregulated regime is that unanimous consent is required: all the members entitled to attend and vote at the meeting must agree, either in person or by proxy[4]. In other respects the procedure is similar to that for a special resolution. At least 21 days' notice in writing must be given of the meeting, stating that an elective resolution is to be proposed and stating the terms of the resolution[5]. Companies do not need any authority in their articles to pass elective resolutions and an elective resolution overrides any contrary provision in the articles[6]. An elective resolution may be revoked by an ordinary resolution[7].

Registration of resolutions

Certain resolutions or agreements then need to be registered with the Registrar of Companies. This involves the company forwarding a copy of the resolution or agreement to the Registrar within 15 days of it being passed or entered into, which the Registrar then records[8]. This requirement applies to all elective, special and extraordinary resolutions[9] and any resolution agreed to by all the members which would otherwise have had to be passed as a special or extraordinary resolution[10]. It also applies to any resolution or agreement of a class of members which has the effect of binding all the members of the class even though some may not have agreed to it[11]. Registration is also required of ordinary resolutions in seven circumstances: voluntary winding up[12]; increasing the authorised share capital[13]; giving, varying, revoking or renewing authority to the directors to issue shares[14]; making a market purchase of the company's own shares[15]; approving certain

---

1 Section 379A(1). They relate to (i) the duration of authority to issue shares, (ii) dispensing with laying accounts before a general meeting, (iii) dispensing with an annual general meeting, (iv) reducing the majority needed to consent to short notice of meetings, (v) dispensing with the annual appointment of auditors.
2 Companies Act 1989, s 117.
3 As the Institute of Directors suggested it should be called.
4 Section 379A(2)(b). It follows that although the new regime is available to all companies, in practice it will be closely-held private companies and wholly-owned subsidiaries which will benefit from it most.
5 Section 379A(2)(a).
6 Section 379(A)(5).
7 Section 379A(3).
8 Section 380(1).
9 Section 380(4)(a) and (b).
10 Section 380(4)(c).
11 Section 380(4)(d).
12 Section 380(4)(j).
13 Section 123(3).
14 Section 380(4)(f).
15 Section 380(4)(h).

acquisitions from subscribers to the company's memorandum of associa-tions[16]; revoking an elective resolution[17]; or treating a meeting called by the Secretary of State as the annual general meeting[18]. Failure to register gives rise to criminal penalties[19] but does not make the resolution invalid although the company may be prevented from relying on the passing of certain resolutions against other persons until they are officially notified which process includes registration[20].

Voting

The normal practice in company meetings is for a vote to be taken first on a show of hands and then, if a valid demand is made, for a poll to be held. The difference is crucial because on a show of hands each member present will have one vote irrespective of the number of shares held[1]; on a poll, members can cast all the votes attached to all the shares they own[2]. A poll therefore will be a far more accurate reflection of the voting strength among the members. It is also provided that on a show of hands, a proxy cannot vote unless the articles allow this[3] and even if a proxy is allowed to vote on a show of hands he can record only one vote even though he represents more than one member[4]. On a poll, a proxy may always vote, a right which cannot be excluded by the articles[5]. Furthermore, on a poll a member or a proxy may split his votes so that he may vote in favour, and against, and abstain on the same resolution, a power which enables proxies or nominee shareholders representing more than one beneficial owner to reflect accurately their instructions[6].

Because of the potential for different results on a show of hands, and a poll, the right to demand a poll is very important. At common law, any member could demand a poll when the result of a show of hands was declared[7] but the articles could exclude or limit that right. The Act therefore now provides[8] that notwithstanding anything in the articles, except on a resolution to elect a chairman or to adjourn the meeting, a poll must be held if demanded by any of the following: not less than five members having a right to vote at the meeting; members holding not less than 10% of all voting rights that could be cast at the meeting; members holding shares conferring a

---

16 Section 111(2).
17 Section 380(4)(bb).
18 Section 367(4). Three resolutions of the board of directors also require registration: s 380(4)(e), (g) and (k).
19 Sections 380(5), 123(4), 111(4) and 367(5).
20 Section 42.
1 See Table A, art 54.
2 The number of votes carried by each share on a poll depends on the memorandum or articles of association or the terms on which the shares were issued but if no other provision is made each share is presumed to carry one vote: s 370(6). See also Table A, art 54.
3 Section 372(2)(c). Table A, art 54 does not allow proxies to vote on a show of hands.
4 *Ernest v Loma Gold Mines Ltd* [1897] 1 Ch 1, CA.
5 Section 372(1).
6 Section 373(3).
7 *R v Wimbledon Local Board* (1882) 8 QBD 459, CA.
8 Section 373(1). On a resolution in connection with an off-market purchase of a company's own shares any one member may demand a poll: s 164(5)(b). Note also that at a class meeting in connection with the variation of class rights, any holder of shares of that class present in person or by proxy may demand a poll: s 125(6)(b).

right to vote at the meeting on which the aggregate sum paid up equals not less than 10% of the total sum paid up on all such shares. Under Table A, the minimum number of members who may demand a poll is reduced from five to two[9]. It is also provided that the chairman may demand a poll[10], a right which he must exercise to give effect to the real sense of the meeting so that he must demand a poll if he has reason to believe the result on a poll would differ from the result on a show of hands[11]. Table A also permits a poll on the election of a chairman and the adjournment of a meeting[12] and allows a demand for a poll to be made before any show of hands[13], thus permitting a show of hands to be dispensed with[14]. Finally the Act provides that a proxy may always join in the demand for a poll[15] and logically a proxy should be able to count for this purpose as representing as many members as he holds proxies for.

The articles of association will usually empower the chairman to direct how a poll is to be conducted, and when[16]. If the meeting is adjourned for a poll to be held then an article allowing proxies to be lodged 'before a meeting or adjourned meeting' will allow further proxies to be lodged. But if the meeting is not adjourned but the holding of the poll merely deferred, such an article will not allow further proxies to be lodged[17] and hence Table A is now drafted so as to allow proxies to be deposited with the company 'not less than 24 hours before the time appointed for the taking of the poll'[18]. At common law, a member may vote on a poll even though he did not attend and was not represented at the original meeting[19].

If the show of hands or poll results in a tie, then at common law such a result stands[20] but articles commonly give a casting vote to the chairman in such circumstances in addition to any vote he may be entitled to as a member[1]. It is also common for articles to attempt to reduce so far as possible uncertainty attending the result of a vote. Thus Table A provides that no objection may be made to the qualification of any voter except at the meeting at which the vote is tendered[2]. If no objection is made, or it is overruled, then the vote is valid. This ties in with the common law rule that if no objection is taken to a form of proxy before the proxy votes are cast,

---

9 Table A, art 46.
10 Ibid.
11 *Second Consolidated Trust Ltd v Ceylon Amalgamated Tea and Rubber Estates Ltd* [1943] 2 All ER 567.
12 Table A, art 51.
13 Table A, art 46.
14 Per Jenkins LJ in *Holmes v Keyes* [1959] Ch 199 at 212, [1958] 2 All ER 129 at 136, CA.
15 Section 373(2).
16 See Table A, arts 49, 51 and 52. It seems likely, at any rate under articles which say 'votes may be given either personally or by proxy' as Table A, art 59 does, that it is not open to the chairman to direct that a postal ballot be held: cf *McMillan v Le Roi Mining Co Ltd* [1906] 1 Ch 331.
17 *Shaw v Tati Concessions Ltd* [1913] 1 Ch 292; *Jackson v Hamlyn* [1953] Ch 577, [1953] 1 All ER 887.
18 Table A, art 62(b). This applies in the case of a poll taken more than 48 hours after it was demanded; otherwise the proxy must be delivered at the meeting at which the poll was demanded: art 62(c).
19 *R v D'Oyly* (1840) 12 Ad & El 139.
20 But if the chairman has not yet cast any vote to which he may be entitled as a member, he may do so to resolve a tie: *Nell v Longbottom* [1894] 1 QB 767.
1 See Table A, art 50.
2 Table A, art 58.

although it may be possible to object to the proxy afterwards, the votes themselves are valid[3]. Under Table A, any objection which is made is referred to the chairman whose decision is final and conclusive[4] and can only be challenged on the grounds of fraud or misconduct[5]. The possibility of uncertainty over the result of a show of hands is particularly acute. As regards special or extraordinary resolutions, the Act itself therefore provides that, unless a poll is demanded, the declaration of the chairman shall be conclusive evidence of the result[6], with the effect that it can only be challenged on the grounds of fraud[7] or that it is wrong on the face of it[8]. Table A extends this principle to ordinary resolutions by providing that unless a poll is demanded, a declaration of the result of a show of hands plus an entry to that effect in the minutes shall be conclusive evidence of the result of the vote[9].

Written and informal resolutions

In the case of companies with a small number of members, the reality of how members decide matters may not reflect very closely the technical requirements of meetings and resolutions outlined above. Provided all the members know about and agree to a decision that is within the capacity of the company, then it is sensible to treat that as binding on the members and the company even though the formal requirements for passing resolutions have not been complied with. This is recognised by an express provision in Table A that a resolution in writing signed by all the members entitled to notice of and to attend and vote at general meetings shall be as valid and effective as if the resolution had been passed at a general meeting[10].

But the common law has developed the principle further, without any need for written resolutions. If it is shown that all the members know of and acquiesce in a decision, they and the company will be bound[11]. At first the principle depended on the members actually having met together[12] but this is no longer necessary provided all of them know of and agree to the decision[13]. As with written resolutions, it will be sufficient if only those members with the right to attend and vote at meetings consent, unless the matter to be decided is one where the Act specifies that others must be notified as well.

---

3 *Colonial Gold Reef Ltd v Free State Rand Ltd* [1914] 1 Ch 382; *Marx v Estates and General Investments Ltd* [1975] 3 All ER 1064, [1976] 1 WLR 380.
4 Table A, art 58.
5 *Wall v London and Northern Assets Corpn* [1899] 1 Ch 550; *Wall v Exchange Investment Corpn* [1926] Ch 143, CA.
6 Section 378(4).
7 *Re Hadleigh Castle Gold Mines Ltd* [1900] 2 Ch 419; *Arnot v United African Lands Ltd* [1901] 1 Ch 518, CA.
8 *Re Caratal (New) Mines Ltd* [1902] 2 Ch 498.
9 Table A, art 47. See *Kerr v John Mottram Ltd* [1940] Ch 657, [1940] 2 All ER 629.
10 Table A, art 53.
11 *Re Express Engineering Works Ltd* [1920] 1 Ch 466, CA. Acquiescence in a procedural irregularity may be inferred in certain circumstances from a failure to use an opportunity to object (*Re Bailey, Hay & Co Ltd* [1971] 3 All ER 693, [1971] 1 WLR 1357) but not where the irregularity could mislead or prejudice the members concerned (*Imperial Bank of China, India and Japan v Bank of Hindustan, China and Japan* (1868) LR 6 Eq 91).
12 *Re George Newman & Co* [1895] 1 Ch 674, CA; *Re Lee, Behrens & Co Ltd* [1932] 2 Ch 46.
13 *Parker & Cooper Ltd v Reading* [1926] Ch 975; *Re Duomatic Ltd* [1969] 2 Ch 365, [1969] 1 All ER 161; *Re Halt Garage (1964) Ltd* [1982] 3 All ER 1016.

Thus a payment to a director under s 312 must be disclosed to all members including, therefore, non-voting preference shareholders and will not be valid just because the voting shareholders know of and agree to it[14].

The principle of unanimous agreement, whether written or informal, has several times been held to bind the company in matters which would otherwise need to be passed by special or extraordinary resolution. Although under s 380(4)(c) such resolutions should be registered, failure to register does not make them invalid though in certain cases it may prevent the company relying on them against other parties[15]. The principle of unanimous assent is non-controversial where it merely cures a procedural irregularity in the passing of a special or extraordinary resolution[16]. It becomes more complicated where the agreement is to do something for which the Act prescribes a special or extraordinary resolution, and no such resolution has been proposed, let alone passed. One approach is to say that shareholders may waive requirements that are purely for their protection so that if no other interests are involved the shareholders may unanimously agree to something which would otherwise require a special or extraordinary resolution[17]. It is submitted, however, that as the Act stands at present, it is also necessary to consider whether the Act's requirement is facilitative, that is, making it possible to do by special or extraordinary resolution what could in any case be done by unanimous agreement, or constitutive, that is, laying down the *only* way in which something can be achieved. In the former case unanimous agreement should suffice[18]; in the latter, not[19].

WRITTEN RESOLUTIONS IN PRIVATE COMPANIES

Although the procedures for written and informal resolutions discussed above are only likely to be relevant to a company with a small number of members, they are applicable to public as well as private companies. Following a report by the Institute of Directors[20] a statutory procedure for passing

14 *Re Duomatic Ltd* [1969] 2 Ch 365, [1969] 1 All ER 161.

15 Section 42(1).

16 *Re Oxted Motor Co* [1921] 3 KB 32 (failure to give notice that resolution to be proposed as an extraordinary resolution); *Re Pearce, Duff & Co Ltd* [1960] 3 All ER 222, [1960] 1 WLR 1014 (notice one day short); *Re Bailey, Hay & Co Ltd* [1971] 3 All ER 693, [1971] 1 WLR 1357 (notice one day short).

17 See Higginson 'Waiver of Requirements of the Companies Acts' (1983) 80 LS Gaz 3085.

18 For example, it was always possible for a company to alter its articles by unanimous agreement. When, therefore, s 9 provides that 'a company may by special resolution alter its articles' that is merely providing an alternative route, one by which a particular majority may bind a minority. See *Cane v Jones* [1981] 1 All ER 533, [1980] 1 WLR 1451. It has similarly been accepted that unanimous agreement of the shareholders can put a company into voluntary liquidation: *Re MJ Shanley Contracting Ltd (in voluntary liquidation)* (1979) 124 Sol Jo 239.

19 For example, s 2(7) prohibits a company from altering the conditions in its memorandum 'except in the cases, in the mode and to the extent, for which express provision is made by this Act'. When, therefore, s 4 provides that 'A company may by special resolution alter its memorandum with respect to the objects of the company' that is the *only* way in which the objects may be changed. Even a unanimous agreement to alter them would not suffice. This explains the reluctance of Nourse J in *Re Barry Artists Ltd* [1985] BCLC 283 to accept a unanimous written agreement by shareholders to a reduction of capital in place of the special resolution required by s 135(1). Section 135 is constitutive of the company's power to reduce its share capital, not facilitative.

20 'Deregulation for Small Private Companies' (1986).

unanimous written resolutions in private companies was introduced by the Companies Act 1989. Anything which a private company may do by a resolution of a general or class meeting may instead be done by written resolution[1]. The procedure is that a written resolution has to be signed by or on behalf of all members who, at the date of the resolution, would be entitled to attend and vote at such a meeting[2]. The signatures may be on separate documents, provided each sets out the terms of the resolution[3]. Once agreed to in this manner a written resolution is as effective as if it had been passed at the appropriate meeting, although no meeting at all need be held and no previous notice of the resolution need be given[4]. It is specifically provided that this statutory written resolution procedure can be used to pass any sort of resolution, whether ordinary, special, extraordinary or elective[5].

How much more can be done under the statutory written resolution procedure compared with using a provision in a company's articles depends in part on how widely the clause in the articles is drafted. Table A, art 53, for example, does not extend to resolutions of class meetings, whereas the statutory written resolution procedure does[6]. Moreover statutory written resolutions can be used in situations where previously the Companies Act itself would have prevented this. Thus, for example, alterations to the objects clause or reductions of capital which can only be done by special resolution and cannot therefore be done merely by unanimous agreement whether under the articles or under the common law doctrine of acquiescence[7], can be carried out by a statutory written resolution[8].

In one respect at least the statutory written resolution procedure will be less flexible than the procedure under the articles. This is because under the statutory procedure a copy of any proposed written resolution must be sent to the auditors[9]. If it concerns the auditors as auditors, they have seven days in which to say that in their opinion the resolution should be considered by a general or class meeting, as appropriate[10]. A written resolution cannot take effect unless either the auditors do not reply within seven days, or they notify the company that the resolution does not concern them as auditors, or if it does concern them as auditors, that nevertheless no meeting is needed[11]. This procedure seems likely to present a serious impediment to the speedy or easy use of written resolutions, unless the auditors are prepared to give some clearance in advance or otherwise indicate the type of resolutions to which they will automatically consent.

---

1 There are two exceptions where it will still not be possible to use written resolutions: Schedule 15A, para 1. These relate to removal of directors or auditors from office before the expiry of their term of office under s 303 and s 391 respectively. The reason for these exceptions is that the director or auditor has the right to make representation at a general meeting of the company: s 304 and s 391(4).
2 Section 381A(1).
3 Section 381A(2).
4 Section 381A(1) and (4). Consequential amendments as to formalities needed for valid resolutions in certain cases are set out in Sch 15A, Pt II.
5 Section 381A(6).
6 Section 381(A)(1)(b).
7 See note 1 above.
8 Section 381A(6).
9 Section 381B(1). This provision was not suggested by the Institute of Directors Report, note 20 above.
10 Section 381B(2).
11 Section 381B(3).

The rights of auditors do not apply to written resolutions under the articles and this raises the question whether it is possible to ignore the statutory written resolution procedure and act under the articles, assuming the resolution falls within the scope of the clause in the articles. It is arguable that for a private company the anser is No, because the written resolution procedure is stated to 'have effect notwithstanding any provision of the company's memorandum or articles'[12]. This may mean merely that it cannot be excluded or subjected to more stringent conditions by a company's memorandum or articles. But if using a provision in the articles enables the statutory written resolution procedure to be ignored altogether, it is hard to see why such trouble was taken to involve the auditors. However, the common law doctrine of unanimous acquiescence is unaffected by the procedure for statutory written resolutions[13]. Maybe it will still be possible for all the members to sign a document setting out a resolution that makes it clear that it is not a statutory written resolution but that each member signing will be regarded as acquiescing in the resolution being treated as passed and precluded from alleging that a resolution in that form has not been duly passed.

12 Section 381C(1).
13 Section 381C(2).

CHAPTER 23

Company officers

DIRECTORS

The articles of association of a company invariably provide that the business of the company shall be managed by the directors[1] who will act collectively as a board although the articles may also provide for the delegation of extensive powers to smaller committees[2] or individual directors[3]. The proceedings of the board will be regulated by the articles[4] which will contain detailed rules covering such matters as the required quorum[5], the passing of resolutions[6] and the chairman's casting vote[7]. Minutes must be kept of all board meetings[8].

'Director' as such is not defined in the Companies Act which limits itself to noting in s 741 that 'director' includes any person occupying the position of director, by whatever name called[9].

A further complication is that an increasing number of provisions, in the Companies Act 1985 and the Insolvency Act 1986[10], particularly those requiring disclosure and regulating certain types of transactions by directors, also apply to 'shadow' directors, defined by s 741(2) of CA 1985 as persons in accordance with whose directions or instructions the directors of a company are accustomed to act. However, a person is not deemed to be a shadow director by reason only that the directors act on advice given by him in a professional capacity. Such 'shadows' will therefore be treated as directors in certain circumstances, despite not being appointed to the board. The use of this category to include individuals who remain backstage, as it were, is designed to prevent the easy evasion of legal liabilities and responsibilities through such obvious manoeuvres. Controlling shareholders are obviously most at risk of being classified as shadow directors[11].

1 Table A, art 70.
2 This is frequently the case in larger companies which may have audit and remuneration committees, for example. The pitfalls of giving too much power to committees are evident from the Guinness saga.
3 Table A, art 72.
4 Ibid, art 88 ff.
5 Ibid, art 89.
6 Ibid, art 93.
7 Ibid, art 88.
8 CA 1985, s 382. There is no provision, however, for inspection of such minutes. The minutes of general meetings, on the other hand, are available for inspection by any member, s 383.
9 It is possible therefore to be a director in legal terms while being described as a manager or governor, for example. Equally, companies may describe employees as technical directors, for example, which does not make them directors in the legal sense.
10 See Pennington Company Law (6th edn, 1990) p 531 for a full list of the relevant provisions.
11 But it is necessary to show that the directors are accustomed to act on their directions or instructions, it is not enough just to show that the directors are their nominees, see Kuwait Asia Bank EC v National Mutual Life Nominees Ltd [1990] 3 All ER 404, [1990] BCLC 868, PC.

However, the scope of this category has not yet been fully determined with attention being focused recently on the question of whether it might in certain circumstances encompass the company's bankers. The problem is that in difficult economic conditions, banks may be very actively involved in the conduct of the affairs of their debtor companies and there is concern that this degree of involvement may result in their being categorised as shadow directors. This is particularly crucial in the context of liability for wrongful trading under s 214 of the Insolvency Act 1986 which applies to shadow directors. Wrongful trading occurs when a company has gone into insolvent liquidation and it is established that there was a point in time before that occurred when the directors or shadow directors knew or ought to have known that there was no reasonable prospect of avoiding insolvent liquidation. In such circumstances a liquidator can ask the court to order such directors to make such contribution to the company's assets as it thinks proper[12]. If it is possible to treat banks as shadow directors for these purposes, then clearly liquidators have a 'deep pocket' from which to recover contributions. The point was first considered in *Re a Company (No 005009 of 1987), ex p Copp*[13], where Knox J refused to strike out the liquidator's claim to treat the bank as a shadow director[14], for in his opinion it could not be said that the claim that the bank acted as a shadow director was obviously unsustainable. Unfortunately the point was not pursued at the full hearing of the case which was decided on other grounds[15]. Nevertheless, the case drew the attention of the banking community to the potential scope of this provision[16].

Another situation which may give rise to a shadow directorship is the relationship between parent and subsidiary companies. It is clearly possible for a parent company to find itself a shadow director of its subsidiary when the level of control which it exercises is such that the directors of the subsidiary are accustomed to act in accordance with its directions or instructions. However, it will be a question of fact in each case as to whether this level of control exists. A limited exemption for holding companies is to be found in s 741(3).

The articles may also provide for the appointment of alternate directors. Such a director is appointed by a director and is entitled generally to perform all the functions of his appointor, as a director, in his absence[17]. Worker directors, on the other hand, are directors appointed to represent the company's employees and are accepted by some but not all the member states of the EC. Efforts continue to harmonise the law governing such representatives[18].

---

12 There is a defence available under s 214(3) if the court is satisfied that the directors took every step to minimise loss to creditors, see discussion of s 214 in Ch 39 post.
13 [1989] BCLC 13.
14 The liquidator alleged that the directors had implemented recommendations contained in a report prepared by the bank on the company's position and were therefore acting on the instructions of the bank.
15 The case was subsequently reported as *Re M C Bacon Ltd* [1990] BCLC 324. The liquidator at that stage abandoned his original claim that the bank was a shadow director, a decision which Millett J described as rightfully abandoned which suggests he was not persuaded of the argument, see [1990] BCLC 324 at 326.
16 There have since been calls for an amendment to the definition to make clear that it is not applicable to financial institutions in such cases. The argument in favour of such an exclusion being that the effect of treating banks as shadow directors will be to impede their rescue efforts when a company is in difficulty.
17 See Table A, arts 65–69.
18 See Chapter 3.

A further distinction is between executive and non-executive directors, ie between those involved in the day-to-day running of the business and those more independent of the actual management of the business who bring an outside perspective to the board's deliberations and who are more concerned with general policy and overall supervision.

Not all companies have non-executive directors although there has been a campaign for increased used of non-executives, particularly in public companies[19]. At the forefront of the campaign has been a body called PRO NED[20] sponsored by such bodies as the Bank of England, the CBI and the Institutional Shareholders' Committee, which has issued a code of recommended practice on non-executive directors[1]. That code, which recommends a minimum proportion of non-executive directors depending on the size of the company, sets out the main tasks of the non-executive as being to contribute an independent view of the board's deliberations, to help the board provide the company with effective leadership, to ensure the continuing effectiveness of the executive directors and management, and to ensure high standards of financial probity on the part of the company. The code also recommends that companies should have audit, appointments and remuneration committees, the majority of whose members should be non-executive directors.

Executive directors, for their part, will generally have extensive powers delegated to them by the articles. They will also have separate service contracts with the company which together with the articles will delimit their powers and responsibilities[2].

It must finally be stressed that while the distinction between executive and non-executive directors is well established as a matter of business practice, the law does not distinguish between the categories and each is subject to the full range of legal duties and responsibilities discussed in greater detail in subsequent chapters.

Appointment

The power to appoint directors is usually vested by the articles in the company in general meeting[3], although the board normally has power[4] to fill casual vacancies[5]. Such an appointment is held only until the next following annual

---

19 The latest annual report of PRO NED (8th, 1990) reports that non-executive directors now occupy 44% of board seats and 99% of Britain's 200 largest companies now have non-executives on their boards.

20 Many other groups and commentators have argued strongly in recent years for increased use of non-executives: indeed some would argue that they should be mandatory. See generally, 'The Role and Duties of Directors – A Statement of Best Practice', Institutional Shareholders Committee (1991); 'The Role and Duties of Directors, A Discussion Paper', Association of British Insurers (June 1990); Carkham 'Corporate Governance and the market for companies: aspects of the shareholders' role', Bank of England Discussion Paper No 44, November 1989; Cadbury, *Owners and Investors in Creative Tension?* (1990). See also Marsh, *Short Termism on Trial* (1990), pp 90–93 who notes that non-executive directors may not actually be particularly independent or effective.

1 Latest version, June 1990. See generally, Jacobs [1987] JBL 269.

2 *Harold Holdsworth & Co (Wakefield) Ltd v Caddies* [1955] 1 All ER 725, [1955] 1 WLR 352, HL.

3 Table A, arts 73–80.

4 Ibid, art 79.

5 Defined as 'any vacancy not occurring by effluxion of time, that is any vacancy occurring by death, resignation or bankruptcy': *York Tramways Co Ltd v Willows* (1882) 8 QBD 685 at 694, CA, per Lord Coleridge CJ.

general meeting when the appointee can be re-elected[6]. As has already been noted, an individual director may appoint an alternate to act in his absence[7].

Board representation is frequently a contractual term on a sale of shares. In *Wilton Group plc v Abrams*[8] the court found such a term objectionable in relation to a public listed company, although it accepted that the position would be different in a private company where all the shareholders agreed. Board appointments are a matter for the company in general meeting, not for the private disposition of vendors and purchasers. In the absence of fraud or bad faith, a shareholder or other person who controls the appointment of a director owes no duty to creditors of the company to take reasonable care that directors so appointed discharge their duties as directors with due diligence and competence[9].

In the case of a public company, each proposed director must be voted on individually unless there is unanimous consent to a block resolution[10]. This is to ensure that shareholders can express their disapproval of any particular director without having to reject the entire board. Failure to comply with this requirement means that the resolution is void[11]. It is not entirely without effect, however, as s 285 will apply. Section 285 provides that the acts of a director or manager shall be valid notwithstanding any defect which may afterwards be discovered in his appointment or qualification. This covers the situation where there has been some innocent, technical, breach of the requirements with the result that the appointment is invalid[12]. It does not validate the acts of someone who has never been appointed at all but who simply purports to fill the office of director[13], although in some circumstances the company may still be bound by the acts of that person[14]. Note also s 42 of the CA 1985 which provides that a company cannot rely against other persons on any change among the company's directors if that change has not been notified in the *London Gazette*[15]. Finally, it should be noted that it is not the case that a director must necessarily be an individual and a company may be appointed[16].

Number

A private company need have only one director whereas a public company must have at least two[17]. The number of directors may, from time to time, be increased or reduced by ordinary resolution[18].

6 Table A, art 79.
7 Ibid, arts 65–69.
8 [1990] BCC 310.
9 *Kuwait Asia Bank EC v National Mutual Life Nominees Ltd* [1990] 3 All ER 404, [1990] BCLC 868, PC.
10 CA 1985, s 292.
11 Ibid.
12 *British Asbestos Co Ltd v Boyd* [1903] 2 Ch 439.
13 *Morris v Kanssen* [1946] AC 459, [1946] 1 All ER 586, HL.
14 See discussion post Ch 24.
15 The effect of the section is purely negative. It does not entitle the company to treat the gazetting of an event as notice to all the world, *Official Custodian for Charities v Parway Estates Developments Ltd* [1985] Ch 151, [1984] 3 All ER 679, CA.
16 *Re Bulawayo Market and Offices Co Ltd* [1907] 2 Ch 458. CA 1985, s 289(1)(b) provides that the register of directors should include the corporate name and registered office of any company holding the office of director.
17 CA 1985, s 282, unless the company was incorporated before 1 November 1929 in which case one director will suffice. Note Table A, art 64, which provides that the number of directors shall not be less than two.
18 Table A, art 64.

Age

A person aged 70 or more cannot be appointed as a director of a public company, or of a private company which is a subsidiary of a public company, unless the appointment is approved by the company in general meeting[19]. A director of such a company who reaches 70 must retire unless his retention as a director is approved by the company in general meeting[20]. These restrictions are all subject to the provisions of the company's articles which may permit the appointment and retention of directors over the 70 year limit[1]. No age restrictions apply to directors of private companies which are not subsidiaries of public companies.

Share qualification

The articles may provide that an individual cannot be appointed a director unless he holds a certain (usually very small) number of shares in the company. The number required will be determined by the company in general meeting and unless and until so fixed no qualification will be required. A share qualification is usually justified on the ground that it ensures that management have a personal commitment to the company and its well-being[2]. In fact, of course, managerial commitment is more likely to be ensured by remuneration packages (bonus payments, etc) linked to the company's performance than by any minuscule share qualification requirement designed to induce a sense of 'ownership'.

If the company's articles do impose a share qualification on would-be directors, then s 291 of CA 1985 provides that the shares must be obtained within two months[3] of the director's appointment or within such shorter time as may be fixed by the articles. If the time limit set by the articles or s 291 elapses without the shares being acquired, then the office of director is vacated; likewise if a director, having initially acquired his qualification shares, thereafter at any time ceases to hold them[4]. If the company increases the amount of shares to be held, the office of director is not immediately vacated but if the director in question continues as a director, he is deemed to have contracted to acquire the necessary shares within a reasonable time[5]. If a director continues in office and continues to act despite being unqualified, by virtue of not holding the requisite shareholding, then he is liable to a fine under s 291(5).

Remuneration

The starting point is that the mere holding of office by itself does not entitle a director to remuneration[6]. That is a matter for the articles. However, the

---

19 CA 1985, s 293.
20 Special notice must be given of any resolution to approve the appointment or retention of any such director: CA 1985, s 293(5).
1 CA 1985, s 293(7).
2 *Re North Australian Territory Co, Archer's Case* [1892] 1 Ch 322 at 337, CA, per Lindley MR.
3 The two month period runs from the date of ascertaining the result of the poll electing the director: *Holmes v Keyes* [1959] Ch 199, [1958] 2 All ER 129, CA.
4 CA 1985, s 291(3).
5 *Molineaux v London, Birmingham and Manchester Insurance Co Ltd* [1902] 2 KB 589, CA.
6 *Hutton v West Cork Rly Co* (1883) 23 Ch D 654, CA.

articles invariably provide, as in Table A, art 82, that remuneration for the directors shall from time to time be determined by the company in general meeting[7]. Alternatively, the power may be delegated to the board and art 84, Table A, provides that the board may determine the remuneration of the managing and executive directors. In larger public companies, the task is frequently delegated to a remuneration committee, usually composed mainly of non-executive directors.

There is a further consideration, namely that directors divide into two categories, those with service contracts and those without, which in practice is often a distinction between executive directors with contracts and non-executive directors without. Where there is a service contract, the company has already identified the appropriate level of remuneration and undertaken contractually to pay it, so few difficulties arise[8].

The position is more complicated where there is no contract thus throwing the director back to the general position as dictated by the articles of the particular company. If there is a provision in the articles which requires either the general meeting or the directors or a committee of the directors to determine the amount of the remuneration and the correct body has not done so, then the director has no claim for payment under the articles[9]. It may be possible, however, for a director to pursue a claim to recover on a quantum meruit basis for services rendered and accepted by the company[10], as in the case where due to some default or other, the director finds that a contract which he had relied on turns out to be non-existent[11]. However, the position on quantum meruit claims has been restrictively stated in *Guinness plc v Saunders*[12].

In this case the board of Guinness had delegated to a committee of the board the power to conduct the takeover bid by the company for Distillers plc. The committee agreed to pay, and the company paid, £5.2m to a member of that committee, Ward, in return for his services in connection with the

---

7 And the general meeting may resolve to pay a director for the mere holding of office, even if he undertakes no specific duties: *Re Halt Garage (1964) Ltd* [1982] 3 All ER 1016.
8 It must be remembered that a director cannot rely on the articles as constituting a contract between himself and the company: *Hickman v Kent or Romney Marsh Sheep-Breeders' Association* [1915] 1 Ch 881; CA 1985, s 14. To allow him to do so would be to enforce an outsider right, something which the courts have refused to do. Occasionally, however, the courts may imply a contract extrinsic to the articles: *Re New British Iron Co, ex p Beckwick* [1898] 1 Ch 324. On the nature of the articles as a contract, see the discussion in Ch 11 above.
9 *Guinness plc v Saunders* [1990] 2 AC 663, [1990] 1 All ER 652, HL.
10 *Craven-Ellis v Canons Ltd* [1936] 2 KB 403, [1936] 2 All ER 1066, CA. *Re Richmond Gate Property Co Ltd* [1964] 3 All ER 936, [1965] 1 WLR 335, noted (1965) 28 MLR 317, (1966) 29 MLR 608, would appear to suggest the contrary but the case had been regarded as being of doubtful authority since the refusal there of quantum meruit arose from the erroneous finding that the articles created a contract between the company and its managing director. *Guinness plc v Saunders* [1990] 2 AC 663, [1990] 1 All ER 652, HL, discussed below, would support the general outcome in *Re Richmond Gate Property Co Ltd*, namely that there may be no room for quantum meruit when the articles have made express provision for the payment of remuneration, but on a different basis. It makes more sense to refuse relief, as Lord Goff did, in *Guinness plc v Saunders* because equity should not provide any encouragement to fiduciaries to put themselves in a position where their duties as fiduciaries conflicted with their interests.
11 *Craven-Ellis v Canons Ltd* [1936] 2 KB 403, [1936] 2 All ER 1066, CA.
12 [1990] 2 AC 663, [1990] 1 All ER 652, HL, noted at [1990] JBL 178, Beatson & Prentice (1990) 106 LQR 365; Hopkins (1990) CLJ 220; Birks [1990] LMCLQ 330.

bid. The articles of association, however, provided that the remuneration of directors, be it annual or special remuneration for additional services, was a matter for the board. The House of Lords found, despite a lack of clarity and various inconsistencies in the articles, that the committee did not have authority to act in this way and could not have entered into a contract to award special remuneration to Ward for services rendered in connection with the bid. There was therefore no contract between Guinness and Ward to pay him £5.2m and the company was entitled to a return of the money.

Ward then sought to recover all or some of the £5.2m on the basis of quantum meruit or an equitable allowance in respect of the services rendered. This was rejected by the House of Lords.

Lord Goff's starting point was that directors must not put themselves in a position where there is a conflict between their personal interests and their duties as fiduciaries, and so they are for that reason precluded from contracting with the company for their services except in circumstances authorised by the articles of association[13]. He went on to say that it would be inconsistent with this long established principle to award remuneration in such circumstances as of right on the basis of a quantum meruit claim. But, he said, the principle does not altogether exclude the possibility that an equitable allowance might be made in respect of services rendered. This equitable jurisdiction could be exercised, however, only if it did not conflict with the policy underlying the rule, ie if it did not provide any encouragement to fiduciaries to put themselves in a position where their duties as fiduciaries conflicted with their interests[14]. He went on to query whether any such allowance might ever be granted in the case of a director of a company (Lord Templeman thought not[15]) which might be said to involve interference by the court in the administration of the company's affairs where the company is not being wound up. In any event, there was no possibility of granting such an allowance in this case. Ward's interests were in stark conflict with his duty as a director of Guinness. If the board of Guinness saw fit, they might still remunerate him for his services but the court would not award an equitable allowance.

Lord Templeman's speech is perhaps more opaque[16] but the overall tenor is the same. His starting point too was the principle that a fiduciary must not place himself in a position of conflict and may not profit from his position except to the extent permitted by the articles. Neither quantum meruit nor equitable allowance should be allowed to dimish that rule and allow recovery of remuneration in circumstances wider than those expressly envisaged by the articles[17].

---

13 [1990] 2 AC 663 at 700, [1990] 1 All ER 652 at 666, HL.
14 [1990] 2 AC 663 at 701, [1990] 1 All ER 652 at 667, HL. He distinguished *Phipps v Boardman* [1964] 2 All ER 187, [1964] 1 WLR 993, where an allowance was awarded, on this basis. See Beatson & Prentice (1990) 106 LQR 365 at 367 on this point, who note the difficulty of reconciling it with the approach in *O'Sullivan v Management Agency & Music Ltd* [1985] QB 428, CA, where an allowance was made. A better distinction, they suggest, is that in *Guinness plc v Saunders*, the profit was made by the fiduciary actually taking company property.
15 It should be noted that Lords Keith, Brandon and Griffiths agreed with Lord Templeman's speech. Lord Griffiths also agreed with Lord Goff.
16 In particular, his reliance on an implied contract approach to quantum meruit claims has been criticised and his interpretation of *Craven-Ellis v Canons Ltd* [1936] 2 KB 403, CA questioned, see Beatson & Prentice (1990) 106 LQR 365 at 367; Birks [1990] LMCLQ 330.
17 [1990] 2 AC 663 at 689, [1990] 1 All ER 652 at 659, HL.

The best method of avoiding all of these difficulties is for executive directors to have express service contracts with the company which provide for their remuneration. Restrictions on the length of such contracts are discussed at the end of this Chapter.

Where remuneration is paid, the courts will not normally concern themselves with the quantum of that remuneration. In particular, they will not attempt to compare the market value of the services rendered with the amount of remuneration actually paid[18]. They will, however, wish to ensure that the payment is genuinely remuneration and not a sham transaction masking an improper return of capital to the shareholders[19]. Excessive payments at a time when the company is in financial difficulties may be the subject of misfeasance proceedings by the liquidator under s 212 of the Insolvency Act 1986 or indeed as a transaction at an undervalue under s 238 of that Act[20]. Such payments may also be the subject of a s 459 petition alleging unfairly prejudicial conduct in the appropriate case[1].

A related issue concerns the payment of (usually large) sums of money to directors as compensation on the loss of, or retirement from, office. This is governed by s 312 which provides that it is not lawful for a company to make any payment by way of compensation for loss of office, or as consideration for or in connection with retirement from office, without particulars of the proposed payment being disclosed to members of the company and the proposal being approved by the company[2]. The section only applies to payments to directors in connection with their office as directors and does not apply, for example, to payments to them in respect of any post they may have had as employees of the company. It only applies to gratuitous, uncovenanted, payments and does not cover any payments which the company is contractually bound to make[3], nor does it apply to any bona fide payments by way of damages for breach of contract, or any payments by way of pension in respect of past services[4]. These exceptions, it can be appreciated, are wide enough to ensure that few of these 'golden handshakes', as they are called, need the approval demanded by s 312.

18   *Re Halt Garage (1964) Ltd* [1982] 3 All ER 1016. See Oliver J at 1039 who notes '. . . assuming that the sum is bona fide voted to be paid as remuneration, it seems to me that the amount, whether it be mean or generous, must be a matter of management for the company to determine in accordance with its constitution which expressly authorises payment for directors' services. Shareholders are required to be honest but . . . there is no requirement that they must be wise and it is not for the courts to manage the company.'
19   Ibid.
20   See *Re Horsley & Weight Ltd* [1982] Ch 442, [1982] 3 All ER 1045, CA. Directors may also find themselves the subject of proceedings under the Theft Act 1968, see *A-G's Reference (No 2 of 1982)* [1984] QB 624, [1984] 2 All ER 216, CA. The level of remuneration paid might, in an appropriate case, be relevant as evidence of unfitness of directors in disqualification proceedings, as where they have maintained their own lifestyle at the expense of the company's creditors, see *Re Keypak Homecare Ltd* [1990] BCLC 440 at 444.
 1   See *Re Cumana Ltd* [1986] BCLC 430, CA.
 2   Similar provisions apply where a payment is made in a take-over situation: CA 1985, ss 313–315. If the payment is made by way of transfer of a non-cash asset then the provisions of s 320, discussed in Ch 26, may also apply, though this has yet to be finally determined. Tolley's *Company Law* (1990) para D5026, relying on an unreported case, *Gooding v Cater* (1989), suggests that this is not in fact the case but as yet no definitive guidance has emerged from the courts.
 3   *Taupo Totaro Timber Co Ltd v Rowe* [1978] AC 537, [1977] 3 All ER 123, PC; Cartoon (1978) 94 LQR 492; Nelson (1978) CLJ 30.
 4   CA 1985, s 316(3). 'Pension' here includes any superannuation allowance, superannuation gratuity or similar payment.

Details of directors' remuneration and compensation for loss of office must be included in notes to the accounts[5] and details of service contracts must be available for inspection by any member at the company's registered office[6].

Disqualification

One of the major concerns of Parliament in passing the Insolvency Act 1985 was to curb the activities of directors who shelter behind the corporate form and limited liability and who, having put a company into insolvent liquidation, promptly set up in business immediately thereafter and start the whole cycle again[7]. The Companies Act 1985 already provided for disqualification on certain grounds but it was decided to strengthen and extend those provisions. This was done in the Insolvency Act 1985 and the provisions were subsequently consolidated and re-enacted as the Company Directors Disqualification Act 1986[8]. It should be noted that many of the provisions of that Act are not limited to directors but they remain the primary group at risk of disqualification.

GROUNDS FOR DISQUALIFICATION

There are several grounds for disqualification. They are:

(a) being convicted of an indictable offence;
(b) persistent default;
(c) fraud;
(d) disqualification when made personally liable;
(e) undischarged bankrupts;
(f)   unfit directors of insolvent companies;
(g) disqualification after investigation.

Each will now be considered in turn.

(a) CONVICTED OF AN INDICTABLE OFFENCE

Section 2 provides that where a person is convicted of an indictable offence (whether on indictment or summarily) in connection with the promotion, formation, management or liquidation of a company, or with the receivership or management of a company's property, then the court may make a disqualification order against that person[9]. This provision is widely drafted and covers any offence 'in connection with' any aspect of the birth, life and

---

5 CA 1985, s 232 and Sch 6, Part 1, as substituted by CA 1989, s 6(3) and Sch 4.
6 CA 1985, s 318, or at any other appropriate pl   specified in CA 1985, s 318(3).
7 The Report of the Review Committee on Insolvency Law and Practice (the Cork Committee), Cmnd 8558, had found widespread concern at the apparent inability of the law to deal adequately with such individuals, see Chapters 43, 45 of that Report. For a recent illustration of the type of conduct which concerned the Committee, see *Re Travel Mondial (UK) Ltd* [1991] BCLC 120.
8 The legislation and the growing body of case law on it has attracted considerable comment, see, in particular, Sealy *Disqualification and Personal Liability of Directors* (3rd edn, 1989); Drake [1989] JBL 474; Finch (1990) 53 MLR 385; Dine (1991) 12 Co Law 6, (1988) 9 Co Law 213; Hicks [1988] JBL 27, (1987) 8 Co Law 243; Hannigan [1987] LMCLQ 188.
9 This provision meant that it was possible in the Guinness trial for the court to have disqualified those convicted and there was some dismay that the court did not avail itself of this option. The trial judge subsequently indicated that he had considered this option but did not think it necessary or appropriate in respect of the individuals concerned.

death of the company and extends to the conduct of both the internal and external affairs of the company[10].

(b) PERSISTENT DEFAULT

Section 3 provides that where it appears that a person[11] has been persistently[12] in default in relation to the provisions of the companies legislation requiring any return, account or other document to be filed with, delivered or sent, or notice of any matter to be given, to the registrar of companies, then the court may make a disqualification order against that person.

The fact that a person has been persistently in default may be conclusively proved by showing that in the five years ending with the date of the application he has been adjudged guilty (whether or not on the same occasion) of three or more defaults[13] in relation to the provisions of the Act[14]. Two cases, *Re Civica Investments Ltd*[15] and *Re Arctic Engineering Ltd (No 2)*[16], illustrate the court's powers under this section.

In *Re Civica Investments Ltd*, A was the sole director of a number of companies, some of which had never traded at all or had traded only on a very limited scale. Nevertheless a large number of defaults had occurred over a period of years and A had been convicted in respect of 59 defaults involving failure to file accounts and annual returns. Nourse J decided that it would be improper not to impose any period of disqualification in view of the extensive number of defaults. However, he limited the disqualification order to one year. The longer periods of disqualification, the court felt, ought to be reserved for cases of a serious nature involving dishonest purpose or a deliberate or wilful default.

Re Arctic Engineering Ltd (No 2)[17] involved proceedings against a liquidator, a busy accountant, who was in default in relation to 35 returns regarding the liquidation/receivership of some 34 companies. Notwithstanding the evidence of persistent default, Hoffmann J decided that a disqualification order was not necessary to protect the public and would have serious consequences for the liquidator, his staff and clients. It was sufficient to caution him as to his future conduct.

(c) FRAUD

Section 4 provides that if, in the course of the winding up of a company, it appears that a person has been guilty of an offence for which he is liable (whether he has been convicted or not) under s 458 of the Companies Act

---

10 *R v Austen* (1985) 1 BCC 99, 528; *R v Corbin* (1984) 6 Cr App Rep (S) 17; *R v Georgiou* (1988) 4 BCC 322, CA.
11 As the provision covers any person, the company secretary will frequently be the person risking disqualification, for his duties will generally include ensuring that the appropriate returns are filed with the registrar of companies and as such he will be the officer in default.
12 'Persistent' means nothing more than that there should be some degree of continuance or repetition; *Re Arctic Engineering Ltd (No 2)* [1986] 2 All ER 346, [1986] 1 WLR 686.
13 CDDA 1986, s 3(3) defines the circumstances in which a person will be adjudged guilty of a default.
14 CDDA 1986, s 3(2), but this is without prejudice to its proof in any other manner.
15 [1983] BCLC 456.
16 [1986] 2 All ER 346, [1986] 1 WLR 686.
17 Ibid.

1985 (fraudulent trading), or has otherwise been guilty, while an officer[18] or liquidator of the company or receiver or manager of its property, of any fraud in relation to the company or of any breach of his duty as such officer, liquidator, receiver or manager, then the court may make a disqualification order against that person.

(d) DISQUALIFICATION WHEN MADE PERSONALLY LIABLE

Section 10 provides that the court may, regardless of whether any application is made or not, disqualify any person against whom a contribution order has been made under s 213 (fraudulent trading) or s 214 (wrongful trading) of the Insolvency Act 1986. Fraudulent trading involves trading with intent to defraud creditors. Wrongful trading occurs if a company goes into insolvent liquidation and at some time before the commencement of the winding up of the company, a director or shadow director knew or ought to have concluded that there was no reasonable prospect that the company would avoid going into insolvent liquidation. In both cases a person may be required to make such contribution to the company's assets as the court thinks proper. Disqualification is then an additional penalty for such offences.

(e) UNDISCHARGED BANKRUPTS

The one instance when disqualification is automatic is in the case of an undischarged bankrupt who by s 11 is prohibited from acting as a director of, or directly or indirectly taking part in or being concerned in the promotion, formation or management of, a company save with the leave of the court by which he was adjudged bankrupt[19].

(f) UNFIT DIRECTORS OF INSOLVENT COMPANIES

The original provision here was s 9 of the Insolvency Act 1976, subsequently amended and consolidated as s 300 of the Companies Act 1985, which provided for disqualification, at the court's discretion, where a person had been a director of at least two companies which had gone into insolvent liquidation within five years of each other and whose conduct made him unfit to be a director. Largely ineffective, few orders were made under the provision and it was repealed by the Insolvency Act 1985.

The Cork Committee[20] had been in favour of some form of automatic disqualification to deal with this problem, a view which the government initially endorsed[1]. Opposed on all sides, that proposal had to be abandoned and less sweeping provisions inserted in its place.

---

18 It should be noted that 'officer' includes a director, manager or secretary, CDDA 1986, s 22(6) applying s 744, CA 1985, and shadow director, CDDA 1986, s 4(2). Shadow directors are persons in accordance with whose directions or instructions the directors of a company are accustomed to act, excluding those persons who give such instructions in a professional capacity, s 22(5).
19 CDDA 1986, s 12 also provides for disqualification where a court under s 429 of the Insolvency Act 1986 revokes an administration order under Part IV of the County Courts Act 1984 where an individual debtor has failed to comply with his obligations under that administration order.
20 Report of the Review Committee on Insolvency Law and Practice, Cmnd 8558, Chapter 45.
1 A Revised Framework for Insolvency Law, Cmnd 9175, Chapter 2. See Hicks [1988] JBL 27 at 39 on the merits and demerits of automatic disqualification.

Basic scheme　Section 7(3) provides that if it appears to an official receiver, liquidator, administrator or administrative receiver (collectively referred to as the office holder) that the conditions mentioned in s 6 are satisfied, i e that in the case of a person who is or has been a director or shadow director[2] of a company which has become insolvent[3], that his conduct as a director, either considered in isolation or taken together with his conduct as a director of any other company, makes him unfit to be concerned with the management of a company, he must forthwith report the matter to the Secretary of State.

Following a report from the office holder, the Secretary of State may apply[4] for a disqualification order if it appears to him expedient in the public interest that an order should be made against any person[5]. An application by the Secretary of State shall not be made more than two years after the day on which the company became insolvent[6] without the leave of the court[7]. If the Secretary of State does decide to apply to the court, then s 6 provides that the court shall make a disqualification order if it is satisfied that that person is unfit to be concerned in the management of a company[8].

Unfitness　In deciding whether a person is unfit s 9 provides that the court shall have regard, in particular, to the matters specified in Schedule 1 to the Act[9], Part 1 of which is applicable in all cases, Part II of which is applicable only if the company has become insolvent. In relation to applications under s 6, therefore, both parts of the Schedule will be relevant.

Part 1 requires the court to have regard to:

(i)　any misfeasance or breach of any fiduciary or other duty;
(ii)　any misapplication or retention by a director of, or any conduct giving rise to an obligation to account for, any money or other property of the company;
(iii)　the director's responsibility for the company entering into transactions liable to be set aside under the Insolvency Act 1986;
(iv)　the director's responsibility for the company's failure to comply with various disclosure requirements;
(v)　the director's responsibility for any failure to comply with accounting requirements.

2　CDDA 1986, s 6(3). See discussion above of who is a shadow director.
3　Defined for these purposes by s 6(2) to include not just a company which has gone into insolvent winding up but also a company in administration or under the control of an administrative receiver.
4　Or the Official Receiver acting on the instructions of the Secretary of State in a case where the company is being compulsorily wound up, s 7(1)(b).
5　CDDA 1986, s 7(1).
6　CDDA 1986, s 7(2). This has been interpreted by the courts to mean two years from the happening of the first of the events specified in s 6(2), *Re Tasbian Ltd (No 1)* [1991] BCLC 54. See Fletcher [1989] JBL 365 at 375 and Finch (1990) 53 MLR 385 at 390 who suggest that this time limit may work to the delinquent directors' advantage and against the public interest.
7　For the circumstances in which leave will be granted or refused, see *Re Crestjoy Products Ltd* [1990] BCLC 677; *Re Cedac Ltd* [1990] BCC 555.
8　270 disqualification orders were made on grounds of unfitness in 1989, 257 in 1988 and 145 in 1987: Annual Reports of the Insolvency Service.
9　As amended by CA 1989, s 139(4), Sch 10, para 35(3); Sch 16, para 4. The Schedule is not exclusive and the Secretary of State retains the power to alter it by statutory instrument, s 9(4)–(5).

Part II requires the court to have regard to:

(i) the director's responsibility for the causes of the company becoming insolvent;

(ii) the director's responsibility for any failure by the company to supply any goods or services which have been wholly or partly paid for;

(iii) the director's responsibility for the company entering into any transaction at an undervalue or giving any preference;

(iv) the director's responsibility for any failure by the directors to comply with the requirements of the Insolvency Act in relation to creditors' meetings;

(v) any failure by the director to supply any statement of affairs or to co-operate with any office holder under the Insolvency Act.

In fact, the courts appear to pay little attention, at least explicitly, to this Schedule[10] but instead, as an increasing number of cases have come before them, have constructed their own schedule of significant factors which must be considered when deciding whether someone should be disqualified.

Before considering the criteria emerging from the cases, it should be noted that many of the cases arose under the old provision, s 300, the requirements of which were slightly different from s 6 although the primary requirement in either case is a finding of unfitness[11]. In considering that requirement there is no discernible difference in judicial attitude depending on whether the section being relied on is s 6 or s 300. It might also be noted that practically all of the cases have presented almost identical facts: most have involved individuals who have been directors of a number of insolvent companies over a relatively short period of time, perhaps four or five companies over four or five years. All of these companies will have suffered from inadequate capitalisation, many will have traded insolvently throughout their existence and Crown debts may have been used to continue trading whilst insolvent.

The starting point for the courts is that disqualification is designed to protect the public against the future conduct of business through companies by persons whose past records as directors of insolvent companies have shown them to be a danger to creditors and others[12]. That this is the key element is evident from the wording of the statute itself which requires that it be expedient in the public interest for them to be disqualified. It is frequently asserted by the courts that disqualification is not intended as a punitive

---

10 Of course, the Schedule does not apply to s 300 cases so it may become more prominent as an increasing number of s 6 cases progress through the courts.

11 The most significant difference between the provisions was that under s 300, even where there was a finding of unfitness, the courts had a discretion as to whether or not to disqualify. Under s 6, once there is a finding of unfitness, there is mandatory disqualification for at least two years, s 6(1), (4).

12 *Re Lo-Line Electric Motors Ltd* [1988] Ch 477 at 486, [1988] 2 All ER 692 at 696, per Browne-Wilkinson V-C. See also *Re Sevenoaks Stationers (Retail) Ltd* [1990] 3 WLR 1165; *Re Cedac Ltd* [1990] BCC 555; *Re Crestjoy Products Ltd* [1990] BCLC 677 at 681; *Re Jaymar Management Ltd* [1990] BCLC 617 at 622; *Re Ipcon Fashions Ltd* (1989) 5 BCC 773; *Re Rolus Properties Ltd* (1988) 4 BCC 446 at 447; *Re Western Welsh International System Buildings Ltd* (1988) 4 BCC 449. See the interesting note by Finch (1990) 53 MLR 385 who questions whether the courts really are concerned with a purely protective principle in these cases.

measure although the courts recognise that removing the privilege of trading through a limited liability company may significantly constrain the freedom of that individual to carry on business and as such has a result which can be described as penal[13].

Equally at the forefront of the judicial approach has been a constant assertion that limited liability is a privilege which carries with it certain duties and obligations which must be carried out[14]. These are duties which fall on each director who cannot, as they have tried to do in a number of cases, pass the blame to another director or employee[15]. As Browne-Wilkinson V-C noted in *Re Lo-Line Electric Motors Ltd*[16], a director cannot consistently with his duties abdicate all responsibility for financial management.

As far as the standard of behaviour indicating unfitness warranting disqualification is concerned, this remains a matter of debate. An initial formulation was that it must be conduct which amounts to a breach of commercial morality[17], a notion which was never fully defined and which was rejected by Peter Gibson J in *Re Churchill Hotel (Plymouth) Ltd*[18].

The approach more commonly adopted now is that of Browne-Wilkinson V-C in *Re Lo-Line Electric Motors Ltd*[19], that the conduct complained of must display a lack of commercial probity, although, he continued, 'I have no doubt that in an extreme case of gross negligence or total incompetence disqualification could be appropriate.'

At one end of the scale, there is the dishonest conduct of a company's affairs, the cynical exploitation of the privilege of trading through limited liability, which would certainly indicate a lack of commercial probity and warrant disqualification. On the other hand, an ordinary commercial misjudgment is in itself not sufficient to justify disqualification[20]. Entrepreneurs must be allowed to take risks without bankrupting themselves. It is the middle ground between these two ends of the spectrum where matters are most uncertain. Certainly, as the cases show, the courts are prepared to disqualify in this middle area where there is no dishonesty as such but nonetheless irresponsible and incompetent management leading to insolvency[1]. However, honesty will often counter-balance lesser incompetence

---

13 Ibid. See Finch (1990) 53 MLR 385 who argues that there is a significant punitive element in many of these decisions. Also Dine (1988) 9 Co Law 213 who discusses this judicial confusion as to the nature of disqualification proceedings and explores its significance.

14 *Re Stanford Services Ltd* [1987] BCLC 607 at 619, per Vinelott J. See also *Re Majestic Recording Studios Ltd* [1989] BCLC 1 at 6; *Re Ipcon Fashions Ltd* (1989) 5 BCC 773 at 775; *Re Bath Glass Ltd* [1988] BCLC 329; *Re Douglas Construction Services Ltd* [1988] BCLC 397; *Re J & B Lynch (Builders) Ltd* [1988] BCLC 376 at 380; *Re Rolus Properties Ltd* (1988) 4 BCC 446 at 447; *Re Western Welsh International System Buildings Ltd* (1988) 4 BCC 449.

15 *Re Majestic Recording Studios Ltd* [1989] BCLC 1; *Re Lo-Line Electric Motors Ltd* [1988] Ch 477, [1988] 2 All ER 692.

16 [1988] Ch 477 at 491, [1988] 2 All ER 692 at 701.

17 *Re Dawson Print Group Ltd* [1987] BCLC 601, per Hoffmann J.

18 [1988] BCLC 341 at 347.

19 [1988] Ch 477 at 486, [1988] 2 All ER 692 at 696. See *Re Keypak Homecare Ltd* [1990] BCLC 440; *Re C U Fittings Ltd* [1989] BCLC 556; *Re Cedac Ltd* [1990] BCC 555.

20 *Re Lo-Line Electric Motors Ltd* [1988] Ch 477 at 486, [1988] 2 All ER 692 at 696, per Browne-Wilkinson V-C, a point emphatically repeated by him in *Re McNulty's Interchange Ltd* [1989] BCLC 709 at 712. See also *Re Douglas Construction Services Ltd* [1988] BCLC 397; *Re Cladrose Ltd* [1990] BCLC 204; *Re Cedac Ltd* [1990] BCC 555; *Re C U Fittings Ltd* [1989] BCLC 556.

 1 See *Re D J Matthews (Joinery Design) Ltd* (1988) 4 BCC 513; *Re Lo-Line Electric Motors Ltd* [1988] Ch 477, [1988] 2 All ER 692; *Re Churchill Hotel (Plymouth) Ltd* [1988] BCLC

and justify the court in not making a finding of unfitness[2]. Two factors which will be significant in deciding on which side of the line the case falls will be the failure to pay Crown debts and to file documents with Companies House.

As far as Crown debts, meaning sums due in respect of VAT, PAYE and national insurance contributions, are concerned, it is often a feature of these cases that a large amount of Crown debts is outstanding. The significance of this has been considered by the courts in a number of cases and, after some initial uncertainty[3], it became generally accepted that the use of moneys which should have been paid to the Crown to finance continuation of an insolvent company's business was more culpable than the failure to pay commercial debts[4], provided the directors knew or ought to have known that the company's continued existence was being financed in this way[5]. The reasons for treating the non-payment of these sums as more culpable had been explained by the courts as arising from the involuntary nature of the Crown as a creditor and the fact that the failure to pay over these sums may have a prejudicial effect on the employees[6].

However, the Court of Appeal in *Re Sevenoaks Stationers (Retail) Ltd*[7] has now criticised this approach, finding that the Crown's position is as it is because of its administrative practice of not pursuing these debts and that employees are not prejudiced because, as far as they are concerned, the Crown treats the sums as paid. Dillon LJ concluded that it is not sufficient to treat non-payment as evidence of unfitness, it is necessary instead to see what, if any, is the significance of that non-payment.

As for the disclosure requirements, in many of the cases the directors will have failed to fulfil their statutory obligations regarding filing annual accounts and returns with the registrar of companies. Such failures are viewed very seriously, for disclosure is part of the price to be paid for the privilege of trading through the limited liability company[8]. Notwithstanding this, a failure to maintain accounts and records is seldom sufficiently weighty

---

341; *Re Sevenoaks Stationers (Retail) Ltd* [1990] 3 WLR 1165; *Re Chartmore Ltd* [1990] BCLC 673. Of course, the absence of dishonesty may affect the period of disqualification imposed and may persuade the court to grant leave to act despite being disqualified, discussed further below.

2 *Re Bath Glass Ltd* [1988] BCLC 329.

3 There was originally some difference of approach between Vinelott J in *Re Stanford Services Ltd* [1987] BCLC 607 and Hoffmann J in *Re Dawson Print Group Ltd* [1987] BCLC 601, although the difference was probably more apparent than real.

4 *Re Lo-Line Electric Motors Ltd* [1988] Ch 477 at 488, [1988] 2 All ER 692 at 698, per Browne-Wilkinson V-C, agreeing with Vinelott J in *Re Stanford Services Ltd* [1987] BCLC 607. See also *Re Cladrose Ltd* [1990] BCLC 204; *Re C U Fittings Ltd* [1989] BCLC 556; *Re McNulty's Interchange Ltd* [1989] BCLC 709; *Re Western Welsh International System Buildings Ltd* (1988) 5 BCC 449; *Re Churchill Hotel (Plymouth) Ltd* [1988] BCLC 341.

5 *Re Bath Glass Ltd* [1988] BCLC 329 at 337, per Peter Gibson J. See also *Re Cladrose Ltd* [1990] BCLC 204; *Re C U Fittings Ltd* [1989] BCLC 556; *Re J & B Lynch Ltd* [1988] BCLC 376 at 379; *Re Churchill Hotel (Plymouth) Ltd* [1988] BCLC 341; *Re Douglas Construction Services Ltd* [1988] BCLC 397. In *Re D J Matthews (Joinery Design) Ltd* (1988) 4 BCC 513 the court found that there was a deliberate policy of not paying Crown debts.

6 *Re Stanford Services Ltd* [1987] BCLC 607; *Re Lo-Line Electric Motors Ltd* [1988] Ch 477, [1988] 2 All ER 692; *Re Cladrose Ltd* [1990] BCLC 204.

7 [1990] 3 WLR 1165.

8 See *Re Rolus Properties Ltd* (1988) 4 BCC 446; *Re Churchill Hotel (Plymouth) Ltd* [1988] BCLC 341; *Re Ipcon Fashions Ltd* (1989) 5 BCC 773; *Re Western Welsh International System Buildings Ltd* (1988) 4 BCC 449.

in itself to justify disqualification and in most of the cases it is simply one of many allegations of misconduct[9].

Redeeming factors which would be considered by the court would include whether the directors have injected their own funds into the company and so have suffered financially as well as the creditors[10], and whether they took professional advice or simply careered on to insolvency without regard to the interests of others[11].

Ultimately, this issue of unfitness is a question of fact[12], and the courts must balance the factors as they appear in an individual case.

(g) DISQUALIFICATION AFTER INVESTIGATION

If it appears to the Secretary of State[13] from a report made by inspectors under s 437 of the Companies Act 1985 or s 94 or s 177 of the Financial Services Act 1986, or from information or documents obtained under s 447 or s 448 of the Companies Act 1985 or s 105 of the Financial Services Act 1986, or s 2 of the Criminal Justice Act 1987 or s 83 of the Companies Act 1989, that it is expedient in the public interest that a disqualification order should be made against any person who is or has been a director or shadow director of any company, he may apply to the court for an order against such a person[14].

The Secretary of State would act under this section if it appeared necessary to do so from inspectors' reports under s 437 following from an investigation into the company's affairs under Part XIV of the Companies Act[15]. Reports under the Financial Services Act 1986 would follow an investigation into the affairs of any collective investment scheme or the managers, trustees or operators of such schemes (s 94), or any investigation into suspected insider dealing offences (s 177). Sections 447 and 448 of the Companies Act 1985 and s 105 of the Financial Services Act 1986 require the production of documents, records, papers, etc by a company, or by persons carrying on an investment business in certain circumstances. Section 2 of the Criminal Justice Act 1987 refers to certain investigations by the Serious Fraud Office and s 83 of the Companies Act 1989 refers to investigations carried out for the purpose of assisting an overseas regulatory authority.

Section 8 permits the Secretary of State to use information obtained in any of these ways as grounds for an application for a disqualification order. On an application being made, the court may make an order if it is satisfied that

---

9 One case where it was sufficient on its own was *Re Cladrose Ltd* [1990] BCLC 204 where the director in question was a chartered accountant who was relied on by the other director to look after these matters. For criticism of that decision, see Finch (1990) 53 MLR 385.

10 *Re Douglas Construction Services Ltd* [1988] BCLC 397; *Re Bath Glass Ltd* [1988] BCLC 329.

11 *Re McNulty's Interchange Ltd* [1989] BCLC 709; *Re Douglas Construction Services Ltd* [1988] BCLC 397; *Re Bath Glass Ltd* [1988] BCLC 329.

12 See Dillon LJ in *Re Sevenoaks Stationers (Retail) Ltd* [1990] 3 WLR 1165 at 1171.

13 Only the Secretary of State may apply under this provision.

14 CDDA 1986, s 8(1).

15 The Secretary of State was urged to use the power under this section to seek to have the Fayed brothers disqualified as directors of House of Fraser Ltd following the critical report of inspectors into the affairs of the House of Fraser, see Inspectors' Report on House of Fraser Holdings plc (HMSO). Despite such a critical report, no application for disqualification was made, the Secretary of State stressing that his role was to act where it was expedient in the public interest to do so and there was no public interest since the House of Fraser is now a private company wholly owned by the Fayeds. This was seen by many commentators as an unnecessarily restrictive view of public interest in this context.

that person's conduct in relation to the company makes him unfit to be concerned in the management of a company[16]. Here the court will normally have regard only to those matters specified in Part 1 of the Schedule for it will not necessarily be the case that the company has gone into insolvent liquidation. If it has, then Part II will also be relevant.

EFFECT OF DISQUALIFICATION

If a disqualification order is made, s 1(1) provides that the person concerned shall not, without leave of the court, be a director, liquidator, administrator, receiver or manager of a company's property or in any way, whether directly or indirectly, be concerned or take part in the promotion, formation or management of a company[17]. In *R v Campbell*[18], a disqualified person was found to be acting as a management consultant to a company and tried to argue that this did not fall within the scope of the prohibition in what is now s 1(1) as he was not in control of the decision-making process within the company. The Court of Appeal found, however, that the wording of the prohibition is widely cast and comprehensively designed to make it impossible for persons to be part of the management and central direction of the company's affairs[19], and that included acting as a management consultant to the company.

It is possible, of course, to apply for leave to act when a disqualification order has been made. For example, in *Re Lo-Line Electric Motors Ltd*[20], having disqualified a director on the grounds of unfitness for a period of three years, the court then gave him leave to be a director of two particular companies, subject to certain conditions. The two companies were family companies, which were both trading profitably and were fully solvent, and another person had primary responsibility for the financial management of those businesses. In *Re Majestic Recording Studios Ltd*[1], leave was granted to act in respect of one particular company, in view of the fact that the director was the moving spirit behind the business and without his presence the jobs of 55 employees would be in jeopardy, and subject to the requirement that he have acting with him as a director an independent chartered accountant approved by the court. In *Re Chartmore Ltd*[2], leave was granted, subject to proper monthly board meetings being held which were to be attended by a representative of the auditors, despite judicial concerns about the under-capitalisation of the company.

Granting leave to act in this way rather diminishes the force of a disqualification order but, perhaps, can be justified if the overriding principle is protection of the public, for leave has usually been granted subject to conditions designed to insulate the public from the possibility of financial mismanagement by the disqualified director.

16 Unlike s 6, this provision is discretionary.
17 Table A, art 81 provides that a director shall vacate his office in the event of being disqualified.
18 [1984] BCLC 83.
19 The scope of this prohibition and its ramifications have not yet been fully explored by the English courts, but see Hicks [1988] JBL 27 at 41 who considers some Australian cases on a similar provision.
20 [1988] Ch 477, [1988] 2 All ER 692.
 1 [1989] BCLC 1.
 2 [1990] BCLC 673.

PERIOD OF DISQUALIFICATION

Where a person is disqualified for persistent default, or on conviction of an indictable offence by a court of summary jurisdiction, or on conviction of summary offences in relation to returns to the registrar, then the maximum period of disqualification is five years[3]. In any other case, the maximum period is 15 years[4]. If the court makes a disqualification order under s 6 on the grounds of unfitness, then a minimum period of two years is prescribed by s 6(4).

The appropriate period of disqualification was considered by the Court of Appeal in *Re Sevenoaks Stationers (Retail) Ltd*[5] which was anxious to lay down some guidelines given the large number of disqualification cases now coming before the courts. Three categories were identified:

(a)   Disqualification for periods over ten years should be reserved for particularly serious cases. These may include cases where a director who has already had one period of disqualification imposed on him falls to be disqualified again.
(b)   Two to five years should be applied where, though disqualification is mandatory, the case is, relatively, not very serious.
(c)   Six to ten years should apply for serious cases which do not merit in excess of ten years.

CONSEQUENCES OF ACTING WHILE DISQUALIFIED

It is a criminal offence to act in breach of a disqualification order, the penalty for which is imprisonment or a fine or both[6]. More importantly, s 15 now imposes personal liability not only on any person who acts in breach of a disqualification order but also on any person who acts or is willing to act on the instructions of a disqualified person[7].

Any disqualified person who is involved in the management of a company becomes personally responsible for such debts and liabilities as are incurred at the time when he was so involved. A person is involved in the management of a company if he is a director or if he is concerned, whether directly or indirectly, or takes part, in the management of a company[8].

Liability is also extended to any person who as a person concerned in the management of the company, acts or is willing to act[9] on instructions given, without leave of the court, by a person whom he knows to be disqualified. Liability in this case is for such debts and other liabilities of the company as are incurred at the time when that person was acting or willing to act on instructions given. In each case liability is joint and several.

---

3 CDDA 1986, ss 3(5), 2(3)(a), 5(5).
4 Ibid, ss 2(3)(b), 4(3), 6(4), 8, 10.
5 [1990] 3 WLR 1165.
6 CDDA 1986, s 13.
7 Hicks [1988] JBL 27 at 45 notes that this self-enforcing device is probably a far greater inducement to compliance than the remote risk of being prosecuted for acting while disqualified.
8 CDDA 1986, s 15(4).
9 Note the presumption in s 15(5) that a person who has acted on the instructions of a person whom he knew to be disqualified is presumed to have been willing at any time thereafter to act on any instructions given by that person, unless the contrary is shown.

PUBLICITY

Court officers are required to provide the Secretary of State with details of disqualification orders made and any cases where the court has granted leave to act, or varied, or quashed any such order. Companies House in turn maintains a register of such information which is available for inspection by the public[10].

Retirement, resignation, vacation and removal

The articles will normally provide for the retirement of all the directors at the first annual general meeting and thereafter may provide for the rotation of directors with a selected number retiring each year, although they remain eligible for re-election and retiring directors are automatically reappointed in default of another appointment[11].

A director may resign at any time. The articles will normally require notice in writing to the board and on so doing the director is deemed to have vacated his office[12].

Article 81 of Table A specifies a number of instances in which a director is deemed to have vacated his office. These include resignation, becoming a bankrupt, or being prohibited by law from being a director. It is always open to a company to add additional vacating circumstances to its articles if it so wishes. A standard provision is that discussed in *Lee v Chou Wen Hsien*[13] where the office of director was vacated if a director was requested in writing by all his co-directors to resign. That power, effectively to expel a director, has to be exercised in the best interests of the company.

Section 303[14] of the 1985 Act provides that a company may, by ordinary resolution, remove a director before the expiration of his period of office, notwithstanding anything in its articles or any agreement between him and the company[15]. Special notice[16] of the resolution must be given and the director concerned is entitled to be heard at the meeting where it is proposed to remove him[17]. He may also require the company to circulate to the members his representations in writing[18], unless this right is being abused to secure needless publicity of defamatory material[19].

There are a number of factors which a company should consider before exercising this power of removal. In particular, the company should consider the amount of damages which may be payable to a dismissed director under s 303(5) which provides that the section is not to be taken as depriving

---

10 CDDA 1986, s 18(2), (4).
11 Table A, arts 73–80. Private companies will frequently dispense with rotation.
12 Ibid, art 81(d).
13 [1984] 1 WLR 1202, [1985] BCLC 45, PC.
14 For two very different views on the value of this provision, see Cartoon [1980] JBL 171, '. . . a vital tool', and Afterman *Company Directors and Officers* (1970) p 20, '. . . of limited value'. On the problems of dismissed directors generally, see Chesterman *Small Businesses* (2nd edn, 1982) pp 191–220.
15 Note that the written resolution procedure provided for private companies by CA 1985, s 381A, inserted by CA 1989, s 113(2), is not available in respect of resolutions under s 303, CA 1985, Sch 15A, inserted by CA 1989, s 114.
16 Defined CA 1985, s 379.
17 CA 1985, s 304.
18 Ibid, s 304(2).
19 Ibid, s 304(4).

a person removed thereunder of compensation or damages payable in respect of the termination of his appointment as director. Problems are most likely to arise when the company attempts to dismiss a managing director or any executive director with a service contract. If a managing director is appointed by contract for a fixed term and the company exercises its power to remove him under s 303 before that term expires, then the company will be liable in damages as the courts will apply a term that the company undertakes to do nothing of its own accord to bring to an end the circumstances necessary to enable a person to act as a managing director, i e by terminating his post as a director[20]. Where a director does not have a separate service contract and has simply been appointed under the articles then his position can be terminated at any time and he cannot recover any damages[1]. Indeed the company may specifically alter its articles to facilitate the removal of such a director and he will not be entitled to any relief[2]. It is clear then that a director without a service contract will be in a somewhat vulnerable position.

A major problem for shareholders wishing to remove directors had been that they frequently found that the directors had such lengthy service contracts with the company that the cost of removing them under s 303 was exorbitant. In practice therefore such directors were irremovable. That cost also deterred would-be takeover bidders which was not necessarily in the best interests of the shareholders. The position is now governed by s 319 of the 1985 Act which requires shareholder approval of any provision whereby a director[3] is to be employed for a period exceeding five years[4] and the contract cannot be determined by the company by notice or it can be terminated only in specified circumstances. Lengthy service contracts then are not prohibited, but must be approved by the company in general meeting after the shareholders have had an opportunity to inspect a memorandum setting out the proposed agreement and identifying the period for which it is to run[5]. If a term is included in contravention of this section and without the approval of the general meeting, then that term is void[6] and will be severed from the agreement which will become one determinable by the giving of reasonable notice. It should be noted that employment is defined to include employment under a contract for services, so consultancy services are also caught by the provision[7]. The section does not apply if the company in question is a wholly-owned subsidiary[8].

Another point which must be considered is the effect of the House of Lords ruling in *Ebrahimi v Westbourne Galleries Ltd*[9] where a dismissed director, who was also a shareholder, was held to be entitled to have the company

---

20 *Shindler v Northern Raincoat Co Ltd* [1960] 2 All ER 239, [1960] 1 WLR 1038; *Southern Foundries (1926) Ltd v Shirlaw* [1940] AC 701, [1940] 2 All ER 445, HL.
1 *Read v Astoria Garage (Streatham) Ltd* [1952] Ch 637, [1952] 2 All ER 292, CA.
2 *Shuttleworth v Cox Bros & Co (Maidenhead) Ltd* [1927] 2 KB 9, CA.
3 Including 'shadow' directors; CA 1985, s 319(7).
4 CA 1985, s 319(2) provides for the aggregation of periods in certain circumstances so that the provision cannot be avoided by a string of contracts. However, the rather obscure wording of the provision offers scope for avoidance.
5 Ibid, s 319(5). The memorandum must be available at the registered office for 15 days before the meeting and at the meeting itself.
6 CA 1985, s 319(6).
7 Ibid, s 319(7).
8 Ibid, s 319(4). The unsatisfactory punctuation of this subsection can give quite the contrary impression but the generally accepted interpretation of it is that stated in the text. See HC Official Report, SC A, 29 November 1979, col 419.
9 [1973] AC 360, [1972] 2 All ER 492, HL; see Chapter 27 post.

wound up on the just and equitable ground under what is now s 122(1)(g) of the Insolvency Act 1986. The House of Lords found that Ebrahimi's dismissal, whilst in accordance with what is now s 303 of the 1985 Act, was nevertheless in breach of the underlying personal relationship which was the basis of the company and which required continued participation by him in the management of the company. Excluding him from management and removing him from the board, in the circumstances, meant that the court was justified in making a winding-up order[10]. The court stressed that a winding-up order will not necessarily be made whenever any company tries to remove a director. Normally compliance with the requirements of the statute and the articles will ensure that the removal is unimpeachable. However, in certain circumstances, the character of the association may be such that the court will subject the exercise by the company of its legal rights (to expel a director) to equitable considerations. Without laying down a definite test, Lord Wilberforce thought this would only occur where one or probably more of the following features were present: where the company was an association founded on the basis of a personal relationship involving mutual confidence; where there were restrictions on the transfer of shares; and where there was an agreement or understanding that all or some of the members should participate in the conduct of the business[11]. In such cases, a decision to expel a director, with its resultant breach of these underlying assumptions, would justify the court in making a winding-up order.

Ebrahimi v Westbourne Galleries Ltd, it should be noted, only entitles a dismissed director to petition for a winding up in the appropriate circumstances. It does not entitle him to an injunction to restrain the company from exercising its statutory right to remove him[12].

In practice, an order for winding up on this basis is unlikely to be sought now, given the availability of more tailored relief under CA 1985, s 459. This section provides that a member of a company may apply to the court by petition for an order on the ground that the company's affairs are being or have been conducted in a manner which is unfairly prejudicial to the interests of the members generally or of some part of its members[13]. It had clearly been the case under s 459's predecessor, s 210 of the Companies Act 1948, that where the petitioner was essentially complaining of removal from the board and exclusion from management he was not entitled to relief for he was not oppressed 'qua member' as required by that section[14]. Indeed it was for this reason that Ebrahimi failed to obtain relief under s 210 and had to resort to a winding-up order[15]. It is now clear, after some initial doubts[16], that the wider interpretation given by the courts to s 459 will ensure that it can apply to the removal of a director in the appropriate case. The issue was considered in *Re Bird Precision Bellows Ltd*[17] where removal from the board was one of the main grounds for complaint. It was accepted by the Court of

10 [1973] AC 360 at 380, [1972] 2 All ER 492 at 501, HL, per Lord Wilberforce.
11 [1973] AC 360 at 379, [1972] 2 All ER 492 at 500, HL.
12 *Bentley-Stevens v Jones* [1974] 2 All ER 653, [1974] 1 WLR 638. An injunction can be obtained if the other directors simply try to exclude a director from board meetings without actually dismissing him: *Pulbrook v Richmond Consolidated Mining Co* (1878) 9 Ch D 610.
13 As amended by CA 1989, s 145 and Sch 19, para 11.
14 *Elder v Elder and Watson Ltd* 1952 SC 49; *Re Lundie Bros Ltd* [1965] 2 All ER 692.
15 See *Re Westbourne Galleries Ltd* [1970] 3 All ER 374.
16 See *Re a Company (No 004475 of 1982)* [1983] Ch 178, [1983] 2 All ER 36.
17 [1984] Ch 419, [1984] 3 All ER 444; affd [1986] Ch 658, [1985] 3 All ER 523, CA.

Appeal that there had indeed been unfairly prejudicial conduct. It was similarly held in *Re Cumana Ltd*[18] and *Re London School of Electronics Ltd*[19] although in these cases, where there are a multitude of allegations, it is not easy to identify the court's view of removal in itself, for it tends to concentrate on the cumulative effect of the behaviour in question. More recently, Hoffmann J in *Re a Company (No 00477/86)*[20] took the view that the interests of a member who had ventured his capital in the business of a small company might include the legitimate expectation of employment as a director so that his dismissal would be unfairly prejudicial to his interests as a member[1]. Where a director/shareholder can establish an interest in employment and participation then s 459 may deter the company from exercising its power to remove him for while it is unlikely that the court would order his reinstatement under the section, it will usually order that he be bought out on a pro rata, and not a discounted, basis in view of his forced expulsion from the company[2]. Section 459 may therefore prove a financial disincentive to exercising the power of removal under s 303. The scope of s 459 and the basis for winding up a company on just and equitable grounds are considered in detail in Ch 27.

Directors can protect themselves to some extent against the possibility that at some date in the future the general meeting will seek to remove them from the board. One possibility is the inclusion of a provision in the articles entitling the director to weighted votes on any resolution to remove him from the board, a practice permitted by the House of Lords in *Bushell v Faith*[3]. In that case the articles of the company provided that on a resolution to remove a particular director, his shares would carry three times the number of votes they normally carried. As a consequence, it was impossible for the other shareholders to pass the required ordinary resolution. Ungoed-Thomas J at first instance refused to permit the practice saying that it made a mockery of the Act but the Court of Appeal and the House of Lords approved it[4] and it remains a valid method of entrenchment for directors[5].

Section 303 then is not the quick, easy and effective curb on directors' conduct which it might appear to be at first sight and companies proposing to use it must carefully weigh up the factors outlined above before proceeding.

---

18 (1986) 2 BCC 99, 453 (where it is reported as *Re a Company (No 002612 of 1984)* Ch D, [1986] BCLC 430, CA.
19 [1986] Ch 211.
20 [1986] BCLC 376.
 1 See also *Whyte, Petitioner* (1984) 1 BCC 99, 044.
 2 See *Re Bird Precision Bellows Ltd* [1984] Ch 419, [1984] 3 All ER 444; affd [1986] Ch 658, [1985] 3 All ER 523, CA.
 3 [1969] 2 Ch 438, [1969] 1 All ER 1002, CA; affd [1970] AC 1099, [1970] 1 All ER 53, HL, noted (1970) 86 LQR 155.
 4 See [1970] AC 1099 at 1109, [1970] 1 All ER 53 at 57, per Upjohn LJ: 'Parliament has never sought to fetter the right of a company to issue shares with such rights or restrictions as it thinks fit'. Note Schmitthoff [1970] JBL 1: '. . . one of the most remarkable instances of judicial interpretation defeating the clear intention of the legislature' and Palmer's *Company Law* (24th edn, 1987) para 60–33 where it is suggested that the decision can be justified in the case of private companies of a quasi-partnership nature but that its ratio may not extend to public companies. See also Hahlo's *Cases and Materials on Company Law* (3rd edn, 1987) p 363.
 5 See the Companies Bill 1973, cl 44 which would have required weighted votes provisions to apply to all resolutions and not just to resolutions removing directors. See *Re Opera Photographic Ltd* [1989] 1 WLR 634, [1989] BCLC 763 for an unsuccessful attempt to use quorum requirements to prevent a s 303 resolution being passed.

THE COMPANY SECRETARY

All companies are required to have a company secretary and a sole director cannot also act in that capacity[6]. Normally appointed by the directors[7], as opposed to the general meeting, their duties are mainly of an administrative nature, in particular ensuring compliance by the company with the disclosure and information requirements of the Companies Acts. They are not mere clerks, however, but officers of the company who may have extensive duties and responsibilities and even authority to enter into contracts on behalf of the company, at least on the administrative side of the company's affairs[8].

Reflecting the important role which the company secretary occupies, s 286 provides that the directors of a public company must take all reasonable steps to secure that the secretary is a person who appears to them to have the requisite knowledge and experience to discharge that position. That person must fall within one of six categories specified in the section which covers persons with experience as a company secretary and members of various professions: accountants, chartered secretaries, solicitors, barristers, etc. However, the directors may appoint someone who appears to them to be capable of discharging the functions of secretary[9], a very wide provision which negates to a large degree the stringent requirements set down earlier in the section.

REGISTERS

Section 288 provides that every company must keep at its registered office a register of its directors and secretaries, giving such details as their names, addresses, nationalities, business occupations, any other directorships held by a director in the preceding five years and their dates of birth[10]. This register must be open to inspection by members of the company, free of charge, and by the public for such fee as may be prescribed[11].

---

6 CA 1985, s 283.
7 Table A, art 99.
8 *Panorama Developments (Guildford) Ltd v Fidelis Furnishing Fabrics Ltd* [1971] 2 QB 711, [1971] 3 All ER 16, CA.
9 CA 1985, s 286(1)(e).
10 Ibid, s 289 as amended by CA 1989, s 145 and Sch 19, para 2.
11 Ibid, s 288(3) as amended by CA 1989, s 143(6).

CHAPTER 24

The distribution of power within a company

In theory, at least, a company acts through two bodies. One is the company in general meeting, ie the shareholders; the other is the board of directors, elected by the general meeting and usually entrusted with the management of the company. This Chapter will consider the division of power between these two bodies and the position when the powers granted are exceeded.

A number of points should be borne in mind when examining this theoretical division of power. First, the extent to which the shareholders can realistically be regarded as electing the directors, given the board's control of the proxy machinery, must always be open to question. In fact boards often become self-perpetuating[1]. Secondly, the board's role in practice is often supervisory rather than managerial as extensive powers are delegated to individual directors and to professional executive managers, a group largely ignored by the basic legal structure[2]. Thirdly, the separation and division of power in this way between the board and the general meeting is often inappropriate to the smaller private company where the individuals concerned may act both as shareholders and directors without differentiating particularly between those capacities, a fact which is not always reflected in the legal regulation of such companies[3].

THE DIVISION OF POWER BETWEEN THE BOARD AND THE GENERAL MEETING

Any discussion must start by looking at the company's articles of association, for it is now clearly established that the relationship between the board and the general meeting is a contractual one based on the articles[4] which will determine the extent of the powers conferred on the board. Normally these

---

1 See Drucker *The New Society* (1950) pp 340–342; Manning 'Review of Livingston's *The American Stockholder*' (1958) 67 Yale LJ 1477.
2 Berle and Means *The Modern Corporation and Private Property* (1932); Eisenberg *The Structure of the Corporation* (1976) pp 140–148.
3 See Manne (1967) 53 Va LR 259; also 'A New Form of Incorporation for Small Firms', Cmnd 8171. The multiple roles of the participants in smaller private companies is increasingly recognised by the courts in the exercise of their powers under s 459, discussed in Chapter 27, post.
4 *Automatic Self-Cleansing Filter Syndicate Co Ltd v Cuninghame* [1906] 2 Ch 34, CA; *Gramophone and Typewriter Ltd v Stanley* [1908] 2 KB 89, CA; *Salmon v Quin & Axtens Ltd* [1909] 1 Ch 311, CA; affd sub nom *Quin & Axtens Ltd v Salmon* [1909] AC 442, HL; *Breckland Group Holdings Ltd v London & Suffolk Properties Ltd* [1989] BCLC 100.

will be extensive, with very few, apart from those conferred by statute[5], retained exclusively by the company in general meeting. As the matter is purely a contractual one, it is open to a company to adopt whatever form of management articles it pleases, but in practice art 70 of Table A will normally be adopted. It provides that:

Subject to the provisions of the Act, the memorandum and the articles and to any directions given by special resolution, the business of the company shall be managed by the directors who may exercise all the powers of the company.

Article 70 therefore permits interference by the shareholders if those holding a sufficiently large stake in the company feel strongly about a particular matter while giving the directors a free hand in the day-to-day management of the company.

This provision replaced art 80 of the 1948 Table A[6], the exact meaning of which had been surrounded by controversy. It had been interpreted to mean that the general meeting could only interfere with the exercise by directors of their management powers by way of a special resolution[7]. Alternatively, the shareholders could alter the articles and the mandate which those articles gave to the directors[8]. The position was stated as follows by Greer LJ in *John Shaw & Sons (Salford) Ltd v Shaw*[9]:

A company is an entity distinct alike from its shareholders and its directors. Some of its powers may, according to its articles, be exercised by directors, certain other powers may be reserved for the shareholders in general meeting. If powers of management are vested in the directors, they and they alone can exercise these powers. The only way in which the general body of the shareholders can control the exercise of the powers vested by the articles in the directors is by altering the articles, or . . . by refusing to re-elect the directors of whose actions they disapprove. They cannot themselves usurp the powers which by the articles are vested in the directors any more than the directors can usurp the powers vested by the articles in the general body of shareholders.

The minority view, on the other hand, was that shareholders could exercise control over the directors by way of an ordinary resolution. Support for this

---

5 For example, the right to alter the memorandum and articles, CA 1985, ss 4 (as substituted by CA 1989, s 110(2)) and 9; certain alterations to the capital structure, CA 1985, ss 121 and 135; the right to petition for a voluntary winding up, IA 1986, s 84(1)(b). Note also CA 1985, s 80 which provides that the power to issue shares, which would normally be vested in the board by virtue of art 70 of Table A, is by s 80 vested in the company in general meeting although the company may restore that power to the directors, either by the articles or by an ordinary resolution. Some powers are customarily given to the general meeting by the articles, for example, the power to determine the number of directors, see Table A, art 64.
6 See CA 1948, Sch 1. Art 80 provided that the business of the company should be managed by the directors who might exercise all the powers of the company subject to such regulations (not being inconsistent with the provisions of the articles) as may be prescribed by the company in general meeting.
7 *Automatic Self-Cleansing Filter Syndicate Co Ltd v Cuninghame* [1906] 2 Ch 34, CA; *Gramophone and Typewriter Ltd v Stanley* [1908] 2 KB 89, CA; *Quin & Axtens Ltd v Salmon* [1909] AC 442, HL; *John Shaw & Sons (Salford) Ltd v Shaw* [1935] 2 KB 113, CA; *Scott v Scott* [1943] 1 All ER 582; *Breckland Group Holdings Ltd v London & Suffolk Properties Ltd* [1989] BCLC 100.
8 Ibid.
9 [1935] 2 KB 113 at 134, CA.

was found in the actual wording of art 80[10]. That the courts will not support this minority interpretation has recently been confirmed by the decision in *Breckland Group Holdings Ltd v London & Suffolk Properties Ltd*[11]. Here a 51% shareholder sought to continue litigation which it had initiated in the company's name despite the company's articles containing art 80 vesting management power in the board of directors[12]. Harman J refused to countenance such an interference with the powers of the board. He stated:

The principle, as I see it, is that art 80 confides the management of the business to the directors and in such a case it is not for the general meeting to interfere. . . . If the board do not adopt it [the unauthorised litigation], a general meeting would have no power whatever to override that decision of the board and to adopt it for itself[13].

Following the decision in *Breckland*, it is unlikely that there is any point in continuing to press the minority interpretation of art 80, and so the position for companies which have retained the old provision is effectively the same as for those which have adopted art 70, ie interference by the company in general meeting with the powers of management vested by the articles in the board must be by way of special resolution.

Under either version of Table A then, it is clear that very little managerial power is retained by the company in general meeting, apart from certain powers conferred by statute and some limited concessions in the articles, although the general meeting does have the ability to alter the directors' mandate by way of special resolution either on an ad hoc basis or on a more permanent basis by altering the articles.

However, the effectiveness of these few constraints is further undermined by new s 35A, inserted by CA 1989, s 108, which allows third parties acting in good faith to prevail where the board acts in breach of constitutional limitations on its authority to bind the company or authorise others to do so[14]. Constitutional limitations obviously encompasses limitations in the memorandum and articles of association but is further defined by s 35A(3) as including limitations deriving from a resolution of the company in general meeting, so it would apply to any directions under article 70. Shareholders do have the option of seeking injunctive relief to prevent such breaches occurring (if they find out about the proposed act in advance[15]) and may seek to hold the directors, or any other person, liable where the transaction has

---

10 See Goldberg (1970) 33 MLR 177; Sullivan (1977) 93 LQR 569; Mackenzie (1983) 4 Co Law 99; *Marshall's Valve Gear Co Ltd v Manning, Wardle & Co Ltd* [1909] 1 Ch 267. It was argued that the cases cited to support the majority view were decided on the basis of the particular articles involved and were not authority for the wider principles of non-interference. In *Breckland Group Holdings Ltd v London & Suffolk Properties Ltd* [1989] BCLC 100 Harman J indicated that he considered that *Marshall's Valve Gear Co Ltd* was overwhelmed by the weight of authorities against it.

11 [1989] BCLC 100, noted Wedderburn (1989) 52 MLR 401; Sealy (1989) CLJ 26.

12 There also was a shareholders' agreement which required that the institution of material legal proceedings by the company had to have the support of two directors representing the two opposing shareholders thus requiring that both the 51% and the 49% shareholder representative be in favour of the action before it could be commenced.

13 [1989] BCLC 100 at 106.

14 A similar provision (although without the good faith requirement) operates when the directors enter into a transaction beyond the company's capacity, see CA 1985, s 35, as substituted by CA 1989, s 108(1).

15 But relief is not available in respect of an act to be done in fulfilment of a legal obligation arising from a previous act of the company, CA 1985, s 35A(4).

already taken place[16], but in practice these remedies may not be very significant. This new provision is discussed in detail below. It suffices here to note that it further erodes the value of the limited restraints which the general meeting is able to impose on the board of directors. Of course, shareholders who find themselves in significant disagreement with their board may wish to exercise, or at least threaten to exercise, their power under s 303 to remove the directors in question. The limitations on the exercise of that power were discussed in Chapter 23.

However, the general meeting is not entirely without power and, in certain limited circumstances, the courts are prepared to hold that there is a residual power of management in the general meeting. For this residual power to arise the board must be deadlocked[17] or unable to act[18] or for all practical purposes has ceased to exist[19]. As Warrington J noted in *Barron v Potter*[20]:

. . . I am not concerned to say that in ordinary cases where there is a board ready and willing to act it would be competent for the company to override the power conferred on the directors by the articles except by way of special resolution for the purpose of altering the articles. But the case which I have to deal with is a different one. For practical purposes there is no board of directors at all.

Faced with such inability to act, it is not surprising that the courts look to the other governing body to resolve it. This the general meeting may do by appointing another director[1], for example, or commencing proceedings[2]. Once a functioning board is again in operation the powers of management revert to it.

The division of power then is predominantly in favour of the board at the expense of the general meeting. Before leaving this discussion, one remaining issue must be considered, namely which body controls the commencement of litigation in the company's name.

This matter had been the subject of a lengthy debate since *Marshall's Valve Gear Co Ltd v Manning, Wardle & Co Ltd*[3], which permitted the general meeting to commence litigation despite the opposition of the board to whom powers of management had been delegated. It had been thought that the answer lay in some sort of parallel authority vested in the board *and* the general meeting[4]. *Breckland* indicates, however, that this issue is no different from any other management matter which under the articles is vested in the board so precluding shareholder intervention in the absence of directions by special resolution or alteration of the articles. As far as *Marshall's Valve Gear* was concerned, Harman J thought it was overwhelmed by the weight of authority against it[5]. However, he did not consider the position of authorities

---

16 CA 1985, s 35A(5).
17 *Barron v Potter* [1914] 1 Ch 895. Such deadlock would justify winding up on the just and equitable ground under IA 1986, s 122(1)(g), see *Re Yenidje Tobacco Co Ltd* [1916] 2 Ch 426, CA.
18 *Foster v Foster* [1916] 1 Ch 532.
19 *Barron v Potter* [1914] 1 Ch 895.
20 [1914] 1 Ch 895 at 902.
1 See *Barron v Potter* [1914] 1 Ch 895.
2 See *Alexander Ward & Co Ltd v Samyang Navigation Co Ltd* [1975] 2 All ER 424, HL, noted Wedderburn (1976) 39 MLR 327.
3 [1909] 1 Ch 267.
4 See Gower *Principles of Modern Company Law* (4th edn, 1979) and supp, p 147; Wedderburn (1976) 39 MLR 327.
5 [1989] BCLC 100 at 105.

such as *Danish Mercantile Co Ltd v Beaumont*[6] and *Alexander Ward & Co Ltd v Samyang Navigation Co Ltd*[7], which have treated the general meeting as having authority to commence litigation in the company's name. Certainly *Danish Mercantile*, in so far as it has given rise to the practice whereby when there is a dispute as to authority to litigate, the court will adjourn the proceedings in order to convene a general meeting to decide the matter, seems to be questionable where the company's articles contain a management article as outlined above[8]. *Alexander Ward & Co Ltd v Samyang Navigation Co Ltd*[9], a House of Lords decision, for its part supports the view that the general meeting may authorise litigation where there is no board capable of acting. That case can be seen as an example of the exercise by the general meeting of residual powers (discussed above) rather than any usurping by the general meeting of management powers vested in the board[10]. This enables the case to be explained consistently with *Breckland* and in keeping with the division of power outlined above.

Equally, the power of the majority in general meeting to institute litigation in the name of the company against the wishes of the board must of necessity be retained where the directors are themselves the wrongdoers[11]. It would be inconsistent with the rule in *Foss v Harbottle*[12] that the majority should be precluded from bringing action against wrongdoing directors by the fact that they had delegated management powers to those who are the wrongdoers[13]. This power in the general meeting also could be treated as an exercise of a residual power of management, for where the wrongdoers are the board then there is no board in existence capable of exercising the power to commence litigation[14]. Alternatively, as Sealy has argued, it could be justified on the basis that the exclusive powers granted to the board under an article such as art 70 relate only to powers to manage the business of the company and do not apply to a matter which is not simply a matter of business but involves an intra-corporate dispute[15].

To sum up, the proper approach to the issue of commencing litigation in the company's name, it is submitted, is that the starting point is the rule in *Foss v Harbottle*[16], which essentially provides that where a wrong is done to the company then the company is the proper person to sue. Which organ of

6   [1951] Ch 680, [1951] 1 All ER 925, CA.
7   [1975] 2 All ER 424, [1975] 1 WLR 673, HL, noted Wedderburn (1976) 39 MLR 327.
8   See Sealy (1989) CLJ 26 at 28.
9   [1975] 2 All ER 424, [1975] 1 WLR 673, HL.
10 See Wedderburn (1989) 52 MLR 402 at 405 and (1976) 39 MLR 327.
11 See Sealy (1989) CLJ 26 at 28; Partridge (1987) CLJ 122 at 130, fn 58. Perhaps this is the true explanation of *Marshall's Valve Gear Co Ltd v Manning, Wardle & Co Ltd* [1909] 1 Ch 267, see Xuereb *The Rights of Shareholders* (1989) p 78. It might be noted that *Breckland* itself concerned litigation against an alleged wrongdoer director, but the facts do not make clear whether that director controlled the board and it seems unlikely that he did. Of course, where the majority in general meeting find the board obstructing their wish to sue wrongdoing directors, the shareholders may decide to exercise their power to remove the directors under CA 1985, s 303 by way of ordinary resolution and install a new board which will commence litigation against the former directors.
12 (1843) 2 Hare 461.
13 See Wedderburn (1957) CLJ 194 at 201–202; Palmer's *Company Law* (24th edn, 1987) and supp, para 65–01.
14 See Sealy *Cases and Materials in Company Law* (4th edn, 1989) p 453, citing *Foster v Foster* [1916] 1 Ch 532.
15 See Sealy, op cit, p 453.
16 (1843) 2 Hare 461.

the company should take that decision depends on the company's constitution. Where the articles are in the form of art 70 or 80, then the matter is vested in the board which may decide as a matter of management not to sue, but this is subject to the general meeting intervening in the ways outlined above and to the general meeting being the appropriate decision-making body when the directors are themselves the wrongdoers. Where the wrongdoers control both the board and the general meeting then the matter may be the subject of a derivative action by an individual shareholder[17].

ACTS BY CORPORATE AGENTS IN EXCESS OF AUTHORITY

We have already seen in Chapter 10 that the CA 1989 has sought to abolish the ultra vires doctrine, at least in so far as outsiders are concerned, thus ensuring the validity of transactions entered into by the company despite any limitations on the company's capacity in the memorandum of association.

Of course, for many third parties difficulties arise, not from any lack of capacity, given the width of most objects clauses, but from a lack of authority, perhaps on the part of the board but more commonly on the part of an individual director or officer with respect to a particular transaction.

It has always been open to the company in general meeting, or to the board, if appropriate, to ratify a transaction entered into in breach of authority[18]. However, on occasion third parties were faced with companies wishing to disown onerous obligations by alleging that the director or directors responsible had no authority to enter into the transaction. Any reforms designed to increase the security of third parties dealing with companies had necessarily to address these questions of lack of authority in addition to issues of capacity and this the 1989 Act did, as far as the board was concerned, by inserting new ss 35A and 35B into the CA 1985. These statutory provisions replace much of the old law in this area but in so doing raise many new uncertainties, both in terms of the wording of s 35A and its relationship with the existing law.

Section 35A

The starting point is s 35A, inserted by CA 1989, s 108, which provides:

In favour of a person dealing with a company in good faith, the power of the board of directors to bind the company, or authorise others to do so, shall be deemed to be free of any limitation under the company's constitution[19].

The provision operates in favour of[20] persons dealing with a company. For the purposes of s 35A, a person deals with a company if he is a party to any

---

17 Subject to *Smith v Croft (No 2)* [1988] Ch 114, [1987] 3 All ER 909 which enables a majority of the independent shareholders to block a derivative action where they believe that litigation is not in the best interests of the company. This decision is discussed in detail in Ch 27.

18 See *Irvine v Union Bank of Australia* (1877) 2 App Cas 366, PC; *Grant v United Kingdom Switchback Railways Co* (1888) 40 Ch D 135, CA.

19 Note that s 35A (and s 35) do not apply to acts of companies which are charities subject to the Companies Act, except in two cases, see s 35(4) and s 35A(6).

20 Unlike s 35, which prevents any challenge to an ultra vires transaction, s 35A only applies in favour of the outsider. The company can hold the outsider to the contract by ratifying it.

transaction or other act to which the company is a party[1]. This ensures that the provision applies to gratuitous as well as commercial transactions.

It should be noted that the application of the section is modified[2] as set out in s 322A, inserted by CA 1989, s 109, where the parties to the transaction[3] include a director of the company or of its holding company, or a person connected with such a director or a company with whom such a director is associated. In such cases the transaction is voidable at the instance of the company but if the parties to the transaction also include a person who is not one of those specified, then that person, provided he is in good faith, will still be able to rely on s 35A[4]. Section 322A is discussed in greater detail in Chapter 26.

To avail of the protection afforded by s 35A(1), the person dealing with the company must have done so in good faith. The statutory provisions go on to ensure that it is very difficult for such a person to be in bad faith. Firstly, a person is presumed to have acted in good faith unless the contrary is proved[5].

Secondly, a person is not to be regarded as acting in bad faith by reason *only* of his knowing that an act is beyond the powers of the directors under the company's constitution[6]. It will be necessary to show something in addition to knowledge to prevent a third party relying on s 35A, such as malicious intent, or fraudulent misrepresentation, or collusion by the third party in the breach by the directors, although the precise factors which the courts will take to be indicative of bad faith remain to be identified[7].

As was the position under the old s 35, third parties dealing with the board are not affected by any doctrine of constructive notice whereby persons dealing with a company were deemed to have notice of the company's memorandum and articles of association and various public documents and any limitations contained therein[8]. This doctrine has now been abolished

---

1 CA 1985, s 35A(2)(a).
2 Ibid, s 35A(6).
3 Defined for these purposes as including any act, see s 322A(8).
4 CA 1985, s 322A(2) and (7). Where the transaction is voidable by virtue of s 322A(2) and valid by virtue of s 35A in favour of the third party, the court may, on the application of that person or the company, make such order affirming, severing or setting aside the transaction on such terms as appear to the court to be just, s 322A(7).
5 CA 1985, s 35A(2)(c).
6 Ibid, s 35A(2)(b). See HL Debs, vol 505, 6 April 1989, cols 1273–74 and vol 512, 7 November 1989, col 682 on this aspect of the provision. This reverses the position under the old provision where knowledge of the defect could be evidence of bad faith, see *Barclays Bank Ltd v TOSG Trust Fund Ltd* [1984] BCLC 1 at 18, per Nourse J.
7 See, for example, the discussion in the recent decision of the High Court of Australia, *Northside Developments Pty Ltd v Registrar-General* (1990) 93 ALR 385, 64 ALJR 427, noted Prentice (1991) 107 LQR 14, as to the position of a third party where the very nature of the transaction is such as to indicate that it is not for the purposes of the company's business or related in any way to that business. The case involved the granting of security in respect of an advance to a third party, not being an advance for the purposes of the company's business or otherwise for its benefit but for the benefit of some of the directors. Obviously the Australian case did not involve an application of s 35A but it is interesting on the position of the third party in these circumstances. The position of the directors as parties to the transaction will be governed by s 322A, as noted above.
8 *Ernest v Nicholls* (1857) 6 HL Cas 401; *Mahony v East Holyford Mining Co* (1875) LR 7 HL 869.

generally by CA 1985, s 711A(1), inserted by CA 1989, s 142. Note, however, s 711A(2) which provides that the abolition of constructive notice does not affect the question whether a person is affected by notice of any matter by reason of a failure to make such inquiries as ought reasonably to be made. However, this has to be read in the light of s 35B which specifically provides that a party to a transaction[9] with a company is not bound to enquire as to any limitation on the power of the board to bind the company or authorise others to do so. So the third party is not deemed to know the contents of the memorandum and articles and is not obliged to enquire as to their content[10].

Assuming that a person is dealing with a company in good faith, the effect of this is that certain limitations imposed by the company's constitution on the power of the directors to bind the company or authorise others to do so may be discarded. The limitations on the directors' powers which may be set aside are those arising under the memorandum and articles of association but also include those limitations deriving:

(a)   from a resolution of the company in general meeting or a meeting of any class of shareholders, or
(b)   from any agreement between the members of the company or of any class of shareholders[11].

The types of limitations which would be covered would include provisions such as those expressly prohibiting the directors from dealing with a particular matter, or requiring directors to execute a transaction in a particular manner. Such provisions are easy to identify as limitations on the power of the directors to act.

The question then arises as to whether it is valid to consider other requirements, such as those relating to quorum requirements or the location of board meetings, as constitutional limitations on the powers of the directors to act, which might be ignored by a third party dealing in good faith. Lord Wedderburn in the House of Lords argued strongly that such requirements are limitations, but the Government's position was that rules as to quorum, for example, are not limitations on the power of the board of directors, but deal with the logically prior question of what constitutes a board of directors and are therefore not within s 35A(1)[12].

The point may be debatable as far as the interpretation of s 35A is concerned but in any event the answer to whether third parties can be adversely affected by breaches of such requirements may lie in the existing law, namely the rule in *Royal British Bank v Turquand*[13].

As mentioned earlier, the relationship between s 35A and the existing common law rules is not altogether clear, and that is particularly true of the rule in *Turquand's* case. The rule essentially provided that third parties were

---

9 Note that s 35B refers to a party to a transaction whereas s 35A is wider and covers dealing with a company defined as any transaction and other acts to which the company is a party.
10 In any event, as we have seen above, if actually consulting the memorandum and articles or making enquiries simply left the third party knowing the transaction was beyond the directors' powers, this alone would be insufficient to establish bad faith and deny him the protection of s 35A.
11 CA 1985, s 35A(3).
12 See HL Debs, vol 512, 7 November 1989, cols 685–687.
13 (1855) 5 E & B 248.

not obliged to inquire into the proceedings of a company but could assume that all acts of internal management had been properly carried out, save where the outsider knew or ought to have known of the failure to adhere to procedures[14]. For example, in *Mahony v East Holyford Mining Co*[15] a bank was entitled to accept cheques drawn and signed by the directors in the manner authorised by the articles and was not obliged to query whether the individuals signing the cheques were validly appointed as directors.

In so far as the rule was in part a response to the constructive notice doctrine, which has now been abolished, it might be thought that there is no room left for its continued application, although the Act does not expressly provide for its abolition. Certainly s 35A will cover many instances which might otherwise have arisen under the rule, as in the *Turquand* case itself. There the board had acted without the resolution required by the articles and that was said to be matter of internal management which the third party could assume had been correctly carried out. That situation would now be within s 35A, but there remain cases, such as those involving inquorate boards which may be outside s 35A (if such quorum requirements are not to be treated as limitations on the board's power to act), where there would seem still to be scope for the rule. It must be assumed therefore that it continues to function in those cases within it but beyond s 35A, although it is narrower than s 35A in that knowledge of the defect will prevent the third party relying on *Turquand*, whereas knowledge of limitations on the directors' powers does not preclude reliance on s 35A.

This freedom from limitations imposed by the company's constitution applies to two categories of power:

(a)   the power of the board to bind the company, and
(b)   the power of the board to authorise others to do so.

In both cases, our concern is with limits to the *power of the board*, be it to act or to delegate to others the power to act.

It is clear from the discussion above of the division of power as between the board and the general meeting that it is possible for the general meeting to reserve to itself certain powers. For example, the consent of the company in general meeting might be needed to authorise the sale of a particular asset, or the articles may limit the power of the board to delegate, or the general meeting might issue special directions to the board by way of special resolution in accordance with art 70. All of these limitations on the directors' powers to act may be ignored, as a result of s 35A, as far as persons dealing in good faith are concerned. The company will be bound by the transaction despite the board lacking authority to enter into it and it is binding without any need for ratification by the company in general meeting.

This obviously increases the security of third parties and expands the

---

14 *B Liggett (Liverpool) Ltd v Barclays Bank Ltd* [1928] 1 KB 48; *Morris v Kanssen* [1946] AC 459, [1946] 1 All ER 586, HL; *Rolled Steel Products (Holdings) Ltd v British Steel Corpn* [1986] Ch 246, [1985] 3 All ER 52, CA. Insiders, ie persons holding positions within the company, are also prevented from relying on the rule: *Morris v Kanssen* [1946] AC 459, [1946] 1 All ER 586, HL; *Howard v Patent Ivory Manufacturing Co* (1888) 38 Ch D 156. A further refinement to the rule was that it would not apply if the document which the outsider sought to rely on was a forgery although this limitation was criticised: see *Ruben v Great Fingall Consolidated* [1906] AC 439, HL; also *Kreditbank Cassel GmbH v Schenkers Ltd* [1927] 1 KB 826, CA.
15 (1875) LR 7 HL 869.

authority of the board, but it further diminishes what little power had been retained by the company in general meeting, by denying shareholders the option of disowning such unauthorised transactions. The statute in recognition of this does go on to offer shareholders some redress, although the practical value of these provisions is open to question.

First, as with ultra vires transactions, a member may bring proceedings to restrain the doing of an act which is beyond the powers of the directors although, as before, no such proceeding shall lie in respect of an act to be done in fulfilment of a legal obligation arising from a previous act of the company[16]. For example, an injunction cannot be obtained to restrain the execution of an executory contract. The obvious difficulty for the members, of course, is discovering the proposed transaction early enough to seek injunctive relief.

Secondly, the validity conferred on the transaction by s 35A(1) does not affect any liability incurred by the directors, or any other person, by reason of the directors exceeding their powers[17]. This raises the possibility of the company, despite being unable to disown the transaction, suing the directors in respect of it and possibly holding a third party liable as a constructive trustee[18]. What is unclear is whether it is possible to hold a third party liable as a constructive trustee despite the fact that he is within the statutory provision and able to hold the company to the transaction.

This is an issue which had arisen with respect to the previous s 35 in *International Sales and Agencies Ltd v Marcus*[19] where Lawson J decided that liability as a constructive trustee can arise separately from and distinct from s 35. It would seem that the same is true of new s 35A. On the point being raised by Lord Wedderburn in the House of Lords debate (in the context of s 35 but the position is the same under s 35A[1]), the Government stated that it would not wish to uphold the constructive trusteeship approach where it arose because the third party knew the directors were exceeding limitations on the company's capacity. This would, it was argued, confound the purpose of new s 35 (equally s 35A, presumably) for it would in effect be saying that knowledge could prejudice the position of the third party which is what the section seeks to exclude. As Lord Wedderburn pointed out, in the absence of express wording in the section to limit the application of constructive trusteeship in this way, this is not necessarily the interpretation which a court would adopt[2].

In theory then the shift in power to the board is compensated for by these provisions enabling a member to obtain injunctive relief and by preserving the liability of the directors and other persons for acting in breach. Given the

---

16 See Lord Wedderburn in HL Debs, vol 512, 7 November 1989, col 681 who argues that this formula means that there will almost never be a case where the proposed right of the shareholder to sue can be operated. By the time the shareholder tries to act, there will always have been an act which creates some legal obligation under s 35A.

17 CA 1985, s 35A(5).

18 See *Rolled Steel Products (Holdings) Ltd v British Steel Corpn* [1986] Ch 246, [1985] 3 All ER 52, CA: a constructive trust can arise not just where a misapplication of company funds was one not authorised by the memorandum but consisted of an application of the company's assets in breach of the company's articles of association.

19 [1982] 3 All ER 551.

1 *Rolled Steel Products (Holdings) Ltd v British Steel Corpn* [1986] Ch 246, [1985] 3 All ER 52, CA.

2 See HL Debs, vol 505, 6 April 1989, cols 1243–1247.

inability to disown the transaction as a result of s 35A(1), it might be thought that this provision will give shareholders an incentive to monitor the conduct of the board in order to ensure that they do not exceed the limitations, such as they are, imposed on the board under the company's constitution. The practical difficulties of doing this, and the natural inertia of many shareholders, mean that this is unlikely to occur in practice and so injunctive relief may be irrelevant. As for actions against the directors after the event, the difficulties involved in pursuing such an action and the reluctance of companies to pursue wrongdoing directors are discussed in Chapter 27. Another possible sanction, again more theoretical than practical, is for the shareholders to remove a board which does not observe the limitations imposed on its activities, but as we saw in Chapter 23, removing directors is itself a difficult exercise.

So far our discussion has focused on the statutory provision removing limits to the authority of the board. In practice this will have only a limited effect outside of ultra vires questions for, as we have seen, the management articles adopted by companies already give the board an almost open-ended authority to manage the company's business and so problems of authority are rare.

What remains a problem is the situation where a third party deals with an individual director whose authority to act on behalf of the company is disputed. The position of third parties dealing with individual directors is not directly addressed by s 35A which is concerned with the powers of the board, and their position remains subject to the rules of agency to which we now turn. Here the issue is not whether the board could have delegated, for that is now governed by s 35A, but whether the board did in fact authorise the individual to act and the extent of that authority.

For a third party to be able to hold the company[3] to a transaction where he has dealt not with the board but with an individual director, officer or employee, it will be necessary for the third party to show that that individual with whom he dealt had authority, actual or ostensible, to bind the company in this way.

Actual authority may be express or implied authority: express, arising from an explicit conferring of authority on a director, perhaps in the articles; implied, arising from the position which the individual holds. If, for example, an individual is appointed as a managing director then implied authority will authorise him to do all such things as fall within the usual scope of that office[4]. In either case, the existence of authority is a matter of fact[5].

Ostensible or apparent authority, on the other hand, is the authority of an agent as it appears to others[6]. The classic example is *Freeman and Lockyer v Buckhurst Park Properties (Mangal) Ltd*[7]. Here the director in question managed the company's property and acted on its behalf and in that role employed the plaintiff architects to draw up plans for the development of

---

3 He may have an action against the director who contracts without authority for damages for breach of an implied warranty of authority: *Hely-Hutchinson v Brayhead Ltd* [1968] 1 QB 549, [1967] 3 All ER 98, CA but he is usually more concerned with holding the company to the transaction.
4 See *Hely-Hutchinson v Brayhead* [1968] 1 QB 549, [1967] 3 All ER 98, CA.
5 *Rhodian River Shipping Co v Halla Maritime Corpn* [1984] BCLC 139.
6 *Hely-Hutchinson v Brayhead Ltd* [1968] 1 QB 549 at 583, [1967] 3 All ER 98 at 102, CA, per Lord Denning.
7 [1964] 2 QB 480, [1964] 1 All ER 630, CA.

land held by the company. The development ultimately collapsed and the plaintiffs sued the company for their fees. The company tried to deny that the director had any authority to employ them. The court found that while he had never been appointed managing director, his actions were within his apparent authority and the board had been aware of his conduct and had acquiesced in it[8]. Diplock LJ identified four factors which must be present before a company can be bound by the acts of an agent who has no actual authority to do so[9]. It must be shown:

(1)   that a representation that the agent had authority to enter on behalf of the company into a contract of the kind sought to be enforced was made to the contractor;
(2)   that such representation was made by a person or persons who had 'actual' authority to manage the business of the company either generally or in respect of those matters to which the contract relates;
(3)   that he (the contractor) was induced by such representation to enter into the contract, ie that he in fact relied upon it; and
(4)   that under its memorandum or articles of association the company was not deprived of the capacity either to enter into a contract of the kind sought to be enforced or to delegate authority to enter into a contract of that kind to the agent.

These criteria must now be considered in the light of the changes brought by the CA 1989 which alter the position somewhat. It remains the case that there must have been a representation of authority (1) which the third party relied on (3). As noted in (2), the agent must have been held out by someone with actual authority to carry out the transaction. Where the third party is relying on a holding out by the board, his position is enhanced by s 35A (providing he is in good faith) since he can ignore limits on the power of the board to authorise others to bind the company. However, it remains the case that there must have been some element of holding out. In other words, the agent cannot create an appearance of authority by means of conduct which is itself unauthorised, since the principal will in that event not have held him out to have the apparent authority which the third party is seeking to invoke against him[10].

(4) is no longer relevant as it reflected the ability of the constructive notice doctrine to cut down an apparent authority by deeming the third party to be aware of limitations contained in the memorandum and articles. Limitations on the company's capacity are no longer relevant following the enactment of new s 35. Limitations on the board's power to delegate are no longer relevant following s 35A. The doctrine of constructive notice has been abolished by s 711A(1) but it remains the position that ostensible or apparent authority cannot be relied upon where the outsider is aware of some

8 Such apparent authority may also be vested in officers other than directors, as in *Panorama Developments (Guildford) Ltd v Fidelis Furnishing Fabrics Ltd* [1971] 2 QB 711, CA where the company secretary as the chief administrative officer of the company was found to have ostensible authority to enter into contracts connected with the administrative side of his company's affairs.
9 [1964] 2 QB 480 at 505, [1964] 1 All ER 630 at 646.
10 *Egyptian International Foreign Trade Co v Soplex Wholesale Supplies Ltd, The Raffaella* [1985] BCLC 404, [1985] 2 Lloyd's Rep 36, CA. See also *British Bank of the Middle East v Sun Life Assurance Co of Canada (UK) Ltd* [1983] BCLC 78, [1983] 2 Lloyd's Rep 9, HL; *Rhodian River Shipping Co v Halla Maritime Corpn*]1984] BCLC 139; *Armagas Ltd v Mundogas SA* [1986] AC 717, [1986] 2 All ER 385, HL.

limitation (other than a limitation on the board's power to authorise since that is within s 35A) which prevents the authority arising, or is put on inquiry as to the extent of the individual's authority[11]. Section 35B does not assist the third party in this instance since it only applies with respect to limitations on the board's power to bind the company.

MONITORING MANAGEMENT

The corporate structure envisages then a strict division of power between the board and the general meeting with extensive power vested in the hands of the former which in turn delegates to individual directors and professional managers. The legal recognition of the concentration of power in the hands of management is consistent with the separation of ownership and control hypothesis and the concept of the corporation as a device for raising large amounts of capital[12]. The problem is that, having accepted this division of power, the law must find ways of monitoring the exercise of that power and curbing abuses arising from it in order that individuals who contribute capital are not exposed to undue risk. The law's response is essentially a four-fold one:

(i)   *Fiduciary duties*   An extensive range of fiduciary duties apply to company directors and officers and are used to control the exercise by them of their powers. These duties are discussed in Chapters 25 and 26. As a rule the company is the proper plaintiff in the event of a breach of those duties but in certain circumstances a minority shareholder can sue. This and other shareholder remedies are discussed in Chapter 27.

(ii) *Disclosure*   Proceeding on the assumption that the full glare of publicity will make directors more circumspect in their activities and will assist shareholders in monitoring those activities, extensive disclosure requirements are imposed on companies with little regard to their cost or efficacy, although recently there have been greater attempts to reduce the regulatory burden[13]. These are considered in Chapter 28.

(iii) *Returning power to the general meeting*   This has been a feature of recent legislation. For example, s 80 of the 1985 Act returns the power to issue shares to the general meeting; ss 164–166 require shareholder approval of any purchase of the company's own shares; ss 319–320 require shareholder approval of directors' service contracts for more than five years and substantial property transactions with the company. This increased monitoring by shareholders is imposed notwithstanding

---

11 *A L Underwood Ltd v Bank of Liverpool* [1924] 1 KB 775, CA; *Rolled Steel Products (Holdings) Ltd v British Steel Corpn* [1986] Ch 246, [1985] 3 All ER 52, CA. In any event, as we saw above, s 711A(2) provides that the abolition of constructive notice does not affect the question whether a person is affected by notice of any matter by reason of a failure to make such enquiries as ought reasonably to be made.

12 See Berle & Means *The Modern Corporation and Private Property* (1932); Manne (1967) 53 Va L Rev 259.

13 See Sealy *Company Law and Commercial Reality* (1984) pp 17–34. For some deregulation proposals, see 'Burdens on Business, Report of a Scrutiny of Administrative and Legislative Requirements' (DTI 1985); 'Accounting and Auditing Requirements for Small Firms' (DTI 1985); 'The Delivery of Annual Accounts and Returns to the Registrar of Companies' (DTI 1986); 'Deregulation for Small Private Companies' (IOD 1986).

the widely held view that shareholders have only a limited interest in monitoring directors' behaviour[14].

Given the inertia, apathy and lack of expertise of individual investors, it has been suggested that this vacuum might be filled by the institutional investors who now own in excess of 70% of listed UK equities. Their role was the subject of much debate in the UK in 1990, both in terms of their contribution to short-termism in British industry rather than long-term planning, and in terms of their contribution to corporate governance[15]. Throughout the last decade, the institutions had focused on specific, relatively narrow issues, such as non-voting shares, pre-emption rights and share option schemes, and relied on takeovers to resolve problems of managerial incompetence (or worse)[16]. The argument now is that they should seek a closer relationship with the companies in which they invest and should press, in particular, for well constructed boards of directors, with the requisite level of non-executive directors, separate chairmen and chief executives, and appropriate audit committees. The question of institutional investment raises a whole range of issues which are discussed in Chapter 34.

(iv)   *Reform of the board*   Many proposals for reform, especially those concerning the involvement of institutional investors as noted above, are directed towards changing the composition of company boards[17], requiring the inclusion of non-executive[18] or worker[19] directors, or subjecting the board as a whole to the scrutiny of an audit committee. But tinkering with the composition of boards is unlikely to be decisive in curbing corporate abuses and may only distract attention from alternative reforms[20]. One possible approach might be to heighten the profile and role of the Department of Trade and Industry as a regulatory body, although there may be political objections to such a course. The powers of the Department are discussed in Chapter 29.

In addition to these legal responses, there are restraining market forces in the markets for investment capital[1], control and management. The idea of the market for corporate control being that inefficient management leaves itself open to takeovers which enables shareholders to displace inadequate

---

14 See Anderson (1978) 25 UCLA L Rev 738 and the extensive literature cited therein; Manne, op cit; Hetherington (1983) 8 Hofstra L Rev 183. As *The Economist* noted recently: '"To shareholders in a typical public company, a share is now little more than a betting slip" A Survey of Capitalism, Punters or Proprietors?', *The Economist* 5 May 1990, p 6. See Charkham 'Corporate Governance and the Market for Companies, Aspects of the Shareholder's Role' Bank of England Discussion Paper, No 44 (1989); Stokes 'Company Law and Legal Theory' in Twining *Legal Theory and Common Law* (1986) p 168.
15 See Marsh *Short-termism on Trial* (1990); National Association of Pension Funds *Creative Tension?* (1990); Charkham, op cit.
16 See Plender 'The Limits to Institutional Power', *Financial Times* 22 May 1990.
17 Some would do away with boards altogether, see Axworthy (1988) 51 MLR 273.
18 See Tricker *The Independent Director* (1978); Brudney (1982) 95 Harv L Rev 597; Axworthy (1988) 51 MLR 273, and the discussion of non-executives in Ch 23, and the references cited there.
19 Although pressure to introduce worker directors is more directed towards improved worker/employer relations than to monitoring directorial misbehaviour and is in response to EC pressures, see Ch 3.
20 See Brudney, op cit.
 1 See Axworthy (1988) 51 MLR 273 at 290.

managers with those better able to run the business[2]. The possibility of such displacement, in theory, encourages existing management to maximise their efforts on behalf of the company and so provides the necessary incentive for efficient management. Others would argue that the use of takeovers to regulate management increases the short-term pressures on management and hinders overall long-term economic growth[3]. The role and regulation of takeovers is discussed in detail in Chapter 35.

2 On the market for corporate control, see Bradley (1990) 53 MLR 170 and the literature noted there.
3 See Sir Gordon White's defence of takeovers as a curb on inadequate management in 'Why Management Must be Accountable', *Financial Times*, 12 July 1990, responding critically to the contrary view by Lipton, 'An End to Hostile Takeovers and Short-termism', *Financial Times*, 27 June 1990.

CHAPTER 25

Directors' duties

Having sanctioned the granting of practically unlimited powers to the board of directors, the next concern is to devise some means of controlling the directors in the exercise of those powers. A balancing act is required: management must not be stifled but neither can unfettered, unsupervised, absolute discretion be permitted. The law's response has been to impose strict prophylactic rules designed to ensure certain minimum standards of behaviour from directors[1], backed up by onerous disclosure rules[2] designed to prevent directors shrouding their transactions in secrecy[3]. The consequences of breach of these rules can be severe[4]. This response by the legal system has not escaped criticism from those who argue that lawyers have simply assumed that the legal rules circumscribing managerial discretion will do so at a cost which is less than the benefit obtained, without any empirical evidence to support this assumption. The critics argue that the markets for management and control effectively constrain managerial discretion within reasonable limits and in a more cost-effective way than the legal rules[5].

Having decided upon the need to regulate directors' conduct, the immediate reaction is to place them into some pre-determined legal category and apply the rules governing that category to them. Thus directors have been regarded as trustees[6], or partners[7], or agents[8] but in reality 'directors of a limited company are creatures of statute and occupy a position peculiar to themselves'[9]. All that can safely be said is that they are

---

1 While, as a matter of convenience, the discussion throughout will refer to directors, the fiduciary duties discussed will apply equally to senior officers occupying important management positions in the company and authorised to act on its behalf. See Gower *Principles of Modern Company Law* (4th edn, 1979) p 574, approved in *Canadian Aero Service v O'Malley* (1973) 40 DLR (3d) 371 at 381, per Laskin J.

2 Discussed post, Chapter 28.

3 See generally, Stokes 'Company Law and Legal Theory' in Twining (ed) *Legal Theory and Common Law* (1986) pp 169–173.

4 See *Regal (Hastings) Ltd v Gulliver* [1967] 2 AC 134n, [1942] 1 All ER 378, HL; *Boardman v Phipps* [1967] 2 AC 46, [1966] 3 All ER 721, HL.

5 See Wolfson (1980) 34 U Miami L Rev 959 at 960–962.

6 *Great Eastern Rly Co v Turner* (1872) 8 Ch App 149 at 152, per Lord Selborne; *Re Lands Allotment Co* [1894] 1 Ch 616 at 631, CA, per Lindley LJ; *Selangor United Rubber Estates Ltd v Cradock (a bankrupt) (No 3)* [1968] 2 All ER 1073 at 1091–1094, [1968] 1 WLR 1555 at 1574–1577, per Ungoed-Thomas J. See also Sealy (1967) CLJ 69.

7 *Re Forest of Dean Coal Mining Co* (1878) 10 Ch D 450 at 453, per Jessel MR.

8 *Ferguson v Wilson* (1866) 2 Ch App 77 at 89; *Aberdeen Rly Co v Blaikie Bros* (1854) 1 Macq 461, HL; *Kuwait Asia Bank EC v National Mutual Life Nominees Ltd* [1990] 3 All ER 404, [1990] BCLC 868, PC.

9 *Regal (Hastings) Ltd v Gulliver* [1967] 2 AC 134n at 147, [1942] 1 All ER 378 at 387, HL, per Lord Russell; *Great Eastern Rly Co v Turner* (1872) 8 Ch App 149 at 152: 'The directors are the mere trustees or agents of the company, trustees of the company's money and property and agents in the transactions which they enter into on behalf of the company', per Lord Selborne.

fiduciaries[10] but as different fiduciaries are subject to different rules, this does not immediately determine what their duties are[11]. However, the following obligations have been identified[12]. Directors must act bona fide in the interests of the company and must not exercise their powers for any collateral purpose. A director must not place himself in a position where his duty to the company and his personal interests conflict and he must not profit from his position as a director. In addition, he must exercise reasonable care and such skill as might reasonably be expected of a person of his knowledge and experience. These duties will be discussed in greater detail later. The initial issue is to ascertain to whom these duties are owed.

TO WHOM ARE DUTIES OWED?

Basically directors owe these duties to the company and not to individual shareholders. The leading authority is *Percival v Wright*[13] where the directors purchased shares from existing shareholders without disclosing that they were in the process of negotiating a takeover bid at a higher price. It was held that since the directors owed no fiduciary duties to the shareholders, they could not be liable for the non-disclosure. This decision has been much criticised[14] and it may be possible to distinguish it on its facts[15]. Nevertheless, the basic principle remains: directors owe their duties to the company and not to individual shareholders. This is equally the position concerning duties to creditors. The orthodox position being as stated by Dillon LJ in *Multinational Gas and Petrochemical Co v Multinational Gas and Petrochemical Services Ltd*[16]: directors owe fiduciary duties to the company though not to the creditors, present or future, or to individual shareholders. The position of creditors is considered further below.

There is nothing, of course, to prevent the shareholders specifically appointing the directors as their agents in any matter, in which case the directors will then owe them the ordinary fiduciary duties arising from that agency relationship[17].

---

10 See Finn *Fiduciary Obligations* (1977) Chapter 1; Sealy (1967) CLJ 69.
11 See *Finn*, op cit, p 64, who regards directors as the most complex fiduciary office; Shepherd *The Law of Fiduciaries* (1981) pp 347–348: 'Nowhere are fiduciary principles applied in a more difficult or complex context than the modern corporation—any attempt to build tidy little theoretical cubbyholes in the corporate context is doomed to failure.'
12 The categories are not exclusive and to some extent overlap with one another. Unsuccessful attempts to reduce the duties to a statutory form have been made in the past, see the Companies Bill 1973, cls 52–53; the Companies Bill 1978, cls 44–46.
13 [1902] 2 Ch 421; *Dawson International plc v Coats Patons plc* [1989] BCLC 233.
14 See the Report of the Committee on Company Law Amendment (the Cohen Committee) Cmnd 6659, paras 86–87; The Report of the Company Law Committee (the Jenkins Committee) Cmnd 1749, para 89; Rider and French *The Regulation of Insider Trading* (1979) p 147; *Coleman v Myers* [1977] 2 NZLR 225.
15 The shareholders had approached the directors, after all, and had named the price at which they wished to sell, and the court was not satisfied that the board ever intended to accept the takeover offer in any event. Indeed the negotiations were ultimately aborted, see [1902] 2 Ch 421 at 426–7.
16 [1983] Ch 258 at 288, [1983] 2 All ER 563 at 585, CA.
17 *Allen v Hyatt* (1914) 30 TLR 444, PC; *Briess v Woolley* [1954] AC 333, [1954] 1 All ER 909, HL. Equally, directors may by agreement or representation assume a special duty to creditors, *Kuwait Asia Bank EC v National Mutual Life Nominees Ltd* [1990] 3 All ER 404 at 421, [1990] BCLC 868 at 889, PC.

That then is the orthodox position regarding directors' duties. However, consideration must be given to the possibility that, in certain limited circumstances at least, directors may owe some duties directly to their shareholders[18].

An important decision in this context is that of the New Zealand Court of Appeal in *Coleman v Myers*[19]. This case involved the takeover, at an undervalue, of a family company by a new company formed by one of the directors of the family company. The New Zealand Court of Appeal accepted that the directors of a company can owe fiduciary duties to their shareholders although the court stressed that the fiduciary relationship would not arise solely by reason of the director/shareholder relationship. Something additional was required. In determining whether that additional element was present regard must be paid to all the surrounding circumstances and the nature of the responsibility which in a real and practical sense the director has assumed towards the shareholder[20]. A number of factors would be relevant: the closely held nature of the company, the dependence of the shareholders upon information and advice from the directors, the existence of a relationship of confidence, the significance of the transaction for the parties and the extent of any positive action taken by or on behalf of the director or directors to promote it[1]. On the facts, the directors did owe a fiduciary duty to the individual shareholders and they were in breach of it by misleading them and withholding information affecting the true value of their shares. They were accordingly liable to account.

Interestingly, the factors considered in *Coleman v Myers* were not unlike the factors which in *Ebrahimi v Westbourne Galleries Ltd*[2] prompted the House of Lords to subject the exercise of legal rights to equitable considerations in the light of the relationship between the parties and the nature of the company and justified the winding up of the company under what is now s 122(1)(g) of the IA 1986. That decision provoked some debate[3] as to whether this approach extended into areas beyond winding up and indeed governed the relationship of the directors and the shareholders while the company was a going concern[4]. One consequence of any such extension might well be the development of fiduciary duties along the lines of *Coleman v Myers*. In all probability, in this jurisdiction, this development will in fact occur under s 459 of the CA 1985, discussed in detail in Chapter 27, which seems to be establishing a basic code of conduct governing the relationship

---

18 See Shepherd, op cit, pp 351–359; Finn, op cit, pp 64–69. For the American position, see *Jones v Ahmanson & Co* 460 P 2d 464 (1969); *Donoghue v Rodd Electrotype Co* 328 NE (2d) 505 (1975), noted 89 Harv L Rev 423 (1975); *Wilkes v Springside Nursing Home Inc* 353 NE (2d) 657 (1976).
19 [1977] 2 NZLR 225 (NZCA), noted Rider (1977) 40 MLR 471; (1978) 41 MLR 585.
20 [1977] 2 NZLR 225 at 324–325, per Woodhouse J.
1 [1977] 2 NZLR 225 at 325, per Woodhouse J. See also the judgment of Cooke J who emphasised the family character of the company, the position of the directors, their high degree of inside knowledge and the way in which they went about the takeover and the persuasion of the shareholders.
2 [1973] AC 360, [1972] 2 All ER 492, HL; revsg sub nom *Re Westbourne Galleries Ltd* [1971] Ch 799, [1971] 1 All ER 561, CA.
3 See Rider (1979) CLJ 148; Burridge (1981) 44 MLR 40 at 57–60.
4 See *Clemens v Clemens Bros Ltd* [1976] 2 All ER 268, noted Joffe (1977) 40 MLR 41; Prentice (1976) 92 LQR 502. Also *Pennell v Venida Investments Ltd* (25 July 1974, unreported), Templeman J, Ch D, discussed at length by Burridge (1981) 44 MLR 40.

between directors and shareholders, and between majority and minority shareholders, at least in the smaller private companies.

Returning to *Coleman v Myers*[5], it will be recalled that it concerned a takeover situation which of its nature frequently results in shareholders relying heavily on the directors for advice. There are a number of English cases where the courts have considered the position of directors vis-à-vis their shareholders in that particular situation. In *Gething v Kilner*[6] Brightman J considered that where a takeover bid had been made, the directors of the offeree company were under a duty to their own shareholders which included a duty to be honest and not to mislead. In *Heron International Ltd v Lord Grade*[7] the directors of the target company were faced with two competing bids. Under the articles the board had power to choose the bidder to whom shares could be transferred. The court found, as a result of that provision in the articles, the directors owed a duty to the current shareholders to obtain for them the opportunity to accept or reject the best price reasonably obtainable. Hoffman J in *Re a Company (No 008699 of 1985)*[8], however, did not accept that the board must inevitably be under a positive duty to recommend and take all steps within its power to facilitate whichever is the highest offer. *Heron International Ltd v Lord Grade*, he emphasised, must be read in the light of the power the board had in that case to choose the bidder to whom the shares could be transferred and the fact that they had chosen the lower bidder. There they had deprived the shareholders of the opportunity of accepting the higher bid. Directors had to refrain, however, from giving misleading advice and from exercising their fiduciary powers in a way which would prevent or inhibit shareholders from choosing the better price[9]. These cases seem to raise the possibility of directors owing duties to shareholders but their true relevance is succinctly explained by Lord Cullen in *Dawson International plc v Coats Paton plc*[10] who stated:

If . . . directors take it on themselves to give advice to current shareholders, the cases cited to me show clearly that they have a duty to advise in good faith and not fraudulently, and not to mislead whether deliberately or carelessly. . . . However, these cases do not, in my view, demonstrate a pre-existing fiduciary duty to the shareholders but a potential liability arising out of their words or actions which can be based on ordinary principles of law. This, I may say, appears to be a more satisfactory way of expressing the position of directors in this context than by talking of a so-called secondary fiduciary duty to the shareholders[11].

As for the significance of *Heron International Ltd v Lord Grade* in this context, he agreed with Hoffman J above, that it was a case which turned on the particular articles applicable in that instance.

Directors may therefore find themselves liable to shareholders under ordinary legal principles if they give misleading advice or abuse their posi-

5 [1977] 2 NZLR 225 (NZCA).
6 [1972] 1 All ER 1166, [1972] 1 WLR 337.
7 [1983] BCLC 244, CA.
8 [1986] BCLC 382.
9 [1986] BCLC 382 at 389. Their conduct may, of course, warrant a petition under CA 1985, s 459 alleging unfairly prejudicial conduct.
10 [1989] BCLC 233, CS (Outer House).
11 Ibid at 244.

tions[12], but that is not to say that they owe fiduciary duties to shareholders as such. This is equally the position as regards creditors, as Lord Lowry pointed out in *Kuwait Asia Bank EC v National Mutual Life Nominees Ltd*[13] '. . . although directors are not liable *as such* to creditors of the company, a director may by agreement or representation assume a special duty to a creditor of the company'[14].

We remain primarily concerned therefore with duties owed by directors to the company. The significance of this is that if such a duty is breached then the wrong is done to the company and the company is the proper person to sue in respect of it. This is the rule in *Foss v Harbottle*[15], discussed in detail in Chapter 27, which generally precludes actions by individual shareholders against wrongdoing directors. These difficulties in enforcement remain a major problem and this should be borne in mind when examining the extent of these duties. After all, there is little point in having onerous duties if they cannot easily be enforced.

THE DUTY TO ACT BONA FIDE IN THE INTERESTS OF THE COMPANY

It is clearly established that directors are under a duty to act bona fide in what they consider, and not what a court may consider, is in the interests of the company and not for any collateral purpose[16]. This is so, even if it means that in so doing they fail to fulfil an agreement entered into with a third party[17].

The overriding nature of this obligation has been stressed recently in two cases concerning takeover bids[18]. In *Dawson International plc v Coats Patons plc*[19] the court accepted that an agreement between a target and a

12 Directors may be liable to existing shareholders in negligence, for example, where the shareholders purchase additional shares pursuant to a rights issue, with respect to erroneous statements in the prospectus inviting those further purchases: *Hedley Byrne & Co Ltd v Heller & Partners Ltd* [1964] AC 465, [1963] 2 All ER 575, HL; *Nocton v Lord Ashburton* [1914] AC 932, HL, per Viscount Haldane; *Al Nakib Investments (Jersey) Ltd v Longcroft* [1990] 3 All ER 321, [1991] BCLC 7.
13 [1990] 3 All ER 404 at 421, [1990] BCLC 868 at 889, PC.
14 Such a liability is not limited to creditors but can extend in appropriate circumstances to other third parties including, possibly, would-be takeover bidders: *Morgan Crucible Co plc v Hill Samuel & Co Ltd* [1991] 1 All ER 148, CA.
15 (1843) 2 Hare 461.
16 *Re Smith & Fawcett Ltd* [1942] Ch 304 at 306, [1942] 1 All ER 542 at 543, CA, per Lord Greene. The test originated in *Allen v Gold Reefs of West Africa Ltd* [1900] 1 Ch 656, CA, a case which concerns the abuse of power by a majority of the shareholders in general meeting, in altering the articles, but which has come to be the test for directors' duties also. The two tests are, of course, different in that shareholders can vote in their own selfish interests (*North-West Transportation Co Ltd and Beatty v Beatty* (1887) 12 App Cas 589, PC) while directors exercising their powers must act in the best interests of the company; see Finn op cit, p 66. See generally, Heydon Directors' Duties and the Company's Interests in *Equity and Commercial Relationships* (1987, ed Finn), pp 120–136; Sealy (1987) 13 Monash Univ L Rev 164.
17 *Dawson International plc v Coats Patons plc* [1990] BCLC 560; *John Crowther Group plc v Carpets International plc* [1990] BCLC 460.
18 For an interesting discussion of the tensions between directors and shareholders and the difficulties of applying a test of what is in the best interests of the company in the takeover context, see Bradley (1990) 53 MLR 170.
19 [1990] BCLC 560.

bidder which provided that the board of the target company would recommend the bid, and would not encourage or co-operate with any other bidder which might emerge, was subject to an implied qualification derived from the law which defines directors' overriding duties to their company and their share holders. The qualification was that the board could, if circumstances altered materially, decide in fulfilment of their continuing duty to the company and its shareholders not to implement the agreement. In the earlier case of *John Crowther Group plc v Carpets International plc*[20] the court likewise accepted that an agreement to secure shareholder consent to one bid had clearly to be read in the light of the fact known to all parties that directors owe a fiduciary duty to act in the interests of the company. The bidders were not therefore entitled to damages when the board recommended that their bid should be set aside after a rival bidder made a more attractive offer.

Shareholder interests

'In the interests of the company' has traditionally meant in the interests of the shareholders and it is the directors' subjective[1] opinion as to the interests of the corporators as a general body[2], balancing the short-term interests of the present members against the long-term interests of future members[3], which counts. Notwithstanding the subjective test a decision by the directors may be set aside if it is such that no reasonable man could consider it to be bona fide in the interests of the company[4] but the courts rarely interfere.

It can be seen therefore that while directors may not owe any fiduciary duties to shareholders as such, the position is redressed to some extent by defining their duty to act bona fide in the interests of the company in terms of the interests of shareholders[5], albeit according to the directors' view of those interests.

Normally the duty requires directors to treat all shareholders equally. For example, they cannot make calls on some members while payment is outstanding on other members' shares[6]. But the equality of individual shareholders does not always require identity of treatment. In *Mutual Life Insurance Co of New York v Rank Organisation Ltd*[7] the court accepted that

---

20 [1990] BCLC 460. See also *Rackham v Peek Foods Ltd* [1990] BCLC 895.
 1 The use of a subjective test has been criticised as entrenching management to an unacceptable degree. If the article conferring the particular power is drafted widely enough, and if a subjective test is applied to the exercise of that power by the directors, then the result can be to confer an absolute and uncontrolled discretion on the directors: see *Re Smith & Fawcett Ltd* [1942] Ch 304, [1942] 1 All ER 542, CA.
 2 *Greenhalgh v Arderne Cinemas Ltd* [1951] Ch 286 at 291, [1950] 2 All ER 1120 at 1126, CA, per Evershed MR.
 3 'Second Savoy Hotel Investigation, Report of the Inspector', (1954) HMSO; *Gaiman v National Association of Mental Health* [1971] Ch 317 at 330, per Megarry J. Sometimes only the interests of the current shareholders will be relevant, as where the directors are considering rival takeover bids, see *Heron International Ltd v Lord Grade* [1983] BCLC 244, CA. It is not therefore the interests of the company as a commercial entity although its interests may be identical with those of its shareholders. See Afterman *Company Directors and Controllers* (1970) p 46; 'it is a well-recognised fact that management . . . do perceive the company as having an independent personality and existence all of its own and they balance its needs as against those of the shareholders, employees, creditors etc'.
 4 See *Shuttleworth v Cox Bros & Co (Maidenhead) Ltd* [1927] 2 KB 9 at 18, CA, per Banke LJ.
 5 See *Finn* op cit, pp 66–67, and Birds (1980) 1 Co Law 67 at 72.
 6 *Galloway v Hallé Concerts Society* [1915] 2 Ch 233.
 7 [1985] BCLC 11.

it was in the best interests of the defendant company to offer its shares for sale on a preferential basis to its existing shareholders other than those resident in North America. This was done in order to avoid the onerous disclosure requirements of the US and Canada and was not unfair to those excluded shareholders whose existing holdings and rights were unaffected.

Where there are different classes of shareholders, so decisions may adversely affect the interests of one class and benefit another, the question is not so much of the interests of the company at all as one of what is fair as between different classes of shareholders[8]. The fact that the decision ultimately taken by the directors also benefits themselves as shareholders does not necessarily mean it is invalid. Directors are not required to live in 'an unreal world of detached altruism'[9].

Where the company is one of a group, the directors must continue to act in the interests of that company and not look solely to the overall interests of the group. This is not to deny, of course, that the interests of the group may be relevant to deciding what is in the interests of the company. The proper approach is to consider whether an intelligent and honest man in the position of the director of the company concerned could, in the whole of the existing circumstances, have reasonably believed that the transaction was for the benefit of the company[10]. Equally where a director is appointed as a nominee of a particular shareholder or class of shareholders, his overriding responsibility remains to the company as a whole[11].

Creditors' interests

As we have seen, directors do not owe duties to shareholders as such. Neither do they owe duties to the company's creditors[12]. The orthodox position being as stated by Dillon LJ in *Multinational Gas and Petrochemical Co v Multinational Gas and Petrochemical Services Ltd*[13]: directors owe fiduciary duties to the company though not to the creditors, present or future, or to individual shareholders.

Winkworth v Edward Baron Development Co Ltd[14], a House of Lords decision, might suggest that there has been a change to that position with Lord Templeman stating[15]:

. . . a company owes a duty to its creditors, present and future. The company owes a duty to its creditors to keep its property inviolate and available for repayment of its

---

8 *Mills v Mills* (1938) 60 CLR 150 at 164, per Latham CJ; *Howard Smith Ltd v Ampol Petroleum Ltd* [1974] AC 821 at 835, [1974] 1 All ER 1126 at 1134, PC.
9 *Mills v Mills* (1938) 60 CLR 150 at 164, per Latham CJ.
10 *Charterbridge Corpn Ltd v Lloyds Bank Ltd* [1970] Ch 62 at 74, [1969] 2 All ER 1185 at 1194. See also *Walker v Wimborne* (1976) 50 ALJR 446; *Lindgren v L & P Estates Ltd* [1968] Ch 572, CA.
11 *Scottish Co-operative Wholesale Society Ltd v Meyer* [1959] AC 324, [1958] 3 All ER 66, HL; *Boulting v ACTT* [1963] 2 QB 606, [1963] 1 All ER 716, CA. See Boros (1989) 10 Co Law 211 for an interesting discussion of the difficulties facing nominee and multiple directors.
12 Although the importance of their role in the company has always been recognised, note the rules governing capital maintenance, Ch 15 ante, and statutory provisions such as s 213 of the IA 1986.
13 [1983] Ch 258 at 288, [1983] 2 All ER 563 at 585, CA. See also *Kuwait Asia Bank EC v National Mutual Life Nominees Ltd* [1990] 3 All ER 404, [1990] BCLC 868, PC.
14 [1987] 1 All ER 114, [1987] BCLC 193.
15 [1987] 1 All ER 114 at 118, [1987] BCLC 193 at 197.

debts. The conscience of the company, as well as its management, is confided to its directors. A duty is owed by the directors to the company and to the creditors of the company to ensure that the affairs of the company are properly administered and that its property is not dissipated or exploited for the benefit of the directors themselves to the prejudice of the creditors.

The case concerned a claim by a wife (a director and shareholder) to be allowed to enforce her equitable interest in the matrimonial home (owned by the company—her husband was the other director and shareholder) against a mortgagee seeking possession. Much of the judgment is devoted to that aspect of the case and it is difficult to assess how much judicial dislike for such equitable interests[16] coloured the court's views on the position of directors vis-à-vis creditors. It is in any event unlikely that Lord Templeman could have intended such a significant restatement of the position as the authorities in this area were not even considered. Given these difficulties[17], this dictum cannot be taken as a statement of the current position which instead remains as stated in *Multinational Gas*.

However, there is support for treating creditors in the same manner as shareholders, ie for defining the duty to act bona fide in the interests of the company as encompassing creditor interests in some circumstances[18].

This process has its origins in Australian and New Zealand decisions[19]. In *Walker v Wimborne*[20] the Australian High Court found the company's directors in breach of their duties to the company and its creditors in guaranteeing loans of another company in the group at a time when the company was itself in serious financial difficulties. The court found the transaction exposed the company to the probable prospect of substantial loss and was undertaken in accordance with a policy adopted by the directors in total disregard of the interests of the company and its creditors. The court thought that creditors' interests should always be relevant given the theoretical possibility of future insolvency[1]. The New Zealand Court of Appeal considered the issue in *Nicholson v Permakraft (NZ) Ltd*[2] where Cooke J thought that current and likely continuing creditors were entitled to consideration if the company was insolvent, or near-insolvent, or of doubtful solvency, or if a contemplated payment or other course of action would jeopardise its solvency. In such situations of marginal commercial solvency he felt creditors may fairly be seen as beneficially interested in the company or contingently so. He did not feel that any duties were owed to future

16 See [1987] Conv 217 on this aspect of the case.
17 For criticism of Lord Templeman's approach, see Sealy (1988) CLJ 175; Riley (1989) 10 Co Law 87; Farrar (1989) 4 Canta L R 12 at 14–15. Drake [1989] JBL 474 at 490 notes that it is a decision best confined to its unusual facts. Despite these criticisms, it was endorsed by the Supreme Court of Western Australia in *Jeffree v NCSC* (1989) 15 ACLR 217, noted Baxt (1989) ABLR 404, but see Grantham [1991] JBL 1 at 12.
18 See generally, Grantham [1991] JBL 1; Prentice (1990) 10 Ox J L S 265; Riley (1989) 10 Co Law 87; Finch (1989) 10 Co Law 23; Hawke [1989] JBL 54; Farrar (1989) 4 Canta L R 12; Heydon Directors' Duties and the Company's Interests in *Equity and Commercial Relationships* (1987, ed Finn), pp 120–136; Sealy (1987) 13 Monash Univ L Rev 164; Dawson (1984) 11 NZULR 68; Barrett (1977) 40 MLR 226.
19 Discussed in Farrar (1989) 4 Canta L R 12.
20 (1976) 50 ALJR 446, noted Barrett (1977) 40 MLR 226.
 1 (1976) 50 ALJR 446 at 449, per Mason J.
 2 [1985] 1 NZLR 242 at 249, noted [1985] JBL 413, (1986) 7 Co Law 39. See also Dawson (1984) 11 NZULR 68; Baxt (1986) 60 Aust LJ 102; *Kinsela v Russell Kinsela Pty Ltd* (1986) 4 ACLC 215, noted Baxt (1986) 14 ABLR 320.

creditors who must take the company as they find it and be guardians of their own interests. He justified such an extension of duties to creditors, restricted in the way outlined, on the basis that limited liability is a privilege which can be used to the prejudice of creditors and that that was a mischief to which the courts should be alive. Somers J agreed that directors must have regard to the interests of creditors where the company is insolvent. Richardson J preferred to reserve to another day what he considered to be the controversial question of the nature and scope of the duties owed to creditors. All three judges, however, were clear that no duty is owed where the company is solvent.

Support here for this approach can be found in *West Mercia Safetywear Ltd v Dodd*[3] where Dillon LJ[4] approved the following statement of the position by the New South Wales Court of Appeal in *Kinsela v Russell Kinsela Pty Ltd*[5]:

In a solvent company the proprietary interests of the shareholders entitle them as a general body to be regarded as the company when questions of the duty of directors arise. If, as a general body, they authorise or ratify a particular action of the directors, there can be no challenge to the validity of what the directors have done. But where a company is insolvent the interests of the creditors intrude. They become prospectively entitled, through the mechanism of liquidation, to displace the power of the shareholders and directors to deal with the company's assets. It is in a practical sense their assets and not the shareholder's assets that, through the medium of the company, are under the management of the directors pending either liquidation, return to solvency, or the imposition of some alternative administration.

In the *West Mercia* case, a director who organised payment by an insolvent company of a debt in respect of which he had given a personal guarantee was in breach of his duty by acting in disregard of the interests of the general creditors of the company.

Creditors' interests were also considered by the House of Lords in *Brady v Brady*[6], a case which concerned the validity of a complicated scheme for the reorganisation of a group of companies. One of the issues before the court was whether the scheme constituted illegal financial assistance contrary to CA 1985, s 151, or whether it was within s 153(2) which permits such transactions in certain circumstances, provided they are done in good faith in the interests of the company. In interpreting this latter requirement, Nourse LJ in the Court of Appeal stated[7]:

The interests of a company, an artificial person, cannot be distinguished from the interests of the persons who are interested in it. Who are those persons? Where a company is both going and solvent, first and foremost come the shareholders, present and no doubt future as well. How material are the interests of creditors in such a case? Admittedly existing creditors are interested in the assets of the company as the only source for the satisfaction of their debts. But in a case where the assets are

---

3 [1988] BCLC 250, CA, noted Finch (1989) 10 Co Law 23. See also *Lonrho Ltd v Shell Petroleum Co Ltd* [1980] 1 WLR 627 at 634, HL; *Re Horsley & Weight Ltd* [1982] Ch 442 at 454, [1982] 3 All ER 1045 at 1055.
4 He distinguished the situation from that which occurred in *Multinational Gas*, noted above, where he had ruled out any duty owed to the creditors, on the basis that there the company was amply solvent and the parties were acting in good faith, see [1988] BCLC 250 at 252.
5 (1986) 4 ACLC 215 at 223, per Street CJ.
6 [1989] AC 755, [1988] 2 All ER 617, HL; revsg [1988] BCLC 20, CA, discussed in greater detail in Ch 15.
7 [1988] BCLC 20 at 40.

enormous and the debts minimal it is reasonable to suppose that the interests of the creditors ought not to count for very much. Conversely, where the company is insolvent, or even doubtfully solvent, the interests of the company are in reality the interests of existing creditors alone.

The House of Lords subsequently overturned the Court of Appeal decision on a number of grounds. As far as the interests of creditors were concerned, Lord Oliver concluded that, on the facts, Nourse LJ was incorrect to suggest that the interests of the creditors had not been considered. The evidence was that the company was solvent so there was no reason to suppose that the position of any present creditor was in the least affected or that the position of future creditors should be considered[8]. So despite this factual disagreement, the overall approach is clearly consistent with the authorities and developments outlined above.

This movement towards increased regard for creditors' interests, at least in situations of insolvency or doubtful solvency, gained some of its impetus from earlier statutory developments in the Insolvency Act 1986 and the Company Directors Disqualification Act 1986.

The Insolvency Act 1986 does not impose duties on directors vis-à-vis creditors but it does assess directors' conduct on a company going into insolvency in the light of, inter alia, the effect of that conduct on the company's creditors. For example, a director's liability for wrongful trading[9] under s 214 of that Act will depend on whether he took every step with a view to minimising the potential loss to the company's creditors as he ought to have taken. He may also be liable under s 213 of that Act if he was knowingly a party to the carrying on of any business of the company with intent to defraud creditors. Any misfeasance or breach of any fiduciary or other duty by a director may be the subject of misfeasance proceedings under s 212 brought on the application of, inter alia, any creditor[10]. Provisions governing prior transactions (especially IA, ss 238–240) are also designed to improve the position of creditors.

The Company Directors Disqualification Act 1986, which is discussed in detail in Chapter 23, also focuses on the creditors' position. Under s 6 of that Act, a director shall be disqualified if the court is satisfied that his conduct as a director of an insolvent company makes him unfit to be concerned in the management of a company. In determining unfitness the court shall have regard to the matters mentioned in Sch 1 to that Act which include the extent of the director's responsibility for the causes of the company becoming insolvent, together with various other factors emphasising the creditors' role. The disqualification cases also emphasise judicial concern that directors

8 [1989] AC 755 at 778, [1988] 2 All ER 617 at 632.
9 Liability for wrongful trading can arise in respect of a person who was a director of a company which has gone into insolvent liquidation and at some time before the commencement of the winding up of the company that person knew or ought to have concluded that there was no reasonable prospect that the company would avoid going into insolvent liquidation. See *Re Produce Marketing Consortium Ltd (No 2)* [1989] BCLC 520; *Re DKG Contractors Ltd* [1990] BCC 903; *Re Purpoint Ltd* [1991] BCC 121 and discussion of s 214 in Ch 39.
10 See *Re Halt Garage (1964) Ltd* [1982] 3 All ER 1016; *Re Horsley & Weight Ltd* [1982] Ch 442, [1982] 3 All ER 1045, CA. An honest attempt to save the business will not warrant misfeasance proceedings alleging that, if the directors had acted differently, the creditors might have received more than they did, *Re Welfab Engineers Ltd* [1990] BCLC 833. For detailed discussion of these provisions and ss 206–219 which also relate to offences against creditors, see Ch 39.

should not feel free to disregard creditor interests, and that directors whose past conduct has shown them to be a danger to creditors and others will be disqualified. Directors will have to pay greater regard to creditors' interests if, on insolvency, they are to avoid the imposition of personal liability and disqualification under these provisions.

All of these factors have combined to result in the common law recognising that creditor interests must now be included as an element in the duty to act bona fide in the interests of the company. Naturally, there are issues which have not yet been fully worked out, not least the difficulty in gauging the point at which shareholders cease to be the dominant concern, as they are when the company is solvent, and creditors become the focus for directors, as they do when the company is insolvent or possibly of doubtful solvency. Identifying the point in time when that shift in emphasis occurs may be difficult[11] and directors may feel that they are not given sufficient guidance. On the other hand, as the courts have made clear in the disqualification cases, directors are not entitled to abdicate all financial responsibility and should keep themselves informed as to the company's financial position. If the company keeps adequate accounting records, as it is required to do, then they should indicate when the company's financial position is worsening, so alerting the directors to the need to consider carefully the interests of the creditors[12].

Another issue is whether it is satisfactory that the creditors should be protected through a duty owed to the company, given the earlier comments about the difficulty of enforcing such a duty. The creditor's position is, of course, different from that of the shareholders, who are often faced with trying to persuade wrongdoers who are still in control of the company to take legal action. If creditor interests have been infringed, then in all probability the company has actually gone into insolvency and so the liquidator will be available to take legal action on their behalf against the directors[13]. Uncertainty also remains as to whether the shareholders could ratify a breach by the directors of the obligation to have regard to the creditors' interests[14].

Employees' interests

The common law definition of 'interests', encompassing only the interests of shareholders, has now been expanded by statute to include employees[15].

11 A problem which also exists under IA 1986, s 214, the wrongful trading provision. See Prentice (1990) 10 Ox J L S 265; Finch (1989) 10 Co Law 23; Hawke [1989] JBL 54.
12 For an indication of the importance of the company's accounts in this context, see *Re Produce Marketing Consortium Ltd (No 2)* [1989] BCLC 520.
13 See Prentice (1990) 10 Ox J L S 265; Riley (1989) 10 Co Law 87.
14 See *Multinational Gas and Petrochemical Co v Multinational Gas and Petrochemical Services Ltd* [1983] Ch 258, [1983] 2 All ER 563, CA; *Re Horsley & Weight Ltd* [1982] Ch 442, [1982] 3 All ER 1045, CA. Also Prentice (1990) 10 Ox J L S 265, Riley (1989) 10 Co Law 87; Heydon Directors' Duties and the Company's Interests in *Equity and Commercial Relationships* (1987, ed Finn), pp 120–136 and Rennard's response to Heydon at p 140; Sealy (1987) 13 Monash Univ L Rev 164.
15 At common law directors were not entitled to take into account employee interests: *Parke v Daily News Ltd* [1962] Ch 927, [1962] 2 All ER 929, now reversed by s 719, CA 1985. See Lofthouse [1984] JBL 320 on the difficulties directors face when trying to balance shareholder and employee interests; also *Xuereb* (1988) 51 MLR 156.

Section 309 of CA 1985 provides that:

The matters to which the directors of a company are to have regard in the performance of their functions include the interests of the company's employees in general as
well as the interests of its members[16].

This provision has attracted a good deal of criticism, not so much for having
included employees within the company 'fold' as for the statutory form
adopted[17]. A major difficulty will be proving that the directors have failed to
comply with the requirements of the section. In any event since the duty, by
sub-s (2), is owed only to the company, the rule in *Foss v Harbottle*[18] will
again come into play and enforcement of the duty will be at the discretion of
the company. It does not seem that a shareholder could bring a derivative
action in the event of a refusal by the company to proceed[19]. It is then a
provision without teeth but nevertheless the section represents the first
tentative steps towards recognising the employees' role in the enterprise[20].

Another often debated issue is whether a company should consider the
interests not just of its shareholders, employees and creditors but also of its
consumers, its local community and indeed in the case of larger companies,
the state as a whole[1]. Little has been achieved on this level in this country,
though lip service is paid to the 'social responsibility' concept in the annual
reports of the larger companies and they are subject to a measure of
enforced responsibility through legislation governing such matters as planning and environmental controls. Given the reluctant recognition of those
bodies most intimately connected with the company, namely its employees
and creditors, it seems unlikely that much progress will be made in terms of
enforced social responsibility.

Ultimately, of course, regardless of what the legal rules are, the directors will
want to balance the differing interests of shareholders, employees, creditors,
consumers and society at large, having regard to the nature and size of the
company and the interests most affected by the particular transaction.

Whatever the interests to which directors have regard, one requirement is
certain. They must come to a decision and must actively exercise their
discretion[2]. Their decisions cannot be taken for them by, for example, the

---

16 Originally introduced by the Companies Act 1980, s 46. For earlier abortive provisions, see
the Companies Bill 1973, cl 53 and the Companies Bill 1978, cl 46. See generally the
'Report of the Committee of Inquiry on Industrial Democracy' (the Bullock Report)
Cmnd 6706; Wedderburn 'The Legal Development of Corporate Responsibility' in Hopt,
Teubner (ed) *Corporate Governance and Directors' Liabilities* (1985).
17 See Boyle and Mordsley (1980) 1 Co Law 280 at 284; Mackenzie (1982) 132 NLJ 688; Birds
(1980) 1 Co Law 67. The value of the provision might be enhanced if progress could be made
within the EC harmonisation programme on the issue of worker directors who would,
presumably, be able to ensure proper consideration of employee interests as opposed to
token compliance with the statutory provision. On harmonisation generally, see Chapter 3.
18 (1843) 2 Hare 461.
19 See Prentice *Companies Act 1980* (1980) pp 138–139. For detailed discussion of the derivative action, see Chapter 27 post.
20 Major reform of the employees' position has been promised by the EEC but there has been
considerable opposition to these developments within the UK, see Docksey (1986) 49 MLR
281; Clough (1982) 3 Co Law 109; Hull and Docksey (1981) 2 Co Law 207.
 1 See generally, Hopt, Teubner (ed) *Corporate Governance and Directors' Liabilities* (1985)
and, in particular, Wedderburn, The Legal Development of Corporate Responsibility,
pp 3–54 and the extensive literature cited therein; also Wedderburn (1985) 5 MULR 4.
 2 See *Brekland Group Holdings Ltd v London & Suffolk Properties Ltd* [1989] BCLC 100 at
103, per Harman J.

majority shareholder who has elected them. They must not fetter their discretion[3] or act as mere puppets on the instructions of another[4]. Sometimes it is not clear whether directors are fettering their discretion (which is prohibited) or exercising their discretion in a way which hampers their future conduct (which is permissible). In *Thorby v Goldberg*[5] the directors of a company agreed as part of a transaction to allot shares in a particular manner at a later date. They failed to do as they had promised and in an action to force them to make the allotment they pleaded that it was an invalid fettering of their discretion on their part. The court rejected this argument, holding that the time for exercising their discretion was at the time of entering into the agreement and provided they had considered the best interests of the company at that time the agreement was valid. It was not the case that they had wrongly fettered their discretion, rather that they had already exercised it[6].

DUTY NOT TO ACT FOR ANY COLLATERAL PURPOSE

It will be recalled that the directors' duty to act in what they consider to be the best interests of the company was qualified by the proviso that they must not act for any collateral purpose[7]. The powers given by the articles to the directors are held in trust for the company and must not be exercised for an improper purpose[8]. If they are so exercised, the transaction may be set aside notwithstanding the directors' assertions that they honestly believed it to be in the best interests of the company[9]. So while directors may have wide managerial powers conferred on them by the articles and may only be constrained by a subjective bona fides test, some measure of control is regained by the use of a proper purpose doctrine which examines objectively the directors' purpose while giving due credit to their business judgment[10].

The rule that they must not exercise their powers for an improper purpose applies to the exercise by the directors of any of their powers, be it the power to make calls on shares[11], to refuse to register transfers[12]; to declare a

---

3 *Motherwell v Schoof* [1949] 4 DLR 812 (Alt SC).
4 *Selangor United Rubber Estates Ltd v Cradock (a bankrupt) (No 3)* [1968] 2 All ER 1073, [1968] 1 WLR 1555.
5 (1964) 112 CLR 597 (Aust HC). See Prentice (1977) 89 LQR 107 at 111–113; Burridge (1981) 44 MLR 40 at 53.
6 (1964) 112 CLR 597 at 618, per Owen J. See also *Ringuet v Bergeron* (1960) 24 DLR (2d) 449.
7 *Re Smith & Fawcett Ltd* [1942] Ch 304 at 306, [1942] 1 All ER 542 at 543, CA, per Lord Greene.
8 'Improper' in the sense of beyond the scope of, or not justified by, the instrument creating the power: *Vatcher v Paull* [1915] AC 372 at 378, PC, per Lord Parker.
9 *Punt v Symons & Co Ltd* [1903] 2 Ch 506; *Piercy v S Mills & Co Ltd* [1920] 1 Ch 77; *Hogg v Cramphorn Ltd* [1967] Ch 254, [1966] 3 All ER 420.
10 It is sometimes argued that there should be no test other than the genuineness of the directors' motives. Once they have acted bona fide then that should end the matter, see Sealy (1967) CLJ 33 and *Teck Corpn v Millar* (1972) 33 DLR (3d) 288.
11 *Galloway v Hallé Concerts Society* [1915] 2 Ch 233; *Alexander v Automatic Telephone Co* [1900] 2 Ch 56, CA.
12 *Re Bennett's Case* (1854) 5 De GM & G 284; *Re Smith & Fawcett Ltd* [1942] Ch 304, [1942] 1 All ER 542, CA; *Heron International Ltd v Lord Grade* [1983] BCLC 244.

dividend[13]; to order the forfeiture of shares[14]; or to expel a member[15]. Most controversy has centred on the exercise by the directors of the power to allot shares, a power which is now restricted by CA 1985, s 80 which provides that the power to allot shares shall not be exercised by the directors unless they are authorised to do so by the company in general meeting or by the articles. Such authorisation can be general or particular, conditional or unconditional, but shall not be for a period longer than five years although it may subsequently be renewed[16]. The five-year limit will not apply to any private company which has passed an elective resolution under s 379A applying s 80A in relation to the authority of directors to allot. In this case, the authority may be given for an indefinite or fixed period[17].

Many attempts by directors to use this power to consolidate their control or prevent a rival body from taking over the company have been held to be invalid, notwithstanding the asserted belief of the directors that they were acting in the best interests of the company[18]. This uncompromising stance by the U K courts has not always been followed by Commonwealth authorities[19] who regard it as too rigid an approach, and in fact as being contrary to the test in *Re Smith & Fawcett Ltd*[20] in that it prevents directors who bona fide believe that a takeover is not in the best interests of the company (perhaps because the offeror is a well known corporate looter, or for some other reason) from doing anything about it. The Supreme Court of British Columbia permitted an allotment to defeat such a takeover in *Teck Corpn v Millar*[1] even though the allotment was made against the wishes of the existing majority shareholder and deprived that shareholder of control of the company. The court was satisfied that the directors had simply been concerned to obtain the best possible deal for the company. Likewise the High Court of Australia, in *Harlowe's Nominees Pty v Woodside (Lake Entrance) Oil Co*[2], permitted an allotment of shares which was made in order to secure the financial support of a large oil company although a

---

13 See *Re a Company (No 00370 of 1987), ex p Glossop* [1988] 1 WLR 1068, [1988] BCLC 570.
14 *Re Agriculturist Cattle Insurance Co, Stanhope's Case* (1866) 1 Ch App 161; *Re European Assurance Society, Manisty's Case* (1873) 17 Sol Jo 745.
15 *Gaiman v National Association for Mental Health* [1971] Ch 317, [1970] 2 All ER 362. See (1970) 33 MLR 700.
16 CA 1985, s 80(3) and (4). The power to issue shares is subject to s 89 which confers pre-emption rights on shareholders although companies may contract out of this provision, see ss 91 and 95, also Chapter 14.
17 CA 1985, s 379A and s 80A are inserted by CA 1989, ss 116 and 115 respectively.
18 See *Fraser v Whalley* (1864) 2 Hem & M 10; *Punt v Symons & Co Ltd* [1903] 2 Ch 506; *Piercy v S Mills & Co Ltd* [1920] 1 Ch 77; *Hogg v Cramphorn Ltd* [1967] Ch 254, [1966] 3 All ER 420; *Ngurli Ltd v McCann* (1953) 90 CLR 425; *Howard Smith Ltd v Ampol Petroleum Ltd* [1974] AC 821, [1974] 1 All ER 1126, PC.
19 See *Teck Corpn v Millar* (1972) 33 DLR (3d) 288, noted Slutsky (1974) 37 MLR 457; *Harlowe's Nominees Pty v Woodside (Lake Entrance) Oil Co* (1968) 121 CLR 483. See also *Pine Vale Investments Ltd v McDonnell & East* (1983) 8 ACLR 199 (Qld SC) where the court found the purchase by the company of an additional business, and the issuing of shares to finance that purchase, commercially justifiable even though its timing was to some extent influenced by a takeover offer by PV. The transactions in question had the effect of impeding that offer. The court took the view that once it was established that action is commercially justified in the corporate interest, directors should not be reduced to inertia just because a takeover offer has been made.
20 [1942] Ch 304, [1942] 1 All ER 542, CA.
 1 (1972) 33 DLR (3d) 288. See Birds (1980) 1 Co Law 68; Ziegel [1974] JBL 85.
 2 (1968) 121 CLR 483.

consequence of the allotment was to block a would-be takeover by an existing shareholder.

The Privy Council in *Howard Smith Ltd v Ampol Petroleum Ltd*[3] has now lent support to this more flexible approach although, on the facts, the allotment was set aside, the court finding that it was made with a view to destroying an existing majority, preventing them taking over the company, while enabling another party to do so[4].

The proper approach, the Privy Council felt, was:

. . . to start with a consideration of the power whose exercise is in question, in this case a power to issue shares. Having ascertained, on a fair view, the nature of this power, and having defined as can best be done in the light of modern conditions the, or some, limits within which it may be exercised, it is then necessary for the court, if a particular exercise of it is challenged, to examine the substantial purpose[5] for which it was exercised, and to reach a conclusion whether that purpose was proper or not[6].

The first step then is to construe the article conferring the power in order to ascertain the nature of the power and the limits within which it may be exercised[7]. In theory, the article could be limitless, permitting the allotment of shares (or indeed the exercise of any other power) for any purpose[8].

Having established the limits, if any, to the power, it is necessary to determine the actual purpose or purposes for which it was exercised. This is not always easy. Here the court:

. . . is entitled to look at the situation objectively in order to estimate how critical or pressing, or substantial or, per contra, insubstantial an alleged requirement may have been. If it finds that a particular requirement, though real, was not urgent or critical, at the relevant time, it may have reason to doubt, or discount, the assertions of individuals that they acted solely in order to deal with it, particularly when the action they took was unusual or even extreme[9].

The court accepted that there are difficulties of proof here which would require crediting the bona fide opinion of the directors if such is found to exist and respecting their judgment as to matters of management[10]. Having done so, the ultimate conclusion must be as to the side of a fairly broad line on which the case falls'[11].

Having identified the substantial purpose for the particular exercise of the

3 [1974] AC 821, [1974] 1 All ER 1126, PC.
4 [1974] AC 821 at 837, [1974] 1 All ER 1126 at 1136, PC.
5 See Farrar (1974) CLJ 221 at 223: '. . . substantial purpose is of course a crypto value judgment of the kind which the courts find useful but which produces flexibility at the price of certainty'.
6 [1974] AC 821 at 835, [1974] 1 All ER 1126 at 1134, PC.
7 See Sealy *Cases and Materials in Company Law* (4th edn, 1989) p 281, who suggests that instead of regarding the matter as one of construction, it would have been better to have considered the matter as a constitutional issue within the control of the general meeting which should decide which shareholders should gain control.
8 See Prentice (1970) 33 MLR 700; also *Re Smith & Fawcett Ltd* [1942] Ch 304 at 308, [1942] 1 All ER 542 at 545, CA, per Lord Greene.
9 *Howard Smith Ltd v Ampol Petroleum Ltd* [1974] AC 821 at 832, [1974] 1 All ER 1126 at 1131–1132, PC.
10 Ibid, at 835, 1134.
11 Ibid. See also *Finn*, op cit, p 72 where he lists the factors which may help the court decide; for example, the existing division of the factions within the company, the indecent haste of the directors' conduct, the hostility of the majority shareholders and the exact nature of the benefit to the company.

power, this purpose must be measured against the permissible purposes for the exercise of that power as indicated by the articles or ascertained by the court. Provided that that substantial purpose is a proper one, then the exercise of the power will not be tainted by the presence of some other improper, but insubstantial, purpose[12]. For example, some incidental benefit obtained by a director will not invalidate the exercise of the power unless his self interest was the substantial purpose for the exercise of the power[13].

Some commentators[14] have suggested that, realistically, it is almost impossible for the courts to determine which is the substantial and which the insubstantial purpose. In the light of the difficulties of establishing the purposes for which the power was exercised and placing those within some hierarchy of permitted purposes, any exercise of a power, it is argued, should be set aside once any improper purpose is established. Anything less than such a strict approach will reduce what little control shareholders have over management. Such an approach while it has the merit of certainty is inflexible and gives little credit to the judiciary's ability to weigh up the case before them. The Privy Council's approach is to be preferred.

As far as a power to allot shares is concerned it seems that such a power is not to be restricted to cases where the company requires additional capital but can be used (unless the articles otherwise provide) to defeat a corporate looter, to foster business connections, or indeed to ensure that the company has the requisite number of shareholders to exercise its statutory functions[15]. On the other hand, it can never be used solely to destroy an existing majority or create a new one[16].

Problems with allotments have arisen even in the case of rights issues. This is unusual for while allotments of shares are inherently discriminatory and can easily alter the balance of power within a company, rights issues are made on the basis of existing shareholdings and do not have the same potential for creating new majorities or destroying old ones. *Pennell v Venida Investments Ltd*[17] shows however that even apparently fair rights issues can be manipulated, something which is particularly pertinent in the light of s 89 of CA 1985 which imposes an obligation on companies to provide pre-emption rights in the event of their making an equity allotment for cash[18]. In this case the directors proposed to make a rights issue in order, so they pleaded, to raise capital to save the company from impending liquidation[19]. At the time

---

12 See, however, *Whitehouse v Carlton Hotel Pty Ltd* (1987) 5 ACLC 421 at 427 where the Australian High Court suggested that regardless of whether the impermissible purpose was the dominant one or but one of a number of significant contributing causes, the allotment will be invalidated if the impermissible purpose was causative in the sense that, but for its presence, 'the power would not have been exercised', per Dixon J, *Mills v Mills*. This was accepted as the correct approach in *McGuire v Ralph McKay Ltd* (1987) 5 ACLC 891 at 894, SC (Vic).

13 *Ngurli Ltd v McCann* (1953) 90 CLR 425 at 440; *Hirsche v Sims* [1894] AC 654 at 660–661, PC; *Mills v Mills* (1938) 60 CLR 150 at 164.

14 Burridge (1981) 44 MLR 40 at 52; Birds (1974) 37 MLR 580 at 585.

15 *Punt v Symons & Co Ltd* [1903] 2 Ch 506.

16 *Howard Smith Ltd v Ampol Petroleum Ltd* [1974] AC 821, [1974] 1 All ER 1126.

17 (25 July 1974, unreported), Ch D, Templeman J, discussed at length in Burridge (1981) 44 MLR 40.

18 The provisions originated in the Companies Act 1980, s 17. Note that companies may opt out of the requirement; see ss 91 and 95.

19 There was evidence of a genuine belief on the part of the directors that insolvency was approaching, see Burridge (1981) 44 MLR 40 at 51. The share capital of the company was held 51% by Venida and 49% by Pennell. After the rights issue Venida would hold 90%.

the majority shareholders knew that the rights issue would not be taken up by the minority shareholder who had financial problems. Applying the tests laid down in *Howard Smith Ltd v Ampol Petroleum Ltd*[20] Templeman J found that the substantial or primary purpose for the rights issue was to enable Venida Investments Ltd to gain total control of the company with a view to using its losses to make tax savings for the Venida group. This was an improper use of their power to raise capital and would not be permitted.

Abuse of power in this way may, in any event, form the basis of a s 459 petition alleging unfairly prejudicial conduct. In *Re a Company (No 002612/84*[1]) Harman J granted an injunction restraining a rights issue which would have reduced the petitioner's shareholding from 33% to 0.33%. He accepted that there was an arguable case that a rights issue, even though pro rata, could be unfairly prejudicial where, for example, it was known that the objecting member could not afford to take up the offer and this had been the reason for making it, or the objecting member was engaged in litigation against the majority shareholder and the offer was designed to deplete the resources available to him to finance that litigation. The Court of Appeal subsequently agreed that the proposed rights issue was unfairly prejudicial to the petitioner's interests[2].

If the directors have exercised their powers for any improper purpose, what is the position? This involves issues of ratification, the rule in *Foss v Harbottle* and any available shareholder remedies. The position on these points will be outlined here and discussed in greater detail in Chapter 27. At its most basic the rule is that if the wrongdoing by the directors is ratifiable (and is ratified) then a minority shareholder cannot bring a derivative action in respect of it. Hence the importance of deciding whether a breach of duty is ratifiable or not. In *Hogg v Cramphorn Ltd*[3], having decided that the directors had exercised their powers for an improper purpose, the court did not set aside the allotment but instead adjourned the proceedings to enable a general meeting to be held which duly ratified the directors' conduct[4]. Support for this approach followed in *Bamford v Bamford*[5]. It is, of course, ratification by the general meeting as it was constituted prior to the invalid allotment which is required, not ratification by the new majority created by the attempted allotment. Permitting ratification of such conduct is out of line with the older cases which regarded such conduct as unratifiable[6]. The ratification debate has become even more interesting with the decision in *Re a Company (No 005136 of 1986)*[7] where Hoffmann J found that an exercise by directors of their fiduciary powers for an improper purpose in this

---

20 [1974] AC 821, [1974] 1 All ER 1126, PC.
1 [1985] BCLC 80. See also *Re a Company* [1986] BCLC 362 and *Re a Company (No 005134 of 1986), ex p Harries* [1989] BCLC 383 where there was a breach of the statutory pre-emption provisions.
2 Reported as *Re Cumana Ltd* [1986] BCLC 430, CA.
3 [1967] Ch 254, [1966] 3 All ER 420.
4 On the question of whether ratification is permissible for all exercises of powers for an improper purpose, see Wedderburn (1967) 30 MLR 77 at 83.
5 [1970] Ch 212, CA, approved in *Winthrop Investments Ltd v Winns Ltd* [1975] 2 NSWLR 666.
6 See *Fraser v Whalley* (1864) 2 Hem & M 10; *Punt v Symons & Co Ltd* [1903] 2 Ch 506; *Piercy v S Mills & Co Ltd* [1920] 1 Ch 77; *Ngurli Ltd v McCann* (1953) 90 CLR 425; *Finn*, op cit, p 73.
7 [1987] BCLC 82.

fashion, while technically a wrong done to the company, is substantially a complaint by a shareholder that his personal rights as a shareholder have been infringed. The basis of the complaint is that the allotment is alleged to be an improper and unlawful exercise of the powers granted to the board by the articles of association which constitute a contract between the company and its members. An abuse of the powers is therefore an infringement of a member's contractual rights under those articles. If that is the case then questions of ratification do not arise and a shareholder will have a personal cause of action. The validity of this approach is considered in Chapter 27.

DUTY OF CARE AND SKILL

This is an area where the common law has failed to keep pace with modern developments and instead presents a lamentably out of date view of directors' duties[8]. In the past the courts have been reluctant to impose onerous standards of care and skill on directors and have been willing to impose liability only when a director's imprudence has been so great and so manifest as to amount to gross negligence[9]. The reasons for this are mainly historical. Many of the cases reflect a time when directors were part-time officers, figureheads, adornments to the corporate Christmas tree[10], titled people with time on their hands. In keeping with this state of affairs, the courts regarded them as pleasant, if incompetent, amateurs[11] who did not possess any particular executive skills and upon whom it would be unreasonable to impose onerous standards of care and skill. Another difficulty was that if a higher degree of care and skill was to be required then this might involve judicial assessment of the managerial skills of the individuals concerned. This would involve investigating the internal management of the company, something which the courts have always been reluctant to do.

In any event, it was argued, the shareholders choose their own directors and if they decide to appoint incompetent amateurs to run their business then that was a matter for them[12]. This argument ignores the extent to which the board has become a self perpetuating body through the directors' control of the proxy machinery and the passive role adopted by the average shareholder. It also ignores the impact which corporate collapse has on creditors, employees, and society at large. This has recently been a major

---

8 See generally Trebilcock (1969) 32 MLR 499; McKenzie [1982] JBL 460; Mitchell *Insider Dealing and Directors' Duties* (2nd edn, 1989) Ch 4; Stanton and Dugdale (1982) 132 NLJ 251; The Conduct of Company Directors (Cmnd 7307).

9 *Overend, Gurney & Co v Gibb and Gibb* (1872) LR 5 HL 480 at 487, per Lord Hatherly LC; *Re Brazilian Rubber Plantations and Estates Ltd* [1911] 1 Ch 425 at 436, per Neville J; *Lagunas Nitrate Co v Lagunas Syndicate* [1899] 2 Ch 392 at 435, CA, per Lindley MR. This reluctance may stem from the difficulty in ascertaining the loss caused to the company by a director's mismanagement, see *Barnes v Andrews District Court* NY 298 Fed Rep 614 (1924).

10 Mace *Directors, Myth and Reality* (1971) p 107.

11 Dwight (1907) 17 Yale LJ 33 at 35 noted the atmosphere of good-humoured tolerance which pervaded the decisions on directors: 'From the gingerly manner in which the question of liability is discussed, one would suppose that directors were all trustees of charitable institutions giving freely of their services and engaged in the most self-denying tasks'.

12 *Turquand v Marshall* (1869) 4 Ch App 376 at 386, per Lord Hatherly LC; *Re Forest of Dean Coal Mining Co* (1878) 10 Ch D 450 at 453, per Jessel MR; *Re New Mashonaland Exploration Co* [1892] 3 Ch 577 at 585, per Vaughan-Williams J.

concern of Parliament in passing the Insolvency Act 1986 and the Company Directors Disqualification Act 1986 and it is as a consequence of these Acts that we are likely to see a raising of the standards expected of directors. As a matter of practice we should see directors bringing greater care and skill to their positions as they attempt to avoid the personal liability and disqualification provided by those Acts for directors who fail to reach an appropriate standard of conduct. The existing case law must now be read in the light of these legislative developments.

The position at common law is dominated by the three propositions set out by Romer J in *Re City Equitable Fire Insurance Co Ltd*[13] which concerned an unsuccessful attempt to make a number of directors, all of whom had acted honestly throughout, liable in negligence for losses resulting from the fraud of the managing director[14].

(i)   A director need not exhibit in the performance of his duties a greater degree of skill than may reasonably be expected of a person of his knowledge and experience[15]. It is a subjective test[16] with no minimum reasonable amount of skill being required. Under such a test the less knowledge and experience a director has, the less skill is expected of him, and the less likely he is to be liable when something goes wrong. Thus in *Re Brazilian Rubber Plantations and Estates Ltd*[17] directors who undertook management of a rubber company in complete ignorance of anything to do with the rubber industry were excused liability for ruinous losses arising from rubber speculation[18]. If a director is acquainted with the company's business, however, then he must give the company the advantage of his knowledge when acting in the company's affairs and if he is employed by the company in a professional capacity then he must attain the standard of a reasonably competent member of that profession in exercising his professional skills on behalf of the company. An executive director appointed under a contract of employment will be obliged, under normal contractual principles, to exercise reasonable skill in the performance of his duties[19]. The standard of care required meanwhile is such care as an ordinary man might be expected to take on his own behalf[20].

---

13 [1925] Ch 407, CA. See also *Fisheries Development Corpn of SA Ltd v Jorgensen* 1980 (4) SA 156 where Margo J suggests that the old rules, as formulated by Romer J, are relevant only to non-executive directors and new rules must be formulated for executive directors.
14 The managing director had been convicted and sentenced in respect of the fraud which had involved the granting of unsecured loans and the making of dividend payments out of capital. Note that some of the other directors were found guilty of negligence but were protected by an exemption clause in the company's articles. Such a clause would be invalid now, see CA 1985, s 310.
15 [1925] Ch 407 at 428.
16 Section 13 of the Supply of Goods and Services Act 1982 would have imposed an objective standard of skill on non-executive directors. However the Supply of Services (Exclusion of Implied Terms) Order 1982, SI 1982/1771 excludes all directors from the operation of that provision, see (1982) 3 Co Law 267.
17 [1911] 1 Ch 425.
18 One director was completely ignorant of business and only consented to act because he was told that the office would give him a little pleasant employment without any responsibility; another was 75 years old and very deaf; a third was induced to join by seeing the names of people he considered good men.
19 *Lister v Romford Ice and Cold Storage Co Ltd* [1957] AC 555, [1957] 1 All ER 125, HL.
20 *Dorchester Finance Co Ltd v Stebbing* [1989] BCLC 498 at 501; *Overend, Gurney & Co v Gibb and Gibb* (1872) LR 5 HL 480 at 487, per Lord Hatherly; *Re Brazilian Rubber Plantations and Estates Co Ltd* [1911] 1 Ch 425 at 437, per Neville J; *Re City Equitable Fire Insurance Co* [1925] Ch 407 at 428, CA, per Romer J.

This first proposition must be re-considered in the light of the wrongful trading provision in s 214 of the Insolvency Act 1986, discussed in detail in Chapter 39, which applies to any director or shadow director of a company which has gone into insolvent liquidation and at some time before the commencement of the winding up of the company, that person knew or ought to have concluded that there was no reasonable prospect that the company would avoid going into insolvent liquidation. In such a case the court, on the application of the liquidator, may declare that person to be liable to make such contribution to the company's assets as the court thinks proper. A disqualification order may also be made[1]. Liability under the section is subject to the defence that no declaration shall be made if the court is satisfied that the person in the position outlined above took every step with a view to minimising the potential loss to the company's creditors as he ought to have taken. The important provision is s 214(4) which provides that the facts which a director of a company ought to know or ascertain, the conclusions which he ought to reach and the steps which he ought to take are those which would be known or ascertained, or reached or taken, by a reasonably diligent person having both—

(a)   the general knowledge, skill and experience that may reasonably be expected of a person carrying out the same functions as are carried out by that director in relation to the company, and

(b)   the general knowledge, skill and experience that that director has.

This subsection sets a standard involving subjective and objective criteria. Meeting a subjective standard alone will be insufficient for the director's behaviour will also be judged against the standard that may reasonably be expected of a reasonable director in that position. The nature of this test was considered by Knox J in *Re Produce Marketing Consortium Ltd (No 2)*[2] who accepted that this requirement to have regard to the functions to be carried out by the director in question, in relation to the company in question, involves having regard to the particular company and its business. He continued:

It follows that the general knowledge, skill and experience postulated will be much less extensive in a small company in a modest way of business, with simple accounting procedures and equipment, than it will be in a large company with sophisticated procedures. Nevertheless, certain minimum standards are to be assumed to be attained[3].

In this case the minimum standards he focused on related to the obligations to keep accounting records, to lay accounts before the general meeting and to file such accounts with Companies House. Had the directors done these things, they would have been aware of the company's financial difficulties. Therefore, he concluded, they ought to have known or ascertained the financial position and ought to have concluded that there was no reasonable prospect of the company avoiding insolvent liquidation by the date when the accounts should have been laid and delivered. They had failed to take every

1 CDDA 1986, s 10.
2 [1989] BCLC 520. See also *Re Purpoint Ltd* [1991] BCC 121; *Re DKG Contractors Ltd* [1990] BCC 903 where the court found the directors' knowledge, skill and experience were hopelessly inadequate for the task they undertook.
3 Ibid at 550.

step with a view to minimising the potential loss to the company's creditors and they were personally liable.

Of course the objective element provided by this provision only arises if the company has gone into insolvent liquidation and so it might be argued it will not affect the behaviour of directors while the company is a going concern. However the fact that the possible personal liability is so extensive and insolvent liquidation always a possibility (however remote) should ensure some raising of standards. This first proposition needs also to be re-considered in the light of the developing case law on unfitness under the Company Directors Disqualification Act 1986 which is discussed in detail in Chapter 23. Suffice it to say here that irresponsible and incompetent management may result in disqualification on the ground of unfitness.

(ii)   A director is not bound to give continuous attention to the affairs of his company. His duties are of an intermittent nature to be performed at periodic board meetings and at meetings of any committee of the board upon which he happens to be placed[4]. He is not bound to attend all such meetings[5] although he ought to attend whenever he is reasonably able to do so[6], nor is he under any obligation to undertake a definitive part in the conduct of the company's business[7]. An extreme example is *Re Cardiff Savings Bank, the Marquis of Bute's* case[8], where the Marquis of Bute (the president of the bank[9]) escaped liability for losses resulting from irregularities in the bank's operations despite having attended only one board meeting in 38 years. There being some 55 trustees and managers, the court did not feel that it could be expected of each of them that they should take a very active part in the management or attend every meeting[10]. The omission to attend the meetings was not the same as the neglect or omission of any duty which ought to have been performed at any such meeting[11]. Likewise in *Re City Equitable Fire Insurance Co Ltd*[12] itself, no blame attached to one director who lived in Aberdeen and who found it difficult to attend board meetings in London, or to another director who had not attended a board meeting for five years due to illness.

Again there are a number of qualifications to the general position, outlined above, which should be noted.

First, not all decisions in the past have been as lenient in the face of such inactivity by directors. One of the oldest cases, *Charitable Corpn v Sutton*[13], imposed some of the highest requirements. Here while only five out of some 50 committee men (directors) were actively involved in the running of the company, the remaining 45 were held guilty of *crassa negligence* because their inactivity enabled the other five to 'lose' some £350,000 (in 1742!). In *Re*

---

4 *Re City Equitable Fire Insurance Co Ltd* [1925] Ch 407 at 429, CA.
5 Afterman *Company Directors and Controllers* (1970) argues that here the law is overly permissive and failure to attend a reasonable number of meetings should be considered prima facie evidence of lack of care and diligence.
6 *Re City Equitable Fire Insurance Co Ltd* [1925] Ch 407 at 429, CA.
7 *Re Brazilian Rubber Plantations and Estates Ltd* [1911] 1 Ch 425 at 437, per Neville J.
8 [1892] 2 Ch 100.
9 He had been appointed president when only six months old!
10 [1892] 2 Ch 100 at 108. But see *Dorchester Finance Co Ltd v Stebbing* [1989] BCLC 498.
11 [1892] 2 Ch 100.
12 [1925] Ch 407, CA.
13 (1742) 2 Atk 400.

Denham & Co[14] (where the director who escaped liability for the fraud of his co-directors had not attended a board meeting for five years) Chitty J, while not finding the director liable, expressed the view that he had been guilty of considerable negligence in not attending meetings and so refused him his costs[15]. More recently Foster J in *Dorchester Finance Co Ltd v Stebbing*[16] held that it was unacceptable for directors not to attend board meetings or take any active interest in the company's affairs. Here all three directors of the company, including two inactive directors who had acted bona fide throughout, were liable for losses incurred when unsecured loans were made which subsequently turned out to be irrecoverable. The very inactivity of the two directors justified their liability because by failing to monitor the conduct of the offending director they had facilitated the fraud.

Secondly, executive directors appointed under service agreements will usually be required to give their exclusive attention to the affairs of their companies and are unlikely to be able to avail of the relaxed regime advocated by the earlier cases. Even non-executive directors may be required to attend board meetings, certainly in public companies, although private companies may still operate a more relaxed regime.

Thirdly, this second proposition of Romer J must also be re-considered in the light of the Insolvency Act 1986. A director who fails to attend board meetings or take any interest in the conduct of his company's affairs may find it difficult to persuade a court (as he may be required to do under s 214(3) if he is to avoid liability for wrongful trading on his company going into insolvent liquidation) that he took every step with a view to minimising the potential loss to the company's creditors. Such non-attendance and inactivity would also be one of the matters for the court to consider in determining whether a director is unfit to be concerned in the management of a company under s 6 of the Company Directors Disqualification Act 1986[17].

(iii)   In respect of all duties which, having regard to the exigencies of business and the articles of association, may properly be left to some other official, a director is, in the absence of grounds for suspicion, justified in trusting that official to perform such duties honestly[18]. It is obvious that a company could not hope to run its business in an efficient manner if the directors were required to do everything themselves and were not permitted to delegate on a wide scale. An intelligent devolution of labour must be possible[19]. Having permitted delegation the law does not require that the directors should distrust and constantly supervise those to whom tasks have been delegated for this would defeat the whole purpose. Thus a director of a gaming club was not negligent in failing to check whether the club had the appropriate licence when the task of obtaining it had been delegated to

---

14 (1883) 25 Ch D 752.
15 (1883) 25 Ch D 752 at 768. It should be noted that under Table A, art 81(e), a director is deemed to have vacated his office if he is absent for six months from directors' meetings without consent and the directors resolve that his office be vacated.
16 [1989] BCLC 498.
17 See discussion Ch 23, and in particular *Re Lo-Line Electric Motors Ltd* [1988] Ch 477, [1988] 2 All ER 692; *Re Majestic Recording Studios Ltd* [1989] BCLC 1.
18 [1925] Ch 407 at 429.
19 *Dovey v Cory* [1901] AC 477 at 489, HL, per Earl of Halsbury LC; *Huckerby v Elliott* [1970] 1 All ER 189.

someone else[20]. Likewise in *Dovey v Cory*[1] the director of a banking company was not negligent in relying on the assertions of the chairman and general manager of the company, whose integrity, skill and competence he had no reason to doubt, with the result that dividends were paid out of capital and advances made on improper security. A director is not required to watch his inferior officers, or verify the calculations of his auditors[2], or examine the entries in the company's books[3]. It is sufficient if the board appoints a competent person to be auditor and has no grounds for suspecting anything to be wrong[4].

On the other hand, directors are not exercising a reasonable amount of care if they blindly accept all documents placed before them[5]. Thus in *Re City Equitable Fire Insurance Co Ltd*[6] Romer J suggested that before declaring a dividend the directors should have a complete list of the company's assets before them and ought not to be guided as to the value of their company's assets merely by the assurances of their chairman, however apparently distinguished and honourable, nor with the expression of belief of the auditor, however competent and trustworthy. Support for this can be found in *Dorchester Finance Co Ltd v Stebbing*[7] where the court rejected the argument that non-executive directors (at least, as here, where they had some accounting experience) could rely on the competence and diligence of the auditors and do nothing themselves[8]. When signing cheques, a director is only required to satisfy himself that the cheque has been authorised by the board. He need not verify that the money is in fact required for the particular purpose specified or is indeed expended on that purpose[9]. Signing blank cheques is, of course, negligent.[10]

As has been mentioned previously, a major problem is the enforcement of directors' duties, in particular overcoming the difficulties posed by the rule in *Foss v Harbottle*[11]. Breach of a director's duties of care and skill will be a wrong done to the company and in respect of which the company should sue. If the company were to decide not to proceed then a shareholder can only bring an action on behalf of the company if he can bring himself within one of the exceptions to the rule. Where negligence is the basis of the petitioner's complaint he will wish to bring himself within the 'fraud of the minority' exception. The cases, however, are not clear as to whether an action will lie for mere negligence[12], or gross negligence which

---

20 *Huckerby v Elliott* [1970] 1 All ER 189.
1 [1901] AC 477, HL.
2 *Dovey v Cory* [1901] AC 477 at 486, HL.
3 *Re City Equitable Fire Insurance Co Ltd* [1925] Ch 407 at 430, CA; *Dovey v Cory* [1901] AC 477 at 493, HL.
4 *Re Denham & Co* (1883) 25 Ch D 752.
5 They are not absolved from the duty of reasonable supervision, nor ought they be permitted to be shielded from liability because of lack of knowledge of wrongdoing, if that ignorance is the result of gross inattention': *Fisheries Development Corpn of SA Ltd v Jorgensen* 1980 (4) SA 156 at 166.
6 [1925] Ch 407 at 472, CA.
7 [1989] BCLC 498.
8 Ibid at 505. Indeed Foster J made it clear that even directors with no accounting experience are not entitled to accept blindly documents laid before them by the auditors.
9 *Re City Equitable Fire Insurance Co Ltd* [1925] Ch 407 at 453, CA.
10 *Dorchester Finance Co Ltd v Stebbing* [1989] BCLC 498.
11 (1843) 2 Hare 461; see Chapter 27, post.
12 *Pavlides v Jensen* [1956] Ch 565, [1956] 2 All ER 518.

inflicts loss on creditors[13], or whether what is required is negligence which also results in some benefit to the wrongdoers[14]. Negligence in the management of the company's affairs may, however, justify a petition under s 459 alleging unfairly prejudicial conduct[15].

A final point to note is the proposed Fifth EC Directive on company law which, as currently drafted[16], provides in art 14 that directors should be jointly and severally liable for damage sustained by a company as a consequence of any wrongdoing by a director. Any director wishing to escape liability would have to prove that no fault was attributable to him personally. The fact that the act giving rise to damage was not within his particular area of responsibility will not of itself suffice to exonerate him. Implementation of this requirement would certainly ensure more active monitoring of directors by directors[17].

13 See *Re Horsley & Weight Ltd* [1982] Ch 442 at 455–456, [1982] 3 All ER 1045 at 1055–56, where Templeman and Cumming Bruce LJJ thought that in such a situation the breach would not be ratifiable, at least where the directors use their own votes to absolve themselves. The Court of Appeal doubted the apparent width of such dicta in *Multinational Gas and Petrochemical Co v Multinational Gas and Petrochemical Services Ltd* [1983] Ch 258, [1983] 2 All ER 563. See also Wedderburn (1984) 47 MLR 87.

14 *Daniels v Daniels* [1978] Ch 406, [1978] 2 All ER 89. On the possibility of shareholder actions in tort, see Sterling (1987) 50 MLR 468.

15 Section 459 is discussed in detail in Chapter 27.

16 This Directive was first proposed in 1972; OJEC 1972 No C 131/49 and followed by a version in 1983, OJEC 1983 No C 240/2. That version was subsequently amended in 1988, see the DTI Consultative Document, Amended Proposal for a Fifth Directive on the Harmonisation of Company Law in the European Community, January 1990.

17 See the DTI Consultative Document, op cit, para 15.2, which indicates the UK's opposition to this proposal.

CHAPTER 26

Controlling self-dealing by directors

THE NO-CONFLICT RULE

Directors must not place themselves in a position where their duties and their personal interests[1] conflict.

It is a rule of universal application that no-one having such (fiduciary) duties to discharge shall be allowed to enter into an engagement in which he has or can have a personal interest conflicting or which may possibly conflict with the interests of those whom he is bound to protect[2].

The most obvious example of a conflict situation is where a director enters into a contract with his company, as in *Aberdeen Rly Co v Blaikie Bros*[3] where the company was entitled to set aside a contract for the purchase of office furniture entered into between it and a partnership when it transpired that one of the directors was also a member of the partnership.

The danger is obvious. The director is obliged to purchase goods on behalf of the company at the lowest possible price while as a member of the partnership he wishes to sell the goods at the highest possible price. Where such a conflict exists, the law recognises that despite his best intentions the director may be swayed by his own self interest. The danger that he will be so swayed requires a general prophylactic rule prohibiting directors from placing themselves in a position of conflict. It should be noted that it is not necessary to prove that there is an actual conflict of duty and interest, it is sufficient if there is a 'real sensible possibility of one'[4].

Where they do place themselves in a position of conflict, the contract is voidable at the instance of the company but the right to avoid the contract will be lost if the company affirms the contract, or delays unduly before rescinding, or restitutio in integrum becomes impossible, or the rights of bona fide third parties intervene[5]. The rule is an inflexible one and the court will not enquire as to the fairness or otherwise of the transaction[6]. In addition to setting aside the contract, the company can call upon the director to account for the gains he has made.

---

1 'Interests' is usually taken by the courts to mean financial interests, see Finn *Fiduciary Obligations* (1977) p 203.
2 *Aberdeen Rly Co v Blaikie Bros* (1854) 1 Macq 461 at 471–472, CA, per Lord Cranworth; *Bray v Ford* [1896] AC 44 at 51, HL, per Lord Herschell; *Boulting v Association of Cinematograph, Television and Allied Technicians* [1963] 2 QB 606 at 635, [1963] 1 All ER 716 at 728, CA, per Upjohn J.
3 (1854) 1 Macq 461.
4 *Boulting v ACTAT* [1963] 2 QB 606, [1963] 1 All ER 716, CA; *Boardman v Phipps* [1967] 2 AC 46, [1966] 3 All ER 721, HL. The English courts have been criticised for this approach, see Oakley *Constructive Trusts* (2nd edn, 1987) p 50; Finn *Fiduciary Obligations* (1977) p 246.
5 *Hely-Hutchinson v Brayhead Ltd* [1968] 1 QB 549, [1967] 3 All ER 98, CA.
6 *Aberdeen Rly Co v Blaikie Bros* (1854) 1 Macq 461 at 471–472.

There are advantages in having such a strict uncompromising rule. First, there is the certainty resulting from the absolute prohibition. Then there are the savings in terms of the time and money which would otherwise be expended if the courts had to be satisfied as to the fairness of each transaction. But there are also disadvantages. Prohibition may in fact force a company to incur costs which could be avoided if the company was permitted to contract with its own directors[7], The company may be forced to contract with an outsider when an insider is the sole or most favourable source of the goods or services which the company requires[8]. A company forced to deal with an outsider must incur costs in finding and negotiating with that outsider, costs which would be substantially reduced if the company were to deal with an insider who is a known quantity[9]. In addition, individuals are often appointed as directors in order to foster business relations between two companies and the very act of appointing may presuppose contracting with the other company and so a possible conflict will exist from the outset.

These disadvantages are regarded as outweighing the advantages and have resulted in the rule being relaxed in a number of ways.

(i) Ratification   As mentioned earlier the contract is voidable, not void. The company can therefore decide to ratify it after full disclosure by the director in question. Ratification cannot be by the board itself[10] but requires the consent of the company in general meeting[11]. A director can vote as a shareholder, however, to ratify a contract in which he is interested for 'every shareholder has a perfect right to vote upon any such question, although he may have a personal interest in the subject matter opposed to or different from the general or particular interests of the company'[12].

(ii) Waiver   It is also open to the company to waive the no-conflict duty in advance by way of a provision in the articles, the standard provision being art 85 of Table A. This is a more convenient way of proceeding, eliminating as it does the need to present each and every contract to the general meeting for ratification.

---

7 Brudney (1982) 95 Harv L Rev 597 at 624; Anderson (1978) 25 UCLA L Rev 738.
8 Brudney, op cit, at 624, although he concedes that this will occur only infrequently.
9 Brudney, op cit, at 624. However you must also offset against any savings the chance that the price at which the insider would contract is an uncompetitive one.
10 Not even if the interested director abstains, for the courts take the view that the company is entitled to the disinterested opinion of the entire board on any transaction. In any event, even if the interested director abstains, it remains possible that he will exert a degree of influence over the rest of his fellow directors: see *Victors Ltd v Lingard* [1927] 1 Ch 323; *Imperial Mercantile Credit Association v Coleman* (1871) 6 Ch App 558; *Aberdeen Rly Co v Blaikie Bros* (1854) 1 Macq 461, HL.
11 Some contracts, as where in reality the director is making a gift of corporate assets to himself, cannot be ratified, for that is a fraud on the minority: *Cook v Deeks* [1916] 1 AC 554, PC; *Menier v Hooper's Telegraph Works* (1874) 9 Ch App 350. Ratification is discussed in greater detail in Chapter 27.
12 *North-West Transportation Co Ltd and Beatty v Beatty* (1887) 12 App Cas 589 at 593, PC, per Sir Richard Baggally; *Northern Counties Securities Ltd v Jackson & Steeple Ltd* [1974] 2 All ER 625, [1974] 1 WLR 1133.

Article 85 provides for disclosure by a director to the board of the nature and extent of any material interest of his in any transactions or arrangements with the company or in which the company is otherwise interested[13]. Provided he has so disclosed, a director may be a party to a transaction or arrangement with his company and shall not, by reason of his office, be accountable to the company for any benefit which he derives from that transaction or arrangement and no such transaction or arrangement shall be liable to be avoided on the ground of any such interest or benefit. In other words, art 85 permits directors to contract out of their fiduciary duty not to place themselves in a position where their duties and their personal interests conflict, provided they disclose the conflict to the board.

Strict compliance with the requirements of the articles is essential if the contracting out is to be effective. So, for example, disclosure to a committee of directors when disclosure to the board is required would not be effective. Equally, a failure to adhere to the provisions in the articles which authorise the no-conflict rule to be set aside may rule out the court permitting a director who has performed services for the company, but allowed himself to be in a position of conflict, from claiming either on a quantum meruit or an equitable allowance for services rendered. The courts are reluctant to encourage directors putting themselves in a position of conflict by allowing them financial recovery.

These issues have all been debated recently by the House of Lords in *Guinness plc v Saunders*[14], which has already been discussed in relation to directors' remuneration. It will be recalled that in this case a committee of the board of Guinness had, without authority, awarded remuneration of £5.2m to one of the Guinness directors, Ward, in return for his services in connection with the bid by Guinness for Distillers plc, despite the power to award remuneration being vested by the articles in the board. Clearly, there was a conflict of interest here, and so potentially a voidable contract on the basis outlined above, namely a failure to strictly comply with the provisions in the articles. But, given that the committee was found to have no authority to act, the court held that there was no contract at all between Guinness and Ward and so the company was entitled to a return of the money. Ward then sought to recover all or some of the £5.2m on the basis of quantum meruit or an equitable allowance in respect of the services rendered. This was rejected by the House of Lords.

Lord Goff's starting point was that directors must not put themselves in a position where there is a conflict between their personal interests and their duties as fiduciaries, and so they are for that reason precluded from contracting with the company for their services except in circumstances authorised by the articles of association[15]. He went on to say that it would be inconsistent

13 The interested directors are normally prohibited from voting in respect of such contracts and from being counted in the quorum present at the meeting: Table A, arts 94, 95, but note also art 96. Some guidance as to the meaning of 'material' can be found in CA 1985, Sch 6, para 17(2): an interest in a transaction or arrangement is not 'material' if in the board's opinion it is not so; but this is without prejudice to the question of whether or not such an interest is material in a case where the board have not considered the matter. This guidance is given for the purpose of determining whether or not information needs to be included in notes to the company accounts but may be of help in the wider context. Sch 6, para 17(2) is as amended by CA 1989, Sch 4, para 4.
14 [1990] 2 AC 663, [1990] 1 All ER 652, HL, noted Hopkins (1990) CLJ 220; Beatson & Prentice (1990) 106 LQR 365; Birks [1990] LMCLQ 330.
15 [1990] 2 AC 663 at 700, [1990] 1 All ER 652 at 666.

with this long established principle to award remuneration in such circumstances as of right on the basis of a quantum meruit claim. But, he said, the principle does not altogether exclude the possibility that an equitable allowance might be made in respect of services rendered. This equitable jurisdiction could be exercised, however, only if it did not conflict with the policy underlying the rule, ie if it did not provide any encouragement to fiduciaries to put themselves in a position where their duties as fiduciaries conflicted with their interests[16]. He went on to query whether any such allowance might ever be granted in the case of a director of a company (Lord Templeman thought not[17]) which might be said to involve interference by the court in the administration of the company's affairs where the company is not being wound up. In any event, there was no possibility of granting such an allowance in this case. Ward's interests were in stark conflict with his duty as a director of Guinness. If the board of Guinness saw fit, they might still remunerate him for his services but the court would not award an equitable allowance.

Lord Templeman's speech is perhaps more opaque[18] but the overall tenor is the same. His starting point too was the principle that a fiduciary must not place himself in a position of conflict and may not profit from his position except to the extent permitted by the articles. Neither quantum meruit nor equitable allowance should be allowed to dimish that rule and allow recovery of remuneration in circumstances wider than those expressly envisaged by the articles[19].

So there is little chance, perhaps no chance, of directors recovering on a quantum meruit or equitable allowance basis for services rendered where they are in breach of the no-conflict rule. *Guinness plc v Saunders*[20] is a strong affirmation by the House of Lords of the fiduciary's duty not to place himself in a position of conflict except as expressly authorised by the articles—the absolute nature of the rule not being tempered by any equitable allowance for fear of encouraging any breach of that fundamental obligation, particularly in the company context where directors are frequently faced with conflicts which can produce significant individual financial gain. The need to deter them from personally taking those gains, other than in strict compliance with the articles, is greater than any concern about a windfall to the company which has had the benefit of the services for which it is not required to pay[1].

---

16 [1990] 2 AC 663 at 701, [1990] 1 All ER 652 at 666. He distinguished *Phipps v Boardman* [1964] 2 All ER 187, [1964] 1 WLR 993, where an allowance was awarded, on this basis. See Beatson & Prentice (1990) 106 LQR 365 at 367 on this point, who note the difficulty of reconciling it with the approach in *O'Sullivan v Management Agency & Music Ltd* [1985] QB 428, CA. A better distinction, they suggest, is that in *Guinness plc v Saunders*, the profit was made by the fiduciary actually taking company property.
17 [1990] 2 AC 663 at 694, [1990] 1 All ER 652 at 662. It should be noted that Lords Keith, Brandon and Griffiths agreed with Lord Templeman's speech. Lord Griffiths also agreed with Lord Goff.
18 In particular, his reliance on an implied contract approach to quantum meruit claims has been criticised and his interpretation of *Craven-Ellis v Canons Ltd* [1936] 2 KB 403, CA questioned, see Beatson & Prentice (1990) 106 LQR 365 at 367; Birks [1990] LMCLQ 330.
19 [1990] 2 AC 663 at 689, [1990] 1 All ER 652 at 661.
20 [1990] 2 AC 663, [1990] 1 All ER 652.
 1 As we shall see, when we consider *Regal (Hastings) Ltd v Gulliver* [1967] 2 AC 134n, [1942] 1 All ER 378, HL and *Industrial Development Consultants Ltd v Cooley* [1972] 2 All ER 162, [1972] 1 WLR 443, below, the courts are not averse to allowing such a windfall where to do so reinforces the fundamental fiduciary obligations.

An additional provision to note is s 317 of the 1985 Act which requires disclosure to the board[2] by the directors and shadow directors[3] of any contract or proposed contract, transaction or arrangement[4] in which they are interested, directly or indirectly. This provision 'merely creates a statutory duty of disclosure and imposes a fine for non-compliance'[5]. Accordingly, a breach of it, or indeed compliance with it, has no effect on the issue of the validity of a contract entered into in breach of the no-conflict rule[6]. That issue is dictated by whether the articles have relaxed the rule and whether there has been strict compliance with the articles.

A director who wishes to contract with his company therefore must first ascertain whether or not the company's articles do include an article in the form of art 85. If such an article is included, then the director must make disclosure to the board (which incidentally also ensures compliance with s 317). Failure to comply with the requirements of the article will deprive the director of the protection afforded by it and will result in the application of the general rule with the result that the contract is voidable and the director may be called to account. It will also, necessarily, mean a failure to comply with s 317 and the director will be liable to a fine under s 317(7).

In the unlikely event that there is no such article, then the director must still comply with s 317, it being a statutory disclosure provision, and the general rule will also apply, so the contract will remain voidable and the director will remain liable to account.

It is clear from the foregoing discussion that the strict no-conflict rule gives way in practice to a more relaxed regime requiring disclosure only to the board and in the accounts. It has as a consequence been necessary to make statutory provision for certain types of transactions, in particular, loans and related transactions, contracts for the purchase or sale of property and directors' service contracts, in order to curb some of the more blatant abuses arising from this permissive regime.

Loans and related transactions

Loans and related transactions in favour of directors and connected persons are the subject of extensive prohibitions contained in s 330 ff of the 1985 Act. Even where transactions are permitted by the legislation, directors may find that more restrictive provisions are included in their company's articles and memorandum. In any event, they must always bear in mind their overriding duty to act in the best interests of the company.

The basic prohibition is contained in s 330(2)(a) which provides that a

---

2 Details of any transaction or arrangement in which a director has a material interest must also be included in a note to the accounts by virtue of CA 1985, s 232 and Sch 6, as inserted by CA 1989, s 6.
3 CA 1985, s 317(8)—disclosure by shadow directors is by notice in writing to the board.
4 Ibid, s 317(5), whether or not that transaction or arrangement constitutes a contract. Included within 'transaction or arrangement' are all the transactions covered by s 330, ie loans, quasi-loans and credit transactions, s 317(6).
5 *Hely-Hutchinson v Brayhead Ltd* [1968] 1 QB 549 at 595, [1967] 3 All ER 98 at 109, CA, per Lord Pearson, endorsed in *Guinness plc v Saunders* [1990] 2 AC 663 at 697, [1990] 1 All ER 652 at 665, per Lord Goff.
6 Ibid. Lord Goff decisively rejecting the clearly erroneous views of the lower courts in the Guinness case that non-compliance with s 317 justified recovery of the money by the company, [1988] 2 All ER 940, [1988] 1 WLR 863, CA; affd [1988] BCLC 43, Ch D.

company shall not make a loan[7] to a director[8] or shadow director[9] of the company or of its holding company[10]. Loans to directors of subsidiary companies are not affected provided that the director is not also a director of the holding company. In addition to the basic prohibition, a relevant company[11], ie a public company or a company which is part of a group which contains a public company, is prohibited from making a loan to a person connected with such a director[12]. It should be stressed that this prohibition applies only to relevant companies. There is no prohibition on private companies, which are not relevant companies, making loans to persons connected with their directors.

Section 346(2) provides that a person is connected with a director of a company if, not being himself a director of it, he is:

(i)   that director's spouse, child or step-child; or

(ii)   a company with which the director is associated, which occurs if the director and persons connected with him together are interested in at least one-fifth of the equity share capital of that company or are entitled to exercise or control[13] the exercise of more than one-fifth of the voting power at any general meeting[14]; or

(iii)   a trustee of any trust, if the beneficiaries of the trust include the director or (i) or (ii) above or if the terms of the trust confer a power on the trustee that may be exercised in favour of the director or (i) or (ii) above[15]; or

(iv)   any partner of a director or a partner of any of the people in (i) or (ii) or (iii) above.

There are a number of exceptions to the general prohibitions.

(I) SMALL AMOUNTS

A loan may be made to a director of a company or of its holding company provided the aggregate of the relevant amounts does not exceed £5,000[16]. It should be noted that this does not permit a relevant company to make a loan to a person connected with a director. That remains totally prohibited.

The aggregate of the relevant amounts is a formula which recurs throughout these provisions and is defined in s 339. Basically the aggregate is determined by adding together the value of the proposed transaction or arrangement and the value of any existing transaction or arrangement of

---

7 Loan is not defined in the Act but see *Champagne Perrier-Jouet SA v HH Finch Ltd* [1982] 3 All ER 713 at 717.
8 It is the individual's status at the time of the arrangement which will determine the legality of the transaction: HC Official Report, SC A, 4 December 1979, col 480.
9 CA 1985, s 330(5).
10 Defined CA 1985, s 736 as substituted by CA 1989, s 144.
11 Defined CA 1985, s 331(6). It was felt that the potential for abuse was much greater in public companies than in private where the relationship between the parties is likely to be more intimate and flexible than in a typical large public company where the directors do not usually combine their managerial functions with a significant degree of ownership: HC Official Report, SC A, 29 November 1979, col 436.
12 CA 1985, s 330(3)(b), the reason being that it was felt that the net had to be cast widely in order to prevent the legislation being circumvented.
13 The circumstances in which a director is deemed to control a company are set out in s 346(5).
14 CA 1985, s 346(4).
15 Ibid, s 346(2)(c).
16 Ibid, s 334, as amended by CA 1989, s 138(b).

that particular type in favour of the person in respect of whom it is proposed to make the new transaction or arrangement, (less any amount by which this has been reduced), together with any amount outstanding in respect of the value of transactions or arrangements of that particular type entered into in favour of persons connected with the person in respect of whom the new transaction or arrangement is being entered into[17]. These provisions are designed to prevent attempts to circumvent the legislation by breaking up a transaction into a number of smaller transactions.

The value of the transaction is determined in accordance with s 340; for example, if the transaction is a loan, then it is the principal of the loan. Where the value of the transaction cannot for any reason be expressed as a specific sum of money, the value is deemed to exceed £100,000[18].

(II) INTRA-GROUP TRANSACTIONS

Where a relevant company is a member of a group of companies, then it is not prohibited from making a loan to another member of the group by reason only that a director of one member of the group is associated with another[19]. A company may also make a loan in favour of its holding company[20]. These exceptions were thought necessary if intra-group business was not to be unduly hampered[1]. Without this exception, the following transaction would have been prohibited: where X is a director of Company A (which is a relevant company) and owns 40% of the shares in Company B, another member of the group, Company A could not have made a loan to Company B as Company B is a person with whom X is associated by reason of s 346 of the 1985 Act.

(III) MONEY-LENDING COMPANIES

Where the company involved is a money-lending one[2] then it may make a loan to any person[3], notwithstanding the prohibitions in s 330, provided certain conditions are met. The loan must be made in the ordinary course of business and the amount of the loan must be no greater than, nor the terms more favourable than, those which it is reasonable to expect the company would have offered to a person of the same financial standing but unconnected with the company[4]. Here the aggregate of the relevant amounts in the case of relevant companies must not exceed £100,000 save in the case of a banking company where there is no monetary limit[5].

A money-lending company may also make a loan to one of its directors or

---

17 Relevant amounts are defined by s 339.
18 CA 1985, s 340(7): this figure was increased from £50,000 by the Companies (Fair Dealing by Directors) (Increase in Financial Limits) Order 1990, SI 1990 No 1393, as from 31 July 1990.
19 Ibid, s 333.
20 Ibid, s 336.
 1 The exception was necessary because a holding company may be a director of its subsidiary or what may be more likely in practice, a director may be such a substantial shareholder of the parent company that it, the parent, is a connected person of that director: HC Official Report, SC A, 29 November 1979, col 448.
 2 Defined CA 1985, s 338(2).
 3 Ibid, s 338(1)(a).
 4 Ibid, s 338(3).
 5 Ibid, s 338(4), as amended by CA 1989, s 138(c) and Sch 10, para 10.

a director of its holding company to enable such a person to purchase their only or main residence, to improve their dwelling house, or in substitution for a loan provided by a third party for any of those purposes[6]. This is so even though the terms are more favourable and the amount more generous than would be offered to a person of the same financial standing but unconnected with the company, provided the loan is made in the ordinary course of business and is of a type ordinarily made by the company to its employees and is on the same terms as would be available to employees. The aggregate amount in this case must not exceed £100,000[7].

Quasi-loans

Quasi-loan is defined by s 331(3) to mean a transaction whereby payments are made by a creditor (the company), on behalf of the borrower (the director), on terms that the borrower or someone on his behalf will ultimately reimburse the creditor, or in circumstances giving rise to a liability on the part of the borrower to reimburse the creditor[8]. It would, for example, cover the provision by the company of a credit card to the director who uses it on the basis that the company will pay the bill initially and the director will reimburse the company later. The provision of goods or services on a receive now, pay later, basis is obviously open to abuse hence the need in the case of relevant companies to extend the prohibitions to such transactions.

Relevant companies are prohibited from making such quasi-loans to directors of their company, or directors of their holding company[9], or persons connected with such directors[10]. The circumstances in which a person is regarded as connected with a director are set out above. There are no restrictions on private companies which are not relevant companies entering into quasi-loan transactions. There are again a number of exceptions.

(I) SMALL AMOUNTS

A quasi-loan may be made to a director of a company or a director of its holding company (but not to persons connected with such a director) provided it contains a term requiring repayment of the expenditure, by the director or a person on his behalf, to the company within two months of its being incurred and the aggregate of the relevant amounts does not exceed £5,000[11]. This would in fact permit the use of the credit card outlined above.

(II) INTRA-GROUP TRANSACTIONS

Where a relevant company is a member of a group of companies then it is not prohibited from making a quasi-loan to another member of that group by reason only that a director of one member of the group is associated with

---

6 Ibid, s 338(6) as amended by CA 1989, s 138(c).
7 Ibid.
8 This provision is designed to cover the abuses in the Peachey Property type situation, where companies in a group laid out money on their own account for goods and services for the chairman's personal use on the basis that reimbursement would be made by him later: HC Official Report, SC A, 29 November 1979, col 436.
9 CA 1985, s 330(3)(a).
10 Ibid, s 330(3)(b).
11 CA 1985, s 332(1)(b), as amended by CA 1989, s 138(a).

another[12]. A company may also make a quasi-loan in favour of its holding company[13]. This relaxation is made for the reasons given above in respect of loans.

(III) MONEY-LENDING COMPANIES

Where the company is a money-lending one[14] then it may make a quasi-loan[15] to any person, notwithstanding the prohibition in s 330, provided certain conditions are met. The quasi-loan must be made in the ordinary course of business and the amount of the loan must be no greater nor the terms of the loan no more favourable than those which it is reasonable to expect that the company would have offered to a person of the same financial standing but unconnected with the company[16]. The aggregate of the relevant amounts in the case of a relevant company must not exceed £100,000 save in the case of a banking company where there is no limit[17].

Credit transactions

Credit transactions are defined by s 331(7) to mean any transaction under which one party, i e the company, supplies any goods or sells any land under a hire purchase or conditional sale agreement; leases or hires any land or goods in return for periodical payments; or otherwise disposes of land or supplies goods or services on the understanding that payment, in whatever form, is to be deferred. An example would be where the company leases a car for use by a director of the company for a specific period, upon the expiry of which the car is returned to the lessor. The danger is presumably that payment will be deferred for a very long time and that the other terms of the agreement will be overly favourable to the director.

Relevant companies are prohibited from entering into a credit transaction as creditor for a director of the company, or a director of its holding company, or a person so connected[18]. There are no restrictions on private companies which are not relevant companies. There are again a number of exceptions.

(I) SMALL AMOUNTS

Credit transactions are permitted provided the aggregate of the relevant amounts does not exceed £10,000[19].

(II) INTRA-GROUP TRANSACTIONS

A company may enter into a credit transaction as a creditor for its holding company[20].

---

12 Ibid, s 333.
13 Ibid, s 336.
14 Defined in CA 1985, s 338(2).
15 CA 1985, s 338(1)(a).
16 Ibid, s 338(3).
17 Ibid, s 338(4), as amended by CA 1989, s 138(c) and Sch 10, para 10.
18 Ibid, s 330(4).
19 Ibid, s 335(1). Figure raised from £5,000 by the Companies (Fair Dealing by Directors) (Increase in Financial Limits) Order 1990, SI 1990 No 1393 which came into force on 31 July 1990.
20 Ibid, s 336(b).

(III) ORDINARY COURSE OF BUSINESS

Credit transactions are permitted if the company enters into the transaction in the ordinary course of business and the value of the transaction is no greater nor the terms no more favourable than those which it is reasonable to expect the company to have offered to a person of the same financial standing but who is unconnected with the company[1].

Related transactions

(I) BACK TO BACK TRANSACTIONS

Section 330(7) provides that a company shall not take part in an arrangement[2] whereby another person enters into a transaction which had it been entered into by the company in the first instance would have been a prohibited transaction within s 330(2), (3), (4) or (6) and that other person, in pursuance of the arrangement, has obtained or is to obtain any benefit from the company or its holding company or a subsidiary of the company or of its holding company.

This provision is designed to cover what are called back to back transactions, e g where Company A makes a loan to X, a director of Company B, in return for Company B making a loan to Y, a director of Company A. The benefit received must be in pursuance of the arrangement and must not be merely incidental to a transaction. Thus it would not cover the situation where Y, a director of Company A, banks with Super Bank plc and receives a personal loan from them, although Company A also banks with Super Bank plc. It does cover the situation where Y is a customer of Super Bank plc and negotiates a loan from the bank on favourable terms in return for his instructing the company to bank with Super Bank plc. It is the element of reciprocity which brings the back to back provisions into play. The prohibition was thought necessary in order to prevent company assets being used, indirectly, to assist or procure financial transactions for a director.

It is important to bear in mind that back to back transactions are only prohibited where they relate to transactions which would contravene s 330(2), (3), (4) or (6). If the transaction therefore is one which does not contravene the general prohibitions, because it is within one of the exceptions set out in ss 332–338, then a back to back transaction is also permitted.

(II) ASSIGNMENT/ASSUMPTION OF LIABILITIES

A company shall not arrange for the assignment to it, or the assumption by it, of any rights, obligations or liabilities under a transaction which, if it had been entered into by the company, would have contravened s 330(2), (3) or (4), i e would have been a prohibited loan, quasi-loan, or credit transaction or the giving of any guarantee or providing of security in respect of such a transaction[3]. This is to prevent the situation where, for example, A makes a loan to B, a director of Company C, and the company either buys A's interest in the loan or takes over the rights and liabilities of Z who is the

---

1 Ibid, s 335(2).
2 Much wider than a binding agreement, 'arrangement' basically means any device which brings about a transaction.
3 CA 1985, s 330(6).

guarantor of B's loan. It was felt that there was too much scope for collusive agreements in these cases[4].

It is important to bear in mind that the prohibition applies only to transactions which are prohibited by s 330(2), (3) or (4). If the transaction is therefore one which does not contravene these provisions because it falls within one of the exceptions in ss 332–338 then an assignment etc will be permitted.

(III) GUARANTEES/SECURITY

The basic position in respect of entering into any guarantee[5] or providing any security in respect of any transaction entered into by a director is that if the company is prohibited from entering into the transaction in respect of which the security is sought, then the company is also prohibited from giving a guarantee or providing security in respect of that transaction where a third party is to provide the loan, quasi-loan, etc[6]. If the company is permitted itself to enter into the transaction, then it will also be permitted to give any guarantee or provide security[7], except apparently under ss 332 or 334 which permit the making of loans and quasi-loans in certain instances but do not permit the giving of guarantees in respect of such transactions which presumably therefore remain prohibited.

Expenditure incurred for the purposes of the company

It should finally be noted that a company may do anything, notwithstanding the prohibitions in s 330, to provide any of its directors (but not the directors of its holding company) with funds to meet expenditure incurred or to be incurred by him for the purposes of the company or for the purpose of enabling him properly to perform his duties as an officer of the company or a company's doing anything to enable any of the directors to avoid incurring such expenditure[8]. This would, for example, permit the company to make a bridging loan to a director where he was required to move residence in the course of his duties. The assistance provided must be approved by the company in general meeting, at which meeting the purpose of the expenditure, the amount to be provided and the extent of the company's liabilities under any connected transaction must be disclosed[9]. Alternatively, approval can be sought at the next following annual general meeting but if it happens that when sought the approval is not forthcoming, then the loan shall be repaid or any other liability incurred shall be discharged within six months from the conclusion of the meeting[10]. If a private company opts to use the written resolution procedure provided by s 381A, as inserted by CA 1989, s 113, then those matters which must be disclosed at the general meeting must be disclosed to each member at or before the time at which the resolution is supplied to him for signature[11]. In the case of relevant companies, the

4 HC Official Report, SC A, 29 November 1979, col 438.
5 Defined in CA 1985, s 331(2), to include any indemnity.
6 CA 1985, s 330(2)(b), (3)(c) and (4)(b).
7 Ibid, ss 333, 336 and 338.
8 Ibid, s 337.
9 Ibid, s 337(3) and (4).
10 Ibid, s 337(3)(b).
11 CA 1985, s 381A(7) and Sch 15A, para 8, as inserted by CA 1989, s 114.

aggregate of the relevant amounts in respect of each director must not exceed £20,000[12].

The various exceptions are not mutually exclusive so careful planning should still enable a director to obtain substantial financial benefits from his association with his company.

DISCLOSURE

It should be noted that s 317 applies to any transaction or arrangement within s 330 which must therefore be disclosed to the board[13]. Details of such transactions must also be included in a note to the company's accounts by virtue of s 232 and Sch 6[14].

THE CONSEQUENCES OF BREACH

Where a company enters into a transaction or arrangement in breach of s 330, the transaction is voidable at the instance of the company[15]. The right to avoid the contract will be lost, however, if restitution is no longer possible; or the company has been indemnified by the parties involved in respect of the loss or damage suffered by it; or an innocent third party has acquired any rights bona fide for value and without actual notice of the contravention of the provisions[16].

Liability of directors   Any director and any person connected with such a director for whom a prohibited transaction was entered into, together with any other director who authorised the prohibited transaction, shall be liable to account to the company for any gains which he has made, directly or indirectly, from the transaction and shall also indemnify the company in respect of any loss or damage resulting from the transaction[17]. This is so whether or not the company has avoided the transaction and without prejudice to any liability which might arise at common law[18].

A director who is liable as a result of the company entering into a transaction with a person connected with the director can escape liability if he can show that he took all reasonable steps to secure the company's compliance with s 330[19]. His liability is absolute when the transaction in question has been entered into between the company and himself. In respect of any prohibited transaction where liability falls on a person connected with a director or on another director who authorised the transaction, they can escape liability by showing that at the time the transaction was entered into they did not know the relevant facts constituting the contravention[20].

---

12 Ibid, s 337(3). Figure raised from £10,000 by the Companies (Fair Dealing by Directors) (Increase in Financial Limits) Order 1990, SI 1990 No 1393, which came into force 31 July 1990.
13 Ibid, s 317(6), whether or not the transaction or arrangement is prohibited, although it is difficult to envisage disclosure of a transaction known to be prohibited.
14 As inserted by CA 1989, s 6 and Sch 4.
15 CA 1985, s 341.
16 Ibid, s 341(1).
17 Ibid, s 341(2).
18 See *Wallersteiner v Moir* [1974] 3 All ER 217, [1974] 1 WLR 991, CA.
19 CA 1985, s 341(4).
20 Ibid, s 341(5).

Criminal penalties   Criminal penalties have been imposed in respect of breaches of the provisions by relevant companies and their directors. This reflects the much tougher line taken in respect of those companies where there has been most abuse of the loan provisions in the past.

A relevant company which enters into a transaction or arrangement for one of its own directors or a director of its holding company in contravention of s 330 is guilty of an offence[1] unless it can show that at the time the transaction was entered into it did not know the relevant circumstances[2]. A director of a relevant company who authorises or permits the company to enter into a transaction or arrangement, knowing or having reasonable cause to believe that the company was thereby contravening s 330, is also guilty of an offence[3]. In addition, any person who procures a relevant company to enter into a prohibited transaction shall be guilty of an offence, provided he knew or had reasonable cause to believe that the company was contravening s 330[4]. Conviction on indictment can result in a term of imprisonment not exceeding two years, or a fine, or both, and on summary conviction in a term of imprisonment not exceeding six months or a fine not exceeding £2,000, or both[5].

Substantial property transactions

The possibility of conflict where directors purchase assets from, or sell assets to, their companies or companies in which they have an interest is so clear that the approval of the shareholders should be sought before the contract is entered into[6].

Section 320 of CA 1985[7] is the legislative response to a problem which was highlighted by a series of inspectors' reports on fraudulent asset stripping by directors in the 1970s[8].

This provision will now cover the *Burland v Earle*[9] type situation where a director was able to sell property to his company for $60,000, making a profit of some $38,000 on the sale. The Privy Council upheld the sale since it could not find any evidence of any commission or mandate to Burland to purchase on behalf of the company or that he was in any sense a trustee for the company of the purchased property[10].

Section 320 provides that, subject to certain exceptions, a company shall not enter into an arrangement whereby a director of the company or its holding company or a person connected with such a director[11] is to acquire

---

1 Ibid, s 342(2).
2 Ibid, s 342(5).
3 Ibid, s 342(1).
4 Ibid, s 342(3).
5 Ibid, s 342(4) and Sch 24.
6 See the White Paper, 'The Conduct of Company Directors' (Cmnd 7037) para 16.
7 Initially introduced by the Companies Act 1980, s 48. See Sealy *Cases and Materials in Company Law* (4th edn, 1989, p 257) who criticises the 'very crude overlap' between this section and the common law position.
8 HC Official Report, SC A, 2 July 1981, col 425.
9 [1902] AC 83, PC.
10 [1902] AC 83 at 98, per Lord Davey. See also *Canada Safeway Ltd v Thompson* [1951] 3 DLR 295 at 322.
11 The same definition applies here as was set out above in relation to loans: see CA 1985, s 346(2).

one or more non-cash assets[12] of the requisite value[13] from the company; or the company is to acquire one or more such non-cash assets from such a director or a person so connected; *unless* the arrangement is first approved by a resolution of the company in general meeting[14]. 'Arrangement' was deliberately chosen with a view to catching a range of transactions which the wily might otherwise have been able to devise to get around 'contract'[15]. It would obviously encompass any scheme whereby an asset was first transferred to a third party and subsequently to a director or a connected person but not any bona fide transaction which ultimately had this outcome. The provision also applies to shadow directors[16]. No approval is required unless the company is a company within the meaning of the 1985 Act or is registered under s 680 of that Act but approval is not required in the case of wholly owned subsidiaries[17]. Note that the section does not prohibit the interested director from voting, as a shareholder, in favour of the arrangement at the general meeting. Note also that the approval required under this section is in addition to disclosing the transaction to the board under s 317 and complying with any other requirements laid down by the company's articles.

There are, as usual, a number of exceptions to the requirement that approval be obtained.

(I) MINIMUM AMOUNTS

Approval is required only if the requisite value of the non-cash asset, at the time the arrangement was entered into, exceeds £100,000[18] or 10% of the company's relevant assets[19]. Where the criterion used is 10% of the relevant assets, the amount involved must exceed £2,000[20]. Relevant assets means the value of its net assets, determined by reference to its last annual accounts, or if no such accounts have been prepared and laid under the 1985 Act, the amount of its called-up share capital[1].

(II) INTRA-GROUP TRANSACTIONS

A feature of all these statutory provisions, as we have seen, has been exemptions designed to permit unhindered intra-group activity. Here again transactions between two companies could be within the prohibitions because one of the companies is a connected person of a director within s 346 and as such is within the general provision. In this instance intra-group

12 Defined in CA 1985, s 739 to mean any property or interest in property other than cash.
13 Defined CA 1985, s 320(2).
14 CA 1985, s 320(1). If the director or connected person is a director of its holding company or a person connected with such a director, then the approval must be given by the general meeting of the holding company.
15 HC Official Report, SC A, 29 November 1979, col 418.
16 CA 1985, s 320(3).
17 Ibid, s 321, the reason being that it was felt that the directors of the holding company would exert sufficient control over the directors of the subsidiaries: HC Official Report, SC A, 29 November 1979, col 419, but this may be a dangerous assumption since they will often be the same people.
18 The amounts specified in this section were increased by the Companies (Fair Dealing by Directors) (Increase in Financial Limits) Order 1990, SI 1990 No 1393.
19 CA 1985, s 320(2).
20 Ibid.
 1 Ibid.

transactions involving the acquisition of assets by holding companies from their wholly-owned subsidiaries or by wholly-owned subsidiaries from other wholly-owned subsidiaries or its holding company are permitted[2]. The exception is limited to wholly-owned subsidiaries since in those instances there are no outside shareholders requiring protection and the holding company will exert control.

(III) WINDING UP

Approval is not required if the arrangement is entered into by a company which is being wound up since if the company is being wound up the shareholders will have little interest in the disposal of its assets and if transactions were prohibited, the liquidator might be unduly hampered in the execution of his duties. This does not apply if it is a members' voluntary winding up because in that case the shareholders will retain an interest in the disposal of the company's assets[3].

(IV) MEMBERS

Approval is not required if the arrangement is one whereby a person is to acquire an asset from the company of which he is a member if the arrangement is made with that person in his character as a member[4]. Note that this exemption does not cover the acquisition of a non-cash asset by the company from a member.

CONSEQUENCES OF NON-COMPLIANCE

Any arrangement entered into by the company without having first obtained the approval of the company in general meeting and any transaction entered into in pursuance of the arrangement, whether by the company or by any other person, is voidable at the instance of the company[5]. A company will lose its right to avoid the transaction if (a) restitution of the subject matter is no longer possible or the company has been indemnified by any other person for the loss or damage suffered by it[6]; or (b) any rights acquired bona fide for value and without actual notice of the contravention by any person who is not a party to the arrangement or transaction would be affected by its avoidance[7]; or (c) the arrangement is, within a reasonable period, affirmed by the company in general meeting[8].

Regardless of whether the company exercises its right to avoid the transaction, the director and any person connected with him and any director who authorised the prohibited transaction shall be liable to:

(i)   account to the company for any gain which he has made directly or indirectly; and

---

2 Ibid, s 321(2)(a).
3 Ibid, s 321(2)(b).
4 Ibid, s 321(3). See Leigh and Edey *Companies Act 1981* (1981) para 376 who express misgivings about this exemption and question whether it is possible in such circumstances to ignore a member's status as a director.
5 CA 1985, s 322.
6 CA 1985, s 322(2)(a).
7 Ibid, s 322(2)(b).
8 Ibid, s 322(2)(c).

(ii)   indemnify the company for any loss or damage resulting from the arrangement or transaction[9].

Certain limited defences are provided. If the prohibited arrangement is between a company and a connected person, the director to whom he is connected will not be liable if he shows that he took all reasonable steps to secure the company's compliance with the section[10]. In any other case, a person so connected and any director who authorised the prohibited transaction shall not be liable if they can show that, at the time the arrangement was entered into, they did not know the relevant circumstances constituting the contravention[11]. The onus is on the party seeking to come within one of these defences to show that he is within it. No defence of lack of knowledge or intent is permitted where the offending party is an actual director. The provisions are designed to strike a balance between the interest of the company and innocent parties who might be prejudiced if companies were allowed too wide a right to recover[12].

Disclosure   Any transaction covered by s 320 must be disclosed to the board under s 317 and by virtue of s 232 (disclosures by directors of material interests) must be included in a note to the accounts.

Invalidity of certain transactions involving directors

A further restriction on transactions between a company and its directors or connected persons has been imposed by CA 1985, s 322A, inserted by CA 1989, s 109. This provision is designed to prevent the new ss 35 and 35A, discussed above in Chapters 10 and 24, being used to validate transactions between a company and such persons. The potential for abuse is such that it was thought that such parties should not be able to avail of the protection afforded by those provisions[13].

The new provision applies where a company enters into a transaction[14], to which the parties include a director of the company or its holding company, or a person connected with such a director[15], or a company with whom such a director is associated[16]. The effect of ss 35 and 35A, as we saw, is that a company may be bound by transactions even though the board exceeds some limitation on its powers under the company's constitution. The effect of s 322A is to treat such transactions as voidable at the instance of the company where the other party to the transaction is one of the parties noted above. The transaction will cease to be voidable if restitution of the subject matter is no longer possible, or if the company has been indemnified for the loss or damage resulting from the transaction, or if any rights acquired bona fide for value and without actual notice of the directors' exceeding their powers by any person who is not a party to the transaction would be affected by its avoidance, or if the transaction is ratified by the company in general

---

9   Ibid, s 322(3).
10   Ibid, s 322(5).
11   Ibid, s 322(6).
12   HC Official Report, SC A, 2 July 1981, col 427.
13   See Furey *The Companies Act 1989* (1990), para 4.24.
14   Defined as including any act, CA 1985, s 322A(8).
15   Defined CA 1985, s 346(2).
16   Defined CA 1985, s 346(4).

meeting, by ordinary or special resolution or otherwise as the case may require[17].

Whether or not the transaction is avoided, any such party as is mentioned above and any director who authorised the transaction is liable to account for any gain which he has made directly or indirectly from the transaction and to indemnify the company for any loss or damage resulting from the transaction[18], although any person other than a director may escape statutory liability by showing that at the time of the transaction he did not know that the directors were exceeding their powers[19]. Liability at common law is also retained[20].

The final point to note is that where the transaction is between the company and two other parties, only one of whom is within s 322A, so that one party wishes to rely on s 35A to validate the transaction which is voidable at the instance of the company under s 322A, then the court must resolve the matter[1]. By s 322A(7) the court has a discretion to make such order affirming, severing, or setting aside the transaction as appears to be just in such circumstances.

Contracts of employment

As has previously been discussed[2], lengthy service agreements were abused by directors and used to defeat the members' power under s 303 of CA 1985 to remove them by an ordinary resolution[3]. Section 319 of the 1985 Act now deals with such contracts and basically requires the prior approval of the company in general meeting where the agreement is for a term exceeding five years. It should be noted that directors' service contracts are open to inspection by the members under s 318 of the 1985 Act.

Competing directorships

Given that the law imposes a strict no-conflict rule, it might have been expected that competing directorships would be precluded, for what could more often give rise to a possible conflict than sitting on the boards of two or more companies in the same line of business? Yet the courts apparently permit competing directorships[4]. Whatever the theory, in practice the problems are obvious. It would seem impossible for a director to act for very long for two competing companies before he would find himself in an intolerable position. He cannot serve two masters at once and would inevitably be in breach of his duties to one or other company. It also seems likely that the

---

17 CA 1985, s 322A(5).
18 Ibid, s 322A(3).
19 Ibid, s 322A(6).
20 Ibid, s 322A(4).
 1 Ibid, s 322A(7).
 2 See discussion in Chapter 23, ante.
 3 By making it too expensive for the company to exercise its statutory powers.
 4 See *London and Mashonaland Exploration Co Ltd v New Mashonaland Exploration Co Ltd* [1891] WN 165; approved in *Bell v Lever Bros* [1932] AC 161, HL. It should be noted that in the *Mashonaland* case no actual conflict had arisen because, at the time of the action, the second company had not in fact commenced business and no damage had therefore occurred. See also *Abbey Glen Property Corpn v Stumborg* (1978) 85 DLR (3d) 35; *Berlei Hestia (NZ) Ltd v Fernyhough* [1980] 2 NZLR 150.

courts would regard competing directorships as in some cases giving grounds for a petition under s 459, alleging unfairly prejudicial conduct in the way in which the company is being run[5]. The easiest solution to the problem is to include a provision in the articles precluding directors from occupying directorships in competing companies. Executive directors with service contracts are in any event prohibited from competing[6].

THE NO-PROFIT RULE

Another inflexible rule of equity is that a person who is in a fiduciary position is not, unless otherwise expressly provided, entitled to profit from that position: where he does so he is liable to account[7]. The rule is often regarded as an element of the no-conflict rule but each rule exists independently of the other although the same fact situation often results in both applying in a particular case[8].

The rule has its origins in the leading trust case of *Keech v Sandford*[9] but the most famous application of the principle in company law is *Regal (Hastings) Ltd v Gulliver*[10]. Regal was the owner of a cinema and wished to acquire a further two cinemas with a view to selling all three as a group. A subsidiary company was established to acquire the additional cinemas. The owner of these cinemas was willing to grant a lease to the subsidiary company but only if the authorised share capital of £5,000 was fully paid up, or if the directors of Regal would give personal guarantees in respect of the rent. Regal was unable to raise more than £2,000 of the £5,000 required and the directors were unwilling to give personal guarantees. In the circumstances it was decided that the directors themselves would subscribe for the remaining shares. Eventually the transaction was carried out by means of a sale of the shares in Regal and the subsidiary with the directors making a profit of almost £3 per share on their shares. The new controllers of Regal promptly sued the former directors to recover these profits and succeeded. The net effect, of course, was to reduce the purchase price paid by them for the companies.

The House of Lords found that the directors had obtained their profits by reason of and in the course of the execution of their office as directors of Regal[11]. They had entered, in the course of their management, into a transaction in which they utilised the position and knowledge possessed by them in virtue of their office as directors[12]. They were thus liable to account, notwithstanding the fact that they had acted bona fide throughout, for that liability:

---

5 See *Scottish Co-operative Wholesale Society Ltd v Meyer* [1959] AC 324, HL and *Abbey Glen Property Corpn v Stumborg* (1978) 85 DLR (3d) 35.
6 *Hivac Ltd v Park Royal Scientific Instruments Ltd* [1946] Ch 169, [1946] 1 All ER 350, HL.
7 *Bray v Ford* [1896] AC 44 at 51, HL, per Lord Herschell; *Parker v McKenna* (1874) 10 Ch App 96; *Boston Deep Sea Fishing and Ice Co Ltd v Ansell* (1888) 39 Ch D 339, CA; *Regal (Hastings) Ltd v Gulliver* [1967] 2 AC 134n, [1942] 1 All ER 378, HL.
8 See, for example, *Guinness plc v Saunders* [1990] 2 AC 663, [1990] 1 All ER 652, HL; also Austin Fiduciary Accountability for Business Opportunities in *Equity and Commercial Relationships* (ed Finn, 1987) pp 146–149.
9 (1726) Sel Cas Ch 61.
10 [1967] 2 AC 134n, [1942] 1 All ER 378, HL.
11 [1967] 2 AC 134n at 147, [1942] 1 All ER 378 at 389, HL, per Lord Russell.
12 [1967] 2 AC 134n at 153, [1942] 1 All ER 378 at 391, HL, per Lord Macmillan.

. . . in no way depends on fraud, or absence of bona fides; or upon such questions or considerations as whether the profit would or should otherwise have gone to the plaintiff, or whether the profiteer was under a duty to obtain the source of the profit for the plaintiff, or whether he took a risk, or acted as he did for the benefit of the plaintiff, or whether the plaintiff has in fact been damaged or benefited by his action. The liability arises from the mere fact of a profit having, in the stated circumstances, been made. The profiteer, however honest and well intentioned, cannot escape the risk of being called upon to account[13].

Notwithstanding the strictness of *Regal* there are some instances when directors will be permitted to retain their profits[14].

(i) *Ratification*   It is clear that the company in general meeting, at least where the shareholders act unanimously[15], can permit a director to profit from his position. The matter is not so clear cut where they purport to ratify such profit making by a simple majority. It was assumed in *Regal* that the directors could, had they wished, have protected themselves by a resolution of the company in general meeting[16]. The difficulty is that it is not easy to reconcile this view with *Cook v Deeks*[17] where the Privy Council refused to accept a purported ratification of profit making by the directors which amounted to the misappropriation by the directors of a contract which belonged in equity to the company. The cases can, perhaps, be reconciled by regarding *Regal* as an instance of merely incidental profit making by directors who acted bona fide throughout[18] while *Cook v Deeks* represents the other end of the spectrum, the actual misappropriation of corporate assets, which is not ratifiable[19]. If the transaction is ratifiable then the interested directors can, as shareholders, vote to ratify their own breaches of duty[20]. Even if the profit making is not ratifiable, an independent majority of shareholders may decide not to pursue a claim against the wrongdoing directors[1].

13 [1967] 2 AC 134n at 144, [1942] 1 All ER 378 at 386, HL, per Lord Russell. The actual decision in *Regal* has been much criticised: see Gower *Principles of Modern Company Law* (4th edn, 1979) p 594: ' . . . carrying equitable principles to an inequitable conclusion'; Jones (1968) 84 LQR 472 at 497. Note Sullivan (1979) 42 MLR 71 who points out that the directors had a would-be purchaser in mind throughout and that there were other shareholders in *Regal* who could have put up some of the money required but who were not invited to do so. See also *Boardman v Phipps* [1967] 2 AC 46, [1966] 3 All ER 721, HL.
14 Indeed the judiciary did not seem to expect that the no-profit rule would become an absolute rule. See *Bray v Ford* [1896] AC 44 at 51, HL, per Lord Herschell: ' . . . satisfied that it might be departed from in many cases without any breach of morality, without any wrong being inflicted and without any consciousness of wrongdoing'.
15 *New Zealand Netherlands Society Oranje Inc v Kuys* [1973] 2 All ER 1222, [1973] 1 WLR 1126, PC. Note also *Queensland Mines Ltd v Hudson* (1978) 52 ALJR 399, PC.
16 [1967] 2 AC 134n at 150, [1942] 1 All ER 378 at 389, HL, per Lord Russell.
17 [1916] 1 AC 554, PC discussed in detail post; see also *Menier v Hooper's Telegraph Works* (1874) 9 Ch App 350.
18 Note Sealy *Cases and Materials in Company Law* (4th edn, 1989) p 265 who says that unless it is thought that this was the crucial finding, it is difficult to say why the impropriety in *Regal* was capable of ratification while that in *Cook v Deeks* was not.
19 See *Gower*, op cit, p 617. It is arguable that *Regal* was a case where the directors appropriated to themselves the opportunity to subsequently profit from the sale of the shares.
20 *North-West Transportation Co Ltd and Beatty v Beatty* (1887) 12 App Cas 589, PC; *Burland v Earle* [1902] AC 83, PC; *Northern Counties Securities Ltd v Jackson & Steeple Ltd* [1974] 2 All ER 625, [1974] 1 WLR 1133.
1 See *Smith v Croft (No 2)* [1988] Ch 114, [1987] 3 All ER 909.

(ii) *Waiver*   The articles commonly include a provision similar to art 85 of Table A which permits the retention of profits made by directors in a *Regal* type situation. The question whether the articles could permit further derogations from the no-profit rule is discussed at the end of this Chapter.

Let us now examine two particular instances of profit making by directors:

(i)   corporate opportunities;
(ii) insider dealing.

Corporate opportunities

A corporate opportunity is regarded as a corporate asset which the directors cannot therefore appropriate to their own use[2]. A classic corporate opportunity case is *Cook v Deeks*[3]. Here three out of four directors of a Canadian railway company diverted a contract in which the company was interested to another company which they had formed. It was held by the Judicial Committee of the Privy Council that the contract was one which in equity belonged to the company and which the directors had acquired for themselves while ostensibly acting on behalf of the company. They were therefore bound to hold it on behalf of the company and were not entitled to make a present of it to themselves[4]. The opportunity to obtain this contract had come to them in their capacity and by virtue of their position as directors of the company. While still retaining that position, while still acting as managers, and with their duties to the company entirely unchanged, they had proceeded to negotiate in reality on their own behalf[5]. The Privy Council refused to sanction such conduct.

Likewise in the Canadian case of *Canadian Aero Service Ltd v O'Malley*[6] the president and executive vice-president of the company[7] were held liable where, having actively pursued a contract on behalf of the company, they resigned, formed a new company and acquired it for the new company.

Such cases are relatively straightforward. The companies were actively seeking the contracts, the opportunities, which their directors instead obtained for themselves. However it is necessary to establish whether directors and officers are prohibited from taking all opportunities which come their way or whether a more limited corporate opportunity doctrine applies. Here again the approach has been to concentrate on the capacity of the profiteers[8], applying Lord Russell's dictum in *Regal* that the profit/ opportunity must have been acquired by reason of their positions as directors and in the course of their fiduciary relationship, rather than engaging in any examination of the nature of the opportunity. An example of the general

---

2 See generally Austin Fiduciary Accountability for Business Opportunities in *Equity and Commercial Relationships* (ed Finn, 1987) pp 141–185, and Kearney, pp 186–210.
3 [1916] 1 AC 554, PC.
4 [1916] 1 AC 554 at 564, PC.
5 [1916] 1 AC 554 at 559–560, PC.
6 (1973) 40 DLR (3d) 371, noted Beck (1975) 53 Can Bar Rev 771; Prentice (1974) 37 MLR 464.
7 The court accepted that senior officers such as these owed duties similar to those owed by directors.
8 It is not without its critics, see Weinrib (1975) 25 UTLJ 1; Beck (1975) 53 Can Bar Rev 771; *Peso-Silver Mines Ltd v Cropper* (1966) 58 DLR (2d) 1.

approach is *Industrial Development Consultants Ltd v Cooley*[9]. Here a director was held liable to account to his former company for the benefits he received under a contract which he had entered into with the Eastern Gas Board. Cooley had been employed as managing director by IDC which was hopeful of obtaining contracts from the Gas Board. He was actively involved in ongoing negotiations to secure these contracts for the company when the Gas Board indicated to him that they were not prepared, under any circumstances, to contract with his company but they were willing to deal with him personally. He promptly resigned[10] and took the contract offered by the Gas Board. He was held liable to account. Roskill J held that he had one capacity and one capacity only at that time and that was as managing director of the plaintiff company[11]. Information which came to him while he was managing director and which was of concern to the plaintiff and was relevant to the company to know was information which it was his duty, because of his fiduciary position, to pass on to the company[12].

The limitations of the capacity approach were appreciated by the Canadian Supreme Court in *Canadian Aero Service Ltd v O'Malley*[13] where Laskin J, noting that such an approach straitjacketed the development of the law in this area, preferred[14] to have regard to a number of different factors and consider whether or not, in the light of all the circumstances, the director in question was in breach of his fiduciary duties. Factors to be considered would include the office or position held, the nature of the corporate opportunity, its ripeness, its specific nature and the director's or managerial officer's relationship to it, the amount of knowledge possessed, the circumstances in which it was obtained and whether it was special or even private information.

The varying approaches have recently been considered in *Island Export Finance Ltd v Umunna*[15]. Umunna was the managing director of IEF Ltd, a company which specialised in seeking business in West Africa, and in 1976 he secured a contract for it from the Cameroon postal authorities. In 1977 he resigned from the company due to general dissatisfaction with it and subsequently obtained orders from the Cameroon postal authorities for his own company. IEF alleged that this was a breach of his fiduciary duty to it for which he was liable to account. Hutchinson J found no breach of fiduciary duty and in his judgment combined elements of the existing English and overseas authorities in a more flexible corporate opportunities doctrine than had previously been applied in this jurisdiction.

The court found that while Umunna may in a general way have contemplated that the Cameroon authorities might be a good source of business for his own company on resignation, the exploitation of that opportunity was

---

9 [1972] 2 All ER 162, [1972] 1 WLR 443.
10 Indeed he deceived the company into thinking he was resigning because of ill health. Note that a director's fiduciary duty does not necessarily come to an end when he ceases to be a director, *Island Export Finance Ltd v Umunna* [1986] BCLC 460.
11 [1972] 2 All ER 162 at 173, [1972] 1 WLR 443 at 451.
12 Ibid.
13 (1973) 40 DLR (3d) 371.
14 (1973) 40 DLR (3d) 371 at 391. This passage was cited with approval in *Island Export Finance Ltd v Umunna* [1986] BCLC 460.
15 [1986] BCLC 460.

not his primary or indeed an important motive in his resignation. Moreover, neither when Umunna resigned nor when he got the orders was IEF actively pursuing further business with the Cameroon authorities. At most it had a hope of obtaining further orders but that could not in any realistic sense be said to be a maturing business opportunity. As it was not a maturing business opportunity of IEF's then it was open to Umunna to take it on his own account.

This decision combined both approaches in that it considered Umunna's capacity as IEF's former managing director but also examined the nature of the opportunity which IEF was claiming as a corporate opportunity. Particularly interesting is the endorsement of the more wide ranging and flexible approach favoured by Laskin J in *Canadian Aero Service Ltd v O'Malley* which is set out above. This may open the door to the development of a more flexible doctrine which, in keeping with other jurisdictions, will go beyond the capacity of the individual concerned to examine the nature of the opportunity in question.

A final problem to consider is the situation where the company is offered an opportunity which the board duly considers but rejects. Can the directors then take that opportunity for themselves? *Regal* suggests they cannot[16]. Commonwealth authorities have decided they can.

The Canadian Supreme Court faced the issue in *Peso-Silver Mines Ltd v Cropper*[17]. In this case a mining company was offered an opportunity to acquire certain mineral claims. The opportunity was turned down by the board because of the company's strained finances and because it felt that the company already had enough land. Three of the Peso directors then personally acquired the claims at the price for which the claims had been offered to Peso. On a subsequent change of management at Peso, an action was brought by the company against the three directors calling on them to account for their gains. The court, while accepting that they were in a fiduciary relationship with Peso, refused to hold them accountable[18]. The decision to reject the opportunity had been taken bona fide and for sound business reasons in the interests of Peso. The opportunity then ceased to be one which they acquired by reason of, and in the course of, the execution of their office as directors of Peso. Thus it was open to them as individuals to acquire the opportunity for themselves[19].

The major criticism of the approach in Peso is that it requires a determination by the court as to whether the board's rejection of the opportunity was

---

16 [1967] AC 134 at 144, [1942] 1 All ER 378 at 386.
17 (1966) 58 DLR (2d) 1, noted Prentice (1967) 30 MLR 450. See also Beck's lengthy analysis of the case in Ziegel (ed) *Canadian Company Law* (1973) p 207.
18 See the strong dissenting judgment of Norris J (1966) 56 DLR (2d) 117 (BCCA) where he argued that the complexities of modern business life and the possibility of abuse required the application of strict principles. See also Beck, in Ziegel, op cit; Shepherd *The Law of Fiduciaries* (1981) p 283; Prentice (1967) 30 MLR 450; *Gower* (4th edn, 1979) p 594. For the opposite view, see Oakley *Constructive Trusts* (2nd edn, 1987) p 75 '. . . approach [in *Peso*] seems preferable in every way to that adopted by the House of Lords in *Regal*'.
19 The Canadian Supreme Court reached this decision by relying on dicta of Lord Greene in the Court of Appeal in *Regal* to the effect that it was carrying duties of directors too far to suggest that if the board, bona fide, rejected an opportunity that an individual director could not acquire it. In the House of Lords Lord Russell declined to approve such a view [1967] 2 AC 134 at 152, [1942] 1 All ER 378 at 391, while Lord Wright felt that it was dead in the teeth of a wise and salutary rule [1967] 2 AC 134 at 156, [1942] 1 All ER 378 at 394.

bona fide or not[20]. The evidence, moreover, which would establish the financial ability or inability of the company to take the opportunity is solely within the control of those who will benefit personally if the company decides to reject the opportunity[1]. It is preferable that they should direct all their energies to obtaining the finance for the company as opposed to preparing to take the opportunity themselves if and when the company rejects it. Anything less than an absolute rule, it is argued, will tempt the directors to be less than totally committed to obtaining the opportunity on behalf of the company. In any event, while rejection by the board may mean that it is no longer a corporate opportunity, the basic conflict remains and the directors should be liable to account[2].

If the decision in *Island Export Finance Ltd v Umunna*[3] does indicate an 'opportunity' rather than 'capacity' orientated doctrine then this may open the door to Peso-like decisions here as the courts develop and refine what is encompassed within a 'maturing business opportunity'. Can something which a company cannot afford to pursue realistically be regarded as a 'maturing business opportunity'? The problem of ascertaining the bona fide nature of the financial inability would, of course, remain.

This approach has been followed in the Australian High Court in *Queensland Mines Ltd v Hudson*[4]. Here a company (Queensland) was formed to exploit mining licences. Hudson, the managing director of the company, was negotiating with the government for the licences when the company ran into severe financial difficulties. He took the licence in his own name, subsequently resigned as managing director, and eventually made considerable profits. The company then sought to hold him to account. The Privy Council held that he was not liable as he had fully discussed the situation and what he proposed to do with the Queensland board and they had resolved not to proceed further in pursuit of the licence.

Perhaps the most appropriate solution to the problems in this area is that suggested by Brudney and Clark[5], namely that different rules should apply depending on whether the company is a public company or a close corporation (a small private company). Public companies should be covered by a categorical rule in view of, inter alia, their widely dispersed shareholdings and the adequate managerial compensation schemes in those companies. Private companies, on the other hand, should be free to regulate this problem as a matter of contract between the parties, given that the people involved are likely to be a closer, more intimate, group and lavish

---

20 The courts themselves are sceptical about their ability to determine the directors' motives: see *Regal (Hastings) Ltd v Gulliver* [1967] 2 AC 134n at 154, [1942] 1 All ER 378 at 392, HL, per Lord Wright; *Ex p James* (1803) 8 Ves 337 at 345: 'no court is equal to the examination and ascertainment of the truth in these cases'. See also Bishop and Prentice (1983) 46 MLR 289 at 303.
1 See *Regal (Hastings) Ltd v Gulliver* [1967] 2 AC 134n at 154, [1942] 1 All ER 378 at 392, HL, per Lord Wright.
2 See Prentice (1967) 30 MLR 450 at 454.
3 [1986] BCLC 460.
4 (1978) 52 ALJR 399, PC, noted Sullivan (1979) 42 MLR 711. Another explanation of this case, however, is that as all the shareholders were completely appraised of the facts throughout, it is simply an example of the general meeting unanimously releasing a director from his liability to account. See also *New Zealand Netherlands Society Oranje Inc v Kuys* [1973] 2 All ER 1222, PC.
5 Brudney and Clark (1981) 94 Harv L Rev 997. See Austin, op cit, pp 166–171, who argues that the case for having different standards has not been made.

managerial compensation plans are not as common. Another suggestion is that in fact no rules are required at all, instead the market will regulate managerial wrongdoing with executives who deflect corporate assets to themselves soon being removed by the shareholders[6] and being identified as wrongdoers in the market.

Where a breach of duty involving a misappropriation of corporate assets does occur, as in *Cook v Deeks*[7], the breach may not be ratified by the company in general meeting[8] and the directors remain liable as constructive trustees of the company's assets[9]. Third parties who knowingly participate in the directors' breach of trust may also be liable as constructive trustees. Liability here depends on the degree of involvement. Third parties who receive corporate assets will be liable if they receive the property with actual notice of the breach of trust or in circumstances in which they ought to have known of the breach[10]. As for third parties who knowingly assist in a dishonest design of the directors without actually receiving any trust property, they will also be liable as constructive trustees if they actually knew of the breach or wilfully shut their eyes to it[11].

Insider dealing

One particular form of profit-making which is greatly criticised is insider dealing[12]. Basically this entails the use by an insider of price-sensitive information (known to him but not generally and which he has acquired by virtue of his position) to trade to his advantage in the securities of a company. This practice is not limited to directors but can be engaged in by anyone who has access to this type of information. It is convenient, however, to discuss insider dealing here since as a matter of practice directors have

6 See Wolfson (1980) 34 U Miami L Rev 959.
7 [1916] 1 AC 554, PC.
8 Subject to the comments made above on the issue of ratification and see Ch 27.
9 *Russell v Wakefield Waterworks Co* (1875) LR 20 Eq 474; *Re Lands Allotment Co* [1894] 1 Ch 616, CA; *Selangor United Rubber Estates Ltd v Cradock (a bankrupt) (No 3)* [1968] 2 All ER 1073 at 1091–2, [1968] 1 WLR 1555 at 1575; *Belmont Finance Corpn Ltd v Williams Furniture Ltd (No 2)* [1980] 1 All ER 393, CA.
10 *Barnes v Addy* (1874) 9 Ch App 244; *Belmont Finance Corpn Ltd v Williams Furniture Ltd (No 2)* [1980] 1 All ER 393, CA; *International Sales and Agencies Ltd v Marcus* [1982] 3 All ER 551; *Rolled Steel Products (Holdings) Ltd v British Steel Corpn* [1986] Ch 246, [1985] 3 All ER 52, CA.
11 *Belmont Finance Corpn Ltd v Williams Furniture Ltd (No 2)* [1980] 1 All ER 393, CA; *Re Montagu's Settlements Trusts* [1987] Ch 264, [1987] 2 WLR 1192; *Lipkin Gorman v Karpnale Ltd* [1989] 1 WLR 1340, [1989] BCLC 756, CA, see note [1989] JBL 255; *Agip (Africa) Ltd v Jackson* [1990] Ch 265; affd (1991) Times, 9 January, Financial Times, 18 January, CA; *Eagle Trust plc v SBC Securities Ltd* (1991) Times, 14 February, Financial Times, 15 February. Harpum, op cit, notes that the authorities on knowing assistance are in a state of considerable disarray, see also *Oakley*, op cit, Chapter 4. There have been suggestions that constructive notice would be sufficient to found liability under the knowing assistance head, see *Selangor United Rubber Estates Ltd v Cradock (a bankrupt) (No 3)* [1968] 2 All ER 1073, [1968] 1 WLR 1555; *Karak Rubber Co Ltd v Burden (No 2)* [1972] 1 All ER 1210, [1972] 1 WLR 602; *Baden, Delvaux and Lecuit v Societe General* [1983] BCLC 325, but this was not accepted in *Belmont* nor in the more recent authorities noted above, and see Millett (1991) 107 LQR 71; Harpum (1986) 102 LQR 114 at 127, (1987) 50 MLR 217; Vroegop [1988] JBL 437; Arora [1990] JBL 217.
12 There is an extensive literature on this issue. See in particular: Ashe and Counsell *Insider Trading* (1990); Suter *The Regulation of Insider Dealing in Britain* (1989); Hannigan *Insider Dealing* (1988); Rider *Insider Trading* (1983); Rider and Ffrench *The Regulation of Insider Trading* (1979); Manne *Insider Trading and the Stock Market* (1966).

most access to this information and are most likely to deal or 'tip' other persons to deal on the strength of it.

Despite the widespread criticism of the practice, the common law provides only very limited relief while statutory intervention is restricted to the Company Securities (Insider Dealing) Act 1985[13] which makes it a criminal offence but only in certain limited circumstances.

This would seem to indicate a certain reluctance to eliminate a practice which even its supporters admit raises the spectre of dishonesty, fraud, exploitation and greed[14]! It is useful therefore to start by considering some of the arguments for and against prohibiting the practice.

Those who argue for prohibition see the practice as being contrary to the demands of fidelity, efficiency and equity[15]. The fidelity argument looks at the problem from the point of view of where the information has come from and the position of the person utilising it[16]. The insider has acquired it from the privileged position he occupies. Loyalty to the company should preclude that insider from taking that information which belongs[17] to the company and using it to his own advantage[18]. Where the insider is a director or senior officer, there is the additional factor that he is in a fiduciary relationship vis-à-vis the company and his appropriation of the information and his profiting therefrom is incompatible with that relationship.

The efficiency argument looks to the effect on the market of the non-disclosure and self-dealing by the insider. The aim of any stock market is to rapidly assimilate all the available information about a company and almost immediately reflect that information in the share price. Investors should be able to identify those companies where their capital is most needed and will most profitably be used. This enables resources to be efficiently allocated and not 'wasted' in companies which are going into decline. An efficient stock market therefore is necessary to ensure an efficient allocation of capital. If however there is information of a price-sensitive nature available which is not disclosed and on the basis of which some people only are trading then they are distorting the market. The price at which those shares are being traded is an artificial one. When this fact subsequently becomes apparent, public confidence in the stock market is diminished. As investors are generally risk averse, if it appears that investing in the stock market is becoming even more of a gamble because of the unknown amount of insider dealing which is occurring, then they may pull out and look to invest elsewhere, perhaps through the financial institutions.

The third argument, of equity, is also related to the available market.

---

13 As amended by the Financial Services Act 1986. The provisions were originally introduced by the Companies Act 1980, ss 68–73. Note also s 323 of CA 1985 which prohibits directors from dealing in options in their company's listed securities.

14 Manne (1970) 23 V and L Rev 547 at 549; Sugarman 'The Regulation of Insider Dealing' in *The Regulation of the British Securities Industry* ed Rider (1979) at p 62 notes that '. . . insider trading has come to symbolise, perhaps more than any other aspect of company law reform, the unacceptable face of capitalism'; Johnston *The City Takeover Code* (1980) pp 155–169.

15 Brudney (1979) 93 Harv L Rev 322 at 344 ff.

16 A view not unlike that expressed in the no-profit cases.

17 Some commentators doubt whether information can belong to the company but the House of Lords in *Boardman v Phipps* [1967] 2 AC 46, [1966] 3 All ER 721 seems to have accepted that it could, see the speeches of Lord Cohen and Hodson but note also the strong dissent by Lord Upjohn.

18 Brudney (1979) 93 Harv L Rev 322 at 346.

American commentators call it the concept of market egalitarianism. This is simply the belief that the law should try to ensure that all individuals in the market are placed on an equal footing, in so far as that is possible. This requires, first, timely and adequate disclosure[19] by companies of price-sensitive information and secondly, the prohibition of dealing on any such information which is undisclosed. Again this is designed to maintain investor confidence in the integrity of the market.

Another often stated view is quite simply that the practice is contrary to good business ethics and morally wrong[20].

However the debate has not been totally one-sided for not everyone is convinced that insider dealing should be prohibited. Professor H Manne, a famous American exponent of the practice, has argued that far from prohibiting it, there should be an unfettered right to trade on the basis of inside information[1]. His view is that insider trading is in fact the only form of compensation which can adequately compensate managers for their entre-preneurial skills[2]. Moreover, it in fact benefits the market since allowing insiders to trade before the information is disclosed will actually accelerate the incorporation of the information in the market price[3]. In any event, there is no evidence that the practice harms anyone since the decision of the outsider to purchase or sell is independent of, and not induced by, the conduct of the insider.

While this debate on the merits and demerits of the practice has been conducted mainly in the US, the last decade or so has seen considerable discussion of the problem within the UK[4]. The initial approach was to rely on disclosure requirements, in particular, requiring disclosure by directors of their interests in the shares of their companies[5], together with a limited prohibition on dealing by a director in options in the listed securities of his company[6]. This was seen as inadequate by the Jenkins Committee which recommended that any director who engaged in insider dealing should be liable to compensate any person who suffered from his action in so doing[7]. Further impetus for change came in the 1970s with The Stock Exchange and the Takeover Panel[8] recommending that the practice be made a criminal offence, as did a Justice Report[9] and a number of White Papers[10]. These views were reflected in the abortive Companies Bills in 1973[11] and in 1978[12].

---

19 On the value of disclosure, see Kripke (1975) 31 BL 293.
20 Justice *Insider Trading* (1972) para 3, but see Kay (1973) 36 MLR 185 at 189; Manne (1970) 23 Vand L Rev 547 at 549.
 1 Manne *Insider Trading and the Stock Market*. For a critical response, see Schotland (1967) 53 Va L Rev 1425, and the spirited debate between Manne and his critics in (1970) 23 Vand L Rev 547.
 2 See Posner *Economic Analysis of Law* (2nd edn, 1977) p 309 who disagrees.
 3 Manne *Insider Trading and the Stock Market* (1966) pp 131–145.
 4 See *Rider and Ffrench*, op cit; *Justice*, op cit.
 5 Originally CA 1967, ss 27–29, now ss 324–329 of the 1985 Act.
 6 Originally CA 1967, s 25, now s 323 of the 1985 Act.
 7 The Report of the Company Law Committee (The Jenkins Committee), Cmnd 1749, para 89.
 8 See *Johnston*, op cit, p 163 ff.
 9 *Justice,* op cit, para 36(ii).
10 Company Law Reform, Cmnd 5391, paras 15–20 although it also recommended civil remedies; 'The Conduct of Company Directors', Cmnd 7037, paras 22–32.
11 Companies Bill 1973, cls 12–16.
12 Companies Bill 1978, cls 57–63.

It was not until 1980 that actual legislation was enacted which is now to be found in the Company Securities (Insider Dealing) Act 1985[13]. This in turn has been amended by the Financial Services Act 1986.

The EC has since adopted a Directive coordinating regulations on insider dealing in 1989[14] which requires member states to make insider dealing unlawful and to co-operate in obtaining and exchanging information about it for enforcement purposes. The Directive is quite similar to the existing UK provisions and would not have required a radical change in position but the Government has decided to use the opportunity created by the need to implement the Directive to simplify and update the 1985 Act. To that end a consultation exercise was undertaken in 1990[15] and it is hoped to bring forward primary legislation at the earliest opportunity. The Directive must be implemented by 1 June 1992.

The Company Securities (Insider Dealing) Act 1985

It is important to stress at the outset that this Act is of limited application and makes insider dealing a criminal offence only in respect of certain classes of individuals, in possession of a certain type of information, and participating in certain types of transactions. It is not a blanket prohibition of all insider dealing in securities transactions. It is important therefore to be able to identify those situations when the Act does apply and dealing would be a criminal offence.

For the purposes of this Act there are basically three categories of insiders:

(i)   individuals connected with a company;
(ii) individuals contemplating takeovers; and
(iii) public servants.

In addition tippees, ie persons tipped off by an insider, may be within the prohibitions. There are a number of exceptions to the prohibitions which are set out in s 3 and will be discussed later.

INDIVIDUALS CONNECTED WITH A COMPANY

Section 1 of the CSA 1985 provides that an individual[16] shall not deal on a recognised stock exchange in securities[17] of a company in certain circumstances. The individual must be, or at any time in the preceding six months[18] has been, knowingly connected with the company in question. Section 9 provides that an individual is connected with a company if but only if:

13 For commentary on the provisions, first introduced by the Companies Act 1980, see Hannigan *Insider Dealing* (1988) Chapters 3 and 4; Rider *Insider Trading* (1983) Chapter 1; Prentice *The Companies Act 1980* (1980) pp 119–136; Naylor (1990) 11 Co Law 53.
14 89/592 EC, see OJ L 334/30 18.11.89.
15 See 'The Law on Insider Dealing, A Consultative Document', December 1989, DTI, hereafter referred to as Con Doc (1989). See Cranston [1990] JBL 444.
16 Note that the provisions apply only to individuals. The Government has reconsidered this requirement and concluded that it would be an unnecessary complication to cover the actions of companies, see Con Doc (1989), para 2.29.
17 Defined CSA, s 12.
18 The Government has concluded that this six month requirement is of little significance and will delete it from the new legislation, see Con Doc (1989), para 2.27.

(a)   he is a director of that company or a related company, i e a subsidiary of that company, or its holding company, or a subsidiary of its holding company[19], or

(b)   he occupies a position as an officer (other than a director) or employee of the company or a related company; or a position involving a professional or business relationship between himself (or his employer or a company of which he is a director) and the first company or a related company.

The position occupied must be one which may reasonably be expected to give him access to information which, in relation to the securities of either company, is unpublished price sensitive information and which it would be reasonable to expect a person in his position not to disclose except in the proper performance of his functions[20]. Executive and non-executive directors, the company secretary, employees, auditors, solicitors, accountants, bankers, and brokers are all conceivably within this provision[1].

It is not sufficient, however, for an individual simply to be knowingly connected for the prohibition in s 1 to apply. He must also be in possession of a certain type of information, i e unpublished price sensitive information, which he knows is unpublished price sensitive information in relation to those securities[2].

This is the key feature of the Act, the misuse of unpublished price sensitive information, defined by s 10 as information which—

(a)   relates to specific matters relating or of concern (directly or indirectly) to that company, that is to say, is not of a general nature relating or of concern to that company; and

(b)   is not generally known to those persons who are accustomed or would be likely to deal in those securities but which would if it were generally known to them be likely materially to affect the price of those securities[3].

Whether information is unpublished price sensitive information in a particular instance will always be a question of fact for the court to decide. The essence of the definition is the distinction between specific and general information. Some guidance as to what would be specific matters may be obtained from the Model Code for Securities Transactions by Directors of Listed Companies issued by The Stock Exchange[4].

---

19 CSA 1985, s 11(b).
20 The Government has accepted that no practical purpose is served by the requirement that the information be such that it would be reasonable to expect a person not to disclose it except in the proper performance of his functions. It will be omitted from the new legislation, see Con Doc (1989), para 2.16.
 1 The 1978 Companies Bill had contemplated including substantial shareholders as well, see cl 63; also *Justice*, op cit, para 21. This would have been particularly relevant to the position of institutional shareholders who may have access to more information than other shareholders. The EC Directive specifically treats shareholders as insiders and this approach is now endorsed by the Government, see Con Doc (1989), para 2.26.
 2 CSA 1985, s 1(1).
 3 For criticism of this definition, see Sugarman & Ashe (1981) 2 Co Law 13.
 4 The Model Code identifies matters such as changes in capital structure, major realisations of assets, proposed mergers or take-overs, the purchase by the company or the group of which the company is part of its listed securities and decisions to change the general character or nature of the business of the company or the group as price sensitive matters.

The information must not be generally known to those persons who are accustomed or would be likely to deal in those securities. This is a more favourable approach from the point of view of insiders than in other jurisdictions which require disclosure to the general public before information loses its unpublished price sensitive characteristics[5]. Here the category 'accustomed or likely to deal' seems more restrictive than that. It will be a question of fact for the court in each case to determine whether this group of investors has received the information in question.

Whether the information will materially affect the price of the securities will likewise depend on the circumstances of the particular case. Examples of information which would have this quality would include the announcement of takeover bids, oil or mineral finds, a marked increase/decrease in earnings, the departure of an important executive to a rival company and so on. In practice it may be that the requirements will be elided with the court looking to see if the information had a material effect on prices after it was disclosed, and if it did, then it follows that it was specific information relating to that company[6].

The individual must hold the information by virtue of being connected with the company[7]. In other words, it is not enough for him to be connected with the company and to have information which is unpublished price sensitive information, he must hold the information by virtue of his position. It must also be reasonable to expect a person so connected, and in that position by virtue of which he is connected, not to disclose that information except for the proper performance of the functions attaching to that position[8]. An objective test will be applied in determining whether an individual should be required to respect the confidentiality of the information which he possesses. At the same time the section does not prevent him disclosing unpublished price sensitive information where that is necessary in the proper performance of his job as, for example, when a financial director is obliged to disclose matters to the company's bank. Finally, it must be established that he knew the information is unpublished price sensitive information in relation to the securities of the company[9].

Where an individual does meet these criteria he is subject to the following prohibitions:

(i)   He shall not deal on a recognised stock exchange in securities of that company[10]. The prohibition is limited to dealing on a recognised stock exchange[11] and does not extend to private transactions not involving a professional intermediary where the onus is on the parties to protect

---

5 The Government has invited views as to whether 'made public' should be defined and, if so, how, see Con Doc (1989), para 2.16.
6 See *Prentice*, op cit, p 129.
7 CSA 1985, s 1(1)(a).
8 Ibid, s 1(1)(b).
9 Ibid, s 1(1)(c).
10 Ibid, s 1(1).
11 A recognised stock exchange means The Stock Exchange and any other investment exchange which is declared by an order of the Secretary of State to be a recognised stock exchange for the purpose of this Act; s 16 as amended by the Financial Services Act 1986, Sch 16, para 28. See also SIs 1990/47, 1989/2165.

themselves[12]. Dealing is defined as buying or selling or agreeing to buy or sell any securities, whether as principal or agent[13].

(ii)　An individual is also prohibited by s 1(7) from counselling or procuring any person to deal in the securities of his company knowing or having reasonable cause to believe that that person would deal in them on a recognised stock exchange. In practice this provision may be more effective than the straight prohibition on dealing for it covers the indirect methods of disclosure which are most likely to occur[14].

(iii)　An individual is also prohibited by s 1(8) from communicating the information to any other person if he knows or has reasonable cause to believe that that or some other person will make use of the information for the purpose of dealing, or counselling or procuring any other person to deal, on a recognised stock exchange.

(iv)　The prohibitions are significantly extended by s 1(2) from dealing in securities of the company with which an individual is connected to dealing in securities of any other company if he has information which he knows is unpublished price sensitive information in relation to the securities of that other company, and relates to any transaction (actual or contemplated) involving both the first company and that other company, or involving one of them and securities of the other, or to the fact that any such transaction is no longer contemplated.

Similar prohibitions on counselling or procuring and on communicating the information to any other person also apply here[15]. This prohibition in s 1(2) is designed to cover the situation where someone who is an insider of one company (as a result of the definition outlined above) acquires information about other companies as a result of actual or contemplated transactions between his own company and those other companies. A number of the cases which have been brought in respect of insider dealing have concerned breaches of this provision. For example, a merchant banker is consulted by a client company about making a takeover bid for a target company. The banker deals in the shares of the target company ahead of the public announcement of the bid[16]. Such dealing is in breach of s 1(2).

(v)　The basic prohibition on dealing on a recognised stock exchange is extended by s 4 to dealing[17] through or as an off-market dealer, provided the securities in question are advertised securities[18] and in certain circumstances to counselling or procuring dealing outside Great Britain on any stock exchange other than a recognised stock exchange[19].

12　This is in contrast with the 1978 Companies Bill which would have required the insider, in private transactions, to identify himself as such to the other party. The Government has recently repeated that in such cases there is no reason for displacing the general rule of caveat emptor, Con Doc (1989), para 2.8. It is doubtful whether parties can be left to protect themselves in face to face transactions, see *Percival v Wright* [1902] 2 Ch 421; Leigh *The Control of Commercial Fraud* (1982) pp 113–116.

13　CSA 1985, s 13(1). See also s 13(1A) added by the Financial Services Act 1986, s 176.

14　These are, of course, difficulties of proof in such cases.

15　CSA 1985, s 1(7) and (8).

16　See *R v Collier* Financial Times, 2 July 1987; see also *R v Jenkins* Financial Times, 18 July 1987; *R v Hales* Financial Times, 9 December 1989.

17　The standard prohibitions on counselling or procuring someone else to deal and on communicating any information to any other person are also included, see s 4(1)(b) and (c).

18　Defined s 12(c) as listed securities or securities in respect of which information indicating the prices at which such securities have been dealt in has been published in the preceding six months before the offence.

19　See CSA 1985, s 5.

INDIVIDUALS CONTEMPLATING TAKEOVERS

Section 1(5) provides that where an individual is contemplating, or has contemplated, making (whether with or without another person) a takeover offer for a company in a particular capacity, that individual shall not deal on a recognised stock exchange in securities of that company in another capacity[20] if he knows that information that the offer is contemplated, or is no longer contemplated, is unpublished price sensitive information in relation to those securities. This is likely to be a very difficult section to apply, given that it will require evidence of a state of mind, that of contemplating a takeover. The standard prohibitions, outlined above, on counselling or procuring and on communicating information also apply.

PUBLIC SERVANTS

Section 2, as amended by s 173 of the Financial Services Act 1986, applies to any public servant or former public servant having any information which is held by him by virtue of his position or former position, and which it would be reasonable to expect him not to disclose except for the proper performance of the functions attaching to that position, and which he knows is unpublished price sensitive information.

A public servant is defined as:

(a)   a Crown servant, ie any individual who holds office under, or is employed by, the Crown,
(b)   members, officers and servants of various regulatory bodies under the Financial Services Act 1986[1], and
(c)   any person declared by an order for the time being in force to be a public servant for the purposes of this section[2].

The standard prohibitions on dealing, counselling or procuring and on communicating information apply here again[3].

TIPPEES

The position of tippees is governed by s 1(3) and (4) which apply to any individual (the tippee) who has unpublished price sensitive information which he knowingly obtained (directly or indirectly) from an insider.

In that situation the tippee is prohibited from dealing in securities of a company on a recognised stock exchange if he knows that the information is

---

20 See Joffe *The Companies Act 1980*, para 11.12, who notes that since the take-over offer will usually be made by a company and not a director, it is uncertain whether a director dealing on his own behalf contravenes the section.
1 See CSA 1985, s 2(4)(b) and (c).
2 See Insider Dealing (Public Servants) Order 1989, SI 1989 No 2164, which declared various members, officers and employees of the Bank of England, Lloyd's and the Monopolies and Mergers Commission to be public servants for these purposes.
3 Only one prosecution has been commenced to date against a public servant. This concerned a secretary in the mergers division of the Office of Fair Trading who was alleged to have supplied her brother with information on the OFT's recommendations concerning references to the Monopolies and Mergers Commission. Both denied all charges and after a lengthy delay the case collapsed when the evidence to establish the charges could not be produced owing to the OFT claiming public interest immunity in respect of OFT documents, see 'Prosecution abandons ship as its case founders', Financial Times, 24 January, 1990.

unpublished price sensitive information in relation to those securities. Similar prohibitions apply where the tippee obtains information from individuals contemplating takeovers[4] or public servants[5].

The whole question of the meaning of 'obtained' in this context was the subject of some controversy following the decision in *R v Fisher*[6]. Fisher was a businessman who was interested in acquiring a controlling interest in Thomson T-Line in 1985. He approached the company's advisers, Kleinwort Benson, but while he was waiting for their response, the company agreed to a rival offer. An officer at Kleinwort Benson informed Fisher of these developments and he subsequently purchased 6,000 shares in the company which he sold a month later for a £3,000 profit. He was charged with dealing as a tippee, having knowingly obtained unpublished price sensitive information from a person connected with the company. However, he was acquitted, on the direction of Judge Butler to the Crown Court jury, for he had not obtained the information which had instead been given to him without any opportunity for him to prevent it being passed on. Judge Butler accepted defence counsel's argument that obtain meant to obtain or procure as a result of purpose and effort and connoted active conduct. On the facts, it was clear that Fisher took no steps whatsoever, by words or conduct, to procure or acquire the information given to him.

Had this ruling prevailed, a significant loophole would have appeared as all tippees, no doubt, would have insisted that they had passively received rather than actively sought the unpublished price sensitive information. The point of law was therefore appealed to the Court of Appeal and then to the House of Lords and is reported as *A-G's Reference (No 1 of 1988)*[7]. The House of Lords, agreeing with the Court of Appeal, accepted that Parliament must have intended 'obtain' to have a wider rather than a narrower meaning if it were to fulfil the object of the legislation. Accordingly, 'obtain' covers the receipt of information whether procured by purpose and effort or received without any positive action on the recipient's part.

The standard prohibitions on counselling or procuring and on communicating information apply here again.

EXCEPTIONS

There are a number of provisions in the Act which permit conduct which would otherwise amount to insider dealing. Once the prosecution has established the elements of the offence, it is for the defendant to bring himself within one of these exceptions[8].

(i) *Profit/loss*   The most controversial exception[9] is s 3(1)(a) which provides that ss 1 and 2 do not prohibit an individual by reason of his having any information from doing any particular thing otherwise than with a view to the making of a profit or the avoidance of a loss (whether for himself or for

---

4 CSA 1985, s 1(6).
5 Ibid, s 2.
6 (1988) 4 BCC 360.
7 [1989] AC 971, [1989] 2 All ER 1, HL; affd [1989] 1 All ER 321, [1988] 2 WLR 195, CA.
8 *R v Cross* [1991] BCLC 125, CA.
9 The Government has indicated that this exception will be retained in any new legislation, see Con Doc (1989), para 2.31.

some other person) by the use of that information. One possible example of this might be where a director, on resigning from the company, has to exercise certain share options within a particular period or lose them, despite being at that time in possession of unpublished price sensitive information.[10] Many commentators have doubted the wisdom of including this provision[11] and one view of it is that it is just the provision to drive a coach and horses through the legislation[12]. The idea behind its inclusion was that, together with the knowledge requirements, it would provide a sufficient safety net for directors who wish to trade in their companies' shares, for it was not the aim of the legislation totally to prevent them from dealing. But there are a number of difficulties. It would seem always possible for the unscrupulous to identify some pressing debt or compelling circumstances as the reason for their trading. Indeed while an individual's motive may well be other than to make a profit or avoid a loss within s 3(1)(a), he will certainly time his transaction, using the inside information, to achieve this result[13]. There will always be an element of making a profit or avoiding a loss. The problem will again be one of proof and the courts will be asked to determine the individual's motive.

(ii) *Other categories*   Sections 3(1)(b), (c) and (d) go on to exempt certain categories of individuals, eg liquidators, receivers and trustees in bankruptcy, jobbers and market-makers, essentially when they are acting in the ordinary course of business.

(iii) *The completion or carrying out of a transaction*   Section 3(2) provides an exemption for individuals who are in possession of information relating to a particular transaction who deal etc in order to facilitate the completion or carrying out of that transaction. This would cover the situation where shares are being bought in pursuance of a takeover bid and the fact of the bid is itself unpublished price sensitive information at this stage. If it were not for this exemption, individuals of the company making the bid would be prevented from carrying out purchases as part of the bid. This does not, of course, permit them to carry out any dealing on their own behalf[14].

(iv) *Price stabilisation*   Section 6, as substituted by s 175 of the Financial Services Act 1986, permits certain price stabilisation activities which might otherwise be prohibited by the CSA provided that those activities conform with the stabilisation rules made under the Financial Services Act 1986.

INVESTIGATIONS

A major omission from the legislation as originally enacted had been any provision for the investigation of alleged offences. Section 177 of the Financial Services Act 1986, as amended by CA 1989, s 74, now provides that if it

---

10 See *R v Cross* [1991] BCLC 125, CA. Another example is provided by the statute, s 7 of which presumes trustees and personal representatives to have acted other than to make a profit or avoid a loss in certain circumstances. The Government has now concluded that s 7 is unnecessary and it will be deleted from the new legislation, see Con Doc (1989), para 2.33.
11 See *Prentice*, op cit, p 131; Tolley's *Company Law* (1990) I 2017.
12 Sugarman and Ashe (1981) 2 Co Law 13 at 17.
13 *Prentice*, op cit, p 131.
14 See *Gower*, op cit, supp pp 636–638; Rider *Insider Trading* (1983) p 35.

appears to the Secretary of State that there are circumstances suggesting that there may have been a contravention of the 1985 Act, he may appoint one or more competent inspectors to investigate the matter[15]. Draconian penalties exist for failing, without reasonable excuse, to co-operate with any such investigation.

Wide ranging powers including the power to examine on oath[16] have been given to these inspectors. Their most important power is that given by s 177(3) which allows the inspectors where they consider any person is or may be able to give information concerning any contravention, to require that person to:

(a)   produce to them any documents[17] relating to the company in relation to whose securities the contravention is suspected to have occurred or to its securities;
(b)   attend before them; and
(c)   otherwise give them all assistance in connection with the investigation which he is reasonably able to give;

and it shall be the duty of that person to comply with that requirement. Any statement made by a person in compliance with a request under this section can be used in evidence against him[18].

Where any person fails to co-operate with the inspectors, s 178 provides that the inspectors may certify that fact in writing to the court. The court, if it is satisfied that that person did *without reasonable excuse* refuse to co-operate, may:

(a)   punish him in like manner as if he had been guilty of contempt of court; or
(b)   direct that the Secretary of State may exercise his powers under s 178 in respect of him.

The question of whether a refusal was without reasonable excuse was considered by the court in *Re an inquiry under the Company Securities (Insider Dealing) Act 1985*[19]. This was an action brought by inspectors investigating the Department of Trade itself in an attempt to identify an alleged insider working within the Department, the Office of Fair Trading or the Mergers and Monopolies Commission (MMC). The investigation was initiated in the light of the apparent unauthorised communication of information about take-over bids to outsiders. The inspectors believed that the business correspondent of a national newspaper, Jeremy Warner of *The Independent*, had information which would help them identify the individual responsible. He had refused to answer their questions on the grounds that he was unwilling to disclose information which might enable his sources to be identified.

On the matter being certified to the court by the inspectors, Hoffmann J

15 The Secretary of State now has powers under s 177(2A) to limit or extend investigations as he thinks fit.
16 FSA 1986, s 177(4).
17 Legal professional privilege is protected, see s 177(7) and there is limited protection for the banker/customer relationship in s 177(8), as substituted by CA 1989, s 74(4).
18 FSA 1986, s 177(6). See *R v Seelig* (1991) Independent, 3 May, CA. *R v Spens* Independent, 8 February, CA.
19 [1988] 1 All ER 203, HL.

decided[20] that the public interest in the protection of the journalist's sources of information outweighed the value of disclosure under s 177 where disclosure had not been shown to be necessary for the prevention of crime. The journalist did therefore have a reasonable excuse for refusing to answer the questions put to him.

The Court of Appeal disagreed[21]. The critical question was whether disclosure had been shown to be necessary for the prevention of crime. The correct approach was that disclosure would be necessary if such disclosure was likely to provide substantial assistance to the inspectors in the conduct of their enquiries and/or if the individual's refusal to disclose was likely substantially to impede them in that process. In the circumstances the conclusion was inescapable that the disclosure of the journalist's sources was necessary for the prevention of crime.

The case then went to the House of Lords which dismissed the appeal and agreed that the inspectors had satisfied the court that disclosure was necessary for the prevention of crime in the general sense. The court was therefore entitled to punish Warner as if he were in contempt of court, for which the penalty includes imprisonment and/or a fine. In Warner's case, no jail sentence was imposed but he was fined £20,000. Alternatively the court may, under s 178(2)(b), direct that the Secretary of State exercise his powers in respect of that individual. These powers are most effective where the unco-operative individual is an authorised person carrying on an investment business under the Financial Services Act. In that case, the Secretary of State may cancel that individual's authorisation, disqualify him from becoming authorised, restrict his authorisation in a particular way, or prohibit him from entering into certain types of business and may direct that any authorised person who proceeds knowingly to transact business with or on behalf of that person, shall be treated as having contravened the conduct of business rules governing authorised persons. That authorised person would then be subject to the penalties provided by the Financial Services Act for contravention of such rules[22].

CONSEQUENCES OF BREACH

Section 8 provides that contravention of ss 1, 2, 4 or 5 shall be a criminal offence resulting in the event of conviction on indictment in imprisonment for a term not exceeding seven years[1] or a fine[2], or both. In the case of summary conviction, the penalty is imprisonment for a term not exceeding six months or a fine not exceeding £2,000 (the current statutory maximum) or both. Proceedings in England and Wales are to be instituted by, or with the consent of, the Secretary of State or the DPP[3]. Contravention of the Act does not make the transaction void or voidable[4].

---

20 [1987] BCLC 506.
21 [1988] AC 660, CA.
22 See FSA 1986, ss 61 and 62.
 1 As amended by the Criminal Justice Act 1988, s 48.
 2 See Sugarman and Ashe, op cit, at p 19, who suggest that, in the absence of any easy means of recovering the insider's ill-gotten gains, the fine should bear a relationship to the amount of that gain.
 3 CSA 1985, s 8(2) as amended by CA 1989, s 209. This has enabled the Secretary of State to consent to prosecutions in less significant cases being brought by the London Stock Exchange.
 4 Ibid, s 8(3).

It was because of the perceived inadequacies of the common law in this area that statutory intervention was called for yet the provisions enacted are unsatisfactory. To judge by press reports they have had little deterrent effect and with the very high standard of proof required, only the most inept and the most blatant have been caught[5].

It is interesting to consider some of the features emerging from the few prosecutions which have been brought. All have involved individual defendants acting apparently on their own initiative. There have been no cases involving professional insider dealing rings operating through off-shore companies and nominee holdings although The London Stock Exchange seems to have no doubts that such rings are operating[6]. In keeping with this type of case, most have involved small amounts of money and the sentences imposed have been remarkably lenient. In only one case has an insider dealer gone to jail[7] and the largest fine imposed has been £25,000 in the *Collier* case. These criminal penalties can be contrasted with the sanctions which are imposed by the American regulatory authorities who in a number of recent cases have recovered profits in each case well in excess of $1m, in addition to imposing jail sentences[8]. In one of these cases, Ivan Boesky was fined $50m and required to disgorge a further $50m in illegal profits. Obviously UK regulation has some way to go before reaching such heights. Indeed the most serious penalty for many insiders is the fact that they invariably loose their positions with their companies. In Collier's case he was also expelled from membership of The Stock Exchange. The possibility of incurring these types of extra-legal sanctions is likely to be a greater deterrent than any legal action.

The other feature of the cases to date has been the difficulty in securing a conviction in any case where the defendant has pleaded not guilty, so obliging the prosecution to establish the numerous elements of each offence[9].

The major omission from the statutory provisions is, of course, any civil remedy whether for the other party to the transaction or for the company itself. This concentration on criminal sanctions, as opposed to civil remedies, has been criticised[10], but the Government has recently repeated that given the remedies available at common law (eg, for breach of fiduciary duty or breach of confidence), it is unconvinced of the need to modify its position on this matter and make statutory provision for civil redress[11].

5 See *Lord Advocate v Bryce* (1981) 2 Co Law 178; *R v Dickenson* (1982) 3 Co Law 185; *R v Titheridge* (1983) 4 Co Law 117; *R v Kettle and Thorneywork* (1985) 6 Co Law 97; *R v Naerger* (1986) Times, 29 April; *R v Collier* (1987) Financial Times, 2 July; *R v Jenkins* (1987) Financial Times, 18 July; *R v Hales* (1989) Financial Times, 9 December.
6 See Observer (1991) 31 March; Financial Times, 10 April 1986; Guardian, 12 December 1986.
7 *R v Goodman* in the *Financial Times*, 1 May 1991. Mr Goodman, chairman of a company, sold 690,000 shares in the company for a price in excess of £1m on the basis of his knowledge of large losses sustained by the company, a fact not generally known at the time. He was sentenced to 18 months' imprisonment with 9 months suspended.
8 For an interesting account of the US position, see Naylor (1990) 11 Co Law 83.
9 See *R v Fisher* (1988) 4 BCC 360; *R v Fitzwilliams, Financial Times*, 21 November 1989; *R v Briggs, Independent*, 9 November 1989; *R v Cross* [1991] BCLC 125, CA; *R v Holyoak, Morl and Hill, Financial Times*, 28 October 1989; *R v Coren and Greenwood, Financial Times*, 24 January 1990.
10 See Gower *Multinational Approaches—Corporate Insiders* ed L Loss (1976) p 241. For the United States approach, see Branson [1982] JBL 342, 423, 536. Prentice 'Insider Trading' (1975) Current Legal Problems 83 at 100.
11 See Con Doc (1989), para 2.12.

RELIEVING DIRECTORS FROM LIABILITY

One final issue which must be considered is the extent to which directors can protect themselves against liability for breach of their duties. Difficulties arise because of s 310 of CA 1985 which provides that any provision, whether contained in the articles or in any contract with the company or otherwise, for exempting any officer of the company or any person (whether an officer or not) employed by the company as auditor from, or indemnifying him against, any liability which by virtue of any rule of law would otherwise attach to him in respect of any negligence, default, breach of duty or breach of trust of which he may be guilty in relation to the company, shall be void[12].

Much academic debate has taken place as to the impact which s 310 has on provisions such as art 85[13]. The issue has now been addressed by Vinelott J in *Movitex Ltd v Bulfield*[14], considering an article equivalent to art 85. He thought it would be startling, or at the lowest very paradoxical, to find that there was a conflict between s 310 and the articles contained in Table A[15], given they are both legislative provisions. Accordingly, it was necessary to seek a solution which would allow the provisions to co-exist[16]. The solution, in his view, lay in the judgment of Megarry V-C in *Tito v Waddell (No 2)*[17], which identified the self dealing rules, not as part of the duties of trustees but as disabilities affecting trustees and other fiduciaries. Directors are not under a duty not to place themselves in a position of conflict; rather if they do so, then certain consequences flow from that. Provisions in the articles, such as art 85, simply modify or exclude the circumstances in which the conflict— and therefore the consequence—arise, but they do not exempt a director from a duty or from the consequences of a breach of a duty owed to the company[18]. An attempt to modify a duty, eg a director's duty to act in the best interests of the company, would infringe s 310[19].

So, provided the rule can be classified as a disability affecting a director's position rather than a duty owed to the company, a provision such as art 85 will be permissible. The question is which of the obligations of directors are disabilities and which are duties? Clearly the no-conflict rule, itself the subject of *Movitex Ltd v Bulfield*, is a disability. On the other hand, Vinelott J himself seemed to rule out the application of that classification to the *duty*

---

12 Companies had developed the practice of including in their articles widely drafted exemption clauses relieving their officers from liability arising from breaches of their duties save in the case of wilful negligence or default, see *Re Brazilian Rubber Plantations and Estates Ltd* [1911] 1 Ch 425; *Re City Equitable Fire Insurance Co Ltd* [1925] Ch 407, CA. The Greene Committee on Company Law, Cmnd 2657, paras 46–47 then recommended that this practice be prohibited. Section 310 gives effect to that recommendation.
13 See Baker [1975] JBL 181; Birds (1976) 39 MLR 394; Parkinson [1981] JBL 335; Gregory (1982) 98 LQR 413.
14 [1988] BCLC 104, noted Sealy (1987) CLJ 217, Birds (1987) 8 Co Law 31.
15 [1988] BCLC 104 at 117.
16 Ibid.
17 [1977] Ch 106, [1977] 3 All ER 129.
18 [1988] BCLC 104 at 120.
19 Ibid at 121. One view, prior to *Movitex*, was that literally interpreted s 310 only restricted clauses which attempted to relieve directors of the consequences of their breaches of duty, but it did not prevent the inclusion of terms which modified or excluded the duty itself, a possibility expressly rejected by Vinelott J as leading to absurd results, see [1988] BCLC 104 at 117–118, also Birds (1987) 8 Co Law 31.

to exercise care and skill[20], or to the *duty* to act in the best interests of the company[21]. Nor would it appear appropriate to the no-profit obligation[1]. The net effect would appear to be simply to validate those provisions modifying the application of the no-conflict rule.

Section 310(3), as substituted by CA 1989, s 137(1), itself goes on to indicate certain other exceptions to the prohibition in s 310. It provides that the section does not prevent the company:

(a)   from purchasing and maintaining for any officer or auditor insurance against any liability which by virtue of any rule of law would otherwise attach to him in respect of any negligence, default, breach of duty or breach of trust of which he may be guilty in relation to the company; or

(b)   from indemnifying any such officer or auditor against any liability incurred

   (i)   where they have successfully defended any civil/criminal proceedings, or

   (ii)   in connection with a successful application under s 727 (general power to grant relief in case of honest and reasonable conduct)[2].

LIABILITY INSURANCE

Much attention in recent years has focused on the effect of s 310 on directors' and officers' liability insurance which on a strict interpretation of the section might well have been found to be void[3]. On a liberal interpretation, however, policies would be unaffected by the section. The uncertainty has now been resolved by the CA 1989, s 137 which makes clear that s 310 does not prevent a company from purchasing or maintaining for any officer or auditor insurance against any liability which by virtue of any rule of law would otherwise attach to him in respect of any negligence, default, breach of duty or breach of trust of which he may be guilty in relation to the company[4].

RELIEF UNDER S 727

Finally, it should be noted that the court has power under s 727 to relieve a director or auditor from liability in certain circumstances. That section provides that where it appears that an officer or auditor may be liable in

---

20 [1988] BCLC 104 at 117.
21 Ibid at 120. See also Finn *Fiduciary Obligations*, (1977) para 106. See Birds (1987) 8 Co Law 31 who makes the point that it is possible to derogate from the proper purpose doctrine, since that arises from the articles itself and so can be modified by the articles, also Sealy (1987) CLJ 217 at 219.
1 See Sealy (1987) CLJ 217 at 219 who describes the no-profit rule as a complex of rules which would not admit of any ready classification without careful analysis; also Birds (1987) 8 Co Law 31. See generally, Butler & Ribstein [1990] 65 Wash L Rev 1 for a very useful review of the American literature on contracting out of duties, also (1989) 89 Colum L Rev 1395–1774.
2 An indemnity may also be provided in respect of liabilities incurred in connection with any successful application under CA 1985, s 144(3) or (4) (acquisition of shares by innocent nominees).
3 See the Law Society's Standing Committee on Company Law: S 310: Effect on Liability Insurance for Directors (1986) 83 LS Gaz 2340.
4 Where the company does purchase or maintain any such insurance, that fact must be stated in the directors' report, CA 1985, Sch 7, para 5A, inserted by CA 1989, s 137(2). See generally, Turnbull and Edwards (1990) 134 Sol Jo 768.

respect of negligence, default, breach of duty or breach of trust, but that he has acted honestly and reasonably, and that having regard to all the circumstances of the case he ought fairly to be excused, the court may relieve him, either wholly or partly, from his liability on such terms as it thinks fit. Section 310(3) allows the company to indemnify such an officer or auditor in respect of liabilities incurred in connection with any successful application under s 727.

The nature of the jurisdiction under s 727 was considered by Knox J in *Re Produce Marketing Consortium Ltd*[5] where the issue was whether the relief available under s 727 might be available in cases where liability arose in respect of wrongful trading under s 214 of the Insolvency Act 1986. Knox J concluded that relief under s 727 was not available in such cases[6]. He decided that the two provisions were mutually exclusive in that if s 214 imposed liability, it did so as a result of an application of an objective assessment of the conduct of the director in question and a conclusion that he had failed to take every step to minimise loss to creditors. Having reached those conclusions, it was not open to the court then to reassess the director's conduct subjectively as required by s 727 for the purpose of relieving him of liability.

5 [1989] 3 All ER 1, [1989] BCLC 513, noted in detail Bradgate & Howells [1990] JBL 249. See also *Customs and Excise Comrs v Hedon Alpha Ltd* [1981] QB 818, CA. Relief under s 727 was sought (rather optimistically) by Ward in *Guinness plc v Saunders* [1990] 2 AC 663, [1990] 1 All ER 652, HL, discussed above, but the court found, on the facts, that there could be no question of relief under s 727, where he was found to be retaining £5.2m paid to him under a void contract. Relief was also refused in *Dorchester Finance Co Ltd v Stebbing* [1989] BCLC 498, discussed in Ch 25. More recently, see *Re Home Treat Ltd* [1991] BCC 165 where administrators appointed under the Insolvency Act 1986 were able to rely on s 727; also *Re Welfab Engineers Ltd* [1990] BCLC 833.
6 But see *Re DKG Contractors Ltd* [1990] BCC 903 where the court refused relief under s 727 but did not rule out its availability as Knox J did.

CHAPTER 27

Shareholder remedies

There are a number of obstacles in the path of any shareholder who decides to pursue an action against alleged wrongdoers, whether on his own behalf or on behalf of the company[1]. Often the suspect transactions are of a complicated financial nature which the shareholder cannot easily unravel. It may be difficult, therefore, to establish precisely what the transaction involves and who the beneficiaries are. The board, if questioned closely at the general meeting, will usually refuse to disclose any information on the basis that the matter is a confidential one, unsuitable for discussion at a public meeting. The non-wrongdoing directors, far from adopting an active policing role, are often quite content to take a back seat and refuse to question the conduct of the other directors although, as we have seen in Chapter 25, there is increasing pressure on directors to take a more active role in their company's affairs. Removing wrongdoing directors, as we have also seen, is not always a readily available option[2]. In any event, their control of the proxy machinery, and in smaller companies their close identi-fication with the majority shareholders, will normally ensure that the appro-priate resolution cannot be passed. Even if a shareholder does decide to proceed, he must also overcome the judiciary's traditional reluctance to second-guess the business judgment of directors or to interfere in the internal management of a company[3]. Add to this, the enormous amount of time and money[4] which must be spent establishing a case and it is little wonder that few shareholders can be persuaded to proceed[5].

For dissatisfied shareholders, the best option is not litigation but simply to withdraw their investment from the company by selling their shares. If the company is a public company, this is quite easily done. If, on the other hand, the company is a private one, then the shareholders' position is more difficult, as there is no readily available market for such shares and so they

---

1 For an excellent account of the difficulties faced by minority shareholder litigants, see Sealy 'Problems of Standing, Pleading and Proof in Corporate Litigation' in *Company Law in Change* (ed Pettet, 1987) cited in this Chapter as Sealy (1987).
2 Discussed in Chapter 23.
3 As Lord Eldon LC stated in *Carlen v Drury* (1812) 1 Ves & B 154: 'the court could not undertake the management of every brewhouse and playhouse in the kingdom'. See also *Burland v Earle* [1902] AC 83 at 93, PC, per Lord Davey; *Hogg v Cramphorn Ltd* [1967] Ch 254 at 268, [1966] 3 All ER 420 at 428, per Buckley J; Sealy (1985) 6 Co Law 21; Sealy (1987); Tunc (1986) 102 LQR 549.
4 Although the position in relation to costs had been eased by the decision in *Wallersteiner v Moir (No 2)* [1975] QB 373, [1975] 1 All ER 849, CA, but see *Smith v Croft* [1986] 2 All ER 551, [1986] 1 WLR 580, noted Prentice [1987] Conv 167.
5 It had been hoped that the institutional investors would take up the challenge, given the resources available to them, but they are likely to have been deterred by the response of the Court of Appeal to the Prudential's efforts in *Prudential Assurance Co Ltd v Newman Industries Ltd (No 2)* [1982] Ch 204, [1982] 1 All ER 354, CA.

may find it difficult to obtain a purchaser[6], although the position has been eased to some extent by the statutory provisions which now permit companies to purchase their own shares[7].

There are three types of action which a shareholder who decides to proceed may bring. First, he may bring a personal action, where some personal individual right has been infringed. It must be remembered, however, that only limited personal rights are recognised by the courts. Secondly, where the same personal right of a number of shareholders has been infringed, then a representative action may be brought on behalf of the group. The third form of action is the derivative action brought by a member of the company where the wrongdoers are in control and prevent the company itself from suing[8]. This is permitted only in exceptional circumstances for the general rule is that the proper plaintiff in an action brought in respect of a wrong done to the company is the company. This is the rule in *Foss v Harbottle* which is discussed below. Where a derivative action is brought the entire benefit of the proceedings will go to the company and not to the shareholder who brings the action.

Statutory alternatives open to an aggrieved shareholder include petitioning under CA 1985, s 459, as amended by CA 1989, where the affairs of the company are being or have been conducted in a manner unfairly prejudicial to the interests of its members generally or of some part of its members, or petitioning under s 122(1)(g) of the Insolvency Act 1986 to have the company wound up on the just and equitable ground, both of which are discussed in greater detail later. First, it is necessary to consider the rule in *Foss v Harbottle*.

THE RULE IN *FOSS V HARBOTTLE*

There are two elements to the rule, the classic statement of which is to be found in the judgment of Jenkins LJ in *Edwards v Halliwell*[9];

First, the proper plaintiff in an action in respect of a wrong alleged to be done to a company or association of persons is prima facie the company or association of persons itself. Secondly, where the alleged wrong is a transaction which might be made binding on the company or association and on all its members by a simple majority of the members, no individual member of the company is allowed to maintain an action in respect of that matter for the simple reason that, if a mere majority of the members of the company or association is in favour of what has been done, then *cadet quaestio*[10].

---

6 In any event there may well be restrictions in the company's articles on a member's right to transfer his shares, discussed ante, Chapter 18.
7 CA 1985, s 162 ff, for while the majority do not need the minority's shares, they may feel it worthwhile to have the company purchase them in order to eliminate a troublesome shareholder from their midst. For a discussion of the American response to the 'market' problem in smaller companies and their use of appraisal statutes, see O'Neal *Oppression of Minority Shareholders* (1975) and cumulative supplement; Hetherington and Dooley (1977) 63 Va L Rev 1. Minority shareholders here may secure the same result through CA 1985, s 459, discussed in detail below.
8 The court will also have to be satisfied that the plaintiff is a proper person to bring the action, that his conduct has not been so tainted as to bar equitable relief and that there has not been an unacceptable delay in bringing the action: *Towers v African Tug Co* [1904] 1 Ch 558, CA; *Nurcombe v Nurcombe* [1985] 1 All ER 65, [1985] 1 WLR 370, CA.
9 [1950] 2 All ER 1064, CA.
10 [1950] 2 All ER 1064 at 1066, CA. See also *Burland v Earle* [1902] AC 83 at 93, PC, per Lord Davey.

The rule, therefore, is basically quite simple. If a wrong is done to a company, it is the company alone which can decide to sue and that decision shall be made by the majority.

The first proposition is clearly based on the separate legal personality of the company and derives from *Foss v Harbottle*[11] itself where the court refused to permit two shareholders to bring an action on behalf of the company against the directors and promoters who had sold property to the company at an inflated value. The court found that it was not open to individual members to assume to themselves the right of suing in the name of the company. The company was the proper person to sue and while that was a rule that could be departed from, it should not be, save for very urgent reasons.

The second proposition, on the other hand, is based on the principle of majority rule and derives from the decision in *Mozley v Alston*[12] where two shareholders tried unsuccessfully to restrain four directors of the company from acting as such when they should have retired in rotation under the articles. The court refused to permit the shareholders to bring their action on the basis that if the alleged wrong is a transaction which might be made binding on the company and all its members by a simple majority then no action will lie. After all:

. . . if the thing complained of is a thing which in substance the majority of the company are entitled to do . . . there can be no use in having litigation about it, the ultimate end of which is only that a meeting has to be called, and then ultimately the majority gets its wishes[13].

There are a number of advantages to the rule. First, it is more convenient that the company should sue, instead of having any number of suits started and subsequently discontinued by individual shareholders. It eliminates wasteful litigation where the only outcome can be that the majority pass a resolution at the next meeting approving the 'wrongdoing'. It also eliminates vexatious actions started by troublesome minority shareholders trying to harass the company[14].

But there is a major drawback. The company is the proper person to sue but a company can only act through its human agents, usually the board of directors (as we saw in Chapter 24), and the directors may well be the actual wrongdoers. They may therefore decide not to sue, a decision which may be challenged in various ways by an independent general meeting[15] but is more likely to be approved by the company in general meeting where the wrong-doers probably control a majority of the votes. The net outcome would be that the wrongdoers would go unpunished and the minority shareholders would be at the mercy of the majority who could loot the company with impunity[16]. This could not be tolerated and so exceptions have been developed whereby, notwithstanding the rule, a minority shareholder might sue. This is done in order to give a remedy for a wrong which would otherwise escape redress[17].

11 (1843) 2 Hare 461.
12 (1847) 1 Ph 790.
13 *MacDougall v Gardiner* (1875) 1 Ch D 13 at 25, CA, per Mellish LJ.
14 Note counsel's statement in *Prudential Assurance Co Ltd v Newman Industries Ltd (No 2)* [1982] Ch 204 at 211, [1982] 1 All ER 354 at 358, CA, that 'it is the concern of the board that the company shall not be killed by kindness', when objecting to a petition by shareholders brought against the wishes of the board.
15 See the discussion in Ch 24 on the division of power between the board and the general meeting.
16 *Wallersteiner v Moir (No 2)* [1975] QB 373 at 395, [1975] 1 All ER 849 at 862, CA.
17 *Burland v Earle* [1902] AC 83 at 93–94, PC, per Lord Davey; *Smith v Croft (No 2)* [1988] Ch 114, [1987] 3 All ER 909.

There are four exceptions[18] (although some are not so much exceptions as merely instances were the rule does not apply):

   (i)   where the transaction is ultra vires or illegal;
  (ii)   where the transaction requires the sanction of a special majority;
 (iii)   where the transaction infringes the personal rights of the share-
          holders; and
 (iv)   where the transaction amounts to a fraud on the minority.

Before considering these exceptions, it has to be said that this is an area of company law where obscurity and inconsistency are the order of the day[19], a position further exacerbated by the latest judicial pronouncements on the rule in *Smith v Croft (No 2)*[20] which, despite a very lengthy judgment, failed to provide clarification and further confused an already blurred picture. The inconsistencies are reflected in the four categories with a degree of overlap, for example, between special majorities and personal rights, while ultra vires and illegality overlaps with personal rights and the fraud on the minority category. They should be regarded therefore as useful starting points rather than definitive statements of exclusive categories. Judicial unwillingness to find a way out of this quagmire surrounding the rule means that we must await parliamentary intervention but unfortunately the opportunity for reform was not taken in the 1989 Act[21].

Having said that, the starting point is that to establish standing to sue a plaintiff shareholder must show a prima facie case that the company is entitled to the relief claimed and that the action falls within the boundaries of one of the exceptions to the rule in *Foss v Harbottle*[1].

---

18 It had been thought that there was a fifth exception to the rule, an all-embracing one which permitted a shareholder to bring an action where the justice of the case so required. The existence of such an exception was accepted by Vinelott J in *Prudential Assurance Co Ltd v Newman Industries Ltd (No 2)* [1980] 2 All ER 841 at 877 which prompted *Gower*, op cit, p 645 to add it as an exception, noting that there was a respectable body of authority supporting it but it was subsequently rejected as an impractical test by the Court of Appeal [1982] Ch 204 at 221, [1982] 1 All ER 354 at 366. See also *Estmanco Ltd v Greater London Council* [1982] 1 All ER 437 at 444, [1982] 1 WLR 2 at 11.
19 Much has been written in an attempt to resolve many of the inconsistencies but the classic exposition of the rule remains that of Wedderburn (1957) CLJ 194, (1958) CLJ 93. See also Partridge (1987) CLJ 122; Sealy (1987); Sullivan (1985) CLJ 236.
20 [1988] Ch 114, [1987] 3 All ER 909.
21 See Sealy (1989) 10 Co Law 52 for an interesting account of the ways in which the Australian courts have minimised the effects of the rule in that jurisdiction.
 1 *Prudential Assurance Co Ltd v Newman Industries Ltd (No 2)* [1982] Ch 204 at 221, [1982] 1 All ER 354 at 366; *Smith v Croft (No 2)* [1988] Ch 114 at 145, [1987] 3 All ER 909 at 922. This is equally the case under CA 1985, s 309, which imposes a duty on directors to have regard in the performance of their functions to the interests of the company's employees as well as the interests of its members. As s 309(2) provides that the duty imposed by the section is owed by the directors to the company and the company alone, a failure to have regard to the employees' interests will be a wrong done to the company and in respect of which the company should sue. If the company declines to proceed against the directors, an employee who was a shareholder would have to bring a derivative action in respect of that breach only if one of the exceptions to the rule could be shown to be applicable. It is not clear that any of the existing exceptions would be appropriate. Problems of proof in this area are almost insurmountable anyway. Employees who are not shareholders have no means of enforcing the provision.

1 Illegality and ultra vires

The position on illegal and ultra vires transactions has been the subject of recent judicial and legislative attention. Actions to restrain threatened ultra vires or illegal actions are outside the rule in *Foss v Harbottle* and matters for personal action[2] for, as Knox J explained in *Smith v Croft (No 2)*, the matter is by definition not a mere question of internal management, nor is the transaction capable of ratification by or on behalf of the company[3]. So an individual shareholder would be able to obtain an injunction to restrain the company proceeding, subject now to the statutory qualification in CA 1985, s 35(2), as inserted by CA 1989, s 108, that no such proceedings shall lie in respect of an ultra vires act to be done in fulfilment of a legal obligation arising from a previous act of the company. The position as regards illegal transactions is unaffected.

It had been thought that an action by a shareholder to recover money or property on behalf of the company in respect of an ultra vires or illegal transaction could equally be a personal action[4]. However, in *Smith v Croft (No 2)* Knox J decided that, in such circumstances, where what is sought is compensation for the company for the loss caused by the ultra vires transaction, the wrong is done to the company and the company is the proper plaintiff[5]. Any action by a shareholder therefore must be a derivative one. This too, as far as ultra vires transactions are concerned, is subject to the amendments made by the CA 1989 which provides that the shareholders may by special resolution specifically relieve the directors from personal liability arising from an ultra vires transaction[6]. In such a case a derivative action clearly would no longer lie. Even where no such special resolution is passed, as we shall see, the decision in *Smith v Croft (No 2)*[7] may prevent a derivative action proceeding where independent shareholders decide that it is not in the best interests of the company. This point is discussed further below.

2 Special majorities

The rule does not apply where the matter is one which could validly be done or sanctioned not by a simple majority of the members but by some special majority. This exception covers the situation where the articles specify a particular procedure which must be followed in respect of a particular transaction. If that procedure is not followed, the majority cannot ratify such conduct for that would be to deny the minority the protection afforded

---

2 See *Simpson v Westminster Palace Hotel Co* (1860) 8 HL Cas 712; *North-West Transportation Co Ltd v Beatty* (1887) 12 App Cas 589, PC; *Parke v Daily News* [1962] Ch 927, [1962] 2 All ER 929.

3 [1988] Ch 114 at 167, [1987] 3 All ER 909 at 943.

4 Wedderburn in his influential article (1957) CLJ 194 at 206 notes that: 'In claims relating to ultra vires acts, however, the plaintiff appears to have, in most cases, a free choice as to the form in which he sues and many actions have been personal.'

5 [1988] Ch 114 at 170, [1987] 3 All ER 909 at 945. Whilst novel, Prentice (1988) 104 LQR 341 at 342 notes that as a matter of principle this approach has much to commend it.

6 CA 1985, s 35(3) as inserted by CA 1989, s 108. Note that the company can also ratify the ultra vires act itself by a special resolution. In either case there is nothing preventing the directors as shareholders voting in favour of the resolution: *North-West Transportation Co Ltd v Beatty* (1887) 12 App Cas 589, PC, provided they do not attempt to ratify something which is fraudulent or illegal.

7 [1988] Ch 114, [1987] 3 All ER 909.

by the initial provision. The only option open to the majority in such a case is to follow the procedure laid down in the articles, or to alter the articles[8]. Where they simply purport to ratify the transaction by an ordinary resolution, the minority shareholder can bring an action to restrain them, as in *Edwards v Halliwell*[9] where two members of a trade union successfully restrained an attempt by the delegate meeting to increase the members' contribution without obtaining the two-thirds majority required under their rules. Likewise in *Quin and Axtens Ltd v Salmon*[10] where the articles of association provided that certain transactions could not be entered into without the consent of both managing directors. In this instance one of the directors dissented but the company in general meeting nevertheless tried to authorise the transaction without that director's consent. It was held that they could not do so. It was an attempt to alter the terms of the contract between the parties by an ordinary rather than a special resolution[11].

3 Personal rights

Obviously if a member can point to the infringement of some personal right[12] then he need not be concerned with *Foss v Harbottle* at all. Here the wrong will be done to him and not to the company and the rule will simply not apply.

The crucial issue is to decide what are the membership rights which will give rise to a personal action if infringed? Membership rights can arise in a number of ways, from the articles, from statute, or from a separate shareholders' agreement. But it is primarily with rights arising from the articles that we are concerned, for that is the grey area where the conflict between shareholder protection and majority rule is most acute. To determine the extent of the membership rights provided by the articles it is necessary to consider the nature of the contract established between the company and its members under s 14[13]. Does a member have a right to have all the articles observed? The answer seems to be no, notwithstanding Wedderburn's arguments to the contrary[14]. Membership rights are more limited than that

---

8 *Automatic Self-Cleansing Filter Syndicate Co Ltd v Cuninghame* [1906] 2 Ch 34, CA; *Quin & Axtens Ltd v Salmon* [1909] AC 442, HL.
9 [1950] 2 All ER 1064, CA.
10 [1909] AC 442, HL.
11 But note the inconsistency between these cases and *Grant v United Kingdom Switchback Railways Co* (1888) 40 Ch D 135 and *Irvine v Union Bank of Australia* (1877) 2 App Cas 366, PC, where the courts permitted the ratification by the majority in general meeting of conduct in breach of the articles. These cases are supposedly distinguishable on the ground that they involved only minor internal irregularities and were not attempts to alter, for all time, the terms of the contract. Drawing the line between the two categories is not easy.
12 This category overlaps to some extent with the previous one: *Edwards v Halliwell* involving the personal right of a member not to have his contribution increased without a special resolution being passed; *Salmon v Quin & Axtens* involving the personal right of a member to have the procedures followed which are specified in the articles. See Wedderburn (1957) CLJ 194, (1958) CLJ 93; Sealy *Cases and Materials in Company Law* (4th edn, 1989) p 463.
13 See Chapter 11.
14 See Wedderburn, op cit, although support for this approach can be found in *Breckland Group Holdings Ltd v London & Suffolk Properties Ltd* [1989] BCLC 100 at 106, where Harman J issued an order restraining a company from acting in a manner unauthorised by its articles at the request of a shareholder owning 49% of the shares. See Wedderburn (1989) 52 MLR 401. *Gore-Browne on Companies* (44th edn, 1986) and supp, para 4.3, notes that the more limited interpretation of the case is that it recognises the division of power as between the board and the general meeting. It does not radically alter the position on personal rights nor sweeep aside the rule in *Foss v Harbottle*.

but include[15] such rights as the right to have your vote recorded[16]; to have a dividend paid in cash if the articles so specify[17]; to enforce a declared dividend as a legal debt[18], and to have the articles observed if they specify a certain procedure to be followed in a particular instance[19]. On the other hand, a member does not have a right to have a poll taken[20]; nor to have accounts prepared in accordance with the requirements of the Companies Act[1]; nor to have directors retire in accordance with the articles[2]; nor do members have the right not to have the value of their shares reduced by the wrongdoing of the directors where that wrongdoing has caused damage to the company and the shareholders' loss is only consequential to that[3].

Many commentators have argued for a liberalisation of the personal rights category[4] since ultimately that would make the rule in *Foss v Harbottle* redundant. One suggestion has been that all the articles should be regarded as conferring personal rights on the shareholders except for those articles which have already been clearly identified by case law as concerning internal procedures only[5]. Another suggestion has been to regard any breach of a director's fiduciary duty as giving a shareholder a personal cause of action[6]. A recent example of the latter approach is *Re a Company (No 005136 of 1986)*[7] where the aggrieved shareholder alleged that the directors had breached their fiduciary duties by using their powers to allot shares for an improper purpose. Hoffmann J said that in this case the true basis of the action is an alleged infringement of the petitioner's individual rights as a shareholder by an improper and unlawful exercise of the fiduciary powers granted to the board by the articles which constitute a contract between the company and its members. An abuse of those powers is an infringement of a member's contractual rights under the articles and so would found a personal action. While any extension of the personal rights category is to be welcomed[8], this decision sits uneasily with that in *Hogg v Cramphorn Ltd*[9] and in *Bamford v Bamford*[10] where improper allotments were referred to the

15 For a more extensive list, see Wedderburn, op cit, at 210–211.
16 *Pender v Lushington* (1877) 6 Ch D 70.
17 *Wood v Odessa Waterworks Co* (1889) 42 Ch D 636.
18 *Mosely v Koffyfontein Mines Ltd* [1904] 2 Ch 108, CA.
19 *Edwards v Halliwell* [1950] 2 All ER 1064, CA.
20 *MacDougall v Gardiner* (1875) 1 Ch D 13, CA.
 1 *Devlin v Slough Estates Ltd* [1983] BCLC 497.
 2 *Mozley v Alston* (1847) 1 Ph 790.
 3 *Prudential Assurance Co Ltd v Newman Industries Ltd (No 2)* [1982] Ch 204 at 223, [1982] 1 All ER 354 at 367, CA, although such conduct may found a derivative action. To found a personal action, the shareholder's loss must be separate and distinct from that of the company. See Sterling (1987) 50 MLR 468 on *Prudential* and possible personal actions. Note *Heron International Ltd v Lord Grade* [1983] BCLC 244 where the Court of Appeal thought that a loss to the shareholders where they were deprived of an opportunity of realising their shares to greater advantage would found a personal action.
 4 Beck (1974) 52 Can Bar Rev 159 at 171–172; Gower *Principles of Modern Company Law* (4th edn, 1979) pp 318–320.
 5 Wedderburn, op cit, at 214–215, also (1958) CLJ 93.
 6 Beck, op cit, at 171–172.
 7 [1987] BCLC 82. See Note (1987) 8 Co Law 131.
 8 This path had seemed closed after the Court of Appeal in *Prudential Assurance Co Ltd v Newman Industries Ltd (No 2)* [1982] Ch 204 at 223, [1982] 1 All ER 354 at 367, CA, had indicated that it would be alert to any attempt to use the personal action as a means of circumventing the rule in *Foss v Harbottle*.
 9 [1967] Ch 254, [1966] 3 All ER 420.
10 [1970] Ch 212, [1969] 1 All ER 969, CA.

general meeting for ratification, something which is irrelevant if an infringement of personal rights is involved.

4 Fraud on the minority[11]

This is the most important, and indeed the only true, exception to the rule. Here the action is a derivative one brought by a shareholder on behalf of the company in respect of a wrong done to the company. There are two elements which must be satisfied before a member can come within this exception: first, he must establish fraud on the minority and, secondly, he must establish wrongdoer control which prevents the company itself bringing an action in its own name.

(I) FRAUD ON THE MINORITY

Fraud in this context includes not just fraud at common law but also fraud in the wider equitable sense of an abuse or misuse of power[12]. Certain categories of misbehaviour are ratifiable by the majority (and so cannot be the subject of a derivative action) while others are not. The difficulty is deciding into which category the conduct in question falls.

Appropriation of corporate property   It is clearly established that the majority cannot 'appropriate to themselves money, property or advantages which belong to the company or in which the other shareholders are entitled to participate'[13]. Such conduct amounts to a fraud on the minority and cannot be ratified; directors holding a majority of votes will not be permitted to make a present of corporate assets to themselves[14]. This clearly covers misconduct such as that in *Cook v Deeks*[15] where the directors appropriated to themselves a contract which the company was actively pursuing. The Privy Council refused to permit the general meeting to ratify such conduct noting that:

. . . a resolution that the rights of the company should be disregarded in this matter would amount to forfeiting the interests and property of the minority of shareholders in favour of the majority and that by the votes of those who are interested in securing the property for themselves. Such use of voting power has never been sanctioned by the courts[16].

The problem of distinguishing such unratifiable misappropriation of corporate assets from the apparently ratifiable profit making in *Regal (Hastings) Ltd v Gulliver*[17] has already been considered[18].

Another aspect of misappropriation has been the willingness of majority shareholders to compromise litigation commenced by the company on terms advantageous to themselves and usually detrimental to the company and the

---

11 As Wedderburn (1958) CLJ 93 noted, this category should more properly be described as a fraud on the company.
12 *Estmanco (Kilner House) Ltd v Greater London Council* [1982] 1 All ER 437 at 445, [1982] 1 WLR 2 at 12, per Sir R Megarry.
13 *Burland v Earle* [1902] AC 83 at 93, PC, see Lord Davey.
14 *Cook v Deeks* [1916] 1 AC 554 at 564, PC.
15 [1916] 1 AC 554, PC. See also *Atwool v Merryweather* (1867) LR 5 Eq 464n.
16 [1916] 1 AC 554 at 564, PC, per Lord Buckmaster.
17 [1967] 2 AC 134n, [1942] 1 All ER 378, HL.
18 See discussion ante Chapter 26.

minority shareholders. The court refused to permit such conduct in *Menier v Hooper's Telegraph Works*[19]. Similarly in *Estmanco (Kilner House) Ltd v Greater London Council*[20] the court held that the decision of the company to discontinue proceedings for breach of contract against the GLC amounted to a fraud on the minority. The company had been set up to manage flats which the GLC were in the process of selling to their tenants. Until such time as all 60 flats in the block were sold, the voting rights in the company were held by the GLC. When only 12 of the flats had been sold, there was a change of control of the GLC and it stopped selling council properties. This was in breach of an agreement between the council and Estmanco that it would use its best endeavours to sell all 60 flats. All the voting shares being held by the GLC, Estmanco voted to discontinue proceedings against the council. A shareholder, one of the 12 purchasers, sought leave to bring a derivative action on the company's behalf against the council. Granting leave, Megarry V-C concluded[1]:

There can be no doubt about the 12 voteless purchasers being a minority; there can be no doubt about the advantage to the council of having the action discontinued; there can be no doubt about the injury to the applicant and the rest of the minority, both as shareholders and as purchasers, of that discontinuance; and I feel little doubt that the council has used its voting power not in order to promote the best interests of the company but in order to bring advantage to itself and disadvantage to the minority.

Negligence   It seems that mere negligence on the part of the controllers is not sufficient to bring the case within the fraud on the minority exception. In *Pavlides v Jensen*[2] the sale of a corporate assets, a mine, at a gross under-value (for £182,000 when it was allegedly worth £1m) was held to be ratifiable. However, self-serving negligence of the *Daniels v Daniels*[3] kind has been held not to be ratifiable. In this case the directors sold an asset at a gross undervalue to one of themselves. The court found that such use by directors of their powers, intentionally or unintentionally, fraudulently or negligently, in a manner which benefits themselves at the expense of the company was within the fraud on the minority exception and so a minority shareholder could bring an action against them on behalf of the company. This decision was regarded by some as signalling the demise of the rule in *Foss v Harbottle*, on the basis that following it very few types of misconduct remained ratifiable[4]. In fact the decision simply reflects a traditional category of non-ratifiable conduct, ie the misappropriation of corporate assets[5].

Abuse of power   Another difficult area is where directors act other than

---

19 (1874) 9 Ch App 350.
20 [1982] 1 All ER 437, [1982] 1 WLR 2. While the decision is based on self-serving conduct of the *Daniels v Daniels* [1978] Ch 406 type, this case can more easily be regarded as an 'appropriation of corporate money, property or advantage' case, similar to *Menier v Hooper's Telegraph Works* (1874) 9 Ch App 350.
1 [1982] 1 All ER 437 at 447, [1982] 1 WLR 2 at 15.
2 [1956] Ch 565, [1956] 2 All ER 518.
3 [1978] Ch 406, [1978] 2 All ER 89. See also *Aveling Barford Ltd v Perion Ltd* [1989] BCLC 626, sale of property to the controlling shareholder at gross undervalue amounted to an unauthorised return of capital which was ultra vires and could not be ratified.
4 See Prentice [1979] Conv 47 at 51.
5 See Boyle (1980) 1 Co Law 3 at 6; Wedderburn (1978) 41 MLR 569.

bona fide in the interests of the company as a whole or for a collateral purpose. Certainly a mala fide exercise of their powers is not ratifiable[6], although a bona fide exercise of their powers for a collateral purpose apparently is, as we saw in *Hogg v Cramphorn Ltd*[7] and *Bamford v Bamford*[8]. Support for the view that an improper allotment cannot be the subject of a derivative action can be found in *Re a Company (No 005136 of 1986)*[9] where Hoffmann J regarded such an abuse of power as an infringement of a member's contractual rights under the articles. In such a case a personal action will lie and the question of ratification is irrelevant.

One final point to consider is whether a wrongdoer director can vote, as a shareholder, to ratify his own misconduct where that wrongdoing is ratifiable. The answer seems to be that he can, for:

. . . every shareholder has a perfect right to vote upon any such question, although he may have a personal interest in the subject matter opposed to, or different from, the general or particular interests of the company[10].

Ratification does not mean ratification by an independent majority[11]. Voting, however, to deprive the company of an asset, as in *Menier v Hooper's Telegraph Works*[12] and *Estmanco (Kilner House) Ltd v Greater London Council*[13], is in itself a fraud on the minority. Ratifying your own wrongdoing may also be grounds for a petition under s 459 of the 1985 Act alleging unfairly prejudicial conduct.

(II) WRONGDOER CONTROL

Establishing wrongful conduct of the requisite type is only one element of the case. The second element which must be established before a member can come within the fraud on the minority exception is wrongdoer control which prevents the company bringing an action in its own name[14]. Wrongdoer control will exist if the wrongdoer has a majority of the votes, or the majority has actually approved a fraud on the minority, or the company has otherwise shown that it is not willing to sue[15]. It is necessary therefore to make some attempt to persuade the company to sue, it is not sufficient to simply allege that the wrongdoers are in control.

It is not altogether clear whether the courts will recognise de facto control, or whether absolute numerical control must be established. Vinelott J in

---

6 *Cook v Deeks* [1916] 1 AC 554, PC.
7 [1967] Ch 254, [1966] 3 All ER 420, see ante, Chapter 25.
8 [1970] Ch 212, [1969] 1 All ER 969, CA, see ante, Chapter 25.
9 [1987] BCLC 82.
10 *North-West Transportation Co Ltd and Beatty v Beatty* (1887) 12 App Cas 589 at 593, PC, per Sir R Baggally; *Pender v Lushington* (1877) 6 Ch D 70; *Burland v Earle* [1902] AC 83, PC. However, the company in general meeting cannot effectively ratify something which is illegal or fraudulent.
11 If it did, then the general meeting would be an effective control over the directors and the courts would have a genuine acceptable reason for not interfering with the decisions of the shareholders; see Afterman *Company Directors and Controllers* (1970) p 140.
12 [1874] 9 Ch App 350.
13 [1982] 1 All ER 437, [1982] 1 WLR 2.
14 *Pavlides v Jensen* [1956] Ch 565, [1956] 2 All ER 518; *Birch v Sullivan* [1958] 1 All ER 56, [1957] 1 WLR 1247.
15 *Russell v Wakefield Waterworks Co* (1875) LR 20 Eq 474 at 482, per Jessel MR.

Prudential Assurance Co Ltd v Newman Industries Ltd (No 2)[16] was prepared to allow the minority to proceed even though the two directors whose
conduct was challenged did not hold a majority shareholding and the rest of
the board was apparently independent, on the basis that control existed if
there was no real possibility that the issue would ever be put to the shareholders in a way which would enable them to exercise a proper judgement on
the issue. The exception, in his opinion, applied wherever the defendants
were shown to be able, by any means of manipulation of their position in the
company, to ensure that an action was not brought by the company. The
Court of Appeal, while not accepting this view, did seem to agree that
control embraces a broad spectrum extending from an overall absolute
majority of votes at one end to a majority of votes at the other end, made up
of those likely to be cast by the delinquent himself plus those voting with him
as a result of influence or apathy[17]. This suggests a willingness to look at the
overall position in each case.

Abandoning or compromising a claim

Once a shareholder has established fraud on the minority and wrongdoer
control, this would normally be the end of the issue and he would have
established standing to sue. This would equally be the case in respect of a
derivative action where it was established that there was a prima facie case of
a past ultra vires or illegal transaction (there being no need to establish
wrongdoer control in those instances[18]). However, Knox J in *Smith v Croft
(No 2)*[19] went on to say that it did not follow from establishing standing to
sue in either category that the minority shareholder necessarily had an
individual and indefeasible right to prosecute the action on the company's
behalf. Relying on a recent trade union case, *Taylor v National Union of
Mineworkers (Derbyshire Area)*[20], he found there is a clear distinction
between the impossibility of ratification (which is the case where the fraud
on the minority category is established and was the case on ultra vires before
the 1989 Act) and the possibility of abandoning or compromising or not
pursuing rights of action. He went on:

Ultimately the question which has to be answered in order to determine whether the
rule in *Foss v Harbottle* applies to prevent a minority shareholder seeking relief as
plaintiff for the benefit of the company is: Is the plaintiff being prevented improperly from bringing these proceedings on behalf of the company? If it is an
expression of the corporate will of the company by an appropriate independent
organ that is preventing the plaintiff from prosecuting the action he is not improperly
but properly prevented and so the answer to the question is No. The appropriate
independent organ will vary according to the constitution of the company concerned
and the identity of the defendants . . .
    . . . I remain unconvinced that a just result is achieved by a single minority
shareholder having the right to involve a company in an action for recovery of

16 [1980] 2 All ER 841 at 875.
17 [1982] Ch 204 at 219, [1982] 1 All ER 354 at 364, CA.
18 A point accepted by Knox J in *Smith v Croft (No 2)* [1988] Ch 114 at 169, [1987] 3 All ER 909
    at 945.
19 [1988] Ch 114 at 177, [1987] 3 All ER 909 at 950.
20 [1985] BCLC 237.

compensation for the company if all the other minority shareholders are for disinterested reasons satisfied that the proceedings will be more productive of harm than good[1].

In deciding whether the decision not to sue was an independent decision votes should be disregarded if, but only if, the court is satisfied either that the vote or its equivalent is actually cast with a view to supporting the defendants rather than securing benefit to the company, or that the situation of the person whose vote is considered is such that there is a substantial risk of that happening[2]. The court should assess whether the decision-making process is vitiated by being or being likely to be directed to an improper purpose.

In *Smith v Croft (No 2)* the view of the majority of the shareholders who were independent of the wrongdoers was that, for disinterested reasons[3], they did not wish proceedings to continue. In such a case, Knox J concluded, the plaintiff minority shareholder, despite having locus standi to sue, should not be permitted to proceed.

This decision seems to reflect the enthusiasm of the English courts for keeping minority shareholders out of court and renders it even more unlikely that derivative actions will be brought[4]. Perhaps the outcome is correct in that litigation which may harm the company should not be pursued but there are many more issues opened than resolved by this case. For example, it further blurs the boundaries between categories (i) and (iv); it may result in even longer preliminary hearings as the court tries to decide if a majority of the disinterested shareholders really are independent[5]; and it further diminishes what little effect the threat of litigation has on the standards of behaviour of those in control of a company's assets. Moreover, time, costs, inconvenience, managerial disruption and natural inertia must combine to dictate that, save in the most extreme of cases, the tendency will be for the independent shareholders to decide that litigation is not in the best interests of the company.

Costs

As mentioned earlier, one of the greatest obstacles to shareholder litigation is the enormous costs which it entails. The position was eased somewhat following the decision of the Court of Appeal in *Wallersteiner v Moir (No 2)*[6] to the effect that where a shareholder has, in good faith and on reasonable grounds, sued as plaintiff in a minority shareholder's action, the benefit of which if successful will accrue to the company and only indirectly to the plaintiff as a member of the company and which it would be reasonable for an independent board of directors to bring in the company name, then the court may order the company to pay the plaintiff's costs[7]. The circumstances

1 [1988] Ch 114 at 185, [1987] 3 All ER 909 at 956.
2 [1988] Ch 114 at 186, [1987] 3 All ER 909 at 958.
3 The defendants were essentially the main assets of the company and to sue them might result in their leaving, thus jeopardising the investment of the shareholders.
4 See Sealy (1987) CLJ 398. Wedderburn (1989) 52 MLR 402 at 406 suggests that the Court of Appeal may not support this restrictive approach.
5 See Prentice (1988) 104 LQR 341 at 345.
6 [1975] QB 373, [1975] 1 All ER 849, CA.
7 [1975] 1 QB 373 at 403–404, [1975] 1 All ER 849 at 868–869, per Buckley LJ. A 'Wallersteiner' order is not available where a shareholder is bringing a personal action, *Re a Company (No 005136 of 1986)* [1987] BCLC 82, nor apparently where the company is insolvent, *Watts v Midland Bank plc* [1986] BCLC 15, criticised by Prentice [1987] Conv 167.

in which a 'Wallersteiner' order should be made and the proper procedure to be followed in applying for an order were reviewed by Walton J in *Smith v Croft*[8]. In the circumstances of that case he concluded that no independent board would have authorised action in the light of an independent accountant's report exonerating the directors whose conduct was at issue. The benefit to the company, which was heavily dependent on the personal services of those individuals, in retaining their services was one which an independent board might have concluded outweighed any benefit in pursuing actions against them, even if wholly well founded. Furthermore, the court could take account of the fact that the company's largest independent shareholder was opposed to any action being brought. More restrictively, Walton J also considered that the plaintiff would have to show that he did not have sufficient resources to finance the action and that he genuinely needed an indemnity from the company[9]. This element was not previously a requirement in order to obtain an indemnity and was not adopted in *Jaybird Group Ltd v Greenwood*[10].

Reform

A somewhat halfhearted attempt to outflank the rule can be found in s 461(2)(c) which permits the court, if satisfied that the petitioner has been unfairly prejudiced as required by s 459, to authorise civil proceedings to be brought in the name and on behalf of the company by such person or persons and on such terms as the court may direct. This provision, which seems never to have been used, is discussed in greater detail later. It may be that statutory reform will have to await the adoption of the Fifth EEC Directive on Company Law which permits an action to be brought against defaulting board members on behalf of the company by one or more shareholders holding 10% of the subscribed capital of a public company[11].

WINDING UP ON THE JUST AND EQUITABLE GROUND

Given the difficulties in bringing a derivative action, shareholders may wish to consider, as an alternative, proceeding under s 122(1)(g) of the Insolvency Act 1986 which permits the court to order that a company be wound up where it is just and equitable to do so. Early attempts to restrict this provision by reading it ejusdem generis with preceding paragraphs of the section[12] (which list a number of instances where the court can order that a

---

8 [1986] 2 All ER 551, [1986] 1 WLR 580. Walton J was critical of the liberal granting of such orders. See Prentice [1987] Conv 167.
9 [1986] 2 All ER 551 at 565, [1986] 1 WLR 580 at 597.
10 [1986] BCLC 319 at 327. See also Prentice [1987] Conv 167.
11 See Amended Proposal for a Fifth Directive on the Harmonisation of Company Law in the European Community, A Consultative Document (January 1990). The Consultative Document notes that this will extend considerably the rights that minority shareholders currently have and the UK will argue for it to be available only in limited circumstances, such as the commission of an ultra vires act.
12 See *Re Agriculturist Cattle Insurance Co, ex p Spackman* (1849) 1 Mac & G 170; *Re Anglo-Greek Steam Co* (1866) LR 2 Eq 1; *Re Suburban Hotel Co* (1867) 2 Ch App 737.

company be wound up) have been rejected[13] and the courts now regard it as providing a very wide discretionary jurisdiction[14].

Procedural matters

Section 124 of the Insolvency Act 1986 permits an application to the court for a winding-up order to be made by any contributory[15], defined by s 79 of that Act to mean every person liable to contribute to the assets of a company in the event of its being wound up. Thus, for example, a partly paid-up shareholder who remains liable to contribute the amount unpaid on his shares in the event of the company being wound up is a contributory. The position is not so clear when the petitioner is a fully paid-up member. Obviously he is not liable to contribute anything on a winding up. How then does he establish a right to bring a winding-up petition? The court's answer has been that he must establish a tangible interest[16] in the winding up, a prima facie probability of surplus assets[17] remaining after the creditors have been paid for distribution amongst the shareholders. An exception is made where the ground for seeking a winding-up order is the management's failure to disclose information, for in such a case it is unlikely that the shareholder will be able to determine whether or not there will be surplus assets[18]. The 'tangible interest' requirement means that if the company is insolvent, a member cannot petition for a winding up[19].

Once a member can establish a tangible interest then he can petition for a winding up notwithstanding the fact that his particular shareholding is very small, as in *Bryanston Finance Ltd v de Vries (No 2)*[20] (where the petitioner held a mere 62 shares out of some 7½ million issued shares), provided that

---

13 *Re Yenidje Tobacco Co* [1916] 2 Ch 426, CA; *Loch v John Blackwood Ltd* [1924] AC 783, PC; *Re Newbridge Sanitary Steam Laundry Ltd* [1917] 1 IR 67.
14 For a useful overview of the jurisdiction, see *Re Wondoflex Textiles Pty Ltd* [1951] VLR 458; *Ebrahimi v Westbourne Galleries Ltd* [1973] AC 360, [1972] 2 All ER 492, HL.
15 Various other parties (including the directors and creditors) may also petition for a winding up, see Chapter 39. Here we will deal only with petitioning shareholders. Note that it may be possible for a person who is not registered as a member to nevertheless be a contributory, for example, where shares have been allotted to a person who has not yet been registered as a member, *Re a Company* [1986] BCLC 391.
16 *Re Rica Gold Washing Co* (1879) 11 Ch D 36, CA; *Re Expanded Plugs Ltd* [1966] 1 All ER 877, [1966] 1 WLR 514; *Re Othery Construction Ltd* [1966] 1 All ER 145, [1966] 1 WLR 69; *Re Instrumentation Electrical Services Ltd* [1988] BCLC 550. This judicial requirement seems to fly in the face of the statute since s 125(1) of the Insolvency Act 1986 provides that a court shall not refuse a winding-up order on the ground alone that the company's assets have been mortgaged to an amount equal to or in excess of those assets or that the company has no assets. The Jenkins Committee, Cmnd 1749, para 503(h) recommended that a contributory's petition should not fail merely because if an order were made there should be no assets available for the contributories.
17 But see *Re Chesterfield Catering Co Ltd* [1976] 3 All ER 294 at 299, [1976] 3 WLR 879 at 885 where Oliver J suggested that tangible interest is not limited to surplus assets but could cover potential liabilities of the shareholder. The advantage however must not be a private one unconnected with the petitioner's shareholding. See also *Re Martin Coulter Enterprises Ltd* [1988] BCLC 12.
18 *Re Newman and Howard Ltd* [1962] Ch 257, [1961] 2 All ER 495; *Re Argentum Reductions (UK) Ltd* [1975] 1 All ER 608, [1975] 1 WLR 186; *Re Commercial and Industrial Insulations Ltd* [1986] BCLC 191.
19 *Re Bellador Silk Ltd* [1965] 1 All ER 667; *Re Othery Construction Ltd* [1966] 1 All ER 145, [1966] 1 WLR 69; *Re Chesterfield Catering Co Ltd* [1977] Ch 373, [1976] 3 All ER 294.
20 [1976] Ch 63, [1976] 1 All ER 25, CA.

what the petitioner hopes to recover in a liquidation is likely to be appreciable in relation to the size of his shareholding[1]. If it is de minimis then the court may regard his application as an abuse of process and throw it out of court. The jurisdiction under s 122(1)(g) is an equitable one and the court will require the petitioner to come before it with clean hands. If the breakdown in the conduct of the company's affairs is a result of his own misconduct[2], or the petitioner has acquiesced in the conduct of which he now complains[3], or if he is presenting the petition merely to put pressure on the company[4], then the court will refuse an order. If, on the other hand, the petitioner can establish sufficient grounds for petitioning, the fact that he also has an ulterior, perhaps personal, motive for pursuing the matter does not render those grounds insufficient[5].

A contributory is not entitled to present a petition unless the shares held by him have been so held for at least six months before the commencement of the winding up unless the number of shareholders has fallen beneath two, or he is an original allottee of the shares, or a person to whom the shares have devolved on the death of a former holder[6]. While this provision is designed to prevent individuals from purchasing shares with a view to winding up a company, the six-month period seems inadequate for this purpose.

It was formerly the case that the court could not grant a winding-up order on the just and equitable ground if there was some alternative remedy available to the petitioner, eg an injunction or an action for breach of contract. Section 125 of the Insolvency Act 1986 now provides that, where the petition is presented by members of the company as contributories, the court can order a winding up notwithstanding that there is some alternative remedy available (a common alternative will be to petition for relief under s 459 of the CA 1985) unless the petitioner is acting unreasonably in not pursuing the alternative. In *Re a Company (No 002567 of 1982)*[7] the refusal of the petitioner to accept an offer by the offending parties to purchase his shares at a fair value to be determined by an independent expert was found to be unreasonable and the petition was struck out, a decision followed in a number of other cases[8]. However, some doubt as to that position has now been cast by the Court of Appeal in *Virdi v Abbey Leisure Ltd*[9]. There the court found that the petitioner's refusal to use the mechanism for purchase in the articles was not unreasonable, given that the value of his shares might be discounted under the articles' scheme when the company's assets were held in cash and therefore a discount was inappropriate[10]. Balcombe LJ

1   [1976] Ch 63 at 75, [1976] 1 All ER 25 at 33, CA, per Buckley LJ; *Re Rica Gold Washing Co* (1879) 11 Ch D 36 at 43, CA, per Jessel MR.
2   *Ebrahimi v Westbourne Galleries Ltd* [1973] AC 360 at 387, [1972] 2 All ER 492 at 507, HL, per Lord Cross. His conduct must be causative of the breakdown in confidence between the parties, *Vujnovich v Vujnovich* [1990] BCLC 227, PC.
3   *Re Fildes Bros Ltd* [1970] 1 All ER 923, [1970] 1 WLR 592.
4   *Re a Company* [1983] BCLC 492, noted (1983) 4 Co Law 163.
5   *Bryanston Finance Ltd v De Vries (No 2)* [1976] Ch 63 at 75, [1976] 1 All ER 25 at 33, CA.
6   IA 1986, s 124(2).
7   [1983] 2 All ER 854, [1983] 1 WLR 927.
8   *Re a Company (No 004377 of 1986)* [1987] BCLC 94 at 103; *Re a Company (No 003843 of 1986)* [1987] BCLC 562; *Re a Company (No 003096 of 1987)* (1988) 4 BCC 80; *Re a Company (No 005685 of 1988), ex p Schwarcz (No 2)* [1989] BCLC 427 at 452.
9   [1990] BCLC 342, CA.
10   In so finding, the Court of Appeal overruled Hoffmann J at first instance, reported at [1989] BCLC 619.

further indicated that, given the just and equitable nature of the jurisdiction, it may be equitable to ignore provisions in the articles obliging the petitioner to sell his shares at a price fixed by the company's auditors and to permit the petitioner to proceed to a winding up[11]. In *Re a Company (No 001363 of 1988), ex p S-P*[12], the petitioner's refusal to accept an offer for his shares was not unreasonable when there was a dispute as to the number of shares to which the petitioner was actually entitled. The court also found that the availability of relief, possibly wider relief, under s 459 does not of itself make it plainly unreasonable to seek a winding up order so as to justify striking out the petition.

It should be noted that the right of a contributory to petition for a winding up is one which is conferred on him by statute and it cannot be taken away or restricted by the articles of association.[13]

Grounds for the petition

Various attempts have been made in the past to categorise the grounds on which a petition will be granted but this has been criticised, most notably by Lord Wilberforce in the leading case of *Ebrahimi v Westbourne Galleries Ltd*[14] who took the view that general words must remain general and should not be reduced to the sum of particular instances[15]. Certainly the categories of conduct within the 'just and equitable' ground are not, and should not, be regarded as closed[16]. There are nevertheless certain well recognised headings which can usefully be relied on when attempting to determine the scope of the just and equitable provision, although all must now be considered in the light of *Ebrahimi v Westbourne Galleries Ltd*[17] which is discussed in detail later.

(1)(a) Quasi-partnership One of the most important grounds for winding up was where the court decided that the company in question was really an incorporated or quasi-partnership. Generally the company would have a small number of shareholders, most if not all of whom would participate in the management of the company and who were prevented by restrictions in the articles from freely transferring their shares[18]. Where the company possessed these characteristics, then the court looked to see if grounds existed for winding up such a 'partnership', in particular whether the personal relationship, so important to the continued existence of a partnership, was still intact. The classic example of this category is *Re Yenidje Tobacco Co Ltd*[19]. Here the relationship between the two shareholders (who were also the directors) had

---

11 [1990] BCLC 342 at 350.
12 [1989] BCLC 579.
13 *Re Peveril Gold Mines Ltd* [1898] 1 Ch 122, CA; *Re American Pioneer Leather Co* [1918] 1 Ch 556.
14 [1973] AC 360, [1972] 2 All ER 492, HL.
15 [1973] AC 360 at 374, [1972] 2 All ER 492 at 496, HL.
16 For example, it has been suggested that failure to comply with a (non-binding) direction of the Panel on Takeovers and Mergers may be evidence to support a winding-up petition, see *Re St Piran Ltd* [1981] 3 All ER 270, [1981] 1 WLR 1300.
17 [1973] AC 360, [1972] 2 All ER 492, HL.
18 Although there was no unanimity amongst the judiciary as to these factors, those stated in the text were the ones which were most commonly relied on. See Chesterman (1973) 36 MLR 129 at 132; Prentice (1973) 89 LQR 107 at 109.
19 [1916] 2 Ch 426, CA. See also *Symington v Symington's Quarries Ltd* (1905) 8 F 121; *Re Davis and Collett Ltd* [1935] Ch 693; *Re Wondoflex Textiles Pty Ltd* [1951] VLR 458.

completely broken down. They refused to talk to one another and all communications were through a third party. The court found that the company was in essence a partnership and that there was such a state of animosity between the parties as to preclude all reasonable hope of reconciliation or friendly co-operation[20]. In such circumstances the court would order that it be wound up.

It was sometimes argued that a separate ground for winding up was deadlock but as it mainly arose in the quasi-partnership cases, being a factor which clearly signified the breakdown of the personal relationship between the parties[1], it is convenient to mention it here. It was unlikely to be accepted as a ground for winding up companies which did not fall within the quasi-partnership category, since in those companies the general meeting would be in a position to exercise its residual powers to resolve any deadlock which might arise[2].

(1)(b) Lack of probity   The classic statement of this ground is to be found in *Loch v John Blackwood Ltd*[3]:

It is undoubtedly true that at the foundation of applications for winding up on the 'just and equitable rule' there must lie a justifiable lack of confidence in the conduct and management of the company's affairs. But this lack of confidence must be grounded on conduct of the directors, not in regard to their private life or affairs, but in regard to the company's business. Furthermore the lack of confidence must spring not from dissatisfaction at being outvoted on the business affairs or on what is called the domestic policy of the company. On the other hand, whenever the lack of confidence is rested on a lack of probity in the conduct of the company's affairs, then the former is justified by the latter and it is, under the statute, just and equitable that the company be wound up[4].

Here the directors failed to hold general meetings or submit accounts or recommend a dividend. Instead the majority shareholder treated the business as if it were his own and ran it down with a view to forcing the minority shareholder to sell out at an undervalue. The court ordered that the company be wound up[5].

(1)(c) Loss of substratum   The position here was that if, at the time of the formation of the company, it was or thereafter became impossible, or illegal, to achieve the main objects for which the company was formed, then the company would be wound up[6]. The theory was that a member had subscribed to the company on the basis of it carrying on a particular business and where the company proposed to pursue some other object, then that member had not agreed to his money being used for that purpose, or to being subjected to the risk of loss in that venture, and was entitled to recover

---

20 [1916] 2 Ch 426 at 430, CA, per Cozens Hardy MR.
1 Deadlock, however, was not a required factor; see *Re Davis and Collett Ltd* [1935] Ch 693.
2 See McPherson (1964) 27 MLR 282; *Barron v Potter* [1914] 1 Ch 895; *Foster v Foster* [1916] 1 Ch 532, discussed ante, Chapter 24.
3 [1924] AC 783, PC.
4 [1924] AC 783 at 788, PC, per Lord Shaw.
5 See also *Re Bleriot Manufacturing Air Craft Co Ltd* (1916) 32 TLR 253; *Re Newbridge Sanitary Steam Laundry Ltd* [1917] 1 IR 67; *Thomson v Drysdale* 1925 SC 311.
6 The doctrine originated in *Re Suburban Hotel Co* (1867) 2 Ch App 737. See also *Re Haven Gold Mining Co* (1882) 20 Ch D 151, CA; *Re Red Rock Gold Mining Co Ltd* (1889) 61 LT 785; *Re Baku Consolidated Oilfields Ltd* [1944] 1 All ER 24.

it by having the company wound up. The fact that the company while formed for a particular purpose had sufficient powers to carry on some other business would not prevent the company from being wound up if that particular purpose failed[7]. In *Re German Date Coffee Co*[8] a company formed to produce coffee under a German patent was wound up when it failed to obtain the patent, even though the company was successfully producing coffee under a Swedish patent and even though the majority of the shareholders were in favour of continuing. An entire case law developed around the problems of loss of substratum[9] but it is not necessary to consider it further. Modern drafting techniques ensure that it would be most unusual now for a company to be wound up for loss of substratum, so varied are the objects conferred on it by the memorandum. Also CA 1985, s 3A now enables companies to have as their object the carrying on of business as a general commercial company[10], so reducing further the relevance of winding up on the ground of loss of substratum.

(2) Ebrahimi v Westbourne Galleries Ltd[11]   In 1958 Ebrahimi and N, having originally traded as a partnership selling oriental carpets, decided to form a company to take over the business. They became the only directors and shareholders, each holding 500 shares. Shortly afterwards N's son A joined the business and E and N both transferred 100 shares to him. He also became a director. Eventually the parties fell out[12] and E was removed from the board by N and A, as they were entitled to do by means of an ordinary resolution under what is now s 303 of the 1985 Act, and excluded from the day-to-day management of the company. As all profits of the company were distributed by way of directors' remuneration and not by way of dividend, he was now deprived of any return on his investment[13]. He petitioned for a winding-up order[14] under what is now s 122(1)(g) of the IA 1986 and eventually succeeded in the House of Lords[15].

The House of Lords found that, as a matter of law, N and A had acted completely within their rights, within the provisions of the articles, and the Companies Act in removing Ebrahimi in this way. But the just and equitable

---

7 *Re Baku Consolidated Oilfields Ltd* [1944] 1 All ER 24; *Re Kitson & Co Ltd* [1946] 1 All ER 435, CA; *Re Perfectair Holdings Ltd* [1990] BCLC 423.
8 (1882) 20 Ch D 169, CA. See also *Re Haven Gold Mining Co* (1882) 20 Ch D 151, CA.
9 See McPherson, op cit, pp 288–293; *Galbraith v Merito Shipping Co Ltd* 1947 SC 446; *Re Crown Bank* (1890) 44 Ch D 634; *Re Kitson & Co Ltd* [1946] 1 All ER 435, CA; *Re Tivoli Freeholds Ltd* [1972] VR 445, noted (1973) 89 LQR 338.
10 Inserted by CA 1989, s 110.
11 [1973] AC 360, [1972] 2 All ER 492, HL.
12 Ebrahimi was particularly concerned that N was importing carpets into the country on his own behalf and then selling them at inflated values to the company.
13 N and A subsequently indicated that they were willing to give an undertaking to the court to alter this in the future.
14 Ebrahimi also petitioned unsuccessfully under s 210 of the 1948 Act, the alternative remedy in cases of oppression. He failed because of the restrictive approach adopted by the courts to that provision, in particular, their insistence that the petitioner be oppressed qua member which Ebrahimi was not since his complaint was about being removed as a director: *Re Westbourne Galleries Ltd* [1971] Ch 799, [1971] 1 All ER 561, CA.
15 A winding-up order was granted at first instance by Plowman J [1970] 3 All ER 374, [1970] 1 WLR 1378; revsd [1971] Ch 799, [1971] 1 All ER 561, CA; and reinstated by the House of Lords [1973] AC 360, [1972] 2 All ER 492.

jurisdiction is not limited to proven cases of mala fides and the legal correctness of their conduct did not make it unassailable. In certain instances, the courts would subject the exercise of legal rights to equitable considerations, ie considerations of a personal character arising between one individual and another which might make it unjust or inequitable to insist on strict legal rights or to exercise them in a particular way[16]. Moreover, a petitioning member was not required to show that the conduct complained of affected him in his capacity as a member of the company but was entitled to rely on any circumstance of justice or equity which affected him in his relationship with the company or with the other shareholders[17].

In this instance E and N had together formed the company on the basis that the character of the association[18] would, as a matter of personal relation and good faith, remain the same[19]. N and A were not entitled in all the circumstances therefore to exercise their undoubted legal power to remove E as a director[20] and having done so, the only just and equitable course was to dissolve the association.

This is not to say that every exercise of majority power will now be restrained by the imposition of equitable considerations. In the vast majority of cases compliance with the Companies Act and the articles of association will ensure the validity of the act (in the absence of bad faith or fraud or any other invalidating ground) but there will be some instances where the rights of the members will not be exhaustively defined in the articles[1] and so equitable considerations may come into play. Such considerations will not arise simply because the company is a small private company, for there are thousands of small private companies which are not of the Westbourne Galleries mould and which are run on strictly commercial lines. Lord Wilberforce suggested that one or more of the following factors should be present[2]:

(i)   that it be an assocation formed or continued on the basis of a personal relationship, involving mutual confidence[3];

(ii) that there be an agreement that all or some of the shareholders shall participate in the management of the business[4]; and

---

16 [1973] AC 360 at 379, [1972] 2 All ER 492 at 500.
17 [1973] AC 360 at 375, [1972] 2 All ER 492 at 496.
18 In particular their joint participation in management.
19 [1973] AC 360 at 380, [1972] 2 All ER 492 at 501.
20 Ibid.
1 *Re Cuthbert Cooper & Sons Ltd* [1937] Ch 392 was disapproved of because of the emphasis placed therein on the articles as being exhaustive of the parties' rights.
2 [1973] AC 360 at 379, [1972] 2 All ER 492 at 500. See Prentice (1973) 89 LQR 107 at 114 where he suggests a fourth criterion, which is that profits are distributed by way of directors' remuneration and not as dividends.
3 Ibid. In many instances the company will formerly have traded as a partnership. But the court stressed that these companies are not to be treated as partnerships. They have adopted the corporate form and will be governed by corporate rules. Those rules, however, may reflect the structure which the parties have adopted and may incorporate partnership concepts such as good faith and probity.
4 There may therefore be sleeping members in the company and that will not preclude it from falling within the *Ebrahimi* criteria. It should also be emphasised that the agreement between the parties may be an unwritten one. See *Tay Bok Choon v Tahawsaw Sdn Bhd* [1987] BCLC 472, PC; *Re a Company* [1988] BCLC 282.

(iii)   that there be restrictions on the transfer[5] of the members' interest in the company.

The approach taken by the House of Lords in *Ebrahimi's* case has since been applied on a number of occasions by the lower courts. In *Re Zinotty Properties Ltd*[6] the court found as evidence of breach of the required trust and confidence that: (i) A had not been appointed as a director as he was entitled to expect; (ii) the company had not been dissolved when the project was completed, as had been originally planned; (iii) there had been interest-free loans to a company in which another of the shareholders was interested; (iv) certain other financial matters needed investigating and (v) the company had not held general meetings and the accounts had not been prepared in time. In all the circumstances, the court felt it was just and equitable that the company be wound up[7]. Another interesting case is *Re a Company (No 00370 of 1987), ex p Glossop*[8] where Harman J thought that if it were established that the directors of a company habitually exercised their powers to retain within the company funds which, subject to proper reserves being maintained, could have been distributed by way of dividend, the members, whose proper and legitimate expectations as to dividends had been defeated, might petition for winding up on the just and equitable ground.

More controversially, *Ebrahimi* was relied on in *Re A and BC Chewing Gum Ltd*[9]. Here the minority shareholder[10] was entitled under the articles and by virtue of a separate shareholders' agreement to appoint one director to the board yet the majority refused to give effect to the appointment. Plowman J, relying on *Ebrahimi*, held that the company should be wound up as the majority had repudiated the minority's right to participate in the management of the company, a right which was the underlying basis of their participation in the company.

One interesting application of the *Ebrahimi* principles is to be found in the New Zealand case, *Re North End Motels (Huntly) Ltd*[11]. Here the court, relying on *Ebrahimi*, ordered the company to be wound up where a minority shareholder/director was being constantly outvoted[12] at board meetings and so had little say in the running of the company. The court found that while it was true that a minority shareholder/director accepts and runs the risk of being constantly outvoted, in this case the petitioner had had no outside advice before joining the company and had little business experience. Moreover, were he to sell his shareholding, the majority shareholder was to

---

5   This would mean that if a shareholder does lose faith with the management, he may find it very difficult to sell his shares and withdraw his investment.
6   [1984] 3 All ER 754, [1984] 1 WLR 1249.
7   This case featured elements of most of the 'old' categories, all of which were subsumed within a more general *Ebrahimi* jurisdiction.
8   [1988] 1 WLR 1068, [1988] BCLC 570.
9   [1975] 1 All ER 1017, [1975] 1 WLR 579.
10 The minority shareholder in this case was in fact an American public company; a reason, Womak argued, for not applying *Ebrahimi*: see (1975) CLJ 208. Note also *Pennell v Venida Investments Ltd* (25 July 1974, unreported), Templeman J, discussed at length by Burridge (1981) 44 MLR 40.
11 [1976] 1 NZLR 446.
12 It will be recalled that mere dissatisfaction at being outvoted was not justification for making an order under the old headings (*Loch v John Blackwood* [1924] AC 783, PC) although here the court seemed to find the entire transaction something of an unconscionable bargain; see Shapira (1977) 93 LQR 22.

be the final arbiter of its value. In the circumstances, the court felt that a winding-up order was warranted.

It would seem that most of the old cases, in particular those dealing with quasi-partnership, deadlock and lack of probity, could all now be subsumed within a more general *Ebrahimi* category; as indeed could the loss of substratum cases, on the basis that they involve the destruction of some underlying fundamental commitment upon which the company was based.

One issue which has generated some debate has been whether the decision in *Ebrahimi* has ramifications for majority rule in areas outside of winding-up proceedings. Judicial support for extending its application can be found in two cases in particular: *Pennell v Venida Investments Ltd*[13] and *Clemens v Clemens Bros Ltd*[14]. In *Pennell's* case the court found that the parties had entered into an understanding that the share ratio in a company would remain at 51:49 and that there would be no increase in share capital without the minority's consent. The company, Templeman J found, was a quasi-partnership founded on mutual trust and confidence and any attempt to alter the agreement through an increase in capital and an ensuing rights issue would be restrained by an injunction. Likewise in *Clemens* an attempt to issue additional shares in order to dilute a particular member's holding was set aside using the *Ebrahimi* principle.

Such an extension of the doctrine to cases where the company is a going concern and no winding-up petition has been presented has been criticised[15]. The orthodox position is that taken in *Bentley-Stevens v Jones*[16] where the court accepted that a director removed from his position could not call into play the *Ebrahimi* principles in the absence of a winding-up petition. The decision in *Ebrahimi* did not, the court said, make it illegal for the majority to exercise their undoubted powers to remove a director but simply said that if they did so they may be subject to a winding-up order[17].

Ebrahimi's case clearly strengthened the position of minority shareholders, at least in the winding-up context, and for a few years it established what is now s 122(1)(g) of the Insolvency Act 1986 as the only effective statutory remedy for aggrieved shareholders. Its importance has now diminished with the emergence of s 459 of the Companies Act 1985 as a valuable shareholder remedy, although, as we shall see, the s 459 jurisdiction itself draws on the approach laid down in *Ebrahimi*.

UNFAIRLY PREJUDICIAL CONDUCT

Section 459, originally s 75 of the Companies Act 1980, replaced the highly unsatisfactory s 210 of the Companies Act 1948 which was intended to provide an alternative remedy to winding up in cases of oppression[18]. It in turn has been amended by the Companies Act 1989.

---

13 (25 July 1974, unreported), Templeman J, noted at length by Burridge (1981) 44 MLR 40.
14 [1976] 2 All ER 268. See Rider (1979) CLJ 148.
15 See Burridge (1981) 44 MLR 40 at 55.
16 [1974] 2 All ER 653, [1974] 1 WLR 638; *Re a Company (No 004475 of 1982)* [1983] 2 All ER 36 at 41, [1983] 2 WLR 381 at 390.
17 [1974] 2 All ER 653 at 655, [1974] 1 WLR 638 at 641, per Plowman J.
18 On s 210 generally, see Rajak (1972) 25 MLR 156; Prentice (1972) Current Legal Problems 124; Wedderburn (1966) 29 MLR 321.

Section 459, as amended, provides that:

A member of a company may apply to the court by petition for an order under this Part on the ground that the company's affairs are being or have been conducted in a manner which is unfairly prejudicial to the interests of its members generally or of some part of its members[19] or that any actual or proposed act or omission of the company (including an act or omission on its behalf) is or would be so prejudicial.

After a somewhat hesitant start, considerable use has been made of s 459 which is proving invaluable to minority shareholders who previously received little redress in the courts. A large number of cases, mainly applications to strike out petitions[1], have now come before the courts, and despite not being full hearings of the issues, provide nevertheless significant judicial guidance as to the scope and nature of the provision[2].

The interests of the members

The initial point to note is that the section is concerned with conduct which is unfairly prejudicial to the *interests* of the members as members[3], which broadens the area of enquiry beyond breach of legal rights[4]. The use of the word 'unfairly' in s 459, like the words 'just and equitable' in s 122(1)(g) of the Insolvency Act 1986, enables the court to have regard to wider equitable considerations in the same manner as indicated by the House of Lords in the *Ebrahimi*[5] case[6].

The courts try to identify the interests of the members by looking beyond the legal entity of the company to the individuals within it and having regard to their rights, expectations and obligations inter se[7]. All the circumstances surrounding their relationship and in particular their expectations at and before the time the business was incorporated must be considered[8].

---

19 As amended by CA 1989, Sch 19, para 11. This replaces the previous requirement which was that the conduct had to be unfairly prejudicial to the interests of some part of the members.
1 The nature of the jurisdiction to strike out is explained in *Re a Company (No 00314 of 1989)* [1990] BCC 221 at 222, per Mummery J.
2 This in turn has attracted much academic comment, see Hannigan [1988] LMCLQ 60; Prentice (1988) 8 Ox J L S 55; Boyle 'The Judicial Interpretation of Part XVII of the Companies Act 1985' in *Company Law in Change* (1987, ed Pettet); Crabb (1982) 3 Co Law 3; and a moot case in (1984) 5 Co Law 264, (1985) 6 Co Law 21. For an interesting account of the equivalent provision in Canada, see Cheffins (1988) 10 U of Pa J of Int Bus L 305, and in New Zealand, Shapira 'Statutory Protection of Minority Shareholders' in *Contemporary Issues in Company Law* (ed Farrar, 1987).
3 *Re a Company (No 004475 of 1982)* [1983] Ch 178, [1983] 2 All ER 36; *Re a Company (No 00477 of 1986)* [1986] BCLC 376; *Re a Company (No 008699 of 1985)* [1986] BCLC 382; *Re a Company (No 00314 of 1989)* [1990] BCC 221.
4 *Re a Company (No 00314 of 1989)* [1990] BCC 221; *Re Sam Weller & Sons Ltd* [1990] Ch 682, [1990] BCLC 80; *Re a Company (No 005685 of 1988), ex p Schwarcz (No 2)* [1989] BCLC 427; *Re Blue Arrow plc* [1987] BCLC 585; *Re a Company (No 00477 of 1986)* [1986] BCLC 376. As we have seen, the courts have determined that members have only limited personal rights, hence the need to expand the section to cover the interests of the members.
5 *Ebrahimi v Westbourne Galleries Ltd* [1973] AC 360, [1972] 2 All ER 492, HL.
6 *Re a Company (No 00477 of 1986)* [1986] BCLC 376 at 378, per Hoffmann J; *Re Posgate & Denby (Agencies) Ltd* [1987] BCLC 8.
7 *Ebrahimi v Westbourne Galleries Ltd* [1973] AC 360, [1972] 2 All ER 492, HL; *Re Posgate & Denby (Agencies) Ltd* [1987] BCLC 8.
8 *Re Bird Precision Bellows Ltd* [1984] Ch 419, [1984] 3 All ER 444, Ch D; affd [1986] Ch 658, [1985] 3 All ER 523, CA; *Re Posgate & Denby (Agencies) Ltd* [1987] BCLC 8.

Obviously, the position will vary greatly from the small private companies, commonly called quasi-partnerships, to public companies of considerable size. As a quasi-partnership, the company will usually have been formed or continued on the basis of a personal relationship involving mutual confidence[9]. There may be an agreement or understanding that all or some of the shareholders are to participate in the conduct of the business[10]. Restrictions on the transfer of shares will be the rule rather than the exception[11]. The individuals involved may also have made relatively substantial capital contributions to the company[12]. Shareholders in such companies will be a small close-knit group, actively involved in many instances in the day-to-day operations and financially and personally committed to the company. Here the scope for legitimate expectations beyond their strict legal rights is obviously greatest.

However, as Lord Wilberforce stressed in *Ebrahimi v Westbourne Galleries Ltd*[13], the case for giving effect to equitable considerations must be made in each instance and it is not sufficient simply to assert that the company is small or private, for in many cases the basis of the relationship will be adequately and exhaustively laid down in the articles. If it is so defined by the articles or, for example, by the articles supplemented by a shareholders' agreement, then there is little room for finding further legitimate expectations beyond those outlined in the documents[14].

The interests of shareholders in larger private and public companies, on the other hand, are likely to be quite different from those of shareholders in quasi-partnerships and considerably more restricted. In these larger companies there is usually no underlying personal relationship, employment is rarely an issue and the shareholders are more interested in such matters as dividend yield and capital appreciation than involvement in the day-to-day running of the company. If they become dissatisfied, especially if it is a

---

9 Some of the factors which help identify a quasi-partnership were set out by Lord Wilberforce in *Ebrahimi v Westbourne Galleries Ltd* [1973] AC 360 at 379, [1972] 2 All ER 492 at 500, HL.

10 *Ebrahimi v Westbourne Galleries Ltd* [1973] AC 360 at 379, [1972] 2 All ER 492 at 500, HL. It is not necessary for an individual to participate in the day-to-day running of the company in order to be a quasi-partner. It is sufficient if he is to participate in all major decisions relating to the company's affairs, *Re Bird Precision Bellows Ltd* [1984] Ch 419, [1984] 3 All ER 444 at 453 per Nourse J.

11 *Ebrahimi v Westbourne Galleries Ltd* [1973] AC 360 at 379, [1972] 2 All ER 492 at 500, HL. This feature, together with the lack of an available market for shares in this type of company, is the source of many of the problems in this area, as it means that when differences arise it is difficult for a shareholder to extricate his investment from the company. Even if a purchaser can be found, the restrictions on transfer often prove insurmountable, particularly if the would-be vendor is a minority shareholder. See Hetherington and Dooley 'Illiquidity and Exploitation: A Proposed Statutory Solution to the Remaining Close Corporation Problem' (1977) 63 Va L Rev 1; also Prentice, Note (1983) 3 Ox J LS 417.

12 See *Re Bird Precision Bellows Ltd* [1984] Ch 419, [1984] 3 All ER 444.

13 [1973] AC 360 at 379, [1972] 2 All ER 492 at 500, HL.

14 In *Re a Company (No 005685 of 1988), ex p Schwarcz (No 2)* [1989] BCLC 427 the court refused to accept that there was a quasi-partnership with various expectations when the relationship was governed by massively detailed and professionally drawn agreements and service contracts with very explicit provisions governing the parties' relationship. See also *Re Posgate & Denby (Agencies) Ltd* [1987] BCLC 8.

public company, they can sell their shares and withdraw from the company. Here the members rarely have expectations beyond their strict legal rights as provided by the articles.

That is not to say that s 459 does not apply to larger private companies and public companies for the section is clearly not limited to quasi-partnerships[15]. The point is that it may be harder to establish conduct which is unfairly prejudicial to the interests of the members in such companies. For example, in *Re Blue Arrow plc*[16] the petitioner failed to establish any expectation that the company's articles would not be altered so as to enable her to remain in office. Vinelott J pointed out that as the company was a public listed company, outside investors were entitled to assume that the whole of the company's constitution was contained in its articles and was not subject to other expectations or agreements which were not disclosed[17]. However, s 459 relief was available in *McGuinness v Bremner plc*[18] to force the directors of a public company to call a general meeting at the request of the shareholders as required by CA 1985, s 368. So the section can still be useful, although in different ways, in a public company.

Finally, when considering the parties' interests, it should not be forgotten that in time the parties' relationship may change, so what may commence as a joint venture and quasi-partnership can change into a purely commercial relationship with a consequent alteration in the parties' expectations inter se[19].

Unfairly prejudicial conduct

As to the meaning of unfairly prejudicial conduct, there is no statutory guidance and it is necessary to consider the large number of cases on the provision to identify the type of conduct which in the court's opinion is unfairly prejudicial to the interests of the members generally or of some part of the members.

Certain criteria have now been established. It is clear that the provision covers conduct which falls short of actual illegality[20], which need not be

---

15 *Re a Company (No 00314 of 1989)* [1990] BCC 221 at 227, per Mummery J.
16 [1987] BCLC 585. Other cases involving public companies include *Re Carrington Viyella plc* (1983) 1 BCC 98, 951 where the petitioner was essentially attempting to enforce an agreement between ICI, a shareholder in CV, and the Government and also challenged the validity of certain service agreements. The petition was dismissed as vexatious and unfounded, see Sealy (1983) 4 Co Law 164. Another case was *Re a Company (No 00477 of 1986)* [1986] BCLC 376 where the public company involved had no assets and its shares were worthless. See also Cheffins [1989] LMCLQ 411.
17 For a discussion of the scope of the section in the case of companies other than quasi-partnerships, see Crabb 'Minority Protection and Section 75' (1982) 3 Co Law 3.
18 [1988] BCLC 673.
19 *Re a Company (No 005134 of 1986), ex p Harries* [1989] BCLC 383. See also *Thomas v H W Thomas Ltd* [1984] 1 NZLR 686.
20 *Re a Company (No 008699 of 1985)* [1986] BCLC 382 at 387, per Hoffmann J; *Re a Company (No 00314 of 1989)* [1990] BCC 221; *Re Sam Weller & Sons Ltd* [1990] Ch 682, [1990] BCLC 80; *Re a Company (No 005685 of 1988), ex p Schwarcz (No 2)* [1989] BCLC 427; *Re Blue Arrow plc* [1987] BCLC 585; *Re a Company (No 00477 of 1986)* [1986] BCLC 376.

discriminatory[1] and while it will usually be the case that the conduct complained of will have damaged or seriously jeopardised the value of the petitioner's shareholding, this is not a requirement[2]. Equally, it is not necessary to show that the respondent acted in bad faith or intended to treat the petitioner unfairly or to harm him, a point considered in *Re R A Noble & Sons (Clothing) Ltd*[3]. There the company was a quasi-partnership formed on the basis that the petitioner would provide capital while the respondent would be responsible for the conduct of the company's affairs. The grounds of the petition were wide-ranging but broadly alleged that the petitioner had been excluded from the running of the company. By way of defence it was argued that, while the petitioner might have been excluded, the respondent had not done so deliberately. He had simply got on with running the business as he had always run it.

The court found that the issue was not whether the respondent intended to harm the petitioner but whether a reasonable bystander observing the consequences of the conduct complained of would regard it as having unfairly prejudiced the petitioner's interests[4]. On the facts, such a reasonable bystander might well have thought that the conduct complained of was prejudicial but would not have regarded it as unfair, for the petitioner by his disinterest in the running of the company had partly brought it on himself.

This highlights another issue, namely the conduct of the petitioner. This may be important in a number of instances, notwithstanding the fact that there is no independent requirement that it should be just and equitable to grant relief or that the petitioner should come with clean hands[5]. First, as *Re R A Noble & Sons (Clothing) Ltd* shows, it may mean that the court is not satisfied that the conduct is both prejudicial and unfair[6]. Secondly, even if the conduct complained of is both unfair and prejudicial, the petitioner's conduct may nevertheless affect the relief which the court is prepared to grant under s 461[7]. It may not grant the specific order which the petitioner has sought and may substitute some lesser remedy instead. It may also affect the basis of valuation if a purchase order is obtained.

Moving on from these more general requirements, it is clear from the

1 Originally there was confusion on this issue, see *Re Carrington Viyella plc* [1983] 1 BCC 98,951; *Re a Company (No 00370 of 1987), ex p Glossop* [1988] BCLC 570 at 575; *Re a Company (No 00789 of 1987), ex p Shooter; Re a Company (No 3017 of 1987), ex p Broadhurst* [1990] BCLC 384 which supported the view that discrimination had to be shown. This had the unsatisfactory consequence of making the provision narrower than the winding up remedy as the Glossop case showed and had not been followed by Peter Gibson J in *Re Sam Weller & Sons Ltd* [1990] Ch 682, [1990] BCLC 80. The issue has now been resolved by the rewording of the provision by the Companies Act 1989 to cover conduct which is unfairly prejudicial to the interests of the members generally or of some part of the members, CA 1989, Sch 19, para 11.
2 *Re R A Noble & Sons (Clothing) Ltd* [1983] BCLC 273; *McGuinness v Bremner plc* [1988] BCLC 673.
3 [1983] BCLC 273.
4 Ibid at p 290, relying on *Re Bovey Hotel Ventures Ltd* (31 July 1981, unreported). See also *Re Sam Weller & Sons Ltd* [1990] Ch 682, [1990] BCLC 80; *Re a Company (No 005134 of 1986), ex p Harries* [1989] BCLC 383.
5 *Re London School of Electronics Ltd* [1986] Ch 211, [1985] BCLC 273.
6 [1983] BCLC 273. See also *Re London School of Electronics* [1986] Ch 211, [1985] BCLC 273 where Nourse J thought the conduct by the petitioner was not relevant, for it did not occur until after the events which amounted to unfairly prejudicial conduct by the respondents and so did not contribute to it in any way.
7 *Re London School of Electronics Ltd* [1986] Ch 211, [1985] BCLC 273.

cases that most complaints fall into certain well defined categories, such as exclusion and removal from the board, improper allotments of shares, and self-dealing by the directors.

As to removal and exclusion, it had clearly been the position under s 210 of the 1948 Act that where the petitioner was essentially complaining of removal from the board and exclusion from management he was not entitled to relief since he was not oppressed 'qua member' as required by that section[8]. No such limitation applies to s 459 and in a number of cases relief has been obtained where the petitioner complained of removal from office. The issue has been considered and unfairly prejudicial conduct established in many instances, such as *Re Bird Precision Bellows Ltd*[9]; *Re Cumana Ltd*[10] and *Re London School of Electronics Ltd*[11], all of which involved removal and exclusion as well as other grounds of complaint.

Removal by itself where there are no allegations of any wrongful conduct such as the misappropriation of corporate assets, but as a result of an irretrievable breakdown in relations, does not ipso facto amount to unfairly prejudicial conduct, particularly if the articles anticipate and deal with that situation and provide a method for the petitioner to dispose of his shareholding, usually at a fair price as determined by the company's auditors[12]. In some instances, the petitioner, dissatisfied with that price, has tried to petition alleging unfair prejudice in the hope of securing a purchase order under s 461 at a more favourable price. The courts have held, however, that where there is an irretrievable breakdown and one party must leave, and the articles provide a method of disposing of his shares, and there is no legitimate expectation that the articles would not apply, then he must abide by the articles[13]. He cannot seek to improve his position by using s 459, unless he can show bad faith or impropriety or an arbitrary or artificial valuation[14]. In the absence of such elements, if he is dissatisfied with the valuation then he must challenge the valuation in the ordinary way, for example, by suing the auditors for negligence[15]. This is equally the case where a fair offer is made independently of the articles[16].

As to the dilution of shareholdings, in a small company the proportionate

8 *Elder v Elder & Watson Ltd* 1952 SC 49; *Re Lundie Bros Ltd* [1965] 2 All ER 692; *Re Westbourne Galleries Ltd* [1970] 3 All ER 374.
9 [1984] 3 All ER 444; affd [1985] 3 All ER 523, CA.
10 (1986) 2 BCC 99,453, Ch D, (reported as *Re a Company (No 002162 of 1984)*; on appeal [1986] BCLC 430, CA.
11 [1986] Ch 211, [1985] BCLC 273. See also *Re a Company (No 00477 of 1986)* [1986] BCLC 376.
12 *Re a Company* [1987] 1 WLR 102, [1987] BCLC 94.
13 *Re a Company (No 007623 of 1986)* [1986] BCLC 362; *Re a Company* [1987] BCLC 94; *Re a Company (No 003096 of 1987)* (1988) 4 BCC 80; *Re Castleburn Ltd* [1991] BCLC 89; *Re a Company (No 006834 of 1988), ex p Kremer* [1989] BCLC 365; *Re Boswell & Co (Steels) Ltd* (1989) 5 BCC 145.
14 *Re a Company* [1987] BCLC 94 at 102; *Re Castleburn Ltd* [1991] BCLC 89. An example can be seen in *Re Boswell & Co (Steels) Ltd* (1989) 5 BCC 145 where the auditor was not thought to be sufficiently independent.
15 On challenging such valuations see Ch 18 above. As we saw there, it is very difficult to do, so it is unfortunate that the courts are closing the door on the use of s 459 in such circumstances.
16 *Re a Company (No 005134 of 1986), ex p Harries* [1989] BCLC 383; *Re a Company (No 006834 of 1988), ex p Kremer* [1989] BCLC 365; *Re a Company (No 003096 of 1987)* (1988) 4 BCC 80; *Re a Company (No 003843 of 1986)* [1987] BCLC 562; *Re a Company* [1986] BCLC 362.

shareholding held by each shareholder is often of great importance. That this is so can be gauged from the number of cases which have involved some deliberate dilution of those holdings by a new issue of shares[17]. Section 459 can be applicable in such a situation. The precise point arose in *Re a Company (No 002612 of 1984)*[18] where Harman J granted an injunction to restrain a proposed rights issue. He accepted that there was an arguable case that a rights issue, even though pro rata and appearing fair and even though it will always benefit a company to increase its equity base, might be unfairly prejudicial. This could be the case where, for example, it could be shown that it was known that the petitioner could not take it up and that that knowledge was a factor leading to the making of the offer. Another instance might be where a person was locked in litigation with the controlling shareholders and the issue was nothing more than an attempt to absorb the cash resources which he will need for that litigation. Here the proposal to make a rights issue followed immediately on the presentation by the minority shareholder of a s 459 petition. Had it gone ahead it would have reduced his 33% holding to 0.33% and was clearly unfairly prejudicial[19]. In *Re a Company (No 005134 of 1986), ex p Harries*[20], Peter Gibson J stated that he could not conceive of a more blatant case of unfairly prejudicial conduct to a member than, as in that case, the unilateral and secret exercise by a director of a power of allotment so as to increase his own shareholding from 60% to 96% and to reduce the petitioner's holding from 40% to 4%.

A great number of complaints relate to the overall way in which the company is run and essentially concern self dealing by the majority shareholders and directors. This may occur in a variety of guises but arises particularly through the payment of excessive remuneration to directors, the existence of conflicts of interests and the diversion of corporate assets. Some of these complaints are difficult to remedy at common law because of the obstacles posed by the rule in *Foss v Harbottle*[1] and, in particular, by the ability of majority shareholders to ratify wrongdoing by directors. All would now appear to be actionable under s 459.

The misappropriation of corporate assets, for example (which may in any case be the subject of a derivative action falling within the fraud on the minority exception[2] to the rule in *Foss v Harbottle*), is clearly within the

---

17 *Clemens v Clemens Bros Ltd* [1976] 2 All ER 268; *Pennell v Venida Investments Ltd* (25 July 1974, unreported) noted (1981) 44 MLR 40. See also *Greenhalgh v Arderne Cinemas Ltd* [1946] 1 All ER 512, CA where the dilution came about by the sub-division of an existing class of shares but the effect is the same.

18 This particular step in the long running legal battle between these parties can be found at [1985] BCLC 80. See also *Re a Company* [1986] BCLC 362 at 367, per Hoffmann J.

19 At the hearing of the main issue in this case Vinelott J, reported as *Re a Company (No 002162 of 1984)* (1986) 2 BCC 99,453 with whom the Court of Appeal subsequently agreed, found that in the circumstances the proposed rights issue was clearly unfairly prejudicial to the petitioner's interests as a member. The Court of Appeal hearing is reported as *Re Cumana Ltd* [1986] BCLC 430.

20 [1989] BCLC 383.

1 (1843) 2 Hare 461.

2 *Cook v Deeks* [1916] 1 AC 554, PC; *Menier v Hooper's Telegraph Works* (1874) 9 Ch App 350; *Atwool v Merryweather* (1867) LR 5 Eq 464; *Estmanco (Kilner House) Ltd v Greater London Council* [1982] 1 All ER 437, [1982] 1 WLR 2; *Daniels v Daniels* [1978] Ch 406. The fact that the conduct complained of would entitle the petitioner to bring a derivative action does not preclude the aggrieved shareholder from proceeding under s 459 if he prefers, see *Re a Company (No 005287 of 1985)* [1986] 2 All ER 253, [1986] 1 WLR 281.

section. Such breaches of fiduciary duty have already been found to be unfairly prejudicial conduct in several cases such as *Re Bovey Hotel Ventures Ltd*[3] (diverting money and property into own pocket); *Re Cumana Ltd*[4] (diverting business into a company owned by the respondent) and *Re London School of Electronics Ltd*[5] (diverting students away from the school into another company owned by the respondents).

As to the problem of excessive remuneration, we saw in Chapter 23 that this has been difficult to challenge, because the courts regard the question of quantum to be a matter for internal management. Now s 459 can be used to challenge these payments, as in *Re Cumana Ltd*[6], where the director and majority shareholder in question had awarded himself remuneration of some £265,000 over a 14 month period. Vinelott J found, and the Court of Appeal agreed, that given the circumstances of the company, such an award was clearly excessive and unfairly prejudicial to the petitioner's interests[7].

The section may also be used to ensure that in any conflict of interest the directors are not too ready to subordinate the company's interest to some personal interest of their own. Thus in *Whyte, Petitioner*[8] proposed alterations to the composition of the board were restrained where there was a danger that the newly composed board would move to compromise litigation which the company had commenced. The would-be new majority on the board were representatives of the party who was the defendant in that litigation. Likewise in *Re a Company (No 008699 of 1985)*[9] the court thought an action would lie if it could be shown that the board's conduct in relation to a particular takeover bid had been motivated by a desire to see it fail in order that a bid of their own might succeed.

Non-payment of dividends is another type of conduct which may in an appropriate case amount to unfairly prejudicial conduct. The use of the section in this context had been hindered by the earlier judicial interpretation of the statutory provision as requiring discrimination[10], although Peter Gibson J in *Re Sam Weller & Sons Ltd*[11] had already decided not to follow that interpretation. The issue of discrimination has now been decided by the CA 1989 which changed the wording of the section to cover conduct which is unfairly prejudicial to the interests of the members generally or some part of the members[12]. Peter Gibson J went on in the *Weller* case to accept that it was certainly arguable that the non-payment or payment of very low dividends could be unfairly prejudicial. In that case the same dividend had been paid for 37 years despite the company being profitable and significant reserves having been built up. The majority shareholder and sole director and his sons were all paid remuneration by the company and so were not

---

3 (13 January 1982, unreported), Ch D; on appeal (10 June 1982), CA, Lexis transcript.
4 (1986) 2 BCC 99,453, Ch D reported as *Re a Company (No 002612 of 1984)*; on appeal [1986] BCLC 430, CA.
5 [1986] Ch 211, [1985] BCLC 273.
6 (1986) 2 BCC 99,453, Ch D reported as *Re a Company (No 002162 of 1984)*; on appeal [1986] BCLC 430, CA.
7 Undeterred by the court's finding, the respondent in this case proceeded, a month after the judgment at first instance, to call an extraordinary general meeting to make a further payment of some £74,000 to himself.
8 (1984) 1 BCC 99,044.
9 [1986] BCLC 382.
10 *Re a Company (00370 of 1987), ex p Glossop* [1988] 1 WLR 1068, [1988] BCLC 570.
11 [1990] Ch 682, [1990] BCLC 80.
12 CA 1989, Sch 19, para 11.

concerned with the level of dividend payments which was a matter of concern, however, to the other shareholders for whom it was their only source of income from the company.

Small private companies notoriously fail to comply with the basic formalities such as holding meetings, passing resolutions, electing directors and filing accounts and annual returns with Companies House[13]. Where all the shareholders are in agreement, little harm arises and the company is often run in this fashion for years. If they are not in agreement, the failure to comply with these elements, particularly to hold meetings and to lay the company's accounts before the general meeting and at Companies House, deprives the members of an opportunity to review how the company is proceeding and the conduct of the directors and the state of the company's finances. In *Re a Company (No 00789 of 1987), ex p Shooter; Re a Company (No 3017 of 1987), ex p Broadhurst*[14] the court accepted that such conduct can be unfairly prejudicial[15].

Finally, it is necessary that the relevant conduct (of commission or omission) relates to the affairs of the company of which the petitioners are members[16]. That the matter complained of is in the conduct of the company's affairs is usually easily established, although on one or two occasions petitioners have complained about the actions of individuals, acting in a personal capacity, outside the course of a company's business[17] and so the petitions have been struck out. The section covers acts and omissions, as in the failure to call meetings[18] or pay dividends[19], and the conduct can be proposed as well as actual conduct[20]. The petitioner must be a member to have locus standi[1] and 'member' for these purposes is as defined in s 22 and expanded by s 459(2)[2].

Court orders

Section 461 provides that if the court is satisfied that a petition under s 459 is well founded[3], it may make such order as it thinks fit for giving relief in

13 This is now recognised by the CA 1989 which provides an elective regime for private companies so that they can decide to dispense with many of these requirements. Until they have done so, however, they remain obliged to adhere to the necessary formalities.
14 [1990] BCLC 384.
15 However, this conduct was not, on the then wording of the section, within s 459 because it affected all of the members. That problem no longer arises as noted above.
16 *Re a Company (No 005685 of 1988), ex p Schwarcz (No 2)* [1989] BCLC 427 at 437, per Peter Gibson J.
17 See *Re a Company (No 001761 of 1986)* [1987] BCLC 141; *Re Castleburn Ltd* [1991] BCLC 89.
18 *Re a Company (No 00789 of 1987), ex p Shooter; Re a Company (No 3017 of 1987), ex p Broadhurst* [1990] BCLC 384.
19 *Re Sam Weller & Sons Ltd* [1990] Ch 682, [1990] BCLC 80.
20 *Re Kenyon Swansea Ltd* [1987] BCLC 514; *Whyte, Petitioner* (1984) 1 BCC 99,044.
1 A petition may also be presented by the Secretary of State, s 460. A similar power was granted to the Board of Trade under s 210 of the 1948 Act but never exercised.
2 'Members' also includes persons to whom shares have been transferred or transmitted by law, ie personal representatives and trustees in bankruptcy, s 459(2). See *Re Nuneaton Borough Association Football Club Ltd* [1989] BCLC 454; *Re Quickdome Ltd* [1988] BCLC 370; *Re a Company (No 007828 of 1985)* (1985) 2 BCC 98,951; *Re a Company (No 003160 of 1986)* [1986] BCLC 391 and discussion in Ch 18.
3 The court must be so satisfied even where the parties consent (without any admission of unfairly prejudicial conduct) to an order being made, as in *Re Bird Precision Bellows Ltd* [1984] 3 All ER 444; affd [1985] 3 All ER 523, CA.

respect of the matters complained of. The court rejected the suggestion in *Re a Company (No 00789 of 1987), ex p Shooter; Re a Company (No 3017 of 1987), ex p Broadhurst*[4] that this requires the courts to limit the remedy to mitigating what has gone wrong. Instead the section is extremely flexible and gives the court power to devise an appropriate remedy[5].

Section 461(2) gives some examples (without prejudice to the generality of the court's power) of the type of orders the court might make.

(i) THE COURT MAY MAKE AN ORDER REGULATING THE CONDUCT OF THE COMPANY'S AFFAIRS IN THE FUTURE

A classic example of this type of order is that made in *Re HR Harmer Ltd*[6], one of only two reported cases where relief was obtained under s 210 of the 1948 Act. Here the court required a sweeping reorganisation of the company's management structure. The court ordered that the 80-year-old founder director should be made president of the company without any rights, duties or powers, and that the company should contract for his services as a consultant for life. The court also ordered him not to interfere in any aspect of the management of the company save in accordance with the decisions of the board. Other typical orders under this heading might include the appointment or removal of directors, the reduction of capital, the alteration of the articles[7] and the calling of meetings, as in *McGuinness v Bremner plc*[8] where the company was ordered to convene an extraordinary general meeting on a set date.

(ii) THE COURT MAY REQUIRE THE COMPANY TO REFRAIN FROM DOING OR CONTINUING AN ACT COMPLAINED OF BY THE PETITIONER OR TO DO AN ACT WHICH THE PETITIONER HAS COMPLAINED THAT IT HAS OMITTED TO DO

Under this provision the court could compel the payment of dividends or order the company not to carry into effect a proposed alteration to the articles or it could order the cessation of payment of excessive salaries to directors. In *Whyte, Petitioner*[9] the court issued an injunction to prevent the majority shareholders exercising their power to remove a particular director from the board while in *Re a Company (No 002612 of 1984)*[10] the court prevented a proposed allotment of shares which would have diluted the petitioner's holding in the company.

(iii) THE COURT MAY AUTHORISE CIVIL PROCEEDINGS TO BE BROUGHT IN THE NAME AND ON BEHALF OF THE COMPANY BY SUCH PERSON OR PERSONS AND ON SUCH TERMS AS THE COURT MAY DIRECT

This provision derives from the recommendation of the Jenkins Committee which felt unable to devise a satisfactory general provision extending the

4 [1990] BCLC 384.
5 See *Ferguson v Maclennan Salmon Co Ltd* [1990] BCC 702; *Re a Company (No 005134 of 1986), ex p Harries* [1989] BCLC 383; *Re a Company (No 005287 of 1985)* [1986] 2 All ER 253, [1986] BCLC 68. For a particularly novel order, see *Re Nuneaton Borough Association Football Club Ltd (No 2)* [1991] BCC 44.
6 [1958] 3 All ER 689, [1959] 1 WLR 62, CA.
7 Section 461(3), (4) and (5) deals with the alteration or entrenchment of the articles or memorandum pursuant to a court order.
8 [1988] BCLC 673, CS.
9 (1984) 1 BCC 99,044.
10 [1985] BCLC 80.

fraud on the minority exception to the rule in *Foss v Harbottle* and instead recommended the enactment of the above provision[11]. It is designed to extend the causes of action open to a minority shareholder and, where he cannot bring himself within one of the exceptions to the rule, permits him instead to petition under s 459 for permission to commence proceedings. There is unlikely to be much demand from petitioning shareholders for this particular remedy as it simply authorises further litigation. They, and the courts, are more likely to prefer an appropriate individual remedy, which will usually be an order that the petitioner is bought out.

(iv) THE COURT MAY ORDER THE PURCHASE OF A MEMBER'S SHARES BY OTHER MEMBERS OR BY THE COMPANY ITSELF AND, WHERE THE PURCHASE IS BY THE COMPANY ITSELF, THE REDUCTION OF THE COMPANY'S CAPITAL ACCORDINGLY

Purchase orders are the remedy most commonly, almost invariably, sought under s 459 and they have been considered by the courts on a number of occasions[12]. Usually the petitioner wishes to recover his investment and depart from the company but on occasion the court has decided that the person responsible for the unfairly prejudicial conduct should be the one to depart[13].

The basis of valuation   The starting point, as established by Nourse J in *Re Bird Precision Bellows Ltd*[14], is that the price fixed by the court must be fair and what is fair will depend on the facts in any particular case. There is no rule that the shares have to be bought on a pro rata basis but nor is there a general rule that they have to be bought on a discounted basis. It all depends on the circumstances of the case.

In general, however, one would distinguish between two types of shareholding in small private companies. First, there is the holding acquired in what is essentially a quasi-partnership. In such a case, if the sale is being forced on the holder because of the unfairly prejudicial manner in which the majority have conducted the affairs of the company, then as a general rule the correct course would be to fix the price pro rata according to the value of the shares as a whole and without any discount—this being the only fair method of compensating an unwilling vendor of the equivalent of a partnership share. Secondly, there is the holding acquired from an existing shareholder at a price which is discounted because the shares represent a minority holding. In such circumstances it would normally be the case that they should be similarly valued under any purchase order, particularly if the purchaser has acquired the shares for investment purposes and has played no part in the affairs of the company. In the circumstances of *Re Bird Precision Bellows Ltd* the facts showed a forced sale in a quasi-partnership. Accordingly, the price to be paid was fixed on a pro rata basis without any

11 Cmnd 1749, para 206.
12 For a more detailed discussion of the valuation rules, see Hannigan (1987) Bus L Rev 21.
13 See *Re a Company (No 00789 of 1987), ex p Shooter; Re a Company (No 3017 of 1987), ex p Broadhurst* [1990] BCLC 384. The court found that the unfairly prejudicial manner in which he had conducted the company's affairs showed that he was unfit to control the company.
14 [1984] 3 All ER 444; affd [1985] 3 All ER 523, CA.

discount to reflect the fact that the shares constituted a minority holding. A case where a pro rata basis was not required was *Re a Company (No 005134 of 1986), ex p Harries*[15] where, although there had been unfairly prejudicial conduct, the minority shareholder had decided to sit it out after the relationship changed from being a quasi-partnership to a more distant relationship and so could not expect to be treated as a quasi-partner when he ultimately sought relief.

The date of valuation As the value of the shares may fluctuate throughout the period in question, the choice of date of valuation will be of great importance to the parties. This is a matter for the exercise of the trial judge's discretion[16], paying due regard to the overriding requirement that the valuation be fair on the particular facts[17]. Essentially there are three options open to the court. It may select (i) the date of the petition, or (ii) a date prior to the date of the petition, or (iii) the date of the judgment. In *Re Cumana Ltd*[18] Vinelott J favoured the date of the petition, on the basis that it is the date on which the petitioner elects to treat the unfair conduct of the majority as in effect destroying the basis on which he agreed to become a shareholder and to look to his shares for his proper reward for participation in a joint undertaking. This approach was subsequently endorsed by the Court of Appeal[19]. Notwithstanding that general approach, fairness may on occasion require that the court select an earlier date. This will frequently be the case where the conduct complained of has altered the position within the company, as in *Re OC (Transport) Services Ltd*[1], or where there was evidence that the majority deliberately took steps to depreciate the shares in anticipation of a petition being presented, as in *Re Cumana Ltd*[2]. Nourse J in *Re London School of Electronics Ltd*[3] thought that, prima facie, an interest in a going concern ought to be valued at the date of the order for purchase and that was the date chosen in *Re a Company (No 005134 of 1986), ex p Harries*[4].

Relationship between s 459 and s 122(1)(g) of the Insolvency Act

As mentioned earlier, the width of the jurisdiction conferred by s 459 means that the winding up jurisdiction under s 122(1)(g) of the Insolvency Act 1986 becomes less important. It will not be entirely redundant, however, as *Re R A Noble & Sons (Clothing) Ltd*[5] shows. Here a businessman excluded from the management of what had been a two man company failed to obtain relief under s 459, for the court found that while his exclusion may have been prejudicial it was not unfair because he had effectively brought it on himself.

---

15 [1989] BCLC 383.
16 *Re Cumana Ltd* [1986] BCLC 430 at 436, CA.
17 *Re Bird Precision Bellows Ltd* [1984] 3 All ER 444; affd [1985] 3 All ER 523.
18 (1986) 2 BCC 99,453, reported as *Re a Company (002612 of 1984)*.
19 [1986] BCLC 430, CA.
 1 [1984] BCLC 251.
 2 [1986] BCLC 430.
 3 [1986] Ch 211, [1985] BCLC 273.
 4 [1989] BCLC 383 at 399.
 5 [1983] BCLC 273.

However, a winding up order was granted because the mutual trust and confidence which was the basis of the company had been destroyed[6].

Impact of s 459

It is clear from the foregoing discussion that s 459 has developed into an extremely valuable remedy for the minority shareholder, particularly but not exclusively for those in the quasi-partnership type of company. The range of conduct covered and the flexibility of the relief offered means that it has rapidly become the most attractive solution for those dissatisfied. It can also be a very effective bargaining counter which prevents many of these disputes reaching the courts and forces the parties to negotiate a solution to their difficulties.

Quite apart from the impact on individual shareholders, the section also has an impact on the development of company law generally. First, in terms of shareholder remedies, it provides a method of side-stepping many of the difficulties surrounding the rule in *Foss v Harbottle*[7] and offers more generous relief than winding up on the just and equitable ground. Secondly, it is rapidly providing a code of conduct for those in the quasi-partnership, not in terms of fiduciary duties imposed on directors but in terms of obligations as between majority and minority shareholders, breach of which warrants relief under s 459, a concept accepted elsewhere but new to this jurisdiction. Thirdly, the jurisdiction highlights a divergence in approach between public and private companies and between large and small companies, a process further advanced by the elective regime provided by the CA 1989. All of these developments must bring closer the possibility of a close corporation statute and the abandonment of the idea that one statute can be appropriate to all. The regulation of public companies will increasingly be the subject of EC Directives and will develop separately.

A final point to bear in mind, however, is that the very width and scope of s 459 may in time attract a judicial reaction. Hoffmann J's dictum in *Re a Company (No 007623 of 1984)*[8] that the provision confers a very wide jurisdiction and discretion which has to be carefully controlled in order to prevent it being used as a means of oppression by a dissident shareholder is now being endorsed in other cases[9]. This may result in a more cautious approach in future years, although it has to be said that there is little evidence of that to date, with one significant exception. The exception is in the reluctance of the courts to permit reliance on s 459 in cases where the articles provide an existing remedy. It was noted above that this is the case in instances where the petitioner complains of his removal/expulsion from the company and the articles provide a mechanism whereby he may sell his shares. It may seem perfectly acceptable not to entertain a claim under s 459

---

6 See also *Vujnovich v Vujnovich* [1990] BCLC 227, PC. We have already noted that the mere availability of s 459 does not make it unreasonable for a petitioner to seek a winding up order, see *Re a Company (No 001363 of 1986), ex p S-P* [1989] BCLC 579.

7 (1843) 2 Hare 461.

8 [1986] BCLC 362.

9 See *Re a Company (No 00314 of 1989)* [1990] BCC 221; *Re Castleburn Ltd* [1991] BCLC 89; *Re a Company (No 005685 of 1988), ex p Schwarcz (No 2)* [1989] BCLC 427; *Re a Company (No 007623 of 1984)* [1986] BCLC 362.

where there is an existing remedy in the articles[10], but the difficulty is that the articles rarely provide a satisfactory buy-out scheme as far as the member is concerned. In particular, he is unlikely to be happy with the non-speaking valuation which the auditor provides which is very difficult to challenge. This insistence on recourse to the articles in those instances may also encourage attempts to make the articles all encompassing on other matters so as to prevent applications to the courts under s 459 and diminish the scope of the provision. Indeed, the whole relationship between the articles and the jurisdiction under s 459 has yet to be fully determined.

10 It should be noted that Balcombe LJ in *Virdi v Abbey Leisure Ltd* [1990] BCLC 342 at 350 thought that given the just and equitable nature of the jurisdiction under s 122(1)(g) of the Insolvency Act 1986, it might be equitable in the appropriate case to ignore buy-out provisions in the articles. Given that s 459 is based on similiar concepts, as the cases have shown, that offers hope that the presence of provisions in the articles will not necessarily defeat a deserving petitioner in an appropriate case.

CHAPTER 28

Public regulation by disclosure of information concerning companies

THEMES UNDERLYING DISCLOSURE OF INFORMATION

Disclosure of information by companies is one of those topics in company law where there is a danger of being overwhelmed by the volume of detailed statutory requirements. It is helpful, therefore, in looking at such a topic to keep in mind certain underlying instrumental themes which can impose some order on the mass of detail[1].

Disclosure as a means of influencing behaviour

The first theme is that the assumption behind many disclosure requirements is that behaviour can be influenced merely by requiring it to be disclosed, without the need of negative prohibition or positive regulation. If those who invest in, or manage, companies know that their activities will be subjected to public scrutiny, their behaviour will be modified to avoid public disapproval[2]. So runs the idea, although in several instances provision for ex post facto disclosure has had to be supplemented by requirements for prior approval by the parties affected or even by outright prohibition. Thus, concern over the terms of directors' service contracts seems to have been the motivation behind a provision introduced in 1967 that companies must keep a copy of any written service contract or, if not in writing, a written memorandum of its terms, available for inspection by members of the company[3]. If the members could see how the directors were providing for themselves, they might be more restrained in their generosity. Perhaps directors are not modest about their worth, however, for in 1980, following a lead given some years earlier by The Stock Exchange, a requirement was introduced for prior approval by the general meeting of any director's service contract which the company might not be able to terminate within five years[4]. Likewise, the provisions requiring directors to disclose dealings in securities of their company and for the company to maintain a register of such dealings

---

1 This chapter is mainly concerned with disclosure via a company's annual report and accounts, although other aspects of disclosure are referred to in this introductory section.
2 See, for example, Company Law Reform (Cmnd 5391) para 10 'openness in company affairs is the first principle in securing responsible behaviour' and para 165 'disclosure of information is the best guarantee of fair dealing and the best antidote to mistrust'. For a less enthusiastic view, see Sealy (1981) 2 Co Law 51–56. See also Loss 'Disclosure as Preventive Enforcement' in *Corporate Governance and Directors' Liability* ed Hopt and Teubner (1985) pp 327–335, Stevenson *Corporations and Information—Secrecy, Access and Disclosure* (1980) pp 79–94 and 157–176 and Grover and Baillie *Proposals for a Securities Market Law for Canada vol 13—Disclosure Requirements* pp 378–389.
3 Section 318.
4 Section 319.

represent the earliest legislative attempt to discourage insider dealing[5]. The theory is that if members of the public generally can see that directors sold shares in the company shortly before a large loss was announced, the directors will feel so embarrassed they will desist from the sale. One of the problems, however, in relying on disclosure to affect behaviour is that the individuals concerned may not even know about the disclosure requirement. At any rate insider dealing on The Stock Exchange has since been made subject to specific prohibitions with criminal penalties for breach.

The type of information to be disclosed

The second underlying theme concerns the type of information that is required to be disclosed. Until 1967, it was invariably information that could be regarded as being of interest to investors in the company whether as shareholders or creditors. It was all information about the financial state of the company and the topic was treated in company law textbooks as one of investor protection. In the Companies Act 1967, provisions were first introduced requiring companies to disclose information that was more obviously in the public interest although still of relevance to investors. Since then requirements have been added for disclosure of information of particular interest to employees and arguments have been put forward for disclosure of information that would more fully reflect companies' social responsibilities[6]. Such information might relate to the interests of consumers of a company's products or of those who live in the locality where a company operates. Disclosure requirements can be seen, therefore, as reflecting, more clearly perhaps than anywhere else in company law, recognition of new interests, besides those of investors, in the way companies operate.

Disclosure to whom

Closely related to developments regarding what information must be disclosed are developments regarding who the information must be disclosed to. This represents a third underlying theme. The main legislative requirements are for disclosure to shareholders and registration at the Companies Registry. Although when the Companies Registry was set up in 1844 there was a requirement for an audited balance sheet to be registered and thus disclosed to the public[7] this was repealed in 1856[8] and even the preparation of accounts and the presentation of them to shareholders

---

5 Sections 323–328 and Sch 13. These sections must not be confused with somewhat similar rules (in ss 198–220) which require public companies to be informed about and maintain a register of any dealings in any class of shares by holders of 3% or more of the class concerned. These were designed to stop substantial stakes in public companies being acquired in secret, a practice often known as warehousing.
6 For two excellent articles setting out detailed proposals, see 'The Case for a Social Audit' Social Audit, vol 1, no 1, p 4 and Imberg and Macmahon 'Company Law Reform' Social Audit, vol 1, no 2, p 3. See also Gray, Owen and Maunders *Corporate Social Reporting* (1987).
7 7 & 8 Vict c 110 (1844) s 43.
8 By the Joint Stock Companies Act 1856.

became optional[9]. The present legislative requirements relating to disclosure began in 1900 with an implicit requirement that an audited balance sheet be presented to the company in general meeting[10]. In 1907, the requirement for registration of an audited balance sheet reintroduced the idea of public disclosure of financial information[11].

The requirements have been added to in most if not all subsequent Companies Acts. The purpose of mandatory disclosure to the shareholders is to promote efficient management by requiring the management to account for their stewardship of the company[12]. In this respect disclosure is just one of a number of techniques used by company law to ensure the accountability of management to shareholders. It should be viewed alongside other techniques designed to facilitate the same end such as the regulation of the relationship of the board of directors to the general meeting, the power of appointment and removal of directors[13], and the duty of directors to act in the best interests of the company and to exercise care and skill[14].

Assuming that the shareholders' interest lies in the most productive use of the company's resources, promoting the accountability of management to shareholders will indirectly serve the public interest in the creation of wealth for society. This public interest is in part the justification for disclosure via registration at Companies House. It seems likely though that this has more to do with prevention of fraud and creditor protection in view of the fact that only limited liability companies are obliged to file their accounts with the registrar of companies[15]. In addition to financial information all registered companies are obliged to file information about the company's constitution, the officers of the company, the address of the registered office, the share capital, charges on company property and an annual return.

In the case of listed companies The Stock Exchange also imposes disclosure requirements. Apart from additional obligations in respect of reports to shareholders[16] The Stock Exchange also requires disclosure to the Exchange immediately 'of any information necessary to enable holders of the

---

9 Provisions were included in the model regulations for management of the company contained in the Schedule to the Joint Stock Companies Act 1856. It has been suggested that the justification for apparently giving shareholders less protection may have been the provisions for Board of Trade Inspectors to be appointed at the request of shareholders that the Act also introduced. See Edey and Panitpakdi 'British Company Accounting and the Law: 1844–1900' in *Studies in the History of Accounting* ed Littleton and Yamey (1956) pp 356–379.
10 Companies Act 1900, s 23.
11 Companies Act 1907, s 21.
12 This view is supported by the evidence about the background to the changes in disclosure implemented in the 1948 consolidation. See Bircher (1988) 18 Accounting and Business Research 107.
13 Representation on the board of directors is a further technique and current demands for inclusion of non-executive directors on the boards of public companies and clarification of their role via the establishment of audit committees are a reflection of this. See [1987] Bank of England Quarterly Bulletin 252 and [1988] Bank of England Quarterly Bulletin 242. One way to encourge such practices is via disclosure: Stevenson *Corporations and Information—Secrecy, Assets and Disclosure* (1980) pp 171–176.
14 Takeovers or the threat of takeovers also serve to keep the management responsive to shareholders' interests. See ch 35 below.
15 Unlimited companies are exempted: s 254.
16 Listed companies must prepare interim reports: Admission of Securities to Listing, s 5, ch 2, paras 23 and 24. There are also additional obligations as regards the contents of the annual accounts: ibid, s 5, ch 2, paras 20 and 21.

companies listed securities and the public to appraise the position of the company and to avoid the establishment of a false market in its listed securities'[17]. The purpose of this form of disclosure is to aid the efficiency of the securities market. Whether it does so or not has been a matter of dispute among economists[18]. It is, however, important to appreciate the difference in function between this form of immediate disclosure to the market[19] and other forms of financial disclosure which are more a matter of record and are intended to serve the other purposes outlined in previous paragraphs.

Two other groups whose interest in the activities of companies may be reflected in future legislative requirements for disclosure of information, are employees and government. Already, several items to be included in the directors' report reflect the interests of employees but as yet there is no legal requirement to provide any form of annual report to the employees[20]. The Industrial Relations Act 1971 contained a provision[1] requiring companies employing more than 350 people to issue an annual statement to each employee covering matters to be specified in regulations by the Secretary of State. The section was never brought into force and following the repeal of the Industrial Relations Act has not been re-enacted. Nevertheless among large companies the practice of supplying a special report to employees is increasingly common[2]. The importance of information in the protection of employee interests is also reflected in the obligations to disclose information relevant to collective bargaining contained in the Employment Protection Act 1975, s 17(1)[3].

The interest of government in the activities of companies was reflected in the provisions of the Industry Act 1975 for disclosure of information relevant to the national economy, provisions which were, however, repealed by the Industry Act 1980 and have not been re-enacted. There is, however, an obligation on companies with South African subsidiaries to report annually to the government on their implementation of the EC Code of Conduct for Companies with Interests in South Africa[4].

---

17 Ibid, s 5, ch 2, para 1.
18 See the material cited in Stevenson *Corporations and Information—Secrecy, Access and Disclosure* (1980) p 210, footnotes 18 and 19 and by Meier-Schwartz (1986) 8 Journal of Comparative Business and Capital Market Law 219. Useful extracts are contained in Posner and Scott *Economics of Corporation Law and Securities Regulation* (1980) chs 10 and 11. See also Keane *Efficient Markets and Financial Reporting* (1987) who suggests certain characteristics a worthwhile disclosure policy in relation to stock markets should possess.
19 This aspect of disclosure relates more to the issues discussed in chapter 33 on raising capital from the public than it does to the issues discussed in this chapter.
20 The Labour government in 1977 was in favour of requiring companies to send the full report and accounts to employees. See The Conduct of Company Directors (Cmnd 7037) para 5. The Conservative government elected in 1979 preferred to allow companies to choose whether and how information should be given to employees. See Company Accounting and Disclosure (Cmnd 7654) p 8.
1 Industrial Relations Act 1971, s 57.
2 *Financial Reporting 1982–83 (A Survey of UK Published Accounts)* from the Institute of Chartered Accountants of England and Wales (ICAEW) shows that in the year ended 30 June 1982, 150 companies out of 196 which responded to the questionnaire (ie 77%) produced reports to employees.
3 See also the revised draft for an EEC Council Directive on procedures for informing and consulting employees. OJ 1983 C 217/3. See Docksey (1986) 49 MLR 281.
4 See Code of Conduct for Companies with Interests in South Africa (Cmnd 9860).

Disclosure according to type of company

We have seen that listed companies are subject to additional disclosure requirements imposed by The Stock Exchange. Gradually the fact that listed companies represent a discrete category with special problems requiring special solutions is also becoming recognised in legislative disclosure requirements[5]. This is just one example of a more general proposition, that disclosure requirements will tend to vary according to the type and size of company and the needs of users of the information. This represents a fourth angle from which to look at disclosure requirements.

ANNUAL REPORT AND ACCOUNTS

Sources of obligations

The most important disclosure of information by companies is that contained in the financial statements and auditors' and directors' reports that together constitute the annual report and accounts. Historically and in terms of extent of coverage, the most important influence on the content of these documents is the companies legislation which in turn now reflects the impact of the Fourth[6] and Seventh[7] Directives on the harmonisation of legislation on company and group accounts in the EC[8]. The Fourth Directive was implemented in 1981 and the Seventh Directive in the Companies Act 1989. Because of the scale of the changes involved, the Companies Act 1989 not only reformed the law but also consolidated the changes with the existing law on company accounts. This has the advantage that all the relevant legislation is together in one statute. However, the Act also reinserts the consolidated material back into Part VII of the Companies Act 1985. Care needs to be taken therefore to check whether a reference to a section in that Part of the 1985 Act (sections 221–262A) is to the old legislation or to that substituted in 1989. Throughout this chapter any references to sections will be to the new substituted legislation unless otherwise made clear.

In addition to legislative requirements, however, there is a growing body of professional accounting requirements affecting the content of company accounts[9]. The professional accountancy bodies first began issuing Recommendations on Accounting Principles in 1942. In 1970 the Accounting Standards Steering Committee was formed, becoming the Accounting

---

5 See s 329 (reporting of substantial interests in shares to the Stock Exchange) and s 251 (summary financial statements).
6 EEC Council Directive 78/660, OJ 1978 L 222/11.
7 EEC Council Directive 83/349, OJ 1983 L 193/1.
8 The Directives have been the subject of various amendments. The financial limits in the Fourth Directive for qualifying as small or medium-sized companies were raised in 1984: EEC Council Directive 84/559, OJ 1984 L 314/28. The Fourth Directive was also amended by the Seventh Directive and both are further amended by two directives which have yet to be implemented by member states. One raises again the financial limits for small or medium-sized companies or groups: EEC Council Directive 90/604, OJ 1990 L 317/57. The other extends the directives to cover partnerships, limited partnerships and unlimited companies where all the partners or members have limited liability themselves: EEC Council Directive 90/605, OJ 1990 L317/60.
9 A third source of obligations for companies listed on the Stock Exchange is provided by Admission of Securities to Listing, s 5, ch 2, para 21.

Standards Committee in 1975, responsible for issuing Statements of Standard Accounting Practice. The importance of these may be gauged from the fact that any significant departure from them must be disclosed and explained in the financial statements and if the auditors agree with the departure they must be in a position to justify it[10]. Doubts, however, arose about the ability of the Accounting Standards Committee to respond quickly and with enough authority to new developments in accounting including the increasing use of creative accounting techniques which some companies and their advisers were prepared to justify by reference to observing the letter of accounting rules while ignoring the purpose behind them[11]. In response to this a committee was appointed, under the chairmanship of Sir Ronald Dearing, to review the process of setting accounting standards, the relationship of standards to company law and the procedures for monitoring compliance with, and enforcement of, standards. As a result of the committee's recommendations[12] a new institutional framework has been set up. At the top, responsible for determining overall policy, is the Financial Reporting Council. Below the Council is the Accounting Standards Board which takes over from the Accounting Standards Committee responsibility for issuing accounting standards[13]. It has a number of advantages over its predecessor. It will have a full-time chairman and full-time technical officer; it will not be reliant solely on the accountancy profession for funding; it can issue new standards on its own initiative without first having to obtain the consent of the six professional accountancy bodies. Its authority is further enhanced by the existence of a third body recommended by the Dearing Committee. This is the Accounting Review Panel which will examine material departures from accounting standards by public or large private companies involving issues of principle or which might result in accounts not giving a true and fair view.

Accounting reference period, accounting reference date and financial year

Before discussing the statutory obligations regarding company accounts there are three terms that need to be defined. The first is the company's *accounting reference period* which is the period between successive accounting reference dates[14]. A company has nine months from its incorporation to nominate its *accounting reference date*[15]; otherwise it will be deemed to fall on the last day of the month in which the anniversary of its incorporation falls[16]. Unless the company alters its accounting reference

---

10 See the Explanatory Foreword to the Statements of Standard Accounting Practice ('SSAPs') in *Accounting Standards* published by the ICAEW. *Financial Reporting 1988–89* Pt I contains an interesting review of developments in financial reporting during the period 1968–1988 showing the influence of accounting standards.
11 See Whittington (1989) 19 Accounting and Business Research 195.
12 *The Making of Accounting Standards* (1988).
13 Accounting Standards (Prescribed Body) Regulations 1990 SI 1990/1667. For discussion of what role accounting standards should fill in the light of current problems in accounting, see Tweedie and Whittington (1990) 21 Accounting and Business Research 87. One of the long-term tasks for the Accounting Standards Board is likely to be involvement in harmonising accounting standards throughout the EC. In this connection the European Commission established an Accounting Advisory Forum in 1990.
14 Section 224(4)(5).
15 Section 224(2).
16 Section 224(3). In the case of a company incorporated before 1 April 1990 the deemed date was 31 March each year.

date[17] then its accounting reference period will remain fixed from year to year. It is by reference to the end of this fixed period that the time limit for the company's obligation to circulate accounts to shareholders, present them to the general meeting and deliver them to the registrar is calculated[18]. The period for which the accounts themselves are drawn up is called the *financial year*[19]. This must end on, or within seven days either side of, the company's accounting reference date, the precise timing being chosen by the directors[20]. The new financial year then begins immediately after the end of the previous one[1]. The effect of this is that unless the company changes its accounting reference date the accounting reference period which fixes the obligation to present accounts to the shareholders and registrar remains static while directors have a limited degree of flexibility in fixing the financial year in respect of which accounts must be drawn up.

Presentation to shareholders and registration

This is a matter which is governed by the Companies Act. The Act requires four documents to be presented to the shareholders and delivered to the registrar each year: the balance sheet, the profit and loss account, the auditors' report and the directors' report[2]. The content of each is discussed below but the disclosure obligations relating to them are linked. Within a specified time after the end of a company's accounting reference period a copy of each document must be laid before the general meeting[3] and at least 21 days before that general meeting, a copy of every such document must be sent to each member and debenture holder in the company[4]. Also, within the time specified for laying the accounts before the general meeting, limited companies must file with the Registrar of Companies a copy of every document comprised in the accounts required to be registered by that category of company[5]. Unlimited companies are exempt from the obligation to file accounts[6] and the advantage of secrecy which this offers must be the main reason why a business opting for the corporate form might nevertheless opt for unlimited liability. The specified time for laying accounts before the general meeting and filing them with the Registrar is ten months after the end of the accounting reference period for a private company and seven

---

17 Section 225.
18 Section 244.
19 Section 226(1).
20 Section 223.
 1 Section 223(3).
 2 The chairman's report, which has become a standard feature of company reports and accounts, is not a matter of statutory obligation.
 3 Section 241(1). As part of the deregulation of private companies the members of a private company may by unanimous elective resolution dispense with laying accounts before the general meeting unless required by a member or the auditors to do so: s 252.
 4 Section 238(1). As to the right of companies listed on the Stock Exchange to offer their members summary financial statements in place of the accounts and directors' report, see below pp 506–508. Where a private company has dispensed with laying reports and accounts before a general meeting they must be sent to shareholders at least 28 days before what would otherwise be the expiry of the period for laying the accounts before the general meeting: s 253(1).
 5 Section 242(1). Which category a company is in depends on its size according to criteria based on turnover, assets and number of employees. See below p 506 ff.
 6 Section 254.

months for a public company[7]. The Stock Exchange, however, requires listed companies to issue accounts within six months of the period to which they relate[8].

The balance sheet and profit and loss account

Every company must prepare a profit and loss account for each financial year[9] and a balance sheet as at the last day of the year[10]. The profit and loss account is essentially a record of the financial fortunes of the company during the period of the account. It will show, therefore, not only the company's trading record for the period but also income received on investments and interest the company has had to pay out to its creditors. The balance sheet, on the other hand, is an indication of the financial state of affairs of the company at a particular date, showing the net assets of the company and how they are financed[11]. The profit and loss account and balance sheet must give 'a true and fair view' of the company's profit or loss for the financial year and of the state of affairs of the company as at the end of the year respectively[12]. They must also comply with the detailed requirements of Sch 4[13].

There are three major issues that arise in relation to the drawing up of a balance sheet and profit and loss account: (i) content ie what must be included; (ii) format ie how must the material be presented; and (iii) valuation ie what rules of measurement must be used. Broadly speaking, legislative requirements until 1981 concentrated on matters of content, leaving companies themselves to decide questions of format and valuation. In the Companies Act 1981, the UK implemented the Fourth Directive on the harmonisation of company accounts. Not only did the Fourth Directive require changes in the content of the accounts but for the first time legislation was required to prescribe the format of the balance sheet and profit and

---

7 Section 244. Following complaints by the Public Accounts Committee in 1984 that only 42% of companies were up to date with filing their annual accounts, the Companies Registration Office mounted an enforcement campaign. As at 30 June 1989, 88% of active companies were up to date in filing annual returns and 84% in filing annual accounts: see the Department of Trade and Industry's Annual Report on Companies. See more generally the Department of Trade and Industry's consultative document 'The Delivery of Annual Accounts and Returns to the Registrar' (1986).
8 Admission of Securities to Listing, s 5, ch 2, para 20.
9 Section 226(1)(b).
10 Section 226(1)(a). Listed companies must also produce half-yearly or interim reports: Admission of Securities to Listing, s 5, ch 2, paras 24 and 25. Interim reports by listed companies are the subject of an EEC harmonisation directive the contents of which are reflected in Admission of Securities to Listing: EEC Council Directive 82/121. Official Journal of the European Communities 1982 L48/26.
11 This refers to how the assets are represented in terms of funds attributable to the shareholders in the form of called-up share capital, share premium account, capital redemption reserve, non-distributable reserves and reserves in the form of accumulations of trading profit.
12 Section 226(2).
13 Section 226(3). A minority shareholder is not entitled to bring proceedings to enforce the provisions of the Companies Act as to the form and content of the accounts: *Devlin v Slough Estates Ltd* [1983] BCLC 497. The company may, of course, decide not to object to proceedings where there is a point of construction it wants resolved: *Henry Head & Co Ltd v Ropner Holdings Ltd* [1952] Ch 124, [1951] 2 All ER 994.

loss account and to include valuation rules. The result is that companies[14] must now prepare balance sheets in accordance with one of two alternative forms and profit and loss accounts in accordance with one of four alternative forms[15]. Moreover the items to be entered must follow the order of the chosen form[16]. Finally, accounting principles are prescribed with alternatives allowing for current cost accounting as well as or instead of historic cost accounting[17]. It should be noted, however, that the obligation to present a true and fair view prevails over the detailed statutory requirements so that if the requirements are insufficient to give a true and fair view additional information must be provided, or in special circumstances, the statutory requirements themselves may be departed from[18].

One of the problems raised by the phrase 'a true and fair view' is whether applicable Statements of Standard Accounting Practice must be followed for the accounts to show a true and fair view[19]. Accounting standards are not legally enforceable although professional practice requires that significant departures from them should be disclosed and explained in the financial statements and the financial effects of such departures estimated and disclosed[20]. The Dearing Committee[1] discussed whether accounting standards should be legally enforceable and concluded for two main reasons that they should not[2]. First, there would be a danger that companies and their advisers might seek ways round the precise letter of legal requirements while ignoring the spirit of the provisions. Secondly, keeping accounting standards not legally enforceable enables them to be drafted in more general terms and makes it possible to respond to new developments in accounting more quickly than would be the case if statutory changes were involved. The Committee did, however, recommend that there should be a legal requirement for public and large private companies to disclose particulars of and the reasons for any material departure from applicable accounting standards[3] and this has now been enacted[4].

The Dearing Committee also recommended that there should be a statutory rebuttable presumption to the effect that compliance with accounting standards is necessary to give a true and fair view[5]. Thus, if there were a material departure from accounting standards the onus would be on those arguing that the accounts nevertheless gave a true and fair view to

---

14 Banking or insurance companies may continue to prepare accounts under the former provisions now contained in ss 255–255D and Schs 9 and 10.
15 Schedule 4, Pt 1, s B.
16 Schedule 4, para 1.
17 Schedule 4, paras 9–34.
18 Section 226(4), (5).
19 As to the impact on interpretation of 'a true and fair view' of the fact that having begun life as a provision of the Companies Act 1948 it is now contained in the Fourth and Seventh Directives, see Lasok and Grace [1988] JBL 235.
20 See the Explanatory Forward to the Statement of Standard Accounting Practice in *Accounting Standards* published by the ICAEW. See also as regards listed companies: Admission of Securities to Listing, s 5, ch 2, para 21(a).
1 *The Making of Accounting Standards* (1988).
2 Ibid, para 10.2.
3 Ibid, para 10.4. The Committee saw three purposes in this requirement. First, to bring to the attention of the whole board of directors any proposed material departure from accounting standards; secondly, to help the user to understand the accounts; thirdly, to facilitate the task of monitoring compliance with accounting standards.
4 Schedule 4, para 36A.
5 *The Making of Accounting Standards* paras 15.14–15.17.

show that they did. Their recommendation, however, was not enacted because it came too close to giving accounting standards legal force with the disadvantages of excessive legalism that might entail. In any case it is doubtful whether such a statutory presumption would make all that much difference. In an opinion given to the Accounting Standards Committee in 1983[6] leading counsel stated that 'the courts will treat compliance with accepted accounting principles as prima facie evidence that the accounts are true and fair. Equally, deviation from accepted principles will be prima facie evidence that they are not'[7].

CURRENT COST ACCOUNTS

The use of the indefinite article before the phrase 'true and fair view' serves as a reminder that the financial position of a company can be viewed from more than one angle. In 'The Corporate Report', a discussion paper published by the Accounting Standards Steering Committee, six different accounting measurement bases are discussed, each valuable for different purposes and all of which could be regarded as giving a true and fair view[8]. Until 1981, legislative requirements assumed that accounts would be drawn up on the basis of historical cost accounting in which the value of assets is taken to be their cost or book value less any provision for depreciation. However, the Fourth Directive allowed member states to permit companies to draw up accounts on the basis of the current cost of assets. In times of high inflation, the profits of a company can appear overstated if no account is taken of the true cost of replacing assets. So taking advantage of the option in the Fourth Directive, Sch 4 now allows companies to continue to present accounts purely on a historical cost basis or to opt instead for a presentation based on current costs. If a current cost basis is chosen, any information necessary to calculate the historical cost figures must also be supplied[9]. It has been emphasised that the legislative requirements are not the only factors bearing on the formulation of company accounts. Standard accounting practice used to require all companies listed on The Stock Exchange and all large companies (in the three-tier classification introduced in 1981 and discussed below) to include accounts drawn up on a current cost basis either as supplementary to accounts based on historical cost principles or as their main accounts[10]. In the latter case, however, accounts drawn up on historic cost principles also had to be published or sufficient information given for comparisons to be worked out.

GROUP ACCOUNTS

Where a business is carried on through subsidiary companies an accurate impression of the overall financial position of the business will not be

---

6 See *Accounting Standards* published by the ICAEW.
7 See also Bird [1984] JBL 480 and *Lloyd Cheyham & Co Ltd v Littlejohn & Co* [1987] BCLC 303.
8 *The Corporate Report* (1975) pp 66–71.
9 Schedule 4, paras 29–34.
10 Statement of Standard Accounting Practice, No 16. This did not prove universally popular and was withdrawn in December 1985 so that auditors' reports no longer need to refer to the omission of current cost accounts. The issue is still under discussion, however. See the Treasury report 'Accounting for Economic Costs and Changing Prices' (1986) and the Accounting Standards Committee booklet *Accounting for the Effect of Changing Prices* (1986).

achieved unless the accounts of all the separate companies are looked at together. In 1948, therefore, legislation was introduced requiring the preparation of group accounts where a company had subsidiaries[11]. The legislation has now been revised as a result of the implementation in the Companies Act 1989 of the Seventh Directive[12] on the harmonisation of group accounts. Because the Directive requires the inclusion of unincorporated subsidiaries the terms now used are parent and subsidiary undertaking. Any company which has one or more subsidiary undertakings must prepare group accounts[13] unless it falls within one of the following three exceptions. First, where the group qualifies as a small or medium-sized group[14]. Before 1989 such groups were entitled to deliver to the registrar modified accounts. They are now exempted from the obligation even to prepare group accounts[15]. Secondly, where the parent is itself a subsidiary and is included in the accounts of a larger group[16]. Previously a holding company was exempt from preparing group accounts if it was the wholly-owned subsidiary of a company incorporated in Great Britain. The immediate parent may now be established anywhere in the EC[17]. The exemption is also extended to cases where the company's immediate parent does not own all the shares but owns more than 50 per cent. In such a case, however, shareholders holding in aggregate more than half of the remaining shares or five per cent of the total shares in the company may none the less demand that the company does prepare group accounts[18]. Thirdly, for the avoidance of doubt, it is expressly stated that if all a parent's subsidiaries are excluded from the group accounts for one reason or another, no group accounts need be prepared[19].

Group accounts must consist of a consolidated balance sheet and profit and loss account[20]. The detailed requirements as to the form and content are set out in Sch 4A[1] but as with individual company accounts the overriding requirement is to give a true and fair view of the state of affairs as at the end of the financial year and of the profit or loss for the financial year[2]. Thus, if the detailed requirements do not provide enough information for a true and fair view, any necessary additional information must be supplied[3]; conversely directors of the parent company must depart from the detailed requirements if in special circumstances they are inconsistent with the requirement to give a true and fair view[4].

Under the definition of holding and subsidiary companies that was laid down in 1948 there were three ways in which one company(s) became the subsidiary of another (P). First, if P was a member of S and controlled the

---

11 Interesting background to the introduction of group accounting is given by Bircher (1988) 19 Accounting and Business Res 3.
12 EEC Council Directive 83/349. OJ 1983 L 193/1.
13 Section 227(1).
14 Section 249.
15 Section 248.
16 Section 228(2).
17 Section 228(1).
18 Section 228(1)(b).
19 Section 229(5).
20 Section 227(2).
 1 Section 227(4).
 2 Section 227(3).
 3 Section 227(5).
 4 Section 227(6).

composition of its board of directors. Secondly, if P held more than half in nominal value of S's equity share capital. Thirdly, any subsidiary of S was also a subsidiary of P. The major problem with this definition, in practice, was that it could exclude situations where one company controlled another which factually, though not legally, would be described as its subsidiary. This led to disagreement as to whether, in order to give a true and fair view, group accounts should reflect the substance of the relationship between companies rather than the formal legal relationship. In 1980 a successful prosecution was mounted against a company for including in its consolidated accounts the results of a company which it factually controlled but which did not legally become its subsidiary until after the end of the financial year[5]. The DTI then reminded auditors that emphasis on substance should never be at the expense of formal legal requirements[6]. Relying on this, companies justified making deliberate use of controlled non-subsidiaries as a means of keeping assets or liabilities off the consolidated balance sheet[7].

As a result of implementation of the Seventh Directive there is now a completely new definition of parent and subsidiary undertakings for accounting purposes. The Seventh Directive provides for mandatory implementation by member states of tests based on legal control[8] while tests based on factual control are optional[9]. However, to help deal with the problem of off-balance sheet financing described above, the UK has implemented the tests based on factual control as well as those based on legal control. There are now six ways in which an undertaking may be a parent undertaking (P) in relation to a subsidiary underating (S). These are where:

(i)   P holds a majority of the voting rights[10] in S[11]. This may be contrasted with the previous test of holding a majority of the equity share capital which might or might not have voting rights attached.

(ii)   P is a member of S and controls alone a majority of the voting rights[12] pursuant to an agreement with other shareholders or members[13].

(iii) P is a member of S and has the right to appoint or remove directors who have a majority of the voting rights at board meetings[14]. This may be contrasted with the previous test of controlling the composition of the board of directors but not necessarily controlling the majority of votes cast at board meetings.

(iv)   P has the right to exercise a dominant influence over S by virtue of a provision in S's memorandum or articles or by virtue of a control contract[15]. The phrase 'the right to exercise a dominant influence' is not defined in the Act. It is, however, laid down by statute that it must at least involve P having the right to direct the operating and financial policies of S and the directors of S being obliged to comply with such

5 See (1981) 2 Co Law 275.
6 See *Tolley's Company Law* (3rd edn 1990) Appendix 3.
7 See Bird [1986] JBL 132.
8 EEC Council Directive 83/349, art 1(1)(a), (b), (d).
9 Ibid, art 1(1)(c), (2).
10 For the meaning of voting rights, see Sch 10A, para 2.
11 Section 258(2)(a).
12 See note 10.
13 Section 258(2)(d).
14 Section 258(2)(b).
15 Section 258(2)(c).

directions whether or not they are for the benefit of S[16]. A 'control contract' is a contract in writing which confers on P the right to exercise a dominant influence over S and which is both expressly authorised by the memorandum or articles of S and permitted by the law under which S is established[17]. Such provisions for control of one undertaking by another are almost completely unknown in the UK and so this test is not likely to be of great significance where the putative subsidiary is incorporated in the UK. This test for establishing the relationship of parent and subsidiary is in fact optional so far as member states are concerned under the Seventh Directive. It has been implemented in the UK, however, because it might be useful if the putative subsidiary is established in, say, Germany, where provisions for control of one undertaking by another are recognised by law[18]. There is also, under discussion in Brussels, a proposed Ninth Directive to harmonise the treatment of groups in areas of company law besides that of consolidated accounts. The Ninth Directive, if it is ever issued, is likely to provide for control contracts to be recognised by member states and including this provision in the accounting legislation could prove helpful in preparing the ground for the Ninth Directive.

(v)   P holds a participating interest in S and either actually exercises a dominant influence over S, or P and S are managed on a unified basis[19]. A 'participating interest' means an interest in the shares of S held[20] on a long-term basis for the purpose of securing a contribution to the activities of any undertaking in the group or of the group as a whole[1]. Neither the term 'dominant influence' nor the term 'managed on a unified basis' is defined in the Act. In particular the statutory provision regarding the interpretation of the phrase 'the right to exercise a dominant influence' referred to above does not apply here[2]. The terms are taken straight from the Seventh Directive and are deliberately left undefined. This test for establishing a parent subsidiary relationship is also an option for member states in the Seventh Directive. It has been implemented in the UK in the hope that it will curb the use of off-balance sheet financing whereby assets or liabilities are acquired by controlled non-subsidiaries with the intention of keeping them off the consolidated balance sheet. Any statutory definition of the relevant terms would merely encourage attempts at evasion.

(vi)   Where P is a parent undertaking of S, it is treated as a parent undertaking in relation to all S's subsidiary undertakings[3].

The inclusion of tests for establishing a parent/subsidiary relationship based on factual control should help to curb the use of off-balance sheet financing and resolve some of the 'substance versus form' disputes between accountants and lawyers. However, there may continue to be cases of

16 Schedule 10A, para 4(1).
17 Ibid, para 4(2).
18 See Wooldridge *Groups of Companies—The Law and Practice in Britain, France and Germany* (1981) pp 5–7.
19 Section 258(4).
20 By or on behalf of P or any of its subsidiary undertakings: s 260(4), (5)(a).
 1 Section 260(1).
 2 Schedule 10A, para 4(3).
 3 Section 258(5).

undertakings which are in fact controlled by the parent but do not fall within the new definition of subsidiary. It may be necessary to give more information about such undertakings than will be shown using the equity method of accounting in order to give a true and fair view of the state of affairs of those undertakings which are included in the group accounts. In such circumstances, in order to comply with the true and fair view requirements, the parent company effectively has two options. It may either give any necessary additional information by way of notes to the accounts[4]; or, in special circumstances, it may override the statutory provisions and include the controlled non-subsidiary in the group accounts[5].

As well as introducing a new definition of parent and subsidiary undertaking for accounting purposes the Companies Act 1989 also revised the definition of holding and subsidiary company for non-accounting purposes[6]. Under the non-accounting definition there are four ways in which a holding company/subsidiary company relationship can be established. Apart from using the terms company instead of undertaking and holding company instead of parent the four ways mirror four of the tests of parent/subsidiary relationship set out above[7]: the first three plus the sixth (the equivalent of the grandparent/grandchild relationship). It will be noticed that these are the tests of legal control and are capable of relatively precise application. The two tests based on factual control are not included in the definition for non-accounting purposes because they depend too much on an element of judgment about the relationship between the two companies. They were included in the accounting definitions because they were important to help control off balance sheet financing for which definitions that enabled the true substance of a relationship to be identified were necessary. In non-accounting contexts the need is far more for precision and certainty.

Statement of source and application of funds

This statement is not required by either the Companies Act[8] or The Stock Exchange but is required by accounting practice for all enterprises with a turnover or gross income of £25,000 per annum and must form part of the audited accounts of such companies[9]. Its object is to show how the operations of the company have been financed, whether from internally generated funds or external short-term borrowings. It usually consists of three segments. The first segment shows the amount of internally generated funds. The second segment shows what the company spent money on during the year. To the extent that any items here increase, that represents a net application of funds which must have been financed from somewhere. To the extent that any items decrease, that represents further funds being released for use elsewhere. If the net total of the second segment is a positive amount (representing an increased application of funds over the year) then to the extent that that sum exceeds the internally generated funds that excess

---

4 Section 227(5).
5 Section 227(6).
6 Sections 736 and 736A.
7 Pages 487–488.
8 But see The Future of Company Reports (Cmnd 6888) paras 22–25.
9 Statement of Standard Accounting Practice, No 10. For a discussion of the use of such statements and an analysis of their presentation, see *Financial Reporting 1987–88* pp 17–41.

must have been financed by externally generated funds shown in the third segment. If instead the net total of the second segment is a negative sum (representing a decrease in the net level of investment during the year) this will represent an additional source of funds. This together with the internally generated funding will be reflected in a decrease in external funding in the third segment.

Value added statement

It is not only by using different bases for valuation that the financial position of a company can be shown in a different perspective. The profit and loss account is only one form in which the income generated by a business can be stated. It is moreover a form which can give the impression that the only point of a company's activities is to generate profits for the shareholders or proprietors. It identifies as profit, or accretions to shareholders' funds, the surplus the business has generated after deducting from the total receipts of the company all the outgoings the company has had to pay except dividends and funds retained for reinvestment. An alternative way of looking at the income generated by a company is to calculate the value added in the course of the company's business. This can be done by subtracting from the gross amount received on sale of the company's products, whether they are goods or services, the sum paid by the company to buy in goods or services from outside, but not deducting the cost of labour i e wages and salaries, nor of capital i e dividends and interest. The resulting figure is the value added or wealth created by the business during the year[10]. The way in which this wealth or value is then divided among employees in the form of wages or salaries, providers of capital in the form of interest or dividends, the government in the form of taxation or is retained in the business for re-investment can then also be shown. This form of account thus views the company's operations as a combined effort by the providers of capital and labour and although there is, as yet, no legal or accounting requirement to publish a value added statement[11] it has become a popular way of presenting a company's financial position[12].

Notes to the accounts

Apart from laying down the format and contents of the profit and loss account and balance sheet, the schedules also list various items that must be included in notes to the accounts. Many of these amplify or explain items in the profit and loss account or balance sheet but others require disclosure of information that goes beyond what would be regarded as being primarily

---

10 Of course, calculating the income generated by a company on a different basis may prompt the question why it is that the law treats the profit or loss to shareholders as the object of the calculation. One answer is that this is the variable figure reflecting the risk taken. This would be altered if all capital received a fixed return. It would then seem natural to deduct the cost of capital in computing the income of the business. Conversely the cost of wages and salaries might not be deducted in which case the variable surplus could then be attributed to employees. An employee co-operative!
11 Cf The Future of Company Reports (Cmnd 6888) paras 13–17.
12 See *Financial Reporting 1983–84* pp 151–163. There is a good account of the computation and uses of value added statements in Morley 'Value Added Reporting' in *Developments in Financial Reporting* ed T A Lee (1981) chapter 11.

relevant to an appreciation of the financial position of the company. Some of these are discussed below but this is not a comprehensive list.

Information about related undertakings   Under Schedule 5 companies must include details of interests of the company or its group in subsidiaries, associates, joint ventures and other entities.

Disaggregation   Where a company has diversified into more than one business, it may be very helpful to users of the accounts to know the relative contribution different businesses make to the company's overall perform-ance. The first legislative requirement[13] to include any form of disaggre-gation was in the Companies Act 1967 which required the directors' report to show the proportion of turnover and profitability in each class of busi-ness[14]. As required by the Fourth Directive[15], this obligation was transferred to the notes to the accounts (the effect being that it is now audited) and was extended to require an analysis of turnover by geographical area[16].

Directors' emoluments   Since 1948, the accounts of a company have had to indicate the aggregate amounts of the directors' emoluments, directors' and past directors' pensions and of any compensation paid to directors or past directors for loss of office[17]. This was added to in 1967 so that now if the aggregate figure for directors' emoluments exceeds £60,000, then the actual remuneration of the chairman must be given and the number of directors remunerated within bands of £0–£5,000, £5,000—£10,000, etc[18].

Particulars of staff   In 1967, a requirement was also introduced for the directors' report to disclose the average number of employees and their aggregate remuneration[19]. In accordance with a provision in the Fourth Directive[20] such information must now be given in the accounts (the effect being, as with figures for disaggregation, that it is now audited) and must include aggregate social security contributions and aggregate pension con-tributions and funding[1].

Loans, quasi-loans or credit transactions   Detailed particulars[2] of trans-actions or agreements to enter into transactions involving loans, quasi-loans

13 The Stock Exchange introduced a requirement for listed companies in 1964. See now Admission of Securities to Listing, s 5, ch 2, para 21(c).
14 Companies Act 1967, s 17. This requirement may still apply to banking or insurance companies: CA 1985, s 255 and Sch 10, para 2C(5).
15 EEC Council Directive 78/660, art 43.1(8).
16 Schedule 4, para 55. For an analysis of disaggregation in published accounts, see *Financial Reporting 1987–88* pp 139–160.
17 Schedule 6, Pt I. The scope of the disclosure obligation was significantly extended by the Companies Act 1989. Under the Companies Act 1929, s 128(1)(c) companies were obliged to include in the accounts aggregate directors' fees and though under s 148 shareholders could demand to know the aggregate remuneration or other emoluments received by directors the company could refuse to tell them.
18 Schedule 6, paras 2–4. Not everyone believes such disclosure is worthwhile. See the observations by Sealy *Company Law and Commercial Reality* (1984) pp 28–29.
19 Companies Act 1967, s 18. This requirement may still apply to banking or insurance companies: CA 1985, s 255(C)(5) and Sch 10, para 3.
20 EEC Council Directive 78/660, art 43.1(9).
 1 Schedule 4, paras 56 and 94.
 2 Schedule 6, para 22.

or credit transactions of a type described in s 330 must be disclosed in notes to the accounts[3], whether or not the transaction or arrangement was prohibited by that section[4]. As regards credit transactions, no disclosure is needed if the aggregate value of the credit granted to the director concerned or persons connected with him did not exceed £5,000[5]. In addition the aggregate amount of any loans, quasi-loans or credit transactions to officers other than directors must be disclosed, except where the aggregate amount outstanding does not exceed £2,500[6].

Other transactions involving directors   Detailed particulars[7] of other transactions in which a director had a material interest must also be disclosed in notes to the accounts[8] unless the aggregate value of such transactions did not exceed £1,000, or, if it did, did not exceed the lesser of 1% of net assets or £5,000[9]. Every transaction between a company and a director of the company or its holding company or a person connected with such a director is deemed to be one in which the director is interested[10]. It is, however, open to a majority of the directors, other than the director interested, when preparing the accounts, to decide that the interest is not material[11].

Securing compliance with obligations in preparation of accounts

Following recommendations made by the Dearing Committee[12] a new set of procedures for dealing with failure to comply with accounting requirements was introduced by the Companies Act 1989. The Committee recognised that the overriding objective should be to ensure that good accounting information is ultimately produced, rather than the punishment of transgressors. Accordingly, the former criminal offence of laying before the general meeting or delivering to the registrar accounts which do not comply with the Companies Act was repealed. It is, however, appropriate for the criminal law to be involved where there has been a deliberate attempt to mislead and a new offence was introduced where directors approve annual accounts which they know do not comply with the requirements of the Act or they are reckless as to whether they comply or not[13].

The more important changes, however, were the introduction of new civil procedures for securing compliance with the accounting requirements. The procedures are based on three stages. First, directors now have an opportunity voluntarily to prepare revised annual accounts or a directors' report[14]. Since it cannot simply be open to directors to change their minds about something and prepare revised accounts, the revisions must be confined to those aspects in which the previous accounts and reports did not comply with

3 Schedule 6, paras 15 and 16.
4 Schedule 6, para 19.
5 Schedule 6, para 24.
6 Schedule 6, Pt III.
7 Schedule 6, para 22.
8 Schedule 6, paras 15(c) and 16(c).
9 Schedule 6, para 25.
10 Schedule 6, para 17(1).
11 Schedule 6, para 17(2). An incentive is thereby given to directors to disclose their interests to their fellow directors.
12 *The Making of Accounting Standards* (1988) Ch 15.
13 Section 233(5).
14 Section 245.

the Act, plus any necessary consequential amendments[15]. Although compliance with accounting standards is not referred to, in so far as the annual accounts fail to comply with the statutory requirement to give a true and fair view because of failure to follow applicable accounting standards, the directors are permitted to make revisions in order to comply with accounting standards.

It may seem strange that if directors have realised the annual accounts or directors' report do not comply with the Act it is not compulsory for them to prepare revised versions. The hope is that by leaving it as a voluntary matter more directors will be encouraged to act in an openly responsible manner. However, the second stage in the new procedure empowers the Secretary of State, where there appears to him to be a question whether a company's annual accounts (but not, it seems, the directors' report) comply with the Act, to require the directors to give an explanation of the accounts or prepare revised accounts[16]. If neither a satisfactory explanation nor revised accounts are produced then under the third stage of the new procedure the Secretary of State may apply for a court order to the directors to prepare revised accounts[17]. The Secretary of State may authorise other bodies to make court applications in respect of defective accounts[18] and the Financial Reporting Review Panel has been so authorised[19]. The Review Panel has been authorised to apply to the court in respect of the accounts of any class of company. It is expected, however, that the Panel will concentrate on the accounts of public and large private companies, leaving responsibility for the accounts of small or medium-sized companies with the Department of Trade and Industry.

The auditors' report

Although the 1844 Joint Stock Companies Act[20] required that registered companies appoint auditors, that the auditors report on the balance sheet to the shareholders and that the balance sheet and report be registered, the Act was repealed in 1856[21]. The provisions about accounts and auditing became optional provisions in the model regulations for the management of company[1]. From 1867, railway companies and from 1879, limited liability banking companies were obliged to appoint auditors but it was not until 1900 that the obligation was re-introduced for all registered companies[2].

---

15 Section 245(2). See also the Companies (Revision of Defective Accounts and Report) Regulations 1990 SI 1990/2570 dealing with such matters as the audit of the revised accounts and whether the same auditors can be used, the manner in which changes in the revised accounts are indicated and explained, and the circumstances in which revised accounts need to be circulated to all shareholders.
16 Section 245A.
17 Section 245B.
18 Section 245C.
19 Companies (Defective Accounts) (Authorised Person) Order 1991 SI 1991/13.
20 7 and 8 Vict c 110 (1844), ss 34–43.
21 Joint Stock Companies Act 1856.
 1 Ibid, Sch, Table B.
 2 Companies Act 1900, s 21.

DUTIES OF AUDITORS

The main statutory duty on the auditors is to report to the members of the company on the company's accounts[3]. The report must state whether the accounts of the company concerned are prepared in accordance with the Companies Acts and whether they give a true and fair view of the state of the company's affairs as at the end of its financial year and of the profit or loss for the financial year[4].

In preparing their report, the auditors must consider whether proper accounting records have been kept, proper returns adequate for their audit have been received from branches not visited by them, and whether the balance sheet and profit and loss account are in agreement with the accounting records and returns[5]. If they find that any of these circumstances is not the case, this must be stated in the report[6]. To enable them to prepare their report, auditors are given a right of access at all times to the books and accounts of the company[7]. They may also require any necessary information or explanations not only from officers of the company itself[8] but also, despite forebodings about the difficulties this might cause[9], from subsidiary companies, if incorporated in Great Britain, and their auditors[10]. If the auditors fail to obtain all the information and explanations necessary for the audit, this too must be stated in the report[11]. Although the directors' report is not audited, the auditors must consider whether information given in the directors' report relating to the financial year in question is consistent with the audited accounts and, if it is not, that fact must be stated in the auditors' report[12].

Apart from the obligations to report on the accounts, the auditors are also under a duty, so far as they reasonably can, to supply certain information if they find the company has failed to supply it. The categories of information relate to the emoluments of directors and certain transactions or arrangements between the company and its officers[13]. Any information which the auditors give in these categories must be included in their report.

Statute, however, is not the only factor governing the content of the auditors' report. The accountancy bodies have issued a series of Auditing Standards and Guidelines, several of which affect the auditors' report[14].

---

3   Section 235(1). See Lee 'A Brief History of Company Audits 1840–1940' in Lee and Parker (eds) The Evolution of Corporate Financial Reporting (1979) p 153.
4   Section 235(2). If the auditors qualify their report on either of these two grounds and the accounts are used as the basis for a distribution, the auditors must state, either in their report or in a separate statement at the time or subsequently, whether in their opinion the qualification is material in determining whether the distribution is lawful: s 271(3),(4). See *Precision Dippings Ltd v Precision Dippings Marketing Ltd* [1986] Ch 447, CA.
5   Section 237(1).
6   Section 237(2).
7   Section 389A(1).
8   Ibid.
9   Report of the Company Law Committee (Cmnd 1749) para 431.
10   Section 389A(3). If a subsidiary undertaking is not a body incorporated in Great Britain the auditors may require the parent company to take steps to obtain necessary information: s 389A(4)
11   Section 237(3).
12   Section 235(3).
13   Section 237(4) and Sch 6.
14   Chiefly, The Audit Report, an auditing standard, issued in April 1980 and revised in March 1989 and Reports of Auditors under Company Legislation in the United Kingdom, an auditing guideline, issued in June 1989.

Thus the auditors must state whether the audit was conducted in accordance with approved Auditing Standards. If the company is one which is obliged by accounting practice to produce a statement of source and application of funds, the statement must be audited and the auditors' report must refer to whether it gives a true and fair view of such matters. Also, if the company's accounting procedures involve any departure from any of the Statements of Standard Accounting Practice, which the auditors do not regard as justified, that fact must be stated in their report. The wording of qualifications in auditors' reports is also governed by an auditing standard. The aim here is to indicate by a consistent use of language whether the qualification relates to a matter of uncertainty or disagreement and whether it is material, in the sense that knowledge of it would be likely to influence the user of the accounts, or fundamental, in the sense that it renders the accounts either meaningless or misleading[15].

QUALIFICATIONS OF AUDITORS

The importance of the auditors' role has been emphasised by developments over the last century and a half designed to ensure their professional competence and independence. In 1844, when for a brief period auditors were first made compulsory for registered companies, it was common practice for the auditors to be shareholders in the company[16]. In 1900, when auditors were again made obligatory for registered companies, it was provided, in an attempt to ensure the auditors' independence from the management, that the auditor should not be an officer of the company[17]. This has been extended to disqualify as auditor of a company anyone who is, or is in partnership with or is the employee of, an officer or employee of the company[18]. In 1929, companies ceased to be eligible for appointment as auditors but it was not until 1948 that a legislative requirement that auditors possess professional qualifications was introduced. The legislation on the qualification of auditors has been revised as a result of the implementation, in the Companies Act 1989, of the Eighth Directive[19] harmonising the rules for approval of persons to act as auditors of limited liability companies[20]. In order to be eligible for appointment as a company auditor, persons must be members of a recognised supervisory body[1] and be eligible under its rules to be appointed as company auditor[2] which requires that they be independent of the company concerned[3] and hold appropriate qualifications[4]. As under the previous legislation, certain relationships with the company concerned which are fundamentally likely to be incompatible with independence are prohibited outright[5]. The Secretary

---

15 For an analysis of auditors' reports see *Financial Reporting 1984–85* pp 13–35.
16 Hadden *Company Law and Capitalism* (2nd edn, 1977) p 137.
17 Companies Act 1900, s 21(3).
18 Companies Act 1989, s 27(1).
19 EEC Council Directive 84/253. OJ 1984 L 126/20.
20 A fuller analysis of the legislation can be found in Furey *The Companies Act 1989* (1990) pp 37–45.
 1 Companies Act 1989, s 25(1)(a). As to recognised supervisory bodies, see ibid, s 30 and Sch 11.
 2 Ibid, s 25(1)(b).
 3 Ibid, s 27.
 4 Ibid, Sch 11, paras 4 and 5. As to the meaning of appropriate qualification, see ibid, ss 31, 32 and Sch 12.
 5 See text at note 18 above.

of State is, however, given a new power to make regulations specifying other connections between auditors and clients that would make a person ineligible[6]. Independence will also be secured by the requirement that recognised supervisory bodies have rules designed to prevent persons from being appointed auditors in circumstances in which they have any interest likely to conflict with the proper conduct of the audit[7].

One of the most significant changes the new regime on auditors introduces is to allow corporate bodies to act as auditors[8]. Where a firm (which in the Act covers a partnership[9] or a corporate body[10]) is appointed company auditor it is the firm which must be a member of a recognised supervisory body and be eligible for appointment as company auditor under the rules of the relevant body. In terms of holding appropriate qualifications this means that the individuals within the firm responsible for audit work must hold appropriate qualifications and the firm must be controlled by qualified persons[11]. The controllers themselves may, of course, be individuals or firms and 'qualified' in this context means, for an individual, holding appropriate qualifications, and for a firm, being eligible for appointment as company auditor[12]. A firm is then 'controlled by qualified persons' if, but only if, a majority of its members and members of its management body are qualified persons[13]. These are minimum requirements and there is nothing to stop a recognised supervisory body imposing more stringent conditions if it wishes[14]. Firms must also have arrangements to prevent individuals who do not hold appropriate qualifications and persons who are not members of the firm being able to exert influence over the conduct of the audit in a way which might affect the independence or integrity of the audit[15]. If partnerships are to take full advantage of these rules enabling them to include as partners persons who are not eligible to act as company auditor a change will need to be made in the exemption from the twenty partner limit in ss 716 and 717. The existing exemption only applies to firms all of whose partners are individually qualified to undertake audits[16]. It is expected that the Secretary of State will make regulations[17] amending the exemption to apply to any firm eligible to undertake audits.

6 Companies Act 1989, s 27(2). It is likely that a corporate auditor will be prohibited from auditing a company which is one of its shareholders.
7 Ibid, Sch 11, para 7. There have from time to time been suggestions that auditors who receive a lot of non-audit work from their audit clients could find their independence jeopardised. The Companies Act 1989 does not restrict non-audit work being undertaken by auditors but auditors' fees must now be disclosed in notes to the accounts and provision is made for regulations requiring disclosure of fees for non-audit work: ss 390A(3) and 390B.
8 Ibid, ss 25(2) and 53(1).
9 Where a partnership which is not a legal person is appointed as company auditor, the appointment is (unless a contrary intention appears) an appointment of the partnership as such and not of the partners: ibid, s 26(1).
10 Ibid, s 53(1).
11 Ibid, Sch 11, para 4(1)(b).
12 Ibid, Sch 11, para 5(2).
13 Ibid, Sch 11, para 5(3)–(6). If a firm consists of only two members, therefore, both of them must be qualified. However, in the case of the management body, if that consists of only two persons, it is sufficient if one of them is qualified: para 5(3)(b).
14 See *Ownership and Control of Firms of Auditors under the Companies Act 1989* a Consultation Paper published by the Department of Trade and Industry in December 1989.
15 Companies Act 1989, Sch 11, para 7(2).
16 Sections 716(2)(b) and 717(1)(b).
17 Under the Companies Act 1989, s 50.

APPOINTMENT, REMOVAL AND RESIGNATION OF AUDITORS

The Companies Act 1989 also made a number of changes to other rules affecting auditors. As with the accounts provisions these changes were consolidated with the existing law and then reinserted into the Companies Act 1985. As before references to the Companies Act 1985 are to the new section numbers as inserted by the Companies Act 1989.

As befits a person whose function is to report to the members and who originally was frequently also a member, the auditor has always been appointed by the members[18]. Apart from the period between 1948 and 1976, when annual reappointment was not necessary, every general meeting at which accounts are presented has had to appoint an auditor to serve until the next such meeting[19]. This is still likely to be the most common method of appointment and is the only one open to public companies. However, as a consequence of the programme of deregulation of private companies two alternative methods of appointment are available to private companies[20]. First, a private company may elect to dispense with laying accounts before a general meeting[1] in which case it must make an annual appointment at a general meeting held within 28 days of sending out the accounts[2]. Secondly, a private company may elect to dispense with annual reappointment of auditors altogether[3] in which case the auditors are automatically deemed to be reappointed[4]. This possibility is open to a private company whether or not it has elected to dispense with laying accounts before a general meeting. It is a particular advantage, however, to a company which has made such an election since it obviates the need to call a meeting at all in connection with the accounts and auditors.

As far as the removal[5], replacement[6] or resignation of auditors is concerned the legislative provisions reflect a trend towards strengthening the position of auditors vis-à-vis the management so that the auditors are in a better position to promote the accountability of management to the shareholders and indirectly thereby to serve the public interest by ensuring the efficient use of company's assets. Although auditors may always be removed by ordinary resolution[7], any resolution to remove or replace auditors requires special notice[8]. Furthermore auditors who for any reason cease to hold office[9] must deposit with the company a statement setting out any relevant circumstances[10] which they consider should be brought to the attention of members or creditors, or, if there are none the statement must

---

18 Section 385(2).
19 Ibid.
20 As under the old law, a private company which has declared itself dormant is exempt altogether from the requirement to appoint auditors: s 388A(1).
1 Section 252.
2 Section 385A(2). If a general meeting to consider the accounts is validly demanded under s 253(2), the appointment is made at that meeting.
3 Section 386(1).
4 Section 386(2). As to terminating the appointment of auditors where such an election is in force, see s 393.
5 In this context this refers to removing auditors before the expiration of their term of office.
6 In this context this refers to appointing as auditor a person other than a retiring auditor.
7 Section 391(1).
8 Section 391A(1).
9 Whether the auditors have been removed, replaced or have resigned.
10 That is, connected with their ceasing to hold office.

say so[11]. If the statement does set out relevant circumstances the company must send a copy to everyone entitled to receive the accounts[12]. If auditors are being removed or replaced a general meeting will necessarily be held but if auditors resign and state that there are relevant circumstances they may requisition a general meeting[13]. Prior to any such meeting the auditors may require the company to circulate a statement[14]. Auditors due to be replaced will have the right to attend and speak at the meeting by virtue of still being auditors until they are replaced[15]. This right is specifically extended to auditors who have been removed[16], or who have resigned[17] notwithstanding that they are no longer in office.

LIABILITY OF AUDITORS FOR NEGLIGENCE[18]

The standard of care and skill auditors must exhibit in carrying out their tasks is that of the ordinary reasonable auditor[19]. The most famous statement about what that standard entails is that of Lopes LJ that an auditor 'is a watchdog but not a bloodhound'[20]. In other words, auditors are entitled to trust the officers and employees of the company they are auditing and to rely on the figures presented to them. If, however, they have reason to be suspicious of any information presented they should make personal inquiries or checks[1]. In view of the professional qualifications now required, and the increased rights to inspect records and demand information and explanations, it may be doubted whether a standard based on nineteenth century case law is still appropriate. There is increasing support for the view that auditors should take on a more active role[2]. In a case involving auditors, although not in relation to the annual accounts, Lord Denning said that an auditor must approach his task 'with an inquiring mind—not suspicious of dishonesty, I agree—but suspecting that somone may have made a mistake somewhere and that a check must be made to ensure there has been none'[3].

---

11 Section 394(1). Any resignation by auditors is ineffective unless accompanied by a s 394 notice: s 392(1).
12 Section 394(3). The company may instead apply to the court for a direction that the statement need not be sent out on the grounds that it secures needless publicity for defamatory matter: s 394(6).
13 Section 392A(2).
14 Where auditors are being removed or replaced: s 391A(3)–(6); where auditors are resigning: s 392A(3)–(7).
15 Section 390.
16 Section 391(4).
17 Section 392A(8).
18 In November 1983, the ICAEW issued a valuable guidance note on 'Professional Liability of Accountants and Auditors'. See also *Professional Liability: Report of the Study Teams* ('The Likierman Report') published by the Department of Trade and Industry (1989) pp 17–40.
19 *Re London and General Bank (No 2)* [1895] 2 Ch 673 at 682–3, CA. On the duty to comply with SSAPs Woolf J has said, 'While they are not conclusive so that a departure from their terms necessarily involves a breach of the duty of care, . . . they are very strong evidence as to what is the proper standard which should be adopted and unless there is some justification, a departure from this will be regarded as constituting a breach of duty.' *Lloyd Cheyham & Co Ltd v Littlejohn & Co* [1987] BCLC 303 at 313.
20 *Re Kingston Cotton Mill (No 2)* [1896] 2 Ch 279 at 288, CA.
 1 *Re Thomas Gerrard & Son Ltd* [1968] Ch 455, [1967] 2 All ER 525.
 2 Baxt (1970) 33 MLR 413.
 3 *Fomento (Sterling Area) Ltd v Selsdon Fountain Pen Co* [1958] 1 All ER 11 at 23, [1958] 1 WLR 45 at 61, HL.

Although the auditors make their report to the members, they will owe a contractual duty of care to the company itself and this is the most likely way in which a negligent audit may give rise to liability. A typical situation might be where profits have been overstated in audited accounts and as a result tax or dividends have been wrongly paid by the company. If the company then goes into an insolvent liquidation, when the likelihood of such errors being uncovered increases, the liquidator can enforce the company's right of action against the auditors and may recover some recompense on behalf of the creditors. Since 1929 what is now s 310 has prevented auditors limiting or excluding their liability, or being indemnified against liability, by contract with the company[4]. The Likierman Report[5] in 1989 recommended that companies and their auditors should be able to agree a limit on the auditors' potential negligence liability which would then be subject to the test of reasonableness under the Unfair Contract Terms Act 1977[6]. The only relevant provision, however, included in the Companies Act 1989 simply made it clear that it is not contrary to s 310 for companies to effect insurance in respect of their auditors' liability in relation to the company[7]. It will in future be possible for auditing firms to adopt the form of limited liability companies[8]. However, this will not prevent the individuals performing the audit from being personally liable for breach of any duty of care imposed upon them under the law of tort[9].

Since the House of Lords' decision in *Hedley Byrne & Co Ltd v Heller & Partners Ltd*[10] the possibility of a wider duty of care in tort has opened up. Although by statute, the auditors' report is specifically made to the members of the company it does not follow that any loss suffered by the members as a result of negligently audited accounts is recoverable. If the loss suffered by the members is in reality just a reflection of a loss suffered by the company it is not recoverable by individual members in actions against the auditors[11]. If, for example, as a result of negligently audited accounts the company paid too much tax, although the company might well have an action against the auditors, it does not follow that if the value of shares in the company fell as a result, individual shareholders could recover any loss suffered[12].

On the other hand, negligently audited accounts may well be relied on by investors in deciding whether to buy shares in or grant credit to the company. Although any loss suffered by such investors is a purely economic loss the decision in *Hedley Byrne & Co Ltd v Heller & Partners Ltd*[13] recognises

---

4 This would not affect exclusions of liability in relation to non-audit work. See Dugdale and Stanton *Professional Negligence* (2nd edn 1989) pp 443–444.
5 *Professional Liability: Report of the Study Teams*.
6 Unfair Contract Terms Act 1977, s 11.
7 Section 310(3)(a).
8 Companies Act 1989, Sch 11, para 13.
9 For analogous cases involving the personal liability of directors: *Fairline Shipping Corpn v Adamson* [1975] QB 180, [1974] 2 All ER 967; *Thomas Saunders Partnership v Harvey* (1989) Times, 10 May; *Kuwait Asia Bank EC v National Mutual Life Nominees Ltd* [1991] 1 AC 187 at 217F–220E, [1990] 3 All ER 404 at 420b–422f, PC. See also Dugdale and Stanton *Professional Negligence* (2nd edn 1989) Ch 27.
10 [1964] AC 465, [1963] 2 All ER 575, HL. See Baxt (1973) 36 MLR 42.
11 *Caparo Industries plc v Dickman* [1990] 2 AC 605 at 626, [1990] 1 All ER 568 at 580, HL.
12 The principle is similar to one of those behind the rule in *Foss v Harbottle* (1843) 2 Hare 461, that the loss is suffered by the company and it is the company therefore that is the only proper plaintiff in any action.
13 See note 10.

that a duty of care to avoid such losses may be owed where a relationship of sufficient proximity can be established. The problem, in the words of Cardozo CJ in *Ultramares Corpn v Touche*[14] is that 'if liability for negligence exists, a thoughtless slip or blunder, the failure to detect a theft or forgery beneath the cover of deceptive entries, may expose accountants to a liability in an indeterminate amount for an indeterminate time to an indeterminate class'. The House of Lords has recently emphasised in *Caparo Industries plc v Dickman*[15] that in deciding whether auditors owe a duty of care to persons who rely on the published accounts in buying shares the proximity of the relationship is vital and this requires more than just foreseeability of reliance. It must be shown that the auditors knew the accounts or any statement made in connection with them would be communicated to the investor, either as an individual or as a member of an identifiable class, specifically in connection with a particular transaction, or transactions of a particular kind, and that the investor would be very likely to rely on them for the purpose of deciding whether or not to enter that transaction or a transaction of that kind[16]. The mere fact that a company is vulnerable to a takeover and that bidders usually rely on the accounts in deciding to launch a bid is not enough to establish proximity; nor is the fact that the bidder is already a shareholder in the company. It might, however, be different where accounts were audited specifically for the purpose of submission to a potential investor[17].

The directors' report

The requirement for directors to make a report to the members was introduced as a result of the changes in the Companies Act 1928. The principal purpose of the report remains its original one of reviewing the progress of the company's business. It is, however, the changes in the contents of the directors' report since 1967, more than changes in any of the other reports and financial statements, which have reflected the recognition of new interests, besides those of shareholders and creditors, in the activities of companies.

CONTENTS

Information about directors   It was not until 1967 that the directors' report was required to give the names of the directors[18]. In addition, the extent of any directors' interest in shares or debentures of the company or any holding

---

14 174 NE 411 at 450, 255 NY Rep 170 at 179 (1931).
15 [1990] 2 AC 605, [1990] 1 All ER 568, HL.
16 As to whether these factors are more easily shown to be present if in a contested takeover bid under the rules of the City Code on Takeovers and Mergers, after an identified bidder has emerged, express representations are made with a view to influencing the bidder to offer a higher price, see *Morgan Crucible Co plc v Hill Samuel Bank Ltd* [1991] 1 All ER 148, [1991] 2 WLR 655, CA.
17 See the discussion in *JEB Fasteners Ltd v Marks, Bloom & Co (a firm)* [1983] 1 All ER 583, CA. The extent of reliance necessary is similar to that for a misrepresentation inducing a contract. The negligently audited accounts must have been an influential factor leading to the investment but they need not have been the only factor. See also *James McNaughton Papers Group Ltd v Hicks Anderson & Co* [1991] 1 All ER 134, [1991] 2 WLR 641, CA.
18 Section 234(2).

or subsidiary company must be given[19] unless such information is given in the profit and loss account or balance sheet[20]. If during the year the company paid for insurance to cover its directors or auditors in respect of possible liability to the company that must be stated in the directors' report[1].

Information about the company's business   The report must state the principal activities of the company and any subsidiaries including any significant changes in those activities during the year[2]. It must also contain a fair review of the development of the business of the company and its subsidiaries and of their position as at the end of the financial year[3]. The directors' report is also useful as a place where companies can be required to amplify information in their balance sheets but in a manner which allows directors flexibility to reflect their companies' particular circumstances[4]. Thus, the directors must report any significant changes during the year in the fixed assets of any of the companies covered by the report[5]. If the market value of any interests in land held by the company differs substantially from its balance sheet value that must be disclosed if the directors think it is significant enough to require the attention of members and debenture holders being drawn to it[6]. As a result of a requirement in the Fourth Directive[7] the directors' report is now also used to draw attention to important events affecting the company or any of its subsidiaries since the date of the balance sheet[8].

Despite the fact that traditionally the accounts are regarded as reports to investors in the company and future prospects are very important to investors, there has until recently been no legal or regulatory requirements for companies to report any forecast of future prospects. A small step in that direction has now been taken, again as a result of a Fourth Directive requirement[9]. Directors' reports must now include an indication of likely

---

19 Section 234(3) and Sch 7, paras 2, 2A and 2B. For companies listed on The Stock Exchange this information must be brought up to date to a date not more than one month before the notice of meeting at which the accounts are to be presented: Admission of Securities to listing, s 5, ch 2, para 21(h).
20 Schedule 7, para 2(1). Companies listed on The Stock Exchange must also give information of substantial (ie 3%) shareholdings: Admission of Securities to Listing, s 5, ch 2, para 21(i). Many listed companies go further and provide a breakdown of the relative size of shareholdings in the company and the number of shareholders in different categories e g pension funds, insurance companies, bank nominees, individuals etc. For an analysis of such disclosure practices, see *Financial Reporting 1984–85* pp 1–12.
 1 Schedule 7, para 5A.
 2 Section 234(2).
 3 Section 234(1)(a).
 4 Thus disaggregation of turnover was to be stated in the directors' report under the Companies Act 1967, s 17. This now has to be given in notes to the accounts (CA 1985, Sch 4, para 55) but the old rule may still apply to banking and insurance companies: CA 1985, s 255C(5) and Sch 10, para 2. Between 1967 and 1981, directors' reports were also obliged to disclose the amount of exports by the company: Companies Act 1967, s 20. This might have been a useful addition to disaggregation (see The Future of Company Reports (Cmnd 6888) paras 45–47) but in fact was introduced to encourage companies in the fight to reduce the balance of payments deficit. In consequence, no thought went into its drafting. It did not distinguish between exports and re-exports, nor was any information about imports ever required to be disclosed.
 5 Schedule 7, para 1.
 6 Ibid.
 7 EEC Council Directive 78/660, art 46.2(a).
 8 Schedule 7, para 6(a).
 9 EEC Council Directive 78/660, art 46.2(b) and (c).

future business developments[10] and of any research and development activities of the company and its subsidiaries[11]. Expenditure on research and development is of interest to shareholders not least because it represents an application of money which would otherwise generally be available to them[12]. This can be regarded, therefore, as complementary to the information directors' reports have always had to contain about the amount recommended as dividend and the amount proposed to be carried to reserves[13].

Information about employment Expenditure on research and development is also of interest to employees since such expenditure is likely to play a large part in maintaining the competitiveness of the company and hence the future employment prospects it offers. The first requirement to report information specifically related to employment was a requirement introduced in 1967 to show the average number of employees and their aggregate remuneration[14]. Then in 1974, the Health and Safety at Work Act[15] provided for the Secretary of State to make regulations for the disclosure of the company's arrangements for securing the health, safety and welfare at work of employees and for protecting other persons against risk to health and safety arising out of or in connection with the activities at work of those employees. No regulations have yet been made but this is an example of how disclosure can be used to back up and indirectly enforce observance of existing regulations. There is, after all, a good deal of legislation governing health and safety at work and the law provides for liability for injury arising from negligently produced goods or negligent production processes. But if the board of directors, in drafting their report, were obliged to consider the company's safety record and perhaps disclose the number of industrial accidents, days lost through such accidents, and successful prosecutions for breaches of health and safety legislation it might result in companies giving more attention to health and safety matters. The exercise would not be expensive since the information will already be available to companies. It is sometimes suggested that information of this sort, not directly related to the financial performance of the company, will not be read by anyone but it is hard to imagine trade unions, consumers' organisations and an army of investigative journalists ignoring it.

The belief that compelling directors to report on a matter may concentrate their minds on it is behind a requirement, introduced in 1980, for directors' reports in companies with over 250 employees to contain a statement of the

10 Schedule 7, para 6(b) and (c).
11 Ibid.
12 It has been suggested that companies should be required to disclose actual expenditure on research and development. It is envisaged that disclosure would encourage such expenditure and help to counteract any tendency of management to concentrate on short-term profitability. See D W Budworth *Rewinding the Mainspring* (1987). For an analysis of present disclosure practices, see *Financial Reporting 1987–88* pp 125–138. SSAP 13 dealing with accounting for research and development was revised in 1989.
13 Section 234(1)(b).
14 Companies Act 1967, s 18. This now has to be given in notes to the accounts (CA 1985, Sch 4, para 56) but the old rule may still apply to banking and insurance companies: CA 1985, s 255C(5) and Sch 10, para 3.
15 Health and Safety at Work Act 1974, s 79 adding what is now CA 1985, Sch 7, Pt IV.

companies' policy about employment of disabled persons[16]. The statement must deal with the company's policy on recruitment of disabled persons, employment and retraining for employees who become disabled and generally with the training, career development and promotion of disabled persons employed by the company.

The most recent addition to the statutory contents of the directors' report is the one that most clearly reflects the changing interests in companies' activities. Where a company has over 250 employees, the directors' report must now contain a statement describing the action taken during the year to promote employee involvement[17]. Specifically the statement must deal with arrangements for providing relevant information to employees, for consulting employees or their representatives on matters likely to affect their interests, for encouraging involvement of employees in the company's performance through an employees' share scheme or by some other means, and for achieving a common awareness on the part of all employees of the financial and economic factors affecting the performance of the company.

Charitable and political donations Provided the payment is intra vires[18] the directors of companies may use the companies' assets to make charitable or political donations without reference to the shareholders. Until 1967, there was no requirement even to inform shareholders about such payments[19]. In that year a provision was introduced whereby if such payments exceeded a certain annual sum, this had to be reported in the directors' report. Currently donations must be disclosed if the aggregate amount exceeds £200 per annum. The purpose of the payment must be stated and in the case of payments for political purposes the recipient must be identified[20].

Particulars of acquisition of a company's own shares As a result of a requirement in the Fourth Directive[1], directors' reports must now include particulars of any acquisition by the company of its own shares, whether through purchase, gift, forfeiture or surrender[2]. In addition, particulars

---

16 Schedule 7, Pt III. The government had announced that it did not intend to introduce legislation requiring the inclusion of detailed employment information in company accounts (Company Accounting and Disclosure (Cmnd 7654) p 5 para 2). It was persuaded to include this requirement for a more general statement, however, by the widespread support for it that emerged in the House of Commons during the Manpower Services Commission's review of the quota system for the employment of disabled people under the Disabled Persons (Employment) Act 1944.
17 Schedule 7, Pt V introduced by the Employment Act 1982, s 1.
18 If the payment is reasonably incidental to the company's business then the company will have an implied power to make it. If it is not the company will need an express power coupled with an independent objects clause and trust that if challenged the court will not rule it incapable of being an independent object. See *Simmonds v Heffer* [1983] BCLC 298 and *Evans v Brunner, Mond & Co Ltd* [1921] 1 Ch 359.
19 Proposals are from time to time introduced into Parliament for companies to be obliged to set up political funds which shareholders could contract out of, analogous to the position governing trade unions. See the debate on the clause proposed to the Companies Bill 1978: HC Official Report, SC F, 15 February 1979, cols 642–689. The debate identified many company law difficulties in making such a clause operate fairly and effectively which had been taken into account when the clause was proposed again to the Companies Bill 1980: see 980 HC Official Report (5th series) cols 58–64.
20 Schedule 7, paras 3–5.
1 EEC Council Directive 78/660, art 46.2(d).
2 Schedule 7, para 7(a).

must be given if the company acquires a beneficial interest in, or a lien or other charge on, its own shares[3]. In the case of a purchase of shares, the particulars must include the aggregate amount of the consideration paid by the company and the reasons for the purchase[4].

AUDITING OF THE DIRECTORS' REPORT

In contrast to the profit and loss account, the balance sheet and the notes attached to those documents, the directors' report is not audited. Where the report consists of interpretation of or commentary in narrative form on the activities of the company, auditing is not necessary, nor would it be practicable. But increasingly the directors' report is required to include factual information and auditing would help to ensure not only the accuracy of the information but establish uniform methods of presentation that would enable comparisons to be made between different companies. A step has been taken in this direction as a result of a requirement in the Fourth Directive[5]. Now the auditors must at least check whether information given in the directors' report relating to the financial year in question is consistent with that given elsewhere in the company's accounts[6].

SHOULD ALL COMPANIES BE SUBJECT TO THE SAME DISCLOSURE REQUIREMENTS?

As the amount of information companies are required to disclose increases, the question is raised as to whether all companies need be subject to the same obligations. There are four levels at which companies might be granted exemption in relation to disclosure requirements. First, at the level of preparation of the information i e what accounting records must be kept and what information must be included in the annual accounts. The second level represents the question whether or not the accounts should be audited. The third level is whether all companies should be subject to the same requirements with regard to disclosure to the shareholders and the fourth level, whether all companies should be subject to the same obligations to publish their accounts via registration at Companies House.

Historical developments

These questions are not new. The first of the present statutory requirements regarding the accounts was the requirement in the Companies Act 1900 for auditors to be appointed who had to sign a balance sheet which by implication was to be placed before the members[7]. The Companies Act 1907 extended this to require registration of the balance sheet but the same Act introduced the private company, the main advantage of which was that it was exempted from the requirement to register its balance sheet and could

---

3　Schedule 7, para 7(b) and (c).
4　Schedule 7, para 8(a).
5　EEC Council Directive 78/660, art 51.
6　Section 235(3).
7　Companies Act 1900, ss 34–43.

thus keep its accounts secret[8]. Private companies were also exempted from the requirement to register the directors' report when this was introduced in 1928. By the same Act, shareholders in public companies had to be sent copies of the balance sheet, and auditors' report, and the directors' report, free of charge, whereas shareholders in private companies remained only entitled to ask for a copy on payment of the company's charges[9].

In 1947, when the profit and loss account was first required to be registered, the advantages flowing from disclosure led to private companies losing their exemptions[10] and thus becoming liable to produce, send to shareholders and register all the documents comprised in the modern accounts on the same basis as public companies[11]. At the same time the necessity for disclosure was felt less strongly in relation to 'the small family business incorporated as a company'. This, coupled with the fact that partnerships, with which such companies would regularly be competing, need not publish accounts[12], led to a category of 'exempt private company' being introduced which was exempted from the obligation to register the documents comprised in the accounts[13]. The complexities associated with the definition of the status of exempt private company led in turn to its abolition in 1967 when unlimited liability companies alone were left without the obligation to register and thus publicly disclose their accounts[14].

Content, audit and registration requirements: small and medium-sized companies

After 1967, both public and private limited companies were therefore subject to the same disclosure requirements. But the impression that this was the culmination of an inexorable progression towards subjecting all companies to the same disclosure requirements can be misleading. For the 1967 Companies Act also began a process of differentiating the disclosure requirements according to the size of the company. Thus certain requirements applied only to companies with a turnover exceeding £50,000. That process of differentiating company accounts at the level of content has been taken further with, for example, certain requirements as to the directors' report being applicable only to companies with more than 250 employees. The real significance of the changes in 1967 is that they represented a switch in emphasis from differentiating disclosure obligations according to the legal classification of the company to one based more on the size of the company.

The differentiation introduced in 1967 was at the level of content. The debate whether differentiation should also be made at the levels of audit, disclosure to shareholders and registration continued, however, and was brought into sharp focus by provisions in the Fourth Directive allowing member states to grant various exemptions at the levels of content[15], audit[16]

8 Companies Act 1907, s 21.
9 Companies Act 1928, ss 39(6)(e) and 41.
10 Report of the Committee on Company Law Amendment (Cmd 6659) para 50.
11 Companies Act 1947, s 54(1).
12 Report of the Committee on Company Law Amendment (Cmd 6659) para 51.
13 Companies Act 1947, s 54(1).
14 Report of the Company Law Committee (Cmnd 1749) paras 55–63.
15 EEC Council Directive 78/660, arts 11, 27, 44, 45 and 46.
16 Ibid, art 51(2). This is only available to small companies.

and registration[17] to companies classified as small or medium-sized[18]. In the end, no advantage was taken of possibilities for exemption at the level of content and the only exemption from auditing requirements that has been introduced is one granted to dormant companies[19]. Exemptions have, however, been introduced from registration requirements[20], differing according to whether the company is classified as small or medium-sized. Certain companies, however, are ineligible for the exemptions: public companies, banking or insurance companies, companies which are authorised persons under the Financial Services Act 1986 and any company in a group which includes an ineligible company[1].

A small company is defined as one which fulfils at least two of the following conditions: its turnover does not exceed £2,000,000; its gross assets do not exceed £975,000; its average number of employees does not exceed 50[2]. The modifications to the requirements for registration of accounts for a small company are that it may file an abbreviated balance sheet with many items aggregated together[3], it need not file a profit and loss account[4] or directors' report[5] at all, and it is exempt from most of the requirements as to notes to the accounts[6].

The exemptions for medium-sized companies are, in comparison, relatively few. A medium-sized company is one which fulfils at least two of the following conditions: its turnover does not exceed £8,000,000; its gross assets do not exceed £3,900,000; its average number of employees does not exceed 250[7]. The exemptions permitted for a medium-sized company are that it may file a modified profit and loss account in which certain items are aggregated[8] and that it need not disclose disaggregated figures for turnover[9].

Disclosure to shareholders: summary financial statements

The Companies Act 1989 introduced two quite different exemptions at the level of disclosure to shareholders. First, the shareholders in private companies, although they must continue to be sent full audited accounts, may by unanimous elective resolution dispense with the requirement that the

17 Ibid, art 47(2)(3).
18 Under the Seventh Directive small and medium-sized groups may be exempted from preparing group accounts: EEC Council Directive 83/349, art 6. This has been implemented in the UK: ss 248, 249.
19 Section 250. See, however, the Department of Trade and Industry consultative document, Accounting and Audit Requirements of Small Firms (June 1985), particularly Section 3. See also the Department of Trade and Industry consultative document on The Delivery of Annual Accounts and Returns to the Registrar of Companies (1986) pp 28–29.
20 Section 246(1).
 1 Section 246(3) and (4).
 2 Section 247(3). Increases in the turnover and gross assets figures were made by SI 1986/1865 in line with EEC Council Directive 84/569. OJ 1984 L 314/28. The thresholds in the Fourth Directive are further increased by EEC Council Directive 90/604. OJ 1990 L 317/57.
 3 Schedule 8, para 1.
 4 Schedule 8, para 2.
 5 Schedule 8, para 4.
 6 Schedule 8, paras 3.
 7 See note 1.
 8 Schedule 8, para 5.
 9 Schedule 8, para 6.

accounts be presented to a general meeting[10]. Secondly, companies listed on The Stock Exchange may send shareholders a summary financial statement instead of the full report and accounts[11], provided certain conditions are satisfied[12]. Listed companies which wish to take advantage of this possibility must ascertain from each of their shareholders whether they wish to receive full accounts before sending them only a summary financial statement[13]. If shareholders were asked to opt for either full accounts or a summary financial statement the likelihood is that the majority would not opt for either—in a few cases by deliberate choice but in most cases through inertia. The legislation, however, does not go that far. It does though entitle companies to assume that shareholders who fail to respond are content to receive the summary financial statement[14]. The consultation that invites shareholders to express a preference must therefore warn them that, unless the company is notified, only a summary financial statement will be sent in future and that this has important consequences. In order that shareholders can see what the choice involves a full set of accounts and report together with a summary financial statement for the same period must be enclosed and a reply paid card must be included on which shareholders can indicate that they wish to receive full accounts for the next financial year and/or succeeding years[15]. A shareholder is entitled at any time to request a full set of report and accounts free of charge and whenever a summary financial statement is sent to a shareholder it must be accompanied by a statement to this effect and a reply paid card must be enclosed on which the shareholder can request a full set of accounts for the current financial year and/or future years[16].

The form and content of a summary financial statement is laid down by regulations[17]. These represent the minimum contents and companies are free to include more information subject to the overriding requirement that all the information is derived from the company's annual accounts and directors' report[18]. Certain statements are also required by statute including one by the auditors as to whether the summary financial statement is consistent with the full accounts and report and complies with the legislative requirements[19]. Companies are free to issue summary financial statements as part of a more wide ranging document which can therefore include information not derived from the annual accounts and directors' report, but it must be clear which part is the summary financial statement and which is not.

The main pressure for the introduction of summary financial statements

---

10 Section 252. As to the right of any member or auditor to require that the accounts and reports be presented to a general meeting, see s 253.
11 Section 251.
12 A company does not need to have authority in its memorandum or articles to send out a summary financial statement but it cannot do so if there is a prohibition or if there is a requirement that full accounts and report be sent to members: Companies (Summary Financial Statement) Regulations 1990, SI 1990/515, reg 4.
13 Ibid, reg 5(a).
14 Ibid, reg 6(1)(b).
15 Ibid, reg 6(3).
16 Section 251(2) and Companies (Summary Financial Statement) Regulations 1990, SI 1990/515 reg 5(g).
17 Ibid, regs 5, 7 and Sch 1.
18 Section 251(3).
19 Section 251(4).

came from companies, particularly recently privatised ones, which have a very large number of small shareholders and for which it may represent a cost saving. However, summary financial statements may also give an opportunity to present information in a way which is more readily understood and more meaningful to the majority of shareholders[20]. The restriction to listed companies is because the inequality of information that arises if some shareholders receive full accounts and others receive a summary matters far less where there is an active market in the shares. The information contained in a company's report and accounts is normally assimilated by the market and reflected in the share price very quickly so that shareholders are unlikely to be prejudiced if they choose to receive only the summary financial statement.

Future developments

The classification of private companies into small and medium-sized and the introduction of summary financial statements for listed companies is a recognition that companies cannot simply be classified as public and private, limited and unlimited as the Companies Acts have tended to do in the past. Companies of different sizes raise different problems requiring different solutions. The developments in the 1980s in relation to disclosure recognise this and have provided a framework for possible further changes.

If statutory obligations are introduced to produce financial statements covering the source and application of funds and value added, it may well be appropriate to apply them, initially at first, to large or medium-sized companies. The largest companies could also more easily accommodate developments in social responsibility reporting, allowing the gradual introduction of further disclosure requirements not related to purely financial matters. Already additional disclosure obligations relating to employment apply to companies with more than 250 employees. These could well be extended, for example, to require information about sex discrimination, equal pay or the employment of minority racial groups, and ultimately to require such companies to circulate a special annual report to all employees.

---

20 It is a comparable development in many ways to the use of mini prospectuses. Both developments reflect disclosure requirements being tailored to the needs of the user.

CHAPTER 29

Public regulation by investigation and inspection of companies

The Department of Trade and Industry has wide powers of investigation into the affairs of a company, its membership and dealings in its securities. In addition it has powers to inspect a company's books and papers[1]. On paper, these are a useful means of curbing misfeasance and oppression. In practice they have not proved so effective.

The original provisions for examination of the affairs of the company by inspectors appeared in ss 48–50 of the Joint Stock Companies Act 1856 and were based on equivalent provisions in the New York Business Corporation Act[2]. These provided that shareholders might apply to the Board of Trade to have their affairs officially inspected at their own expense. They were later amended by the 1947 and 1948 legislation to include an obligation on the Board of Trade to appoint where there was a special resolution of the company or a court order to that effect and additional powers of appointment. Henceforth, subject to what is said below, the cost of investigation was to fall on public funds. The judicial interpretation of the inspectors' role was that it was essentially fact-finding[3]. Subsequent cases have recognised that the proceedings are administrative but have established an obligation of fairness[4] which we shall examine later. The wording of the grounds for appointment and powers of an inspector has changed, particularly as a result of recent legislation. To these has been added the power to investigate ownership of shares and certain dealings in shares and debentures. The Companies Act 1967 extended the power to call for books and papers to companies generally. The Companies Act 1981 extended the powers of inspectors and gave them access to directors' private bank accounts in certain cases. The present law is now contained in Pt XIV of CA 1985.

---

1 See Department of Trade Handbook of the Companies Inspection System 1990; also R D Fraser (1971) 34 MLR 260; R Instone [1978] JBL 121; J Hull (1979) NLJ 825; G Nash (1965) 38 ALJ 111 and (1967) 8 UW Aust L Rev 143; J S Lockhart (1971) 45 ALJ 504 and the commentaries thereon; T. Hadden *The Control of Company Fraud* (1968) (PEP); D Chaikin (1982) 3 Co Law 115; L H Leigh *The Control of Commercial Fraud* (1982) chapter 11, p 165 ff. For a recent critique see Third Report of the House of Commons Trade and Industry Committee: 1989–90 Session and the Government's Reponse, *Company Investigations* Cm 1149 (1990).
2 See B C Hunt *The Development of the Business Corporation in England 1800–1867* (1936) p 135 Cf Instone, op cit, p 121 and see B Rider and H L Ffrench *The Regulation of Insider Trading* (1979) pp 184–190.
3 *Re Grosvenor and West End Rly Terminus Hotel Co Ltd* (1897) 76 LT 337, CA.
4 *Re Pergamon Press Ltd* [1971] Ch 388, CA; *Maxwell v Department of Trade and Industry* [1974] QB 523, CA. See RR Pennington 'Investigations under the Companies Acts and the Pergamon Affair' (1974) 118 Sol Jo 507. Cf however *Testro Bros Pty v Tait* (1963) 109 CLR 353. Noted by R A Sundberg (1964) 4 MULR 413. See also J B Kluwer and R H Woellner *Powers of Investigation in Revenue, Companies and Trade Practices Law* (1983) pp 147, 181.

Section 177 of the Financial Services Act 1986 gave the Secretary of State power to appoint inspectors to investigate suspected insider dealing. The Companies Act 1989 revised and generally extended the powers to order investigations and to obtain information. This was done by textual amendment of the earlier legislation.

We shall now deal with the law and practice under the Pt XIV procedures.

INVESTIGATIONS INTO THE AFFAIRS OF A COMPANY

Sections 431(1) and (2) and 432(2) specify grounds on which the Secretary of State *may* appoint an inspector or inspectors. Section 432(1) specifies grounds on which he *must* appoint.

The grounds where the Secretary of State *may* appoint are:

(a)   in the case of a company having a share capital, on the application either of not less than 200 members or of members holding not less than one-tenth of the shares issued;

(b)   in the case of a company not having a share capital, on the application of not less than one-fifth in number of the persons on the company's register of members;

(c)   in any case, on the application of the company;

(d)   if it appears that the company's affairs are being or have been conducted with intent to defraud its creditors or the creditors of any other person or otherwise for a fraudulent or unlawful purpose or in a manner which is unfairly prejudicial to some part of its members;

(e)   that any actual or proposed act or omission of the company (including an act or omission on its behalf) is or would be so prejudicial, or that it was formed for any fraudulent or unlawful purpose;

(f)   if it appears that persons concerned with its formation or the management of its affairs have in connection therewith been guilty of fraud, misfeasance or other misconduct towards it or towards its members; or

(g)   if it appears that its members have not been given all the information with respect to its affairs which they might reasonably expect.

Where inspectors are appointed under (d)–(g) they may be appointed on terms that any report they make is not for publication (s 432(2A)). This departs from the normal practice under s 437(3) which provides for the availability and publication of inspectors' reports.

Section 431(3) provides that the application in the case of (a), (b) and (c) shall be supported by such evidence as the Secretary of State requires for showing good reason for the investigation. Presumably this means a prima facie case. It may be an onerous obligation for a minority shareholder who may not have access to the necessary evidence. On the other hand, it is necessary in order to protect the company from the adverse publicity and expense involved. Section 431(4) also provides that the Secretary of State may require the applicant to give security of an amount not exceeding £5,000 or such other sum as the Secretary of State may specify by order for payment of the cost of the investigation.

The power conferred in respect of (d), (e), (f) and (g) may be exercised even where the company is already being wound up voluntarily[5].

The only ground under s 432(1) where the Department *must* now appoint inspectors is where the court orders it[6].

It was held by the Court of Appeal in *Norwest Holst Ltd v Secretary of State for Trade*[7] that the Secretary of State cannot be ordered to give reasons why he has ordered an investigation under s 432(2) and the court will not interfere in the absence of bad faith or improper purpose[8]. The proceedings were struck out as frivolous, vexatious and an abuse of the process of the court.

The conduct of the investigation

In *Re Pergamon Press Ltd*[9] and *Maxwell v Department of Trade and Industry*[10] the Court of Appeal was called upon to consider how company investigations should be conducted. It held that the proceedings were administrative, not judicial, and stopped short of requiring a full compliance with the rules of natural justice. However in view of the wide repercussions of their report, the inspectors must act fairly 'in that if they were disposed to condemn or criticise anyone in a report they must first give him a fair opportunity to correct or contradict the evidence against him'. 'Inspectors do not have to put all the evidence against him to the person concerned in precise detail; it suffices to indicate the substance of the evidence on which the criticism would be based.' The House of Lords refused leave to appeal in the second case. Opinions differ strongly as to the wisdom of requiring a legal duty to act fairly in proceedings which are neither judicial nor quasi-judicial. Some criticise the vagueness of the duty, while others see this very vagueness as a positive virtue. Some regard it as an unnecessary impediment to getting at the truth while others regard it as a necessary safeguard against star chamber practices. A useful discussion of the duty to act fairly took place at an Australian Law Conference in 1971. Mr Justice Mason said[11]:

Now, the duty to act fairly is one which accomodates itself to the particular situation. It does not without more carry an obligation to imitate judicial procedures—that is clear enough. Indeed, it seems that in many cases it will be sufficient if the party who may be affected by the investigation and any decision subsequently reached, is given an opportunity to answer to explain his position. That, certainly, in many cases will be sufficient. But in other cases more may be required. Thus, it is evident that even if there is a legal duty to act fairly imposed upon the inspectors, they are under no obligation to afford the rights that are customarily involved in court hearings.

The procedure by way of enquiry and report is quite different from the traditional common law adversary system. It does not involve the formulation of a case against a party, the right of cross-examination by the party of those witnesses who speak

---

5 Section 432(3).
6 Formerly this also included a special resolution by the company and mandamus lay on the Department once it had been passed: *R v Board of Trade, ex p St Martins Preserving Co Ltd* [1965] 1 QB 603.
7 [1978] Ch 201. Noted [1977] JBL 349, [1978] JBL 179.
8 See DT Handbook.
9 [1971] Ch 388.
10 [1974] QB 523.
11 See [1971] 45 ALJ 513 at 520.

against him, the right to examine evidence presented against him, or the right to present evidence in support of his own case. Nor does it involve a right to address. In these respects it lacks elements which have been regarded as essential to the rights of the party who is involved in adversary litigation. The absence of these rights is the more significant when it is recalled that an aggrieved party has no right of appeal against adverse reflections made upon him in an inspector's report, and that the report may well attract very considerable publicity. It is these considerations that led to criticism of company investigations by lawyers. This criticism proceeds, in part at least, from a conviction that any substantial departure from established procedures in a court hearing may involve an element of injustice to individuals. It views with suspicion any such departure and regards it as an intrusion into the basic rights of the individual. In truth, those rights are in-built in the adversary system, which is the usual means of trying issues between opposing parties in a court hearing. But the adversary system is singularly inappropriate when the task is not that of deciding issues between contending parties but is one of investigating a matter of public interest, the misconduct of individuals being an aspect incidental and subordinate to the general investigation. It has always been recognised that the adoption of the inquiry procedure is essential to the investigation of complicated matters, where the material facts are not known and can only be established by investigation. Company investigations are of this kind. The traditional procedure involving public and private examinations in bankruptcy and in company windings up and the reports of official receivers and liquidators show that there is simply no practical alternative to company investigations by inquiry and report.

Sir Richard Eggleston[11], another distinguished Australian judge, who was Chairman of a Company Law Reform Committee, said that the duty to act fairly in proceedings which were not even quasi-judicial was a novel idea and continued:

If I may say so again with the greatest respect, a very impractical one, because when you are conducting one of these investigations, you don't know when you are getting evidence from the witnesses whether anybody has done anything wrong or whether it is just bad luck and it may not be until you have examined the fifty-fourth witness that you suddenly get the information which enables you to discover that the second, third or fourth witness has told you a pack of lies and that, in fact, he is the man who has stolen all the company's funds.

Of course, I am not suggesting that a fair investigator would not, in those circumstances, seek to recall the man whom he examined second, third or fourth. Of course, he would, but he is under a duty to, and more importantly, if he does not, what is the legal remedy for the breach of this legal duty to act fairly, because the first time that the second, third or fourth witness is going to find out that he has not been given an opportunity to repel the criticism is when the report is published, and the only consequence that is going to flow . . . is that the only real damage that is going to be done is the publication of the report. And so, I think that one has to analyse a little more closely than perhaps has been done hitherto to see what kind of remedy you can have for a breach of a duty to act fairly in a proceeding which is not a quasi-judicial proceeding.

His Committee took the view that the duty to act fairly was a moral not a legal duty.

Except for the duty to act fairly the inspectors are not subject to any set rules or procedure[12]. However, it was held in *Re Gaumont-British Picture Corpn Ltd*[13] in 1940 that an inspector should not hold an inquiry in public but

---

12 But see the DT Handbook.
13 [1940] Ch 506.

should only admit persons whose presence was reasonably necessary to enable him to carry out his duty under the statutes.

Formerly, an inspector could only examine on oath a person other than an agent or officer of the company if he obtained a court order under s 167(4) of the Companies Act 1948. Thus The Stock Exchange and City Takeover Panel would only give evidence under a court order[14]. Indeed the latter somewhat proudly declaimed the fact in its rather patronising Notes for Inspectors. Now, however, s 434 gives the inspector power to investigate any person or body corporate whom the inspector considers is in possession of any information concerning the company and to examine them under oath. Section 435 also gives the inspector access to directors' private bank accounts in certain circumstances[15]. This applies to directors and former directors of the company or an associated company and requires him to produce all documents in his possession relating to a bank account at home or abroad. However, the power is only exercisable where the inspector has reasonable grounds for believing that money has been paid in in respect of any of the following:

(1)   *a failure to disclose directors' emoluments* contrary to Sch 5, paras 24–26; or
(2)   any money which has resulted from or been used in the financing of any transaction, arrangement or agreement:
 (i)   in respect of *substantial contracts* between a company and its directors *not disclosed* contrary to s 232 and Sch 6, Pt I; or
 (ii)   in respect of *outstanding loans*, quasi-loans and credit transactions between a recognised bank and its directors *not disclosed* contrary to s 234 and Sch 6, Pt III or not recorded in the register of transactions contrary to s 343; or
(3)   any money connected in any way with any act or omission or series of acts or omissions, which constituted misconduct (whether fraudulent or not) towards the company or associated company or its members[16].

Although the power is wide it is subject to some limitations[16]. First, there is the 'reasonable ground' requirement which can lead to judicial review. Secondly, the inspector needs to know and specify the particular account. Thirdly, the inspector is limited by the bank's duty of secrecy to its customers and the reluctance of the court to exercise its discretion to allow inspection of bank records under the Bankers' Books Evidence Act 1879 although to some extent this is now qualified by the 1989 amendments to s 435 and the Secretary of State's powers under s 452(3). Fourthly, there are practical problems where the director uses a nominee, particularly if the bank account is kept overseas.

Section 433 empowers inspectors to investigate the officers of any subsidiary or holding company of the company under investigation. The power extends to former relationships. Where the inspector wishes to examine a pre-acquisition matter it may be necessary to obtain an express separate appointment over the related company[17].

Normally the Secretary of State expects investigations to be concluded

---

14   See Chaikin, op cit, p 116.
15   See Chaikin, op cit, p 115.
16   See Chaikin, op cit.
17   DT Handbook.

within a year[18]. In practice, a lawyer and an accountant are jointly appointed. The information relating to a body investigated must not be disclosed, without the previous consent in writing of that body, except to a competent authority unless publication or disclosure is required for certain further proceedings (s 449).

Results of an investigation

There are five main possible consequences of an inspector's report which makes findings of misconduct. These are:

(1)   the Secretary of State may bring civil proceedings in the name of the company under s 438 where it appears to be in the public interest to do so;

(2)   the Secretary of State may bring proceedings under s 8 of the Company Directors Disqualification Act 1986 for disqualification of a director where it is considered expedient in the public interest that such an order should be made;

(3)   the Department of Trade and Industry or another competent authority may institute criminal proceedings;

(4)   the Secretary of State may bring a petition to wind up the company; or

(5)   the Secretary of State may bring a petition under s 460 for conduct unfairly prejudicial to the members.

The Secretary of State thus has wide powers. Unfortunately, he does not regularly exercise them for reasons which we shall explore later.

INVESTIGATIONS INTO MEMBERSHIP

Section 442 gives the Secretary of State power to appoint inspectors to investigate the true ownership and control of a company. Section 444 gives power to require information as to persons interested in shares or debentures and s 445 gives the power to impose restrictions on shares or debentures.

Section 442(1) is widely worded. It provides:

Where it appears to the Secretary of State that there is good reason to do so, he may appoint one or more competent inspectors to investigate and report on the membership of any company, and otherwise with respect to the company, for the purpose of determining the true persons who are or have been financially interested in the success or failure (real or apparent) of the company or able to control or materially to influence its policy.

The Secretary of State is bound to appoint an inspector where an application is made by one of the minorities referred to in s 431(2)(a) and (b) but the restrictions which there apply do not apply to s 442(1). The Secretary of State under s 442(3)(a) and (b) may refuse to appoint if satisfied that the application is vexatious or unreasonable. He may require the applicants to give security for costs (s 442(3B)). In addition, the Secretary of State under s 442(1) may appoint where it appears that there is good reason to do so. He may also make an order under s 444 instead of s 442 (s 442(3c)). The power

---

18 DT Handbook (statement by the Secretary of State).

under s 444 is exercisable without the appointment of inspectors. The power again is wide and non-compliance is an offence.

Section 445, when read with Pt XV, gives the Secretary of State very wide powers to combat any obstruction of his investigations. While the restrictions are in force:

(a) any transfer of those shares, or in the case of unissued shares any transfer of the right to be issued with them and any issue of them, is void;

(b) no voting rights are exercisable in respect of the shares;

(c) no further shares shall be issued in right of the shares or in pursuance of any offer made to the holder;

(d) except in a liquidation, no payment shall be made of any sums due from the company on the shares, whether in respect of capital or otherwise[19].

INVESTIGATIONS INTO DEALINGS

Section 446 gives the Secretary of state power to appoint inspectors to investigate contraventions of ss 323 or 324 or 328(3)–(5), relating to option dealings by directors and their families or disclosure of interests by directors in their own company.

INSPECTIONS OF BOOKS AND PAPERS

Section 447, which was originally introduced in 1967 as a result of the Jenkins Report[20], gives the Secretary of State power to require companies (including overseas companies carrying on business in Great Britain) to produce documents if there is good reason. It enables the Secretary of State to carry out enquiries discreetly including enquiries which would justify a full-scale investigation. In practice, good reason is taken to include grounds for suspicion of fraud, misfeasance, misconduct, minority oppression or failure to give shareholders the information which they might reasonably expect. The strength of evidence required is less than that required for appointment of inspectors[1]. In *R v Secretary of State for Trade, ex p Perestrello*[2] in 1981 it was held that the notice must not be excessively wide or unreasonable and that the officers must act fairly.

Under s 448, the Secretary of State may obtain a warrant for entry and search of premises for which there are reasonable grounds for suspecting that there are documents whose production has been required under Part XIV and which have not been produced in compliance with the requirement. The section was extended by the CA 1989.

Section 452, however, retains solicitor's privilege and bank's confidentiality unless in the case of the latter the customer has been required to

---

19 See generally *Re Lonrho plc* (1987) 3 BCC 265 for a discussion of the court's powers. Cf also *Re F H Lloyd Holdings plc* [1985] PCC 268.
20 (Cmnd 1749) para 218 (1962).
 1 DT Handbook.
 2 [1981] QB 19.

produce documents under ss 434, 443 or 446 or consents or the making of the requirement is authorised by the Secretary of State.

Section 449 restricts the use of the information. It may only be used in connection with proceedings specified in s 449(1)(a) to (m).

Section 450 imposes penalties for destruction or concealment of documents.

Section 447 is an addition to s 721[3], which gives the court power to order production of books where an offence is suspected.

The powers conferred for inspection of books and papers are often used in practice as a preliminary to a full-scale investigation of the affairs of the company.

OTHER LEGISLATION

In addition to the Companies Acts 1985 and 1989, the Financial Services Act 1986, the Insolvency Act 1986 and the Insurance Companies Act 1982 contain provisions dealing with the appointment of inspectors and investigators.

CONCLUSION

The Secretary of State has wide ranging powers. However, recent reforms may be somewhat cosmetic as the relevant section of the Department of Trade and Industry is inadequately staffed and there is pressure to reduce this number[4]. In the past the Department has not made great use of its powers. In the period 1919 to 1947, there were 131 applications for the appointment of inspectors resulting in only 23 appointments[5]. The position between 1948 and 1989–90 is shown on the next pages[6]. The number of appointments is still very small compared with the number of applications. Recently there has been mounting criticism of this apparent inactivity[7]. However, in by far and away the majority of cases the Department has chosen to use the powers under s 447. The Department prefers to use this procedure, since it avoids potential damage to the company which the appointment of inspectors might produce, and may avoid expense and delay. On the other hand, it does not give general power to question officers of the company and its utility depends on the information to be found in the company's records[8]. The Companies Act 1989 amendments also signal an intention to make more use of s 444 in these circumstances.

The companies investigation system has become increasingly complex

---

3 See *Re Racal Communications Ltd* [1981] AC 374, HL.
4 Chaikin, op cit, at pp 115, 120.
5 DT Handbook.
6 These statistics are taken from the DT Handbook and the Department's annual reports for companies for 1980 to 1990.
7 See e g *Wallersteiner v Moir (No 2)* [1975] 1 All ER 849, CA and the Memorandum on Department of Trade Inspectors by the Consultative Committee of the Accountancy Bodies 1978. See also the useful article by David Foulkes 'The Supervision of Companies—The Parliamentary Commissioner's Reports' [1974] JBL where he discusses complaints to the Ombudsman. See also the reports cited on p 517.
8 DT Handbook.

with recent reforms and has been the subject of continuing criticism. The Third Report of the House of Commons Trade and Industry Committee in the 1989–90 session made a number of recommendations for reform. First, they recommended that broader public interests than just the duties of directors and the rights of shareholders should be reflected in company law in the way in which it was applied. Secondly, auditors should be obliged to disclose confidential information to the supervisory authorities. Thirdly, obligations should be imposed in the United Kingdom on intermediaries to exercise reasonable care to ensure that they did not facilitate dishonest transactions. Fourthly, the Committee made a number of recommendations with a view to improving the companies investigation system. They favoured the recruitment of more qualified people both to carry out investigations and to support outside inspectors. Outside inspectors should be required to devote at least three quarters of their professional time to the inquiry. Fifthly, the Committee recommended that the Handbook should be updated annually to give more information on the practical conduct of investigations. Sixthly, inspectors should continue to draw conclusions from the evidence they took and make recommendations for action against individuals. Seventhly, the Committee made a number of recommendations to improve the procedure including the introduction of a central clearing house for information regarding malpractice.

The report met with a characteristically complacent response from the Department of Trade and Industry. While the Department accepted responsibility for maintaining what it described as 'a fair level of protection for the individual consumer and investor', it nevertheless thought that there had to be some realism about what any regulatory system could be expected to achieve. It could not prevent all company failures or defalcations. Also it was not the regulators' job to duplicate the private system of remedies. The financial services area was a particularly attractive target for fraud and the objective should be simply to set a framework within which investors can make their own judgments about risk and reward. The Department thought that the Committee had given little consideration to the bulk of the investigatory work of the Department which in the main was carried out by in-house investigators primarily under s 447 of the Companies Act 1985. The Department would continue to look for ways of recruiting appropriate personnel to enable more work to be done in-house. The Government has no plans for further review and updating of the investigations legislation but will consider the question again when further companies legislation is under consideration. Consolidation was a matter for the Law Commission[9].

---

9 See Department of Trade and Industry, *Company Investigations:* Government's response to the Third Report of the House of Commons Trade and Industry Committee: 1989–90 session (Cm 1149 August 1990).

Investigations under the Companies Acts: a statistical summary 1948–1979

1	2	3	4	5	6	7
			Appointments			
Year	Applications	Outside inspectors	Departmental officers			
		Companies Act 1948: ss 164, 165 and 172	Companies Act 1948: ss 164, 165 and 172	s 334	Companies Act 1967: s 109	s 32
1948	49	2(2)	–(–)	–		
9	64	2(2)	3(7)	–		
1950	87	6(6)	2(2)	2		
1	72	3(3)	–(–)	–		
2	79	–(–)	1(1)	–		
3	97	3(3)	–(–)	2		
4	88	1(2)	1(1)	7		
5	74	–(–)	2(2)	8		
6	74	1(2)	5(4)	3		
7	74	2(2)	–(–)	1		
8	72	1(1)	2(2)	2		
9	73	2(2)	1(1)	1		
1960	74	2(13)	1(1)	1		
1	81	2(2)	1(3)	–		
2	88	2(9)	2(2)	–		
3	91	–(–)	3(7)	–		
4	122	5(9)	4(5)	–		
5	149	2(3)	1(1)	–		
6	160	5(9)	1(5)	5		
7	246	1(12)	4(6)	4	27	–
8	346	–(–)	14(16)	–	47	–
9	403	3(8)	15(18)	–	62	–
1970	408	4(6)	7(9)	–	61	–
1	442	5(16)	4(8)	–	103	–
2	403	1(3)	3(3)	–	109	–
3	408	6(8)	2(2)	–	81	1
4	438	8(17)	6(9)	–	130	–
5	456	7(14)	5(5)	6	150	–
6	447	2(6)	3(4)	14	130	–
7	374	9(11)	2(4)	9	89	–
8	343	1(8)	4(4)	20	69	1
9	263	1(1)	2(3)	1	74	–

The numbers in columns 3 and 4 are the totals of investigations and (in brackets) of individual companies. Some of the latter refer to investigations started in earlier years.
Source: DT Handbook of the Companies Inspection System 1985.

Company investigations: 1980–1990

	1980	1981	1982	1983	1984	1984–85	1985	1985–86	1986	1986–87	1987–88	1988–89	1989–90
Applications:													
Outstanding at end of previous year	164	188	165	117	89	77	106	63	74	79	90	55	129
Received	395	412	408	374	449	474	528	517	496	495	441	640	6.6
Approved	81	103	91	112	101	132	116	117	138	134	135	151	167
of which under:													
(i) s 164 of the 1948 Act (now s 431, CA 1985)	–	–	–	–	–	–	–	–	–	–	–	–	–
(ii) s 172 of the 1948 Act (now s 432)	2	–	–	3	1	1	1	1	1	1	2	7	5
(iii) s 165 of the 1948 Act (now s 442)	1	2	9	6	1	–	3	4	3	3	–	6	4
(iv) s 334 of the 1948 Act (now s 446)	4	2	3	–	–	–	–	1	1	–	–	–	1
(v) s 109 of the 1967 Act (now s 447)	74	98	79	103	99	130	111	111	133	130	133	138	157
(vi) s 36 of the Insurance Companies Act	–	1	–	–	–	1	1	–	–	–	–	–	–
Not proceeded with or refused	209	332	365	290	331	325	444	384	356	350	341	415	459
Outstanding at end of year	188	165	117	89	106	63	74	79	76	90	55	129	119

Sources: *Companies in 1980, 1981, 1982, 1983, 1986/7–1989/90.*

PART V

Structural problems and change

CHAPTER 30

Structural problems and change—
the issues

Almost all companies start small. Why they are started is arguably a matter
for psychological and sociological rather than legal analysis, why they manage to survive is primarily an economic question—the availability of a local
market, specialism, sometimes the development of a new idea. The small
incorporated business is usually a one man or family concern with many of
the characteristics of the sole trader or partnership. Unlike the public listed
company, it is not peculiarly a capital-raising device but a means of organising production and limiting liability[1]. Although theoretically possessed of
limited liability for its shareholders, in practice as a result of contract this
does not extend to liability to commercial finance providers. As an economic
unit it is vulnerable.

If the company survives and grows, it will usually adopt a group structure
of parent and subsidiary companies with the proprietors holding shares in
the former. This new relationship engenders complications of its own. To
whom does the management of parent and subsidiaries owe duties? Whose
interests should prevail? Can the parent company allow a subsidiary to go to
the wall? What measure of disclosure should be required in relation to the
group? From the point of view of a commercial finance provider, what
security should it take[2]?

Whether or not a company adopts a group structure, problems of organisation tend to increase with size. Communication and co-ordination prove
more difficult as the firm expands and an appropriate management control
system is needed. The basic choice is between a highly centralised pyrami-
dical structure or a decentralised system. Much will depend on the historical
development of the firm, the technology involved and the management
philosophy adopted. The law has little to say on these questions.

Another stage of growth will be where the company considers a flotation
of its shares on The Stock Exchange. The main reasons for doing this are
principally to obtain finance for expansion from the market for investment
capital and to enable the proprietors to realise some of their investment in
the company. This represents a time of dispersal of share ownership, and a
subjection of management to additional legal regulation and the self regulatory controls of City of London institutions. The relationship of legal and
self regulation of flotations is a problematic one.

The company or group may expand further by vertical or horizontal
integration. Vertical integration, as we saw in Chapter 1, is where the two
companies occupy adjacent stages in some vertical chain of production and
distribution. Horizontal integration is where the companies are actual

---

1 H G Manne (1967) 53 Va L Rev 259.
2 J M Landers (1975) 42 U Chi L Rev 589; cf R A Posner's comment (1976) 43 U Chi L Rev
499.

competitors in some relevant market. Conglomerate integration is where the companies are in essentially unrelated fields. The company participates in the market for control by merging with or taking over or being the target of a bid by another company. There are various reasons for expansion—the availability of mass markets, economies of scale in production, marketing and financing, the desire to diversify the companies with strong cash flows, international competition and sometimes managerial ambitions[3]. The first discernible period of growth by merger was in the late nineteenth century, which was a period of rapid technological change, declining profits and growing international competition. After the First World War there was an increase in mergers due to depression and the need to reduce competition and rationalise production. In this period we see the emergence of the High Street banks, the four main railway companies and ICI. In the late 1960s and 1970s, there was a big increase in mergers due to rapid technological change and economic growth followed by recession due to the oil crises. During this latter period, there was increased government intervention to encourage mergers. The benefits or detriments of mergers have been the subject of much debate. Those in favour tend to stress the benefits to consumers, employees and the community by the more efficient reallocation of resources. These benefits will occur with economies of scale in production by greater specialisation in plant, plant scale economies enabling particular plant to operate to optimum size, and marketing economies through a reduction of advertising costs and distribution outlets[4]. On a larger plan, mergers affect allocative efficiency by transferring resources from one industry to another to ensure that the right type and quantity of goods are produced. Growth by merger will be faster. It is easier to buy an established business than to expand an existing one or to diversify—the structure is already there. It is arguably safer to do so since there is an existing track record. The larger unit[5] gives greater market power and access to finance. Those against mergers stress the insufficient competition for control or the detriment from particular mergers[6]. The first arises largely because the stock market is essentially a market for minority parcels of shares and reflects expectations of earnings rather than asset values. The second arises because some mergers have failed due to managerial shortcomings and with others, growth sometimes leads to a contraction in the market which may result in higher prices, inefficiencies and curtailment of choice[7]. There are, however, contradictions in the arguments for and against industrial expansion and this no doubt accounts for the differing government policies over the years[8].

The law had developed three main procedures for dealing with mergers—the takeover bid, amalgamation and reconstruction, although the historical evolution was in reverse order. Takeover bids whereby a bidder can if necessary appeal over the heads of a hostile management are the most common method in practice and are the subject of both legal and self-

---

3 See Edith T Penrose *The Theory of the Growth of the Firm* (1959) chapter VIII; D A Hay and D J Morris *Industrial Economics, Theory and Evidence* (1979) chapter 14.
4 K D George and C Joll *Industrial Organisation* (3rd edn, 1981) p 71 ff.
5 Ibid.
6 See New Zealand Securities Commission *Company Take-overs—A Review of the Law and Practice* (1983) vol 1, p 31.
7 A Singh *Takeovers* (1971); G Meeks *Disappointing Marriage: A Study of the Gains from Merger* (1977).
8 See *George and Joll*, op cit, chapter 14.

regulation of the securities market. An elaborate code of self-regulation and institutional framework has been evolved by the City of London financial bodies, whereas in many other English-speaking countries it is left to a system of legal regulation through a securities commission. Now as a result of the Financial Services Act 1986 there is a system of self-regulation within a statutory framework but still no securities commission. Reconstructions whereby there is a merger of undertakings or businesses rather than companies are the oldest method in English law and still the most common method in Europe. Amalgamation, whereby two companies of approximately equal standing join together to form a third which becomes their holding company, was very common in the inter-war period but is less common today.

The main benefits of legal regulation of mergers are first, to promote confidence in the market, secondly, to promote competition for control and thirdly, by the pricing mechanism to achieve a rational reallocation of resources. The main costs are, first, loss of freedom and flexibility in the market place for some market participants, secondly, the risk of reducing the number of takeovers and thirdly, the administrative costs borne by participants or the community at large[9].

One recent American study found that the transaction costs of making a take-over by tender offer in the USA were on average 13% of the post offer market price of the shares[10] and another study shows how the costs have increased as a result of a recent federal reform[11].

Sometimes a company may wish to reorganise its capital structure—for instance, it may wish to replace loan capital by shares or vice versa. Originally it was necessary to wind up the company, and start again. Later, companies were given the power to reduce their share capital as we saw in Chapter 16. In addition, a procedure which was originally introduced as a means of enabling a company in financial difficulties to enter into a scheme with its creditors was later extended to cover arrangements with shareholders. The resulting provision, now s 425 of CA 1985, is very flexible and is used for a wide variety of purposes. Another structural change which may take place is where the original company has served its purpose or has become undesirable because of fiscal rules. Here, provided the company is not insolvent, it can be put into members' voluntary winding up which gives the members control over the initiation of the proceedings and choice of a liquidator. The ultimate stage of dissolution is the corporate equivalent of death. Winding up by the court is also possible but is rare in the case of a solvent company unless it is the result of a petition to wind up the company on the just and equitable ground. This has been dealt with already as a minority shareholder's remedy in Chapter 27. The whole topic of company insolvency is dealt with later in Part VI.

---

9 New Zealand Securities Commission, op cit.
10 R Smiley (1976) 58 Rev Econ & Stat 22.
11 D R Fischel (1978) 57 Tex L Rev 1.

CHAPTER 31

Small incorporated firms

Most companies start as small businesses although the majority of small businesses do not in fact incorporate. They remain as sole traders or partnerships[1]. However, the extent to which the corporate form is used depends on the sector of industry in which the business operates. As we saw in Chapter 4, in manufacturing industry, according to the research findings of the Bolton Report, over 80% of small firms were incorporated whereas in non-manufacturing firms, only 33% were incorporated and these were dominated by construction and wholesale distribution.

We are not concerned here with the problems of small firms in general but only with the problems which are solved or exacerbated by the use of the corporate form[2]. Small firms are characteristically managed by the people who own them which takes them outside the Berle and Means hypothesis of corporate development. In Marxist terms, the separation of ownership and control is the natural development of capitalism and small businesses represent an anachronism[3]. It is certainly true that small business has declined over the last hundred years and continues to do so at an annual death rate of over 5% despite some assistance from the government. Those who support small business either rest their case largely on it as the source of innovation and capitalist development or on the broader social grounds of the greater contribution of small business to the community at large. It is interesting that small business reveals contradictions in both the Conservative and Labour policies. Conservatives believe in free enterprise and the laws of the market. It is precisely the latter if not the former which are driving many small businesses out of existence. Socialists believe in state capital and the growth of larger, more efficient units yet they are committed to cutting down unemployment. Small firms surveyed by Bolton employed 4.4 million people which was over 30% of the persons employed in the industries surveyed and it was estimated that small business as a whole gave employment to 25% of the total employed population[4]. A more recent statistic shows that they still represent 20% of the gross national product[5]. The classic legal problems of small firms are choice of an appropriate legal structure, financing, coping with government requirements, and providing for continuity in the ownership and control of the business. Looked at from an economic point of view small incorporated firms have common characteristics with sole traders and moderately sized partnerships—they have

---

1 See 'Small Firms—Report of the Committee of Inquiry on Small Firms', Cmnd 4811 (the Bolton Report) p xv.
2 For useful discussions of those problems, see the Bolton Report and M Chesterman *Small Business* (2nd edn, 1982).
3 *Chesterman*, op cit, pp 39, 40.
4 Bolton Report, pp 33 and XIX.
5 The Times, 27 January 1983, p 15. In the USA, the figure is 40%.

relatively few managers who tend to be the largest shareholders; they need to restrict the alienability of a business interest; they lose the benefit of specialisation of function; the proprietors lack a public market for their business interest. The lack of a public market makes valuation difficult; it may lead to problems over distributions; and it precludes the use of the market as a monitoring device on management[6]. We shall examine each of these problems in turn looking at the matter primarily from a company law perspective[7].

DEFINING SMALL INCORPORATED FIRMS[8]

So far we have spoken fairly generally. Let us be a little more precise. While one should not make a fetish of definition and much depends on the immediate purpose of defining, it will be helpful if we at least take our bearings by reference to existing nomenclature. The Bolton Committee identified three characteristics of small firms—a relatively small share of the market, personal management by the owners, and independence. They then adopted shifting relativist criteria for different sectors of industry, as we saw in Chapter 4. In manufacturing industry there was widespread use of the corporate form which increased with the number of employees. In non-manufacturing, the trend was not so pronounced. Catering small firms tended not to use the corporate form and the two sectors which did—construction and wholesale distribution—probably did so because of the risks involved. In this chapter we shall basically follow the same relativism as the Bolton definition and concentrate on those small firms which are incorporated. Since 90% of incorporated small firms according to Bolton are close companies, the kind of company we are considering is the U K-resident company controlled by five or fewer persons or by its directors, provided at least 35% of its voting power is not held by the public and listed and dealt in on a stock exchange. However, we are only concerned with a subclass of close company which is characterised by independence and owner/management.

THE USE OF THE CORPORATE FORM FOR SMALL FIRMS

Although the majority of small firms are not incorporated, a sufficient number are for us to consider what motivates the adoption of the corporate form and whether the present legal form is appropriate.

The main reasons for choosing the corporate form are undoubtedly limited liability and the ability to give a floating charge. However, a private company's bank will usually insist on personal guarantees by the controlling directors which, to this extent, removes the advantage of limited liability. Nevertheless, there remains limited liability as far as trade creditors and involuntary creditors such as claimants in tort are concerned. A floating charge will primarily benefit the bank. Thus the proprietors of a small

---

6 See Frank Easterbrook and D Fischel (1986) 38 Stanford L Rev 271.
7 See generally S J Naude (1982) 4 Modern Business Law 6; D S Ribbens (1982) TSAR 49, (1983) TSAR 118; M C Sheehan (1985) 2 Canta LR 374.
8 See the Bolton Report, chapter 1 and also *Chesterman*, op cit, chapter 2.

business may be advised to incorporate by their bank to grant a floating charge but will then immediately sign away limited liability. For a number of small businesses, the tax results of incorporation are neutral or disadvantageous. For such companies, then, one must question whether the cost and artificiality of incorporation and maintaining the corporate form are justified. Small businesses are not usually very concerned with the other advantages of incorporation such as ownership of property and capacity to be sued. The early Companies Acts were probably not intended in any event to be used by small businesses. The statutory minimum number of members was prescribed at seven and it was not until the decision of the House of Lords in *Salomon v A Salomon & Co Ltd*[9] that the legitimacy of the use of six nominees or dummy shareholders was recognised[10]. Prior to that date the practice had been adopted and the term 'private company' was occasionally used to describe in commercial language the incorporated small business[11]. That term was later adopted as a term of art in the Companies Act 1907 (later embodied in the Companies (Consolidation) Act 1908) to exempt them from certain requirements of publicity including the obligation to file accounts. The criteria of a private company were originally a restriction on the transfer of shares, basically 50 members and a prohibition on raising capital from the public. Out of this class was created the subclass of exempt private company by the Companies Act 1948 as a result of the Cohen Report, and this alone of limited companies continued to enjoy the old privileges of not filing accounts and of making loans to directors. The definition of exempt private company was complex and produced anomalies. It was abolished by the Companies Act 1967. Now all private companies whose members' liability is limited by shares must file accounts. In the Companies Act 1980, s 1(1) a new definition of private company was introduced which involved not being a public company. The principal characteristics of a public company under s 1(3) of CA 1985 are a provision in its memorandum to that effect and compliance with the requirements of the Companies Acts. These include having a minimum share capital, a common requirement in Europe for private companies as well.

This approach of defining a private company by negation is even more unsatisfactory than the old approach of defining a public company by negation. It is arguable that private companies, particularly those which are small incorporated firms, have definite characteristics which need to be recognised. These characteristics are not adequately defined by not being public companies especially when the definition of the latter is so patently inept. Small incorporated firms have more in common with sole traders and partnerships than this approach recognises. Size is one important factor. The absence of capital raising from the public is the other.

The Companies Act 1981 introduced the new concept of small company for the purpose of filing modified financial statements which need not comply with all the provisions of the Companies Acts. Under s 248(1) (as amended), a company qualifies as a small company if it satisfies for that financial year any *two* of the following *three* conditions:

9 [1897] AC 22.
10 See L C B Gower (1953) 18 Law & Contemporary Problems 535 at 538.
11 Thus Sir Francis Palmer, the Victorian company law specialist, first published his book on private companies in 1877. See also judicial usage in *Re British Seamless Paper Box Co* (1881) 17 Ch D 467 at 478, CA.

(a)   the amount of its turnover is not more than £2m;
(b)   the balance sheet total is not more than £975,000;
(c)   the average number of employees employed by the company in the financial year does not exceed 50.

It can be seen that (a) at least is a reasonably generous figure although in some businesses, turnover is high but profit margins low. This shift from an a priori general approach to classification to a more pragmatic relativist approach based on size as far as accounts are concerned is welcome. With this can be compared some Canadian reforms such as the Canada Business Corporations Act[12] which has abandoned the public/private dichotomy altogether in favour of a variety of different definitions depending on the circumstances in which it is thought appropriate to draw distinctions between different types of company. The main distinctions are between those raising capital from the public and those which do not, although some jurisdictions have adopted specific close corporation provisions on US lines. These pay particular attention to the needs of small incorporated firms which are closed held and recognise the unity of management and ownership. The ways in which this has been done are:

(a)   to relax procedures;
(b)   to allow special redeemable shares;
(c)   to allow and in some cases require pre-emption provisions;
(d)   to introduce appraisal rights to prevent fundamental changes without consent;
(c)   to allow unanimous shareholder agreements which also fetter directors' discretions; and
(f)   to provide for application to the court for dissolution as in the case of a partnership.

The most relaxed procedure is perhaps contained in the Delaware statute in the USA and in s 10 of the Statutory Close Corporation Supplement to the Model Business Corporation Act in the US[13]. This allows direct shareholder management. The corporation need not elect directors but may be managed by shareholders who are deemed to be directors. This in effect is a subclass of close corporation and would suit the incorporated partnership type of company. (b) was facilitated in English law by the 1981 Act reforms. (c) is permissible and for new issues the rule unless excluded. (d) would involve a change in English law insofar as it allows fettering of directors' discretion although there is some latitude under the case law already[14]. (e) would be in addition to winding up on the just and equitable ground and might prejudice the interests of employees and creditors.

Given that all or some of these are desirable reforms, one is still left with the threshold problem of definition unless one adopts the approach of the Canada Business Corporations Act. It is difficult to produce a definition

---

12 See Iacobucci, Pilkington and Prichard *Canadian Business Corporations* (1977) p 75 ff.
13 Ibid, p 80; see Report of the Committee on Corporate Laws 'Proposed Statutory Close Corporation Supplement to the Model Business Corporation Act' (1981) 37 Bus Law 269–311; (1983) 38 Bus Law 1031. Cf the South African Close Corporations Act 1984, ss 42 and 46.
14 See Chapter 24, ante.

which is much better than the 1948 Act definition of private company, possibly reducing the number of members to less than 15.

In Chapter 4 we mentioned certain trends in the case law which indicated that the courts are beginning to recognise distinctive traits of the small incorporated firm. These were:

(1)   the tendency to pierce the veil where the interests of justice required it;
(2)   the trend to recognition of something like a *personellgesellschaft*;
(3)   the willingness to bypass strict legalities;
(4)   in some, but not all, cases, the willingness to look at a group of associated companies as a whole.

It is difficult to give conceptual unity to these trends but there are perhaps two alternative ways in which they can at least be partially explained. One is by reference to contract, the other by reference to equity. One can ask, what was the basic contract agreed between the parties and of which the company is the expression? Do the company constitution and machinery give adequate reflection to it? This helps to explain (2) and (3) but not necessarily (1) and (4). (4) in fact will be relatively rare although it is surprising how often problems arise because there is not a group in the strict sense but a motley collection of small incorporated firms owned by the same person or persons. The equity approach is capable of covering most of the field. Many instances of (1) are cases where it would be inequitable to enforce the strict letter of *Salomon's* principle although it is noteworthy that the courts have not readily disregarded the corporate form in favour of creditors. (2) arises because of the recognition of equitable considerations under the just and equitable formula in winding up. There have been a few faltering steps taken by first instance courts in the Commonwealth to extend this to non-winding up situations. Many instances of (3) can be explained in terms of acquiescence, waiver or estoppel which can be the subject of equitable intervention. (3) and (4) can be explained in terms of equity's regard for the substance rather than the form in legal transactions. Of course, to say that these trends can be explained by reference to equity begs the question of why there has been equitable intervention. It is submitted that there are two reasons—first, the traditional personal equity which is rooted in a concept of conscience or fairness and secondly, and perhaps more importantly, what might be described as commercial equity—the willingness to look to the substance and not the form of legal transactions. Sometimes this is simply described as commercial construction but it seems to have been of equitable origin either in equity properly so called or the Law Merchant. However, there are limits. There is no general doctrine of small firms which overrides established equitable doctrines such as fiduciary obligations. There are certain things, to use Churchill's powerful phrase in another context, 'up with which' equity 'will not put'. The blurring of function between shareholder and director, for instance, while the most natural thing in the world for small incorporated firms, is frowned upon if it amounts to a fetter of the director's discretion although there is an increasing tendency in the cases to adopt a restricted approach to the doctrine[15]. Where greater latitude has been felt necessary, it has resulted from statutory reforms in the USA and

15 Ibid.

Canada. English law has not yet found the impetus in either the case law or statute to recognise the full implications of the small incorporated firm.

The financing of small incorporated firms

Small firms are at a greater disadvantage than larger firms in raising finance[16]. External equity finance is difficult to find although the power to issue redeemable shares and to purchase its own shares may now assist the small incorporated firm. Nevertheless the terms will often be unfavourable. Loan capital is more expensive and the security requirements are more onerous.

According to the Bolton Report[17] a smaller proportion of the finance of small business comes from external borrowings than is the case with larger firms. Long term debt together with bank loans and overdrafts provided finance for about 14% of total assets for the firms surveyed compared with 19% for quoted companies. A substantial number of small firms do not borrow at all. There are variations between sectors of industry. According to a survey by ICFC, faster growing firms rely to a much greater extent on external borrowing than slower growing firms. Bank credit nevertheless forms the greater part of the *external* finance for small businesses. Many small businesses are financed by the owners either out of their own capital or by ploughed back profits. Additionally further finance may be raised in the family.

Another important source of finance is trade credit, although in a time of recession suppliers are insisting on accounts being settled in shorter periods. For small businesses with some growth potential there are specialist City of London financial institutions who often mix equity and loan participation. Hire purchase and plant hire is indirectly a source of finance.

The disadvantages faced by small firms do not necessarily represent any distinct bias against them. The cost to the finance provider is higher and the risks more difficult to assess. The Wilson Committee[18] thought that if any bias did exist it might be in the banks' excessive caution in assessing risk, particularly where the customer had no capital of his own.

Recently, largely as a result of the Report of the Wilson Committee, there has been an attempt at reshaping the financing of small firms[19]. Some of this is tied in with regional development, some with more information and advice, while government guarantees and tax concessions have been given to investors and the relevant thresholds for corporation tax and VAT have been increased. The high street banks have set up specialist departments and specialist firms have grown up in the City. Sometimes one is left with the impression that there is now a bewildering range of choice open to small firms. It is remarkable, however, how this diminishes at the point of contact. A lot of the change is cosmetic.

Disclosure and the small incorporated firm

We have already dealt with disclosure in Chapter 28. We shall briefly recapitulate. The private company was exempt from many disclosure

---

16 Wilson Report (Cmnd 7937) App 2.
17 Bolton Report, chapter 17.
18 See the Wilson Report, op cit.
19 *Chesterman*, op cit.

requirements until 1948. Between 1948 and 1967, exempt private companies were exempt from filing accounts. Between 1967 and 1981, all private limited companies had to file accounts but had a limited relaxation of certain disclosure requirements. Since 1981, small companies have been subject to a more lenient regime as regards financial reports. They are now wholly exempt from filing a profit and loss account and directors' report and are permitted to file a modified balance sheet. This still requires the same flow of information to shareholders but not to the general public including creditors.

Some would argue that this does not go far enough and that we should have a return to the pre-1967 days but this seems undesirable from the point of view of creditor protection. We have seen in earlier chapters how the corporate form can be abused. Obligations to file accounts afford some, albeit an imperfect, index of solvency. The availability of public accounts makes credit reporting easier and cheaper[20]. It also facilitates the more macro-economic objective of implementation of an incomes policy as well as providing useful economic data to government.

Transitional problems of small incorporated firms

Small firms perhaps more than larger firms are fraught with transitional problems. These centre around the death or retirement of the founder or controller shareholder, expansion, disputes between the controllers and financial instability and insolvency[1].

Some small incorporated firms are in reality 'one man companies'—incorporated sole traders. Other small firms have been called 'little business' by an American writer[2]. They are really forms of self-employment where employees other than the proprietor are members of his family. When he dies or wishes to retire the impetus might disappear. The alternatives are that the business is; (1) sold, (2) wound up, or (3) is taken over by another member of the family. Where (1) occurs there will either be an agreement to sell the shares in the company or its undertaking and assets. (2) will be a members' voluntary winding up unless the company is insolvent. (3) will involve a member of the family taking over the proprietor's shares. Another alternative now made possible is for the employees or the company itself to buy the proprietor's shares. This has been possible since the Companies Act 1981.

Many small incorporated firms are in reality incorporated partnerships where the corporate form has been used primarily for reasons of limiting liability to third parties. Disputes can arise between the proprietors in innumerable ways. Michael Chesterman in his useful study, *Small Businesses*, includes the following as examples[3]:

1 dismissal of one of the proprietors from his position as director, manager or employee;
2 expulsion;

20 Bolton Report, chapter 17.
1 For a useful discussion of this, see *Chesterman*, op cit, chapter 7. See also Frank Easterbrook and Daniel Fischel (1986) 38 Stanford L Rev 271.
2 Edward D Hollander *The Future of Small Business* (1979).
3 *Chesterman*, op cit, pp 151–152.

3 setting up a rival enterprise;
4 denying access to books and accounts;
5 failure to give notice of meetings;
6 denying a vote at meetings;
7 payment of excessive remuneration to others;
8 refusal to pay dividends;
9 issuing shares to others at less than full value;
10 refusal to register a person as member.

The remedies available to the injured party in such a case are to bring an action under one of the exceptions to the rule in *Foss v Harbottle* or under s 459 of CA 1985 or to petition to wind up the company on the just and equitable ground under s 122(1)(g) of the Insolvency Act 1986. Many of the cases discussed in Chapter 27 concerned small incorporated firms. Indeed *Ebrahimi v Westbourne Galleries Ltd*[4] laid down principles which seem to be based on a paradigm of such a company. Lord Wilberforce said:

It would be impossible, and wholly undesirable, to define the circumstances in which these considerations may arise. Certainly the fact that a company is a small one, or a private company, is not enough. There are very many of these where the association is a purely commercial one, of which it can safely be said that the basis of association is adequately and exhaustively laid down in the articles. The superimposition of equitable considerations requires something more, which typically may include one, or probably more, of the following elements:
(i) an association formed or continued on the basis of a personal relationship, involving mutual confidence—this element will often be found where a pre-existing partnership has been converted into a limited company;
(ii) an agreement, or understanding, that all, or some (for there may be 'sleeping members'), of the shareholders shall participate in the conduct of the business;
(iii) restriction upon the transfer of the members' interest in the company—so that if confidence is lost, or one member is removed from management, he cannot take out his stake and go elsewhere . . .

At the moment there is Commonwealth authority[5] in favour of applying this to a non-winding-up situation and the English courts have begun to apply it in s 459 cases and in relation to controlling shareholders' duties. In *Re Bird Precision Bellows Ltd*[6] Nourse J applied it to the question of valuation of a minority interest for a buy out under s 459. This resulted in no discount being made for a minority interest.

Lastly, we come to financial instability and insolvency. Small firms are vulnerable. Some simply fail. Some are not viable from the start. Others are outstripped by their rivals. A fast growing small firm may find problems in expanding too quickly and may be tempted to overtrade. It may take on extra staff or purchase extra plant to meet a current demand which later drops. The company's bank may be prepared to tide it over a temporary illiquidity; this depends on the vagaries of banking policy. Otherwise, it is likely that the bank will appoint a receiver under its debenture if the company has assets. Alternatively, the Inland Revenue or a trade creditor may petition for its compulsory winding up. The proprietors may, however, take the initiative and put the company into creditors' voluntary winding up

---

4 [1973] AC 360 at 379, HL.
5 See Chapter 27, ante and BAK Rider [1979] CLJ 148.
6 [1984] Ch 419. However see Chapter 27, ante.

by calling the appropriate meetings. Sometimes this is done to remove the intolerable pressure from creditors.

Deregulation of private companies

The Thatcher Government has been keen to cut down on Government expenditure and reduce the regulatory burden on small firms. This was the subject of the White Paper, *Lifting the Burden* (Cmnd) 9571, July 1985. This stated that:

. . . regulations have grown over the years to a stage where many of them are too heavy a drain on our national resources. To the extent that regulations go further than necessary, there were lower profits for firms or raised prices, or both. Output and employment will tend to be lower. Regulations can also stifle competition and deter new firms from entering the market or prevent others from expanding. Too many people in central and local Government spend too much of their time regulating the activities of others. Some regulations were framed a century and more ago, have been added to or amended, and now bear little relevance to the modern business world. Other regulations are too complex and confusing even to professional advisors (and sometimes to the people who administer them, too). Many regulations are necessary and it is, of course, Government's responsibility to ensure that flexibility and freedom are not abused by those who would flout the proper interests of customers, consumers and employees. We must maintain our quality of life, but we have to strike the right balance.

The Institute of Directors also commissioned Dr L S Sealy of Gonville and Caius College, Cambridge to produce a report on deregulation of private companies which influenced the CA 1989.

The main reforms of the CA 1989 as we saw in Chapter 22 are:

(1)   the possibility of written resolutions by all the members without notice or a meeting (s 381A of the CA 1985). There are two exceptions—resolutions to remove directors under s 303 and resolutions under s 391 to remove an auditor before the expiration of his term of office. Copies of the written resolutions must be sent to the auditors and if it concerns them they may require it to be considered by a general meeting (s 381B). The resolution is ineffective until the auditors indicate that it does not affect them or they have no objection.

(2)   the right for members to elect by resolution in general meeting to dispense with certain requirements of company law. These cover: duration of authority to issue shares; dispensing with laying of accounts and reports before general meetings; dispensing with holding of annual general meetings; dispensing with annual appointment of auditors.

PROPOSALS FOR A NEW FORM OF INCORPORATION

Early in the nineteenth century, John Austin, the jurist, called for an incorporation similar to the French *commandite*[7]. These proposals were toyed with throughout the nineteenth century and then Pollock's work at the end of the century resulted in not only the Partnership Act 1890 but also

---

7 [1825] Parliamentary History Review 711.

eventually the Limited Partnership Act 1907 and the Registration of Business Names Act 1916. The 1907 Act has not been a great success and the 1916 Act has now been repealed.

In 1969 in *Companies Legislation in the 1970s*, four of the main accountancy institutes called for a new classification of proprietary as opposed to stewardship companies. A proprietary company would be defined as one[8]:

(a)   which is managed and controlled by substantially the same persons;
(b)   which is not under the control of another company which is not itself a proprietary company;
(c)   which limits the right to transfer its shares;
(d)   which prohibits any offer of its shares to the public;
(e)   which limits the number of its members to 25;
(f)   whose average number of employees per week does not exceed 200; and
(g)   which has an annual turnover not exceeding £500,000.

The object of the new classification was to exempt them from the more onerous accounting requirements, some of which purposes have been achieved by the 1981 Act.

In 1981, the Department of Trade published a consultative document entitled 'A New Form of Incorporation for Small Firms'[9] which included in Annex A a scheme devised by Professor L C B Gower for a new form of incorporation which is in effect an incorporated partnership with legal personality, the members of which might enjoy a measure of limited liability. It would be available to firms with a membership of between two and ten. It would be registered by filing a simple document. This would not be its constitution. The firms would not be dissolved on the death or retirement of members. It would have the power to buy out the outgoing members' interest and, failing this, the other members would have the right. There would be no share capital as such but simply interests in the net worth. The right of participation in management would be given to all members and would not be capable of being taken away. Management as in partnership would be by majority rule except where there was to be a change in the nature of the business where there would be a need for unanimity.

The proposals avoid strict capital maintenance and argue a case for liberality in disclosure. Solvency was the most important thing and an annual certificate of solvency would be necessary.

Liability would not be totally limited since there would be a prescribed amount and withdrawals at less than full consideration would be repayable. The firm would be able to grant a floating charge.

Such a reform would avoid the distortion which results from forcing small firms into the private company mould and would yet achieve some of the advantages of legal personality and limited liability. Unfortunately only the National Chamber of Trade, the Institute of Chartered Secretaries and the National Farmers' Union among the larger interest groups expressed any support for the proposal and according to research done by the Confederation of British Industry in 1980, the directors of private companies have

---

8 The Bolton Report, p 314; cf 'Company Accounting and Disclosure' (Cmnd 7654) p 1.
9 Cmnd 1871 (1981). See *Chesterman*, op cit, chapter 9 and R Baxt (1984) 2 C & SLJ 248. See too the Australian Companies and Securities Law Review Committee's 'Report on Forms of Legal Organisation for Small Business Enterprises', September 1985.

little enthusiasm for the introduction of any new form of incorporation and it appears that few will opt for it if introduced. As the CBI did not invite replies from sole traders or partnerships (other than a few professional ones) it is uncertain how much this reflects their views also. In the absence of some general support, it is unlikely that any reform will be carried out[10]. In the meantime the private limited company form will remain as the most viable method of incorporation of a small firm. Given the reforms of the CA 1989 it is unlikely that there will be a new form of incorporation. While the 1989 reforms are to be welcomed, there still remains the complex structure of UK company law as a whole. Compared with the relative simplicity of the Canada Business Corporations Act the UK model seems distinctly dated and not very 'user friendly'. This has an inevitable effect on transaction costs. There either needs to be a simplification of the Act as a whole on the Canadian model or the enactment of a whole new Close Companies Act or Chapter. The latter does not necessarily involve a new form of incorporation but an attempt to have a self-contained compendium of the rules applicable to small incorporated firms.

10 See LCB Gower 'Proposals for Reform' in *The Abuse of Limited Liability*, Transcript of a Seminar at Monash Law School on 30 August 1983, 1, 4–5; F Wooldridge 'A New Form of Incorporation—Reponding to the Gower Proposals' (1982) 3 Co Law 58. Compare also the proposals of J R M Lowe *The Incorporated Firm*, winner of the 1974 Jordan competition; T Hadden *Company Law and Capitalism* (2nd edn, 1977) pp 222–230; the South African Close Corporations Act 1984 and the Australian Close Corporations Act 1989. The Australian Act is a bad precedent. It is far too complex.

CHAPTER 32

Groups

THE GROUP ENTERPRISE

A company is a species of undertaking. Undertaking is wide enough to include a partnership and an unincorporated association carrying on a trade or business, with or without a view to profit (s 259(1)). The extended concept is for the purposes of consolidated accounts.

A group of undertakings is in general terms a holding or parent undertaking and its subsidiaries. Instead of a single company, we are concerned with the inter-relationships of a number of undertakings and the ways in which the parent exercises control over the business of its subsidiaries. We are also concerned with their relationship with the outside world. Holding companies originated in the USA as early as 1832 and were one of a number of devices used to pool resources and share profits. When the Sherman Anti-Trust Law of 1890 outlawed trust agreements, the holding company became more commonly used. Concern over the inability of existing accounting requirements to cover the group enterprise was expressed in 1904 by Sir Arthur Lowes Dickinson, a partner in Price Waterhouse, a leading firm of accountants. In 1922, his partner, Sir Gilbert Garnsey, drew the attention of the English accounting profession to the problems in detail in a public lecture which was later published. The first consolidated balance sheet was published by Nobel Industries Ltd in 1920 and the first consolidated profit and loss account by Dunlop Rubber Co Ltd in 1933. The Greene Committee in 1925–26 generally agreed with the Institute of Chartered Accountants that the matter was better left to the companies themselves, except that shareholders were entitled to know whether the dividends to be declared by the holding company were justified by the results of the group as a whole. The first legal obligation to produce group accounts was introduced by the Companies Act 1947, and is now contained in ss 229 and 230 of CA 1985[1]. The question of group accounts was addressed by the Seventh EC Directive which was implemented by CA 1989. Steps were taken to broaden the scope of groups to deal with evasion of the accounting requirements. The group relationship is currently the subject of a proposal for a Ninth Directive which is a matter of controversy.

Groups arise in different ways. They may be founded as such. A company is incorporated to carry on business as a holding company and then proceeds to incorporate trading subsidiaries. Alternatively, a company which is a trading company may grow and convert itself into a holding company, later hiving down its trading activities into subsidiaries. Again, a group relationship may

---

1 For the history, see J Kitchen 'The Accounts of British Holding Company Groups' in T Lee and R Parker *The Evolution of Corporate Financial Reporting* (1979). See also R M Wilkins *Group Accounts* (2nd edn, 1979) p 16 et seq.

arise as a result of a takeover. One company takes over another which then becomes its subsidiary when its shares have been acquired by the first company. Takeovers may arise from reasons of trade expansion but many conglomerates today represent horizontal expansion and diversification. There are various reasons why the subsidiaries are kept in business. The bidder will wish to preserve the goodwill of the business. There are costs involved in transferring the actual business. The subsidiary may constitute a convenient unit of management or accounting within the group[2].

It is interesting to note that British based groups tend to be typically more complex than their American or European counterparts. The complexity arises from the numbers of operating subsidiaries and dormant companies and the low priority given to rationalisation[3]. This complexity makes it more difficult for shareholders and employees to monitor the affairs of the group.

Now, whereas the rational goal of investors in a single company is to gain the largest return on their investment consistent with the risks which they are prepared to take, the goal of investors in a group of undertakings will be to maximise the profitability of the group enterprise as a whole[4]. The interests of any one undertaking are irrelevant except insofar as they increase the overall profitability. There may be commercial or fiscal advantages in running one or more undertakings at a loss or on a break-even basis. The economic rationale of the group enterprise may, therefore, generate a conflict with legal norms which approach the group in a more atomistic way. This produces the contradiction that management pursuing rational economic ends may be in breach of their fiduciary duties to the companies of which they are directors[5]. Lest one dismiss this as an instance of the irrationality of the law, one should remember that each constituent company has its own creditors who will look to its assets for recovery in the case of default and insolvency. We shall say more about these topics later.

NO GENERAL LAW OF GROUP ENTERPRISE

Unlike German law, English law has not developed a distinct body of rules applicable to groups. The ordinary rules of company law apply to the companies in the group and to their relationship with outsiders.

A holding company, while the owner of whole or part of the share capital of a subsidiary, is not regarded as the owner of the assets of the subsidiary in the absence of an express agency or trust relationship[6]. Sometimes a more liberal attitude, looking to the economic enterprise as a whole, has been manifested by the English courts when dealing with compensation cases as we saw in Chapter 7 but that can perhaps be explained as a desire not to allow the doctrine of separate legal personality to be used to produce manifest injustice.

---

2 See T Hadden *Company Law and Capitalism* (2nd edn, 1977) p 389.
3 See the valuable study by T Hadden *The Control of Corporate Groups* (1983) p vii. For the use of a complex corporate form to evade creditors see *Re a Company* [1987] BCLC 333, CA.
4 Jonathan M Landers (1975) 42 U Chi L Rev 589 at 591. See generally H Collins (1990) 53 MLR 731.
5 See generally C M Schmitthoff [1978] JBL 218; R Baxt and D Harding 'Duties of Directors and Majority Shareholders in Groups of Companies—Tension between Commercial Convenience and Legal Obligations' [1977] 9 Comm Law Association (Australia) Bulletin 127; R Baxt (1976) 4 ABLR 289.
6 *Salomon v A Salomon & Co Ltd* [1897] AC 22, HL.

In *Littlewoods Mail Order Stores Ltd v IRC*[7] Lord Denning MR made a very sweeping statement. He said:

The doctrine laid down in *Salomon v A Salomon & Co Ltd* [1897] AC 22, HL, has to be watched very carefully. It has often been supposed to cast a veil over the personality of a limited company through which the courts cannot see but that is not true. The courts can and often do draw aside the veil . . . They look to see what really lies behind. The legislature has shown the way with group accounts and the rest. And the courts should follow suit.

He made similar remarks in *DHN Food Distributors Ltd v London Borough of Tower Hamlets*[8] but in both cases there were special features such as trusteeship which justified the decisions. A different and more orthodox view has been taken in the New Zealand Court of Appeal[9] and the House of Lords dealing with a Scottish appeal[10]. This view is that the principle of separate legal personality must be observed unless there are compelling reasons to discard it. Similarly in the Australian case of *Industrial Equity Ltd v Blackburn*[11] where the High Court of Australia held that a company had breached its articles in declaring dividends out of profits earned by a subsidiary, Mason J said:

It can scarcely be contended that the provisions of the Act operate to deny the separate legal personality of each company in the group. Thus in the absence of contract creating some additional right, the creditors of company A, a subsidiary company within a group, can only look to that company for payment of their debts. They cannot look to company B, the holding company, for payment.

A holding company and other companies in the group are not liable for the debts incurred by a member of the group unless they have guaranteed them or have participated in the carrying on of the subsidiary's business with intent to defraud its creditors within what is now s 213 of the Insolvency Act 1986[12] or are the only member when the subsidiary's membership has remained below the statutory minimum for more than six months within s 24 of the CA 1985.

The directors of a parent company as such owe no duties to protect the interests of its subsidiaries when the subsidiaries have independent boards. This view of the law was accepted by the Court of Appeal in *Lindgren v L and P Estates Ltd*[13] in 1968, in spite of a cogent counter argument by counsel that the property of a holding company consists of the investment in the shares of its subsidiaries and the duty of a director of a holding company is to promote the interests of the subsidiaries representing that investment[14]. It is also arguable that directors of a holding company who sacrifice the interests of creditors of a subsidiary may, in appropriate circumstances, be parties to

7 [1969] 1 WLR 1241 at 1254, CA. See C M Schmitthoff [1976] JBL 305, [1978] JBL 218 at 219–222; see also *Walker v Wimborne* (1976) 50 ALJR 446; R Baxt [1976] 4 ABLR 289; Baxt and Harding, op cit.
8 [1976] 3 All ER 462, CA.
9 *Re Securitibank Ltd (No 2)* [1978] 2 NZLR 136.
10 *Woolfson v Strathclyde Regional Council* (1978) 38 P & CR 521.
11 (1977) 17 ALR 575.
12 See *Re Augustus Barnett & Son Ltd* (1986) 2 BCC 98,904. Noted by D D Prentice (1987) 103 LQR 11.
13 *Lindgren v L and P Estates Ltd* [1968] Ch 572 at 595 e and 604 e-f, CA. See also *Walker v Wimborne* (1976) 50 ALJR 446. See Baxt, op cit; Baxt and Harding, op cit.
14 [1968] Ch 572 at 582 d-e (Mr Ralph Instone).

the carrying on of the subsidiary's business with intent to defraud its creditors within the fraudulent trading provisions of s 213[15]. If this is the case they can be made personally liable for its debts. In the USA, there is a duty to treat a subsidiary with fairness[16] and it has been argued that there should be a tougher rule requiring sharing of opportunities within the group[17]. Under English law, the directors of a subsidiary are as such under no fiduciary duties to the holding company merely as a majority shareholder[18]. It is not possible for the directors of a member of a group to rely on a transaction as being for the good of the group as a whole or other members of the group when it is not in the interests of the particular company of which they are directors. In the absence of evidence of what they did in fact consider, the test of their obligations is what they or an honest and reasonable director would consider to be in the interests of the subsidiary[19]. English law has not yet developed a concept of group interest or a coherent doctrine of fairness in respect of group transactions for the purposes of directors' fiduciary duties. The emphasis is still on the interest of individual companies. Indeed, the directors of a subsidiary must not simply act as puppets of the holding company or obey the holding company[20] where this will constitute a breach of their duties to the subsidiary[1]. Where the directors of a subsidiary who are nominees of the holding company sacrifice its interests for those of the holding company, minority shareholders may have a remedy for oppression under s 459. In *Scottish Co-operative Wholesale Society Ltd v Meyer*[2] in 1958, the House of Lords held that the Scottish CWS had acted towards the minority in an oppressive manner and that this conduct through its nominee directors who were also directors of the Society amounted to conduct of the affairs of the company within the section (then s 210 of the Companies Act 1948) since the transactions could not be separated. Viscount Simonds, following Lord President Cooper and Lord Keith of Avonholm in the Court of Session, formulated a principle that where a subsidiary is formed with an independent minority of shareholders, the parent company, if it is engaged in the same class of business, is under an obligation to conduct its own affairs in such a way as to deal fairly with its subsidiary[3]. Lord Keith added that even where such directors are conducting the affairs of the parent they may by neglect be misconducting the affairs of the subsidiaries[4]. A liberal interpretation of the nominee director's role was

---

15 Cf *Re Sarflax Ltd* [1979] Ch 592; see Barrett [1977] 40 MLR 226; Baxt and Harding, op cit; Russell [1982] 1 Canta LR 417.
16 *Sinclair Oil Corpn v Levien* 290 A 2d 717 (1971). Noted at (1971) 57 Va L Rev 1223.
17 Brudney and Chirelstein (1974) 88 Harv L Rev 297.
18 *Bell v Lever Bros Ltd* [1932] AC 161 at 228, HL.
19 *Charterbridge Corpn Ltd v Lloyds Bank Ltd* [1970] Ch 62. See also *Re Halt Garage (1964) Ltd* [1982] 3 All ER 1016; *Re Horsley & Weight Ltd* [1982] Ch 442, CA and *Rolled Steel Products (Holdings) Ltd v British Steel Corpn* [1986] Ch 246, [1985] 3 All ER 52, CA, discussed in Chapter 10. See also the New Zealand Court of Appeal decision in *Nicholson v Permakraft* [1985] 1 NZLR 242. Cf the US case law discussed in R Nathan (1986) 3 Canta LR 1, 11 et seq. See further H W Ballentine (1925) 14 Calif L Rev 12; A Berle Jr (1947) 47 Col L Rev 343; B Cataldo (1953) Law & Contemp Problems 473; GMB (1971) 57 Val Rev 1223; J Landers (1976) 43 Chi L Rev 527; Note (1984) 74 Yale L J 338.
20 *Selangor United Rubber Estates Ltd v Cradock (a bankrupt) (No 3)* [1968] 2 All ER 1073.
1 *Lonrho Ltd v Shell Petroleum Co Ltd* [1980] 1 WLR 627, HL.
2 [1959] AC 324, HL. See too *Re National Building Maintenance Ltd* (1971) 1 WWR 8; affd sub nom *National Building Maintenance Ltd v Dove* (1972) 5 WWR 410 (Controlling shareholder selling company's major asset to associated company).
3 Ibid, at 343.
4 Ibid, at 363.

given in the Australian case of *Re Broadcasting Station 2GB Pty Ltd*[5] where Jacobs J held that conduct in pursuit of the dominant company's interests is not reprehensible unless it can also be inferred that the directors would so act even if they were of the view that their acts were not in the best interests of the company.

LIMITED RECOGNITION OF THE GROUP IN THE COMPANIES ACTS

Section 736 defines 'holding company' and 'subsidiary'. Section 736(1) defines a subsidiary of another company 'its holding company' if that other company—

(a) holds a majority of the voting rights in it, or
(b) is a member of it and has the right to appoint or remove a majority of its board of directors, or
(c) is a member of it and controls alone, pursuant to an agreement with other shareholders or members, a majority of the voting rights in it,

or if it is a subsidiary of a company which is itself a subsidiary of that other company.

Section 736(2) amplifies s 736(1) and provides (inter alia) that:

(1) In section 736(1)(*b*) the reference to the right to appoint or remove a majority of the board of directors is to the right to appoint or remove directors holding a majority of the voting rights at meetings of the board on all, or substantially all, matters; and for the purposes of that provision—

(a) a company shall be treated as having the right to appoint to a directorship if—
     (i) a person's appointment to it follows necessarily from his appointment as director of the company, or
     (ii) the directorship is held by the company itself; and
(b) a right to appoint or remove which is exercisable only with the consent or concurrence of another person shall be left out of account unless no other person has a right to appoint or, as the case may be, remove in relation to that directorship (s 736A(3)).

(2) Rights which are exercisable only in certain circumstances shall be taken into account only—

(a) when the circumstances have arisen, and for so long as they continue to obtain, or
(b) when the circumstances are within the control of the person having the rights;

and rights which are normally exercisable but are temporarily incapable of exercise shall continue to be taken into account (s 736A(4)).

(3) Rights held by a person in a fiduciary capacity shall be treated as not held by him (s 736A(5)).

(4) Rights held by a person as nominee for another shall be treated as held by the other; and rights shall be regarded as held as nominee for

5 [1964–5] NSWR 1648. Noted (1965–7) 5 Sydney LR 288.

another if they are exercisable only on his instructions or with his consent or concurrence (s 736A(6)).

(5) Rights attached to shares held by way of security shall be treated as held by the person providing the security—

(a)   where apart from the right to exercise them for the purpose of preserving the value of the security, or of realising it, the rights are exercisable only in accordance with his instructions;

(b)   where the shares are held in connection with the granting of loans as part of normal business activities and apart from the right to exercise them for the purpose of preserving the value of the security, or of realising it, the rights are exercisable only in his interests (s 736A(7)).

(6) Rights shall be treated as held by a company if they are held by any of its subsidiaries; and nothing in subsection (6) or (7) shall be construed as requiring rights held by a company to be treated as held by any of its subsidiaries (s 736A(8)).

(7) The voting rights in a company shall be reduced by any rights held by the company itself (s 736A(10)).

So far these definitions have concentrated on corporate groups. However, the key provisions of s 258 deal with groups of undertakings which are the basis of the new consolidated accounts requirements under the Seventh Directive. Here the references to dominant influence and control contracts echo German Law. The relevant provisions are as follows:

(1) An undertaking is a parent undertaking in relation to another undertaking, a subsidiary undertaking, if—

(a)   it holds a majority of the voting rights in the undertaking, or

(b)   it is a member of the undertaking and has the right to appoint or remove a majority of its board of directors, or

(c)   it has the right to exercise a dominant influence over the undertaking—
        (i) by virtue of provisions contained in the undertaking's memorandum or articles, or
        (ii) by virtue of a control contract, or

(d)   it is a member of the undertaking and controls alone, pursuant to an agreement with other shareholders or members, a majority of the voting rights in the undertaking (s 258(2)).

(2) For the purposes of subsection (1) an undertaking shall be treated as a member of another undertaking—

(a)   if any of its subsidiary undertakings is a member of that undertaking, or

(b)   if any shares in that other undertaking are held by a person acting on behalf of the undertaking or any of its subsidiary undertakings (s 258(3)).

(3) An undertaking is also a parent undertaking in relation to another undertaking, a subsidiary undertaking, if it has a participating interest in the undertaking and—

(a)   it actually exercises a dominant influence over it, or

(b)   it and the subsidiary undertaking are managed on a unified basis (s 258(4)).

A right to exercise a dominant influence is a right to give directions with respect to the operating and financial policies of another undertaking which the latter's directors are obliged to comply with whether or not they are for its benefit (CA 1989, Sch 9, para 4(1)).

A control contract is a contract in writing confirming such a right of a kind authorised by the memorandum or articles of the undertaking in question and permitted by the law under which that undertaking is established (CA 1989, Sch 9, para 4(2)).

The primary reasons for the Companies Act definitions which differ from some other statutory definitions e g in some tax statutes, are first for the purpose of disclosure. Section 227 requires consolidated group accounts to be prepared, combining the information contained in the separate balance sheets and profit and loss accounts of the holding company and of the companies which were its subsidiaries at the end of the financial year to show the profitability and solvency of the group as a single unit. This is in addition to separate accounts for each member of the group which has limited liability. The group accounts must give a true and fair view of the state of affairs at the end of the year and the profit and loss for the year of the undertaking included in the consolidation. They must comply with Schedule 4A. Where such compliance would not show a true and fair view, additional information must be given in the accounts or notes to the accounts. If compliance with any of these requirements fails to show a true and fair view the company must depart from them to show a true and fair view[6].

There are a number of exemptions and exclusions which are dealt with in Chapter 28. The directors' report must also contain details about the group. In the Australian case of *Industrial Equity Ltd v Blackburn*[7] Mason J, commenting on the equivalent provisions in the Australian Uniform Companies legislation, said:

The purpose of these requirements is to ensure that the members of, and for that matter persons dealing with, a holding company are provided with accurate information as to the profit or loss and the state of affairs of that company and its subsidiary companies within the group, information which would not be forthcoming if all the shareholders received was limited to the accounts of the holding company disclosing as assets the shares which it holds in its subsidiaries. It is for this purpose that the Companies Act treats the business group as one entity, and requires that its financial results be incorporated in consolidated accounts to be circulated to shareholders and laid before a general meeting (ss 162(4) and 164(1)) and requires that the accounts and other documents shall accompany the annual return . . .

The second reason for the Companies Act definition is that s 23 prohibits a subsidiary or its nominee from being a member of its holding company and any allotment or transfer to it is void. This was introduced as a result of the Greene Committee's Report to bolster the rule in *Trevor v Whitworth*[8] which has since been modified by statute. The prohibition does not apply if the subsidiary is merely concerned as personal representative or trustee and is not beneficially interested. Voting rights on shares already held are suspended. Certain residual interests under pension schemes or employees share schemes are disregarded until they vest in possession. In addition as a

6 See Ch 28 ante and C Swinson *A Guide to the Companies Act 1989* (1990) Ch 3.
7 (1977) 17 ALR 575.
8 (1887) 12 App Cas 409, HL.

result of CA 1989, s 129 the prohibition does not apply if the shares are held as a 'market maker' as defined by CA 1985, s 23(3). Thirdly, there are a number of provisions in the Companies Act where obligations imposed on companies are extended to other members of the group or at least the holding company and their, or its, directors[9]. Conversely, there are provisions to exempt intra-group transactions which would otherwise be prohibited[10].

Thus it can be seen that, unlike the German *Aktiengesetz*, English law has not produced a coherent comprehensive law relating to groups[11]. The legislative provisions are sporadic and the case law underdeveloped. The result is unsatisfactory, as the courts are beginning to realise. In *Re Southard & Co Ltd*[12] in 1979, Templeman LJ said:

English company law possesses some curious features, which may generate curious results. A parent company may spawn a number of subsidiary companies, all controlled directly or indirectly by the shareholders of the parent company. If one of the subsidiary companies, to change the metaphor, turns out to be the runt of the litter and declines into insolvency to the dismay of its creditors, the parent company and other subsidiary companies prosper to the joy of the shareholders without any liability for the debts of the insolvent subsidiary.

The imposition of the Seventh Directive requirements upon the old group provisions has added to the complexity and incomplete character of English law. The broader concepts of control and the reference to control contracts echo German law and have an ill-defined relationship to English law.

REFORM

The draft proposal for a Ninth Directive on Groups, which is based on the German model, provides for a legal structure for unified mamagement of a public limited company and any other undertaking which has a controlling interest in it whether or not that undertaking is a company. It prescribes rules for the conduct of groups which are not managed on a unified basis but only in respect of public limited company members. Unless the relationship is formalised by one of the two methods specified, the controlling undertaking is liable for losses of the subsidiary resulting from the controlling influence and attributable to a fault in management or action taken which is not in the subsidiary's interest.

The draft has been strongly criticised[13] and no further steps are to be taken in the forseeable future[14].

Short of a comprehensive code of law relating to groups on the lines of the

---

9 For example, s 151 and s 330 of CA 1985. See also R R Pennington *Company Law* (6th edn, 1990) chapter 20.

10 In the loan prohibitions for directors in Pt X there are exemptions for intra-group transactions.

11 See F Wooldridge *Groups of Companies—The Law and Practice in Britain, France and Germany* (1981).

12 [1979] 1 WLR 1198 at 1208, CA.

13 See for instance Yves Guyon, 'Examen Critique des Projets Européens en matière de Groupes de Sociétés (le paint de vue français) in *Groups of Companies in European Laws*, Vol II (ed by Klaus J Hopt) (1982) p 155; R. Rodière, 'Reflexions sur les Avants-Projets d'une Directive de la Commission des CEE concernant les Groupes de Sociétés', D 1977, 136.

14 'The Single Market Company Law Harmonisation' (DTI) Sept 1989, p 17.

German *Aktiengesetz* which might be forced upon us as a result of EC influences, there are pressures on the one hand to legitimate the group interest and on the other hand to make members of a group liable for the debts of other companies in the group[15] and to protect employees. In the USA this takes place to some extent through equitable subordination, piercing the corporate veil and consolidation of related bankrupts[16]. In New Zealand and the Republic of Ireland, reforms have recently been adopted providing for a discretion to be conferred on the courts to order payment of the debts of one group member by another and pooling of assets. The Cork Committee shrank from making such radical proposals but favoured the tightening-up of the law on connected persons and the deferment of the debts owed to other companies in the group of directors' loan accounts to the debts of external creditors, where the former appear to be part of the long-term capital structure of the debtor company[17].

The Cork Report favoured a more comprehensive review of groups by a committee charged with reform of company law in general. If such a review was undertaken, it would be necessary to go back to basics and to ask what are the underlying economic purposes of limited liability and to what extent do they require the doctrine to apply to groups of companies[18]. Also what restrictions on control and group behaviour are justified in the interests of minority shareholders and of general creditors? It is almost instinctive for reformers to consider that the answer lies in whole or in part in increased disclosure. Thus the preamble to a draft EC Directive states that 'it is necessary in the interest not only of shareholders, creditors and employees but also of the general public that clear insight be afforded into their ownership and power structures by means of the most extensive disclosure measures possible'. However, in this context, disclosure is frequently not enough and the cost exceeds any likely benefit. There is a need for substantive reform but its precise form is a matter of controversy.

---

15 See the Conference on Harmonisation of Company Law in Europe—The Draft Directive on the Conduct of Groups, issued by the Department of Trade, March 1981. See generally J Welch (1986) 7 Co Law 29; R Nathan (1986) 3 Canta LR 1.
16 Landers, op cit (see footnote 5 supra); Hadden *The Control of Corporate Groups*, op cit, chapter 5; Nathan, op cit.
17 Cmnd 8558, ch 51.
18 See D D Prentice 'Groups of Companies: The English Experience' in *Groups of Companies in European Laws* (1982), vol II, ed Klaus J Hopt, pp 99, 128.

CHAPTER 33

Raising capital from the public

INTRODUCTION

Capital raising by the company

The basic function of companies is to provide a vehicle for entrepreneurial activity. Large scale entrepreneurial activity may, however, require amounts of capital which can only be provided by inviting outside investors to pool their resources and invest in an enterprise over which they may have relatively little control. To persuade such investors to come forward two incentives are needed. One is limited liability[1]. The other is a market in which investors can realise their investment. Without such a market investors will require a higher return on their investment to compensate for the lack of liquidity. The existence of a market for shares thus not only makes it possible for companies to raise external funding but makes it cheaper for them to do so as well. This chapter is concerned with the rules governing the operation of securities markets and in particular the rules regulating the invitation the company issues when it offers shares to the public.

Under the rules of company law only a public company may offer its shares or debentures to the public[2]. Being a public company, however, is not synonymous with being listed or quoted on a stock market. The company will, therefore, need to join a stock market if it is to be able to offer the attraction of liquidity to its investors[3]. It may be that the scale of a new project to be undertaken is such that capital has to be raised by inviting outside investors to pool their resources. In such a case the company may be formed at the outset as a public company[4]. More commonly it is likely that an existing enterprise has expanded to the point where further growth cannot be funded from either retained profits or borrowing from the bank. So the decision is taken to 'go public' and convert what may until then have

---

1 On this aspect see Halpern, Trebilcock and Turnbull 'An economic analysis of limited liability in corporation law' (1980) 30 Univ of Toronto Law Jo 117.
2 At the time of writing this restriction is contained in the Companies Act 1985, s 81. This will be repealed and replaced by s 170(1) of the Financial Services Act 1986 when that section is brought into force. As at 31 March 1990 there were 10,608 active public companies in England and Wales, compared with 947,793 active private companies: Department of Trade and Industry's Annual Report on Companies.
3 Of the 10,608 public companies between 3,000 and 3,500 are listed or quoted on one of the markets run by The Stock Exchange.
4 A recent example might be the formation of Eurotunnel plc together with its French counterpart, Eurotunnel SA, to build the channel tunnel. 1,166 public companies were incorporated in England and Wales in the 12 months to 31 March 1990: Department of Trade and Industry's Annual Report on Companies.

been a private company into a public one, to seek admission to one of the markets in securities and to offer shares in the company to the public[5].

The process of launching a public company by offering its shares to the public, whether it is a brand new company or a former private company, is known as flotation[6]. One must not think though of raising capital from the public as just comprising flotations. Existing public companies may also use the stock market to raise further capital from outside investors rather than retained profits. This may be by means of an offer to the public generally. More probably it will be by means of a rights issue, in which the new shares are offered to existing shareholders in proportion to their existing holding, or by a placing, in which shares are placed with certain selected investors who have agreed to take them. The company may be raising capital to expand its existing business or it may be planning to expand through acquisition of other businesses. Or the company may decide, instead of raising outside capital, to offer shares in itself as the consideration for the acquisition of another business or in exchange for the shares in a target company it is seeking to take over. This ability of companies to expand through acquisition by offering shares is one of the main advantages of converting a private company into a public one listed on a stock exchange.

Share sales by existing shareholders

So far we have referred to situations in which the company is raising capital for its own expansion. In many cases though the reason for shares in the company being offered to the public is because the existing shareholders wish to sell some of their shares, rather than the company raising fresh capital. It may be that in a family business the existing family members are all reaching retiring age and there is no one within the family to carry the business on. The family may wish to convert their capital into a more liquid form so they are prepared to sell their shares. If there is no single buyer ready to take over the company then it will be sensible to float the company and for the family to realise their shares through a public offering. Even if the present owners are not retiring they may still wish to diversify their investments by selling part of their shareholdings or it may just be they wish to realise their investment so as to have money available to use for a different purpose.

Formation of public companies

If the decision is taken to form a company as a public company, in addition to the requirements for registration of the company, the company will need to obtain a commencement of business certificate. Without one the company will not be entitled to commence business or exercise any borrowing

---

5 In the 12 months to 31 March 1990, 1087 companies converted from private to public in England and Wales: Department of Trade and Industry's Annual Report on Companies. There is some evidence that commercial advantages may flow from public company status and that it may be adopted even though there is no intention to raise capital from the public: *Financial Times*, 12 December 1989.

6 For light relief the reader is recommended to read, preferably aloud, *The Times* leading article of 22 March 1844, quoted in Hunt *The Development of the Business Corporation in England 1800–1867* (1936) pp 90–92.

powers[7]. To obtain such a certificate a director or secretary must make a statutory declaration that the minimum requirements for paid up share capital in public companies have been complied with[8]. When the company receives its commencement of business certificate that, like the certificate of incorporation, is conclusive evidence that the company is entitled to do business and exercise borrowing powers[9]. If the company has entered transactions without such a certificate, the company and any officers may be liable to a fine[10]. Furthermore, if the company fails to obtain a certificate within 21 days of being called upon to do so the directors are liable to compensate the other party to the transaction for any loss suffered by the company's failure to obtain such a certificate[11].

Conversion of private companies to public

Where a private company is converted into a public one, besides the members passing a special resolution to alter the memorandum etc[12], various documents must be delivered to the Registrar[13] and the company must show that it meets the more stringent rules on the raising and maintenance of share capital applicable to public companies[14].

Conversion of public companies to private

Not all public companies find the status an advantage. There are more requirements for the disclosure of its activities; it is less easy to organise the company's affairs to suit the interests of the family who may still own a large percentage of the equity; and there is the cost of dealing with large numbers of new shareholders. So sometimes companies convert back from public to private status[15]. This may happen, of course, where a company is taken over and becomes the wholly owned subsidiary of another company. But it does happen occasionally that the majority decides to buy out the minority and then revert to private status. The members must pass a special resolution altering the memorandum[16] and there is provision for a certain minority of members to object by application to the court[17]. In practice any dissenting minority are more likely to have been bought out before the change of status is made.

7 Section 117(1).
8 Section 117(3).
9 Section 117(6).
10 Section 117(7).
11 Section 117(8). It is difficult to envisage what loss may result since it is specifically provided that breach of the section shall not affect the validity of the transaction.
12 Sections 43(1)(a), (2) and 48(2).
13 Section 43(1)(b), (3).
14 Section 45.
15 277 companies converted from public to private status in England and Wales in the 12 months to 31 March 1990: Department of Trade and Industry's Annual Report on Companies.
16 Section 53(1)(a), (2).
17 Section 54.

THE STOCK EXCHANGE MARKETS

We have already seen that for a company effectively to raise capital from the public it must have its shares listed or quoted on a stock market. Apart from developments in the way securities are traded associated with Big Bang and the passing of the Financial Services Act 1986, two other developments during the 1980s had a particular impact on the organisation of stock markets in the UK. One was the opening of new markets for shares designed to cater for smaller companies with shorter trading records. The other was the move towards EC harmonisation of the requirements for admission to listing on the main stock market or 'official list' in each member state[18].

The Stock Exchange Official List

As a result companies joining the main market of the Stock Exchange are said to be admitted to the Official List and are correctly described as 'listed' rather than 'quoted' companies. A company may only be admitted to the Official List if it has agreed to abide by certain conditions imposed by the Exchange and contained in a book called Admission of Securities to Listing[19]. The market value of the shares being listed must be at least £700,000[20], though in practice it will usually be far greater than that. The company must have at least a three year trading record[1] and at least 25% of any class of shares being listed must be held by the public, ie persons who are not associated with the directors or major shareholders[2]. The company will have to publish listing particulars when it joins the Official List[3] and must publish interim reports to its shareholders as well as the statutory report and accounts[4]. In addition the company must abide by a number of continuing obligations the principal object of which is to secure immediate release of information which might have a material effect on market activity in, and prices of, listed securities[5].

The Unlisted Securities Market

In the early 1970s a number of licensed dealers in securities began to create a market outside the control of The Stock Exchange by offering to match buyers and sellers, or, in some cases, by dealing in shares as principals, a practice known as market-making. This Over The Counter Market or OTC as it was known grew steadily, one of its advantages being that it could offer a market for shares in companies that were too small to be admitted to The Stock Exchange. The Wilson Committee in its interim report on the

---

18 The motives for harmonisation are to provide equivalent minimum investor protection in different member states and to promote cross-border listings of companies.
19 But usually referred to as the Yellow Book because of the colour of its cover.
20 Admission of Securities to Listing, s 1, ch 2, para 3.
 1 Ibid, s 1, ch 2, para 5. The period was reduced from five years to bring it into line with the minimum requirement for official listing in other EC member states. A three year trading record is the minimum required under EEC Council Directive 79/279.OJ 1979 L66/21, Sch A, para 13.
 2 Ibid, s 1, ch 2, para 12.
 3 Ibid, s 1, ch 2, para 17.
 4 Ibid, s 5, ch 2, paras 23 and 24.
 5 Ibid, s 5, ch 1 and ch 2, para 1.

Financing of Small Firms[6], recommended that the government should consider how to promote the facilities of the OTC market. In anticipation of this The Stock Exchange launched in November 1980 the Unlisted Securities Market or USM[7] which was designed to provide a market for shares in smaller companies which did not qualify or did not choose listing on the main exchange. The minimum market capitalisation for shares quoted on the USM is £500,000[8]. The company need only have a two[9] year trading record and a minimum of only 10% of any class of quoted shares need be in public hands. In place of the Admission of Securities to Listing companies joining the USM must enter into the USM General Undertaking, a simpler set of obligations though it does include the obligation to send a half yearly interim report to shareholders. One of the functions of the USM was to provide a stepping stone onto the Official List for suitable companies and of the 839 companies that had joined the USM by the end of February 1991, 418 remained and 169 had graduated to the Official List.

The Third Market

Prompted by the success of the USM The Stock Exchange added a third tier to the market structure when it launched the prosaically named Third Market in January 1987. This was open to companies with only a one year trading record and there was no requirement that any particular percentage of shares be in public hands. The Third Market never repeated the success of the USM and when the minimum trading record for admission to the Official List was reduced from five years to three years it was decided to reduce the minimum period for entry to the USM from three years to two and to wind up the Third Market altogether.

METHODS OF MARKETING SHARES

When a company wishes to raise fresh capital by issuing shares there are a number of factors to be considered. Among these will be the method of marketing, who the shares are to be offered to, how the price is to be fixed, and what professional services the company should make use of. It may also be the case that it is not the company marketing the shares at all but an existing shareholder offering shares for sale. Many of the same considerations, however, arise here too. The final factor to bear in mind is whether the shares being marketed are in a company already listed or quoted on one of the markets run by The Stock Exchange, or whether the marketing accompanies a new entry into the particular market by the company concerned. In this section we look at these different considerations, at the various methods of marketing shares and the different transactions involved[10].

---

6 Cmnd 7503.
7 For an excellent account of the operation of the USM and OTC see G Bannock and A Doran *Going Public: the Markets in Unlisted Securities* (1987).
8 The conditions are set out in *Unlisted Securities Market*, published by The Stock Exchange, and known as the Green Book.
9 The period was reduced from three years when the minimum trading record for admission to the Official List was reduced from five years to three. See note 1 above.
10 See also *Initial Public Offers* the report of a Stock Exchange Review Committee published in February 1990 and New Equity Issues in the United Kingdom [1990] Bank of England Quarterly Bulletin 243.

Offers for subscription and offers for sale

Where the company itself offers the shares this is known as an offer for subscription and the persons who acquire the shares directly from the company are known as subscribers. Where the offer is not by the company itself but by an existing shareholder it is called an offer for sale and the persons who acquire the shares are known as purchasers[11]. In practice both the company and existing shareholders will often make use of the services of an issuing house which will acquire the shares from the company[12] or the existing shareholders and then offer them for sale to the public. Alternatively, the company or existing shareholders may use the issuing house purely as an agent without the shares concerned being allotted or transferred to the issuing house.

Whichever method is used, the price at which the shares are sold may either be that fixed by the seller (a fixed price offer) or that fixed by a system of tendering by interested buyers (a tender offer). The problem with a fixed price offer is judging the appropriate price. It is not unknown for the market value of shares, when dealings in them begin, to be at a considerable premium to the fixed offer price. To try and curtail this a tender offer may be used. Under a tender offer system the seller invites prospective purchasers to tender whatever price they wish for the shares, provided it is above a minimum or reserve figure indicated by the seller. The price at which the shares will actually be sold (known as 'the striking price') will be the highest price at which all the shares on offer will have been applied for and thus will be sold[13].

Where shares are sold at a fixed price the difficulty of predicting a price that will precisely match supply and demand means that offers will almost certainly be either under or oversubscribed. Since the seller and its advisers, in order to make the offer a success, will have agreed a price slightly below what they anticipate the market price will be, most fixed price offers are oversubscribed to a greater or lesser extent. Even a tender offer does not avoid this problem because at the striking price there may in fact be more

---

11 All the privatisations are of this type since it is usually the appropriate government minister who is selling the shares vested in his office. In some cases it is a parent company selling shares in a subsidiary. An example of this type was the privatisation of Jaguar where the shares were sold on behalf of BLMC Ltd which then used some of the proceeds to reduce its indebtedness to the government.

12 Hence this too is called an offer for sale since the company has allotted the shares to the issuing house which then offers them for sale. The sale of shares in TSB was an example of this since the TSB was not owned by the government and the entire net proceeds of the sale of shares went ultimately to the TSB itself. Where a company is joining one of the markets for the first time the most common pattern is for the company itself and its existing shareholders each to sell some shares. Only in so far as the company issues new shares will fresh capital be raised for the business and even then part of the proceeds may be being used to repay borrowings from existing shareholders rather than for fresh investment.

13 Under this system people may tender at a very high price safe in the knowledge that they will only end up paying the striking price which ought fairly to reflect the market value. They will of course have to write out a cheque for the number of shares applied for multiplied by the price tendered. If the cheque is dishonoured not only will they receive no shares but they may face criminal prosecution for attempting to obtain property by deception. In the privatisation of BAA an offer for sale by tender *without a common striking price* was used for a part of the shares being sold. Under this method all tenders above the level at which all the shares offered will be sold, are accepted *at the price tendered*.

applications than there are shares on offer[14]. Where the offer is oversubscribed the seller and its advisers will decide how to scale down or ballot the
applications. The fact that many offers are oversubscribed and that the
market price when dealings begin is often at a premium to the offer price has
led to the practice of 'stagging'. This term refers to applying for new issues of
shares with the intention of selling any shares acquired immediately dealings
begin. Although stags help to provide liquidity in the market when dealings
begin sellers usually try and discourage stagging, preferring no doubt that
any premium on the shares should go to longer term shareholders rather
than short term speculators[15].

If an offer by a public company is not fully subscribed then the company
cannot proceed to allot any of the shares offered unless the terms of the offer
allowed for allotment in any event, or, in the event of certain specified
conditions, which have been satisfied[16]. In practice sellers do not take the
risk of an offer not being fully taken up. Instead they will insure the risk with
underwriters who agree to take up any shares not applied for in the offer[17].
The underwriter will be paid a fee for the service which, however, cannot
exceed 10% of the issue price of the shares or such lesser sum as is authorised
by the company's articles of association[18].

In terms of the law of contract advertising an offer of shares constitutes an
invitation to treat. A person interested in acquiring shares fills in an application form which constitutes an offer which will then be accepted or rejected

---

14 Usually tenders will only be invited in figures rounded to the nearest 5 or 10p. It is not
impossible therefore that while, for example, at 180p not all the shares on offer would be
sold, at 175p the shares could be sold, say, four times over.
15 One way sellers do this is by requiring all applications to be accompanied by a cheque for the
full amount which must be capable of being met on first presentation. If the application is
accepted in part the company then sends a return cheque to the applicant for the balance. In
R v Greenstein; R v Green [1976] 1 All ER 1, [1975] 1 WLR 1353, CA the defendants
regularly applied for more shares than they could afford in the expectation that their
application would be scaled down. They relied on receiving the return cheques and having
them specially cleared so that their account would be in sufficient credit when the cheque
they had sent with their application was presented for payment. Using this method they
made 136 applications in 1971 and 1972 and their cheques were only dishonoured on 14
occasions. They were, however, charged under the Theft Act 1968, s 15 with obtaining
property by deception and convicted. If it is anticipated that the basis of allocation will
favour small applications then stags will be tempted to put in multiple applications. The
seller will usually reserve the right to consolidate suspected multiple applications or to reject
them altogether. However, in the case of government privatisations the price was fixed in
the expectation that there would be a premium when dealings began in order to encourage
wider share ownership. It was also known that the allocation basis would favour small
applications. It would partly defeat this objective if, by putting in multiple applications,
people could obtain more than their fair share. So in the case of privatisation issues persons
putting in multiple applications have sometimes been prosecuted, again under the Theft Act
1968, s 15. See, for example, *R v Best* (1987) Times, 6 October.
16 Section 84(1). An allotment in breach of s 84(1) is voidable provided steps are taken within
one month of the allotment. The directors may also be liable to compensate the applicant
and proceedings may be taken against them for up to two years: s 85.
17 It is slightly curious that the underwriters are often institutions which might be expected to
apply for shares as ordinary applicants or which may already own shares in the company
concerned.
18 Section 97. This figure may be amended when rules are made under the Financial Services
Act 1986, s 169(2). See ibid, Sch 16, para 16. It is possible the limit will be removed
altogether, the only control then being via disclosure obligations. See the consultative
document *Listing Particulars and Public Offer Prospectuses* published by the Department of
Trade and Industry in July 1990.

by the person selling the shares[19]. The successful applicant will then be sent a letter of acceptance which will normally be renounceable. At this stage the applicant will not be registered as a shareholder in the company. For an interim period of two or three months if applicants wish to sell any of their holdings they may renounce their right to be registered as shareholders in favour of someone who buys that right from them. In other words a renounceable letter of acceptance is marketable in the same way as shares themselves. At the end of the interim period the company will enter in the register of members those persons now entitled to the letters of acceptance and will send them share certificates[20].

Placings

Offering shares to the public at large is inevitably a lengthy process. It is also expensive not only in terms of printing costs, advertising costs, underwriting and other professional fees but also in terms of the discount to the anticipated market price that must be built in to make sure the offer is a success. For these reasons companies will often prefer to raise capital via a procedure under which the broker sponsoring the issue finds persons interested in acquiring shares in the company and places the shares with them. This process is known as placing. The Stock Exchange, however, is concerned that raising capital in this selective way may prevent a wide spread of shareholdings in the company and inhibit the development of a market in the shares. For this reason it is provided that companies being listed for the first time may only raise a maximum of £15m via a placing by the sponsor with its own clients[1]. There must also be at least 100 placees[2]. If the issue is raising between £15m and £30m then the sponsoring broker may place up to 75% of the total or £15m whichever is less[3] and must allocate to at least five placees per £1m placed[4]. The balance of the issue must then be marketed either by an offer for sale or through other brokers[3]. Issues raising over £30m must include an offer for sale[5] but up to 50% of the issue may be 'taken firm', that is either placed or reserved to the institutions underwriting the offer[6]. If this is done the allocation of the remainder must favour non-institutional applicants[7].

---

19 One advantage to the investor of acquiring shares this way, rather than through a market purchase, is that there will be no broker's commission or stamp duty to add to the purchase price. If an application is made through a broker the company, rather than the broker's client, will pay commission to the brokers out of the proceeds of sale. This is authorised under s 98(3).
20 The company must also make a return of allotments to the Registrar of Companies: s 88.
 1 Admission of Securities to Listing, s 1, ch 3, para 2.2.
 2 Ibid, s 1, ch 3, para 2.5(a). There must also be at least one market maker independent of the sponsoring broker and at least 5% of the issue must be offered to independent market makers: ibid, s 1, ch 3, para 2.5(b).
 3 Ibid, s 1, ch 3, para 2.6.
 4 Ibid, s 1, ch 3, para 2.7(a). In this case there must be at least two independent market makers and at least 5% of the shares placed must be offered to independent market makers: ibid, s 1, ch 3, para 2.7(b).
 5 Ibid, s 1, ch 3, para 1.1.
 6 Ibid, s 1, ch 3, para 1.2. Again there must be at least two independent market makers and at least 5% of the shares taken firm must be offered to the independent market makers: ibid, s 1, ch 3, para 1.4.
 7 Ibid, s 1, ch 3, Introduction.

Rights issues and open offers

A rights issue is where a company offers shares to its existing shareholders in proportion to their existing shareholding. In the case of companies listed on The Stock Exchange the procedure for a rights issue is for the company formally to allot the new shares to the shareholders. They are informed of this by means of a letter of allotment which, however, must be renounce-able[8]. In other words shareholders who do not wish to take up their rights must be able to sell these rights to someone else. Furthermore, there is protection for shareholders who neither take up their rights nor sell them. Unless specifically agreed by the general meeting, the company must arrange to sell any shares not taken up, for the benefit of the shareholders entitled to them[9].

An open offer, like a rights issue, is an offer of shares to existing share-holders. But, unlike a rights issue, it is not pro rata to existing sharehold-ings[10]. In other words existing shareholders may apply for as many shares as they wish and the offer may, of course, be oversubscribed which a strict rights issue cannot be. In procedural terms it is an offer for subscription addressed only to existing shareholders. It will not be done by a letter of allotment and no shares will automatically be sold on behalf of any share-holders who do not apply[10].

Under s 89 companies issuing new equity shares for purely cash considera-tion are normally[11] obliged to do so via a rights issue, unless the directors and shareholders have agreed to dis-apply the section[12]. From the point of view of the company management a rights issue is seen as a relatively expensive way of raising capital compared with a placing. In order to ensure that the shares are taken up the discount to the current market price on a rights issue will be greater than that on a placing[13]. There will also be the cost of underwriting a rights issue as well as greater printing and advertising costs. Because the shareholders must consent to any dis-application of s 89, The Stock Exchange no longer places any restriction on existing listed companies using placings instead[14]. However, in response to concern by the institu-tional shareholders about dis-application of s 89, The Stock Exchange agreed certain guidelines with representatives of corporate treasurers and institutional shareholders as to when dis-application would be acceptable[15].

---

8 Ibid, s 1, ch 3, para 4.2.

9 Ibid, s 1, ch 3, para 4.3.

10 Ibid, s 1, ch 3, para 5.1.

11 Section 89 does not apply to an issue of shares for cash to an employee share scheme: s 89(5). Nor does it apply to a capitalisation or bonus issue: s 94(2). Finally, a private company may exclude s 89 altogether: s 91.

12 Under s 95. There are two methods of dis-application but both entail the consent of the directors and of the shareholders given by special resolution.

13 It is only the management who will see the greater discount on a rights issue compared with a placing as expensive. To the shareholders it does not matter what the discount is on a rights issue since the wealth that flows out of the company goes to the people entitled to that wealth in the first place. Whereas on a placing any discount to the market price represents a transfer of wealth away from the existing shareholders.

14 Admission of Securities to Listing, s 1, ch 3, para 2.2.

15 See the Pre-emption Guidelines published in October 1987 (replacing those published in 1981). Under the 1987 guidelines the institutional shareholders have agreed to support dis-applications provided they increase the issued share capital by not more than 5% in any one year or 7½% over three years. For listed companies dis-application resolutions can only last for one year: Admission of Securities to Listing, s 5, ch 2, para 37.1.

Other methods of marketing shares

Offers for subscription, offers for sale, placings and rights issues are the main methods of marketing shares where the company's purpose is to raise money. But companies may also offer shares to their employees as part of an employee share scheme[16], they may offer shares to the shareholders in another company as consideration for a takeover[17] or they may issue shares to their existing shareholders as a capitalisation or bonus issue[18]. Finally, there is one important transaction which needs to be mentioned in this context although it does not involve the company in issuing any shares at all. This is where a company merely seeks a listing or quotation on one of the markets run by The Stock Exchange. This is a process known as an Introduction[19].

THE NATURE AND FUNCTION OF SECURITIES REGULATION

The purposes of securities regulation

Before looking at the detail of how the marketing of securities is regulated in the U K it may be helpful to consider the purposes behind securities regulation and, in the light of that, to consider the various techniques available. As we have seen the reasons why stock markets develop is to provide a forum in which shares can be traded. The existence of a market in which shares can be sold will encourage such investment to take place. Without a market in which to realise their investment, investors would require a higher return to compensate them for this lack of liquidity. So the existence of a market also makes it cheaper for companies to raise externally generated funds for investment.

If the market is operating efficiently then the price of a company's shares, quoted on the market, will reflect the profitability of the use to which the assets of the company are currently being put. This is important to the overall national economy in that it will enable successful companies to raise further funds more easily, allowing them to expand their operations and ultimately increase the overall wealth of society by ensuring that assets are allocated to their most productive use. It also means that companies with poor management become vulnerable to takeover bids which may result in the assets being put to a new, more productive, use or in the management being replaced. Conversely, successful managements will be able to expand their operations because it will be cheaper for such companies, relative to others, to raise money for acquisitions or to offer their own equity as consideration for an acquisition.

These, admittedly very basic, propositions about the operation of the stock market are intended to show how the stock market plays a role in the national economy. The fundamental objective of securities regulation must be, therefore, to help the stock market operate more efficiently in fulfilling the functions just described. There are other objectives as well[20]. Promoting

---

16 Admission of Securities to Listing, s 1, ch 3, para 9.
17 Ibid, s 1, ch 3, para 8. See also Chapter 34 below.
18 Admission of Securities to Listing, s 1, ch 3, para 6.
19 Ibid, s 1, ch 3, para 3.
20 See the White Paper Financial Services in the United Kingdom (Cmnd 9432) ch 3.

the U K as a financial centre by ensuring that investors have confidence in the U K securities market is one. Stimulating competition and innovation in the financial services sector itself, so that the assets it employs are used efficiently could also be described as one of the objectives.

Particular aspects of securities regulation may be seen as furthering these broad objectives. For example, providing a regulatory framework will discourage dishonesty and encourage those who wish to adopt high standards to do so. Dishonest trade practices represent a form of unfair competition which leads ultimately to a misallocation of resources. In theory market forces may be expected to discourage dishonesty because in the long run investors will shun the dishonest trader. However, a regulatory structure may help to reveal dishonesty more quickly. It will also encourage honest traders to realise that they do not need to adopt the same tactics in order to compete with the dishonest, by reassuring them that dishonesty will result in a sanction. A regulatory structure may also aim to promote professional competence among the personnel in the securities market[1]. Finally, a specific influence on the regulation of the securities market in all member states of the EC has been the desire to achieve harmonisation of such regulation within the EC in order to promote an equivalent level of investor protection and to facilitate cross-border listings by companies.

Securities regulation in the context of investor protection

One way to look at the controls on the marketing of shares in the U K is as part of the overall pattern of investor protection. Purchasing shares is, after all, only one method people may choose to invest their savings. For the private investor other methods include investments such as building society deposits, unit trusts, life assurance policies, pensions and perhaps even commodities. The variety and complexity of new methods of investment since the first Prevention of Fraud (Investment) Act was passed in 1939[2], together with a number of financial frauds, led the Department of Trade in 1981 to appoint Professor Gower to conduct a review of investor protection[3]. This culminated in the passing of the Financial Services Act 1986, Pts IV and V of which deal specifically with the marketing of shares and debentures[4].

The Act as a whole, however, provides a comprehensive framework for the regulation of investment business and investor protection. The basic control imposed by the Act[5] is the prohibition on carrying on investment

---

1 See Report of the Review of Investor Protection, Pt 1 (Cmnd 9125) pp 59–61.
2 The Prevention of Fraud (Investments) Act 1958 was largely a re-enactment of the 1939 Act.
3 Professor Gower's reports are an invaluable aid to understanding the problems the Financial Services Act deals with and the solutions it adopts. He first produced a discussion document *Review of Investor Protection* (1982). His report, under the same title, was published in two parts (Cmnd 9125) in 1984 and 1985. Between the publication of Pts I and II the government published its White Paper, see footnote 20 above.
4 There are useful historical surveys of investor protection in BAK Rider, C Abrams and E Ferran *Guide to the Financial Services Act 1986* (2nd edn 1989) chs 1 and 2 and R Pennington *The Law of the Investment Markets* (1990) ch 2.
5 Financial Services Act 1986, s 3.

business in the U K except by authorised[6] or exempt persons[7]. Authorisation can be achieved by membership of a self-regulating organisation[8] recognised for the purposes of the Act[9] by the Securities and Investments Board[10], or through certification by a similarly recognised professional body[11], or via direct authorisation by the Board itself[12]. In practice those whose main investment business is in relation to shares will be authorised by virtue of being members of The Securities and Futures Association, one of the recognised self-regulating organisations.

Techniques of regulation

The most important method of achieving the aims and objects of securities regulation outlined above is requiring full disclosure of information about the company involved and the securities being marketed. For the stock market to operate efficiently as much information as possible must be available to the market. For this reason there are rules requiring the publication of certain information whenever new securities are introduced or marketed and containing obligations to notify any information which might have a material impact on the valuation of securities[13]. Some economists argue that market forces will induce companies voluntarily to provide information to the market and that elaborate disclosure requirements are unnecessary[14]. Neither The Stock Exchange nor Parliament, however, has been prepared to rely on market forces alone. We shall be looking at the detailed provisions on disclosure of information in listing particulars and prospectuses in the next section.

The second major aspect of regulating the marketing of securities is controlling the personnel involved so as to ensure their integrity and financial standing. This is achieved in the first place by restricting the carrying on of investment business to those authorised under the Financial Services Act[15]. This is buttressed by a specific prohibition on publishing advertisements offering to buy or sell investments, including shares, except by authorised persons or where the contents have been approved by an

---

6 Ibid, ss 7–34. Companies in issuing their own shares or debentures are not, however, regarded as carrying on investment business: ibid, Sch 1, para 28(3).

7 Ibid, ss 35–46. Exempt persons will include, among others, the Bank of England, Lloyds, investment exchanges and clearing houses.

8 Ibid, s 7.

9 Ibid, s 10.

10 The Act refers to recognition by the Secretary of State but it is part of the self-regulatory basis of the controls that many of the Secretary of State's powers can be transferred to an independent, non-statutory agency: ibid, s 114. The Securities and Investments Board is a private company limited by guarantee. Although its members are appointed jointly by the Secretary of State and the Governor of the Bank of England they are not Crown servants. The system of regulation is paid for by a levy on recognised self-regulating organisations and professional bodies and on those directly authorised. There is also an 80p levy on stock market transactions over £1,000 of which 50p goes to the Securities and Investments Board and 30p to finance the Takeover Panel.

11 Financial Services Act 1986, s 15.

12 Ibid, s 25.

13 See W M H Grover and J C Baillie *Proposals for a Securities Market Law for Canada – Disclosure Requirements* (1976) pp 389–393.

14 For a discussion of the economic basis for disclosure requirements see R A Posner and K E Scott *Economics of Corporation Law and Securities Regulation* (1980) chapter 10.

15 Financial Services Act 1986, s 3.

authorised person[16]. There are, however, exceptions to this prohibition[17]. Most cases where listing particulars or prospectuses are required to be published are excepted[18] because they are governed by separate rules[19] which impose a stricter regime that permits their form, content, scrutiny and distribution to be regulated. The final question in relation to techniques of regulation is whether, if breaches of the rules do occur, the sanctions should be based in the civil or criminal law, or should take the form of disciplinary measures imposed by a self-regulating organisation[20].

REGULATING SECURITIES OFFERINGS

Development of legislative controls

PERIOD UP TO 1985

Until 1985 offers of company securities were regulated by either the Companies Act[1] or the Prevention of Fraud (Investments) Act[2]. These applied whether or not the company was listed on The Stock Exchange, although if it was listed The Stock Exchange's own requirements, contained in Admission of Securities to Listing, also had to be complied with. The central requirement of the Companies Act provisions was that any offer of securities to the public had to be made via a prospectus containing certain statutory information. As was pointed out earlier[3], part of the EC programme to establish a common market includes the harmonisation of rules relating to the admission of securities to listing in member states. Three directives, covering the conditions for admission of securities to listing[4], requiring the publication of listing particulars containing certain prescribed information[5] and requiring the publication of interim financial statements[6] were implemented via the Stock Exchange (Listing) Regulations 1984[7]. Since in the UK offers to the public of securities for which admission to listing is being sought usually happen at the same time as the application for listing, when the directives were implemented in the UK the requirement to publish a prospectus was subsumed within the requirement to publish listing particulars so that only

---

16 Ibid, s 57. There is also a ban on making unsolicited calls to promote investments, even for authorised or exempted person, unless an exemption applies: ibid, s 56.

17 The Secretary of State may grant exemptions: ibid, s 58(3)(4). See the two Financial Services Act 1986 (Investment Advertisements) (Exemption) Orders 1988, SI 1988/316 and SI 1988/716.

18 Financial Services Act 1986, s 58(1)(d), (2).

19 Ibid, Pts IV and V. See also Sch 15, para 8 which exempts prospectuses under the Companies Act 1985 until Pt V is brought into operation.

20 See, for example, ibid, s 171.

1 The Companies Act 1985, Pt III and Sch 3 (replacing the Companies Act 1948, ss 37–46 and Sch 4) applied to offers for cash made by the company itself.

2 The Prevention of Fraud (Investments) Act 1958, ss 13, 14 applied inter alia to offers by existing shareholders or offers of shares in exchange for other shares as on a takeover.

3 See above, p 549.

4 EEC Council Directive 79/279. OJ 1979 L 66/21 ('The Admissions Directive').

5 EEC Council Directive 80/390. OJ 1980 L 100/1 ('The Listing Particulars Directive').

6 EEC Council Directive 82/121. OJ 1982 L 48/26 ('The Interim Reports Directive').

7 SI 1984/716.

one document need be published[8]. This was achieved by the Stock Exchange (Listing) Regulations excluding most of the Companies Act rules[9] so that offers of securities to be admitted to the Official List of the Stock Exchange became governed by a discrete set of rules, a situation that has continued despite the repeal of the Regulations by the Financial Services Act 1986.

PERIOD FROM 1985 ONWARDS

One of the problems with the legislation as it existed in 1985 was the variety of sources and differing applications of rules governing offers of company securities[10]. Part of the purpose behind the Financial Services Act 1986 was thus to bring all the controls under one statutory umbrella. As far as listed companies are concerned the contents of the three harmonisation directives are now incorporated into the rules in Admission of Securities to Listing. The directives are nonetheless implemented in a legally binding way because all applications for admission to the Official List must comply with Pt IV of the Financial Services Act[11]. Part IV in turn requires that companies comply with, and continue to abide by, the rules in Admission of Securities to Listing[12]. Offers of securities which are, or are to be, listed on The Stock Exchange are now, therefore, governed by Pt IV of the Financial Services Act together with the requirements in Admission of Securities to Listing. Offers of securities which are not to be admitted to The Stock Exchange Official list are to be governed by Pt V of the Financial Services Act and the regulations to be made under the Act. As yet Pt V has not been brought into force and no regulations have been made[13]. Until that happens public offers of unlisted securities continue to be governed by the Companies Act[14].

One reason Pt V has not yet been brought into operation is because two further EC harmonisation measures have been promulgated and it is sensible to make any necessary changes to the legislation before bringing it into force[15]. The first measure consists of a directive[16] providing for the harmonisation of rules relating to the publication of a prospectus whenever securities are offered to the public for the first time. This applies whether the securities are to be listed on an exchange or not but in the case of securities to be listed there are provisions to avoid duplication between listing particulars and prospectuses which are examined below. The second measure is the introduction of the principle of mutual recognition of listing particulars and

8 It is helpful though to remember that listing particulars thus often fulfil two separate functions: as listing particulars on the admission of securities to listing and as a prospectus containing statutory information to be published when securities are offered to the public.
9 Stock Exchange (Listing) Regulations 1984, SI 1984/716, para 7(1).
10 See the Gower Report (Cmnd 9125) Pt I, ch 9 and Pt II, ch 6.
11 Financial Services Act 1986, s 142(1). Part IV of the Act came into force for privatisations on 12 January 1987 and for other listed securities on 16 February 1987.
12 Ibid, ss 144(1) and 153(1).
13 March 1991.
14 Companies Act 1985, Pt III, ie ss 56–79 and Sch 3.
15 The government had hoped to have the necessary legislative changes in place by 17 April 1991 which is the date for implementation of the directives but this was not achieved. A helpful discussion as to the form of possible changes, however, is contained in a consultative document *Listing Particulars and Public Offer Prospectuses: Implementation of Part V of the Financial Services Act 1986 and Related EC Directives* published by the Department of Trade and Industry in July 1990.
16 EEC Council Directive 89/298. OJ 1989 L 124/8 ('The Prospectus Directive').

prospectuses[17]. Under this principle where applications for listing or public offers of securities are made simultaneously or within a short interval[18] in two or more member states an issuer of securities need only comply with the rules of one member state in order for the listing particulars or prospectus to be acceptable in the other member states. The member state whose rules the issuer must comply with is the one where the issuer has its registered office provided that the issuer is seeking a listing or making an offer in that member state; if not then the issuer can choose one of the member states in which it is seeking a listing or making an offer[19]. In the case of a public offer of shares which is not to be accompanied by an application for listing, the issuer must, however, choose a member state which provides for the pre-vetting of prospectuses, assuming that the rules of one of the member states in which a public offer is to be made do so provide[20]. At present in the UK pre-vetting is only carried out by The Stock Exchange and only where securities are to be admitted to listing. In order to ensure that prospectuses issued by UK registered companies will be acceptable in other member states provision will be made for companies to request that a prospectus be pre-vetted by the Stock Exchange even though the shares are not to be listed on the Stock Exchange[1].

Offers of securities to be listed on The Stock Exchange

ADMISSION TO LISTING

The directives harmonising the treatment of securities admitted to official listing provide that supervision of the requirements may be devolved by governments to a so-called 'competent authority'. Under Pt IV of the Financial Services Act the competent authority is the Council of The Stock Exchange[2]. The Council is given wide powers to make and enforce listing rules. It may in certain circumstances refuse applications for listing[3]; it may

17 As to listing particulars, see EEC Council Directive 80/390 art 24a (as inserted by art 1 of EEC Council Directive 87/345. OJ 1987 L 185/81). As to prospectuses, see EEC Council Directive 89/298 art 21. See the Companies Act 1985 (Mutual Recognition of Prospectuses) Regulations 1991, SI 1991/823.
18 The Stock Exchange has interpreted 'a short interval' as six weeks: Admission of Securities to Listing, s 8, ch 2, para 2(b).
19 As to listing particulars, see EEC Council Directive 80/390 art 24 (as inserted by art 1 of EEC Council Directive 87/345). As to prospectuses see EEC Council Directive 89/298, art 20(1).
20 EEC Council Directive 89/298, art 20(2).
 1 See consultative document *Listing Particulars and Public Offer Prospectuses* pp 19–20.
 2 Ibid, s 142(6).
 3 Ibid, s 144(3). All applications for listing must have the consent of the company. A major shareholder could not apply, therefore, independently of the company, to have the shares listed: ibid, s 143(2). No private company may apply for listing: ibid, s 143(3). It has been pointed out that a literal interpretation of s 143(3) might allow a private company to apply for an introduction to The Stock Exchange in respect of already issued shares: Rider, Abrams and Ferran *Guide to the Financial Services Act 1986* (2nd edn 1989) p 163. However, the Stock Exchange rules prohibit private companies applying for listing: Admission of Securities to Listing, s 1, ch 2, para 1. It would in any case undermine the basis on which companies are classified as either public or private if private companies could be listed. Much of the legislation which applies only to public companies, such as disclosure of substantial shareholdings under the Companies Act 1985 Pt VI, does so on the assumption that public companies are the appropriate vehicles for investment by the public at large and additional measures of investor protection are therefore provided only in relation to that type of company.

suspend listings[4] and may discontinue[5] them altogether where there are special circumstances which preclude normal regular dealings in the securities[6]. A decision of the competent authority to refuse admission to listing or to discontinue a listing must be subject to judicial review[7] but in common with other regulatory bodies under the Financial Services Act[8], the competent authority is granted limited immunity from liability in damages[9]. Neither the Council nor any members, officers or servants may be made liable in damages for anything done or omitted in the discharge or purported discharge of any functions of the Council under Pt IV, unless the act or omission is shown to have been in bad faith.

FORM AND CONTENT OF LISTING PARTICULARS AND PROSPECTUSES

The Council is specifically empowered to include in the listing rules a requirement for the publication of listing particulars as a condition of admission to listing[10]. The listing rules, in fact, require the publication of listing particulars for any application for listing of securities unless the case falls within one of the exceptions[11]. Examples of excepted cases are: a capitalisation issue to holders of existing listed shares[12]; where the new shares will increase the size of an existing class of listed shares by less than 10%[13]; or, where shares are allotted to employees, if shares of the same class are already listed[13]. In contrast listing particulars are required where a company is introduced on to the Official List even though no new shares are being issued. The introduction carries an implicit invitation to investors to acquire existing shares and the necessary background information about the company must therefore be made available.

The detailed contents of the listing particulars are governed by the Admission of Securities to Listing[14]. In addition the Financial Services Act lays down a general duty for listing particulars to contain all the information that investors and their professional advisers would need to make a fair assessment of the value of the securities[15]. If material changes occur or new

---

4 Ibid, s 145(2). Admission of Securities to Listing, s 1, ch 4.
5 Ibid, s 145(1).
6 These requirements seem more appropriate to the power of suspension rather than discontinuance. In relation to discontinuance these requirements seem to place too great a restriction on the powers of The Stock Exchange.
7 EEC Council Directive 79/279 art 15. See also Beatson (1987) 8 Co Law 34.
8 Financial Services Act 1986, s 187(1), (3), (6).
9 Ibid, s 187(4). The immunity covers liability to investors as well as liability to companies who claim to have been wrongly refused admission or which claim to have had their listing wrongly suspended or discontinued. In relation to investors there may be immunity at common law anyhow: *Yuen Kun Yeu v A-G of Hong Kong* [1988] AC 175, [1987] 2 All ER 705, PC. See also Feldman 'Liability of Regulatory and Disciplinary Bodies' (1987) 3 Professional Negligence 23.
10 Financial Services Act 1986, s 144(2). Under the Listing Particulars Directive the publication of listing particulars is obligatory except in specified circumstances: EEC Council Directive 79/279, arts 3, 6. If the competent authority does not comply with the directive the Secretary of State may direct it to do so: Financial Services Act 1986, s 192.
11 Admission of Securities to Listing, s 3, ch 1, para 1.1.
12 Ibid, s 3, ch 1, para 5.3.
13 Ibid, s 3, ch 1, para 5.4.
14 Ibid, s 3, ch 2.
15 Financial Services Act 1986, s 146. In the Listing Particulars Directive it is clear that the general duty of disclosure is the primary obligation and the detailed rules are secondary: EEC Council Directive 80/390, arts 4.1 and 5.1. It is appropriate therefore that the general duty is contained in the Act itself.

information becomes available after publication of the listing particulars, supplementary listing particulars are required to be published[16]. One of the crucial respects in which investor protection by The Stock Exchange has been in advance of that of the Companies Act is in the requirement for pre-vetting of prospectuses[17]. No listing particulars may be issued unless they have been approved by The Stock Exchange[18]. The listing particulars must also be registered before they are published[19]. Finally, The Stock Exchange lays down minimum levels of publication[20] in terms of national newspaper coverage, availability in brochure form and circulation in the statistical services.

The rules governing admission to listing and the publication of listing particulars reflect the requirements of the Admissions Directive and the Listing Particulars Directive. When it is implemented listed companies will also be required to comply with provisions of the Prospectus Directive[1]. This requires publication of a prospectus containing prescribed information whenever securities which are not already listed are offered to the public for the first time[2]. However, if the securities are the subject of an application for listing the requirements as to content, pre-vetting and publication are the same as for listing particulars[3]. Furthermore if a prospectus complying with those requirements was drawn up in the three months prior to the application for listing it must be recognised as fulfilling the requirements for listing particulars[4]. In most cases, therefore, the present practice whereby a single document serves as both listing particulars and prospectus will continue.

Offers of unlisted securities

FRAMEWORK OF CONTROLS

Offers of securities which are not to be admitted to The Stock Exchange Official List are due to be governed by Pt V of the Financial Services Act and

---

16 Financial Services Act 1986, s 147. As to the power of the Council to grant exemptions from disclosure requirements, see ibid, s 148.
17 See Review of Investor Protection (Cmnd 9125) Pt I, paras 9.16–9.23. In practice some of the most effective enforcement of high standards of disclosure comes from the requirement that every company listed on The Stock Exchange must be sponsored by a member of the Exchange: Admission of Securities to Listing, s 1, ch 1, paras 4, 5.
18 Admission of Securities to Listing, s 3, ch 1, para 2.1. Recently it has become increasingly common to produce abbreviated or mini-prospectuses and separate application forms. These must also be approved by The Stock Exchange unless their issue has been authorised without approval: Financial Services Act 1986, s 154(1). See Admission of Securities to Listing, s 2, ch 1, para 9 and s 2, ch 3, paras 3.10 and 3.11. Breach of s 154 as well as carrying criminal penalties may also give rise to civil liability under ss 61, 62 and 62A: ibid, s 154(2), (3).
19 Financial Services Act 1986, s 149.
20 Admission of Securities to Listing, s 2, ch 3.
1 EEC Council Directive 89/298.
2 Ibid, arts 1 and 4.
3 Ibid, art 7.
4 Listing Particulars Directive: EEC Council Directive 80/390, art 24b (as inserted by EEC Council Directive 90/211, art 1). As to the recognition of listing particulars and prospectuses approved in other member states, see above pp 559–560.

the regulations to be made under the Act[5]. The basis of the controls is the requirement that a prospectus must be registered containing certain prescribed information. The way this requirement is imposed is by prohibiting the publishing of advertisements offering shares unless a prospectus has been registered[6]. The Secretary of State is also permitted to make rules regulating the terms and conduct of the offer[7]. In imposing the registration obligation, and the provisions as to the contents of the prospectus, the Act draws a distinction between offers of securities to be quoted on an approved exchange[8] and other offers[9]. An approved exchange for this purpose means[10] a recognised investment exchange[11] which has been approved by the Secretary of State for the purpose of Pt V of the Act[12]. We will therefore deal with the two types of offer separately and begin with offers where shares are to be quoted on an approved exchange.

OFFERS OF SECURITIES TO BE QUOTED ON AN APPROVED EXCHANGE

No advertisement[13] offering securities[14] to be quoted on an approved exchange is to be issued[13] unless either (i) a prospectus containing certain specified information has been submitted to and approved by the exchange and delivered for registration to the Registrar of Companies, or (ii) the advertisement is such that it cannot lead to an agreement until such a prospectus is so

5 As at March 1991 Pt V of the Financial Services Act 1986, ie ss 158–171 had not been brought into force and no regulations had been made. Until then offers of unlisted securities continue to be governed by the Companies Act 1985, Pt III, ie ss 56–79 and Sch 3. This work is written, however, on the assumption that the Financial Services Act 1986, Pt V, will be brought into operation, at which time the Companies Act provisions will be repealed. However, before Part V is brought into force it is likely to be amended to take account of the Prospectus Directive. Reference will therefore also be made to the consultative document *Listing Particulars and Public Offer Prospectuses* published in July 1990.
6 This compares with the Companies Act provisions under which the prospectus which is registered is also the offer document. Under the Financial Services Act the offer document and prospectus are separate, only the latter being registered.
7 Financial Services Act 1986, s 169. The possible content of such rules is discussed in the consultative document *Listing Particulars and Public Offer Prospectuses* pp 20–22. Under the statute the purpose of the conduct rules must be to ensure that persons to whom the offer is addressed are treated fairly and equally. The government's provisional intention is to impose this as a general requirement and leave the courts to determine what does constitute fair and equal treatment. The statute does allow the rules to include provision for priority among applicants and it is likely that the rules will permit preference to be given to employees and to applicants for smaller numbers of shares. Listed companies making an offer for sale may normally only give preferential allocation to existing shareholders, directors or employees and preferential allocations must not account for more than 10% of the shares offered to the public: Admission of Securities to Listing, s 1, ch 3, para 1.3. The present rules in the Companies Act 1985, s 82, restricting the acceptance or revocation of applications, and which will be repealed when Part V is brought into force, are unlikely to be included in any new rules. Any benefits they confer are outweighed by the constraint they impose on issuers.
8 Financial Services Act 1986, s 159.
9 Ibid, s 160.
10 Ibid, s 158(6).
11 Ibid, s 37.
12 Presumably the Unlisted Securities Market is a likely candidate for approval.
13 Financial Services Act 1986, s 207(2).
14 Ibid, s 158(4).

submitted, approved and delivered for registration[15]. It will be noted that these provisions cover advertisements in which the company itself is offering shares and those in which an existing shareholder offers shares. The requirement for approval of the prospectus before it may be published also means that its contents will have been pre-vetted. In this respect investors in shares to be quoted on an approved exchange are protected in a similar manner to investors in shares which are to be admitted to the Official List[16]. The Prospectus Directive is drafted in terms of 'securities which are offered to the public for the first time'[17]. It would be possible therefore to exclude from Part V offers which are not to the public even though the securities are to be quoted on an approved exchange. However, as the consultative document points out 'the admission of securities to dealings implies an expectation that a subsequent market will exist in the securities. The issue of a prospectus establishes a basis for valuation of the securities and underpins the development of a market in them, irrespective of the precise circumstances of the initial offer. Accordingly there is a strong case for requiring all prospectuses and other selling documents issued under s 159 of the Financial Services Act to comply with the requirements of the Prospectus Directive, even if the offer concerned is not an offer to the public[18].

OTHER OFFERS OF SECURITIES

Where the offer is of securities which are not to be quoted on an approved exchange then no advertisement for the securities must be published unless either (i) a prospectus containing certain specified information has been delivered for registration to the Registrar of Companies[19], or (ii) the advertisement is such that it cannot lead to agreement until such a prospectus is registered[20]. In this case the Act specifically makes these restrictions apply both to offers by the company itself and to offers by existing shareholders in certain circumstances. An offer by the company itself is called a primary offer and the persons acquiring the shares are called subscribers[1]. The section applies whether the shares are offered for cash or non-cash consideration[2].

---

15 Ibid, s 159(1). There is an exception where a prospectus relating to the securities has been registered in the previous 12 months and the exchange certifies that investors have enough information: ibid, s 159(2). Other exceptions are contained in s 161.

16 See above, footnote 15. It is possible that pre-vetting will be restricted to cases where issuers wish their prospectuses to be recognised in other member states and that pre-vetting will only be carried out by The Stock Exchange: see the discussion of mutual recognition on pp 559–560 above.

17 EEC Council Directive 89/298, art 1.

18 *Listing Particulars and Public Offer Prospectuses* pp 18–19. There does not, however, appear to be any intention to extend Part V to apply to mere introductions to quotation on approved exchanges, not accompanied by any offer.

19 Note that here there will be no pre-vetting of contents. Even so it is doubtful that any modern prospectus would rival the audacity of one eighteenth century prospectus entitled 'For an undertaking which shall in due time be revealed'. The public was so keen to invest in any enterprise that despite the lack of candour, or perhaps because of it, the promoter received 1,000 subscriptions on the morning of publication, with which he disappeared in the afternoon: Stanhope's *History of England*, vol II, p 11, quoted by Napier in *A Century of Law Reform* (1901) p 383.

20 Financial Services Act 1986, s 160(1).

1 Ibid, s 160(2). It also applies to offers inviting persons to underwrite an issue of securities.

2 Under the Companies Act 1985 the prospectus provisions only applied where the offer of shares was for cash consideration: *Governments Stock and Other Securities Investment Co Ltd v Christopher* [1956] 1 All ER 490, [1956] 1 WLR 237. This will be reversed under the

An offer by an existing shareholder is called a secondary offer[3]. The prohibition on advertising securities unless a prospectus has been registered applies to offers by existing shareholders in three circumstances. The first is where the offer is by a person who acquired the securities from the company concerned with a view to advertising them for sale[4]. This will apply, for example, where the company uses the services of an issuing house because the company will usually allot the shares to the issuing house which then offers them for sale. It will also apply where a company issues shares to its existing shareholders so that they can realise part of their investment by selling shares. There is a rebuttable presumption that a person acquired securities with a view to advertising them for sale if they are advertised for resale either within six months of the acquisition or before the person has paid for them[5]. Secondly, a prospectus must be registered where the shares are acquired from an existing shareholder, and not directly from the company, unless the shares are quoted on an approved exchange or the shares have been held as an investment[6]. The point of this provision is simply to prevent avoidance of the first situation by introducing an intermediate holder of the shares. The third situation is where the sale is by a controller of the company acting with the company's consent or participation[7].

EXCEPTIONS AND EXEMPTIONS

Under the Financial Services Act as at present drafted there are a number of situations where offers of securities are either excepted or exempted[8] from the scope of sections 159 and 160[9]. The excepted cases are all situations in which sufficient information will already be available making it unnecessary for a full prospectus to be published[10]. The exemptions are cases where the offer is only made to a restricted class. In most of these the exemption is related to the type of advertisement. They include advertisements which are of a private character because of a connection between the issuer and recipient[11]. This would probably cover offers to existing members, debenture holders[12] or employees[13]. Advertisements issued to persons sufficiently

Financial Services Act so that, for example, a prospectus will have to be registered when a company making a takeover bid offers shares in itself in exchange for shares in the target company.
3 Financial Services Act 1986, s 160(3).
4 Ibid, s 160(3)(a).
5 Ibid, s 160(4).
6 Ibid, s 160(3)(b).
7 Ibid, s 160(3)(c). A controller is, basically, anyone holding 15% of the voting power at general meetings: ibid, s 207(5).
8 The difference seems to be that exceptions are provided for in the Financial Services Act itself and are relatively unconditional while exemptions depend on regulations being made which may impose conditions.
9 It is probable that the Financial Services Act 1986, s 160, and possibly s 159, will be redrafted to reflect the wording of the Prospectus Directive so as to require delivery of a prospectus to the Registrar prior to the issue of an advertisement offering securities to the public for the first time. There will then be provisions explaining when an offer is *not* to the public and these will replace the present exemptions. See the consultative document *Listing Particulars and Public Offer Prospectuses* pp 27–31 and Annex F.
10 Financial Services Act 1986, ss 159(2), 160(5) and 161.
11 Ibid, s 160A(1)(a).
12 At present exempted under the Companies Act 1985, s 56(5)(a).
13 At present exempted under the Companies Act 1985, ss 56(3)(b) and 60(1).

expert to understand any risks involved may be exempted[14] and this will probably be used to exempt underwriting offers[15]. In addition there may be an exemption[16] for advertisements in connection with private placings involving a limited number of persons[17]. Offers of securities which do fall outside the scope of section 159 or 160 will instead be regulated as investment advertisements under section 57[18]. The necessary level of investor protection will be achieved through the involvement of authorised persons in the approval or issue of advertisements in accordance with the rules[19] of the Securities and Investment Board or the appropriate self-regulating organisation or recognised professional body[20].

FORM AND CONTENT OF PROSPECTUSES UNDER PART V

The Secretary of State is empowered to make rules as to the form and content of prospectuses[1]. The Secretary of State may also direct that the prospectus shall instead comply with the rules laid down by the appropriate approved exchange, if satisfied that the rules and practices of the exchange provide investors with at least equivalent protection[2]. Any rules, whether laid down by the Secretary of State or an approved exchange must include the information required by the Prospectus Directive[3] but the government's provisional view is that the rules should not impose any further obligations[4]. In addition to the detailed contents there is an overriding duty to supply all the information that investors and their professional advisers would need to make a fair assessment of the value of the securities[5]. Finally, if material changes occur or new information becomes available after publication of the prospectus, a supplementary prospectus is required to be published[6].

BREACH OF THE PROSPECTUS PROVISIONS

This part deals with the consequences of offering securities without having first registered, and, if the securities are quoted on an approved exchange, obtained approval for, a prospectus. It also covers the consequences of breach of any regulations, for example, as to the terms and conduct of offers,

---

14 Financial Services Act 1986, s 160A(1)(c). Advertisements relating to securities normally only bought or dealt in by experts may also be exempted: ibid, s 160A(2).
15 At present exempted under the Companies Act 1985, s 56(3)(a).
16 Under the Financial Services Act 1986, s 160A(1)(d).
17 A maximum of 50 is suggested in *Listing Particulars and Public Offer Prospectuses* Annex F.
18 Unless the offer is exempted from the Financial Services Act s 57 as well, under regulations made under s 58(3). See the two Financial Services Act 1986 (Investment Advertisement) (Exemptions) Orders 1988 SI 1988/316 and SI 1988/716.
19 Financial Services Act 1986, s 48(2)(e).
20 See the consultative paper *Listing Particulars and Public Offer Prospectuses* p 17. Compliance with the prospectus rules under the Financial Services Act 1986, Pt V is likely to be an acceptable alternative: ibid, p 18.
1 Financial Services Act 1986, s 162(1). These will replace the present requirements contained in the Companies Act 1985, Sch 3.
2 Ibid, s 162(3).
3 EEC Council Directive 89/298 art 11.
4 Consultative document *Listing Particulars and Public Offer Prospectuses* pp 13–15 and p 22. The Secretary of State has power to ensure that an approved exchange complies with the directive: Financial Services Act 1986, s 192.
5 Financial Services Act 1986, s 163.
6 Ibid, s 164. An approved exchange can in certain circumstances grant exemptions from disclosure requirements: ibid, s 165.

made by the Secretary of State. It does not cover a failure to comply with the rules as to the form and content of the prospectus itself. Just because the prospectus is deficient in some respect does not amount to a failure to register a prospectus at all[7]. If the breach is by an authorised person it is treated as a breach of the rules granting authorisation[8]. It will thus be dealt with as a disciplinary matter. A breach by an unauthorised person, on the other hand, constitutes a criminal offence punishable by a fine and/or imprisonment[9]. Whether the breach is by an authorised or an unauthorised person it is also actionable at the suit of a person who suffers loss as a result of the contravention in an action for breach of statutory duty[10].

Prohibition on private companies advertising securities

When private companies were first introduced in 1907 one of the three restrictions they had to accept to qualify as private companies was a prohibition on offering shares or debentures to the public[11]. That prohibition had to be contained in the company's articles. With the recasting of the definitions of public and private companies in 1980 the prohibition was put into statute and breach became a criminal offence[12]. With the passing of the Financial Services Act the prohibition takes yet another form although it fundamentally remains enforceable by criminal sanctions. First of all, as we have seen, no private company may apply for admission to The Stock Exchange Official List[13]. Secondly, no private company may issue an advertisement offering securities to be issued by that company unless it falls within an exemption under regulations made by the Secretary of State[14]. The sanctions for breach of these provisions are the same as for breach of the prospectus provisions, ie a disciplinary matter for authorised persons[15] and a criminal offence for unauthorised ones[16]. So far as the company itself is concerned it will be a criminal offence[17]. The company will also be unable to enforce any resulting contract and will be liable to make restitution and pay compensation[18] for any loss unless it can show that the advertisement had no material influence or was not misleading[19]. In the case of any breach of these provisions there is also the possibility of a civil action for breach of statutory duty[20].

7 Ibid, s 171(5). As to the circumstances in which omission of required information may give rise to civil liability, see ibid, s 166(1), (2).
8 Ibid, s 171(1).
9 Ibid, s 171(3).
10 Ibid, s 171(6).
11 The last form of this on the statute book was in the Companies Act 1948, s 28(1)(c).
12 Companies Act 1985, s 81.
13 Financial Services Act 1986, s 143(2).
14 Ibid, s 170. The prohibition and exemption may be redrafted yet again if the suggestion of framing legislation around the term 'offer to the public' is followed up. See the consultative document *Listing Particulars and Public Offer Prospectuses* p 25 and Annex F.
15 Ibid, s 171(1).
16 Ibid, s 171(3).
17 Ibid, s 57(3) applied to this situation by s 171(2).
18 Ibid, s 57(5), (7), (9) applied by s 171(2).
19 Ibid, s 57(8) applied by s 171(2).
20 Ibid, s 171(6).

REMEDIES FOR MISSTATEMENTS IN PROSPECTUSES

Civil remedies

In this section we consider the remedies available to persons who have acquired shares on the basis of a prospectus containing false statements or which has omitted prescribed information[1]. The problem for a student of company law in this area is the number of different and often overlapping remedies that can arise. The explanation for the overlapping lies in the historical development of liability for misstatements and misrepresentations in tort and contract. The liabilities and remedies in themselves are not difficult to understand and if the reader keeps in mind the historical developments the overlapping should cause no confusion.

There are three other general considerations which if borne in mind will help clarify the situation. The first is the type of remedy being sought and here the distinction lies between seeking rescission of the contract under which the shares were acquired and seeking money compensation from the persons responsible for the false statements. The second consideration, which as we shall see is closely related to the question of rescission or damages, is whether the plaintiff is seeking a remedy against the other party to the contract under which the shares were acquired, or against other persons responsible for the prospectus. Thirdly, it makes a difference to what remedies are available and against whom, whether the plaintiff is a subscriber who acquired shares directly from the company, or a purchaser who acquired shares from an existing shareholder. If these three considerations are borne in mind the apparent plethora of liabilities and remedies will present no difficulties.

RESCISSION AGAINST THE OTHER PARTY TO THE CONTRACT

If it is available, the most effective remedy for a person induced to acquire shares on the basis of a false representation is to rescind the contract of acquisition. Rescission is possible for misrepresentations whether made fraudulently, negligently or innocently[2]. It is important to remember that rescission is a remedy which can obviously only be exercised against the other party to the contract. In the case of subscribers this will mean rescinding their contract with the company; in the case of purchasers it will mean rescinding their contract with the transferor[3].

The difficulty with this, however, is that a person can only rescind a contract if the other party to the contract was responsible for the misrepresentation. In the case of misrepresentations contained in a prospectus[4], if the prospectus is issued by the company then the subscriber can rescind against

---

1 In the remainder of this chapter the term prospectus includes listing particulars where these are serving as a prospectus. It should be remembered also that the common law remedies for misrepresentation or misstatement inducing persons to acquire shares may be available whether the misrepresentation or misstatement was contained in a prospectus or not.

2 *Re Metropolitan Coal Consumers' Association, Karberg's Case* [1892] 3 Ch 1 at 13, CA.

3 It used to be the case that a contract entered into on the basis of a misrepresentation could not be rescinded once it was executed: *Seddon v North Eastern Salt Co Ltd* [1905] 1 Ch 326. This rule, which never applied to contracts between the company and subscribers, was repealed by the Misrepresentation Act 1967, s 1.

4 An omission of particulars required to be included in the prospectus does not give rise to a right of rescission: *Re South of England Natural Gas and Petroleum Co Ltd* [1911] 1 Ch 573.

the company[5]. If the prospectus is issued by an issuing house then the purchaser from the issuing house can rescind against the issuing house. But if the purchaser has bought shares from a person who is not responsible for the prospectus, albeit having been induced to buy by reading the prospectus, the purchaser will be unable to rescind[6]. The usual limits on exercising the right of rescission of affirmation[7], lapse of time[8] or intervention of third party rights all apply. In particular it will be too late to rescind, as against the company, once the company has gone into liquidation[9]. The reason is that the rights of the creditors and other members are regarded as having intervened because they will inevitably be prejudiced if any members are allowed to withdraw their money from the company and thus deplete the fund available for paying creditors.

DAMAGES FROM THE OTHER PARTY TO THE CONTRACT

If it is no longer possible to rescind, or if the plaintiff does not wish to do so, or if the plaintiff has suffered consequential loss which would not be reimbursed by mere rescission, the question arises whether the plaintiff can claim damages instead of or as well as rescission. We will consider first the possibility of claiming damages from the other party to the contract ie the company in the case of a subscriber and the transferor in the case of a purchaser. If the other party to the contract has been responsible[10] for fraudulent[11] misrepresentations which have induced the plaintiff to acquire shares then there may be liability in damages in the tort of deceit. Since 1967 the Misrepresentation Act[12] has also made it possible for the other party to

---

5 Problems can arise over whether the company is responsible for statements in the prospectus. For example, if the prospectus is issued before the company is incorporated as in *Karberg's Case,* supra. There, after the company was incorporated, the directors approved the prospectus and accepted applications which had been sent in before incorporation. It was held the contract could be rescinded. Where the false statement is in a report set out in the prospectus the company will be responsible unless it makes clear that it does not vouchsafe the accuracy of the report: *Re Pacaya Rubber and Produce Co Ltd* [1914] 1 Ch 542; *Mair v Rio Grande Rubber Estates Ltd* [1913] AC 853, HL. As to whether the company is responsible for statements made by individuals purportedly on its behalf, see *Lynde v Anglo-Italian Hemp Spinning Co* [1896] 1 Ch 178 at 182–3.
6 In *Collins v Associated Greyhound Racecourses Ltd* [1930] 1 Ch 1, CA, the court was prepared to find that there was a contract between a purchaser under a renounceable letter of allotment and the company. However, although the purchaser had read the prospectus and on that basis had agreed to become a sub-sub-underwriter of the issue, the court held that this prospectus had exhausted its effect once it had attracted original allottees and could not be relied on by a purchaser. It might have been different if the company had known at the time it registered the plaintiff as a member, that he had agreed when the prospectus was first issued to participate in the sub-underwriting. As to the prospectus exhausting its effect see further below.
7 In the case of shares this may be indicated by acting, after the false statements are revealed, in a manner inconsistent with exercising a right of rescission: *Ex p Briggs* (1866) LR 1 Eq 483; *Crawley's Case* (1869) 4 Ch App 322 (selling or trying to sell shares); *Sharpley v Louth and East Coast Rly Co* (1876) 2 Ch D 663, CA (attending meetings).
8 *Scholey v Central Rly Co of Venezuela* (1868) LR 9 Eq 266n (seeking rescission only after reading that another shareholder in the same company had successfully done so).
9 *Oakes v Turquand and Harding* (1867) LR 2 HL 325. But cf s 85(1).
10 *Briess v Woolley* [1954] AC 333, [1954] 1 All ER 909, HL.
11 Ie a false statement 'made knowingly, or without belief in its truth, or recklessly, careless whether it be true or false' per Lord Herschell in *Derry v Peek* (1889) 14 App Cas 337 at 374, HL.
12 Misrepresentation Act 1967, s 2(1).

the contract to be liable in damages for so-called 'negligent' misrepresentations[13].

The amount of damages which plaintiffs will recover in deceit or 'negligent' misrepresentation will be based on the tort measure of putting the plaintiffs back in the position they were in prior to the misrepresentation. If the damages are in addition to rescission their main function will be to compensate the plaintiffs for consequential losses flowing directly from the misrepresentation[14]. If the plaintiffs are not exercising a right of rescission, the damages will also cover[15] the difference between the price paid by the plaintiffs for the shares and the real value of the shares on the date of the allotment or transfer[16].

Plaintiffs may argue, however, that in acquiring shares they not only did not want to lose the money invested but were led by statements in the prospectus to expect to receive an income or make a profit on the investment. Such expectation losses will not be compensated by the tort measure of damages but might be compensated by the contract measure, which aims to put innocent parties in the position they would have been in had the contract been properly performed. In order to achieve this, however, the plaintiff will have to show a breach of contract. This will involve showing that the statements in the prospectus became a term of the plaintiff's contract for the acquisition of the shares. Until recently, however, there was an important limitation on the availability of a claim for damages against the company itself, even if misrepresentation or breach of contract could be established. This was the rule laid down by the House of Lords in *Houldsworth v City of Glasgow Bank and Liquidators*[17] that shareholders could not claim financial compensation from a company while remaining as shareholders. In that case the plaintiff had subscribed for shares in the company on the basis of a fraudulent prospectus which concealed the fact that the company was insolvent. As the company had gone into liquidation it was too late for the plaintiff to rescind[18]. The House of Lords held that unless the plaintiff could and did rescind he was unable to claim damages.

The precise reason for the rule has never been clear[19]. The City of Glasgow Bank was an unlimited liability company and there is an obvious practical difficulty in allowing shareholders to claim damages from the company in such circumstances. Allowing their claims would add to the liabilities of the company to which they, as shareholders, have to contribute. That increases their loss and thus their claim against the company, which adds to the liabilities of the company, and so on, ad infinitum. But in *Re*

13 The onus is on the makers of representations to prove that they reasonably believed them to be true ie that they were not negligent. Under s 2(2) the court may award damages in lieu of rescission. This covers any misrepresentation other than one made fraudulently but including therefore an innocent misrepresentation, ie one reasonably believed to be true.
14 *Archer v Brown* [1985] QB 401, [1984] 2 All ER 267.
15 If, under the Misrepresentation Act 1967, s 2(2), the court awards damages in lieu of rescission in respect of an innocent misrepresentation, ie one reasonably believed to be true, no damages for consequential losses will be awarded.
16 See *McConnel v Wright* [1903] 1 Ch 546 at 554–5, CA (a case involving damages against directors, rather than the other party to the contract).
17 (1880) 5 App Cas 317, HL.
18 *Oakes v Turquand and Harding* (1867) LR 2 HL 325.
19 See the discussion between Hornby and Gower (1956) 19 MLR 54, 61 and 185.

Addlestone Linoleum Co Ltd[20], the rule was held to apply to a shareholder in a limited liability company as well. The justification here may have been a fear that allowing shareholders to claim money from their company involved the risk of payment being made to the shareholders out of capital. Whatever its justification, the rule has now been abrogated by s 111A of the Companies Act 1985[1]. However, the issue of capital maintenance is likely still to be a concern of the courts in any case in which the question of the company paying compensation to a shareholder arises[2].

DAMAGES FROM PERSONS OTHER THAN THE OTHER PARTY TO THE CONTRACT

As we have seen, where the plaintiff is a subscriber for shares directly from the company and rescission is no longer possible, the plaintiff used to be left without any remedy at all against the company. In such circumstances attention naturally focused on whether the plaintiff could proceed against anyone else responsible for misstatements in the prospectus, other than the company itself. This question will also be important where the misstatements are made by individuals in circumstances such that the company is not responsible for them. In these cases the only possibility will be a remedy against the individuals concerned.

Where statements are included in a prospectus, because the directors will have authorised its issue, they will potentially be liable if the statements are false[3]. If the directors know that the statements are untrue then they may be liable in the tort of deceit[4]. However, in *Derry v Peek*[5], the House of Lords held there could be no liability in the absence of fraud[6]. It was not sufficient to show that the directors were negligent. That decision has now been superseded by the decision in *Hedley Byrne & Co Ltd v Heller & Partners Ltd*[7] under which persons may be liable for negligent statements provided there is a sufficient degree of proximity between them and the plaintiff. So far there is no case law to indicate what would be regarded as a sufficient

---

20 (1887) 37 Ch D 191, CA.
 1 Inserted by the Companies Act 1989, s 131. The initiative for the change originated in a report by the Law Society's Standing Committee on Company Law published in September 1988. Whilst it is clear that shareholders who were creditors of the company could always sue in their capacity as creditors, it is not clear whether the rule prevented any claim for financial compensation arising in a shareholder capacity or only claims relating to the allotment of the particular shares. However, the placing of s 111A within a group of sections dealing with allotment of shares may restrict abrogation of the rule to claims arising out of the allotment of shares.
 2 It is possible that any compensation would fall within the definition of distribution in s 263(2) and thus only be payable if the company has available distributable profits as defined in s 263(3). The question is also likely to arise as to whether in liquidation any payment of compensation is deferred to the claims of creditors under the Insolvency Act 1986, s 74(1)(f) as a sum due to a member 'by way of dividends, profits or otherwise'.
 3 In the case of shares to be listed on The Stock Exchange the listing particulars must include a statement that the directors accept responsibility for the information it contains. Admission of Securities to Listing, s 3, ch 2, para 1.7. Similar provisions apply in relation to shares quoted on the Unlisted Securities Market.
 4 *Edgington v Fitzmaurice* (1885) 29 Ch D 459, CA. The measure of damages in such a case will be the difference between the price paid by the plaintiff and the real value of the shares on the day the plaintiff acquired them, together with any direct consequential loss: *McConnel v Wright* [1903] 1 Ch 546, CA.
 5 (1889) 14 App Cas 337, HL.
 6 For the definition of fraud see footnote 11 above.
 7 [1964] AC 465, [1963] 2 All ER 575, HL.

degree of proximity in relation to statements in prospectuses. The arguments against imposing liability include the possibility that it will open the floodgates of litigation. It is not difficult, therefore, to envisage the courts being more prepared to find a duty of care where a prospectus is circulated among only a few people than they would be in the case of a major public offering where the prospectus is published in several national newspapers. Still less are the courts likely to impose liability where the plaintiff read newspaper comments on the prospectus rather than the prospectus itself.

There is another rule which the courts already use to restrict the scope of liability arising out of false statements in prospectuses. It is that a prospectus is presumed to be intended to enable the issuer simply to find a person willing to acquire the shares. Thus if it is issued by the company it will be presumed to be exhausted once it has served its purpose of obtaining subscribers. If it is issued by an existing shareholder offering shares for sale it will be exhausted once the shareholder has found purchasers for the shares. In neither case therefore can transferees from the initial subscriber or initial purchaser sue in respect of false statements in the prospectus even though they had read the prospectus and that induced them to acquire the shares. This rule was established in relation to prospectuses by the House of Lords in *Peek v Gurney*[8] in which the plaintiff, having obtained a copy of the prospectus in the flotation of Overend Gurney & Co, which contained fraudulent misstatements, bought shares in the company a few months later. His action against the directors[9] for deceit failed because the prospectus was presumed to have exhausted its effect once the shares had been issued to subscribers. It may be possible, however, given suitable facts, to rebut the presumption and show that part of the purpose of the prospectus was to create a buoyant market in the shares after they were issued[10]. In such a case a purchaser will be able to sue in respect of misstatements in the prospectus. However, the rule in *Peek v Gurney*[8] was recently re-affirmed in relation to liability in negligence in *Al Nakib Investments (Jersey) Ltd v Longcroft*[11]. In this case a company offered its shareholders the right to subscribe for shares in a subsidiary it was promoting, issuing to them a prospectus which it was alleged contained false or misleading statements. The plaintiff shareholder not only took up its rights but also purchased shares in the subsidiary in the market. It was held that the plaintiff's action in respect of shares acquired in the market should be struck out. Mervyn Davies J applied the decision in *Caparo Industries plc v Dickman*[12] in holding that no duty of care could exist

---

8 (1873) LR 6 HL 377 at 410–413.
9 Formerly the question whether a prospectus was exhausted in relation to the liability of the company itself was less likely to arise because a transferee from a subscriber will not normally have a contract for the acquisition of shares with the company. The transferee will therefore be unable to seek rescission against the company and until recently if shareholders could not rescind they could not claim damages either: *Houldsworth v City of Glasgow Bank and Liquidators* (1880) 5 App Cas 317, HL. That restriction has now been removed by s 111A. In one case in which the court did find a contract between the company and the transferee it was held that the prospectus had exhausted its function in obtaining subscribers: *Collins v Associated Greyhound Racecourses Co Ltd* [1930] 1 Ch 1, CA, see above p 569.
10 *Andrews v Mockford* [1896] 1 QB 372, CA, described as 'a case of continued systematic fraud from its commencement to its end' per A L Smith LJ at 381.
11 [1990] 3 All ER 321, [1990] 1 WLR 1390.
12 [1990] 2 AC 605, [1990] 1 All ER 568, HL.

in relation to a statement unless the defendant knew or ought to have known that the plaintiff would rely on it for the purpose of such a transaction as the plaintiff in fact entered into. Whilst the defendant knew the plaintiff might rely on the prospectus to subscribe for shares it had no knowledge that the plaintiff would rely on it to make market purchases.

STATUTORY COMPENSATION FOR FALSE STATEMENTS OR OMISSIONS

In *Derry v Peek*[13] we saw that the House of Lords held that directors could not be liable for negligent false statements in prospectuses. The general principle behind that decision was not superseded at common law until the decision in *Hedley Byrne & Co Ltd v Heller & Partners Ltd*[14]. However, as far as directors' liability for false statements in prospectuses was concerned, the effect of *Derry v Peek*[13] was reversed the very next year by the Directors' Liability Act 1890. These provisions, which have formed part of the companies legislation ever since[15], are now contained in the Financial Services Act. The provisions actually appear twice in almost identical form in the Financial Services Act. The first time is in relation to listing particulars[16] and the second in relation to those prospectuses which are governed by Pt V of the Act[17]. In discussing this liability it is proposed, as before, to refer only to prospectuses but in this context that must be understood to refer to prospectuses within Pt V of the Act and all listing particulars.

The basic provision is as follows:[18]

. . . the person or persons responsible[19] for a prospectus shall be liable to pay compensation[20] to any person who has acquired[1] any of the securities in question and

13 (1889) 14 App Cas 337, HL.
14 [1964] AC 465, [1963] 2 All ER 575, HL.
15 In the Companies Act 1985 the provisions were contained in ss 67–69. However, the effect of the Stock Exchange (Listing) Regulations 1984, SI 1984/716, reg 7(1)(b) was to prevent these provisions applying to listing particulars issued in respect of shares to be listed on The Stock Exchange. As Professor Gower observed at the time, 'we have repealed in relation to the most important type of prospectus, sections 43 and 44 of the Companies Act 1948 . . . Section 43, it should be said, is the successor of the trend-setting Directors' Liability Act 1890 which has been our main claim to international acclaim for reforming zeal in this area': Report of Review of Investor Protection: Pt II (Cmnd 9125), para 6.13. The hiatus was ended when the Financial Services Act 1986, s 150 came into force on 16 February 1987.
16 Financial Services Act 1986, ss 150–152.
17 Ibid, ss 166–168. As at March 1991 Pt V had not yet come into force. Until it does liability in relation to prospectuses continues to be governed by the Companies Act 1985, ss 67–69. The text is written on the assumption that Part V is in force but the important differences between the Companies Act 1985, ss 67–69 and the Financial Services Act 1986, ss 166–168 are pointed out.
18 Financial Services Act 1986, s 150(1) (listing particulars) and s 166(1) (prospectuses).
19 See below.
20 The measure of compensation is the tort measure rather than the contract measure. This is because the section was originally designed to provide the remedy that was denied in *Derry v Peek*. See *Clark v Urquhart* [1930] AC 28 at 56–57, 67 and 76, HL.
 1 In all previous versions, including the Companies Act 1985, s 67, the remedy was restricted to subscribers, leaving purchasers to rely on *Hedley Byrne & Co Ltd v Heller & Partners Ltd*. Even when restricted to subscribers the potential liability was extremely wide but it does not appear to have opened the floodgates of litigation.

suffered loss in respect of them as a result of[2] any[3] untrue[4] or misleading statement in the prospectus or the omission from it of any matter required to be included by section 163[5].

The person or persons responsible for a prospectus are defined by statute[6]. Under the Financial Services Act this includes, for the first time, the company itself[7]. Shareholders will thus be able to receive compensation in respect of their shareholding from the company, while remaining as shareholders[8]. In addition to the company, the current directors[9], except those who did not know of or consent to the publication[10], and persons named in the prospectus as having agreed to become directors, are persons responsible for the prospectus[11]. Likewise any persons who accept responsibility for any part of the document[12] and are stated as doing so or who authorise the contents of any part of the document[13] will be liable in respect of that part for which they are responsible[14].

There are then a number of defences open to persons who are otherwise responsible for the prospectus. The most important is that persons will not be liable if they can show that they reasonably believed any statement for which they are responsible to be true or not misleading or that an omission of information was proper[15]. The section thus only imposes liability if no

---

2　Boyle and Birds point out that there is no requirement that the false statement or omission induced the plaintiff to invest or was relied on by him. The plaintiff need not therefore have read the prospectus. He may suffer a loss through paying more for his shares than they are really worth because there is a higher demand for the shares as a result of the false statements or omissions: Boyle and Birds *Company Law* (1987, 2nd edn) p 176.

3　The section does not, as it might appear to, impose liability for completely innocent misstatements. See the discussion of defences below.

4　Where the rules require a positive or negative statement about a matter, silence equals a negative statement. If that is incorrect then it will be an untrue statement: Financial Services Act 1986, ss 152(2) and 166(2).

5　This is the section which imposes the general duty to disclose relevant information. The equivalent section in relation to listing particulars is s 146. Omission of information required to be included by the rules governing the content of prospectuses or listing particulars will result in a deemed negative statement which if it is false will result in an untrue statement. See footnote 4 above. In relation to omissions this replaces liability previously based on the Companies Act 1985, s 66.

6　Financial Services Act 1986, ss 152 and 168.

7　Ibid, ss 152(1)(a) and 168(1)(a). The company itself is not a person liable to pay compensation under the Companies Act 1985, s 67.

8　This change made the rule in *Houldsworth v City of Glasgow Bank and Liquidators* (1880) 5 App Cas 317, HL, look even more anomalous and prepared the way for its abrogation in s 111A. In order not to undermine the rules relating to the raising and maintenance of share capital it is provided that any compensation payable by the company under these provisions is to be ignored in determining the amount paid up on the shares: Financial Services Act 1986, ss 152(9) and 168(8).

9　It is possible for a prospectus under the Financial Services Act 1986, Pt V to be issued by an existing shareholder without the company's consent. Where this happens neither the company nor the directors are liable: ibid, s 168(2). The problem cannot arise in relation to listing particulars since every application for shares to be admitted to The Stock Exchange Official List must be with the company's consent: ibid, s 143(2).

10　Ibid, ss 152(2) and 168(2).

11　Ibid, ss 152(1)(b), (c) and 168(1)(b), (c).

12　A person is not responsible by reason only of giving advice on contents in a professional capacity: ibid, ss 152(8) and 168(7)(d), (e).

13　Ibid, ss 152(1)(d), (e) and 168(1)(d), (e).

14　Ibid, ss 152(3) and 168(3).

15　Ibid, ss 151(1) and 167(1). This formula was followed in the drafting of the Misrepresentation Act 1967, s 2(1).

reasonable belief can be shown, which effectively imposes liability for negligent or fraudulent but not for innocent false statements. That defence will not only apply to directors, who basically accept responsibility for the whole prospectus, but also apply to those experts who have contributed reports etc to the prospectus for which they must accept responsibility. In addition persons who authorise the inclusion of an expert's statement[16] will not be liable for that statement if they reasonably believed that the expert was competent and had consented to the inclusion of the report[17]. Finally, persons will not be liable if a timely correction is made of any false statements[18], if the false statement arises from the accurate and fair reproduction of an official statement or document[19], or, if they can prove that the plaintiff was aware of the falsehood[20].

Criminal liabilities

When the Financial Services Act 1986 is fully in force the principal criminal liability that may arise in relation to the marketing of securities will be under s 47(1)[1]. Under this section it is an offence (i) knowingly or recklessly (dishonestly or otherwise) to make a statement, promise or forecast which is misleading, false or deceptive, or (ii) dishonestly to conceal material facts, provided in either case, that this is done to induce, or reckless as to whether it induces, a person to enter or to offer to enter, an investment agreement, or to refrain from so doing, or to exercise, or refrain from exercising, rights conferred by the investment[2].

Offences may also arise under the Theft Act 1968, s 19. This makes it an offence for an officer of the company, or person purporting to act as such to publish a written statement or account[3] which he knows is or may be misleading, false or deceptive with intent to deceive members or creditors of the company. It was under the predecessor of this section that Lord Kylsant was convicted[4]. He was the chairman of a company which issued a prospectus stating, truthfully, that dividends had been paid for a number of years. The prospectus did not, however, state that these dividends had only been possible by drawing on secret reserves and it was held that this omission made the otherwise true statement about dividends into a misleading one.

---

16 In this context an expert includes any engineer, valuer, accountant or other person whose profession, qualifications or experience give authority to the statement: Financial Services Act 1986, ss 151(7) and 167(7).
17 Ibid, ss 151(2) and 167(2).
18 Ibid, ss 151(3) and 167(3).
19 Ibid, ss 151(4) and 167(4).
20 Ibid, ss 151(5) and 167(5).
 1 The section replaces the offence under the Prevention of Fraud (Investments) Act 1958, s 13. The offence under the Companies Act 1985, s 70 will also be repealed and not replaced.
 2 The offence is drafted in terms of investment agreements rather than securities because it applies to all forms of investment and not just shares or debentures.
 3 The section does not cover promises or forecasts or any oral statements.
 4 *R v Lord Kylsant* [1932] 1 KB 442.

CHAPTER 34

Problems of ownership and control of the listed public company

In Chapter 1 we identified seven major economic themes in the development of modern company law. These were of particular relevance to public limited companies and were:

(1) the growth of larger business units;
(2) the development of increasingly elaborate structures;
(3) the shift from ownership to control;
(4) the increase in institutional investment;
(5) the increasing amount of government intervention;
(6) the growth of multinational companies; and
(7) the development of a transnational economy and the international financial revolution.

In this chapter we return to themes (3) and (4) and discuss the impact which they are having on company law and particularly on the division of power in listed public companies. In doing so, we shall consider in more detail some general topics which assume greatest significance in the case of such companies. However, before we do so we will examine changing conceptions of the company and corporate benefit.

CHANGING CONCEPTIONS OF THE COMPANY AND CORPORATE BENEFIT

The concept of the good of the company crops up in the law of ultra vires[1], in alteration of articles[2] and in directors' duties[3]. It also arises in an oblique form in fraud on the minority[4] and is beginning to feature as an aspect of a duty on controlling shareholders. It does not mean in English law the good of the company as a community or enterprise. It does not even mean the economic benefit of the company. It means the interests of the shareholders of the particular company as a general body, or put in another way the interests of the individual hypothetical shareholder[5]. Loan creditors are disregarded unless their security is jeopardised by a proposed course of action or unless the company is on the verge of liquidation[6]. This approach is remarkably out of date when compared with current management thinking about corporate responsibility in the larger companies. German law has recognised wider interests in company law and the corporate structure since

---

1 See Chapter 10.
2 See Chapter 11.
3 See Chapters 25 and 26.
4 See Chapter 27.
5 See *Greenhalgh v Arderne Cinemas Ltd* [1951] Ch 286, CA.
6 See Chapter 39.

the Weimar Republic and as long ago as 1951, an English writer, George Goyder[7], argued for a general objects clause setting out the objects of the company in terms of its obligations:

(a)   to the company itself: its development, financial stability and future growth;
(b)   to the shareholders (to pay regular dividends in accordance with the company's articles);
(c)   to the workers in the company (to provide stable employment under good conditions as far as possible); and
(d)   to the consumers of the company's products (to make good bread or shoes or whatever it may be at fair and reasonable prices).

In 1980, the employee interest was included by statute as a legitimate interest for directors and the company to consider[8]. In Australia, there was a proposed reform to the same effect. In New Zealand, there has been no such change except in relation to ultra vires[9]. In all these jurisdictions there is increasing recognition by the courts of the need to take account of the interests of creditors[10] and a longer term view of the interests of the company[11]. In surveys based on randomly selected US and New Zealand public company directors each holding two or more directorships, the majority in both countries placed the traditional legal concept of the company as the lowest of four concepts of accountability[12]. The majority thought that the company's duty was to serve as fairly and equitably as it could the interests of shareholders, employees, customers and the public. One US commentator has written[13]:

The long term advancement of shareholder interests is accepted as a satisfactory justification for corporate behaviour, if such advancement could conceivably be a reasonable outcome. With so vague a standard, it is apparent that the directors are free to respond to social expectations and demands, notwithstanding a short-term adverse impact on earnings, because of the inability of any shareholder challenging such policies to demonstrate that the conduct would not in the long run prove advantageous to the advancement of corporate interests.

This recognition of the business judgment rule is stronger in the USA than in the UK where the proper purpose doctrine acts as a brake. On the other hand, shareholder action under the exceptions to the rule in *Foss v Harbottle* or s 459 is rare in the case of listed companies. Even the procedural innovations of *Wallersteiner v Moir (No 2)*[14] have not had any noticeable impact on shareholder initiative to bring legal proceedings to keep management in line. This is no doubt due to the separation of ownership and control and the rational decision of the small investor to leave well alone. Even where a

---

7 G Goyder *The Future of Private Enterprise* (1954) p 93.
8 Companies Act 1980, ss 46 and 74; now CA 1985, ss 309 and 719.
9 See J H Farrar and M Russell *Company Law and Securities Regulation in New Zealand* (1985) chapter 7.
10 See Chapters 25, 32, 37.
11 See Chapters 10 and 25.
12 R F Chandler 'The Control and Accountability of New Zealand's Public Corporations' (1982) 4 NZ Journal of Business 1; R F Chandler and B D Henshall *Corporate Directorship Practices in NZ Listed Public Companies* (1982).
13 P I Blumberg *The Megacorporation in American Society* (1975).
14 [1975] QB 373, CA.

larger shareholder takes initiative in the case of patent management misconduct, the results may be problematic. The monitoring of management in the case of a solvent listed company today owes less to legal proceedings than the economic forces of the market for investment capital and the market for control[15]. It is otherwise when the company goes into receivership or insolvent winding up[16].

THE CONCEPT OF CONTROL

Control, like power, with which it is almost synonymous, is an ambiguous concept and the ambiguities assume greatest significance in the case of public listed companies. A principal ambiguity is between power in the sense of the probability that one will be in a position to carry out one's will despite resistance, regardless of the basis on which this probability rests, and what has been called imperative control or authority, which is the probability that a command with a specific content will be obeyed by a given group or person[17]. In *Prudential Assurance Co Ltd v Newman Industries Ltd (No 2)*[18] the Court of Appeal said that control for the purpose of fraud on the minority embraces a broad spectrum extending from an overall absolute majority of votes at one end to a majority of votes at the other end made up of those likely to be cast by the delinquent himself plus those voting with him as a result of influence or apathy.

In Chapter 1, we saw how Berle and Means[19] argued that control of a large company can be separated from ownership of its shares although they seemed to equivocate between the two senses of control. They identified five different species of control:

(1)   control through almost complete ownership;
(2)   majority control;
(3)   control through legal devices without majority ownership;
(4)   minority control;
(5)   management control.

In earlier chapters we have examined (1), (2) and (3) and now we must say more about (4) and (5), since they are most common in the case of the listed public company. One can perhaps express the distinction most clearly in percentage terms of voting rights as follows:

Absolute	99–100%
Substantial	75–99%
Simple majority	51%
Negative	26%
Minority	up to 25%?

15 See Chapter 21, ante.
16 See Chapters 37 and 39.
17 Max Weber *The Theory of Social and Economic Organisation* (1947). Cf E Herman *Corporate Control, Corporate Power* (1981). See the useful chapter on 'Control' concepts under the SEC statutes in L Loss *Fundamentals of Securities Regulation* (1983) chapter 6. See further J H Farrar 'Ownership and Control of Listed Public Companies in Revising or Rejecting the Concept of Control' in *Company Law in Change* (1987) ed B Pettet, p 39.
18 [1982] Ch 204, CA.
19 *The Modern Corporation and Private Property* (revised edn, 1968). See generally the June 1983 issue of the Journal of Law and Economics.

Obviously someone with 99% or 100% of the issued voting shares of a company can completely control it. He can pass any resolution he wishes in general meeting and can appoint or remove the board. The same results will follow in the case of substantial control since 75% enables a person to get a special resolution passed and only 51% is needed to remove a director under s 303 of CA 1985. Simple majority control means that one can remove the board and get an ordinary resolution passed. It means, however, that one cannot get a special resolution passed. Negative control is the ability to block a special resolution. In *Clemens v Clemens Bros Ltd*[20] which was considered in Chapter 11 the niece had negative control and a right of pre-emption which would have eventually given her the possibility of absolute or substantial control, but the aunt had simple majority control and attempted to dilute the niece's holding. Foster J held that the aunt could be restrained from doing so. Minority control is a much more amorphous term based on the facts of the case and means that the control rests on ability to attract enough support which when combined with the shareholder's own holdings will procure a majority of votes at general meetings and particularly at the annual general meeting. Conversely, it means that no other shareholding is sufficiently large to act as a nucleus around which to gather a majority of votes. Control of this kind is really control in the first of our two general senses—power or influence rather than authority[1].

Management control which is not absolute, substantial or simple majority control may sometimes be either negative or minority control, but Berle and Means used it in a further sense of control where ownership is so widely distributed that no individual or small group has even a minority interest large enough to dominate the affairs of the company. Today as we have seen and will explore in some detail later, the largest shareholders in the largest listed companies tend to be financial institutions, especially insurance companies who generally adopt a passive role. It is, then, difficult to say categorically whether there is management control or minority or negative control vested in the institutions. The position is further complicated in the case of some listed companies by nominee shareholdings, interlocking directorships and crossholdings. The best approach, therefore, in any given case is to regard control as a relative concept—control in respect of what and for what purpose[2]?

Recently, the matter has been raised in the context of consolidated accounts and the implementation of the Seventh EEC Directive. There the emphasis has shifted from company to the broader concept of an undertaking and a key definition for the purpose of the parent/subsidiary relationship is a right to exercise a dominant influence. This is a right to give directions with respect to the operating and financial policies of another undertaking which its directors are obliged to comply with whether or not they are for the benefit of that other undertaking (CA 1989, Sch 9 para 4(1)). Although this concept of control is in respect of accounts and disclosure it

---

20 [1976] 2 All ER 268.
  1 *Berle and Means*, op cit, p 66. See also the useful article by M Zeitlin 'Corporate Ownership and Control: The Large Corporation and the Capitalist Class' (1973–74) 79 American Journal of Sociology 1073.
  2 Cf Zeitlin, op cit, at 1090: 'Control (or power) is essentially relative and relational: how much power, with respect to whom?' See further Farrar, op cit (footnote 17 supra).

indicates a looser approach which may prove influential in other contexts. The questions of disclosure and accounts are dealt with in Chapter 28, post.

The nature and extent of the shift from ownership to control in the UK

The Berle and Means hypothesis of separation of ownership and control was tested in the UK by Sargant Florence of Birmingham University using 1930s data[3]. His main findings were:

(1)   At least half of the largest companies were still controlled by a dominant ownership interest.
(2)   Most of the marginal cases were companies in which the top 20 shareholders held more than 20% of the voting shares.

In 1951[4] the proportion had fallen to about a third of all industrial and commercial companies of over £3 m nominal capital. The proportion of shares held by the 20 largest shareholders had fallen. The average percentage fell from 30% to 19% and the percentage held by corporate shareholders increased. Thus majority control declined and minority control increased. There was, however, less evidence of a managerial revolution than of a managerial evolution[5].

These results were confirmed by two later studies in the 1950s[6] and 1960s,[7] but in work carried out in 1975 by Nyman and Silberston[8], using Florence's definitions, the percentage of owner-controlled companies was 45% as a whole and 35% of the top 100 companies. Using their own criteria, Nyman and Silberston[9] arrived at a figure of 56.25% under ownership-control which they considered to be an underestimate partly because of the use of nominee shareholdings. We set out below a table based on their research.

This may mean that ownership control has increased since 1951. Certainly since this category includes institutional investment and thus takes in a wide variety of proprietorial interests, this seems to be the case, although institutional investment raises a whole congeries of problems which we shall consider later in this chapter.

J H Farrar[10] carried out research into the top ten listed companies by market capitalisation in 1984 and the main findings were:

(1)   The very low personal holdings of directors.
(2)   The absence of a notifiable interest of 5% or more in the issued equity capital of five out of the ten companies. The UK government had a 31.73% holding in British Petroleum Company plc and the Prudential Assurance group had notifiable interests in the General Electric Company plc and Marks and Spencer plc. The 'Shell' Transport and Trading Company plc is a multinational with a complex relationship with Royal Dutch Petroleum Company through crossholdings in Shell Petroleum NV and The Shell Petroleum Company Ltd.

3   *The Logic of British and American Industry* (3rd edn, 1972).
4   Florence *Ownership, Control, and Success of Large Companies* (1961).
5   Florence *The Logic of British and American Industry*, op cit.
6   S Hall et al 'The Insiders' (1957) 1 Universities and Left Review 3.
7   M Barratt Brown 'The Controllers of British Industry' in *Can the Workers Run Industry?* ed K Coates (1968).
8   'The Ownership and Control in Industry' (1978) 30 Oxford Economic Papers 74.
9   Op cit.
10   Farrar, op cit, p 48 et seq.

TABLE 1   Major shareholders in the largest British non-financial companies (1975)

Proportion held by a single large interest or by directors	*No of Companies*	*% of Companies*
No dominant interest	98	39.2
0–5%	15	6.0
5–10%	10	4.0
10–20%	32	12.8
20–30%	12	4.8
30–40%	11	4.4
40–50%	8	3.2
More than 50%	22	8.8
Unquoted	16	6.4
Unknown	26	10.4
TOTALS	250	100.0

Source: Nyman and Silberston (1978), table 1; Scott *Corporations, Classes and Capitalism* (1979) p 67. (Cf Table 18 of Scott's second edition, 1985.)
Note: In the 10%–12% category, we have included six companies which had in excess of 10% of their shares held by single interests but for which the authors could give no precise figures.

(3) The fact that financial institutions usually appear as the largest share-holders. Although individual holdings are seldom higher than 5%, institutions collectively have potential minority control or negative control of many companies.
(4) The wide dispersal and relatively small holdings of shares amongst non-institutional shareholders.
(5) The use of US nominee companies and American Depository Receipts for US-based holdings in companies such as ICI plc and Glaxo Holdings plc.

However, we must add some notes of caution to these research findings. First, these results do not take into account option schemes, employee share schemes and the extent to which executive remuneration is tied to the results of the company. Secondly, they are based on the largest listed companies by market capitalisation. Medium-sized and smaller companies tend to have higher holdings by directors and executives. Thirdly, to quote Nyman and Silberston[11]:

To locate control in any given corporation, it is not adequate to set up arbitrary statistical criteria such as the percentage of shares which must be owned by the largest holder or the largest twenty holders. Rather a case-by-case approach is necessary. Any individual firm may be related to other corporations, banks, financial institutions, and family owners via complex patterns of shareholdings, interlocking directorates, and kinship networks.

The control of a public listed company can only be determined if it is examined in relation to the 'concrete situation within the [company] and the constellation of intercorporate relations in which it is involved'[12]. Strategic control is 'mediated through a complex of social forms. While the legal

---

11 'The Ownership and Control in Industry' (1978) 30 Oxford Economic Papers 74.
12 Zeitlin, op cit, at 35.

structure of property relations is a central part of this institutional media-
tion, it is never the sole part'[13].

Ascertaining the extent of control

The 1967 and 1976 Companies Acts laid down rules for disclosure of interests in shares in listed public companies to enable the extent of control to be
ascertained. Those provisions were replaced by further provisions in the
Companies Act 1981 which were more stringent and the present provisions
are now contained in CA 1985, Pt VI[14].

DETAILS REQUIRING NOTIFICATION[15]

The provisions apply to all public companies, but will assume their greater
significance in relation to listed public companies. A person has a notifiable
interest under s 199 when he is interested in shares in the relevant share
capital of such a company of an aggregate value equal to, or more than 3%
of, the nominal value of that share capital. Under s 198(2), 'relevant share
capital' means the company's issued share capital of a class carrying rights to
vote in all circumstances at general meetings of the company.

Changes of more than 1% in any notifiable interest have to be notified to
the company as well as the acquisition or termination of such an interest.
Notification has to be made not only when the acquisition and disposals take
place, but also when the holder becomes aware of the acquisition or termination of a notifiable interest or a change therein.

Under s 203, a person is taken to be interested in certain family or
corporate shareholdings. Also included are interests as a beneficiary under a
trust, the property of which includes shares. Certain interests are to be
disregarded. These are set out in s 209 and include an interest in reversion or
remainder or as a bare trustee, and any discretionary interest under an
English or Welsh trust, and an interest in fee or of a simple trustee and a
discretionary interest under a Scottish trust.

Section 204 contains a provision whereby persons are taken to be acting
together for the provisions of Pt VI if there is an agreement between them
for the acquisition by any one or more of them of interests in shares of a
target company. The section applies where such an agreement imposes
obligations or restrictions on any one or more of the parties concerning the
use, retention or disposal of an interest in shares of the target company
acquired in pursuance of the agreement, and an interest is in fact acquired by
any one or more of those persons. The term 'agreement' includes any
agreement or arrangement but the section does not apply to an agreement
which is not legally binding unless it involves mutuality in undertaking,
expectations or understandings of the parties to it. The section also does not
apply to a simple underwriting or sub-underwriting agreement. Under
s 206, persons acting together are under an obligation to keep each other
informed.

---

13 J Scott *Corporations, Classes and Capitalism* (1979) pp 46–7. Cf chapter 2 of the second
    edition.
14 See *Re Geers Gross plc* [1988] 1 All ER 224.
15 See M Hatchard (1990) 38 LS Gaz 24. See too the Directive 88/627/EEC discussed ibid, at
    p 27.

REGISTER OF INTERESTS

Under s 211, a public company must keep a register for the purposes of ss 198–202 and record therein the information disclosed under those provisions. The register must be kept at the same place as the register of directors' interests. Under s 219, the register of interests is to be available for inspection to any member of the company or any other person without charge. However, under s 211(9) and Sch 5, paras 3 and 10, disclosure is not required if it would be harmful to the company's business.

INVESTIGATION BY A COMPANY OF INTERESTS IN ITS SHARES

Under s 212, a public company may by notice in writing require a person whom the company knows or has reasonable cause to believe to be or, at any time during the three years immediately preceding the date when the notice was issued, to have been interested in shares in the company's relevant share capital, to indicate whether he holds or has held such an interest. When the company receives such information, it must record it in the register. Where a person has been incorrectly entered in the register, he can apply to the company to have the entry removed (s 217).

Members holding not less than one-tenth of the paid-up share capital carrying voting rights may requisition the company to exercise its powers under s 212 (s 214). On receipt of such a requisition, it is the duty of the company to carry out an investigation. The report must be made available for inspection at the registered office within a reasonable time not exceeding 15 days after the conclusion of the investigation.

Section 216 imposes penalties for failure to provide information. The company may apply to the court for an order imposing restrictions on the shares in question[16]. These restrictions which are set out in Pt XXV cover transfer, exercise of voting rights, issue of further shares or payments to the shareholder. In addition, s 216(3) makes a failure to comply a criminal offence. The restrictions imposed under s 216(1) may be lifted if the court or the Secretary of State is satisfied that the relevant disclosure has been made, and no unfair advantage has accrued as a result of the earlier failure to make disclosure, or the shares are to be sold[17] and the court or the Secretary of State approves the sale.

It can be seen from the above that these provisions go some way to ascertaining control, particularly where people act in concert. The concept of an agreement for this purpose is quite wide but will not cover every kind of collusive device. In particular, these provisions do not extend to a person who has control in the sense of a dominating influence without any provisions for acquisition of the relevant shares (s 204). Such a person may, however, be a shadow director, within CA 1985, s 741(2).

In addition to these provisions, there are rules governing substantial acquisitions of shares which are now contained in the City Code on Take-Overs and Mergers and the rules governing substantial acquisitions of shares issued by the Panel on Take-Overs and Mergers and effective from 29 April 1985. These are dealt with in Chapter 35.

---

16 See *Re Geers Gross plc* [1988] 1 All ER 224, CA. Such restrictions cannot be avoided by a sale on the open market.
17 This requires the transfer of shares for cash and does not cover the transfer of shares in exchange for other shares; see *Re Westminster Property Group plc* [1985] 2 All ER 426, CA.

Legal obligations of control[18]

THE CONVENTIONAL VIEW

The conventional view, rooted in Victorian individualism, is that individual shareholders are not fiduciaries for each other and the company and do not owe any duty to the company or other shareholders in the absence of fraud or some contractual obligation. The *locus classicus* is perhaps the judgment of Jessel MR in *Pender v Lushington*[19] in 1877 where he said:

> In all cases of this kind, where men exercise their rights of property, they exercise their rights from some motive adequate or inadequate, and I have always considered the law to be that those who have the rights of property are entitled to exercise them whatever their motives may be for such exercise—that is as regards a court of law and distinguished from a court of morality, if such a court exists . . . A man may be actuated in giving his vote by interests entirely adverse to the interests of the company as a whole. He may think it more for his particular interest that a certain course may be taken which may be in the opinion of others very adverse to the interests of the company as a whole, but he cannot be restrained from giving his vote in what way he pleases because he is influenced by that motive. There is . . . no obligation on a shareholder of a company to give his vote merely with a view to what other persons may consider the interests of the company at large. He has a right, if he thinks fit, to give his vote from motives or promptings of what he considers his own individual interests.

However, Jessel MR, true to his adage 'I may be wrong, but I never have any doubts[20]', was wrong even in 1877. It has never been recognised that shareholders constituting the majority have unbridled powers. Indeed in Adam Smith the rational pursuit of self-interest was led by the 'invisible hand' to the common good[1]. It is arguable that a similar—almost mechanistic—assumption applies in company law and may indeed have been influenced by prevailing economic and political theory.

THE DUTY TO ACT BONA FIDE FOR THE GOOD OF THE COMPANY[2]

Under company law the majority of shareholders act as the company general meeting and the majority of directors act as the board, hence the term, majority rule. In a sense both the majority and minority are themselves organs of the company. Obviously this is true only in a less formal sense than the general meeting and the board of directors, but it is possible to see the majority and minority as weight and counter-weight in the structure of corporate decision making[3]. The existence of the minority is a necessary check on the power of the majority to exercise the corporate will. In a number of cases on alteration of articles of association, it has been recognised that the majority are subject to an overall equitable obligation to exercise their votes bona fide for the good of the company as a whole[4]. This is

---

18 What follows is based on J H Farrar 'Duties of Controlling Shareholders' in *Contemporary Issues in Company Law* (1987) ed Farrar. See also P Anisman (1987) 12 Can Bus LJ 473.
19 (1877) 6 Ch D 70.
20 See James Bryce *Studies in Contemporary Biography* (1903) p 181.
1 'An Inquiry into the Nature and Causes of the Wealth of Nations' (NY 1937) 423.
2 See F G Rixon 'Competing Interests and Conflicting Principles; An Examination of the Power of Alteration of Articles of Association' (1986) 49 MLR 446 at 448–454.
3 See D Schmidt *Les Droits de la Minorité dans la Société Anonyme* (1970) p 257.
4 See the authorities reviewed by Rixon, op cit.

a concept which company law inherited from partnership via the Deed of Settlement constitution which operated between 1844 and 1856. The company was a partnership on which certain corporate attributes had been conferred by the legislation. Hence it was appropriate to transpose partnership ideas and equitable principles to the company[5]. The first coherent discussion of the duty was formulated, appropriately enough, by the great partnership lawyer Lindley MR in *Allen v Gold Reefs of West Africa Ltd*[6]. The concept was used in numerous cases on alteration of articles since 1900. There are analogous concepts in class and creditors' meetings[7]. There has, however, been crucial equivocation in the meaning attributed to the concept by the courts. It has been said to refer to the present shareholders[8], the present and future shareholders[9], the company as an institution[10], and at least in some cases, the creditors as well[11]. The legislative reforms of 1980 made it legitimate to consider the interests of employees as well, without necessarily imposing a duty to do so[12]. Dr Rixon in a recent illuminating article has referred to it as[13]:

a Delphic term employed by different judges in different circumstances to signify different things: it has been used to signify, on the one hand, the corporate entity distinct from the corporators, and, on the other hand, to import a reference to the doctrine of fraud on a power.

The concept falls short of a fiduciary relationship. At most it is a fragment of a fiduciary obligation. In *Peter's American Delicacy Co Ltd v Heath*[14] the High Court of Australia recognised the ultimate inadequacy of the concept to deal with every conflict which arose within a company. It was recognised that in some cases it was necessary to resort to a more general obligation of fairness between different classes of shareholders. It is submitted that there is much sense in this approach. Indeed it is implicit in the statutory rights given to the minority to object to alteration of objects and class rights. The inadequacy of the concept of the good of the company to provide a satisfactory basis for duties of controlling shareholders probably springs from the fact that it represents an incoherent attempt to reconcile fairness and the business judgment rule. It is significant that the concept is seldom used by the US courts which distinguish very clearly between the two doctrines. It will be suggested later that if any progress is to be made in the development of a coherent law on the duties of controlling shareholders it will be necessary to turn openly to these doctrines.

THE BROADENING EQUITABLE BASE

In *Clemens v Clemens Bros Ltd*[15] Foster J applied the concept of the good of the company to a case which did not involve alteration of articles but did

---

5 See Chapter 11 ante.
6 [1900] 1 Ch 656, CA.
7 See B H McPherson 'Oppression of Minority Shareholders', Part 1: Common Law Relief (1962–3) 36 ALJ 404, 409.
8 *Greenhalgh v Arderne Cinemas Ltd* [1951] Ch 286 at 290–291, CA.
9 R R Pennington *Company Law* (6th edn) pp 76, 82.
10 *British Equitable Assurance Company Ltd v Baily* [1906] AC 35 at 39, HL.
11 *Kinsela v Russell Kinsela Pty Ltd* (1986) 10 ACLR 395.
12 Now restated in the Companies Act 1985, ss 309 and 719.
13 Rixon, op cit, p 454.
14 (1938–39) 61 CLR 457.
15 [1976] 2 All ER 268.

involve an abuse of directors' powers and powers in general meeting in connection with a share issue under one of the exceptions to what is now s 151 of the CA 1985. Foster J recognised that the concept of the good of the company, fraud on the minority and oppression did not assist in formulating a principle to provide some means of restraint on abuse of power by a controlling shareholder. He preferred to refer generally to 'equitable considerations' which may make it unjust to exercise one's powers in a particular way. In doing so he made reference to the underlying equitable relationship of confidence which Lord Wilberforce had spoken of in *Ebrahimi v Westbourne Galleries Ltd*[16] in 1973. Lord Wilberforce had, of course, formulated the principles as a paradigm case for intervention by the court in the case of winding up on the just and equitable ground. The decision and reasoning of Foster J have either been criticised as being unorthodox and a mis-application of the basic concepts[17] or alternatively, as a 'first swallow which heralds the new spring'[18]. However, even the latter commentators tend to question its adequacy as a conceptual base for developing a coherent law of duties of controlling shareholders. Again this falls short of recognition of a fiduciary relationship.

THE GOOD OF THE COMPANY, ABUSE OF POWER AND THE LINK WITH FOSS
V HARBOTTLE

In the past there has been an assumption that anything that was not for the good of the company constituted a fraud on the minority for the purpose of the exception to the rule in *Foss v Harbottle*[19] and that anything that was for the good of the company could not constitute fraud on the minority[20]. The neat fit of these two concepts was, however, doubted by Sir Robert Megarry V-C in *Estmanco (Kilner House) Ltd v Greater London Council*[1] in 1982. Sir Robert recognised that acts could be carried out for the good of the company and still constitute fraud on the minority[2]. His reasoning seems convincing and provides another step in the clarification of the underlying conceptual framework in this area of law. It is arguably a step towards the recognition of a coherent doctrine of fraud on a power in this context. It is often said, as Jessel MR inferred in *Pender v Lushington*[3], that English law recognises no general doctrine of abuse of rights. In broad terms this is undoubtedly true. However, it is not to say that abuse of *power* is not recognised in particular contexts in equity[4]. The power of the majority to bind the minority is a corporate, not an individual, power. As the Ontario Court of Appeal said in obiter remarks in *Goldex Mines Ltd v Revill*[5] in 1974:

---

16 [1973] AC 360, HL.
17 See D D Prentice (1976) 92 LQR 502; L S Sealy [1976] CLJ 235; V Joffe (1977) 40 MLR 71.
18 B A K Rider [1979] CLJ 148; J H Farrar, op. cit.
19 (1843) 2 Hare 461.
20 Cf Gower, op cit, p 620 et seq.
1 [1982] 1 WLR 2.
2 Ibid.
3 (1877) 6 Ch D 70.
4 See *Peter's American Delicacy Co Ltd v Heath* (1938–9) 61 CLR 457.
5 (1975) 7 OR (2d) 216 at 224. Described as 'a most unfortunate statement' by B Welling *Corporate Law In Canada—The Governing Principles* (1984) p 602. His main complaint, however, seems to be their later suggestion that this might be a fiduciary obligation.

The principle that the majority governs in corporate affairs is fundamental to corporation law, but its corollary is also important—that the majority must act fairly and honestly. Fairness is the touchstone of equitable justice, and when the test of fairness is not met, the equitable jurisdiction of the Court can be invoked to prevent or remedy the injustice which misrepresentation or other dishonesty has caused.

THE GOOD OF THE COMPANY AND UNFAIR PREJUDICE

The revised wording of the statutory minority shareholders' remedy in s 459 of the CA 1985 makes unfair prejudice the key concept and arguably within the key concept the emphasis should now be on fairness. In other words some prejudice is unavoidable through membership of a limited liability company and the courts will not interfere unless the prejudice can be said to be unfair. The question arises, as in the case of the rule in *Foss v Harbottle*[6] and its exceptions, of the relationship of the concept of the good of the company to unfair prejudice. It would seem that an act which is for the good of the company may still nevertheless constitute unfair prejudice. To say that an act was done in good faith and for a purpose within the relevant power is relevant but not conclusive for the purposes of relief under the section. Richardson J said, in the New Zealand case of *Thomas v H W Thomas Ltd*[7] that it is not necessary to point to a want of good faith. The test is whether there was some unfairly detrimental effect on the interests of the complaining member. This was to be assessed by a balancing of interests in the light of the history of the company and the policies underlying the companies legislation. This was also recognised by Brennan J in the High Court of Australia in the case of *Wayde v New South Wales Rugby League Ltd*[8]. He thought that the decision to intervene was a question of fact and degree which the court should answer by inquiring whether reasonable directors (possessed of any special skill, knowledge and acumen of the actual directors) would have decided that the action was unfair. His Honour said:

The test assumes (whether it be the fact or not) that reasonable directors weigh the furthering of the corporate object against the disadvantage, disability or burden which their decision will impose, and address their minds to the question whether a proposed decision is unfair. The Court must determine whether reasonable directors, possessing any special skill, knowledge or acumen possessed by the directors and having in mind the importance of furthering the corporate object on the one hand and the disadvantage, disability or burden which their decision will impose on a member on the other, would have decided that it was unfair to make that decision.

The other judges who were parties to a single judgment (Mason ACJ, Wilson, Deane and Dawson JJ) also recognised an objective test but stressed the need for caution in exercising the statutory discretion in such circumstances[9].

---

6 (1843) 2 Hare 461.
7 (1970–1985) 1 BCR 648 at 657–8.
8 (1986) 10 ACLR 87 at 95. See G Shapira 'Minority Shareholders' Protection—Recent Developments' (1982) 10 NZULR 134; I Cameron 'Rugby League Footballers and Oppression or Injustice' (1985) 8 UNSWLJ 236.
9 (1986) 10 ACLR 87 at 95. See too Slade J in the unreported English case of *Re Bovey Hotel Ventures Ltd* (31 July 1981, unreported) cited by Nourse J in *Re R A Noble & Sons (Clothing) Ltd* [1983] BCLC 273 at 290. See A J Boyle 'The Judicial Interpretation of Part XVII of the Companies Act 1985' in B Pettet (ed) *Company Law in Change* (1987) p 23.

OTHER POSSIBLE BASES[10]

a. Special facts fiduciary relationship[11]   Even though no general fiduciary relationship exists between controlling shareholders and the company and its minority shareholders it is possible for there to be a special facts fiduciary relationship arising from the circumstances. In most cases this will only be possible in the case of a private company. The majority of authorities deal with private companies or their equivalent. The existence of such a relationship was recognised by the Supreme Court of the US in *Strong v Repide*[12] in 1909 and by the New Zealand Court of Appeal in *Coleman v Myers*[13] in 1977. Most commentators have limited the concept to special facts arising out of a small incorporated firm but in the US case of *Dunnett v Arn*[14] it was recognised that there could be a special facts fiduciary relationship in the case of a larger company whose shares are widely held. In that case Phillips J said[15]:

Persuasive reasons may be given for applying the minority rule to officers and directors of a large corporate organisation, where its stock is widely distributed and held in comparatively small units. The officers and directors of such a corporation, because of their official connection therewith, have a knowledge of its assets and liabilities, the condition of its business, its prospects for the future, and the value of the stock which it would be difficult if not practically impossible for the ordinary stockholder to obtain. In such a case it seems reasonable to require such officers or directors to make full disclosure of all pertinent facts when selling to, or purchasing individual stock from, a shareholder in the corporation.

The advantage of a special facts fiduciary relationship is that it contains within itself, like the duty of care in negligence, a judicial filter. There is a necessity to establish special facts in each case.

b. Constructive trust[16]   It has been recognised in a number of cases that where a third party acts in complicity with a director in breach of his fiduciary duties the third party can be liable as a constructive trustee. A fortiori a controlling shareholder acting in such circumstances can be liable. A common situation will be where a controlling shareholder puts its nominee on the board and he feeds confidential information to it which the shareholder then takes advantage of. This may be a case of corporate opportunity or insider trading[17]. Alternatively a controlling shareholder could himself be regarded as something approximating to a 'shadow director'. In other words his obligations could be primary rather than secondary. However the duty will normally be owed to the company and not to individual shareholders.

10 See *Farrar*, op cit.
11 Ibid, p 393.
12 213 US 419 (1909).
13 [1977] 2 NZLR 225.
14 71 F (2d) 912 (1934).
15 Ibid, at 918.
16 For a recent case see *Aveling Barford Ltd v Perion Ltd* [1989] BCLC 626.
17 See the New Zealand Securities Commission's Report on Takeovers, Vol 2.

c. Conspiracy[18]   In recent years there has been an increasing tendency in company law cases to plead conspiracy in tort[19]. However, the use of conspiracy in this context is problematic since the Court of Appeal decision in *Prudential Assurance Co v Newman Industries Ltd (No 2)*[20]. In that case the English Court of Appeal held that where wrongs were done to the company the individual shareholders could not sue for any consequential diminution in the value of their shares. The denial of such a right means that conspiracy cannot be used as a means to by-pass the rule in *Foss v Harbottle*.

A COMPARISON WITH US CORPORATION LAWS[1]

It can be seen from the above that Commonwealth company laws are in a state of development. Old orthodoxies are being challenged but as yet the law lacks a coherent conceptual base. The concept of the good of the company has proved inadequate and it is only recently that its relationship to the developing areas of minority protection have been fully explored. There are signs of an emerging doctrine of fairness or abuse of power and there are alternative bases of a more particular kind which are being explored. However, since this has been the subject of a much greater volume of litigation in the US it is interesting and useful to make comparisons with US corporation laws to see if these provide a better frame-work for future development.

US corporation laws generally start from a similar base to Commonwealth laws—they will not interefere with legitimate exercise of majority rule[2]. However in almost every state the majority, dominant or controlling shareholders are under some duties to the minority and to the corporation which are often described as fiduciary duties and in some cases are comparable to the obligations of the directors and officers of the corporation[3]. The basic standard is that of *fairness* encompassing obligations of good faith, loyalty, honesty, and full disclosure of material facts[4].

Unfairness is predicated on majority control or domination and self dealing. It consists of fraud or other wrongful conduct although what constitutes unfairness depends on the facts of each case[5]. Clearly oppression or fraud on the minority is encompassed as too is the equivalent of unfair prejudice in advanced Commonwealth systems[6]. In addition there are a variety of transactions which almost defy precise categorisation and which

---

18 See M J Sterling (1987) 50 MLR 468.

19 See *Belmont Finance Corpn v Williams Furniture Ltd (No 2)* [1980] 1 All ER 393, CA; *Prudential Assurance Co Ltd v Newman Industries Ltd (No 2)* [1982] Ch 204, CA; *Rogers v Bank of Montreal* [1985] 5 WWR 193.

20 *Prudential Assurance Co Ltd v Newman Industries Ltd (No 2)* [1982] Ch 204, CA. See also *Rogers v Bank of Montreal* [1985] 5 WWR 193.

1 See generally 18A Am Jur 2d para 762 et seq.

2 Henn and Alexander *Laws of Corporations* (3rd edn) p 653 et seq.

3 *Hyams v Old Dominion Co* 113 Me 294, 93 A 747; *Iwasaki v Iwasaki Bros Inc* 58 Or App 543, 649 P(2d) 598; *Boss v Boss* 98 RI 146, 200 A(2d) 231.

4 See the authorities listed in 18A Am Jur 2d para 764 especially in footnotes 17 and 20.

5 *Re Reading Co* 551 F Supp 1205; affd 709 F (2d) 1494–5; revsd on other grounds 711 F (2d) 509; *Jones v H F Ahmanson & Co* 460 P (2d) 464; *Singer v Magnavox Co* 380 A (2d) 969; overruled on other grounds 457 A (2d) 701; *Knaebel v Heiner* 663 P (2d) 551; later app 673 P (2d) 885.

6 *Coduit v Hellwig* 469 NE (2d) 220.

differ from state to state but which can loosely be subsumed under the concept of unfairness to the minority[7].

Thus there is an increasing body of case law on the sale of control to a third party[8]. Then there are some restrictions on the abuse or sale of voting power[9]. However shareholders as such are not subject to the same conflict of interest rules as directors and thus are usually able to vote in favour of ratification of their own self dealing transactions[10].

Interlocking directorships

In Table 2 below, we show the number of directors from the largest 50 manufacturing companies who also had other directorships in that sector as well as in other sectors, especially finance. Ninety-two directors held a total of 150 other directorships in other large companies in the sectors shown. Particularly noticeable is the number of links between the largest manufacturers and the clearing and merchant banks. These accounted for two-thirds of all interlocks[11].

TABLE 2: Interlocking directorships by the 50 largest manufacturing companies, 1976

Largest companies in:	*Numbers of the 92 directors of the largest 50 companies also holding directorships in the following*
Manufacturing (50)[1]	38
Retailing/wholesaling/services (25)	4
Shipping (10)	5
Clearing banks (6)	32
Finance (17)	24
Insurance companies (50)[2]	40
Other[3]	7
Total	150

Source: Utton *The Political Economy of Big Business* (1982) p 32.
1 Numbers in parentheses refer to the number of companies in each category included in the compilation of the table.
2 Includes one directorship in a large building society.
3 This category includes four directorships in the largest construction companies, two in property companies and one in an international merchant company.

Interlocking directorships, particularly between a financial institution and a trading company, have always been a feature of the corporate scene. From the point of view of empirical research into corporate control they are significant as an indicator of intercorporate cohesion and interdependence. Certain institutions may be found to be central to a number of relationships and therefore occupy an important position in the constellation of interests.

From a company law point of view, the principal question is whether this

7 *Jackson v St Regis Apartments Inc* 565 SW (2d) 178. See the useful checklist in 18A Am Jur 2d para 768.
8 See Henn and Alexander *Laws of Corporations* (3rd edn) p 654 et seq.
9 18A Am Jur 2d para 788–796.
10 See e g *Insuranshares Corpn of Delaware v Northern Fiscal Corpn* 35 F Supp 22.
11 M A Utton *The Political Economy of Big Business* (1982) p 31 et seq.

gives rise to a conflict of interest[12]. The older authorities saw nothing wrong in the holding of competing directorships. In *London and Mashonaland Exploration Co Ltd v New Mashonaland Exploration Co Ltd*[13] Chitty J held that a director would not be restrained from acting as a director of a rival company, except where there is a prohibition in the articles, or where the director is about to disclose confidential information. Also the director can be restrained where there is a term in his contract of service prohibiting him from so acting[14].

Later cases have undermined the multiple director's apparently secure position. In the Canadian case of *Abbey Glen Property Corpn v Stumborg*[15] McDonald J thought that the *Mashonaland* dicta were too widely expressed, and that 'there might well be cases in which a director breaches his fiduciary duty to Company A merely by acting as a director of Company B[16], even where there is no question of passing on confidential information.'

In New Zealand, the matter was considered by Mahon J in *Berlei Hestia (NZ) Ltd v Fernyhough*[17]. The learned judge thought there was 'a wide distinction between asking a director to account for a profit made out of his fiduciary relationship, and asking a director not to join the board of a competing organisation in case he should, at some future time, decide to act in breach of his fiduciary duty'[18]. Only the former was regulated. However, Mahon J appears to overlook the point that the making of a profit is only one facet of the conflict of interest rule which can apply to render a director in breach of his fiduciary duty even where he makes no profit.

The cases thus take a surprisingly lax approach which some would argue is justified from the point of view of commercial convenience. However, in certain circumstances interlocking directorships may give rise to an action for breach of confidence or to a petition under s 459[19].

In a Staff Report of the Antitrust Subcommittee of the U S Committee on the Judiciary in 1965[20] it was stated that there were three objections to corporate management interlocks: (1) matters of antitrust significance; (2) conflicts of interest; and (3) debasement of the quality of available business leadership. The antitrust objections were said to be the avoidance of competition, the promotion of common action and the possibility that if the proportion of interlocking directors is sufficient, competition between the two firms may be eliminated entirely.

Interlocking relations between companies in closely related industries may tend to forestall the development of competition which otherwise would occur in the normal expansion and diversification of each of the respective companies. Common directors

---

12 D E McLay (1980) 10 VUWLR 429; R Carroll, B Stening and Kal Stening (1990) 8 C & SLJ 290.

13 [1891] WN 165. See also *Bell v Lever Bros* [1932] AC 161 at 195, HL but cf *Scottish Co-operative Wholesale Society v Meyer* [1959] AC 324 at 366, HL.

14 *Hivac Ltd v Park Royal Scientific Instruments Ltd* [1946] Ch 169, CA; *Thomas Marshall (Exports) Ltd v Guinle* [1979] Ch 227.

15 (1976) 65 DLR (3d) 235.

16 Ibid, at 278.

17 [1980] 2 NZLR 150.

18 Ibid.

19 On breach of confidence see L Thomson 'Nominee and Multiple Directors and Breach of Confidence' in *Contemporary Issues in Company Law* (1987) ed J H Farrar, p 159. On s 459 see *Scottish Co-operative Wholesale Society v Meyer*, supra.

20 Interlocks in Corporate Management, Staff Report, Antitrust Subcommittee, Committee on the Judiciary, Washington 1965.

between companies that are in a supplier-purchaser position to each other may result in preferential treatment in periods of short supply to the impairment of competition generally throughout the affected industry. Similarly, preferential treatment may occur in access to market outlets. An interlock between a manufacturing corporation and banks and insurance companies or other sources of financial services may establish a community of interest that would tend to assure adequate credit to a favoured company and a withholding of credit and capital from disfavoured competitors.

The report identified two types of conflict of interest problem. It argued that 'when a director serves on boards of different corporations, there is the narrow problem that the interests of stockholders may be subordinated to the opportunity for personal gain that is afforded the director because he has an opportunity for "inside dealings". The second problem extends beyond the effects of the director's divided loyalties for his own private gain. The structure of the interlock also divides his loyalties to the stockholders of each of the respective corporations. The incentive of the director to serve each is lessened in any course of dealing that involves both of the combined companies. Although in his official capacity a director is a fiduciary to his stockholders and is required to act in their interests, a director of two companies having business dealings with each other, or whose interests may conflict with each other, is placed in the anomalous position of being a fiduciary with respect to each'.

Even when the common director attempts to harmonise the conflicting interests this may be at the expense of both companies. The tendency is to blunt the rivalry between the companies and compromise opposing interests.

The third objection arises from the fact that the restriction of opportunities for management experience caused by the practice of interlocks may result in the deterioration of service on the boards of listed companies. A director who undertakes to serve on the boards of too many companies may be too busy to serve them effectively and may consequently be an absentee director. Younger executives may be denied the opportunity to be active at senior board level. In the light of this, it is submitted that there should be a presumption that interlocking directorships are against the public interest and the onus should be on those who seek to justify them.

Insider trading

The topic of insider trading assumes its greatest significance in connection with price-sensitive information concerning public listed companies. Insider trading has been discussed at Chapter 25.

INSTITUTIONAL INVESTMENT AND MONITORING OF MANAGEMENT[1]

Extent

Institutional investors increased their market share of UK-listed equities from 17.9% in 1957 to 54.1% in 1981, and are acquiring about 2% of the UK

---

1 See J H Farrar and M Russell (1984) 5 Co Law 107, on which what follows is based.

equity market each year[2]. It has been estimated that they will hold 69%–84% by the year 2000, although it is uncertain whether this trend will be sustained[3]. Institutions held 63.8% of listed loan capital in 1981[4]. There are similar trends in Australia, New Zealand, Canada and the USA[5]. These facts revolutionise the concept of control. Ownership is regrouped but still generally passive. The relationship between institutions and portfolio companies and between institutions and their constituents is not uniform and is in fact quite complex[6]. Whereas the separation of ownership from control is a relatively simple movement, this further stage of a regrouping of ownership with the potential of control is not so simple. Yet its impact on our understanding of the listed company and the whole conceptual framework of company law is potentially profound. Hence one American writer, Paul Harbrecht, has referred to the 'paraproprietal society[7]'.

We set out in Tables 3–5 details of ownership of listed UK securities. Table 3 gives the beneficial ownership of listed UK ordinary shares, 1957–75, while Table 4 gives the ownership of listed UK securities by financial institutions, 1957–78. In Table 5 (on p 596), we show the distribution of beneficial holdings. These document the trend. In Table 6 (on p 597), we set out a projection of the future pattern in UK share ownership to 1990.

THE REASONS FOR THE GROWTH OF INSTITUTIONAL HOLDINGS

The first and paramount reason for the growth of institutional holdings is the growth of pension and superannuation schemes since 1945. Originally in private pension plans, pension obligations were satisfied by the purchase of annuities from life insurance companies. Thus the funds were included in the insurance companies' assets. Later, non-insured plans became popular because of the possibility of investment of the fund in ordinary shares.

A second reason is the relaxation of the trustee investment rules by the Trustee Investments Act 1961 which allowed trustees to invest part of the trust funds in equities.

A third reason is the rise of insurance-linked investment schemes to take advantage of the insurance tax relief. (This relief has now been withdrawn.)

A fourth reason is the favourable tax treatment of insurance companies and unit and investment trusts.

It is noticeable how none of these reasons is company-oriented. In other words, the company is simply the outlet for these investment urges. This, combined with the passivity of institutions as shareholders, probably accounts for the fact that such investment has almost caught the corporate world unawares and company lawyers have failed to appreciate its full significance.

2 R J Briston and R Dobbins *The Growth and Impact of Institutional Investors* (1978) p 24; J Coakley and L Harris *The City of Capital* (1983) pp 106–7.
3 R Dobbins and T W McRae *Institutional Shareholders and Corporate Management* (1975).
4 *Coakley and Harris,* op cit.
5 *Farrar and Russell,* op cit, and materials cited.
6 *Farrar and Russell,* op cit, at 66–67.
7 'Pension Funds and Economic Power: The Paraproprietal Society': Preface to D J Baum and N B Stiles *The Silent Investors* (1965).

TABLE 3: Beneficial ownership of listed UK ordinary shares, 1957–75

At end December[1]; % of total
shareholdings at market value

Category of beneficial shareholder	1957[1]	1963	1969	1975
Persons	65.8	54.0	47.4	37.5
Charities and other non-profit making bodies serving persons	1.9	2.1	2.1	2.3
Stockbrokers and jobbers	0.9	1.4	7.4	0.4
Banks	0.9	1.3	1.7	0.7
Insurance companies	8.8	10.0	12.2	15.9
Pension funds	3.4	6.4	9.0	16.8
Investment trust companies[2]	5.2	7.4	7.6	6.1
Unit trusts	0.5	1.3	2.9	4.1
Other financial companies[3]	1.6	2.6	1.1	4.0
Industrial and commercial companies[4]	2.7	5.1	5.4	3.0
Public sector	3.9	1.5	2.6	3.6
Overseas sector	4.4	7.0	6.6	5.6
TOTAL	100.0	100.0	100.0	100.0
£ billion	11.6	27.5	37.9	44.6

1 Except 1957, which at 1 July.
2 In 1957–69 includes listed investment trust companies.
3 Includes property companies; in 1975 includes unlisted investment trust companies.
4 Excludes property companies.
Source: JP Moyle The Pattern of Ordinary Share Ownership, 1957–1970 (Cambridge University Press, 1971); The Ownership of Company Shares: A Survey for 1975 (HMSO, 1979).

INSTITUTIONAL INVESTMENT AND THE ELUSIVENESS OF INSTITUTIONAL POWER

While the growth of institutional holdings and their *potential* power is well documented there is little evidence that such power has been exercised in any significant way. One, therefore, hesitates to talk in terms of control except perhaps in the sense of constraint[8].

In the UK, the two best documented cases of institutional intervention are the Thalidomide and the Newman Industries cases. In the former the management of Distillers Company Ltd foolishly resisted public pressure to settle on more generous terms with the victims. In the end, their shares fell and the institutional investors together with the company's merchant banks met senior management on 4 January 1973. Two days later, the company increased its offer from £3.25 m to £21.75 m which formed the basis of the ultimate settlement[9]. In the Newman Industries[10] case, the Prudential Assurance Co Ltd litigated in individual and derivative form as a minority shareholder and the costs of the proceedings at first instance were reported

8 Herman Corporate Control, Corporate Power (1981).
9 See The Times, 5 and 6 January 1973; The Economist, 6 January 1973, p 9; P I Blumberg The Megacorporation in American Society, op cit.
10 Prudential Assurance Co Ltd v Newman Industries Ltd (No 2) [1982] Ch 204, CA. See also Vinelott J [1980] 3 WLR 543. See also (1980) Sunday Times, 24 February; (1980) Times, 19 June; (1981) Times, 31 July and 1 August.

TABLE 4: Ownership of listed UK securities by financial institutions, 1957–78

	At end year; % of total market value in issue					
	1957	*1962*	*1967*	*1972*	*1977*	*1978*
All financial institutions[1]						
British government securities	44	49	56	61	63	68
UK local authority securities[2]	39	39	50	70	56	59
UK company securities:						
Loan capital	75	79	77	53	49	47
Preference shares	36	38	59	53	72	76
Ordinary shares	21	26	33	37	47	50
Investing institutions[3]						
British government securities	17	24	27	34	41	46
UK local authority securities[2]	23	26	21	10	16	20
UK company securities:						
Loan capital	75	79	77	51	45	42
Preference shares	36	37	59	52	69	72
Ordinary shares	19	24	31	35	44	47

1 Investing Institutions, banks in UK and discount market, building societies, saving banks' investment accounts, finance houses and special finance agencies.
2 Listed stocks and negotiable bonds.
3 Insurance companies, pension funds, investment trust companies and unit trusts.
Source: The Financial Interdependence of the Economy; Bank of England: Central Statistical Office.

to be £¾ m. The case later went on appeal before being eventually settled. The judgment of the Court of Appeal was rather critical of the cost involved in their initiative.

In numerous cases, institutional support has assisted a bidder in a takeover bid. The voting strength of institutions was demonstrated in the UK in the GEC-AEI, Capitarium-Duple Motor Bodies and American Tobacco-Gallagher mergers. In the latter, the institutions immediately accepted American Tobacco's offer which was only open for a few hours, thereby making acceptance impossible for private shareholders[11]. The main aim here has been gain. In the US, the SEC's Institutional Investor Study Report, vol 5 in 1971[12] documented institutional involvement in transfers of corporate control. They instanced the following as the two main strategies which had been adopted:

(1) Purchase of shares in anticipation of a bid.
(2) Financial assistance to the bidder.

Amongst the special inducements which they had received in return for advance information about a bid were a higher price for their shares and assurances of contingent benefits if the bid succeeded.

In the UK, advance information may now be caught by the insider trading provisions of the Companies Securities (Insider Dealing) Act 1985 and the City Takeover Code will regulate the terms of a bid.

---

11 *Briston and Dobbins,* op cit, p 61.
12 House Doc 64 Pt 5, 92d Cong 1st Session, 2847–9.

TABLE 5: Distribution of registered and beneficial shareholdings

A survey produced by the Economics Department of The Stock Exchange shows that personal shareholdings accounted for 35% of the total holdings in the 357 companies included in the survey. Weighting the figures by the market capitalisation of the individual companies concerned increases the overall figure to 36%. These figures contrast with the Department of Industry's figure of 37.5% for personal shareholders in 1975, and a lower figure (of 28–30%) which has been calculated from it as the current figure. Comparisons between the two sets of data should not be too closely drawn because of the differences in methods of compilation.

The percentage of personal sector involvement showed few marked differences between large and small companies, although in the capitalisation group £101m–£150m the personal sector hold only 30% while two other groups recorded a figure of 33%. Among the institutions, a number of interesting factors emerge. One is the surprisingly large percentage of shares of small companies (below £20m market capitalisation) held by insurance companies, while investment and unit trusts have a large proportional holding in companies in the £21m–£25m group. 'Other institutional' holdings are proportionately high in the £150m–£200m market capitalisation group, but comparatively low above that level.

BENEFICIAL HOLDINGS: PERCENTAGE

	Valuation group	Insurance companies %	Investment & unit trusts %	Pension funds %	Other institutions %	Individual shareholdings %
A	Over £500m	18	12	19	13	38
B	£210m–£500m	21	13	19	10	37
C	£151m–£200m	17	11	18	21	33
D	£101m–£150m	19	13	20	18	30
E	£76m–£100m	18	14	16	14	38
F	£51m–£75m	17	14	17	14	38
G	£36m–£50m	20	14	14	13	39
H	£26m–£35m	19	17	14	11	39
I	£21m–£25m	19	19	14	15	33
J	£0m–£20m	20	12	13	17	38
	Average Market value	19	15	17	14	35
	Weighted average	18	13	18	15	36

Source: The Stock Exchange Offical Year-Book 1983–84.

TABLE 6: The future pattern of UK share ownership

	Point estimates			95% 1974	Confidence 1977	Intervals 1990
	1974	1977	1990			
Private pension funds	8.3	9.0	—	7.8–8.7	8.3–9.7	—
Public pension funds	4.2	5.1	—	3.7–4.7	4.3–5.9	—
Local authority pension funds	2.1	2.6	—	1.9–2.4	2.2–3.0	—
Combined pension funds	14.6	16.7	—	13.5–15.8	14.9–18.6	—
Insurance companies	17.5	19.8	—	16.4–18.6	18.6–21.0	—
	32.1	36.5	—	—	—	—
Investment trusts	8.1	8.4	—	7.8–8.4	7.0–8.8	—
Unit trusts	4.4	5.2	—	4.0–4.7	4.7–5.8	—
Combined institutions	44.6	50.1	68.0	42.8–46.6	47.4–53.0	63.9–72.3
Persons, executors, trustees	38.9	34.2	14.0	36.5–41.3	30.6–37.8	9.7–18.9
Other investors	17.5	15.7	18.0	16.4–18.6	13.9–17.6	12.0–23.8
	100	100	100			

Source: R Dobbins and M J Greenwood, 'The Future Pattern of UK Share Ownership' *Long Range Planning* vol 8, no 4, 1975.

However, two further points must be mentioned. There is enormous potential for exercise of power. The fact that it has not been exercised much in the past does not mean it will not be exercised in the future. Secondly, the absence is of documented and acknowledged exercise of power or influence. Institutional investors are notoriously reticent in acknowledging initiatives which they take. Behind the scenes in the UK and the USA, institutional investors have been known to investigate unprofitable contracts, management incentive and share option schemes and influence management changes.

The prevailing view hitherto has been that the primary responsibility of the institutional investor is to achieve maximum investment performance. If this is not present in a portfolio company the rule is to sell. This rule has two aspects—first, it denies the existence of any duty to fellow shareholders and other groups such as employees and consumers and secondly, it maintains that in any event the overriding duty is to sell rather than incur costs and further risks[13].

Institutional investors are worried about the political consequences of an exercise of power. They eschew public criticism and fear public intervention. Some consider that their expertise is finance and investment rather than management and this does not necessarily equip them to pursue an interventionist role. They are also worried about the risks involved. Lastly, they are reluctant to offend the companies in which they invest. There may be more than one relationship between the company and institutions and in any event the institutions continue to rely on the companies for current information in spite of the new prohibitions on insider trading.

This conservatism of institutions in the exercise of their power has, however, been criticised by Adolf Berle Jr in the following terms[14].

In effect, the position of the institutional managers is that they will not exercise their voting power so as seriously to affect the choice or the policies of corporate managements. The individuals for whom the institutions are fiduciaries, holders of rights in pension trusts, of shares in mutual funds, or of insurance policies, have surrendered their voting power. The institutional managers, therefore, by their policy of non-intervention, merely insulate the corporate managements from any possible action by or influence of the ultimate, beneficial 'owners' of the stock. A policy of non-action by the institutions means that the directors and managements of the corporations whose stock they hold become increasingly self-appointed and unchallengeable; while it continues, it freezes absolute power in the corporate managements.

It is submitted that any rational policy for exercise of power by institutions should first, confine influence to areas of expertise and possibly some areas of social policy, and secondly, refrain from making a profit at the expense of non-institutional shareholders[15]. The first part of the first rule is predicated on legal caution. To act otherwise might result in liability for negligence. Social policy is a controversial area. Nevertheless, there are some matters which speak for themselves. Thalidomide was such a case. The second rule again is based on evolving standards of legal and self-regulatory prescription

13 *Blumberg,* op cit.
14 Berle *Power without Property* (1960) pp 55–56. See also E Herman and C Stafanda 'Proxy Voting by Commercial Bank Trust Departments' (1973) 90 Banking LJ 91.
15 See 'Mutual Funds, Portfolio Companies and the Small Investor: The Role of Institutional Influence' (anonymous note) (1969) 5 Columbia Journal of Law and Social Problems 69 at 82–3.

of insider trading and the existing fiduciary obligations. It is submitted that in any event maxims of prudence should be in advance of the law. We now turn to the present state of the law before assessing the movement towards legislative intervention.

Legal implications of institutional power

(a) Institutions and control   The institutions still show most interest in listed public companies, although an interest in small firms has recently become evident. In the former, a 20% holding or less will often be sufficient to secure minority control. This in turn affords to the controlling shareholder the power to influence not only such matters as dividend policy, but also the whole management of the company. As well as the potential for what might be termed control de jure, there is the equally important ability to influence management through threats to sell shareholdings or to work against management at general meetings. In the sense that the institutions merely provide another example of a power bloc within a company, this is nothing remarkable. However, what is unique about the present trend is first, that it applies across the board. It is not limited to one company or even a sector of industry. It is the scale and extent of the present trend which is distinctive. Secondly, there is a unity arising not from collusion but from broadly similar objectives and approximately equal access to information amongst the institutions irrespective of their legal structure[16]. This brings into sharper relief the need to anticipate difficulties which may arise from the increased dominance of the institutions. The matter may be becoming of more than theoretical interest in the light of a more interventionist tendency. If so, then the question is whether the potential power of the institutions should carry with it legal responsibilities governing the exercise of such power. Of course, one must be realistic and recognise that a reaction against any participation in management could set in, once it was realised that the active exercise of power carried burdens with it. We have already considered the extent to which the law imposes duties on those who control companies.

Given that the arrival or departure of an institution as shareholder may substantially affect share prices, it is not surprising that it has been argued that the institutions have a duty not to sell their holdings should dissatisfaction with management arise, but to stay on and work to remedy any wrongs[17]. It is said that a controlling shareholder has responsibilities to the other shareholders, to employees, even to consumers. This is one area where the question must at least be raised whether company law should adapt so as to redefine the role of the controlling shareholder in general, and/or institutional shareholders in particular. There are indications that some institutions see themselves as playing a wider role in the future[18]. No doubt there are powerful arguments that could be raised against such a proposal, particularly on the ground that it would constitute an unwarranted fetter on the institutions' freedom to manoeuvre. On the other hand, it can

16 See P Harbrecht's introduction to Baum and Stiles *Silent Investors*, op cit.
17 *Blumberg,* op cit, at p 136; *Baum and Stiles*, op cit, at p 159 ff.
18 P E Moody 'A More Active Role for Institutional Investors' The Banker, February 1979, p 49.

be argued that where a particular institution has a large holding it may find itself locked in unless it is prepared to sell at a loss. This may force institutions into some greater involvement in the affairs of a portfolio company.

(b) Institutions and conflicts of interest   Problems may arise in the area of conflicts of interest. As we have seen, in theory any shareholder may vote in his own self-interest, even if that does not coincide with the company's interests. At the same time, however, it is established that a majority of shareholders must use their votes in the best interests of the company as a whole[19], when voting e g on a proposed alteration to the articles of association. The relationship between these two apparently conflicting principles is not an easy one in theory or in practice. For our purposes, it is sufficient to note that power accruing to institutional shareholders as members of a majority must be exercised for the good of the company. Any duty which an institution owes to its investors ranks behind that owed to the company in which the institution holds shares, at least as far as company law is concerned.

Clearly, therefore, the potential exists for what might colloquially be termed a 'no-win' situation. A similar sort of dilemma faced trustees in the case of *Re Holders Investment Trust Ltd*[20], where Megarry J (as he then was) refused to confirm a proposed reduction of capital, on the ground that the trustees, who held preference shares, had voted, at a class meeting of preference shareholders, not in the best interests of that class as a whole, but rather to benefit their total holdings in the company. Megarry J thereby affirmed that the trustees' first duty was to the company, and not to their beneficiaries.

Two principles compete here:

(1)   Institutions owe it to their constituent investors, as a matter of trust or contract or at least legitimate expectation based on sales literature and the like, to safeguard returns, providing either wealth maximisation or steady income. The trust deed or contract will usually confer unlimited freedom to *dispose* of securities but will not envisage subjecting the investors to the possibility of reduced returns pending solution of the corporate problems in issue, or to increased risk in the event that solutions were not achieved.

(2)   Institutions must act, as a majority or controlling shareholder, in the interests of the company as a whole. This could restrict a right of disposal. This is sometimes linked with a wider social responsibility of institutions. Whether such duties would lead to reluctance on the part of institutions to continue holding voting shares is another matter. Some institutions would no doubt argue that their interest is exclusively financial.

(c) Access to inside information   Another major area of concern is access to inside information. Any major shareholder may have advantages over small shareholders in respect of, for instance, 'unpublished price-sensitive information' about the share market. In the case of the institutions, much of this may derive simply from expertise in the financial markets. Some may

19 See note 18.
20 [1971] 2 All ER 289.

come from closer contact with portfolio companies. However, some of it may also derive from nominees appointed to the board of directors[1].

In law, a 'nominee' director is not recognised as being in a special category. What this means is that he must not have regard primarily to the interests of those who appointed him when he exercises his directorial functions[2]. He must, like any other director, place the interests of the company first. He should not pass on to his appointor information which may affect the price of the company's shares, so as to enable the latter to steal a march over other shareholders[3]. Neither should he place in the appointor's hands information relating to a corporate opportunity[4]. While there is some evidence to suggest that directors nominated by institutions adopt an independent stance upon appointment[5], the unease remains.

The problem arises in another way, through interlocking directorships[6]. It is possible for a large investment institution to place nominees on the boards of several companies, perhaps operating in the same industry. In the case of conglomerates this is almost inevitable. What if these nominees work closely together as a matter of habit? What if the same person occupies these board positions? What must such person or persons do if he or they learn of a corporate opportunity whilst not acting specifically as director of any of the companies? If more than one of the companies is capable of taking up the opportunity, then to which must he communicate details of it? His dilemma would seem to be insoluble. The available case law does not seem to have fully confronted this problem. For instance, Roskill J in *Industrial Development Consultants v Cooley*[7] spoke of a director's obligation as simply one to pass on relevant information regarding a corporate opportunity to his company. This is no help in the above situation. Furthermore, the law still permits a director of one company to act as a director of another competing company[8], except where there is a prohibition in the company's articles, or the director is about to use confidential information. A director's duties will be clear cut if he acquires 'corporate opportunity' information whilst actively engaged in directorial functions on behalf of one of the companies. It is inconceivable that he would be permitted to divert such information to another company. However, the matter is simply not so easy to solve. If the

---

1 There are other possible advantages to be gained from having a nominee on the board, for example, knowledge of a company's intention to make a takeover offer for shares of a target company. Information about negotiated acquisitions can, of course, be particularly sensitive. See generally L Thomson 'Nominee Directors and Confidential Information' in *Contemporary Issues in Company Law* (1987) ed J H Farrar.
2 See *Scottish Co-operative Wholesale Society v Meyer* (1959) AC 324, HL. Cf however, the Australian cases of *Levin v Clark* [1962] NSWR 686 at 700 and *Re Broadcasting Station 2GB Pty Ltd* [1964–5] NSWR 1648 at 1663 which postulate a more pragmatic test.
3 See Chapter 25. For information partly public, partly private see *Baker v Gibbons* [1972] 2 All ER 759 at 764–5.
4 *Cook v Deeks* [1916] 1 AC 554, PC.
5 'Of course, it is improper to speak of any company director as a representative of institutional interests unless the director does, in fact, have a dominant allegiance to the institution and its interests. Few, if any, such directors would concede that their only function was the furtherance of institutional objectives, to the exclusion of corporate policies and purposes. Most directors conceive of their role as that of independent servant to both the institution and the company, acting in the best interests of each in the fulfilment of their respective fiduciary obligations.': SEC Institutional Investors Study, op cit, p 2716, note 70.
6 Ibid.
7 [1972] 2 All ER 162.
8 See note 5.

same person is appointed by an institutional shareholder to the board of several companies then of course information may pass, with the resultant possibility of abuse.

The solution would be to create rules which will provide, for example, that the same person would not be eligible for appointment to more than one board. This should be coupled with a 'Chinese Wall' type of system to prevent information from being exchanged between nominees. Chinese Walls have been the subject of detailed study both in the US and the UK[9] in relation to merchant banks and it seems that it is possible to segregate different departments of an institution in order to shut off an exchange of such information between them. The use of such a system would have the advantage of rendering recourse to more draconian solutions, such as complete divestiture of shareholdings, unnecessary. The difficulty with Chinese Walls lies in policing them. It seems unworkable to attempt any form of statutory enactment. A suitable compromise might be to give some sort of credit for the existence of such a system as a defence to any action alleging wrongful use of inside information. The US courts have shown some approval of the system[10].

(d) Self-investment   A particular difficulty exists in the case of pension and superannuation funds. There is at present no legal prohibition on a fund investing in its employing or related companies[11]. Obviously, the potential exists for using such investment as a control device, but according to the Wilson Report, self-investment is rare[12] because of the potential risk that an employee's pension could then be at stake, as well as his job, if the company got into difficulties[13]. Another factor is the difficulty that conflicts of interest about self-investment can arise where trustees are also employees, scheme members, and even shareholders in the company concerned. Finally, there is the feeling that a company seeking external funds should have to subject itself to the scrutiny of the market[14].

The Wilson Committee nevertheless felt that self-investment, carefully monitored, could be a useful source of finance for a company. It recommended that pension funds should be required to disclose more information about their assets, including the extent of self-investment, and that the Occupational Pensions Board should issue a code of practice about self-investment[15].

9 See B A K Rider, 'Conflicts of Interest and the Chinese Wall' in *The Regulation of the British Securities Industry*, ed Rider (1979) chapter 5; B A K Rider and H Leigh French *The Regulation of Insider Trading* (1979) pp 173–4; Herzel and Collings 'The Chinese Wall Revisited' (1983) 4 Co Law 14; Lipton and Mazur. 'The Chinese Wall Solution to the Conflict Problems of Securities Firms' (1975) 50 NYULR 459.
10 See *Briston and Dobbins*, op cit.
11 Indeed the law recognises the desirability of assisting company employees to acquire shares, by providing for an exemption from the controls on a company providing financial assistance for the purchase of its own shares, in the case of employee share schemes.
12 See the Wilson Report—The Committee to Review the Functioning of Financial Institutions, Report Volume 1 (Cmnd 7939) para 322.
13 Apparently, however, it is not so rare in the US. In *The Unseen Revolution* (op cit) Peter F Drucker reveals that in 1975 'the pension funds of New York City employees were used to bail out their employer, New York City . . .', p 8.
14 Wilson Report, ibid.
15 Ibid, chapter 23.

Future regulation of institutional investment

Existing company law thus contains isolated rules which may on occasion be used to regulate particular acts of misconduct by institutional investors. It is increasingly felt that these are not enough. Some argue that the company is merely a legal abstraction embodying a standard form of contract which supersedes individual contracts and the price system in the process of production and the raising of finance[16]. Ownership is a dead end and no longer has any functional meaning[17]. New forms of relationship and new forms of control are evolving which need regulation. Shareholders are not the working democracy which they seem. Control of the shares is often not with the legal or beneficial owners but with specialist financial managers. The links between financial institutions and management are not adequately analysed in traditional company law concepts. What is needed is a more sophisticated analysis of the concept or concepts of control which takes account of latent control and financial control[18]. The absence of such an analysis has not, however, prevented detailed proposals being made for regulation of institutional investment.

One major proposal of more significance in the USA than in the UK is to limit the proportion of shares in a particular company which can be held by a single institution[19]. Such restrictions already exist for investment trusts and unit trusts in the UK. While this will be effective to prevent control by a single institution it will not necessarily lead to a diminution of institutional investment in the company.

Another proposal is to curtail the rights of shares held by institutions while they are in their hands or alternatively to limit them to non-voting shares[20]. It is submitted that this may well lead to a vacuum which would further concentrate power in the board. This would be undesirable.

A number of related proposals have been put forward for removing the possible information advantage of institutions[1]. The main philosophy here seems to be to mandate companies to disseminate information to the market place as soon as possible. Control over the so-called Chinese Walls within merchant banks between banking and trust departments is difficult to enforce in the absence of separate institutions. Further disclosure by institutions of the precise nature of their holdings and details of how they vote is being called for. The question of investment activities and disclosure by pension schemes to members is a specialist topic which as such lies outside the scope of this book. The answer here may lie in a Pension Fund Act[2]. Such

---

16 See Ronald Coase 'The Nature of the Firm' (1937) 4 Economica 386.

17 See P Harbrecht *Towards the Paraproprietal Society* (1960) p 16.

18 For a very useful start by an economist see Edward Herman *Corporate Control, Corporate Power* (1981) chapter 2. Herman distinguishes between active and latent power and the mechanisms and the locus of control. He emphasises strategic position as the crucial underpinning of management control. He sees institutional investors as latent power and influence.

19 See M E Blume and I Friend *The Changing Role of the Individual Investor—A Twentieth Century Fund Report* (1978) chapter 5; see also *Voting Rights in Major Corporations*—a staff study prepared by the Sub-Committee on Reports, Accounting and Management of the Committee on Government Affairs, US Senate, January 1978, p 576.

20 *Blume and Friend,* op cit.

1 See the Wilson Report—The Committee to Review the Functioning of Financial Institutions, Report Vol 1 (Cmnd 7939) 1980.

2 See the Wilson Report, op cit; see also *Drucker,* op cit.

legislation has been passed in the USA and was recommended by the Wilson Report. In the meantime the pension funds themselves move towards some elementary system of self-regulation.

A more radical proposal was put forward in 1971 by Robert M Soldofsky in 'Institutional Holdings of Common Stock, 1900–2000', a study published by the University of Michigan. This was for the votes of institutional holdings to be transferred to an impartial Stockholders' Voting Council. This would be financed by the institutions but a third of its membership would be government appointments. The remaining two-thirds would be appointed by the institutions and their constituents with the latter electing a majority. This would remove a burden from institutions and a source of friction with governments on the left. It would confer some meaningful franchise on the constituents of institutional investment. It would, however, leave control in the private sector while allowing for some representation of the public interest. As an idea it is worth further thought and it is unfortunate that it does not appear to have been considered by the Wilson Committee. As a reform, it would need implementation by legislation because of the uncertainty regarding the separation of votes from share ownership.

Another radical idea is to take away management's control of the proxy voting system and to give control of it to a committee of the company's largest shareholders. In this way there would be a reunification of ownership and control[3]. This is a simple but interesting idea which would probably prove practically unworkable as the largest shareholders changed or reduced their holdings.

The simple panacea put forward by some commentators, and supported by the present government of encouraging a return of the small shareholder to the market does not seem very realistic. The fact is that for good financial reasons, many small investors find indirect investment preferable and thus the market is being made accessible to millions by institutional investment. It is a trend which cannot be reversed unless there is a considerable amount of government intervention. As an economic mechanism, it achieves the rational end of reallocation of resources with possibly greater expertise and a lowering of transaction costs. Nevertheless, there is some cause for concern. The matter cannot be assessed solely by the tenets of economic rationality. Indeed, there is mixed evidence of economic advantage in any event. The dominant issue is control of portfolio companies. Who is to control them and who is to control the controllers? This is essentially a political issue of power.

---

3 See George W Dent, 'Toward Unifying Ownership and Control in the Public Corporation' (1989) Wisconsin L Rev 883.

CHAPTER 35

Takeovers and mergers

INTRODUCTION

In this chapter we shall examine the more important aspects of the legal and extralegal regulation of takeovers and mergers[1]. Takeovers form one of the most interesting and exciting parts of company law; interesting, because they usually involve the practical application of rules from a variety of different areas of company law; exciting, when the context in which the rules come to be applied is that of a fiercely contested battle between the bidder and the subject of the bid[2].

TAKEOVERS AND THE MARKET FOR CORPORATE CONTROL

There are a number of different levels at which rules, whether legal or extralegal can be studied. One of these is simply understanding how the rules themselves operate. For example, the rules protecting minority share-holders in the event of compulsory acquisition of their shares[3] need to be understood from the point of view of the minority shareholder and how the rules can be used. It is also important, however, to appreciate why there are rules allowing for compulsory acquisition at all and to understand in what circumstances those running the company would make use of them. This second level of understanding is particularly important in relation to

---

1 The terms 'takeover' and 'merger' have become almost synonymous and are treated as such in this chapter. The clearest distinction between the two terms is provided by the accounting definitions of merger and acquisition. In a merger not only are the assets of the previously separate businesses merged but the owners of the separate businesses all remain and become owners of the merged business. The value of the merged business is basically the sum of the original businesses. No value has been paid out because no owner has left. In contrast, in an acquisition the increase in the value of the acquiring company will be the value of the business acquired less any consideration paid for its acquisition. Both company law and competition law are thus concerned with acquisitions and mergers but it has become almost conventional to speak of takeovers in relation to company law and mergers in relation to competition law. For more detailed accounts see Terence E Cooke *Mergers and Acquisitions* (1986), *Weinberg and Blank on Takeovers and Mergers* (5th edn, 1990) and Paul Davies *The Regulation of Takeovers and Mergers* (1976). Two works which, as well as covering the regulation of mergers, deal with merger trends and the economic function of takeovers are P F C Begg *Corporate Acquisitions and Mergers* (2nd edn, 1987) and B Chiplin and M Wright *The Logic of Mergers* (1987) published by the Institute of Economic Affairs. See also *Mergers and Merger Policy* eds J A Fairburn and J A Kay (1989), a collection of papers commissioned by the Institute of Fiscal Studies.
2 The first edition referred to how takeover battles were often carried on in the form of full-page advertisements in the national press. After a series of unedifying, though enter-taining, slanging matches the City Code on Takeovers and Mergers was amended to prohibit argument or invective in advertisements: r 19.4.
3 See below p 623.

takeovers. It sets the managerial decision, whether to make or to recommend a takeover bid, in the context of the overall management of the company's business. Takeovers tend to be associated in the public mind with aggressive or predatory management. In practice a management that wishes to expand a company's business may have a choice of doing so via organic growth or through an acquisition or merger and may choose the latter simply because of the advantage it offers. The apparent surge in takeover activity in the U K in the years 1985–1987[4] revived the debate about whether takeovers and mergers are generally beneficial or harmful to the overall economy. A third level, therefore, at which the rules on takeovers and mergers may be studied is whether, in the light of this debate, the rules should encourage or discourage takeovers and mergers[5].

As with any major investment decision there may be a variety of motives for a company seeking a takeover. A company may, for example, be concerned about its access to raw materials or vital components and thus seek a merger with one of its suppliers; or it may be concerned to safeguard outlets for its products and so seek to merge with or take over one of its distributors or dealers. Such mergers or takeovers between different stages in the production process are referred to as vertical integration. Horizontal integration occurs when a firm merges with another firm at the same stage of production, perhaps to achieve economies of scale or, more mischievously, a monopoly profit. Or a company may be concerned to diversify its activities and merge with or take over a company in a completely different field, thus creating what is often described as a conglomerate. But equally companies may be motivated less by economic considerations and more by financial or fiscal ones of improving the appearance of their balance sheet or reducing their liability to tax[6].

The normal outcome of a successful takeover, however, will be that assets are brought under new management. It may be that the successful offeror will not provide all the new management itself but will sell off parts of the business to persons who will provide new management; or the offeror may go further and put the assets it has acquired to a completely new use. In each case the economic argument for the takeover is that the offeror believes the assets can be managed more productively than the existing management were doing. The offeror therefore offered a price which the existing shareholders were persuaded was higher than anything the existing management could achieve. Takeovers thus enable less productive or less efficient management to be replaced by more efficient management and it is in this way that takeovers are said to form part of the market for control of corporate assets. Even an unsuccessful takeover bid, or the mere threat that a takeover bid could be made, acts as a spur to efficiency by ensuring that management make the most productive use of resources under their control.

If the economic argument in favour of takeovers is correct and assets are

---

4 There are a variety of ways of measuring the number of takeovers and different sources of statistics. For a helpful summary see Chiplin and Wright *The Logic of Mergers* (1987) chapter 2. See also Department of Trade and Industry *Mergers Policy* (1988) pp 1–3 and Benzie (1989) 29 Bank of England Quarterly Bulletin 78.

5 For an introduction to the economic aspect of the legal issues that arise in relation to takeovers, see Posner and Scott *Economics of Corporation Law and Securities Regulation* (1980) Ch 7. See also Gillen (1986) 24 Osgoode Hall Law Journal 919, King and Roell [1989] National Westminster Bank Quarterly Review 2 and Bradley (1990) 53 MLR 170.

6 This is discussed further below footnote 18.

put to more productive use then the overall wealth of society increases. Various studies have tested whether this is true using two main methods of study[7]. The first examines the effect of takeovers on share prices, by comparing the combined share price of the offeror and offeree with the price movement of comparable shares during the period before and after the takeover. Such studies assume that stock markets themselves are efficient and that stock market prices take account of all known information accurately to reflect expected returns on the given use of assets. There have been a large number of such studies and the general conclusion from them is that, even allowing for market changes, the combined value of offeror and offeree companies was significantly greater than that of the constituent parts. If the assumption that stock markets are efficient is correct this implies that the market places a higher value on the assets under their new management and supports the view that takeovers do create wealth. The second main method of studying the effects of takeovers has been to study the accounting rate of return on the assets involved. Studies using this method have tended to be less sanguine about the benefits of takeovers. The methodology has been criticised, however, as being biased against takeovers and the measurement of accounting rate of return involves more subjective criteria than the measurement of stock market values[8].

Fears have increasingly been expressed, however, that takeovers, or the threat of takeovers, far from leading to productive use of assets, compel managements to concentrate too much on short-term profitability[9]. If the existing management of a company feels threatened by a takeover they may take measures which in the short-term will boost the current share price of the company and thus ward off the threat of a takeover. An example of such a measure might be reduction in expenditure on research and development. This would give the appearance that profits were increasing. In the long term, however, such reduction might adversely affect the efficient use of the company's assets, to the detriment of the shareholders in the company and resulting in less wealth for society as a whole. In fact research has shown that investors, far from being only concerned with the short-term, react favourably to announcements of increases in expenditure on research and development and that share prices go up; conversely share prices fall following announcements of cut backs in research and development[10]. Criticism that investors take a short term view of profitability has been levelled particularly at institutional shareholders[11]. It is said that they are unwilling to

---

7   There are reviews of the main methods of study and summaries of their findings by C Lorenz, Financial Times, 6 January 1986 and in Chiplin and Wright *The Logic of Mergers* (1987) at pp 65–73. See also Department of Trade and Industry *Mergers Policy* (1988) Annex E.

8   See Marsh *Short-termism on Trial* (1990), a report published by the Institutional Fund Managers Association, p 112 n 36.

9   See *Takeovers and Short-termism in the UK* (1990) published by the Institute for Public Policy Research.

10   McConnell and Muscarella 'Corporate Capital Expenditure Decisions and the Market Value of the Firm' (1985) 14 Journal of Financial Economics 399.

11   Marsh *Short-termism on Trial* (1990) pp 52–63 suggests that if there is a problem of short-termism it is managerial short-termism or the tendency of corporate managers to favour the short-term quite independently of any spur from the financial markets. This is encourged by remuneration systems which reward short-term performance improvements and the fact that executives may stay with the same employer for only a relatively short

support existing management in their long-term plans and are quick to accept a higher offer for their shares in takeovers. Again the research does not bear out the criticism. In fact where the existing management advises shareholders to reject a bid they are normally supported by the institutional shareholders[12].

A different criticism of takeovers is that they are an expensive way of ensuring that management has an incentive to be efficient[13]. Suggestions have accordingly been made to make the takeover market itself more efficient by requiring for example disclosure of fees paid to advisers and commissions paid to underwriters of shares issued in connection with the takeover[14]. Likewise concentration on takeovers must not be to the exclusion of other ways of making sure management is efficient by increasing their accountability to existing shareholders[15]. In this connection, the critics who are less convinced of the value of takeovers, emphasise the importance of having non-executive directors on the boards of companies[16]. There is also increasing support for the suggestion that companies should include an 'innovation report' in their annual report to shareholders[17]. This would be designed to encourage expenditure on research and development by requiring companies to state, for example, the amount of expenditure geared to bringing new products to market over, say, the next one, two or five years. One final consideration concerning takeovers as providing an efficient market for corporate control is that measures may need to be taken from time to time to ensure that takeovers for the 'wrong' reasons are discouraged. If takeovers are carried out for purely financial[18] or fiscal reasons and

period. The fact that even with the same employer executives may change jobs and that performance goals are divisional rather than company wide aggravates the problem. For the possible contribution of company law in helping to solve the problem, see Stocks (1991) 12 Co Law 21.

12 See the results of a survey of fund managers in (1987) 27 Bank of England Quarterly Bulletin 253–260. The City/Industry Task Force set up by the Confederation of British Industry also found that accusations of short-termism among institutional shareholders were misplaced. See their report, *Investing in Britain's Future* (1987). See also Marsh *Short-termism on Trial* (1990) pp 94–97.

13 See the Introduction by the editors in *Mergers and Merger Policy* (1989) eds Fairburn and Kay.

14 See Clive Wolman, Financial Times, 24 July 1986.

15 See *Creative Tension* (1990) a collection of essays on issues arising from the relationships between the management of public companies and institutional investors published by the National Association of Pension Funds. On the question of institutional shareholders becoming more involved with the management of companies, see Marsh *Short-termism on Trial* pp 85–90.

16 See David Walker (1987) 27 Bank of England Quarterly Bulletin 247. See also Charkham *Corporate Governance and the Market for Corporate Control* (1989) published by the Bank of England. There is also a useful discussion in Marsh *Short-termism on Trial* (1990) pp 90–94.

17 See David Walker (1987) 27 Bank of England Quarterly Bulletin 247. See also DW Budworth *Rewinding the Mainspring* (1987).

18 It has been suggested that the methods of accounting for mergers and takeovers give offeror companies advantages unrelated to any increase in efficient use of assets. There is a useful account of the problem and possible solutions in *Merger and Acquisition Accounting* (1987), a consultation paper published by the Confederation of British Industry. See also Carty 'Accounting for Takeovers' in *Takeovers and Short-termism in the UK* (1990). New provisions in the Companies Act 1985, Sch 4A, paras 7–15, inserted by the Companies Act 1989, have restricted the freedom to choose between acquisition and merger accounting. For an attempt by a mere lawyer to unravel these mysteries, see Furey *The Companies Act 1989—a Practitioners' Guide* (1990) pp 19–25.

not because the offeror company believes it can improve the management of the offeree company's assets this may distort the operation of the market for corporate control.

CONTROL OF MERGERS IN THE PUBLIC INTEREST

UK controls

We have seen that one reason businesses may be tempted to combine together is to achieve a monopoly. The first statutory controls of monopolies in 1948 also provided for restrictive trade practices including cartels to be investigated by the Monopolies and Restrictive Practices Commission[19]. In 1956 cartels became subject to the jurisdiction of the Restrictive Practices Court and were presumed to operate against the public interest unless they could be shown to come within a number of narrow exceptions[20]. The control of cartels encouraged a spate of mergers in the late 1950s and led to demands for powers to assess the economic impact of mergers. These resulted in the Monopolies and Mergers Act 1965 which enabled the Secretary of State to refer mergers and prospective mergers to the enlarged and renamed Monopolies and Mergers Commission. With the establishment of the Office of Fair Trading, headed by the Director General of Fair Trading, the legislation was re-enacted in amended form in Pt V of the Fair Trading Act 1973[1]. This is not the place for a detailed analysis of the provisions or of their operation[2]. In relation to takeovers and mergers that fall within the ambit of the provisions, however, they can play an important part in the conduct of a bid[3] and form a possible defence against unwelcome bids.

A merger, other than a newspaper merger in respect of which there are separate provisions[4], is liable to be referred to the Monopolies and Mergers Commission if two or more enterprises cease to be distinct[5], at least one of which was carried on in the UK or by or under the control of a body

---

19 Monopolies and Restrictive Practices (Inquiry and Control) Act 1948.
20 Restrictive Trade Practices Act 1956.
 1 The Fair Trading Act 1973, Pt V was itself amended by the Companies Act 1989, Pt VI and Sch 20. Many of the changes were foreshadowed in *Mergers Policy* published by the Department of Trade and Industry in 1988.
 2 For fuller accounts, see Whish *Competition Law* (2nd edn, 1989) chapter 20; Korah *Competition Law of Britain and the Common Market* (3rd edn, 1982) chapter 3; Opie 'Merger Policy in the United Kingdom' in *European Merger Control* ed Hopt, vol 1, pp 25–41; Merkin and Williams *Competition Law* (1984) chapter 6.
 3 See, for example, the rival takeover bids for Distillers by Guinness and Argyll Group. The Guinness bid was referred to the Monopolies and Mergers Commission, which under the City Code meant it lapsed and could not be renewed during the reference: r 12. Guinness thereupon requested the chairman of the Monopolies Commission to exercise the Commission's power to lay aside the reference and not proceed with the reference, as Guinness intended to make another bid on different terms which it hoped would not be referred by the Secretary of State. The chairman exercised the power to lay aside the reference whereupon Argyll Group sought judicial review of his decision: *R v Monopolies and Mergers Commission, ex p Argyll Group plc* [1986] 2 All ER 257, [1986] 1 WLR 763, CA. Guinness was criticised for what is in effect a form of plea-bargaining with the Office of Fair Trading. There is now, however, a statutory power for the Secretary of State to accept undertakings from parties to divest part of a merged business as an alternative to referring the merger: Fair Trading Act 1973, ss 75G–75K inserted by the Companies Act 1989, s 147.
 4 Fair Trading Act 1973, ss 57–62.
 5 Ibid, s 65.

incorporated in the U K and either (i) it results in or enhances a 'monopoly situation' with regard to the supply of goods or services or (ii) the value of assets taken over exceeds £30m[6]. A 'monopoly situation' exists for this purpose if in relation to goods or services of any description at least 25% of the total supply in the U K or in a substantial part of the U K are either supplied by or to one person, or by or to the persons by whom the enterprises are carried on which have ceased to be distinct[7]. The legislation also permits proposed mergers which would fall within the above tests to be referred[8].

The reference to the Commission is made by the Secretary of State, but the Director General of Fair Trading is under a duty to keep himself informed about actual or prospective mergers and to make recommendations to the Secretary of State[9]. There is no obligation to notify the Office of Fair Trading of mergers that might qualify for investigation[10], but in practice, information comes frequently from the parties to the takeover bid themselves. This may be because they are seeking informal clearance that the bid will not be referred or sometimes, as a defensive tactic by the offeree, in the hope that the bid will be referred. The Secretary of State is not bound to accept the recommendation of the Director General and has on occasion not referred bids which the Director General had recommended should be referred or referred a bid which the Director General had recommended should not be referred[11]. Although as part of a policy of more open government the Secretary of State now makes it explicit when he disagrees with the recommendations of either the Director General or the Monopolies and Mergers Commission, there have been suggestions that the Secretary of State should be legally obliged to give reasons in such circumstances and that fuller and clearer guidelines should be published relating to both the pre-reference vetting process and deliberations of the Commission itself[12].

6 Ibid, s 64(1). The figure for the value of assets taken over was raised to £30m by the Merger References (Increase in Value of Assets) Order 1984, SI 1984/932. For the valuation of assets, see Fair Trading Act 1973, s 67.
7 Fair Trading Act 1973, s 64(2) and (3).
8 Ibid, s 75. In practice most references occur before the merger takes place.
9 Ibid, s 76.
10 There is now a voluntary notification procedure, the incentive being that, in clear cases, after four weeks the merger will receive automatic clearance: ibid, ss 75A–75F inserted by the Companies Act 1989, s 146. For a proposal that certain mergers should have to be notified, see Labour Finance and Industry Group *A Market with Rules: Regulating Takeovers, Mergers and Monopolies* (1988).
11 In July 1984 the Secretary of State announced that mergers would be referred principally on the grounds of their effect on competition: Office of Fair Trading *Mergers: a Guide to the Procedures under the Fair Trading Act 1973* (2nd edn, 1985) Annex 2. This was reaffirmed by the Secretary of State in October 1987. Department of Trade and Industry *Mergers Policy* (1988) Annex B. See also ibid, chapter 2 for a broader discussion of the policy on merger references. References are still made on other grounds. For example, the Elders IXL bid for Allied Lyons was referred because of concern over takeovers being financed by a high level of borrowed money: see Cmnd 9892, pp 81–86. On the financing of takeovers in this way see Chiplin and Wright *The Logic of Mergers* (1987) pp 58–61. See also City Code r 24.2(c).
12 *Financial Times*, 2 March 1983. The Secretary of State's decision not to refer a merger is not subject to judicial review: *Lonrho plc v Secretary of State For Trade and Industry* [1989] 2 All ER 609, [1989] 1 WLR 525, HL. The application for judicial review arose because of allegations that the Secretary of State was misled by false information into not making a reference. For one of the sequels, see *Lonrho plc v Fayed* [1990] 2 QB 479, [1989] 2 All ER 65, CA. It is now a criminal offence knowingly or recklessly to supply information to the

When a merger is referred to the Commission, it investigates and reports whether it qualifies for investigation and, if it does, whether it operates or may be expected to operate against the public interest[13]. The Commission is charged to take into account all matters that appear to be relevant in considering the public interest but in particular it must have regard to the desirability of maintaining and promoting competition, the interests of consumers, efficiency and innovation, the balanced distribution of industry and employment, and exports[14]. The Commission must reach definite conclusions and if it finds the merger operates against the public interest, it must specify the particular adverse consquences, consider what action should be taken and may make recommendations for action either by the government or by the companies concerned[15].

The Secretary of State has power to preserve the status quo pending the report of the Commission[16]. On receiving the report, a copy must be sent to the Director General[17]. If the Commission has concluded that the merger qualified for investigation and that it operates or may be expected to operate against the public interest and have specified particular adverse effects, the Secretary of State may exercise a number of powers[17] to remedy or prevent the adverse effects[18]. These include power to order the break-up of mergers, to prohibit proposed mergers from taking place or to regulate the behaviour of enterprises after they have merged. In practice, the Secretary of State tries a voluntary approach first and there is provision for the Director General to seek undertakings from the various parties as to their future conduct[19]. If these are not forthcoming, then the Secretary of State may, taking account of any recommendations by the Commission or advice of the Director General[20], use compulsory powers. If undertakings are given or orders made it is the duty of the Director General to supervise their implementation[1]. The Secretary of State is not, however, bound to accept the recommendations of a Commission report that a merger should be

Secretary of State, or the Director General of Fair Trading or the Monopolies and Mergers Commission which is false or misleading in a material particular: Fair Trading Act 1973, s 93B inserted by the Companies Act 1989, s 151 (replacing offences under ss 46(3) and 85(6)(b) which covered only the Monopolies and Mergers Commission).

13 Fair Trading Act 1973, s 69(1). For an argument that there should be a presumption against certain mergers and that the onus should be on those seeking the merger to justify it, see Labour Finance and Industry Group *A Market with Rules: Regulating Takeovers, Mergers and Monopolies* (1988).

14 Fair Trading Act 1973, s 84(1).

15 Ibid, s 72.

16 Ibid, s 74(1) and (2). There is now an automatic ban on share dealing once a reference to the commission is made: ibid, s 75(4A)–(4M) inserted by the Companies Act 1989, s 149. This followed an incident in which Elders IXL used the time between the announcement of a reference of its bid for Scottish and Newcastle Breweries and the making of an order banning further shares purchases to increase its holding in Scottish and Newcastle Breweries by nearly 10%.

17 Ibid, s 86(1).

18 Ibid s 73(1) and (2) and Sch 8, Pts I and II.

19 Ibid, s 88(1)–(3).

20 Ibid, s 73(3).

 1 Ibid, s 88(4) and (5). Such undertakings and those given under s 75K to avoid a reference to the Commission are given to the Secretary of State and are enforceable by injunction: ibid, ss 93 and 93A. Whether breach of an undertaking given by one company to reduce its shareholding in a second company was actionable by shareholders in the second company was left open in *Re Carrington Viyella plc* (1983) 1 BCC 98,951, see especially 98,956–98,958.

halted[2]. It is in his unfettered discretion[3], though in exercising it he must take into account any advice he is given on the matter by the Director General[4].

EC controls

Apart from control under the Fair Trading Act there is also the possibility of a merger being investigated by the Commission of the European Communities. The Treaty of Rome provided for the control of cartels under art 85 and dominant positions under art 86. As in the U K the demand to control mergers was not felt until later. It was held in the *Continental Can*[5] case that the Commission has power to control mergers under art 86 of the Treaty if they constitute an abuse of a dominant position within a substantial part of the Common Market. The Commission's view is that art 85, which deals with agreements between parties which prevent, restrict or distort competition within the Common Market, also gives them powers in relation to mergers[6]. There is now, however, a regulation[7] giving the Commission exclusive jurisdiction[8] to evaluate the largest[9] cross-border[10] mergers in the EC[11]. The basic criterion of evaluation will be the impact on competition. The creation or strengthening of a dominant position will be incompatible with the common market if effective competition is impeded to a significant extent, whether within the common market as a whole or in a substantial part thereof.

2 The Secretary of State has no powers under this legislation to intervene if the Commission recommends that a merger should not be halted. There is power under the Industry Act 1975, s 13 to stop transactions involving the transfer to non-residents of control of important manufacturing undertakings if this would be contrary to the national interest.
3 *R v Secretary of State for Trade, ex p Anderson Strathclyde plc* [1983] 2 All ER 233.
4 Fair Trading Act 1973, s 86(1).
5 Case 6/72 *Europemballage Corpn and Continental Can Co Inc v EC Commission* [1973] ECR 215, [1973] CMLR 199, ECJ. Breach of arts 85 and 86 can entitle an injured party to sue. One of the ways in which Argyll Group sought to stop the Guinness takeover of Distillers was on the grounds of breach of art 86: *Argyll Group plc v Distillers Co plc* [1986] 1 CMLR 764, 1987 SLT 514.
6 The view is said to be supported by the decision in joined cases 142, 156/84 *British American Tobacco Co Ltd and R J Reynolds Industries Inc v EC Commission*, [1988] 4 CMLR 24, ECJ. Because of the need for an agreement, art 85 may only apply to mergers agreed between the managements of each side.
7 EEC Council Regulation 4064/89, OJ 1989 L395/1. The regulation and various associated measures, including a short introduction summarising the regulation, are conveniently collected together in the Bulletin of the European Communities Supplement 2/90.
8 There are derogations from this allowing member states to invoke legitimate interests including public security, media plurality and prudential rules mainly relevant to the provision of financial services. However, this only allows members states to prohibit mergers or impose further conditions for approval; member states may not authorise mergers which have been prohibited by the Commission. A matter may also be referred to national authorities if a dominant position exists in a distinct market in a member state and application of the regulation would not achieve a satisfactory solution.
9 The aggregate world wide turnover of the undertakings concerned must be at least ECU 5,000m and at least two of the undertakings must have Community-wide turnovers of at least ECU 250m. It is intended these limits will be progressively reduced to ECU 2,000m and ECU 100m respectively.
10 The regulation does not apply if each of the undertakings concerned achieves at least two-thirds of its turnover within one and the same member state.
11 Qualifying mergers must be pre-notified to the Commission. It is anticipated that the present thresholds will result in about 50 cases being examined a year. Under the City Code an offer must lapse if the Commission initiates proceedings itself or refers the offer to the Monopolies and Mergers Commission: r 12.

FORMS OF REGULATION OF TAKEOVERS

Company law is about the problems that arise in the regulation of companies. Sometimes those problems have a legal solution; sometimes a legal solution has been consciously avoided or the problem has not yet arisen in a way which seeks a legal solution; at other times extralegal regulatory agencies have provided an answer. All of these represent a part of company law. It is as much a part of company law to know and understand why a legal solution is not provided to a particular problem as it is to know the detail of a legal solution where one is provided. Likewise, a knowledge of the extralegal regulatory solution to problems is not only important for its practical effect but forms a part of company law because it creates the context in which legal rules apply and represents a potential solution for the law to adopt.

The City Code on Takeovers and Mergers

Takeovers are one of those areas where the legal solution of problems is comparatively rare[12]. The UK has no statutory code dealing with takeovers. Instead since 1959 there has been developed an extralegal code of conduct for the regulation of takeovers known as the City Code on Takeovers and Mergers[13]. Although the City Code applies principally to public companies[14], the rules it contains provide a starting point for considering how the same problems could be approached in relation to companies not covered by the Code. The restricted application of the City Code, however, must be borne in mind in reading this chapter.

The origins of the Code lie in the Notes for the Amalgamation of British Businesses drawn up by the Issuing Houses Association in 1959. The Notes were revised in 1963 and again in 1968 when they were given their present name and revised editions of the City Code have been issued in 1969, 1972, 1976, 1981, 1985, 1988 and 1990. From the outset, the Notes distinguished between principles and procedure and this distinction is maintained in the present Code consisting as it does of 10 general principles and 38 more detailed rules supplemented by notes which amplify and explain the operation of a number of the rules.

The City Code is not legally enforceable though its existence is taken into account by the courts and on occasion may be recognised as representing the required or desirable practice by directors[15]. As a result, its provisions can be drafted in a manner that enables them to be applied flexibly to a variety of situations. The spirit of the rules is intended to be observed as much as the

---

12 The main areas covered by legislation are compulsory acquisition of shares, payments of compensation to directors for loss of office and secret acquisition of shares. All are dealt with in this chapter.
13 See Johnston *The City Takeover Code* (1980). See also Prentice 'Take-over Bids and the System of Self-regulation' (1981) 10 Oxford Journal of Legal Studies 406, Lord Alexander 'Takeovers: the Regulatory scene' [1990] JBL 203 and Calcutt 'The Work of the Takeover Panel' (1990) 11 Co Law 203.
14 City Code, Introduction, para 14.
15 See, for example, *Dunford & Elliott Ltd v Johnson & Firth Brown Ltd* [1977] 1 Lloyd's Rep 505, CA and *Morgan Crucible Co plc v Hill Samuel Bank Ltd* [1991] 1 All ER 148, [1991] 2 WLR 655, CA. It may also be enforceable indirectly via the obligation on persons authorised to carry on investment business under the Financial Services Act 1986 to observe the City Code under the Securities and Investment Board's Conduct of Business Rules.

letter[16]. The rules themselves often include words like 'normally' or allow for the rules to be waived with the consent of the Panel on Takeovers and Mergers. The Panel was established to administer the Code in 1968 and consists of part-time representatives of various financial institutions with a full-time executive[17]. The executive operates in an active supervisory capacity, often at the end of a telephone, advising the parties to a takeover how to proceed in accordance with the spirit of the Code and giving rulings on interpretation of the Code[18]. If parties wish to contest rulings of the executive they may appeal to the Panel and the executive may itself refer a question where there is a particularly difficult or important point at issue[19].

The Panel also conducts inquiries into alleged breaches of the Code[20] and administers sanctions where appropriate. Because the Code is not legally enforceable, the investigation of breaches of the Code and the application of appropriate sanctions can present a problem. The sanctions to which the Panel has recourse include private reprimand, public censure or depriving the offender of the facilities of the securities market. The Panel may also refer aspects of a case to the Department of Trade and Industry, The Stock Exchange or other appropriate body[1]. Where the Panel finds a person in breach of the Code and proposes disciplinary action, the person may appeal to an Appeal Committee consisting of the Panel Chairman and two members of the Panel not previously involved in the case[2]. When the procedure before the Panel or the Appeal Committee is completed their conclusions and the reasons for them are usually published so that their operations are thus subject to public scrutiny[3].

In an important decision affecting the legal status of the Code, it was held in *R v Panel on Take-overs and Mergers, ex p Datafin plc*[4] that the rulings of the Panel are subject to judicial review. The Panel's objection that court applications in the course of takeovers would create delay and uncertainty was met in two ways[5]. First, the need for the court's leave before applying for judicial review will enable the court to exclude unmeritorious or trivial cases. In exercising its functions the Panel should therefore ignore, for the time being, the fact that an application for leave has been made. Secondly, the Panel and those affected should treat the Panel's decisions as valid and binding, unless and until they are set aside. Because of the flexibility of the Code and the role of the Panel in amending the rules of the Code, the cases

---

16 City Code, General Principles, Introduction.
17 City Code, Introduction, para 2.
18 The Code contains a reminder that taking legal, or other professional, advice on the interpretation or application of the Code is not an appropriate alternative to obtaining a view or
   ruling from the executive: City Code, Introduction, para 3(b). The Panel re-emphasised this
   in a statement arising out of the offer by Turner & Newall plc for AE plc: [1987] JBL 140.
19 City Code, Introduction, para 3(b)(c).
20 The Panel is protected by qualified privilege in relation to the law of defamation in
   conducting its investigations: *Graff v Lord Shawcross* (10 October 1980, unreported but see
   (1981) 2 Co Law 33).
1 City Code, Introduction, para 3(d).
2 City Code, Introduction, para 3(f).
3 City Code, Introduction, para 3(f).
4 [1987] QB 815, [1987] 1 All ER 564, CA. See also *R v Panel on Take-overs and Mergers, ex p
   Guinness plc* [1990] 1 QB 146, [1989] 1 All ER 509, CA, which contains a useful account of
   how the Panel operates.
5 See especially [1987] QB 815 at 839–842, [1987] 1 All ER 564 at 577–580.

in which the court will intervene are likely to be very rare. When the court does intervene it may well be via a declaratory judgment for the future rather than an intervention affecting the substantive issue between the parties to the takeover[6].

A system of self-regulation ultimately depends on those affected by it voluntarily abiding by its rules. Such voluntary co-operation, however, may be less forthcoming if a few individuals are able to breach the Code and go unpunished. One of the themes running through the whole topic of takeovers is whether self-regulation should be replaced by some form of legally enforced regulation. Particular attention should therefore be paid to the effectiveness or otherwise of any sanctions the Panel has imposed. The issue of self-regulation versus a statutory code is also raised by the proposal for a Thirteenth Directive[7] harmonising the rules for takeovers within member states[8]. At present differing or non-existent rules on takeovers in various member states represent a barrier to cross border takeovers[9]. The lack of protection for shareholders in some member states makes them reluctant to open the way to foreign acquisitions and inhibits the full realisation of a common market[10].

Other forms of regulation

Besides the City Code, The Stock Exchange's Admission of Securities to Listing contains a number of provisions relating to the content of takeover offer documents and procedure on takeovers[11] and requires drafts of all documents connected with takeovers to be submitted to The Stock Exchange for approval[12]. In addition some aspects of takeovers may be regulated by provisions of the Financial Services Act 1986.

MECHANICS OF TAKEOVERS AND MERGERS

The term takeover is normally used to refer to the acquisition of the shares in a company. It is, of course, possible to acquire a company's business by acquiring its undertaking or assets rather than the company itself. The legal considerations affecting such a transaction may involve questions of ultra

---

6 According to Sir John Donaldson MR, the court is likely 'to allow contemporary decisions to take their course, considering the complaint and intervening, if at all, later and in retrospect by declaratory orders which would enable the Panel not to repeat any error and would relieve individuals of the disciplinary consequences of any erroneous finding of breach of the rules'. See, ibid at 842, 579–580.
7 Amended proposal for a Thirteenth Council Directive on Company Law, OJ 1990 C 240/7. On an earlier draft see Bulletin of the European Communities Supplement 3/89. See also an excellent article by Hahn (1990) 10 Int Rev of Law and Economics 131.
8 The directive requires member states to designate an authority to discharge the functions specified in the directive. This authority may, however, delegate its powers to a private body provided such authority or body has all the powers necessary for the exercise of its functions including ensuring that parties comply with their obligations: art 6.
9 See *Barriers to Takeovers in the European Community* (1989) a report by Cooper & Lybrand commissioned by the Department of Trade and Industry.
10 The proposed Thirteenth Directive includes provision for the mutual recognition of offer documents. In other respects it is heavily influenced by the City Code.
11 Stock Exchange Admission of Securities to Listing, s 6, ch 2.
12 Ibid, s 6, ch 2, para 2.

vires[13] and how within a company's constitution a decision to transfer part or all of a company's undertaking may be arrived at. In the case of a company listed on The Stock Exchange, the size of the transaction in relation to the size of the company involved may require announcements to be made to The Stock Exchange and the press, a circular to be sent to shareholders and, in some cases, the consent of the shareholders in general meeting to be obtained[14]. Although some of the statutory provisions affecting takeovers also relate to the acquisition of undertakings or assets, for the most part, this chapter is concerned with the regulation of takeovers by the acquisition of shares.

Whether shares or assets are acquired the offeror company will usually pay for them either in cash or by issuing shares in itself or by offering shares or cash in combination or in the alternative[15]. If shares are offered as consideration, the offeror will need to ensure it has the authority of its shareholders under s 80. Section 89, which otherwise requires shares to be offered first to existing shareholders, will not apply because under s 89(4) the obligation does not apply where shares are issued for non-cash consideration. Provided also that certain conditions are fulfilled, the shares or assets acquired will not need to be valued under s 103 despite the fact that they represent non-cash consideration for the issue of shares. The conditions are that any offer for shares was made to all the holders of the class of shares involved (other than shares held by or on behalf of the offeror, its holding company or any subsidiary thereof)[16] or any acquisition of assets involved the acquisition of all the assets and liabilities of the offeree company[17].

If shares are offered as consideration then, particularly where there are rival share exchange offers, the market value of any shares offered can be crucial to the success of a bid. This has led to practices being employed to support the share price of the offeror. There is a strong objection to this in economic theory in that it may distort the market for corporate control thus denying to the takeover its fundamental economic function. Nevertheless the controls on such practices in the rules regulating takeovers are uncoordinated and imprecise[18]. They fall into three categories. First, there are controls under the Companies Act itself. Any buying of its own shares by the offeror would, of course, have to comply with the statutory provisions on companies buying their own shares[19]. To avoid this the offeror may instead

---

13 It will not be implied in a trading company's objects that it has power to sell its entire undertaking. When s 4 stated specific grounds on which objects could be altered, it was recognised that a company could amend its objects to incorporate such a power. It is also doubtful whether selling its entire undertaking is within the powers of a general commercial company under s 3A.

14 Stock Exchange Admission of Securities to Listing, s 6, ch 1.

15 Shareholders may prefer to receive shares in exchange because in certain circumstances the exchange is not a disposal for the purposes of capital gains tax: Capital Gains Tax Act 1979, s 85. In certain circumstances under the City Code a cash alternative *must* be offered: r 11. See below p 635.

16 Section 103(3).

17 Section 103(4), (5).

18 Many of the controls are also relevant to a different, defensive, share buying operation. This is where shares in the offeree company are purchased for the sole purpose of defeating a takeover bid. An example of this occurred where somebody spent £4m buying ten million shares in Amalgamated Engineering just before a takeover bid by Turner & Newall plc closed and sold them three days later at a loss of 40p per share: see [1987] JBL 140.

19 Sections 159–181.

arrange for third parties to buy shares in the offeror[20]. Here the danger is that the arrangement may result in the offeror giving unlawful financial assistance to a third party to buy its own shares[1]. Secondly, under the City Code as it existed until April 1985, third parties with an interest in the bid were prohibited from dealing in the shares of either company[2]. This was repealed because the Panel found it impossible to enforce. It was replaced by provisions requiring prompt disclosure of any such dealing by a party having a material trading arrangement with the offeror or offeree company[3]. The third category of controls are possible criminal offences[4]. Here the crucial provision is likely to be the Financial Services Act 1986, s 47(2)[5]. This makes it an offence to do anything which creates a false or misleading impression as to the value of shares if this is done for the purpose of creating that impression and of thereby inducing another person to acquire the shares in question[6].

20 After the Guinness plc offer for Distillers plc had succeeded it emerged that a number of third parties had bought shares in Guinness as a result of various inducements or payments from Guinness.

 1 Contrary to s 151. One of the problems raised by this section is that it does not apply where the acquisition of shares is not the principal purpose for the financial assistance, or, if it is, the acquisition is part of a larger purpose of the company and, in either case, the assistance is given in good faith in the interests of the company: s 153(1)(2). However, in *Brady v Brady* [1989] AC 755, [1988] 2 All ER 617, HL Lord Oliver observed that where a takeover is financed using the target company's own funds the purpose of the financial assistance is to complete the takeover. The reason for the takeover or the benefits to flow from it cannot constitute a larger purpose for which the provision of assistance is merely an incident. 'The purpose and the only purpose of the financial assistance is and remains that of enabling the shares to be acquired and the financial or commercial advantages flowing from the acquisition, whilst they may form the reason for forming the purpose of providing assistance, are a by-product of it rather than independent purpose of which the assistance can properly be considered to be an incident' at 780, 633. Section 151 was also raised in connection with another aspect of the Guinness bid for Distillers. The board of Distillers invited Guinness to bid rather than see the company taken over by Argyll Group plc. At Guinness's request Distillers promised to indemnify Guinness for the costs of their bid should it fail. Argyll, as a shareholder in Distillers, began proceedings to challenge the indemnity agreement as being in breach of s 151. Quite apart from such an indemnity coming within the possible exception in s 153(1)(2) referred to above, it is also possible that an indemnity agreement like that is not caught by s 151 at all. Whilst such an indemnity might have constituted financial assistance 'in connection with' the acquisition of shares, and hence been unlawful under the pre-1981 legislation, that phrase was dropped in 1981 so that only financial assistance given 'for the purpose of' the acquisition of shares is now unlawful.

 2 City Code, 1981 edition, r 37.

 3 City Code, r 8.1 and the definition of 'associate'. Following amendments to the Code in February 1987 an arrangement by anyone with any party involved in a bid or their associates, relating to dealing in shares of the relevant companies, must be disclosed, whether or not any dealings actually take place. Arrangement includes, in addition to indemnity or option arrangements, any agreement or understanding which may be an inducement to deal or refrain from dealing: r 8, note 6. The Stock Exchange has also introduced rules to try and control the giving of indemnities to others in connection with the buying of shares. A listed company must now obtain prior shareholder approval if, other than in the ordinary course of business, it agrees to accept liability for costs, expenses, commissions or losses by third parties where liability is either unlimited or equals or exceeds 25% of average audited pre-tax profits over the past three years: Admission of Securities to Listing, s 6, ch 1, para 3.3.

 4 Ie other than technical offences under provisions of the Companies Act.

 5 Other possible offences include obtaining property by deception contrary to the Theft Act 1968, s 15 and the common law offence of conspiracy to defraud.

 6 It is a defence for a person to show that he reasonably believed his act or conduct would not create a false or misleading impression as to the value of shares: Financial Services Act 1986, s 47(3).

Statutory procedures used for takeovers and mergers

Just as there is no comprehensive set of legal rules governing the conduct of takeovers in the UK so there is no statutory framework within which takeovers and mergers may take place. Instead, the legal framework for takeovers is largely provided by the law of contract rather than company law. A takeover bid in the form of an offer for shares is in law made to and accepted or rejected by, not the offeree company, but the offeree company's shareholders. There are, however, two statutory procedures which came into existence in connection with other purposes, but which can be used as mechanisms for effecting takeovers and mergers.

RECONSTRUCTION IN THE COURSE OF VOLUNTARY LIQUIDATION

Since 1862 the companies' legislation has included a provision, currently contained in the Insolvency Act 1986, s 110[7], whereby a company in voluntary liquidation may by special resolution[8] authorise the liquidator to sell the whole or part of its business or property to another company in return for shares in that other company which are then distributed among the members of the company in liquidation[9]. In its simplest form, where one company transfers its business to a new company, this is called reconstruction. Historically, this was usually done either because the new company had wider or different objects than the old company, or to change the rights of different classes of shareholders by giving them shares with altered rights in a new company, or to raise fresh capital by giving the shareholders partly-paid shares in the new company. But the provisions can also be used to amalgamate two existing businesses into one company. This can be done either by putting one company into liquidation and transferring its business to the other in return for shares in that other, or by putting both companies into liquidation and transferring both their businesses to a third company, which issues shares to the two liquidators for distribution to the shareholders in the two companies now in liquidation.

The crucial effect of the section is that the sale or arrangement is binding on all the members of the company[10] subject to the right of any members who did not vote for the resolution, to give notice in writing to the liquidator, within seven days after the passing of the resolution, requiring the liquidator either to abstain from carrying out the resolution or to purchase their interest at a price to be determined by agreement or arbitration[11]. This does not, however, mean that shareholders who neither assent nor give formal notice or dissent are bound to take the shares in the transferor company.

---

7 The provisions are in the Insolvency Act because the procedure involves the company going into liquidation. The company may well, of course, not be insolvent.
8 Insolvency Act 1986, s 110(3)(a). In a creditors' voluntary liquidation, the consent of either the court or the liquidation committee is required also: s 110(3)(b).
9 Ibid, s 110(2). The requirement for voluntary liquidation means that the transferor company must be one registered under the Companies Act since an unregistered company can only be wound up by court order: s 221(4). The transferee company need not be registered under the Companies Act.
10 Ibid, s 110(5).
11 Ibid, s 111(2). A shareholder may also be able to halt the transaction by obtaining a winding-up order: s 110(6) and *Re Consolidated South Rand Mines Deep Ltd* [1909] 1 Ch 491.

They may instead forfeit their interest in the company altogether[12] or the scheme may provide for the shares of such shareholders to be sold and the proceeds paid to them[13]. The consideration received by the liquidator must be distributed among the shareholders entitled to it strictly in accordance with their respective rights as shareholders[14]. In other words, although their rights as shareholders in the new company may be very different from their rights in the old company, the shares in the new company must somehow be distributed in a way that exactly reflects the rights of shareholders in the old company.

The sale or arrangement agreed to by the special resolution is also binding on the creditors of the old company[15]. They are not transferred with the business to the new company but remain creditors of the old company. So they must look to the liquidator of the old company to retain sufficient assets or to realise sufficient of the consideration received from the transferee company to be able to pay them[16]. If they doubt whether the liquidator will be able to pay them, their remedy is to petition for the compulsory liquidation of the company. If an order for winding up is made within a year of the special resolution being passed, the resolution is not valid unless sanctioned by the court[17]. Liquidators will therefore usually make adequate provision for creditors since they will not want to run the risk of the whole transaction being invalidated, as would be the case if the special resolution were invalidated.

SCHEME OF ARRANGEMENT

The second statutory provision under which mergers can be effected was originally introduced in 1870 to enable companies in liquidation to make compromises and arrangements with their creditors. In 1900 it was extended to apply to arrangements between companies and their members, and, in 1907, the requirement that the company be in liquidation was removed. The provision is now contained in s 425 and is far wider in application than the Insolvency Act 1986, s 110. First, because the company need not be in liquidation, reconstructions can be effected within the company. Thus, shareholders' rights can be varied in the same company, in contrast to the Insolvency Act 1986, s 110, where they had to be strictly observed[18]. Secondly, creditors' rights can be altered which is not possible under the Insolvency Act 1986, s 110. Thirdly, the range of transaction within the phrase 'compromise or arrangement' includes more than just the reconstruction or amalgamation that can be achieved under the Insolvency Act 1986, s 110. The limitations that have been recognised on the scope of s 425 are that the transaction must not be ultra vires the company[19], nor contrary to the

---

12 *Re Bank of Hindustan, China and Japan Ltd, Higgs's Case* (1865) 2 Hem & M 657; *Burdett-Coutts v True Blue (Hannan's) Gold Mine* [1899] 2 Ch 616, CA.
13 *Fuller v White Feather Reward Ltd* [1906] 1 Ch 823.
14 *Griffith v Paget* (1877) 5 Ch D 894; (1877) 6 Ch D 511.
15 *Re City and County Investment Co* (1879) 13 Ch D 475, CA.
16 *Pulsford v Devenish* [1903] 2 Ch 625.
17 Insolvency Act 1986, s 110(6).
18 Whether rights attaching to a class of shares and set out in the memorandum are alterable under s 425 without obtaining the consent of all members, if required under s 125(5), raises a question analogous to that left open in *Re Palace Hotel Ltd* [1912] 2 Ch 438 and *Re JA Nordberg Ltd* [1915] 2 Ch 439.
19 *Re Oceanic Steam Navigation Co Ltd* [1939] Ch 41, [1938] 3 All ER 740; *Re Bramall & Ogden Ltd* [1981] LS Gaz R 813.

general law[20], and must involve some element of give and take on the part of each of the parties involved[1]. But, provided these limits are observed, any form of compromise or arrangement may be included.

It will be apparent that any transaction that could come within the Insolvency Act 1986, s 110 could in principle come within s 425 as well. The courts have, however, held that the special protection afforded to dissenting shareholders, of compelling the liquidator to buy them out or drop the transaction[2], must be made available to dissenting shareholders if a similar scheme is effected under s 425[3]. Where, however, the company is transferring only part of its undertaking or assets and is continuing in existence with the remaining assets rather than going into liquidation, so that the Insolvency Act 1986, s 110 would not apply, there is no necessity for dissenting shareholders to be given a cash option[4]. Section 425 can therefore be used for reconstructions or amalgamations, but it can also be used for straight takeover bids provided the bid has the consent of the directors of the offeree company because their co-operation will be needed in calling the various meetings necessary under s 425[5]. If s 425 is available, it seems it can also be used for compulsory acquisition of dissenting shareholders[6] on a wider scale than the orthodox provisions. It has the further advantage over a conventional takeover in which the offeror acquires the existing share capital of the offeree company in that the existing share capital of the offeree company can be cancelled instead, and new shares issued to the offeror, thus saving stamp duty on the transfer of shares.

The procedure under s 425 is begun by an application to the court by the company, a creditor or a member, or the liquidator if the company is in liquidation. The court then directs meetings of the classes of the members or creditors concerned[7]. The responsibility for deciding the appropriate classes rests on the company[8] and if they are not correct, the court will not approve the scheme at least in cases where it can be shown the scheme would not have received the necessary majority had the meetings been properly constituted[9]. The notice calling the meeting must be accompanied by a circular

20 *Re St James' Court Estate Ltd* [1944] Ch 6.
 1 *Re National Farmers' Union Development Trust Ltd* [1973] 1 All ER 135, [1972] 1 WLR 1548.
 2 Insolvency Act 1986, s 111(2).
 3 *Re Tea Corpn Ltd, Sorsbie v Tea Corpn Ltd* [1904] 1 Ch 12, CA; *Re General Motor Cab Co Ltd* [1913] 1 Ch 377, CA; *Re Sandwell Park Colliery Co Ltd* [1914] 1 Ch 589; *Re Anglo-Continental Supply Co Ltd* [1922] 2 Ch 723.
 4 *Wall v London and Northern Assets Corpn* [1898] 2 Ch 469, CA; *Re Bramall & Ogden Ltd* [1981] LS Gaz R 813.
 5 *Re Savoy Hotel Ltd* [1981] Ch 351, [1981] 3 All ER 646.
 6 *Re National Bank Ltd* [1966] 1 All ER 1006, [1966] 1 WLR 819; *Singer Manufacturing Co v Robinow* 1971 SC 11.
 7 Section 425(1).
 8 *Practice Note* [1934] WN 142.
 9 *Re United Provident Assurance Co Ltd* [1910] 2 Ch 477; *Re Hellenic and General Trust Ltd* [1975] 3 All ER 382, [1976] 1 WLR 123. The definition of a class for these purposes is 'those persons whose rights are not so dissimilar as to make it impossible for them to consult together with a view to their common interest' per Bowen LJ in *Sovereign Life Assurance Co v Dodd* [1892] 2 QB 573 at 583, CA. In *Re Hellenic and General Trust Ltd* (supra) Templeman J held that a 53% stake in the offeree held by a wholly-owned subsidiary of the offeror constituted a separate class even though all the shares in the offeree had identical rights. The decision is criticised by Hornby (1976) 39 MLR 207 and has not been followed in

explaining the scheme, disclosing any material interests of the directors and whether the compromise or arrangement affects them differently from others with a similar interest[10].

The scheme will be approved by the appropriate meetings of shareholders or creditors if it is agreed to by a majority in number representing 75% in value of those present and voting in person or by proxy[11]. There follows a second application to the court, and, if the court sanctions the scheme, then once an office copy of the court order has been registered it becomes binding on all the members or class of members or creditors or class of creditors as the case may be[12]. It is this capacity to bind dissenting or apathetic members which makes s 425 such a formidable section. The protection for dissenters lies in the majority both in number and value that is required and in the need for the court's approval. The test most often applied by the courts in deciding whether to approve schemes of arrangement is that of Maugham J, where he said the function of court is to see 'whether the proposal is such that an intelligent and honest man, a member of the class concerned and acting in respect of his interest, might reasonably approve'[13]. In practice, the courts are reluctant to interfere if a proper majority has approved the scheme, preferring to reject inappropriate schemes on the grounds that they fall outside the scope of the section or on the grounds of procedural irregularity.

It has been observed that s 425 can be used for the transfer of the whole or part of one or more companies' businesses to another company. Another advantage s 425 has over carrying out a similar reconstruction or amalgamation under the Insolvency Act 1986, s 110 is that under s 427, the court may effect certain transactions by a single court order, dispensing with the need for separate deeds and conveyances and in some cases, with the need to obtain the consent of other interested parties. Under the Insolvency Act 1986, s 110, when an undertaking is transferred, the creditors remain creditors of the old company. Under s 427, the court can by order transfer not only the whole or any part of a company's undertaking or property but also its liabilities[14]. Creditors could, of course, agree to be transferred and, if appropriate meetings of creditors were held, a majority in number representing 75% in value could bind them all. But in cases where the company is solvent and there is no risk to creditors, the courts will not require meetings of creditors to be held but will transfer the liabilities by court order[15]. It has been held that property rights which are not assignable by law cannot be transferred[16] nor can functions which are personal to the

---

South Africa: *Borgelt v Millman NO* 1983(1) SA 757. It is supported, however, by Prentice (1976) 92 LQR 13. Perhaps it is 'impossible' for a wholly-owned subsidiary to even consider rejecting its parent company's offer but what would the position be if the subsidiary were not wholly-owned?

10 Section 426. Failure to comply with these requirements may preclude approval by the court. *Scottish Eastern Investment Trust Ltd—Petitioners* 1966 SLT 285. As to the effect of a change in the directors' interests between the notice and the meeting, see *Re Jessel Trust Ltd* [1985] BCLC 119; cf *Re Minster Assets plc* [1985] BCLC 200.

11 Section 425(2).

12 Section 425(2)(3).

13 *Re Dorman, Long & Co Ltd, South Durham Steel and Iron Co Ltd* [1934] Ch 635 at 657.

14 Section 427(3)(a).

15 A separate application is usually made for an order under s 427 and in the case of transferring liabilities the court will consider whether any protection for creditors is needed: *Clydesdale Bank Ltd, Petitioners* 1950 SC 30; *Re Bramall & Ogden Ltd* [1981] LS Gaz R 813.

16 *Re L Hotel Co Ltd and Langham Hotel Co Ltd* [1946] 1 All ER 319.

company concerned[17]. But the former rule, that contracts of employment could not be transferred[18] is now reversed for they are automatically transferred when the undertaking or part thereof is transferred[19] whether the transfer is effected by sale or by some other disposition or by operation of law[20].

Impact of the Third and Sixth Directives   Two of the directives issued as part of the programme for the harmonisation of company law within the European Community have modified the procedures for certain schemes of arrangement[1]. The Third Directive[2] applies where two or more public companies merge by the transfer of the undertaking, property and liabilities[3] of one or more public companies, either to another public company[4] or to a new company[5]. The Sixth Directive[6] applies to the division of a public company where its undertaking, property and liabilities[3] are transferred to two or more public companies or to new companies[7]. Both directives also only apply where the transfer is in exchange for the allocation to the shareholders of the transferor company or companies of shares in the transferee company or companies, with or without an additional cash payment[8].

Where a merger or division falls within these provisions, Sch 15B will apply as well as ss 425–427. The Schedule requires[9] approval of the scheme by each class of members of the transferee company involved[10], as well as by those in the transferor company[11]. The draft terms of the merger or division are subject to the official notification procedure[12] at least one month before the court sanctions the scheme[13]. The directors' report on the proposed scheme[14] must include, among other matters, information on the legal and

---

17 *Re Skinner* [1958] 3 All ER 273, [1958] 1 WLR 1043.
18 *Nokes v Doncaster Amalgamated Collieries Ltd* [1940] AC 1014, HL.
19 Transfer of Undertakings (Protection of Employment) Regulations 1981, SI 1981/1794, reg 5(1).
20 Ibid, reg 3(2).
 1 The Directives have been implemented, via statutory instrument, by inserting s 427A and Sch 15A into the Companies Act 1985: The Companies (Mergers and Division) Regulations 1987, SI 1987/1991. The new provisions apply where the initial application to the court was made after 31 December 1987.
 2 EEC Council Directive 78/855. Official Journal of the European Communities 1978 L 295/36. There is also a proposal to harmonise procedures where a merger of the type that falls within the Third Directive takes place between companies in different member states. See proposal for a Tenth Directive: Official Journal of the European Communities 1985 C 23/11.
 3 It follows that these provisions do not apply to a reconstruction under the Insolvency Act 1986, s 110, because there liabilities are not transferred. Furthermore these provisions do not apply where the transferor company goes into liquidation: s 427A(4).
 4 Section 427A(3) Case 1.
 5 Section 427A(3) Case 2. The new company need not be a public company nor does it matter that other transactions involving private companies are involved.
 6 EEC Council Directive 82/891. Official Journal of the European Communities 1982 L 378/47.
 7 The new companies need not be public companies.
 8 Section 427(1)(c).
 9 Section 427(1).
10 Schedule 15B, para 1.
11 This is already required by s 425(2).
12 Delivery to the Registrar who then publishes a notice in the Gazette.
13 Schedule 15B, para 2.
14 See also s 426.

economic grounds for the terms, in particular, for the share exchange ratio[15]. A report, by an independent expert, setting out such matters as how the share exchange ratio was arrived at and whether it is reasonable[16] must also be made available to the shareholders[17].

The problem of the dissenting minority

COMPULSORY ACQUISITION OF MINORITY SHAREHOLDINGS

Where a company makes an offer for the shares in another company, it may be content just to acquire sufficient shares to give it control of the offeree company. But in many circumstances, it will want to acquire 100% of the shares in the offeree company. This would be the case, for example, if the offeror intended to invest large sums of fresh capital in the offeree company, but could not expect other shareholders to invest a proportionate amount. The profitability of the company would be expected to increase to the advantage of all the shareholders including the minority who had not invested any of the extra capital. In such circumstances, it might be felt to be fair that before investing the extra capital the majority should have the opportunity to buy out the minority at a fair price. Another example is that of a holding company which may legitimately wish to operate its subsidiaries in the interest of the enterprise or group as a whole. It will be able to do so more easily if the subsidiaries are wholly owned, so that the interests of minority shareholders do not need to be considered. So although the notion of compulsory acquisition has overtones of squeeze out and oppression, making a company a wholly-owned subsidiary can be a perfectly legitimate objective and provided a fair price is paid for the shares acquired, it should be unobjectionable[18].

Alteration of the articles   Although there are few illustrations in the reported cases it is apparent that provided the appropriate majorities could be obtained, both reconstruction in the course of voluntary liquidation and a s 425 scheme of arrangement could result in the compulsory elimination of minority shareholdings[19]. However, in cases where it was desirable, rather than acquire assets, to take over a company by the acquisition of shares[20] there was no mechanism for the elimination of the minority who did not accept the offer. An attempt to achieve this by altering the articles, to incorporate a clause that minority shareholders had to sell their shares at a

15 Schedule 15B, paras 3 and 4.
16 Schedule 15B, paras 3 and 5.
17 Schedule 15B, para 6.
18 For an economic analysis of compulsory acquisition, see Yarrow (1985) 34 Journal of Industrial Economics 3.
19 *Castello v London General Omnibus Co Ltd* (1912) 107 LT 575, CA is a case where the equivalent of the Insolvency Act 1986, s 110 was used for the compulsory acquisition of minority shareholders' interests for cash.
20 See the Report of the Company Law Amendment Committee (1926) (Cmd 2657) which gives as examples the necessity of preserving the goodwill associated with the name of the company taken over and in other cases that part of its property (eg a licence to utilise a patent assignable only with a consent which cannot be obtained) cannot be assigned: para 84.

fair value if requested to do so by holders of 90% of the issued shares, failed on the grounds that the alteration was not 'bona fide for the benefit of the company as a whole'[1].

Part XIIIA Instead, in 1929, a specific statutory power was introduced whereby an offeror, whose offer has been accepted by holders of 90% or more of the shares to which the offer relates, can compulsorily acquire the remaining shares, unless the court upholds an objection by a dissenting shareholder. The drafting of the provisions was criticised over many years[2] and eventually revised provisions were introduced with effect from 30 April 1987[3], though the basic principles remain unaltered.

The revised provisions operate only where an offeror[4] has made a 'takeover offer'[5]. To qualify as a takeover offer, an offer must fulfil two important conditions[6]. First, the offer must be to acquire all the shares, or all of a particular class of shares, not already held at the date of the offer[7] by the offeror or its associates[8]. Secondly, the offer must be on the same terms[9] for all the shares of the same class. Where the offer is accepted within four months by holders of 90% in value of the shares to which the offer relates[10], the offeror may within two months serve notice to acquire the remaining shares[11]. The recipient of the notice then has six weeks in which to apply to the court which may allow or disallow the acquisition or specify terms different from those in the offer[12]. If no application is made to the court then the offeror is entitled and bound to acquire the shares on the terms of the offer[13].

1   *Brown v British Abrasive Wheel Co Ltd* [1919] 1 Ch 290. The majority had acquired 98% of the shares in a takeover but were not prepared to put fresh capital into the company unless they owned 100%. One example of a shareholder putting fresh capital into a business without owning all the shares, and thus benefiting the minority shareholders was the government in relation to British Leyland. In 1975 the government offered the equivalent of 100p per share compared with a stock market price when the shares were suspended equivalent to 62.5p (these prices allow for a subsequent consolidation). The offer was accepted by holders of 78% of shares. Subsequently the government invested £2.98bn, mostly in the form of equity, increasing its stake to 99.8% by 1988 when the government accepted an offer from British Aerospace of 2.7p per share compared with a current stock market price of 67p. British Aerospace then compulsorily acquired the remaining 0.2% at 100p per share, the same as the government's offer in 1975. Allowing for inflation, however, shareholders who declined the government's offer in 1975 would have needed an offer of 307p to match the offer they had turned down in 1975.
2   See especially the Report of the Company Law Committee (Cmnd 1749) paras 283–293.
3   The revised provisions were enacted via the Financial Services Act 1986, s 172 and Sch 12.
4   Note that an offeror may be a company, an individual or any combination: s 430D. The provision had previously been restricted to offers made by a single company: *Blue Metal Industries Ltd v Dilley* [1970] AC 827, [1969] 3 All ER 437, PC.
5   Section 429(1)(2).
6   Section 428(1).
7   Section 428(5).
8   Shares held by the offeror or associates are excluded altogether so that they count neither for nor against the 90% acceptance level. The important definition of 'associate' is contained in s 430E(4)–(8).
9   Section 428(3)(4).
10   Where more than one class of shares is involved separate offers must be made for each class. The 90% acceptance level is thus calculated separately for each class.
11   Section 429(1)(3).
12   Section 430C(1). The power to specify different terms was new in 1987.
13   Section 430(1)(2).

Under the provisions operating before 30 April 1987 many problems arose in establishing the 90% acceptance level. These are now dealt with by the legislation. The first is where the offeror continues to buy shares in the offeree company during the period of the offer. The difficulty here is that shareholders who sell during the bid are people who might otherwise have accepted the offer, thus making it harder to obtain a 90% acceptance of the actual offer as a result. This problem is resolved by providing that shares acquired during the offer by the offeror or its associates can be counted as acceptances of the offer provided that the consideration does not exceed the offer price, or if it does, that the offer price is correspondingly increased[14]. The second problem was that a revised offer would sometimes constitute a fresh offer, so that acceptances of the original offer could not count as acceptances of the fresh offer, again making it more difficult to achieve the 90% acceptance level. This in turn is dealt with by providing that a revised offer is not a fresh offer as long as the original offer allowed for revision, and, for acceptance of previous terms to be treated as acceptance of revised terms[15]. The third problem was that of the untraceable shareholder which is now dealt with by allowing the court to deem shareholders to be acceptors of the offer if certain conditions are met[16].

If dissenting shareholders wish to object to the compulsory acquisition the onus is on them to convince the court that compulsory acquisition would be unfair[17]. The test of whether the offer is fair, moreover, is whether the offer is fair to the shareholders as a body and it will not be relevant that the dissenting shareholders will be forced to sell at a loss[18]. So the dissenter must try and convince the court that the judgment of those who have accepted the offer is somehow at fault[19]. Where the shares are quoted on The Stock Exchange, if the offer price is above the market price, that raises a presumption that the price is fair. More than once in such cases dissenters have pointed out that The Stock Exchange price of shares is theoretically the price at which one share in the company could be bought. Such a share would not give control of the company whereas the offeror is acquiring control and hence the price of shares should reflect this. In the circumstances in which the argument has been put, this has always been rejected by the courts[20]. This might seem to imply acceptance by the courts that control of the company belongs to the controlling shareholders rather than to the company. It is thought, however, that this is not so and that evidence that some shareholders were paid a higher price than other shareholders for identical shares would probably be a ground for the court to refuse compulsory acquisition[1]. It seems likely that the principle embodied in the City Code

---

14 Sections 429(8), 430E(2). The problem used to be solved by having a third party buy the shares during the bid who would then accept the offeror's offer.
15 Section 428(7).
16 Section 430C(5).
17 *Re Sussex Brick Co Ltd* [1961] Ch 289n, [1960] 1 All ER 772n; *Re Grierson, Oldham and Adams Ltd* [1968] Ch 17, [1967] 1 All ER 192.
18 *Re Grierson, Oldham and Adams Ltd*, supra.
19 Knowing what advice the directors were given with regard to different classes of shares may be important in this: *Re Lifecare International plc* [1990] BCLC 222.
20 *Re Press Caps Ltd* [1949] Ch 434, [1949] 1 All ER 1013, CA; *Re Grierson, Oldham and Adams Ltd*, supra.
 1 *Re Fras Hinde & Sons Ltd* (1966) Times, 23 April. Since 30 April 1987 the definition of takeover offer has required that the same terms be offered to shareholders of the same class.

that shareholders must be treated equally would be given effect to by the courts under Part XIIIA.

Although normally the onus of proof is on the dissenting shareholders to show that the offer is unfair, in *Re Bugle Press Ltd*[2] the 90% acceptances in the offeree company came from two persons who owned all the shares in the offeror company and it was held that the onus of proof was on them to show positively that the offer was fair rather than on the dissenter to show the offer was unfair. Since they had produced no evidence at all the court refused to allow the compulsory acquisition of the dissenter. In that case there was only one other shareholder. If there had been more and a majority of them had accepted the offeror's offer, thus suggesting that to a majority at least of the independent shareholders the offer was fair, it is possible the onus of proof would have remained on the dissenters[3].

Section 425   We have seen that s 425 covers any form of arrangement including a straightforward takeover bid for the shares in the offeree company. Provided a majority in number representing 75% in value of the shares voting in person or by proxy accept the arrangement it is binding on abstainers or dissenters. In *Re National Bank*[4] the question arose whether if a s 425 scheme or arrangement involves the compulsory elimination of minority shareholders the court should impose a 90% acceptance level as a condition for approving the scheme. Plowman J rejected the argument stating that '. . . the two sections, section [425] and [Part XIIIA] involve quite different considerations and different approaches. Under section [425] an arrangement can only be sanctioned if the question of its fairness has first been submitted to the court. Under [Part XIIIA], on the other hand, the matter may never come to the court at all. If it does come to the court, then the onus is cast on the dissenting minority to demonstrate the unfairness of the scheme. There are, therefore, good reasons for requiring a smaller majority in favour of a scheme under section [425] than the majority which is required under [Part XIIIA] if the minority is to be expropriated.'[5]

The same conclusion was reached in *Singer Manufacturing Co v Robinow*[6] in which the offeror company, which already owned 92% of the shares in the offeree company, used s 425, with its far lower acceptance level requirement, to compulsorily acquire the remaining 8% of shares, rather than comply with the conditions in Part XIIIA. However, in *Re Hellenic and General Trust Ltd*[7], Templeman J had to consider the position where a

2 [1961] Ch 270, [1960] 3 All ER 791, CA.
3 This might arise in circumstances like those in *Singer Manufacturing Co v Robinow* 1971 SC 11 where one shareholder owned 92% of the shares in a company and wished to acquire the remainder. The normal way would be for the shareholder to make an offer for the remaining 8% but this would require that holders of 90% of that 8% accept. Could the shareholder instead form a new company to make an offer for all the shares, distinguishing *Re Bugle Press Ltd* on the grounds that the independent shareholders are a large enough body for a majority of them to give a clear indication whether the offer is fair? It is possible the court might treat the shareholder connected with offeror as a separate class and thus require a 90% acceptance from the independent shareholders. What the shareholder in *Singer v Robinow* did was to use s 425. See below.
4 [1966] 1 All ER 1006, [1966] 1 WLR 819.
5 Ibid, at 1013 and 829–830.
6 1971 SC 11. Section 425 was also used by British Aerospace to compulsorily acquire the remaining private shareholders in British Leyland.
7 [1975] 3 All ER 382, [1976] 1 WLR 123.

dissenting shareholder could not have been compelled to sell under Part XIIIA because it owned more than 10% of the shares and therefore no 90% acceptance level could ever have been achieved. He held that in such circumstances 'there must be a very high standard of proof on the part of the petitioner to justify obtaining by section [425] what could not be obtained by [Part XIIIA]'[8]. Until the matter is considered by a higher court it should not perhaps be regarded as settled that compulsory acquisition can be achieved under s 425 without requiring a 90% acceptance level.

Section 135   It has even been held that compulsory elimination of minority shares can be achieved by means of a reduction of capital under s 135[9]. The court did, however, emphasise that where such transactions involve treating some shareholders differently from other shareholders of the same class the transactions should normally be effected under s 425[10]. The decision to allow the reduction in that particular case was no doubt influenced by the fact that although one shareholder voted against the special resolution no one turned up in court to oppose the application for the court's approval[11].

RIGHT OF MINORITY TO BE BOUGHT OUT

Those shareholders who do not accept the takeover bid may well have rejected it because they thought some other plan for the company's future preferable[12]. When it turns out the takeover bid has been overwhelmingly successful they may not wish to remain minority shareholders in a company which has new controlling shareholders and when the alternative plan they had in mind for the company can no longer be put into effect. Part XIIIA therefore also includes provisions allowing them a period of time in which to insist on being bought out by the offeror at the price paid to the other shareholders or such other terms as may be agreed or the court may fix[13]. The provisions operate where a takeover offer relates to all, or all of any class, of the shares in a company. If, before the offer expires, someone accepts it and in consequence the offeror and its associates own at least 90% in value of all the shares or of the shares in the class concerned, then any shareholder who has not accepted the offer may require the offeror to acquire his shares[14]. Within one month of the above conditions being satisfied the offeror must give non-acceptors notice of their right to sell, specifying a closing date not less than three months after the expiry of the offer[15].

---

8 Ibid, at 388 and 129.
9 *Re Robert Stephen Holdings Ltd* [1968] 1 All ER 195n, [1968] 1 WLR 522. See also *Re Rank Radio and Television Ltd* (1963) Times, 19 November.
10 The difference would be that a majority in number of shareholders as well as 75% in votes would need to support the resolution. Since *Re Hellenic and General Trust Ltd* [1975] 3 All ER 382, [1976] 1 WLR 123 it is also possible that shareholders being treated differently would form separate classes, requiring the majority to be obtained in each class.
11 Reduction of capital under s 135 can, of course, be used if it is intended to eliminate an entire class of shares but on the same terms: *Re Saltdean Estate Co Ltd* [1968] 3 All ER 829, [1968] 1 WLR 1844; *House of Fraser plc v ACGE Investments Ltd* [1987] AC 387, HL.
12 It is thought that many of those shareholders in British Leyland who did not accept the government's offer in 1975 believed that if the company were wound up it would produce a higher return than the government's offer.
13 Sections 430B(2) and 430C(3).
14 Section 430A(1)(2),
15 Section 430A(3)(4).

CONTROLS OVER TAKEOVER DOCUMENTS

Controls over issue

Section 57 of the Financial Services Act 1986 prohibits the issue of 'investment advertisements' unless the issuer is an authorised person under the Act[16] or the contents have been approved by an authorised person[17]. Since, under the Act, 'investment advertisement' covers inviting persons to dispose of or convert investments[18], investment includes shares or debentures[19] and advertisement includes circulars[20], it follows that takeover offer documents fall within the prohibition of s 57[1]. They must therefore only be issued either by authorised persons or after the contents have been approved by an authorised person[2]. There is an exemption covering recommended offers for private companies provided certain detailed conditions are fulfilled[3].

If the terms of the takeover bid include an offer of shares in the offeror then the document giving details of the shares offered will also be an investment advertisement[4]. Hence it too would be regulated by s 57. Since, however, documents offering shares will in many cases also be regulated by Pt IV or Pt V of the Financial Services Act there are exemptions from s 57 to reflect this. If the offer is of shares to be listed on The Stock Exchange or quoted on an approved exchange then the issue of listing particulars or prospectuses, or any part of such documents, is exempted from s 57[5].

Control over contents

Both the City Code[6] and The Stock Exchange Admission of Securities to Listing[7], in relation to the offers to which they apply, contain detailed

---

16 Ie under the Financial Services Act 1986, Pt 1, Ch III. The commonest route to authorisation is membership of a self-regulating organisation recognised by the Securities and Investments Board.
17 Financial Services Act 1986, s 57(1).
18 Ibid, s 57(2). But defence documents that recommend shareholders to reject the offer are not covered by s 57.
19 Ibid, s 1(1) and Sch 1, Pt 1.
20 Ibid, s 207(2).
 1 Telephone calls to persuade shareholders to accept an offer may be subject to the rules on unsolicited calls: ibid, s 56. Telephone campaigns are also regulated by the City Code, r 19.5.
 2 In practice merchant banks send out the majority of offer documents. See the statistics in the Annual Report of the Panel on Takeovers and Mergers. The criminal consequences of breach of the prohibition are contained in s 57(3)(4) and the civil consequences in s 57(5)–(10). Although advising on investments is a form of investment business for which a person needs to be authorised under the Financial Services Act, the directors of the offeree company may advise their shareholders about the offer without being authorised because the advice is given to persons as shareholders, not as investors and because the directors are not carrying on any business. See Rider, Abrams and Ferran *Guide to the Financial Services Act 1986* (2nd edn 1989) p 56.
 3 Financial Services Act 1986 (Investment Advertisements) (Exemption) (No 2) Order 1988, SI 1988/716, art 4 and the Schedule.
 4 The term covers invitations to acquire investments as well as dispose of them.
 5 Financial Services Act 1986, s 58(2)(d).
 6 See especially City Code, rr 24 and 25. Note also that each document must state that the directors have taken all reasonable care to ensure that the information contained is in accordance with the facts: ibid, r 19.1.
 7 See especially Admission of Securities to Listing, s 6, ch 2, para 3. See also the Financial Services Act 1986 (Investment Advertisements) (Exemptions) (No 2) Order 1988, SI 1988/716, art 4(3) and Sch Pt IV.

provisions as to the contents of both the offer document and any documents issued by the offeree company advising shareholders whether to accept the offer[8]. Many of the rules are designed to ensure that shareholders can gauge the impact of the takeover on the directors themselves and thus better assess the quality of any advice the directors give them[9]. As a further safeguard the directors must obtain independent advice which must be passed on to the shareholders[10]. In addition the shareholdings and dealings in the previous 12 months in either of the parties by the other party, or by any persons acting in concert or having other arrangements with them must be disclosed. Likewise shareholdings and dealings in the previous 12 months in either of the parties by directors of either party must be disclosed[11]. Apart from financial information about the offeror and offeree companies the offer document must also set out the offeror's intentions regarding the continuation of the business of the offeree company, any major changes to be introduced including redeployment of fixed assets, the long-term commercial justification for the offer and its intentions regarding the continued employment of employees of the offeree company and of its subsidiaries[12].

If the offer includes an offer of shares in exchange then listing particulars or a prospectus will need to be published as well. If the shares offered are to be listed on The Stock Exchange listing particulars are required unless the issue increases the class of existing listed shares by less than 10%[13]. The contents are governed by the Admission of Securities to Listing[14] and must be approved by The Stock Exchange[15]. After which they must be registered[16], published as required by The Stock Exchange[17] and a copy sent to each of the offeree company's shareholders[18]. If, instead of being listed on The Stock Exchange, the shares offered are to be quoted on an approved exchange then a prospectus, approved by the exchange, must be regis-

---

8 Profit forecasts may be crucial to the outcome of a takeover bid and are subject to special rules: City Code, r 28. They may persuade existing shareholders to reject the offer, the offeror to make a higher offer or a rival bidder to emerge. As to whether the directors of the offeree company and their advisers owe any duty of care in tort to existing shareholders, the offeror or potential rival bidders, see *Morgan Crucible Co plc v Hill Samuel Bank Ltd* [1991] 1 All ER 148, [1991] 2 WLR 655, CA. Following *Caparo Industries plc v Dickman* [1990] 2 AC 605, [1990] 1 All ER 568, HL, normally no such duty is owed in respect of the publication of financial statements but different considerations may apply once a bid has been made.
9 Thus, for example, directors of the offeree company must indicate whether they intend to accept the offer in respect of any shares beneficially held by them in the offeree company, City Code, r 25.3(a)(vi).
10 City Code, r 3.1.
11 This is important because the statutory requirement on directors to disclose share dealings in s 324 only applies to dealings in the company of which they are director.
12 City Code, r 24.1. The directors of the offeree company should comment on these points in their statement: ibid, r 25.2.
13 Admission of Securities to Listing, s 6, ch 2, para 5.1. The requirements of the Admission of Securities to Listing regarding listing particulars have statutory authority by virtue of the Financial Services Act 1986, s 144(1)(2).
14 Admission of Securities to Listing, s 6, ch 2, paras 5.3 and 5.4. Listing particulars must also comply with the general duty of disclosure in the Financial Services Act 1986, s 146.
15 Admission of Securities to Listing, s 3, ch 1, para 2.1.
16 Financial Services Act 1986, s 149.
17 Admission of Securities to Listing, s 6, ch 2, paras 5.3 and 5.4.
18 Ibid, s 6, ch 2, para 5.2.

tered[19]. The prospectus must comply as to form and content with rules made by the Secretary of State[20] or, if so directed by the Secretary of State, with rules made by the approved exchange[1]. Even if the shares are neither to be listed nor quoted a prospectus must still be registered[2], complying as to contents with the rules laid down by the Secretary of State[3].

OBLIGATIONS ON DIRECTORS

DUTY OF DIRECTORS IN ADVISING SHAREHOLDERS

Although a takeover of a company by acquisition of shares consists legally of an offer to the shareholders which they decide whether to accept or reject, the City Code is based on the premise that the shareholders are entitled to receive the advice of their directors about the offer. The City Code thus establishes that an offer should be put forward in the first instance to the board of the offeree company or its advisers[4]. The advice the directors give may well be crucial in determining the success or otherwise of the offer and the board of the offeree company is obliged to seek competent independent advice in the interests of shareholders and make the substance of such advice known to its shareholders[5] at the same time as it circulates its own views[6]. General principle 9 restates the common law position that, in advising shareholders, directors must always act only in their capacity as directors and not have regard to their personal or family shareholdings or their personal relationship with the company.

It is not just in relation to takeover offers for shares that the directors advice to shareholders can be important. Companies listed on The Stock Exchange will need to obtain the consent of their shareholders in general meeting for any acquisition or disposal that affects 25% or more of the company's assets or profits etc[7]. Any contract the company enters which requires such approval must necessarily be conditional upon approval being given[8]. In such cases, as in takeover offers[9], the time-lag between the

---

19 Financial Services Act 1986, s 159(1).
20 Ibid, s 162(1). Any prospectus must also comply with the general duty of disclosure in the Financial Services Act 1986, s 163.
1 Ibid, s 162(3).
2 Ibid, s 160(1). It is specifically provided that a prospectus must be registered even though the shares offered will be issued for non-cash consideration; s 160(2). This reverses the effect of *Governments Stock and Other Securities Investment Co Ltd v Christopher* [1956] 1 All ER 490, [1956] 1 WLR 237.
3 Financial Services Act 1986, s 162(1). It must also comply with the general duty of disclosure: s 163.
4 City Code, r 1(a).
5 City Code, r 3.1.
6 City Code, r 25.1. In *Gething v Kilner* [1972] 1 All ER 1166, [1972] 1 WLR 337 the offeree directors did not send out the advice of stockbrokers against the bid until ten days after the offer document had been sent and then indicated that they disagreed with the advice. Brightman J nevertheless refused an injunction to stop the takeover being declared unconditional.
7 Admission of Securities to Listing, s 6, ch 1, paras 2 and 3.
8 See *Rackham v Peek Foods Ltd* [1990] BCLC 895, a purchaser needing approval for the acquisition of a property company; and, *John Crowther Group plc v Carpets International plc* [1990] BCLC 460, a vendor agreeing to dispose of a subsidiary company.
9 *Dawson International plc v Coats Paton plc* [1990] BCLC 560.

takeover offer and its acceptance or the conditional contract and its approval may cause problems if, for example, market conditions change[10] or rival bidders[11] emerge. The techniques have therefore developed to try and ensure, so far as possible, that shareholders accept the offer despite the changed circumstances. Thus the directors may promise that the company will use its best endeavours to obtain shareholder approval[12]. However, the overriding duty on directors is to give their best advice. So if circumstances do change, and the deal is no longer in the best interests of shareholders, it has been accepted that the duty to use their best endeavours does not require directors to recommend what they genuinely and reasonably believe not to be in the best interests of shareholders nor to give advice which is genuinely believed to be bad advice. If, in the changed circumstances, the transaction could not be beneficial and might be a disaster for shareholders the duty on the directors is to so advise and use their influence and powers to ensure that the transaction is not approved[13].

A second technique[14] to try and ensure shareholders' approval is the so-called 'lock-out' contract whereby a company agrees to cease negotiations with rival bidders or agrees not to encourage or co-operate with other bidders[15]. If higher offers are made, however, then again it has been accepted that the duty of directors is to make full and honest disclosure of such offers, even if the higher offer arose as a result of a breach of the 'lock-out' agreement[16]. It might be thought that a company could not validly agree to a 'lock-out' contract in view of the directors' duty to act in the best interests of the shareholders. Whilst the directors' duty might rule out a contract that prevented higher offers even being put to shareholders, it does not prevent companies agreeing not to encourage or co-operate with rival bidders and if the company breaks such an agreement it may potentially be liable in damages[17].

An analogous problem concerning the duty of directors in advising shareholders, and also in voting as shareholders themselves, may arise where a company has agreed to an unconditional contract but a resolution of the shareholders is needed in order to fulfil the company's obligations. In

---

10 A change in the taxation of property companies in *Rackham v Peek Foods Ltd*, above.
11 *John Crowther Group plc v Carpets International plc*, above; *Dawson International plc v Coats Paton plc*, above.
12 As in *Rackham v Peek Foods Ltd*, above, and *John Crowther Group plc v Carpets International plc*, above.
13 See *Rackham v Peek Foods Ltd* [1990] BCLC 895 at 916.
14 Another technique used by offerors is to obtain irrevocable undertakings to accept their offer. Normally there can be no objection to directors giving such undertakings in respect of their own shareholdings but see the very special facts of *Heron International Ltd v Lord Grade* [1983] BCLC 244, CA.
15 As in *John Crowther plc v Carpets International plc*, above and *Dawson Interntional plc v Coats Paton plc*, above. It is important to distinguish between 'lock-out' agreements made before a deal has been concluded and a concluded agreement which is subject to shareholder approval. The former are contracts to negotiate and are not enforceable: *Walford v Miles* (1991) Independent, 15 January, CA.
16 *John Crowther Group plc v Carpets International plc* [1990] BCLC 460 at 464–465.
17 *Dawson International plc v Coats Paton plc*, above. The City Code states that any information given to one offeror must, on request, be given equally and promptly to other offerors even if that other offeror is less welcome: r 20.2. The Code now warns directors of the risk of entering into commitments with offerors which restrict their freedom to advise shareholders: general principle 9.

Northern Counties Securities Ltd v Jackson & Steeple Ltd[18] the defendant company had agreed to issue shares to the plaintiff with permission to deal in and quotation for such shares on the Stock Exchange. When it failed to fulfil its obligation an order of specific performance was granted ordering the company to use its best endeavours to obtain the quotation and permission to deal on The Stock Exchange. Under The Stock Exchange rules, however, that required the defendant company to pass an ordinary resolution but the directors persistently failed to call a meeting to do this, believing that it was in the best interests of the shareholders not to pass the resolution. Eventually the plaintiff obtained a court order directing a meeting to be held. In granting the order Walton J stated that the directors' duty was to do everything to help the company comply with the order of specific performance. Otherwise both the directors and the company would be in contempt of court. Furthermore the circular from the directors must not be neutral but must invite a positive response from the shareholders. The shareholders, however, including the directors in respect of their shareholdings, were not subject to the order made against the company and were free therefore to vote as they pleased. If they defeated the resolution to apply to The Stock Exchange neither they nor the company would be in contempt of court.

Problems as to how directors should advise shareholders and how much information about the company they are obliged to disclose arise in a particularly acute form where the directors themselves make an offer for the shares in the company, as for example in a management buyout. Under the City Code 'Shareholders must be given sufficient information and advice to enable them to reach a properly informed decision . . . No relevant information should be withheld from them'[19]. If there is a competing offer to the management buyout the obligation to give information equally and promptly to competing offerors requires that information generated by the offeree company which is passed to external providers of finance must also be passed to the competing offeror[20]. In *Re a Company (No 008699 of 1985)*[1] where there were rival bids for a private company, one of which was by the directors, Hoffman J adapted the City Code in stating that he did not think 'fairness can require more of the directors than to give the shareholders sufficient information and advice to enable them to reach a properly informed decision and to refrain from giving misleading advice or exercising their fiduciary powers in a way which would prevent or inhibit shareholders from choosing to take the better price'[2], adding that 'Particularly in a private company, there may be cases in which the board's duty to provide sufficient information and advice is satisfied by saying nothing'[2].

Ordinarily directors do not owe a fiduciary duty to individual shareholders and are thus not under an obligation to disclose all material facts[3]. However, it was held in the New Zealand case of *Coleman v Myers*[4] that the existence

---

18 [1974] 2 All ER 625, [1974] 1 WLR 1133.
19 City Code, general principle 4.
20 Ibid, r 20.2 note 2.
 1 [1986] BCLC 382.
 2 [1986] BCLC 382 at 389.
 3 *Percival v Wright* [1902] 2 Ch 421. But compare *Allen v Hyatt* (1914) 30 TLR 444, PC. See also *Heron International Ltd v Lord Grade* [1983] BCLC 244 at 261–263 where it was accepted that a duty could be owed by directors to individual shareholders.
 4 [1977] 2 NZLR 225 (NZCA).

of a fiduciary relationship with the shareholders must depend on all the facts of the particular case including the shareholders' dependence on information and advice, the existence of a relationship of confidence, the significance of some particular transaction for the parties and the extent of any positive action by the directors to promote it[5]. In that case a father and son who were chairman and chief executive of a family company bought out the rest of the family and then sold some assets of the company at a price that effectively reimbursed the cost of the takeover. It was held that the family character of the company, the position of the father and son in the company and the family, their high degree of inside knowledge and the way they went about the takeover and the persuasion of shareholders meant that a fiduciary relationship did arise[6].

PAYMENTS TO DIRECTORS FOR LOSS OF OFFICE

Because of the directors' powerful position in being able to advise shareholders whether to accept or reject an offer, there are statutory obligations on directors to disclose certain payments for loss of office so that shareholders are aware of factors that might influence the directors' attitude. It should be noted that these are the only statutory provisions governing payments to directors in such circumstances, that they only apply to ex gratia payments[7] and that they only apply where a director retires from office[8]. If

---

5 [1977] 2 NZLR 225 at 325.
6 [1977] 2 NZLR 225 at 330.
7 Thus neither damages for breach of contract nor a contractual right to compensation is covered: s 316(3) and *Taupo Totara Timber Co Ltd v Rowe* [1978] AC 537, [1977] 3 All ER 123, PC. The Jenkins Committee recommended that any such payment should, however, be disclosed at the time an ex gratia payment is approved so that shareholders are aware of the total payment which it is proposed to make to a director: Report of the Company Law Committee (Cmnd 1749) para 93. See also the Gower Report: Review of Investor Protection Report—Pt I (Cmnd 9125) para 9.33. Listed companies are required to disclose any payment proposed for loss of office in the offer document: Admission of Securities to Listing, s 6, ch 2, para 3(c)(i).
8 Each of ss 312, 313 and 314 refer just to 'loss of office'. In *Taupo Totara Timber Co Ltd v Rowe* supra, the Privy Council interpreted this phrase where it appears in s 312 as referring only to loss of office as director and not covering loss of any other office or employment with the company. The Cohen Committee, on whose recommendations the sections are based, understood the phrase to cover loss of any office. This is shown by the fact that they recommended that the phrase in what is now s 312 (but not where it appears in ss 313 or 314) be expressly restricted to loss of office as director by referring specifically to 'loss of office as director' and loss of 'such office': Report of the Committee on Company Law Amendment (Cmnd 6659) para 92. Parliament, in enacting the section, did not adopt the recommended restriction, presumably because they did not intend s 312 to be restricted only to loss of office as director. Cf the Victorian Companies Act 1961, s 129 which did adopt the Cohen Committee recommendation: *Lincoln Mills (Australia) Ltd v Gough* [1964] VR 193. In *Taupo Totara Timber Co Ltd v Rowe*, supra, Lord Wilberforce, at 545, 127, dismisses evidence as to the intention of the legislature, pointing out that, 'The belief of the draftsman as to what the section was intended to mean is of course not decisive'. The Jenkins Committee recommended that the provisions be extended to loss of any office in connection with the management of the affairs of the company or any subsidiary, and to payments to former directors: Report of the Company Law Committee (Cmnd 1749) para 93. See also the Gower Report which goes further in recommending removal of the requirement of retirement altogether: Review of Investor Protection Report—Pt I (Cmnd 9125) para 9.33.

there is no loss of office then any payment to the directors is unaffected, by statute at least.

The provisions vary according to whether it is a sale of assets or a sale of shares in the offeree company. Section 313 provides that if in connection with the sale of the whole or any part of the undertaking or property of a company any payment is made to directors of the company in connection with retirement from office, it must be disclosed to and approved by shareholders in general meeting[9]. If this is not done, then the money is held on trust for the company[10]. Section 314 applies to payments relating to the retirement of directors from office in connection with the transfer by anyone of shares in the company resulting from certain types of offer. The section provides that directors concerned must take all reasonable steps to ensure that any such payment is disclosed with the notice of the offer and are liable to criminal penalties for failing to do so[11]. In addition, the payment must be approved by a meeting of the class of shareholders to which the offer relates[12]. If it is either not properly disclosed, or not approved, then the directors cannot keep the money. But who gets it? If the money is held on trust for the company as under the previous section then the people who have sold their shares (and who may have sold for less than their shares were worth if the directors' judgment was influenced by the payment and the shareholders followed their advice) will be the very people who have no share in the remedy since by definition they have ceased to be shareholders in the company. So the section provides that the money shall be on 'trust for any persons who have sold their shares as a result of the offer made'[12].

Although they are not by their terms restricted to such payments, the crucial aspect of ss 313 and 314 is that they cover payments made by the offeror. Payments to directors as compensation for loss of office made by their own company may fall within ss 313 or 314 but will be required to be disclosed to and approved by the shareholders in general meeting in any case under s 312 which is not restricted to payments connected with the sale of assets or shares. Sections 313 and 314 apply to payments by way of compensation for loss of office or as consideration for or in connection with retirement from office. It is expressly provided that if in connection with retirement from office of directors they receive a price for selling their shares in the company in excess of what could have been obtained by other holders of like shares or receive any gift, the excess or the money value of the gift is deemed to be a payment as compensation for loss of office[13]. The onus of proving that a payment falls within ss 313 or 314 would normally lie on those seeking to recover it but there is a rebuttable presumption that the payment was within the sections if certain conditions are fulfilled[14].

---

9 Section 313(1). At present an ordinary resolution is sufficient. The Jenkins Committee proposed it should be a special resolution: Report of the Company Law Committee (Cmnd 1749) para 93. The Gower Report suggested instead that neither the director concerned nor any person connected with him nor the offeror should be allowed to vote: Review of Investor Protection Report—Pt I (Cmnd 9125) para 9.33.
10 Section 313(2).
11 Section 314(2) and (3).
12 Section 315(1).
13 Section 316(2).
14 Section 316(1).

THE CONDUCT OF TAKEOVERS UNDER THE CITY CODE

Equal treatment of shareholders and the sale of controlling shares

Perhaps the most fundamental issue in the regulation of takeovers is whether control of the company is to be regarded as an asset belonging to the company or to the shareholder who, because of the size of its shareholding, is able to control the company. If control is regarded as belonging to the company, then it ought to follow that the controlling shareholder should not receive more for its shares than minority shareholders do for theirs. If, on the other hand, control is regarded as belonging to the controlling shareholder, then it will be entitled to keep the higher price which a purchaser may be prepared to pay for its block of shares because they give control of the company. The argument in favour of the latter view is that the controller will only receive a higher price when someone particularly wants to buy the shares. At other times, when the controller wants to sell it may be compelled to accept a lower price than a small shareholder because the very size of the controller's shareholding depresses the market.

The basic principle on which the City Code is founded requires that all shareholders of the same class in an offeree company be treated similarly by an offeror[15]. If, in the three months prior to the offer, the offeror purchases shares in the offeree company, the offer to shareholders of the same class must be on not less favourable terms[16]. Likewise, if, during the offer, the offeror buys shares at above the offer price, the offer price must be correspondingly increased[17]. The principle of equal treatment is also reflected in r 11 which requires a cash offer to be made in certain circumstances[18]. The cash offer must be not less than the highest price paid in cash by the offeror during the offer or in the preceding 12 months.

The second basic principle underlying the City Code is that a shareholder should have a right to sell if control of the company changes[19]. Thus, if a shareholder acquires control where no single shareholder had control before or if control of a company changes hands, under the Code shareholders are given the chance to sell. Control is regarded as established under the City Code by holding 30% or more of the voting shares in a company. If such control is established or changes hands the right to sell arises in two ways. First, partial bids, ie bids for over 30% but less than 100%, are strongly discouraged and cannot be made without the Panel's consent[20]. Secondly,

---

15 City Code, general principle 1. For a comparison of shareholder protection in the regulations of takeovers in the UK, USA and Australia, see Sappideen (1986) 8 Journal of Comparative Business and Capital Market Law 281.
16 City Code, r 6.1.
17 City Code, r 6.2.
18 The cash offer may be as an alternative to an offer of shares. A cash offer is required if the offeror has purchased for cash more than 10% of the voting shares in the offeree in the 12 months prior to the offer or during the offer. If there are rival bids the market price may rise well above the value of any cash offer and if an offeror has already purchased 9.9% for cash it cannot buy anymore without increasing its offer under r 11. In such circumstances attention naturally focuses on whether parties who do buy blocks of shares in the market are associates of an offeror. See *R v Panel on Take-overs and Mergers, ex p Datafin plc* [1987] QB 815, [1987] 1 All ER 564, CA and *R v Panel on Take-overs and Mergers, ex p Guinness plc* [1990] 1 QB 146, [1989] 1 All ER 509, CA.
19 Johnston *The City Takeover Code* (1980) p 254.
20 City Code, r 36.1. Where partial offers are allowed they must be open to all shareholders to accept in full for the relevant percentage of their shareholdings: r 36.7. The Stock Exchange

the mandatory bid rules mean that a shareholder cannot acquire a 30% stake without making an offer at all. Once a shareholder reaches the 30% threshold, the shareholder is obliged to make a general offer for all the remaining shares of any class in which the shareholder holds shares[1]. If a shareholder already owns between 30% and 50% it similarly becomes obliged to make a mandatory bid for all shares if it strengthens its control by increasing its stake by 2% or more within 12 months[2]. If the shareholder already owns over 50% it can continue to acquire shares without making a general offer since strengthening a controlling stake which is already over 50% is not regarded as affecting the minority shareholder to the same extent. The offer, which a shareholder obliged to make a mandatory bid must make, is a cash offer at not less than the highest price paid by it or persons acting in concert with it for shares of the class concerned in the preceding 12 months[3].

The reason for the Code discouraging partial bids and requiring a shareholder who acquires or enhances a controlling stake in a company to extend a similar offer to all shareholders is, as we have seen, because it is felt to be wrong to compel shareholders to become minority shareholders in a company without giving them the option of selling their shares. Nor should shareholders who are already minority shareholders under one controlling shareholder be compelled to continue under a different controlling shareholder, as would happen if a controlling block of shares were sold, without having the chance here too of selling their shares. The effect of r 9 and of r 6, however, is to enshrine within the City Code the principle that normally if a shareholder acquires or enhances a controlling stake in a company, then a similar offer must be extended to all shareholders. The price paid for control is thus extended to all shareholders and control is effectively treated as an asset of the company, reflected in the value of each share rather than as an asset of the controlling shareholder.

So far the common law has not had to consider in the context of takeovers whether control belongs to the controlling shareholders or to the company[4]. Where the question has arisen, in relation to the valuation of shares, it has been accepted that control belongs to controlling shareholders and thus enhances the value of a controlling block of shares[5]. Similarly, where shareholders objecting to being compulsorily acquired under Part XIIIA have argued that the offer price is not a fair one because it does not include an element for the value of control, the argument has been rejected[6]. The courts have, however, endorsed the principle that shareholders with equal rights should receive equal treatment[7] and with the same principle stated so

Admission of Securities to Listing requires the reason for not making a full offer to be set out in the offer document: s 6, ch 2, para 3(c)(ii). See further D Gross (1983) 1 Company and Securities Law Journal 251.
1 City Code, r 9.1(a).
2 City Code, r 9.1(b).
3 City Code, r 9.5(a).
4 The question has arisen in the US: *Perlman v Feldman* 219 F (2d) 173 (1955). See generally Boyle (1964) 13 ICLQ 185.
5 *Dean v Prince* [1953] Ch 590; revsd on other grounds [1954] Ch 409, [1954] 1 All ER 749, CA.
6 *Re Press Caps Ltd* [1949] Ch 434, [1949] 1 All ER 1013, CA; *Re Grierson, Oldham and Adams Ltd* [1968] Ch 17, [1967] 1 All ER 192. See also *Short v Treasury Comrs* [1948] 1 KB 116, CA; affd [1948] AC 534, [1948] 2 All ER 509, HL where the entire share capital of a quoted company was acquired on nationalisation under provisions that provided for payment 'as between a willing buyer and a willing seller'. It was held the valuation should not include an element for control.
7 *Re Fras Hinde & Sons Ltd* (1966) Times, 23 April.

strongly in the City Code, it is not impossible that the courts will sooner or later accept that control is an asset of the company. One of the problems if they do is that the normal remedy would be to compel the controlling shareholders to account to the company for any additional benefit received for selling control. But if that were done, the benefit would go to the remaining shareholders who would include the purchaser and might well *not* include minority shareholders who had also sold their shares but at a lower price than the controlling shareholders received. What is needed is a principle similar to that in s 315(1) whereby the additional benefit received by controlling shareholders is held on trust for those shareholders who accepted a lower price from the offeror.

POSTSCRIPT ON R 9

It is instructive at this juncture to digress slightly and relate the saga of Mr J J Raper and St Piran Ltd[8] which arose out of alleged breaches of r 9 and which more than any other case tested the effectiveness of self-regulation. Mr Raper acquired 34% of the voting shares of St Piran Ltd in 1974, but the Panel released him from his obligation to bid for all the rest of the shares provided he reduced his holding below 30%. There followed a series of transfers to exotically named companies, but in 1978 the question arose whether these were really Mr Raper in disguise and whether in fact he had not increased his holding rather than reduced it. 29.9% of the voting shares in St Piran Ltd were held by Gasco Ltd, a Hong Kong registered company whose only asset was its stake in St Piran. Gasco was controlled by another Hong Kong company in turn controlled by a Bermudan company. Two other companies, one registered in Luxembourg, the other in Panama, also held a total of 10% of the voting shares in St Piran Ltd.

The Panel investigated and concluded that all the companies referred to were controlled by Mr Raper and they ordered him to bid for the rest of the shares at 85p per share. Mr Raper denied controlling the companies concerned and forthrightly refused to comply with the Panel's instructions. The Panel's normal range of sanctions such as reprimands or disciplinary action were clearly going to be ineffective and so ultimately they suspended the quotation of shares in St Piran Ltd on The Stock Exchange when the shares stood at 63p each. Finally in April 1981, Gasco did offer 50p per share and many shareholders, frustrated at being unable to sell their shares on The Stock Exchange, accepted this offer. The offer was then increased to 60p per share but meanwhile Department of Trade inspectors appointed to investigate the ownership of shares in St Piran Ltd had confirmed the Panel's findings and recommended that the Department of Trade petition for the company to be wound up on the just and equitable ground. The government refused, preferring to leave it to any concerned shareholder to do so and eventually one did[9]. But all this time shareholders, unable to sell their shares on The Stock Exchange, were being tempted by Gasco Ltd's offer and when

---

8 [1980] JBL 270 and 358. The further adventures of Mr Raper would take too long to recount in a book of this size but the interested reader is referred to the report of the Department of Trade and Industry inspectors *Milbury plc: Westminster Property Group Ltd* (1988).

9 In *Re St Piran Ltd* [1981] 3 All ER 270, [1981] 1 WLR 1300 it was held that the Department of Trade report could be admitted as evidence thus avoiding the necessity of producing the evidence the inspectors had relied on. It was also accepted that breaches of the City Code would be relevant in deciding whether it was just and equitable to wind up the company.

Gasco Ltd announced that they had over 90% acceptances the winding-up petition was withdrawn.

The Panel has pointed out[10] that there were many aspects of the affair in which their executive could take pride. The Department of Trade inspectors were not able to add substantially to the evidence that had been collected, despite their powers to summon witnesses and examine them on oath, and their conclusions broadly confirmed those of the Panel. The Panel recognised that the City Code works best when dealing with professional practitioners in the UK who can readily be persuaded of the advantages of complying with established best practice and that persons operating principally abroad and who may not be much concerned about their reputation in the City, cannot be brought against their will to observe its requirements. Nevertheless, the Panel was disappointed at the failure of the government to use powers open to it in connection with the takeover. It may well be that the mandatory bid provisions in r 9, since they govern the substantive question of when a bid must be made, as opposed to merely regulating the procedure of how a bid is carried out, would be more appropriately contained in legislation enforceable in the courts.

Conditional offers

In practice, the offeror will usually make its offer conditional on receiving a certain minimum level of acceptances and on the offer not being referred to the Monopolies and Mergers Commission or under the EC Mergers Regulations[11]. But the offer will usually leave open the possibility of the offeror declaring the offer unconditional at a lower level of acceptances. If shareholders agreed to sell on the basis that the offeror was going to acquire control, they should not be obliged to sell if the offeror has not in fact received sufficient acceptances to give it over 50% of the voting rights and r 10 so provides.

Frustrating action by the offeree

One of the key issues in any takeover which is contested by the management of the offeree company is the extent to which they can take defensive measures to frustrate the bid. It is a cardinal principle of the City Code that any defensive measures which, of course, may have the effect of keeping the existing management in office, may only be taken with the consent of the shareholders in general meeting[12]. Thus[13] during the offer, or even beforehand if the board of the offeree company has reason to believe an offer might be imminent, the board of directors must not, without the approval of a general meeting (i) take steps to increase the share capital[14] (ii)

---

10 Annual Report of the Panel on Takeovers and Mergers 1981, pp 3–4.
11 City Code, r 12.
12 City Code, general principle 7.
13 City Code, r 21.
14 Similar protection is achieved at common law under the 'proper purposes' doctrine. See *Howard Smith Ltd v Ampol Petroleum Ltd* [1974] AC 821, [1974] 1 All ER 1126, PC and *Hogg v Cramphorn Ltd* [1967] Ch 254, [1966] 3 All ER 420.

sell, dispose of, or acquire assets of a material amount, or, (iii) enter into contracts otherwise than in the ordinary course of business[15].

Withdrawal of offers by the offeror

Another of the central features of the City Code is that once an offer has been announced, the offer cannot be withdrawn without the consent of the Panel[16]. The Panel is anxious to prevent offerors making opportunistic bids based on particular market conditions and thus will not normally give consent to the withdrawal of a bid merely because market conditions have altered and the offer is now at an unrealistically high price. One case where the Panel ordered a company to proceed with a mandatory bid, despite a change in market conditions which made the bid overpriced, raised the question of the directors' duty to observe the City Code where this might conflict with the best interests of the shareholders in the company. When the Panel ordered Crest International Securities Ltd to make a full bid for Ashbourne Investments Ltd[17], a shareholder in Crest sought an injunction to prevent the directors complying with the Panel's instruction on the ground that the directors would not be acting in the best interests of the company. In order to ensure that the case for the bid to proceed was properly presented, the Panel arranged to be joined as co-defendants with the company[18]. The proceedings never resulted in a concluded judgment but it is submitted that although the courts would not compel directors to observe the terms of the City Code they would never hold directors to be in breach of their duty to act in the best interests of their company merely because they did observe the City Code.

Timetable of the offer

One of the features of the City Code is that it lays down a timetable for the conduct of bids. The object is to avoid the process being so hurried that there is inadequate time for advice and information to be obtained and considered. At the same time the process must not be so drawn out that uncertainty is created in the market. The timetable runs from the posting of the offer document, known as Day 1, which must be within 28 days of the announcement of the offer[19]. The board of the offeree company must give advice to their shareholders by the end of Day 14, ie within 14 days of the posting of the offer document[20]. To ensure shareholders in the offeree have time to consider the offer and are not rushed into acceptance an offer must

---

15 Buying back any shares acquired by an unwelcome bidder, probably at an inflated price, a practice known as 'greenmail' in the United States, cannot occur under U K legislation without the consent of the shareholders. In the case of an off-market purchase specific authority via a special resolution, not counting the votes on the shares to be bought, is needed: s 164(2)(5). A market purchase is unlikely but although it needs only a general authority by ordinary resolution under s 166(1)(7) the price payable is strictly controlled by reference to the quoted market price: Admission of Securities to Listing, s 5, ch 2, para 30.4.
16 City Code, r 2.7.
17 [1975] JBL 44.
18 Johnston *The City Takeover Code* (1980) App A, pp 288–296.
19 City Code, r 30.1.
20 City Code, r 30.2.

remain open for at least 21 days so that Day 21 is the first possible closing date[1]. After Day 39 there must be no further material announcements by the offeree[2]. Shareholders who have accepted the offer are entitled to withdraw their acceptances, provided the offer has not become unconditional, after the expiry of 21 days from the first closing date, which is usually therefore Day 42[3]. Day 46 is the last date for revision of the offer by the offeror[4] and finally Day 60 is the last possible closing date[5]. No offer may be left open for more than 60 days without the consent of the Panel which may be granted, for example, if a competing offer is announced[6]. Where an offer has not become unconditional and has therefore been withdrawn or lapsed, the offeror may not make another offer for the offeree during the next 12 months nor acquire any shares which would oblige it to make an offer under r 9[7]. This can be of crucial importance to a company which has successfully resisted an unwelcome bid in securing a breathing space before the bidder returns.

WAREHOUSING AND DAWN RAIDS

Warehousing or secret acquisitions

The policy behind the law relating to warehousing or the secret acquisition of shares through nominees is that shareholders and the public generally are entitled to know promptly of the acquisition of significant shareholdings in public companies. The aim of the acquirer may be to influence policy or mount a takeover bid and members of the company and those dealing with it are entitled to protect their interests; nor should the conduct of the company be prejudiced by uncertainty as to who controls it. There may also be dangers in companies passing secretly into foreign ownership, particularly since the abolition of exchange control which had required Bank of England permission if 10% of a UK company passed out of UK control[8].

The first legislation to control warehousing was introduced in 1967 and was considerably strengthened in 1976 and 1981[9]. The basic obligation is that as soon as persons know they have 3%[10] of any class[11] of voting shares[12] of a

---

1 City Code, r 31.1.
2 City Code, r 31.9.
3 City Code, r 34.
4 City Code, r 32.1.
5 City Code, r 31.6. Any offer which has become unconditional as to acceptances must, however, remain open for acceptance for at least 14 more days; r 31.4.
6 City Code, r 31.6.
7 City Code, r 35.1.
8 The whole issue of nominee shareholdings, and whether they should be allowed at all, was highlighted by the battle for control of Westland plc in 1986. See Second Report from the House of Commons Trade and Industry Committee: Westland plc HC 176 (1986–87) paras 15–20.
9 The European Commission have issued a directive to harmonise the disclosure of significant shareholdings in listed companies: EC Council Directive 88/627. OJ 1988 L348/62. The disclosure requirements already in the Companies Act are considerably stricter than those set out in the directive. See consultative document *Disclosure of Interests in Shares: The EC Major Shareholdings Directive* (1991) published by the Department of Trade and Industry.
10 Section 199(2). The percentage may be varied by statutory instrument: s 210A(1).
11 Section 198(2)(a).
12 Section 198(2).

public company[13], they must inform the company within 2 days[14] and there-after of any acquisition or disposal which takes their holding through a whole per cent or below 3%[15]. The company must then enter the information in a register[16] kept for the purpose which must be open to public inspection[17]. There are complex provisions[18] dealing with what constitutes an interest in shares for the purposes of this disclosure requirement. It extends to any form of beneficial interest in shares[19] and includes the situation where a person has the right to acquire or control shares[20]. Persons are also taken to be inter-ested in any shares in which their spouse or any infant child or stepchild is interested[1], and also in any shares in which a body corporate is interested if the body corporate or its directors usually act under their directions or they can control more than one-third of the voting power at general meetings of the body corporate[2]. In addition, where two or more persons act together in the acquisition of interests in shares in a particular company they may constitute a group acting in concert (commonly referred to as 'a concert party'). In such a case any acquisition or disposal of an interest in shares by any member of the concert party is treated as an acquisition or disposal by every member of the concert party[3]. Members of concert parties are accord-ingly obliged to keep each other informed of relevant acquisitions and disposals[4].

Persons may, of course, choose to ignore their obligations to notify the company and hope not to be found out. Since 1948, the Department of Trade and Industry has had power to investigate the ownership of com-panies via the appointment of inspectors[5] or requests for information[6] and to impose restrictions[7] on the rights enjoyed by the shares if the information is

13 The legislation does not apply to private companies.
14 Section 202(4).
15 Section 199(5).
16 Section 211(1).
17 Section 211(8)(b). The disclosure provisions in the City Code used broadly to repeat the statutory requirements. Following revelations of share buying during takeovers, notably in connection with Guinness's takeover of Distillers, these provisions were strengthened. Now anyone owning or controlling 1% or more of a company involved in a takeover must disclose any dealings in shares of the companies involved to The Stock Exchange, the Panel and the press not later than 12 noon on the business day following the transaction: r 8.3.
18 Sections 203–209.
19 Section 208(2) and (3).
20 Section 208(4)–(6).
 1 Section 203(1).
 2 Section 203(2)–(4).
 3 Section 205(1). This is so however the interest in shares was acquired, ie whether pursuant to the concert party or not. It can be difficult to establish that a concert party exists. See, for example, the interim report of an inspector appointed by the Department of Trade and Industry to investigate share dealings in the House of Fraser plc (1984). One problem is distinguishing a concert party, which presupposes some measure of mutual understanding, from a 'fan club'. The latter describes a situation in which a group of investors claim to be so impressed by the investment decisions of another person that they will buy shares in a company just because that other person has done so, but without any understanding that they would do so.
 4 Section 206.
 5 Section 442.
 6 Section 444.
 7 See s 454.

not supplied[8]. Companies can therefore request the Department of Trade and Industry to investigate but the Department has a discretion and the number of such investigations each year is extremely low[9]. So in 1976 public companies were given their own statutory power to require shareholders to state whether they own shares beneficially and, if not, to identify on whose behalf they are held[10]. Again, the company must keep a register of information received which must be open to public inspection[11]. It is still, however, the company which must make the request and if what shareholders want to know is who owns the controlling block of shares in the company, the company is unlikely ever to ask the question. Shareholders could ask the Department of Trade and Industry to investigate but as we have seen such a power is discretionary. So in 1981 shareholders holding between them 10% of the voting paid-up capital were given the right to requisition the company to ask the question[12].

Failure to supply information properly requested by the company either of its own volition or following a requisition by shareholders is a criminal offence[13]. But far more importantly, restrictions can be imposed on the shares concerned. If the Department of Trade and Industry investigates, it can impose restrictions itself[14] and since 1981 companies have had the power to apply to the court to impose the same range of restrictions[15]. Companies may, of course, incorporate power to impose such restrictions in their articles of association and the statutory right to apply to the court to impose restrictions is in addition to the company's constitutional powers[16].

Dawn raids

A dawn raid is the colloquial term given to the rapid acquisition of a large number of shares in a listed company[17]. If the acquisition takes the acquirer's holding to 30% there is no real problem because the acquirer will then be obliged to make a bid for the remaining shares in the company, thus ensuring the equal treatment of shareholders[18]. But if the acquisition leaves the acquirer's holding below 30% then the City Code does not apply at all. Since the acquirer is acquiring a large number of shares rapidly, the price offered

---

8 Section 445(1). See, for example, *Re Ashbourne Investments Ltd* [1978] 2 All ER 418, [1978] 1 WLR 1346 and *Re Geers Gross plc* [1988] 1 All ER 224, [1987] 1 WLR 1649, CA.

9 Since 1974 when the Department of Trade and Industry began to indicate separately the number of investigations under s 442 there have never been more than three in any one year: Annual Report of the Department of Trade and Industry on Companies.

10 Section 212.

11 Section 213.

12 Section 214.

13 Section 216(3).

14 Section 445(1).

15 Section 216(1).

16 Section 216(2). See also Admission of Securities to Listing, s 9, ch 2 para 14.

17 The practice achieved notoriety when in the course of a few minutes after The Stock Exchange opened on the morning of 12 February 1980 (hence the reference to 'dawn') brokers acting for Anglo-American Corporation and De Beers Consolidated Mines acquired 11.4% of the shares in Consolidated Gold Fields. They had during the previous six month secretly acquired 13.6% of the shares in Consolidated Gold Fields but the means used would today constitute a 'concert party' and require disclosure under s 205. See [1980] JBL 422.

18 City Code, r 9.

will probably be considerably higher than the prevailing market price[19]. But since the acquisition will usually be a well planned affair carried out at great speed, the majority of shareholders in the target company will never have an opportunity to sell their shares at this premium price[20]. Because, in terms of the City Code, control does not change hands, strictly speaking dawn raids are not part of the topic of takeovers. But, along with warehousing, dawn raids are tactics used by prospective bidders to build up their holdings in target companies[1] and they raise many of the same issues of equal treatment for shareholders so that it is convenient to discuss them in this context.

In order to ensure the equal treatment of shareholders, the Council for the Securities Industry produced Rules Governing Substantial Acquisitions of Shares[2]. Under these Rules a person shall not within any period of seven days acquire 10% or more of the voting rights in a listed company if such acquisition would give the buyer more than 15% of the voting rights in the company[3] unless the acquisition:

(a) would take the buyer's holding beyond 30% (in which case the City Code would require an offer for all other shares at a not less favourable price); or

(b) immediately precedes and is conditional on the buyer announcing its intention to make an offer for the company which is publicly recommended by the board of the offeree company; or

(c) is from a single shareholder and is the buyer's only acquisition of such shares within the seven days; or

(d) is pursuant to a tender offer under the Rules[4].

The making of a tender offer under the Rules involves the buyer in giving notice by advertisement in two national newspapers of its offer to acquire shares[5]. The advertisement must state, among other matters, the maximum number of shares or proportion of voting capital offered for and the fixed or maximum price offered[6]. It must also state the closing day and time for tenders[6] which must not be for at least seven days after the advertisement appears[5]. This gives any shareholders who wish to sell the chance to accept the buyer's offer by tendering some or all of their shares either at the fixed

---

19 The price offered for the shares in Consolidated Gold Fields was 18% above the market price.

20 It is estimated that only 200 of the 40,000 shareholders in Consolidated Gold Fields could have accepted the offer.

 1 In fact, shareholders have become reluctant to sell to dawn raiders because they believe an even higher premium will be offered when the takeover bid comes.

 2 The Rules Governing Substantial Acquisitions of Shares (revised 1987) are published together with the City Code on Takeovers and Mergers. They are now administered by the Panel on Takeovers, following the demise of the Council for the Securities Industry.

 3 Ibid, r 1.

 4 Ibid, r 2.

 5 Ibid, r 4.1(a).

 6 Ibid, r 4.2. As a result of amendments made in 1987 a tender offer may only be in cash, not an offer of shares in exchange. Offerors are also forbidden to promise to make up to shareholders who accept the tender offer, the difference between that offer and any subsequent general offer for the company. The reason for these changes was to prevent tender offers becoming too complicated and involving lengthy documentation. Shareholders typically have seven days in which to decide whether to tender. This is not long enough to consider the documentation and for their board of directors to make a recommendation. If an offeror wishes to offer shares in exchange it should seek the Panel's permission for a partial offer which would then have to be open for at least 21 days.

price set by the buyer or if the buyer has set only a maximum price at whatever price the shareholder would be prepared to sell at. Where the tender offer is at a fixed price and is oversubscribed, then all tenders are scaled down pro rata[7]. If the tender offer was at a maximum price then the shares will be sold at the lowest price (known as 'the striking price') at which the number of shares sought by the buyer can be acquired and all shareholders who tender at or below the striking price will receive that price[7].

7 Ibid, r 4.1.(c).

PART VI

Company collapse

CHAPTER 36

Corporate failure in the UK

Firms not only expand. Sometimes they contract and sometimes they fail. Their contraction and failure are not necessarily bad things in themselves since they may result in a rational reallocation of resources by enabling the assets to be acquired by another company which will use them more efficiently. However, this assumes a lot, particularly within a national economy. It assumes that the market operates efficiently, that the resources are not too specialised and that the costs of transfer are not excessive. It also assumes that there are alternative uses for the resources[1]. In practice these factors are often not present due to macro-economic conditions and the assets are eventually sold for a greatly reduced price or men and plant lie idle. The number and rate of business failures in the UK are very high, and over the period 1971–1980, the failure rate averaged over twice that of the USA[2].

PREDICTION OF BUSINESS FAILURE

Management because of its strategic position has a greater opportunity to forecast insolvency than investors. Investors can, however, by diversification reduce some of the risks for them of company failure. Nevertheless, they have to rely on financial data provided by companies which will fall short of all the information in the hands of management. Creditors will either depend on security or high interest charges and careful monitoring. Trade creditors will often rely on knowledge of the company's business and adjust their credit terms accordingly.

Attempts have been made to develop formulas or ratios for predicting business failure to aid all three groups but most of the empirical work has been based on a population of failed companies which gives an immediate bias to the findings. The early work was based on univariate analysis whereas the later work such as that of Edward Altman[3] makes use of multivariate analysis. Using this technique Altman concentrates on the following ratios:

working capital/total assets;
retained earnings/total assets;
earnings before interest and taxes/total assets;
market value of equity/book value of long term debt;
sales/total assets.

---

1 See J Freear *The Management of Business Finance* (1980) chapter 14.
2 See E Altman *Corporate Financial Distress* (1983) p 339.
3 E Altman *Corporate Bankruptcy in America* (1971). See also Altman *Corporate Financial Distress*, op cit, p 339.

To these he assigned weights to give an overall score known as the Z factor. A variation on this theme has been produced in the UK by R J Traffler[4].

Without going into the detailed operation of these ratios and the resulting analysis, the following general points can be made. First, there is no unanimity amongst the studies as to which ratios offer the best guide. Secondly, the predictive accuracy of the models improves as the failure approaches. Thirdly, there seems to be a time about one to two years ahead of the predicted failure after which management is unlikely to be able to reverse the decline. Fourthly, while they provide information the models do not necessarily aid in devising the appropriate strategy. They are based on static or comparative static, not dynamic, calculations but Altman argues that this is because the science is underdeveloped[5].

The causes of business failure

Apart from such work, the causes of business failure have been inadequately studied. Most professional receivers and liquidators have their own theories but there is usually little settled consensus.

It is interesting to note that the first Report of the Select Committee on Joint Stock Companies in 1844 divided what it described as 'bubble companies' into three categories:

(1)   'Those which, being faulty in their nature, inasmuch as they are founded on unsound calculations, cannot succeed by any possibility';
(2)   'Those which, let their object be good or bad, are so ill constituted as to render it probable that the miscarriages or failures incident to management will attend them'; and
(3)   'Those which are faulty, or fraudulent in their object, being started for no other purpose than to create shares for the purpose of jobbing in them, or to create, under pretence of carrying on a legitimate business, the opportunity, and means of raising funds to be shared by the adventurers who start the company'.

We may regard this as an apt description of business failure before the introduction of the modern form of incorporation. Remarkably little seems to have changed with the introduction of incorporation under general Companies Acts and limited liability.

Clearly, inadequate capital is a common failing. Many businesses are started up with insufficient working capital. Bank finance, which is usually sought, has its drawbacks. The interest has to be found whether or not the company makes profits unlike dividends on ordinary shares which are only paid out of profits. Bank surveillance and the changes in banking policy from time to time can inhibit the company's freedom to manoeuvre. Buying goods on hire purchase is a great temptation but the true cost of such goods is rarely taken into account. Another factor is inadequate control over working capital. Imprudent business judgment in one form or another is another common failing which in fact covers a multitude of sins. One has only to walk

---

4 Finding those firms in danger using discriminant analysis and financial ratio data: a comparative UK-based study, City University Business School Working Paper 4. See also J Argenti *Corporate Collapse* (1976).
5 See *Freear*, op cit, pp 348–349.

regularly through any shopping centre in any town to see the rise and fall of small businesses.

Fraud is another factor although its incidence is often exaggerated. Some businesses are fraudulent by nature, others are basically lawful but are carried on fraudulently. Others again are lawful and are carried on in a lawful manner but there are management frauds committed against the company.

In a survey carried out in the U S A in 1973, Dun and Bradstreet[6], the commercial intelligence specialists, identified 'management inexperience and incompetence' as the major cause of failures. Fraud accounted for a mere 2%. In a 1967 survey of 100 U K private companies which had been wound up and almost all of which were small incorporated businesses, 71% failed due to mismanagement. A high proportion had a low share capital of £100 or less in 52% of the cases, and of £1,000 or less in 78% of the cases[7].

The most interesting and thorough analysis of company failure in the U K has been done by a financial journalist and management consultant, John Argenti, in his book *Corporate Collapse*[8]. Argenti lists the following causes or symptoms—management shortcomings, lack of accountancy information, failure to respond to change, constraints, recession, big expensive projects, 'creative' (ie cosmetic) accountancy and excessive gearing. Let us examine each of these in turn.

Under management shortcomings, Argenti lists one-man rule, a non-participating board, unbalanced top team, lack of management depth, weak financial function and where there is a combined office of chairman/chief executive. He instances the former Rolls-Royce as having five out of six of these shortcomings. These are all pretty self-explanatory.

As examples of accountancy failings he instances lack of budgetary control, cash flow forecasts, costing systems and unrealistic valuation of properties.

He gives five examples of change—competitive trends, political change, economic change, social change and technological change. A company must be capable of responding to change. Included under economic and social change would now be changes in industrial relations.

Constraints covers a wide range of things. Some matters such as monopolies and restrictive practices are caught by legal and administrative mechanisms. Some corporate activities may be penalised by tax provisions, eg the retention of profits in close companies. Trades unions also represent a powerful constraint on a company's freedom of manoeuvre and some of their de facto rights were made de jure by the Employment Protection Act 1975, eg right of consultation on redundancy and closures. Again, public opinion, especially through the media or in the form of organised pressure groups, operates as an increasingly powerful check on companies. This is particularly true in the area of pollution. Recession and inflation both represent considerable threats to business. To these can be added strikes and the oil crises which created havoc in their time. The increased cost of oil and transport is still having repercussions across the world. The big project often brings a company down. It is frequently accompanied by little or no

6 *Freear*, op cit, p 349.
7 R Brough (1967) Business Ratios 8.
8 J Argenti *Corporate Collapse* (1976).

realistic costing of research and development. Rolls-Royce was a classic case. Royston Industries, manufacturers of the Midas black box for aeroplanes, was another. In both cases, profitable aspects of the group were brought down by over-ambitious research projects.

Creative accounting is usually a symptom rather than a cause. It has frequently occurred in the past with the over-valuation of properties or work in progress. The accountancy profession is seeking to establish controls over this kind of activity.

Excessive gearing ie excessive loan capital in relation to share capital again is usually a symptom rather than a cause. In some cases the blame can be laid at the door of the banks for encouraging this kind of improvidence but for small incorporated businesses, it can be the only available source of finance.

In a survey published in the Bank of England Quarterly Bulletin[9] two other factors are mentioned—low and declining profitability often marked by historic cost accounts which may show a steady but in reality inadequate return, and increased import penetration of home markets.

ECONOMIC AND LEGAL PERSPECTIVES

Economists and lawyers tend to view the insolvency systems from different perspectives[10]. Economists on the whole have shown relatively little interest in insolvency. Most standard texts deal with it in a very cursory way and it usually receives most treatment in books on finance. Where they are interested, economists tend to concentrate on the allocative impact of bankruptcy and winding up. Thus bankruptcy and winding up are viewed simply as an aspect of the money market mechanisms. Lawyers, on the other hand, tend to be more concerned with equity and distribution issues. Is there fairness between different classes of creditor and between debtor and creditor? Recently there has been a greater interest in the rehabilitation of consumer debtors and businesses. This sense of fairness and interest in the salvation of individuals and firms is not necessarily consistent with what some economists regard as efficient reallocation. Such economists tend to play down the welfare aspects of legal procedures and look forward to the day when the market will take care of such matters. It is arguable that many of the insolvencies of small firms which are classified as company failures have more in common with personal bankruptcy than large scale corporate collapse[11]. At the same time many personal bankruptcies result from giving guarantees for company debts. The legal form is often not the distinguishing feature so much as the size of the firm.

The legal procedures for dealing with corporate failure

At present the law provides four basic procedures to deal with corporate business failure—receivership administration, a voluntary arrangement and liquidation or winding up. Receiverships are a loan creditor's remedy for

9 (1980) 20 Bank of England Quarterly Bulletin 430.
10 See P Schuchman (1977) 41 Law and Contemporary Problems 66.
11 Compare W H Meckling (1977) 41 Law and Contemporary Problems 13.

enforcing his or her security, although sometimes the better type of receiver attempts a company doctor role as well. Usually the company will subsequently be wound up, although the viable parts of the business will be hived off and sold. Administration is a new procedure introduced in 1985 to facilitate a moratorium to aid the rehabilitation of a company experiencing financial difficulties. Schemes of arrangements are possible in solvent as well as in insolvent circumstances as we have seen. The reforms of 1985 introduced the possibility of a less formal and less expensive procedure. Winding up will either be a compulsory winding up, usually on a creditor's petition, or a creditor's voluntary winding up. In the case of the former, the Companies Court of the Chancery Division or the local County Court having jurisdiction performs a supervisory role.

Receiverships, administration and winding up involve collecting in and realisation of assets, and payment of debts. Winding up, however, is followed by dissolution which is the corporate equivalent of death. Unlike a personal bankrupt an insolvent company does not live to resume its former status.

The objectives of corporate insolvency law

Professor R M Goode in his *Principles of Corporate Insolvency*[12] states that corporate insolvency law embodies a variety of objectives some of which are mutually exclusive while other apply in combination. He identifies the following as the principal purposes of the law and we comment on them:

1. *To facilitate the recovery of companies in difficulty*—At a time of recession many companies face financial difficulties. Some of these companies are salvageable. This can be achieved as a result of the appointment of an administrator or administrative receiver. In some cases the company can be restored to profitable trading and then handed back to the directors but in many other cases administration or receivership leads to the hiving off of the viable part of the business and the winding up of the remainder.
2. *To suspend the pursuit of rights and remedies by individual creditors*— The effect of administration and winding up but not receivership is to suspend the rights of individual creditors. This is done in a variety of ways. In winding up unsecured creditors rank pari passu in competition with each other but secured creditors' rights are unaffected unless they fall within the winding up provisions which vitiate certain securities. On the other hand an administration order freezes the enforcement of real rights and judicial remedies while not barring other forms of self help such as set-off. An administrative receivership does not terminate other creditors' rights but because of the assumption of control by the administrative receiver it creates practical restrictions on the enforcement by unsecured creditors of their rights.
3. *To divest the directors of their management powers*—The directors of a company are displaced by the appointment of an administrator,

---

12 (1990), pp 5 et seq. See generally J Ziegel (1990) Alberta L Rev 191 for an interesting recent survey and review of the US law and economics literature on secured creditors' rights. See also R M Goode (1983–84) 8 CBLJ 53.

administrative receiver or liquidator. Unlike Chapter 11 of the American Bankruptcy Act, English law does not recognise the concept of the debtor in possession, leaving existing management in office subject to the supervision of the court and creditors.

4. *To provide for the avoidance of transfers and transactions which unfairly prejudice the general creditors*—We refer above to the provisions which apply to vitiate certain securities. English law contains provisions whereby transfers made by an insolvent company in the period before winding up or administration are clawed back into the assets available to the general body of creditors.

5. *To procure an orderly distribution of the estate*—Winding up involves the ascertainment of liabilities, the collection and realisation of assets and the distribution of the proceeds by way of dividend according to the statutory order of priority. Although the other procedures involve the payment of preferential debts in certain circumstances they do not involve the full gamut of the procedures of winding up.

6. *To provide a fair and equitable system for the ranking of claims*—Winding up provides detailed rules for the ranking of claims and certain claims are given preference on the grounds of public policy. These claims also have priority over the holder of debentures secured by a floating charge where possession is taken or a receiver is appointed.

7. *To provide for investigation of the causes of the company's failure and impose responsibility for culpable management by its directors and officers*—There is a public interest in the investigation of the causes of business failure and the allocation of responsibility where it is due. This aspect of company insolvency procedure has received more attention since 1985 and considerable emphasis has been put on the disqualification of directors involved in the management of insolvent companies in certain circumstances. The basis on which civil redress can be obtained against directors personally has also been changed to allow for easier recovery.

8. *To protect the public against future improper trading by delinquent directors*—This overlaps with 7 and is achieved through the disqualification process.

9. *To ensure the integrity and competence of insolvency practitioners*—Since 1985 insolvency practitioners have been required to be qualified by authorisation from a recognised professional body, the Secretary of State or a competent authority designated by the Secretary of State.

10. *In the case of liquidation, to dissolve the company*—Winding up does not involve dissolution of the company. The company continues to exist until formal dissolution. This takes place when all the assets have been collected, claims established and dividends distributed. It is marked by striking the company off the Register of Companies.

Incidence of corporate failure

Statistics published in *Economic Trends* of March 1975, p 122 show a general upward movement in the number of insolvent liquidations since 1960 and a similar (although less clear) increase can probably be explained by reference to the growth of the economy between 1960 and 1973 and the increased use of the corporate form of business. However, since 1972 we have had the successive oil crises, world economic stagnation and recession, high interest rates and at times high rates of inflation, which have all affected the liquidity of businesses and there has been a sharp rise in insolvencies since 1973. The numbers are still high although legal changes introduced by the Insolvency Act 1976 and the fee increases had a disturbing effect on the statistics. In the period 1970–74, the London clearing banks appointed on average receivers in some 150 cases a year; there was a slight rise in insolvencies in 1975–79 but a sharp increase in 1980 which continued until 1986–7 when it began to subside.

We set out below a table based on the CSO Annual Abstract of Statistics 1986[13], which we have updated, giving statistics of company liquidations from 1974–1989/90, together with a graph based thereon. Liquidations as a whole increased from 7,956 in England and Wales in 1971 to 15,100 in 1989/90. They reached 18,962 in 1986/87. Compulsory and creditors' voluntary liquidations, however, more than doubled in this period. Similar trends were present in Scotland and Northern Ireland. These figures may overstate the number of firms becoming insolvent because a business may be carried on through a number of separate companies. Although the trend has now been reversed the figures are still high compared with twenty years ago. This puts immense power in the hands of finance creditors and English law has yet to develop adequate checks and balances[13]. In the meantime, finance creditors are gradually learning that with such power comes social responsibility ultimately predicated on enlightened self-interest.

The legal procedures for dealing with company failure have been the subject of mounting criticism in recent years. They were the subject of a detailed report[14] by a Departmental Committee chaired by Sir Kenneth Cork, a leading insolvency specialist. This was followed by a White Paper[15] and the Insolvency Acts of 1985 and 1986. Although the law and practice is much improved the law is still too complex and there is a lack of coherence in the unified scheme established by the 1985–6 legislation.

13 For statistics back to 1960, see J H Farrar [1976] JBL 214 at 232–233.
14 'Insolvency Law and Practice'–Report of the Review Committee (Cmnd 8558).
15 'A Revised Framework for Insolvency Law' (Cmnd 9175).

TABLE   Company liquidations

	1974	1975	1976	1977	1978	1979	1980	1981	1982	1983	1984	1985	1986	1986–7	1987–8	1988–9	1989–90
England and Wales																	
Compulsory liquidations	1,395	2,287	2,511	2,425	2,265	2,064	2,935	2,771	3,745	4,807	5,260	5,761	5,204	4,882	3,700	3,600	4,300
Voluntary liquidations:																	
Creditors'	2,325	3,111	3,428	3,406	2,821	2,473	3,955	5,825	8,322	8,595	8,461	9,137	9,201	9,198	6,900	5,800	6,800
Members'	3,746	3,917	4,173	3,650	3,615	4,030	3,970	3,638	3,908	3,808	3,772	3,946	4,525	4,882	2,700	3,800	4,000
Total liquidation modified (all types)	7,466	9,315	10,112	9,481	8,701	8,567	10,860	12,234	15,975	17,214	17,493	18,844	18,930	18,962	13,200	13,200	15,100
Scotland																	
Compulsory liquidations	42	53	84	67	78	56	135	158	177	263	272	306	299	281	200	200	200
Voluntary liquidations:																	
Creditors'	113	151	145	204	196	182	244	280	326	258	251	231	212	214	200	200	200
Members'	264	276	299	222	230	214	242	248	253	263	234	233	251	233	200	300	200
Total liquidations notified (all types)	419	480	528	493	504	452	621	686	756	764	757	770	762	728	600	700	700

Sources: CSO Annual Abstract of Statistics, Department of Trade and Industry. The Registrar of Companies, Edinburgh. *Companies in 1989–90.*

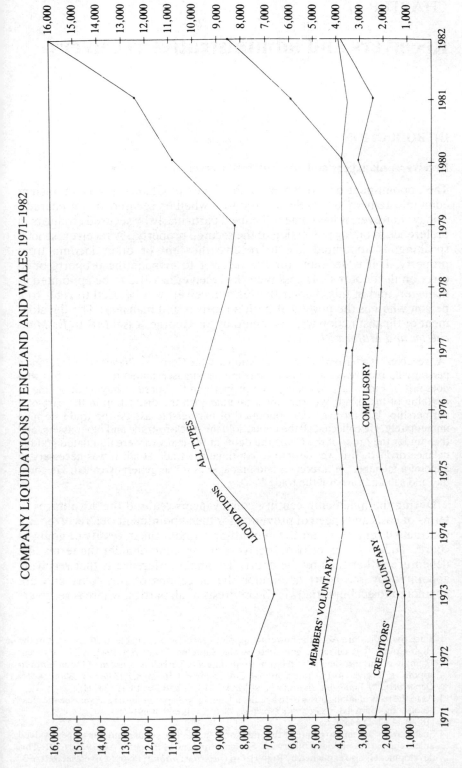

COMPANY LIQUIDATIONS IN ENGLAND AND WALES 1971–1982

Sources: CSO Annual Abstract of Statistics 1983; Companies in 1982.

CHAPTER 37

Receivers and administrative receivers

INTRODUCTION

Receivers, managers and administrative receivers

The appointment of a receiver by the Court of Chancery was an ancient equitable remedy available to creditors whether secured or unsecured[1]. Today, however, it has come to be used particularly by secured creditors in preference to taking possession of the secured property[2]. A receiver, strictly speaking, is appointed just to receive the rent or other income from property. If it is desirable for the receiver to manage the property or to carry on the debtor's business then the receiver has also to be appointed as manager, and in this chapter the term 'receiver' will be used to refer to a person who has the powers of both a receiver and manager. The development of the distinction was explained by Sir George Jessel MR in *Re Manchester and Milford Rly Co*[3]:

'A "receiver" is a term which was well known in the Court of Chancery, as meaning a person who receives rents or other income paying ascertained outgoings, but who does not, if I may say so, manage the property in the sense of buying or selling or anything of that kind. We were most familiar with the distinction in the case of a partnership. If a receiver was appointed of partnership assets, the trade stopped immediately. He collected all the debts, sold the stock-in-trade and other assets, and then under the order of the Court the debts of the concern were liquidated and the balance divided. If it was desired to continue the trade at all, it was necessary to appoint a manager, or a receiver and manager as it was generally called. He could buy and sell and carry on the trade.'

During the nineteenth century conveyancers realised the advantages in terms of costs and speed of providing for the appointment of a receiver as a contractual remedy under the debenture, without the necessity of going to court[4]. Today the majority of receivers are appointed under the terms of a debenture rather than by the court. The main difference is that receivers appointed by the court are under the directions of the court and are appointed to act impartially in the interests of all parties, whereas receivers

---

1 Since the Judicature Acts, the power to appoint a receiver is available in all divisions of the High Court. It is currently governed by the Supreme Court Act 1981, s 37. A recent example of the jurisdiction in relation to an unsecured creditor concerned the attempt to appoint a receiver to the International Tin Council: *J H Rayner (Mincing Lane) Ltd v Department of Trade and Industry* [1990] 2 AC 418, [1989] 3 All ER 523, HL.
2 As to the risks of taking possession and the advantages of appointing a receiver, see the clear account by Rigby LJ in *Gaskell v Gosling* [1896] 1 QB 669 at 691–693.
3 (1880) 14 Ch D 645 at 653.
4 Such powers became so common that they were implied by statute into mortgages by deed unless the parties provided otherwise. See now the Law of Property Act 1925, s 101. This development is also explained by Rigby LJ in *Gaskell v Gosling* [1896] 1 QB 669 at 691–693.

appointed under debentures are appointed principally to realise the debentureholder's security. For the most part, however, the position of receivers is the same whether they are appointed by the court or under the debenture. Where the distinction is relevant this will be made clear.

The Cork Report contained a number of recommendations designed to improve the competence, independence and effectiveness of receivers[5]. The report also contained a series of proposals designed to provide better mechanisms for rescuing businesses in financial difficulty[6]. It was realised that in some cases, although the company running the business might have incurred debts it could no longer meet, the business itself was still a viable and profitable enterprise. One outcome of these proposals was the introduction of the administration order and new procedures for voluntary arrangements discussed in the next chapter. Another was the special position accorded to a receiver appointed under a debenture secured by a floating charge over the whole or substantially the whole of a company's property. Such receivers are now known as *administrative receivers*[7] and are given considerable new powers and responsibilities to enable them to keep potentially successful enterprises intact. In this chapter we will refer simply to receivers but this must be understood as including administrative receivers and where special rules apply to administrative receivers this will be made clear. The function of a receiver is to receive income or realise property in order to pay off a particular secured creditor or creditors[8]. There is nothing to stop either other creditors petitioning the court for a compulsory winding up order to be made or the members resolving to put the company into voluntary liquidation. Where a company in receivership also goes into liquidation the receiver remains in office and continues to manage the business and realise the assets. The liquidator monitors the receivership on behalf of the other creditors and if assets still remain after the receivership is completed these will be dealt with by the liquidator[9].

Appointment of receiver

Although it is common to hear of companies 'calling in the receiver', not all receivers are appointed with the consent of the existing management or the owners of the company. Since a receiver who has been invalidly appointed will be a trespasser, it is important to ensure that the power of appointment has arisen and is validly exercised[10]. As we have seen, receivers can be appointed either by the court or under the terms of the debenture. The

---

5 See Insolvency Law and Practice (Cmnd 8558) chapter 8.
6 Ibid, para 1500–1515.
7 Insolvency Act 1986, s 29(2). The reference to administrative receivers being appointed 'by or on behalf of' debentureholders probably confines the definition to appointments under a debenture and excludes appointments by the court.
8 Subject in the case of a floating charge to the claims of preferential creditors.
9 Quite often nothing is left for the unsecured creditors. The Cork Report recommended that 10% of net realisations under a floating charge should be made available for distribution among the unsecured creditors: Insolvency Law and Practice (Cmnd 8558) paras 1538–1549. The proposal has not been enacted.
10 A receiver who is a trespasser will be personally liable: *Windsor Refrigerator Co Ltd v Branch Nominees Ltd* [1961] Ch 375, [1961] 1 All ER 277, CA. A receiver will normally therefore insist on an indemnity from the debentureholder before accepting office. The court may also order the debentureholder to indemnify the receiver: Insolvency Act 1986, s 33 implementing a recommendation of the Jenkins Committee (Cmnd 1793) para 299.

circumstances in which a receiver can be appointed under a debenture will depend on its terms. There is no automatic right to appoint under a debenture merely because the security is in jeopardy[11], although the court can make an appointment on such a ground[12]. A debentureholder who is uncertain whether the circumstances permit appointment under the debenture may be advised as a precaution to apply to the court to make the appointment. The usual precondition for appointment under a debenture is that a demand for repayment has not been met. Such a demand need not specify the amount of the debt and need only give the company enough time to get the money rather than time to raise or find the money[13]. In deciding whether or not to appoint a receiver, debentureholders owe no duty of care to the company or to guarantors or other mortgagees and thus may ignore the fact that negotiations are taking place with a view to rescuing the business in some other way[14]. An administrative receiver must be a qualified insolvency practitioner[15]. Apart from that, no qualifications are needed for appointment as receiver, although a company may never be appointed[16] and an undischarged bankrupt can only be appointed by the court[17]. In order to be effective, an appointment as receiver must be accepted before the end of the business day following that on which the instrument of appointment was received[18]. Provided it is so accepted, however, the appointment is deemed to be effective from the moment the instrument of appointment was received[19].

RECEIVERS AND CONTRACTS OF THE COMPANY

Existing contracts in general

The general rule is that, in itself, the appointment of a receiver has no effect on existing contracts of the company. The contract continues as one entered into by the company and the receiver will incur no personal liability in relation to the performance of the contract. The receiver takes over the management of the company but, as regards the other party to any existing contracts with the company, the receiver is in the same position as the company in deciding whether to perform the contract or whether to break it

---

11 *Cryne v Barclays Bank plc* [1987] BCLC 548, CA.
12 *Re London Pressed Hinge Co Ltd* [1905] 1 Ch 576.
13 *Bank of Baroda v Panessar* [1987] Ch 335, [1986] 3 All ER 751. See also *ANZ Banking Group (NZ) Ltd v Gibson* [1986] 1 NZLR 556 and Ziegel 'The Enforcement of Demand Debentures–Continuing Uncertainties' (1990) 69 CBR 718.
14 *Shamji v Johnson Matthey Bankers Ltd* [1991] BCLC 36, CA.
15 Insolvency Act 1986, ss 230(2), 388(1)(a).
16 Ibid, s 30.
17 Ibid, s 31.
18 Ibid, s 33(1)(a).
19 Ibid, s 33(1)(b). The appointment of a receiver must be notified to the Registrar of Companies: s 405. Under the new Pt XII of the Companies Act 1985 to be inserted by the Companies Act 1989, Pt IV, this becomes s 409. Appointment of a receiver is only one, although the most usual, method of crystallising a floating charge. The new s 410 of the Companies Act 1985 will allow regulations to be made providing for: (i) notice to be given to the Registrar of the occurrence of crystallising events or action taken to crystallise a charge; and (ii) the consequences of failure to give such notice which may include treating the crystallisation as ineffective.

and leave the other party to a remedy in damages[20]. Any proprietary rights acquired by the other party to the contract which were binding on the company before receivership continue to bind it in receivership[1]. Thus, where before receivership a company had exchanged contracts for the sale of land, the purchaser was entitled to specific performance against the company in receivership[2]. Similarly where a pre-receivership contract created a lien over company property, the lien was binding on the company in receivership even though the events causing the lien to arise only occurred after the receivership began[3]. Other equities existing at the commencement of the receivership, which effectively give the other party a prior claim to an asset of the company, also bind the company in receivership. Thus a right of set-off is exercisable against the company in receivership provided the mutual obligations existed at the date of receivership, even though the amounts only became quantified later[4]. It is submitted that a right of rescission against the company that had arisen before the receivership would likewise be exercisable against the company in receivership.

Specific performance, lien, set-off and rescission are all examples of equities that continue to bind the company in receivership. In principle it ought to follow that where the other party is entitled to an injunction to prevent a breach of contract by the company, the injunction will also be granted against the company in receivership. Thus if a company grants a lease giving the right to extract minerals from the company's quarry, the company will be restrained by injunction from breaking the lease and it is submitted it would make no difference if the company had gone into receivership. That is a strong case, because it is accepted that property rights are unaffected by the receivership. It is submitted though, that a right to extract minerals granted as a purely contractual licence, if the circumstances are such that it would be protected by an injunction, will continue to be so protected even after the company is in receivership.

The case which is difficult to reconcile with this proposition is *Airlines Airspares Ltd v Handley Page Ltd*[5] which is often cited as authority for the proposition that the company in receivership is in a better position than the company before receivership. The defendant company had agreed to pay the plaintiff £500 for every 'Jetstream' aircraft the defendant sold. When the defendant went into receivership, the receiver transferred all the assets to a newly-formed subsidiary and negotiated a sale of the shares in the

---

20 Thus a receiver who causes a company to break a contract will not be liable to the other party for the tort of inducing breach of contract: *Lathia v Dronsfield Bros Ltd* [1987] BCLC 321. See also *Edwin Hill & Partners v First National Finance Corpn plc* [1988] 3 All ER 801, [1989] 1 WLR 225, CA.

 1 The debentureholder will not be in any better position, because the assignment of the company's property that occurs on crystallisation of the floating charge will be subject to proprietary rights existing against company property. Conversely a Mareva Injunction, which does not create proprietary rights, will not bind a debentureholder: *Cretanor Maritime Co Ltd, The Cretan Harmony v Irish Marine Management Ltd* [1978] 3 All ER 164, [1978] 1 WLR 966, CA.

 2 *Freevale Ltd v Metrostore (Holdings) Ltd* [1984] Ch 199, [1984] 1 All ER 495.

 3 *George Barker (Transport) Ltd v Eynon* [1974] 1 All ER 900, [1974] 1 WLR 462, CA. *Re Diesels and Components Pty Ltd* [1985] 2 Qd R 42, 9 ACLR 825.

 4 *Rother Iron Works Ltd v Canterbury Precision Engineers Ltd* [1974] QB 1, [1973] 1 All ER 394, CA. It is different if the transaction which is claimed to give rise to the set-off takes place after the receivership has begun: *N W Robbie & Co Ltd v Witney Warehouse Co Ltd* [1963] 3 All ER 613, [1963] 1 WLR 1324, CA.

 5 [1970] Ch 193, [1970] 1 All ER 29n.

subsidiary[6]. Since the defendant would not be manufacturing any more 'Jetstream' aircraft the plaintiff sought an injunction to prevent the sale of the shares going ahead until satisfied that provision had been made for the payment of their commission in respect of all future sales.

The court accepted that it was a breach of an implied term of the contract for the defendant company to put it out of its power to perform the contract, and seems to have assumed that, had the company not been in receivership, an injunction to prevent the breach would have been granted. However, because the company was in receivership an injunction was refused and it was accepted that the receiver could be in a better position in relation to breaking the company's contracts than the company itself. This reasoning is inconsistent with the other cases so far considered in this section. One possible explanation is that the decision is wrong and that an injunction ought to have been granted against the company in receivership. The other possibility is that no injunction would in fact have been granted against the company, even without a receivership. The agreement seems to have been drafted very loosely. Only if there was an express term that the defendant company was not to transfer production of the 'Jetstream' to any other person without obtaining a promise by that person also to pay the plaintiff's commission, or if the court implied a term to that effect, would an injunction be granted. And if there was such a term in the contract, express or implied, surely the appointment of a receiver would make no difference to whether or not breach of the term would be restrained by injunction. Whatever the merits of the actual decision in *Airlines Airspares Ltd v Handley Page Ltd*[7] it is submitted that the proposition that a receiver is in a better position than the company is inconsistent with principle[8].

New contracts

Where a receiver enters into new contracts in the course of carrying on the company's business, the position is that the receiver will be personally liable on the contract but will have a right of indemnity out of the assets of the company. The legal rules that lead to this result, however, vary according to the type of receiver involved. Receivers appointed by the court are personally liable, because as independent officers of the court they are not agents of either the company or the debentureholder, but contract as principals[9]. A receiver appointed under a debenture, on the other hand, might be expected to act as agent of the debentureholder. However, it is almost invariably agreed that the receiver will not be agent of the debentureholder but will be agent of the company[10]. Even so, an agent would not normally be personally

---

6 This is an example of a transaction known as 'hiving-down'. It is a convenient means of preparing the viable parts of a business for sale as a going concern while leaving the debts and other liabilities with the parent company.

7 [1970] Ch 193, [1970] 1 All ER 29n.

8 The proposition was described as 'plainly wrong' in *Schering Pty Ltd v Forrest Pharmaceutical Co Pty Ltd* [1982] 1 NSWLR 286 in which an injunction was granted to prevent a receiver breaking an exclusive distributorship the company had granted.

9 *Moss SS Co Ltd v Whinney* [1912] AC 254, HL.

10 It is expressly provided by statute that an administrative receiver is agent of the company: Insolvency Act 1986, s 44(1)(a). In accordance with the general rule applicable to agents of the company, the agency terminates if the company goes into liquidation. Thereafter a receiver still has power to sell company property but does so as principal. The Insolvency Act 1986, s 127, which invalidates dispositions of company property in compulsory liquida-

liable. However, it is also provided by statute that a receiver appointed under a debenture, whether an administrative receiver or not and whether agent of the company or the debentureholder, is personally liable on new contracts, except in so far as the contract provides otherwise, and has a right of indemnity from the assets of the company[11]. The position thus reached reflects the economic realities of the situation. If it is in the interests of the debenture-holder that the business should be carried on, new contracts will need to be entered into and yet persons will not be prepared to enter new contracts with a company in receivership unless they are assured of being paid. The effect of making the receiver personally liable but with a right of indemnity is to treat liabilities under new contracts as if they were expenses of the receivership with the highest priority to be met out of the assets of the company[12].

Contracts of employment

EFFECT OF RECEIVER'S APPOINTMENT

Contracts of employment existing when the receiver is appointed are subject to special rules different from those applicable to other existing contracts. The appointment of a receiver by the court automatically terminates existing contracts of employment because employment is a personal relationship and the appointment of a receiver by the court substitutes a new party in place of the company[13]. A receiver appointed out of court and who is made agent of the company will not be a new party substituted in place of the company, and thus will not terminate contracts of employment[14]. The result at common law is that such receivers will not be personally liable on contracts of employment which are kept going after the receivership[15]. However, under the Insolvency Act 1986, receivers appointed under debentures will be personally liable on contracts of employment which are adopted by them but with a right of indemnity out of the assets of the company[16]. There is no definition of what adopting a contract of employment involves, but it is provided that nothing done in the 14 days after appointment amounts to adoption of a contract and so it seems likely that merely continuing with the contract after 14 days amounts to adopting it[17]. In practice, whether the receiver is personally liable

---

tion without court sanction, does not apply, because the receiver is only carrying out a disposition made on creation of the floating charge: *Sowman v David Samuel Trust Ltd* [1978] 1 All ER 616, [1978] 1 WLR 22; *Re Margart Pty Ltd* [1985] BCLC 314, NSW Supr Ct.
11 See Insolvency Act 1986, s 44(1) as to administrative receivers and s 37(1) as to other receivers.
12 Normally the debentureholder will not incur liability on new contracts. However, the receiver may insist on an indemnity from the debentureholder in case the assets are insufficient. The debentureholder may also become liable if it intervenes in the receiver's work by giving instructions etc to such an extent that the receiver becomes its agent: *Standard Chartered Bank Ltd v Walker* [1982] 3 All ER 938, [1982] 1 WLR 1410, CA.
13 *Reid v Explosives Co Ltd* (1886) 19 QBD 264, CA.
14 *Re Mack Trucks (Britain) Ltd* [1967] 1 All ER 977, [1967] 1 WLR 780. A contract of employment which is inconsistent with the appointment of a receiver, eg that of a managing director where the receiver will be managing the business, may be terminated by the receiver's appointment: *Griffiths v Secretary of State for Social Services* [1974] QB 468, [1973] 3 All ER 1184.
15 *Nicoll v Cutts* [1985] BCLC 322, CA.
16 Insolvency Act 1986, s 44(1) as to administrative receiver and s 37(1) as to other receivers.
17 Ibid, ss 44(2) and 37(2).

on a contract of employment or not, employees are unlikely to work without payment and so the receiver will ensure that funds of the company are available to pay employees being retained. Receivers may be less happy at the prospect of incurring personal liability for accrued statutory entitlements and, although the legislation does not appear to permit receivers to contract out of personal liability on contracts adopted by them, it was held in *Re Specialised Mouldings Ltd*[18] that receivers could write to employees during the 14 days after their appointment indicating that they were not adopting the contract and that continued employment was only offered on that basis.

EFFECT OF TRANSFER OF THE BUSINESS

One aim of the receiver may be to realise the assets by selling the business as a going concern. The purchaser, however, may not want to take on all the employees and might prefer that those that are taken on start fresh contracts without accrued statutory employment rights. The practice has grown up therefore of dismissing any remaining employees immediately before the transfer of the business, leaving the purchaser to re-employ those it wishes to take on[19]. This practice continued despite the Transfer of Undertakings (Protection of Employment) Regulations 1981[20] which provide that on the transfer of a business the contract of employment of persons employed by the transferor immediately before the transfer shall be transferred to the purchaser[1]. It was held[2] that if employees were dismissed, even a matter of a few hours, before the transfer took place, then the regulations had no effect because the employees were not employed immediately before the transfer. A dismissal in such circumstances would be an unfair dismissal under the regulations[3] but would nevertheless be effective as a dismissal. However, the European Court of Justice held[4] that under the Directive[5] which the regulations implement, a dismissal effected before the transfer and solely because of the transfer of the business is, in effect, prohibited and is for the purposes of the Directive required to be treated as ineffective. In *Litster v Forth Dry Dock and Engineering Co Ltd*[6], a case in which all the employees were dismissed at 3.30pm so that they were no longer employed when the transfer took place at 4.30pm, the House of Lords applied that reasoning in the construction of the regulations. Now, therefore, any employees dismissed before and solely because of the transfer of the business are not

---

18 (13 February 1987, unreported), but see G Stewart *Administrative Receivers and Administrators* (1987) pp 96–99.
19 For criticism of the practice, see *Pambakian v Brentford Nylons Ltd* [1978] ICR 665, EAT.
20 SI 1981/1974.
1 Ibid, reg 5. Where the receiver hives down the business to a subsidiary, that transfer is ignored for the purposes of the regulations until the subsidiary is sold or the subsidiary transfers the business: SI 1981/1974, reg 4.
2 *Secretary of State for Employment v Spence* [1987] QB 179, [1986] 3 All ER 616, CA.
3 Transfer of Undertakings (Protection of Employment) Regulations 1981 SI 1981/1974, reg 8(1).
4 Case 101/87 *P Bork International A/S v Foreningen af Arbejdsdere i Danmark* [1989] IRLR 41, ECJ.
5 EEC Council Directive 77/187. OJ 1977 L 61/26.
6 [1990] 1 AC 546, [1989] 1 All ER 1134, HL. See Collins (1989) 18 ILJ 144 and McMullen (1990) 87 Law Soc Gaz, No 5 p 27 (7 February 1990).

dismissed at all but are transferred to the purchaser[7]. The effect of the decision is that if any employees so transferred are not kept on by the purchaser they are treated as dismissed by the new solvent employer rather than by the old insolvent employer. Since many of the accrued employment rights against insolvent employers are payable out of government funds[8], with the government being subrogated to the claim of the employee against the insolvent company[9], one effect of the decision is to save the government money by giving the employee a claim against a solvent employer. Although this increases the liabilities of the new employer it will presumably be matched by a reduction in the price paid for the business. However, the element of uncertainty it introduces may make purchasers marginally more reluctant to buy businesses from receivers[10].

Leases and other rental agreements

The lessor of property to a company in receivership is not entitled to payment of the rent in respect of the period of receivership ahead of other creditors, including the debenture holder, as an expense of the receivership. As a lease is a continuing obligation it is not a new contract on which the receiver would be personally liable[11]; neither will the court order a receiver to pay rental for the period of receivership out of the proceeds of sale of the assets[12]. However, the lease may provide for forfeiture on the grounds of non-payment of rent or on other grounds such as crystallisation of a floating charge which the lessor will be entitled to exercise. In the case of land, relief against forfeiture may be available under the Law of Property Act 1925, s 146 but this will usually be on condition that arrears are paid or future liability undertaken by the debentureholder[13]. In addition, a landlord will be entitled to levy distress for arrears of rent arising both before and during the

---

7 There is an exemption for dismissals by reason of economic, technical or organisational reasons which receivers may be expected to use if they are closing down parts of the business or disposing of any assets piecemeal: Transfer of Undertakings (Protection of Employment) Regulations 1981, SI 1981/1974, reg 8(2). The House of Lords in *Litster* [1990] 1 AC 546, [1989] 1 All ER 1134, HL, was thus able to approve the decision in *Secretary of State for Employment v Spence* [1987] QB 179, [1986] 3 All ER 616, CA, on the basis of the facts found in that case. These were that when the decision was taken at 11.00am to stop trading and dismiss all the employees, there was no guarantee that negotiations for the sale of the business would succeed. In fact the negotiations were successful and a deal was signed at 2.00pm that day. It was accepted, however, that the reason for the dismissals was not one connected with the transefer but was due to economic considerations.
8 Employment Protection (Consolidation) Act 1978, s 122. It does not include the compensatory element in an award for unfair dismissal which an employee therefore had to claim as an unsecured creditor against the insolvent company. Such a claim may now be made against the purchaser as the new employer.
9 Ibid, s 125.
10 Ideally the purchaser would like an indemnity against liabilities under contracts of employment. However, an indemnity given by the insolvent transferor company will be worthless and the debentureholder and receiver may not be prepared to give such an open-ended commitment.
11 *Hay v Swedish and Norwegian Rly Co Ltd* (1892) 8 TLR 775.
12 *Hand v Blow* [1901] 2 Ch 721, CA.
13 See the discussion in G Lightman and G Moss *The Law of Receivers of Companies* (1986) pp 159–165.

receivership by seizing property on the premises notwithstanding that the debentureholder's charge has attached to the property[14].

Liability for rates

When a receiver is appointed, the company normally continues in occupation of any premises; the receiver does not normally replace the company as occupier and thus does not become personally liable for rates payable during the receivership[15]. The assets of the company are, however, liable to be distrained in respect of rates due for the period prior to the receivership and during the receivership[16]. As long as there is property of the company on the premises, therefore, it is advisable for the receiver to ensure that the rates are paid.

Supply of gas, electricity, water and telecommunications

The suppliers of public utilities like gas, water, electricity and telecommunications have a statutory duty to supply. A new occupier of premises, therefore, cannot be refused supply on the grounds that the previous occupant has left an outstanding account. However, since at common law a receiver does not normally become a new occupier of the company's premises, public utility suppliers can legitimately threaten to cut off the supply unless outstanding arrears are paid[17]. This may hamper attempts to keep the business intact and to realise it as a going concern[18]. Accordingly, Parliament has protected administrative receivers from such threats. Under the Insolvency Act 1986, s 233 administrative receivers are entitled to the supply of gas, electricity, water and telecommunications without having to pay the arrears which remain as a debt due from the company[19]. The administrative receiver may, however, be required personally to guarantee

14 *Re Roundwood Colliery Co* [1897] 1 Ch 373 at 392–394, CA. The Law Commission has recommended the abolition of distress for rent: Law Commission Report No 194 (HC 138).
15 *Gyton v Palmour* [1945] KB 426, [1944] 2 All ER 540. *Ratford v Northavon District Council* [1987] QB 357, [1986] 3 All ER 193, CA.
16 *Re Marriage, Neave & Co* [1896] 2 Ch 663, CA. The assets liable to be taken in distress for rates are only those of the occupier, unlike distress for rent at common law which extends to assets on the premises. It does not matter, however, that the company's assets have in equity become those of the debentureholder on crystallisation of the floating charge: G Lightman and G Moss *The Law of Receivers of Companies* (1986) pp 218–219.
17 *Paterson v Gas Light and Coke Co* [1896] 2 Ch 476, CA. Cf *Husey v London Electricity Supply Corpn* [1902] 1 Ch 411, CA. It is sometimes suggested that receivers appointed under the debenture do not become new occupiers whereas receivers appointed by the court do. It is submitted, however, that it is question of fact in each case and that the presumption is that a receiver does not become a new occupier. This provided a further reason for hiving-down the business to a new subsidiary which would constitute a new occupier: *Re Fir View Furniture Co Ltd* (1971) Times, 9 February.
18 See the Cork Report (Cmnd 8558) paras 1451–1462. Another objection was that threatening to cut off the supply ensured that sums due to public utility suppliers were paid in full ahead of all other creditors.
19 A similar privilege is extended to liquidators, administrators and supervisors of voluntary arrangements, each of whom acts in the interests of all parties. Granting the privilege to administrative receivers, who act in the interests of debentureholders, is a sign that in future administrative receivers will more and more be expected to have regard to the interests of other creditors as well.

the payment of charges during the receivership[20]. This is logical since the continued supply is effectively being treated as a new contract in which case the receiver would be personally liable. The effect is therefore to treat the cost of gas, electricity, water and telecommunications during the receivership as expenses of the receivership.

POWERS OF ADMINISTRATIVE RECEIVERS

Besides protection from public utility suppliers cutting off the supply[1], adminstrative receivers are given a number of crucial new powers to enable them to carry on the company's business. First, the same powers which are made available to the administrator are also deemed to be included in any debenture under which an administrative receiver is appointed[2]. Second, where this is likely to promote a more advantageous realisation of the company's assets, the administrative receiver may, with the sanction of the court, dispose of property subject to a security ranking in priority to the floating charge as if it were not subject to the security[3]. The sanction of the court will be conditional on the net proceeds of disposal of the secured property, or its open market value if that is greater, being applied to discharging sums secured by the property[4]. Third, some of the statutory powers previously only available to liquidators but now made available to administrators are also made available to administrative receivers[5]. However, unlike liquidators and administrators, the statutory powers[6] to reopen or set aside transactions at an undervalue, preferences, extortionate credit transactions and certain floating charges are *not* made available to administrative receivers. Nor do they have power to take proceedings for fraudulent or wrongful trading, although they are obliged to report on whether the directors of the company may merit disqualification[7].

RECEIVER'S DUTY TO THE COMPANY AND OTHER CREDITORS

Duties in realising the company's assets

Although the receiver's principal function is to realise the debentureholder's security, how this is achieved may be of concern to other creditors of the company, guarantors of the company's debts and ultimately to the members

---

20 Insolvency Act 1986, s 233(2)(a).
 1 Insolvency Act 1986, s 233. See above.
 2 Ibid, s 42 and Sch 1.
 3 Ibid, s 43(1). See the Cork Report (Cmnd 8558) paras 1500–1515. Compare the far more extensive powers of the administrator under the Insolvency Act 1986, s 15. See below p 674.
 4 Insolvency Act 1986, s 43(3).
 5 Ibid, ss 234–237. Section 246 of the Insolvency Act 1986, which enables liquidators or administrators to override liens on books, papers or other records of the company, does not apply to administrative receivers. They may nevertheless inspect documents subject to a lien using s 236: *Re Aveling Barford Ltd* [1988] 3 All ER 1019, [1989] 1 WLR 360.
 6 Insolvency Act 1986, ss 238–241 and 244–246.
 7 Company Directors Disqualifications Act 1986, s 7(3).

of the company. Any duties mortgagees or receivers appointed to realise mortgaged property may owe are governed by principles of equity[8] rather than the common law and are of older origin than the duty of care in negligence at common law recognised in *Donoghue v Stevenson*[9] and *Hedley Byrne & Co Ltd v Heller & Partners Ltd*[10].

The first issue the receiver is likely to face is whether to keep the business of the company going or whether to close it down with the inevitable damage to any goodwill the business may still retain. A receiver appointed by the court has been held to be appointed as an impartial administrator of the company's assets who must therefore consider the interests of all parties and not just those of the debentureholder. Such a receiver may therefore be restrained from breaking an existing long-term contract to supply one of the company's customers with coal, even though the receiver could now sell the coal at a higher price elsewhere[11]. In contrast, a receiver appointed under a debenture is appointed primarily to realise the debentureholder's security. Any duty to preserve the company's goodwill for the benefit of other creditors or members exists only in so far as it is consistent with performance of the primary duty to the debentureholder. Such a receiver is, therefore, free to decide whether to carry on the company's business or whether to close it down and sell off the assets[12]. And in selling the assets the receiver is free to choose when to sell and is not obliged to wait while the market rises[13]. In conducting the sale, however, the receiver does owe a duty to take reasonable care to obtain the proper price or true market value on the date of the sale[14]. Furthermore, if the purchaser is a company controlled by the receiver the burden of proof will be on the receiver to show that reasonable care was taken[15].

Exclusion of liability

It is not uncommon for a debenture to contain a clause limiting or excluding a receiver's liability for breach of duty. Problems of privity of contract may arise because the receiver will not be a party to the debenture. Various

---

8   *China and South Sea Bank Ltd v Tan Soon Gin* [1990] 1 AC 536, [1989] 3 All ER 839, PC. The debentureholder is unlikely to be under any liability since a receiver appointed under the debenture will almost always be acting as agent of the company and a receiver appointed by the court is an officer of the court and not the agent of the debentureholder. Liability may arise if the debentureholder intervenes to such an extent as to constitute the receiver its agent: *Standard Chartered Bank Ltd v Walker* [1982] 3 All ER 938, [1982] 1 WLR 1410, CA.
9   [1932] AC 562, HL.
10   [1964] AC 465, [1963] 2 All ER 575, HL.
11   *Re Newdigate Colliery Co Ltd* [1912] 1 Ch 468, CA.
12   *Re B Johnson & Co (Builders) Ltd* [1955] Ch 634, [1955] 2 All ER 775, CA. *Kernohan Estates Ltd v Boyd* [1967] NI 27.
13   *Cuckmere Brick Co Ltd v Mutual Finance Ltd* [1971] Ch 949, [1971] 2 All ER 633, CA. Conversely a receiver who chooses to wait will not be liable if the value of the security declines: *China and South Sea Bank Ltd v Tan Soon Gin* [1990] 1 AC 536, [1989] 3 All ER 839, PC.
14   *Cuckmere Brick Co Ltd v Mutual Finance Ltd* [1971] Ch 949, [1971] 2 All ER 633, CA. It has been held that the duty also extends to guarantors of the company's debt: *Standard Chartered Bank Ltd v Walker* [1982] 3 All ER 938, [1982] 1 WLR 1410, CA; *American Express International Banking Corpn v Hurley* [1985] 3 All ER 564.
15   *Farrar v Farrars Ltd* (1888) 40 Ch D 395, CA; *Tse Kwong Lam v Wong Chit Sen* [1983] 3 All ER 54, [1983] 1 WLR 1349, PC.

solutions to this problem have been canvassed[16], and it may be that in some circumstances the company at least may be treated as having consented to any breach of duty by the doctrine of *volenti non fit injuria*. However, an exclusion clause will not normally be construed as covering liability for breach of a duty to take reasonable care[17]. Furthermore, under the Unfair Contract Terms Act 1977 a clause which excludes or restricts such liability in relation to a party to the contract[18] can only be relied on to the extent that it is fair and reasonable[19].

Duty to pay preferential creditors

As a general proposition, the preferential creditors[20] rank ahead of a floating charge. Where a floating charge is enforced by the appointment of receiver, therefore, the receiver is under a duty to pay the preferential creditors out of assets subject to the floating charge in priority to the debt secured by the floating charge[1]. If the remaining assets subject to the floating charge are insufficient to pay the debentureholder in full, the debentureholder is recouped out of assets available for payment of the general creditors[2]. Failure to pay the preferential creditors in priority makes the receiver personally liable to them for breach of statutory duty[3] and in certain circumstances the debentureholder can also become liable[4]. If, however, the debentureholder's debt is also secured by a fixed charge and is fully paid out of the proceeds of the fixed charge then no preferential debts arise[5].

Enforcement of duties

During the receivership the duty owed by the receiver to the company is enforceable in proceedings brought by the company, not by a derivative action brought by individual shareholders[6]. If the company is put into liquidation, then the summary procedure under the Insolvency Act 1986, s 212 will be available against administrative receivers though not against any other type of receiver[7]. This is part of the process that is leading to administrative receivers being recognised as having to consider the interests of other persons besides those of the debentureholder. It can be seen also in

16 See the discussion in G Lightman and G Moss *The Law of Receivers of Companies* (1986) pp 75–80.
17 See *Bishop v Bonham* [1988] 1 WLR 742, CA, where a charge authorising the chargee to sell 'in such manner and upon such terms and for such consideration . . . as you may think fit' and which provided that the chargee 'shall have no liability for any loss howsoever arising in connection with any such sale' did not exclude liability for negligence.
18 Unfair Contract Terms Act 1977, s 2(2). The Act does not apply to exclusion of liability in relation to the creation, transfer or termination of interests in land: ibid, s 1(2) and Sch 1, para 1.
19 Ibid, s 11(1).
20 See the Insolvency Act 1986, ss 386, 387 and Sch 6.
1 Ibid, s 40(1)(2). See also the Companies Act 1985, s 196 (debentureholder taking possession) and Insolvency Act 1986, s 175(2)(b) (liquidation).
2 Insolvency Act 1986, s 40(3).
3 *Westminster Corpn v Haste* [1950] Ch 442, [1950] 2 All ER 65.
4 *IRC v Goldblatt* [1972] Ch 498, [1972] 2 All ER 202.
5 *Re G L Saunders Ltd* [1986] 1 WLR 215.
6 *Watts v Midland Bank plc* [1986] BCLC 15.
7 Cf *Re B Johnson & Co (Builders) Ltd* [1955] Ch 634, [1955] 2 All ER 775, CA.

the duty administrative receivers are under to keep all other creditors of the company informed about their conduct of the receivership[8]. Finally, to ensure that administrative receivers are not put under pressure by the debentureholder when they do give consideration to other interests, administrative receivers can only be removed from office by court order[9].

8 Insolvency Act 1986, s 48.
9 Ibid, s 45.

CHAPTER 38

Administration orders and voluntary arrangements

INTRODUCTION

For a variety of reasons an insolvent company and its creditors may prefer to try and deal with the company's assets and affairs without putting the company into liquidation. Obviously if the company itself is to survive as a distinct legal entity, as opposed to just saving the business by transferring it to a new legal entity, then liquidation must be avoided. But there may be other advantages. It may be cheaper. It may allow the company's business to be carried on and then sold as a going concern or at least allow for a more advantageous disposal of the company's assets. If the company owes money to its directors or shareholders, they may be persuaded not to press their claims in competition with those of outside creditors in return for the company not being placed in liquidation. Finally, a not uncommon situation is where a company is making a profit on current trading and yet through a disastrous business venture has incurred debts it cannot repay immediately. What such a company may do is have a moratorium on debts whereby creditors with debts contracted before a certain date agree not to enforce those debts for a specified period in return for receiving regular instalments on their debts. Meanwhile, new debts incurred by the company will be paid as and when they fall due, thus allowing the company to continue trading. Or a company may wish to compromise one or more of its debts whereby the creditor or creditors concerned agree to take a smaller sum in full satisfaction of their debt. A compromise may be combined with a moratorium and either may also be used by a liquidator to ensure an orderly realisation of assets or to resolve complicated questions of creditors' rights without wasteful litigation or time consuming calculations.

A number of difficulties can arise, however, in making any arrangement to deal with an insolvent company's affairs outside of a liquidation. First, how are creditors to be dissuaded from enforcing their claims against the company's assets while the terms of the arrangement are being negotiated? Secondly, is there any procedure for binding dissenting creditors? For any compromise or arrangement to work it is necessary for all the creditors affected by it to be bound by it and unless the creditors concerned unanimously agree to the arrangement there will need to be a mechanism to bind dissenters. Thirdly, is it possible to make a binding arrangement without the court being over-involved as this would just add to the costs and delay implementation? Fourthly, to what extent are the creditors foregoing powers a liquidator would have to investigate the past running of the company and to re-open past transactions? In order to provide greater opportunities for dealing with a company's affairs outside of liquidation two new procedures were introduced in the Insolvency Act 1986 which, it is hoped, will avoid some of the difficulties just outlined.

ADMINISTRATION ORDERS

Making the order

The more radical of the two new procedures is the administration order. This is a court order that, for the duration of the order, the affairs, business and property of a company shall be managed by an administrator[1]. The administrator, who must be a qualified insolvency practitioner[2], thus replaces the board of directors for the duration of the order. In this respect an administrator fulfils a role similar to that of an administrative receiver appointed by the holder of a floating charge, except that the administrator is appointed by the court to manage the company in the interests of everyone involved whereas the administrative receiver's principal duty is still to the debentureholder. The new administration order procedure will therefore be of particular benefit where there is no floating charge or where for one reason or another the holder of a floating charge is reluctant to appoint an administrative receiver. Essentially the purpose of an administration order is to provide a breathing space, free from the pressure of creditors' claims, in which to take stock of the situation, to decide whether the business can profitably be rescued or whether it should be broken up and to negotiate with creditors regarding any possible moratorium or composition[3].

As the number of potential procedures for dealing with insolvent companies increases it is important to see how they differ from one another and how they may interrelate. For an administration order to be made it must be shown that the company is, or is likely to become, unable to pay its debts[4]. The company must not, however, be in liquidation[5]. Nor may it be in administrative receivership, unless the debentureholder has consented to the appointment of an administrator or the debenture itself is liable to be

---

1 Insolvency Act 1986, s 8(2). The number of administration orders has been: 1987–131; 1988–198; 1989–135; 1990–211: Insolvency Annual Report published by the Department of Trade and Industry. For an interesting survey of administration orders, see M Homan *The Result of Administration Orders Made in 1987* (1988) published by the Institute of Chartered Accountants for England and Wales.

2 Ibid, ss 388(1), 389(1).

3 The provisions are based on recommendations of the Cork Committee. See Report of the Review Committee on Insolvency Law and Practice (Cmnd 8558) ch 9. In some respects it resembles judicial management which was invented in South Africa in 1926. South Africa, however, does not recognise the floating charge and so there was no possibility of a receiver being appointed to take over management of a company in financial difficulties. A somewhat similar procedure was introduced in Australia in 1961 which does recognise floating charges and receiverships and perhaps for this reason the new procedure has not been widely used. French law has a procedure known as *suspension provisoire des poursuites* which allows a moratorium while a plan for recovery is formulated. This procedure is limited, however, to cases where it is in the public interest. See generally on overseas comparisons: Farrar [1976] JBL 214, 217–223, Sealy (1986) 2 IL & P 70 and Wooldridge *Administration Procedure* (1987) pp 1–4. In the US chapter XI of the Federal Bankruptcy Code provides a framework for company reorganisation as an alternative to liquidation. Chapter XI is compared with administrative receivership and the administration order in a Bank of England Occasional Paper 'Company Reorganisation' (1983). See also the entertaining and interesting article by Westbrook 'A Comparison of Bankruptcy Reorganisation in the US with the Administration Procedure in the UK' (1990) 6 IL & P 86.

4 Insolvency Act 1986, s 8(1)(a).

5 Ibid, s 8(4).

avoided[6]. Furthermore, the court must be satisfied that the administration order is likely to achieve[7] one or more of the following[8]:

(i)   the survival of the company[9], and the whole or any part of its undertaking, as a going concern;
(ii) the approval of a voluntary arrangement under the Insolvency Act[10];
(iii) the sanctioning of a scheme of arrangement under the Companies Act, s 425; or,
(iv) a more advantageous realisation of the company's assets than would be effected on a winding up.

An application for the making of an administration order is begun by a petition being presented to the court by[11] the company, its directors, a creditor or by the supervisor of a voluntary arrangement[12]. Merely making the application ensures that the status quo is preserved regarding the company's assets while the hearing is pending[13]. Thus the company may not be put into liquidation; nor, without leave of the court, may any steps be taken to enforce any security over the company's property, to repossess any goods in the company's possession which are on hire purchase[14], or to levy execution or distress on the company's property[13]. One thing which may be done, however, is the appointment of an administrative receiver[15]. The legislation is designed so that if a debenture holder with the right to appoint an administrative receiver wishes to do so, that right prevails over any application for an administration order[16]. If, however, an administration order is

6   Ibid, s 9(3).
7   In *Re Consumer and Industrial Press Ltd* [1988] BCLC 177 at 178 Peter Gibson J suggested that 'likely to achieve' meant 'more probably than not'. However, a more relaxed test interpreting the phrase as meaning 'a real prospect', suggested by Hoffman J in *Re Harris Simons Construction Ltd* [1989] 1 WLR 368, has come to be accepted: see *Re Primlaks (UK) Ltd* [1989] BCLC 734 and *Re SCL Building Services Ltd* [1990] BCLC 98. It must be remembered that even after the conditions are satisfied the judge still has a discretion whether to make an order: *Re Imperial Motors (UK) Ltd* [1990] BCLC 29.
8   Insolvency Act 1986, s 8(1)(b), (3).
9   The requirement that the company survive as a legal entity, as well as its undertaking, could inhibit the use of the administration procedure for facilitating the sale of the business as a going concern: *Re Rowbotham Baxter Ltd* [1990] BCLC 397.
10 Insolvency Act 1986, ss 1–7.
11 Ibid, s 9(1).
12 Ibid, s 7(4)(b).
13 Ibid, s 10(1).
14 References to hire purchase include conditional sales, chattel leases and retention of title agreements: ibid, s 10(4).
15 Ibid, s 10(2)(b). A holder of a floating charge must therefore be served with notice of the petition as must the company. Other creditors are not notified, however, at this stage, the idea being to avoid a protracted hearing and to try and emulate the speed with which administrative receivers are appointed: Homan, op cit, paras 4.23–4.26. As to the advisability of notifying parties who might, with leave of the court, be entitled to appear at the hearing, see Goldring [1990] 7 JIBL 284.
16 In order to ensure that the debentureholder has the right to appoint an administrative receiver, it should be made a default condition under the floating charge for a petition for an administration order to be presented in relation to the company. In respect of a floating charge created before 29 December 1986 (when this part of the Act came into force) it is deemed to be a default condition precedent to the appointment of an administrative receiver: ibid, Sch 11, para 1. Because of the adminstrator's powers to deal with charged property, holders of fixed charges have on occasion deliberately also taken a nominal floating charge in order to be able to prevent the making of an administration order by putting the company into administrative receivership: *Re Croftbell Ltd* [1990] BCLC 844. However, Homan found that in 40% of administration order there was a floating charge but

made not only do all the above restrictions on enforcing claims against the company continue for the duration of the order but also no administrative receiver may now be appointed[17]. If the court makes an administration order it appoints the administrator[18] who, within three months, must draw up and put to a meeting of creditors proposals as to how to achieve the purpose for which the administration order was made[19]. The proposals are accepted by the creditors if a majority in value of those present and voting, in person or by proxy, vote in favour[20]. It is the creditors' decision therefore whether the administration order is put into effect or not[21].

Implementing the proposals

In order to put the proposals into effect the administrator is empowered to do all such things as may be necessary for the management of the affairs, business and property of the company[1]. Essentially the administrator replaces the directors in the management of the business[2]. The appointment in itself has no effect on existing contracts of the company. Subject to the need to obtain the court's consent for proceedings, any right to specific performance, lien, set-off, rescission or injunction available against the company before administration continues to be available against the company in administration[3]. However, as an office holder under the Insolvency Act 1986, an administrator is protected against suppliers of gas, electricity, water or telecommunications cutting off the supply until outstanding accounts are paid[4]. Although the creditors' meeting is supposed to decide whether the administrator's proposals are implemented or not it may happen that the administrator must decide at short notice whether to accept an offer for the company's business. In such circumstances the administrator

the holder had presumably chosen not to appoint an administrative receiver: Homan, op cit, para 4.07.
17 Insolvency Act 1986, s 11(3).
18 On being appointed the administrator must send a notice of the administration order to the company, advertise it, register it and send a copy to every creditor: ibid, s 21. This will be the first time the majority of creditors formally hear anything. The administrator is entitled to receive a statement as to the affairs of the company: ibid, s 22.
19 Ibid, s 23(1). The administrator must also send a copy of the proposals to the Registrar of Companies, to every creditor and to every member or advertise where members may obtain a copy free of charge: ibid, s 23.
20 Insolvency Rules 1986, r 2.28(1). In valuing debts for voting purposes, see, as to secured creditors: ibid, r 2.24; as to hire purchase, chattel lease and retention of title creditors: ibid, rr 2.26, 2.27(1). Any resolution passed only as a result of votes of creditors 'connected with the company' is deemed defeated: ibid, r 2.28(1A).
21 The result of the meeting is reported to the court but this just involves filing the report. There is no hearing and, in particular, no requirement for the court to approve the proposals: Insolvency Act 1986, s 24(4). The remedy of any creditor, or member, who feels aggrieved by the approval of the proposals is to petition the court on the grounds that the company's affairs, business or property, are being managed in an unfairly prejudicial way: ibid, s 27.
1 Ibid, s 14(1). An administrator also has the powers set out in Sch 1 to the Insolvency Act.
2 See ibid, s 14(4). Where management powers are conferred by contracts outside the memorandum and articles, see *Re P & C and R & T (Stockport) Ltd* [1991] BCC 98.
3 *Astor Chemicals Ltd v Synthetic Technology Ltd* [1990] BCLC 1.
4 Insolvency Act 1986, s 233.

can apply to the court to sanction the sale under the court's power to give directions to the administrator[5].

One of the problems the administrator may face in carrying on the company's business or selling it as a going concern is that some of the assets used by the company may be subject to security interests; others may not be owned by the company, as for example, where they are the subject of hire purchase or conditional sale agreements[6]. The administrator will be helped by the Insolvency Act 1986, s 11(3)(c) which provides that, while the administration order is in force, no security[7] may be enforced against the company, nor may goods on hire purchase etc be repossessed, without the consent of either the administrator or the court[8]. Thus a lessor may not exercise a right of forfeiture for non payment of rent without consent[9]. In *Re Atlantic Computers plc*[10] the Court of Appeal laid down guidelines as to the granting of such consent. Since the justification for the prohibition in s 11 is to help achieve the purpose for which the administration order was made, leave will be granted if enforcement is unlikely to impede achievement of that purpose. In other cases the court has to balance the interest of the lessor with those of the other creditors of the company. So far as possible administration for the benefit of unsecured creditors should not be conducted at the expense of creditors with proprietary rights and therefore leave will be granted if significant loss would be caused to the lessor by refusal[11]. If leave is refused it may be on terms that the administrator pay the current rent which should be possible since if the administration order has been rightly

---

5 Insolvency Act 1986, ss 14(3) and 17(2). In *Re Charnley Davies Ltd (No 2)* [1990] BCLC 760 at 767 Vinelott J is reported to have expressed the view that an administrator had authority to sell the entire undertaking in advance of the creditors' meeting and without obtaining the sanction of the court. However, this must be doubted in the light of the judgment of Peter Gibson J in *Re Consumer and Industrial Press Ltd (No 2)* (1987) 4 BCC 72. An administrator can sell particular assets under the general authority conferred by s 14, without applying to the court, as this does not deprive the creditors' meeting of all point: *Re NS Distribution Ltd* [1990] BCLC 169. *Re Charnley Davies Ltd (No 2)*, above, concerned a claim by creditors for compensation on the basis of an alleged sale at an undervalue by the administrator. The proceedings were brought under the Insolvency Act 1986, s 27 but it was held that such a claim was in reality one of professional negligence and not one of unfair prejudice. The correct procedure would be to put the company into liquidation and bring proceedings under the Insolvency Act 1986, s 212.

6 The Act refers to hire purchase agreements but included in this term are conditional sale agreements, chattel leasing agreements and retention of title agreements: ibid, s 15(9).

7 Security is defined as 'any mortgage, charge, lien or other security': ibid, s 248. In *Bristol Airport plc v Powdrill* [1990] Ch 744, [1990] 2 All ER 493, CA, security was held to include the right of an airport to detain aircraft under the Civil Aviation Act 1982, s 88.

8 Under the Insolvency Act 1986, s 11(3)(d) other proceedings, execution or other legal process and levying distress are prohibited without the consent of the court or the administrator. Proceedings refers to proceedings by creditors and does not include the hearing of an application to revoke an airline's air transport licence: *Air Ecosse v Civil Aviation Authority* [1988] PCC 252, [1987] SLT 751. Nor is an application for the late registration of a charge within the mischief the section is aimed at although such applications are subject to the court's discretion in any case: *Re Barrow Borough Transport Ltd* [1990] Ch 227.

9 *Exchange Travel Agency Ltd v Triton Property Trust plc* [1991] 12 LS Gaz R 33.

10 [1990] BCC 859, CA, (1990) Times, 18 September. The company in administration had leased computers from the owners and sub-leased them to end users. It was held they were still in the possession of the company for the purposes of the Insolvency Act 1986, s 11(3).

11 Thus secured creditors who are fully secured are unlikely to obtain leave. See *Re Meesan Investments Ltd* (1988) 4 BCC 788.

made the business should generally be sufficiently viable to hold down current outgoings[12].

Even more significant for secured creditors or creditors with proprietary rights, however, are the powers of the administrator to deal with certain assets as if the company had an unencumbered title to them. The powers fall into two categories, depending on whether or not the administrator also needs the consent of the court. First, without the consent of the court, the administrator may dispose of or otherwise exercise powers in relation to property of the company subject to a floating charge as if it were no longer subject to the charge[13]. Where such property is disposed of the charge holder has the same priority in respect of the proceeds as it would have had in respect of the property[14]. Secondly, with the court's consent, the administrator may dispose of assets subject to other forms of security or goods in the possession of the company which are subject to hire purchase agreements[15].

As regards setting aside or re-opening transactions the administrator has the same powers as a liquidator[16]. Thus charges which are not registered as required by the Companies Act 1985 are void against the administrator[17]. Likewise, the administrator has powers to reopen or avoid transactions at an undervalue[18], preferences[19], extortionate credit transactions[20] and certain floating charges[1]. The administrator, however, has no power to take proceedings for fraudulent or wrongful trading but does have to report on whether directors' conduct may merit a disqualification order[2].

Discharge

The administration order ends when the court discharges it which the court may do in four circumstances. First, following an application by the

---

12 The Court of Appeal rejected the lessor's claim that current rentals should be treated as expenses of the administration and thus given priority, as would happen in winding-up. The concept of administration expenses was inappropriate to a temporary phase like administration.
13 Ibid, s 15(1)(3). If the floating charge holder objects it can do so by applying to the court on the grounds of unfair prejudice: ibid, s 27.
14 Ibid, s 15(4). Presumably if the administrator has exercised powers other than disposal, e g by using up the assets in the production process, the floating charge holder's priority is lost.
15 Ibid, s 15(2)(3). The court's consent will be on condition that the net proceeds (or open market value, if higher) are applied towards discharging the sums secured by the security or payable under the hire purchase agreement: ibid, s 15(5). See *Re ARV Aviation Ltd* [1989] BCLC 664.
16 Certain procedural powers, previously only available to the liquidator are also available to the administrator: ibid, ss 234–237 and 246.
17 At present see s 395. Under the new Pt XII of the Companies Act 1985, to be inserted by the Companies Act 1989, Pt IV, see ss 399(2)(a), 402(2)(a) and 419(5). Under the present law either party can apply for late registration of a charge but it has been held that once an administration order has been made, if it is clear an insolvent liquidation cannot be avoided, no order allowing registration will be granted: *Re Barrow Borough Transport Ltd* [1990] Ch 227. When the new provisions are in force registration can take place at any time but a charge registered more than 21 days after its creation will for a limited period remain vulnerable to the making of an administration order: s 400.
18 Ibid, s 238(1).
19 Ibid, s 239(1).
20 Ibid, s 244(1).
1 Ibid, s 245(1).
2 Company Directors Disqualification Act 1986, s 7(3).

administrator which may be made at any time[3] but which must be made if it appears to the administrator that the purpose of the order has been achieved, or has become incapable of achievement, or if he is required by the creditors' meeting to apply[4]. Secondly, if the creditors' meeting rejects the administrator's proposals[5]. Thirdly, following an application by a creditor or member of the company on the grounds that the company's affairs, business or property are being managed by the administrator in an unfairly prejudicial way[6]. Fourthly, if the creditors and members agree to a voluntary arrangement[7], although as we shall see it may be in the interests of the creditors and supervisor of such arrangements to keep the administration order in place.

VOLUNTARY ARRANGEMENTS

Historical context

One of the most important powers for those managing an insolvent or financially pressed company, whether or not it is yet in liquidation, is the power to make binding compromises or arrangements with one or more of the creditors of the company. For any compromise or arrangement to work it is necessary for all the creditors affected by it to be bound by it. This can either be achieved by ensuring that the creditors concerned unanimously agree to the plan or by making use of statutory provisions that enable a specified majority to bind the minority. The first such statutory provisions were introduced in 1870 and were only available if the company was in liquidation. In 1900 the provisions were extended to include arrangements between the company and its members, as well as arrangements between the company and its creditors. Then in 1907 the requirement that the company be in liquidation was removed.

Unfortunately these provisions, which are now contained in ss 425–427, have proved complicated, time-consuming and expensive to operate and their use today has become remarkably infrequent[8]. In an attempt to find a cheaper alternative, the liquidator in *Re Trix Ltd*[9] tried to use the liquidator's power[10] of agreeing a compromise or arrangement with creditors, to compel a whole list of creditors to accept a composition without consulting

---

3 Ibid, s 18(1).
4 Ibid, s 18(2). If the purpose has been achieved the administrator will no doubt be handing the business back to the management of the directors. If the purpose has become impossible to achieve the application for discharge of the order may be coupled with a petition that the company be compulsorily wound up. In at least one case the court has discharged the administration order conditionally on the members passing a resolution for voluntary winding up. The order was also conditional on the unsecured creditors waiving their rights so far as necessary to enable the preferential creditors to be in the same position in the voluntary winding up as they would have been in a compulsory winding up. In the latter case the relevant date for the accrual of preferential creditors' rights would be the date of the administration order; ibid, s 387(3)(a). *Re Scot Lane Ltd* (unreported but see (1987) 8 Co Law 273, 276).
5 Ibid, s 24(5).
6 Ibid, s 27(4)(d).
7 Ibid, s 5(3)(a).
8 See the Cork Report (Cmnd 8558) ch 7, Pt II especially paras 404–418.
9 [1970] 3 All ER 397, [1970] 1 WLR 1421.
10 Under what is now the Insolvency Act 1986, Sch 4, para 2.

them as to whether they agreed or not. The court refused, holding that the only way apathetic or dissenting creditors can be bound to such a compromise or arrangement is under statute. As a result it became increasingly common for companies to enter into compromises or arrangements at common law and not under the statutory provisions at all. Since, at common law, there is no power for a majority to bind a dissenting minority, agreement must be unanimous and in practice this may mean paying off smaller creditors in full, leaving a few large creditors to agree to a moratorium or composition. To remedy this a new statutory procedure was introduced in the Insolvency Act 1986[11]. In the following paragraphs we shall compare the procedure under the Companies Act, ss 425–427 with that under the Insolvency Act, ss 1–7 and we shall see the advantages of using the Insolvency Act provisions. It is likely that because of these advantages the Insolvency Act provisions will be the ones used where a company wishes to make an arrangement with its creditors[12]. One major reason is that creditors are likely to prefer an arrangement under the Insolvency Act because it must be under the supervision of a qualified insolvency practitioner[13], with the assurance of professional competence and independence that that implies.

Maintaining the status quo

Under both procedures arrangements may be proposed whether the company is in liquidation or subject to an administration order or not. If, however, the company is not in liquidation or subject to an administration order, there may be a problem, once the proposal has been announced, in preventing creditors from pursuing their claims against the company while the proposal is being considered[14]. The solution is to apply for an administration order, because merely applying for such an order will itself preserve the status quo[15]. Since two of the four reasons for which application may be made for an administration order are to facilitate approval of arrangements with creditors[16] it seems the legislation envisages that administration orders and statutory procedures for arrangements with creditors will frequently be used in conjunction with each other.

Approving the arrangement

Before any proposals become binding they must be approved by meetings of creditors and of members of the company. Under the Companies Act the entire procedure begins with an application to the court which then orders

---

11 See the Insolvency Act 1986, ss 1–7. The provisions are closely modelled on the reformed provisions for voluntary arrangements for individual debtors contained in the Insolvency Act 1986, ss 252–263.
12 If the company wishes to amend the rights of its members then it will continue to use ss 425–427.
13 Insolvency Act 1986, s 1(2). The number of Insolvency Act voluntary arrangements has been: 1987–21; 1988–47; 1989–43; 1990–58: Insolvency Annual Report published by the Department of Trade and Industry.
14 As to whether the court has power to stop the enforcement of a judgment against the company in the absence of a petition for either an administration order or a winding-up order, see below p 703, footnote 5.
15 Insolvency Act 1986, s 10(1).
16 Ibid, s 8(3).

the meetings to be held[17]. Futhermore, separate meetings will be needed of each class of creditors or class of members whose rights are affected[18]. In contrast, under the Insolvency Act, the meetings are called by the proposed supervisor[19]. If the proposed supervisor is anyone other than the liquidator or administrator the supervisor must first notify the court whether such meetings should be held and if so when[20]. This, however, is a mere matter of filing and, unless there is an objection, does not involve a court hearing. Furthermore, only two meetings will be held, one of creditors and one of members; no distinctions are made between different classes of creditors or members.

Under the Companies Act procedure the proposal is only accepted by the meeting if it receives the support of a majority in number representing 75% in value of those present and voting in person or by proxy[1]. Under the Insolvency Act the creditors' meeting accepts the proposal if the majority is over 75% in value of the creditors present in person or by proxy and voting on the resolution[2]. The members' meeting accepts the proposal if there is a simple majority vote in favour of the resolution. How many votes each member may cast depends on whether such rights are set out in the articles of association. If they are then members vote in accordance with such rights[3]; if not then a simple majority of members[4] present in person or by proxy and voting on the resolution suffices[5]. Under the Companies Act the proposal must then return to court for the court's sanction which will involve another court hearing[6]; under the Insolvency Act the result of the meeting is merely reported to the court[7].

Effect on dissenting creditors

The crucial aspect of both procedures is that once the appropriate approvals have been obtained the proposal binds dissenting creditors. Under the Companies Act this takes effect when the proposal, having been sanctioned by the court, is delivered to the registrar for registration[8]; under the Insolvency Act approval by the appropriate meetings binds all creditors with notice of and entitled to vote at the creditors' meeting[9]. The rights of dissenting creditors are protected under the Companies Act by the majority both in number and value that is needed at the relevant meetings and by the need for the court's approval. In the case of the Insolvency Act no court approval is needed. Instead it is up to the dissenting creditor to use the available power to apply to the court, within 28 days of the report of the

17 Section 425(1).
18 As to what constitutes a class of creditors, see *Sovereign Life Assurance Co v Dodd* [1892] 2 QB 573, CA.
19 Insolvency Act 1986, s 3.
20 Ibid, s 2(2).
 1 Section 425(2).
 2 Insolvency Rules, 1986, r 1.19(1) ie a majority in number of creditors is not required.
 3 Ibid, r 1.18.
 4 Excluding any member holding only non-voting shares: ibid, r 1.20(2).
 5 Ibid, r 1.20(1).
 6 Section 425(2).
 7 Insolvency Act 1986, s 4(6).
 8 Section 425(2).
 9 Insolvency Act 1986, s 5(2)(b).

meetings being filed. The grounds on which such an application can be made are that the arrangement is unfairly prejudicial or that there was a material irregularity at or in relation to either of the meetings[10]. In the case of secured or preferential creditors, under the Companies Act they will form separate classes from the unsecured creditors generally and from each other; their class rights therefore cannot be affected unless their class meeting approved the scheme by the appropriate majority. Under the Insolvency Act there is only one meeting of creditors but it is provided that the rights of secured or preferential creditors cannot be affected without their consent[11].

Powers of the supervisor of an arrangement

Compared to those of a liquidator or administrator the powers of a supervisor of a voluntary arrangement under the Insolvency Act to re-open or set aside past transactions are very meagre. The prohibition on suppliers of gas, electricity, water and telecommunications from threatening to cut off supplies unless their outstanding accounts are paid applies[12] but none of the other powers to re-open transactions is available. If such powers are needed then, if the company is not yet subject to an administration order, the supervisor should consider applying for one[13]. If the company is already in liquidation or already subject to an administration order then the powers will be available. Although on approval of a voluntary arrangement the court may order a stay in the winding up or discharge the administration order[14], the supervisor of the voluntary arrangement may ask that this should be without prejudice to powers to re-open past transactions[15].

Problems where liquidation ensues

Where creditors do accept a moratorium or composition whether at common law or under statute, a problem may arise if the company subsequently goes into liquidation. To take the simplest example: suppose existing creditors of a company agree to compromise their debts so as to enable the company to continue trading. If the company subsequently goes into liquidation before the compromise is paid, are the creditors who agreed to the compromise restricted to proving for the lesser sum they promised to accept? The answer is No, because the accord represented by their agreement to accept a lesser sum only discharges the original debt when satisfied by payment of the lesser sum. This is so whether the compromise was at common law[16] or under statute[17].

A related problem may arise where creditors agree to a moratorium on the enforcement of existing debts for, say, 12 months and during that time

---

10 Ibid, s 6. See *Re Primlaks (UK) Ltd (No 2)* [1990] BCLC 234.
11 Ibid, s 4(3)(4).
12 Ibid, s 233(1)(c).
13 Ibid, s 7(4)(b). The supervisor can also apply to the court for directions: ibid, s 7(4)(a). For an example of how useful this power can be, see *Re FMS Financial Management Services Ltd* (1988) 5 BCC 191.
14 Ibid, s 5(3)(a).
15 Ibid, s 5(3)(b).
16 *Ex p Bennet* (1743) 2 Atk 527.
17 *Re Alfred Shaw & Co, Bank of Australia's Claim* (1897) 8 QLJ 48.

agree to give priority to current creditors. If the company goes into liquidation during those 12 months the current creditors will rank ahead of the creditors who agreed to the moratorium[18]. But if the company goes into liquidation after 15 months but while some people who became creditors during the 12 month moratorium are still unpaid, do the latter group still have priority[19]?

In some cases it has been argued that any agreement to forego rights in a liquidation is not binding because it is contrary to the statutory principle that creditors be treated pari passu[20]. Though this may prevent creditors contracting for better rights than they would obtain under a pari passu principle[1], it should not prevent people contracting out of their rights by agreeing to defer their debts to those of other creditors. The only case where it is not apparently possible for a creditor to agree to defer his debt is where he has a right of set-off. The set-off rule is mandatory[2] and must be applied even if the effect is to raise to the status of an ordinary creditor someone who had agreed to rank as a deferred creditor[3].

CONCLUSION

Whether the new procedures for administration orders and voluntary arrangements will be used remains to be seen. On its own the administration order may prove useful in those cases where there is no floating charge under which an administrative receiver can be appointed. It is possible, however, that the most valuable function of an administration order will be in conjunction with a voluntary arrangement, as a means of maintaining the status quo while the proposal is considered. These new procedures must also be looked at in the light of other recent changes to insolvency law, in particular the potential liability of directors for wrongful trading[4]. Under those provisions directors may find themselves personally liable to contribute to the assets of the company if, once they should have realised the company was heading towards insolvent liquidation, they failed to take every step to minimise loss to the creditors they ought to have taken. One aim of the wrongful trading provision is to encourage directors to face up to a financial

---

18 *Re Walker Construction Co Ltd (in liquidation)* [1960] NZLR 523.
19 The answer must depend on construing the terms of the moratorium. In *Rendell v Doors and Doors Ltd (in liquidation)* [1975] 2 NZLR 191, it was held that the creditors who became creditors during the moratorium had priority in a liquidation occurring after the moratorium had ended. But an opposite construction would have seemed equally plausible.
20 It was so held by Mahon J in *Re Orion Sound Ltd* [1979] 2 NZLR 574. When he was counsel for the liquidator in *Re Walker Construction Co Ltd (in liquidation)* supra, note 6, Mahon J had put forward the same argument, unsuccessfully. See also Johnston [1991] JBL 225.
 1 As in *British Eagle International Airlines Ltd v Cie Nationale Air France* [1975] 2 All ER 390, [1975] 1 WLR 758, HL.
 2 *National Westminster Bank Ltd v Halesowen Presswork and Assemblies Ltd* [1972] AC 785, [1972] 1 All ER 641, HL, obiter per Viscount Dilhorne, Lord Simon and Lord Kilbrandon relying on the use of the words 'shall be set off' in the Bankruptcy Act 1914, s 31. Lord Cross thought the set-off rules were not mandatory because of the need for creditors to forego their rights of set-off in agreeing on compromises. The Cork Committee recommended that contracting out of set-off should be permitted. See Cmnd 8558, para 1342.
 3 *Rendell v Doors and Doors Ltd (in liquidation)* [1975] 2 NZLR 191.
 4 Under the Insolvency Act 1986, s 214.

crisis before it is too late and to inform creditors at an early stage what the problems are. That way it is hoped more businesses can be saved from liquidaton with the waste of resources that may often entail. It is as new, realistic, options for the directors and creditors together to consider that the administration order and voluntary arrangement procedures should be judged.

CHAPTER 39

Winding up

TERMINOLOGY

Winding up is a term commonly associated with the ending of a company's existence. In fact winding up or liquidation (the terms are synonymous) is the process by which the assets of the company are collected in and realised, its liabilities discharged and the net surplus, if there is one, distributed in accordance with the company's articles of association. Only when this has been done is the company's existence finally terminated, by a process known as dissolution. If one thinks of the company in terms of an individual, the equivalent of winding up is the administration of a deceased person's estate; the dissolution of the company is equivalent to the death of the individual. The obvious difference is that in the case of companies the winding up or administration of assets precedes the dissolution or death.

Just as an individual's estate at death may be solvent or insolvent, so a company being wound up may be solvent or insolvent. Insolvency is not a process like winding up but a state of affairs in which persons, whether individuals, partnerships or companies, are unable to pay their debts in full[1]. When a company cannot pay its debts in full, delicate problems arise over how the assets that are available should be distributed. Broadly speaking, as we shall see, the law tries to maintain an equality between creditors so that assets are distributed pari passu ie rateably according to the size of each creditor's claim. At the same time the law recognises that certain creditors, for a variety of reasons, need to be given an advantage over the general body of creditors. How these conflicting objectives are reconciled is a fascinating story and so this chapter will concentrate mainly on the winding up of insolvent companies. But it must be remembered that winding up as a process may be applicable to either solvent or insolvent companies.

One common confusion of terminology occurs in the use of the term 'bankruptcy'. Bankruptcy is a legal process by which the assets of an insolvent individual or partnership are realised and the proceeds distributed to the creditors. Companies cannot be made bankrupt[2]. The equivalent procedure in the case of a company is winding up, but whereas bankruptcy in the case of an individual or partnership necessarily presupposes insolvency, winding up may apply to solvent as well as to insolvent companies. It is

---

1 The draftsman of the 1986 insolvency legislation has, however, used the term insolvency to describe a variety of proceedings rather than the state of affairs of being unable to pay debts in full. There is also no consistency about which proceedings are referred to. Compare the different definitions of 'onset of insolvency' in the Insolvency Act 1986, s 240(3) and s 245(3) with the definition of 'insolvency' in s 247(1) which in turn is different from the meaning of 'becomes insolvent' in the Company Directors Disqualification Act 1986, s 6(2).
2 Insolvency Act 1986, s 265.

therefore important to distinguish between bankruptcy, a process applicable to insolvent individuals or partnership, and the winding up of an insolvent company. Part of the problem in distinguishing them is that insolvent debtors, whether they are individuals or companies, will frequently face the same problems over such questions as what assets are to be made available to which creditors and in what order. From time to time the similarity of these problems has led Parliament to apply the bankruptcy solution in the winding up of insolvent companies but, as will be seen, this has led to its own difficulties.

Another contrast in terminology is between winding up and receivership. A receiver, as we have seen, will typically be appointed to a company by a secured creditor e g a debenture holder under a floating charge[3], and the receiver's function will be to pay off the debt of that secured creditor either from income receipts or asset realisations. A liquidator, on the other hand, represents the interests of all creditors but, in particular, the unsecured creditors. It is very likely that a company which has defaulted on a secured debt, leading to the appointment of a receiver, will be unable to pay its unsecured debts in full. The unsecured creditors may then choose to protect themselves by putting the company into liquidation and appointing a liquidator. When this happens the receiver continues to act in the exercise of receivership powers but no longer as agent for the company[4], and the liquidator will watch over proceedings on behalf of the other creditors of the company until the secured debt in respect of which the receiver was appointed has been discharged.

It is also necessary to distinguish from winding up two other procedures which may be used in relation to insolvent companies. The first, called an administration order, is a court order that, for the duration of the order, the affairs, business and property of a company shall be managed by a third party called an administrator[5]. Such an order will be made in the hope of saving the company from liquidation or of obtaining a more advantageous realisation than would be effected on a winding up. The second procedure, known as a voluntary arrangement, allows a company and its creditors to agree on a composition in satisfaction of its debts or a scheme of arrangement of its affairs[6]. Like the administration order this will also provide a way of managing the company's business or realising its assets without liquidation. If the administration order or voluntary arrangement is successful in restoring the company to solvency the company will be returned to the management of its directors. If solvency is not restored then whether the business has been sold or not the administration order or voluntary arrangement is likely to be followed by liquidation as the process by which any remaining assets can be realised and the proceeds distributed to the creditors.

3 If, as often will be the case, the appointment of a receiver by a debenture holder under a floating charge comprises the whole or substantially the whole of a company's property, the receiver is referred to as an 'administrative receiver': Insolvency Act 1986, s 29(2).
4 *Gosling v Gaskell* [1897] AC 575, HL and Insolvency Act 1986, s 44(1).
5 Insolvency Act 1986, s 8(2).
6 Insolvency Act 1986, s 1(1).

REFORM OF INSOLVENCY LAW

In 1977 the government appointed a committee headed by Sir Kenneth Cork to review the whole of insolvency law[7]. Many of the Committee's recommendations were implemented in the Insolvency Act 1985. They involved amending many of the winding-up and receivership provisions in the Companies Act 1985 as well as introducing the new administration order and voluntary arrangement procedures referred to above. It was then decided to consolidate all the winding-up and receivership provisions contained in the Companies Act 1985 together with the legislation governing the new procedures, in the Insolvency Act 1986. It is this Act which now provides the legislative background to most of this chapter.

TYPES OF WINDING UP

Winding up may be either compulsory or voluntary[8]. A compulsory winding up is where a court orders that the company be wound up, a voluntary winding up is where the members of the company resolve that the company be wound up.

Compulsory winding up

The process of obtaining a winding-up order begins with a petition alleging that one or more of the seven grounds exists on which a compulsory winding-up order may be made. The seven grounds are set out in the Insolvency Act 1986, s 122(1). The seventh of these, winding up on the just and equitable ground, is important as a means of minority shareholder protection and has been dealt with earlier[9]. Of the other six, it is the sixth one, that the company is unable to pay its debts, which is the most important. This can be seen from the fact that the vast majority of petitions are presented by creditors to whom the fact that the company is unable to pay its debts will be the important consideration[10]. Besides creditors, petitions can be presented by the company itself[11] or by its directors[12] or by members[13],

---

7 Report of the Review Committee on Insolvency Law and Practice (Cmnd 8558). See also the White Paper outlining the government's reaction to the Report: A Revised Framework for Insolvency Law (Cmnd 9175).
8 Insolvency Act 1986, s 73(1).
9 See Chapter 27, ante.
10 The annual report on Companies published by the Department of Trade and Industry last gave figures showing who presented winding-up petitions in 1977. In that year, of 4,213 petitions presented in England and Wales, 4,060 were presented by creditors.
11 Insolvency Act 1986, s 124(1).
12 An amendment made in the Insolvency Act 1985 reversing the effect of the decision in *Re Emmadart Ltd* [1979] Ch 540, [1979] 1 All ER 599 which had held that the directors could not present a petition in the name of the company. A petition by the directors must be presented by all the directors: *Re Instrumentation Electrical Services Ltd* (1988) 4 BCC 301.
13 The legislation uses the term 'contributory' which encompasses members of the company as well as others not registered as members but who are liable to contribute to the assets of the company: Insolvency Act 1986, s 79.

provided basically that they have held their shares for at least six months[14] and that they have an interest in the winding up[15].

The ways in which a company can be shown to be unable to pay its debts are defined in the Insolvency Act 1986, s 123. Provided the debt is then due, and exceeds £750, a creditor can serve on the company a notice demanding payment within 21 days. If the company then fails either to pay the debt or to secure or compound it to the reasonable satisfaction of the creditor, that establishes that the company is unable to pay its debts[16]. If the company satisfies the court that the debt is disputed in good faith and on substantial grounds then a petition based on a statutory demand will be dismissed and the creditor can be restrained by injunction from presenting a petition[17]. On the other hand if the debt is due and is undisputed the petition will proceed to hearing and adjudication in the normal way. The company is not entitled to have the petition struck out, or prevent its being issued, merely because it is in fact solvent[18]. Alternatively if, having obtained judgment against a company, a creditor enforces the judgment but the execution is returned unsatisfied, that also establishes that the company is unable to pay its debts[19]. The advantage of serving a statutory notice or executing a judgment is that if the notice is not complied with or execution unsatisfied that will establish that the company is unable to pay its debts. But it is not necessary to take these steps. It is sufficient if the creditor can satisfy the court by whatever means that the company owes a debt which is due and unpaid[20].

All the three methods considered so far are based on petitioning creditors who have debts which are immediately due and payable. It might be the case that a creditor has lent money to a company which is not due to be repaid until some date in the future but the creditor is afraid that the present financial position of the company suggests it will not be able to repay the debt when payment is due. Such a creditor could rely on the general ground of showing that the company is now unable to pay its debts as they fall due[1]. Alternatively the creditor might make use of the fourth way of establishing that a company is unable to pay its debts, known as the balance sheet test: on this test a company is also deemed unable to pay its debts if it is proved to the court that the value of a company's assets is less than the

14 Ibid, s 124(2), More precisely, the number of members must have dropped below two, or the member must be an original allottee, or have held the shares for 6 of the 18 months prior to commencement of the winding up, or have succeeded to the shares of a deceased shareholder.
15 A member who is liable to contribute (because, for example, he holds partly-paid shares or the members have unlimited liability) will have an interest as will any member if there is going to be a surplus for distribution to members. But a holder of fully paid shares in a limited company who cannot show that there may be a surplus cannot petition: *Re Rica Gold Washing Co* (1879) 11 Ch D 36, CA. The Jenkins Committee recommended the rule be abolished: Report of the Company Law Committee (Cmnd 1749) para 503(h).
16 Insolvency Act 1986, s 123(1)(a).
17 *Stonegate Securities Ltd v Gregory* [1980] Ch 576, [1980] 1 All ER 241, CA.
18 *Cornhill Insurance plc v Improvement Services Ltd* [1986] 1 WLR 114.
19 Insolvency Act 1986, s 123(1)(b). The judgment must normally be for at least £750: *Re World Industrial Bank Ltd* [1909] WN 148.
20 Insolvency Act 1986, s 123(1)(e). *Taylors Industrial Flooring Ltd v M & H Plant Hire (Manchester) Ltd* [1990] BCLC 216, CA.
 1 Insolvency Act 1986, s 123(1)(e).

amount of its liabilities, taking into account the contingent and prospective liabilities of the company[2].

Having grounds for the presentation of a petition does not necessarily entitle the creditor to the making of a winding-up order. Winding up is a collective or class remedy and an order may be refused if the petitioner is merely seeking to obtain some private advantage[3]. If the purpose of the petition is legitimate, however, it does not matter that the motive of the petitioner is malicious. Purpose here relates to the future: what the petitioner seeks to obtain by the order; motive relates to the past: why the petitioner is motivated to seek winding up. An unsecured creditor does not have to show an interest in the outcome of the winding up. Investigation of past conduct is a legitimate purpose for seeking a winding-up order and one will be granted for that purpose even though it may not produce a return for the unsecured creditors. The test is whether a winding-up order will be useful, not whether it will be fruitful to the unsecured creditors[4].

There may well be differences of opinion among the creditors as to whether winding up should be ordered in which case the court can direct meetings to be held to ascertain the creditors' wishes[5]. A particular aspect of this clash may arise where a company is already in voluntary liquidation and the court is being asked to replace that by a compulsory winding up order. Again the court takes account of the wishes of creditors but it also looks carefully at the quality of the creditors on either side as well as the quantity. It may well happen that some of the creditors are also shareholders or directors of the company or their associates in which case their views may be given far less weight or disregarded altogether[6].

Voluntary winding up

TYPES OF RESOLUTION

A voluntary winding up begins with a resolution passed by the members. An ordinary resolution is sufficient in the rare case of a company whose articles specify that it shall be dissolved after the expiration of a fixed period of time or on the happening of a particular event, and that time has passed or event occurred[7]. More usually a special resolution will be passed[8]. Alternatively, where a company cannot continue its business by reason of its liabilities, an extraordinary resolution will suffice[9]. The reason for this is that in such circumstances it may be desirable to pass a resolution commencing the winding up quickly and it was formerly the case that an extraordinary resolution could be passed far more quickly than a special resolution. Until 1929, a special resolution had to be confirmed at a second general meeting held not less than 14 days and not more than one month after the meeting at

2 Ibid, s 123(2).
3 *Re A Company (No 001573 of 1983)* [1983] BCLC 492. *Re Greenwood & Co* [1900] 2 QB 306. Cf *Re Compania Merabello San Nicholas SA* [1973] Ch 75, [1972] 2 All ER 448.
4 *Re Crigglestone Coal Co Ltd* [1906] 2 Ch 327, CA.
5 Insolvency Act 1986, s 195.
6 *Re Falcon R J Development Ltd* [1987] BCLC 437. *Re H J Tomkins & Son Ltd* [1990] BCLC 76.
7 Insolvency Act 1986, s 84(1)(a).
8 Ibid, s 84(1)(b).
9 Ibid, s 84(1)(c).

which the resolution was first passed. Since the abolition of the requirement for confirmation of a special resolution the only difference between a special and an extraordinary resolution is that a meeting at which a special resolution is to be proposed requires 21 days' notice[10], whereas any other meeting requires only 14 days' notice[11] (except an annual general meeting which requires 21 days)[12]. So even in a case where notice is not waived the difference in the speed with which the two resolutions can be passed is the difference between 21 days and 14 days. Furthermore, the period of notice for meetings (other than annual general meetings) at which extraordinary or special resolutions are to be proposed can be waived with the consent of a majority of members who together hold at least 95% in nominal value of the shares giving a right to attend and vote at the meetings[13]. In cases where the members consent to short notice therefore, there is today no difference at all in the speed with which a special or an extraordinary resolution can be passed so as to commence winding up.

MEMBERS' VOLUNTARY WINDING UP

If in the five weeks before the resolution to wind up the company is passed[14] a majority of the directors[15] make a statutory declaration of solvency[16], the winding up is known as a members' voluntary winding up[17]. Solvency here means that the directors have made a full enquiry into the affairs of the company and have formed the opinion that the company will be able to pay its debts in full within, at most, 12 months of the date of the resolution[18]. The advantage to the directors in making such a declaration will be seen later, particularly in relation to the appointment of the liquidator. The risk in doing so is that if the declaration is made by any directors without reasonable grounds they commit a criminal offence[19] and if the debts are not paid in full within the specified time, that raises a rebuttable presumption that the directors did not have reasonable grounds for making the declaration[20].

CREDITORS' VOLUNTARY WINDING UP

If the directors do not make a statutory declaration of solvency then the winding up is referred to as a creditors' voluntary winding up[1]. In addition to

---

10 Section 378(2).
11 Section 369(1)(b).
12 Section 369(1)(a).
13 Section 378(3) and s 369(4).
14 Insolvency Act 1986, s 89(2)(a).
15 Ibid, s 89(1).
16 The statutory declaration must be delivered for registration within 15 days after the resolution is passed: Insolvency Act 1986, s 89(3). Failure to do so gives rise to criminal penalties but, on the analogy of the treatment of other resolutions requiring registration, probably does not make the declaration itself invalid or ineffective: Insolvency Act 1986, s 89(6).
17 Insolvency Act 1986, s 90.
18 Ibid, s 89(1).
19 Ibid, s 89(4).
20 Ibid, s 89(5).
 1 Ibid, s 90. Creditors' voluntary liquidations and compulsory liquidations, which we may assume are nearly all on the grounds that the company cannot pay its debts, together constitute the insolvent liquidations. According to the Department of Trade and Industry Annual Report on Companies, in the 12 months to 31 March 1990 there were 6,782 creditors' voluntary liquidations and 4,289 compulsory liquidations which would give a total of 11,071 insolvent liquidations compared to 3,984 members' voluntary liquidations.

the meeting of members called to pass a resolution for the company to go into liquidation, a meeting of creditors must be summoned to take place not more than 14 days after the members' meeting[2] and the directors must lay before the meeting a statement of the company's affairs together with a list of creditors and their debts[3].

THE LIQUIDATOR

Appointment

In a compulsory winding up, if, on the hearing of the winding-up petition the court makes a winding-up order[4], the Official Receiver will become the liquidator[5]. If he considers it worthwhile, or if 25% in value of creditors request it, the Official Receiver then calls separate meetings of creditors and of members[6]. Each meeting may then nominate a liquidator, though, in the event of different nominations, the creditors' nominee will be appointed[7]. If no meetings are held or no nominations made the Official Receiver remains as liquidator[8]. In a members' voluntary winding up, the members appoint the liquidator[9]. In a creditors' voluntary winding up, if the members and creditors cannot agree then the creditors' nominee is appointed[10]. This illustrates one of the real differences between a members' and creditors' voluntary winding up because the members' nominee as liquidator, as often as not probably a person chosen by the directors, may be expected to be far less inquisitive about the directors' past conduct of the company's business. Since 1986, whoever is appointed as liquidator, whether in a compulsory or voluntary liquidation, apart from the Official Receiver[11], must be a qualified insolvency practitioner in relation to the company concerned[12]. This means, among other things, that he or she must be an individual[13], in respect of

2 Insolvency Act 1986, s 98(1)(a).
3 Ibid, s 99.
4 The court has power to appoint a provisional liquidator prior to the making of the winding-up order: ibid, s 135.
5 Ibid, s 136(2). Official Receivers are employees of the Department of Trade and Industry. There is one nominated to every court having winding-up jurisdication.
6 Ibid, s 136(4)(5).
7 Ibid, s 139(2)(3).
8 There is provision for the Secretary of State to appoint a liquidator in certain circumstances: ibid s 137. In a compulsory winding up the Official Receiver has certain investigative functions designed to protect the public interest by ensuring that fraud or other malpractice is detected and dealt with: ibid, ss 131–134.
9 Ibid, s 91(1).
10 Ibid, s 100. Since the members' meeting will have taken place first any nominee of that meeting will have become liquidator prior to the creditors' meeting being held. Until the creditors' meeting is held, however, such a liquidator, without the consent of the court, has power only to protect and preserve the company's property or to dispose of perishable items: ibid, s 166. Before this change was made it was not unknown for unscrupulous members and directors to appoint a liquidator who would dispose of the company's assets, often to nominees or friends of the directors or members, before the creditors' meeting could be held: see the Sunday Times, 26 April 1981, p 62.
11 Insolvency Act 1986, s 388(5).
12 For the background to these changes see the Report of the Review Committee on Insolvency Law and Practice (Cmnd 8558) ch 15.
13 Insolvency Act 1986, s 390(1).

whom appropriate financial security is in force[14], who is authorised either as a member of a recognised professional body[15] or as an individual by the Secretary of State[16] and who is independent of the company concerned[17].

Powers and duties

The basic duty of the liquidator in all types of liquidation is to collect in and realise the company's assets. In a compulsory liquidation, the directors' functions cease and the liquidator takes into his custody and control the company's property[18]. In a voluntary winding up, the power of the board ceases save in so far as they are allowed to continue by the liquidation committee in a creditors' voluntary winding up[19] or by the general meeting or the liquidator in a members' voluntary winding up[20]. In the event of any of the members still being liable to pay sums to the company on partly-paid shares, or shares with unlimited liability, these will be paid to the liquidator[1].

In connection with collecting contributions from shareholders it is remarkable that it is still uncertain exactly what is the limit on the liability of a shareholder in a limited liability company. Since 1856 successive Companies Acts have contained a statement, presently found in the Insolvency Act 1986, s 74(2)(d), that 'in the case of a company limited by shares, no contribution is required from any member exceeding the amount (if any) unpaid on the shares'. In *Niemann v Smedley*[2] shares with a nominal value of five shillings were issued to various subscribers at ten shillings each. When the company went into liquidation some subscribers had paid ten shillings, some five shillings and some nothing. In the liquidator's application to recover ten shillings from each subscriber it was held he could recover only up to the nominal value of five shillings. He could not recover the full ten shillings despite each subscriber having promised to pay that sum. The court relied on dicta of the House of Lords in *Ooregum Gold Mining Co of India v Roper*[3] although in that case the House of Lords was concerned with a purported issue of shares at below the nominal value and did not have in mind the situation where shares are issued at above the nominal value. Furthermore since 1948 companies have been obliged to credit any premium received on the issue of shares to the share premium account and to treat such sum as part of the capital to be maintained. Although, where shares are issued on a partly paid basis, the share premium account will only be

---

14 Ibid, s 390(3).
15 Ibid, ss 390(2)(a) and 391.
16 Ibid, ss 390(2)(b) and 393.
17 Ibid, s 419(2)(b) together with the Insolvency Practitioners Regulations 1990, SI 1990/439.
18 Insolvency Act 1986, s 144(1).
19 Ibid, s 103. The liquidation committee which may be set up in either a compulsory or creditors' voluntary winding up consists of creditors' and members' representatives and exercises various functions in relation to the liquidation: see ibid, ss 141 and 101. Provision as to the functions, membership and proceedings of such committees is included in the Insolvency Rules, SI 1986/1925 rr 4.152 ff.
20 Insolvency Act 1986, s 91(2).
1 As to the order in which members' contributions are collected, see ibid, s 74(2). In compulsory winding up the court settles the list of contributories: ibid, s 148; in voluntary winding up it is done by the liquidator: ibid, s 165(4)(a).
2 [1973] VR 769, Victoria Supreme Court.
3 [1982] AC 125 at 135–6 per Lord Watson.

credited when the premium is received by the company it is likely that creditors will rely on the fact that shareholders have promised to pay up a sum in excess of the often very low nominal values that shares have nowadays. Even if creditors are not misled it is submitted that it was unfair in *Niemann v Smedley* on those shareholders who had paid up the full issue price to allow other shareholders to avoid paying more than the nominal value. In the event of there being a surplus to return to shareholders it would surely be wrong, in calculating the surplus, to disregard amounts unpaid on shares, just because the nominal value had been paid[4].

The office of liquidator was first introduced in the Joint Stock Companies Act 1856, which replaced an earlier system of official managers in whom the property of the company had vested[5]. In the case of the liquidator the property is not automatically vested in him unless the court so orders under the Insolvency Act 1986, s 145. Liquidators are in a fiduciary relationship with the company. Thus they must not make any unauthorised profit from their position[6] and any purchase by them of the company's property is liable to be set side[7]. Liquidators may also be liable for negligence in realising the company's property[8]. While the liquidation is in progress individual contributories or creditors can apply to the court to control the exercise of any of the liquidator's powers[9] or they may use the summary procedure under the Insolvency Act 1986, s 212[10] to ask the court to compel the liquidator to restore property to the company or compensate it for breach of duty. The power to make an application under s 212 continues after the winding-up is completed and notwithstanding the release of the liquidator from all liability connected with the liquidation[11], but any application in these circumstances need the court's consent[12]. Although the liquidator's duty is thus enforceable on the application of individual contributories or creditors, the duty is owed to the company. Ordinarily liquidators owe no duty to individual contributories or creditors. So in *Knowles v Scott*[13] a liquidator was not liable

---

4 This conclusion is supported by provisions of the Second Directive 77/91/EEC OJ 1977 L 26/1. Whilst art 8 makes clear the 'Shares may not be issued at a price lower than their nominal value' art 12 states that 'the shareholders may not be released from the obligation to pay up their contributions'. Unless the 'contribution' referred to could be a figure higher than the nominal value, art 12 adds nothing to what is stated in art 8. It is submitted that contributions refers to the issue price and that shareholders are therefore liable to pay up the nominal value plus the premium and must not be released from that liability.

5 See further Dr B H Mcpherson, *The Law of Company Liquidation* (3rd edn, 1987) pp 205–206.

6 *Re R Gertzenstein Ltd* [1957] Ch 115—solicitor liquidator not entitled to profit costs for doing work in his professional capacity in the liquidation. Compare Insolvency Rules 1986, SI 1986/1925, r 4.128(3) which allows such profit costs provided they are authorised by the liquidation committee, the creditors or the court.

7 *Silkstone and Haigh Moor Coal Co v Edey* [1900] 1 Ch 167. See also Insolvency Rules 1986, SI 1986/1925, r 4.149.

8 *Re Windsor Steam Coal Co (1901) Ltd* [1928] Ch 609.

9 Under the Insolvency Act 1986, ss 167(3) or 168(5) in compulsory liquidation and s 112(3) in voluntary liquidation. The court will not grant an injunction to retrain a proposed transaction on a mere allegation of negligence by the liquidator: *Leon v York-O-Matic Ltd* [1966] 3 All ER 277, [1966] 1 WLR 1450; *Harold M Pitman & Co v Top Business Systems (Nottingham) Ltd* [1984] BCLC 593.

10 Contributories need the court's consent to apply: Insolvency Act 1986, s 212(5).

11 Ibid, ss 173(4) and 174(6).

12 Ibid, s 212(4).

13 [1891] 1 Ch 717.

for loss caused by delay in making a distribution to a contributory. During the liquidation the remedy for contributories or creditors who are aggrieved by the way their own claims are being dealt with by the liquidator is to apply to the court for an order under its jurisdiction to control the exercise of the liquidator's powers[14]. This remedy is not available after the liquidation is completed and the company dissolved. In these circumstances the courts have been prepared to recognise a right of action against the former liquidator by an individual creditor whom the liquidator had negligently failed to inform about the liquidation and who thus did not discover about the liquidation until after the company had been dissolved[15].

In order to fulfil their duties liquidators are given a wide range of powers, some of which can be exercised of their own volition entirely, others of which need the appropriate consent. In a compulsory or creditors' voluntary winding up, the consent needed is that of either the court or the liquidation committee if one has been appointed[16]. In a members' voluntary winding up the consent is given by the members by extraordinary resolution[17]. One of the most important decisions liquidators will have to take is whether to keep the company's business going and if so, for how long. It should be noted that liquidators may only do so, so far as may be necessary for the beneficial winding up of the business[18]. This has been interpreted to mean they may do so if this may be expected to produce a better return for the creditors but not if the object is to seek to continue or resuscitate the business for the benefit of the members[19]. Furthermore in a compulsory winding up liquidators must obtain the consent of the court or the liquidation committee to a decision to carry on the business[20].

Where liquidators do carry on the business for its beneficial winding up they do so as agents of the company. Any contracts a liquidator makes will be between the company and the outsider and the liquidator will incur no personal liability[1]. Any claims by outsiders against the company will also rank as expenses of the winding up and thus be paid first out of any available assets[2]. If, however, the liquidator carries on the business when it was not

---

14 Insolvency Act 1986, ss 167(3) and 168(5) in compulsory liquidation and s 112(3) in voluntary liquidation. For a recent example see *Re Linda Marie Ltd* [1989] BCLC 46. It may also be possible to apply under the Insolvency Act 1986, s 212 because an amendment made in 1986 makes clear that the section covers breach of any duty in connection with the carrying out of the liquidator's functions: s 212(2). However, the remedies the court can grant under s 212 are all remedies in favour of the company, not in favour of individual creditors: s 212(3).

15 *Pulsford v Devenish* [1903] 2 Ch 625.

16 Insolvency Act 1986, ss 167(1) and 165(2)(b). Consent should be sought first from the liquidation committee and application to the court made if consent is refused or given subject to conditions the liquidator will not accept. The liquidator should tell the committee of his application to the court so that their views may be heard as well: *Re Consolidated Diesel Engine Manufacturers Ltd* [1915] 1 Ch 192.

17 Insolvency Act 1986, s 165(2)(a).

18 Ibid, Sch 4, para 5.

19 *Re Wreck Recovery and Salvage Co* (1880) 15 Ch D 353, CA.

20 The committee's sanction cannot be given retrospectively and if the liquidator contracts without consent he will be personally liable to the other party for breach of warranty of authority. The court, however, has power to give a retrospective sanction: *Re Associated Travel Leisure and Services Ltd* [1978] 2 All ER 273, [1978] 1 WLR 547.

1 *Re Anglo-Moravian Hungarian Junction Rly Co, ex p Watkin* (1875) 1 Ch D 130, CA; *Stead, Hazel & Co v Cooper* [1933] 1 KB 840.

2 *Re Great Eastern Electric Co Ltd* [1941] Ch 241, [1941] 1 All ER 409.

necessary for its beneficial winding up it seems the creditors have no claim against the company at all, although presumably they could sue the liquidator for breach of warranty of authority. On the other hand, the company may enforce claims against the creditors, at least where the contract has been performed by the company[3].

DISSOLUTION OF THE COMPANY

Dissolution after winding up

After completion of the winding-up process, the company will cease to exist by being removed from the register at Companies House, a process known as dissolution. In both compulsory[4] and voluntary[5] liquidations this occurs automatically three months after the registration of the liquidator's final return at Companies House. Because Official Receivers in the past frequently ended up having to deal with compulsory liquidations where there were very few, if any, assets they now have the power to apply to the Registrar for dissolution without winding up, if the assets are insufficient to cover the expenses and the affairs of the company do not warrant investigation[6].

Striking off the register

The majority of companies that are dissolved in England and Wales each year are never formally wound up at all. Instead they cease to exist when the Registrar strikes them off the register which can be done if the Registrar has reasonable cause to believe the company is not carrying on business or is not in operation[7]. The procedure is for the Registrar to write, enquiring about the company's activities, to the company and anyone whose names appear as officers of the company on the company's file or who have filed documents on behalf of the company. The Registrar naturally picks companies which have failed to file annual returns and accounts because that may suggest the company has ceased trading. Frequently, however, it reveals no more than that the company has an idle management and the threat of being struck off the register concentrates the minds of those running the company on the need to fulfil filing obligations. But in many cases, companies have become moribund and are struck off the register.

Restoration to the register

After a company has been removed from the register having been wound up, it may be discovered that the company owned other property or owed other debts. It is therefore provided that the company may be revived within two

---

3 *Bateman & Co v Ball* (1887) 56 LJ QB 291; *Hire Purchase Furnishing Co v Richens* (1887) 20 QBD 387, CA.
4 Insolvency Act 1986, s 205(1)(2).
5 Ibid, s 201(1)(2).
6 Ibid, s 202(1)(2)(5).
7 Section 652. According to the Department of Trade and Industry's Annual Report on Companies, in the 12 months to 31 March 1990, 68,963 companies were struck off under s 652.

years of the dissolution by order of the court and on such terms as the court orders[8]. Once the two year period is over, it seems there is very little a creditor whose debt has only just come to light can do[9]. An attempt to argue that the declaration of solvency was invalid, since of necessity it did not take account of the complainants' debt, failed[10]. Likewise, an attempt to make the members, as overpaid recipients, liable in equity to reimburse the underpaid newly discovered creditor also failed[11]. On the other hand, where the company is struck off without winding up then the court may restore the company to the register at any time within 20 years[12]. When a company is restored to the register, property which had vested in the Crown as bona vacantia[13] re-vests in the company but any disposition of the property in the meantime is valid, the Crown being liable to account for any consideration received[14].

DISTRIBUTION OF ASSETS

Proof of debts

Contrary to what might be supposed, the administration of an insolvent debtor's estate does not involve the payment and discharge of *all* the debts owing by the debtor. Instead, it is only those debts which are provable in the insolvency and which are proved which will receive any payment. In the case of an individual debtor who is made bankrupt the hardship on a creditor who has a non-provable debt is alleviated by the fact that the discharge of a debtor from bankruptcy does not release the debtor from any non-provable debts[15]. The creditor who will not have been able to claim in the bankruptcy can therefore enforce his claim against the debtor notwithstanding the debtor's discharge from bankruptcy. The concept of discharge from winding up, however, is unknown. Instead, when the winding up is complete, the company is inexorably dissolved. The company will thereafter not even

---

8 Section 651(1). A limited amendment to s 651 was made by the Companies Act 1989, s 141 which extends indefinitely the period for declaring void a dissolution of a company after winding up. The extension, however, only applies for the purposes of bringing proceedings against the company in respect of death or personal injuries and does not apply if it appears to the court that the proceedings would in any case be statute barred. The reasons for allowing such proceedings are two fold. First the death or personal injury may not have become apparent until after the company had been dissolved (for example in the case of disease). Secondly, the proceedings will be worthwhile if the company was insured for such liability because the proceeds will go to the plaintiff under the Third Party (Rights Against Insurers) Act 1930 (see below p 701). The amendment deals with the problem highlighted by *Bradley v Eagle Star Insurance Co Ltd* [1989] AC 957, [1989] 1 All ER 961, HL.

9 Where the liquidator negligently failed to notify a creditor that the liquidation was taking place an action against the liquidator may be possible: *Pulsford v Devenish* [1903] 2 Ch 625. Any liability of the liquidator for breach of duty remains enforceable under the Insolvency Act 1986, s 212 notwithstanding the liquidator's general release from liability, but proceedings may only be brought with leave of the court: s 212(4).

10 *De Courcy v Clement* [1971] Ch 693, [1971] 1 All ER 681.

11 *Butler v Broadhead* [1975] Ch 97, [1974] 2 All ER 401. It may be that had the predecessor of the Insolvency Act 1986, s 159 been cited to the court the decision would have been different: see Goff and Jones *The Law of Restitution* (3rd edn, 1987) p 576.

12 Section 653.

13 Section 654.

14 Section 655.

15 Insolvency Act 1986, s 281(1)(b).

exist, let alone possess any assets out of which a creditor with a non-provable debt might seek payment. Nevertheless there are rules which specify which debts are provable and what procedure is to be followed in establishing the claim[16].

The principal rule restricting which debts are provable is that the company must have been liable on the debt before going into liquidation[17]. In a compulsory liquidation this is the date of the winding-up order and in a voluntary liquidation the date of the resolution putting the company into liquidation[18]. It does not matter that at the time when the debt was incurred the creditor knew that a winding-up petition had been presented or that a meeting had been called to vote on a resolution putting the company into liquidation[19]. Nor does it matter that the actual debt or liability arose after the company had gone into liquidation provided this is in respect of an obligation incurred before the company went into liquidation. Thus a contractual promise, entered into before going into liquidation, to pay a sum of money at a date occurring after the company has gone into liquidation gives rise to a provable debt. Similarly a contractual obligation undertaken by the company before going into liquidation, but which is broken and thus gives rise to liability in damages only after the company is in liquidation, also creates a provable liability[20]. In contrast tortious obligations only arise when the damage occurs. Accordingly, a claim will not be provable against the manufacturer of a defective product who put it in circulation before going into liquidation if the injury only occurred after the company had gone into liquidation. Provided, however, a tortious injury occurred before the company went into liquidation the liability in respect of it is provable and it does

---

16 The Companies Act 1862 had provided that in the winding up of a company *all* debts were provable: 25 & 26 Vic c 89, s 158. This was modified by the Judicature Act 1875, s 10 which provided that in the case of insolvent companies the bankruptcy rules as to proof of debt should apply. The reason for the modification was to extend to insolvent winding up the bankruptcy rule that secured creditors could only prove in respect of any unsecured portion of their debt. The wording, however, was considerably wider than that. For the history of how the modification came about and the difficulties it gave rise to, see the first edition of this work pp 569 ff. Although both provisions were repeated in every subsequent Companies Act, including the Companies Act 1985, they were repealed by the Insolvency Act 1985. The provisions as to proof of debt in winding up now appear in the Insolvency Rules 1986, SI 1986/1925, rr 4.73–4.94 with the rules as to proof by secured creditors in rr 4.95–4.99.

17 Oddly this is not stated expressly anywhere in the Insolvency Rules, though it is apparent from the prescribed form for Proof of Debt (Form 4.25). It follows that if a creditor lends money to a company after it has gone into liquidation the creditor cannot prove for that sum, even though the creditor was unaware of the liquidation at the time of the loan. The creditor may, however, be able to trace the money: *Re Thellusson, ex p Abdy* [1919] 2 KB 735, CA. The priority this gives the creditor in the insolvency is, however, unjustifiable if the creditor intended to be an unsecured creditor and was therefore taking the normal risk as to the debtor's solvency.

18 Insolvency Act 1986, s 247(2).

19 Until 1986 such knowledge would have prevented the debt being provable: Bankruptcy Act 1914, s 30(2) applied to companies by Companies Act 1985, s 612. The provision was repealed following a recommendation of the Cork Committee (Cmnd 8558) para 1294. The new rule may seem to be open to abuse but any fraudulent collusion between the company and a creditor would be open to attack under other provisions. See below p 705ff.

20 *Re Charge Card Services Ltd* [1987] Ch 150, [1986] 3 All ER 289, cf *Carreras Rothmans Ltd v Freeman Mathews Treasure Ltd* [1985] Ch 207 at 230, [1985] 1 All ER 155 at 171 where, however, the earlier decision of *Re Asphaltic Wood Pavement Co* (1885) 30 Ch D 216, CA was not cited.

not matter that the damages are not quantified until after the company is in liquidation[1]. The liquidator is, in fact given specific power to estimate the value of contingent liabilities or debts of an uncertain amount[2]. In the case of secured creditors, if they are content to rely solely on their security they do not submit a proof of debt at all. Alternatively they may value their security and prove for any unsecured balance[3] or realise their security and prove for any unsecured balance[4] or surrender their security and prove for the whole amount[5].

A further restriction on the amount for which creditors may prove arises from the rules of set-off[6]. The effect of these rules is that if creditors of a company also owe money to the company they must set off the debts against each other and can only prove for the balance[7]. In practice, set-off benefits creditors because the debts they owe the company are assets of the company, the proceeds of which would normally be made available to all creditors. To the extent that creditors can set off debts they owe the company against debts the company owes them, creditors are able to use assets of the company exclusively for their own benefit in a way which is akin to security[8]. Creditors will therefore seek to acquire rights of set-off[9] but again there are limitations. Thus, the dealings giving rise to the set-off must occur before the company goes into liquidation[10]. Likewise there can be no set-off where the creditors, at the time the sums became due to them from the company, knew of the summoning of the meeting of creditors (in the case of a creditors' voluntary winding up) or the presentation of the petition (in the case of a compulsory winding up)[11].

Order of distribution of assets

A second popular conception which in practice rarely turns out to be correct is that in the case of an insolvent company, the creditors rank equally and are paid rateably according to the size of their debts. In fact, there is a strict hierarchy in which the assets must be applied. Top of the list are the costs, charges and expenses of the winding up[12]. The expenses of the winding up will include items such as rent on premises which the liquidator uses to store

---

1 Insolvency Act 1986, s 382(2). This was a reversal of the previous rule, as recommended by the Cork Committee (Cmnd 8558) paras 1310–1318. For the problems the previous rule presented and the contortions it required see the first edition of this work p 570.
2 Insolvency Rules 1986, SI 1986/1925, r 4.86.
3 Insolvency Rules 1986, SI 1986/1925 r 4.75(1)(g). As to the liquidator's right to redeem the security at the creditor's valuation see ibid, r 4.97.
4 Ibid, r 4.88(1).
5 Ibid, r 4.88(2).
6 Ibid, r 4.90.
7 Provided both debts arise out of mutual dealings; for example, that both transactions were entered into in the same capacity. A creditor who is owed both secured and unsecured debts by the company is entitled to exercise the right of set-off against the unsecured part of the total debt since it is only in respect of that amount that the creditor will be submitting a proof: *Re Norman Holding Co Ltd* [1990] 3 All ER 757, [1991] 1 WLR 10.
8 Despite this creditors are not allowed to contract out of their right of set-off: *National Westminster Bank Ltd v Halesowen Presswork and Assemblies Ltd* [1972] AC 785, [1972] 1 All ER 641, HL.
9 For example, *Re Eros Films Ltd* [1963] Ch 565, [1963] 1 All ER 383.
10 Insolvency Rules 1986, SI 1986/1925, r 4.90(1). See also footnote 13 above.
11 Ibid, r 4.90(3).
12 Insolvency Act 1986, ss 115 and 156.

assets pending realisation[13] and, if it is necessary to carry on the business of the company for the beneficial winding up of it, any debts incurred in so carrying on the business[14]. It will also include the remuneration of the liquidator.

PREFERENTIAL DEBTS

Next in order of priority comes a group of claimants whose debts Parliament has felt have a claim to priority over other unsecured creditors. In so far as there are insufficient assets to meet these preferential claims in full, they all rank equally and abate proportionately[15].

The creditors granted preferential status consist chiefly of central government and employees. Thus sums due from the company to the Inland Revenue in respect of deductions of income tax from emoluments paid during the 12 months before winding up[16] are preferential[17]. Various duties for which the company is liable to Customs and Excise are also treated as preferential[18]. The Department of Health and Social Security is given priority for social security contributions[19] payable in the 12 months before winding up and employers' contributions to occupational pension schemes and state pensions have similar priority[20].

Employees are entitled to claim as a preferential debt wages or salary for services rendered in the four months[1] before winding up[16] but up to a maximum amount of £800 per employee[2]. Four further species of payment are to be treated as wages for this purpose and are thus accorded priority but are subject to the four-month and £800 limits[3]. In addition all accrued holiday remuneration has priority and is not counted towards the £800 limit[4]. If any wages or accrued holiday pay which would have had priority have been paid with money advanced for that purpose by someone else, the lender is subrogated to the claim so paid and thus enjoys the same priority[5].

---

13 *Re ABC Coupler and Engineering Co Ltd (No 3)* [1970] 1 All ER 650, [1970] 1 WLR 702; *Re Downer Enterprises Ltd* [1974] 2 All ER 1074, [1974] 1 WLR 1460.
14 *Re Great Eastern Electric Co Ltd* [1941] Ch 241, [1941] 1 All ER 409.
15 Insolvency Act 1986, s 175(2)(a). The preferential debts also have priority over the claims of holders of debentures under a floating charge: s 175(2)(b). A creditor owed preferential and non-preferential debts must exercise any right of set-off proportionately against each class of debt: *Re Unit 2 Windows Ltd* [1985] 3 All ER 647, [1985] 1 WLR 1383.
16 For the precise point from which the 12 months runs back in a winding-up, see Insolvency Act 1986, s 387(3).
17 Ibid, Sch 6, paras 1 and 2. As recommended by the Cork Committee (Cmnd 8558) paras 1409–1427, all rates and assessed taxes ceased to be preferential under the Insolvency Act.
18 Insolvency Act, Sch 6, paras 3–5.
19 Ibid, Sch 6, paras 6, 7.
20 Ibid, Sch 6, para 8.
 1 Ibid, Sch 6, para 9.
 2 The Insolvency Proceedings (Monetary Limits) Order 1986, SI 1986/1996, art 4.
 3 Insolvency Act 1986, Sch 6, para 13.
 4 Ibid, Sch 6, para 10.
 5 Ibid, Sch 6, para 11. The money used to pay wages must have been lent for that purpose but it does not matter that it was not lent only for that purpose; *Re Primrose (Builders) Ltd* [1950] Ch 561, [1950] 2 All ER 334; *Re Rampgill Mill Ltd* [1967] Ch 1138, [1967] 1 All ER 56. This is wider than the right of a surety to be subrogated to the preferential status of a creditor paid off by the surety, whether at common law or under the Mercantile Law Amendment Act 1856. The right of subrogation by a surety depends on the surety being liable directly to the creditor concerned; *Re Lamplugh Iron Ore Co* [1927] 1 Ch 308.

Although giving wages and salaries preferential status is likely to go a long way towards ensuring that employees receive unpaid arrears it does not ensure that they will receive them quickly. It was to deal with this problem that a major innovation was made in 1975 whereby certain payments to employees of insolvent companies are guaranteed by the state[6]. The payments, which must not exceed £198[7] per employee per week, are made out of the National Insurance Fund and include arrears of wages or salaries for up to eight weeks and up to six weeks' holiday pay to which the employee may have become entitled in the 12 months before winding up. Both these payments could rank as preferential in the winding up and once a payment has been made out of the redundancy fund, the fund is subrogated to the employee's claim, including any preferential status[8].

ORDINARY UNSECURED DEBTS

If there is any money left after discharging the costs and expenses of the winding up and paying the secured and preferential creditors, it must be used to pay the ordinary creditors who will rank equally and whose debts therefore abate proportionately, if there is insufficient to pay them in full[9]. So strong is the principle that the creditors rank equally that a rule (known as 'the rule in *Ex p Mackay*'[10], after the bankruptcy case in which it was laid down) developed that any contractual provision designed to prefer one unsecured creditor ahead of the others is void. Provided, however, that the provision was not designed to prefer one creditor it did not matter that it incidentally had the effect of doing so. Thus, a provision in a standard form building contract whereby if the main contractor unduly delays payment to a sub-contractor the employer may make a direct payment to the sub-contractor out of money due to the main contractor, would not be invalidated even if the delay was due to the main contractor's insolvency and the direct payment had the effect of giving the sub-contractor more money than it would have received as a creditor in the winding up of the main contractor[11]. However, by a majority of 3:2, the House of Lords held in *British Eagle International Airlines Ltd v Cie Nationale Air France*[12] that the rule in *Ex p Mackay*[10] did not depend on intention but invalidated any provision that had the effect of preferring one creditor or group of creditors over the rest. Whether this will continue to be the law and what its impact will be remains to be seen. Its effect can be avoided if the contract can be drafted so that the asset diverted to the creditor preferred does not belong to

6 Employment Protection (Consolidation) Act 1978, s 122.
7 Employment Protection (Variation of Limits) Order 1991, SI 1991/464.
8 Employment Protection (Consolidation) Act 1978, s 125.
9 This is specifically stated in regard to voluntary liquidation in the Insolvency Act 1986, s 107 but there is no doubt that it applies to compulsory liquidation as well.
10 *Re Jeavons, ex p MacKay, ex p Brown* (1873) 8 Ch App 643.
11 *Re Wilkinson, ex p Fowler* [1905] 2 KB 713; *Re Tout and Finch Ltd* [1954] 1 All ER 127, [1954] 1 WLR 178.
12 [1975] 2 All ER 390, [1975] 1 WLR 758, HL. See also *Carreras Rothmans Ltd v Freeman Mathews Treasure Ltd* [1985] Ch 207 at 227–229, [1985] 1 All ER 155 at 169–170 where, however, the same decision would have been reached applying the principle in *Re Jeavons, ex p Mackay, ex p Brown* because the debtor had the intention of preferring a specific group of its creditors.

the debtor and is not therefore available for distribution among the creditors generally[13].

The principle of pari passu distribution is further reinforced by a provision introduced in 1986, restricting public utilities from claiming preferential payment of pre-winding-up debts[14]. After a company has gone into liquidation the suppliers of gas, electricity, water or telecommunications cannot make it a condition of any further supply that charges outstanding for supplies given before winding up are paid; neither can they do anything which has the effect of making further supply subject to such a condition[15]. Any such supply given after the company is in liquidation will normally rank as an expense of winding up and thus is likely to be paid in full but the supplier is permitted to make it a condition of such supply that the liquidator personally guarantees payment of the charges[16].

DEFERRED DEBTS

Next in priority come a number of debts which rank in order after the ordinary debts have been paid. The first of these is interest on all proved debts, whether or not the debt was an interest bearing debt, from the company going into liquidation until the date of actual payment[17]. It is specifically provided that for the purposes of interest under this provision all debts rank pari passu and it makes no difference, for example, whether the debt was preferential[18]. The rate of interest payable under this provision is that payable on judgment debts or, if the debt carried interest at a rate higher than that, such higher rate[19].

The second deferred debt arises where a company has contracted to redeem or purchase some of its own shares and although completion is due the company has not completed the transaction when it commences winding up. The company may be compelled to complete[20] the bargain but only after all other debts and liabilities of the company (other than any due to members in their character as such) have been paid[1].

The third and final deferred payment is any debt or liability due to the members in their character as such whether by way of dividends, profits or otherwise[2]. It will be apparent that debts to members in other capacities such as trade creditor or lender rank alongside similar debts due to non-members. This can be a source of abuse. A company may be incorporated with a share capital of, say, two £1 shares and the shareholders then lend the company all

---

13 See e g *Carreras Rothmans Ltd v Freeman Matthews Treasure Ltd* supra at 224–226, 167–169. Avoiding the consequences of the *British Eagle* decision is one of the purposes behind the introduction, in the Companies Act 1989, Part VII, of an entirely new legislative structure to govern the settlement of a defaulter's debts on financial markets, although the new structure goes further and isolates such clearance schemes and default procedures from general insolvency law altogether.
14 See the Cork Report (Cmnd 8558) paras 1451–1466.
15 Insolvency Act 1986, s 233(2)(b).
16 Ibid, s 233(2)(a).
17 Ibid, s 189.
18 Ibid, s 189(3).
19 Ibid, s 189(4). Where the debt carried interest it may, however, be vulnerable as an extortionate credit transaction: ibid, s 244.
20 Section 178(4).
1 Section 178(6).
2 Insolvency Act 1986, s 74(2)(f). *Re L B Holliday & Co Ltd* [1986] 2 All ER 367.

the money it needs for its business. Morever, since they control the company it will be a simple matter for them to secure their loan on the assets of the company. So when the crunch comes, the shareholders, in their capacity as secured creditors, will be the first to be paid. This is the more remarkable bearing in mind that loans by one spouse to another are postponed to other creditors[3] as are loans by a partner to a partnership[4] and loans by a non-partner for use in a business at a rate of interest varying with profits[5]. The Cork Committee considered this vital question and recommended that 'on the winding up of a company those of its liabilities, whether secured or unsecured, which are owed to connected persons or companies, and which appear to the court to represent all or part of the long term capital structure of the company, shall be deferred to the claims of other creditors and be paid only after all such claims have been met in full'[6]. Regrettably the Committee's recommendation was not enacted in the form they proposed. The courts have, however, been given the power to defer debts due from the company to persons found liable for fraudulent or wrongful trading in relation to it[7].

It is submitted that there is no actual authority that loans by shareholders which in reality represent the capital of the company cannot be deferred to the claims of outside creditors. The only reported decision directly on the question of deferring shareholder loans is *Re Overend, Gurney & Co, Grissell's Case*[8]. The trial judge did in fact order that repayment of a loan to a creditor who was also a shareholder should be postponed to the claims of outside creditors on the analogy of the position in partnership law. The Court of Appeal reversed this and held that in company law repayment of loans due to shareholders is not postponed. But on the facts any other result would have been very unfair. The company's business was that of banking and the shareholder, one of several hundred if not several thousand, became a creditor by virtue of being a depositor with the bank. It is hard to imagine a case further removed from that of the one-man company or wholly-owned subsidiary financed entirely out of loan capital provided by its sole shareholder, and provided moreover on terms that no commercial lender would have accepted. Given the right set of facts, therefore, it is not impossible that an enterprising liquidator might still persuade a court to do justice to the outside creditors and order the postponement of debts which were essentially the risk capital of the company.

---

3 Ibid, s 329.
4 Partnership Act 1890, s 44(b), r 2.
5 Ibid, s 3.
6 Cmnd 8558, para 1963. The Cork Committee suggested that a change would require legislation because it involves breaching the pari passu rule which, as we have seen, cannot be contracted out of. But while legislation may be desirable, the courts have managed to develop similar principles in bankruptcy in cases like *Re Beale* (1876) 4 Ch D 246 and *Re Meade (Bankrupt)* [1951] Ch 774, [1951] 2 All ER 168 despite an equivalent statutory pari passu rule in the Insolvency Act 1986, s 328(3).
7 Insolvency Act, 1986, s 215(4). In fraudulent trading this covers persons knowingly party to the carrying on of business. In wrongful trading it covers directors and shadow directors. Arguably the latter might in certain circumstances include parent companies which have financed subsidiaries through loans rather than shares. This was one of the situations the Cork Committee were particularly concerned about.
8 (1866) 1 Ch App 528.

ASSETS AVAILABLE FOR DISTRIBUTION

Rules governing what property is available for creditors

There is not space here for a detailed discussion of all the rules governing what property is available to the creditors of an insolvent debtor[9]. This section therefore concentrates on the most important of the rules as they affect companies. The basic proposition in insolvency is that all the property of a debtor must be made available to the creditors. A company cannot therefore validly agree that on its insolvency its property shall be applied in a particular way and not made available to its creditors generally[10]. However, a transferor of property to the debtor can validly provide that the debtor only has an interest until insolvency[11]. Thus it has long been accepted that a condition in a lease terminating the lease on the tenant going into liquidation or making a composition or arrangement with creditors is valid[12], even though the effect may be to remove a valuable asset from the creditors[13].

SECURED CREDITORS

The rights of secured creditors do, of course, deprive the creditors generally of a large part of the assets but this is not an exception to the basic rule set out above. The property remains the debtor's, with the secured creditors merely having a right to a prior claim on the proceeds of realisation. Nevertheless, the fact that the claims of secured and preferential creditors frequently leave the unsecured creditors with very little has led to the adoption of new devices to protect unsecured creditors and led the Cork Committee to recommend that 10% of the net realisations of assets subject to a floating charge should be put aside for the unsecured creditors[14]. The White Paper, however, rejected this proposal[15] and it has not been implemented.

TRUST PROPERTY

It is only property to which the company is beneficially entitled that is available to its creditors. If the company holds property on trust for others, that property is not available to the company's creditors[16]. This has led to the

---

9 See R M Goode *Principles of Corporate Insolvency Law* (1990) Ch 4.
10 *Higinbotham v Holme* (1811–12) 19 Ves 88.
11 *Dommett v Bedford* (1796) 3 Ves 149.
12 *Roe d Hunter v Galliers* (1787) 2 Term Rep 133. The particular justification for allowing the landlord to forfeit the lease was that he should be able to control who became tenant of his property. The obvious way to do that, by a covenant prohibiting assignment without consent, was not possible because such covenants were not binding on those administering the estates of insolvent debtors: *Goring v Warner* (1724) 2 Eq Cas Abr 100. Ironically, they are now binding on both liquidators (*Re Farrow's Bank Ltd* [1921] 2 Ch 164, CA) and trustees-in-bankruptcy (*Re Wright (Bankrupt)* [1949] Ch 729, [1949] 2 All ER 605).
13 The liquidator may be entitled to seek relief against forfeiture: Law of Property Act 1925, s 146(10). See also 'Forfeiture of Tenancies' (Law Com, no 142).
14 Cmnd 8558, ch 34 and paras 1523–1549.
15 Cmnd 9175, para 26.
16 Unlike bankruptcy where this rule is expressly stated in the Insolvency Act 1986, s 238(3)(a), it is not expressly stated in relation to winding up. It has nevertheless been applied consistently to companies. See, for example, the statutory trust in *Re Nanwa Gold Mines Ltd* [1955] 3 All ER 219, [1955] 1 WLR 1080, and the resulting trust in *Barclays Bank*

use of the trust as a means of protecting unsecured creditors by making them beneficiaries under a trust. The most notable example of this is *Re Kayford Ltd*[17] where a mail order company in financial difficulties in November 1972 opened a separate bank account into which it paid money sent in advance for goods by its mail order customers. When the company went into liquidation in December 1972, it was held that the £11,000 in the account was held on trust for those customers whose money had been deposited there and was not available for the general creditors. This result appeals to a sense of fair play because the customers would be unaware of the financial circumstances of Kayford Ltd and therefore of the risk they were running. Trade creditors on the other hand are aware of the risks of insolvency, and can check the creditworthiness of the company they are dealing with[18].

It is crucial to the decision in *Re Kayford Ltd* that the money in the account never became the company's money beneficially. Placing the company's own money on trust with the desire of preferring a particular group of creditors would be voidable as a preference if done within six months before winding up and at a time when the company was unable to pay its debts[19]. It has, however, been cogently argued that since the customers knew nothing of the proposed trust deposit account when they sent money to Kayford Ltd, the money was free of any trust obligations[20]. It was Kayford Ltd which therefore declared itself trustee of its own money and since this was within six months of the winding up, it was voidable as a preference[1].

GOODS SUBJECT TO RESERVATION OF PROPERTY

Although almost all the reported cases have concerned receivership[2], a clause in a sale of goods contract that prevents property passing to the purchaser will not only mean that the goods are not available to the secured creditors who appointed the receiver, but also that they are not available to any unsecured creditors in a winding up[3].

RIGHTS OF ACTION AND INSURANCE CLAIMS

Among the assets available to the company's creditors generally are the proceeds of rights of action belonging to the company[4]. So, for example, any

Ltd v Quistclose Investments Ltd [1970] AC 567, [1968] 3 All ER 651, HL. See also *Carreras Rothmans Ltd v Freeman Mathews Treasure Ltd* [1985] Ch 207 at 220–224, [1985] 1 All ER 155 at 164–167; *Re EVTR Ltd* [1987] BCLC 646, CA and *Re E Dibbens & Sons Ltd* [1990] BCLC 577.

17 [1975] 1 All ER 604, [1975] 1 WLR 279. See also *Re Chelsea Cloisters Ltd (in liquidation)* (1980) 41 P & CR 98, CA.
18 Megarry J remarked that 'Different considerations may perhaps arise in relation to trade creditors' [1975] 1 All ER 604 at 607, [1975] 1 WLR 279 at 282. It is difficult, though, to see what other considerations on the present law might arise. For an excellent discussion of the issues involved see Ogus and Rowley *Prepayments and Insolvency* (1984) an occasional paper prepared for the Office of Fair Trading. See also a report by the Director General of Fair Trading *The Protection of Consumer Prepayments* (1986).
19 Insolvency Act 1986, ss 239 and 240.
20 Goodhart and Jones (1980) 43 MLR 489.
 1 Ibid at p 496.
 2 See Chapter 36, ante.
 3 See generally A L Diamond *A Review of Security Interests in Property* (1989), a report published by the Department of Trade and Industry.
 4 This is why the right of set-off, which entitles a creditor to treat the company's right of action against him as available to satisfy his own claim against the company, is so anomalous.

damages recovered by the company go into the pool for the creditors generally even though the company's claim may only have arisen because of its own liability to a particular creditor[5]. It is different if the company's claim is for an indemnity rather than damages for then the proceeds are not pooled but go direct to the creditor concerned[6]. Even so, it was held at common law that the proceeds of a claim on an insurance policy should be pooled regardless of the fact that the claim was in respect of a liability the company was under to a third party and which the company had not met[7]. Parliament, however, intervened and the Third Parties (Rights Against Insurers) Act 1930 provides that if the insured company becomes subject to one of the specified types of insolvency procedure[8] its rights against the insurer vest in the third party. The Act only transfers rights once a company is subject to one of the insolvency procedures. If the insurance proceeds are paid to the company before the relevant procedure begins then under the common law rule they form part of the pool for the creditors generally.

DISCLAIMER OF ONEROUS PROPERTY

This is a means by which a liquidator can terminate certain obligations on the company or disclaim ownership of unsaleable assets[9]. One purpose behind the power is simply to enable the winding up to be completed without undue delay, or, in some cases, to be completed at all. But disclaimer also enables the liquidator unilaterally to terminate onerous contracts so that, for example, the other party to a contract cannot insist on performing the contract and adding unnecessarily to the debts of the company but can be compelled to sue for damages as an unsecured creditor.

The effect of a disclaimer is to terminate the rights and liabilities of the company in the property disclaimed[10]. But, it does not, except so far as is necessary for the purposes of releasing the company from any liability, affect the rights or liabilities of any other person[11]. There is no time limit within which the liquidator must decide whether to disclaim property except that any person with an interest in the property can serve a notice on the liquidator requiring the liquidator to disclaim within 28 days or lose the right to do so[12].

---

5 Thus a company which buys goods from a manufacturer and resells them to a customer will be liable to the customer if they are badly manufactured but will itself have a claim for damages against the manufacturer. If the company becomes insolvent it may only be able to pay a small dividend on the damage due to the customer. Nevertheless, the damages recovered from the manufacturer will be for the full amount (*Ashdown v Ingamells* (1880) 50 LJQB 109, CA) and will be available to the creditors generally and not the particular customer: *Anglo-Baltic and Mediterranean Bank v Barber & Co* [1924] 2 KB 410, CA. The customer may be able to recover in full by suing the manufacturer directly in tort as in *Junior Books Ltd v Veitchi Co Ltd* [1983] 1 AC 520, [1982] 3 All ER 201, HL.
6 *Re Richardson* [1911] 2 KB 705, CA.
7 *Re Harrington Motor Co, ex p Chaplin* [1928] Ch 105, CA.
8 Third Party (Rights Against Insurers) Act 1930, s 1(1)(b).
9 Insolvency Act 1986, s 178.
10 Ibid, s 178(4)(a).
11 Ibid, s 178(4)(b). Despite the clear wording of the section it has been held that disclaimer does terminate the liability of a guarantor of the company's obligations: *Stacey v Hill* [1901] 1 KB 660, CA. Cf *Tempany v Royal Liver Trustees Ltd* [1984] BCLC 568, High Ct (Ireland).
12 Insolvency Act 1986, s 178(5).

PRESERVATION OF THE COMPANY'S PROPERTY FOR THE CREDITORS

The property of the company that is available to the creditors includes the property owned by the company at the commencement of the winding up. Since a compulsory winding up commences with the presentation of the petition[13] property which should be available to the creditors may have been disposed of in the period before the winding-up order is made. In order to preserve such property for the creditors, it is provided that all dispositions of the company's property after the commencement of the winding up are void unless the court orders otherwise[14].

In exercising their discretion to validate dispositions, the courts have refused to validate payments which have the effect of preferring pre-insolvency creditors[15] unless either the payment confers a benefit on creditors generally[16] or the creditor did not know of the insolvency at the time of receiving payment[17]. In the latter case, though, the payment will still not be validated if the intention of the debtor was to prefer that creditor[18].

It is open to either company or creditor to apply to the court to validate a transaction in advance of it taking place[19] and this is particularly useful where the company carries on business in the period between the presentation of a winding-up petition and the making of a winding-up order. In such circumstances the courts have taken into account the benefit to the creditors generally of keeping a business going with a view to selling it as a going concern[20]. The same consideration has led the courts to validate the repayment of or the grant of security for loans made to the company after the commencement of insolvency[1]. Conversely, where a company repaid money it had been lent after the presentation of a winding-up petition but where no decision had been reached that keeping the company's business going was in the interests of creditors, and no application was made for validation in advance of any transaction, the lender was ordered to pay the additional loss suffered by the company as a result of its loan keeping the business going[2].

Control of legal proceedings and enforcement of remedies

When a business becomes insolvent it is necessary to strike a balance between encouraging creditors to enforce their claims promptly and ensuring equal treatment for all creditors. This is done by giving the courts a discretion to stop both legal proceedings[3] and the enforcements of

---

13 Ibid, s 129(2).
14 Ibid, s 127. As to what is property of the company, see *Re French's (Wine Bar) Ltd* [1987] BCLC 499.
15 *Re Civil Service and General Store Ltd* (1887) 57 LJ Ch 119.
16 *Re A I Levy (Holdings) Ltd* [1964] Ch 19, [1963] 2 All ER 556.
17 *Re Gray's Inn Construction Co Ltd* [1980] 1 All ER 814, [1980] 1 WLR 711, CA.
18 *Re J Leslie Engineers Co Ltd* [1976] 2 All ER 85, [1976] 1 WLR 292.
19 See *Re A I Levy (Holdings) Ltd*, supra, where the history is reviewed.
20 *Re Wiltshire Iron Co, ex p Pearson* (1868) 3 Ch App 443.
 1 *Re Steane's (Bournemouth) Ltd* [1950] 1 All ER 21; *Re Clifton Place Garage Ltd* [1970] Ch 477, [1970] 1 All ER 353, CA.
 2 *Re Gray's Inn Construction Co Ltd (in liquidation)*, supra.
 3 In compulsory winding up the court has power to stay any legal proceedings after the presentation of the petition, but the onus is on those who wish to stop the proceedings to apply and show cause: Insolvency Act 1986, s 126(1). When the winding-up order has been made or a provisional liquidator appointed all pending proceedings are automatically halted and no new proceedings may be commenced, unless an application is made and cause shown

remedies[4] once the winding up has commenced[5]. So far as legal proceedings are concerned, the courts allow proceedings relating to property rights to continue[6] but in relation to other matters will decide whether there is any sensible point in allowing the proceedings to continue[7].

EXECUTION OF JUDGMENTS

Where legal proceedings have already resulted in a judgment against the company, the discretion to stop enforcement of the judgment after the commencement of winding up is supplemented by the Insolvency Act 1986, s 183. This provides that, unless the court orders otherwise[8], the proceeds of an execution against the goods or land of a company or the attachment of a debt due to the company cannot be retained by the creditor unless completed before the commencement of winding up[9]. The court thus has a discretion whether to allow the enforcement to proceed or, if it already has proceeded but was not completed in time, whether to allow the creditor to keep the proceeds. The court also has a discretion arising from the fact that two methods of enforcement, a charging order on goods or land and a garnishee order attaching a debt due to the company both require the court's approval before being made absolute.

The strong presumption in exercising all these discretionary powers is not to allow the individual creditor the benefit of enforcing the judgment if this

why proceedings should be allowed to continue or new ones commence: ibid, s 130(2). This power is also available in voluntary winding up under s 112(1), but here again the onus is on the party who wants the proceedings stopped to apply and show cause.

4 In compulsory winding up after the presentation of the petition, the court has a discretion to stop the enforcement of remedies, upon an application being made: Insolvency Act 1986, s 126(1). Once a winding-up order has been made, s 128(1) appears to make the enforcement of a remedy put in force after the commencement of the winding up void. It is, however, invariably treated as subject to the court's discretion under s 130(2) to allow the enforcement to continue; the onus, here, is on those seeking the enforcement to show cause why it should continue. The power to halt existing or new enforcements is also available in voluntary liquidation under s 112(1) with the onus on those seeking to halt the enforcement to apply and show cause.

5 Whether the courts have a discretion to stop enforcement of judgments before commencement of winding up is a moot point. In *Booth v Walkden Spinning and Manufacturing Co Ltd* [1909] 2 KB 368 it was held there was no power unless winding up had commenced, a view supported by Scrutton LJ in *Bowkett v Fuller's United Electric Works Ltd* [1923] 1 KB 160 at 165, CA. However in *Prestige Publications Ltd v Chelsea Football and Athletic Co Ltd* (1978) 122 Sol Jo 436 the Court of Appeal used RSC Ord 47, r 1 to stop the enforcement of a judgment even though no winding up or scheme of arrangement was proposed. Furthermore under the Charging Orders Act 1979, when considering whether to grant a charging order the court must consider the effect on other creditors of the debtor.

6 *Re David Lloyd & Co, Lloyd v David Lloyd & Co* (1877) 6 Ch D 339, CA and *Re Aro Co Ltd* [1980] Ch 196, [1980] 1 All ER 1067, CA (secured creditors enforcing security); *Re Coregrange Ltd* [1984] BCLC 453 (creditor suing for specific performance).

7 Leave will not be given if the issues can conveniently be decided in the winding up (*Craven v Blackpool Greyhound Stadium and Racecourse Ltd* [1936] 3 All ER 513, CA; *Re Exchange Securities and Commodities Ltd* [1983] BCLC 186) but will be given if the issues are better decided by an action (*Currie v Consolidated Kent Collieries Corpn Ltd* [1906] 1 KB 134, CA).

8 Insolvency Act 1986, s 183(2)(c).

9 Or notice to the creditor that a meeting has been called to consider a resolution for voluntary winding up: ibid, s 183(2)(a). There are still circumstances where the liquidator may wish to *stop* the execution of a judgment as opposed to merely claiming the proceeds when the execution is completed; for example, if the assets being seized were needed to help the liquidator sell the business as a going concern.

will prejudice the equal treatment of creditors generally[10]. Thus, even where a creditor sought to garnishee a debt due to the company that had arisen entirely as a result of liability to that creditor[11] or entirely through the work of that creditor, the court would not make the order absolute[12]. Nor would the court make absolute a charging order in favour of involuntary creditors who had not therefore taken the risk of the debtor becoming insolvent which other creditors had done[13]. On the other hand, the court has allowed the individual creditor to succeed where the debtor forced[14], tricked[15] or persuaded[16] the creditor into abstaining from enforcing a judgment sometime before the winding up commenced.

LEVYING DISTRESS

The lack of sympathy for individual judgment creditors is in marked contrast to the courts' attitude to the levying of distress by creditors to whom that particular remedy is available. Where the distress is in progress at the commencement of the winding up the courts will allow it to continue[17], unless there are exceptional circumstances[18], notwithstanding that the consequence is to prefer one creditor ahead of the rest. The Insolvency Act 1986, s 183 does not apply to distress so that even though it is completed after the commencement of winding up the creditor levying the distress will be allowed to keep the proceeds. Where the distress is only levied after the commencement of the winding up, however, the courts will not normally allow it to continue[19] unless the distrainor is not able to prove as a creditor in the insolvency[20]. In a compulsory winding up where the distress is levied in the three months before a winding-up order the preferential debts constitute a first charge on the proceeds of the distress[1].

---

10 *Roberts Petroleum Ltd v Bernard Kenny Ltd* [1983] 2 AC 192, [1983] 1 All ER 564, HL.
11 *Anglo-Baltic and Mediterranean Bank v Barber & Co* [1924] 2 KB 410, CA.
12 *D Wilson (Birmingham) Ltd v Metropolitan Property Developments Ltd* [1975] 2 All ER 814, CA.
13 *Rainbow v Moorgate Properties Ltd* [1975] 2 All ER 821, [1975] 1 WLR 788, CA.
14 *Re London Cotton Co* (1866) LR 2 Eq 53.
15 *Armorduct Manufacturing Co Ltd v General Incandescent Co Ltd* [1911] 2 KB 143, CA.
16 *Re Grosvenor Metal Co Ltd* [1950] Ch 63; *Re Suidair International Airways Ltd* [1951] Ch 165.
17 *Herbert Berry Associates Ltd v IRC* [1978] 1 All ER 161, [1977] 1 WLR 1437, HL; *Re Bellaglade Ltd* [1977] 1 All ER 319. The jurisdiction to halt a distress is apparently under s 126(1) although it is far from clear that distress is an 'action or proceeding' within that section. It was originally held to be so by Knight Bruce and Turner LJJ in one of their pieces of creative statutory interpretation: *Re Exhall Coal Mining Co Ltd* (1864) 4 De G J & Sm 377.
18 *Re G Winterbottom (Leeds) Ltd* [1937] 2 All ER 232.
19 *Shackell & Co v Chorlton & Sons* [1895] 1 Ch 378.
20 *Re Regent United Service Stores Ltd* (1878) 8 Ch D 616, CA.
 1 Insolvency Act 1986, s 176(2)(3). This does not apply in voluntary winding up because of the reference to winding-up order. *Re Herbert Berry Associates Ltd* [1976] 3 All ER 207, [1976] 1 WLR 783. In two respects the old law, as interpreted by *Re Memco Engineering Ltd* [1986] Ch 86, has been changed by the Insolvency Act. The preference creditors' prior claim on the proceeds of distress now appears to apply only if the distress is levied in the three months before the winding-up order; under the former provision if the distress was levied earlier but was still in the process of being levied within the three months period, that was subject to the preference creditors' claim. The second change is that, to the extent that proceeds are taken by preference creditors, the distrainor ranks as a preference creditor but only against the *remaining* assets.

Avoidance of transactions prior to winding up

Besides being entitled to the property the company owns at the commencement of the winding up, the creditors are in certain circumstances given specific powers to go back earlier than the commencement of winding up and recover property transferred, or avoid transactions entered into, by the company[2]. To see how these powers relate to one another it may help to remember certain factors which often determine the scope of the particular power. The first factor is the type of disposition the power applies to. Sometimes, for example, only secured transactions or even a particular form of security is caught; other powers apply to anything done by the company at all. The second factor is the time zone within which the transaction must have been entered into for it to be vulnerable. Thirdly, there is the question whether any particular intention or motive must be established on the part of those who caused the company to enter the transaction. And fourthly, there is the question whether it must be shown that the company was insolvent at the time of the transaction. Finally, a factor which will be noticed in relation to many of the powers is that they apply more strictly where the transaction or disposition is with a person connected with the company. This development was based on recommendations by the Cork Committee[3]. The precise definition of persons connected with the company is complex[4] but broadly it includes any directors or shadow directors of the company[5], employees of the company[6], those who control the company[7] and other companies under the same control[8].

TRANSACTIONS AT AN UNDERVALUE

It has been mentioned earlier that many of the problems faced by insolvent debtors are the same whether the debtor is an individual or a company. Unfortunately, because of the different regimes of bankruptcy and winding up applicable respectively to individuals and companies, some of the solutions that have been developed for similar problems are radically different. One of the most glaring is that since 1603[9] it has been possible for a trustee in bankruptcy to recover gratuitous dispositions of the bankrupt's property made within a certain period before the bankruptcy. No equivalent provision was made available to liquidators[10] and they therefore attempted to achieve equivalent protection using company law doctrines, none of which had been intended for the protection of creditors of insolvent companies and which produced predictably inconsistent results.

---

2 See Prentice 'The Effect of Insolvency on Pre-Liquidation Transactions' in Pettet (ed) *Company Law in Change* (1987) p 69.
3 Cmnd 8558, ch 21.
4 Insolvency Act 1986, ss 249 and 435.
5 Ibid, s 249(a). Shadow directors include persons in accordance with whose directions or instructions the directors are accustomed to act: ibid, s 251. For discussion of the circumstances in which a holder of a floating charge might become a shadow director, see *Re a Company (No 005009 of 1987), ex p Copp* [1989] BCLC 13 at 14–18.
6 Ibid, s 435(4).
7 Ibid, s 435(7).
8 Ibid, s 435(6)(a).
9 1 Jac 1 c 15, s 5. Subsequently this became the Bankruptcy Act 1914, s 42.
10 Interestingly in *Re Lee, Behrens & Co Ltd* [1932] 2 Ch 46 counsel for the liquidator, in challenging an ex gratia pension seems to have tried to argue by analogy from the Bankruptcy Act 1914, s 42.

Because none of the various doctrines on which liquidators have relied or attempted to rely was specifically intended for the protection of creditors they are all subject to factors which can result in the liquidator failing to recover property in a particular case, even though the transaction was prejudicial to creditors. Thus liquidators have relied on the ultra vires doctrine. But whether a transaction is ultra vires depends on the drafting of the objects clause[11], a matter which is entirely for the members not the creditors[12]. In other cases liquidators may fail because any wrong to the company has been ratified by the consent of shareholders. Lack of authority of an agent[13], breach of directors' duty[14] and procedural irrgularity[15], though sometimes pleaded successfully, are all vulnerable to the possibility of ratification. A further problem with procedural irregularity as a ground for invalidating transactions is that the courts have often proceeded without regard to whose interests the procedural requirement was designed to protect. An example of this is *Re Duomatic Ltd*[16] where the liquidator succeeded in recovering a golden handshake from a former director on the grounds that the payment had not been disclosed to non-voting preference shareholders[17]. It is obviously questionable whether such disclosure would have made any difference to the payment being made[18]. The point, however, is that the disclosure requirement was designed to protect shareholders whereas the non-disclosure to the shareholders was used as the basis for allowing creditors to recover the money. The issue of real concern to creditors, whether the company could afford the payment at the time it was made without prejudicing its creditors, was not apparently raised in the case because there was no remedy in relation to which it became a relevant question. Finally, recovery of gratuitous payments to shareholders out of non-distributable profits[19], although it cannot be ratified, is obviously restricted to cases where the payments have been made to shareholders[20]. None of these grounds for re-opening transactions could therefore be consistently relied upon by liquidators. The effect

---

11 Thus in both *Re Horsley & Weight Ltd* [1982] Ch 442, [1982] 3 All ER 1045, CA, and *Rolled Steel Products (Holdings) Ltd v British Steel Corpn* [1986] Ch 246, [1985] 3 All ER 52, CA, the claims based on ultra vires failed.
12 Section 4.
13 The liquidator succeeded in *Rolled Steel Products (Holdings) Ltd v British Steel Corpn*, note 11 above, but would probably not have done so if British Steel Corporation had been allowed to argue and had succeeded in proving that all the shareholders in *Rolled Steel Products (Holdings) Ltd* knew of and agreed to the giving of the guarantee.
14 *Kinsela v Russell Kinsela Pty Ltd* [1986] 4 NSWLR 722; *Re Clasper Group Services Ltd* [1989] BCLC 143 at 148–153. In these cases the liquidator used breach of fiduciary duty to seek to recover property or re-open transactions on the basis that the recipient was a constructive trustee. As to liquidators seeking compensation for the breach of duty from the directors themselves, see pp 718–720 below. Recent developments which have emphasised the importance in relation to shareholders' ratification of whether the company was solvent or insolvent at the time of the breach of duty are also discussed at pp 720–721 below.
15 In both *Re Horsley & Weight Ltd*, note 11 above, and *Rolled Steel Products (Holdings) Ltd v British Steel Corpn*, note 11 above, the liquidator argued that the decision to enter the transaction had not been validly taken by the board of directors. The argument failed in the former but succeeded in the latter.
16 [1969] 2 Ch 365, [1969] 1 All ER 161.
17 As required under s 312.
18 The judge, Buckley J, took the view that the non-voting members might have persuaded the voting members, who had to approve the payment, not to do so.
19 *Re Halt Garage (1964) Ltd* [1982] 3 All ER 1016.
20 In *Aveling Barford Ltd v Perion Ltd* [1989] BCLC 626 the doctrine was extended to permit recovery from a company controlled by a shareholder.

was that before 1986 the protection of creditors in company law, at least in relation to the re-opening of transactions was uncertain, if not capricious. However, as a result of a recommendation by the Cork Committee[1], liquidators of insolvent companies do now have a power, albeit a modest one, to seek to recover gratuitous dispositions made by insolvent companies. The great advantage of the new power is that it raises directly the question of balancing the interests of unpaid creditors against those who have received gratuitous benefits from the company, instead of raising it indirectly via remedies that were not designed for the protection of creditors.

The new power liquidators have is to challenge transactions at an undervalue[2]. A transaction is at an undervalue if the company makes a gift or enters a transaction for no consideration or for significantly less consideration than the company itself provides[3]. Such a transaction may be set aside by court order if it was entered into in the two years[4] before the onset of insolvency[5] and the company was unable to pay its debts at the time or became unable to do so as a result of the transaction[6]. It will be noticed that

1 The Cork Committee were not entirely conviced the power was needed 'since in almost every case a transaction liable to be challenged under these provisions would, . . ., be ultra vires and void against the liquidator, as well as constituting a probable misfeasance on the part of the directors responsible': (Cmnd 8558) para 1237. What has been said so far in this section suggests that, perhaps, this view was rather optimistic.

2 The power applies only to transactions entered into after 28 December 1986: Insolvency Act 1986, Sch 11, para 9.

3 Ibid, s 238(4). Difficult questions may arise here in assessing whether a payment by the company was a gift, or, even, if it was not, whether the company received significantly less than it provided. Consider the following examples: remuneration for directors' services as in *Re Halt Garage (1964) Ltd* [1982] 3 All ER 1016; an ex gratia pension for the past services of a director as in *Re Horsley & Weight Ltd* [1982] Ch 442, [1982] 3 All ER 1045, CA; a golden handshake to a director who might otherwise have involved the company in acrimonious litigation as in *Re Duomatic Ltd* [1969] 2 Ch 365, [1969] 1 All ER 161; a guarantee of a related company's debts as in *Rolled Steel Products (Holdings) Ltd v British Steel Corpn* [1986] Ch 246, [1985] 3 All ER 52, CA; whether dividends are gifts or consideration for the shareholders investing their capital, which might arise on facts like those in *Precision Dippings Ltd v Precision Dippings Marketing Ltd* [1986] Ch 447, CA. In *Re M C Bacon Ltd* [1990] BCLC 324 at 340–341 it was held that giving a bank security for an existing unsecured overdraft in return for the bank not calling in the overdraft was not a transaction at an undervalue. As to how the costs of challenging the validity of security are dealt with, see *Re M C Bacon Ltd* [1991] Ch 127.

4 Insolvency Act 1986, s 240(1)(a).

5 The statute uses the term 'onset of insolvency' but as will be seen from the remainder of the sentence the company must have been insolvent at the date of the transaction. It is suggested a term like 'relevant date' would have been less misleading. Except where there was a prior administration order the onset of insolvency is the commencement of the winding up: Insolvency Act 1986, s 240(3).

6 Ibid, s 240(2). The onus of proof is on the liquidator except where the transaction was with a person connected with the company, otherwise than only as an employee, when there is a rebuttable presumption that the company was unable to pay its debts. The approach under s 240(2) has an advantage over the embryonic common law duty on directors towards creditors. The common law duty arises, 'if the directors should at the time have appreciated that the payment was likely to cause loss to the creditors': *Re Horsley & Weight Ltd* [1982] Ch 442 at 455, [1982] 3 All ER 1045 at 1055, CA per Cumming-Bruce LJ. See also Templeman LJ at pp 455 and 1056. Under s 240(2) the test whether the company was unable to pay its debts at the time is objective. It is submitted the latter approach is the correct one in these circumstances. By definition the company is now in liquidation and the creditors are not being paid in full. It is right that the creditors' challenge should depend on objective criteria about whether they were prejudiced by the payment, rather than on the subjective opinion of optimistic directors.

the power does not depend on establishing any particular intention or motive on the part of the company in entering the transaction. This accords with the position as it has been in bankruptcy since 1603. However, in the course of the passage of the Insolvency Bill through Parliament, a defence was introduced whereby those seeking to uphold the transaction can do so if they show that the company entered into it in good faith, for the purpose of carrying on its business and that there were reasonable grounds for believing it would benefit the company[7].

The existence of this defence adds considerably to the uncertainty regarding the effectiveness of this new power to set aside transactions at an undervalue[8]. It would presumably not be possible to defend the payment of excessive remuneration under such a provision. But the provision of a golden handshake or an ex gratia pension to a retiring director, the payment of a dividend, the guarantee of another company's debt or the grant of security for an existing unsecured loan could arguably satisfy all three requirements and so be immune from attack under the provision. It is submitted, however, that in many cases it would be very unfair were this to be the case. By definition the court will be balancing the interests of creditors, for whom there are insufficient assets to pay them in full, against the recipients of gifts or other largesse from the company, given moreover at a time when the company was unable to pay its debts. In such circumstances the court should apply the maxim that 'persons should be just before they are generous and that debts must be paid before gifts can be made'[9].

A separate statutory remedy, introduced in bankruptcy in 1571[10] and already available to liquidators, was completely revised in the Insolvency Act[11] and now hinges on the same definition of transaction at an undervalue[12]. There are crucial differences, however, between this provision and the one already discussed. First, this provision has no time zone beyond which the liquidator cannot go. Nor is it necessary that the company was insolvent at the time of the transaction. However, it must be shown that the company's intention was to put assets beyond the reach of the claimant or otherwise prejudice a claimant[13]. There is also a difference in the power of

---

7 Insolvency Act 1986, s 238(5). It must be shown that all three conditions are satisfied.

8 Assuming the examples discussed in footnote 3 above were all held to be transactions at an undervalue it is then interesting to consider which, if any of them, might satisfy the tests in s 238(5).

9 *Freeman v Pope* (1870) 5 Ch App 538 at 540 per Lord Hatherley LC. Giving a bank security for an existing overdraft could in circumstances like those in *Re M C Bacon Ltd* [1990] BCLC 324 satisfy the three tests but it is likely in that case that the transaction will not be at an undervalue.

10 13 Eliz c 5, ss 1, 5. The remedy dealt with what were formerly known as fraudulent conveyances. The provisions were revised in the Law of Property Act 1925, ss 172, 173.

11 Based on recommendations of the Cork Committee (Cmnd 8558) paras 1210–1220. The provision does not depend on the company being in liquidation (nor in the case of an individual, being bankrupt). The circumstances, of there being unpaid creditors and powers to investigate the debtor's affairs, however, make it likely that the main use of the section will be in liquidation or bankruptcy.

12 Insolvency Act 1986, s 423(1). This may, in fact, narrow the scope of the former provision. A transaction like that in *Lloyds Bank Ltd v Marcan* [1973] 2 All ER 359, which was held to be a fraudulent conveyance, may not be a transaction at an undervalue. The new rules apply to transactions entered into after 28 December 1986: Insolvency Act 1986, Sch 11, para 9. It follows that the old rules may continue to be relevant for some years to come.

13 Insolvency Act 1986, s 423(3). *Arbuthnot Leasing International Ltd v Havelet Leasing Ltd (No 2)* [1990] BCC 636. Perhaps out of respect for the uncertainty 400 years of litigation about fraudulent conveyances produced, the draftsman has not thought it advisable to add

the court depending on which provision is used to attack a transaction at an undervalue[14]. If the transaction is successfully challenged under s 238 'the court *shall* . . . make such order as it thinks fit for restoring the position to what it would have been if the company had not entered into the transaction'[15]. This will almost always mean that any property recovered goes into the pool of assets for the benefit of creditors generally. In contrast if the undervalue transaction is challenged under s 423 'the court *may* . . . make such order as it thinks fit for (a) restoring the position to what it would have been if the transaction had not been entered into, and (b) protecting the interests of persons who are victims of the transaction'[16]. In other words, here the court may also order property to be handed over or reimbursement made to the particular party prejudiced by the transaction.

PREFERENCES

One of the main objectives in the winding up of an insolvent company is to ensure the equal treatment of creditors. To help achieve this the court is given a power to set aside things the company has done or suffered to be done[17] which have the effect of preferring a creditor[18] or creditors ahead of others. Certain crucial conditions, however, must be satisfied[19]. First it must be shown that the company was influenced by a desire to achieve the preference[20]. It does not matter whether the creditor was aware of the company's desire or not[1], nor is it any defence for those making the payment on behalf of the company to show that they believed ultimately all the creditors would be paid in full and therefore no one would be prejudiced if

any guidance on issues like whether the company's purpose must be proved objectively or subjectively nor about whether the company must intend to prejudice the specific claimant or whether prejudice to claimants generally will suffice. It is likely, however, that the section will not apply, for example, to a transaction that merely prefers one creditor ahead of others. In other words the section cannot be used to extend the time zone for attacking preferences: *Re Lloyd's Furniture Palace Ltd, Evans v Lloyd's Furniture Palace Ltd* [1925] Ch 853. But cf *National Mutual Life Assurance Society v Tee and Whiten and J Mead Ltd* (30 November 1981, unreported), CA where the creditor being preferred was the parent company of the debtor.

14 The specific powers of the court under each provision are identical: see Insolvency Act 1986, ss 241(1) and 425(1). Under both provisions the good faith, or lack of knowledge of the relevant circumstances, of the other party to the transaction are irrelevant, but subtransferees acquiring interests or benefits in good faith, for value and without notice of the relevant circumstances are protected: ss 241(2)(3) and 425(2)(3).
15 Insolvency Act 1986, s 238(3).
16 Ibid, s 423(2).
17 For example, not opposing an application for late registration of a charge can constitute a preference: *Peat v Gresham Trust Ltd* [1934] AC 252, HL.
18 *Re Clasper Group Services Ltd* [1989] BCLC 143 at 146–148.
19 Insolvency Act 1986, s 239(3)(4). These conditions were considerably strengthened as a result of recommendations by the Cork Committee (Cmnd 8558) paras 1241–1277. For the earlier history see J H Farrar [1983] JBL 390.
20 Ibid, s 239(5). Under the old law intention to prefer had to be shown which meant preference had to be the dominant motive. In contrast, desire to achieve a preference probably covers cases where preference is one of the aims but not necessarily the main one. If the preference is of a person connected with the company, otherwise than only as an employee, there is a rebuttable presumption that the company desired to achieve the preference: ibid, s 239(6). See the Cork Report (Cmnd 8558) paras 1247–1258. *Re Beacon Leisure Ltd* [1991] BCC 213.
1 Insolvency Act 1986, s 241(2)(3).

one creditor was paid ahead of the rest[2]. Nevertheless establishing the desire to prefer is still likely to prove one of the difficulties in applying the provision. For example, the harder a creditor presses for payment the less likely any eventual payment is to constitute a preference; the company having paid because of the pressure rather than out of a desire to prefer[3]. On the other hand, it has been held that if, in return for a loan, a company agrees to give a charge on demand in future, and the charge is actually given within six months of the winding up[4], it is presumed that the company desired to prefer the creditor, if the reason for not executing the charge at the outset was so that the company's creditworthiness would not be affected[5].

The second condition that must be satisfied is that it must be shown that the company was unable to pay its debts at the time the preference was given or that it became unable to do so as a result of the preference[6]. Thirdly, the preference must have been given within six months before[7] the onset of insolvency[8], or within two years before that date in the case of a preference given to a person connected with the company[9]. If these conditions are fulfilled then the court is under a duty to make an order restoring the position to what it would have been but for the preference[10]. One of the most common forms of preference occurs where directors have guaranteed the company's bank overdraft and/or secured it with a charge on their own property. If, to release the guarantee or security, the directors cause the company to discharge the overdraft that is a preference of the bank, even though the bank was paid in order to benefit the directors. The bank can be ordered to repay the money to the liquidator[11] but the court also has the power to impose on the directors such new or revived obligations towards the bank as it thinks appropriate[12].

---

2 *Re F P and C H Matthews Ltd* [1982] Ch 257, [1982] 1 All ER 338, CA. It will not be a preference if those making the payment believed that all the creditors would get paid as and when their debts fell due.

3 Thus a charge given to secure an existing overdraft, although its effect is to prefer the lender, will not be given from a desire to achieve that preference if the alternative was the lender calling in the overdraft and the motive for giving the charge was to prevent that happening in the interests of the creditors generally: *Re M C Bacon Ltd* [1990] BCLC 324 at 334–336.

4 I e within the time zone that makes a preference vulnerable; see below.

5 *Re Eric Holmes (Property) Ltd* [1965] Ch 1052, [1965] 2 All ER 333.

6 Insolvency Act 1986, s 240(2).

7 If the preference is given *after* the commencement of a compulsory winding up the question may arise whether it should be validated under s 127: *Re J Leslie Engineers Co Ltd (in liquidation)* [1976] 2 All ER 85, [1976] 1 WLR 292.

8 Ibid, s 240(1)(b). The misleading nature of the phrase 'onset of insolvency' has already been commented on: see p 707 footnote 5.

9 Ibid, s 240(1)(a), unless the person is connected only as an employee.

10 Ibid, s 239(3). It follows that the normal rule is that any money recovered goes into the pool for the creditors generally. The range of orders the court can make is the same as in relation to a transaction at an undervalue: ibid, s 241(1). Money or other property recovered as a preference does not form part of the property covered by a floating charge, if there is one over the company's assets. Instead it forms part of a pool of unencumbered assets available to all creditors. This is because the company itself could not have recovered the preference; only a liquidator or administrator can do so: *Re Yagerphone Ltd* [1935] Ch 392.

11 Ibid, s 241(1)(d).

12 Ibid, s 241(1)(e). Although there appears to be no power under s 241(1) to order the guarantor or surety to pay directly to the company, where the guarantor is also a director of the company the liquidator may recover the amount of the preference from the director as a breach of fiduciary duty: *West Mercia Safetywear Ltd v Dodd* [1988] BCLC 250, CA. It

EXTORTIONATE CREDIT TRANSACTIONS

Section 244 of the Insolvency Act 1986[13] gives liquidators the right to challenge any credit transactions entered into by the company in the three years[14] before going into liquidation[15]. It will then be for those who seek to uphold the transaction to show that it was not an extortionate credit transaction[16]. The test for whether a transaction is extortionate is whether, having regard to the risk accepted by the person providing the credit, either its terms required grossly exorbitant payments in respect of the provision of credit, or it otherwise grossly contravened ordinary principles of fair dealing[17]. If the liquidator's challenge is successful the court can exercise a range of powers. These include setting aside the whole or part of any obligations created by the transaction, varying any of its terms, or requiring the creditor to repay any sums to the liquidator[18].

UNREGISTERED SECURITIES

One of the consequences of failure to register a charge on property of the company which is registrable under s 395 is that the charge becomes void against the liquidator. This applies to all registrable charges falling within s 395 whenever created[19].

AVOIDANCE OF FLOATING CHARGES

Even if a floating charge is duly registered it will still be invalid, subject to the exception mentioned below, if it fulfils the conditions laid down in the Insolvency Act 1986, s 245[20]. If the charge was granted to a person not connected with the company[1] the conditions are that the charge was granted

seems that giving any preference is a breach of duty by the directors even if they are not beneficiaries, directly or indirectly, of the preference: *Re Washington Diamond Mining Co* [1893] 3 Ch 95, CA.
13 Based on recommendations by the Cork Committee (Cmnd 8558) ch 31.
14 Insolvency Act 1986, s 244(2).
15 Ie the making of a compulsory winding-up order or passing of a resolution for voluntary winding up: ibid, s 247(2).
16 Ibid, s 244(3). This is the same onus of proof as under the Consumer Credit Act 1974, s 171(7) which, however, does not apply to companies.
17 Insolvency Act 1986, s 244(3). This is the same as under the Consumer Credit Act 1974, s 138(1) but there are no guidelines comparable to those in s 138(2)–(5).
18 Insolvency Act 1986, s 244(4)(5). One of the functions of this section is to prevent companies in effect preferring a creditor by agreeing artificially high rates of interest on the creditor's debt. If arrears of interest are allowed to build up the creditor's proof of debt will be artificially increased. This abuse used to be prevented by restricting arrears of interest that could be proved to a maximum of 5% per annum but this was repealed on the Cork Committee's recommendation (Cmnd 8558) ch 31.
19 Under the new Pt XII of the Companies Act 1985, to be inserted by the Companies Act 1989, Pt IV, see ss 399(2)(a), 402(2)(a) and 419(5).
20 Only the charge is rendered void. The underlying debt remains valid and, if the debt has been repaid before winding up, the fact that the charge would have been void in the winding up does not affect the repayment. In appropriate circumstances the repayment may, of course, be voidable as a preference: *Mace Builders (Glasgow) Ltd v Lunn* [1987] Ch 191, CA.
 1 The conditions for the application of s 245 were amended as a result of recommendations made by the Cork Committee (Cmnd 8558) paras 1550–1556. The amended version applies to charges created after 28 December 1986.

within 12 months before the onset of insolvency[2] and that, at the time, or as a result of the transaction, the company was unable to pay its debts[3]. Where the charge was granted to a person connected with the company the time zone is extended to two years before the onset of insolvency[4] and it is irrelevant whether or not the company was able to pay its debts at the time[5]. The exception referred to above is that even if the above conditions are satisfied and regardless of whether the charge was granted to a person connected with the company or not, the floating charge will nevertheless be valid to the extent that fresh cash, goods or services are provided to the company or any debt of the company is reduced or discharged[6].

Many of the problems with the section in the past have concerned the question of whether fresh cash has been provided to the company. If a person lends money to a company in return for a floating charge, but on condition that the money is used to pay off specified unsecured debts, has the company been provided with fresh cash? The object of the section is to prevent the substitution of a secured debt for an unsecured so that if that is the essence of the transaction, no fresh cash will have been provided[7]. On the other hand, if the payment of the unsecured debts is clearly for the company's benefit and that is the motive for the transaction and not the mere substitution of a secured for an unsecured debt, then the court will treat the money needed to pay off the debts as fresh cash[8].

A similar problem arose where a company granted a floating charge to secure a current account overdraft of £65,000 and thereafter paid into the account £111,000 and withdrew £110,000 before a winding-up petition was presented 353 days later. At that stage therefore the overdraft stood at £64,000 and arguably the bank had not lent the company any fresh money. It was held[9], however, applying the rule in *Clayton's Case*, that sums paid into the account discharged the earliest indebtedness and hence the whole of the £65,000 had been repaid. The £64,000 overdraft at the commencement of the winding up was therefore all fresh money.

---

2 Insolvency Act 1986, s 245(3)(b). The meaning of 'onset of insolvency' is contained in s 245(5). It is the same as that for transactions at an undervalue and as has been pointed out it is not equivalent to the company becoming unable to pay its debts. A neutral term like 'relevant date' would have been better.
3 Insolvency Act 1986, s 245(4). Bearing in mind the exception dealt with below it is arguable that any charge which actually fell within this section would also constitute a transaction at an undervalue within s 238 under which the time zone for setting it aside is two years before the onset of insolvency. But see *Re M C Bacon Ltd* [1990] BCLC 324 at 340–341.
4 Ibid, s 245(3)(a). See footnote 2 above.
5 This means that s 245 still has a wider application than s 238 because under the latter it is a requirement that the company be unable to pay its debts, albeit there is a rebuttable presumption that it is unable to do so.
6 Insolvency Act 1986, s 245(2). The extension of the exception to cover provision of fresh goods or services or the payment of a debt was a result of a recommendation by the Cork Committee.
7 *Re Destone Fabrics Ltd* [1941] Ch 319, [1941] 1 All ER 545, CA; *Re G T Whyte & Co Ltd* [1983] BCLC 311, but see the comment on this case in Picarda *The Law Relating to Receivers and Managers* (2nd edn, 1990) p 210.
8 *Re Matthew Ellis Ltd* [1933] Ch 458, CA.
9 *Re Yeovil Glove Co Ltd* [1965] Ch 148, [1964] 2 All ER 849, CA.

REMEDIES FOR MISMANAGEMENT

Introduction

The issue of misuse of limited liability was one of the central concerns of the Cork Commitee in their review of insolvency law[10]. Two particular problems had become the subject of regular complaints. The first concerned typically a one man business carried on via a limited liability company selling double glazing, loft conversions, house insulation materials or the like. The company would take deposits or even full payment in advance from customers and then go into liquidation without delivering the goods and apparently with no assets left. Soon afterwards the same individual could be discovered doing the same or similar tricks via another limited liability company. The other area of difficulty, although one without the same overtones of dishonesty or fraud, was that of groups of companies where the parent company put a subsidiary into an insolvent liquidation and, taking advantage of limited liability, did not provide funds to pay the subsidiary's creditors in full. There are three broad approaches company law can take in dealing with these problems: first, imposing liability on persons to contribute to the company's assets; secondly, disqualifying persons from managing companies in future; and thirdly, prohibiting the use of similar names for future businesses. Each of these is dealt with in the following pages.

Liability to contribute towards the assets of the company

FRAUDULENT TRADING

Imagine a director has lent money to the company, has secured the loan by a floating charge over the company's entire undertaking and assets and has avoided the Insolvency Act 1986, s 245 by keeping the company afloat for at least two years thereafter. The company, however, has no assets so that the director's security is worthless. To remedy this, the director causes the company to buy stock on credit. The company will become the owner of the stock which will thus become subject to the floating charge. The director as debenture holder then appoints an administrative receiver and the stock is sold to satisfy the floating charge, leaving the suppliers as unsecured creditors. It was particularly to prevent this abuse of 'filling up' a floating charge that fraudulent trading provisions[11] were introduced in 1929 whereby in certain circumstances those responsible for carrying on a company's business after it has become insolvent may be made personally liable for the company's debts[12] and may also be liable to criminal penalties[13].

Today, these provisions have a vital function in persuading those in control of companies in debt to stop carrying on business once the company cannot pay 100 pence in the pound on its debts and when in reality the business is being carried on at the expense of the creditors. Unfortunately the provisions are blunted in their impact by the conditions that need to be fulfilled for their application. Typical of these conditions is the requirement

---

10 Cmnd 8558, ch 43 and paras 1922–1952.
11 Insolvency Act 1986, s 213. See J H Farrar [1980] JBL 336.
12 Insolvency Act 1986, s 213(2).
13 Section 458.

that the company must be in the course of winding up. Although this has been repealed for the purposes of criminal liability[13], it still applies to civil proceedings. It means that a creditor who has lost money to an insolvent company and who wishes to make the controllers personally liable may first have to incur further expense and inconvenience in putting the company into liquidation.

The central requirement in the section is that the 'business of the company has been carried on with intent to defraud creditors'. It has been held that 'carrying on business' can include a single transaction designed to defraud a single creditor[14]. But, perhaps because the section can involve criminal liability, it has been said that the test of intent will only be satisfied in cases where there is 'actual dishonesty, involving, according to current notions of fair trading among commercial men, real moral blame'[15]. Although this is a strict standard it will clearly be satisfied where directors allow a company to incur credit when they have no reason to think the creditors will ever be paid[16]. However it has been held that it can also be satisfied where the directors have no good reason to think funds will become available to pay the creditors when their debts become due or shortly thereafter[17].

When the provisions were introduced in 1929, only directors could be made liable, but since 1948 the provisions have applied to any persons 'knowingly parties to the carrying on of the business' with intent to defraud creditors. It has been held that this involves taking at least some active steps in the management of the business. Thus a company secretary who merely carries out the administrative functions of such an office is not concerned in the management of the company or in carrying on its business[18]. So also a floating charge holder who merely waits until the company is rich in assets before appointing a receiver is not liable for fraudulent trading. Nor are creditors who press for payment liable for fraudulent trading merely because they know the debtor company will have no money to remain in business if it is honest. But creditors can be party to fraudulent trading if they accept money knowing it has been procured by carrying on business with intent to defraud creditors and for the very purpose of paying their debts[19].

The recent case of *Re Augustus Barnett & Son Ltd*[20] raised both the issue of being party to the carrying on of business and of the necessary intent to defraud, in the context of parent companies giving financial support to their ailing subsidiaries. The directors of Augustus Barnett Ltd, a wholly owned subsidiary of a Spanish company, Rumasa S A, were advised that they were at risk of personal liability for fraudulent trading and that unless additional funds to pay current debts were obtained, the company should cease trading. Additional finance was obtained from another subsidiary of Rumasa and Rumasa itself gave suppliers assurances of continued support which were given wide publicity at a press conference. When a few months later Rumasa withdrew its support and Augustus Barnett went into liquidation the liquidator sought to make Rumasa liable for fraudulent trading. The

---

14 *Re Gerald Cooper Chemicals Ltd* [1978] Ch 262, [1978] 2 All ER 49.
15 Per Maugham J in *Re Patrick & Lyon Ltd* [1933] Ch 786 at 790.
16 *Re William C Leitch Bros Ltd* [1932] 2 Ch 71.
17 *R v Grantham* [1984] QB 675, [1984] 3 All ER 166, CA.
18 *Re Maidstone Building Provisions Ltd* [1971] 3 All ER 363, [1971] 1 WLR 1085.
19 *Re Gerald Cooper Chemicals Ltd*, supra.
20 [1986] BCLC 170. The case concerned the liability of a parent company for its subsidiary's debts. See generally on this *Hofstetter* (1990) 39 ICLQ 576.

claim was pursued in two ways, both of which failed. The first was on the basis that the business had been carried on by the directors of Augustus Barnett but that Rumasa had been a party to this. This failed because, while there was no doubt that the board of Augustus Barnett had carried on the company's business they had not done so with intent to defraud. The board had honestly believed Rumasa would continue to support the company and they would not have continued to trade without such belief. There were therefore no relevant acts to which Rumasa could be a party. The second argument was that Rumasa itself was carrying on the business with intent to defraud. Whilst Hoffmann J was prepared to accept as arguable that Rumasa was carrying on the business the evidence did not point cogently enough to the conclusion that it was intending thereby to defraud creditors. The evidence was consistent, for example, with Rumasa intending to support Augustus Barnett to enable it to stand on its own feet. The case illustrates the difficulties of seeking to make parent companies liable for the debts of subsidiaries and we shall refer to it again when considering liabilities for wrongful trading.

The case of *Re Sarflax Ltd*[1] is also worth looking at in some detail because it illustrates the interplay of various of the remedies open to liquidators. In this case the company, which was being sued in Italy by an Italian company, ceased trading on 30 April 1971. It thereupon began realising its assets and distributing them to its creditors. This included selling its fixed assets, stock in trade and work in progress at their book value to its parent company in settlement of a debt due to the parent company. On 23 September 1973, i e more than two years later, the company went into voluntary liquidation and in November 1973 the Italian creditor obtained judgment. By now there were insufficient assets left to satisfy the Italian judgment. The Italian creditor's obvious ground of complaint would be that the other creditors of the company had been preferred at its expense. However, the time zone that makes a preference liable to be set aside, then and now, is six months before the commencement of the winding up[2]. Today the Italian creditor might have a better chance of setting aside preferences to persons connected with the company such as its parent company, because in such cases the time zone is two years before commencement of winding up[3]. Even that, however, would only enable the Italian creditor to go back to November 1971. A second possibility today is that some of the distributions might be transactions at an undervalue but here again the time zone under s 238 is restricted to two years before the commencement of winding up[3].

Although there is no time zone under s 423 it is likely that preferring one creditor to another would not constitute putting assets beyond the reach of a claimant or otherwise prejudicing a claimant[4]. So the liquidator was left to argue instead that the directors were guilty of fraudulent trading in distributing the assets to the creditors while knowing that an action was proceeding against the company. After an extensive review of the law Oliver J held that, although distributing the proceeds of the realisation of assets could constitute carrying on business, the mere preference of one creditor over another did not constitute intent to defraud for the purposes of fraudulent trading.

---

1 [1979] Ch 592, [1979] 1 All ER 529.
2 Insolvency Act 1986, s 240(1)(b).
3 Ibid, s 240(1)(a).
4 *Re Lloyd's Furniture Palace Ltd, Evans v Lloyd's Furniture Palace Ltd* [1925] Ch 853.

The possibility has been raised as to whether a government department which kept an ailing company going for economic or social reasons could find itself liable for the debts of the company[5]. It might be thought there was some justification for such a result in that while there may be sound economic or social reasons for public money being used to help an ailing company, the effect of government support may be that private creditors then give credit to the company, which they lose if the company finally does go into liquidation. It could turn out therefore that private finance is thus used to serve a public purpose for which it might be felt the government should accept responsibility.

The extent of liability of those responsible for fraudulent trading is subject to the court's discretion. Maugham J stated in *Re William C Leitch Bros Ltd*[6] that it is not necessary to consider how many debts were incurred during the period of fraudulent trading nor whether any particular creditors were misled. Although a definite sum must be fixed by the court, the object of the section is penal rather than compensatory. Furthermore the liability is to contribute to the company's assets[7] which means that any money recovered will be available for creditors generally and not allocated to particular creditors[8]. Again, therefore, no inquiry will be necessary to determine which creditors, if any, were misled[9]. Finally, the court was given a new power in 1986 to defer any debts owed by the company to any person guilty of fraudulent trading in relation to the company[10].

WRONGFUL TRADING

The difficulties in establishing liability for fraudulent trading led the Cork Committee to recommend the introduction of a new provision under which civil personal liability could arise without proof of fraud or dishonesty and without requiring the criminal standard of proof[11]. This has now been implemented in the Insolvency Act 1986, s 214. As with fraudulent trading, applications can only be made once the company is in liquidation and if successful result in the court declaring persons liable to make such contributions towards payment of the company's debts as the court thinks fit[12]. The liquidator making the application must satisfy the court that at some

5 See Ganz *Government and Industry* (1977) pp 97–100. Rumasa SA had been nationalised by the Spanish government just before it gave the letters of comfort concerning the financing of Augustus Barnett & Son Ltd. In relation to British Leyland successive Secretaries of State gave assurances to the effect that the government would ensure that the obligations of British Leyland to its creditors were met. The assurances expired on 29 March 1988 when the sale of the government's holding in British Leyland (now Rover Group) to British Aerospace was announced.
6 [1932] 2 Ch 71. There is a helpful summary of the relevant principles in *Re a Company (No 001418 of 1988)* [1990] BCC 526 at 531–533.
7 Insolvency Act 1986, s 213(2).
8 Until 1986 the court had a discretion to order payment to particular creditors. See the discussion in *Re Cyona Distributors Ltd* [1967] Ch 889, [1967] 1 All ER 281, CA.
9 *In Re a Company (No 001418 of 1988)* (note 6 above) the court fixed a compensatory maximum by reference to the amount of the debts of the creditors proved to be defrauded by the fraudulent trading and then added to that figure a punitive element.
10 Insolvency Act 1986, s 215(4).
11 Cmnd 8558, ch 44.
12 Insolvency Act 1986, s 214(1).

time before commencement of the winding up, at a time when the persons were directors[13], they knew or ought to have concluded that there was no reasonable prospect of the company avoiding going into insolvent liquidation[14]. The court can then make the directors liable unless they in turn can satisfy the court that thereafter they took every step with a view to minimising potential loss to creditors they ought to have taken[15]. What a director ought to know or have concluded or done depends on two things: what a reasonable director carrying out similar functions in that type of company would know, conclude or do, and, the general knowledge, skill and experience of that director[16].

In the first reported case[17] on wrongful trading it was held[18] that in having regard to the functions of the directors in question in relation to the company in question the court will take account of whether it is a small company with simple accounting procedures and equipment or a large company with sophisticated procedures. Nevertheless there are certain minimum standards for all directors: keeping accounting records, preparing annual accounts and laying them before the general meeting and registrar. In deciding whether directors knew or ought to have concluded that there was no reasonable prospect of the company avoiding insolvent liquidation it is therefore appropriate to take account of knowledge the directors would have had, had the requisite accounts been prepared on time.

It is likely that liquidators will now rely on wrongful trading rather than fraudulent trading for making persons liable to contribute towards the company's assets. The first point of comparison in the two provisions is as to who can be made liable. In fraudulent trading it is persons who are party to the carrying on of business. In wrongful trading it is directors or shadow directors, the latter being persons in accordance with whose instructions the directors are accustomed to act[19]. As to the conduct needed to establish liability, under fraudulent trading the onus is on the liquidator to show that the business was carried on with intent to defraud. In wrongful trading the onus is on the directors or shadow directors to show that they took positive steps to minimise the loss to creditors. Once liability is established, the extent of any contribution to the company's assets is, in both sections, a matter for the court's discretion but unlike fraudulent trading the aim here is primarily compensatory rather than penal. Subject to relevant factors in the particular case the appropriate sum is the amount by which the company's

---

13 Or shadow directors: ibid, s 214(7).
14 Ibid, s 214(2).
15 Ibid, s 214(3).
16 Ibid, s 214(4).
17 *Re Produce Marketing Consortium Ltd (No 2)* [1989] BCLC 520. See comments by Prentice [1990] 10 Ox JLS 265 and Oditah [1990] LM & CLQ 205. See also *Re DKG Contractors Ltd* [1990] BCC 903.
18 [1989] BCLC 520 at 550.
19 Section 741(2). However, a person is not deemed a shadow director by reason only that the directors act on advice given by him in a professional capacity. One of the issues about which there is likely to be much litigation is the circumstances in which a parent company is a shadow director of its subsidiary. Would Rumasa SA have been a shadow director of Augustus Barnett & Sons Ltd? See above, pp 714–715. Another possibility is that a secured lender could become a shadow director: see *Re a Company (No 005009 of 1987), ex p Copp* [1989] BCLC 13 at 14–18.

assets were depleted by the conduct which amounted to wrongful trading[20]. As in fraudulent trading, however, the court also has the power to defer debts owing from the company to any person found liable for wrongful trading[1].

It is noticeable that neither fraudulent nor wrongful trading liability breaches the principle of limited liability for shareholders as such. It has been convincingly shown that the economic arguments in favour of limited liability for investors are less strong when the number of persons who might be made liable is small and their ability to influence the conduct of the business concerned is relatively high[2]. The provisions imposing liability in both fraudulent and wrongful trading are consistent with these economic arguments. Liability is imposed under both sections potentially on a relatively small group of people who are, however, instrumental in the running of the business.

LIABILITY FOR BREACH OF DUTY

The other route a liquidator may use for seeking to make persons liable generally to contribute to the company's assets is through liability for breach of duty to the company[3]. The duty may be either the fiduciary duty or the duty of care and skill. The content of such duties has been examined already[4] but it may be helpful to consider them briefly in relation to liquidation, a context in which they often become relevant.

In one respect it is easier to bring actions in respect of breaches of fiduciary duty or negligence once the company is in liquidation. This is because the Insolvency Act 1986, s 212 provides a summary procedure by which such actions may be brought[5]. This enables the court, on the application of the

---

20 *Re Produce Marketing Consortium Ltd (No 2)*, above note 17, at 553–554. Knox J held the two directors jointly and severally liable to pay the liquidator £75,000 but ordered one of them, D, to indemnify the other fully for the first £50,000. This was because D had guaranteed the company's bank overdraft which was also secured by a floating charge and the judge seems to have assumed the charge would cover the contributions paid under s 214. This, however, may not be correct. On the analogy of recovering a preference, because the company itself could not have recovered the money as only the liquidator can take proceedings for wrongful trading, the money does not form part of the assets of the company subject to the floating charge but forms a fund available to the unsecured creditors: *Re Yagerphone Ltd* [1935] Ch 392.

1 Insolvency Act 1986, s 215(4). This could have particular significance if a parent company was held to be a shadow director of its subsidiary. It could represent a modest implementation of the more far reaching proposals of the Cork Committee (Cmnd 8558) paras 1953–1965. See also *Re Purpoint Ltd* [1991] BCC 121.

2 See the very clear article by Halpern, Trebilcock and Turnbull (1980) 30 University of Toronto Law Journal 117.

3 Where the company is insolvent the possibility of individual creditors having rights of action against the directors personally in respect of particular debts becomes very significant. For a thorough analysis of the circumstances in which such liability may arise, see Pennington *Directors' Personal Liability* (1987) paras 10.01–10.10. See also *Thomas Saunders Partnership v Harvey* (1989) Times, 10 May. The question whether shareholders as well as directors could be liable is raised in *Metall und Rohstoff AG v Donaldson Lufkin & Jeurette Inc* [1990] 1 QB 391 and *Kuwait Asia Bank EC v National Mutual Life Nominees Ltd* [1991] 1 AC 187, [1990] 3 All ER 404, PC.

4 See Chapter 25 above.

5 For an outline of the procedural advantages see Pennington *Directors' Personal Liability* (1987) para 11.06. The section does not provide a new cause of action but merely provides a summary procedure.

official receiver, the liquidator or any creditor or contributory[6] to examine the conduct of any promoter or officer[7] of the company, or any liquidator, administrator or administrative receiver of it. The court examines their conduct to see if they have misapplied or retained or become accountable for money or other property of the company or been guilty of any misfeasance or other breach of duty to the company[8]. If the court finds that this is the case, it can order the person to repay, restore or account for it or to make contribution to the assets of the company of such sum as the court thinks just.

However, it frequently happens that the shareholders in the company had no objection to, or even authorised, the conduct which the liquidator is now complaining of as a breach of duty. The question then arises whether the consent of the shareholders amounts to consent by the company so that the company can no longer complain of any breach of duty and neither therefore can the liquidator on behalf of the creditors. In the *Multinational Gas*[9] case it was held that in relation to allegations of negligence and where the company was solvent at the time the relevant decisions where taken, the consent of the shareholders did bind the liquidator[10]. The court was influenced by the argument that unsecured creditors have no interest in the way debtors look after their assets and in this they equated companies with individuals. Thus Lawton LJ[11] said that, 'Just as an individual can act like a fool provided he keeps within the law so could the plaintiff, but in its case it was for the shareholders to decide whether the plaintiff should act foolishly'. Likewise Dillon LJ[12], 'An individual trader who is solvent is free to make stupid, but honest, commercial decisions in the conduct of his own business. He owes no duty of care to future creditors. The same applies to a partnership of individuals. A company, as it seems to me, likewise owes no duty of care to future creditors'[13]. It might be different where the allegation is one of

---

6 Two changes to applications by contributories were made in 1986. They no longer need to show that they will benefit from any order the court might make but applications by contributories do need the leave of the court: Insolvency Act 1986, s 212(5). Minority shareholders are, however, potentially free from the restrictions imposed by the rule in *Foss v Harbottle* (1843) 2 Hare 461.
7 Ie director, manager or secretary; s 744.
8 Since the Insolvency Act 1986, the summary procedure does now cover allegations of negligence, implementing a recommendation of the Jenkins Committee: Report of the Committee on Company Law Reform (Cmnd 1749) para 503(d). The courts have traditionally resisted adjudicating allegations of negligence against directors where it involves the court in reviewing business decisions. *Re Welfab Engineers Ltd* [1990] BCLC 833 is an interesting recent illustration of the difficulties. Were the directors negligent in accepting an offer for the business as a going concern which would enable all the employees and directors to keep their jobs and rejecting a potentially higher offer for the premises alone?
9 *Multinational Gas and Petrochemical Co v Multinational Gas and Petrochemical Services Ltd* [1983] Ch 258, [1983] 2 All ER 563, CA.
10 See, ibid, Lawton LJ at 268–269, 571 and Dillon LJ at 288–291, 585–587; cf the dissenting judgment of May LJ at 280–282, 579–580.
11 Ibid, at 268, 571.
12 Ibid, at 288, 585.
13 Whilst it is true that neither individual nor corporate debtors owe a duty of care to their creditors it is submitted that the courts have been too slow to recognize that the different rules that apply to limited liability companies for the purpose of creditor protection ought to permit creditors locus standi to enforce them. The decisions in *Mills v Northern Rly of Buenos Ayres Co* (1870) 5 Ch App 621 and *Lawrence v West Somerset Mineral Rly Co* [1918] 2 Ch 250 refusing creditors locus standi to seek injunctions to restrain dividends being paid

misfeasance involving misapplication of the company's funds rather than just negligent decision making causing loss to the company[14]. It will certainly be different if at the time of the alleged breach of duty the company was insolvent because in such circumstances the shareholders have no financial interest in what becomes of the remaining assets of the company. The company is essentially trading now at the risk of the creditors' money and the consent of the shareholders to any breach of duty should not deprive the creditors of any remedy[15].

Disqualification of directors of insolvent companies

As a further deterrent to irresponsible directors a provision was introduced in 1976[16] whereby directors of companies which went into insolvent liquidation could in certain circumstances be disqualified for a period from future management of companies. These provisions have since been revised[17] and are now contained in the Company Directors Disqualification Act 1986, ss 6 and 7. Under the revised provisions the court *must* make a disqualification order[18] against any person, if it is satisfied that the person was a director[19] of a company which, while he was a director or subsequently, has become insolvent[20] and that his conduct as director of that company (either alone or together with his conduct as director of other companies) makes him unfit to be concerned in the management of a company[1]. The crucial question is whether a person is unfit to be concerned in the management of a company and in deciding this the court is given certain factors that it must have particular regard to[2]. These include: breaches of duty by the director; responsibility for any failure by the company to comply with Companies Act requirements as to production of accounts and registration of documents; responsibility for the company becoming insolvent, failure by the company to supply goods or services which have been paid for or the company entering into transactions at an undervalue or giving voidable preferences. Although it has been held that the primary purpose of disqualification is not penal but protection of the public, it does involve a substantial interference with the freedom of the individual. Accordingly it has been accepted that,

from non-distributable profits is in marked contrast to the statutory recognition of creditors locus standi in s 136(2)–(6) (reduction of capital) and ss 176, 177 (private company redeeming or purchasing shares out of capital).

14 See, for example, *Re Horsley & Weight Ltd* [1982] Ch 442, [1982] 3 All ER 1045, CA per Cumming Bruce LJ at 455, 1055 and Templeman LJ at 456, 1056.

15 *West Mercia Safetywear Ltd v Dodd* [1988] BCLC 250, CA. Note particularly the passage from the judgment of Street CJ in *Kinsela v Russell Kinsela Pty Ltd* [1986] 4 NSWLR 722 at 730 which was cited with approval in *West Mercia Safetywear Ltd v Dodd*. As to when a company counts as insolvent for this purpose see the analysis in *Nicholson v Permakraft (NZ) Ltd* [1985] 1 NZLR 242 at 249 per Cooke J.

16 In the Insolvency Act 1976, s 9 which subsequently became the Companies Act 1985, s 300.

17 See the discussion by the Cork Committee (Cmnd 8558) ch 45.

18 For the scope of a disqualification order see Company Directors Disqualification Act 1986, s 1(1). It prohibits being 'concerned in or taking part' in management, as to which see *R v Campbell* [1984] BCLC 83, CA (management consultant advising the board).

19 Or shadow director: Company Directors Disqualification Act 1986, s 6(3).

20 This covers not only insolvent liquidation but also being subject to an administration order and having an administrative receiver appointed: ibid, s 6(2).

1 Ibid, s 6(1).

2 Ibid, s 9(1) and Sch 1.

'ordinary commercial misjudgment is in itself not sufficient to justify disqualification. In the normal case, the conduct complained of must display a lack of commercial probity although . . . in an extreme case of gross negligence or total incompetence disqualification could be appropriate'[3]. The period of disqualification must be for a minimum of two years and may extend to a maximum of 15[4]. Applications for disqualification orders on these grounds can be made only by the Secretary of State or in compulsory liquidation by the Official Receiver[5] and must be made within two years of the company becoming insolvent[6], unless leave of the court is obtained[7]. It is also open to a court which has found a person liable for fraudulent or wrongful trading to make a disqualification order against the person for up to 15 years[8]. This is a matter for the court's own initiative and no application by the Secretary of State or anyone else is needed. The effect of disqualification orders generally was also strengthened in 1986 by a provision exposing disqualified persons to personal liability for debts incurred by companies operating under their direction while disqualified[9].

Prohibition on the use of company names

One of the tricks of those who abused limited liability was to form several companies with very similar names which could then be used to confuse creditors. A common variant of this was quietly to liquidate one company while continuing to trade via another company with an almost identical name. It would often be a long time before creditors of the old company realised what had happened and probably too late to bother doing anything

---

3 Per Browne-Wilkinson V-C in *Re Lo-Line Electric Motors Ltd* [1988] Ch 477 at 486, [1988] 2 All ER 692 at 696. The statement was later approved by the Court of Appeal but with the observation that the incompetence or negligence need not be 'total' but that a 'very marked degree' would suffice: *Re Sevenoaks Stationers (Retail) Ltd* [1990] 3 WLR 1165 at 1178. The Court of Appeal also resolved a difference of opinion among the judges by holding that trading while running up Crown debts is no different from trading while running up other debts.

4 Ibid, s 6(4). If the matter is dealt with summarily then the maximum period of disqualification the court will impose is five years: Insolvent Companies (Disqualification of Unfit Directors) Proceedings Rules 1986, SI 1986/612.

5 Company Directors Disqualification Act, s 7(1). One of the problems with the old law was that the liquidator who knew about the past failings of directors had little incentive to seek a disqualification order to protect future creditors of other companies. Now rules require the office holder of each insolvent company to send a report to the Secretary of State listing all directors or shadow directors in the three years before insolvency stating whether the conduct of any of them makes them unfit to be concerned in the management of companies and if so giving details of such conduct. Even if no adverse report is made on the conduct of a director the Secretary of State may notice if the same names regularly appear in relation to insolvent companies: The Insolvent Companies (Report on Conduct of Directors) No 2 Rules 1986, SI 1986/2134. According to the Department of Trade and Industry Annual Report on Insolvency, in 1989 proceedings were instituted in 440 cases and 270 orders were made of which 240 were for 5 years or less.

6 Where the appointment of an administrative receiver or the making of an administration order is followed by winding up, the two year period begins with the earlier event. No separate two year period commences on winding up unless the company has been restored to solvency in the meantime: *Re Tasbian Ltd (No 1)* [1991] BCLC 54, CA.

7 Company Directors Disqualification Act 1986, s 7(2). For a case where leave was refused, see *Re Crestjoy Products Ltd* [1990] BCLC 677.

8 Ibid, s 10.

9 Ibid, s 15.

about it. This practice is now prevented by a provision whereby when a company has gone into insolvent liquidation any name by which the company was known in the previous 12 months, or which is so similar as to suggest an association with it, is a prohibited name in relation to a person who was a director or shadow director of it at any time in those 12 months[10]. The effect of the prohibition is that the person must not, without leave of the court or in such circumstances as may be prescribed[11], for five years, be a director of or concerned in the promotion, formation or management of a company using such a prohibited name[12]. Nor must he be concerned in the carrying on of a business carried on otherwise than by a company, under such a prohibited name[13]. Breach of this prohibition is a criminal offence[14] but in addition it will result in the director being personally liable for debts incurred during the period of the breach[15].

10 Insolvency Act 1986, s 216(1)(2).
11 Insolvency Rules 1986, SI 1986/1925, rr 4.226–4.230.
12 Insolvency Act 1986, s 216(3).
13 Ibid.
14 Ibid, s 216(4).
15 Ibid, s 217.

PART VII

The international dimension

CHAPTER 40

International dimensions of company law

THE EXTENSION OF CORPORATE ACTIVITY BEYOND NATIONAL FRONTIERS

We saw in earlier chapters how some of the earliest English companies were international enterprises. They were formed to exploit international trade. Indeed, some of them were the earliest vehicles for colonisation. A classic case is the East India Company.

Later, in the nineteenth century, many English companies carried on business in the Empire through local branches taking advantage of the favourable trading conditions. Some like the British South Africa Company performed a colonising role. In this century companies like ICI and the major oil companies like BP and Shell have carried on business in many countries through local subsidiaries. Since the end of the First World War there has been a phenomenal increase in overseas subsidiaries of US companies. Since the formation of the EEC there has been an increase in overseas subsidiaries of European companies and more recently there has been a large increase in overseas subsidiaries of Japanese companies[1].

The development of a transnational economy shaped by money flows as much as trade in goods and services has stimulated faster economic and legal integration. The aim is now not so much profit maximisation as market maximisation, and trade follows investment and is becoming a function of investment[2].

The extension of corporate activity beyond the frontiers of the country of incorporation has sometimes given rise to complex problems of private international law. In general, English law tends to solve these by the application of the law of incorporation or English law[3]. However, this is not the place for a detailed discussion of such problems. The reader is referred to the specialist works on private international law such as *Dicey, Cheshire* and *Graveson*.

There are separate company registries for each part of the UK. England and Wales are assimiliated and share one registry. Scotland has a separate registry but is governed by most of the provisions of the Companies Act, although it has separate case law and statutory provisions on matters such as company charges and receivership and winding up. Northern Ireland has a separate registry and separate legislation although the provisions are virtually the same as English law. For Northern Irish and foreign companies,

---

1 Se L G Franko *The European Multinationals* (1976) p 10, Table 1.2 for comparative data until 1970.
2 Peter Drucker, *The New Realities* (1989) pp 115–17.
3 See L C B Gower *Modern Company Law* (4th edn, 1979) chapter 29 for a useful summary. See also the discussion in the context of cross-frontier mergers in Chapter 41.

Pt XXIII of CA 1985 provides special disclosure provisions for companies establishing a place of business in Great Britain.

Disclosure by overseas companies

Under s 691 such a company establishing a place of business here must file:

(1)   a certified copy of its constitution;
(2)   a list of directors and secretary;
(3)   the names and addresses of one or more persons authorised to accept service.

Any alterations must be notified within 21 days after notice could with reasonable diligence have been received in Great Britain[4]. The requirement of (3) goes to jurisdiction as well as disclosure and is intended to protect creditors[5].

Accounts must also be prepared and filed[6] and particulars of charges registered[7]. The company must exhibit its name and the fact of limited liability[8].

In addition to these requirements, which only apply to a company which has established a place of business here, the provisions of the Financial Services Act 1986[9] apply to issues of, or dealings in, foreign company securities in the UK[10].

Lastly, foreign companies which are carrying on business in Great Britain or have at any time done so can be the subject of an investigation by the Department of Trade and Industry and most of the powers discussed in Chapter 29 apply to them.

COMPANY LAW FAMILIES

We saw how American and European influences were at work in the early nineteenth century English legislation. Of course, it was a two-way process. The UK was the leading commercial nation at that time and was a major initiator as well as borrower of ideas regarding corporateness.

Nevertheless, one can discern an interesting phenomenon from an early period. The USA from the beginning of its independence was an experimenter with the corporate form. It did not slavishly follow English ideas. It moulded the law to suit local conditions. However, there was a close affinity between English and American company law which survived until the 1930s. Since then, particularly with the growth of legislation on securities regulation, there has been substantially a parting of the ways[11]. The UK remained a close influence on the development of Commonwealth company laws until

4 Section 692.
5 *Gower*, op cit, p 747.
6 Section 700.
7 Part XXIII, Chapter III.
8 Section 693(b) and (d).
9 See generally B Rider, D Chaikin and C Abrams, *Guide to the Financial Services Act 1986*.
10 See ss 142(1), 159, 160 as amended by the CA 1989, s 212 and Sch 24.
11 See generally L C B Gower (1956) 69 Harv L Rev 1369.

relatively recently. This was inevitable given its cultural dominance and the close economic ties between the UK and the Commonwealth. However, by the late 1960s, Canada and Australia were branching out on their own and were more subject to American influences. New Zealand continued in closer association with the UK until the 1970s. The major change has been the UK's membership of the European Economic Community since 1973. This is still dominated by the original six states who were members of a different legal tradition and company law inheritance which in some respects was more advanced but generally lagged behind the UK in the scope and sophistication of its disclosure requirements and securities markets.

Germany, the leading company law jurisdiction of the Six, for instance, developed three important company law concepts—the private company as a distinct species, the dual board system and the principle of co-determination[12]. The other original member states adopted the German model of the private company but the UK and Republic of Ireland have not. Even the recent developments in *Ebrahimi v Westbourne Galleries Ltd*[13] fall short of the European concept and are of uncertain scope outside the area of winding up. The two-tier board has not been universally adopted in the Six but has dominated EC thinking until recently. Co-determination, a product of an unusual and distinctly German history, has likewise appealed to EC policy makers who have seen it in some way as a formal solution to an essential contradiction in labour relations. It is generally treated with scepticism or hostility by both management and labour in the UK. France has tended to follow the German reforms in recent years. In comparison, Italy, the Netherlands and the Benelux countries have been more conservative.

This membership of the EC means that there has been a complete parting of the ways with the USA and a growing detachment from Commonwealth company law reforms. Even if it wished to follow these reforms, the UK has lost the right to do so. The result since 1973 has been to bog down UK company law reform, and to re-orientate it.

Within the Commonwealth, it seems inevitable that Canada will move closer to the US model and that New Zealand will be influenced by Australia. Unfortunately, Australian Company Laws have become almost gratuitously complex and are the subject of active constitutional controversy which has not been finally resolved. The approach has become very 'black letter' with inadequate attention being paid to underlying principle and policy. Like the United Kingdom practitioners, Australians seem to be swamped by more and more technical reforms which there is little time to reflect upon. Recently, New Zealand has been looking closely at Canadian reforms as an alternative model but the logic of the Closer Economic Relations Agreement with Australia leads perhaps inexorably towards harmonisation between the two countries. All these jurisdictions have opted for a statutory system of securities regulation rather than the UK system of self-regulation.

Japan is an interesting subject of comparison. When it began to industrialise, it based its company law on the German model but after the Second World War it adopted a system of securities regulation based on US laws.

---

12 See Clive Schmitthoff 'The Future of the European Company Law Scene' in *The Harmonization of European Company Law*, ed C Schmitthoff (1973).
13 [1973] AC 360, HL.

Recently it has adopted close corporation and insider trading laws based on the US models. It would be a mistake, however, to put too much emphasis on the law since the Japanese system can only be understood as part of the larger picture of Japanese society in which tradition is perhaps more important than statute. Japan is increasingly active in international capital markets as a participant although it has been cautious in the movement towards regulation of capital markets.

Company law as a subject of international unification

The rules of private international law and problems of recognition and establishment of companies in different states have traditionally been the subject of bilateral and multilateral treaties between states, and, indeed, there are many such treaties[14]. On the other hand, there has only been a very limited record of international unification of municipal laws. This may be due partly to the difficulty of the task since company law is not entirely a discrete topic which can be separated from other fields of municipal law and partly because governments have not felt that there was a pressing need. Also, companies are an integral part of the economic and fiscal structure of a particular state and it may have been thought dangerous to tamper in the absence of a moving economic or political force. Such attempts as have been made to unify municipal law have been on a regional basis—the EC, the Council of Europe, the Central American Common Market and the Nordic Council. The greatest progress to date outside the EC has been in the Nordic Council where there is a greater degree of homogeneity[15].

Both the EC and the United Nations are actively at work in attempting to standardise company accounts. This is, of course, a formidable task. Traditions of accounting, the role of accounts, the status of the accounting profession and indeed basic standards of commercial honesty differ from country to country. Nevertheless, the task is worthwhile and it will facilitate more meaningful group accounts for companies with international operations.

THE GROWTH AND REGULATION OF MULTINATIONALS AND TRANSNATIONALS

Companies like ICI, BP and Shell are multinationals and transnationals. Although the parent company is registered here, they operate with subsidiaries all over the world. Production is increasingly diversified.

In terms of Gross National Product, a multinational like General Motors would rank fourteenth in the world if it were a state. Organisations of this size are inevitably a political force in the world. They raise problems for nation states which individual states find it difficult to solve. While multinational companies enable most countries to exploit their assets and provide capital and jobs, they tend to operate either in their own corporate interests or the interests of their parent country. They can switch funds and capital with alarming speed and produce instability in their wake. Sometimes they

---

14 E Stein *Harmonization of European Company Laws* (1971) p 68.
15 Ibid.

represent a latter-day vestige of a former colonial regime. There is a need for international regulation.

So far the EC has attempted rather unsuccessfully to tackle the problem on a regional level. The United Nations has also turned its attention to it on a global basis, spurred on by Third World countries who fear exploitation. This in its turn has forced Western countries to begin to think seriously of devising their own system of controls through the OECD. The regulatory problems encompass not only company law and accounting but also monopolies and restrictive practices, revenue law and labour law. At a time of growing international interdependence, these problems loom large and must be dealt with.

THE PRESENT CONTRADICTION

We detect a certain contradiction in present trends. There is, on the one hand, the movement towards greater harmonisation of company laws. This is due partly to economic integration which has superseded colonialism to some extent as a harmonising force and partly due to the fact that the basic problems of corporate enterprise are the same throughout the western world and the mixed economies of the Third World. On the other hand, economic integration through regionalism tends to separate off countries into geographical units and to make the reform process slower, more conservative and less responsible to outside influences. The EC and North America are developed regions and a third region is forming centred around the Pacific Rim. These have an increasingly uneasy relationship with each other which is exacerbated by the international financial revolution which has led to a semi-autonomous world economy of money. Add to this the complications arising from the developments in Eastern Europe and the impact of the war in the Middle East, and we have a very unstable situation. Perhaps the fallacy is to seek for stability and consistency in such a dynamic subject matter at a time of great economic and political flux.

While unification and harmonisation of municipal systems is involved in such a contradiction one sees in the regulation of multinational enterprise the beginning of an attempt to develop the international legal order. While it is a mistake to expect too much of such a development, such discussion as has taken place has provided a forum for smaller countries of the Third World and a way of monitoring corporate activities. This has enabled discussion to take place at a more rational level. At the present stage of international law, this is as much as one can reasonably expect.

CHAPTER 41

Cross frontier mergers

THE CONCEPT OF A CROSS FRONTIER MERGER

In spite of the globalisation of financial and other markets, domestic and international law do not greatly facilitate cross frontier co-operation. Each country has its own corporate laws, securities regulation, foreign ownership laws, antitrust, taxation law and system of industrial relations. Apart from limited regional integration, bilateral treaties and ad hoc contracting promoted or encouraged by governments, there has been little in the way of international co-operation. Within a particular state co-operation can usually take place. The form that particular co-operation takes will be determined by the domestic law, and particularly by its business organisations, antitrust and tax laws. Some states have been slow to facilitate co-operation in the form of mergers.

In economics and antitrust there are three general types of merger: horizontal, vertical and conglomerate[1]. A horizontal merger occurs when two firms in the same industry are merged. Both firms must have been rivals in the sense of selling the same product in the same geographic market. A vertical merger occurs whe a firm merges with one of its suppliers or one of its customers. The first is called backward integration, the second forward integration. A conglomerate merger can be one of three types. A product extension merger occurs where a multiple product firm acquires a producer of a further commodity. A market extension merger involves firms in the same product but not the same market. A pure conglomerate merger involves two firms which are wholly unrelated. Merger, however, is an ambiguous legal term[2]. In English law it is used loosely to cover *reconstruction* which involves fusion of enterprise, *amalgamation* which involves the formation of a new holding company to take over the two original companies and a *takeover* whereby one company takes a controlling interest in the shares of another[3]. Sometimes co-operation short of a full merger takes the form of a *joint venture* agreement[4], which is either a form of partnership or a looser agreement or co-operation, or a *consortium*[5] where a number of companies join together to form a joint company for a particular, usually limited, purpose. In a consortium no single company has control.

---

1 See Roger D Blair and David L Kaserman *Antitrust Economics* (1985) p 227–228 on which this classification is based.
2 Cf *Weinberg and Blank on Takeovers and Mergers* (5th edn, 1989) para 1–004.
3 Ibid, para 1–003 et seq.
4 See Jesse H Choper, John C Coffee Jr and C Robert Morris Jr *Cases and Materials on Corporations* (3rd edn, 1989) p 50.
5 See F Wooldridge 'Consortium and Related Operations in the United Kingdom' [1978] 3 LMCLQ 427; A H Boulton 'Construction Consortia—their Formation and Management' [1959] JBL 234; J T Brown 'International Joint Venture Contracts in English Law' (1979) 5 Droit et Pratique du Commerce International 193.

In US corporation and tax laws the following transactions are commonly referred to as mergers[6].

(i)   A statutory merger or consolidation, known as an 'A' reorganisation under section 368(1)(a)(A) of the Internal Revenue Code. This involves one firm merging into another firm or a consolidation involving two firms merging into a newly created third firm.

(ii) A stock for stock exchange (a B reorganisation). Here one corporation becomes the subsidiary of the other.

(iii) An exchange of voting stock for substantially all of the assets of a target corporation (a C reorganisation).

(iv) The purchase of assets of the target corporation for cash or non-voting securities.

(v)   The purchase of the stock of the target for cash or non-voting securities.

There are tax advantages in (i)–(iii)[7].

In most of the continental European member states of the EEC a merger is effected by either:

(1)   an absorption of one company by another and the transfer of all the assets of the absorbed company to the other. The latter issues shares to the shareholders of the absorbed company which is then dissolved (this resembles an A reorganisation in US laws and a reconstruction in English law); or

(2)   the formation of a new company which absorbs two other companies as in (1), with the latter companies being dissolved rather than becoming members of a group as they would in an English amalgamation. This resembles a consolidation in US laws[8].

Most continental European countries have not hitherto recognised the hostile takeover as a means of achieving a merger[9]. In most countries 100% approval is necessary and the company acquired needs to be wound up[10]. Mergers there are thus essentially co-operative in nature[11]. This is also the position which prevails in Japan where recent attempts by US corporations to take over Japanese companies by hostile tender offers have been frustrated[12].

The topic of corporations in general receives fragmented treatment in private international law[13] and questions of merger are rarely (if ever)

6 See Bruce Wasserstein *Corporate Finance Law* (1978) Ch 15.

7 Ibid, pp 203 et seq.

8 See R R Pennington and F Wooldridge *Companies in the Common Market* (3rd edn); S N Frommel and J H Thompson *Company Law in Europe* (1975).

9 For the changing scene see Simon MacLachlan and William Mackesy, 'Acquisitions of Companies in Europe—Practibility, Disclosure and Regulation: An Overview' 23 Int Law 373 (1989).

10 See *Internal Market and Industrial Cooperation—Statute for the European Company* Internal Market White Paper, point 137, Commission of the European Communities Com (88) 320 final, Brussels, 15 July 1988 (hereinafter called 'EC White Paper'), p 13.

11 See Deborah DeMott 'Comparative Dimensions of Takeover Regulation' 65 Wash ULQ (1987).

12 H Boone Pickens, the notorious US corporate raider, recently had this experience.

13 See Thomas C Drucker 'Companies in Private International Law' (1968) 17 ICLQ 28. The matter receives token treatment in most works on conflicts of laws. A valuable exception is C M Schmitthoff *The Conflict of Laws* (2nd edn) Ch XIII.

discussed[14]. In Anglo-American systems a company is governed by the law of the place of incorporation[15] and this law governs merger of the company with another company of the same domicile[16]. The position is less clear with a cross frontier merger although a corporation validly incorporated in one jurisdiction will normally be recognised in other jurisdictions[17]. It may, however, be subjected to special local formalities[18]. With regard to mergers, US laws operate choice of law rules which are based on the law of the place of incorporation except in unusual cases where, with respect to a particular issue, another state has a more significant relationship to the event and the parties[19]. The law of the place of incorporation normally governs the exercise of power within the corporation and the public issue of its securities[20] except that in the case of the latter the requirements of the place of issue have also to be complied with[1]. Different rules may apply to debt financing[2]. In Anglo-American laws a state may wind up the business of a corporation within its jurisdiction without necessarily terminating the existence of the foreign corporation[3]. Dissolution otherwise is a matter for the law of the place of incorporation[4].

Within a federal system the law relating to mergers between corporations incorporated in different states within the federation is usually determined partly by the constitution and partly[5] by state laws. Most constitutions contain full faith and credit clauses in respect of state laws and legal acts but some require licensing of out-of-state corporations. Canada requires licensing but has provisions for continuance where a corporation wishes to shift residence between jurisdictions[6]. In the USA a liberal regime exists which has facilitated capital accumulation. Many of the leading corporations are registered in Delaware, a permissive state, whose Corporation Code expressly provides for a merger or consolidation of a Delaware corporation with a foreign corporation[7]. By contrast in the looser-knit union of the European Community many of the member states have put a number of obstacles in the way of cross frontier mergers. It is the attempts to overcome these obstacles against a background of different corporate law and even conflict of laws philosophies which makes the EC such an interesting case study of regional co-operation, which may provide a model for further international co-operation.

---

14 See *National Bank of Greece and Athens SA v Metliss* [1958] AC 509, HL. However, the corporations in this case were of the same domicile. See Drucker, op cit, p 33. For the position in US laws see *Restatement of the Law 2d, Conflict of Laws* Ch 13, para 302, Comment.

15 Schmitthoff, op cit, p 336; Drucker, op cit, p 28.

16 See note 14, supra.

17 Schmitthoff, op cit, pp 334–335.

18 See eg Restatement, op cit, para 297, comment.

19 Ibid, para 302.

20 *Banco de Bilbao v Sancho* [1938] 2 KB 176, 194–195, CA; Drucker, op cit, p 47.

 1 Drucker, op cit, p 51.

 2 Ibid (proper law of the contract of loan as well as country of issue—quaere questions of security).

 3 See Schmitthoff, op cit, pp 339 et seq.

 4 *Lazard Bros & Co v Midland Bank Ltd* [1933] AC 289 at p 297, HL per Lord Wright.

 5 See eg US Constitution, Act IV Section 1.

 6 See for instance Ontario Business Corporations Act 1982, s 179; Canada Business Corporations Act 1985, s 187.

 7 General Corporation Law of the State of Delaware, section 252.

OBSTACLES TO CROSS FRONTIER MERGERS

A recent report by the EC Commission[8] has identified the following obstacles to transnational mergers.

1. The difficulty under present laws of carrying out cross frontier mergers[9]. At the moment within the EC mergers take the form of participation in capital by minority holdings and joint ventures. The European Economic Interest Grouping (EEIG) was introduced to facilitate certain aspects of cross frontier joint ventures but is not intended as the vehicle for the merger itself.
2. Tax problems resulting from (a) taxation of hidden reserves, (b) double taxation of dividends, (c) economic double taxation which might arise from cross frontier transactions between associated companies if the profits of one of the companies have been adjusted upwards without a corresponding downward adjustment in the other country, (d) distortions arising because of the different corporation tax systems[10].
3. The differences in company laws and their administration between member states[11].
4. The difficulties under present laws of integrating a group of enterprises as a single economic unit. The law of most member states adopts a rather fragmented approach to the corporate group, except for disclosure purposes[12].
5. Administrative difficulties surrounding the establishment of companies. This is exacerbated by the unfamiliarity of foreign businessmen with the requirements of a particular country[13].

Although the Commission does not discuss them in this context there are the additional complications of the different anti-trust regimes[14] and industrial relations systems[15] which are also very significant factors.

Faced with these obstacles, cross frontier co-operation in Europe has taken a variety of forms of which the most significant are as follows.

(a) *Royal Dutch/Shell*   This was set up in 1907. Here Shell formed a wholly-owned English holding company. Royal Dutch formed a Dutch holding company. Each company transferred shares in subsidiaries to the respective holding companies then exchanged shares in the holding companies so that the picture was:

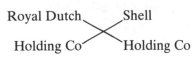

Royal Dutch   Shell

Holding Co   Holding Co

8 EC White Paper, pp 7 et seq.
9 Ibid, pp 7–8.
10 Ibid, pp 8–9.
11 Ibid, p 9.
12 Ibid.
13 Ibid.
14 See Klaus J Hopt, *European Merger Control*, Vol 1 (1982) passim.
15 See the *Green Paper on Employee Participation and Company Structure in the European Communities*, EEC Bull Supp 8/75; J Welch (1983) 8 ELR 83.

(b) *The Unilever type of agreement*   This merger was set up in 1927 and involves complex agreements between the UK company and the Dutch company for a pooling of assets and profits, treatment of shareholders pari passu and identical boards.

(c) *Agfa-Gevaert*   This was an example of intricate corporate structures between the German Agfa-Gevaert and the Belgian Gevaert NV set up to avoid the nationalist opposition which would have resulted if one company had been absorbed by the other.

(d) *Dunlop-Pirelli*   This left the parties as they were but gave each partner a distinct stake in the operations of the other. In essence this involved both companies creating subsidiaries to which were transferred the operations and assets of the parent companies. Each then exchanged an interest in its subsidiary for a corresponding interest in the other's subsidiary. Thus the structure is two headed. The merger experienced a number of difficulties, which are commercial and financial as much as structural.

(e) *Variations on the theme of joint ventures*   There has been an increasing number of joint venture agreements, particularly in the automobile industry. In the automobile industry these frequently provide for pooling of research and design and patents etc; rationalisation of production; common specifications for sub-contractors and suppliers; common machine tools; and joint financing. Examples are Renault-Peugeot, Ford, Chrysler, and BAC and Sub-Aviation on Concorde. An example in 1990 was the announcement by Volvo and Renault that they intend to make sizeable investments (20–25%) in each other in the hopes of making both companies more competitive. In addition to the equity investments the two companies intend to enter into an extensive co-operation agreement to co-ordinate elements of product development, purchasing and investment plans. However, each company will retain its separate identity, trademarks and distribution organisations and will continue assembling and marketing its own cars, trucks and buses. The co-operation structure is described by Pehr Gyllenhammar, the Volvo president, as 'an alliance, not a merger or an acquisition'.

A successful joint venture outside the automobile and aircraft industries is Polygram, jointly run by Siemens and Philips.

All of these five methods are essentially horizonal contractual arrangements which are attempts to cope with the absence of a truly international structure. At the same time the flexibility of ad hoc contracting is not without advantages.

EC STEPS TO FACILITATE CROSS FRONTIER MERGERS

A number of proposals to facilitate cross frontier co-operation has been put forward within the EC although the proposals have been marked with lack of success at the stage of implementation. Apart from the Right of Establishment of agencies, branches and subsidiaries without discrimination on grounds of nationality, there are no specific provisions in the Treaty of Rome on this but the treaty provides for law making in the form of regulations, directives and decisions. Under art 189, a regulation takes immediate internal effect in the member states. A directive is binding on the member states but leaves it to them to choose the method of implementation. A decision is only binding on the parties to whom it is addressed.

Initial efforts to facilitate cross frontier mergers within the EC were concentrated on a convention. This project was eventually dropped. The *European Economic Interest Grouping*[16] (EEIG) was created as a new legal form of co-operation between individuals, companies, firms, and other legal bodies from different member states by a EC regulation of 25 July 1985. The EEIG has a limited purpose, namely to facilitate or develop the economic activities of its members and to improve the results of these activities. It is not in itself a profit making venture. Its activities are only ancillary to the economic activities of its members. It has no power of management over its members' activities and can only hold shares in their undertakings, to the extent necessary to achieve its objectives. It must not employ more than 500 people and it must not be a member of another EEIG. It cannot be used by a company to make a loan to a director or transfer property between a company and a director except as allowed by national law. An EEIG is formed by contract between the members of the grouping. There are various registration and disclosure requirements and an EEIG has basically two organs, the members and the managers. Each member has to have the power to vote. If profits are made, they are to be apportioned to the members in accordance with the contract or, in the absence of any express provision, in equal shares. The members of the EEIG have unlimited joint and several liability for all its debts and other liabilities. Admission of new members is allowed by unanimous decision. In these latter respects an EEIG resembles a partnership under English law. Although an EEIG looks a somewhat limited innovation, its existence has been welcomed by some EC businessmen and this probably indicates the inadequacy of current EC laws to facilitate cross frontier co-operation[17]. It is significant that in a recent discussion of the topic the point was also made that there is a real need for a simplified European company statute.

Following the adoption of the Third Directive of 9 October 1978[18] on mergers of companies within the same member state, the intention was to build on this and to adopt *a directive on cross frontier mergers*[19]. This is now the Draft Tenth Directive. Since the mechanics of national and cross frontier mergers are identical the proposed Tenth Directive of the EC refers to the Third Directive extensively and is itself limited to additional requirements for cross border mergers and to those aspects of cross border mergers which differ from national mergers. The justification of this was that all mergers, both national and cross frontier, involved the following steps:

(a)   the drawing up of joint draft terms of merger;
(b)   the approval of the merger by the appropriate organs of each of the companies involved;

---

16 Regulation No 2137/85, 25 July 1985 (OJL 199/31 July 1985); S Israel (1988) 9 Co Law 14; 25th Report of the HLSC 1984.
17 See Janet Dine, 'The Community Company Law Harmonisation Programme' (1988) 13 ELR 322 at 323.
18 OJ 1978, L295/36. See Pierre van Ommeslaghe, 'La Proposition de Troisième Directive sur L'Harmonisation des Fusions des Sociétés' in P Zonderland, *Quo Vadis, Jus Societatum* (1972), p 123.
19 Proposal for a Tenth Directive submitted by the Commission to the Council 14 January 1985 (OJ 1985 C23 28/11).

(c)   the drawing up of a report by the administrative or management bodies of each of the companies;

(d)   the drawing up of an expert's report for each of the companies involved;

(e)   either the judicial or administrative supervision of the legality of the merger and completion of the formalities.

The special feature of cross frontier mergers is that the merging companies are governed by the laws of different member states. However, the significance of this should not be exaggerated since a number of the preparatory acts are taken individually by the companies involved and are conducted in accordance with the law of each member state. Nevertheless it is necessary to synchronise certain steps in the procedure. This is the case with the supervision of the drawing up and completion of the formalities of the merger and the publicity surrounding the completion of the merger. In addition certain rules in connection with cross frontier mergers have to be harmonised to a great degree than is necessary for national mergers. These are in respect of (a) the contents of the draft terms of merger, (b) the protection of creditors of acquired companies, (c) the date on which the merger takes place and (e) the causes of nullity of mergers.

Article 1 of the draft states that the directive is limited to public limited companies and does not apply to companies in insolvency proceedings. Article 2 states that the aim is to require member states to provide for cross frontier mergers both by the acquisition of one or more companies by another and by the formation of a new company. Articles 3 and 4 provide the definition of a cross frontier merger either by acquisition or by the creation of a new company and this is identical with that of the national merger under the Third Directive with the exception that two or more of the companies involved must be governed by the laws of different member states. Article 5 provides that the draft terms of merger must be drawn up in writing in the appropriate form required by the laws of the member states. Article 6 requires the draft terms to be published in the same way as the national merger but in addition the cross frontier aspects must be emphasised. Article 7 provides that member states may not impose stricter requirements as regards general meetings approving a cross frontier merger than they impose on a national merger. Article 8 provides that the report of an expert or experts is required for each of the merging companies. Article 9 provides that the protection of creditors provisions of the Third Directive also apply. Article 10 deals with the examination of the legality of mergers and again applies the provisions of the Third Directive but contains additional provisions for synchronisation of the judicial or administrative supervision of the drawing up of the terms of merger. Article 11 deals with the date on which the merger take effect. This is to be determined according to the law of the member state governing the acquiring company. Articles 12 and 13 deal with publicity and special formalities. Article 14 deals with the civil liability of the members of the administrative bodies and the experts involved. Article 15 sets out nullity rules.

In January 1989, the Commission adopted a proposal for a Thirteenth Directive on Takeovers and Other General Bids[20]. The need for harmonisation

---

20 Proposal for a Thirteenth Directive on Company Law Governing Takeover and other General Bids (OJ 1989, c 64/8). Department of Trade and Industry (UK) *EC Proposal for a*

in the area of takeovers was recognised in the Commission's White Paper on completion of the internal market and is also supported by the European Parliament. The Commission takes the view that the economic climate supports the Directive. There is an increasing number of takeovers especially cross frontier takeovers and the legal arrangements, if any, in member states are very varied. It is inconsistent that there should be EC controls on certain types of mergers and divisions but not on takeover bids. The principal aims of the draft Directive are the protection of shareholders and the regulation of disclosure requirements.

The main features of the draft are the rules relating to the timetable for offers, the content of offer and defence documents, the obligation on a bidder to bid for the remainder of the shares when he has acquired a certain percentage, the prohibition of certain types of defences and the independent supervision of the takeover process. The proposals are less flexible than the City of London takeover code in that they rely more on rules than principles.

Article 3 sets out the fundamental axiom of the draft Directive. This is that 'shareholders who are in the same position shall be treated equally'. Article 3 deals with the obligation to make a bid. This imposes an obligation to make a bid for all the voting shares and convertible securities of a company when a person (and those acting in concert with them) aims to bring his or her holdings above a specified percentage. The percentage is to be set by the member state concerned but it must not be any higher than one-third (33⅓%). The obligation only applies to public listed companies and it does not apply to bids for small and medium-sized enterprises which are not listed.

Articles 7, 10, 11, 14 and 19 set out the provisions dealing with contents and publication of offer and defence documents. These lay down the procedure prior to the publication of documents, the information that must be included in them and the means of publication. Article 14 requires the report of the board of the target company to be accompanied by an expert's valuation of consideration consisting of unlisted securities. Article 19 requires the offer documents to be communicated to employee representatives of the target company.

Article 8 prohibits the target company from issuing new voting shares and convertible securities and from engaging in exceptional transactions during the period of an offer unless approval to do so is given in a general meeting of shareholders. This is aimed at regulating takeover defences by the management of target companies.

Articles 10, 12, 13, 15 and 20 deal with the period of an offer which must be between 4 and 10 weeks. They also deal with the circumstances where a bid may be withdrawn, the circumstances for revision of a bid, and the treatment of competing bids.

Article 16 provides for the price of the offer to be the highest price paid for shares in the target company during the offer period by the offerors or those acting in concert with them.

Article 6 requires member states to designate a supervisory authority which must have the necessary powers to ensure compliance with the

Thirteenth Company Law Directive Concerning Takeovers. A Consultative Document August 1989 ('the Consultative Document'). See MacLachlan and Mackesy, op cit (footnote 9, supra); Jeffrey P Greenbaum, 'Tender Offers in the European Community: The Playing Field Shrinks' 22 Vanderbilt J of Transnational L 923 (1989).

directive. It is, however, left to member states to determine whether the authority should be a public and private body. In certain circumstances, the supervisory authority will have discretion to modify some of the requirements of the Directive.

The United Kingdom Government has several major concerns over the draft directive[1]. These relate to the method of implementation and its apparent lack of flexibility and the increased risk of litigation which it may occasion. It argues that the Directive should be based on a wider range of general principles than are currently provided by Article 3 and for the supervisory authority to be given adequate flexibility to waive or adapt the more specific rules provided that it operates within those general principles. The wider general principles for which the UK delegation argue are:

1.   holders of securities who for all practical purposes are in the same position should be treated similarly;
2.   holders of securities should be given adequate time, information and advice to enable them to reach a properly informed decision on the offer;
3.   the Board of a target company must not, after it has reason to believe that an offer might be imminent, take any action without the approval of the holders of its securities which could result in the offer being frustrated or those holders of securities being denied an opportunity to consider it on its merits;
4.   all parties to an offer must use every endeavour to prevent the creation of a false market in relevant securities of the target or bidding company;
5.   target companies should not remain under siege from an unwanted bidder beyond a reasonable time[2].

The UK delegation also argues for the Directive to be framed in a way which reduces the scope for litigation or some other form of outside review during the course of a bid. The fear here is that such litigation or review would bog down takeover bids. Such delay would create a powerful barrier to takeovers at a time when it is vital to the development of more open capital markets that existing barriers should be eliminated.

As a result of UK initiative the Commission is currently making a comprehensive study of various takeovers in the EC[3]. The UK delegation thinks more needs to be done than the regulation of certain takeover defences to remove barriers in other member states in the interest of achieving a single, open and efficient market.

It is understood that some member states are objecting to the idea of a threshold and a compulsory bid. The UK delegation is arguing that the threshold should be retained and that there should be a requirement for a full bid in order that minority shareholders should not be locked into a company under new managerial control without the opportunity to realise their share bid premium[4].

Takeovers are becoming an increasing widely-used technique in the EC and one whose importance is growing with the gradual liberalisation of capital markets.

1 The Consultative Document, pp 7 et seq.
2 Ibid, p 9.
3 Ibid, pp 10–11.
4 Ibid, p 11.

Other proposals now under consideration include *three directives on tax*[5] which deal with the tax treatment of mergers in similar operations; the tax treatment of parents and subsidiaries; and an arbitration procedure to eliminate double taxation arising from transactions between associated companies. In addition to the latter, the Commission proposed as far back as 1975 the harmonisation of corporation tax systems on the basis of the 'partial imputation system' and it is also considering another proposal for harmonisation of the determination of taxable profits. The object of these proposals is to reduce tax distortions on commercial transactions.

Mergers may lead to economies of scale and increased efficiency but they also have the capacity to impede effective competition. The international perspective arises in two main ways. The first is in the definition of concept of the market in question and the second is in the international application of domestic antitrust laws. Most antitrust regimes concentrate on their own domestic markets and restrict horizontal mergers, are mixed in reaction to vertical mergers but generally permissive in respect of conglomerate mergers. In the EC the main concern in the present period of low growth is to achieve faster growth through dynamic competition[6]. Anti-competitive forces may result from market dominance or the creation of a cartel. Dominance occurs where one company gains control of a competitor thus reducing the number of independent competitors and increasing concentration in the particular industry. A cartel typically occurs where two independent competitors create an arrangement likely to reduce competition or enter into a consortium to make a takeover bid which has the effect of an auction ring for the target company's shares or an arrangement to divide up its assets or which leads to a joint venture which restricts competition[7]. In all these cases everything depends on the structure of the particular market. There has been an increasing feeling in the Commission that the provisions in Articles 85 and 86 of the Treaty of Rome are inadequate to deal with mergers[8]. There has consequently been a growing recognition of the need for a specific merger regulation. A regulation[9] has been prepared which defines concentration widely as occurring when two or more undertakings merge or when one or more persons or undertakings acquire direct or indirect control of the whole or part of another undertaking. The definition of control is wide. It encompasses not only de jure control, ie more than 50% of voting rights, and de facto control, but also the power to influence the composition, voting or decisions of the board or general meeting. The regulation only applies to concentrations having a 'community dimension', in other words, involving cross frontier concentration within the EC. There are financial tests which are to be applied: the aggregate *world-wide* turnover of all the undertakings concerned must be not less than 1 billion ECUs. Acquisitions will escape control if (a) the aggregate world-wide turnover of the target is less than 50 million ECUs, *or* (b) each of the undertakings effecting the concentration have more than 75% of the aggregate *community-wide*

5 EC White Paper pp 10–11.
6 See Ingo L L Schmidt and Jan B Rittaler *A Critical Evaluation of the Chicago School of Antitrust Analysis* (1989) p XIV.
7 Stanley Berwin & Co *Company Law and Competition* Mercury Books London (1989) Ch 9.
8 Clifford Chance *1992 An Introductory Guide* 1988, paras 5.7, 5.8.
9 Regulation on the Control of Concentrations between Undertakings OJC 22/89. Adopted 21 December 1989.

turnover within one and the same member state. Thus small acquisitions by large companies will escape control as will mergers of substantial companies whose business remains confined to one member state. In the latter case they will, of course, be subject to the individual member states' antitrust laws.

Under the regulation concentrations are regarded as incompatible with the common market when they create or strengthen a dominant position in the common market or a substantial part of the common market. On the other hand such concentrations will be allowed if they improve production or distribution or promote technical or economic progress. There is a rebuttable presumption that concentrations are compatible with the common market when the aggregate market share of the undertakings concerned in the common market, or a substantial part of the common market, is less than 20%.

The Commission has sought exclusive jurisdiction to apply the regulation, subject only to review by the Court of Justice, and that such matters should be governed by the regulation alone and not by national laws. This reduces the risk of double jeopardy and ensures uniformity of application. States are reluctant to enforce antitrust laws which work to the detriment of local firms while at the same time paying lip service to the principle of world free trade.

Industrial relations differ considerably in the member states ranging from adversarial collective bargaining on the one hand to worker participation on the other. Negotiations on these topics have been long and controversial especially since the United Kingdom joined the EC. We will return to this matter later.

The most elaborate proposal to date is that of the *European company*[10] project. The European company is sometimes called *societas europae* (SE) and we will use that abbreviation. This would be a genuine transnational corporation which would provide a suitable vehicle for cross frontier mergers within the EC.

There are four possible legal bases for the SE project[11]. These are (i) a uniform statute (ii) an international convention and (iii) a regulation under two separate provisions of the Treaty of Rome. As regards (i) the problem is to ensure uniform interpretation since uniform statutes such as the 1930 Geneva Convention on Bills of Exchange leave interpretation entirely to the national courts. There are two possible ways of overcoming this difficulty. The first is a provision along the lines of 'Questions concerning matters regulated by the present law that are not expressly decided by it shall be

---

10 EC White Paper passim; *European Stock Corporation Text of Draft Statute with Commentary* by Prof P Sanders, CCH Inc, New York (1969); Yvon Loussouarn 'La Proposition d'un Statut des Sociétés Anonyme Européennes et le Droit International Privé' (1971) Rev Critique DIP 383; Jean Van Ryn 'Le Projet de Statut des Sociétés Européennes' (1971) Rev Trim de Droit Europ 563; see, generally P Zonderland (editor) *Quo Vadis, Jus Societatum* Kluwer (1972), which is a festschrift for Prof Sanders, especially the papers by Dabin, Rotondi, Vasseur and Vogelaar; Guy Keutgen *Le Droit des Groupes de Sociétés dans la CEE* Bruylant Bruxelles 1973, Titre II Chapitre II; F A Mann 'The European Company' (1970) 19 ICLQ 468; D Ranier 'The Proposed Statute for a European Company' 10 Texas Int LJ 90 (1975). For the latest text of the draft see OJ C 263/41. Proposal for a Council Regulation on the Statute for a European Company (16 October 1989). For comment see J Dines (1990) 11 Co Law 208.

11 European Stock Corporation Text (supra note 50) pp 8 et seq.

governed by the general principles on which it is based' such as is found in art 17 of The Hague Convention relating to a Uniform Law on the International Sale of Goods. The second is the provision for interpretation by a single court as the French Government advocated on 15 March 1965. The main disadvantage with a uniform statute is that it is enacted in each state as a domestic law and can be amended or repealed as such. As regards (ii)—the international convention—there are precedents such as the Warsaw Convention on International Transportation by Air and CMR (the Convention Relating to Contracting for the International Transport of Goods by Road) and this was the original idea. Here the problem is the differing approaches to international treaties in the member states—in some member states treaties take internal effect and take precedence over national law. This is not of course the case in English and Irish law.

As far as (iii)—the two possibilities are articles 235 and 100a of the Treaty of Rome. Article 235 is couched in very general terms and provides that if action by the Community proves necessary to attain one of the objectives of the Community and the Treaty of Rome has not provided the necessary powers, the Council shall, acting unanimously on a proposal from the Commission and after consulting the European Parliament, take the appropriate measures. Article 100a provides inter alia that:

1. The Council shall, acting by a qualified majority on a proposal from the Commission in co-operation with the European Parliament and after consulting the Economic and Social Committee, adopt the measures for the approximation of the provisions laid down by law, regulation or administrative action in member states which have as their object the establishment and functioning of the internal market. 2. Paragraph 1 shall not apply to fiscal provisions, to those relating to the free movement of persons nor to those relating to the rights and interests of employed persons.

The Commission favoured Article 235 in its 1975 report but now favours Article 100a. The UK Government considers that this is inappropriate and that the only possible legal basis is Article 235. In its Consultative Document of December 1989 the UK Government states:

The Government consider that Article 100a does not provide an appropriate basis for the regulation because that Article is concerned with measures to approximate provisions of law in Member States whereas the ECS proposal is not about the approximation of national laws but about the creation of a Community-wide legal framework for a new supranational entity. Further, even if this were not the case, Article 100a would be an inappropriate treaty basis because, by virtue of Article 100a(2), it cannot be used for provisions on fiscal or worker participation matters. Provisions on both matters are included in the proposed regulation. The Government also consider that Article 54 is an inappropriate Treaty basis for the provisions contained in the proposed directive. Those provisions are regarded as an integral part of the ECS proposal and, just as Article 54 could not provide a basis for the proposal as a whole, so it cannot be used for a part of that proposal.

The original SE concept was put forward by French legal practitioners in 1959 and the idea was developed by Professor Pieter Sanders of the University of Rotterdam in the same year[12]. Professor Sanders advocated a new corporate form, a European limited liability company registered on a European Commercial Register and incorporated under an alternative EC company regime, uniform in each member state and interpreted by the

---

12 Ibid, p vii.

European Court of Justice. By this means he hoped to solve the conflict of laws problems such as the transfer of the seat of an enterprise across frontiers, which generally involved a change of nationality, liquidation and reconstitution under the other law, and the problem of mergers of companies incorporated under different legal systems. The Commission set up a committee of experts which assisted Professor Sanders in elaborating the concept. This led to a Commission proposal in 1970 which followed its complex EC path ending before the Council in 1975[13]. There it languished before an ad hoc working party and got bogged down in the discussion of the proposals on groups. It was shelved in 1982. However, as part of the 1992 programme, the proposal was resurrected in 1988 and is now being pursued in earnest in spite of lukewarm support from the UK Government and business community[14].

THE PROPOSED EUROPEAN COMPANY

The European company proposal is ambitious. It has to overcome the current legal difficulties inherent in the domestic laws and constitute a valid alternative to the present techniques. The Internal Market White Paper *Internal Market and Industrial Cooperation—Statute for the European Company* gives the following example to show how it will work[15]:

(a)   Let us imagine that two groups merge their activities because they complement each other and on account of the economies of scale secured by merging together their three respective subsidiaries which pursue the same activities:

Group governed by the Law of State A	Group governed by the Law of State B
Company A	*Company B*

(b)   because of the current impossibility from a legal standpoint (consent of 100% of shareholders under most national laws) and from the standpoint of taxation (the companies which are acquired have to be wound up), of cross frontier mergers between companies, the simplest organisation plan which meets the wishes of those directing or managing the companies is, at present, the following:

Holding company made up of shareholders of A and B

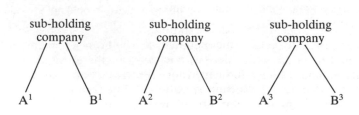

13 See generally EC White Paper, p 11.
14 Ibid, p 22.
15 Ibid, pp 12–13 (this is set out verbatim).

(c)   The alternative of the European Company would afford considerable simpli-
fications:

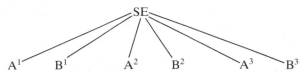

While the company law aspects are important and the European Company Statute will itself provide a code of law for the operation for the
company which will serve as a blueprint for the harmonisation programme,
the question of the tax status of the SE is also vital and and tax regime will
have to be consistent with the logic underlying the concept of the SE.

Specific issues which have to be addressed in the European company
project are, (1) co-existence with national systems of company law, (2)
worker participation, (3) the question of disclosure of information and
consultation of workers, (4) the problem of groups and (5) tax treatment.
The latest proposals consist of two documents:

(a)   a proposal for a Council regulation on the statute for a European
Company, and
(b)   a proposal for a Council directive complementing the statute with
regard to the involvement of employees in the SE. It is intended that
the two will operate as an integrated whole.

The regulation relies heavily on previous directives or proposed directives
and at the same time refers a number of things back to the member state in
which the SE is registered. Article 7 provides that matters within its scope
not expressly mentioned are to be determined by the general principles of
the Regulation or, failing that, by the law applying to public limited companies
in the state of registration. This will give scope to differences between SEs.
Matters outside the scope of the regulation such as antitrust, employment
law and intellectual property law are to be governed by existing national and
community law[16].

The essential structure is that of commercial public limited company
which will have a minimum capital of 100,000 ECUs (approximately
£70,000) which is higher than the £50,000 required for a public limited
company in the UK. The SE's capital will be in ECUs. The SE will have its
registered office in the place of central administration and will have either a
two-tier board (management and supervisory boards) or a one-tier board
(an administrative board).

1. Co-existence with national systems of company law

The Commission argues that the statute will have to establish a single system
of company law, totally independent of national systems. It will have to
contain provisions which deal with legal problems which differ from those
arising in national law or which do not exist in any member state's legislation.
Since the statute will be entirely optional, the arguments against its inconsistency with national law are of less weight. This goal has not been
completely realised by the latest draft.

16 This is based on EC White Paper, pp 14 et seq.

2. Worker participation

The Commission takes a strong view that it is necessary to lay down rules governing worker participation in the structure and decision-making process of the European company. This is for a variety of reasons. It will be necessary to be compatible with national systems and the statute should not provide a means for contracting out of more rigorous obligations in individual member states. The Commission's argument is that worker participation is essential, not simply as a matter of social rights, but as an instrument of promoting the smooth running and success of the enterprise through promoting stable relationships between managers and employees in the workplace.

There are three main approaches for dealing with worker participation in the European Company Statute.

(a)   The model laid down in the 1975 version of the statute which consisted of a supervisory board composed of ⅓ of shareholder representatives, ⅓ of worker representatives and ⅓ of members co-opted by these two groups representing general interests.

(b)   The rule of the country of establishment.

(c)   A choice from the principal schemes provided in the Fifth Company Law Directive which are (i) the workers elect no less than ⅓ and no more than half of the members of the supervisory board which is the German system; (ii) worker participation through a body representing the employees quite separate from the company organs; (iii) worker participation through collectively agreed systems to be determined within the company[17].

(a) represents the most ambitious form of participation but it has not yet been applied in any member state and is likely to meet with considerable resistance from companies. (b) runs contrary to the basic idea of the SE being independent of national systems. For these reasons it (c) has been the option chosen and the option of co-option by the board has been added. The Commission considers that the provisions must be based on principles governing systems in the states that have so far developed them and yet be flexible enough to allow for a consensus. It is thought that the system need not be uniform. It would be appropriate to allow companies a choice between different schemes which reflect accepted practices in most member states, such choice being subject to consultation with the workers affected. Nevertheless there should be a provision that member states can restrict the choice. In this way the fear that the Germans have that companies might be inclined to use an SE to evade the provisions of the national law regarding worker participation is addressed.

3. Disclosure and consultation with workers

The Commission takes the view that the employees of the SE should benefit from the same disclosure and consultation rights which are enjoyed in other firms in the EC. The inclusion of more stringent rules in the statute is not thought to be desirable at this stage.

---

17   OJ 1983, C 240/2; see J Welch (1983) 8 ELR 83.

4. The group problem

In many systems within the EC the group is simply recognised de facto and not de jure. Except in Germany and Portugal the laws of member states is based on the principles of the economic and legal independence of each company which is a member of the group which is an idea which is not always easy to reconcile with a degree of concentration. In England the courts have already been faced with the conflict between the interests of the company and the interests of the group. This was in the context of ultra vires and gratuitous payments.

The problem arises within the context of the European Company Statute because two of the means of creating a European company—the creation of a holding company or a joint subsidiary—automatically entail the formation of a group. The aim of the original draft was to enable those setting up the SE to opt for a special group status facilitating management of the company as a single economic unit while at the same time protecting the interests of third parties such as minority shareholders and creditors. The Commission now takes the view that it is open to question whether the European Company Statute is the proper place to create a body of rules governing groups. Under Article 114 where an undertaking controls an SE, that undertaking, rights and obligations relating to minority shareholders and third parties are to be governed by the law of public limited companies of the state where the SE has its registered office. This does not, however, affect the obligations imposed on the controlling undertaking by the legal system which governs it.

5. Tax treatment

The European company will be subject to the tax regime of the state in which it is domiciled in the same way as any other company. In this way it will also be subject to any bi-lateral agreements against double taxation made between that state and other member states. In addition there will be certain favourable provisions for enterprises which differ from normal tax treatment. There will be provisions whereby losses suffered by permanent establishments of the European company situated in another member state or by foreign subsidiaries can be deducted from the profits in the member state of domicile. At the same time the Commission takes the view that it would not be desirable to lay down any other tax provisions favourable to the European company which derogate from the normal tax treatment of companies. To do so would create a distortion in its favour which is detrimental to small or medium-sized enterprises which are unlikely to opt for this method of incorporation. The UK Government favours a system of tax neutrality for SEs.

The Department of Trade and Industry was sceptical whether the SE would provide any real assistance in helping companies in the community to restructure in response to changing market forces in the developing single market. There were three main reasons for their scepticism. First, the proposal as drafted will still be closely identified with the member state in which the SE was registered. Second, the proposal would not result in a single body of European Company Law and the law applicable to an SE would vary according to the member state in which it was based. Third, there was no real evidence that companies wanted to adopt the new form proposed, particularly if it involved compulsory employee participation.

The Department of Trade and Industry and the Department of Employment carried out consultations and received 41 responses. Three of the responses were favourable; 26 were opposed to the company law aspects of the current draft; 9 were opposed to the whole idea of a European company; and 10 were in favour of the general idea but opposed the detailed proposals. Only 31 of the 41 responses commented on the worker participation question and of these only 3 favoured compulsory worker participation or did not see difficulties in the present proposal. The Minister of State for Employment said that the Government did not believe that the draft directive was necessary and this view was shared by British industry generally. His Department rejected the forms of worker participation proposed in the European Company Statute as being in no way superior to the UK voluntary system. The Confederation of British Industry said that they were unable to identify the problem for which the European company statute was a solution. It did not think that the European company statute would enhance business activity nor facilitate cross border investment. The statute would not help the single European market in relation to the free movement of capital, goods, services and people. Far from simplifying matters the statute presented a more complicated situation. It would not make life easier for British companies wishing to merge with European companies nor would it lead towards the harmonisation of European company law.

The Select Committee on the European Communities reporting on the European company statute said that in its present form proposal would not be attractive. It would be unfortunate if this attempt failed for lack of adequate consideration of all the factors involved. The Committee made a number of proposals with a view to making the statute acceptable in the UK and in the EC[18].

CROSS FRONTIER MERGERS, INTERNATIONAL COMPETITION AND INTERNATIONAL CO-OPERATION

In the 1960s the main argument advanced for co-operation within the EC was economic integration under a policy of planned growth[19] and this, of course, remains valid today but in a time of slower growth and increasing international competition. Today, a more pressing reason and that which is the basis of the 1992 programme and the advancement of the cause of the European Company Statute is to improve the EC's competitive position in world markets characterised by ever-increasing global capitalism[20]. Such co-operation is regarded as absolutely vital, especially in high technology industries and for companies which are highly specialised in financial services. Only by means of EC level co-operation will it be possible to bring together the large amounts of capital and technical know-how required to ensure competitiveness in world markets. Without such competitiveness there will be an erosion of living standards and a diminution of social and economic status[1]. In the lead-up to 1992 many EC companies

18 See Select Committee on the European Communities—*European Company Statute Report* (House of Lords Session 1989–90 19th Report HL Paper 71–I).
19 EC White Paper, p 5; Schmidt and Rittaler, op cit, p XIV.
20 EC White Paper, p 5.
 1 See Robert L Heilbroner *The Nature and Logic of Capitalism* (1985) p 58.

are looking for merger partners and many US corporations are seeking a European partner[2]. The table shown overleaf gives the top 30 cross frontier acquisitions in Europe in the second quarter of 1990. This is a tendency which is likely to increase and the progress of the European Company Statute as the means of facilitating cross frontier mergers is, therefore, important on a European level.

Although we have referred to the position in private international law and have concentrated on the EC position as an interesting case study of regional co-operation, the question of cross frontier mergers is also a topic of public international law. Some of the earliest examples of cross frontier co-operation in Europe involved the creation of corporate bodies by international treaty. Thus the 'Societé Internationale de la Moselle' was created in 1956 by an international convention between France, Germany and Luxembourg to make the Moselle River navigable between Thionville and Coblence, and EUROFIMA was set up to assist railways in the financing of purchase of rolling stock[3]. Such bodies were created by treaty and mainly regulated by by-laws or 'statutes' accompanying the treaties. In matters not covered by the treaty and by-laws, the treaties provide for them to be governed by the law of the country of registration or by rules common to the countries involved. However, where there is an inconsistency between the treaties and by-laws and the latter the treaties and by-laws prevail[4]. The Euratom Treaty provides rules for the creation of 'common enterprises' but the EC treaty does not contain such a provision with the exception of articles 129 and 130 which create the European Investment Bank. Foreign investment laws have been the subject of a number of international treaties, of a bi-lateral nature[5]. Thus the USA has entered into numerous treaties, imbued with the spirit of international co-operation under GATT but largely in pursuit of its own self-interest. Similarly, there are even more numerous double taxation agreements between different countries.

Each country is concerned with such international issues as the mutual recognition of the decisions of courts and administrative agencies of other countries. Within the British Commonwealth[6] and within the EC[7] the question of the mutual recognition of judgments and orders has been the subject of international co-operation. Elsewhere it is the subject of bi-lateral treaties or often nothing at all. Recently since the stock market crash of 1987, there has been an increase in informal co-operation between national securities regulators, futures markets and financial institutions. Legislation has been passed in a number of jurisdictions to allow international co-operation[8]. IOSCO is working actively in this field with its annual conferences and

---

2 See Tim Hindle 'Cross-border Takeovers—Proof That the Single Market is Here' (1990) 2 EuroBusiness 13.
3 See Hans Smit and Peter Herzog *The Law of the European Economic Community* Vol 2.
4 Ibid.
5 *Bilateral Trade Treaties* (UN).
6 See K W Patchett *Recognition of Commercial Judgments and Awards in the Commonwealth* (1984).
7 L Collins *The Civil Jurisdiction and Judgments Act 1982* (1983).
8 See H Williams and L Spencer, 'Regulation of International Securities Markets: Towards a Greater Cooperation', 4 J Comp Corp L & Sec, Reg 55 (1982); P Merloe 'Internationalisation of Securities Markets: a Critical Survey of US and EEC Disclosure Requirements', 8 J Comp Bus and Cap Market L 249 (1986); Daniel L Goelzer, Robert Mills, Katherine Gresham and Anne H Sullivan, 'The Role of the US Securities and Exchange Commission in Transnational Acquisitions' 22 Int Law 615 (1988) pp 635 et seq.

TOP 30 CROSS-BORDER ACQUISITIONS IN EUROPE ANNOUNCED DURING SECOND QUARTER 1990

Buyer		Target		% Acq'd	Local Price (m)	Ecu Price (m)
Name (Nationality)	*Business*	*Name (Nationality)*	*Business*			
Philip Morris (US)	Tobacco, foods	Jacobs Suchard (Swi)	Confections, coffee	80	SFr 5,400.0	3,091.1
Svenska Cellulosa (Swe)	Paper	Reedpack (UK)	Paper	100	£1,050.0	1,474.6
Stora (Swe)	Forest products & mining	Feldmuhle Nobel (WG)	Paper, steel, armaments	75	DM 2,980.0	1,457.3
LVMH (Fr)	Luxury goods	Guinness (UK)	Drinks	12	£822.7	1,155.3
Group AG (Bel/Fr)	Insurance	Amev (Nth)	Insurance	50	B Fr 45.4 bn	1,071.7
Amev (Nth)	Insurance	Groupe AG (Bel)	Insurance	50	B Fr 34.7 bn	818.9
SPP (Swe)	Insurance	London & Edinburgh Trust (UK)	Property	99	£495.0	672.5
Patrica (Swe) G	Wallenberg group vehicle	Feldmuhle Nobel (WG)	Paper, steel, armaments	25	DM 988.54	483.2
Gamlesladen (Swe)	Financial services	Bricom (UK)	Commercial Services	100	£337.5	474.0
Cogefin (Bel/Fr)	SGB/Accor holding co.	Wagons Lits (Bel)	Tourism, leisure	27	B Fr 18.8 bn	444.9
GTH (US)	Electricals, lighting	Thorn Lighting (UK)	Lighting	100	£300.0	415.9
Corroon & Black (US)	Insurance Broker	Willis Faber (UK)	Insurance broker	40	£274.0	384.8
Bidermann (Fr)	Fashion	Cluett Peabody (UK)	Clothes	100	£256.3	348.3
Nobel (Swe)	Armaments, chemicals	units of Crown Berger (UK)	Paint activities	100	£227.7	315.6
Joh. A. Benckiser (WG)	Detergents	Ian/M. Astor/Mon/Parera (Eur)	Cosmetics	100	£210.0	291.0
Norwich Union (UK)	Insurance	Plus Ultra (Sp)	Insurance	90	Pta 36.6 bn	280.9
CPE International (US)	Foods	Ambrosia, Bovril & Marmite (UK)	Food spreads brands	100	£157.0	216.8
Klockner-Werke (WG)	Engineering, steel	Eurotec Plastics (UK)	Plastic auto components	100	£155.0	214.9
SE Banken (Swe)	Banking	Scandinavian Bank Group (UK)	Banking	78	£152.7	214.4
Midland & Scottish (UK)	Offshore drilling	Tortin Investments (Tt/UK)	Holding co. for oil & gas dist.	100	£155.9	211.8
Euroc (Swe)	Building materials	CVCP (Sp)	Cement	13	Pta 25.4 bn	200.7
Norse Partners (Nor)	Consortium of shipping firms	nine ships (UK)	Refrigerated cargo vessels	100	£141.5	196.2
Cadbury Schweppes (UK)	Confections, drinks	Oasis, Bali, Atoll (Fr)	Soft drink brands	100	FFr 1,200.7	173.3
Old Bond Street (US)	Holding company	Units of Yardley-Lentheric (UK)	Cosmetics businesses	100	£110.0	151.9
British Steel (UK)	Steel	Klockner-Mannstadt (WG)	Steel	100	DM 300.0	145.6
HPH Industries (UK)	Plasterboard	Inveryeso (Sp)	Plaster	65	Pta 17.3 bn	136.4
Saint-Gobain (Fr)	Glass	Solaglas (UK)	Building glass	100	£96.5	133.8
Viscofan (Sp)	Sausage casings	Naturin Werk, Becker (WG)	Sausage casings	100	DM 260.2	126.3
Blue Circle (UK)	Cement	activ.. of Aalborg Portland (Den)	Cement, aggregates, fly ash	50	DKr 980.0	125.1
Corange (WG)	Healthcare & Drugs	Chas K Thackray (UK)	Hip joints	100	£75.0	104.0

Note: This table includes acquisitions made in European nations by US and Japanese companies as well as acquisitions between European nations.

Source: Translink's European Deal Review

various committees[9]. The question of comprehensive regulation of multi-national enterprises is being considered by the United Nations at great length as well as by various regional bodies[10]. Cross frontier mergers, like multi-national securities and financing operations in general, present a complex range of issues. At the present time international co-operation is still in its infancy but, in fostering extensive and varied debate and regional co-operation within its borders, one hopes that the EC will ultimately provide a model or series of models for international co-operation, rather than an impregnable Fortress Europe.

---

9 IOSCO is based in Montreal. It hosts a number of specialised committees and an annual conference. The recent conferences in Melbourne and Venice have been important gatherings of securities and financial regulators.
10 See Ch 42 post.

CHAPTER 42

Multinational and transnational companies

We have used the terms multinational and transnational companies[1] in the title to this chapter, although this belies definitional problems which we shall have to consider in a moment. Until then we shall simply use both terms loosely to cover any company which carries on directly or indirectly business in more than one country. This kind of activity is obviously not new. Some of the earliest trading companies such as the East India Company and the Hudson's Bay Company were set up for this purpose[2]. However, this meant a home-based company which carried out overseas commercial operations. In more recent times, modern companies such as ICI have set up hundreds of foreign subsidiaries to carry out such operations[3]. Since the Second World War we have seen the rise of multinational corporations which generally have the following characteristics:

(1) they extend production and marketing across national frontiers usually through foreign subsidiaries or joint venture companies;
(2) they are large in size;
(3) they tend to have centralised management and integrated production and marketing[4].

The main reasons for the growth of multinationals are the growth of technology and the improvement of communications and transport. In particular, the use of computers and telecommunications has facilitated global management[5].

The rapid growth of multinationals in Europe since 1945 can be attributed to the recovery of the European economy with US assistance, the greater political stability, the return of European currencies to convertibility and the formation of the EC[6].

Whereas the traditional multinational consisted of a parent company and foreign subsidiaries which produced goods locally the transnational designs and produces goods anywhere within the system. As Peter Drucker has said in transnationals, 'Top management is transnational, and so are the company's business plans, business strategies, and business decisions'[7].

In a Round Table on the Code of Conduct of Transnational Corporations held in Montreux, Switzerland, in October 1986 a statement was issued

---

1 See generally K Simmonds (ed) *Multinational Corporations Law* for a useful compilation of important data and documents.
2 See Chapter 2, ante.
3 See Chapter 1, ante.
4 See J E Spero *The Politics of International Economic Relations* (3rd edn, 1985) chapter 4. See also C M Schmitthoff [1970] JBL 177.
5 See J H Dunning 'Multinational Business and the Challenge of the 1980s' in EIU Special Report No 79 *Ten Years of Multinational Business* (1980) pp 2, 3–4.
6 *Spero*, op cit.
7 Peter Drucker *The New Realities* (1989) p 125.

noting the fundamental changes in the world economy which had taken place over the previous decade. Included in these fundamental changes was the role that multinational corporations had come to play in international economic relations. Foreign direct investment is now one of the most common forms of international economic activity. The total value of such investment in 1986 amounted to over \$700 billion. Multinationals are involved in all economic sectors and are dominant in a number of industries[8].

CLASSIFICATION AND LEGAL STRUCTURE

In a useful, if now somewhat dated, study entitled *Multinational Enterprise,* Dr Robert Tindall[9] defines a multinational enterprise as a combination of companies of different nationality, connected by means of shareholdings, managerial control or contract and constituting an economic unit. He then distinguishes between national multinationals and international multi-nationals.

When a multinational has one parent company of a particular nationality it is a national multinational. When it has two or more controlling parent companies of different nationalities, it is called an international multi-national or transnational. The term transnational has, however, recently acquired a much looser meaning.

Examples of the first are ICI, Ford Motor Co and Mitsubishi. Examples of the second are Royal Dutch/Shell, Unilever and the former Dunlop/Pirelli. Royal Dutch/Shell was formed in the following way[10]:

English parent formed wholly owned English holding company.

Dutch parent formed wholly owned Dutch holding company.

Each parent company transferred shares in subsidiaries to the respective holding companies.

Then each parent exchanged shares in the holding companies so that the picture was:

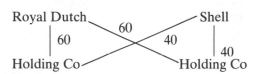

The management was unified and the group operates as a single economic unit.

Dunlop/Pirelli was formed in an analogous fashion[11].

In the case of Unilever, the international multinational was constituted by an equalisation agreement, various other agreements and common directors.

---

8 See UN Economic and Social Council Organisational Session for 1987 Adoption of the Agenda and Other Organisational Matters E/1987/9 30 Jan 1987.
9 Tindall *Multinational Enterprise* (1975) p xvi; C M Schmitthoff 'The Multinational Enter-prise in the UK' in H R Hahlo, J G Smith and R W Wright *Nationalism and the Multi-national Enterprise* (1973) chapter 2.
10 *Tindall*, op cit, xxi.
11 *Tindall*, op cit, xxii.

The equalisation agreement guarantees equal rights to shareholders of each parent company[12].

Transnationals bear an ill-defined relationship with multinationals. Some of this is due to the increased use of joint venture agreements sometimes coupled with a significant but not controlling interest in the other company. This kind of structure is very common for instance in the automobile industry as we saw in the last chapter.

The question of definition of multinational or transnational corporations has presented difficulties for a member of international bodies. In the United Nations the Group of Eminent Persons defined transnational corporations as 'Enterprises which own or control production or service facilities outside the country in which they are based. Such enterprises are not always incorporated or private; they can also be co-operatives or state-owned entities[13]'.

In the Guidelines for Multinational Enterprises produced by the OECD the following approach was adopted using flexible, non-legal language.

A precise legal definition of multinational enterprises is not required for the purposes of the Guidelines. These usually comprise companies or other entities whose ownership is private, state or mixed, established in different countries and so linked that one or more of them may be able to exercise a significant influence over the activities of others and, in particular, to share knowledge and resources with the others. The degree of autonomy of each entity in relation to the others varies widely from one multinational enterprise to another, depending on the nature of the links between such entities and the fields of activity concerned. For these reasons, the Guidelines are addressed to the various entities within the multinational enterprise (parent companies and/or local entities) according to the actual distribution of responsibilities among them on the understanding that they will co-operate and provide assistance to one another as necessary to facilitate observance of the guidelines. The word 'enterprise' as used in these Guidelines refers to these various entities in accordance with their responsibilities[14].

A similar approach was adopted by the International Labour Organisation in its Tripartite Declaration of Principles Concerning Multinational Enterprises and Social Policy[15].

In the United Nations the Commission of Transnational Corporations has used a variety of definitions in its draft Code of Conduct for Transnational Corporations. In 1984 the following proposal was put forward:

This code is universally applicable to enterprises, irrespective of their country of origin and their ownership, including private, public or mixed, comprising entities in two or more countries, regardless of the legal form and fields of these entities, which operate under a system of decision-making, permitting coherent policies and a common strategy through one or more decision-making centres, in which the entities are so linked, by ownership or otherwise, that one or more of them may be able to exercise a significant influence over the activities of others and, in particular, to share

---

12 *Tindall*, op cit, xxi-ii.
13 *The Impact of Multinational Corporations on Development and on International Relations* (UN pub E74 IIA 5) p 25.
14 *Guidelines for Multinational Enterprises*, para 8.
15 *Tripartite Declaration of Members Concerning Multinational Enterprises and Social Policy* (1982) para 6.

knowledge, resources and responsibilities with the others. Such enterprises are referred to in this code as transnational corporations[16].

So far no final agreement has been reached. As can be seen the latest drafts transcend law and the corporate form.

THE CASE FOR AND AGAINST MULTINATIONALS[17]

The main case for multinational enterprise is that it increases economic efficiency and stimulates growth, thereby improving welfare. There are those who argue the contrary but the existing data suggests that the overall effect is positive in countries such as the UK, Canada and France[18]. The presence of a multinational is said to enhance competition, break local monopolies and to provide better products at lower cost. It is the most effective instrument for transferring technology and managerial know-how. It is a means of investing capital in developing countries and management are becoming more sensitive to local conditions. As a truly international enterprise, it breaks down barriers between nations.

However, the activity of multinationals is not without costs for the host state, particularly where the host state is a developing country. Decisions which are rational for the multinational enterprise may be suboptimal for the host country. In terms of power, a multinational represents an invasion of sovereignty and removes a significant part of the economy from responsible political control. It is capable of exercising excessive political influence and sometimes it gives priority to the interests of its country of origin. It is capable of impeding the implementation of national economic policies. It almost inevitably sacrifices the interests of its subsidiaries to those of the parent company. Its size may represent unfair competition to local companies.

Although it represents a transfer of technology, know-how and capital, this may not always be in the interests of the host country. The training will be to suit the interests of the parent company and not necessarily the host country. The real control will usually lie outside the host country and the costs for the host country are usually high—most multinationals demand preferential treatment in terms of setting up grants, low taxation and exchange control latitude.

The critics of multinationals often end their arguments by summing up the position as neocolonialism, and it is noticeable how most multinationals are based in former colonial powers.

16 United Nations Economic and Social Council *Work on the Formulation of the United Nations Code of Conduct on Transnational Corporations – Outstanding Issues in the Draft Code of Conduct on Transnational Corporations*, E/C10/1985/5/2, 22 May 1985.
17 See *Tindall*, op cit, chapter 6; *Spero*, op cit; M Crawford, EIU Unit Special Report No 79, p 9 ff; Unterman and Swent, *The Future of the US Multinational Corporation* (1975) pp 136–138; H R Hahlo, J G Smith and R W Wright *Nationalism and the Multinational Enterprise*, op cit, Pt II.
18 See *Tindall*, op cit, p 154; D M Steuer and others *The Impact of Foreign Direct Investment on the United Kingdom*, ed W Friedmann (1973) HMSO.

REGULATION OF MULTINATIONALS

The multinational enterprise represents the latest stage of development of the national company group which evolved from a local corporate enterprise which in its turn evolved from a local non-corporate enterprise. Just as the issues of ownership and control are important in relation to national enterprises they are crucial in relation to multinational enterprise where the resolution of the question necessarily has a political significance. The multinational enterprise poses additional problems because it is not simply one discrete legal form but many. As the late Wolfgang Friedman wrote: 'It is the complexity of its legal structure, or rather of the interplay of legal entities and relationships constituting that structure, no less than the size of its resources or the scale of its operations, which makes its power so elusive and so formidable a challenge to the political order and rule of law. It is therefore inherent in the nature of the multinational corporation that there is no simple solution for the problem of its relationship to states, the world of states, or an organised world community. . . .'[19]

The political and legal regulation of multinational enterprise can be classified under three headings which approximately correspond to stages of historical development. These are:

(1)   national;
(2)   bilateral;
(3)   regional; and
(4)   international regulation.

Let us deal with each in turn.

National regulation

A liberal regime to domestic companies by the countries of origin created the economic conditions which favoured the growth of multinational enterprise.

For host states there is often a dilemma of regulating conduct against the national interest yet not discouraging foreign investment. Canada in the past has been faced with this dilemma because of its proximity to the USA. On the whole it has favoured the presence of subsidiaries of foreign corporations although since 1972 it has screened new direct foreign investment[20].

The UK has generally favoured a very liberal regime like other European states. To a large extent this has been based on enlightened self interest since the UK is the headquarters of a number of multinationals and the City of London has traditionally financed many multinational operations.

The main worries apart from loss of control that the individual nation has is that multinationals may reduce the effectiveness of national monetary policy, evade taxation and injure labour relations.

The most effective and systematic form of regulation seems to be the control over initial capital investment. Control over later behaviour seems to be more ad hoc.

---

19 *Transnational Law in a Changing Society* (1972) pp 79, 80. See also C M Schmitthoff [1972] JBL 103.
20 *Tindall*, op cit; *Spero*, op cit.

Bilateral regulation

In the last decade there has been a growth in bilateral arrangements. These have taken the form of investment protection and promotion treaties and reflect the desire of home country governments to protect the investment of their companies abroad and the desire of host countries to attract foreign direct investment. Such treaties normally provide for legal protection of foreign subsidiaries and aim to produce a stable environment for development. In the period between 1945 and the mid 1960s the USA was the first country to seek to achieve its objectives in this manner. Many of the bilateral treaties were concluded with developed countries. The emphasis of the early treaties, however, was more to do with international trade and protection of citizens abroad rather than foreign direct investment. From the 1960s onwards the treaties tended to be more concerned with foreign direct investment and many of these were concluded with developing countries. In this period the Federal Republic of Germany concluded more than 50 agreements of this kind by the end of 1983. There are today more than 200 such treaties in force and many of these have been initiated between OECD countries and developing countries. It should be noted that such treaties do not normally contain obligations on home country governments to promote foreign direct investment. The mere existence of an investment protection treaty is unlikely to lead to increased flows of investment unless there are other inducements. Conversely the absence of such a treaty where there are such other investments will not necessarily deter foreign investment. The role of such treaties, therefore, is simply marginal in the decision making of the multinational and the host country[1].

Regional regulation

The USA, Canada and Australia are all federations, yet each effectively operates as one economic unit. Since 1954, there have been a number of looser economic groupings of states such as EFTA and the EC. Other groupings such as OPEC have been established on the basis of specialised markets.

Of these groupings of states the most important for our purpose is the EC. Here, the lack of any provision in the Treaty of Rome has hindered progress. The member states have consistently refused to yield any national authority to the EC. Various attempts – the adoption of a regulation for EC regulation of foreign investment in 1965, a Commission proposal to protect employees in the event of takeovers, the formulation of common industrial policy and the adoption of a convention on internal mergers – have all been unsuccessful[2].

---

1 See *Bilateral, regional and international managements on matters relating to transnational corporations. Report of the Secretariat of the UN Economic and Social Council* E/C10/1984/8 6 Feb 1984 on which this is substantially based.
2 *Spero*, op cit. See Multinational Undertakings and Community Regulations EEC Bull Supp 15/73; Industrial Policy in the Community 1970; Draft Convention on Internal Mergers EEC Bull Supp 13/73; J H Dunning and P Robson (1987) 26 JCMS 103.

International regulation

The International Monetary Fund (IMF), the General Agreement on Tariffs and Trade (GATT) and the Organisation for Economic Co-operation and Development (OECD) all have some bearing on the activities of multinationals. The IMF provides for convertibility of currency and repatriation of funds. GATT facilitates international production and transfers. The OECD facilitates freedom of establishment.

On the other hand, the special attempts to deal with multinational enterprise have not been successful. The Havana Charter which was to have provided for a liberal regime of foreign investment was later amended by Third World countries to protect host countries and was opposed by the USA[3].

In 1976, the OECD adopted voluntary guidelines for conduct by multinationals[4]. The guidelines are recommendations jointly addressed by the member countries to the multinationals operating within their territories. They are not legally binding. There is no precise definition given of 'multinational', although the guidelines refer to groups which 'comprise companies and other legal entities having private, public or mixed capital, established in various countries and linked in such a manner that one or more of them are in a position to exercise significant influence on the countries of others, and in particular to share knowledge and resources amongst themselves'. The guidelines contain a statement of general policies and then deal with six topics—disclosure of information; competition; financing; taxation; employment and labour relations; and service and technology.

With regard to disclosure, the number and scope of the items of information called for is extensive while at the same time an attempt is made to protect the legitimate requirements of business secrecy.

An acute problem which the guidelines address is the question of transfer pricing, and here it is provided that multinationals shall refrain from making use of transfer pricing which does not conform to an arm's length standard.

A third problem is the question of bribes. Here the guidelines draw the line at what is legal although even this is questionable since some payments which are legal may still be grossly immoral.

In the 1970s, the United Nations set up a Centre on Transnational Corporations to gather and disseminate information on multinationals and an inter-governmental Commission on Transnational Corporations to act as a forum for discussion of issues relating to them and to supervise the centre[5]. Of these two bodies, the first will probably prove the most practical since ignorance of empirical data impedes rational debate and leads to perpetuation of myth.

Since 1977, a Working Group of the Commission has been engaged in the

---

3 *Spero*, op cit
4 See *Review of the 1976 Declaration and Decisions on Guidelines for Multinational Enterprises* (OECD, 1979); H Schwamm (1978) 12 JWTL 342. See now *The OECD Guidelines for Multinational Enterprises* (1986).
5 See P D Maynard (1980) 2 Co Law 226; (1983) 4 Co Law 103. (1983) 9 Commonwealth Law Bulletin 259. See the materials collected in Simmonds (ed) *Multinational Corporations Law*.

formulation of a code of conduct as its highest priority. It decided against taking the OECD guidelines as its starting point[6].

The benefits of such a code were considered by the Round Table on the Code of Conduct of Transnational Corporations held in Montreux, Switzerland in October 1986. The Round Table saw the benefits as being as follows:

(a) It would establish a balanced set of standards of good corporate conduct to be observed by multinationals in their operations and of standards to be observed by governments in their treatment of multinationals.

(b) It would help to ensure that the activities of multinationals were integrated in the development policies of the developing countries.

(c) It would establish inter alia the confidence, predictability and stability required for development of foreign direct investment in a mutually beneficial manner.

(d) It would contribute to a reduction of friction and conflict between multinationals and host countries.

(e) It would 'encourage positive adjustment through the growth of productive capacities'.

One cannot but admire the skill of international diplomats in developing plasticity of language. It helps on occasion to hide the unacceptable truth, albeit it at the cost of sacrificing meaning[7].

Progress on the code has been slow. It is of course easy to dismiss such codes as unimportant since they are not legally binding. This would, however, be a mistake. Such codes may form the basis of subtle diplomacy by the UN towards a consensus among governments which in turn will be embodied in national legislation. Such a consensus will in any event help host countries in negotiating with multinationals and may assist trade unions in both the home countries to oppose outward investment and the host countries to seek regulation of multinational practices against the interests of their members[8].

CONCLUSION

The multinational and transnational enterprise represents the latest and most complex version of the corporate form. In fact, it frequently transcends the corporate form in terms of legal structure and economic and political

---

6 See *The United Nations Code of Conduct on Transnational Corporations* UNCTC Current Studies (1988). For some discussion see Maynard (1983) 4 Co Law 103 at 104; Sanders (1982) 30 Am J Comp L 241.

7 See Economics and Social Council – Adoptions of the Agenda and other organisational matters – code of conduct on transnational corporations – Report of the Secretary General, E/1987/9 30 Jan 1987; 17th Plenary Meeting 28 May 1987 E/1987/INF/5; see too E/1988/39/ Add 1; E/C 10/1990/6.

8 See M Crawford 'The Case against Multinationals: The Main Criticism Re-examined' in EIU Special Report No 79 *Ten Years of Multinational Business*, p 15. See also the very useful paper by T H Reynolds 'Clouds of Codes: The New International Economic Order through Codes of Conduct: A Survey' in Simmonds (ed) *Multinational Corporations Law*, vol 4; *North-South: A Programme for Survival*, The Report of the Independent Commission on International Development Issues under the chairmanship of Willy Brandt (1980) chapter 12.

significance. These problems are compounded by increased freedom which has come as a result of the International Financial Revolution. At the moment attempts are being made at the level of the nation state to curb the powers of multinationals and transnationals, but in many cases the nation state competes on unfavourable terms. Economic regional regulation lacks the political will to supersede national interests and international attempts have not been particularly successful. There is the risk that in this hiatus the multinationals and transnationals will develop themselves as an additional form of government responsible to no democratic constituency other than the loose-knit assemblage of shareholders in the country of origin. Amongst these shareholders, financial institutions feature prominently but appear to perform a passive role. As Berle and Means wrote: 'The future may see the economic organism now typified by the corporation, not only on an equal plane with the state, but possibly even superseding it as the dominant form of social organisation[9].' While this may represent a triumph of economic rationality, it will represent a political regression.

---

9 *The Modern Corporation and Private Property* (revised edn, 1968) p 313.

APPENDIX

The alter ego or organ theory in tort and criminal law

For the most part English law adopts an agency analysis to directors. Where, however, the question arises in tort or in criminal law as to whether the company was personally at fault, the courts sometimes adopt the organ theory and regard the acts or omissions of a director or responsible official as the act or omission of the company.

The leading case is *Lennard's Carrying Co Ltd v Asiatic Petroleum Co Ltd* [1915] AC 705, HL, which concerned a cargo claim which Lennards sought to defend by arguing s 502 of the Merchant Shipping Act 1894 which exonerated the owner from losses arising without his actual fault. The House of Lords held that they could not rely on that defence since the fault of the appropriate organ such as the board of directors or managing director could be attributed to the company. Viscount Haldane said at 713:

My Lords, a corporation is an abstraction. It has no mind of its own any more than it has a body of its own; its active and directing will must consequently be sought in the person of somebody who for some purposes may be called an agent, but who is really the directing mind and will of the corporation, the very ego and centre of the personality of the corporation. That person may be under the direction of the shareholders in general meeting; that person may be the board of directors itself, or it may be, and in some companies it is so, that that person has an authority co-ordinate with the board of directors given to him under the articles of association, and is appointed by the general meeting of the company, and can only be removed by the general meeting of the company.

In recent cases the courts have been prepared on occasion to regard non-director managers as the alter ego of the company where all relevant powers of control have been vested in them (see, eg, *Lady Gwendolen* [1965] P 294, CA. Cf *Tesco Supermarkets Ltd v Nattrass* [1972] AC 153, [1971] 2 All ER 127, HL.

In *Tesco Supermarkets Ltd v Nattrass* [1972] AC 153, [1971] 2 All ER 127, HL, the defendant company was charged under s 11(2) of the Trade Descriptions Act 1968 with advertising goods at a price less than that at which they were in fact available. The store branch had run out of specials and had replaced them by similar items at the normal price. The employee in question should have notified the store manager but had failed to do so. The manager therefore failed to discharge his responsibilities. The defendant company had in place an extensive system designed to ensure compliance with the Act. Section 20 of the Act provided:

where an offence under this Act which has been committed by a body corporate is proved to have been committed with the consent and connivance of, . . . any director, manager, secretary or other similar officer of the body corporate, . . . he as well as the body corporate shall be guilty of that offence . . .

Section 24 of the Act provided the following defence:

In any proceedings for an offence under this Act it shall, . . . be a defence for the person charged to prove—(a) that the commission of the offence was due to . . . the act or default of another person, . . . and (b) that he took all reasonable precautions and exercised all due diligence to avoid the commission of such an offence . . .

The defendant company successfully pleaded the defence. Lord Reid said at 170 D-G:

I must start by considering the nature of the personality which by a fiction the law attributes to a corporation. A living person has a mind which can have knowledge or intention or be negligent and he has hands to carry out his intentions. A corporation has none of these: it must act through living persons, though not always one or the same person. Then the person who acts is not speaking or acting for the company. He is acting as the company and his mind which directs his acts is the mind of the company. There is no question of the company being vicariously liable. He is not acting as a servant, representative, agent or delegate. He is an embodiment of the company or, one could say, he hears and speaks through the persona of the company, within his appropriate sphere, and his mind is the mind of the company. If it is a guilty mind then that guilt is the guilt of the company. It must be a question of law whether, once the facts have been ascertained, a person in doing particular things is to be regarded as the company or merely as the company's servant or agent. In that case any liability of the company can only be a statutory or vicarious liability . . .

Normally the board of directors, the managing director and perhaps other superior officers of a company carry out the functions of management and speak and act as the company. Their subordinates do not. They carry out orders from above and it can make no difference that they are given some measure of discretion. But the board of directors may delegate some part of their functions of management giving to their delegates full discretion to act independently of instructions from them. I see no difficulty in holding that they have thereby put such a delegate in their place so that within the scope of the delegation he can act as the company. It may not always be easy to draw the line but there are cases in which the line must be drawn . . . (171 E-G)

For a detailed critique of *Tesco*, see WB Fisse 'Consumer Protection and Corporate Criminal Responsibility' (1971) 4 Adel L Rev 113. *Tesco* was applied in *R v Andrews Weatherfoil Ltd* [1972] 1 All ER 65, [1972] 1 WLR 118, CA. See also *Nordik Industries Ltd v Regional Controller of Inland Revenue* [1976] 1 NZLR 194 at 199–202; *Taxation Comr v Whitfords Beach Pty Ltd* (1982) 56 ALJR 240 at 245; *R v McNamara* (1981) 56 CCC (2d) 193 (Ont CA); *R v N Paterson & Sons Ltd* (1980) 117 DLR (3d) 517; *R v Roffel* (1985) 9 ACLR 433. See also the Massachusetts case of *Commonwealth v Beneficial Finance Co* 275 NE (2d) 33 (1972) for a wide ranging discussion of the issues. Generally on corporate criminal liability, see L. H. Leigh *The Criminal Liability of Corporations in English Law* (1969); 'The Criminal Liability of Corporations and other Groups' (1977–78) 9 Ottawa LR 247. See also A Vincent 'Can Groups be Persons?' (1989) 42 Review of Metaphysics 678; P French *Collective and Corporate Responsibility* (1984); C Wells 'Manslaughter and Corporate Crime' (1989) 139 NLJ 931; S Field and N Jörg 'Corporate Liability and Manslaughter: Should We be going Dutch?' [1991] Crim LR 156.

Index

Page references in italics indicate tables or diagrams.